DESERTS OF THE WORLD

DESERTS OF THE WORLD

AN APPRAISAL OF RESEARCH INTO THEIR
PHYSICAL AND BIOLOGICAL ENVIRONMENTS

Edited by
WILLIAM G. McGINNIES
BRAM J. GOLDMAN
PATRICIA PAYLORE

A United States Contribution to the
International Hydrological Decade

THE UNIVERSITY OF ARIZONA PRESS

Information in Pertinent Publications lists coded BA is used with permission of BioSciences Information of *Biological Abstracts*. Certain information in those lists (coded CA) is reprinted with permission of *Chemical Abstracts*. The editors and publisher express appreciation to these organizations for their cooperation.

First printing 1968
Second printing 1970

THE UNIVERSITY OF ARIZONA PRESS

Copyright © 1968
The Arizona Board of Regents
All Rights Reserved
Manufactured in the U.S.A.

S. B. N. 8165-0181-5
L. C. No. 68-9338

FOREWORD

SINCE ITS BEGINNINGS in the latter years of the 19th century, the University of Arizona has recognized, by reason of its location on the semiarid border of the desert, a special responsibility for basic and applied research relating to problems of the arid and semiarid regions of the earth. Research in arid-lands agriculture was a concern of the University of Arizona even before the first undergraduate students were admitted. Since that time many other departments and laboratories, directly and indirectly concerned with the field of water problems, have given these areas increasing attention. These include the Agricultural Experiment Station, the Laboratory of Tree-Ring Research, the Institute of Atmospheric Physics, the Geochronology Laboratories, the Water Resources Research Center, and the Office of Arid Lands Studies.

The Office of Arid Lands Studies, with the assistance of a major contract from the U.S. Army Research Office, undertook in 1964 the preparation of a compendium publication to result from a project entitled "An Inventory of Geographical Research on Desert Environments." The purpose of the project was to determine in detail what topics had been or were being investigated for the world's deserts, to appraise the reported work, and to disclose areas of study where further work was needed. Rather than recapitulate all information known about the deserts of the world, the results were to comprise a compendium-guidebook to past and present research based upon critical review of the published literature augmented by consultations with specialists.

With the completion of this project, the Publications Committee of the University of Arizona approved a decision to revise and publish formally the material originally submitted to fill the contract obligation to the U.S. Army Research Office. I believe that this publication provides a working tool for many people seriously interested in advancing the state of knowledge of arid lands. The Office of Arid Lands Studies, under the direction of Dr. William G. McGinnies, has therefore prepared this information to be of maximum use to those planning, managing, and executing future research efforts.

It is my hope and intention that the University of Arizona, through education, training, research, and publication associated with arid lands, one of its fields of special competence, will continue to carry out its local, national, and international service responsibilities.

RICHARD A. HARVILL
President

About the Editors and Authors . . .

WILLIAM G. MCGINNIES, editor of this volume and author of the section on Vegetation, in 1964 became director of the Office of Arid Lands Studies at the University of Arizona — the same institution at which he acquired as an undergraduate his consuming interest in the desert. A doctoral graduate of the University of Chicago in 1932, he then served as head of the botany department at the University of Arizona. During this early part of his career he was a protégé of the late Homer Shantz, renowned student of arid lands. For twenty-five years McGinnies served with the United States government in such varied capacities as district manager for the Soil Conservation Service on the Navajo Reservation, as supervisor of a project to extract rubber from a dry-lands plant during World War II, and as director of the Rocky Mountain Forest and Range Experiment Station and the Central States Forest Experiment Station.

McGinnies returned to the University of Arizona in 1960 as director of the Laboratory of Tree-Ring Research and coordinator of the University's arid-lands program, then moved to the Office of Arid Lands Studies. He has been a member of two FAO-UNESCO committees on range problems and afforestation, and has published extensively since 1928, including four works that appeared in the UNESCO Arid Zone Research series.

BRAM J. GOLDMAN, on the editorial team for this volume, since 1964 has been editor for the Office of Arid Lands Studies at the University of Arizona. Following completion of a bachelor's degree in business administration from the University of Michigan, he pursued a varied business career that focused later on becoming technical writer and editor on programs involving large missile silos, an electronics test facility, and the Falcon air-to-air missile. He joined the University of Arizona in 1963 as assistant to the director of the Lunar and Planetary Laboratory, where his duties included editing the *Communications* series of the laboratory. He later shifted to the University's Orbiting Astronomical Observatory. The move to the Office of Arid Lands Studies followed. There he assumed not only the editorial function but also managerial responsibility for publications, including the present volume.

PATRICIA PAYLORE, also one of the editors, was primarily responsible for uncovering bibliographic sources and verifying the mass of citations for the authors of this project. The bibliographer for the Office of Arid Lands Studies at the University of Arizona since 1965, Miss Paylore joined the University in 1930, following completion there of her bachelor's and M.A. degrees. She served the University Library as head of the acquisitions department, Special Collections librarian, and assistant and acting head librarian. Her extensive indexing experience backgrounded her taking charge also of the three comprehensive indexes of this volume. The only native of the American Southwest among the authors and editors of this book — she was born in New Mexico Territory — Miss Paylore has been oriented all her life toward arid lands.

She has published extensively, especially in library journals, and has won numerous awards. Among them are the Life Patron Award of the Oklahoma City Libraries, the Librarian of the Year award from the Arizona State Library Association, and the Woman of the Year in Research Award (1967) from the Tucson *Arizona Daily Star*.

CLAYTON H. REITAN, coauthor of the chapter on Weather and Climate, in 1968 was a researcher and a doctoral student at the Center for Climatic Research, University of Wisconsin. Previously, he had been with the University of Arizona since 1955, where he was on the staff of the Institute of Atmospheric Physics and also taught meteorology. The holder of a bachelor's degree from Iowa State University and of an S.M. degree from the University of Chicago, he has done research work on atmospheric water vapor, and is widely interested in matters pertaining to the climatology of arid regions. The project that resulted in the coauthorship of the chapter in the present volume was his first internationally oriented work, and it confirmed his interest in arid regions which had been reinforced by his living in Arizona.

CHRISTINE R. GREEN is the coauthor of the section on Weather and Climate. A statistical climatologist, she was for eleven years a staff member of the University of Arizona's Institute of Atmospheric Physics until 1968. Although she majored in French at Kent State University, aptitude tests taken later revealed she had unusual ability in mathematics and statistics. A varied career followed, including employment as a statistical supervisor for North American Aviation on work involving missile aerodynamics, with RCA in the field of statistics, in The University of Arizona's computer department on programs involving the Institute of Atmospheric Physics, and finally with the Institute itself. There one of her more interesting projects with an international flavor was that of applying formulas to derive construction data for solar-energy-fueled water desalting installations. These data were applicable to San Diego and Tucson in the United States, to Puerto Peñasco, Mexico, and to the Peruvian coast, Jerusalem, and the island of Curaçao, West Indies. She is author or coauthor of a number of scientific papers on climatology.

LAWRENCE K. LUSTIG, the section on Geomorphology and Surface Hydrology's author, since mid-1968 has been senior editor for the Earth Sciences with the *Encyclopedia Britannica,* a position involving responsibility for all articles about the Earth, its atmosphere, and its hydrosphere. He has done extensive work in the Basin and Range area of the western United States. A 1963 doctoral graduate of Harvard University, where his dissertation was on an investigation of the alluvial fans in arid Deep Springs Valley, California, his specialty is the fluvial geomorphology of arid lands.

This specialty has resulted in his traveling to many parts of the world, including the Mideast, South and southwestern Africa, the nations of northern Africa, Southeast Asia, and England. His interest in other nations is inherent in his career as an arid-lands geomorphologist, but it originally sprang from his service with the U.S. Army, during which he traveled though much of the Caribbean and Central America, went across and around the Pacific, and served in Japan and Korea. Lustig has worked as a geophysicist for Shell Oil in New Mexico and Arizona, as a geologist for ARAMCO, with the U.S. Geological Survey as a research hydrologist, and for four years was a member of the University of Arizona's geology faculty.

HAROLD E. DREGNE, the contributor of the section on Surface Materials, wrote from his vantage point as professor of soil chemistry at New Mexico State University. His interest in arid lands stems from his doctoral studies at Oregon State University, where he worked in the arid and semiarid lands of the American Northwest. Throughout his professional career — at the University of Idaho, Oregon State University, Washington State University, with the U.S. Soil Conservation Service in Colorado, and at New Mexico State — he has carried on investigations in arid lands. His particular area of expertise is soil and water salinity.

This field has enabled him to combine soil chemistry with his other interests in soil classification, soil fertility, and soil physics. The international implications of his work have led Dregne to Chile, where he served as a United Nations Food and Agriculture Organization specialist, on a State Department-sponsored trip through the arid lands of the Soviet Union, and to the University of Sind in Pakistan for two years in an intercollegiate exchange program.

CHARLES H. LOWE, who wrote the section on Desert Fauna, became a faculty member of the University of Arizona in 1950 after receiving the Ph.D. degree from the University of California, Berkeley. His research interests are the biology of the poisonous and harmless cold-blooded vertebrates, and the general and physiological ecology of desert animals and plants. In connection with the project that led to this volume, he has traveled widely, visiting — among countless places — Australia, Southeast Asia, the Mideast, northern, southern and South West Africa, Malaysia, France, and England. Lowe's interest in various animals, ecology, science in general, and in communicating his findings to both scientists and laymen is far-reaching. His numerous publications cover such subjects as aquatic snakes, pseudoherpetology, the Gila monster, aggressive behavior in male sidewinders, the discovery and study of eight species of whiptail lizards with populations consisting of only females, the limits of the Sonoran Desert, thermal stress, correlation of vegetation climaxes with soil, and comments on ecology and evolution.

Although he spends as much time as possible in the field, he has also found time to edit *The Vertebrates of Arizona* (University of Arizona Press), and to serve as scientific consultant and manuscript editor for *The Desert* in the *Life* Nature Library Series.

JOSEPH F. SCHREIBER, JR., compiler of the section on Desert Coastal Zones, manages to combine professional and recreational activities in both desert and marine environments. He is particularly interested in ancient and modern sedimentary environments, and his joining the University of Arizona — where he became a member of the Geology Department in 1959 — gave him a chance to work extensively in the sedimentary basins of the Basin and Range province. Previously, Schreiber had taken two degrees at The Johns Hopkins University, and was also involved in geological oceanography for the Chesapeake Bay Institute. His experience in obtaining shallow-water cores in Chesapeake Bay was paralleled by later research taking cores from Great Salt Lake in an attempt to clarify the sedimentary history of this unique environment.

The latter project was the subject of his doctoral dissertation for the University of Utah. While pursuing a career in the oil industry prior to his doctoral studies, Schreiber continued to investigate sedimentary environments in the Rocky Mountain states, west Texas, and the Louisiana Gulf Coast. Completing a full circle of his ocean-oriented work, he turned his later attention to marine geological studies of the arid Sonoran coast of the Gulf of California.

EUGENE S. SIMPSON, author of the appendix on Ground-Water Hydrology, joined the University of Arizona faculty in 1963. Always interested in the problem of dispersion and mixing of contaminants in subsurface waters, for many years he devoted himself exclusively to the problem of contamination of subsurface waters by radioactivity, although his basic background is the general field of ground-water hydrology. Much of Simpson's professional career has involved classified information, for he started with the U.S. Geological Survey in 1945, where he worked on projects involving disposal of radioactive wastes in the ground and in evaluating the hazards of radioactivity for prospective nuclear-facility sites. He used much of this research for his dissertation at Columbia University, from which he received the Ph.D. degree in hydrology in 1960. Simpson has also worked — on loan from the U.S.G.S. — for the Atomic Energy Commission, and at the Belgian Nuclear Research Center where he helped organize a group charged with the responsibility of protecting water supplies from radioactivity.

More recently, he has widened his interests to include studies of contaminants of underground water supplies, and his laboratory and field research has involved the use of existing common and trace elements from irrigation and sewage water to determine how they move through stream bottoms and other points of recharge and then enter and disperse through aquifers.

PREFACE

This book is intended for those seriously interested in planning, managing, and executing research or development efforts in the arid parts of the world. It contains evaluative comments on the work that has been accomplished in those areas, statements about how well known subjects are for each desert, and recommendations for filling gaps in the state of knowledge and research. Our coverage includes investigations of the natural environment; we do not treat such subjects as agriculture or economics directly. The term "appraisal of research" in the title may deserve further explanation here. When authors discuss, for example, investigations of the fauna or climate of the Thar Desert, they do not, except incidentally, tell the reader the names and numbers of the fauna or describe the climate. They *do* name the best sources of information on facets of the subject, and they *do* give an estimate of the general state of knowledge for that subject and desert.

Some of man's earliest recorded habitats were in areas we now know as deserts. His migrations into more temperate environments have served for centuries to keep the world's deserts the places of solitude and silence that give them the special ambience by which they are universally characterized. Even today, with population presures beyond what Malthus himself may have foreseen, the deserts remain the lonely places of the Earth.*

Threatening the solitude of the quarter of the world's land surface classified as semiarid or drier are inexorable population growth and the advanced technology that makes possible comfortable living in that quarter. Research on desalination, discovery of little-known underground sources of water, advances in weather modification, and applications of research to food and fuel production, transportation, and air conditioning—elements such as these are likely, before this century is out, to combine to make obsolete Webster's use of "desert" to illustrate the word "solitude."

The world's travelers do not always wait for technological perfection. Already crowds ride camels to the rosy ruins of Petra, French sand yachts make race runs into Tombouctou, and bronzed sun worshippers threaten to make a Jones Beach of the arid Sonoran coast on the Gulf of California. The accommodations and services these travelers expect and will demand may provide a relatively unconventional basis for economic development.

Are we ready for a revolution in land use and demography in the arid world? As is brought out in the chapters that follow, the gaps in knowledge of various aspects of the physical features of arid lands are enormous, in part because of the inaccessibility of many areas, in part because of the inhospitable nature of deserts, in part because priorities for studying a country are usually drawn so that other potentials are developed before deserts. Yet we must have basic knowledge if we are to avoid the improvisation which pell-mell economic development often foists upon us, with its attendant waste, error, spoliation, and environmental hazards.

What are the prospects for an orderly and scientific development of the arid lands on every continent? For the many countries that are almost entirely arid or semiarid, the only hope of creating viable societies seems to lie in understanding the potentials of their environments, then moving quickly to build into their governmental structures provisions for research and its subsequent applications. Such actions world-wide will require massive infusions of international assistance. It is our hope that the present publication, bringing together critical appraisals of the research and state of knowledge on the world's deserts, will give all concerned a basis for a real understanding of the urgent schedule and the need for research efficiency.

Much useful knowledge does exist, and it is to this that we have addressed ourselves first in this work. The authors have attempted to sift it and to evaluate it, and the very extent of the considerable body of information thus described does provide a usable base. The deficiencies in literature coverage may be ameliorable by more intensive searches for native-language reports not always accessible to our

---

* *Webster's Third New International Dictionary:* "solitude: a lonely place (as a desert)."

authors. There is arid-lands literature in the language of each country in which the world's deserts lie. The problem is to locate and identify it as pertinent, then to evaluate it, and finally to disseminate information about it, all to the end that the most important of such publications and reports be made more accessible to those who an use it in the attack on the world-wide problems of arid lands.

The three editors of this publication have been fortunate. The combination of physical proximity (we are all faculty members at the Office of Arid Lands Studies, University of Arizona) and temperamental compatibility enabled us to work together closely through a long and sometimes frustrating program with mutual respect undiminished. Dr. McGinnies served as scientific editor, planner, advisor, and authority for all major decisions; Mr. Goldman aided in the planning, performed the day-to-day managerial tasks, and assumed responsibility for copy and production editing (exclusive of the functions of the University of Arizona Press); Miss Paylore developed new sources of information for our authors, assumed responsibility for bibliographical editing, took charge of indexing, and, upon occasion, performed the managerial tasks.

It might be useful at this juncture to supply the standard plan used by the editors and authors for outlining, investigating, writing, and producing each chapter. Unfortunately we cannot do so. The work plan developed for each chapter was unique, reflecting to varying extents the subject matter of the chapter, the locations of main bodies of published and unpublished information on the subject, the work preferences of the authors, and the period of time that each author could free himself from other academic duties.

Some of our authors were required to travel extensively overseas; others were able to limit their travel to United States sites. Some were able to make use of much graduate student help; others were not. Almost all authors used extensive contacts within the United States or throughout the world to provide reviews of parts or entire chapters. When an extraordinary amount of writing or reviewing was required from an outside expert, he was employed as a consultant or a subcontract was executed. All the predictable difficulties of trying to manage a project such as this within a univeristy were experienced, and yet none of the editors, if offered the choice, would hesitate to begin tomorrow a similar task for the semiarid areas.

We have attempted to keep the terminology consistent from chapter to chapter. Our authority for place names was *The Times Atlas of the World,*

5 vols., 1955-1959; when place-name terminology could not be ascertained in the Times Atlas, the editors used *U.S. Board on Geographic Names Gazetteer.*

Geographic areas covered by the publication are generally those classified as arid or extremely arid by Peveril Meigs in his Unesco maps, *Distribution of Arid Homoclimates.** A number of the smaller areas classified as arid by Meigs are not treated in any of our chapters for reasons of time, space, and money, and the coverage of such nations as the Soviet Union, Outer Mongolia, and mainland China varies from chapter to chapter depending upon each author's assessment of the efficiency of investigating material on these nations in the time available.

We have tried to compile and produce a publication containing a comprehensive, evaluative inventory of research activities and the state of current knowledge about desert environments. The authors have identified gaps and suggested future research to fill the gaps. Because of limitations in our original contract, it was not possible to include items specifically related to the needs of man for food, clothing, shelter, and industry, nor could we concentrate to any extent on the semiarid zones. We hope that appraisals like the present publication covering those subjects and areas can be compiled and published, because we believe that a pressing need for such work exists.

Authors of the chapters were faculty members of the University of Arizona at the time of writing except for Harold E. Dregne of New Mexico State University, a colleague of long standing. Cooperating faculty from other institutions throughout the world contributed greatly to the chapters. Funding has been provided by the University of Arizona and the U.S. Army under contract DA49-092-ARO-71. Army clearance has been secured for this publication (TP-517), but the findings in the report are not to be construed as an official Department of the Army position. Particular thanks are due to Dr. Lester W. Trueblood, now Director of the Earth Sciences Laboratory at the U.S. Army Natick Laboratories, Dr. William C. Robison, head of the Geography Division of that Laboratory, and Dr. Guy N. Parmenter, now Chief, Research Division, Tropical Test Center, Ft. Clayton, C.Z., all of whom contributed not only as official technical monitors on the contract but also as professional colleagues interested in the collection and dissemination of valuable scientific information. Advice given by Dr. Peveril Meigs, a guiding spirit

---

*Original maps dated 1952 accompanied "World Distribution of Arid and Semi-Arid Homoclimates" in *Reviews of Research on Arid Zone Hydrology* (Unesco, Paris, 1953). Maps were revised in 1960.

on this program, has proven invaluable since its inception. Of the Unesco officials who helped and encouraged us, special thanks are due to personnel of the Natural Resources Division (Paris): M. Batisse, Chief, and Miss I. R. Dudeney. Thane A. Riney of the Food and Agriculture Organization (Rome), Dr. J. Marçais, Director of the Centre de Recherches sur les Zones Arides (Paris), and John Wickham of the World Meteorological Organization (Geneva) were extraordinarily helpful, as were Miss B. McHugo of the Directorate of Overseas Surveys (Surbiton, Surrey), H. A. Izant of the World Health Organization (Geneva), Dr. M. Y. Nuttonson of the American Institute of Crop Ecology (Washington), and Savel Kliachko, Lecturer in Russian at the University of Arizona, whose keen interest in language and science unraveled some of the mysteries of Russian terminology.

In addition to those whose contributions have been acknowledged in the individual chapters, thanks are due Sherwood Carr, Comptroller of the University of Arizona, who always found ways to get the essential actions accomplished on this unorthodox program; Miss Dorothy J. Cramer, in charge of travel, who patiently aided our authors in planning their foreign journeys and filing the extensive reports required; and Mrs. Kathryn J. Gloyd of the University of Arizona Library, who provided efficient cooperation in solving bibliographic problems before the staff of the Office of Arid Lands Studies was expanded to include such capability internally. Indeed, University Library personnel were of great help throughout the program. The contribution of University of Arizona Press, which cooperated during the report phase as well as the stage resulting in the present publication, should not go unrecognized, for without the professional and financial help of that organization publication in book form would not have been possible.

The brunt of the monumental manuscript typing and proofreading tasks was borne gallantly by Mrs. D. Genice Dickerson; other contributions in this field were made by Mrs. Marilyn Bresnahan, Mrs. Virginia Richardson, Miss Karen Stroman, and Mrs. Charlene W. Shultz. Special bibliographic work was accomplished by Miss Mary Lu Moore and Mrs. Elizabeth J. Wall and clerical work by Mrs. Beverly S. García and Mrs. Nancy C. Hitchcock.

The U. S. Government's Work-Study program, and its University of Arizona administrators, provided us with a surprisingly well-qualified group of assistants, among whom we wish to thank Miss Jerri Freedman, Miss Ethel S. Black, Mrs. Valerie Temple Siegel, and the present incumbent, Miss Karin Metrock, who will shortly leave for India on a Fulbright grant.

Perhaps it would not be amiss to pause on the threshold of this look into the future and point out that we ourselves, in preparing this work for publication, share with our authors a sense of gratitude to those who went before, not just in earlier books but in pioneer field investigations under conditions far more inhospitable than now prevail, to lay the groundwork which is still so useful to the modern investigator with his satellites, airplanes, Land Rovers, portable refrigeration, packaged foods, and sophisticated instrumentation for field work. These latter advances, together with prior research, should accelerate the studies which still will be required to make the deserts habitable and productive, so that in the end we may say, with the Psalmist, that together we have turned a wilderness into a pool of water, and a dry land into watersprings, and there made the hungry to dwell.

WILLIAM G. McGINNIES
BRAM J. GOLDMAN
PATRICIA PAYLORE
Office of Arid Lands Studies
The University of Arizona
Tucson, Arizona, U. S. A.

CONTENTS

LOCATOR MAPS OF EXTREMELY ARID, ARID, AND SEMIARID REGIONS BY CONTINENTS (AFTER MEIGS)

INTRODUCTION
Staff, Office of Arid Lands Studies, University of Arizona

APPRAISAL OF RESEARCH ON WEATHER AND CLIMATE OF DESERT ENVIRONMENTS
Clayton H. Reitan and Christine R. Green

APPRAISAL OF RESEARCH ON GEOMORPHOLOGY AND SURFACE HYDROLOGY OF DESERT ENVIRONMENTS

Lawrence K. Lustig

APPRAISAL OF RESEARCH ON SURFACE MATERIALS OF DESERT ENVIRONMENTS

Harold E. Dregne

APPRAISAL OF RESEARCH ON VEGETATION OF DESERT ENVIRONMENTS
William G. McGinnies

APPRAISAL OF RESEARCH ON FAUNA OF DESERT ENVIRONMENTS

Charles H. Lowe

APPRAISAL OF RESEARCH ON DESERT COASTAL ZONES
Joseph F. Schreiber, Jr.

APPENDIX: GENERAL SUMMARY OF THE STATE OF RESEARCH ON GROUND-WATER HYDROLOGY IN DESERT ENVIRONMENTS

Eugene S. Simpson

INDEXES

LOCATOR MAPS OF THE ARID LANDS

On the pages that follow are general-location maps of the deserts of the world. The Extremely Arid, Arid, and Semiarid areas are delineated in accordance with Peveril Meigs' 1960 revision to his 1952 maps that accompanied "World Distribution of Arid and Semi-Arid Homoclimates" in *Reviews of Research on Arid Zone Hydrology* (UNESCO, Paris, 1953). We have repeated Meigs' codes in the Extremely Arid and Arid portions where space permitted, and we have also included some of his coding for the Semiarid zones. The names and location of the subdeserts do not necessarily coincide with those used by Meigs; they of necessity reflect the usage of our chapter authors and their consultants worldwide.

— The Editors

KEY

■ Extremely Arid

▨ Arid   Maps by Cartographic Service
                          Goode's Homolosine
▨ Semiarid   Equal-Area Projection

Sc13
Sc13
Ac13
Ac23
Ac24
Sc23
Ac23
Ac23
Ac14
Ac23
Ac23
Ea23
Ac24
Ea24
Ac23
Ac23
Ea24
S A H A R A
Ac34
Ab23
Ab34
Sb33
Sb34
Sb23
Sb34
Aa34
Sb22
Sb33
Sb33
Ab33
Ab34
SOMALI - CHALBI
Sb33
Sb23
0 500
MILES
KEY
Extremely Arid
Arid
Semiarid
30°
20°
10°
0°
10°
MEIGS CLASSIFICATIONS
E — Extremely arid
A — Arid
S — Semiarid
a — no marked season of precipitation
b — summer precipitation
c — winter precipitation
Digits
1st digit indicates mean temperature of coldest month
2nd digit indicates mean temperature of warmest month
0 = less than 0°C
1 = 0° to 10°C
2 = 10° to 20°C
3 = 20° to 30°C
4 = more than 30°C

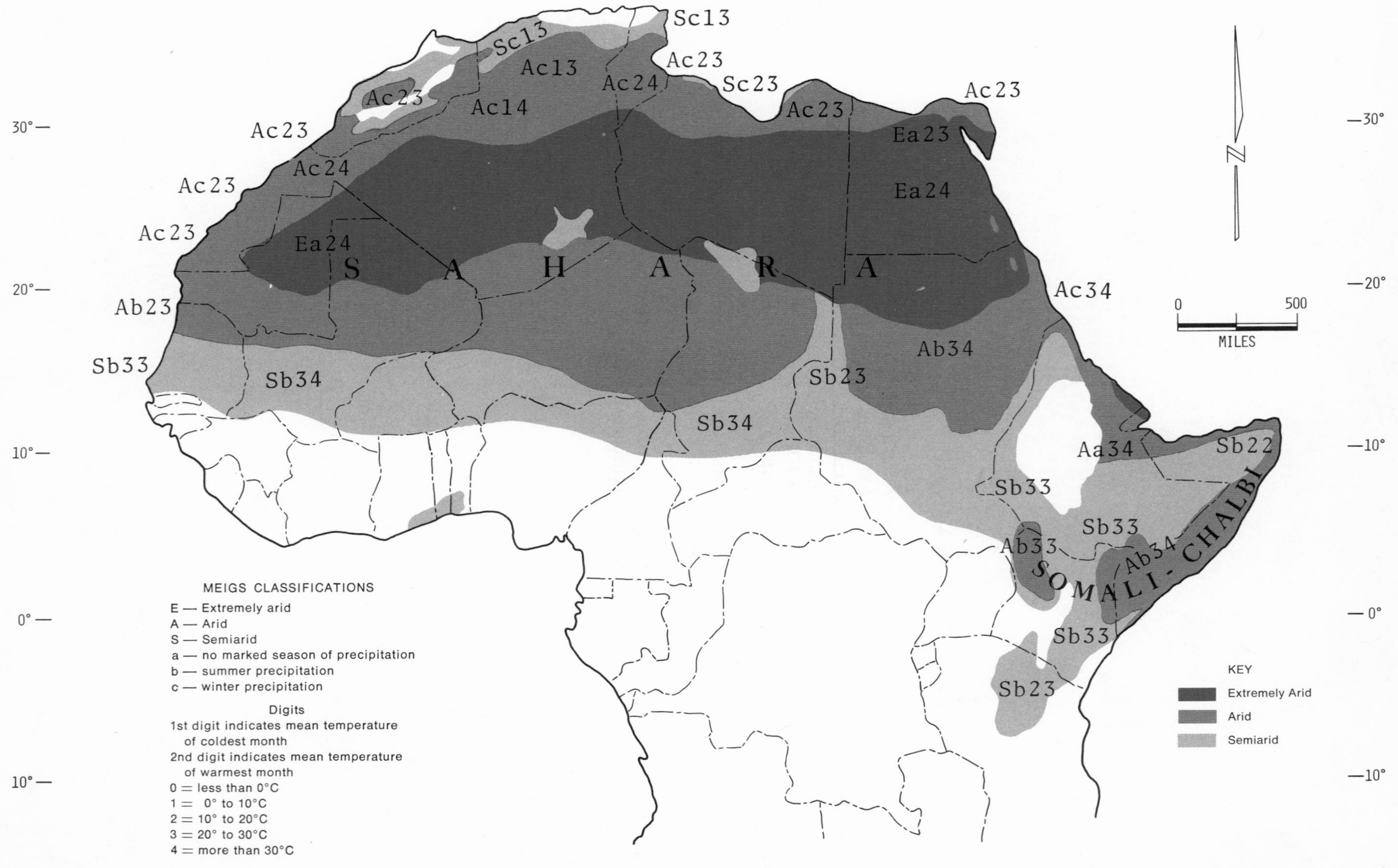

Arid Lands of Northern Africa (after Meigs)

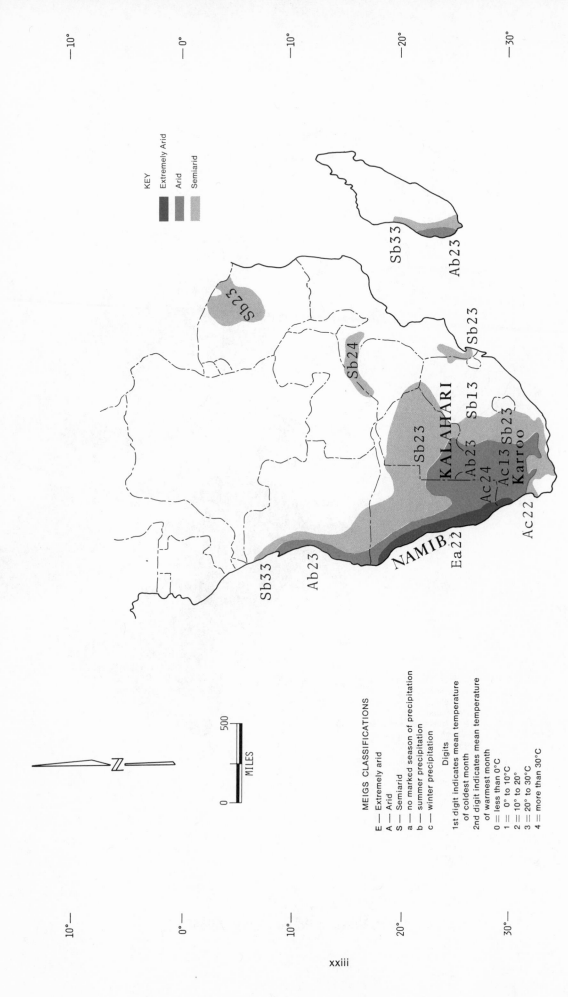

MEIGS CLASSIFICATIONS

E — Extremely arid
A — Arid
S — Semiarid
a — no marked season of precipitation
b — summer precipitation
c — winter precipitation

Digits

1st digit indicates mean temperature
  of coldest month
2nd digit indicates mean temperature
  of warmest month

0 = less than 0°C
1 = 0° to 10°C
2 = 10° to 20°C
3 = 20° to 30°C
4 = more than 30°C

KEY

Extremely Arid
Arid
Semiarid

MILES

0   500

Arid Lands of Southern Africa (after Meigs)

xxiii

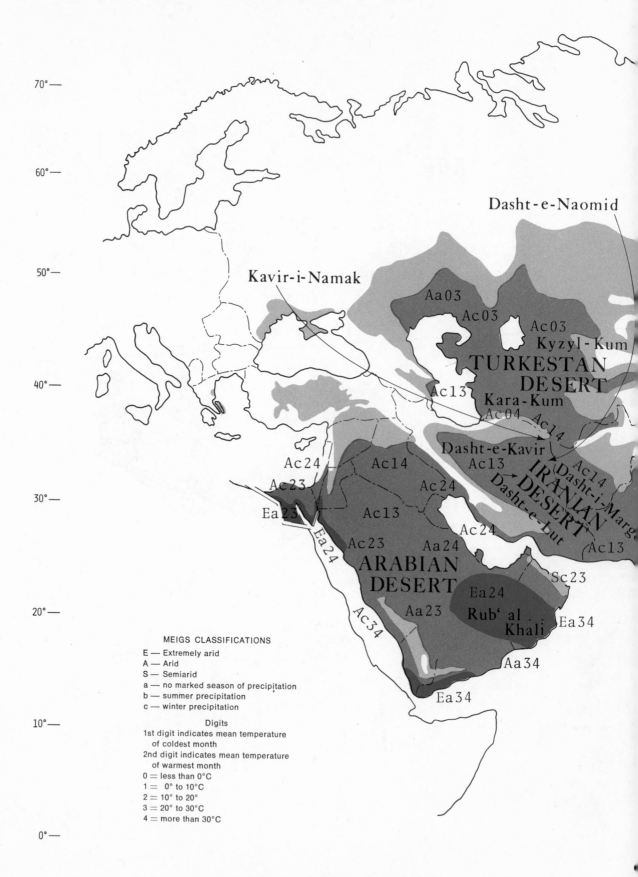

Dasht-e-Naomid

Kavir-i-Namak

Aa03

Ac03   Ac03
                 Kyzyl-Kum
           TURKESTAN
              DESERT
Ac13   Kara-Kum
      Ac04   Ac14

Dasht-e-Kavir
Ac24   Ac14   Ac13   IRANIAN   Ac14
Ac23   Ac24   DESERT   Dasht-i-Marg
Ea23   Ac13   Dasht-e-Lut
                                      Ac24   Ac13
        Ea24   Ac23   Aa24
                                            Sc23
        ARABIAN   Ea24
        DESERT   Rub' al   Ea34
Ac34   Aa23   Khali
                                      Aa34

Ea34

MEIGS CLASSIFICATIONS

E — Extremely arid
A — Arid
S — Semiarid
a — no marked season of precipitation
b — summer precipitation
c — winter precipitation

                Digits
1st digit indicates mean temperature
  of coldest month
2nd digit indicates mean temperature
  of warmest month
0 = less than 0°C
1 =   0° to 10°C
2 = 10° to 20°
3 = 20° to 30°C
4 = more than 30°C

Arid Lands of Asia: Western Portion (after Meigs)

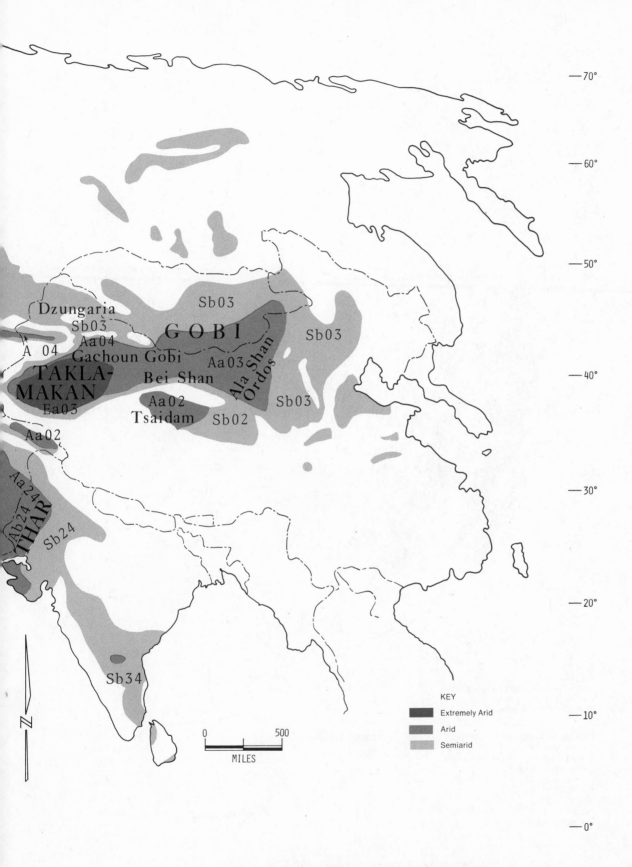

Dzungaria
Sb03
Aa04
A 04
Gachoun Gobi
TAKLA-
MAKAN
Ea03
Aa02
Aa24
Ab24 THAR
Sb24

Sb03

G O B I

Sb03

Bei Shan
Aa03
Ala Shan
Ordos

Sb03

Aa02
Tsaidam
Sb02

Sb03

Sb34

KEY

Extremely Arid

Arid

Semiarid

N

0   500

MILES

Arid Lands of Asia: Eastern Portion (after Meigs)

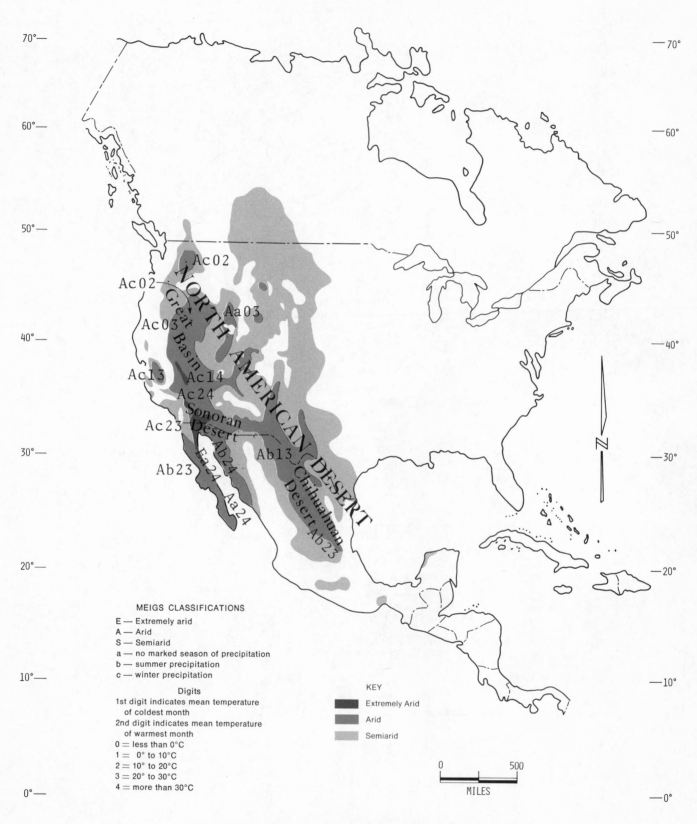

MEIGS CLASSIFICATIONS

E — Extremely arid
A — Arid
S — Semiarid
a — no marked season of precipitation
b — summer precipitation
c — winter precipitation

Digits

1st digit indicates mean temperature
   of coldest month
2nd digit indicates mean temperature
   of warmest month

0 = less than 0°C
1 = 0° to 10°C
2 = 10° to 20°C
3 = 20° to 30°C
4 = more than 30°C

KEY

Extremely Arid
Arid
Semiarid

0   500
MILES

Arid Lands of North America (after Meigs)

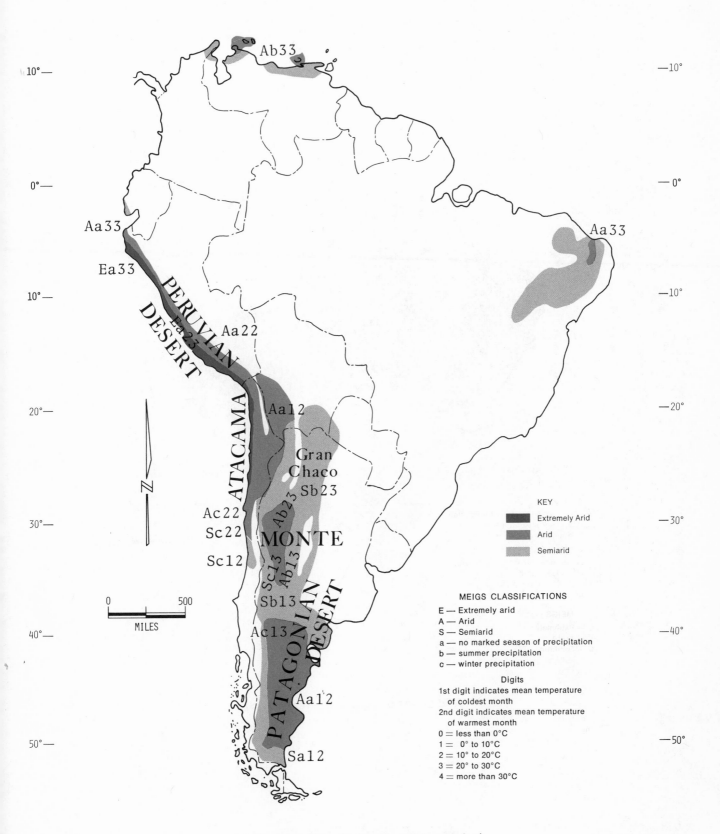

Ab33

Aa33

Ea33

Aa33

PERUVIAN
DESERT

Ea23

Aa22

ATACAMA

Aa12

Gran
Chaco
Sb23

Ac22
Sc22

Ab23

MONTE

Sc12

Sc13
Ab13

Sb13

PATAGONIAN DESERT

Ac13

Aa12

Sa12

N

0   500
MILES

KEY

Extremely Arid

Arid

Semiarid

MEIGS CLASSIFICATIONS

E — Extremely arid
A — Arid
S — Semiarid
a — no marked season of precipitation
b — summer precipitation
c — winter precipitation

Digits
1st digit indicates mean temperature
    of coldest month
2nd digit indicates mean temperature
    of warmest month
0 = less than 0°C
1 =   0° to 10°C
2 = 10° to 20°C
3 = 20° to 30°C
4 = more than 30°C

Arid Lands of South America (after Meigs)

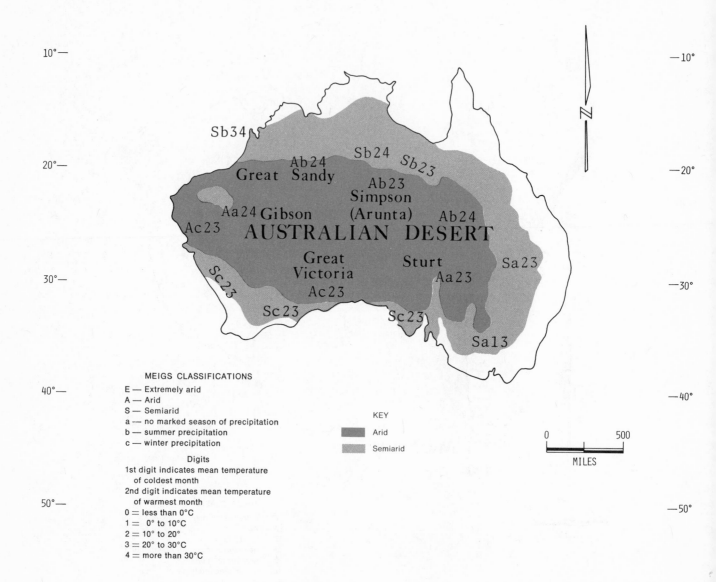

INTRODUCTION

STAFF, OFFICE OF ARID LANDS STUDIES
THE UNIVERSITY OF ARIZONA

PROBLEMS AND RESULTS
OF APPRAISING DESERT RESEARCH

A. LACK OF BASIC DATA COLLECTION

Each author in this compendium decries the lack of basic data in his field. An analysis of the chapter sections on deficiencies in information and recommendations reveals the interlocking handicaps under which arid-lands scientists everywhere labor: the geomorphologist is hampered by the lack of basic climatic data, the ecologist points out the disadvantage imposed on his vegetation studies by the absence of complete soils information, the climatologist calls attention to the lack of satisfactory systems for determining water need and water use. Other examples can be found detailed in the chapters themselves.

In a way, our lack of basic information on deserts is not surprising. Until recently desert travel has been so difficult that only the hardy traveler would attempt it. Impeding scientific exploration were the vastness of the Sahara, the remoteness of the central Asiatic deserts, and the absence, in many desert areas, of water and vegetation to support men and animals. Since there appeared little economic justification for such exploration, few studies were made in the past.

More recently, with the discovery of unsuspected underground resources, exploration increased; unfortunately the investigations too often took the form of "prospecting" where the searches were sporadic and did not result in comprehensive studies. Population pressures sent investigators scurrying for potential food-producing areas, necessitated development and expansion of irrigation systems, required reclamation of waterlogged and saline areas, and caused concentration on sand-control operations; these kinds of efforts and other studies initiated out of direct economic need have served to provide additional information. Unfortunately, most of the results are scattered and unorganized as far as geographic synthesis is concerned.

The exciting possibilities of improving our knowledge of basic data through continuing technological improvement of remote-sensing devices are noted by several of our authors. Other improvements are in the offing, but no prospective improvement approaches the magnitude of the major problem.

For the immediate future lack of basic data about desert environments remains our largest single category of arid-lands problem.

B. LACK OF RESEARCH INTO NATURAL PROCESSES AND MECHANISMS

To the extent that we have experienced widespread desert encroachment within historic times, we are far from unanimous as to its causes. A clearer understanding of the conditions under which vegetation can survive desertic environments, for instance, would be most helpful, as would more comprehensive knowledge of the relative importance of climatic factors that influence precipitation, wind, temperature, and evaporation. Certain elementary steps toward the rehabilitation of arid lands for the benefit of man's great needs go forward almost blindly now, because the basic research into such processes has not been accomplished.

C. DEFINITION OF "DESERT"

As glibly as scientists and laymen use the term, there is, nevertheless, no common agreement as to what constitutes a desert. This fact becomes important when one searches the literature, and one author limits publications on the desert to areas with less than 2 inches of rainfall annually, while others include areas with 10 inches, 15 inches, or even more. In addition, it is recognized that rainfall alone is not an adequate criterion for a desert; however, adding other parameters is not a complete solution, because opinion diverges widely about the elements to be included and the relative weight of each in the aridity formula.

Establishing boundaries on the basis of vegetation offers false hope of improvement, as here again there are no universally accepted criteria as to boundary lines. The situation is still further complicated, as is the case for much terminology, by the lack of consistency in the use of the term "steppe." The usage may overlap with "desert" as defined by some authors, it may be restricted to areas in which grasses and other herbs are the dominant features of the landscape, or it may include any dry areas, some of which may be dominated by shrubby species. Such terms as "subdesert" and "semidesert" add to the confusion, especially since these may be the equivalent of "desert" in some cases and "steppe" in others.

Soils offer little help in drawing the desert boundary, especially since there appear to be many areas where the characteristics of soils now supporting desert vegetation indicate that they developed under more humid conditions.

While there are certain geomorphological characteristics associated with arid regions, these are not sufficiently sensitive to biological and physical conditions to serve as boundary markers for the desert.

The imprints of past climatic changes show on the present landscape, including geomorphology, soils, vegetation, and fauna. Finally man entered the picture, and his activities have reduced or increased plant and animal life and have changed physiographic and edaphic conditions.

D. COMMUNICATIONS AND ACCESSIBILITY

One of the most heartening developments toward disseminating knowledge about world deserts is the increasing emphasis being placed upon international programs. Beginning with Unesco's arid zone program, the World Meteorological Organization's World Weather Watch, FAO's Freedom from Hunger campaign, the present International Hydrological Decade, and the International Biological Program, such projects serve to acquaint scientists with their counterparts in comparable research elsewhere and to permit a freer exchange of information and publications among all levels of research personnel. Without the counsel which these international agencies provided the authors of the chapters that follow, who requested the help of the various secretariats, it is doubtful that the authors could have established the broad bibliographical base supporting this publication.

The student of deserts should theoretically have ability to read at least in Arabic, Chinese, English, French, German, Portuguese, Russian, and Spanish. Because he does not, language often proves another barrier. In this context, attention should be called to the Israel Program for Scientific Translations specifically, and to the several U.S. agencies with an interest in this matter, particularly the Joint Publications Research Service. Despite the fine start made

on translation services, electronic bibliographic control of the products of those services, now scattered throughout the world, is an urgent matter requiring a high priority of attention from international bodies, for wasteful duplication in translation efforts undoubtedly exists. Only a skilled bibliographer, as things now stand, can work his way through the thickets of present uncoordinated proliferation of translations. Unless we are willing to allow each investigator to stumble upon pertinent translations by accident, electronic bibliographic control of translations must be greatly increased.

It is not only translations that require such control. Much of the information obtained from arid-lands investigations throughout the world does not get beyond reports lost in government files or is restricted in distribution because of industrial competition. If it is released, it may be reproduced in a local language or in a journal or other publication of limited distribution, and if it gets beyond that stage it may appear in any one of a number of subject-matter periodicals in which desert reports make up a very minor portion of the contents. Such information thus requires a great deal of searching to find, and when it is encountered it is often unrecognized because of the lack of desert identity in its title and vehicle for publication.

All our chapter experts, then, look forward to use of modern electronic developments to provide the access to all possible arid-lands information, in original language or in translation, whatever the sources, by means of accurate, complete, and analytical retrieval systems. Our own Office of Arid Lands Studies is now embarking on a pilot experiment, under the sponsorship of the National Science Foundation, in an effort to contribute to the achievement of this desirable objective.

E. SUMMARY OF INFORMATION GAPS BY FIELD OF STUDY

Many specific problems were found in the course of the investigations that led to this book. These are covered in the various chapters, but a brief review here might serve to bring them into focus as related to the desert environment.

The difficulty of relating climatic data to deserts, because of paucity of data, is almost universal. Recording stations are usually outside or on the edge of desert areas, and hence little definite information is available about interior conditions. Such data as are available are often for short periods and restricted to precipitation and temperature. Little or no information is available for evaporation, evapotranspiration, or radiation; hence common methods of arriving at aridity indexes cannot be used.

In synoptic climatology, systems covering large areas are usually studied without particular reference to included deserts, and as desert areas may be peripheral to these regions and subject to great variability, the general observations fail to provide needed information for the desert areas. Portions of the central Asiatic deserts lie at the extremity of the Indian monsoon influence, and the Sahara lies between the Mediterranean climatic region and the intertropical convergence zone. The Sonoran Desert in North America feels the influence of Pacific storms in winter and convective storms resulting from moisture movements from the Gulf of Mexico in summer. Because of these conditions, the vegetation of the Sahara tends to vary more along a north-south transect than an east-west, while the much smaller Sonoran Desert varies more along an east-west transect than a north-south.

Information gaps and communication problems are stressed in the chapter on geomorphology. In most of the desert areas there has been too little attention given to landscape features as a basis for universal classifications. The plains have received the least attention, probably because they lack features of interest, whereas topographic highs catch the attention of travelers. Even about these higher portions of the landscape hover unsolved problems concerning geological processes and the classification of physiographic features. While many studies have been concerned with sand dunes, not enough is known about them as physiographic features of the landscape. The low areas, including playas, pans, flats, sinks, sebkhas, deflation basins, and depressions, need much more attention to determine their origins and processes of development; both categories have an important bearing on soil formation, salinity, and use for agricultural purposes.

The information on arid-zone soils is generally inadequate throughout the world. Although there is information on desert soils as a general subject, many areas in the interiors of deserts are practically unknown. The best known are those of the United States and the Soviet Union. There is not any recognized universal definition of a "desert" soil, and complications arise from the use of such terms as "semidesert," "subdesert," and "semiarid." The state of knowledge on physical and chemical properties and water relationships is generally inadequate for all desert areas.

In the chapter on vegetation an attempt has been made to assess the adequancy of state of knowledge. The specific deficiencies range from a knowledge of what species occur, through ecological and phytosociological relationships, to application of this basic information to human needs. The problems of defining "desert" are reiterated, and the deficiencies in communication are stressed. Because of these problems and information deficiencies, there is little common ground for comparing the vegetation of one desert with another with any degree of precision; hence the usefulness of research results that might be widely applied is severely curtailed.

Only the North American Desert has a "good" rating as far as knowledge of the fauna is concerned. For the Australian, Thar, Arabian, Sahara, and Turkestan, the rating is subadequate. A fair rating is given the Kalahari-Namib, Monte-Patagonian, Atacama-Peruvian, Iranian, and Somali-Chalbi, while the Gobi and Takla-Makan are least known.

Surface hydrology and drainage are intimately involved in all aspects of the physical and biological features of the arid regions, and hence what has been stated in regard to those various features applies with perhaps even greater force to the subject of surface water. What has been said for surface hydrology holds true for ground-water hydrology, but with the additional problems related to the source and depth of water resources. Often the water beneath the desert or flowing through it is not of desert origin, so that knowledge of the outside source conditions becomes important, which further complicates the acquisition and communication of information. This situation is especially difficult to work with when the source lies outside the country in which the desert occurs.

Desert shorelines are the least known of all oceanic shorelines because of the general low occupation levels and economic production in these desert areas. The problems are those borne in common with all coastal areas, intensified by unfavorable onshore conditions such as lack of potable water, sparseness or absence of vegetation, and sometimes unstable terrain.

GENERAL DESCRIPTION OF DESERTS

The delineation of deserts in this compendium was that developed by Peveril Meigs (1953). Cold arid regions, such as Antarctica, are excluded. According to Meigs, many distinctive environmental traits distinguish the dry lands of Earth but the essential trait, and the one upon which all others depend, is the lack of precipitation. Just how little precipitation places an area in the desert category is not self-evident. Trewartha (1954) stated that the essential feature of a dry climate is that the potential evaporation from the soil surface and from the vegetation should exceed the average annual precipitation.

Meigs noted that, as temperature is a climatic factor that affects rate of evaporation most strongly, and as temperature observations are widely available, some sort of ratio involving precipitation and temperature is most useful in expressing the aridity of an area. Meigs therefore followed the system developed by Thornthwaite (1948) (discussed in chapter II), which uses an index based upon the adequacy of precipitation in relation to the hypothetical evapotranspiration of natural vegetation. Where the precipitation analyzed month by month is just adequate to supply all the water that would be needed for maximum evaporation and transpiration in the course of a year, the moisture index would be 0. Climates with an index between 0 and minus 20 are considered subhumid, between minus 20 and minus 40 semiarid, and below minus 40 arid. Meigs noted that within deserts there are many degrees of dryness; such terms as "arid," "desert," "semiarid," "semidesert," "absolute desert," "total desert," and "extreme desert," are used in many ways by many authorities. He followed Emberger and others in defining the true or extreme desert as one in which in a given locality at least 12 consecutive months without rainfall have been recorded, and in which there is not a regular seasonal rhythm of rainfall.

In mapping the world distributions of arid and semiarid climates, Meigs indicated the season of precipitation by use of the letters "a" (no distinct seasonality of precipitation), "b" (summer concentration of precipitation), and "c" (winter concentration). Noting that heat as well as water is essential to the growth and reproduction processes of plants, he also included a consideration of temperature, indicating on his maps the mean temperatures of the coldest and warmest months respectively. It is therefore possible to indicate, by means of his system, for each desert area the degree of aridity (extremely arid or arid), the season of the year when most of the precipitation occurs, and the temperatures of the hottest and coldest months.

In general he showed that the dry climates of the continents occur in five great provinces separated from one another by oceans or by wet equatorial zones. The bulk of the desert lies between 15° and 35° latitude (in both the northern and southern hemispheres), although extending to 55° N latitude in some cases. Of these five provinces the North Africa-Eurasia province is larger than all the remaining dry areas of the world combined. It includes the world's largest desert, the Sahara, and a series of other hot deserts and semiarid areas continuing eastward through the Arabian Peninsula, along the Persian Gulf, to Pakistan and India. To the north lie the milder cool-winter dry areas of the Mediterranean coast and Iran, while farther northward and eastward lie the vast deserts and steppes of the U.S.S.R., China, and Mongolia, with subfreezing winters and warm or hot summers. In East Africa lie the hot lowlands of the Somali-Chalbi, which bear certain affinities to much of the southern part of the Arabian Peninsula.

The South African dry province consists chiefly of the narrow elongated coastal desert of the Namib, and the Karroo and Kalahari and steppe uplands. The Australian dry province occupies a large portion of the continent, with hot climates prevailing in the northern half of the province and mild climates in the southern.

The South American dry province is confined to a strip along the west coast and an area on the east side of the Andes toward the southern portion of the continent.

The North American dry province resembles the North Africa-Eurasia province in variety of subdivision types, although the subdivisions are much smaller in North America. Dry upland areas analogous to those of Iran, Turkestan, and upland Arabia make up much of the province of the United States and Mexico. A small area bordering the Gulf of California is comparable to the Sahara by virtue of its scanty and irregular precipitation.

Reitan and Green, in their chapter on weather and climate, have made particular note of the fact that arid lands are found over a wide range of latitudes and come under the influence of nearly all the major wind and pressure belts. A variety of weather systems prevail and a variety of reasons for aridity exist. These include separation of the region from the oceanic moisture sources by topography or distance, the formation of dry, stable air masses that resist convective currents, and the lack of storm systems that create conditions favorable for precipitation.

THE MAJOR DESERTS

In this compendium thirteen major desert areas are recognized: Kalahari-Namib, Sahara, Somali-Chalbi, Arabian, Iranian, Thar, Turkestan, Takla-Makan, Gobi, Australian, Monte-Patagonian, Atacama-Peruvian, and North American. In the following pages these desert areas are briefly discussed as to location, climate, and landscape features including topography, soils, and vegetation. The general orientation material presented in this introductory chapter has for the most part been abstracted from the chapters that follow or other material supplied by the chapter authors. More detailed information on each of these subjects is to be found in the chapters.

The generalizations in the present chapter should be taken as gross orientation material; clearly statements such as those on the aridity of the southern Arabian Peninsula could be modified, when one looks more closely, by noting as exceptions the Asir, the ranges of Yemen and Aden, and the ranges of Muscat and Oman. Indeed, orographic effects that prevail in many desert mountain ranges make them exceptions to generalizations about aridity in many desert areas.

The extent and location of these desert areas is roughly indicated on pp. xxi-xxviii. Most of these major desert areas include more than one individual desert of somewhat distinctive character. For example, the small Iranian Desert, occupying portions of Iran, Afghanistan, and Pakistan, itself includes five main desert units: the Dasht-e-Kavir, the Kavir-i-Namak, the Dasht-e-Lut, the Dasht-i-Naomid, and the Dasht-i-Margo.

A. KALAHARI-NAMIB

According to Meigs (1966) the Namib extends 1,750 miles from Luanda (8° 45′ S) in Angola to St. Helena Bay (32° 45′ S) in the Republic of South Africa (see p. xxiii). The extreme desert extends from about 18° to 29° S latitude, or less than half the total length of the desert; its width from the coastline to the Great Western Escarpment is about 100 miles at most places. The Namib receives an average of less than 2 inches of rainfall but benefits from sea fog and dew, and in some areas it supports a scanty vegetation. Extreme desert conditions are found along the west coast and semiarid conditions inland toward the escarpment. In the northern and central portions it is bordered by the grasslands and thornbush country of the plateau. In the south it merges eastward into the Kalahari and Karroo. In the indistinct transition belt, widespread extension of xerophytic vegetation has occurred during the past 300 years.

The Kalahari, in popular concept, occupies Botswana (formerly Bechuanaland) and eastern South West Africa, from the Okavango River in the north to the northern border of South Africa in the south. The northern part, however, has neither the climate nor the vegetation of true desert; referred to locally as "thirstland" and lacking surface water because of deep layers of subsurface sand, it supports a year-round stand of trees and grass, and luxuriant growths of ephemerals following the December-to-March rains.

From 22° S latitude southward to the Orange River, however, the Kalahari is more truly desert, receiving only little and unreliable rainfall in the summer, and supporting scattered small trees, bushes, and, in occasional wet years, summer grasses. South of the Orange River the Karroo subdesert receives both summer and winter rains, and the wooded grassland gives way to scattered low succulent shrubs.

The Kalahari-Namib desert of southern Africa lies in a transition zone with a tropical storm pattern on its equatorward margins and winter cyclonic precipitation on its poleward borders.

The Namib varies from extreme desert conditions to desert and from hot to mild (but it is mostly mild). In the northern part there is no seasonality to precipitation; in the southern portion winter precipitation is the rule.

The Kalahari is arid according to the Meigs classification, with summer precipitation and mild-to-hot temperatures in the north, and with winter precipitation and cool-to-warm winters and warm-to-hot summers in the south.

The northern terrain subdivision comprising about 60 per cent of the entire length of the Namib, and extending from Luanda to Walvis Bay, consists principally of bedrock and extensive flat gravel surfaces, with scattered sand accumulations along the coast. The central subdivision from Walvis Bay to Lüderitz is a vast extent of tremendous sand dunes with some crests 800 feet above the troughs. They occur in windrows with a northwest-southeast orientation. Near the coast the sands are yellow-white becoming brick red 20 to 80 miles inland. The southern terrain subdivision between Lüderitz and St. Helena Bay is mostly a flat rock platform with low rock ridges and shallow deposits of sand and gravel.

The true Kalahari is a huge sand-filled basin. The landscape is dominated by gentle dunes 100 to 500 feet apart and often miles in length. There are no large areas of rock.

The soils of the Kalahari-Namib desert area are generally weakly developed. In the Namib, soil development is nonexistent on the dunes and the bedrock surfaces. Cementation of subsurface layers by lime occurs beneath the gravel or stone pavements of the northern Namib. The soils vary from slightly alkaline to slightly acid, and are dominantly reddish-brown in color. Deep soils are the rule with soil textures ranging from sand to clay. Saline soils are found in depressions in the south, bordering pans or dry lakes.

The Namib has very little vegetation. Many plants are leafless, most are succulent, and some are halophytic. The higher plants do not show any visible adaptation to fogs, but their locations and spacings indicate that they make much use of condensed moisture, especially from the radiation fogs. Lichens, subsisting on condensed moisture, grow conspicuously on the windward (seaward) side of most rocks. In the inner Namib, a short grass develops in the autumns (April-June) following rainier summers.

In the Kalahari, trees, tall shrubs (chiefly *Acacia* species) and grasses (both perennial and annual) dominate in the north, while the south is a land of low, scattered shrubs, with scattered acacias along the dry watercourses and grasses in rainy years.

B. SAHARA

The Sahara, largest desert in the world, extends from the Atlantic coast of Africa to the Red Sea (see p. xxii). It measures more than 3,000 miles from east to west and 800 to 1,200 miles from north to south. Its northern boundary starts near the Wadi Dra on the Atlantic Coast near Goulimine, follows eastward along the Saharan Fault to Erfoud, Figuig,

and Biskra, and there dips southward to the Gulf of Gabès. The southern boundary, which generally follows the 16th parallel (north), is not as well defined, being a broad transition area between desert and semidesert. The total area of the Sahara is between 3,000,000 and 3,500,000 square miles.

The Sahara is not only the largest desert on Earth, but also includes some of the hottest and driest areas and the greatest expanses of sand. The Great Tanezrouft has an annual precipitation of less than 1 inch and may experience several years without appreciable precipitation. The highest temperature recorded anywhere is 136.4° F in the shade at El Azizia in Libya. Libya also has the most extensive sand desert in the Sahara, covering an area of about 750 by 300 miles.

The Sahara has a Mediterranean climate in the north and a tropical climate in the south. The Mediterranean climate, with an emphasis on winter precipitation, is the predominant influence extending from Spanish Sahara through Morocco, Algeria, Tunisia, Libya, and Egypt. The central portion of this area is extremely dry and hot. The northern portion has cool-to-warm winters and warm-to-hot summers.

The southern Sahara falls in the intertropical convergence zone. Countries containing tropical desert portions of the Sahara are Cameroon, Chad, Mali, Mauritania, Niger, Nigeria, Sudan, and Upper Volta. This area has warm winters, hot summers and predominantly irregular and scanty summer rainfall.

The Sahara embraces a variety of landscapes, including mountain massifs, great flat areas of stone and gravel, and huge expanses of sand. Geologically it is a series of elevated areas and closed basins. The great chotts or depressions are filled with saline silt and sand deposited by rivers that seldom flow now.

The elevated areas include the foothills of the Atlas on the north, the great Ahaggar (Hoggar) massif in southern Algeria and the 11,000 foot Tibesti massif in northern Chad, as well as lesser plateaus and mountain ranges. The elevated plateaus or hamadas are often very extensive. Outwash material from them eroded by wind into rocky desert pavement is the source of regs, which often cover large areas. Extensive sand dune areas, called ergs, have formed from wind blown sand. The largest of these ergs, located in the Libyan desert, embraces an expanse of sand as large as France. Second in size is the Grand Erg Occidental in Algeria.

For the Sahara as a whole, sandy and stony materials are dominant, vegetative cover is very sparse, susceptibility to wind erosion is high, water infiltration rates are good, soils of depressions are saline, water erosion is locally severe near mountainous areas, stony desert plains (regs) and dune chains (ergs) are widespread, fine-textured material is rare outside of depressions, and soil development is weak; compact and indurated layers (crusts) are largely restricted to the northwest section of the desert in association with calcareous bedrock. Ergs and regs are neutral to slightly alkaline, soils of the depressions are moderately to strongly alkaline, and grey is the dominant soil color, although in some places, mostly in the south, soils have a reddish color. In the extremely arid parts of the Sahara the surface materials have been little altered by vegetation and climate and properly should not be called soils. The regs are similar to the gobi of China and the stony plains of Australia.

The Sahara is essentially a desert of herbs and small shrubs, with larger shrubs and trees appearing where moisture is most abundant. Ephemerals are common, particularly in the northern portion. Halophytes are found in saline areas. Succulents are not prominent. A large portion of the central part of the Sahara is almost devoid of any plant life. With increasing precipitation plant life increases, appearing first in wadis, depressions, and other sites where the precipitation is augmented by flow from adjacent or perhaps remote areas.

C. SOMALI-CHALBI

Delineations of the Somali-Chalbi (see p. xxii) vary according to scientists; Trewartha (1954), in his application of Köppen's system, extended the *BW* (desert) climate classification in a narrow band along the African shores of the Red Sea and Gulf of Aden and, in a slightly wider band, southward along the east coast bordering the Indian Ocean to just south of the equator, with an extension inland near the southern extremity. Meigs (1966) includes an area along the coast of the Red Sea extending northward to approximately 12° north latitude. The western boundary of his *A* (arid) area starts at the coast at approximately 40° east and extends southward, bearing slightly to the east, to a point at approximately 10° N, then eastward nearly to Cape Guardafui, then in a southwesterly direction, following along the western boundary of Somali and extending into Kenya to the South. He also shows an *A* area surrounding Lake Rudolf.

The Somali-Chalbi area, like the southern Sahara, is under the intertropical convergence influence, but the low rainfall is related to orography, thermal low pressure, and coastal upwelling. The (light) precipitation season varies from winter or no seasonality in the north of the area to summer in the

south, with a lack of definite seasonality in between. The climate is generally hot with little temperature variation from winter to summer.

The geology of this region is noteworthy for its diversity. The coastal-zone strip consists chiefly of raised coral reefs. Inland are extensive eolian and alluvial deposits; limestone areas include the Danakil Alps. In the west and south are large areas of crystalline rocks; volcanic rocks of various ages are also encountered.

The soils of the Somali-Chalbi are largely undeveloped. There are some deep soils in the upland areas and in river flood plains. Stony plains are common, but sand dunes are largely restricted to coastal areas. Many of the skeletal soils are saline and may contain gypsiferous layers.

The vegetation of the Somali-Chalbi resembles that of the warmer parts of the Sahara and the southern Arabian desert. Scanty vegetation grows in the area where annual precipitation falls below 4 inches and the dry period lasts six months or more. Widely spaced herbs, grasses, undershrubs, and dwarf trees are found in slightly more favorable locations. In areas where conditions are more favorable, the shrubs are larger, more closely spaced, and intermixed with grasses. Where average annual rainfall reaches or exceeds about 8 inches, shrub and tree savannas are found.

D. ARABIAN DESERT

The Arabian Desert (see p. xxiv) includes the nations of the Arabian Peninsula and Jordan, Iraq, Israel, Syria, and a small part of Iran; roughly a rectangle, its longer axis extends from southeast to northwest through the Arabian Peninsula to the Mediterranean Sea. It includes the Syrian, Saudi, Aden and Tihama deserts, and the very dry Rub' al Khali.

The Arabian desert area has been classified in slightly differing ways by Meigs (1953) and by Emberger *et al.* (Unesco, 1963). Meigs (1953) classified most of the area either *E* (extremely arid) or *A* (arid) except for high elevations in the southwest of the Arabian Peninsula, a small area bordering the Gulf of Oman, the northernmost part of Iraq, and the northern two-thirds of Syria. The bioclimatic map prepared by Emberger and his associates shows the area varying from "sub-desertic" to "true desert" with xerothermic indexes ranging between 200 and 365.

The southern portion of the Arabian Desert is much like the Sahara, with a small area of extreme aridity along the southwest coast of the Arabian Peninsula and a larger area in the southeast. Practically all of the peninsula is arid or extremely arid. A Mediterranean influence and winter precipitation govern in the northern third; scanty rainfall occurs any season of the year in the southern half. The southern portion is hot in all seasons; moving northward the winters gradually change to milder, but without much, if any, relief from summer heat.

The western corner of this desert is characterized by a coastal plain and a mountainous belt with elevations up to 3,600 feet dropping off on the east side to deep valleys, which are bordered on the east by plateau country. There are sand dunes along the sea coast, but most of the area has a cover of desert soils.

The Arabian Peninsula has a basement of crystalline rocks that reaches an altitude of more than 9,300 feet in the western highlands. It is overlaid in places with sedimentary rocks and by great sand desert areas, including the great An Nafud (Nefud) in the north and the Rub' al Khali in the south-central area.

Except for Israel, eastern Iraq, and southwestern Iran there is little detailed information available on soil. In general, surficial deposits of the Arabian Desert consist of sandy and stony materials, with fine-textured (largely silt) saline sediments occurring extensively in the lower Mesopotamian plain and in the plains of central Saudi Arabia. Sand dunes of the erg type occur in a broad arc extending from southern Jordan through northeastern and eastern Saudi Arabia to the vast expanse of the Rub' al Khali. Stony and gravelly plains cut by wadis, along with barren and rocky desert mountains, form another arc beginning in western Iraq and curving through Jordan, the Negev in Israel, Sinai, western Saudi Arabia, Yemen, and South Arabia. Calcrete is locally important in the Ad Dahna' and As Summan areas of Saudi Arabia.

The same general type of vegetation as that found in the Sahara extends eastward across Asia to India. There is general agreement that this is a phytogeographical region with common characteristics. It has been called the Saharo-Sindian Region, extending from the Atlantic coast of North Africa through the Sahara, the Sinai Peninsula, extratropical Arabia, southern Iraq, Iran, West Pakistan, Afghanistan, and into India to Sind. Also, portions of the Arabian desert are included within two other phytogeographical regions, the Irano-Turanian and Sudano-Deccanian. The former includes deserts and steppes in the cooler part of the desert and the latter in the tropical portion.

In the north *Zygophyllum dumosum* is the key plant, along with a large number of winter annuals and some succulent perennials. In the southern part the vegetation consists largely of ephemeral plants that grow only following rains. Perennials include many halophytes but almost no true succulents. Some vegetation is found in the driest portion, even in the Rub' al Khali.

E. IRANIAN DESERT

The Iranian Desert (see p. xxiv), which includes parts of Iran, Afghanistan, and Pakistan (the Baluchistan area), is one of the smallest desert areas and one of the least known. Meigs (1953) has classified this desert as *Ac*13 and *Ac*14 (arid with cool winters, winter precipitation, and warm-to-hot summers). It includes five major units: the Dasht-e-Kavir in the northwest, the Kavir-i-Namak in the north, the Dasht-e-Lut in the southwest, the Dasht-i-Naomid in the east, and the Dasht-i-Margo in the southeast.

Petrov (1966-1967) has shown that it is useful to view the Iranian desert as the southwestern end of a zone that includes the Turkestan Desert and extends to eastern China. In the present compendium, however, we have chosen what we feel is an equally fruitful method in discussing the Thar immediately following the Iranian Desert; we then return to treat the Turkestan-thru-Gobi. In Petrov's terminology (as translated) the Iranian and Turkestan deserts are in "Middle Asia"; we use "Central Asia" to cover Turkestan-thru-Gobi.

The Iranian Desert has primarily a Mediterranean type climate with winter rainfall produced by cyclonic storm systems. The winters are cool and the summers hot.

Grey desert soils, sierozems, lithosols, regosols, and saline soils constitute the majority of the surface materials in the Iranian Desert. Soils are generally coarse-textured and undeveloped. Commonly they are calcareous throughout the profile, deep except on rough, broken land, very low in organic matter, frequently covered with desert pavement, grey in color, and saline in local depressions and in extensive salt marshes.

Very little is known botanically about the Iranian Desert. The major phytogeographical regions are the Irano-Turanian and Saharo-Sindian. The vegetation tends toward Mediterranean types on the west. Many of the desert areas at the higher elevations with cold winters are dominated by *Artemisia herba-alba* communities similar in appearance to those found in the Great Basin Desert of the United States. In the south where summers are very hot the plant population is quite scanty.

F. THE THAR

The Thar (see pp. xxiv, xxv), sometimes called the Indian Desert, includes the arid portions of western India and eastern West Pakistan. Some authors identify the area eastward to the Aravalli Range and southward into Sind as arid. There is some question, however, as to how much of this area is naturally arid and how much of its arid appearance has resulted from the activities of man.

The Thar is in a transition zone between major wind belts. Midlatitude cyclones produce moderate amounts of winter precipitation in the northern and western portions, while the eastern portion receives its rainfall from the monsoon circulation that dominates the subcontinent in summer. The monsoon movement of moist air terminates in western India, resulting in a small and irregular rainfall in the Thar. Summers are hot and winters warm throughout the area.

The entire desert consists of level to gently sloping plains broken by some dunes and low barren hills. For the Thar as a whole, interspersed sandy and medium- and fine-textured surface materials are dominant. Gravelly and skeletal soils are restricted to mountains, hills, footslopes, and water courses, none extensive. Soil salinity is high in the uncultivated fine-textured soils and in much of the irrigated land. Sand dunes occur within the Thar Desert area of the Indus plain and more widely outside the plain.

The Thar lies near the eastern end of the Saharo-Sindian region. The vegetation is influenced strongly by edaphic conditions, with communities varying distinctively among sand, gravel, and rock areas. Trees and shrubs appear to be more common, especially on open soils, than is average for the Saharo-Sindian region.

The vegetation can be divided into five plant communities: salt desert, clay desert, stone desert, sand desert, and riverside thickets. The vegetation of the salt desert is extremely scanty, dominated by *Halostachys caspica* bushes and a few summer annuals. The clay deserts are very dry with grasses dominating along with some bulb and tuberous plants. The stone-desert areas are unfavorable to plants and support only a sparse growth of small woody plants. The sand deserts invaded by the grass *Aristida pennata* later support a variety of shrubs and trees. The riverside thickets include several species of trees and shrubs.

G. CENTRAL ASIA: THE TURKESTAN DESERT

The Turkestan Desert (see p. xxiv) lies in the U.S.S.R. between 36° and 48° N and between 50° and 83° E. It is bounded on the west by the Caspian Sea, on the south by the mountains bordering Iran and Afghanistan, on the east by the mountains bordering Sinkiang, and on the north by the Kirgiz Step'. The region is an immense undrained basin with parts below sea level. Very young dry land areas are encountered, formed as a result of drying up of lake basins and the drop in the level of the Caspian Sea. The average precipitation varies from 3 to 8 inches, falling in winter or spring, leaving the summer months without precipitation. Except in the far north, the Turkestan Desert has a Mediterranean type of moisture distribution but with colder winters than in typical Mediterranean climates. Throughout the area winters are mostly cold and the summers hot or very hot. The temperature range is great: summer high temperatures reach 115° F and winter low may drop to minus 40° F.

Petrov (1966-1967) uses a term translated as "Middle Asia" to include the Turkestan Desert and the Iranian Desert, with "Central Asia" reserved for the Takla-Makan, Gobi, and associated desert areas. In this compendium we include the Turkestan-to-Gobi as Central Asia; we do not use the other term.

Two great sandy expanses are included: the Kara-Kum (meaning black sands), covering about 86 million acres, and the Kyzyl-Kum (meaning red sands) covering about 49 million acres.

Elevations within the basin vary from 85 feet below sea level near the Caspian Sea to about 1200 feet toward the eastern boundary.

The Turkestan Desert includes extensive sand dunes, loessial or alluvial plains, fine-textured depressions or river terraces, and flood plains. The sand dunes of the Kara-Kum and Kyzyl-Kum Deserts are interspersed with medium- and fine-textured depressions with saline and sodium-affected soils. Stony and gravelly soils are confined to the footslopes of the mountains on the south and east and the plateaus in the northwest.

Two large rivers, the Amu-Dar'ya and Syr-Dar'ya, rise in the high mountains southeast of the Kyzyl-Kum and flow northwestward into the Aral Sea. The Ili River rises in the Ala-Tan Mountains and flows into Lake Balkhash. The Amu-Dar'ya and the Syr-Dar'ya support extensive streambank vegetation (tugai). To some extent other vegetation is supported by underground water, especially in salt flats.

The vegetation varies with soil conditions. *Poa bulbosa* is the dominant spring plant in the clay desert portion, which is the driest of all habitats. The stone deserts, which are also unfavorable for plant growth, support a sparse stand of small shrubs. On the sandy areas *Aristida pennata* is the first invader, followed by shrubs and trees. The salt desert areas have shallow water tables and an extremely scanty vegetation dominated by halophytic shrubs and a few summer annuals. The animal life is richer in the Turkestan than in the Takla-Makan and Gobi group.

H. CENTRAL ASIA:
THE TAKLA-MAKAN AND GOBI GROUP

Desert and semidesert comprise the most extensive natural region of China, more than 675,000 square miles extending to the middle course of the Hwang Ho (Yellow River) in the east (see p. xxv). The Gobi, largest desert in Asia, lies in Outer Mongolia (Mongolian Peoples' Republic) and mainland China's Inner Mongolian Autonomous Region. The deserts of Outer Mongolia change gradually, going northward into desert steppes and then into steppes. To the southwest of the Gobi lies the Takla-Makan; between them and south of the Gobi lie other desert areas, including notably the Bei Shan (Peishan, Beichan), Tsaidam, Ala Shan (Ala-Chan), and Ordos. For Central Asia, in addition to the place-name sources given in the introduction to this chapter, the maps in Petrov's publications of 1962 and 1966-1967 were required.

The desert areas of Asia represent diverse conditions. The mean elevations are: Dzungaria, 500 to 2000 feet; Takla-Makan, 2300 to 4600 feet; Bei Shan (Beichan), 3300 to 6600 feet; Ala Shan, 2600 to 5300 feet; Ordos, 3600 to 4600 feet; and Tsaidam, 8900 to 10,200 feet. Some of the oldest geological formations are represented, with some sedimentary deposits and extensive Quaternary materials including alluvial and extensive eolian deposits. The Bei Shan and Ordos, like the Kazakh hilly area, are very ancient dry land areas (from the Cretaceous). The areas with the largest expanses of sands are the Dzungarian, Takla-Makan, and Ala Shan. "Gobi" surfaces of varying types are widely distributed in the following lowlands and mountains: Ordos, Ala Shan, Gachoun Gobi, Bei Shan, Nan Shan, Kunlun, Gobi Mongol, western Tsaidam, Holan Shan, Dzungaria, and eastern Tyan-Shan. Rocky and pebbly deserts predominate in this part of the world, in contrast to the Turkestan Desert. In general, the area lacks external drainage and receives very little rainfall; mean annual precipitation seldom exceeds 4 inches and may be below 2 inches. The driest parts are eastern Kashgaria, Bei Shan, and Tsaidam. In the Turfan and Hami depressions, both below sea level, the summers are hotter than in the tropics and the frost-free season is 240 days; elsewhere the vegetation must contend with extremely low winter temperatures (January

means from minus 6° C to minus 19° C) and warm summers (July averages of 24° C to 26° C).

Of the Gobi and Takla-Makan group, organic life is most developed in the Ordos. Only in the deserts of Dzungaria does the vegetation approach the character and abundance of that in eastern Kazakhstan. Many other areas are barren. The valley of the Tarim River contains dense and in some places impassable forests similar to the tugais of the Amu Dar'ya as they might have been before the trees were felled.

The animal life, both wild and domesticated, is rich in the eastern portion of the Gobi and Takla-Makan group, but not in other parts of the group.

1. Takla-Makan

The Takla-Makan (see p. xxv), in common with other Central Asian deserts, owes its dry climate to the high mountains and great distance separating it from moisture sources. The Tibetan plateau, 2,000 miles in length and with an average elevation of 12,-000 feet, forms an effective barrier to moisture moving northward from the Indian Ocean. It is an area of hot summers and cold winters with no particular seasonality for the scanty precipitation. A large portion of the Takla-Makan is extremely arid. The remainder of the area is arid as far as can be determined from available records.

The southward-moving, shifting sands occupy much of the central part of the Takla-Makan. Soils vary from coarse-textured sandy and gravelly material, with surface stones (gobi) on the footslopes of the mountains, to sandy to medium-textured alluvial fans and plains becoming fine-textured in the river flood plains, and finally to the dunes of loose sand in the center. A similar variety of soils occurs in the Dzungarian area. The soils at the base of the mountains are low in soluble salts, with salinity becoming greater toward the center of the basin.

Adjacent to flowing streams grows a lush tugai vegetation. Elsewhere the vegetation is sparse. The sand deserts, which make up the greatest part of the area, support sparse herbaceous vegetation where moisture is low and a scanty woody vegetation on larger more stabilized dunes. Halophytic vegetation occurs in the old valleys, lake depressions, and river deltas.

2. Gobi

The Gobi is a repeating sequence of mountains, gravelly and stony footslopes, plains, and gentle slopes and depressions, giving a mountain-and-basin landscape with some basins up to 5-20 miles across. Sand dunes are extensive in some parts of the Gobi and may be found nearly anywhere on the plains;

they are not nearly as extensive, however, as within the Takla-Makan. In addition to the widespread sand dunes, brown gobi soils are the most extensive types. The soils are nonsaline, nongypsiferous, coarse-textured, with lime accumulations in the subsoil. Saline soils occur in the many closed depressions, and sodium-affected soils are common on the slopes.

The vegetation of the Gobi has eastern and western affiliations, with the latter dominating. The vegetation of the Gobi plains is characterized by shrubs and semishrubs. On unstabilized dunes grasses and some widely spaced shrubs are found. The vegetative cover is greatest on stabilized dunes and is dependent upon depth to the water table.

I. AUSTRALIAN DESERTS

Records are lacking for much of the arid portion of Australia, and a considerable difference of opinion exists among Australians about the extent and nature of aridity there (e.g., Keast, Crocker, and Christian, 1959; note especially the statement therein by Wood, p. 291). It would appear that at least half and perhaps considerably more of the Australian continent is arid. Some deserts are sandy; the others are stony. The three largest deserts, the Great Sandy, the Great Victoria, and the Simpson (Arunta) consist of parallel sand ridges sometimes more than 100 miles long. The stony desert areas include the Gibson desert in Western Australia, the desert area west of Lake Eyre in South Australia, and the Sturt desert in the northeast corner of South Australia extending into Queensland.

The arid land of Australia (see p. xxviii) is affected by tropical weather in the north and by mid-latitude cyclones in the south. The climate is of the monsoonal type north of about 20° S, and Mediterranean type south of about 32° S. The intermediate area receives little benefit from either system. The entire arid area has mild winters and warm-to-hot summers.

The desert area of Australia lies mostly on the Great Plateau (1,000 to 2,000 feet elevation) constituting the pre-Cambrian shield of a basement complex of Archean rocks; lying above this are longitudinal sand ridges of great extent. Some of these were formed in a previous period of aridity, but most are active and trend parallel with the direction of the dominant sand-shifting wind. There is no external drainage, except close to the edge of the continent.

The variety of soils found in Australia is similar to those of other arid regions, with the exception that loose, eroding sand dunes appear to be limited in extent. Rather, the sand dunes, which are common, are fixed by a fairly dense vegetative cover. Among the more important soils are stony tablelands, sand

plains having ironstone gravel, coarse-textured and deep brown soils, red and brown hardpan soils, deep red earths of medium to fine texture, and saline- and sodium-affected soils.

The landscape of arid Australia gives the appearance of a vast plain interrupted by occasional desert mountains, large and small tablelands, and sand dunes, with many saline depressions and flood plains of intermittent streams. The dominant soil colors are red and reddish brown. Surface soil textures range from coarse to fine; surface-soil pH frequently is on the acid side of neutrality; calcareous, saline, and gypsiferous subsoils are common; and organic matter content is very low. The red-earth soils are more highly leached and show much more development than would be expected under present climatic conditions; siliceous hardpans and silicified surface stones occur extensively in the interior; and sand dunes and sandy soils in general are stabilized in position unless the surface is disturbed. Arroyos and wadis are less common than in North America, North Africa, and the Middle East. All in all the soils are rather infertile.

Australian deserts have no succulents and very few spiny plants. The most characteristic plants are perennial evergreen tussock grasses called "spinifex" and small trees or shrubs belonging to the genus *Acacia*. In depressions and on more saline soils, salt bushes and various members of the Chenopodiaceae family are characteristic.

J. MONTE-PATAGONIAN DESERT

The Monte-Patagonian Desert (see p. xxvii), is located in the rain shadow of the Andes Mountains. The northern portion, the Monte, is an area of mountains, valleys, and extensive depressions occupied by saline deposits. Its extension into Bolivia is sometimes treated with Atacama information for convenience. The southern portion, the Patagonian Desert, consists of low tablelands dissected by stream valleys.

1. Monte

According to Morello (1958) the Monte phytogeographical province extends from 24° 35′ S to 44° 20′ S in the center of Patagonia, and from 62° 54′ W on the Atlantic coast to 69° 50′ W inland. It is located in the pre-Andean region occupying intermountain bolsons (flat valleys) where the moist air currents rarely penetrate. Precipitation, which occurs mostly in summer, is generally less than 8 inches. Winters are cool and summers are mild. No permanent streams reach the ocean from this area.

Monte type conditions develop in depressions, which are typically circular or elliptical. They are flat-bottomed and often limited by very high mountain ranges. Main landscape types are muddy depressions (barrioles), salt pans, dunes, slopes, badlands, permanent rivers, mountains torrents, brackish soils, alluvial cones, and tablelands.

Mountain and hill soils in and near the Andes are lithosols. The soils grade from coarse to medium in texture toward the plains; in the valleys the soils are usually gravelly or sandy, with saline soils occupying the small (and large) closed basins.

Much of the Monte has a cover of resinous bushes, with Zygophyllaceae bushes being dominant. Many species are totally or partially aphyllous. Trees, if present at all, are found on river borders where they form gallery forests. Perennial grasses are limited to moist places.

2. Patagonian Desert

Meigs (1966) delineates an arid zone along the entire length of Argentina, bordering the eastern base of the Andes Mountains to the west, stretching eastward an average distance of about 350 miles into the plains, and extending southward all the way to the sea. It forms a coastal desert and steppe for 1000 miles from approximately 39° to 53° S. Meigs states that the Patagonian Desert (see p. xxvii), the only high latitude east-coast desert, has no counterpart among the Earth's deserts. It owes its dryness to the Andes Mountains, which form a barrier to the rain-bearing air masses from the west, and to the cold Falkland current off the east coast.

The climate is cold temperate, very dry, and windy. Precipitation varies from 6 to 12 inches, falling principally during the warm season. The terrain consists of extensive plateaus more than 3000 feet high in many places. The plateaus slope toward the sea and end in cliffs along the coast. The rivers flow through deeply incised narrow valleys. Surface soils are generally medium textured over lime-cemented gravels and slightly acid. Because of the gravelly surface, wind erosion is slight in spite of the continuously strong winds. Low-lying soils tend to be marshy and remain wet throughout most of the year. The vegetation is dominated by widely spaced clumps of xerophytic grasses and low cushion-type shrubs.

K.   ATACAMA-PERUVIAN

The recent Unesco publication (Meigs, 1966) on the geography of coastal deserts summarizes a great amount of information on the deserts of this area (see p. xxvii). Meigs describes the Atacama as the driest coastal desert in the world; the vegetation must contend with an annual rainfall at Arica and Iquique of less than 0.04 inches. At the southern limit of the Atacama, near the town of Copiapó, the annual rain-

fall is 2.52 inches. On the basis of rainfall and vegetation, the Río Limari, 60 miles south of La Serena, is taken as the southern limit of the "regular" desert. To the north the desert of Chile merges into the Peruvian coastal desert which extends northward nearly to Ecuador.

The Peruvian coastal desert becomes slightly less arid northward as does the Atacama southward. The whole area has a mild climate year-round with little variation in temperature from summer to winter. Heavy fogs and high humidity are the rule. East of the coast range, especially in Chile, the climate becomes more continental with greater range in temperature, but it remains arid eastward to the lower slopes of the Andes.

The Peruvian portion is a narrow band dissected by more than 40 transverse valleys with a substantial flow of water from the Andes from October to April. The Atacama section of Chile is characterized by coastal ranges rising sharply almost from the water's edge to summits of 3000 to 3500 feet. East of this is the Longitudinal Depression, consisting of a series of undrained basins 25 to 50 miles wide. The floors of these basins are made up of alluvial fans from material washed down the canyons from the Andes, and vary from 2000 to 3500 feet in altitude.

The soils of northern Chile include skeletal soils of mountains and plains, recent alluvial soils of the river valleys, and old lacustrine soils. The central plains have weakly developed coarse-textured soils and stony deposits. Marine coastal terraces continue into Peru; they are undeveloped in the south but show moderate development northward. Sand dunes are common.

The Atacama-Peruvian Desert is almost without vegetation except along streams. On slopes moistened by mist or drizzle during the winter a sparse stand of *Tillandsia* may exist with a few lichens in association. Lomas, barren mist-bathed slopes with ephemeral vegetation, occur between 500 and 5000 feet above sea level.

L.   NORTH AMERICAN DESERTS

According to Shreve (1942) the North American desert extends southward from central and eastern Oregon, embracing nearly all of Nevada and Utah except the higher mountains, into southwestern Wyoming and western Colorado, reaching westward in southern California to the eastern base of the Sierra Nevada, the San Bernardino Mountains, and the Cuyamaca Mountains. From southern Utah, the desert extends into northeastern Arizona and also into western and southwestern Arizona.

Desert areas extend southward along the eastern coast of northern Baja California, in the lee of the (mountain ranges) Sierra de Juárez and Sierra de San Pedro Mártir. South of these ranges it extends across the peninsula as far south as the northern end of Sierra de la Giganta; farther southward, it is limited to the Pacific coast, a very narrow strip along the coast of the Gulf of California, and parts of the lower elevations in the cape region at the tip of Baja California. On the mainland of Mexico, it occupies the lowlands of Sonora as far south as the delta of the Yaqui River.

On the highlands of southeastern Arizona and southern New Mexico, the continuity of the desert is broken by a desert-grassland transition. At a slightly lower elevation it reappears in the valleys of the Río Grande and the Pecos River, extending as far east into Texas as the lower course of Devils River. Southward into Mexico, the desert extends continuously through eastern Chihuahua state and nearly all of Coahuila, being broken only by a few higher mountains and elevated areas of grassland. Farther south, the desert is confined to eastern Durango, northern Zacateca, the western margin of Nuevo León, and the northern part of San Luis Potosí.

In the north an isolated area of desert occupies part of the Columbia River basin in eastern Washington and southern Idaho, while in the south several detached areas occur in Hidalgo and Puebla, notably the valleys of Ixmiquilpán, Actopán, Mezquital, and Tehuacán.

The deserts of North America owe their aridity to a variety of conditions. Orographic barriers are most important in the north, and in such local areas as the San Joaquin Valley of California, while the southern portion comes under the influence of a subtropical high pressure cell. The southern portion of the arid region has a summer maximum of precipitation. The intermediate regions, such as central Arizona, receive some precipitation in both seasons. There is an extremely arid area around the north end of the Gulf of California with limited extension northward in California, including Death Valley. The Chihuahuan and Sonoran deserts have a mild to hot climate and the Great Basin desert has cold winters and warm summers.

The soils of the deserts of North America belong to the red desert, desert, sierozem, calcisol solonchak, solonetz, lithosol, regosol and alluvial great soil groups. Because of the great variations of climate, physiography and geology, there is also a great diversity of soils. Sand dunes and hummocks are smaller and cover much smaller proportions of the desert areas in North America than in desert areas of North Africa and Arabia.

The vegetation of the North American deserts is of two general types, sagebrush and saltbushes in the cooler portions, and mixed shrubs and succulents in the warmer portions. The two communities which are most widespread in the Great Basin Desert are those dominated by sagebrush (*Artemisia tridentata*) and saltbush (*Atriplex confertifolia*). The two are often associated but the latter appears chiefly at lower elevations and in more alkaline soil. These communities apear in pure stands forming monotonous gray-green communities, with their boundaries determined by changes in soil conditions. Although the southern deserts may have large communities dominated by creosotebush (*Larrea tridentata*), which gives a darker green but equally monotonous appearance, the variable topography gives rise to mixed stands of vegetation including large shrubs, small trees, and a variety of succulents.

PERTINENT PUBLICATIONS

Keast, A., R. L. Crocker, and C. S. Christian, eds.
1959 Biogeography and ecology in Australia. Monographiae Biologicae 8:1-640.
A comprehensive discussion of biogeography and ecology in Australia by a group of 40 scientists, covering the environment, man, native flora and fauna, pests, conservation, and agricultural uses. It includes 37 topics prepared by individual writers. The book points out the problems as well as the resources. It also brings out the differences of opinion as to what constitutes the arid portion of Australia.

Meigs, P.
1953 World distribution of arid and semi-arid homoclimates. *In* Reviews of research on arid zone hydrology. Unesco, Paris. Arid Zone Programme 1:203-209.
On the basis of Thornthwaite's (1948) classification of climates, Meigs categorized and mapped the arid and semiarid areas of the world by season of rainfall, maximum temperature of the hottest month, and minimum temperature of the coldest month. The original maps which accompanied this paper were dated 1952 and revised in 1960.

────

1966 Geography of coastal deserts. Unesco, Paris. Arid Zone Research 28. 140 p. 14 maps.

Morello, J.
1958 La Provincia fitogeográfica del Monte. Universidad de Tucumán, Instituto Miguel Lillo, Opera Lilloana 2. 155 p.
A very comprehensive publication on the phytogeographical province of the Monte; the best available reference for this area. The paper gives information on the limits, physiography, climatology, floristic composition, ecological types, and types of vegetation of the Monte. The climate of the Monte is discussed in detail in relation to the response of plants to climatological factors. The autecology of the dominant species in each community is discussed in detail. The author states that an effort has been made to gather, in the present paper, the largest possible quantity of exact data on the climate physiography, ecological types, and types of vegetation of the Monte—this in order to provide other scientists in arid zones such data as will permit them to make comparative studies with other similar regions of the world.

Paylore, P.
1967 Arid-lands research institutions, a world directory. University of Arizona Press, Tucson. 268 p.

Petrov, M. P.
1962 Types des déserts de l' Asie centrale. Annales de Géographie 71:131-155.
An excellent discussion of the types of deserts of Central Asia, starting from the Ordos in the far east and ending with the Tarim depression and Tsaidam on the west. Most of the rain in this area occurs from June to September. The precipitation is tied to the Pacific ocean and dryness due to the high mountains increases from east to west. Provides a comprehensive discussion of climate, soils, and vegetation of the desert area, and identifies 11 principal types of desert landscapes.

────

1966- Pustyni TSentral'noi Asii. Nauka, Leningrad. 2
1967 vols. (Translation of Vol. 1 available from JPRS as 39,145; of Vol. 2 as 42,772).
(The deserts of Central Asia)
The two volumes on the deserts of Central Asia were received too late to be covered in full in the various chapters, but they are worthy of special attention since they provide very complete and comprehensive information on the Iranian Desert and those of the Soviet Union, Outer Mongolia, and China. Volume 1 covers the Ordos, Alashan, and Peishan (Bei Shan) deserts and Volume 2 the Hohsi Corridor, Tsaidam, and Tarim Basin. For each of the major subdivisions Petrov includes a physical geographic description; review of literature; basic features of the geological structure; topography; the origin, character, and distribution of sands; climate; surface and ground waters; soil cover; and vegetation cover. The texts include many illustrations, Cyrillic and non-Cyrillic bibliographies, indexes of geographic names, and Latin plant names. All in all they represent an excellent source of information for these deserts.

Shreve, F.
1942 The desert vegetation of North America. Botanical Review 8(4):195-246.
A basic study and discussion of the desert vegetation of North America; contains the best overall description, particularly of the warmer desert areas. Desert vegetation, life forms, structure, floristic composition, and geographic areas are discussed for each of the four great desert regions of North America: the Great Basin, the Mojave, Sonoran, and the Chihuahuan.

Thornthwaite, C. W.
1948 An approach toward a rational classification of climate. Geographical Review 38(1):55-94.
A key paper in which Thornthwaite advanced the idea of potential evapotranspiration and the methods for computing it. The concept is discussed and illustrated with the use of water balance studies for several stations. Meigs' later classification and distribution of arid homoclimates (Meigs, 1953) uses this concept and the related index derived by Thornthwaite. This article is reviewed in the chapter on weather and climate.

Trewartha, G. T.
1954 An introduction to climate. 3rd ed. McGraw-Hill Book Company, Inc., New York. 402 p.
A standard text with a full treatment of Köppen's climatic classification.

Unesco
1963 Bioclimatic map of the Mediterranean zone, explanatory notes. Unesco, Paris. Arid Zone Research 21. 60 p.

WEATHER AND CLIMATE OF DESERT ENVIRONMENTS

CLAYTON R. REITAN*
Department of Meteorology
University of Wisconsin

and

CHRISTINE R. GREEN
Institute of Atmospheric Physics
The University of Arizona

*Formerly of the Institute of Atmospheric Physics, The University of Arizona

INTRODUCTION

In a survey of what is known about the weather and climate of deserts, it quickly becomes apparent that few aspects of meteorology or climatology are unique to deserts and that many aspects are pertinent to deserts. Unlike some other climatic types (Mediterranean climate, tropical rainforest) deserts are not confined to a particular latitude belt or position on a continent but range from the equator well into the midlatitudes and may be found on various parts of land masses. In his discussion of the causes and distribution of aridity, Hare (1961) points out that the major deserts result from global or at least hemispheric wind patterns; they arise from the whole general circulation. Petterssen (1964), in his paper on the climatological problems of deserts, notes that the effects of aridity could be reduced through extended range forecasts which would lessen the importance of the characteristically low rainfall reliability of deserts, but that this vast problem, for which the behavior of the whole atmospheric shell must be considered, cannot be solved on a regional basis. Thus the weather and climate of deserts is integrally involved with that of most of the major wind belts. It includes tropical meteorology, monsoon circulations, and the dynamics of the midlatitude westerlies.

An example of a general meteorological problem of particular pertinence to desert meteorology is the definition of aridity, the relationship between the water supply and the water need of an environment. Deacon, Priestley, and Swinbank (1958), in their review article for Unesco on evaporation and the water balance, point out that the emphasis on the arid zone must be incidental in determining the content of a discussion article on their subject, which, although important to arid lands, has developed without any special reference to desert climatology. In this and numerous other ways, desert climatology and meteorology encompass aspects of the science which are not unique to arid lands.

Interest in Weather and Climate of Deserts

Although the meteorology of deserts has not been the subject of a Worldwide Arid Pentad or an International Desert Year, arid-zone meteorology has progressed about as fast as the meteorology of other

climatic types, due in a large measure to the special interest of the arid-zone program of Unesco. The total Unesco effort is being reviewed throughout this report, but it should be emphasized here that the state of knowledge of the weather and climate of deserts has benefited from the Unesco program.

Recognizing the large part of the Earth's surface classified as semiarid or arid and the increasing pressure from a growing population on the vegetative resources of the Earth, the Unesco program was organized to improve economic and living conditions through the application of scientific research. From its beginning, Unesco has encouraged the publication of reviews covering the information available about a particular subject, reviews that have also served as background documents for scientific symposia sponsored by Unesco. Weather and climate have been the subjects of several of the reviews. Some of those in the Arid Zone Research series primarily devoted to climatology are:

No. 10. *Climatology. Reviews of Research* (Unesco, 1958*a*);

No. 11. *Climatology and Microclimatology. Proceedings of the Canberra Symposium* (Unesco, 1958*b*);

No. 20. *Changes of Climate. Proceedings of the Rome Symposium* (Unesco-WMO, 1963);

No. 21. *Bioclimatic Map of the Mediterranean Zone* (Unesco-FAO, 1963).

Some Unesco publications devoted primarily to other subjects include articles contributing notably to the understanding of the meteorology of deserts. Unesco's *Arid Zone Research No. 25, Methodology of Plant Eco-Physiology*, contains several articles in this category. The proceedings of Unesco's Paris symposium, which was called to review and evaluate the state of arid-zone research, were published as *Arid Zone Research No. 18, The Problems of the Arid Zone;* they include notable review articles on climatology (Wallén, 1962) and microclimatology (van Wijk and de Wilde, 1962). Cooperation between Unesco and other agencies has resulted in contributions to the arid-zone program. The interagency project on agroclimatology in the arid zones of the Near East conducted by the Food and Agriculture Organization (FAO), World Meteorological Organization (WMO), and Unesco is an important piece of work relevant to the weather and climate of the area. A second project has been organized for a similar study of the arid zone of Africa south of the Sahara and north of the equator. Although this study is not yet complete, it was pointed out in review that the main results have been informally presented and that the investigators have obtained very important and useful knowledge about deserts with summer rainfall.

Problems of the Field

What are the major problems of weather and climate important to deserts? Two main subjects emerge: (*a*) the paucity of climatic data, and (*b*) the definition of aridity. The lack of weather observations is not necessarily unique to the deserts; other parts of the world suffer the same problem, but because of small populations and low levels of economic activity, the data are generally less adequate for deserts than for more humid and prosperous regions. Since the climate exerts a greater stress on the life in deserts than in humid regions, the immediate need for observed data is in some ways greater for deserts than for less severe climatic types.

The second major problem is to express the degree of aridity as an element of climate. Since eventual use of desert regions will depend on the ability to modify or endure their aridity, a thorough understanding of this condition is required. Historically, the definition of aridity has been an ecological problem, but there is now an indication that it may be definable in terms of the basic elements of weather and climate, as a meteorological characteristic of an area, through the use of equations such as proposed by Penman and Budyko.

Subjects Discussed

The discussion portion of this chapter on weather and climate begins with a review of the present state of knowledge. The first general topic considered is the availability of climatic data: what is known about climatic conditions. In the broadest sense this latter can be determined from world charts of temperature and rainfall. But when attention is directed towards a more restricted area, such as a specific desert, it is clear that the information is often inadequate to describe the climate more precisely than required for broadscale mapping, or to evaluate the degree of variability. The concern of this study then shifts from consideration of what it is, climate in terms of available data, to consideration of why it is,

the state of knowledge of the regional weather systems. This state of knowledge is highly variable also, known in the broadest sense in terms of hemispheric and global considerations, but often lacking the detail necessary for a complete understanding of regional weather.

Following the discussion of these two general subjects, attention is directed to a major arid-land problem, the expression of aridity. This problem has historically concerned natural scientists. Just as the determination of what a desert is has been basically a problem of mapping the vegetation and soils, geographers, ecologists, soil scientists, and agrometeorologists have expressed aridity in qualitative terms. Meteorologists have had an interest for years in measuring evaporation from water or land surfaces. Thornthwaite and Holzman (1939) outlined and summarized early attempts to measure evapotranspiration by direct means, but this interest did not lead to expressions for degrees of aridity.

Not until the concept of potential evapotranspiration was formulated could measurements of water use, with abundant water available, be combined into measures of aridity. The physical processes at the Earth's surface then became the important considerations rather than the relationships between the elements of climate and the responses attributable to them. The physical sciences began to replace the natural sciences as a basis for determining aridity.

The theoretical methods for determining evapotranspiration or potential evapotranspiration did not develop from arid-lands problems or in response to any need to define aridity, but rather as part of the advance of general meteorology. When Thornthwaite (1948) formulated the concept of potential evapotranspiration, he used it to determine a moisture index or index of aridity. His method of computing water need was empirical, but certainly his combination of water need, water availability, and soil moisture into an index was a great improvement over the use of relationships between climate and responses to climate. Refinements in the techniques for computing water use, such as the semiempirical but fundamentally founded methods of Budyko (1956) and Penman (1948), hold promise of giving good estimates of water needs, which may eventually give rise to new measures of aridity.

In addition to the major topics covered in this survey, lesser topics having application to the deserts are discussed. Weather modification is an example. Although the major emphasis in weather modification in recent years has been in cloud-seeding and rainmaking, this type of research appears to be relatively unimportant to the world's deserts. The basis of this statement requires further review. Micrometeorological problems such as dew, shelter belts, and effects of irrigation are pertinent to deserts in some degree. The measurement or estimation of radiation may take on new importance as a required observation for the more sophisticated methods of determining potential evapotranspiration. And no survey of knowledge would be complete without a survey of previous surveys.

Agricultural meteorology, aviation meteorology, and the relation of arid climate to human physiology are not treated in this chapter.

Emphasis

Because of the vast amount of world information pertinent to this study, some compromises were inevitable. The choice as to what to cite is based on several factors: the contents of the articles themselves, the total available information on an area or subject, the advice of meteorologists and climatol-ogists who are area specialists and subject-matter experts, and the availability of the literature. Some papers simply could not be obtained to meet schedules. Literature in English, the language of the authors, has been emphasized; the criterion of accessibility was construed to allow such emphasis. When a work is cited without an explicit evaluation, it may be assumed that we consider it a competent effort.

Acknowledgments

The authors wish to recognize the generous help received from colleagues during the study period. The text was reviewed by C. C. Wallén and Peveril Meigs, both of whom made pertinent contributions. We also wish to record our appreciation for the less formal contributions made by W. D. Sellers and J. R. Hastings of the University of Arizona and by M. Blanc, E.S.S.A. (Environmental Science Services Administration), Phoenix, Arizona.

DISCUSSION OF STATE OF KNOWLEDGE

A. CLIMATIC DATA

Any assessment of the state of knowledge of the weather and climate of deserts must consider the availability of climatic data. Wallén (1962), in his excellent review of climatology problems of arid lands, refers to data collections as the fundamental task in arid-lands research and makes the point that the study of these areas depends upon the existence of sufficient data. Bilham (1957) refers to a climatological service as a prime necessity to the further development and use of any extensive area and points out several connections between climatological data and economic activity in an area. If the climate is unknown, it is unlikely that large capital investments will be made in enterprise sensitive to climate.

Data collection and publication are usually accomplished by the national weather services of the individual countries, and one would expect the quality and quantity of climatic data to vary just as the economic and social development of countries varies. Arid-land nations tend to be relatively underdeveloped, and often little economic support is available for activities that do not obviously and immediately contribute to the welfare of the country. The degree of organization of national weather services varies greatly from country to country, since arid lands are found within the borders of established world powers as well as newly emerging nations.

Another reason that we have very little climatic data for some arid lands is that many of these regions are nearly uninhabited. It appears unlikely that the expense of installing automatic observing stations or of maintaining an observing staff will be met until economic usefulness of the data is apparent. An additional reason for lack of observing personnel in the low-latitude countries is that the benefits of a synoptic observing network are small compared to the importance of daily weather to the midlatitudes; thus, the establishment of observing networks has tended to lag in those areas.

1. Need for Data

Climatic data cannot be collected in the abstract, and certain elements of weather and climate may be more important to know for arid than for humid areas. What needs to be known? Rainfall variability is usually more important for the fringes of the deserts than for the humid tropics. The same elements do not have equal importance in all parts of the arid zone. Frost frequency is important to deserts bordering the midlatitude climates — but is completely irrelevant in some of the low-latitude regions. Some elements of weather and climate are more basic than others. Temperature and precipitation are more fundamental than cloud cover. Some elements require a denser observing network than others. For example, observations of solar radiation and cloud cover at a few stations allow for estimations of radiation at locations where cloud cover alone is observed. The expense of installation and the problems of maintenance of a dense network of radiation observations need not be assumed. Some economic limit must govern the amount of data that can be summarized and published.

The question of what needs to be known has not been answered. Gilead and Rosenan (1958), Wallén (1962), Brann (1958), and especially Bilham (1957) discuss the question but do not or cannot answer it. A study is needed to establish general priorities for the elements to be measured and recommend the practical density of the network for each element. The WMO Working Group on Climatological Networks is currently centering its attention on networks in the less-populated areas such as the arid, tropical, and polar zones. Results of this committee's discussions should be of help. Effective summarizing and publishing is as important as identifying and collecting the needed data. Monthly and yearly summaries that present the data by days and months seem desirable, but again, what is to be included? Relative humidity, which undergoes a wide diurnal variation, needs a well-defined, standard time for its observation: for example, local noon or an average of a morning and an evening observation. Comparisons are possible only when standardization exists. Perhaps relative humidity should not be reported at all, but rather some element such as vapor pressure should be used as a measure of atmospheric moisture. There is a need for uniformity in what is observed, what is published, and what publication format is

24

used. But since the problems and environmental conditions of deserts are largely different from those of more humid areas, the importance of observation of certain elements of climate in deserts will vary from the importance of observation of similar elements in more humid areas.

2. Availability of Climatic Data

A discussion of availability of climatic data can be divided into two sections: *(a)* what is currently being collected and published, and *(b)* what is already available in terms of published means, normals, and the like.

Current Collection

Most arid-lands nations have national weather services. The name and address of each permanent representative to the World Meteorological Organization (WMO), usually the director of the national weather service, is routinely listed in the annual report of the World Meteorological Organization. Almost all arid-lands countries are members. The national weather service is ordinarily responsible for collecting and publishing current climatological data, usually monthly and annual summaries, though this arrangement varies. Table I, Known Publications of Climatic Data, has been prepared on the basis of direct contact with most of the national weather services and a survey of climatological data available at the U. S. Weather Bureau Library in Washington, D. C. Table I indicates availability of current data and shows that the publication of periodic summaries is common. Publications of climatic data for individual countries are not listed here. That information changes from time to time, can be irregular, and may lag by years from being current. Information regarding the availability of current publications should be obtainable, upon request, from the national weather service of each country.

A recent publication of the World Meteorological Organization (1965*a*) is a catalog of publications of meteorological data. For each country, this catalog lists the current, former and occasional publications of climatic data and gives a brief description of the contents of each. Some idea of the regularity and lag in publication can be gained from the descriptive information. It should be noted that 38 of the 46 arid-lands countries (as defined for this compendium) are members of the WMO and that only two-thirds (25 of 38) submitted information for the WMO catalog.

Publication of Mean Data

The availability of mean or normal data can be more important to research activity than the availability of current data. National weather services often

Table I
KNOWN PUBLICATIONS OF CLIMATIC DATA

Country	Monthly Summary	Annual Summary	Compiled Mean or Normal Data
	(x = published)		
Aden	–	–	–
Afghanistan	x	–	–
Algeria	x	–	–
Angola	x	x	x
Argentina	x	–	x
Australia	x	–	x
Bahrain	–	–	–
Bechuanaland (Botswana)	x	x	x
Bolivia	–	x	–
Cameroon	x	x	–
Chad	x	–	–
Chile	–	x	x
China	–	–	x
Ethiopia	x	–	–
French Somaliland	x	–	–
India	x	x	x
Iran	x	x	–
Iraq	x	–	x
Israel	x	x	x
Jordan	x	–	–
Kenya	x	x	x
Kuwait	x	x	–
Libya	x	–	x
Mali	x	–	–
Mauritania	–	–	–
Mexico	x	x	x
Morocco	x	x	–
Muscat & Oman	–	–	–
Niger	–	–	–
Nigeria	x	–	x
Outer Mongolia	–	–	–
Pakistan (West)	x	x	–
Peru	x	x	–
Qatar	–	–	–
Saudi Arabia	x	x	–
Somalia	–	–	–
South Africa	x	x	x
South West Africa	x	x	x
Spanish Sahara	–	–	–
Sudan	x	x	x
Syria	x	x	–
Trucial Coast	–	–	–
Tunisia	x	x	x
U.S.S.R.	x	–	–
United Arab Republic (Egypt)	x	x	x
U.S.A.	x	x	x
Upper Volta	–	–	–
Yemen	–	–	–

publish reports containing average values of the elements of climate for the country. For many countries this kind of climatic data is not as readily available as are current publications because the history of the observing networks (or of the nation itself) is not long enough to have generated many data on which to base a publication of means. Another type of paper often available is one that incidentally contains tabulations of mean data. This type of publication is usually a descriptive survey of the climate of a country and may contain extensive tabulations of climatic data.

Finally, other more general compilations of climatic data should be noted. One of the best collections has been published by the British Meteorological Office (1958). A collection of six individual parts, it presents climatic data for the world. A second collection of worldwide data is the WMO set of climatic normals for CLIMAT and CLIMAT SHIP stations (World Meteorological Organization, 1962). The U. S. Weather Bureau is currently involved in the publication of a new edition of the World Weather Records, extending the current available data by publishing records for the 1951-1960 period. The first volume for North America has been published (U. S. Weather Bureau, 1965). Six more volumes covering the rest of the world are to follow.

Length of Record

One of the questions that arises with respect to mean data is the length of record necessary for establishing average values. McDonald (1956) has studied the characteristics of precipitation data for the arid southwestern United States and concludes that 50 years of data are necessary to establish precipitation means that are within 10 per cent of the population mean at the 95 per cent confidence level. Over this long a period, however, long-term trends may distort the concept of the mean. In tropical areas, but with some application to arid lands, de Queiroz (1955*b*) has studied the representativeness of various lengths of records for Angola and concludes that 5 years of record are sufficient for monthly or annual means of most elements of climate, but that 10 years at least are required for precipitation even when variability is low, not a usual characteristic of deserts. In Unesco-FAO (1963, page 19), it is stated that 25- and 10-year periods produce satisfactory means for precipitation and temperature, respectively. However, useful studies can be made with short-term records if care is exercised; and where long-term records do not exist, approximation based upon the short-term records available may be more useful than no estimate at all.

Typical Study to Fill Gaps

Before proceeding to a discussion of the data available for the individual deserts, it is pertinent to consider a paper by Beckett and Gordon (1956), which is interesting in several respects. The purpose of the study was to examine the climatic factors relevant to the agricultural development of a region in central Iran. The sources of the climatic data were for the most part local manuscripts; some data were obtained from British diplomatic and consular reports, some unpublished data from sources in England, and some from collections of the Indian government. Most of the observations were taken during the early 1900's. One indication from Beckett and Gordon's study is that many climatic data for regions such as Iran or Afghanistan must be sought locally if they are to be obtained at all. Data such as these probably will remain inaccessible to foreign scientists until a specific need justifies the expense of a personal, on-the-spot search for them.

These authors used to the fullest the fragmentary data available to them, though their conclusion about wind velocity may indicate the danger of using limited amounts of data. Throughout their paper, they make pertinent comments about the local climate, stating, for example, that rare summer thunderstorms can have catastrophic effects on the landscape, and that this area probably marks the westward extent of the Indian monsoon. This paper is cited because it illustrates a type of study that probably could be made anywhere in the world's deserts where an on-the-spot search for local data can be justified.

It should be pointed out that Beckett and Gordon published their study about the same year that the Iranian Meteorological Department was established. This was also about the time that the WMO began to stress the importance of having each national weather service collect all the available climatological data in its country, a program that has been quite successful.

3. Climatic Data for Each Desert

Kalahari-Namib Data

The meteorological service of Angola publishes monthly and annual summaries of climatological data. A general discussion of meteorology in Angola and the climate of the region has been given by Angola Serviço Meteorológico (1955). Rainfall and its variability have been discussed by Leal and de Queiroz (1952) and de Queiroz (1955*a*). In the latter paper de Queiroz contrasts the high variability of the arid section to the low variability in the more humid regions.

Climatic data are available in quantity for areas governed by South Africa. Monthly and yearly summaries are published. In addition, the weather bureau of South Africa has been issuing a series of publications entitled *Climate of South Africa*. The individual issues have dealt with different climatic elements. A general discussion of the climate of South Africa is found in part 8 of the series (South Africa Weather Bureau, 1965). Nuttonson's (1961c) analogy study of South Africa and Israel is another good source of climatic data for this region. Gellert (1955) has written a comprehensive study of rainfall variability in South West Africa. Climatic data for South West Africa and Bechuanaland are now routinely included in publications of the weather bureau of South Africa.

Sahara Data

Climatic data for the Sahara can best be discussed by dealing with those nations south of the core of the Sahara and bordering the tropical climates separately from those countries with Mediterranean climates. One general source of information about weather, climate, and climatic data for this area is the bibliography prepared by Rodier (1963b), which lists some general references and many references on climatic data for the individual countries. Rodier (1963a) also lists present sources of climatological data for African nations.

Some general publications contain a great deal of climatic data for the Sahara. Two papers by Nuttonson (1961a, b) are concerned with the comparison of regions in North Africa with those in Israel. Climate is one of the elements for which analogies are made. A recent major study of the climate of the Sahara has been made by Dubief (1959, 1963a). These two volumes constitute an excellent survey of the distribution of general climatological elements over this region. A publication appropriate to the Sahara as well as the Somali-Chalbi and Kalahari-Namib deserts is the *Climatological Atlas of Africa* by Jackson (1961). This magnificent collection of 55 plates depicts rainfall, temperature, humidity, and upper-air data for the continent. Another paper of importance by Dubief (1953a), contains a detailed discussion of the distribution of rainfall and its variability. The dynamic climatology of the precipitation is discussed, and the equatorward limits of the cyclonic rains and the poleward extent of the monsoons are noted. The climate of elevated regions has been recently studied by Dubief (1963b); he notes that minimum temperature is the climatic element most affected by changes in elevation.

The Institut Scientifique Chérifien, Service de Physique du Globe et de Météorologie, publishes some climatic data for Morocco, and individuals from that organization have summarized some of the data: Debrach, Ousset, and Michel (1956, 1958) discussed precipitation and the distribution of temperature in Morocco, and Bidault (1953) summarized data for eastern Morocco.

The climate of Algeria is the subject of a study by Seltzer (1946) that presents data as well as an extensive bibliography. Seltzer (1953) discusses the distribution of annual rainfall and probable annual rainfall, and Isnard (1950) shows the several types of seasonal rainfall regimes found in Algeria. Much of the work in the meteorology and climatology of the country was done by the Institut de Météorologie et de Physique du Globe, part of the University of Algiers.

Tunisia's national weather service publishes daily, monthly, and annual weather bulletins and issues publications on meteorological or climatological subjects from time to time; see Tunis, Service Météorologique (1954a, b) for example. Berkaloff (1949) and Isnard (1952) have discussed the statistical properties of Tunisian rainfall. Tixeront's (1956) general discussion of rainfall variability in arid lands utilizes data from Tunisia.

The meteorological service of Libya publishes some current data for a limited number of stations. Two papers by Fàntoli (1952, 1954) are pertinent to the distribution of temperature and rainfall of Libya.

The meteorological department of Egypt (United Arab Republic) publishes monthly and annual reports. An additional paper which can be mentioned is that of Soliman (1953a) in which the distribution of rainfall is mapped and its occurrences are related to upper cold lows and troughs.

Papers with any reference at all to the Spanish Sahara are rare. During the investigation period, only three papers (Font Tullot 1948, 1949, 1955) were found that referred to this particular area.

Extensive climatic data were found to be available from the four countries on the equatorward side of the Sahara. Other than a small amount of current data, few publications were found dealing with the climate of this region. The National Weather Service of Upper Volta, in a private communication, stated that monthly summaries are published. A general discussion of the climate as well as mean data are found in Haute-Volta, Service Météorologique (1964). The Mali Weather Service, also in a private communication, stated that a monthly bulletin is published. For Mauritania, no publications are available, but the national weather service provided typed copies of mean data (5 years of record) for twelve stations. Some mean data are found in Chabra (1959). No data were found that applied specifically to Niger. Historically, these countries were included in what was known as French West Africa and serviced by the meteorological service of France. That organization (Météorologie Nationale) has published monthly summaries in its *Annales des Services Météorologiques de la France d'Outre-Mer.* Summaries for 1951 through 1958 have been issued, and 1959 and 1960 are to be published next. Reports were irregular prior to 1951.

Nigeria's weather service dates to 1961. Prior to that time, the administrative office was the British West African Meteorological Service. Although not in the arid zone, the Department of Geography of Ibadan University College maintains a record of many climatic elements. For some of the area that includes Chad and Cameroon, older data are available from the Service Météorologique de l'Afrique Equatoriale Française in Brazzaville.

One country south of the core of the Sahara with a well-developed meteorological service is Sudan. Monthly and annual publications of climatic data are published. Useful mean data in quantity are available in a series of pamphlets published by the Sudan Meteorological Service (each entitled simply "Pamphlet No. . . ."). Rainfall averages and parameters, average pentad rainfalls, and wind-speed statistics are some of the subjects covered in this series of publications. Other series by the meteorological service that deal with meteorology beyond the collection of climatic data are their "Memoirs," "Scientific Notes," and "Technical Notes."

A by-product of the second FAO/Unesco/WMO agroclimatological study of the arid lands south of the Sahara was the collection of all available climatic data for this region by the principal investigator, J. Cochemé, Plant Production Division, FAO, Rome.

Somali-Chalbi Data

Monthly weather summaries for Ethiopia are published by the meteorological service of that country. A general climatology of the region has been given by Sivall (1951). Some of the long-term and better climatic data of the region have been included in papers by Fàntoli (1960a, 1961). Weather data are published monthly by the Service Météorologique in French Somaliland. According to the weather service of the Somali Republic (private communication), meteorological observations are not regularly published by that country. General information about the weather service and about the climate of the country has been given by Fàntoli (1960b). General discussions of the weather and large amounts of detailed climatological data are available for French

Somaliland, Somalia and Ethiopia in reports of the Great Britain Meteorological Office (1962a, b).

The best meteorological service in the area is the East African Common Services Organization, Meteorological Department, which provides regional weather services. Monthly and annual publications of climatological data are available as well as mean and normal summaries, of which the 1931-1960 normals for Kenya should be noted (East African Common Services Organization, Meteorological Department, 1965). This weather service also issues "Pamphlets," "Technical Memoranda," and "Memoirs" in which research papers and reports, usually pertinent to the area, are published. Some papers of importance are Thompson (1957b), Griffiths and Hemming (1963), and Griffiths (1958). These are but a few of the many reports available. In addition to the publications of the main source, the East African Meteorological Department, Johnson's (1962) rainfall analysis and Griffiths' (1962) general climatic discussion contribute to the state of knowledge of the climate of the area. Although much of the area is not classified as arid, a great deal of work in the region deals with characteristics of precipitation. It is interesting to note that Griffiths' *Climate of East Africa* (1962) points out that more than 70 per cent of Kenya receives less than a reliable 20 inches of rainfall per year.

Arabian Data

The well-organized meteorological service of Israel has been active in studying the problems that climate poses to that region. The list of publications of the Israel Meteorological Service contains numerous papers in several classifications, most of which deal directly with the weather and climate of Israel. In particular, recent issues of normal data can be cited (Israel Meteorological Service, 1961, 1965; Katsnelson, 1959). Papers published by Israeli meteorologists in journals are also often issued as Meteorological Service publications. Katsnelson's study of the variability of annual rainfall was published in a conventional periodical (Katsnelson, 1964) as well as issued as No. 17, Series D, *Contributions of the Israel Meteorological Service.*

Jordan has at least two agencies that publish climatic data: the Meteorological Department and the Central Water Authority, which is concerned with irrigation and hydrology. Saudi Arabia publishes both a monthly and an annual summary of climatic data. On the Arabian peninsula, oil companies have made climatological observations; for example, the Arabian-American Oil Company at Dhahran has kept a meteorological record since 1935 and kindly supplied a copy of their record and some summaries of the data in it. Companies such as Aramco collect the data as a matter of local necessity, and records such as the one at Dhahran exist only because of the continued personal interest of a long succession of employees. In the Persian Gulf a private weather service, operated by IMCOS Ltd. of London, provides sea and weather forecasts for offshore operations of oil companies in this region. Observations are provided by weather stations established by this service, by the oil companies, and by the local governments. In the 7 years of its operation, a valuable backlog of information has been built up. The scope of the operation was provided in a personal communication from David Hibbert, IMCOS.

Climatological data from Iraq are readily available through the Iraq Meteorological Department. In addition to currently available data, a whole series of compilations of mean data has been published. This series, put out under the title of "Publications" by the Meteorological Department, Ministry of Communications, Republic of Iraq, provides an excellent source of mean climatic data. Publications 13 and 14, a new climatic atlas and a new issue of normal data, respectively, are recent examples of the type of material available. Volume 2 of the *Meteorological Memoirs* (Iraq Meteorological Department, 1964) is a collection of papers dealing with the characteristics of temperature and rainfall in Iraq. A general discussion of the climate of Iraq has been given by Khalaf (1956).

Climatic data for the Middle East were studied and collected for the first FAO/Unesco/WMO agroclimatological study of the semiarid and arid zones of the Near East by de Brichambaut and Wallén (1963). These data are available at FAO in Rome.

Iranian Data

The government of Iran publishes both a monthly summary of weather data and an annual yearbook. The current issues of the yearbook contain only climatic data; however, the issues for 1956 and 1957 also contained general papers about weather and climate in Iran. Historically, the 1956 yearbook is of special interest (Iran Meteorological Department, 1958). Two general discussions of the climate of Iran are available (Adle, 1960; Ganji, 1955).

The Afghan weather service, like the Iranian national weather service, has been organized recently. Veydner (1962) outlines the history and the continuing activities of this weather service. Current meteorological data are published on a monthly basis only. Some collection of weather data has been done by the U. S. Weather Bureau (1943, 1955) but

other than that, mean data do not seem available. Stenz (1957) discusses, among other subjects, precipitation in Afghanistan.

Thar Data

Both of the nations that share the Thar Desert, India and Pakistan, have well-developed weather services and routinely publish climatological data. Mean data are not readily available from Pakistan, but three papers, Khan (1953), Butt (1950), and Naqvi and Rahamatullah (1962) give general discussions of the climate. Husain (1950) discusses the general characteristics of rainfall at Quetta. This Pakistan information applies to its portion of the Iranian Desert as well as the Thar Desert.

Regular publications of climatic data and mean data are available from India; for example, India Meteorological Department (1962), an excellent source of mean data, contains mean rainfall data for the period 1901-1950 for about 2700 stations. Chatterjee (1953) has compiled a general discussion of climate and has also edited the national atlas of India, which contains some maps of mean climatic data. Studies dealing with the distribution of rainfall are available: Naqvi (1949) and Govindaswamy (1953). Rao (1958) and Naqvi (1958) have discussed historical records of rainfall and conclude that significant changes have not occurred. Lettau and White (1964) have used harmonic analysis to note the regions with a secondary maximum of rainfall in winter.

Turkestan Data

Political and language problems have limited the amount of information on the Turkestan Desert obtained for this study. It is likely that climatic data are regularly and routinely published on a scale comparable to any country in the world. The amount of interest in problems in climatology in the Soviet Union seems to exceed that of all other countries. Our lack of knowledge about regularly published data is compensated for by the large number of good climatologies available. The climate of the state of Kazakhstan has been discussed by Uteshev (1959). A 7-volume work on the climate of the Soviet Union has been published by the A. I. Voeikov Main Geophysical Observatory in Leningrad, Glavnaya Geofizicheskaya Observatoriya im. A. I. Voyenkova (1958-1963). Parts of this major work of Russian climatology have been translated into English. (See publications list for coverage of original and translations.)

Balashova, Zhitomirskaia, and Semenova (1960) have published a climatological description of the republics of Middle Asia. A 1-volume climatology by Borisov (1965) has recently been translated into English. Klykova (1959) has discussed the rainfall regime of the Alma-Ata region of Kazakhstan.

Takla-Makan and Gobi Data

The problems of language and politics have proven effective barriers to the assessment of current sources of climatic data for these two deserts of eastern Asia. A letter from D. Tuvdendorj, director of the hydrometeorological service of the Mongolian People's Republic, states that although climatological observations are made, collected, and summarized, they are not published. Mean data are sometimes found in other publications, but the length of record is usually short. The above-mentioned letter states that the length of record is now 29 years for an unspecified number of stations. A recent Russian paper by Kuznetsov (1962) presents a map of mean annual rainfall as part of a study of river runoff. Pond (1954) discusses the climate in the Gobi on the basis of available, but fragmentary data. The data available from the Takla-Makan desert are at best fragmentary, and the existing records are short. A recently available climatic atlas of China (China, Central Meteorological Bureau, Office of Climatological Data Research, 1960), translated by the U. S. Joint Publications Research Service (J.P.R.S.), used data from less than 20 stations in this area, with the longest temperature record being 5 years. Isolines on maps were not extended into this region. A collection of meteorological maps has been compiled by Lu (1946). A general discussion of the climate of this area has been given by Chu (1958), while Ch'en (1961) has presented a general climatology of all of China. Chiao-min Hsieh of the Catholic University of America is preparing an atlas of China using the data from the aforementioned Chinese atlas translated by J.P.R.S. He believes it to be the best available. Although data are not exchanged by the Peking government and the United States, exchanges do take place with other Western countries. Chinese data are available at the Library of the British Meteorological Office at Bracknell.

Australian Data

The Australian Bureau of Meteorology is responsible for the collection and publication of data for this desert. Monthly summaries are published and climatic averages determined. A general source of mean data is the *Official Yearbook of the Commonwealth of Australia,* published annually, which contains detailed data for the major cities in the country. Two papers that contain large amounts of climatic data, though their main purposes are not data publication, are Gentilli (1955) and Nuttonson (1958). Climatic averages, or means, have been published by Australia, Bureau of Meteorology (1956), and a climatological atlas of Australia dated 1940 is also available. Selected rainfall data and a statistical analysis have been issued by the Australia Director of Meteorology (1960).

Monte-Patagonian Data

The meteorological group for Argentina that collects and publishes climatic data is the Servicio Meteorológico Nacional. Monthly publications are available, but annual summaries are not issued. Mean data have been compiled in a series of publications entitled "Estadísticas Climatológicas," which present detailed climatological data for varying periods of time. Six volumes published from 1958 through 1963 are available in this important series. A climatic atlas has also been prepared for the country, dated 1960. Analyses of the characteristics of the distribution of rainfall have been made by several authors. Marchetti (1951, 1952*a, b*) has dealt with the general characteristics and the variability of rainfall regimes in Argentina, Olascoaga (1950) has discussed the per cent daily distribution, and Prohaska (1961) has analyzed the characteristics of rainfall in the pampas region.

Climatic data and publications about the climate of Bolivia were not generally found. The national weather service published an annual compilation of climatic data until 1960; efforts are being made to resume publication. Long-term means are not available; however, precipitation summaries for 10 years from 35 stations have been recently prepared for the Hydrological Decade. A small general discussion on the climate of Bolivia by Prada Estrada (1948) contains some short-period climatic records. Negretty (1949) investigated annual variations in Bolivian rainfall.

Atacama-Peruvian Data

The National Weather Service of Chile, a part of that country's air force, is the agency concerned with the publication of climatic data. An annual summary for the current year is published; it contains detailed data for about 50 stations and rainfall for several hundred additional locations. Two collections of mean data are published by the national weather service. Detailed data for the period of record up to 1945 have been summarized for 36 selected stations (Chile, Oficina Meteorológica, 1964), and rainfall data only for 135 stations in Chile have been published for their period of record (Chile, Oficina Meteorológica, 1965). Additional sources of rainfall data are found in papers by the late Almeyda Arroyo (1949, 1954).

The National Weather Service of Peru publishes both monthly and annual climatological summaries. In addition, the Servicio de Agrometeorología e Hidrología started a new publication of mean climatic data in 1965. This same agency has begun a collection of pre-1960 climatic data and is publishing them in a series of bulletins by catchment basins. About 25 have been done so far. A new climatological network of about 700 stations is being established through a WMO/Special Fund project, to be administered by the Servicio de Agrometeorología e Hidrología. There appears to be no readily available publication of mean climatic data for Peru. A private communication from R. Gervasi B. of the Peruvian General Office of Meteorology implies that mean and normal data have been compiled but are not published. Guerra T. (1959) has studied the distribution of temperature, and Valdivia Ponce (1955) has discussed some of the effects of the ocean on climate.

North American Data

Two countries share the deserts of North America: Mexico and the United States. In contrast to the abundant climatological data available for the United States is the paucity of published data for Mexico. Climatological data are collected by two main agencies: the Secretaría de Recursos Hidráulicos (the hydrological service) and the Servicio de Meteorológica Nacional (the national weather service). The history and organization of meteorology in Mexico has been reviewed by Lebrija Celay (1963). The national weather service has just recently resumed publication of climatic data on a current basis. The latest data to be published were for 1960, issued in 1963. This can be considered a resumption of the publication suspended in 1943. Monthly summaries were presented in four reports of three months each, plus an annual report. The hydrological service has published a series of bulletins that present climatic data for various sections of Mexico. Data for the Sonoran Desert are presented in Volumes 12 and 13 of the *Boletines Hidrológicos de la Secretaría de Recursos Hidráulicos*. Two recent publications by Hastings (1964*a, b*), which present temperature and precipitation data for the northwestern region of Mexico in more detail and amount than heretofore, are the best collections available for the northwestern deserts of Mexico. Climatological data are also available in Vivó and Gómez (1946) and Contreras Arias (1942). Wallén (1955) notes the availability of precipitation data and discusses its variability.

In the state of Chihuahua, climatological data are collected by the association of ranchers in the area in cooperation with the state weather service. A daily weather bulletin is published listing mean, maximum, and minimum temperatures for the day and the daily rainfall for about 50 stations. An annual report summarizes the data for the year. The annual report for the year 1962 (Unión Ganadera Regional de Chihuahua, 1963) also contains mean data for the period 1958-1962. It is interesting to note that climatic data collection and publication are not concentrated in the national weather service but are scattered among different agencies in the constituent states. The literature search turned up a recent publication from an obscure source of an atlas of monthly temperature and precipitation for the Mexican state of Vera Cruz, for example. This publication is apparently not associated with any national or state weather service.

No doubt the climatic data available for the United States are equal in quality and quantity to those of any country in the world; however, since the United States is not primarily a desert region, no emphasis is placed on arid-zone data. Collection and publication of climatic data is almost exclusively the function of the United States Weather Bureau in Washington, D. C. Although many publications apply to the entire United States, data are usually grouped by constituent state. It is not necessary to list here the vast amount of published data and regularly issued reports available from the U. S. Weather Bureau for the area of interest. Monthly and annual reports are issued for each state. For the major cities within states, detailed summaries are published monthly and means are issued yearly. A national summary for all states is issued monthly and yearly. Mean and normal weather information have been published, and data have been compiled for a large number of individual years.

In addition to the data regularly available from the Weather Bureau, some other publications should be noted. Green and Sellers (1964) and Smith (1956) have published descriptions of climate and summaries of data for Arizona. A series of scientific and technical reports by the Institute of Atmospheric Physics of The University of Arizona have been in part devoted to the analysis of climatological data for that state. Of these reports, McDonald (1956) and Green (1959) are particularly noteworthy. The New Mexico State Engineer Office (1956*a, b*) has published long-term records of basic data for that state. A recent paper by Orton (1964) contains much climatological data for Texas.

4. General Comments, Climatic Data

Availability of climatic data is one of the major problems of arid lands, though it varies in importance from desert to desert. As illustrated in the atlas by Jackson (1961) and indicated by Griffiths and Hemming (1963), data are available for generalized mapping. It is in the realm of specific climatological data that gaps exist. As will be discussed in a later section, a meaningful definition of aridity will depend upon the measurement or estimation of such factors as radiation balance and the knowledge of such rarely observed and published parameters as vapor pressure. Those approaching problems such as definition of aridity, or, as in the case of the problem facing Beckett and Gordon (1956), of assessment of the potential for agricultural development in an arid region, will face the reality that detailed climatic data are not generally available. Even where detailed climatic data are available, new schemes will be needed to apply results.

Some mean data containing such information as cloud type and cloud amounts, wind direction and velocity, vapor pressure, and occurrence of special phenomena exist, but have not been formally published. They are available at and obtainable from individual national weather services; however, the number of locations for which this type of information is available will be small.

B. SYNOPTIC CLIMATOLOGY

1. Weather Systems

Synoptic climatology is the study and analysis of climate in terms of synoptic weather systems. The average climate of a region is given in terms of weather systems and atmospheric motions rather than in mean values of the usual parameters. The study of the synoptic climatology of an area, a particular desert for example, could emphasize the relationship of that desert to the features of the general circulation or could concentrate on the frequency of tropical cyclones. This branch of climatology attempts to describe weather and to give the "why" of climate.

The purpose of a review of research related to the synoptic climatology of a desert is to be able to determine the state of understanding of the weather systems of the region. In some respects, this understanding is more important to arid lands than to humid regions because of the greater climatic variability associated with deserts. Since rainfall is the important element, there tends to be an emphasis on the relationship between rainfall and storm systems. Basically, the synoptic climatology of most desert regions is tied to a study of storm systems or systems of atmospheric motions larger than the area in question. (The exception to this generalization may be that extensive arid area extending from west Africa eastward to Afghanistan and including parts of the Sahara, Arabian, and Iranian deserts.) For example, one would not study the cyclones of the Sonoran Desert, but rather the study area would more likely be the size of one-fourth of North America. The

summer rains in the Thar Desert are associated with the Indian monsoon, an atmospheric system affecting an area many times the size of that desert. Studies of these large-scale systems are clearly outside the scope of this compendium. Rather the emphasis here will be on studies that tend to concentrate on the deserts and the climatology of those regions in particular.

Causes of Aridity

A general discussion of the weather systems of deserts is not possible because these arid lands are found over a wide range of latitudes and come under the influence of nearly all the major wind and pressure belts. A variety of weather systems prevail and a variety of reasons for aridity exist. Aridity can be thought of as arising from three general causes acting individually or in combination. One of these causes is the separation of the region from oceanic moisture sources by topography or by distance. Part of the desert area of the United States and the Monte-Patagonian Desert to the leeward of the Andes in South America can be thought of as arising from the aridifying effect on air masses of moving over a major mountain barrier. One of the causes of the Takla-Makan, Turkestan, and Gobi deserts of Central Asia is the great distance from major moisture sources. A second general cause of aridity is the formation of dry, stable air masses that resist convective currents. The Somali-Chalbi desert probably owes its existence to a stable environment produced by large-scale atmospheric motions. Deserts dominated by the eastern portions of subtropical high-pressure cells originate in part from the stability produced by these pressure and wind systems. Aridity can also result from the lack of storm systems, the mechanisms that cause convergence, create unstable environments, and provide the lifting necessary for precipitation. The paths, frequencies, and degrees of development of midlatitude cyclones or tropical cyclones are crucial factors in the production of rainfall. The deserts of the subtropical latitudes are particularly sensitive to the climatology of cyclones. The Arabian and Australian deserts and the Sahara are examples of regions positioned between major wind belts with their associated storm systems.

Works of Broad Application

Since there is no universal desert weather system, we will consider here the weather systems of individual regions, especially rainfall. It should be recognized that many pertinent synoptic studies are not really concerned with deserts or with aridity. One such paper is Klein's (1957) study of the frequency and formation of cyclones and anticyclones over the Northern Hemisphere. This paper is pertinent to all the deserts poleward of about 25°N, yet would hardly be cited as a key paper in the synoptic climatology of deserts. From several symposia not emphasizing desert climatology have come conference publications that make real contributions to the understanding of pressure and wind belts important to deserts. Particularly important are *Tropical Meteorology in Africa,* proceedings of the symposium jointly sponsored by WMO and the Munitalp Foundation, Nairobi, Kenya, 1959 (World Meteorological Organization, 1960); and *Proceedings of the WMO/FAO Seminar on Meteorology and the Desert Locust,* Tehran, Nov.-Dec. 1963 (World Meteorological Organization, 1965*b*).

Systems of the Kalahari-Namib

The Kalahari-Namib Desert of southern Africa is a transition zone with tropical summer rains on its equatorward margins and winter cyclonic rainfall on its poleward borders. Two weather services are concerned with this region, those of Angola and of South Africa.

The weather and climate of South Africa have been well described in publications of their Weather Bureau in the series "Climate of South Africa" (South Africa Weather Bureau, 1965); Part 8, General Survey, should be especially mentioned. Other papers of interest are regularly published in the scientific periodical *Notos.* Summertime precipitation in South Africa is related to equatorial westerlies by Gellert (1962). Logan (1960), in his discussion of the geography of the Namib Desert, discusses climate, the causes of the desert, and the differences between coastal and inland regions. Rubin's (1956) study of rainfall related to circulation anomalies seemed to show that the wet and dry extremes are related not only to number of rain days but also to intensity of precipitation.

Systems of the Mediterranean Climate Region

The Mediterranean climate, with its emphasis on winter rainfall originating in midlatitude cyclones, applies to a region that extends from western Africa eastward along the northern fringe of the continent and north of the core of the Sahara through the Middle East and into the Iranian Desert. Although specific papers do apply to individual countries or portions of this broad area, it is also useful to consider the total area in a discussion of synoptic climatology.

The area under discussion is extensively studied and its weather and climate are well documented; this is not to say that the climatology of the area has been completely defined (contributions are still being made), but rather that the subject is well in hand. It

is a region in which the important rain-producing system is the cyclone that moves through or forms in the Mediterranean area in winter. A definitive paper on the weather systems of the areas has been prepared by Biel (1944). Although written for use in the teaching of forecasting during World War II, the paper is also an important contribution to the climatology of the region. Biel's extensive bibliography lists the papers pertinent to the area prior to about 1940. A more recent review of the winter cyclones of the Mediterranean area has been presented by Butzer (1960). Other studies dealing with the region are by Gleeson (1953, 1956), Baum and Smith (1953), and Rosenthal and Gleeson (1956). The previously cited paper by Klein (1957) on the cyclone frequency is also particularly pertinent to this region because of the dominance of cyclonic systems in producing weather. The recent FAO/Unesco/WMO project on agroclimatology for the Near East by de Brichambaut and Wallén (1963) has a good general discussion of the climatic characteristics of the region. The papers and reports for the Unesco/WMO seminar on Mediterranean synoptic meteorology edited by Bleeker (1960) are another reliable general source of basic synoptic meteorological literature.

Northern Sahara Portion

The northern African portion of the Mediterranean climate zone extends from Spanish Sahara through Morocco, Algeria, Tunisia, Libya, and Egypt. Taha (1963), in his review of the state of meteorology and climate for North Africa, was considering essentially this area (Africa north of the Tropic of Cancer). As for papers dealing with the synoptic climatology of individual countries, Pédelaborde and Delannoy (1958) have related weather types and rainfall for Algeria in a study relevant to much of North Africa. Mayençon (1961*a*) has described the weather types associated with hailstorms in Algeria, and the synoptic conditions for heavy rains and their importance are analyzed in Mayençon (1961*b*). Isnard (1958) has analyzed the seasonal distribution of rainfall in Morocco and differentiated between the maritime regime of the coast and the continental regime of the Atlas Mountains and the interior. Debrach (1953) presents a general discussion of the climate of Morocco. A complete discussion of the climate of Spanish Sahara has been given by Font Tullot (1949). Soliman (1950, 1953*b*), el-Fandy (1948, 1950) and Sayed (1949) have discussed aspects of the synoptic climatology pertaining to the United Arab Republic. Berenger (1960) has outlined the weather of the Sahara in terms of polar front disturbances and systems that originate in the south.

Northern Arabian Portion

The northern portion of the Arabian Desert, in the Mediterranean climate region, is under the influence of winter cyclones and dry summers. In this area Israel leads in developing a meteorological service and making research contributions to synoptic climatology. The list of publications from the Israeli weather service illustrates the large amount of work done by their meteorologists in defining the weather and climate of the area. Aelion (1958) has related storm types and precipitation, Amiran and Gilead (1954) have related excessive rainfall to specific synoptic situations, Shaia (1964) has related upper-air patterns to the occurrence of rain, and Levi (1963) has analyzed the dry winter of 1962-63. These cited papers are examples of the many from Israel that pertain primarily to the relationship of rainfall to synoptic weather patterns. Papers about other countries in the region are not nearly so common. al-Shalash (1957) has written a climatology of Iraq, Hassoon (1962) has noted the main synoptic features associated with squalls at Baghdad, and Kheder (1962) has outlined the climatic features of Iraq. Few papers were found for the remaining countries, but they are included in the study of storm systems for the Mediterranean region in general.

Iranian Portion

The Iranian Desert, encompassing parts of Iran and Afghanistan, has primarily a Mediterranean-type climate: important winter rainfall produced by cyclonic storm systems. The area is dominated by an extension of the storm systems of the Mediterranean Sea; knowledge of the synoptic climatology of the region has benefited somewhat from the large amount of work that has been done on the Mediterranean cyclones. This benefit is marginal, however, because of distance from the main study area. Studies of the synoptic climatology of this desert in particular are not abundant: neither country's national weather service was organized until the mid-1950's. M. H. Ganji, Director General of the Iranian Meteorological Department, writing in the introduction to the new *Meteorological Publications,* Series A, No. 1, expresses very well the publication problems of relatively new weather services. He justifies publishing the results of local investigations and studies to stimulate further research and to form a base of information upon which future projects may build.

Ludwig Weickmann has served in the Middle East for several years as a meteorological advisor. Weickmann (1958, 1960) has discussed rainfall and the paths of lows, especially as related to Iran. Weickmann (1963) has further investigated the relationship between cyclones and rainfall amounts and has summarized (1961) what is known about the subtropical jet stream, particularly as it affects Iran.

Ganji (1955) has presented a general discussion of the climate of Iran. Early editions of the Iran Meteorological Department's publication, *Meteorological Yearbook,* also contain a few papers pertinent to the synoptic climatology of Iran. On rare occasions, it appears that the Indian monsoon can extend into the region. In a specific example discussed by Ramaswamy (1965), the interaction between low- and middle-latitude systems during July, 1956, produced extremely heavy rains and resulted in both property damage and loss of life.

Systems of the Southern Sahara

For several reasons, the weather systems of the arid lands south of the core of the Sahara are not as well documented as those of the Mediterranean regions. Tropical weather is seemingly much more constant than that of midlatitudes, the forecast problem is less important, and therefore there seems less need to understand the forces producing it. In addition, this area is in a state of development that would make it difficult for governments of many of these countries to justify the expense of meteorological research not purporting to give immediate economic return. Walker (1963) has reviewed the problems of weather and climate for this region of the Sahara. Countries containing deserts are Cameroon, Chad, Mali, Mauritania, Niger, Nigeria, Sudan, and Upper Volta. The region is best discussed as a whole, since no local research has been conducted in many of the individual countries.

The climate of the region is related to the shift of the intertropical convergence zone and therefore also falls in the general field of tropical meteorology. A collection of papers pertaining to the meteorology of the region is contained in the previously mentioned publication, *Tropical Meteorology in Africa,* Nairobi, Kenya, 1959 (World Meteorological Organization, 1960). The purpose of this symposium was to review the state of knowledge of tropical meteorology in Africa and to identify the main problems and the means for solving them. Many papers are pertinent in that their discussions bear directly on the structure and development of the intertropical convergence zone. It is worth noting again that the second FAO/Unesco/WMO agroclimatological study conducted by J. Cochemé of FAO, Rome, is an important contribution to the synoptic climatology of this area (Cochemé and Franquin, 1967).

Another avenue of research that has contributed to the available knowledge of the meteorology of Africa and the Middle East in general is the effort to control the desert locust. The movement and reproduction of the locust are related to winds and rainfall; thus the study of this pest has contributed to the meteorological literature of the area. An interesting aspect of this problem is the attempt to use the meteorological satellite as a tool to combat the locust. It is believed that the satellite can detect areas where rainfall has recently occurred by the changes in color produced by the fresh vegetation. Since locust breeding and hatching are related to rain areas, the regions of reproduction can be determined. This work is being done at the National Satellite Center in Washington, D. C., under the direction of V. J. Oliver. Locusts and meteorology have been extensively reviewed in two particularly noteworthy publications of the World Meteorological Organization (1963, 1965*b*). Other papers on this problem are Sayer (1962) and Rainey (1958, 1959). Kraus (1958) points out that ameliorating the locust problem is basically a task for entomologists, who can specify the conditions that affect the locust population. Meteorology's value possibly lies in being able to state when and where the specific conditions exist.

A particularly good collection of papers on the synoptic meteorology of Africa and the Middle East is contained in the proceedings of the WMO/FAO seminar on meteorology and the desert locust held in Tehran in November and December of 1963, published as a technical note of the World Meteorological Organization (1965*b*). The papers presented there indicate the great progress made in understanding the weather of the region. Most of the emphasis is on tropical meteorology and the intertropical convergence zone, but weather systems for the whole locust invasion area from southwest Asia westward to most of Africa are discussed. This is one of the finest collections of papers available on the synoptic meteorology of the area. Walker (1960) has discussed several aspects of the intertropical belt as it affects weather in West Africa. Solot (1950) provides a general discussion of the weather systems of the area.

Tschirhart (1956) has discussed the unusual February, 1954, rain produced by a frontal system in Chad. Some synoptic examples of the weather of different seasons are discussed by Dhonneur (1957) in a study of aerial routes into Fort Lamy. Leluin's (1949) study of weather at Port Etienne is one of the few papers noted that discusses weather and climate in Mauritania. The now-defunct British West African Meteorological Service published a series, "Meteorological Notes," that described some aspects of the climatology of the region; however, it emphasized the humid south.

The Nigerian Meteorological Service is publishing a series of "Technical Notes" making significant contributions to the climatology of this region.

Although there is no arid-lands emphasis, all contributions to the knowledge of the climate in this relatively unknown area are important to the entire region. Obasi (1965) has given an up-to-date review of the general climatological features of the area, both at the surface and in the upper levels. Adejokun (1965) has studied the position of the intertropical discontinuity over an 8-year period. The analysis of its 3-dimensional structure suggested a classification of four weather zones, which the author describes. An earlier paper by Hamilton and Archbold (1945) describes the general synoptic features of the area. Eldridge (1957) presents a study of disturbance lines, which move through the area and generate stormy conditions and rainfall. He notes that in Ghana there seems to be an increase in the proportion of the total rainfall associated with these systems as one goes northward, which suggests greater importance of these systems to the arid regions than to more humid locations. A general article on Nigeria's climate has been written by Miller (1952).

The meteorological service apparently most concerned with the climate of the area is that of Sudan. This service publishes several different series: its "Memoirs" are most applicable to the subject of synoptic climatology. A name associated with the synoptic climatology of Sudan, and Africa in general, is that of M. G. el-Fandy. His study of the Sudan summer weather (el-Fandy, 1949*a*) is an example of his work. Solot (1950) has studied the air flow over the area during four local seasons and shows that the intertropical convergence zone is the major climatic control.

Systems of the Somali-Chalbi and Southern Arabian Deserts

Little is known of the synoptic climatology of the entire sector from the Somali-Chalbi desert northeastward across the Arabian Sea and the southern Arabian Peninsula into West Pakistan, yet the reasons for the aridity of this area are very complex. Orography, thermal low pressure, coastal upwelling, and the monsoon circulation of the Indian subcontinent in summer combine to produce an environment in which rainfall is rarely recorded. Ramage (1966) has discussed the dynamics of the subsidence in the region and the causes of the dryness in general. Flohn (1965) in his 3-part study of rainfall anomalies, the intertropical convergence, and the causes of the aridity of the area has made an important contribution to the synoptic climatology of the lower Red Sea region. H. Flohn has been a major contributor to the understanding of the climatology of this region. His papers appear in collections such as the *Tropical Meteorology in Africa* (World Meteorological Organization,

1960) and WMO Technical Note 69 on meteorology and the desert locust (World Meteorological Organization, 1965*b*).

Parts of the Somali-Chalbi desert of east Africa lie in four countries: Somalia, Ethiopia, French Somaliland, and Kenya. It is an area in which little work has been done. One weather service, Meteorological Department of the East African Common Services Organization (Nairobi) is active in research. Its activities and organization are outlined in East African Common Services Organization, Meteorological Department (1963*a*). Research activities are published in its "Memoirs," "Technical Memoranda," and "Pamphlets." Works by Griffiths (1958), Griffiths and Hemming (1963), and Thompson (1957*a*) are all relevant to our subject. The general discussion of the climate of East Africa by Griffiths (1962) has been mentioned previously.

For the other countries, few papers deal with synoptic climatology. Sivall (1951) provides some general information about Ethiopia. El-Fandy (1952) discusses aspects of the synoptic climatology of this region in a paper dealing with the forecasting of thunderstorms.

Systems of the Thar

The Thar Desert of northwest India and Pakistan is a transition zone between major wind belts. Midlatitude cyclones produce moderate amounts of winter precipitation in the northern and western portions of the region while the eastern sector receives its rainfall from the monsoon circulation that dominates the subcontinent in summer. The monsoon movement of moist air north and west generally terminates in western India, marking the westward extension of rains.

Because of the importance of the monsoon to India, numerous studies of the monsoon circulation have been made, dating from the 1800's; they become more definitive in later years with the increase in upper-air observations in the tropics. One need only scan the list of titles in such publications as the *Memoirs of the Indian Meteorological Department* or the *Indian Journal of Meteorology and Geophysics* to note a great interest in these weather systems of the subcontinent. Pant's (1964) study of the 700-millibar patterns associated with the onset of the monsoon is an example of the kind of synoptic study readily available.

Ananthakrishnan and Bhatia (1960) have discussed the movement of summer monsoon depressions over western India and Pakistan as controlled by upper-level winds. The climatology of storms and depressions in the Arabian Sea for about 60 years has been discussed by Ray Choudhuri, Subramanyan,

and Chellappa (1959). During the winters, western disturbances sometimes cause unseasonably cold weather in northwestern India and northern Pakistan. Rai Sircar and Datar (1963) and Hariharan (1956) have discussed these systems in general, and Bhalotra (1956) and Kumar and Bhullar (1956) have discussed synoptic examples of these cold waves. Mooley (1956) has contrasted the circulation and temperature distribution between the monsoon and winter seasons.

It should be emphasized for the Thar Desert that the synoptic climatology of the region has been extensively studied, but that these studies are related primarily to the structure and development of the monsoon rather than specifically directed toward arid-lands problems. The major interest has, however, contributed to a basic understanding of the weather systems of the entire region of which the Thar Desert is a part. A good collection of papers on monsoons in general, with the majority of them referring to the Indian subcontinent, has been published as the proceedings of a symposium on monsoons of the world held in India in 1958 (India. Meteorological Department, 1960).

Systems of the Turkestan

The Turkestan Desert of the Soviet Union presents a striking contrast to most of the desert regions: much work has been done on problems of weather and climate. The weather systems of this region have been extensively studied. The oft-stated goal of opening the arid regions to a more efficient agriculture has produced a wealth of information on the weather occurrences in the region. The local wind of importance is the sukhovei, a desiccating wind of the arid lands. An impressive volume on this wind has been edited by Dzerdzeevskii (1957). This book is a collection of papers prepared from reports read at a U.S.S.R. Academy of Science conference in 1953; the editor regards the collection as a fairly extensive and complete exposition of the subject. This work contains a bibliography of 415 entries relating to the sukhovei wind as well as individual bibliographies for the 30 separate papers. A general review of this wind in English literature has been given by Lydolph (1964). The impressive feature of Russian literature from the arid regions, referring both to steppes and deserts, is the large number of papers concerned with the weather systems and their relationship to aridity, dry winds, and drought. Works by Bachurina and Gus'kova (1956) and Bezverkhniaia (1955) can be cited as examples.

Cold-air invasions into southern Kazakhstan and a late spring snow storm have been discussed by Shchukina and Kuvaldina (1956) and Nikolaev

(1958). Cyclones and anticyclones in central Asia have been the subjects of papers by Romanov (1955, 1959). A special wind of the region, the ursat'ev wind of the Golodnaya Steppe, is described and its origins discussed by Aizenshtat (1959), Chanysheva (1959), and Listrovoi (1959), among others.

The climate of central Asia has been discussed in a translation by Bugaev *et al.* (1962). The synoptic climatology of Kazakhstan was the subject of papers by Golubov (1956) and Puzyreva (1960). An analysis of cyclones for the region has been given by Komissarova (1955).

Systems of the Takla-Makan and Gobi

The Takla-Makan and Gobi deserts can be considered as a unit in a discussion of synoptic climatology, the unit broadly defined as central Asia. This is an area separated from major moisture sources by orographic barriers or by great distance. The Tibetan plateau, roughly 2000 miles in length with a mean elevation of about 12,000 feet, forms an effective barrier to moist air moving northward from the Indian Ocean. Mountain barriers and distance are important to the exclusion of moisture from sources to the west.

Papers that deal with the weather systems of these two areas specifically seem to be rare or unavailable. Chi (1955) has written a short paper on the surface winds in the Sinkiang region. Frequencies of wind direction based on 4 years of data are given. In general in midlatitudes, weather systems are discussed in terms of scales of distance greater than the desert regions. Yeh and Ku (1964) have summarized a great deal of work by Chinese meteorologists on the effect of the Tibetan plateau on the circulation over Asia. One of the aspects of the study is the relationship of cyclone formation and movement under the effects of upper-level flows modified by the presence of the plateau. Chang (1960*a, b*) has discussed the synoptic climatology of China in both winter and summer in papers having some applications to the desert areas. As other examples of the kind of work available, two papers by staff members of the Academia Sinica (1957, 1958) can be mentioned. Gherzi's (1951) 2-volume work on the climate of China contains some discussion of synoptic climatology. It is old (essentially 1939) and does not extend its discussion to cover the desert regions, yet it can be a useful general reference on Chinese climatology. It appears from a review of Chinese literature that the major emphasis of research is in general circulation problems and forecasting, and that the research applies mostly to the densely settled eastern portion of China.

Systems of the Australian Deserts

The arid land of Australia is affected by tropical weather on the equatorward side and by midlatitude cyclones on the poleward side. Aridity then results from the deserts' positions relative to the two regions of convergent lifting mechanisms. Bond (1960) discusses the importance of tropical weather to northern Australia. He notes that the severe drought of 1951-52 was caused by the failure of the northwest monsoon and the low incidence of tropical cyclone activity, and he believes that seasonal conditions are related to the anticyclonic circulations in the temperate zones of both hemispheres. The tropical cyclones of one season, 1955-56, have been discussed by Newman, Martin, and Wilkie (1956). This article is pertinent because of its discussion of individual storms, one of which was the most destructive cyclone ever to affect the west coast of Western Australia.

Moriarty (1955) has studied the synoptic behavior of the continental (thermal) low pressure area in summer and has classified the summer lows and determined the frequencies of classes. Karelsky (1961) has determined the cyclonic and anticyclonic characteristics of Australian weather. Foley (1956) has described the synoptic conditions associated with widespread rains, primarily as related to 500-millibar flow patterns. A general discussion of the climate of the Alice Springs area in the heart of the desert has been presented by Slatyer (1962).

The papers cited are but a selection of those available that describe and explain the weather patterns and systems of this continent. Again for Australia, the available literature is not usually directed to the arid regions, but rather is concerned with a much larger area than just the desert. Australia's well-developed weather service and its national research group, the Commonwealth Scientific and Industrial Research Organization (C.S.I.R.O.), have produced many studies of the synoptic situation for this part of the world.

Systems of the Monte-Patagonian Desert

The Monte-Patagonian desert of Argentina and Bolivia can be thought of as a rainshadow desert. The high mountain barrier induces a ridge-trough configuration that prevents cyclones that cross the mountain barrier from regenerating until they have passed beyond the limits of the narrow land (Boffi, 1949). Serra and Ratisbonna (1960) have written a thorough analysis of the air masses of South America. It is interesting to note that these authors felt it worthwhile to republish, essentially, a study first done in 1942. Prohaska (1952) has defined rainfall regimes for South America and related them to pressure and circulation patterns. The drought of 1960 was related to features of the large-scale pressure systems by Prohaska (1960). Burgos (1963) has discussed the climate of the arid regions in general and Capitanelli (1955) has studied the aridity of the province of San Luis and contributed in general to the climatology of Argentina. Diaz (1953) has studied anomalies of precipitation related to other variables such as temperature and pressure gradients. In contrast to the west coast of South America, the literature from the meteorologists of the arid countries east of the Andes is much more abundant. As is true in all of the southern hemisphere, synoptic studies are handicapped by the lack of upper-air data.

Systems of the Atacama-Peruvian Desert

The coastal deserts of South America west of the Andes owe their existence to the combined effects of the cold ocean currents and the stable eastern portion of a subtropical high-pressure cell. Although papers dealing with the climate of this area are not generally available, a good general discussion of the climate was given by Trewartha (1961) in his excellent book on the Earth's "problem climates." Another source of descriptive material has been the forecasting studies prepared by airlines, although their principal problem is that of fog and stratus in the coastal regions. One of these groups that has been active is Pan American Grace Airways (Panagra). Graves (1954) has summarized the research into the fog and stratus problem along the Peruvian Coast. Larson (1954) has prepared a bibliography, with abstracts, of local and general forecast studies by Panagra meteorologists for air routes over much of South America. Panagra in Lima kindly provided the titles of many research bulletins and reports, some of which contribute to the understanding of the meteorology of these arid lands. A personal communication from M. E. Graves (formerly with Panagra, now with the Department of Aerospace Engineering, University of Michigan) indicated that the published work about the meteorology of this desert was meager. A general discussion of the arid zone of Peru by de Reparaz (1958) is in part devoted to a discussion of climate. Howell (1953) described the complex mechanism of rainfall formation over some watersheds in the Andes which drain toward the coastal deserts. Graves, Schweigger, and Valdivia P. (1955) describe the abnormally cool coastal conditions of 1954. The number of papers that deal with the synoptic climatology of Chile is, as with Peru, small. A recent general discussion of the weather systems and rainfall of the arid zone of Chile has been given by Pizarro and Rivas (1965), and the general climatological features of the Chilean desert region have been discussed by

Weischet (1966) with special reference to the distribution of cloudiness. The climate for all of South America discussed by Serra (1963) has some application to the arid zones.

One weather phenomenon of the Peruvian Desert needs to be mentioned, the "el niño" effect of the equatorward portions of the desert. El niño is a replacement of the cold ocean currents and south winds along the coast by warm equatorial waters and northerly winds that bring in humid and unstable tropical air. The weather change has been described as dramatic, and torrential rains result. The frequency of occurrence of this event is about once every 10 years. A general discussion of the event has been given by Trewartha (1961, pages 31-33). Flohn and Hinkelmann (1952) relate the event to the shifting of the equatorial wind belts. (Flohn and his collaborators are currently engaged in studies of this area.) A serious effect of the change in ocean temperature is a reduced supply of fish as food for the guano birds found in the region. The importance of this phenomenon and coastal weather in general was reflected in the activities of the Compañía Administradora del Guano, Lima (now disbanded), with which the late Dr. Erwin Schweigger, a prominent authority of the coastal region, was associated. Schweigger's (1959) general geographical study of the area contains a chapter on climate (p. 181-246) with a good general discussion on the main elements of weather.

Systems of the North American Deserts

The deserts of North America span a latitude range of about 20°, extending from the Tropic of Cancer on the south to about 40°N. All three causes of aridity contribute to the formation of these deserts. Orographic barriers are most important on the northern boundaries where they affect the distribution of winter rainfall. The orographic barrier continues to be a factor as far south as Baja California, but the decreasing frequency of winter cyclones and decreasing rainfall amounts tend to mask the effect. In summer, the Pacific region of the desert comes under the influence of the stable eastern portion of a subtropical high pressure cell as cyclone frequencies decrease and cyclone tracks shift northward. The seasonal shift of the wind belts from winter to summer brings a flux of moisture from the Gulf of Mexico, extending westward across Mexico and northward into the southwestern United States. Its westward extent is to about the Arizona-California border and to parts of Baja California. Convective precipitation originates in this moist air mass. The southern portion of the North American deserts has a summer maximum in rainfall, the northern and western regions have a winter maximum, and the intermediate regions, such as central

Arizona, receive some precipitation in both seasons.

Papers that discuss the weather systems of North American deserts are in general not specifically directed toward arid-zone problems. Klein's (1957) previously cited discussion of tracks and frequencies of cyclones and anticyclones is pertinent to the synoptic climatology of winter rains. The summer rains in the southwestern United States have been described by Bryson and Lowry (1955), Bryson (1957a, b), and Jurwitz (1953). Carr (1951) has described unusually heavy summer rains and the synoptic weather patterns associated with them. Leighly (1953) deals in part with the explanation of the origin of rains in the arid regions of North America. Green and Sellers (1964) also include some descriptive material on the origins of climate in Arizona.

Although the synoptic climatology of the deserts in Mexico has been the subject of only a few papers, good general discussions of the synoptic climatology of Mexico as a whole do exist. Surface weather patterns and upper-air flow patterns are the subject of a paper by Mosiño A. (1964) in which weather types are recognized and related to rainfall. In an earlier paper, Mosiño A. (1959) related rainfall to upper-air flow patterns. Wallén (1956) made suggestions about the relationship of the atmospheric circulation to the rainfall over all of Mexico. Noble and Lebrija Celay (1956) have studied the synoptic patterns associated with drought in Mexico. Hastings and Turner (1965) have analyzed the seasonal distribution of rainfall in Baja California. They emphasize variations and discuss the origin of rainfall in the different seasons in this major contribution to the climatology of the Sonoran Desert.

2.   Desert Storms

Desert storms can be defined as atmospheric phenomena in the desert that produce some extraordinary effect on the environment or require the inhabitants of a region to alter significantly their normal routine in response to the storm. A midlatitude cyclone in the southwestern United States would not be considered a desert storm because such systems are relatively common. If such a system moved far south of its usual track, however, and produced unusual cold or wind in Mexico, it could be classified as a desert storm. Desert storms can be roughly subdivided into three groups: sand and dust storms, special winds, and tropical cyclones. Sand and dust storms are the most commonly mentioned special phenomena, and the literature abounds with references to these events; their frequency and effects are important factors to consider. Tropical storms are important to only a few deserts and unimportant to most. Special winds have a variety of different names but in fact are relatively similar in their genesis from desert to desert.

Dust and sand storms seem to be the storm phenomena most important to the desert areas, for arid lands are environments where the factors conducive to the formation of these storms are found. The vegetation is sparse, exposing the bare soil, usually dry. Wind speed tends to be high, because surface friction is small and the intense heating at the Earth's surface results in a large thermal coupling with the air aloft. The strong thermal heating also produces instability in the lowest layers, which leads to the development of the vertical eddies required to transport the dust aloft. The term "dust" is used to include material of such a particle size that terminal velocity is small in relation to the turbulent vertical motions of the air; dust can therefore remain airborne. On the other hand, "sand" includes particles with greater fall velocities that ordinarily are not kept aloft by wind currents. Sand moves at most only a few feet away from the Earth's surface; dust can be carried thousands of feet upward.

The processes by which dust and sand become airborne are probably best outlined by Bagnold (1941) in his excellent study of the processes going on at the Earth's surface. Chepil (1965), Belly (1964), and Hilst and Nickola (1959) have also written on this same general subject, the physics of blowing sand and dust. Dust and sand movement are important in several respects. For deserts, dust is the major phenomenon in the reduction of visibility. Moving sand can drift and cause dune formation, or it can blow with such an intensity as to halt essentially all human activity in an area. There are other interesting aspects of the effect of particulate matter in the atmosphere. Bugaev, Dzhordzhio, and Dubentssov (1952) describe the warming effect in the lower atmosphere (300-500 meters height) due to the lifting of hot dust and sand particles from the Earth's surface. Moreover, these particles absorb solar radiation, which increases their heating effect. El-Fandy (1949b) gives a theoretical discussion of this effect with data to support the theory. On the other hand, Bryson and Baerreis (1965) suggest that radiational cooling by dust in the atmosphere may have a stabilizing effect on the environment.

Importance of Sand and Dust

How important are the phenomena of blowing sand and dust to the deserts? One way in which this importance can be assessed is by examining the published climatological data from desert countries and noting whether or not the occurrence of these phenomena is usually given. Although data from all countries were not examined, it can be stated that, in general, the occurrence of blowing sand and dust is a climatic statistic ordinarily but not universally published. For example, the annual climatological summary of Kuwait does list the number of days with rising dust and sand. The annual report for Sudan does not list occurrences of dust storms but includes visibility data. The yearly summary for Saudi Arabia identifies reasons for the reduction of visibility and notes the hours of various degrees of visibility reduction due to sand, dust, or haze, as opposed to rain and mist. Sand and dust storms are also included under "Number of days of occurrence." Data for Libya make no specific mention of dust storms. Iran data make no mention of sand and dust, but Israel's annual summary does, and blowing sand and dust are mentioned in Afghanistan's monthly reports. This phenomenon is important enough to be noted frequently in published data. It is probably more apt to be specifically mentioned in summaries of countries that are primarily arid and less often for those primarily humid.

Strong Winds

Since dust storms result from strong winds, it is worthwhile to classify broadly the causes of these winds as large-scale storm systems or small-scale storm systems (local winds). Many names are used to describe essentially the same type of wind. As an indication of the numerous terms, Levi's (1965) excellent summary of the local winds of the Mediterranean area can be examined. A cleverly-designed map indicates the local region of each wind, its name, its direction, and the season in which it is found. Examples of the main types of winds may serve to illustrate the point. The sirocco is a wind of the Mediterranean area that occurs during the cold half of the year. It is a south or southeast wind and is the continental tropical air in the warm sector of an easterly-moving cyclonic system. It is dry and dusty, since the source region is the arid Sahara of North Africa. Other names are used to describe this wind. "Leste" is a general term used in North Africa, and "samum" is used in Algeria and Syria. An excellent study of the sirocco, made by Sivall (1957), deals primarily with Israel, Lebanon, Egypt, and Syria and the meteorological conditions involved in this wind system.

In Egypt, the term used to describe this wind is "khamsin" — not that it blows for 50 days but rather because it occurs most frequently in the 50-day period following the spring equinox. If this wind crosses mountains or descends a slope in such a manner that katabatic warming takes place, extremely hot and arid conditions can result. The ghibli of Libya, the sahat of Morocco, and the chili of Tunisia are examples.

Frequent and steady winds of the eastern Mediterranean region are the etesians, associated with the large thermal low over the Middle East in summer. The shamal or shimal of Iraq and the seistan of Iran are etesian winds.

High winds also originate in small-scale storm systems such as thunderstorms. The downdraft of a thunderstorm, in descending from the high cloud base typical of deserts, arrives at the Earth's surface much colder than the surrounding environment and spreads out across the desert as a miniature cold front. This process generates the habbob of Egypt and Sudan. Dust devils, of a scale smaller than thunderstorms, are small whirlwinds, caused by intense heating of the desert surface. They are ordinarily short-lived, and since they are usually moving with the general air flow will usually affect a given location for only a few seconds to at most a minute. They are sometimes called "sand devils" in North Africa and Arabia. Lacaze (1958) describes sand devils in the Sahara and the meteorological conditions of their formation. Sinclair (1966) has made a thorough theoretical study of dust devils over a desert surface.

Frequency and Formation

It is worthwhile to mention here a few papers treating the frequency and reasons for the formation of dust storms, but it is unnecessary to note the many papers that describe individual dust and sand storms because these are a usual part of the weather and climate of deserts and their effects are generally known.

Von Eschen (1961) has determined the frequency of dust storms for Albuquerque, New Mexico. Elser (1959) describes the origin of a severe dust storm at El Paso, Texas, as being the high-based thunderstorm of the region. Loewe (1943) has described the conditions for the occurrence of Australian dust storms. Seredkina (1960) and Zhirkov (1964) have written about dust storms in the Kazakhstan region of Russia in terms of frequencies and origins. Roy's (1954) discussion of the expansion of the Rajasthan Desert of India contains a discussion of types, origins, and frequencies of dust storms in northwest India. Awad (1962) investigated the frequency of dust at Baghdad and concluded that there had been an increase in incidence from 1950 to 1960. Frequencies of reduced visibilities at Bahrain due to dust have been discussed by Houseman (1961); he found that most dust originated in the shamal wind of the Persian Gulf region.

Dubief (1942, 1953b) has tabulated dust-storm and sand-wind frequencies for numerous Sahara stations. Freeman (1952) has written about the frequencies and origins of dust storms at Khartoum. A good general discussion of dust storms for the Sudan has been given by Bhalotra (1958). Lunson (1950) gives a general discussion of khamsin dust storms along the coast of Libya and Egypt and describes a specific example.

Tropical Storms

Tropical cyclones of the tropical storm and hurricane class are important to the North American, the Australian, and the Thar among the world's deserts. They are of minor concern to the Iranian and Arabian deserts. Ramage (1959) provides a summary of hurricane (typhoon) frequency for the Earth by region and season. Tropical cyclones important to the North American deserts occur off the west coast of Mexico and generally move westward. Occasionally they move with a northerly component and affect the coastal regions of Mexico. Only rarely has one of these tropical storms reached the United States. Rosendal (1962) and Ives (1952) have discussed the climatology of these storms. Kalstrom (1952) has discussed some of the effects of these storms along the coastal regions. Although infrequent, these west-coast hurricanes have been major weather disasters, causing both loss of human life and property destruction. It is interesting to note that the TIROS satellites have revealed that the frequency of tropical storms in the eastern north Pacific is about three times as large as had been previously thought (Sadler, 1964), but this incidence is of little consequence to the land areas.

Tropical storms are important to the northwestern coast of Australia and occur during the summer and fall seasons, December through May. The tropical cyclones for each season have been summarized in *Australian Meteorological Magazine;* see, for example, Australia Meteorological Office (1963). An article by Brunt and Hogan (1956) gives rather complete data on frequency of occurrence and seasonal behavior of these storms. The papers by Bond (1960) and Newman, Martin, and Wilkie (1956) cited in the synoptic section should also be noted here as contributions to the climatology of these storms in Australia.

The last region in which tropical cyclones are important is centered on the Arabian Sea, affecting in part the Thar, Iranian, and Arabian deserts. Khan (1957) has made a thorough study of the climatology of tropical cyclones that affect West Pakistan. Koteswaram (1961) has used TIROS satellite data to study the cloud patterns and tropical cyclones in the Arabian Sea. Sadler (1962) also utilized TIROS data to determine a hurricane track in the Arabian Sea which moved onto land and dissipated over southwestern Arabia.

Other Severe Winds

Occasional severe winds are also to be considered under the subject of desert storms. For example, Ives (1962a) mentioned the importance of cold winter air masses, which are relatively common in the United States, as they move south across the Gulf of California bringing unseasonably cold weather to the region. Obruchev (1950) and Poufir'ev (1958) discuss two local winds of the Russian deserts. Riaguzov (1955) has defined the fundamental synoptic situations associated with strong winds on Lake Issyk Kul' and has determined the frequencies and distribution of storm winds. Clark (1963) has surveyed tornadoes for all of Australia, though mostly with reference to the humid zone.

3. Upper-Air Circulations

Although it is the layer of air near the ground that is critical to the life cycle of plants and the water balance of the Earth's surface, it is also important to understand the relevance of the upper air to arid lands, or, more specifically, how the upper atmosphere of deserts is related to the problems of deserts.

In general, the farther one goes from the Earth's surface, the more there is a tendency to dissociate from a particular region and become more concerned with hemispheric and global considerations of the atmosphere. In the same manner that the synoptic climatology of the Thar Desert in summer is related to a wind system which dominates a much larger region, the Indian monsoon, so the upper-air motions over deserts are a part of a global- or at least hemispheric-scale system. In some ways the knowledge of the upper air over a particular desert is pertinent to that desert. The analysis of a particular storm, the computation of precipitable water, the problems of aeronautical meteorology, all depend upon local upper-air data. But the problems of climatic variability, of forecasting beyond a few days, and of determining the factors of the general circulation important to climate are related to large-scale considerations of atmospheric motions.

Since upper-air climatology tends to be a study of atmospheric processes of large areas, this topic may be subdivided into three geographic sectors. One such sector is the southern hemisphere poleward of the tropics, which contains all or part of four desert regions. A second general area is the region encompassing the Sahara of North Africa and extending eastward through the Middle East to the Thar Desert of western India. The third general region, which can be classified as the northern-hemisphere sector, contains the deserts of North America and the three desert areas in central Asia.

Worldwide and Hemispheric Upper-Air Data

Few publications contain upper-air data on a worldwide or hemispheric basis. The World Meteorological Organization (1965c) has published short-period averages of upper-air data at selected levels for CLIMAT stations based on a 10-year (1951-1960) period when available. Some of these stations are in the deserts. For the northern hemisphere, the U. S. Weather Bureau publishes the historical weather map series and accompanying data tabulations that contain upper-air sounding on a daily basis. Mean monthly data are published in *Monthly Climatic Data for the World,* issued by the U. S. Weather Bureau.

Southern-Hemisphere Sector

The southern hemisphere suffers most from the lack of upper-air observations. During the International Geophysical Year (IGY) about 66 radiosonde stations took data poleward of 20°S, obviously not enough stations to establish reliably the hemispheric upper-air patterns and their variations. Obasi (1963), in his analysis of southern-hemisphere angular momentum flux for 1958, used a total of 143 stations, 22 of which were in the northern hemisphere, a net of 121 in the southern hemisphere from equator to pole. The total existing record of analyzed upper-air data begins with the 18 months of the IGY and has been extended into the year 1959 by the South African weather service in its publications, *Notos.*

For Australia, mean monthly upper-air wind and radiosonde data have been tabulated by Lamond (1959) and Australia, Bureau of Meteorology (1958). Gibbs and Hounsell (1961) have discussed stratospheric winds over Australia. An examination of a paper such as Hutchings' (1961) illustrates that Australia does have a well-developed upper-air observational network. A second southern-hemisphere country with a well-developed network for upper-air observations is that of South Africa. Its weather bureau was responsible for the publication of the set of IGY weather maps for the southern hemisphere. South Africa's current radiosonde and rawin data are routinely published. Hofmeyr (1961) has analyzed the variability of upper-level winds and temperature for all of Africa up to 1960. For this continent, only 21 of the stations used had records for longer than 3 years. Taljaard (1963) has determined mean monthly 500-mb data for the IGY period plus 1959 for the 66 southern hemisphere upper-air stations. Mean surface and 500-mb charts based on about seven years of records have been prepared by van Loon (1961).

South America extends as a narrow shaft into the midlatitudes, so that upper-air observations from this continent are somewhat like a longitudinally oriented cross section through the westerlies. Alvarez (1962) has used data from the IGY period to study the jet stream over South America. About ten radiosonde stations were available. Double that number of stations would be expected in an area of that size and shape extending through the United States and Canada. In addition, the radiosonde stations in North America would be supplemented by a dense observing network upwind and downwind of the area; comparable regions of South America are essentially void of observations. The problems of studying the dynamics of the motions in regions of scant data are illustrated in a recent paper by Gutman and Schwerdtfeger (1965). This study describes an upper-level anticyclone over the Bolivian Andes and explains its origin as thermal due to the release of latent heat by thunderstorms in the region. The only upper-air data available were outside the study area. Routine summarization of upper-air data does not seem to have been made for Argentina, Bolivia, Chile, or Peru.

Tropical and Mediterranean Sector

The Tropical and Mediterranean sector is somewhat better observed than the southern-hemisphere sector because of the more favorable ratio of land to water and the distribution of land and water. An interesting paper by Sadler (1965) examines the availability of data in the tropics. In his study, Sadler collected the output of all the national weather services in the low latitudes and examined the amount of data available. He concluded that enough data are now routinely available for a reliable analysis of the large-scale global circulation of the tropical troposphere. His maps extended to about 40 degrees of latitude from the equator. Since this latitude belt contains a major portion of the world's deserts, it can be concluded that on global scale the density of reports is acceptable. Closer examination of Sadler's maps discloses, however, that the arid regions in particular are areas of limited coverage. Little surface data are available from the western and central Sahara and the Takla Makan Desert. At 700 mb the deserts are also areas of few observations, yet it appears that an acceptable hemispheric analysis can be made despite these shortcomings.

Sahara Circulations

The upper winds of the Sahara are mentioned mostly in studies of the upper winds of the Mediterranean regions; however, some summaries are available. Mean upper-air winds for French West Africa have been published by Afrique Occidentale Française Service Météorologique (1958), and frequencies of wind directions and of velocity determined. Austin and Dewar (1953) give mean data for eight stations in the Mediterranean area and Africa. Eltantawy (1964) has treated the tropical easterly jet stream over Africa. Dettwiller (1963) used data for 1958 through 1961 to define the subtropical jet stream over the western Sahara. Olintseva-Nebrat (1962) has studied the evolution of the subtropical jet over eastern Africa. The large-scale nature of the factors affecting development is brought out in the article. The proceedings of a symposium particularly pertinent to this region are available in World Meteorological Organization (1964a). The subject of the symposium, high-level forecasting over Africa and the Middle East, resulted in the presentation of several papers that contribute to an understanding of the upper-air circulations over this region.

Somali-Chalbi Circulations

The East African Common Services Organization, Meteorological Department (1963b) has summarized the radiosonde observations of a 6-year period for Nairobi Fàntoli (1963) has made an analysis of 3 years of pilot balloon runs at Addis Ababa, while Berges (1962) has used data from Aden, Khartoum, and Djibouti to describe upper-level winds over the Red Sea area.

Arabian Circulations

For the Arabian Desert, some summarizing of radiosonde data has been done by the Meteorological Office of Great Britain for Bahrain and Aden as part of a series of publications of upper-air data for stations maintained by the Great Britain Meteorological Office. Data for 1946-1950 and 1951-1955 have been published in two volumes. Murray (1960) has made a few comments on 200-mb winds at Aden. Shaia (1962) has summarized radiosonde data taken at Beer-Ya'akov in Israel for 1957-1959. This radiosonde station, established in 1956, was the first radiosonde station of the Israel Meteorological Service.

Iranian Circulations

A survey of available data shows that few observations of the upper-air circulation are made in Iran and Afghanistan. Weickmann (1961, 1962) has reviewed and summarized the characteristics of the subtropical jet stream in the Middle East. Kaka, Sakka, and al-Basri (1962) discuss an example of the activity of the subtropical jet over the Middle East in which they relate surface weather to the jet-stream development.

Thar Circulations

The upper-level circulations associated with western disturbances over the Thar Desert have been discussed by Singh (1963). The state of knowledge of the upper air over India is related to the study of the monsoon circulation. Ramakrishnan, Sreeniva-saiah, and Venkiteshwaran (1960) present the mean distribution of temperature and wind over India for May, June, and July to illustrate the start of the summer monsoon, and for November to represent the winter monsoon. Pisharoty and Asnani (1960) describe the 500-mb flow patterns during the summer monsoon (July). The variability of upper winds over India in terms of the steadiness and standard vector deviation has been determined by Krishnan, Pant, and Ananthakrishnan (1961). A general discussion of both the westerly jet stream of the dry season and the easterly jet of the summer monsoon has been given by Koteswaram (1962). Ramaswamy (1956, 1962) has related upper-air circulations to surface weather, convection, and breaks in the monsoon, and shows the relationship between large-scale atmospheric motions in the upper air and rainfall. The available material on upper-air circulations is clearly directed toward the understanding of the monsoon circulations. In the near future, results of the International Indian Ocean Expedition, reviewed by Ramage (1962), may be expected to contribute to the basic understanding of large-scale wind systems of the region.

Northern-Hemisphere Sector

The upper-air climatology of the midlatitude deserts of the northern hemisphere can be thought of as part of the studies of the upper air of the entire hemisphere. Availability of data does not present the problem that it does in the tropics and the southern hemisphere, although Mexico is one country with few upper-air stations, and the upper-air climatology of this region suffers from this lack. The radiosonde station at Guaymas on the east coast of the Gulf of California is the only one in the desert or in the north. Mosiño A. (1959, 1964) has made the most significant contributions to the knowledge of upper-air circulations in Mexico. For the United States, mean upper-air data for a 10-year period have been published in the Series *Technical Papers* by the U. S. Weather Bureau, and mean monthly values are published routinely.

One publication in particular should be mentioned for the Soviet Union. One of the series *Climate of the U. S. S. R.* is *Climate of the Free Atmosphere* (Nakorenko and Tokar', 1959). This volume discusses the upper-air circulations for all of the Soviet Union and in terms of more localized regions. The section entitled "Central Asia and Kazakhstan" is particularly pertinent.

It has been mentioned that problems of the general circulation and forecasting have been a main concern of Chinese meteorologists, and papers have been cited as examples of their work.

C. ARIDITY

1. Measures of Water Use

One of the first impressions received from an examination of the climatological literature of arid lands is the importance of the concept of aridity. Aridity can be thought of as an expression in a qualitative or quantitative manner of the dryness of an area. It is not surprising that a measure of dryness is an important topic, for if eventual use of deserts is a goal of those who study them, a critical factor will be the ability to moderate or endure their basic aridity. Aridity must therefore be understood, defined, and explained.

Aridity is basically a comparison between water *supply* and water *need*. Water can be naturally supplied, by rain for example, or artificially supplied, by irrigation. Measurement of *supply* does not pose any real problem to the evaluation of aridity; rather, it is water use or water *need* that challenges adequate definition. Water use of a region (evapotranspiration) and water need (potential evapotranspiration) are separate quantities, but closely related in the search for a definition of aridity. The concern in these next several sections is with methods of actual measurement or estimation of water use or water need in the quantitative sense. We are not here concerned with indexes of aridity that attempt to express the dryness of a region as observed in the relationship between natural responses and the elements of climate.

Historically, there have been three major approaches to the problem of expressing evapotranspiration and potential evapotranspiration. One line of investigation has been the direct measurement of water lost from some evaporating surface. Pan evaporation, the evaporation from a small surface of water freely exposed to the atmosphere, is the most common direct measurement. In addition to pan evaporation, other methods have been devised to measure the water loss from some more representative surface than that of plain water. Many instruments have been designed, from the complex and elaborate weighing lysimeters to the Piche porous paper wick evaporimeter.

A second approach to the definition of water need was the development of empirical expressions that used commonly available climatological data in a formula that, according to the formulator, gave an estimate of the amount of potential evapotranspiration from a surface. These formulas were derived from the observed water use of irrigated fields, lakes, watersheds, or instruments and the accompanying meteorological conditions. Thornthwaite's formula is an example of this approach. Other equations based on fundamental physical principles but using empirically determined constants were also formulated, but these systems, of which Penman's is the most familiar,

require climatic data usually available only from synoptic class weather stations.

The third general approach to the determination of water use can be termed theoretical, in that the water movement from ground to air is determined from the physical processes going on at the Earth's surface. Two different processes have been used. In one, the energy balance at the Earth's surface is investigated and that portion of the heat that goes into the evaporation of water is determined. In the second theoretical approach, the turbulent transfer of water vapor away from the Earth's surface is measured either by measuring the turbulent eddies that pass through a level near the Earth's surface or by measuring the gradient of water vapor near the Earth's surface and computing the transport by turbulent diffusion. These turbulent transfer methods suffer from the necessity for elaborate instrumentation and from the uncertainty of assumptions that must be made about some factors in the equations. Both theoretical methods provide direct measurements of actual water use.

Measurement by Instruments

Pan Evaporation

The oldest methods of investigation of water use have involved the direct measurement of water loss from environments. The most common is that of pan evaporation; the loss from a small surface of water, usually under 10 square feet, freely exposed to the atmosphere. Although pan evaporation is a measure of something, investigators are not unanimous in their analyses of what that "something" is. Pans have been used to represent lake evaporation, but it has been found that pans and lakes have differing evaporation rates and seasonal variations. The ratio of lake to pan evaporation, sometimes called the pan coefficient, is probably about the order of 0.6 for arid areas and increases in more humid climates. Hounam (1958) has given an outstanding discussion of pan coefficients. Among other things, he concludes that there is no justification for the adoption of a universal coefficient for Australia and suggests that lake evaporation might be more reliably measured by Penman's equation.

A second problem with pan evaporation measurements is the lack of standardization of pan designs. Different types of pans will give different results. Robertson (1955) discusses the need for a standard evaporation pan, and Hounam (1961) also notes the need for a standard pan and points out the necessity for careful attention to observational technique. This latter paper is an excellent example of the detailed analysis required to assure that pan evaporation records are meaningful. Nimmo's (1964) paper is another that thoroughly discusses many aspects of pan evaporation.

Pan evaporation measurements are commonly made worldwide. Kohler, Nordenson, and Baker (1959) have published pan evaporation maps for the United States. Long (1948) presents data for about 40 stations in the arid Southwest. McCulloch (1961) discusses pan evaporation data for parts of Africa, while Kriel (1961) and Roberts (1961) have contributed general discussions on pan evaporation based upon their work in South Africa. The 1961 Hounam paper cited above presents extensive data for Australia.

Lysimeters

A second method of measuring water use is with the lysimeter, a large tank filled with vegetation and soil similar to the surroundings and equipped with a mechanism that allows the tank to be weighed precisely or otherwise equipped so that its water use can be accurately measured. By adjusting the water available to the tank or the surface of the tank, water use under a variety of conditions can be measured. Two of the lysimeter installations in the United States are in the West, one in a Mediterranean climate at Davis, California, described by Pruitt and Angus (1960), and the other in the desert at Tempe, Arizona (van Bavel and Myers, 1962). A major lysimeter installation abroad is in Australia, described by McIlroy and Angus (1963). An excellent review discussion of lysimeters — their forms and applications — has been published by the International Association of Scientific Hydrology (1959).

As an example of the use of lysimeters, a paper by McIlroy and Angus (1964) can be cited. This study has multiple objectives and produced several interesting conclusions. For example, it was found that evaporation from well-watered grass could exceed that of a free water surface. It was shown that the lysimeter grass evaporation could be well estimated from pan evaporation or by empirical formulas. Another example of the use of lysimeters is given in a paper by Fritschen and van Bavel (1962). The purpose of their study was to investigate the components of the energy balance of evaporating surfaces in arid lands. Fritschen and van Bavel (1963) used their lysimeter to investigate evaporation from small and extended bodies of water, again as a study of the energy balance equation.

Lysimeters are expensive pieces of equipment to build and operate, and the experimental technique requires careful attention to detail. For this reason there will probably be few operated in the arid zones; however, observations in large numbers are not required, because the real usefulness of lysimeters is in determining relationships between water need or water use and more commonly or more easily observed meteorological factors.

Other Direct Measurements

There are other methods of measuring evaporation, the Piche evaporimeter being one instrument commonly used because of its small size. It is convenient and inexpensive and is used for comparing regions. It does not give absolute results because it is very sensitive to differences in exposure to the atmosphere. Both its absolute accuracy and its degree of correlation to actual water use are poor.

Standardization of equipment and technique are both necessary in evaporation measurements. It appears that the U. S. Class A pan is gradually being accepted as some sort of a standard, not because it is noticeably superior to other evaporating instruments but because it has been used extensively and a backlog of records has been accumulated.

Theoretical Measurement of Water Use

Theoretical measures of water use are methods based upon the physical processes going on at the Earth's surface and the layer of atmosphere adjacent to it. There is no need to review the details of the theoretical methods of estimating water use or water need; several excellent articles are available. One of the best is a chapter on the loss of water to the air by Thornthwaite and Hare (1965). A less technical and more descriptive review has been written by Sibbons (1962). This well-written discussion emphasizes critical comparison and evaluation of the several processes. Both of these reviews contain excellent bibliographies. If a review of the details of the processes were in order in this study, either of these two papers could be inserted in this report almost unchanged. An older review concerned with the outline of basic ideas is the now-classic paper on evaporation by Penman (1956). A review of the water balance and evaporation with special reference to the arid zone has been made by Deacon, Priestley, and Swinbank (1958) in their excellent article for Unesco's Canberra Symposium on Arid Zone Climatology and in part by van Wijk and de Wilde (1962) for Unesco's 1960 Symposium on Arid Zone Problems. A new textbook on physical climatology by Sellers (1965) presents a thorough treatment of all aspects of these methods.

Turbulent Diffusion

Theoretical approaches have been carried out along two separate lines. One method has been to investigate the turbulent diffusion of water vapor from the Earth's surface; it is based upon the fact that the flux of moisture can be determined from a known vertical gradient of water vapor and measurement of a mass of air passing through some level. The basic mathematical treatment can be found in Sutton (1953); general review articles have already been noted. Major work along this line has been done by Australian meteorologists at C.S.I.R.O., as evidenced by several articles in Unesco's Arid Zone Research XI, *Climatology and Microclimatology.* One of the major problems with this aerodynamic approach has been to devise instruments capable of measuring the rapid fluctuations in temperature, wind, and moisture content of the air as the eddies pass vertically through the measurement level. Not only are the instrumentation requirements demanding, but the analysis of the data is laborious and time-consuming. An effort to reduce the amount of data analysis has been made by dealing with deviations from the means of the several variables. Instrumentation that essentially measures deviations from the mean has been developed. "Evapotron" is the name given by Dyer and Moher (1965) to a device for eddy flux measurements. An example of the use of the instrument is given by Dyer and Pruitt (1962) and Dyer (1965). The usefulness of the turbulent diffusion method is limited by the neglect of advection terms and by assumptions that must be made about turbulent transfer coefficients. Also, the mechanics of operating an installation are usually beyond the capabilities and resources of most research programs.

Energy Balance

The energy-balance approach to the measurements of evaporation seeks to determine that portion of the available heat going into the evaporation of water by determining all the energy sources and sinks at the evaporating surface. The energy balance is usually expressed in an equation of the form

$$R = G + LE + H$$

where R = radiation balance,
   G = heat transfer to the soil,
   LE = energy expended in evaporation
   H = sensible heat transfer to the air.

Radiation balance, R, and heat transfer to the soil, G, are relatively easy to measure, and the continued development of instrumentation, particularly in the field of net radiometers, has contributed to a good determination of these quantities. Latent heat and sensible heat transfer are more difficult to determine, and they are usually investigated by assigning the relative amounts of heat that go into each by some scheme such as the use of the Bowen ratio. The energy-balance approach probably leads to an experimental system easier to operate than the turbulent diffusion system, but it suffers from the fact that advection terms can be far from negligible and that

certain assumptions must be made about turbulent transfer coefficients.

The two theoretical schemes of measuring actual evapotranspiration would not be used routinely to arrive at values of water use because of the high cost and large amount of effort required to operate these systems. Rather they provide a means of studying the processes of evaporation, evaluating the basic theories, and acquiring data for the formulation of empirical relationships between measured evaporation and commonly observed meteorological factors. The Evapotron holds some hope of being an operational instrument in the future, but it still requires too much in the way of skills, experience, and initial cost to be practical for routine use.

Empirical Measurement of Water Use

The empirical methods of estimating evaporation, usually potential evapotranspiration, are based on use of commonly observed climatological data in formulas that give the evaporation from a surface of water or from a land surface with abundant water available for evapotranspiration.

Potential evapotranspiration has never been precisely defined. Is it water evaporated from a short green crop, completely shading the ground, of uniform height and never short of water? This only leads to the problem of specifying the uniform height and deciding whether crop type makes a difference. Since there is no exact definition, there can be no exact method of computing it. It has been suggested by Robertson (1955) that the standard for evaporation be based on regularly observed climatic data, which would allow for direct comparison of water need from one area to another. The problem is to define a standard instrument and then be able to estimate accurately the water loss from it in terms of the meteorological elements affecting it.

The best known, most widely used, and least understood equations are those devised by Thornthwaite (1948). Although evapotranspiration must depend upon many factors, these equations were, in the final analysis, based upon temperature and day length only. Thornthwaite's work with potential evapotranspiration did result in an index of aridity in which the water surplus in a given year was combined in an expression with the water deficits and potential evapotranspiration to give a number that could be used as a measure of aridity. This index is discussed in Thornthwaite and Mather (1955). It was this index, or the earlier 1948 expression, that was used by Meigs (1953*a*) in the preparation of his now classic maps of the arid zone. The index has been used repeatedly for climatic classification. Thornthwaite and Mather (1955) list an extensive bibliography of articles that used the Thornthwaite system in climate classification. Not all of the articles refer to arid lands, although many do. Further discussion of the Thornthwaite method is found in Pelton, King, and Tanner (1960) and van Wijk and de Vries (1954).

From this beginning, other empirical formulations were devised. Sibbons (1962) lists 12 additional papers that present empirical methods for calculating potential evapotranspiration. A concept related to potential evapotranspiration is the idea of consumptive use, defined by Blaney and Criddle (1962, and in earlier papers), as a measure of the amount of water necessary to produce maximum economic yields of a certain crop. Relationships were based upon temperature and daylight hours during the growing season and, in addition, an empirical constant for individual crops.

Somewhere between the theoretical methods of determining evapotranspiration and the strictly empirical methods for estimating potential evapotranspiration, such as Thornthwaite's, are methods founded on the theoretical methods but also relying on empirical relationships. Two methods identical to one another in essence were independently suggested by Penman (1948) and Budyko (1956). The methods combine the turbulent-transfer and heat-balance methods, some reasonable approximations, and empirical constants to arrive at expressions for evaporation from moist surfaces. The previously mentioned review articles discuss these methods completely, in particular Penman's because of its greater familiarity to Western meteorologists and agriculturists. Penman's equations were devised for evaporation from a water surface, but were later modified with an empirical constant to be applicable to a "short green crop, completely shading the ground, of uniform height and never short of water." In its computational form, the observational data needed are duration of bright sunshine, mean air temperature, mean humidity, and wind speed, quantities usually available at synoptic class weather stations.

Oasis Effect

The measurement of evapotranspiration in arid lands suffers from another problem not so important to more humid regions. This is the "oasis" effect. When dry air moves over a surface having an abundant supply of water, for example an irrigated field or a lysimeter, the radiational energy may not be sufficient to supply all the latent heat required for evaporation. Energy must then be supplied from the air itself, energy advected over the evaporating surface. If evapotranspiration is being measured from a lysimeter in order to determine the water require-ments for large irrigated fields, a buffer zone must be maintained around the instrument in order to eliminate or modify the advection effects. Available evidence indicates the required distance to be approximately 200 meters. If, however, the purpose of the measurement is to gain an idea of the water stresses on natural vegetation, then the oasis effect is not important.

An attempt to analyze the oasis effect has been made by de Vries (1959), who develops a theory that takes into account the advective energy in determining the potential evapotranspiration rate for irrigated areas of limited extent. The solution of the oasis effect problem awaits development of appropriate climatic correction factors.

Evaluations of the Methods

Since empirical methods provide the only practical ways of estimating water need on a large scale, evaluations of the various methods are needed. As an example of the type of work which should be done, several papers by G. Stanhill of the National and University Institute of Agriculture, Rehovot, Israel, can be cited. In one study (Stanhill, 1961a) a comparison was made between evaporation from lysimeters (assumed actual) and that computed from other empirical equations (four methods) or measured with instruments (four methods). The correlation between actual potential evapotranspiration and computed or measured was about 0.95 on a monthly basis and about 0.75 on a weekly basis. Penman's open-water equation gave the highest correlation and the slope of the regression line was nearly unity. Other methods had high correlations but slopes of regression lines varied. Tank and pan evaporation methods also gave good results. A cost analysis of the operation of the various systems was given, in which it was concluded that pan evaporation was the most practical method. This paper presents a systematic evaluation of the most commonly used methods of determining potential evapotranspiration carried out in an arid environment.

Stanhill has also compared the usefulness of different techniques in different climatic regions. In three different papers he has made comparisons of the accuracy of different methods in England (Stanhill, 1958) Israel's Negev (Stanhill, 1961b) and in Nigeria (Stanhill, 1963). The actual evapotranspiration, determined by lysimeters, was compared with that computed from Penman's equation, by Thornthwaite's method, and measured from evaporation pans. In the desert, Penman's equation compared well with pan evaporation and was highly correlated to actual evapotranspiration. The same was true in England. Thornthwaite's method gave underestimates in the desert but worked well in England. In Nigeria, Penman's method did not work particularly well and was less accurate than the pan evaporation method. Thornthwaite's method gave good annual results, although there were seasonal variations in accuracy.

The specific results of studies such as Stanhill's are not of prime importance here, but his approach to the problem is noteworthy. Here are systematic efforts to assess the relative merits of each scheme for determining water need. This work is important for the deserts, but it is equally important to know the variation among different climatic types. The fact that the different methods did not work as well in different climatic types suggests the probability that no one measure will work equally well in all latitudes. It is necessary to expand the research done in the deserts to define more completely the relative merits of the various systems. It is equally important to determine why a system may work well under some conditions and less satisfactorily in other instances. Such evaluations should lead to eventual improvement in the forms and types of equations available.

The discussion of the various methods to measure or estimate water use and water need does not imply that this subject is a unique problem of deserts. There seems to be no indication that these methods were developed in connection with the problems of deserts. Rather they evolved as a result of a general meteorological and climatological problem; however, the concepts do seem to have greater application in deserts than in more humid regions. It is important to look at some applications of these schemes of measurement of water consumption in desert environments.

Sellers (1964) used Budyko's method to compute potential evapotranspiration at Yuma, Arizona. Comparisons were made with the amounts computed from Penman's equations and by Thornthwaite's method. The latter method gave values much lower. One of the aims of the study was to determine the effects of different relative humidities on the rate of evaporation; increased relative humidity decreased evaporation. Sellers also showed how the variation in relative humidity would affect the temperature difference between the air and the evaporating surface. For low relative humidities, radiation does not meet the latent-heat requirements for evaporation, and energy must be drawn from the air. Stork (1959), reporting on evapotranspiration problems in Iraq, found that Penman's method seemed to be in agreement with observed water use. Mention is made of the fact that Blaney and Criddle's method has been used extensively in Iraq. Hussain, Ahmad, and Aziz (1962) compared pan and Penman evaporation in Pakistan and presented 9 years of data.

Gentilli (1953) has reviewed some of the empirical formulas for determining potential evapotranspiration. A formula by Halstad based on duration of daylight, temperature range, and moisture content of the air was found to agree with Australian data better than Thornthwaite's or Blaney's methods.

In the U.S.S.R. there seems to have been less use of systems of estimating evapotranspiration familiar to the Western nations and greater use of formulas developed by Russian climatologists. Molchanov (1955) has used a modified form of a formula by Ivanov (based on temperature and relative humidity) to compute evapotranspiration in Central Asia. Ivanov (1959) has used his formula to estimate potential evaporation in the Russian plains.

In water balance maps of West Africa presented and discussed by Garnier (1960), potential evapotranspiration is computed using a modified Thornthwaite formula.

An interesting evaluation has been made by Brutsaert (1965) working in low latitudes. He points out that formulas based on temperature and day length, such as those of Thornthwaite or Blaney and Criddle, will not work in latitudes where both of these factors have small annual variations but where evaporation does vary because of seasonal variations in humidity and wind speed. Penman's method worked fairly well, but the highest correlation between actual measured evapotranspiration and that found by other methods was with a standard evaporation pan.

Pan Evaporation as a Measure of Potential Evapotranspiration

It is pertinent to examine some of the results of comparing actual evapotranspiration (usually designed to be potential) from a lysimeter to that from an evaporation pan. Pan evaporation usually exceeds lysimeter evapotranspiration with a ratio of lysimeter to pan of about 0.75, although this number varies from study to study and is not always constant among seasons at a given location. The relationship between the two different measures of water loss is usually very good, as good if not better than that found when comparing lysimeter values to empirical estimates determined with equations such as Penman's. These empirical equations usually give estimates that are better answers in the quantitative sense than that from pan evaporation, but not superior when used in regression equations.

Pan evaporation is advantageous in that the instrumentation is easy to build and install, though as Hounam (1961) points out, it must be properly maintained in order to produce good data. Pans can be used where the climatological data necessary for computations using Penman's methods are not available, and, as Stanhill (1961a) has shown, they are more economical to use than other methods. Pans alone do not give accurate quantitative estimates, and relationships need to be established between pan and lysimeter values. There is no evidence of any universal relationships; however, it would be expected that the same regression equation would apply within the same general climatic region.

In view of the high correlation between pan evaporation and the water use of lysimeters, it seems worthwhile to investigate all aspects of the relationships between these two elements, the variations of regression equations and the reasons for variations in different climatic regions. If regression techniques can be used to obtain good quantitative estimates of potential evapotranspiration, existing pan data can be used to determine aridity at many locations. Not only would this be valuable in a climatological sense, but it would establish the usefulness of this relatively inexpensive instrument for practical use where an estimate of potential evapotranspiration is needed.

2. Climatic Typing and Indexes of Aridity

Climatic typing or classification is an attempt to designate regions of the Earth where the elements of weather and climate tend to be relatively uniform. The bases of typing systems are usually temperature, precipitation, and their seasonal distribution, in some simple or complex combination. The difference between climatic types is some specific characteristic of climate that has significance because it marks the change or transition from one response of the environment to another, when the response can be attributed to climate. Classifications are devised for a variety of reasons, and the motivation behind the formulation will determine which elements are deemed important. Vernet (1958) has included an excellent discussion of the basis of climatic typing and a detailed description of three systems.

Classifications of Climate

The best-known classification of climate is that of Köppen (1931) in which climatic types were recognized mainly by differences in vegetation. This classification has been used widely as a teaching aid and has considerable merit in distinguishing the general world patterns of climate. Many modifications have been made to this basic system, but for the most part these changes do not alter the system in any fundamental manner. It is still a descriptive system, that is, terms or phrases can be used to describe the different responses of the environment to the climate. A second general classification has been formulated by Thornthwaite (1931), who used complex functions of temperature and rainfall combined with such concepts as temperature efficiency and precipitation effectiveness to define his climatic types.

Meigs System

General classifications of climates such as Thornthwaite's or Köppen's are not of concern here. Rather our interest lies in classifications that emphasize the concept of aridity or are directed toward arid lands. The classification that best fits that category is that of Meigs (1953a). At the onset of Unesco's interest in arid lands in the early 1950's, Meigs' maps were constructed to fill an immediate need to delineate the arid zone. The system used was to compute the index of aridity suggested by Thornthwaite (1948) and to choose specific values of this index to define different degrees of aridity. In addition, at the suggestion of others, areas classified "extremely arid" not only displayed a high index of aridity but also showed no seasonal rainfall distribution and had a history of at least one 12-month period without recorded rain. Besides using the basic index of aridity, the system also included the use of seasonal distributions of rainfall and temperature. An area classified *Sb24* on Meigs' map is a semiarid region with summer precipitation; the coldest month has a mean temperature between 10 and 20°C, and the mean of the warmest month is greater than 30°C. Meigs' system has proven useful, providing a sort of analogy system, in that an *Sb24* area in one part of the world would have a climate similar to an *Sb24* area elsewhere. It is interesting to note that Meigs wrote that the choice of his temperature limits is not self-apparent, but he explains that he chose values which were already in widespread use due to their probable significance. It is easy to visualize an expanded Meigs system that could have much wider application without much increase in complexity. The system is applied in Meigs (1953b) and further explained in Meigs (1957).

Unesco Bioclimatic System

The second climatic classification to be discussed here is not strictly an arid-zone classification, but emphasizes the importance of aridity. This is a recent scheme for bioclimatic mapping of the Mediterranean Zone (Unesco-FAO, 1963). The essential factors considered were temperature, precipitation, the number of days with rain, atmospheric humidity, dew, and mist. Hot, cold, and dry seasons are also terms used in the system. Ombrothermic diagrams indicate the duration and severity of drought, and an index of hot-weather drought (xerothermic index) takes into account humidity and the character of rainfall during the drought season. The choice of several threshold temperatures and the value of the xerothermic index define the types of climate. It is of interest to observe that the basis of the definition of a dry month is an empirical relationship between temperature and rainfall, specifically $P<2T$, where P is the monthly mean precipitation in millimeters and T is the monthly mean temperature in degrees centigrade. The xerothermic index takes into account such factors as mist or dew days (counted as half a dry day each) and various values of relative humidity, which modify the computed dryness. The classification is based upon proper choice of the magnitude and influence of the pertinent factors, and the choice is based upon past experience. For example, dryness is defined as a condition wherein the precipitation in millimeters is less than 2 times the temperature in degrees centigrade; this rule-of-thumb relationship has been found by many authorities to be useful in plant ecology and to work well in parts of the Mediterranean region.

The Meigs system and the Unesco bioclimatic system both emphasize the importance of aridity and are therefore particularly applicable to arid lands. They both use a similar principle, the division of a major climatic type into many subtypes based upon degree of aridity (primarily) and upon other characteristics of the climate (secondarily). Both systems are designed to provide comparisons of areas within major climatic type. The Unesco system for the Mediterranean zone can be applied to high latitudes also, but it appears to be of most use for areas experiencing dry, hot summers. These systems seem to be of the type needed, but their usefulness is dependent on the proper choice of temperatures and seasonal distribution of precipitation in their formulation. If one can isolate the important factors, then systems such as these seem to have real application for arid-zone research.

Indexes of Aridity

The two systems already mentioned are designed to provide climatic classification. Beyond these systems, numerous indexes of aridity have been proposed, formulas that combine the elements of weather and climate into expressions for the degree of dryness of a region. The best-known index of aridity is probably that of Thornthwaite (1948), which has been slightly revised by Thornthwaite and Mather (1962). The moisture index is $I_m = [(S\text{-}d)/PE]\ 100$, where S is the excess of monthly rainfall over potential evapotranspiration and storage into the soil during wet months, d is the deficit of rainfall plus available soil moisture below potential evapotranspiration during dry months, and PE is potential evapotranspiration. Values of −67, −33, and 0 separate "arid," "semiarid," "dry subhumid," and "moist subhumid," terms used in Thornthwaite's nomenclature. Potential evapotranspiration is computed using the complex equations derived by Thornthwaite, based essentially on temperature and hours of daylight. This is probably the most widely used index of aridity.

One of the early, simple indexes was developed by de Martonne (1926). He used precipitation and temperature to obtain an expression for dryness, $P/(t+10)$, where P is precipitation in millimeters and t is temperature in degrees centigrade. Another one of the better-known empirical relationships is that of Emberger (1955 and earlier papers) in which his quotient of dryness, $100\ P/(M+m)\ (M-m)$, is based on precipitation (P), the mean maximum temperature in the hottest month (M), and the mean minimum temperature in the coolest month (m). This expression has been used extensively for Mediterranean-type climates. According to Davitaya (1964), one of the indexes most widely used by Russian agrometeorologists is Selianinov's expression $10P/\Sigma t$, where P is total precipitation in millimeters and t is the monthly mean temperature, both for the period of the year when the average daily temperature exceeds $10°C$.

Prescott (1949), as discussed in Prescott (1958), related rainfall, P, to s.d., saturation deficit, in the expression $P/\text{s.d.}^{.75}$. A value of rainfall in inches equal to 5 (s.d.$^{.75}$) is a measure of evapotranspiration for the limiting condition of an arid region. Critical values of the index were chosen on the basis of soil formation and the distribution of vegetation. Budyko (1956) established a relationship for a radiational index of dryness, R.I.D. $= R/LP$, which is the ratio of the radiative balance at the Earth's surface, R, to the amount of energy required to evaporate the rainfall P, where L is the latent heat of vaporization. Steppes are characterized by values of the index between 1 and 2, semiarid areas by values between 2 and 3, and deserts typically by values 3 or greater.

Discussion of Index Systems

Under "Indexes of Aridity" above, six of the more common indexes have been mentioned. Dzerdzeevskii (1958) lists 19 different expressions. In addition to the basic indexes, numerous minor modifications of these expressions have been made to fit the particular purposes and data of other authors. Comparisons have shown that all give about the same answers, though some work better than others in particular climatic types (for example, in Mediterranean climates, or in humid as contrasted to arid regions). An interesting review of some of the more common indexes and their usefulness in the Mediterranean zone has been given by Meigs (1964).

Maps using the various indexes of aridity have proven useful in vegetation studies and agrometeorological work. There is, however, something unsettling about a procedure that uses relationships without a clear understanding of the physical processes involved in those relationships. Thornthwaite's scheme of the interaction of rainfall, potential evapotranspiration, and soil moisture seems sound, although he computes potential evapotranspiration as a function of existing temperature records and day length only. Other expressions such as de Martonne's $P/(t+10)$, Emberger's $100P/(M+m)(M-m)$, or Prescott's $P/s.d.^{.75}$ seemingly do not have the same sound, fundamental basis on which to base a system of climatic classification. On the other hand, Budyko's R/LP appears well founded and has proven useful in widely varying locations.

Discussions and Applications of Climatic Classification Schemes

Numerous papers discuss classifications of climate for the world and for the arid zones. Some of the authors use the conventional systems of classification, while others have derived their own particular criteria that seldom seem to have widespread use. A few of these papers should be mentioned specifically because of their application to arid zones or their discussions of classifications in general. For Mexico, Stretta and Mosiño A. (1963) have used a modified Emberger index of aridity to delineate the arid zones of that country. A map of distribution of aridity shows that about 38 per cent of Mexico is classed as desert. García (1964) has applied a Köppen classification of climate modified to fit the conditions in Mexico, particularly with respect to the boundaries of the desert, steppe, and humid climates. Soto Mora and Jauregui O. (1965) has published monthly average daily maximum and minimum temperatures for 578 climatological stations in Mexico and have used these data to construct maps of aridity based on Emberger's index of aridity.

Burgos and Vidal (1951) applied Thornthwaite's classification to Argentina and concluded that it provided the best correspondence with vegetation zones when compared with other systems. Papadakis (1954) discussed various methods of expressing the degree of moisture or aridity and concluded that a formula based on saturation deficit produced the best results. Prada Estrada (1948) used Thornthwaite's system to map climates in Bolivia, but on the basis of only a few stations with short periods of record. Prescott (1958) and Gentilli (1953) have compared different systems in classifying the climates of Australia. Prescott's paper emphasizes the use of saturation deficit as a parameter for delineating deserts.

Zhegnevskaia (1954) and Dzerdzeevskii (1958) have compared different measures of aridity in the Soviet Union. M. S. Ahmad (1958) and K. S. Ahmad (1951) have both compared systems in Pakistan. M. S. Ahmad preferred Penman's method to that of Thornthwaite and found good correspondence between measured and computed values of evaporation. India's climate has been investigated by Subrahmanyam (1956a, b) using the Thornthwaite scheme. Bhatia (1957) has made a comparative study with several systems and concluded that Thornthwaite's methods give realistic values in India. Ganji (1954) has made comparative classifications for Iran. South Africa's climate has been classified by Schulze (1958) using Thornthwaite's system. For Morocco, Joly (1958) has used Thornthwaite's system to classify climate and Bryssine (1949) has used several different systems in a study mainly concerned with relating aridity to soil formation.

Classification of climate requires climatic data; systems of classification are generally based on the data that are available, and as yet only temperature and precipitation data exist in sufficient quantity for climatic mapping. The purpose of most climatic classifications is to delineate the different climates in terms of vegetational responses. Since vegetation responds primarily to temperature and precipitation, it is reasonable then to expect that these two elements will form the basis of most systems of climatic classification. In terms of the arid zones, however, it is also reasonable to suppose that the degree of aridity is the fundamental problem for desert vegetation; therefore, systems that tend to emphasize this aspect seem to have greater application in arid zones than those that do not. Systems such as Thornthwaite's, based upon the potential evapotranspiration, or Budyko's index, based upon radiation balance compared to rainfall, have a physical basis that suggests that they have greater usefulness than strictly empirical formulations. While some of these strictly empirical formulations seem to give excellent correspondence with vegetational forms, a recurring theme seems to be that this index or that index works better in one general climatic type than another. If indexes were based upon physically sound concepts, however, it would seem that these indexes should work in all types of climates.

Climatic Analogs

When considering only one climatic type, such as deserts, it can be useful to find the similarities and differences from area to area. Several studies have been made to determine to what extent various parts of the world are analogous. The U. S. Army Quartermaster Corps series of analogs was constructed to find areas with climates similar to the Army's desert test center at Yuma, Arizona. Several climatic elements were chosen as significant, and then areas with about the same values as Yuma were rated as analogous or semianalogous depending upon the degree of similarity. Some of the areas studied were:

Middle East	East Central Africa
Northeast Africa	South America
Northwest Africa	Southern Africa
South Central Asia	Australia
Soviet Middle Asia	North America
Chinese Inner Asia	

Two of the studies, Robison and Dodd (1955) and Ohman (1961) can be cited as examples of the technique.

A second type of climatic analogy, this developed by M. Y. Nuttonson of the American Institute of Crop Ecology in Washington, D. C., has been prepared as part of a group of studies undertaken to develop agricultural activities in Israel by the introduction of plants and farming techniques from regions climatically and latitudinally analogous to Israel. The material on analogous regions is but one part of the report, but it illustrates a useful technique. In the reports, Israel is compared with Australia; with the Union of South Africa; with Libya and Egypt; with Morocco, Algeria, and Tunisia; and with California and Arizona. Similarities are based upon the growing season and temperature and rainfall through the year; the growing season analogy is considered the most important. In addition to indicating areas with similar climatic characteristics, these studies contain excellent general discussions of the weather and climate of the countries that are compared. Nuttonson's studies are interesting because of their similarity to the Yuma analogs. They have limited usefulness, since they have little application beyond the original areas of comparison. A climatic classification such as Meigs' scheme or the Unesco bioclimatic system for the Mediterranean zone has more general value.

D. OTHER TOPICS

1. Weather Modification

Weather modification can be defined as acts of man that produce changes in weather and climate. By his existence, modern man has inadvertently changed the weather. Industrialization has increased the carbon-dioxide content of the atmosphere and consequently may have changed the radiation balance of the Earth and atmosphere. Through urbanization, air pollution has increased the local incidence of fog and may even affect the distribution of clouds and rain. These and other unintentional alterations in weather and climate are problems of worldwide concern, not peculiar to the deserts, and are outside the scope of this review. Rather deliberate acts of man designed to change weather are of more concern, especially

when these acts have applications to the arid zone. Three general scales of weather modification activity can be recognized: microclimatological, intermediate, and macroclimatological.

Examples of man's modification of the climates of small areas are the use of frost protection devices such as heaters or wind machines, the effects of irrigation, and the maintenance of shelterbelts. When they are pertinent to deserts, these schemes are discussed in the section on microclimates and are not discussed here. At the large end of the size scale are proposals to change the general circulation. Using carbon black to melt the Greenland ice cap or pumping of water over a dammed Bering Strait to melt the Arctic ice pack are examples of proposals for macroclimatological modification.

The focus of this section on weather modification is on the intermediate-scale acts or proposals, the modification of local or regional climates primarily by the manipulation of clouds and storm systems. As with most arid-zone problems, precipitation is the element primarily considered. Cloud seeding is the subject most prominent in weather modification activity in recent years, but there are other proposed schemes to encourage cloud growth.

Cloud Seeding

Cloud seeding is a general meteorological field that could have more application to arid regions than to the more humid climates. In general, it can be said that modern rainmaking has not produced large amounts of rainfall beyond what would have occurred naturally; however, the kinds of increases found (10 to 15 per cent are the numbers usually given) can be economically important. Because of the highly variable character of natural rainfall, increases can ordinarily be detected only by statistical analysis of a large number of seeding trials. Two recent surveys of the state of weather modification that include discussions of cloud seeding have been issued by the National Academy of Sciences (1966) and by Gilman, Hibbs, and Laskin (1965) for the U. S. Weather Bureau.

For the most part, cloud seeding has not been carried on in the world's deserts. This situation has come about because modern cloud-seeding techniques seek to modify the microphysics of clouds, and arid lands are characterized by large-scale atmospheric motions that inhibit cloud formation: deserts lack clouds. Contrary to what might seem a logical solution to the lack of rainfall over deserts, it is unlikely that cloud seeding will ever be really important to desert areas directly; however, indirect results can be important. Cloud seeding in humid regions that provide runoff for more arid areas could greatly affect the economy of the dry areas. Cloud seeding in the Rocky Mountains of the western United States might increase the water available in the Colorado River for use in California and Arizona. Seeding in the humid Ethiopian highlands might increase water available in the Nile.

An indirect cloud-seeding project conducted in the Andes Mountains, which has apparently resulted in economically important irrigation water for the Peruvian desert, has been described by Howell (1965). Howell reported economically important increases in rainfall were produced during 12 years of seeding in Peru. Orographic convective clouds associated with moist air masses from the intertropical convergence zone east of the Andes were seeded with silver iodide over watersheds draining toward the arid western slopes of these mountains. Increases of about 10 to 15 per cent were found. This is an example of an indirect result, because it was the run-off from seeding over humid areas (the mountains) that produced surface water important to the arid regions.

Although few cloud-seeding experiments have been conducted in the world's deserts, summer cloud seeding in Arizona has been done in orographic cumulus clouds by the Institute of Atmospheric Physics of the University of Arizona. Seven summers of seeding with silver iodide produced no increases in rainfall (Battan, 1966). Other cloud-seeding projects, commercial in nature, have been carried on in the United States portion of the North American deserts. These projects date from the early and middle 1950's. Increases were reported by the cloud seeders, but their statistical significance was disputed. Although some cloud seeding has been done in Mexico, none of it seems to have been conducted in the desert areas.

Australians have engaged in many cloud seeding projects, primarily by scientists at C.S.I.R.O. These projects have been carried out in the humid eastern portion of the continent rather than in the deserts. China has engaged in cloud-seeding activity, but it is believed that these projects were not carried on in the arid zones. Ku (1959) discusses in general the progress in rainmaking in China, but propaganda articles such as this are of little scientific value.

Cloud seeding in the Soviet Union has been carried on at a fairly high level of activity. Soviet work in this field has been reviewed by Battan (1961, 1963). Battan notes that Soviet experiments do not seem to be designed for statistical evaluation of the results, but he indicates that Russian meteorologists believe that increases of about 10 to 15 per cent are usually obtained. Cloud seeding has been carried on in India, though not particularly directed toward the desert portion of the country. Rao and Desai (1955) have discussed the suitability of clouds for seeding in various parts of India. Roy (1962) has discussed the seeding program of the National Physical Laboratory. In Pakistan, cloud seeding does not seem to be important at this time, although some work was done in the 1950's with salt seeding (Fournier d'Albe *et al.,* 1955).

A major program in cloud seeding is being carried out in Israel, but it is being conducted in the subhumid northern rather than the arid south. Results summarized by Gabriel (1965) for 3½ years indicate that seeding of winter cumuli increased the rainfall by 15 to 18 per cent. This project is financed by the Israel Ministry of Agriculture and its design and evaluation are the result of work at the Hebrew University of Jerusalem.

Cloud Formation

Weather modification consists of more than cloud seeding. Some attempts have been made to create clouds where they did not originally exist. Black and Tarmy (1963) have proposed the paving of arid lands with asphalt to produce thermal convection that would increase the sea-breeze circulation and promote cloud formation. It is reported by the National Academy of Sciences (1966) that Black has plans to test the scheme in the coastal deserts of western Australia. Lettau (1965) has suggested that the thermal heating of an extended mountain slope, for example the Pacific slopes of the Andes, can give rise to a low-level jet stream that acts to suppress vertical motions by frictionally induced downslope motions. It is suggested that the suppression of surface heating, perhaps by moistening the Earth's surface, would destroy the low-level jet-stream circulation but still allow for convection to proceed and clouds and rain to form. Bryson and Baerreis (1965) have speculated that the dust in the lowest levels of the atmosphere over the Rajputana Desert contributes to the formation of a stable atmosphere by its radiational cooling. If the dust were removed or prevented from entering the atmosphere, convectional rainfall might be increased. If it is true that man's activities have formed this desert, as Bryson believes is very possible, stabilization of the soil may be all that is required to ameliorate the aridity.

Modification for Arid Lands

Weather modification for arid lands is closely related to weather modification work in general. It is of interest to examine the possibilities of success as outlined by Gilman, Hibbs, and Laskin (1965). It appears that cloud seeding of the winter orographic precipitation situation will produce modest increases in rainfall, but that large increases are less likely.

Rainfall increases from cumulus clouds do not seem as likely as from the orographic types. Prospects for changing climate on a small scale by modifying the surface layer of the atmosphere are only moderately good. Chances for purposeful large-scale modification are rated as low.

There seems to be little interest in weather modification specifically directed toward arid lands. Three examples of proposed projects were mentioned, but they have no universal application to deserts. The major project, that of increasing rainfall, probably has less value in the deserts than in any other climatic type because of the lack of clouds. There seems to be interest in cloud seeding as a tool to increase rainfall over humid areas that might provide runoff for more arid regions, but little interest in cloud seeding as a source of direct moisture to the desert areas.

The present state of knowledge of the effects of cloud seeding is one of confusion. If results are difficult to evaluate in the humid climates, the statistical problems are harder to cope with in the more arid regions. In view of the successes reported in orographic winter storms, this type of seeding activity may be economically important to some deserts. But the large number of unanswered questions suggest that other types of seeding need to be conducted on an experimental rather than operational basis.

The lack of clouds in deserts is again a pertinent consideration. As the seedable weather situations become more infrequent, the time required to obtain significant results becomes longer, and the economic return for an investment in a cloud-seeding project becomes less. As total rainfall amounts decrease, the percentage increases become less and less important. For example, a 15 per cent increase in the *summer* rainfall at Tucson, Arizona, changes the new Thornthwaite moisture index $I_m = 100[(P/PE)-1]$, where P = precipitation and PE = potential evapotranspiration (see Thornthwaite and Mather, 1962), from -75 to -73; a 15 per cent increase in the *annual* rainfall total produces a change from -75 to -71. Both calculations assume no change in temperature. This is not to suggest that small changes do not have effects on natural vegetation, for studies of climatic variation indicate that ecosystems can change with relatively small changes in climate; however, from an agricultural point of view, the economic returns from such increases would seem to be small.

2. Microclimate

Dew and Fog

The study of dew may be more important to the deserts than to the humid regions because of the unfavorable moisture balance of arid lands. Dew may

be important in three general ways. In one case, it may affect the heat balance of the Earth's surface. The evaporation of dew will retard the heating of the Earth and vegetation. This retardation may eliminate or reduce excessive heat loads, or it may keep the plant temperature below that required for optimum growth. Dew may be a direct source of water, since some plants may be able to use directly the water condensed on them. Dew may also be important because it contributes to the formation of an environment suited to the growth of fungus diseases and the development of some insects.

How much dew is deposited at any given location? Data from Israel indicate that it may be about 30 mm per year distributed over about 200 nights per year, an average fall of tenths of a millimeter per night. Dew formation is highly variable, depending a great deal upon the character of the surface, the local topography, the plant cover and the soil moisture and atmosphere conditions. The measurement of dew has been discussed by Angus (1958) and Masson (1958) in Unesco's *Proceedings of the Canberra Symposium*. Nagel (1962a) has given comparisons between different devices for measuring dew. Slatyer and McIlroy (1961) include a comprehensive discussion of dew and water absorption by leaves in their volume on practical microclimatology.

The desert country that seems to have done the most work on the problem of dew is Israel. At one time the Israel Meteorological Service published an annual summary of dew measurements in Israel. Gilead and Rosenan (1954) have summarized much of the data. Duvdevani (1953) has discussed the occurrence and variability of dew in Israel with an emphasis on the effects of climate and topography. Neumann (1956) has developed a means for estimating dew based on commonly observed meteorological parameters. Monteith (1957) has discussed the physics of dew in general, and Baier (1966), in his study of dew formation under semiarid conditions, showed the importance of the placement of the dew instrument in relation to the crop canopy.

General publication on the meteorological processes of dew are not abundant. Zikeev (1952) has compiled a bibliography on dew, limited in usefulness by the few papers listed in recent years. A comprehensive general review of the subject has been presented by Masson (1954), who reviews all facets of the subject and includes an extensive bibliography. An interesting aspect of dew formation is reported by Ives (1962b). In the Sonoran desert of North America he has found that dew forming on a somewhat larger area collects in depressions in the rocks. These depressions, which may contain from a few ounces to a few cups of water, are known as "kiss tanks" and in other parts of the world as "dew ponds." They have been found in Utah, California, Baja California, and Sonora in the North American deserts.

Is dew important to arid lands? Its possible effects on vegetation are considered in the vegetation chapter. While the literature available does not suggest that it is of major significance to deserts, Duvdevani (1964) in studies carried on in Israel shows that plants deprived of dew did not grow as well as those on which dew formed naturally. It is interesting to note, however, that dew was considered a factor in the definition of a dry day when determining the xerothermic index for Unesco's bioclimatic map of the Mediterranean zone. Possibilities for the use of dew can be envisioned; for example, the creation of specific microclimates might increase dew formation to the benefit of certain crops.

Related to the topic of dew is the study of precipitation that results from fog. The movement of fog by wind through vegetation will result in liquid water being captured by the vegetation; a considerable amount can be collected. Nagel (1962b) discusses the amount of water captured from fog and estimates that along the coastal regions of the Kalahari-Namib desert the total fog precipitation is equivalent to about 150 mm per year. The importance of the effect decreases rapidly with distance from the sea. In addition to the Kalahari-Namib coasts, the Atacama-Peruvian desert and the part of the Sonoran desert that borders the Pacific coast of Baja California also have a high incidence of fog. According to a personal communication from J. R. Hastings, the vegetation along the coast reflects the presence of the fog. Epiphytes can be found growing on cacti, and certain plants have root structures indicating use of the fog drip from the plant itself. Data on the incidence of fog are not available for this region.

Shelterbelts

The subject of shelterbelts can be mentioned briefly, although it is recognized that they are more important to subhumid and semiarid regions than to deserts. The main purpose of shelterbelts is to reduce wind speed. The change in microclimate and the resulting effect on plant and animal life arise primarily from this decrease in wind velocity. Shelterbelts increase snow retention both within the shelterbelt and in the protected region. Significant increases in soil moisture can result, especially in climates with severe winters and dry summers.

The starting point for any study of shelterbelts is the review article on windbreaks and shelterbelts published by the World Meteorological Organization (1964b). In addition to a complete review of the subject, the article contains an extensive bibliography.

This review contains no emphasis on the deserts. The desert country that seems to have done the most work with shelterbelts is the U.S.S.R. Two Russian agroclimatologists, Razumova (1963) and Kas'yanov (1961), have written general articles on the subject. Another general review was published in Unesco's Arid Zone series (Hall, Russell, and Hamilton, 1958).

Shelterbelts have not been used extensively in desert regions; one reason given is that the water and land used to grow the trees could be used more profitably for actual crop production. Lorch (1959) has reported an interesting example of the usefulness of shelterbelts. Banana plantations in Israel were protected by windbreaks to reduce wind speed and physical damage to the leaves of the banana trees. Hand-tearing of protected leaves confirmed that tearing of the leaves by wind was a significant problem. Lomas (1965) reports that the use of shelterbelts to reduce winds in southern Israel increased the yield of tomatoes or permitted their introduction into areas where they could not be grown without protection from the wind.

Effect of Irrigation

A minor micrometeorological problem of arid lands is the effect of irrigation on climate. Irrigation, through its effect on heat and water balances, certainly changes the climate of the field, but does it have much effect on the neighboring areas? Two reports on this subject have been published by the Environmental Protection Research Division of the U. S. Quartermaster Research and Development Command. Ohman and Pratt (1956) studied the effect of irrigation on daytime humidities near Yuma, Arizona. They found that dew points increased 6° to 8° F within the immediate area of cultivation if wind speeds were low, but that irrigation in the whole Yuma region had a negligible influence on the atmosphere humidities in the region. Bennett and Nelson (1960) examined the influence of irrigation on nighttime humidities in the Yuma oasis region. Increases in dew point were noted within the irrigated land but no effects were noted more than a few hundred yards from the edge of the irrigated land. Smirnova (1963) reported effects of irrigation on humidity up to about 100 feet from an irrigated field for only a few days following irrigation, five days in one instance. Irrigation of land does not appear to have any effect on the climate except within the irrigated fields and the areas immediately adjacent to them. No effect on large-scale areas is noted. Another question often raised is whether or not the creation of large bodies of water in arid lands would augment the atmospheric supply of water vapor and lead to increased rainfall. This concept has been discussed by McDonald (1962). He shows that it is simply not reasonable to expect to increase precipitation by constructing large bodies of water, nor is it practical to attempt it. McDonald cites the case of the Caspian Sea just upwind of the Turkestan Desert as an example of the fallacy of expecting rainfall to increase due to the evaporation from nearby large bodies of water.

One important aspect of irrigation is that it changes the basic properties of the air moving over the irrigated area in terms of temperature, humidity, and the like. Thus if data from the natural and arid environment were used to compute potential evapotranspiration, for example, through the use of Penman's equation, the computed results for a large irrigated area would be different from what would actually occur, since the basic data would be changed by the evaporation of the irrigation water. This aspect should be considered when using empirical equations to estimate water needs. This problem is essentially that of the oasis effect and how to correct for it.

3.   Radiation

Radiation, solar and terrestrial, is a general meteorological subject of particular importance to the arid regions of the Earth. It affects the heat and water balance, which in turn is important to the determination of aridity. As more sophisticated techniques are developed for the determination of evapotranspiration and potential evapotranspiration, it is likely that radiation and the radiation balance will play an important part in the formulation of the equations.

The importance of solar radiation to our Earth and the physics of radiation have been covered adequately in numerous texts and review articles. Sellers (1965) has a particularly good section on radiation and the radiation balance. A recent monograph by the American Meteorological Society (1965) on agricultural meteorology has a chapter on radiation by D. M. Gates. Drummond's (1958*a*) Unesco review article is a well-written and comprehensive discourse on many aspects of radiation and was specifically written as a background summary for arid-zone climatology. A review article by Godson (1955) might also be given special mention.

Since radiation is a general problem in meteorology, only the aspects of particular importance to the weather and climate of arid lands need be considered here. The questions posed to meteorology can be broadly stated as: (1) How much? (2) Where? (3) How often? The concern, then, of this discussion of radiation is with the measurement of radiation, and

with techniques of estimation where measurements are lacking. The distribution of solar radiation over the arid lands and the Earth as a whole is also of importance.

Measurement of Radiation

Instrumentation for the measurement of solar radiation is fairly well developed and is not generally considered to be a particularly bothersome problem. Although reasonably accurate instrumentation is available, the devices are usually expensive. Furthermore, present-day instrumentation must be continually maintained by trained personnel to secure accurate measurements. These two factors combine to limit the amount of data available. Worldwide solar radiation is measured at about 800 locations. Budyko and Efimova (1964) have stated that 829 stations exist and tabulated the number of stations with records of 1 to 5, 6 to 10, and over 10 years duration. Daniels (1964) has estimated that there are about 700 stations with available records of some years duration. Black (1956) used only 150 stations for his worldwide distributions of solar radiation. Landsberg *et al.* (1965) have based their world distribution on about 300 stations, many of which had short records and had been established during the period of the International Geophysical Year. Budyko (1963) has presented data based on 300 measuring stations. It should be noted here that the sparseness of the data is not as critical as might be supposed considering the very few direct observations available over an area as large as the Earth; the accuracy of estimations based upon more commonly observed meteorological parameters is really quite good.

What elements of radiation need to be measured? Solar radiation, both direct beam and for the hemisphere (direct plus diffuse) are basic quantities to be determined. In addition, cloudiness and duration of bright sunshine should be determined to supplement the radiation data. Terrestrial radiation also should be measured, because it is radiation balance that is important to heat budget problems and, combined with albedo, is probably one of the important climatological factors in terms of the general circulation in the atmosphere. A new tool for the measurement of radiation is the meteorological satellite. Some of the TIROS series have been designed to measure long-wave radiation emitted from the Earth as well as short-wave radiation reflected by the Earth. These measurements are most useful to global heat-balance studies. They are probably less useful to the problems of arid lands involving radiation; however, contributions have been made to radiation climatology by satellites. For example, the albedo of the North African deserts was measured as between 25 and 30 per cent by TIROS III, as reported by Nordberg *et al.* (1962).

Estimation of Solar Radiation

As stated above, few stations record solar radiation, a few hundred at best. Radiation climatologies are based on these few actual measurements of radiation, but because of the high degree of reliability of systems of estimating radiation, additional points can be added. Solar radiation can be estimated accurately because the primary factor affecting how much radiation reaches the surface is the amount of cloud cover. Absorption and scattering effects are relatively constant compared to the larger variations produced by changes in sky cover. Since the amount of radiation at the top of the atmosphere is known for any place for any day, the relationship between this quantity and cloudiness provides a good estimate of actual radiation at the surface. Equations of the form

$$Q/Q_a = a + b\ (n/N),$$

where

Q = radiation at the Earth's surface,
Q_a = radiation at the top of the atmosphere for the day and place,
a, b = constants in a regression equation,
n = duration of sunshine,
N = possible duration of sunshine,

are usually determined. Q_a is sometimes replaced by Q_o, which is radiation to the Earth's surface under a clear-sky condition, but this has to be a measured quantity and can be obtained for a nonrecording location only by interpolation from some nearby place for which the quantity has been previously determined.

Black, Bonython, and Prescott (1954) computed a regression equation (for 32 stations, with sunshine and solar radiation data) which they suggested could be generally applied. For Australia, de Vries (1958) has determined an equation for one station for a period of 2 years; his work agrees with an equation by Hounam (1963) based upon a large amount of Australian radiation data. Hounam justifies the use of one equation for all Australian observations. Bennett (1964) has given a complete discussion of his method of determining mean radiation over the western United States; he has expanded the method (Bennett, 1965) in order to compute the distribution of solar radiation over the entire United States.

Distribution of Solar Radiation

One of the main concerns of meteorology with respect to solar radiation is to determine its distribution. Since only a small number of stations regularly measure solar radiation, the distributions are based upon both direct and estimated data. Mean distribu-

tions over the Earth have been given by Black (1956), Landsberg *et al.* (1965), and Budyko (1963). Black, for example, has used 160 stations, of which only 88 had more than a 3-year record. For specific areas, the U. S. Weather Bureau (1964) has published annual and mean monthly values for the United States. These maps are based upon measured data only, from about 120 stations. Bennett (1964, 1965) has published data for the western states and for the entire United States. South Africa's distribution has been given by Drummond and Vowinckel (1957). Hounam (1963) has published mean maps for Australia. It is clear that the measured radiation data available in the arid zones and for most of the world is insufficient for determining distributions to more than the crudest estimates.

Illumination

"Illumination" refers to the intensity of light, in the wavelengths detectable by the human eye, on a material surface. "Illumination climate" or "light climate" is the study of the distribution of natural light from the sun and sky. There seems to be no emphasis on this subject in arid-lands literature. A survey of *Meteorological and Geoastrophysical Abstracts* for the 1950-1965 period revealed no articles treating illumination as a problem of deserts. A map of the illumination climate of Russia was included in a recent collection of papers on the subject, Vsesoiuznaia Konferentsiia po Svetovomu Klimatu, 2d, Moscow 1960 (1961). The emphasis of this conference was on the importance of natural illumination as it affects the planning of buildings. Drummond (1958b) has presented data for Pretoria and made comparisons with other regions.

For the most part, illumination depends upon the amount and type of cloudiness and the sun's elevation angle. The duration of bright sunshine is the climatic element that gives the best estimate of illumination. Barteneva and Guseva (1957) have related illumination to various types of cloud cover and showed that it is not a function of latitude. Shifrin and Guseva (1957) have devised a scheme for estimating illumination from sun elevation data and observations of cloudiness. Although it is assumed that illumination in deserts is relatively high, there is no evidence that it has been studied as a meteorological problem. Since illumination is a function of duration of bright sunshine, it should be computable for the locations where this climatic element is observed.

4. Bibliographies

In a study to determine the state of knowledge, a useful tool is a compiled bibliography, especially if annotated. The bibliography represents the author's attempt to delineate the important literature; thus a subject-matter bibliography prepared by an expert in the field or a regionally oriented bibliography done by a local meteorologist has special value because it tends to define important matters beyond the scope of the general literature review. The researcher can frequently get a good start toward locating the pertinent literature by examining the bibliographies of books on the subject or those contained in monographs and review articles. Many review articles are available, especially in the various Unesco publications. Though these are useful, specialized annotated bibliographies on specific areas or subject matter are much more valuable.

The major source of bibliographical information in meteorology is a publication by the American Meteorological Society, entitled *Meteorological Abstracts and Bibliography* from 1950 through 1959 and since 1959 entitled *Meteorological and Geoastrophysical Abstracts.* This publication annotates current meteorological literature on a worldwide basis. In addition, it prepares special bibliographies on specific subjects. Some of the subjects covered of particular interest to arid lands are given in Table II.

A particularly good series of annotated bibliographies has been published by the Foreign Area Section, Office of Climatology, U. S. Weather Bureau. Each issue treats a country and is titled either "An Annotated Bibliography of the Climate of . . . ," or "An Annotated Bibliography of Climatic Maps of

Table II
ARID-LANDS BIBLIOGRAPHIES OF THE AMERICAN METEOROLOGICAL SOCIETY

Year	Vol.	No.	Title
1950	1	11	Evaporation
1951	2	5	Climate of the Near East
1951	2	6	Climate of the Middle East
1951	2	7	Climate of Northeast Africa
1952	3	1	Climate of Northwest Africa
1952	3	3	Climate of Paraguay, Uruguay, and Argentina
1952	3	8	Climate of Central Africa
1953	4	4	Climate of Australia
1955	6	1	Bibliography of Bibliographies
1955	6	2	Bibliography of Textbooks and Monographs Containing Subject Bibliographies
1959	10	8	Evaporation Measurement
1959	10	9	Evapotranspiration (-1955)
1959	10	10	Evapotranspiration (1956-59)
1959	10	11	Evaporation

. . . ." Of the more than 100 bibliographies in this series, 38 apply to arid-lands countries (covering 36 of the 50 arid-lands countries). Sources of information for these bibliographies were mainly the U. S. Weather Bureau Library and the Library of Congress, both in Washington, D. C. These bibliographies are well-indexed in terms of subject matter, authors, and usually year of publication. They should be considered a major source of information about published arid-lands literature. Table III illustrates the country coverage of these bibliographies.

Other general bibliographies have application to arid lands, although they are not specifically oriented toward the world's deserts. Aniol and Schlegel (1963) have published a bibliography of climatic atlases and climatic charts containing 434 references. Zimmerman and Wang (1961) have published a bibliography of agrometeorological studies for South America that covers most of the arid countries on that continent. The bibliography of Wang and Barger (1962) on agricultural meteorology is generally useful. This volume lists titles only, but is well-indexed by subject and author. An example of a regional bibliography is the compilation of about 250 items concerning the Mediterranean area by Gleeson (1952). Venter (1950) has compiled a bibliography of literature for southern Africa. A regional bibliography by Rodier (1963b) on the subject of African hydrology is another example of a general bibliography that contains many references to meteorology and climatology.

Other than the extensive series of bibliographies compiled by the Foreign Area Section, Office of Climatology, U. S. Weather Bureau, bibliographies by country dealing with meteorology and climatology have not generally been prepared. In bibliographies covering the general scientific literature of countries, meteorology will often be included, but specific bibliographies related to weather and climate are usually not available. Some, however, do exist and should be mentioned. For example, Indacochea (1946) has prepared a meteorological bibliography of Peru; Miagkov (1957) has compiled one for the Turkmen Republic; Ghani (1951) for Pakistan; the British West Africa Meteorological Services (1954) has prepared one for that particular region; and Ferreira (1957) has prepared a meteorological bibliography for Angola.

5. Depositories

Published climatological data is routinely exchanged between most countries of the world. The U. S. Weather Bureau Library in Suitland, Maryland, has copies of almost all published data for the world. Data that have not been published are accessible at most national weather services. No central depositories are recommended beyond the U. S. Weather Bureau Library and the national weather services as having holdings stronger than these sources in any portion of the weather and climate of the arid world identifiable on the basis of geography or subject matter.

It is indeed doubtful that any libraries could be classified as depositories of arid-lands information as contrasted to depositories of meteorological and climatological information in general. Several libraries in addition to that of the U. S. Weather Bureau are outstanding depositories of general meteorological literature. The Library of Congress and the library of the U. S. Department of Agriculture are in the Washington, D. C. area, the greatest center for meteorological literature in the world. Foreign scientists rate the U. S. Weather Bureau Library an excellent depository of general meteorological information. A major depository abroad is the British Meteorological Office Library in Bracknell, Berkshire. For the French (and former French) deserts, the library of Météorologie Nationale in Paris has an extensive collection of published information.

A private library in this country with a good collection of meteorological literature is the Linda Hall Library in Kansas City, Missouri. This depository cooperates in the Farmington Plan by concentrating on the subject matter area of meteorology and climatology. The holdings in meteorological periodicals are extensive. Another group collecting meteorological publications is C. W. Thornthwaite Associates, Laboratory of Climatology, Centerton, New Jersey. This laboratory holds an impressive number of reports and reprints, many of which are not generally available. The organization has been collecting climatic data also, under a program initiated by the late C. W. Thornthwaite when he was president of the Commission for Climatology of the World Meteorological Organization.

Table III
ARID-COUNTRY COVERAGE, BIBLIOGRAPHIES OF FOREIGN AREA SECTION, OFFICE OF CLIMATOLOGY, U. S. WEATHER BUREAU

	C*	M**		C*	M**
Aden	42†	15†	Morocco	—	19
Afghanistan	—	—	Muscat and Oman	42†	15†
Algeria	—	—	Niger	—	—
Angola	8	50	Nigeria	—	24
Argentina	—	—	Pakistan (West)	—	71
Australia	44	16	Peru	5	—
Bahrain	42†	15†	Qatar	42†	15†
Bechuanaland (Botswana)	—	42†	Saudi Arabia	42†	15†
Bolivia	74	47	Somali Republic	—	17†
Cameroon	3	24†	South Africa	—	42
Chad	4†	—	South West Africa	—	42†
Chile	23	—	Spanish Sahara	—	—
China	71, 82	30	Sudan	80	43
Ethiopia	—	17	Syria	—	57
French Somaliland	—	—	Trucial Coast	42†	15†
India	—	65	Tunisia	—	21
Iran	31	51	U.S.S.R.	—	—
Iraq	35	5	United Arab Republic (Egypt)	—	53
Israel	57	—	U.S.A.	—	—
Jordan	49	35	Upper Volta	—	—
Kenya	7†	—	Yemen	42†	15†
Kuwait	42†	15			
Libya	—	28			
Mali	—	—			
Mauritania	—	—			
Mexico	—	59			
Mongolia	—	—			

Legend
* *Annotated bibliography of the climate of the country has been compiled.
** *Annotated bibliography of the climatic maps for the country has been compiled.
Numbers in *C* and *M* columns are serial numbers of the annotated bibliographies.
†Information for this country is included under another title.

CONCLUSION

A. PROBLEMS AND RECOMMENDATIONS

A logical result of a survey such as this is to ask if there are any special climatological problems unique to or important to deserts in general, not specifically related to particular regions. It has already been noted that the activities of national weather services are highly variable, and for a variety of reasons. It would be presumptuous to write, for example, that the Somali Republic should publish detailed climatic summaries, that the Iranian Meteorological Department should expand its research into problems of the interaction of troughs in the westerlies and the monsoon circulation of southern Asia, or that Peru and Chile should cooperate on the construction of a set of lysimeters to investigate the effect of latitude on various methods of estimating potential evapotranspiration. Such suggestions are clearly out of order. But several essentially unsolved problems associated with the definition of aridity are pertinent to deserts, and their solution would apparently lead toward a better understanding of desert climates.

1. Definition of Aridity

One of the main climatological problems of arid lands is the lack of a satisfactory system for determining water need and water use, and for expressing aridity in those terms. On the one hand, there is a need to know actual evaporation for immediate applications; it would be useful to know the water loss from existing or planned water storage facilities. It would also be useful to know the actual evapotranspiration from the land to help determine water needs for irrigation projects. On the other hand, a reliable potential-evapotranspiration figure would facilitate expression of aridity and quantitative comparisons of aridity.

Aridity has usually been expressed as some more-or-less complex function of temperature and rainfall which is related to observed responses of the environment to climate. The indexes of Köppen, Emberger, de Martonne and others are examples of the technique. Although this technique is still useful, there is probably little to be gained from continuing to pursue that approach to the problem. While these indexes are useful for mapping the gross features of

climate, they are not usually applicable in all climatic types and often fail when used to compare aridities at different locations. Further progress in meeting the challenges that the deserts pose will probably depend upon the ability to estimate water need quantitatively.

It should be emphasized that evaporation in nature is a very complex process dependent on factors such as vapor pressure difference, wind velocity, and available energy. Existing indexes of aridity can use temperature as an estimator of evapotranspiration because temperature is related to radiation balance or available energy, but schemes based upon only one factor do not work equally well in all climates. Those indexes based upon saturation deficit seem to give good results in regions of high aridity, but their usefulness decreases in more humid regions such as in the critical boundaries between the semiarid and subhumid climates. In humid climates they cannot be expected to function well at all. Seasonality of rainfall is an important factor to consider in assessing the aridity of a region, so again no single expression should be expected to work well in all climatic types. The expression $P < 2T$ used in the Unesco-FAO bioclimatic classification is said to work well in some parts of the Mediterranean region, but it could not be expected to give a good measure of aridity where the rainfall distribution is not of the dry-summer type.

It is not practical to secure routinely direct measurements of actual evapotranspiration. The two theoretical approaches, the aerodynamic and the energy-balance methods, are not practical on an operational basis. The instrumentation and data analysis are so complex that these methods can be used only by the trained scientist. Lysimeters are also not generally practical because of the high cost of an installation and the large amount of effort required to operate a system. Evapotranspiration, potential evapotranspiration, and aridity must be estimated, and for widespread applications, they must be estimated using generally available climatic data: temperature and precipitation.

The empirical equations of Penman and Budyko are the most practical methods of estimating water need. The required data are either measured at or estimated from observations made at major weather stations. Since the methods require the use of empirical constants and relationships, the accuracy of the estimates must be evaluated. An evaluation would ordinarily be accomplished by comparing the computed results to the water use of a lysimeter. Evaluations should be carried out under a variety of conditions, so that the effects of latitude, season, and different climatic types can be determined. Only when the degree of accuracy of the equations is known and the reasons for variations in results are explained can the methods be confidently applied. A certain amount of comparative evaluation has been done, but there is a need to evaluate systematically the available results and initiate research directed toward any unanswered questions.

Once the usefulness of the empirical techniques has been established for a location, their use can be extended (see Sellers, 1965, p. 174) to a climatologically homogeneous region through the use of a relationship of the form $E = at$, where E is mean monthly potential evapotranspiration, a is an empirical coefficient that has seasonal and regional variations, and t is mean monthly temperature. This method allows for the estimation of water need over areas where the data required for its direct computation are not available. Once potential evapotranspiration has been determined, it needs to be combined into an index of aridity. Thornthwaite's moisture index seems to be the type of expression needed, and it may be the best index to use if potential evapotranspiration is accurately determined. As Sellers (1965, p. 90) points out, Thornthwaite's index is basically the aridity index of Budyko, the ratio of radiational energy available for evaporation to the total energy required to evaporate the actual rainfall.

It has been suggested that the Penman- and Budyko-type equations be used to estimate values of potential evapotranspiration upon which indexes of aridity can be based. However, it is recognized that the climatic data necessary to make those determinations of potential evapotranspiration are not generally available, so that other techniques will be required to extrapolate from the few locations where the necessary data are available to nearby areas where only temperature and precipitation data are available. The extrapolation can take place only within climatically homogeneous areas, so it is necessary to be able to define climatologically homogeneous regions. Existing systems may already fulfill this requirement. Meigs' system differentiates on the basis of seasonal temperature and rainfall and may provide sufficiently homogeneous regions; however, the bioclimatic system suggested by Unesco-FAO for the Mediterranean region may be better suited to defining the areas over which the climate is homogeneous. This system is based upon different degrees of aridity for the dry season, which is probably of some importance to the regional application of the classification.

It has been stated that the usefulness of the theoretically sound empirical techniques is limited by the availability of the necessary data, but that these techniques probably can be used by extrapolation over climatically homogeneous regions. Homogeneous regions can be delineated by some sort of typing scheme or can be related to the general circulation of the atmosphere over the desert regions. Although it has been stated earlier that atmospheric motions are usually of a scale larger than the desert area and their study is not a unique problem of deserts, the understanding of these motion systems does need to be focused on the deserts. For example, the state of knowledge of the intertropical convergence zone in Africa has increased greatly in the past 5-10 years. As the understanding of the development and movement of this system increases, the selection of climatically homogeneous regions may be based in part upon the dominance of this weather system in different months and seasons.

If aridity and quantitative estimates of water need are to be defined and determined in terms of equations of the Penman or Budyko type, climatological data that are not ordinarily available will be needed. Radiation measurements, cloud cover, and vapor pressure are some of the elements of climate necessary to conduct these studies. Much of this information has been summarized and is available from the national weather services although it has not been published. There exists a need to collect and compile arid-zone climatic data, not just the usual means of temperature and precipitation data, but also these more uncommon observations that are rarely published. The trouble and effort sometimes necessary to acquire these data preclude their routine acquisition by individual scientists; however, their compilation should be no obstacle within a well-organized and properly funded study.

A choice would have to be made of the elements to include in the collection, how they are to be expressed, and what is to be the standard observational period. It is easy to visualize that the years 1931-1960 might be the preferred period; however, much existing mean data is based upon other periods, some longer and many shorter than this normal span. Collection and publication of these less commonly reported elements of climate in some sort of handbook of arid-lands climatic data may fill a real need in arid-zone research by making available data that are sometimes extremely difficult to acquire.

2. Field Studies

A number of field studies should be made within the deserts to determine the variations of climate that occur on the micro or meso scale of distance. As examples, studies by Dodd and McPhilimy (1959) and Ohman and Pratt (1966) can be cited. In these studies, temperature, wind, and some radiation measurements were made on three sites with different soils and elevations. Differences were found to exist among the three sites, and between the surface layer and the standard (2 meter) climate at all sites. The authors noted that the differences were great enough to warrant consideration when planning tests at the Yuma Test Station (Arizona) or in other hot deserts. Logan (1961) has made a study of the winter temperatures around a desert mountain. Although the study was based on only 8 days of record, useful information was obtained about the temperature distribution.

Studies such as these suggest that much can be done to define more closely meso and micro variations of climate in deserts. It is clear that important differences exist, and their general character and magnitudes should be known. Temnikova (1959) describes what seems to be a practical and sensible approach. Detailed microclimatic investigations are made on locations with specific exposures, elevations, and general climates. Once the microclimatic characteristics of these typical locations are known, then the same characteristics should be found on similar locations that have not been studied. Temnikova feels that this system might be useful in adjusting the local agriculture to the natural conditions, but it may have usefulness beyond that application. A system could include the differences among the bottoms, slopes, and crests of canyons, north- and south-facing slopes, soil types, and other factors that might cause micro and meso variations in climate important to activities in the deserts.

Somewhat akin to studies of small-scale variations in climate are studies that concentrate on the idea of the weather of "typical days." Descriptions of the weather of actual days, the instantaneous typical situations, from a variety of different desert types would be an important contribution to the general knowledge of deserts. The actual weather events at a specific location can sometimes be lost in the usual presentation of the long-term means, but one should not overlook the fact that long-term data are needed to assure that the weather during the data-gathering period (perhaps 2 weeks) was not atypical. Anyone who has taught survey courses in general meteorology or climatology to undergraduates has probably been made aware of the misconceptions that can exist if one's ideas of weather at a location are based upon experiences during a limited visit when the weather deviated greatly from the normal.

B. LEVEL OF CURRENT RESEARCH AND AUTHORITIES (BY AREAS)

The purpose of a regional evaluation is to gain an idea of the quality and quantity of research and general meteorological activity in the individual deserts and the countries in which they are located. In general, it is the national weather service of a country that determines the degree of meteorological activity; however, there are cases where other agencies or institutes engage in important research. The number of these other agencies devoted solely or mainly to meteorological problems is very small. Most arid-zone institutes seem to be more concerned with ecology, agricultural problems, and surface- and ground-water resources.

This evaluation is based upon indirect sources of information. The scientific literature gives some idea of the problems being studied by individuals or groups. Correspondence with national weather services and reviews of their publications of climatic data as well as the results of their meteorological studies serve as a useful measure of general meteorological activity. Correspondence with individuals within the countries was also helpful, but often the amount and type of information exchanged was less than adequate. Critical evaluation depends, in part, upon the opportunity to observe, listen, and discuss; since this direct method was possible to only a limited extent, less-direct methods have been used.

In this section, an individual's name in *italics* indicates that he is considered an authority for the purposes of this project.

Kalahari-Namib

The Kalahari-Namib desert area of southern Africa is shared by Angola, the Republic of South Africa, South West Africa, and Botswana. Only a small part of Angola is arid or semiarid. There is no evidence of any research in desert meteorology in Angola, though it should be pointed out that regular publication of climatic data is carried on and that the climate of Angola has been studied by local meteorologists and by Portuguese scientists. A bibliography of the meteorology of Angola was available from the national meteorological service in Lisbon.

The Weather Bureau of South Africa (W.B.S.A.) has been very active in the study of weather and climate in South Africa and the southern hemisphere. There is no active arid-lands research in the meteorological problems of deserts other than the collection and publication of records from a fairly well-represented climatological network. The Weather Bureau of South Africa ranks with that of Australia as pre-eminent in the southern hemisphere. In addition to its extensive publications on the climate of South Africa and the upper-air circulation of the southern hemisphere, W.B.S.A. publishes *Notos,* a periodical for scientific papers in meteorology. The Namib Desert Research Station, Walvis Bay, does some meteorological work. Climatological data are collected, the first reliable data for the inner portion of the desert. Comparative studies on the profile of climate between the inner Namib and the coast are also being made using four automatic weather stations.

There seems to be no significant research concentrating on arid-lands meteorology or the weather and climate of the Kalahari-Namib in South Africa or Angola. Individuals who have made substantial indirect contributions to the understanding of the Kalahari-Namib through their general research activities are listed as authorities in weather and climate of the Kalahari-Namib. They are *S. P. Jackson,* Faculty of Science in Geography, University of Witwatersrand, Johannesburg; and *J. J. Taljaard* and *W. L. Hofmeyr,* South Africa Weather Bureau, Private Bag 193, Pretoria.

Sahara

The Sahara covers a large area and is a climatically heterogeneous region. On the north, it has a Mediterranean climate dominated by midlatitude meteorology, while on its equatorward borders it is dominated by the intertropical convergence zone and tropical meteorology. It is convenient for discussion purposes to divide the region into two parts based on the major wind belts, although it is recognized that some comments apply to the whole.

The Mediterranean countries of the Sahara include Egypt, Libya, Tunisia, Algeria, Morocco, and Spanish Sahara. Although there seems to be little organized research into the meteorological problems of the deserts, individuals have contributed to the basic understanding of the weather and climate of the region. *M. G. El-Fandy* of Cairo University is an authority who has contributed to the climatology and synoptic meteorology of the Sahara in numerous papers for more than a generation. He ranks as one of the more prolific authors for the area. *K. H. Soliman* of the Meteorological Department of the United Arab Republic (U.A.R.) is an authority on the synoptic climatology of the region. The recently organized Meteorological Institute for Research and Training in Cairo has just begun its activities. Its research has included a study of khamsin winds and methods of forecasting them. *M. H. Omar* (Meteorological Department) is an authority specializing in micro-

meteorological problems and irrigation. Other knowledgeable meteorologists are *G. Tschirhart* of Paris and *J. Cochemé* of the Food and Agriculture Organization in Rome, who is currently working on an agro-climatological study for the semiarid zone south of the Sahara.

Correspondence with the Libya Meteorological Department suggests that there is no significant research being carried on in the field of arid-lands meteorology in Libya. In Tunisia, the Service Météorologique has been active in regular publication of climatic data and undertakes occasional studies of a general nature. Nine of its publications deal with the weather and climate of this arid country. The major project of the Service at present is the preparation of a climatic atlas for the whole of Tunisia.

The degree of current research in meteorology in Algeria is uncertain. The Institut de Recherches Sahariennes, Météorologie et Physique de Globe, at the Université d'Alger has in the past been active in research and has published the climatological work of *J. Dubief,* who until recently was associated with that organization. It has been indirectly reported that there is some work being done at this Institute on the relationship between rainfall and runoff in the Sahara, probably the only recent use of climatological data in Algeria. Both *J. Dubief* and *R. Capot-Rey* have left Algeria; Dubief is currently in Paris. The national weather service of Algeria is apparently not engaged in meteorological or climatological research.

As far as can be determined, little or no research into arid-lands weather and climate is in process in Morocco or Spanish Sahara. Spanish Sahara is administered by the meteorological service of Spain, and the few papers noted that applied to this region usually originated in Madrid.

The tropical countries of the Sahara are Sudan, Chad, Cameroon, Nigeria, Niger, Upper Volta, Mali, and Mauritania. Only two countries, Nigeria and Sudan, seem to be active in meteorological research, and most of this is climatological or concerned with the synoptic meteorology of the intertropical convergence zone. The publications of the Nigerian Meteorological Service show an active interest in the meteorology of the area; the papers, although not focusing on arid-lands problems, do contribute indirectly to the understanding of the climate of deserts. *G. O. P. Obasi,* with the Meteorological Service in Lagos, has been most helpful, though he is not an arid-zone specialist. *B. J. Garnier* of the Department of Geography, McGill University, Montreal, Quebec, Canada, is an authority who served as climatologist in the southern Sahara area for some years.

The Sudan Meteorological Service has been very active in meteorological and climatological research.

Its list of publications includes climatological summaries, papers on the synoptic climatology of the region, and water-balance investigations. *G. Mustafa,* head of the climatological section, and *A. A. S. Sayed* and *Y. P. R. Bhalotra* of the Meteorological Service have been contributors to these publications; all three should be considered authorities on the area.

Tropical meteorology in Africa has also profited from the interest of meteorologists from the midlatitudes. In particular, *H. Flohn,* Meteorologische Institut der Universitat Bonn, and *R. C. Rainey* of the Anti-Locust Center in London are authoritative on the subject of tropical meteorology with special reference to arid-lands problems. Waldemar Haude of the Flugwetterdienst, Hanover, Germany, has studied evapotranspiration in Egypt, particularly as it relates to irrigation problems.

One of the ways that the state of knowledge of the weather and climate of the tropical Sahara could be advanced is through the standardization of weather observations and the publication of climatic data. Atmospheric processes do not respect national boundaries and the study of them cannot be confined to individual countries. Standardization has been a project of the World Meteorological Organization for some time. The WMO Regional Association I (Africa) has been working to establish a basic synoptic network, particularly with regard to observations during the nighttime hours.

Further research on the problem of the seasonal forecasting of rainfall might produce results of practical importance. In an area dependent upon agriculture, where rainfall variability is high, the usefulness of a seasonal rainfall forecast would be great. We have not determined how much work has been done on this problem in tropical meteorology. It has not been very successful in middle latitudes, but this does not mean that reliable systems could not be devised for equatorial regions.

Somali-Chalbi

Only one weather service in this desert studies the weather and climate of the area, the East African Meteorological Department, which has Kenya in its jurisdiction. The climatology of the area has been investigated by meteorologists from this organization and has been reported mainly in the publications of the East African Meteorological Department. *B. W. Thompson,* who recently retired as director of this department and is now in Canada, has been very interested in the climatology of eastern Africa and Africa in general. In addition to other meteorologists in Kenya, such as *H. W. Sansom* and *D. H. Johnson, J. F. Griffiths,* a climatologist formerly in Kenya and

now at Texas A. and M. University, is an authority on the climatology of the Somali-Chalbi.

Correspondence with meteorologists in Somalia and Ethiopia reveals that research into the weather and climate of the deserts is nonexistent in these countries. *H. J. Sayer,* a meteorologist at the Asmara Center of the Desert Locust Control Organization at Asmara, should be considered an authority. *A. Fantoli,* Rome, has access to most of the climatological data for Ethiopia, observations that date back to the Italian occupation period. *A. Gizaw Attlee* of the Ethiopian Weather Service is a meteorologist knowledgeable about the weather and climate of Ethiopia, although he has not emphasized the arid zone. At press time we have not yet seen his "Weather at Asmara," which reportedly contains information pertinent to the arid area of Ethiopia.

Arabian

Of the twelve nations that share the Arabian Desert, only two, Iraq and Israel, evidence any interest in the weather and climate of the desert. Israel has an active interest in many problems of the arid lands. Two groups, the Department of Meteorology at Hebrew University and the Israel Meteorological Service, have carried on extensive studies in the climatology of the area. The list of publications of the Israel Meteorological Service indicates a wide scope of interest and the quality of the research is very good. Climatology, synoptic climatology, investigations of evapotranspiration, and the use of shelterbelts are a few of the topics considered. Cloud seeding is also conducted in the semiarid regions.

Individuals who have been concerned with the weather and climate of Israel and the Arabian Desert in general are *J. Neumann, D. Ashbel,* and *D. H. K. Amiran* of the Hebrew University in Jerusalem. People of note in the Israel Meteorological Service, Bet Dagan, are *M. Gilead, N. Rosenan, J. Katsnelson,* and *J. Lomas.* At the National and University Institute of Agriculture, Rehovot, *G. Stanhill* has done research in comparing methods of estimating evapotranspiration. Current research at that institute is centered on the search for a better understanding of the physics of water loss from evaporating surfaces, varying from free water surfaces and irrigated fields to natural vegetation. The research by this group can be considered the most comprehensive into the evaluation of methods of determining water use. The staff at Rehovot feels that Class A pan data with *properly determined crop coefficients* is the best empirical index of crop water requirements, while Penman's formula is the most practical theoretically sound method.

It should be noted that the British Meteorological Office maintains weather stations in this desert region. Its publication, *Daily Weather Report Overseas Supplement,* contains data from the Persian Gulf, Aden, and Saudi Arabia; and its summaries of upper-air data include stations such as Aden and Bahrain. This organization has produced a series of summaries of weather over the oceans and coastal regions, including two volumes covering the Indian Ocean, Red Sea, and Persian Gulf.

Correspondence with the weather services of Jordan and Kuwait revealed that no meteorological research is conducted in those countries. Baumer (1964) writes that there is no arid-zone meteorological work in Saudi Arabia. In Jordan and Syria, there is an increasing interest in agroclimatology resulting from the basic foundation laid by the FAO/Unesco/WMO agroclimatological study of the Near East.

Iraq has published a climatological atlas and publishes its climatological data in rather complete form. In addition, the "Memoirs" of the Iraq weather service contain studies about the local weather and climate. The Arid Zone Research Institute of the University of Baghdad is doing some work on evapotranspiration, but mainly as it applies to soils. Jan Barica of this institute is studying evaporation in the presence of a high ground-water table and is investigating the usefulness of evaporation from a free water surface for estimating losses from irrigated fields.

Iranian

The relatively young meteorological services of Iran and Afghanistan have not generated much research into the problems of the arid zone. The Iranian Meteorological Department under *M. H. Ganji,* its Director General, has published climatological data and a few research papers in its yearbooks. There seems to be little if any research into the meteorological problems of deserts. Dr. Abdul Khalek of the Afghan meteorological department writes that they conduct no research into the problems of arid lands.

The Iranian Desert lies to the east of the core of Mediterranean climate and west of the major monsoon circulation of the Indian subcontinent. As such it either benefits from the study of both systems or it suffers from its position on the fringe of major study areas. The latter is more probable. For the most part the weather and climate of the area is not well known. There is not a large backlog of climatic data to support climatological research, and current data, particularly upper-air, is not abundant. There is a need for studies in the synoptic climatology of the area.

It is interesting to note the influence of one man on the state of knowledge of the region. During the period from about 1955 to 1964, *Ludwig Weickmann* (now with the Deutscher Wetterdienst) was a meteorological advisor in the area for the International Civil Aviation Organization (I.C.A.O.). Although his main concern was aeronautical meteorology, he did work in the synoptic climatology of the region and studied the subtropical jet stream in the Middle East; he should be considered a regional authority on those subjects. His papers stand out as major contributions to the state of knowledge of the region, and his efforts illustrate the importance of encouraging the local meteorologist to publish the results of his personal experience with weather and climate.

Thar

India's excellent weather service has contributed extensively to the knowledge of the weather and climate of the area. A review of the *Indian Journal of Meteorology and Geophysics* reveals a variety of meteorological interests and quality research. In addition to this journal, the India Meteorological Department publishes research results in its "Memoirs."

The Indian publications do not indicate any special emphasis on arid-zone meteorology. The Central Arid Zone Research Institute at Jodhpur is making climatological studies of rainfall and is investigating the distribution of aridity. This organization has had some success in predicting actual evapotranspiration using Thornthwaite's method when actual runoff is measured and included in water balance calculations. The Penman and Budyko methods are to be tried next to get quantitative estimates of potential evapotranspiration. These investigations are associated with the Division of Basic Resources Studies headed by *B. B. Roy. A. Krishnan* is the climatologist associated with the group.

L. A. Ramdas of the National Physical Laboratory in New Delhi has an interest in the problems of meteorology related to deserts and has been very active internationally in arid-lands meteorology. He is a world authority on the subject. In addition to Dr. Ramdas, other Indian authorities on the meteorology and climatology of deserts are *A. K. Roy* of the National Physical Laboratory in New Delhi, and *Sujan B. Chatterjee* of the geography department of Calcutta University. At the Meteorological Office, Poona, some investigations on climatic data are being carried out.

Our direct information about meteorological activity in Pakistan is nearly nonexistent. Some information was gathered from *Pakistan.* a yearbook of that country. The yearbook for 1963 had a section (pages 84-87) on the meteorological activities of the national weather service. A general review article on the weather service also appeared in *Pakistan Quarterly,* Volume 10, 1960, an issue which was devoted to a review of science in that country. Meteorological research is carried on at the Geophysical Institute at Quetta. Work is being done on the heat and water balance problem using "Naqvi's evapotranspiration balance." Also under study are cloud seeding and the use of solar radiation.

In addition to the Geophysical Institute at Quetta, Pakistan has a research and training center at Karachi, the Institute of Meteorology and Geophysics. This group is concerned with the forecast problem, synoptic meteorology, and instruction and training.

Pakistan scientists concerned with arid-lands problems are *Qaiyum Hamid* and *M. Shafi Ahmad* of the Meteorological Service, and *Kazi S. Ahmad* of Punjab University. *S. N. Naqvi,* recently retired Director of the Pakistan Meteorological Service, has long been an authority on arid-lands problems, including those of the Thar Desert. He is currently a WMO expert in Iraq.

Turkestan

The Soviet Union has a well-developed meteorological service and other state and national research institutes competent and active in meteorology and climatology. Much of this research has been directly concerned with problems of aridity, though mostly with the semiarid rather than the arid regions. It is the oft-stated aim of the Soviet government to increase the productiveness and the extent of agricultural activity in the dry regions of Russia, and the vast amount of work done to study drought, aridity, and heat and water balance of the Earth's surface illustrates the concern of Soviet scientists with this problem.

Within the Soviet Union, the Academy of Sciences is the main research organization. One of the eight divisions of the organization is the Division of Geology and Geography, which contains the Institute of Geography. Its section of Climatology and Hydrology is headed by *B. L. Dzerdzeevskii.* The main emphasis has been on synoptic or dynamic climatology, but some work has been done on heat and water balance.

The principal scientific institution in the Soviet Union in the field of atmospheric physics and climatology is the A. I. Voeikov Main Geophysical Observatory, Leningrad; however, this is not an "arid-lands" research group (that is, it does not emphasize the problems of deserts). Important research has been done in the heat and water balance of the Earth's surface by *M. I. Budyko* and his co-workers at this

observatory. The recent atlas of heat and water balance of the Earth's surface resulted from these studies, and the 7-volume climatology noted earlier in the text originated from this institute.

The Hydrometeorological Service does not seem to be active in research in arid-lands problems. One of its projects has been the publication of agroclimatological handbooks for about 125 regions of the Soviet Union, 66 of which pertain to semiarid and arid zones.

A third expert on climatological research is *F. F. Davitaya,* now with the Academy of Science branch at Tbilisi. Davitaya has been mainly concerned with agroclimatological problems of the semiarid and arid regions, particularly in regard to drought and its effects. Other climatologists of note are *B. P. Alisov* of the geography faculty of Moscow State University and *A. A. Borisov* of the geography faculty at the University of Leningrad, though neither seems to have any particular interest in desert climates or their meteorological problems. Reviews of the extent of arid-zone studies in the Soviet Union have been written by Sinelshikov (1965) and Davitaya (1961).

Takla-Makan and Gobi

China's interest in meteorology has been growing in recent years. Translations of general articles on many aspects of weather and climate have been prepared by the U. S. Joint Publication Research Service and are available through the Office of Technical Services of the U. S. Department of Commerce. These papers seem to indicate that the major interest of Chinese meteorologists is in forecasting and general circulation problems. There is no evidence of emphasis on arid-lands research, but it may be that such emphasis exists without being evident to Western observers.

The development of meteorology in China has been discussed by Rigby (1961) as part of a volume devoted to a review of science in mainland China. The organization of the field of meteorology is outlined, publications are noted, and the general emphasis of Chinese meteorology is reviewed. It is stated that the importance of meteorology to the development of the national economy is fully realized by the Chinese government. Rigby writes "This meteorological program in China being basic to all other programs, was evidently given such a high priority and assistance at all levels that impressive results were actually achieved in record time." In view of such an observation, it seems unlikely that meteorological and climatological research directed toward use of the arid lands is not taking place. The appended bibliography, however, indicated no emphasis on water-balance studies or other meteorological or climatological problems of deserts. General review articles on the extent of meteorological activity in China, as have been written by Ho and Peng-fei (1959) and Kuo (1963), make no mention of a special interest in desert meteorology, indirect evidence that no major research effort is in progress in this subject. No authorities are named for these deserts.

There was no information available to make any judgment of meteorological activity in Outer Mongolia, other than that the national weather service stated that climatological data are not published.

Australian

Australia has a well-developed meteorological service carrying on the routine activities of data collection and publication. In addition, its staff has contributed to the general knowledge of the weather and climate of Australia, which includes the desert regions; however, there seems to be no particular interest or organized effort into the meteorological problems of deserts.

One of the major research groups that contributes indirectly to the weather and climate of deserts is the C.S.I.R.O. Division of Meteorological Physics, located at Aspendale, Victoria. Although this division would not be classified as an organization doing arid-lands research, scientists from this group have made major contributions to the basic theory of the measurement of evapotranspiration through their theoretical and experimental work on the turbulent transfer of water vapor from the surface to the air. Authorities who have worked on this problem include *C. H. B. Priestly, W. C. Swinbank,* and *E. L. Deacon.* This division also operates a battery of lysimeters at Aspendale to study evapotranspiration under natural conditions. Fundamental contributions have been made to the study of evapotranspiration by *I. C. McIlroy* and *D. E. Angus,* who should be considered authorities on this subject.

C. E. Hounam of the Australian Meteorological Bureau in Melbourne is an authority who has contributed to the knowledge of arid lands through his early studies of the rainfall in marginal areas, his analysis of pan evaporation data, and most recently his work with solar radiation. In addition to the Division of Meteorological Physics of C.S.I.R.O. the Division of Land Research and Regional Survey is doing an increasing amount of climatological work in its Australian studies. *R. O. Slatyer* is a climatologist with this organization.

Research results are published in the *Technical Papers* of the Division of Meteorological Physics, C.S.I.R.O., in the *Australian Meteorological Magazine* published by the Bureau of Meteorology of the Commonwealth, and in the standard English-language meteorological periodicals.

Monte-Patagonian

Weather and climate research is more advanced in Argentina than in Peru and Chile. The available literature indicates a good understanding of the meteorology of Argentina, though there is no special emphasis on the meteorology and synoptic climatology of the arid zone. The national meteorological service has compiled mean and normal data. *J. J. Burgos* in Buenos Aires and *F. J. Prohaska* and *W. Schwerdtfeger* of the University of Wisconsin, Milwaukee, are authorities on the weather and climate of Argentina.

Bolivia apparently is not doing any arid-lands research. The arid zone is a neglected area since there are no population pressures to have it developed. Publication of climatological data has lapsed: the latest available year is 1960; however, the Bolivian weather bureau is taking steps to resume the series.

Atacama-Peruvian

Meteorology and climatology do not seem to be important fields of study in Peru and Chile; however, changes seem to be in process: a WMO/Special Fund project is seeking to establish a new climatological network. Data publication is carried on in Chile, but Peru lags in this important aspect of meteorological research. In Santiago, Chile, a hydrometeorological project operates in cooperation with the United Nations, and some work is being done at the Universidad del Norte in Antofagasta in solar energy and obtaining water from mist.

Peru apparently has no organized research in arid-lands weather and climate. Correspondence with scientists in the country indicates that meteorological research in general is almost nonexistent, and that published work on this desert area is very meager. The reports and papers written by Panagra meteorologists are a source of general meteorological information for the Peruvian desert, although the emphasis is on forecasting for aviation activities.

One organization in Peru that, before its recent termination, was interested in the coastal areas was the Compañía Administradora del Guano, Lima. Although its main interest was in oceanography as it related to the guano industry, occasional climatological studies were made by this group. Scientists from other countries who are considered to be knowledgeable about this desert area are *H. Flohn,* Universitat Bonn, Germany, and *C. C. Wallén,* Sveriges Meteorologiska och Hydrologiska Institut, Stockholm.

North American

The state of knowledge for the North American deserts varies depending upon the country under consideration. For the United States, climatic data is abundant, and it has been summarized and published. The general features of the synoptic climatology are well known; however, there is no special emphasis on problems of the deserts since they are a small part of a generally humid country.

Several groups within the arid zone have made and are making contributions to the state of knowledge; the individuals named below should be considered authorities. The Institute of Atmospheric Physics of the University of Arizona has produced many contributions to the climatology of that state and the synoptic climatology of the Southwest. *J. R. Hastings* (bioclimatologist) and *R. M. Turner* (U.S.G.S. botanist) are working in the field of plant-climate relationships with a special interest in the Sonoran Desert. They have collected and published previously unavailable climatic data from Mexico. *J. E. McDonald,* primarily concerned with theoretical cloud physics, has done work in the climate of the area. *W. D. Sellers* is doing experimental research in the heat balance of a desert soil and is engaged in studies to evaluate the transfer coefficients in terms of different lapse rates of temperature in the surface layers.

C. H. M. van Bavel is associated with the U. S. Water Conservation Laboratory at Tempe, Arizona. This organization has used a weighing lysimeter to measure evaporation and evapotranspiration under a variety of conditions and has investigated the "oasis" effect. Lysimeter work is also being done in a semi-arid climate by the University of California at Davis. A project of the Department of Meteorology at the University of Wisconsin is concerned with a possible method of reversing the advance of the Rajputana Desert in India. The theory is that infrared cooling of the air due to the dust contributes to subsidence, which might be eliminated by stabilizing the soil with an adequate grass cover.

In Mexico, the publication of climatological data has been irregular, though real progress has been made in recent years in establishing a climatological network in the arid northwest. There is no evidence of any interest in the meteorology of the deserts, though by virtue of his good work in the synoptic climatology of Mexico as a whole, *Pedro Mosiño A.,* head of the Department of Meteorology at the Universidad Nacional Autonoma de México (Mexico City), is listed as an authority. Other Mexican authorities with interests in the weather and climate of arid lands are *J. A. Vivó* and *M. Maldonado-Koerdell* of the Instituto Panamericano de Geografía e Historía, Mexico City.

World Authorities

Arid-lands meteorology has benefited in general from the interests of several individuals. People such as *Peveril Meigs,* Wayland, Mass., and *C. C. Wallén,* Sveriges Meteorologiska och Hydrologiska Institut, Stockholm, have contributed to the understanding of the meteorological problems of arid lands as productive scientists and as eminent students who have brought their insight and understanding to bear on arid-lands problems in general. *J. Cochemé,* an agroclimatologist with the Food and Agriculture Organization, Rome, is another scientist who has specialized in arid-zone climatology, particularly of the Sahara.

C. OVERVIEW

One point made in this report is that desert meteorology and climatology is a rather limited field. Weather and climate exist as part of global or hemispheric systems of air motions, and desert areas are often small in relation to the wind systems that dominate them. In such subject-areas as evapotranspiration, the basic theory and most of the experimental work developed without any emphasis on their application to deserts. In fact, it would probably be preferable to the scientists in this field if the arid lands with their bothersome advection effects or their excessively unstable surface layers did not exist.

The availability of climatic data from the 50 or so countries containing deserts is highly variable. Some of the reasons for this situation are the impoverished economic status of many arid-lands countries, the fact that many of the nations have had short and often chaotic histories, and the backwardness of many of the areas in general. Personal correspondence with individuals in certain countries confirms what literature searches reveal, essentially a void in available information. It is difficult to accept the conclusion that there has been almost no significant work done on the weather and climate of some desert areas, but such is the case. It is also true that many climatic data are collected but never summarized and published. If no need for the data is communicated, there is little reason to make them available.

While in some cases it is difficult to accept the lack of information about an area, it should also be pointed out that excellent summaries of climatic data do exist for many countries. Although the quality of the data cannot be assessed, the quality of their presentation is often good. Climatic atlases are frequently available, as well as descriptive discussions of the climate. This report has purposely avoided a discussion of current data publication from the individual countries. This information is so subject to change that it is felt that, when a need for data exists, the current availability has to be determined from the primary source and the U. S. Weather Bureau Library in Washington, D. C.

The weather events that combine to form climate are known, in general, for they are part of the whole general circulation of the atmosphere. Emphasis in this review is placed on the rainfall of an area. No attempt is made here to write a synoptic climatology for each country or each desert; but we believe that significant and useful references to the weather and climate of countries and deserts are mentioned. In many cases, the papers to be included were suggested by local scientists, individuals well able to judge the significant contributions.

Desert storms are discussed in terms of the several main types that occur. Dust storms are the most important storms characteristic of deserts; their frequency is probably the most important climatic element. Upper-level winds are properly considered large-scale phenomena of little relevance to the deserts as deserts.

The most fruitful area for research in the problems of deserts probably lies in the application of methods for measuring or estimating potential evapotranspiration. This subject has been discussed under "Problems and Recommendations." In review, the essential problem is to evaluate the usefulness of equations of the Penman or Budyko types under difficult climatic conditions and then extrapolate to those areas where only temperature is available. The extrapolation can only be within climatically homogeneous regions. Intratype climatic classification becomes a prerequisite to the extrapolation. Needed are systems such as Meigs used for the Unesco Arid Zone Project or such as were proposed by the Unesco-FAO study of bioclimatic mapping of the Mediterranean area.

Weather modification seems to have no particular significance to the deserts. Although the effect of cloud seeding seems to be modest increases in rainfall, the fact that the deserts tend to be cloudless means that the essential prerequisite to effective cloud seeding is missing.

The measurement of radiation and radiation balance, and the estimation of these quantities, will take on an increasing importance. The application of new methods for estimating potential evapotranspiration will require estimates of radiation where it is not usually measured. Empirical equations for radiation balance will need to be tested for latitude, cloud type, and general climatic conditions. Accurate estimation of radiation becomes necessary in low latitudes where annual variation is small.

We have engaged in bibliographical investigations of the meteorological and climatological literature of significance to deserts. Two major bibliographical sources were of immense help to this review, the *Meteorological and Geoastrophysical Abstracts* published in the United States by the American Meteorological Society, and the country bibliographies compiled by the Foreign Area section of the U. S. Weather Bureau. The review articles written for the Unesco Arid Zone Research series are also excellent sources of bibliographical information. That series represents a major contribution to the state of knowledge of the weather and climate.

PERTINENT PUBLICATIONS

This bibliography combines in one alphabetical sequence for simplicity both an annotated bibliography and a more inclusive reference list. Those works which it has been possible to determine are of particular significance or interest to this study within the limitations discussed in the chapter are annotated. Other competent works and best-available works on specific subjects and areas are listed without annotation; lack of annotation should not be construed as *necessarily* indicating a less important publication. The abbreviation MGA indicates that an abstract of the listed publication can be found in *Meteorological and Geoastrophysical Abstracts.*

Academia Sinica, Peking
1957   On the general circulation over Eastern Asia (I). Tellus 9:432-446.

_____

1958   On the general circulation over Eastern Asia (II). Tellus 10:58-75.

Adejokun, J. A.
1965   The three dimensional structure of the intertropical discontinuity (I.T.D.) over Nigeria. Nigerian Meteorological Service, Lagos, Technical Note 39. 7 p.

Adle, A. H.
1960   Climats de l'Iran. Université Téhéran, Publication 586. 38 p.
Presents data and an analysis for an area where almost no climatological studies have been made. The general climatic controls, geographic factors, and the elements of weather and climate are discussed.

Aelion, E.
1958   A report on weather types causing marked storms in Israel during the cold season. Israel Meteorological Service, Series C, Miscellaneous Papers 10. 7 p.

Afrique Occidentale Française. Service Météorologique
1958   Les vents en altitude en Afrique Occidentale Française, période 1941-1955. Paris. 181 p.
(Upper-air winds in French West Africa, 1941-1955. MGA 13:11-576.)

Ahmad, K. S.
1951   Climatic regions of West Pakistan. Pakistan Geographical Review 6:1-35.
One of the features of this paper is a comparison of the climatic zones of Pakistan according to a variety of the standard schemes. The author's own system of classification based upon temperature and rainfall regimes is also given.

Ahmad, M. S.
1958   Précipitation, évapotranspiration et aridité en Pakistan Occidental: essai d'interprétation géo-graphique. Université Rennes, Faculté des Lettres & Sciences Humaines, Laboratoire de Climatologie, Travaux 1. 91 p.
Aridity in Pakistan is estimated using potential evapo-transpiration computed by Thornthwaite's and Penman's methods. Penman's method is preferred.

Aizenshtat, B. A.
1959   Issledovanie granits rasprostraneniia ursat'evskogo vetra. Sredneaziatskii Nauchno-Issledovatel'skii Gidrometeorologicheskii Institut, Trudy 2:3-16. (Investigation of the limits of propagation of Ursat'ev winds. MGA 13.2-392.)

Almeyda Arroyo, E.
1949   Pluviometría de las zonas del desierto y las estepas calidas de Chile. Editorial Universitaria, Santiago, Chile. 162 p.
(Rainfall in the zones of the desert and hot, dry plains of Chile. MGA 2.7-135.)
Presents monthly precipitation data for Chile for the period of record of all stations in the rainfall network. The data have been carefully checked, and a rainfall map of Chile is given.

_____

1954   Estaciones pluviométricas de Chile. Revista Geográfica de Chile 11:89-94.
(Rainfall stations in Chile. MGA 6.1-261.)

Alvarez, J. A.
1962   Some features of jet-streams over the southern parts of South America. Notos 11:67-75.

American Meteorological Society
1965   Agricultural meteorology. Meteorological Monographs 6(28). 188 p.
Several articles in this monograph are excellent reviews of subjects pertinent to arid-zone climatology ("Radiation," Gates; "Transport by Wind," Chepil; "Evapotranspiration," Thornthwaite and Hare).

Amiran, D. H. K. and M. Gilead
1954   Early excessive rainfall and soil erosion in Israel. Israel Exploration Journal 4:286-295.

Ananthakrishnan, R. and K. L. Bhatia
1960   Tracks of monsoon depressions and their recurvature towards Kashmir, p. 157-172. *In* Symposium on Monsoons of the World, New Delhi, Feb. 19-21, 1958, Proceedings.

Angola. Serviço Meteorológico
1955   O clima de Angola. Luanda. 53 p.
(Climate of Angola. MGA 8.3-292.)
A complete discussion of the climate of Angola. Meteorological data from about 53 stations are tabulated and discussed in the text. The climatic zones of the country have been delineated using the Köppen and Thornthwaite systems.

Angus, D. C.
1958   Measurement of dew. *In* Climatology and microclimatology, Proceedings of the Canberra Symposium. Unesco, Paris. Arid Zone Research 11: 301-303.

Aniol, R. and M. Schlegel
1963   Klimaatlanten und neuere klimakarten. Deutscher Wetterdienst, Bibliographien 14.
(Climatic atlases and recent climatic charts. MGA 15:7-87.)

Austin, E. E. and D. Dewar
1953   Upper winds over the Mediterranean and Middle East. Great Britain, Meteorological Research Committee, M.R.P. 811. 10 p.

Australia. Bureau of Meteorology
1956   Climatic averages, Australia; temperature, relative humidity, rainfall. Melbourne. 107 p.
Mean monthly temperature, rainfall, and relative humidity data by months are presented for about 200 stations in Australia, each with about 10 years of record.

———
1958   Upper air data, Australia: mean of geopotential and temperature and median values of mixing ratio. Director of Meteorology, Melbourne. 238 p.

Australia. Director of Meteorology
1960   Selected tables of Australian rainfall and related data. Melbourne. 146 p.

Australia. Meteorological Office
1963   Tropical cyclones in the northeastern and northwestern Australia regions, 1962-1963 season. Australian Meteorological Magazine 43:40-43.

Awad, A.
1962   Dust phenomena at Baghdad airport. Meteorological Department of Iraq, Meteorological Memoirs 1:1-6.

Bachurina, A. A. and V. G. Gus'kova
1956   Issledovanie sukhoveia, nabliudavshegosia v iiune 1948 g. na iugo-vostoke Evropeiskoi Territorii S.S.R. Tsentral'nyi Institut Prognozov, Moscow, Trudy 46:64-78.
(An investigation of the dry winds observed in June 1948 over S. E. European U.S.S.R. MGA 9.1-228.)

Bagnold, R. A.
1941   The physics of blown sand and desert dunes. Methuen and Co., London. 265 p.
Bagnold's treatise on the effect of wind on sand is considered to be the definitive work on this subject. A shorter review article is found in Chepil (1965).

Baier, W.
1966   Studies on dew formation under semi-arid conditions. Agricultural Meteorology 3:103-112.

Balashova, E. N., O. M. Zhitomirskaia, and O. A. Semenova
1960   Klimaticheskoe opisanic respublik Srednei Azii. Gidrometeoizdat, Leningrad. 240 p.
(Climatological description of the Republics of Middle Asia. MGA 12.5-12.)

Barteneva, O. D. and L. N. Guseva
1957   Rezhim estestvennoi osveshchennosti v zavisimosti ot meteorologicheskikh uslovii. Glavnaia Geofizicheskaia Observatoriia, Trudy 68:120-131.
(Regime of natural illumination as influenced by meteorological conditions. MGA 13:4-466.)

Battan, L. J.
1961   Soviet research in radar meteorology and cloud modification. American Meteorological Society, Bulletin 42:755-764.

———
1963   A survey of recent cloud physics research in the Soviet Union. American Meteorological Society, Bulletin 44:755-771.
Soviet work in cloud seeding is extensively reviewed in this paper and in Battan (1961).

———
1966   Silver iodide seeding and rainfall from convective clouds. Journal of Applied Meteorology 5:669-683.
The total experience (7 years) of seeding convective clouds over an isolated mountain range in an arid area (Southeastern Arizona) did not indicate that seeding increased the amount of rainfall.

Baum, W. A. and L. B. Smith
1953   Semi-monthly mean sea-level pressure maps for the Mediterranean area. Archiv für Meteorologie, Geophysik und Bioklimatologie, Serie A: Meteorologie und Geophysik 5:326-345.

Baumer, Michel
1964   Scientific research aimed at developing the arid zone of Saudi Arabia. Unesco, Paris. Arid Zone (Newsletter) 24:4-12.

Beckett, P. H. T. and E. D. Gordon
1956   The climate of Kerman, South Persia. Royal Meteorological Society, Quarterly Journal 82:503-514.

Belly, P.
1964   Sand movement by wind. With addendum II by Abdel-Latif Kadib. U. S. Corps of Engineers, Technical Memorandum 1. 38 p.

Bennett, I.
1964   A method for preparing maps of mean daily global radiation. Archiv für Meteorologie, Geophysik und Bioklimatologie, Series B, 13:216-248.

———
1965   Monthly maps of mean daily insolation for the United States. Solar Energy 9:145-158.
Solar energy measurements from 59 stations were used to estimate insolation of the 139 locations where more-usually-observed meteorological variables were available. Regression equations were devised.

Bennett, I. and R. A. Nelson
1960   Nighttime influence of irrigation upon desert humidities. U. S. Quartermaster Research and Engineering Center, Natick, Mass., Environmental Protection Research Division, Technical Report EP-136. 42 p.

Berenger, M.
1960   Quelques remarques sur les perturbations intéressants le Sahara. Météorologie 58:325-334.
The weather of the Sahara is composed of polar front disturbances and also disturbances that originate in the south. Synoptic examples of the two types are given.

Berges, R.
1962   Flux de vent sur le sud de la Mer Rouge aux niveaux 300, 200, 150 mb. France, Météorologie Nationale, Monographies 27. 35 p.
(Wind flow over the southern part of the Red Sea at 300, 200, 150 mb levels. MGA 14:12-503.)

Berkaloff, E.
  1949   Fréquence des pluies en Tunisie. Service Météoro-
         logique, Tunis. 4 vols.
  Gives the frequencies of different rainfall amounts.

Bezverkhniaia, R. Ts.
  1955   Sinopticheskie usloviia atmosfernoi za sushlivosti
         v zapadnom Kazakhstane. Nauchno-Issledovatel'-
         skii Gidrometeorologicheskii Institut, Alma-Ata,
         Kazakhstan, Trudy 5:77-88.
         (Synoptic conditions of atmospheric aridity in
         western Kazakhstan. MGA 13.5-526.)

Bhalotra, Y. P. R.
  1956   A spell of exceptionally low temperatures over
         Western Pakistan and Northwest India from May
         6-12, 1955. Indian Journal of Meteorology and
         Geophysics 7:204-205.

  ———

  1958   Dust storms at Khartoum. Meteorological Service
         of Sudan, Memoir 1. 74 p.
  Winter and summer dust storms are studied and discussed
  separately. Their frequencies, durations, and directions are
  tabulated, as are their effects on visibility. Synoptic charts
  have been used to study the mechanisms of the different
  types of dust storms.

Bhatia, S. S.
  1957   Arid zone of India and Pakistan: a study in its
         water balance and delimitation. Indian Journal of
         Meteorology and Geophysics 8:355-366.
  Thornthwaite's aridity and moisture indexes were computed for about 60 stations in India and Pakistan. These
  values gave better results than Köppen's and de Martonne's indices.

Bidault, G.
  1953   Notes sur le climat du Maroc Oriental. Institut
         Scientifique Chérifien, Rabat, Service de Physique
         du Globe et de Météorologie, Recueil des Publi-
         cations 6.

Biel, Erwin
  1944   Climatology of the Mediterranean area. University
         of Chicago, Institute of Meteorology, Miscella-
         neous Report 13. 180 p.
  Although based primarily on prewar data, this report is
  an excellent summary of the climatological conditions
  existing in the Mediterranean area. The main elements of
  climate (pressure and wind, precipitation, cloudiness, and
  fog and temperatures) are discussed. A particularly good
  section is devoted to the discussion of local winds in the
  Mediterranean area.

Bilham, E. G.
  1957   Climatology. *In* Guide book to research data for
         arid zone development. Unesco, Paris. Arid Zone
         Research 9:26-43.
  This is one of the Unesco review articles which presents
  good general discussions of some aspects of arid zone
  climatology, in this case the subject of climatological
  observations in arid lands.

Black, J. F. and B. L. Tarmy
  1963   Use of asphalt coatings to increase rainfall. Journal
         of Applied Meteorology 2:557-564.

Black, J. N.
  1956   The distribution of solar radiation over the Earth's
         surface. Archiv für Meteorologie, Geophysik und
         Bioklimatologie, Serie B, 7:165-189.
  One point to be gained from this article is that the amount
  of actual measured solar radiation data is very small.

Black, J. N., C. W. Bonython, and J. A. Prescott
  1954   Solar radiation and the duration of sunshine. Royal
         Meteorological Society, Quarterly Journal 80:231-
         235.

Blaney, H. F. and W. D. Criddle
  1962   Determining consumptive use and irrigation water
         requirements. U. S. Department of Agriculture,
         Technical Bulletin 1275.
  Consumptive use is defined as the amount of water used
  by growing crops. It is based on the relationship between
  temperature and daylight hours during the growing season
  and the empirical constant for individual crops.

Bleeker, W. (ed.)
  1960   The Unesco/WMO seminar on Mediterranean
         synoptic meteorology, Rome, 24 November to 13
         December 1958. Freien Universität, Berlin, Institut
         für Meteorologie und Geophysik, Meteorologische
         Abhandlungen 9. 226 p.

Boffi, J. A.
  1949   Effect of the Andes Mountains on general circula-
         tion over the southern part of South America.
         American Meteorological Society, Bulletin 30:242-
         247.

Bond, H. G.
  1960   Drought of 1951-52 in Northern Australia, p. 215-
         222. *In* Symposium on monsoons of the world,
         New Delhi, Feb. 19-21, 1958, Proceedings.

Borisov, A. A.
  1965   Climates of the U.S.S.R. Oliver and Boyd, London.
         255 p.
         (This volume is a translation of the 2nd edition
         of Klimat CCCR by A. A. Borisov, 1959.)
  This general climatology of the Soviet Union is rated as
  the most comprehensive book on the subject available
  today. The factors that form climate, the distribution of
  climatic elements, and regional climates of the U.S.S.R.
  are the three main divisions in the book.

Brann, H. N.
  1958   Meteorological measurements in arid zones. *In*
         Climatology and microclimatology, Proceedings of
         the Canberra symposium. Unesco, Paris. Arid
         Zone Research 11:304-306.

Brichambaut, G. P. de and C. C. Wallén
  1963   A study of agroclimatology in semi-arid and arid
         zones of the Near East. World Meteorological
         Organization, Technical Note 56.
  Although the emphasis of this report is on agroclimatology, it can be considered a major contribution to the
  understanding of the meteorology of the Mediterranean
  region with an emphasis on the eastern portion. A general
  picture of the climatic conditions in the region is given.
  The report deals with the general circulation and discusses
  various causes of rainfall during the winter and spring
  seasons. Of special interest is a study of the length of the
  reliable rainfall season.

British Meteorological Office
  1958   Tables of temperature, relative humidity, and pre-
         cipitation for the world. Her Majesty's Stationery
         Office, London. 6 pts.
  This publication of climatic data is probably the most
  comprehensive 1-volume collection of world climatic data
  recently published. There is no arid-lands emphasis, but it
  is a ready reference for standard climatological data.

British West Africa. Meteorological Services
1954 Bibliography of publications relating to the meteorology of British West Africa. Lagos.

Brunt, A. T. and J. Hogan
1956 Occurrence of tropical cyclones in the Australian region, p. 5-18. *In* Tropical Cyclone Symposium, Brisbane, December 1956, Proceedings.

Brutsaert, W.
1965 Evaluation of some practical methods of estimating evapotranspiration in arid climates at low latitudes. Water Resources Research 1:187-191.
Brutsaert's evaluation is noteworthy for his observations that systems of estimating evapotranspiration based on latitude and day-length (annual variation in radiation) cannot be expected to work well in low latitudes.

Bryson, R. A.
1957*a* Some factors in Tucson summer rainfall. University of Arizona, Institute of Atmospheric Physics, Technical Reports on the Meteorology and Climatology of Arid Regions 4. 26 p.

_____
1957*b* The annual march of precipitation in Arizona, New Mexico, and Northwestern Mexico. University of Arizona, Institute of Atmospheric Physics, Technical Reports on the Meteorology and Climatology of Arid Regions 6. 24 p.

Bryson, R. A. and D. A. Baerreis
1965 Possibilities of major climatic modification and their implications; Northwest India, a case study. Conference on social and economic implications of weather modification, Boulder, Colorado, July 1965, Proceedings.
The authors suggest that radiational cooling by dust in the air contributes significantly to the average subsidence that inhibits convection and rainfall in the region. They suggest that the climate would be different if the dust in the lower atmosphere were reduced, and that the advance of the Rajputana Desert could be reduced.

Bryson, R. A. and W. P. Lowry
1955 Synoptic climatology of the Arizona summer monsoon. American Meteorological Society, Bulletin 36:329-339.
It is noted that there is a large increase in the amount of rainfall from late June to early July in Arizona. This paper relates this sharp increase to a change from dry air masses in June to moist air masses from the Gulf of Mexico in July. The occurrence appears to be related to a hemispheric singularity.

Bryssine, G.
1949 Les facteurs climatiques de la pédogénèse au Maroc. Service de la Recherche Agronomique et de l'Expérimentation Agricole, les Cahiers de la Recherche Agronomique 2:41-70.

Budyko, M. I.
1956 Teplovoi balans zemnoi poverkhnosti (The heat balance of the Earth's surface, translated by N. A. S. Zikeev, U. S. Weather Bureau, Washington, 1958.) Gidrometeorologicherkoe Izdatel'stov, Leningrad. 255 p.
The English translation of this monograph was the means by which the Budyko method of estimating potential evapotranspiration became generally known to the Western world. The method of estimating potential evapotranspiration is discussed and the radiation index of

aridity is presented. In addition, data for the heat and water balance of the world are presented.

Budyko, M. I., ed.
1963 Atlas Teplovogo Bolansa. Mezhduvedomstvennyy Geofizicheskiy Komitet pri Prezidiume AN S.S.S.R. Moscow. 6 p., 69 maps.
This atlas of the heat balance of the Earth's surface is a major contribution to the field in general. The text and map legends have been translated by the U. S. Weather Bureau, Washington, D. C., and issued in December, 1964, as *Guide to the Atlas of the Heat Balance of the Earth,* WB/T-106.

Budyko, M. I. and N. A. Efimova
1964 Izmenchivost' radiasionnykh factorov teplovogo balansa zemnoi poverkhnosti. Meteorologiia i Gidrologiia 4:9-15.

Bugaev, V. A., V. A. Dzhordzhio, and V. R. Dubentsov
1952 O termicheskom effekte pyli pri pyl'nykh i peschanykh buriakh. Akademiia Nauk S.S.S.R., Izvestiia, Ser. Geograficheskaia 3:44-45.
(The thermal effect of dust during dust and sand storms. MGA 5:11-129.)

Bugaev, V. A. *et al.*
1962 Synoptic processes of Central Asia. World Meteorological Organization, Geneva. 645 p.
This is the major work on the subject available in English translation. Many different types of weather patterns are discussed.

Burgos, J. J.
1963 El clima de las regiones áridas en la República Argentina. Revista de Investigaciones Agrícolas, Buenos Aires, 17:385-405.

Burgos, J .J. and A. L. Vidal
1951 Los climas de la República Argentina, según la nueva clasificación de Thornthwaite. Meteoros 1:3-32.
Translated in full: Association of American Geographers, Annals 41:237-263.

Butt, M. T.
1950 Climate of the Pak Punjab. Pakistan Geographical Review 5:52-58.

Butzer, K. W.
1960 Dynamic climatology of large-scale European circulation patterns in the Mediterranean area. Meteorologische Rundschau 13:97-105.

Capitanelli, R. G.
1955 Régimen de aridez de la provincia de San Luis. Boletín de Estudios Geográficos 2:291-317.

Carr, J. A.
1951 The rains over Arizona, August 26-29, 1951. Monthly Weather Review 79:163-167.

Chabra, A.
1959 Aperçu climatologique de la Mauritanie. Service Météorologique, République de Mauritanie. 10 p.
Chabra's short general discussion of climate contains some mean climatic data and was the only publication received from the Mauritania Meteorological Service.

Chang Chi-chia
1960*a* Mnogoletnie srednei kharakteristiki nekotorykh meteorologicheskikh elementov i tsirkuliatsii nad kitaem v simnem polugodii. Glavnaia Geofizicheskaia Observatoriia, Leningrad, Trudy 90:11-26.
(Long period average characteristics of certain

meteorological elements and circulation over China during winter. MGA 13.1-355.)

―――

1960*b* Srednie mnogoletnie kharakteristiki atmosferoi tsirkuliatsii i rezhima pogody nad Kitaem v letnee polugodie. Glavnaia Geofizicheskaia Observatoriia, Leningrad, Trudy 90:43-62.
(Long period average characteristics of atmospheric circulation and weather regime over China in summer. MGA 13.3-423.)

Chanysheva, S. G.
1959 Aerologicheskaia kharakteristika ursat'evskogo vetra. Sredneaziatskii Nauchno - Issledovatel'skii Gidrometeorologicheskii Institut, Trudy 2:26-40.
(Aerological characteristics of Ursatev winds. MGA 14.2-621.)

Chatterjee, S. B.
1953 Indian climatology: climostatics, climatic classification of India with special reference to the monsoons. Calcutta University. Ph.D. thesis.
Although not a book in the general sense, this collection of reprints and connecting text presents a fairly complete climatology of India. Many features of the synoptic climatology of India are discussed, and seasonal and regional descriptions are included.

Ch'en Shih-hsun
1961 Klimat Kitaia. Izd-vo Inostrannoi Lit-ry, Moscow. 343 p.
A general discussion of the climate of China emphasizing three major factors: climatic controls, characteristics of climatic elements, and analysis of the climate in eight regions, one of which is the Sinkiang area. (A translation from Chinese into Russian.)

Chepil, W. S.
1965 Transport of soil and snow by wind. Meteorological Monograph 6:123-132.
This short, well-referenced article is a good review of the effect of wind on soil.

Chi, C. H.
1955 Surface air currents in Sin-Kiang. Meteorological Bulletin, Taipei, Formosa, 1:33-38.

Chile. Oficina Meteorológica.
1964 Climatología de Chile. Fasc. I: Valores normales de 36 estaciones seleccionadas, periodo 1916-1945. Proyecto Hidrometeorológico, Naciones Unidas-Gobierno de Chile. Santiago. 12 p., tables.
Mean data for 36 stations are presented. Items included in these detailed summaries are temperature at selected hours, relative humidity, precipitation, frequency of occurrence of meteorological phenomena such as fog, thunderstorms, etc., and wind statistics.

Chile. Oficina Meteorólogica
1965 Pluviometría de Chile. Fasc. II. Santiago. 268 p.
This volume contains the monthly and yearly rainfall for the period of record of 137 stations and computed values of the 1931-1960 normals (when appropriate). Along with Chile, Oficina Meteorológica (1964), these two publications comprise good sources of climatological data.

China. Central Meteorological Bureau. Office of Climatological Data Research (ed.)
1960 Chung-kuo Ch'i-hou T'u. Map Publishing Society, Peiping. 582 p., charts, tables.
(Atlas of Chinese climatology. Translated by the U. S. Joint Publications Research Service, Washington, as JPRS 16,321.)

This translation of a Chinese climatological atlas is apparently the best available source of climatic data in the English language. Most of the data are up to the year 1950, though a few stations have data through 1955. Most of the maps do not extend their isolines into the Takla Makan Desert. Lengths of record of stations in this area are usually short, on the order of 5 years for temperature and 8 years for precipitation.

Chu Bao-tsian
1958 Izuchenie osobennostei klimata Sin'tsziana. Priroda 11:79-82.
(Climatic features of Sinkiang Province. MGA 11.1-280.)

Clark, R. H.
1963 Severe local wind storms in Australia. Commonwealth Scientific and Industrial Research Organization, Division of Meteorological Physics, Technical Paper 13. 45 p.

Cochemé, J. and P. Franquin
1967 An agroclimatology survey of a semiarid area in Africa south of the Sahara. World Meteorological Organization, Geneva, Technical Note 86. 136 p.

Contreras Arias, A.
1942 Estudios climatológicas. Area geográficas de dispersión. *Parthenium argentatum, Hevea brasiliensis, Castilloa elastica.* Mexico. 112 p.
One of the early Mexican publications of the study of that climate, this paper contains some tabulations of climatic data. More recent publications such as Hastings (1964*a, b*) largely replace it as an arid-zone data source.

Daniels, F.
1964 The direct use of the sun's rays. Yale University Press, New Haven. 374 p.
This is a general discussion of the possibilities of the utilization of solar radiation. It is a popular as contrasted to a technical discussion.

Davitaya, F. F.
1961 Arid-zone studies in the U.S.S.R., 1956-60. Soviet Geography 2:69-71.
A general discussion of some of the research being carried on dealing with the weather and climate of the Soviet arid zone.

―――

1964 Climatic resources of arid zones and their agricultural use in the U.S.S.R. *In* Land use in semi-arid Mediterranean climates. Unesco, Paris. Arid Zone Research 26:31-36.

Deacon, E. L., C. H. B. Priestley, and W. C. Swinbank
1958 Evaporation and the water balance. *In* Climatology, reviews of research. Unesco, Paris. Arid Zone Research 10:9-34.
Written as a review article with special reference for arid zones, this paper discusses the evaporation of water from the Earth's surface and reviews the methods of determination: the aerodynamic, heat balance, and empirical approaches. This is an excellent, critical review of all aspects of the problem of measuring or estimating evapotranspiration and potential evapotranspiration.

Debrach, J.
1953 Notes sur les climats du Maroc Occidental. Institut Scientifique Chérifien, Rabat, Service de Physique du Globe et de Météorologie, Recueil des Publications 5. 15 p.
(Notes on the climate of western Morocco. MGA 6.9-314.)

Debrach, J., J. Ousset, and M. Michel
1956 Précipitations atmosphériques au Maroc. Institut Scientifique Chérifien, Rabat, Service de Physique du Globe et de Météorologie, Annales 16:77-108. (Atmospheric precipitations in Morocco. MGA 10M-136.)

1958 Données nouvelles sur la température de l'air au Maroc. Première partie. Institut Scientifique Chérifien, Rabat, Service de Physique du Globe et de Météorologie, Annales 18:17-115.

Dettwiller, J.
1963 Vents forts dans la haute troposphère au dessus du Sahara. Météorologie 72:403-417.
Sahara upper-wind data for the 1958-1961 period are used to study the characteristics of the subtropical jet stream in the western Sahara.

Dhonneur, M.
1957 Étude climatologique des routes aériennes aboutissant à Fort-Lamy. France, Météorologie Nationale, Monographies 2. 49 p.
(Climatological study of the aerial routes ending at Fort-Lamy. MGA 9.9-77.

Diaz, E. L.
1953 Interrelaciones entre anomalías mensuales de lluvias, temperatura, presión, gradientes y variaciones. Meteoros 3:342-382.
(Correlation between monthly anomalies of rain, temperature, pressure, gradients, and related variables. MGA 6.1-329.)

Dodd, A. V. and H. S. McPhilimy
1959 Yuma summer microclimate. U. S. Army Quartermaster Research and Engineering Center, Natick, Mass., Environmental Protection Research Division, Technical Report EP-120. 34 p.

Drummond, A. J.
1958a Radiation and the thermal balance. In Climatology, reviews of research. Unesco, Paris. Arid Zone Research 10:56-74.
The main purpose of this review is to provide a background summary of the field of radiation for the Unesco Australia Symposium on Arid Zone Climatology. The major concern is therefore on radiation as it affects the problems of arid lands. Data from South Africa, South West Africa, and Bechuanaland (now Botswana) are used for examples.

1958b Notes on the measurement of natural illumination. Pt. 2: Daylight and skylight at Pretoria: the luminous efficiency of daylight. Archiv für Meteorologie, Geophysik und Bioklimatologie, Serie B, 9:149-163.

Drummond, A. J. and E. Vowinckel
1957 The distribution of solar radiation throughout southern Africa. Journal of Meteorology 14:343-353.
Sufficient data are now available to present the general features of the distribution of radiation in South Africa. Data are estimated from a solar radiation network using percent of possible sunshine.

Dubief, J.
1942 Sur les vents de sable du Sahara algérien. Académie des Sciences, Paris, Comptes Rendus 215:374-376.
This short paper contains frequencies of dust storms for numerous Sahara stations. Summarized in tables.

1953a Essai sur l'hydrologie superficielle au Sahara. Direction du Service de la Colonisation et de l'Hydraulique, Service des Etudes Scientifiques, Algiers, Algeria. 457 p.
Has been cited as a key paper on the climatology of the Sahara with an emphasis on the distribution of precipitation. The synoptic climatology of the sources of precipitation is discussed showing the southern limits of rain originating from the polar front and the northern limit of monsoon rains. A detailed map shows the distribution of annual rainfall, and extensive amounts of precipitation data are tabulated.

1953b Les vents de sable au Sahara français. Centre National de la Recherche Scientifique, Paris, Colloques Internationaux 35:45-70.

1959 Le climat du Sahara, vol. 1. Université d'Alger, Institut de Recherches Sahariennes. 312 p.
This is the first volume of Dubief's 2-volume "Climatology of the Sahara" (Dubief 1963a is Vol. 2). This study is rated the most comprehensive climatology available for this region.

1963a Le climat du Sahara, vol. 2. Université d'Alger, Institut de Recherches Sahariennes. 275 p.
The second volume of Dubief's 2-volume "Climatology of the Sahara" (Dubief 1959 is Vol. 1). This study is rated the most comprehensive climatology available for this region.

1963b Résultats tirés d'enregistrements automatiques récents dans des stations élevées du Massif Central Saharien. Geofisica e Meteorologia 11:119-125.
(Results derived from recent automatic recording at elevated stations of the Central Sahara Range. MGA 15.3-440.)

Duvdevani, S.
1953 Dew gradients in relation to climate, soil and topography. In Desert research, proceedings of the International Symposium held in Jerusalem, May 7-14, 1952, sponsored by the Research Council of Israel and Unesco. Research Council of Israel, Special Publication 2:136-152.
A rather complete article on the measurement of dew. Numerical and graphical data are given for several stations in Israel. Average values are also presented. The variation of dew with elevation is discussed.

1964 Dew in Israel and its effects on plants. Soil Science 98-14-21.
The general processes of dew formation are discussed, and data for Israel are presented. It is shown that plants deprived of dew did not grow as well as those on which dew was allowed to form naturally.

Dyer, A. J.
1965 The flux-gradient relation for turbulent heat transfer in the lower atmosphere. Royal Meteorological Society, Quarterly Journal 91:151-157.

Dyer, A. J. and F. J. Moher
1965 The "Evapotron": An instrument for the measurement of eddy fluxes in the lower atmosphere. Commonwealth Scientific and Industrial Research Organization, Division of Meteorological Physics, Technical Paper 15. 31 p.

Dyer, A. J. and W. O. Pruitt
1962 Eddy-flux measurements over a small, irrigated area. Journal of Applied Meteorology 1:471-473.

Dzerdzeevskii, B. L. (ed.)
1957 Sukhovei ikh proiskhozhdenie i bor'ba s nimi. Akademiya Nauk S.S.S.R., Institut Geografii, Moskva. 366 p.
(Sukhoveis and drought control. Translated from the Russian by the Israel Program for Scientific Translation, 1963, and available from U. S. Department of Commerce, Office of Technical Services, Washington, D. C.)
Collected papers of a conference convened by the Institute of Geography at the U.S.S.R. Academy of Sciences in December, 1953, to study the sukhovei or dry wind. Contains a bibliography of 415 papers on sukhovei from the period 1917-1955. The editor regards this volume as the definitive work on this atmospheric phenomenon.

1958 On some climatological problems and microclimatological studies of arid and semi-arid regions in U.S.S.R. *In* Climatology and microclimatology, Proceedings of the Canberra Symposium. Unesco, Paris, Arid Zone Research 11:315-325.
A noteworthy feature of this article is that it lists 19 different expressions for aridity, many common ones as well as many due to Russian authors (generally less-well-known).

East African Common Services Organization. Meteorological Department.
1963a Annual Report, 1961/1962. Nairobi, Kenya. 36 p.

1963b Summaries of radiosonde observations of temperature and humidity and of radar wind measurements at standard pressure levels, 1957-1962. Nairobi, Kenya.

1965 Monthly and annual rainfall in Kenya during the 30 years, 1931-1960. Nairobi, Kenya.

Eldridge, R. H.
1957 A synoptic study of West African disturbance lines. Royal Meteorological Society, Quarterly Journal 83:303-314.

Elser, H. L.
1959 A desert dust storm strikes El Paso, Texas. Weatherwise 12:115-116.

Eltantawy, A. H. I.
1964 The tropical easterly jet stream over Africa. U.A.R. Meteorological Department, Cairo, Scientific Paper 1.

Emberger, L.
1955 Afrique du nord-ouest. *In* Plant ecology, reviews of research. Unesco, Paris. Arid Zone Research 6:219-249.
Emberger's index of aridity is applied to stations in the western Sahara, and a map of the distribution of aridity is given. This paper is useful as a recent discussion of Emberger's index of aridity.

el-Fandy, M. G.
1948 The effect of the Sudan monsoon low on the development of thundery conditions in Egypt, Palestine, and Syria. Royal Meteorological Society, Quarterly Journal 74:31-38.

1949a Forecasting the summer weather of the Sudan and the rains that lead to the Nile floods. Royal Meteorological Society, Quarterly Journal 75:375-398.
Summer thunderstorms in the Sudan are classified into four types. Each type is discussed and illustrated by a synoptic example.

1949b Dust — an active meteorological factor in the atmosphere of northern Africa. Journal of Applied Physics 20:660-666.

1950 Troughs in the upper westerlies and cyclonic developments in the Nile valley. Royal Meteorological Society, Quarterly Journal 76:166-172.

1952 Forecasting thunderstorms in the Red Sea. American Meteorological Society, Bulletin 33:332-338.

Fàntoli, A.
1952 Le pioggie della Libia, con particolare riguardo alle zone di avvaloramento. Ministero dell'Africa Italiana, Ispettorato Meteorologico. Rome. 528 p.
Has been classified as a magnificent climatological study in terms of the statistical analysis of climatic data and the descriptive and analytic material presented about the distribution of rainfall.

1954 I valori medi della temperature in Libia. Societá Geografica Italiana, Bollettino, Series 8, 7:59-71.
Concentrates on the analysis of average temperature in Libya based on 48 stations with varying lengths of record.

1960a Contributi preliminari alla climatologia dell' Etiopia, III: Neghelli, Bonga, Lechémti, Oletta, Dessiè. Rivista di Meteorologia Aeronautica 20:3-32.
(Preliminary contribution to the climatology of Ethiopia, part 3. MGA 12.4-298.)

1960b Alcuni elementi relativi alla climatologia della Somalia. Rivista di Meteorologia Aeronautica 20:3-21.
(Certain elements of the climatology of Somaliland. MGA 12.6-410.)

1961 Caratteri climatologici di alcune località dell' Eritrea. Rivista di Meteorologia Aeronautica 21:21-46.
(Climatic characteristics of some Eritrean localities. MGA 13.4-547.)

1963 Le correnti aeree al suolo e in quota ad Addis Abeba, Etiopia. Rivista di Meteorologia Aeronautica 23:3-29.
(Surface and upper air current at Addis Ababa, Ethiopia. MGA 15:3-385.)

Ferreira, H. A.
1957 Bibliografia meteorológica e geofísica de Angola. Angola, Serviço Meteorológico, Luanda. 14 p.

Flohn, H.
1965 Contributions to a synoptic climatology of the Red Sea trench and adjacent territories. University of Bonn, Institute of Meteorology. U. S. Department of Army contract No. DA-91-591-EUC-3201, Technical Report 1. 33 p.

Flohn, H. and K. Hinkelmann
1952 Aquatoriale zirkulationsanomalien und ihre klimatische auswirkung. Deutscher Wetterdienst, Berichte 42:114-121.
(Equatorial circulation anomalies and their climatic effect. MGA 15L-39.)

Foley, J. C.
1956 500 mb contour patterns associated with the occurrence of widespread rains in Australia, Australian Meteorological Magazine 13:1-18.

Font Tullot, I.
1948 El régimen de lluvias del Sáhara Español. Revista de Geofísica 7:380-393.
(Rainfall regime of the Spanish Sahara. MGA 3A-271.)

1949 El clima del Africa Occidental Española. Servicio Meteorológico Nacional, Madrid, Publicación, Series A, 21. 88 p.
This study of the climate of Spanish Sahara is mainly descriptive. The elements of weather to be found in this region such as thunderstorms, sandstorms, special winds, and weather types, are discussed.

1955 El clima del Sáhara, con especial referencia a la Zona Española. Consejo Superior de Investigaciones Científicas, Madrid. 112 p.
(Climate of the Sahara, with special reference to the Spanish Zone. MGA 8.4-291.)
A monograph on the climate of the Sahara's Spanish Zone, sometimes called Río de Oro, contains a description of the physical geography and overall climate of the Sahara. A detailed description of the climate of the Spanish Zone is given with special reference to the effects of the Canaries Current. The water problems of the Spanish Sahara are also discussed. Data are presented and climatological summaries are given in tables.

Fournier, d'Albe, E. M. *et al.*
1955 The cloud-seeding trials in the central Punjab, July-September 1954. Royal Meteorological Society, Quarterly Journal 81:574-581.

Freeman, M. H.
1952 Duststorms of Anglo-Egyptian Sudan. Great Britain Meteorological Office, Meteorological Reports 11. 22 p.
Types of dust storms at Khartoum are classified and described. Their frequencies are discussed and synoptic conditions associated with them are described.

Fritschen, L. J. and C. H. M. van Bavel
1962 Energy balance components of evaporating surfaces in arid lands. Journal of Geophysical Research 67:5179-5185.

1963 Evaporation from shallow water and related micrometeorological parameters. Journal of Applied Meteorology 2:407-411.
Lysimeter measurements were combined with computations of the energy balance equation over isolated shallow water and extended shallow water to illustrate the "oasis" effect.

Gabriel, K. R.
1965 The Israeli artificial rainfall stimulation experiment. An interim statistical evaluation of results. Hebrew University, Department of Statistics, Jerusalem, Israel. 23 p.

Ganji, M. H.
1954 A contribution to the climatology of Iran. Clark University, Worcester, Mass. Ph.D. dissertation. 334 p.
This general discussion of the climate of Iran presents climatic data and a bibliography. Climatic classifications are given based on several different schemes.

1955 The climates of Iran. Société Royale de Géographie d'Egypte, Bulletin 28:195-299.

García, E.
1964 Modificaciones al sistema de clasificación climática de Köppen (para adaptarlo a las condiciones de la República Mexicana). Universidad Nacional Autónoma de México, Instituto de Geografía, México, D. F. 71 p.
The author modifies the Köppen classification of climate to fit the conditions in Mexico. She then uses her revised boundary conditions to construct a map for this classification.

Garnier, B. J.
1960 Maps of the water balance in West Africa. Institut Français d'Afrique Noire, Bulletin, Series A, 22: 709-722.

Gellert, J. F.
1955 Die Niederschlagsschwankungen im Hochland von Südwestafrika. Meteorologischer und Hydrologischer Dienst, Abhandlungen 4:69.
(Rainfall variation in the highlands of South West Africa. MGA 8.1-18.)

1962 Wetterlagen und Niederschlagsschwankungen in Süd- und Südwestafrika. Zeitschrift für Meteorologie 16:103-109.
Weather situation and precipitation fluctuations in South and South West Africa are treated. Synoptic studies by the author show that summer rains in South West Africa can be traced to the equatorial westerlies. Yearly variations are related to shifts in the general circulation.

Gentilli, J.
1953 Die Ermittlung der möglichen oberflächen-und pflanzenverdunstung, dargelegt am beispiel von Australien. Das suchen nach einer formel. Erdkunde 7:81-93.
(The estimation of the possible evapotranspiration, with Australia as an example: the search for a formula. MGA 10I-70.)

1955 Australian climates. University of Western Australia, Perth. 18 p.

Ghani, A. R.
1951 Pakistan: a select bibliography. Pakistan Association for the Advancement of Science, University Institute of Chemistry, Lahore. 339 p.

Gherzi, E.
1951 The meteorology of China. Serviço Meteorológico, Macao. 2 vols.
This old publication is still useful as a general discussion of the climate of China. There is little emphasis on the arid zone.

Gibbs, W. J. and W. K. Hounsell
1961 Stratospheric winds over Australia. Australia, Bureau of Meteorology, Working Paper 60/2612.

Gilead, M. and N. Rosenan
1954   Ten years of dew observation in Israel. Israel Exploration Journal 4. 4 p.

———
1958   Climatological observational requirements in arid zones. *In* Climatology, reviews of research. Unesco, Paris. Arid Zone Research 10:181-188.

Gilman, D. L., J. R. Hibbs, and P. L. Laskin
1965   Weather and climate modification. Weather Bureau, Washington, D. C. 41 p.
Part of the current thought in the United States on this changing and controversial subject is here summarized.

Glavnaya Geofizicheskaya Observatoriya im. A. I. Voyenkova
1958-   Klimat S.S.S.R. Gidrometeorologicheskoye Izda-
1963   tel'stvo, Leningrad. 7 vols.
A major work on the climate of all of the U.S.S.R. Four of the 7 volumes are known to have been translated by the Foreign Technology Division, Air Force Systems Command, Wright-Patterson Air Force Base, Ohio. The four translated volumes discuss:
Issue 2.   The Caucasus (1961, 290 p.)
Issue 4.   Western Siberia (1962, 360 p.)
Issue 5.   Eastern Siberia (1961, 300 p.)
Issue 8.   Climate of the free atmosphere (1959, 220 p.)
The other three known volumes are
Issue 1.   The European territory of the U.S.S.R.
Issue 3.   Central Asia
Issue 6.   Far East
There is apparently no Issue 7.

Gleeson, T. A.
1952   Bibliography of the meteorology of the Mediterranean, Middle East and South Asia areas. Florida State University, Department of Meteorology, Scientific Report 1 (Appendix). 37 p.

———
1953   Cyclogenesis in the Mediterranean Region. Archiv für Meteorologie, Geophysik und Bioklimatologie, Serie A: Meteorologie und Geophysik 6:153-171.
A statistical study of cyclones originating in the Mediterranean region in the months of October through May. Some of the features summarized are regions of origin, type, displacement, filling, deepening, and trajectories. The relationships between the surface cyclone and 3-km wind motions are also noted.

———
1956   A comparison of cyclone frequencies in the North Atlantic and Mediterranean regions. Archiv für Meteorologie, Geophysik und Bioglimatologie, Serie A: Meteorologie und Geophysik 9:185-190.

Godson, W. L.
1955   Atmospheric radiation (current investigations and problems). World Meteorological Organization, Technical Note 8.

Golubov, R. S.
1956   Sinoptiko - klimaticheskoe opisanie Kazakhstana. Nauchno-Issledovatel'skii Institut, Alma-Ata, Trudy 6:3-21.
(Synoptic-climatological description of Kazakhstan. MGA 13.5-664.)

Govindaswamy, T. S.
1953   Rainfall abnormalities, week by week, in India during 1908 to 1950. Irrigation and Power 10: 128-129, 207-244.

Graves, M. E.
1954   Summary of research at Limatambo, Peru, 1939-1954. Pan American-Grace Airways, Inc., Lima, Peru. 26 p.
Graves' summary is one of several publications put out by Pan American-Grace Airways concerning their publications pertinent to the weather and climate of South America. This group is one of the few sources of meteorological literature for the west-coast deserts.

Graves, M. E., E. Schweigger and J. Valdivia P.
1955   Un año anormal. La Compañía Administradora del Guano, Lima, Boletín Científico 2:49-71.

Great Britain. Meteorological Office
1962a   Ethiopia (including Eritrea). Investigations Division, Climatological, Bracknell, Report 60. 66 p.

———
1962b   The Somali Republic and French Somaliland. Investigations Division, Climatological, Bracknell, Report 61. 100 p.
This is one of two general descriptions of climate (1962a) for the Somali-Chalbi Desert put out by this group. They contain general descriptions of the climate and some climatic data.

Green, C. R.
1959   Arizona statewide rainfall. University of Arizona, Institute of Atmospheric Physics, Technical Reports on the Meteorology and Climatology of Arid Regions 7. 14 p.

Green, C. R. and W. D. Sellers
1964   Arizona climate. Revised edition. The University of Arizona Press, Tucson, Arizona. 503 p.
The climate of Arizona contains a general discussion of the climate of the state and climatic data for the period of record for about 100 stations. It is an excellent source of mean climatic data and essentially replaces Smith (1956).

Griffiths, J. F.
1958   An initial investigation of the annual rainfall in East Africa. East African Meteorological Department, Memoirs 3(5).

———
1962   The climate of East Africa, p. 77-87. *In* The natural resources of East Africa. D. A. Hawkins, Ltd., Nairobi, Kenya.
In this general discussion of the climate of East Africa, the author notes that the factors that produce the climate are not fully understood, but that the classical pattern associated with the intertropical convergence zone is not followed. Rainfall variability is high.

Griffiths, J. F. and C. F. Hemming
1963   A rainfall map of eastern Africa and south Arabia. East African Meteorological Department, Memoirs 3(10). 42 p.
This noteworthy publication presents a rainfall map for eastern Africa for annual averages. Tabulations of data, lists of stations used, maps of monthly regions of heavy rain, and a proability graph of rainfall occurrence are presented. The authors suggest that there may be a decrease in rainfall with height above 3,000 or 4,000 meters. They drew their isolines on the basis of elevation and observed vegetation as well as the rainfall data.

Guerra T., J. C.
1959 Temperaturas de las costas central y norte del Perú. Revista Meteorológica del Perú 4:9-11. (Temperatures on the central and northern coasts of Peru. MGA 13.3-392.)

Gutman, G. J. and W. Schwerdtfeger
1965 The role of latent and sensible heat for the development of a high pressure system over the subtropical Andes in the summer. Meteorologische Rundschau 18:69-75.

Hall, N., V. S. Russell, and C. D. Hamilton
1958 Trees and microclimate. *In* Climatology and microclimatology, Proceedings of the Canberra Symposium. Unesco, Paris. Arid Zone Research 11:259-264.

Hamilton, R. A. and J. W. Archbold
1945 Meteorology of Nigeria and adjacent territory. Royal Meteorological Society, Quarterly Journal 71:231-264.

Hare, F. K.
1961 The causation of the arid zone. *In* A history of land use of the arid zone. Unesco, Paris. Arid Zone Research 17:25-30.

Hariharan, P. S.
1956 A study of the extension of cold waves at the surface in relation to upper winds at 3,000 ft. in India. Indian Journal of Meteorology and Geophysics 7:363-370.

Hassoon, K.
1962 An analysis of a violent squall at Baghdad airport. Meteorological Department of Iraq, Baghdad, Meteorological Memoirs 1:112-121.

Hastings, J. R.
1964a Climatological data for Baja California. University of Arizona, Institute of Atmospheric Physics, Technical Reports on the Meteorology and Climatology of Arid Regions 14. 132 p.
This publication and Hastings (1964b) present climatic data for part of the Sonoran Desert in Mexico to an extent and in a form heretofore unavailable.

_____
1964b Climatological data for Sonora and northern Sinaloa. University of Arizona, Institute of Atmospheric Physics, Technical Reports on the Meteorology and Climatology of Arid Regions 15. 152 p.

Hastings, J. R. and R. M. Turner
1965 Seasonal precipitation regimes in Baja California, Mexico. Geografiska Annaler, Series A, 47:204-223.
The distribution of precipitation in Baja California is discussed with an emphasis on its seasonal distribution and the meteorological factors which determine it. Statistical techniques are used to rank the importance of the various seasons in terms of the total rainfall amounts.

Haute-Volta, Service Météorologique
1964 Aperçus sur le climat de la Haute-Volta. Ouagadougou. 12 p.
A short discussion of the climate of Upper Volta, plus maps of mean climatic values and tables of norms and means.

Hilst, G. R. and P. W. Nickola
1959 On the wind erosion of small particles. American Meteorological Society, Bulletin 40:73-77.

Ho Lu and Wang Peng-fei
1959 Development of meteorological services in China in the past decade. Ch'i-hsiang Hsueh-pao 30:197-201. (Translation by U. S. Joint Publications Research Service, published 1960 by U. S. Office of Technical Services as JPRS 2452.)

Hofmeyr, W. L.
1961 Statistical analyses of upper air temperatures and winds over tropical and subtropical Africa. South Africa Weather Bureau, Notos 10:123-149.

Hounam, C. E.
1958 Evaporation pan coefficients in Australia. *In* Climatology and microclimatology, Proceedings of the Canberra Symposium. Unesco, Paris. Arid Zone Research 11:52-60.

_____
1961 Evaporation in Australia; a critical survey of the network and methods of observation together with a tabulation of the results of observations. Australia, Bureau of Meteorology, Bulletin 44. 34 p.
One of several points made in this paper is the necessity for standardization of evaporation pans. Since the water loss from different sized pans will vary under different conditions, it is essential that comparisons be made between similar instruments. Observations should be conducted only by observers who will devote proper attention to such items as the observational technique and maintenance. In addition to the discussion of the use of evaporation pans, pan data for Australia are completely analyzed, evaluated, and tabulated.

_____
1963 Estimates of solar radiation over Australia. Australian Meteorological Magazine 43:1-14.
Equations developed for the estimation of solar radiation are discussed, and an equation is developed for Australia. Maps showing the January and July radiation are drawn based on this equation. Terrestrial radiation is computed and a map of radiation balance is given.

Houseman, J.
1961 Dust haze at Bahrain. Meteorological Magazine 19:50-52.

Howell, W. E.
1953 Local weather of the Chicama Valley (Peru). Archiv für Meteorologie, Geophysik und Bioklimatologie, Serie B, 5:41-51.

_____
1965 Twelve years of cloud seeding in the Andes of Northern Peru. Journal of Applied Meteorology 4:693-700.

Husain, A. A.
1950 A workable analysis of the precipitation data for Quetta. Karachi Geographical Society, Journal 2:30-40.

Hussain, M., N. Ahmad, and S. Aziz
1962 Evaporation from free water surface. Pakistan Journal of Science 14:308-316.

Hutchings, J. W.
1961 Water-vapor transfer over the Australian continent. Journal of Meteorology 18:615-634.

Indacochea G., A. J.
1946 Bibliografía climatológica del Perú. Instituto Geológico del Perú, Boletín 4. 81 p. (Bibliography on the climatology of Peru. MGA 2:10-156.)

India. Meteorological Department
1960   Symposium on monsoons of the world. Manager of Publications, Government of India, New Delhi. 270 p.
This volume contains about 35 papers dealing with monsoon circulations, many referring to the Indian subcontinent. The quality of the papers is generally good and presents a review of the problem as it stood in 1958.

1962   Monthly and annual normals of rainfall and of rainy days based on records from 1901-1950. Memoirs 31:63-208.

International Association of Scientific Hydrology
1959   Symposium of Hannoversch - Munden. Vol. 2, Lysimeters. Gentbrugge, Belgium, Publication 49.

Iran. Meteorological Department
1958   Meteorological Yearbook, 1956. Tehran. 68 p.

Iraq. Meteorological Department
1964   Studies of rainfall and temperature conditions in Iraq. Meteorological Memoirs 2. 55 p.
A collection of seven papers, four of which deal with the characteristics of rainfall, two with temperature, and one with the use of climatic records for Iraq.

Isnard, H.
1950   La répartition saisonnière des pluies en Algérie. Annales de Géographie 59:354-361. (The seasonal distribution of rain in Algeria. MGA 2.9-136.)

1952   La répartition saisonnière des pluies en Tunisie. Annales de Géographie 61:357-362. (Seasonal distribution of rainfall in Tunisia. MGA 5.2-207.)

1958   La répartition saisonnière des pluies au Maroc. Annales de Géographie 67:39-42. (Seasonal distribution of rain in Morocco. MGA 10M-109.)
The analysis of the seasonal variation of precipitation for Moroccan climatic stations shows that along the Moroccan Atlantic Coast about 30 per cent of the rain occurs during the spring and summer, while in the interior of the Atlas Mountains and in eastern Morocco more than 40 per cent of rain occurs in the spring and summer months.

Israel. Meteorological Service
1961   Climatological normals, Pt. 1, B: Temperature and relative humidity. Series A, Meteorological Notes 3B. 17 p.

1965   Climatological normals. Pt. 1, A: Rainfall. 3rd edition. Series A, Meteorological Notes 3A. 20 p.

Ivanov, N. N.
1959   Karta ispariaemosti v ravninnoi chasti S.S.S.R. Universitet, Uchenye Zapiski, No. 269:160-166. Leningrad. (Potential evaporation map for the plains region of the U.S.S.R. MGA 10K-146.)

Ives, R. L.
1952   Hurricanes on the west coast of Mexico. Pacific Science Congress, 7th, 1949, Proceedings 3:21-31.

1962a   "Pestiferous winds" of the upper Gulf of California. Weatherwise 15:196-199, 201.

1962b   Kiss tanks. Weather 17:194-196.

Jackson, S. P.
1961   Climatological atlas of Africa. Compiled and edited in the African Climatology Unit of the University of the Witwatersrand, Johannesburg, under the direction of S. P. Jackson. With the collaboration and assistance of the African Regional Association of the World Meteorological Organization and the cartographic services of member governments of the Commission for Technical Cooperation in Africa South of the Sahara. Lagos. 55 fold col. maps. (CCTA/CSA, Joint Project 1.)
This atlas contains 55 plates depicting the climate of Africa. It can be rated as a key volume for this continent and for the arid zones on it.

Johnson, D. H.
1962   Rain in East Africa. Royal Meteorological Society, Quarterly Journal 88:1-19.
A method that emphasizes distribution of rainfall rather than rainfall amounts was used as a tool to accomplish synoptic research and to examine the usefulness of rainfall forecasting. It is noticed that rainfall in East Africa is not unpredictable, but that organized rain systems exist and persist for several days. The characteristics of the rainfall patterns are such that there seems to be a good prospect of explaining and predicting their changes synoptically and dynamically.

Joly, F.
1958   Etude des indices de Thornthwaite pour quelques stations du Maroc. Institut Scientifique Chérifien, Rabat, Service de Physique du Globe et de Météorologie, Annales 18:119-128.

Jurwitz, L. R.
1953   Arizona's two-season rainfall pattern. Weatherwise 6:96-99.

Kaka, G., R. Sakka, and A. W. M. al-Basri
1962   A case of jet stream activity over eastern Mediterranean Sea and the Middle East. Iraq Meteorological Department, Meteorological Memoirs 1:149-158.

Kalstrom, G. W.
1952   El Cordonazo — the lash of St. Francis. Weatherwise 5:99-103, 110.

Karelsky, S.
1961   Monthly and seasonal anticyclonicity and cyclonicity in the Australian region, 15 year (1946-1960) averages. Australia. Bureau of Meteorology, Meteorological Study 13. 11 p.

Kas'yanov, F. M.
1961   Quantitative and qualitative significance of shelter belts. Translated from the Russian by the Israel Program for Scientific Translation. Office of Technical Services, Washington, D. C. OTS 60-21888.

Katsnelson, J.
1959   Rainfall in the Negev, distribution and intensity. Israel Meteorological Service, Series E, 11.

1964   The variability of annual precipitation in Palestine. Archiv für Meteorologie, Geophysik und Bioklimatologie, Serie B, 13:163-172.

Khalaf, J. M.
1956   The climate of Iraq. Union Géographique Internationale. Congrés International de Géographie, 18e, Rio de Janeiro, 1956, Comptes Rendus 2:507-525.

Khan, A.
1953   Contributions to the study of the climate of the Punjab and the North West Frontier Province (Pakistan). Clark University, Worcester, Massachusetts. Ph.D. dissertation. 195 p.

Khan, M. I.
1957   A study of structure, behaviour and effects of tropical cyclones in West Pakistan. Karachi University, Karachi, West Pakistan. Thesis.

Kheder, J.
1962   A note on some climatic features of Iraq. Meteorological Department of Iraq, Baghdad, Meteorological Memoirs 1:53-86.

Klein, W. H.
1957   Principal tracks and mean frequencies of cyclones and anticyclones in the Northern Hemisphere, U. S. Weather Bureau, Washington, D. C., Research Paper 40. 60 p.

Klykova, Z. D.
1959   Rezhim atmosfernykh osadkov Alma-Ata. Nauchno-Issledovatel'skii Gidrometeorologicheskii Institute, Trudy 11:30-39.

Köppen, W.
1931   Grundriss der klimakunde. 2d edition. Walter de Gruyter Co., Berlin. 388 p.
A standard reference for Köppen's system of climatic classification.

Kohler, M. A., T. J. Nordenson, and D. R. Baker
1959   Evaporation maps for the United States. U. S. Weather Bureau, Technical Paper 37. 13 p.
Contains maps of pan evaporation and pan coefficients for the United States.

Komissarova, L. N.
1955   Povtoriaemost' iuzhnykh tsiklonov nad Srednei Aziei i Kazakhstanom. Kazakhskii Nauchno-Issledovatel'skii Gidrometeorologicheskii Institut, Alma-Ata, Kazakhstan, Trudy 5:116-121.
(Recurrence of southern cyclones over Central Asia and Kazakhstan. MGA 12N-268.)

Koteswaram, P.
1961   Cloud patterns in a tropical cyclone in the Arabian Sea viewed by TIROS I meteorological satellite. University of Hawaii, Institute of Geophysics, Scientific Report 2. 34 p.

————
1962   Jet streams over India and neighbourhood, p. 101-108. *In* Symposium on Meteorology in relation to high level aviation over India and surrounding areas, New Delhi, December 7, 1957.

Kraus, E. B.
1958   Meteorological aspects of desert locust control. *In* Climatology and Microclimatology, Proceedings of the Canberra Symposium. Unesco, Paris. Arid Zone Research 11:211-216.

Kriel, J. P.
1961   Correlation of evaporation loss from tanks and large water surfaces, p. 144-151. *In* Inter-African Conference on Hydrology, Nairobi, 1961, Proceedings.

Krishnan, A., P. S. Pant, and R. Ananthakrishnan
1961   Variability of upper winds over India. Indian Journal of Meteorology and Geophysics 12:431-438.

Ku Chen-ch'ao
1959   Artificial precipitation work in Communist China in 1959. Office of Technical Services, Washington, D. C. (JPRS 3053.)

Kumar, S. and G. S. Bhullar
1956   Unusual cold wave over Northwest India from April 13 to 23, 1955. Indian Journal of Meteorology and Geophysics 7:88-91.

Kuo Cheng
1963   China's meteorological services today. Weather 18:366, 371-372.

Kuznetsov, N. T.
1962   Rechnoi stok na territorii Mongol'skoi Narodnoi Respubliki. Akademiia Nauk S.S.S.R., Izvestiia, Ser. Geogr. 5:111-118.
(River run-off in the Mongolian People's Republic. MGA 14.6-535.)

Lacaze, J.
1958   Tourbillons atmospheriques d'axes verticaux. (Tourbillons de sable.) Journal Scientifique de la Météorologie 10:133-147.

Lamond, M.
1959   Tabulated upper wind data for Australia. Australia, Bureau of Meteorology, Project Report 55/688. 18 p.

Landsberg, H. E. *et al.*
1965   World maps of climatology. 2d edition. Springer-Verlag, New York. 28 p.

Larson, R. J.
1954   Meteorological research from Panama to Buenos Aires; an abstract of Panagra's meteorological files. Pan American-Grace Airways, Inc., Lima, Peru. 16 p.

Leal, F. A. and D. X. de Queiroz
1952   Distribuição da precipitação na Província de Angola. Esbôço da carta udmétrica. Luanda, Angola. 9 p.
(Precipitation distribution in Angola Province. Rainfall charts. MGA 6.1-271.)
Annual and monthly rainfalls are presented in a series of isohyetal charts. A brief text gives basic information about the records and the rainfall in various sections of Angola. The maps are based on the records from about 100 stations with lengths of record of 5 years or more.

Lebrija Celay, M.
1963   Brief history of meteorology in Mexico and the present organization of the services. Weatherwise 16:208-211.
The history and organization of the Mexican Weather Bureau are outlined in this short article. Information is given on the present services and the extent of the climatological network.

Leighly, J.
1953   Dry climates, their nature and distribution. *In* Desert research; proceedings of the International Symposium held in Jerusalem. Research Council of Israel, Special Publication 2:3-18.

Leluin, P.
1949   Le temps à Port-Etienne. Météorologie 15:147-156.
(The weather at Port-Etienne. MGA 9-97.)

Lettau, H.
1965   On the meteorological causes of coastal deserts. Lecture presented at U. S. Army Natick Laboratories, 9 July 1965, in honor of Dr. Earl E. Lackey.

Lettau, K. and F. White
1964   Fourier analysis of Indian rainfall. Indian Journal of Meteorology and Geophysics 15:27-38.

Levi, M.
1963   The dry winter of 1962-63: a synoptic analysis. Israel Exploration Journal 13:229-241.

———
1965   Local winds around the Mediterranean Sea. Israel Meteorological Service, Bet Dagan, Series C, Miscellaneous Papers 13. 6 p.
This descriptive paper lists numerous local winds of the Mediterranean region. A clever map shows where the name is used, the usual direction of the wind, and the season during which it blows. Each wind and its origin is described in the text.

Listrovoi, A. A.
1959   Ursat'evskie vetry. Sredneaziatskii Nauchno-Issledovatelskii Gidrometeorologicheskii Institut, Trudy 2:54-84.
(Ursat'ev winds. 12.8-346.)

Loewe, F.
1943   Duststorms in Australia. Australia, Meteorological Branch, Bulletin 28. 16 p.

Logan, R. F.
1960   Central Namib Desert, South West Africa. National Academy of Sciences — National Research Council, Publication 758. 162 p. (ONR Foreign Field Research Program, Report 9.)
Although this work is not mainly concerned with the discussion of climate, the section on climatology of the Namib is relatively complete. The deserts are described, their causes are explained, and the differences between coastal and inland climates are pointed out. The effects of the Benguela Current on the climate are also noted.

———
1961   Winter temperatures of a mid-latitude desert mountain range. Geographical Review 51: 236-252.

Lomas, J.
1965   The effects of windbreaks on the yields of tomatoes grown during the winter in the southern Araba. Israel Meteorological Service, Agrometeorological Bulletin September:7-9.

Long, A. R.
1948   Evaporation; New Mexico and contiguous areas. U. S. Weather Bureau, Albuquerque, New Mexico. 37 p.

Lorch, J.
1959   Windbreaks and windbreak effects in the banana plantations of the Jordan Valley, Israel. Israel Meteorological Service, Meteorological Notes, Series A, 17. 25 p.

Lu, A.
1946   The climatological atlas of China. Central Weather Bureau, Chungking, China.
This collection of meteorological maps shows mean monthly or seasonal averages of many different meteorological variables, such as cyclone frequency, pressure, and diurnal temperature range.

Lunson, E. A.
1950   Sandstorms on the northern coasts of Libya and Egypt. Great Britain, Meteorological Office, Professional Note 102. 12 p.
The worst sand storms occur between October and July and are associated with khamsin depressions. The storm of March 23-25, 1942, is analyzed with the use of synoptic charts.

Lydolph, P. E.
1964   The Russian sukhovey. Association of American Geographers, Annals 54:291-309.
Sukhovei are dry winds of the Russian plains, important for its desiccating effects on crops. This system has been extensively studied by Russian climatologists, and Lydolph reviews the system in an article in English.

Marchetti, A. A.
1951   Oscilaciones extremas de la cantidad de precipitación en la República Argentina. Meteoros 1: 46-54.

———
1952a Variability of the rain-fall in the Argentine Republic. International Association of Scientific Hydrology, Brussels, 1951, Transactions 3:76-80.
A statistical study is made of precipitation data for about 60 stations in Argentina during the period 1905-1946. Maps of variability are included.

———
1952b Estudio del régimen pluviométrico de la República Argentina. Meteoros 2:243-309.
(Study of the rainfall regime of Argentina.)
A more detailed analysis, in Spanish, of the rainfall variability of Argentina than found in Marchetti (1952a).

Martonne, E. de
1926   Aréisme et indices d'aridité. Académie des Sciences, Paris, Comptes Rendus 182:1395-1398.

Masson, H.
1954   La rosée et les possibilités de son utilisation. Institut des Hautes Etudes, L'Ecole Supérieure des Sciences, Dakar, Sénégal. Annales. 44 p.
A general review of the literature on dew and the instrumentation for measuring it. The meteorological factors controlling dew formation and the microclimatological factors which have effects on its occurrence are discussed. An extensive bibliography is included.

———
1958   La mesure de la rosée. In Climatology and microclimatology, Proceedings of the Canberra Symposium. Unesco, Paris. Arid Zone Research 11: 309-314.

Mayençon, R.
1961a Conditions météorologiques synoptiques propices aux chutes de grêle importantes en Algérie. Météorologie 61:41-54.
(Synoptic weather conditions promoting heavy hail-showers in Algeria. MGA 13.8-761.)

———
1961b Conditions synoptiques donnant lieu a des précipitations torrentielles au Sahara. Météorologie 62:171-180.
Infrequent, heavy rains are of great importance in the Sahara. The causes of dryness are examined and then the synoptic conditions for heavy rain are analyzed with case studies.

McCulloch, J. S. G.
1961 Evaporation pans in East and Central Africa, p. 159-163. *In* Inter-African conference on hydrology, Nairobi, 1961, Proceedings.

McDonald, J. E.
1956 Variability of precipitation in an arid region: a survey of characteristics for Arizona. University of Arizona, Institute of Atmospheric Physics, Technical Reports on the Meteorology and Climatology of Arid Regions 1. 88 p.
The importance of this paper is not mainly the analysis of rainfall data for an arid region, but rather McDonald's discussion of the statistical aspects of the analysis.

1962 The evaporation-precipitation fallacy. Weather 17:168-170; 172-177.

McIlroy, I. C. and D. E. Angus
1963 The Aspendale multiple weighted lysimeter installation. Commonwealth Scientific and Industrial Research Organization, Division of Meteorological Physics, Technical Paper 14. 27 p.
A description of the lysimeter installations by the Division of Meteorological Physics at Aspendale, Victoria, Australia. One of the conclusions is that although the initial requirements for lysimeter installation are complicated, the reliability and ease of subsequent operations are such that lysimeters can be recommended for routine operations as well as research purposes.

1964 Grass, water and soil evaporation at Aspendale. Agricultural Meteorology 1:201-224.
The results of three years of operations of lysimeters at Aspendale. Net radiation over the crop is the important factor in evaporation. An empirical formula based on meteorological observations gave good results, and it is suggested that lysimeter data be used to calibrate simpler methods of computing potential evapotranspiration.

Meigs, P.
1953a World distribution of arid and semi-arid homoclimates. *In* Reviews of research on arid zone hydrology, Unesco, Paris. Arid Zone Programme 1:203-210.
The arid zones of the Earth are divided into three main groups, "extremely arid," "arid," and "semiarid," using Thornthwaite's index of aridity. Other factors are also considered. The degree of aridity is combined with the distribution of precipitation and temperature through the year to form the basis for a system of climatic classification for the arid zone. Large-scale maps are included.

1953b Design and use of homoclimatic maps; dry climates of Israel as example. *In* Desert research, proceedings of the International Symposium held in Jerusalem, May 7-14, 1952, sponsored by the Research Council of Israel and Unesco. Research Council of Israel, Special Publication 2:99-111.

1957 Arid and semiarid climatic types of the world. *In* International Geophysical Union, 17th Congress, Washington, D. C., 8th General Assembly, Proceedings, p. 135-138.

1964 Classification and occurrence of Mediterranean-type dry climates. *In* Land use in semi-arid Mediterranean climates. Unesco, Paris. Arid Zone Research 26:17-21.

Miagkov, N. I.
1957 Bibliograficheskii ukazatel' literatury po klimatu Turkmenii. Upravlenie Gidrometsluzhby Turkmenskoi S.S.R. Ashkhabadskaia Gidrometeorologicheskaia Observatoriia, Ashkhabad. 104 p.
(Bibliography on the climate of the Turkmen Republic. MGA 11:8-295.)

Miller, R.
1952 The climate of Nigeria. Geography 37:198-213.

Molchanov, L. A.
1955 Novaia karta ispariaemostina territorii Srednei Azii, p. 35-39. *In* Meteorologiia i gidrologiia v Uzbekistane. Akademiia Nauk Uzbekskoi S.S.R.
(New potential evaporation map for Central Asia. MGA 9:11-230.)

Monteith, J. L.
1957 Dew. Royal Meteorological Society, Quarterly Journal 83:322-341.
An excellent review of the process important to dew. A distinction is made between dewfall (moisture from the air) and distillation (moisture diffused upward from the soil).

Mooley, D. A.
1956 Zonal wind circulation and vertical temperature distribution along the Indian longitudes during the monsoon and winter seasons. Indian Journal of Meteorology and Geophysics 7:113-128.

Moriarty, W. W.
1955 The synoptic behaviour of the summer low. (Pt. 1 of Large-scale effects of heating over Australia.) Commonwealth Scientific and Industrial Research Organization, Division of Meteorological Physics, Technical Paper 7. 31 p.

Mosiño A., P. A.
1959 La precipitación y las configuraciones del flujo aéreo en la República Mexicana. Ingeniería Hidráulica en México, México, D. F. 12 p.

1964 Surface weather and upper-air flow patterns in Mexico. Geofísica Internacional 4:117-168.
Surface and upper-air flow patterns are classified and their frequencies are noted. Persistence of weather types is examined and found to be remarkably high. The various weather types are related to the amounts of precipitation.

Murray, R.
1960 Mean 200-millibar winds at Aden in January 1958. Meteorological Magazine 89:156-157.

Nagel, J. F.
1962a On the measurement of dew. Archiv für Meteorologie, Geophysik und Bioklimatologie, Serie B, 11:403-423.

1962b Fog precipitation measurements of Africa's southwest coast. South Africa Weather Bureau, Notos 11:51-60.
The instrumentation for measuring the liquid water intercepted from a wind-carried fog is described and the amounts are discussed. The contribution of fog precipitation can exceed rainfall in some locations.

Nakorenko, N. F. and F. G. Tokar'
1959 Klimat svobodnoy atmosfery. Klimat S.S.S.R., Vpusk 8. Glavnaya Geofizicheskaya Observatoriya im. A. I. Voyenkova. Leningrad. 220 p.
(Climate of the free atmosphere. Issue 8, Climate

of the U.S.S.R. Full translation available from D.D.C., Cameron Station, Alexandria, Virginia, as Document AD-613 988.)

Naqvi, S. N.
1949   Coefficient of variability of monsoon rainfall in India and Pakistan. Pakistan Geographical Review 4:7-17.
The mean rainfall, standard deviation, and coefficient of variability are given for 68 individual stations in India and Pakistan. Coefficient of variability of monsoon rainfall is small in regions where it is due to orographic lifting, and is large in regions where monsoon rainfall is small.

1958   Periodic variations in water balance in an arid region — a preliminary study of 100 years' rainfall at Karachi. *In* Climatology and microclimatology, Proceedings of the Canberra symposium. Unesco, Paris. Arid Zone Research 11:326-345.

Naqvi, S. N. and M. Rahamatullah
1962   Weather and climate of Pakistan. Pakistan Geographical Review 17:1-18.

National Academy of Sciences
1966   Weather and climate modification, problems and prospects. Vol. 2: Research and development. Publication 1350. 198 p.
Weather and climate modification, especially cloud seeding, is a controversial subject. This study is a comprehensive analysis of the current status of this general field.

Negretty, J. J. R.
1949   Variaciones de las precipitaciones anuales en Bolivia. Revista Meteorológica 8:277-296.
(Annual precipitation variations in Bolivia. MGA 4.1-183.)

Neumann, J.
1956   Estimating the amount of dewfall. Archiv für Meteorologie, Geophysik und Bioklimatologie, Serie A, 9:197-203.

New Mexico. State Engineer Office
1956a   Climatological summary of New Mexico; temperature 1850-1954; frost 1850-1954; evaporation 1912-1954. Technical Report 5. 277 p.

1956b   Climatological summary of New Mexico: precipitation 1849-1954. Technical Report 6. 407 p.

Newman, B. W., A. R. Martin, and W. R. Wilkie
1956   Occurrence of tropical depressions and cyclones in the Australian region during the summer of 1955-56. p. 25-55. *In* Tropical cyclones symposium, Brisbane, December 1956, Proceedings.

Nikolaev, A. V. A.
1958   Maiskie kholoda v iuzhnom Kazakhstane. Priroda 5:124-125.
(May cold in southern Kazakhstan. MGA 12.1-308.)

Nimmo, W. H. R.
1964   Measurement of evaporation by pans and tanks. Australian Meteorological Magazine 46:17-53.
An excellent general article on the subject of pan evaporation, particularly with reference to Australia. Several different types of pans and the problems associated with each are discussed.

Noble, G. and M. Lebrija Celay
1956   La sequía en México y su previsión. Ingeniería Hidráulica en México 10:85-98.

Contains an analysis of synoptic patterns and especially of those situations which result in drought in Mexico. Examples of the most serious droughts are given. Variations in annual precipitation at several stations in Mexico are given for the period 1901-1950.

Nordberg, W. *et al.*
1962   Preliminary results of radiation measurements from the TIROS III meteorological satellite. Journal of Atmospheric Sciences 19:20-30.

Nuttonson, M. Y.
1958   The physical environment and agriculture of Australia with special reference to its winter rainfall regions and to climatic and latitudinal areas analogous to Israel. American Institute of Crop Ecology, Washington, D. C. 1124 p.
One of several studies compiled by Nuttonson relating the characteristics of various regions to Israel. One of the features of these reports is a discussion of the climate of the analogous region, in this case Australia, and a compilation of climatic data.

1961a   Introduction to North Africa and a survey of the physical environment and agriculture of Morocco, Algeria, and Tunisia with special reference to their regions containing areas climatically and latitudinally analogous to Israel. (Vol. 1 of a Survey of North African Agro-Climatic Counterparts of Israel.) American Institute of Crop Ecology, Washington, D. C. 608 p.
This volume and Nuttonson (1961b) are part of a series of reports comparing the climate of Israel to other arid regions. These reports are characterized by good general discussions of climate and the presentation of large amounts of climatic data.

1961b   Physical environment and agriculture of Libya and Egypt with special reference to their regions containing areas climatically and latitudinally analogous to Israel. (Vol. 2 of a Survey of North African Agro-climatic counterparts of Israel.) American Institute of Crop Ecology, Washington, D. C. 452 p.

1961c   The physical environment and agriculture of the Union of South Africa with special reference to its winter-rainfall regions containing areas climatically and latitudinally analogous to Israel. A study based on official records, material, and reports of the Department of Agriculture and of other government and provincial agencies of the Union of South Africa. American Institute of Crop Ecology. Washington, D. C. 459 p.
One of a series of reports that feature good general discussions of the climate and the inclusion of large amounts of climatic data, in this case for South Africa.

Obasi, G. O. P.
1963   Poleward flux of atmospheric angular momentum in the southern hemisphere. Journal of Atmospheric Sciences 20:516-528.

1965   Atmospheric synoptic and climatological features over the West African region. Nigerian Meteorological Service, Lagos, Technical Note 28. 45 p.
The most significant of the tropospheric, synoptic and

climatological features over the West African region are briefly reviewed. These features are the vortices and associated upper-level waves, the intertropical discontinuity, the West African squall lines, Harmattan haze, and the summer easterly jets. This paper is an excellent review of the current state of knowledge of the weather systems of this part of Africa.

Obruchev, V. A.
1950 Zametki o dvukh raionakh neobychainykh bur' v Tsentral'noi Azii, p. 7-25. *In* A. K. Leonov, ed., Pamiati IUlia Mikhailovicha SHokal'skogo, Moscow.
(Notes on unusual storms in two districts of Central Asia. MGA 5:9-197.)

Ohman, H. L.
1961 Analogs of Yuma climate in southern Africa. Yuma analogs 10. U. S. Quartermaster Research and Engineering Center, Natick, Mass., Environmental Protection Research Division, Research Study Report RER-35. 21 p.

Ohman, H. L. and R. L. Pratt
1956 The daytime influence of irrigation upon desert humidities. U. S. Quartermaster Corps Research and Development Command, Natick, Mass., Environmental Protection Research Division, Technical Report EP-35. 30 p.

———
1966 Yuma winter microclimate. U. S. Army Natick Laboratories, Earth Sciences Division, Technical Report ES-24.

Olascoaga, M. J.
1950 Some aspects of Argentine rainfall. Tellus 2:312-318.
This study of Argentine rainfall is mainly concerned with the percentage of days that account for most of the rainfall in different regions in Argentina.

Olintseva-Nebrat, G. G.
1962 Issledovanie evoliutsii subtropicheskikh struinykh techenii. Meteorologiia i Gidrologiia 5:29-33.
(A study of the evolution of subtropical jet streams. MGA 13:12-492.)

Orton, R. B.
1964 The climate of Texas and the adjacent Gulf waters. U. S. Government Printing Office, Washington, D. C. 195 p.

Pant, P. S.
1964 Onset of monsoon over India. Indian Journal of Meteorology and Geophysics 15:375-380.

Papadakis, J.
1954 Contribución al estudio de los climas argentinos: tipos de regimen hídrico. Instituto de Suelos y Agrotecnia, Buenos Aires, Publicación 33.

Pédelaborde, P. and H. Delannoy
1958 Recherches sur les types de temps et le mécanisme des pluies en Algérie. Annales de Géographie 67:216-244.
(Research on weather types and rain mechanism in Algeria. MGA 10.11-247.)

Pelton, W. L., K. M. King, and C. B. Tanner
1960 An evaluation of the Thornthwaite and mean temperature methods for determining potential evapotranspiration. Agronomy Journal 52:387-395.

This article along with van Wijk and de Vries (1954) reviews the Thornthwaite method of computing potential evapotranspiration (based on mean temperature).

Penman, H. L.
1948 Natural evaporation from open water, bare soil and grass. Royal Society of London, Proceedings, Series A, 193:120-145.
In this classic paper, the Penman method of estimating potential evapotranspiration through a combination of the heat balance method, the aerodynamic method, and empirical relations is presented. The computations are described and the technique is discussed.

———
1956 Evaporation: an introductory survey. Netherlands Journal of Agricultural Science 4:9-29.
This survey of evaporation as an agricultural phenomenon was limited to an outline of basic ideas. The aerodynamic method, energy balance method, and the empirical method are discussed and described. An excellent review paper ranking with that of Thornthwaite and Hare (1965).

Petterssen, S.
1964 Meteorological problems: weather modification and long-range forecasting. American Meteorological Society, Bulletin 45:2-6.

Pisharoty, P. R. and G. C. Asnani
1960 Flow pattern over India and neighbourhood at 500 mb during the monsoon, p. 112-117. *In* Symposium on monsoons of the world, New Delhi, February 19-21, 1958, Proceedings.

Pizarro Callejas, H. and R. Rivas
1965 Irregularidad de las precipitaciones en el Norte Chico. Oficina Meteorológica de Chile, Santiago. 15 p., charts, tables.

Pond, A. W.
1954 Climate and weather in the central Gobi of Mongolia. U. S. Arctic, Desert and Tropic Information Center, ADTIC Publication D-101. 11 p.

Poufir'ev, I. F.
1958 Duet "evgei." Meteorologiia i Gidrologiia 4:34-35.
(The "evgei" blows. MGA 12:4-207.)

Prada Estrada, R.
1948 Climas de Bolivia. Dirección General de Meteorología, La Paz. 52 p.
This small paperback book is one of the few publications that discuss the climate of Bolivia. It is mostly text, but a few maps and tables of data are included.

Prescott, J. A.
1949 A climatic index for the leaching factor in soil formation. Journal of Soil Science 1:9-19.

———
1958 Climatic indices in relation to the water balance. *In* Climatology and microclimatology, Proceedings of the Canberra Symposium. Unesco, Paris. Arid Zone Research 11:48-51.

Prohaska, F. J.
1952 Regímenes estacionales de precipitación de Sudamérica y mares vecinos (desde de 15°S hasta Antártida). Meteoros 2:66-100.
(Seasonal precipitation regime for South America and neighboring seas, from 15°S to the Antarctic. MGA 4.6-172.)

Prohaska F. J.
1960   El problema de las sequías en la región semiárida pampeana y la sequía actual. Idia 115:53-67.
(Problems of droughts in the semi-arid pampas and the present drought. MGA 14.4-706.)

1961   Las características de las precipitaciones en la región semiárida pampeana. Instituto de Suelos y Agrotecnia, Buenos Aires, Publicación 72.

Pruitt, W. O. and D. E. Angus
1960   Large weighing lysimeters for measuring evapotranspiration. American Society of Agricultural Engineers, Transactions 3:13-18.

Puzyreva, A. A.
1960   Klimaticheskii ocherk Iuzhno-Kazakhstanskoi oblasti. Akademiia Nauk Kazakhoskoi S.S.R., Alma-Ata, Sektor Geografi, Trudy 6:168-177.
(Climatic outline of the south Kazakhstan region. 13.5-658.)

Queiroz, D. X. de
1955a Variabilidade das chuvas em Angola. Serviço Meteorológico, Luanda, Angola. 4 p.
(Variability of rainfall in Angola. MGA 8.6-295.)

1955b Valores médios mensais e anuais representativos de elementos climáticos em Angola. Serviço Meteorológico, Luanda, Angola. 8 p.
(Monthly and annual means of climatic elements in Angola. MGA 8.9-287.)

Rainey, R. C.
1958   Some observations on flying locusts and atmospheric turbulence in eastern Africa. Royal Meteorological Society, Quarterly Journal 84:334-354.

1959   Application of synoptic meteorology to problems of desert locust control: Some recent findings, 6 p. *In* Joint Symposium on Tropical Meteorology in Africa, Nairobi, Kenya, December, 1959.

Rai Sircar, N. C. and S. V. Datar
1963   Cold waves in northwest India. Indian Journal of Meteorology and Geophysics 14:315-319.

Ramage, C. S.
1959   Hurricane development. Journal of Meteorology 16:227-237.
Although this paper summarizes hurricane and typhoon frequencies for the whole Earth, its completeness makes it applicable to arid lands, in that it illustrates the variations among deserts and the relative frequencies in deserts as compared to the more humid climates.

1962   The United States meteorology program for the International Indian Ocean Expedition. American Meteorological Society, Bulletin 43:47-51.

1966   The summer atmospheric circulation over the Arabian Sea. Journal of Atmospheric Sciences 23:144-150.
The heat low over Somalia and southern Arabia is maintained through interactions with the monsoon rain systems to the east and south. The complexity of the processes that seem to operate in this area is illustrated.

Ramakrishnan, K. P., B. N. Sreenivasaiah, and S. P. Venkiteshwaran
1960   Upper air climatology of India and neighbourhood in the monsoon seasons, p. 3-34. *In* Symposium on monsoons of the World, New Delhi, February 19-21, 1958, Proceedings.

Ramaswamy, C.
1956   On the subtropical jet stream and its role in the development of large-scale convection. Tellus 8:26-60.

1962   Breaks in the Indian summer monsoon as a phenomenon of interaction between the easterly and the subtropical westerly jet streams. Tellus 14:337-349.

1965   On a remarkable case of dynamical and physical interaction between middle and low latitude weather systems over Iran. Indian Journal of Meteorology and Geophysics 16:177-200.
During the second half of July, 1956, heavy rains over Iran were caused by an extension of the Indian Southwest monsoon into the region. An added factor was frontal lifting on the most active rain days. The flooding caused great damage and loss of life. This study of the synoptic conditions suffers from lack of upper-air data.

Rao, K. N.
1958   Some studies on rainfall of Rajasthan with particular reference to trends. Indian Journal of Meteorology and Geophysics 9:97-116.
The Rajasthan desert is said to be expanding. This analysis of rainfall for the period 1901-1955 does not show any significant change in the area rainfall.

Rao, Y. P. and B. N. Desai
1955   Possibilities of artificial rain in the states of Bombay, Saurashtra and Kutch. p. 121-126. *In* Symposium of artificial rain, New Delhi, February 1953, Proceedings and Papers.

Ray Choudhuri, S. N., Y. H. Subramanyan, and R. Chellappa
1959   A climatological study of storms and depressions in the Arabian Sea. Indian Journal of Meteorology and Geophysics 10:283-290.

Razumova, L. A.
1963   Izmenenie agrometeorologicheskikh uslovii pod viliianiem polezashchitnogo lesonasazhdeniia. Tsentral'nyi Institut Prognozov, Trudy 131:64-100.
(Changes in agrometeorological conditions due to shelter belts. MGA 15:8-72.)

Reparaz, G. de
1958   La zone aride du Pérou. Geografiska Annaler 40:1-62.
Although the major emphasis of this paper is not on climate, it does contain a good discussion of the general climatic controls affecting the distribution of climatic elements in this particular area. Emphasis is on the coastal zone.

Riaguzov, V. N.
1955   Shtormy ozera Issyk-Kul', p. 163-177. *In* Meteorologiia i gidrologiia v Uzbekistane, Akademiia Nauk Uzbekskoi S.S.R., Tashkent.
(Storms on Lake Issyk Kul. MGA 10.1-166.)

Rigby, M.
1961   Meteorology, hydrology, and oceanography, 1949-1960. *In* Sciences in Communist China. American Association for the Advancement of Science, Publication 68:523-614.

The organization of the science of meteorology in Communist China is outlined. Major research institutes and journals are named. The extensive bibliography gives a review of the type and kind of work being done. There is no evidence of any special interest in arid-lands problems.

Roberts, D. F.
1961 A comparison of the evaporation loss from Symons and Class A pans in South Africa, p. 152-158. *In* Inter-African Conference on Hydrology, Nairobi, 1961, Proceedings.

Robertson, G. W.
1955 The standardization of the measurement of evaporation as a climatic factor. World Meteorological Organization, Technical Note 11. 10 p.

Robison, W. C. and A. V. Dodd
1955 Analogs of Yuma climate in South Central Asia (India — Pakistan — Afghanistan — Iran). Yuma analogs 4. U. S. Quartermaster Research and Engineering Center, Natick, Mass., Environmental Protection Research Division, Research Study Report RER-4. 24 p.
One of a series of reports designed to define areas climatically analogous to Yuma, Arizona. The analogy is based primarily on temperature, precipitation, and dew point. Depending upon the values of the elements in the area studied, it is classified as analogous or semianalogous. Maps of the analogous areas are shown. The analogs in this series usually contain good discussions of the climates of the areas.

Rodier, J.
1963*a* Hydrology in Africa. *In* A review of the natural resources of the African continent. Unesco, Paris. Natural Resources Research 1:179-220.
Contains a bibliography devoted in part to the subject of general climatic data and to evaporation. A listing of sources of climatological data by country is compiled.

——— 1963*b* Bibliography of African hydrology. Unesco, Paris. Natural Resources Research 2. 166 p.

Romanov, N. N.
1955 Nekotorye osobennosti divizheniia antitsiklonov nad Srednei Aziei i smezhnymi s nei territoriiami. p. 151-157. *In* Meteorologiia i gidrologiia v Uzbekistane. Akademiia Nauk Uzbekskoi S.S.R. Tashkent.
(Certain characteristics of the movement of anticyclones over central Asia and adjacent territories. MGA 9.8-174.)

——— 1959 Makrosinopticheskaia kharakteristika periodov s povyshennoi tsiklonicheskoi deiatel'nost'iu v Srednei Azii. Sredneaziatskii Nauchno-Issledovatel'skii Gidrometeorologicheskii Institut, Trudy 1:76-87.
(Macrosynoptic characteristics of increased cyclonic activity periods in Central Asia. MGA 12L-135.)

Rosendal, H. E.
1962 Eastern North Pacific tropical cyclones. 1947-1961. Mariners Weather Log 6:195-201.
A descriptive article on the occurrence of tropical storms off the west coast of Mexico. Tracks of known storms during the 15-year period are shown on monthly maps.

Rosenthal, S. L. and T. A. Gleeson
1956 Sea-level anticyclogenesis affecting Mediterranean weather, Archiv für Meteorologie, Geophysik und Bioklimatologie, Serie A: Meteorologie und Geophysik 9:185-190.

Roy, A. K.
1962 Rain stimulation experiments by present contemplated techniques of cloud nucleation. Indian Journal of Meteorology and Geophysics 13:219-225.

Roy, S. C.
1954 Is the incidence of unusually dusty weather over Delhi in May and June for the two consecutive summers of 1952 and 1953 an indication that the Rajasthan Desert is advancing towards Delhi? Indian Journal of Meteorology and Geophysics 5:1-15.
The two main types of dust storms in northwest India are described. The frequency of the various types is tabulated for May and June at Delhi airport. The synoptic conditions favorable for the formation of dust are illustrated by a series of charts.

Rubin, M. J.
1956 The associated precipitation and circulation patterns over southern Africa. South Africa Weather Bureau, Notos 5:53-59.

Sadler, J. C.
1962 The first hurricane track determined by meteorological satellite. Indian Journal of Meteorology and Geophysics 13:29-44.

——— 1964 Tropical cyclones of the eastern North Pacific as revealed by TIROS observations. Journal of Applied Meteorology 3:347-366.

——— 1965 The feasibility of global tropical analysis. American Meteorological Society, Bulletin 46:118-130.

Sayed, A. M. M.
1949 Khamsin and khamsin conditions. Egypt Meteorological Department, Paper 1. 57 p.

Sayer, H. J.
1962 The desert locust and tropical convergence. Nature 194:330-336.

Schulze, B. R.
1958 The climate of South Africa according to Thornthwaite's rational classification. South African Geographical Journal 40:31-53.

Schweigger, E.
1959 Die westküste Südamerikas im bereich des Perustroms. Keysersche Verlagsbuchhandlung. Heidelberg. 513 p.
(The west coast of South America in the vicinity of the Peru Current. MGA 12.9-6.)

Sellers, W. D.
1964 Potential evapotranspiration in arid regions. Journal of Applied Meteorology 3:98-104.
The system of Budyko is applied to arid regions to investigate the effect of relative humidity over a field on the evaporation from it. A 50 per cent increase in relative humidity caused a 10 to 15 per cent decrease in potential evapotranspiration and an increase in surface temperature. Budyko's system gave results 30 to 50 per cent higher than Thornthwaite's method. Penman's and Budyko's methods gave essentially the same result, about 70 per cent of the evaporation from a Class A pan.

Sellers W. D.
1965   Physical climatology. University of Chicago Press, Chicago, Illinois. 272 p.

Seltzer, P.
1946   Le climat de l'Algérie. Institut de Météorologie et de Physique du Globe de l'Algérie, Travaux, Hors série. 219 p.
A comprehensive and detailed study of the Algerian climate. Each element of climate is thoroughly discussed and substantiated with extensive observations. The relationship of the climate of Algeria to that of all North Africa is also presented. An extensive bibliography is included.

———
1953   Un essai: la carte des pluies annuelles probables en Algérie. Météorologie 29: 73-75.

Seredkina, E. A.
1960   Pyl'nye buri v Kazakhstane. Nauchno-Issledovatel'skii Gidrometeorologicheskii Institut, Alma-Ata, Kazakhstan, Trudy, 15:54-59.
Data are presented on the frequency of dust storms in the state of Kazakhstan. The synoptic situations associated with the occurrence of these storms are also discussed.

Serra, A.
1963   Clima da América do Sul. Revista Geográfica 33: 99-126.

Serra, A. B. and L. R. Ratisbonna
1960   As massas de ar da América do Sul, pts. 1-2. Revista Geográfica 25:67-128; 26:41-61.
(Air masses of South America. MGA 15.7-435.)

Shaia, J. S.
1962   Upper air data for Beer-Ya'aqov: summaries of radiosonde observations of temperature, humidity and wind at standard isobaric surfaces (1957-1959). Israel Meteorological Service, Series A, Meteorological Notes 19. 38 p.

———
1964   Characteristics of the 500 millibar surface over Beer-Ya'aqov on raindays. Israel Meteorological Service, Series A, Meteorological Notes 20. 35 p.

al-Shalash, A. H.
1957   The climate of Iraq. University of Maryland, Baltimore. M.S. Thesis. 82 p.

Shchukina, N. F. and E. D. Kuvaldina
1956   Sinopticheskie usloviia severnykh vtorzhenii na lugo-vostochnye raiony Kazakhstana. Nauchno-Issledovatel'skii Gidrometeorologicheskii Institut, Alma-Ata, Kazakhstan, Trudy 6:83-100.
(Synoptic conditions leading to northerly outbreaks into the southeastern regions of Kazakhstan. MGA 12.10-326.)

Shifrin, K. S. and L. N. Guseva
1957   Prognoz estestvennoi osveshchesnnosti. Akademiia Nauk S.S.S.R., Izvestiia, Ser. Geofiz. 6:827-830.
(Forecasting natural illumination. MGA 13:7-116.)

Sibbons, J. L. H.
1962   A contribution to the study of potential evapotranspiration. Geografiska Annaler 44:279-292.
An excellent review article on the concept of potential evapotranspiration. It is more descriptive and less technical than the review article by Thornthwaite and Hare (1965).

Sinclair, P. C.
1966   A quantitative analysis of the dust devil. University of Arizona, Department of Meteorology. Ph.D. dissertation. 292 p.

Sinelshikov, V. V.
1965   Agroclimatological trends in the U.S.S.R., problems, methods and scientific and practical results. Agricultural Meteorology 2:73-77.

Singh, M. S.
1963   Upper air circulation associated with a western disturbance. Indian Journal of Meteorology and Geophysics 14:156-172.

Sivall, T.
1951   Nagot om vädar och klimat i Etiopien och Eritrea. Ymer 71:32-44.
(Weather and climate of Ethiopia and Eritrea. MGA 3.5-258.)

———
1957   Sirocco in the Levant. Geografiska Annaler 39: 114-142.

Slatyer, R. O.
1962   Climate of the Alice Springs area. Commonwealth Scientific and Industrial Research Organization, Melbourne, Land Research Series 6:109-128.

Slatyer, R. O. and I. C. McIlroy
1961   Practical microclimatology with special reference to the water factor in soil-plant atmosphere relationships. Prepared and reproduced by C.S.I.R.O., Australia. Unesco. 7 sections, separately paged.

Smirnova, S. I.
1963   Meteorologicheskii effeckt orosheniia na sosednikh nepolivnykh uchastkakh. Meteorologiia i Gidrologiia 11:40-42.
(Meteorological effect of irrigation on the neighboring non-irrigated areas. MGA 15:7-434.)

Smith, H. V.
1956   The climate of Arizona. Arizona Agricultural Experiment Station, Tucson, Bulletin 279. 99 p.

Soliman, K. H.
1950   Air masses and quasistationary fronts in spring and summer over the Middle East. Mathematical and Physical Society of Egypt, Proceedings 4:15-30.
This study is concerned with the classification of air masses prevailing over the Middle East during times of excessively high temperature. Föhn effects were found to play an important role in the occurrence of dryness and high temperature in some of these air masses.

———
1953a   Rainfall over Egypt. Royal Meteorological Society, Quarterly Journal 79:389-397.

———
1953b   Heat waves over Egypt. Mathematical and Physical Society of Egypt, Proceedings 1:91-101.
Heat waves are classified and their frequency of occurrence at Cairo in each month of the year is given. The nature and causes of these heat waves over Egypt are discussed. They are found to be connected with the movement of the quasistationary fronts separating hot air, forming in the thermal lows of the Sudan and the interior of northwest Africa, from the air north of it.

Solot, S. B.
1950   General circulation over the Anglo-Egyptian Sudan and adjacent regions. American Meteorological Society, Bulletin 31:85-94.

Soto Mora, C. and E. Jauregui O.
1965   Isotermas extremas e índice de aridez en la República Mexicana. Universidad Nacional Autónoma de México, Instituto de Geografía. 119 p.
Mean monthly maximum and minimum temperatures are determined for over 500 stations in all of Mexico. These data are used to determine and map Emberger's index of aridity. This is one of several recent papers (García, 1964; Stretta and Mosiño, 1963) that have mapped aridity in Mexico.

South Africa. Weather Bureau
1965   Climate of South Africa, Part 8: General Survey Pretoria. 330 p.
This volume is a complete discussion of the surface climate of South Africa. Major elements of climate are discussed by chapters. One chapter is devoted to a general discussion of climatic controls and another to a classification of climates into 15 regions.

Stanhill, G.
1958   The accuracy of meteorological estimates of evapotranspiration. Institution of Water Engineers, Journal 12:377-383.

———
1961a   A comparison of methods of calculating potential evapotranspiration from climatic data. Ktavin 11:159-171.
Comparisons are made between several empirical or instrumental methods of computing or measuring potential evapotranspiration and the actual value determined from lysimeters. Penman's formulation gives the best results. A cost analysis of the eight methods tested shows that the U. S. Class A pan is the most practical.

———
1961b   The accuracy of the meteorological estimates of evapotranspiration in arid lands. Institution of Water Engineers, Journal 15:477-482.
This is one of Stanhill's papers on the comparison of the potential evapotranspiration determined by several different methods, done here in the Negev.

———
1963   The accuracy of meteorological estimates of evapotranspiration in Nigeria. Institution of Water Engineers, Journal 17:36-44.

Stenz, E.
1957   Precipitation, evaporation and aridity in Afghanistan. Acta Geophysica Polonica 5:245-266.
The geographical and temporal variation of rainfall in Afghanistan is discussed in terms of mean monthly and mean annual precipitation, number of rain days, frequency of thunderstorms, and snow. An analysis is made of calculated evapotranspiration and the distribution of aridity.

Stork, C.
1959   Evapotranspiration problems in Iraq. Netherlands Journal of Agricultural Science 7:269-282.

Stretta, E. J. P. and P. A. Mosiño A.
1963   Distribución de las zonas áridas de la República Mexicana. Ingeniería Hydráulica en México, México, D. F. 8 p.
Emberger's index of aridity is revised to suit the conditions in Mexico. Maps of climate and of distribution of aridity are presented.

Subrahmanyam, V. P.
1956a   Climatic types of India according to the rational classification of Thornthwaite. Indian Journal of Meteorology and Geophysics 7:253-264.

———
1956b   The water balance of India according to Thornthwaite's concept of potential evapotranspiration. Association of American Geographers, Annals 46:300-311.

Sutton, O. G.
1953   Micrometeorology. McGraw-Hill, New York City. 333 p.

Taha, M. F.
1963   Climate and meteorology in Africa; Africa north of the tropic of cancer. *In* A review of the natural resources of the African continent. Unesco, Paris. Natural Resources Research 1:153-164.
Discusses the state of knowledge of weather and climate in North Africa. The two main handicaps to the advancement of knowledge are the vast uninhabited areas and the political situation and economic problems in newly independent nations. General problems are reviewed and specific topics such as climatology, synoptic meteorology, and agricultural meteorology are discussed. Taha concludes there is much to be done in this field. Walker (1963) has written a closely related paper.

Taljaard, J. J.
1963   Monthly mean 500 mb data for radiosonde and rawinsonde stations south of 15°S for the IGY and IGC 1959. Notos 12:51-65.

Temnikova, N. S.
1959   O metodakh izucheniya mikroklimata. Meteorologiya i Gidrologia No. 5:45-48.
(Methods of investigating microclimate.) Also available in translation from the Office of Technical Services, U. S. Department of Commerce, Washington, D. C., as publication number OTS 60-51018.

Thompson, B. W.
1957a   Some reflections on equatorial and tropical forecasting. East African Meteorological Department, Nairobi, Technical Memorandum 7. 14 p.

———
1957b   The diurnal variation of precipitation in British East Africa. East African Meteorological Department, Nairobi, Technical Memorandum 8. 70 p.

Thornthwaite, C. W.
1931   The climates of North America according to a new classification. Geographical Review 21:633-655.

———
1948   An approach toward a rational classification of climate. Geographical Review 38:55-94.
A key paper in which Thornthwaite advanced the idea of potential evapotranspiration and the methods for computing it. The concept is discussed and illustrated with the use of water balance studies for several stations.

Thornthwaite, C. W. and F. K. Hare
1965   The loss of water to the air. Meteorological Monographs 6(28):163-180.
An excellent review article on the subject of evapotranspiration. The authors discuss the evaporation process in general, particularly the theoretical means of determining it. They then proceed to discuss some of the methods of estimating evapotranspiration such as those of Penman, Budyko, and Thornthwaite. There is some discussion of direct methods of measurement of evapotranspiration.

Thornthwaite, C. W. and B. Holzman
1939   The determination of evaporation from land and water surfaces. Monthly Weather Review 67:4-11.
Thornthwaite, C. W. and J. R. Mather
1955   The water balance. Drexel Institute of Technology, Laboratory of Climatology, Centerton, New Jersey, Publications in Climatology 8(1). 86 p.

_____
1962   Average climatic water balance data of the continents. Part 1, Africa. C. W. Thornthwaite Associates, Centerton, New Jersey. 287 p.
Tixeront, J.
1956   Water resources in arid regions. *In* The future of arid lands. American Association for the Advancement of Science, Washington, D. C. Publication 43:85-113.
Trewartha, G. T.
1961   The earth's problem climates. University of Wisconsin Press, Madison, Wisconsin. 334 p.
Tschirhart, G.
1956   Etude de l'évolution particuliére d'une masse d'air. Météorologie 43:243-258.
       (Study of an unusual development of an air mass. MGA 9.10-187.)
Tunis. Service Météorologique
1954a Climatologie de la Tunisie, Vol. 2: Vent au sol. Etudes Météorologiques. 342 p.
       (Climatology of Tunis, Vol. 2, Surface wind. MGA 8.3-24.)

_____
1954b Le climat de la Tunisie; évapotranspiration, bilan, hydrologique, zones climatiques. Tunis. 8 p.
Unesco
1958a Climatology. Reviews of research. Unesco, Paris. Arid Zone Research 10. 190 p.
One of several titles in the Unesco Arid Zone Research series devoted to weather and climate. The 8 papers in this volume were written as review reports for the Canberra symposium of 1956 on arid-zone climatology with special reference to microclimatology. Four particularly noteworthy papers:
1) "Evaporation and the water balance" (Deacon, *et al.,* 1958),
2) "Radiation and the thermal balance" (Drummond, 1958a),
3) "Climates and vegetation" (Vernet, 1958),
4) "Climatological observational requirements in arid zones" (Gilead and Rosenan, 1958).

_____
1958b Climatology and microclimatology, Proceedings of the Canberra Symposium, October 1956. Unesco, Paris. Arid Zone Research 11. 355 p.
One of several titles in Unesco's Arid Zone Research series devoted to weather and climate. Fifty papers presented at the Canberra symposium on climatology and microclimatology are contained in this volume. Evaporation and the water balance, radiation, and requirements for climatological observations are three pertinent sections. Proceedings such as this are also valuable for their lists of participants and their affiliations.
Unesco-FAO
1963   Bioclimatic map of the Mediterranean zone — Explanatory notes. Unesco, Paris. Arid Zone Research 21. 58 p., 6 maps.

This study presents a system of climatic classification based on subjective criteria and emphasizes the degree of aridity as a major factor in the determination of different climatic types.
Unesco-WMO
1963   Changes of climate, Proceedings of the Rome Symposium organized by Unesco and the WMO. Unesco, Paris. Arid Zone Research 20. 488 p.
Unión Ganadera Regional de Chihuahua
1963   Boletín Meteorológica. Chihuahua, Chihuahua, México.
One of a series of annual publications of mean monthly climatic data for Chihuahua. Number 6 also contains mean data for the 1958-1962 period.
U. S. Weather Bureau
1943   Climatic data for selected stations in and near Afghanistan and Turkey. Special Report 242. 19 p.

_____
1955   A collection of Afghanistan climatic data to 1953.

_____
1964   Mean daily solar radiation, monthly and annual. A sheet of the National Atlas of the United States. U. S. Government Printing Office, Washington, D. C.

_____
1965   World weather records, 1951-1960. Volume 1: North America. U. S. Government Printing Office, Washington, D. C. 535 p.
Uteshev, A. S.
1959   Klimat Kazakhstana. Gidrometeoizdat, Leningrad. 366 p.
       (Climate of Kazakhstan. MGA 12.5-11.)
A complete discussion of the characteristics of climate in this semiarid and arid part of the Soviet Union. The general climatic characteristics and the synoptic climatology of the region are discussed. In addition an analysis is made of separate climatic elements such as temperature, pressure, and wind. Numerous maps and tables of climatic data are included.

Valdivia Ponce, J.
1955   Estudio climatológico de Puerto Chicama. Compañía Administradora del Guano, Lima, Boletín Científico 2:5-23.
       (Climatological study of Puerto Chicama. MGA 9.3-258.)
van Bavel, C. H. M. and L. E. Myers
1962   An automatic weighing lysimeter. Agricultural Engineering 43:580-583, 586-588.
A description of the lysimeter installation at Tempe, Arizona. The instrument is accurate to about 0.01 to 0.02 mm of water. It is 1 meter square and 1.5 meters deep.
van Loon, H.
1961   Charts of average 500 mb absolute topography and sea-level pressure in the Southern Hemisphere in January, April, July, and October. South Africa Weather Bureau, Notos 10: 105-112.
Venter, R. J.
1950   Bibliography of regional meteorological literature. Vol. 1: South Africa 1486-1948. Union of South Africa Weather Bureau. 412 p.
Vernet, A.
1958   Climates and vegetation. *In* Climatology, reviews of research. Unesco, Paris. Arid Zone Research 10: 75-101.

Veydner, I. N.
1962 The meteorological service in Afghanistan. U. S. Department of Commerce, Office of Technical Services, Washington, D. C. JPRS 12,468. 9 p.

Vivó, J. A. and J. C. Gómez
1946 Climatología de México. Instituto Panamericano de Geografía e Historia, Publicación 19. 73 p.
This standard work on the climate of Mexico begins with a short general discussion of the climate but consists mostly of tables and maps. It contains a very large and detailed Köppen map of the climatic regions of Mexico.

Von Eschen, G. F.
1961 Dust sorms in Albuquerque, N. M. U.S. Weather Bureau, Albuquerque, N. M. 2 p.

Vries, D. A. de
1958 Two years of solar radiation measurements at Deniliquin, Australia. Australian Meteorological Magazine 22:36-49.

1959 The influence of irrigation on the energy balance and climate near the ground. Journal of Meteorology 16:256-270.

Vsesoiuznaia Konferentsiia po Svetovomu Klimatu, 2d, Moscow, 1960
1961 Trudy Konferentsii Akademiia Stroitel'stva i Arkhitektury S.S.S.R., Moscow. 94 p.

Walker, H. O.
1960 Monsoon in West Africa, p. 35-42. *In* Symposium on monsoons of the World, New Delhi, February 19-21, 1958, Proceedings. New Delhi.

1963 Climate and meteorology in Africa; Africa south of the Tropic of Cancer. *In* A review of the natural resources of the African continent. Unesco, Paris. Natural Resources Research 1:165-177.
This review and the article by Taha (1963) provide a survey of the problems of weather and climate in Africa. The problems are those resulting from the state of the economic and political development, rather than with the scientific aspects of the problems.

Wallén, C. C.
1955 Some characteristics of precipitation in Mexico. Geografiska Annaler 37:51-85.
The author discusses the nature of available precipitation data in Mexico. He then investigates variability of annual rainfall and the causes of the variability. Frequency distributions of rainfall amounts are also described.

1956 Fluctuations and variability in Mexican rainfall. *In* The future of arid lands. American Association for the Advancement of Science, Washington, D. C. Publication 43:141-155.

1962 Climatology and hydrometeorology with special regard to the arid lands. *In* The problems of the arid zone. Unesco, Paris. Arid Zone Research 18:53-81.
This review outlines the essential meteorological problems of the arid zones and gives an overall picture of the climatological research that needs to be directed toward them.

Wang, J. Y. and G. L. Barger
1962 Bibliography of agricultural meteorology. University of Wisconsin Press, Madison, Wisconsin. 673 p.

Weickmann, L.
1958 A synoptic study of the occurrence of precipitation at Teheran. Iranian Meteorological Department, Meteorological Year-book 1956:12-25.

1960 Häufigkeitsverteilung und zugbahnen von depressionen im mittleren osten. Meteorologische Rundschau 13(2):28-33.
(Frequency distribution of paths of depressions in the Middle East. MGA 12.11-228.)
The distribution and paths of cyclonic systems over Iran are investigated on the basis of new meteorological data. It is shown that the distribution of lows is influenced by the terrain and the season. The tracks are markedly concentrated in some regions.

1961 Some characteristics of the sub-tropical jet stream in the Middle East and adjacent regions. Iran, Meteorological Department, Meteorological Publications, Series A, 1. 29 p.
Summarizes the available information on the subtropical jet stream in the Middle East. The seasonal shifts and the jet core are described.

1962 Beitrag zur klimatologie des subtropischen strahlstroms in Nordafrika und Asien. Beitrage zur Physik der Atmosphare 35:165-183.
(Contribution to the climatology of subtropical jet stream in North Africa and Asia. MGA 14:11-676.)

1963 Meteorological and hydrological relationships in the drainage area of the Tigris River north of Baghdad. Meteorologische Rundschau 16:33-38.

Weischet, W.
1966 Zur klimatologie der nordchilenischen Wüste. Meteorologische Rundschau 19:1-7.

Wijk, W. R. van and D. A. de Vries
1954 Evapotranspiration. Netherlands Journal of Agricultural Science 2:105-119.
Noteworthy for its review of the Thornthwaite method of computing potential evapotranspiration.

Wijk, W. R. van and J. de Wilde
1962 Microclimate. *In* The problems of the arid zone, Proceedings of the Paris Symposium. Unesco, Paris. Arid Zone Research 18:83-113.

World Meteorological Organization
1960 Tropical Meteorology in Africa: Papers presented at the joint symposium of Tropical Meteorology in Africa, Nairobi, Kenya, December 1959. World Meteorological Organization, Geneva. 446 p.
(Sponsored by Munitalp Foundation and WMO.)
The purpose of this symposium was to review the state of knowledge of tropical meteorology in Africa and to identify the main problems and means of solving them. Tropical meteorology is important to the equatorward borders of the Sahara, the Somali-Chalbi and the Namib-Kalahari. The symposium is reviewed in the WMO Bulletin for 1960, Volume 9, p. 71-75.

1962 Climatological normals (CLINO) for CLIMAT and CLIMAT SHIP stations for the period 1931-1960. WMO 117. T.P. 52. 17 p., tables.

1963   Meteorology and the migration of desert locusts. Technical Note 54.

1964a   High-level forecasting for turbine-engined aircraft operations over Africa and the Middle East. Proceedings of the Joint ICAO/WMO Seminar, Cairo-Nicosia, 1961. World Meteorological Organization, Technical Note 64.

1964b   Windbreaks and shelter belts. World Meteorological Organization, Technical Note 59. 188 p.

1965a   Catalogue of meteorological data for research, Part 1. WMO 174. T.P. 86 (loose-leaf).
Lists the current publications of meteorological data by countries, usually with a short description of the material contained in each publication. It should give researchers useful information about sources of climatological data. A good review of the catalog is found in the WMO Bulletin of April, 1966 (Vol. 15, No. 2, p. 89-90).

1965b   Meteorology and the desert locust. Technical Note 69. 310 p.
A current review of the synoptic climatology of the desert locust area of Africa through the Middle East to the Thar Desert. Although the emphasis is on the weather systems important to locusts, the collection into one volume of the ideas and thoughts of so many meteorologists interested in this area results in a particularly useful report.

1965c   Short-period averages for 1951-1960, and provisional average values for CLIMAT TEMP and CLIMAT TEMP SHIP stations. World Meteorological Organization, Geneva. WMO 170. T.P. 84.

Yeh Tu-cheng and Chen Chao Ku
1964   The effect of the Tibetan Plateau on the circulation of the atmosphere and the weather of China. U. S. Weather Bureau, Foreign Area Section, Washington, D. C. 20 p.
(A translation of an article from Akademiia Nauk Izvestiia Seriia Geograficheskaia, 2:127-139, Moscow, 1956.)

Zhegnevskaia, G. S.
1954   K voprosu o klimaticheskikh faktorakh uvlazhneniia iuga evropeiskoi chasti S.S.S.R. Vsesoiuznoe Geograficheskoe Obshchestvo, Izvestiia 86:537-542.
(Climatic humidity factors affecting the south of the European U.S.S.R. MGA 8:4-253.)

Zhirkov, K. F.
1964   Dust storms in the steppes of western Siberia and Kazakhstan. Soviet Geography 5(5):33-41.
An English version of an article originally published in a Russian journal. Frequencies of dust storms are given for several stations and the synoptic conditions are identified.

Zikeev, T.
1952   Annotated bibliography on dew. Meteorological Abstracts and Bibliography 3:360-391.

Zimmerman, A. and J.-Y. Wang
1961   Bibliography for agrometeorological studies on South America: the first collection, 1960. University of Wisconsin, Departments of Meteorology and Soils, Madison. 23 p.

GEOMORPHOLOY AND
SURFACE HYDROLOGY
OF DESERT ENVIRONMENTS

LAWRENCE K. LUSTIG
Senior Editor
Encyclopaedia Brittanica

*Formerly of the Department of Geology, The University of Arizona

INTRODUCTION

This report on the state of knowledge of geomorphology and surface hydrology of the arid regions is but one part of a much larger work on the state of knowledge of the desert environment. The guidelines for this compendium required separate treatment for such topics as surface materials, vegetation, climate, and desert regional types, among others. These are worthy of mention here because such topics are germane to geomorphology and each would normally be accorded treatment in a report on general geomorphology. Hence, it is necessary at the outset to indicate the nature of the subject matter that will be treated in this report and, further, the meaning of "arid lands" as used here.

Basically, those aspects of surface configuration and drainage features that are cited in the guidelines will be treated. Significant omissions will be noted under "Report Limitations," but the nature of the coverage and discussion to be accorded surface configuration and drainage features can best be provided by outlining the primary goals of this report. These goals are as follows:

1) To survey the adequacy and availability of pertinent information on the topics considered.

2) To outline existing deficiencies of information and fundamental problems within the field of inquiry.

3) To provide suggestions for future research which will meet the deficiencies revealed in the course of the study and which will serve to enlarge our understanding of the desert environment.

As implied by these goals, the intent of this report is to provide a summary of the work that has been done in an attempt to determine what needs to be done. The production of a catalog of the landforms of the arid regions is not contemplated here. The evaluation that is presented, with respect to both current work and existing literature, is based upon both academic and practical considerations. It might be well to state at once that these are not so divergent in purpose as might be imagined.

In order to understand some of the ramifications of the criteria for this chapter, the writer visited the Yuma Test Station in May 1965 and subsequently examined several U. S. Army research reports. The visit to the Yuma facilities made clear at once the nature of one basic problem of a practical nature, namely, whether the passing of a test by a given item of equipment at Yuma signifies that the item is truly desert-worthy or whether it is simply "Yuma-worthy." The answer to this question obviously depends, in part, upon the extent to which the terrain features at the Yuma Test Station are comparable to the features of the deserts of the world. This question, however, is also of considerable academic interest, and the problem therefore illustrates the alliance between academic and governmental aims.

The Army research reports that were subsequently examined largely pertained to terrain analysis and landform geometry. Here, again, one is confronted with the fact that many aspects of quantitative geomorphology are involved and that similar studies, although not on a worldwide scale, have been and are being undertaken for purely academic reasons.

Several of these reports will be cited and discussed in this chapter. The reasons for this inclusion are several. First, if a basic requirement is to assess the status of knowledge of the arid regions, then one must consider all pertinent information, regardless of its source. Second, as previously noted, an evaluation of research in terms of practical significance to U. S. governmental agencies requires that the investigator understand fully the possible relationships involved. Third, terrain analysis is intimately interwoven with quantitative geomorphology and modern methods of landform description. As such, it is extremely pertinent in any report on geomorphology.

The treatment of geomorphology in this chapter will therefore be concentrated upon, but not limited by, the aspects of surface configuration and drainage features outlined in the guidelines. There may be some overlapping of the material dealt with in other sections of the compendium, particularly those on climate, soils, and desert regional types, but no fundamental duplication of effort is envisaged. Treatment of these allied subjects is largely confined to the section of this chapter that evaluates the available information. Basic problems associated with climatic factors and soils and weathering are included therein.

The Pertinent Publications list at the end of this chapter should be consulted for bibliographic information on works cited in the text. The list is divided into 15 sections: Sections II through XV include works cited in portions of the text that treat specific geographical areas. Publications cited in the general part of the text (before specific desert areas are treated) are listed in Pert. Pubs. Section I (Historical Background and General). For example, works cited in the text discussion of the Arabian Desert will be listed in Section VI (Arabian Desert) of the list of pertinent publications.

Each publication appears only once in the list. In the event of duplicate citations in the text, the secondary citations would be of the following form: (Jones, 1964; see Pert. Pubs. Sec. I).

Those works listed in the Pertinent Publications list which it has been possible to determine are of particular significance or interest to this study within the limitations discussed under Report Limitations below are annotated. Other competent and best-available works on specific subjects and areas are listed without annotation.

Those works pertinent to the United States that are annotated according to the above criteria are also of general applicability and are listed in Section I of the Pertinent Publications list rather than in Section XIV.

The literature and current work that will be cited and discussed are of several types and these may be classified according to content, as follows:

1) Information of a descriptive or qualitative nature.
2) Quantitative data on desert landforms or drainage features.
3) Information on geomorphic mapping.
4) Information on Army research efforts.
5) Information on general principles of landform or drainage development and the empirical relationships involved.

The categories are largely self-explanatory, but it should be emphasized here, particularly with reference to (5) above, that information will not be restricted solely to that obtained in arid areas. Certain types of problems in arid areas may be amenable to solution only by application of general principles derived with respect to semiarid or even humid environments. Moreover, the lack of information on vast regions of the deserts of the world can in many cases be overcome only by subjective decision. This is true,

for example, of the preparation of terrain analogs of the world's deserts. Hence, it is advisable to supplement such necessary subjectivity with empirical formulae or relationships, despite their derivation from nonarid areas.

With respect to the parts of the world called "arid" in this chapter, they conform with the usage adopted by participants from the University of Arizona at the outset of the project. Basically, it was agreed to include those areas of the world that are designated as "arid" or "extremely arid" on the homoclimatic maps of Meigs (1953). As is true of climatic, terrain, and any other manmade classifications, none can be said to be a "true" classification. All are arbitrary and have been established to serve certain specific purposes. The homoclimatic maps in question will be discussed in this chapter in several respects, but, within the limitations described below, Meigs' boundaries accord with the areas discussed in this chapter.

Report Limitations

Any treatment of the literature, current work, outstanding problems, and future needs of a given subject or field of inquiry is inevitably limited by several factors. Chief among these factors is the availability of time, and this is particularly true of the present report because academic duties could not be set aside for the duration of the project. For these reasons, no pretense is made with respect to the completeness of the literature review for all countries that are wholly or partially within the arid regions of the world. The same may be said with respect to current research that is pertinent to the arid regions in general. Every effort was made to obtain information on the most relevant work in both categories, and it is hoped that the inadvertent omissions that do occur in this report are not of fundamental significance.

The time available to the writer was approximately apportioned as follows, without regard to concomitant academic requirements. Three months were largely devoted to correspondence with various individuals abroad who were known or thought, either personally or by reputation, to be involved in investigations pertinent to the geomorphology of the arid regions. Nearly four months were consumed by travel for the purpose of personally interviewing individuals in various agencies, institutions, universities, and private corporations who had substantial knowledge of the work and problems in the arid regions. Firsthand experience, through such contacts and/or by means of field trips, was gained in the following countries: England, Senegal, Bechuanaland (now Botswana), South West Africa, South

Africa, Ethiopia, Sudan, Egypt, Saudi Arabia, Iran, Afghanistan, West Pakistan, India, and Australia. Experience in the deserts of North America was gained prior to this project. Equivalent time was not devoted to each of these countries during the four months of travel, but they are cited here in order to provide the reader with the means by which to assess evenness of coverage or lack of same in this chapter. Finally, the major portion of an academic year was devoted to literature review and the preparation of this text.

Aside from the limitations imposed by lack of personal contact and observation in all parts of the world, several specific chapter limitations should be noted here. Deserts of the U.S.S.R. and China are not treated in this chapter because of insufficient time and translation difficulties. No specific consideration is given to bodies of standing water. Irrigation canals, ditches, and water regulation and control structures are to be covered in another chapter by J. R. Healy. Early-traveler type reports have been cited, but with selectivity, because their number is quite large and because references to these descriptive accounts can be obtained from more recent works in most instances.

Usually throughout the text, general evaluations of the work that has been done are presented, rather than evaluations of the legion of individual reports available; but numerous specific works are evaluated in statements in the chapter text and in annotations in the Pertinent Publications list. The mere citation of a report in this chapter is an indication that the work is considered useful, but it is not necessarily assurance that the entire work is competent.

In sections treating the various deserts under "Discussion of Availability of Information" the names of depositories, or institutions where classes of information about that desert area are stored, are given and (in italics) the names of authorities, who are individuals of special competence in some field of knowledge. If such information is omitted, the reader may assume that this writer was unable to verify the existence of authorities or depositories.

Acknowledgments

The writer was materially assisted in the task of information compilation for this report by many individuals, agencies, institutions, and private corporations in most parts of the world. The efforts of all cannot be cited here, but the assistance rendered is collectively acknowledged. Specific mention is clearly due in several instances, however, by reason of the many field trips arranged, illuminating discussions, or valuable information on current activities that were provided in the countries visited by the writer. In this

category the efforts of Professor R. F. Peel, University of Bristol; Mr. R. J. Chorley, Cambridge University; Professor Charles Toupet and Dr. Hughes Faure, University of Dakar and IFAN; Mr. Colin Boocock, Director of the Geological Survey, Lobatsi; Dr. W. L. van Wyk and Mr. Klaus Linning, Geological Survey, Windhoek; Dr. P. A. Mohr, Geophysical Observatory, Addis Ababa; Dr. A. R. Bayoumi, Director of Land Use and Rural Water Development, Khartoum; Mr. John Groman, U. S. AID, Khartoum; the Arid Lands Research Group, University of Khartoum; Mr. A. J. Ibrahim, Ministry of Irrigation, Khartoum; Mr. A. Shata, Director of the Desert Research Institute, El Matarîya; Mr. Has'san Yassin and Mr. Abdul Derhally, Ministry of Petroleum and Mineral Resources, Jiddah; Mr. William Overstreet, U. S. Geological Survey, Jiddah; Dr. Friedrich Vinck, Ministry of Agriculture, Riyadh; Mr. Thomas Barger, President of the Arabian American Oil Company, Dhahran; Mr. David Andrews, Manager of the Geological Survey Institute, Teheran; Mr. Albert Plummer, U. S. AID, Teheran; Dr. Davoud Hariri, Ministry of Water and Power, Teheran; Mr. Arthur Westfall, U. S. AID, Kabul; Dr. Alfred Schreiber, Chief of the German Mission to Afghanistan, Kabul; Mr. Zamir-uddin Kidwai and Mr. W. Raoof Siddiqi, WAPDA, Lahore; Dr. A. F. M. M. Haque, Director General of the Geological Survey, Quetta; Dr. A. R. Mohajir, Director of PANSDOC, Karachi; Dr. S. N. Naqvi, Director of the Meteorological Department, Karachi; the Oil and Gas Development Corporation, Karachi; Dr. Wolfgang Swarzenski, U. S. AID, Lahore; Dr. L. A. Ramdas, Physical Laboratory, New Delhi; Professor G. H. Dury and Dr. T. Langford-Smith, University of Sydney; Dr. T. G. Chapman, C.S.I.R.O., Canberra; Professor J. A. Mabbutt, University of New South Wales (formerly C.S.I.R.O., Canberra); and Mr. Ian Douglas, Australia National University, are gratefully acknowledged.

Within the United States, Mr. George Taylor, Jr., Chief of the Foreign Hydrology Branch, U. S. Geological Survey, Mr. J. R. Jones of the same organization, and Dr. R. L. Nace, U. S. Geological Survey, each provided information on certain individuals and organizations engaged in hydrological activities abroad. Dr. D. L. Bryant, University of Arizona, provided much of the information on South American desert areas, and Dr. J. W. Harshbarger, University of Arizona, served as topic director in planning the physical features chapters of this program. Mr. Thomas Maddock, Jr., U. S. Geological Survey, read several sections of the manuscript, and his valuable comments and the efforts of those individuals cited above were of substantial benefit to the writer.

Professor R. F. Peel, University of Bristol, Professor J. A. Mabbutt, University of New South Wales, and Dr. W. B. Langbein, U. S. Geological Survey, kindly consented to read the manuscript and offer review comments. The several suggestions of these reviewers would, if complied with, clearly have improved this report. Unfortunately, insufficient time remained to accomplish substantial revision of the manuscript. For this reason, although the time-consuming efforts of the reviewers are gratefully acknowledged, it should be made clear that the author is solely responsible for the views expressed in this chapter.

Finally, the bibliographic assistance rendered by Gretchen Luepke during the summer of 1965, and the excellent performance of Alice Cooper, who typed both the text and bibliography, must be acknowledged here. In the absence of this aid it is doubtful that this report would have been completed on schedule.

BACKGROUNDS OF MODERN GEOMORPHIC CONCEPTS

Because much of the literature on the geomorphology of arid areas, as well as current research effort, is inextricably enmeshed in basic concepts or working hypotheses of debatable validity, it is appropriate to consider here the evolution of geomorphic thought. The treatment that follows is primarily intended to indicate the conceptual frameworks within which various investigators today operate and the relationship between modern and earlier ideas. Citations will be selective rather than all-inclusive.

The roots of modern geomorphic thought can be traced to the ancients, but their ideas need not be considered in detail here. It should suffice to point out that such concepts as sea-level fluctuation and the formation of flood plains by rivers were anticipated by Herodotus, who also considered the question of the source of the Nile. The general importance of flowing water in landscape evolution was also recognized during the pre-Christian era; Aristotle, Strabo, and Seneca were the most noteworthy contributors in this regard.

Pursuit of these topics was greatly neglected for more than 1,000 years until Avicenna enlarged upon the idea that the Earth's topography was the result of running water and that changes in landforms could occur by erosion. After his 11th century treatment the subject again fell dormant, and it is to Leonardo da Vinci that the most cogent early statements on fluvial processes may be attributed. The notebooks of Leonardo da Vinci (1906) provide a description of the consequences of uplift of the land surface in terms of climatic effects and an attendant increase in runoff. Further, he clearly stated that valleys were the products of their contained streams and refuted the widespread concept that the Earth's topography could be interpreted in terms of the biblical flood.

It is unfortunate that his contemporaries, and succeeding generations as well, failed to read Leonardo's work objectively. Indeed, even among 18th and 19th century writers it is a commonplace to encounter the supposition that the waters of the "deluge" were responsible for scattering boulders about and carving valleys, and had left terraces, beaches, and other features exposed during their supposed retreat.

Schools of Thought

Aside from those concerned with a literal interpretation of Genesis, two schools of thought developed in Europe during the 18th and 19th centuries, and the conflict involved is of direct relevance here. Werner (1787) and his many adherents championed a point of view that may best be termed "catastrophic." Essentially, the argument was that the rocks and landforms of the earth may be attributed to causes or forces that are catastrophic, with respect to both their magnitudes and time duration.

The opposing view, namely, that present processes are representative of those which have been operative in the past, and that these processes have acted through time to produce the visible landscape, was well-argued by Hutton (1788, 1794), Playfair (1802), and Lyell (1872). These men were champions of the concept, which is today termed "uniformitarianism" and is taught to every student.

The conflict between the catastrophic and uniformitarian viewpoints is, in slightly revised form, germane to present arguments about the development of landforms in arid regions. This is true, for example, because of the decrease in the frequency of runoff of low and moderate magnitudes in arid regions in general. This raises the question of whether catastrophic events, or those of large magnitude and infrequent return period, are not in fact of greatest importance in molding the desert landscape. The uniformitarian view would be quite different. Still a third viewpoint is that the present desert landscape is to some extent relict, that is, that the present features are a product of previous climatic and hydrologic regimes which differ completely from those of today. This matter will be discussed later, but it serves to indicate the relevance of the concept of climatic change within the context of this historical review.

The peasants of the Swiss Alps had long been cognizant of the boulders that were strewn through their meadows, the presence of striations or grooves

99

on bedrock, and many other features now known to be glacially inherited. Several investigators drew the proper conclusion around 1800, but the concept that the Alps had formerly been occupied by much larger glaciers was first outlined in detail by Venetz-Sitten in 1821. This idea of large-scale, former glaciation was subsequently strengthened by other authors, but Louis Agassiz, who discussed a great ice age associated with climatic change (Agassiz, 1840), is commonly given credit for the concept. Evidence for climatic changes in nonglaciated areas, including the present deserts of the world, is unquestioned today.

Importance of Climatic Change

Climatic change is of considerable importance in the evolution of geomorphic thought for two reasons. First, it serves to provide one important qualification to the concept of uniformitarianism, namely, that although it is quite true that present landforms are the result of processes which have operated through time and which are of the same kind as those now operative, the intensities and rates of these processes may have been quite different in the past. This qualification is applicable to all regions, whether they be presently ice-covered or desertlike in aspect. Second, knowledge that climatic changes had in fact occurred allowed Jamieson (1863) to infer correctly that the saline lakes of Asia must formerly have attained higher levels than those which occur today. Similar conclusions, with respect to the Dead Sea, were presented by Lartet (1865). The basic thesis was that climatic changes serve to alter the hydrologic balance among precipitation, evaporation, and runoff, and thus induce changes in lake level. This thesis pertains to any lake, playa, pan, or similar feature in the arid regions of the world. Moreover, it is important to recognize that the concept of climatic change is a part of the operational framework within which many workers approach desert geomorphology in modern investigations.

Geomorphic Thought in 19th Century North America

Following the development of the ideas of uniformitarianism and climatic change in Europe, the evolution of geomorphic thought progressed rapidly in North America. The early explorations of the West in the 19th century served as a vehicle for three men, above others, to introduce other concepts. These three are Powell, Dutton, and Gilbert. Powell (1875, 1876, 1961) is largely responsible for introduction of the genetic system of classification, which stemmed from his field work in the Uinta Mountains, and the concept that a base level exists beneath the land surface which, he argued, represents the ultimate

limit for processes of subaerial erosion. Both Powell and Dutton (1880-1881, 1882) emphasized the role of fluvial processes in the development of the Grand Canyon, and the latter recognized the occurrence of erosion surfaces within the stratigraphic sequence. Dutton also contributed to the development of geomorphic thought by calculating recession rates for canyon walls and by introducing the idea that prior drainage paths may influence the ultimate courses of streams. The ideas of Powell and Dutton were subsequently assimilated by Davis, as discussed below, but of all the pioneers of the western explorations, G. K. Gilbert was most outstanding.

The most important and often-cited contributions by Gilbert are his explanation of basin-and-range topography by block faulting (1875), his monograph on Lake Bonneville (1880-1881), and his quantitative treatment of the competence of streams to transport their loads (1914). For purposes of the present discussion, however, it seems clear that Gilbert's treatment of the Henry Mountains (1877) provided an analysis of the conditions of grade and of the dynamic equilibrium between form and processes that serves as a basis for much current geomorphic discussion. In essence, Gilbert stated that any slope can be regarded as a member of a series, each of which receives both water and waste from that above, and that any increase in the rate of erosion of one such member will be compensated for by accelerated erosion of the member above and diminished erosion of the member below. These effects would be propagated through every slope member to the drainage divide, and thus the entire sequence of slope members would adjust to the initial disturbance and a state of dynamic equilibrium be established.

It should be mentioned in passing that several of the early civil engineers in Europe had anticipated Gilbert, as well as others to be cited in this review, with respect to the equilibrium concept. Surell (1841), for example, provided many observations on the tendency toward adjustment between rivers and their channels which have a distinctly modern ring, and even Dausse (1857), who reiterated the concept, published on this subject about 20 years in advance of Gilbert's paper (1877).

Cycles of Erosion

The relation between these ideas on equilibrium and current research in geomorphology will be elaborated upon later. One might say that the intervening years were largely devoted to the ideas of W. M. Davis, who dominated the subject by reason of his prolific writing and his numerous students and adherents. Davis adopted the ideas of Powell, Dutton, and other early workers, and in a series of papers from 1884 onward he set forth the concept of the cycle of erosion (Davis, 1889).

According to Davis' view, the landscape evolves through a series of stages, termed "youth," "maturity," and "old age," which follow an initial uplift. Both the landforms and the streams which flow upon them are said to exhibit distinct characteristics during each such stage, and a cycle of erosion is concluded by peneplanation, or the bevelling of the land surface to base level in "old age." Accompanied by a vast and ever-growing descriptive terminology of purported genetic significance, and supported by numerous illustrative block diagrams, this easily-grasped, deductive approach to landform development soon occupied the whole of geomorphic investigation. Literally thousands of articles have come from all countries, produced by authors who believe that one need simply view an area, match it to some suitable block diagram, and then proceed to write a treatise on the history of that region. Even today, such supporters of the cycle-of-erosion concept are unfortunately numerous and texts that serve to propagate the idea are also abundant. (See Fenneman, 1931; Lobeck, 1939; Thornbury, 1954; Strahler, 1965; Abul-Haggag, 1961; Brown, 1960.)

Because the cycle of erosion is unquestionably one of the conceptual frameworks of reference of some authors, their work must be evaluated in light of the degree of validity of the hypothesis. Hence, there is some purpose in outlining some of the arguments here. First, it must be noted that terms such as "youth," "maturity," "old age," and other anthropomorphic stage names lack the degree of precision which is required of any definition. Scientific purposes cannot be well-served by descriptions of "adolescent" sand dunes, for example.

Aside from this matter, however, serious question can be raised on several counts. Davis believed that the streams of a given region also passed through an evolutionary sequence of stages, and this is basically incorrect in reference to any large region as a whole. A river system can, in most instances, be described in Davis' own terms as exhibiting the successive stages of "youth," "maturity," and "old age" between the basin divide and the river mouth. No river can properly be said to represent a single "stage" throughout its length, however. Likewise, the peneplain becomes improbable when large areas are considered.

The size of such a hypothetical surface has never been defined, but it seems clear from the writings of Davis (1954) and others that an area of at least subcontinental dimensions is intended. If such an area is considered, then it is probable that the interior portions will be at a somewhat higher elevation than the peripheral portions and, in the classical view, might easily be interpreted as two separate surfaces that are supposedly related to two cycles of erosion. Moreover, the degree of departure from a plane surface has been ignored, good examples of undissected peneplains are lacking, and relatively flat surfaces can be produced by means other than subaerial processes within a cycle of erosion, assuming that such cycles actually run to completion in nature. The evidence provided by Davis for his classic area in the Appalachians (Davis, 1889) basically consisted of (1) the statement that accordant elevations occurred on ridges of different lithology, and (2) the claim that the stream courses, which flow to the southeast across the northeast structural trend, could be explained only by the assumption that they formerly flowed across a peneplain (which no longer exists). His interpretation of the history of the Appalachians in terms of multiple erosion cycles was termed a triumph of geomorphic analysis at that time, and the impact of his logic was such that the present drainage pattern in much of Great Britain, for example, is still interpreted on the basis of formerly existing peneplains, which now parallel the horizon in diagrammatic reconstructions.

The advent of large-scale topographic maps, however, enabled Denny (1956) to reconstruct the former surface in the Appalachian region. He showed that this surface closely corresponds to the structure of the rocks and would, in fact, exhibit relief on the order of a thousand feet if it were intact. The former surface, which is depicted in block diagrams as a smooth and horizontal plain, appears therefore to consist of ridges and valleys of considerable relief. Moreover, Denny found that the regional dip of this surface would range to about 5 degrees. This example demonstrates the virtue of an approach to a geomorphic problem via measurement, mapping, and field work rather than by the use of deductive logic by those of classical bent. Denny did not, however, explain the present course of the drainage of the region; he simply demonstrated that Davis' appeal to antecedent stream courses would not suffice because the reconstructed topography would be much the same as the present topography.

The seeming logic of the cycle of erosion was further eroded by Hack (1957) in the following year. Hack demonstrated by careful field work and mapping that the slopes of stream channels in the Appalachians are inversely proportional to drainage area when the median size of the bed material is equal, and are directly proportional to bed-material size in areas of equal drainage area. His empirical formula for this relationship is $S = 18 (M/A)^{0.6}$ where S is slope, M is the median size of bed material, and A is drainage area. Furthermore, he clearly showed that all the streams in the area are graded, or in equilibrium, and that the longitudinal profiles vary with rock type. Davis, however, essentially argued that river grade was a function of stage in the cycle of erosion.

In this same report, Hack rebuts the central argument of Davis and his adherents, namely, that accordant summits and discordant rock types constitute evidence of former peneplanation. Hack points out that because different rock types weather at different rates, two hills of equal elevation and different rock types must necessarily be of different age, rather than erosional remnants of the same surface.

With regard to the drainage course of streams in this area, Hack and Young (1959) subsequently showed that the entrenched meanders of the Shenandoah River are a function of differential rock structure and resistance and need not be related to superposition from a hypothetical former surface. Finally, Hack (1960, 1965) has adapted the long-ignored work of Gilbert, previously cited, and has reinterpreted this entire classic area in terms of the concept of dynamic equilibrium; erosion cycles are wholly omitted in this view. The landforms are related to a balance between processes and rock structure, and are time-independent.

Although the example cited is in a humid area, it is of relevance to arid regions as well because Davis (1954) applied his same basic approach to the basin-and-range area of the western United States. Once he had "solved" the problems in the Appalachians, Davis set forth the cycle of erosion in arid regions, and this differed from the original chiefly by reason of the different block diagrams and descriptive terminology. Initial uplift was considered the all-important factor, and through time a series of young, mature, and old mountain ranges were depicted. As before, an ultimate stage is said to exist; according to Davis, this will occur when the basins fill with sediment to a sufficient height to blanket the former ranges and a plain of regional extent is formed. Processes are almost totally ignored, and, in fact, in any area so described nothing is said about drainage development during the considerable time period required for an initial uplift; one is presented with block-faulted mountains that are full-blown, as it were.

Davis' concept of the cycle of erosion was challenged by a few authors during his lifetime, but most workers were content to seek new areas, look for accordant levels, and thus "discover" the numbers of peneplains present and the numbers of cycles of erosion involved. One notable protagonist was Penck (1953), who sought to deduce the tectonic history of an area from its aspect, particularly from the nature of the hillslopes.

Penck believed that hillslopes were a function of the balance, or lack of same, between uplift and denudation. He argued that when these opposing processes were equal, straight hillslopes would form. A rate of uplift that was greater than the rate of denudation would lead to convex slopes, and, last, reversal of these rates would lead to concave hillslopes, in Penck's view. As was true of Davis, Penck based his argument on deductive logic and presented illustrative diagrams rather than careful field measurements. Moreover, he totally ignored the effects of climate and rock type, which are two of the more important factors that govern the slopes of hillsides.

In refutation of the Penck concept, Strahler (1950, 1952a) found that hillslopes are in dynamic equilibrium with the processes that are operative upon them, as originally argued by Gilbert (1877); Schumm (1963) has attempted to investigate the rates of uplift and denudation that may be involved. Although some of the rates that are used by Schumm in this argument are open to debate, and although it is necessary to extrapolate present rates through time, it seems likely that his basic contention is valid, namely that rates of uplift generally exceed rates of denudation by a considerable margin; for this reason, two of the three cases for hillslope development postulated by Penck are not applicable in nature.

One additional concept which warrants mention because of its influence upon some workers is that of pediplanation, as advocated by King (1950, 1953, 1962). In this scheme, large planar areas of the sort termed "peneplains" by Davis, are presumably produced by mountain-front retreat through time and are termed "pediplains." One difficulty with application of this concept is that if extensive areas are exposed in this manner, then one is requiring increasing work, in terms of distance of sediment transport, of the streams draining a mountain scarp through time, whereas the catchment areas for these streams must diminish through the same time interval.

Recent Geomorphic Thought

Geomorphic thought in recent time has been strongly dependent upon (1) evidence which suggests that hillslopes are in dynamic equilibrium (Hack, 1960; Strahler, 1950, 1952a; Culling, 1963), (2) evidence which suggests that most streams are presently at grade, and (3) the adaptation of general systems theory (Von Bertalanffy, 1950, 1951, 1952) to geomorphology.

As previously noted (Surell, 1841; Dausse, 1857), the concept of the graded river can be traced back more than a hundred years. A review of the subject has been provided by Mackin (1948), but much impetus for subsequent field, laboratory, and theoretical investigation stemmed from the work of Leopold and Maddock (1953). These authors examined the available gaging-station data for Midwestern streams in the United States and found a series of empirical relationships among such factors as channel width and depth, and velocity of flow, with water discharge, for a given stream cross section and in a downstream direction. The water discharge involved is that which occurs at a given stage, namely bankfull discharge, and this has a particular frequency of occurrence, or return period, which will not be identical in all regions.

The empirical relations provided by Leopold and Maddock were subsequently found to pertain to all streams, despite divergences of topography and climate. This hydraulic geometry of stream channels is supported by the work of Wolman (1955) in the eastern United States, Hack (1957) and Hack and Young (1959) as previously discussed, Miller (1958) in the high mountain streams of New Mexico, Leopold and Miller (1956) in ephemeral stream channels, Myrick and Leopold (1963) in tidal estuaries; indeed, it is supported in all natural environments where a demonstration of this geometry was investigated, including the Amazon, the largest river in the world. In a truly arid area one is faced with the problem of the absence of knowledge of the magnitude and frequency of the dominant or channel-forming discharge, but Denny (1965) has investigated the relations of width, depth, and slope of the principal washes on alluvial fans and has found that these channels may be steeper and wider than those in humid regions but appear to be roughly comparable: a similar relationship among the variables is implied but the precise relationship is not known.

The essential point to this discussion is that, contrary to the classical view, it has been demonstrated that most channels in nature are either in dynamic equilibrium with present processes or are tending to adjust to this condition. Moreover, in easily erodible material the adjustment is quite rapid and has little to do with the "stage" of a large area, contrary to the conclusions of Davis and his supporters. Finally, it has been argued by Leopold and Langbein (1962), from entropy-energy considerations, that river channels tend toward the most probable state in nature. Entropy is, in this treatment, equated to the sum of the logarithms of the probabilities of all possible states and thus is used in the statistical sense. The thesis was supported by analogy with random-walk models of stream profiles and drainage development. The latter received corroboration by Schenk (1963) and the theoretical argument was supported by Scheidegger (1964b), but debate (Kennedy, Richardson, and Sutera, 1964) and rebuttal (Langbein, 1965) have continued. The theory has recently been applied to the general problem of river meanders by Langbein and Leopold (1966) and to channel cross sections, drainage nets, and drainage systems of a landmass of continental dimensions by Langbein (1966). The burden of each of these excellent reports is that models based upon the principle that stochastic processes prevail have successfully simulated the characteristics of natural rivers and their channels. For purposes of this discussion, however, it should suffice to point out an obvious, but not trivial, conclusion. That is, whether one wishes to consider streams and their channels from the viewpoint of the summation of forces acting upon particulate matter or in statistical-probabilistic terms, to refute the claim that streams tend toward the most probable paths in nature, one is forced to entertain the illogical position that they follow improbable paths.

The third influence upon geomorphic thought in recent times is, as stated previously, the adaptation of general systems theory to geomorphology. The entropy consideration cited above (Leopold and Langbein, 1962) stems from an adaptation of Von Bertalanffy's (1950, 1951, 1952) treatment of open and closed systems in physics and biology. These two types of general systems differ chiefly by reason of the fact that open systems are maintained by the addition and subtraction of energy and material, whereas closed systems are not. As summarized so well by Chorley (1962), the Davisian cycle of erosion is essentially a closed-system framework of reference wherein the initial conditions (uplift) determine the final product (peneplain). The open system, in contrast, embraces natural drainage basins wherein a dynamic equilibrium of form (hillslopes and channel profiles) and processes results. It is apparent that the classical or Davisian view tends to exclude the equilibria which have been demonstrated in nature, whereas the open-system viewpoint is reconciled only with some difficulty with the facts of continuous denudation through time.

Conceptual Frameworks

The foregoing background material may best be summarized by stating that three general viewpoints are represented. These are actually conceptual frameworks within which any given worker operates, and they serve to influence, to a great extent, his approach to a given problem as well as the conclusions that are reached. First, there is the classical view, within which the hypotheses of Davis, Penck, King, and those who investigate denudation chronologies may be accommodated. Although the hypotheses involved will vary, any investigator who embraces them will tend to conclude that some single, dominant process has operated through time to produce an observed natural phenomenon and will probably ignore the multivariate nature of the factors involved. Moreover, the tendency to describe features in qualitative terms which connote some presumed genetic significance is inescapable because the "proof" of the validity of such hypotheses resides largely in comparisons with block diagrams that need not be quantitative.

The second school of thought relies heavily upon the equilibrium concept, as enunciated by Gilbert and enlarged upon by many authors previously cited. An investigator harboring this conceptual framework must of necessity gather basic data of a quantitative nature, with respect to form, process, and rates of processes, in order to demonstrate that an equilibrium condition actually exists.

Aside from the merits of one approach above the other, it is clear that those who desire to obtain basic data for practical or academic purposes would be wise to support investigators within the second category. But as previously mentioned, the conflict between those who seek for time-independent landforms (Hack, 1960) and those who seek the historical imprint of time is everpresent. Accordingly, there is a third group of investigators who tend to occupy the middle ground and are difficult to categorize.

Schumm and Lichty (1965), for example, have argued that the "correct" view of landform development is highly dependent upon the length of time involved and the extent of the area that is considered. In the view of these authors, dynamic equilibrium, even where demonstrated to exist, is referable to a short segment of time within a cycle of erosion and to certain portions of drainage basins rather than to any large basin in its entirety. Howard (1965) also has argued that the imprint of time may well be present in a given landform despite the tendency toward equilibrium. Lustig (1965a) and many others hold an equivalent view, and Chorley's (1962) treatment of open and closed systems specifically provided the space for this middle-ground view with respect to the impress of past climatic events in the arid areas. Similarly, the consideration of the magnitude and frequency of events of geomorphic significance by Wolman and Miller (1960) demonstrates an awareness that in the deserts of the world events of large magnitude and slight frequency may be of greatest significance, although this is not true in humid areas.

The arid lands therefore provide the best proving ground for those investigators who occupy the middle ground with respect to these conceptual frameworks. It is in such areas that the imprint of time may be best represented or, on the other side of the coin, that the visible landforms may retain features that more closely reflect an equilibrium with certain former processes. It is probably incorrect to entertain an extreme view in treating deserts that erosion by either wind or water is dominant, for example. The proper question in this instance is what proportion of the work done may be attributable to either agent. Or, in the case of drainage systems in the midst of vast deserts today, it also may be incorrect to hold that all such features are Pleistocene relics on the one hand, or are in adjustment with modern discharges on the other. This will be discussed later in this report but it is, in general, important to recognize that the position, or the conceptual framework, of a given investigator may vary between the limits outlined and that the merit of the intermediate view is enhanced when arid lands are the subject of research.

The foregoing discussion of conceptual frameworks may seem to be irrelevant to some readers, but within the scope of geomorphology today one encounters an array of such diverse investigations that it is profitable to organize them in some convenient scheme. The tendency is clearly toward the quantitative in all modern work, and whether the approach involves field, laboratory, or theoretical studies it is referable to one of the three broad groups of hypotheses which have here been termed "conceptual frameworks." Those who desire additional information on the historical backgrounds of modern concepts in geomorphology may consult the excellent work by Chorley, Dunn, and Beckinsale (1964), and additional information on the Pleistocene and on climatic change is available from several standard sources (Flint, 1957; Woldstedt, 1958; Butzer, 1961; Wright and Frey, 1965b).

Quantitative Studies

It will be apparent to the initiated reader of this review that one important area of geomorphology has thus far been ignored, namely, the quantitative treatment of landforms proper and drainage-basin analysis. Quantitative studies of rivers and drainage networks are most numerous in the literature, perhaps because they were undertaken earlier than studies of other features. The work of Surell (1841), cited previously, is an example of this fact. Additional references to the early work in river hydraulics that led to the establishment of many empirical formulas still in use can be obtained from the works of Rouse

(1950), Leliavsky (1955), and Chorley, Dunn, and Beckinsale (1964), among others. More pertinent considerations, perhaps, began with the treatment of drainage networks by Gravelius (1914), who attempted to apply an ordinal system of description to rivers and their tributaries.

The first complete exposition of this subject was provided by Horton (1945), who laid the foundation for all subsequent investigations of this topic. Horton set forth the laws of stream order, length, and slope, provided several quantitative parameters for expressing the degree of drainage development and the branching habit of streams, and related these and other variables to hydrologic factors. Basically, he swept away "youth," "maturity," "old age," and a vast array of accompanying qualitative terms; it would not be an overstatement to claim that all modern morphometric investigations are to some extent dependent upon Horton's original work. Shreve (1966), Scheidegger (1966), and Woldenberg (1966) have each reexamined Horton's laws of stream order and stream number in theoretical papers and have concluded, as did Leopold and Langbein (1962), Langbein and Leopold (1966), Schenk (1963), and other authors, that in the absence of constraints the laws describe drainage nets that can develop through random processes. Hence, the drainage geometry seen in nature is a reflection of the most probable geometry, and it can be shown that the branching pattern exhibited by trees is analogous (Leopold, *in press*).

The basic concepts that were introduced by Horton (1945) were subsequently enlarged upon and extended to a wide variety of geologic and climatic environments by other workers. Most notable among these are Strahler (1950; 1952*a, b*; 1954; 1956; 1957) and several of his students: Miller (1953), Schumm (1956), Melton (1957, 1958), Coates (1958), Broscoe (1959), Morisawa (1959), and Maxwell (1960). The methods illustrated by their work have, with certain variations, been applied by Rzhanitsyn (1960) to rivers in the U.S.S.R., by Leopold and Miller (1956) to ephemeral streams, by Lustig (1965*b*) to problems of sediment yield from drainage basins, and by many others, some of whom are cited in the recent review article by Strahler (1964) and in the excellent text by Leopold, Wolman, and Miller (1964).

The relation of quantitative drainage-basin analysis to hydrology is well illustrated by many of the papers cited in the previous section as well as above. In addition to Horton's (1945) demonstration, it is worthy of note that Sherman (1932) first showed that the unit hydrograph will vary with basin size and shape and that Langbein *et al.* (1947) provided a quantitative relationship between stream discharge and drainage area. The application of multiple-regression analysis to the problem of runoff from drainage basins largely stems from the work of Anderson (1949) and Anderson and Trobitz (1949), but Maxwell's (1960) sophisticated treatment of variables and the recent work of Benson (1962, 1964) should also be mentioned in this regard.

Hillslopes have not been ignored because of undue concentration upon drainage networks. In fact, studies of the quantitative aspects of drainage basins and their hydrology often, of necessity, treat the subject. The papers by Coates (1958), Schumm (1956), and several of Strahler's works, for example, devote attention to hillslopes, and their development. Moreover, papers by Melton (1960, 1965*a, b*) relate slope gradients to several climatic or geologic variables, and Culling (1963), Rapp (1960), Segerström (1950), White (1949), Ruxton (1958), Mammerickx (1964), Savigear (1956), Scheidegger (1961*a, b*; 1964*a*), and Bakker and Strahler (1956) have considered problems associated with hillslope development from different viewpoints and in a diversity of environments. Indeed, it is sometimes argued that the two dominant facets of geomorphology are hillslopes and their retreat, which provide debris for removal by streams, and the drainage nets which accomplish the necessary removal; thus, these aspects of geomorphology are intimately related.

Although drainage-basin analysis and hillslope development are the two topics which dominate quantitative geomorphology, a third category of interest also exists. Within this category are quantitative descriptions of a single given landform, or some aspect thereof, and the quantitative relationships that may emerge from such studies.

A good example of the description of an individual landform is provided by the work of Chorley (1959) with respect to drumlins. Chorley found that the shape of a drumlin could best be approximated by fitting a lemniscate to its outline. Although the drumlin is not a landform which occurs in arid regions, the method may nevertheless have some application because certain types of sand dunes resemble the drumlin in configuration. Moreover, a subsequent paper by Chorley, Malm, and Pogorzelski (1957) demonstrated that this same function could be employed as a descriptive measure of drainage basin shape. The work of Yasso (1965), who fitted a logarithmic spiral to certain shorelines, and Troeh (1965), who applied the simple expression $Z = P + SR + LR^2$ to the configuration of alluvial fans, are examples in a similar vein.

The treatment accorded river meanders by Leopold and Wolman (1957, 1960) and that of river and valley meanders by Dury (1964*a, b*; 1965) is illustrative of a type of quantitative description of one aspect of a larger subject. Subsequently, Langbein and Leopold (1966) showed that a sine-generated curve could be fitted to any river meander, regardless of shape. It is interesting to note that although these authors were basically concerned with so academic a question as why a river meanders and, again, with entropy considerations, the identical problem of finding the curve of best fit for river meanders had been undertaken previously for practical reasons (Remson *et al.,* 1962).

With respect to quantitative relationships that may emerge from various studies, numerous pertinent examples are available. Hack's (1957) equation relating channel slope, bed-material size, and drainage area can be used to estimate one of these variables when the others are known; the relation of drainage area to discharge (Langbein *et al.,* 1947), the basic hydraulic geometry of stream channels (Leopold and Maddock, 1953), and the host of parameters that have emerged from drainage basin studies are all relevant in this sense. Another relationship worthy of mention here is that between the area of an alluvial fan and the area of its associated drainage basin. This was originally established by Bull (1964) and subsequently employed by Denny (1965) and Hooke (1965) in arguments concerning dynamic equilibrium and alluvial fans. It is obvious that whether or not one is concerned with the matter of equilibrium, the empirical relationship between fan area and drainage area may prove to be of practical value in desert terrain studies.

In summary, several types of quantitative studies have been undertaken and any of these may be of relevance to academic or governmental affairs. Because modern geomorphology is, in fact, increasingly quantitative, it is a subject worthy of both consideration and support. The gathering of basic, quantitative data is a continuing function of several agencies in the United States; among these, the U. S. Geological Survey is perhaps foremost. A network of hydrologic bench marks (Leopold, 1962) is in the process of establishment in the United States and many of these stations will be located in arid or semiarid regions. Slaymaker and Chorley (1964) have proposed a similar network for Great Britain and have described the nature of the observations on hillslopes and stream channels that may be made; Miller and Leopold (1963) have described the basic procedures involved. With the passage of time the accrual of data will increase, hopefully in other parts of the world as well. In any event, the data gathered will surely be applicable to many divisions of human affairs. As is true of the present literature on quantitative geomorphology, however, one limiting factor with respect to application is knowledge of the existence of applicable information. The references supplied by this report should serve, in part, to meet this need.

DISCUSSION OF AVAILABILITY OF INFORMATION

The sources of information on the geomorphology of the arid lands and related topics include the following categories: (1) military reports, maps, and documents, (2) reports of other governmental agencies, ministries, and departments, (3) publications of international organizations or their sponsored symposia, (4) books of various types, (5) scientific periodicals that treat aspects of geology, geography, or hydrology, (6) popular journals and magazines, (7) publications of universities and student theses, (8) reports of private corporations, (9) reports of research institutes or organizations, (10) bibliographic or abstracting services, and (11) unpublished information possessed by individuals or any organization.

Given this great diversity with respect to sources of information, it is clear that any complete list of references on this subject must remain an unattainable goal. Indeed, it would be accurate to state that information retrieval or compilation poses a problem that is at least equal in magnitude to that of information evaluation. Nevertheless, because it is desirable to essay a listing of the principal sources of information, this will be presented below on a desert-by-desert or country-by-country basis.

Because certain sources of information are sufficiently general or broad in scope, they are not amenable to treatment in terms of individual deserts or countries. These general sources will be considered at the outset of the following discussion.

A. GENERAL SOURCES OF INFORMATION

Material that may be categorized as general in character is well illustrated by Unesco reports, several of which provide excellent sources of information. Of particular relevance to this report are the reviews of research on arid-zone hydrology (Unesco, 1953a), the proceedings of the Ankara symposium (Unesco, 1953b), and subsequent treatment (Schoeller, 1959) of arid-zone hydrology. Data on geomorphology and hydrology of the arid regions are also presented in the guide book to research (Dickson, 1957), the proceedings of the Jerusalem symposium (Israel Research Council, 1953) which was jointly sponsored by Unesco and the host country, and in the excellent volume entitled *The problems of the Arid Zone* (Unesco, 1962). Two additional works in this vein, which supply intimately related material, are the history of land use in the arid regions (Stamp, 1961) and the Rome symposium on climatic changes (Unesco, 1963a). Unesco has also published a directory of institutions that are engaged in arid-zone research (Unesco, 1953c) which is still useful despite the passing of more than a dozen years since the compilation was made; an updating is in preparation at the Office of Arid Lands Research, University of Arizona. Finally, the bibliography of African hydrology (Rodier, 1963) and review of the natural resources of that continent (Unesco, 1963b) provide unparalleled sources of general information on Africa. Mention should also be made of Unesco's *Arid Zone Newsletter,* and *Nature and Resources,* which was first issued in 1965. Both publications contain useful summary papers on the status of knowledge and problems in various countries, news of current symposia and programs, and reviews of current publications that pertain to hydrology, geomorphology, and allied subjects.

The articles contained in all of the Unesco reports cited above commonly include extensive reference lists. Hence, any investigation of the work that has been done can profitably be begun by consulting these works.

The United Nations has published reports in the "Flood Control" series since 1951, although in 1962 the series title was changed to "Water Resources Research." Certain of these reports are germane here by reason of either (1) their treatment of the hydrology of countries that are partially located in the arid zone, or (2) their treatment of general hydrologic principles which, as indicated in the introduction of this report, may be pertinent to investigations in arid regions. Moreover, useful reference lists accompany many of the contained articles.

The United Nations reports* that are worthy of mention here for one or more of these reasons include the treatment of flood damage and flood control in Asia (United Nations, 1951), the sediment

---

*These reports list the United Nations as corporate author.

problem (1953), water-resources development in Burma, India, and Pakistan (1956), and in Afghanistan, Iran, Korea, and Nepal (1961). Similarly, the proceedings of other regional conferences on water resources in Asia and the Far East (United Nations, 1962a, 1963) provide relevant information on the hydrology of certain areas in southern Asia which are partially arid. Finally, there are two useful publications on methods and equipment in hydrologic studies (United Nations, 1960, 1962b) which provide information of potential application to arid-zone research.

Aside from Unesco publications and those of the United Nations proper, there are other reports of an international nature which are excellent sources of information. Included in this category are the published proceedings and reports of the International Geological Congress, the International Geographical Union, and the International Association of Scientific Hydrology.

Although some papers that specifically treat either the geomorphology or hydrology of the arid regions may be found in nearly all of the publications of these three organizations, certain of the publications may be mentioned as likely to be of greatest benefit. Among these are (1) the reports of the XIX and XX Geological Congresses (International Geological Congress, 1952, 1956), which were held in Algeria and Mexico, respectively, (2) the reports of the International Geographical Union which treat terraces and erosion surfaces (Union Géographique Internationale, 1948, 1952a), slopes and slope development (1956), and the application of aerial photography to geomorphology (1951, 1952b), and (3) the reports of the Scientific Hydrology General Assembly of Rome (International Association of Scientific Hydrology, 1954), Toronto (1958a, b), and Berkeley (1964a, b) which treat surface waters and land erosion, among other topics.

Three publications clearly deserve inclusion among these references by reason of their content, namely, the supplemental volumes to the *Zeitschrift für Geomorphologie* which treat slope morphology and development (Birot and Macar, 1960, 1964), and the publication of the Polish Academy of Sciences on problems of geomorphological mapping (Polish Academy of Sciences, 1963). Each of these works contains international contributions and excellent references on the subjects that are covered therein.

This leads to a consideration of scientific journals in general as sources of information. Those journals that present a preponderance of articles on some aspect of the country of issue will be cited later, as appropriate. Journals that contain articles on the geomorphology of various parts of the world and

are therefore of importance as general information sources include the *Zeitschrift für Geomorphologie, Journal of Geomorphology, Revue de Géomorphologie Dynamique, Geografiska Annaler, Erdkunde, International Geology Review, Revue de Géographie Physique et de Géologie Dynamique, Bulletin de l'Association de Géographes Français, Bulletin de la Société Géologique de France, Annales de Géographie, Petermanns Geographische Mitteilungen, Geologische Rundschau, Geographical Review, Annals of the Association of American Geographers, Quarterly Journal of the Geological Society of London, Geography, Geographical Journal, Transactions of the Institute of British Geographers,* and the *Geological Magazine.*

Although the European periodicals listed above also contain a preponderance of articles that pertain to the country of issue, these countries have no arid zones and for this reason one can encounter, within their covers, pertinent articles on nearly any area of the world. Thus, the journals in question are truly general sources of information for purposes of this report.

Bibliographies or abstracts on general geomorphology, or on the geomorphology of the arid regions, are not abundant. The most important general information sources in this respect are the *Geomorphological Abstracts,* published by the Department of Geography, London School of Economics, which provide broad but somewhat uneven coverage of the literature, the *Bibliography of Geology Exclusive of North America,* published by the Geological Society of America, two of the Unesco reports previously cited (Rodier, 1963; Unesco, 1963b), and the extensive compilations of the Military Geology Branch of the U. S. Geological Survey. Also worthy of note are the abstracts and critiques of current literature that are presented in individual issues of *Revue de Géomorphologie Dynamique* and the *Zeitschrift für Geomorphologie,* and the specialized bibliographies on Quaternary shorelines (Richards and Fairbridge, 1965) and sand dunes (Warren, 1966) of the world. Finally, the *Bibliographique Géographie Internationale,* published by Colin, Paris, and the abstracts being compiled at the Office of Arid Lands Research, University of Arizona, may be useful. There are a few additional bibliographies, such as that on British geomorphology (Clayton, 1964) or the recently published list of reports resulting from the U. S. Technical Assistance Program from 1940-1965 (Heath, 1965), but these contain relatively few items of direct interest here.

Many pertinent references can be obtained by recourse to (1) the indices of the periodicals previously cited, (2) the bibliographies that accompany review articles in the Unesco volumes and elsewhere, and (3) books that treat geomorphology or hydrology. Within this last category a number of excellent works are available. *Das Relief der Erde* (Machatschek, 1955) covers the globe, as the title implies, and King's book, *Morphology of the Earth* (King, 1962) also contains a considerable array of useful references in addition to the data presented in the text. The work of Leopold, Wolman, and Miller (1964) previously cited, includes a number of pertinent references in addition to the American citations, but books on geomorphology by Derruau (1965), Tricart (1965), Tricart and Cailleux (1955), Louis (1960), and Birot (1959) are particularly noteworthy in this respect. Additionally, King's book on geomorphic techniques (King, 1966) and the collection of papers presented in the work edited by Chorley and Hagget (1965) should be cited here.

The subject of general hydrology has received more complete attention in many countries, and standard works that contain an abundance of references include those by Tonini (1959), Streck (1953), Wundt (1953), Roche (1963), Chebotarëv (1955, 1960), and Sokolovskii (1959). Of particular relevance is the recent compendium edited by Chow (1964). The work of equal magnitude on man's role in changing the face of the Earth (Thomas, 1956) should not be omitted as a general source book; extensive reference lists are included and the topics covered are of relevance to changes in landforms through time.

With respect to maps, the best general coverage of the world can be obtained by recourse to the aeronautical charts of the U. S. Coast and Geodetic Survey (19—) and the extensive collection of the U. S. Army Map Service (1946-). Also worthy of note are the landform maps of various parts of the world by Raisz, examples of which are those of the Near East (Raisz, 1951), North Africa (1952), the United States (1957), and Mexico (1959). The various maps of this series present an amazing amount of detail, particularly if one considers the relatively small scales involved. Of even greater relevance to geomorphic studies, perhaps, is the monumental physical-geographic atlas of the world; this unique work was issued as a limited edition but the explanatory text which accompanies the maps has been made available by the American Geographical Society (Akademiya nauk S.S.S.R. . ., 1964).

General Authorities

Individuals who possess considerable information on one or more aspects of the geomorphology of arid regions will be cited in the discussions of this report either by topic or by geographic area, as may be appropriate. Those who may profitably be consulted for general information, but who represent countries without an arid zone, include several individuals in England or western Europe. *R. F. Peel,* University of Bristol, can supply information on the general activities of many geomorphologists who are currently engaged in arid-lands research and is personally expert on Saharan problems. *J. Dresch* of the Sorbonne is similarly well qualified. *R. J. Chorley,* Cambridge University, should be regarded as an authority on quantitative geomorphology and general interpretive problems. In the area of geomorphic mapping, the application of aerial photography to geomorphic problems, and aspects of terrain analysis, many individuals could be cited here. *J. Tricart,* University of Strasbourg, has wide knowledge of research on these topics in many parts of the world and on the strength of their works, *R. A. G. Savigear* (1965), University of Sheffield, *J. P. Bakker* (1960, 1963), University of Amsterdam, *P. H. T. Beckett* (Beckett and Webster, 1962), Soil Science Laboratory, Oxford, and *C. W. Mitchell,* Cambridge University, are each worthy of designation as an authority. Mitchell is engaged in important research on landform classification and terrain analysis of the arid regions of the world, and, although his work is not yet published, he has much information on topics that are quite germane to the purposes of this report.

In other countries outside the arid zone, *H. Schiffers,* University of Cologne, can supply information on the activities of his German colleagues and on a current compendium on all aspects of the Sahara which he is editing. *Ake Sundborg,* University of Uppsala, is a general authority on aspects of sediment transport and fluvial processes and may profitably be consulted on these matters. Additional authorities on geomorphology or surface-water hydrology will be cited elsewhere in this report, in discussions of the availability of information on a given desert or country. Several of these individuals are acknowledged world authorities on arid-zone problems, and their omission at this point should not be construed otherwise.

General Depositories

General depositories within the United States for information on geomorphology and surface hydrology of the world's deserts are the Library of Congress and the libraries of Harvard University, Yale University, Stanford University, University of Southern California, and the University of California system. Other depositories of world stature are in London and Paris; these are especially strong in holdings on the deserts of Africa, the Middle East, and southern Asia. In London, the Directorate of Overseas Surveys should be consulted; in Paris, the Institut Géographique National, the Bureau de Recherches Géologiques et Minières, and the Office de la Recherche Scientifique et Technique Outre-Mer. For the topics treated in this chapter, depositories supplementary to the world centers mentioned above are, in general, the working and publishing organizations in the desert countries. Valuable holdings of unpublished materials are present in the institutions mentioned in the text as carrying out research, as sources of current information, and as having staff members considered to be authorities. For certain of the deserts and constituent nations, additional depositories are specifically mentioned.

B.   AFRICA

The desert area of Africa is extensive, and for ease of treatment in the discussion of available information which follows, some subdivision is required. Before essaying a regional or country-by-country division, however, a few references on the continent as a whole should be provided. Publications cited in the following text on Africa (in general), unless otherwise noted where cited, are listed in Section II of the Pertinent Publications list.

In addition to relevant portions of the books by King (1962) and Machatschek (1955, see Pert. Pubs. Sec. I) on the morphology of the Earth, the Russian atlas of the world (Akademiya nauk S.S.S.R. . . ., 1964, see Pert. Pubs. Sec. I) and the Unesco volumes on the hydrology (Rodier, 1963, see Pert. Pubs. Sec. I) and natural resources (Unesco, 1963a, see Pert. Pubs. Sec. I) of Africa should be consulted. Three review papers of particular importance appeared in the natural resources volume, namely that on topographic mapping by Rumeau (1963), on geology and geophysics by Dixey (1963), and on hydrology by Rodier (1963). An excellent outline of the geology of Africa also has been provided by Furon (1960), in a book which is itself a source of much additional geological information by reason of the contained references on individual countries.

Geologic maps of the continent of Africa have been compiled by Katchevsky (1933), the Association of African Geological Surveys (1936-1952), and, most recently, Unesco (1964). Several special maps of such items as mineral locations are also available, but only one additional map need be noted here. Because several of the African desert areas extend to, or occupy, coastal regions, McGill's work (1958, see Pert. Pubs. Sec. I) is pertinent. This includes a map of the coastal landforms of the world, and it

depicts a coastal strip of about 5 to 10 miles in width around the African and other continents. The scale of publication is unfortunately small (1:25,000,000) but the original compilations were on larger bases. Chapter III of the present series, *An Inventory of Geographical Research on Desert Environments,* may be consulted for information on desert coastal zones.

1.   Southern Africa

The arid portion of southern Africa is essentially a contiguous area. It extends from south-central Botswana (Bechuanaland) southward and westward, into South Africa and South West Africa, respectively, and then northward along the coastal region of South West Africa into Angola. The coastal part of the desert, the Namib, in Angola is locally designated as "the Moçâmedes Desert." The interior part of the arid region, the Kalahari, is termed "the Karroo Desert" in portions of South Africa. Meigs' map (1953, see Pert. Pubs. Sec I) of the arid regions of the world reveals two separate and relatively small areas in southern Africa which are also classified as deserts. One area extends from western Mozambique to the west and the second desert area is depicted along the southwestern coast of Madagascar. The delimitation of these areas depends, in part, upon the arbitrary criteria that are used to distinguish between a semiarid and arid environment; the two regions in question are not with unanimity classified as arid desert. In any event, time limitations precluded an investigation of these dry areas and it should be noted here that the discussion of available information on southern African deserts pertains solely to the Kalahari and Namib and to their respective extensions, the Karroo and Moçâmedes desert areas. For simplicity, only the terms "Kalahari" and "Namib" will be used here. Publications cited in the following text on Southern Africa, unless otherwise noted where cited, are listed in Section III of the Pertinent Publications list.

Pertinent maps that show the southern African deserts include those by Du Toit (1959) and King (1951) in their books on (respectively) the geology and morphology of South Africa, the provisional geological map of Bechuanaland (Bechuanaland Geological Survey Department, 1964) on a scale of 1:2,000,000, and the geological map of South West Africa (South West Africa, Surveyor-General, 1963) on a scale of 1:1,000,000. Portions of the area occupied by the Namib Desert in Angola are shown on geologic maps on a scale of 1:250,000 (Portugal, Província de Angola, 1961) and 1:2,000,000 (Mouta, 1933, 1954).

The Kalahari

The Kalahari has been the subject of many reports that treat some aspects of geology or geomorphology; in some instances these accounts were published prior to 1900. Publications cited in the following text on the Kalahari, unless otherwise noted where cited, are listed in Section III of the Pertinent Publications list. The descriptive treatment of François (1892, 1893*a*) is an example of the information gained via early travels but Passarge (1904) produced the classic and most often cited report on the Kalahari of this approximate vintage. His work, *Die Kalahari,* provides a good early account of the geology and geography of the northern part of the region and a previous paper by Passarge (1901) is also worthy of note.

Other authors also contributed to general knowledge of the Kalahari in the early 1900's however. Both Hermann (1908) and Range (1910, 1912, 1914), for example, discussed geology and geography, and the description of travels by Schultze (1907) might be mentioned in this context. The Kalahari expeditions of 1925 and 1945 have been reported by Du Toit (1926) and MacKenzie (1946), respectively. These reports, combined with the basic geologic work of Rogers (1934, 1935, 1936) and the morphologic treatment by Dixey (1939, 1943, 1956) through the years, have provided the basis for modern considerations of the general character of the Kalahari. In this vein, the discussion of physiographic provinces in South Africa by Taljaard (1945) and the outline of the geology and geomorphology of Bechuanaland by McConnell (1959) should be noted. The best modern review paper on the central Kalahari region has been provided by Boocock and van Straten (1962), but with respect to individual topics of interest some additional references will be cited here.

The pans of the Kalahari constitute one of the relatively few departures from featureless plains in the region, and this fact, combined with the complex interpretive problem they pose, provides the reason for the many studies of pans. Pans were discussed by Passarge both in his major work cited above (1904) and in a subsequent paper (1943) but early reports on pans in the western Kalahari also were provided by Michaelson (1910) and Jaeger (1926, 1936). The latter subsequently expanded the scope of his considerations to include the pans or pan-like features of the world (Jaeger, 1939), and this effort was reviewed by Rogers (1940). Wellington (1938, 1939) has discussed the Etocha region, which is a bit northwest of the arid Kalahari proper, and MacGregor (1930) has described the Makarikari pan in northeastern Bechuanaland which is similarly in a semiarid environment. In both cases, however, these extremely large features are intimately related to the historical development of Kalahari pans everywhere. A classification of pans, based on the presence or absence of grass and degree of salinity of the contained sediments, has been set forth by van Straten (1955), and, again, the best modern review of the general problems posed by the pans has been provided by Boocock and van Straten (1962). Mr. A. T. Grove of Cambridge University is currently investigating the pans and adjacent terrain by means of aerial photographs.

With respect to hillslopes and pediments and similar topics, pertinent information on the southwestern Kalahari is contained in papers by Fair (1948) and Mabbutt (1955*a, b*). Some information of less substantial character was provided by Schwartz (1926) on the northern Kalahari.

The Kalahari sands, which are ubiquitous, and the sand dunes that border the pans on the south and southeast or occur in longitudinal patterns in the western Kalahari, have been the subject of remarkably few studies of merit. Lewis (1936*a*) discussed the sand dunes in South Africa and the phenomenon termed "roaring sand" or "musical sand" in the Kalahari (Lewis, 1936*b*). This topic was pursued by Van der Walt (1940), but the finest paper on musical sand in the literature is that by Brown *et al.* (1961), who devised an acoustical experimental procedure which allowed precise correlation of the sound frequency emitted and the size, shape, arrangement, and other characteristics of the sands considered. In addition to this work, Poldervaart (1957) investigated the heavy-mineral distribution of the surficial Kalahari sands in order to deduce fossil wind directions. His results accord with the known distribution of the stabilized dunes that rim the Kalahari pans on the southeast. Mabbutt (1955*a, b*) has outlined some physiographic evidence that is pertinent to considerations of the age of the sands.

Other reports of geomorphic relevance on parts of the Kalahari include descriptions of the Fish River canyon in South West Africa by Jaeger (1932) and Simpson and Davies (1957), a review of the evidence on erosion cycles in Bechuanaland by Jennings (n.d.), and a few papers on climatic changes. Among the latter, most notable are Flint's review paper on the evidence for climatic change in eastern and southern Africa (Flint, 1959), Wayland's discussion of climatic change in Bechuanaland (1954), and Kokut's treatment of the hydrologic data relevant to recent changes in southern African climate (1948). In an allied vein, the report of the Desert Encroachment Committee (Union of South Africa, 1959) is informative. On this point, Bosazza, Adie, and Brenner

(1946) have taken the position that no climatic changes have occurred and that desert encroachment is produced by the activities of man, overgrazing and migration of animals, and the like.

Pertinent reports on the surface-water hydrology of the Kalahari are rare. In common with most desert regions, efforts have been directed largely toward development of ground-water resources or the study of major rivers that flow through nonarid regions. Boocock and van Straten (1962) have compiled the most recent information on water-resources activities in Bechuanaland and, in addition, have presented a description of the mokgachas or fossil river valleys that occur in the Protectorate. Martin (1961) had previously reviewed the hydrology of part of the Kalahari, and earlier discussions were presented by Schwartz (1920), Pfalz (1944), and Wellington (1955), and by Debenham (1948) and Wayland (1953) on the question of whether the Kalahari sands constitute an aquifer. The areas considered in these reports are largely semiarid, and, in any event, neither drainage patterns nor channel geometry was treated. Insight into the current status of available information on surface-water hydrology in the Kalahari proper can best be gained by consulting the paper by Boocock and van Straten cited above (1962), the report of the Kalahari expedition of 1945 (Union of South Africa, 1946), and hydrologic papers by Roberts (1952, 1954). Mackenzie (1949), Menne (1958), Modgley (n.d.), and Wicht (1947), all of which treat some aspect of surface-water resources and research in South Africa.

In summary, it may be said that the gross aspects of the geomorphology and geology of the Kalahari are fairly well known and that specific features such as pans, fossil drainage, and sand dunes have been studied. There is a great need for detailed mapping; however, and as will be made clear in the section of this report entitled "Evaluation and Recommendations," much more work of a quantitative nature should be undertaken. This statement applies not only to the pans, drainage systems, and dune sands that have been studied previously but to precipitation-runoff relations and surface-water hydrology in general. Few data on this subject are actually available for the truly arid portions of the Kalahari.

Authorities and Depositories

Authorities on the Kalahari largely consist of individuals who have worked and traveled in the desert region for many years, and among these *Colin Boocock,* Director of the Geological Survey in Lobatsi, is particularly knowledgeable on all aspects of geology, geomorphology, and trafficability problems. *O. J. van Straten,* of this same organization, is expert

in matters of water resources, particularly with respect to water quality. Last, *Henno Martin,* of the University of Göttingen, Germany, should be cited as a general authority on both the Kalahari and the Namib.

Sources of information on the Kalahari include the *South African Geographical Journal, Transactions of the South African Geological Society,* and unpublished reports and data in the files of the Geological Survey in Lobatsi. Information on mapping and aerial photographs can be obtained from the Directorate of Overseas Surveys in London and the Director of Trigonometrical Surveys of the Republic of South Africa. Finally, an unpublished bibliography of geology of South West Africa has been compiled by the Geological Survey of South West Africa (n.d.); it is currently being revised. The bibliography contains many pertinent references on that part of the Kalahari within or adjacent to South West Africa and references to the Namib Desert which will be next discussed.

The Namib

Publications cited in the following text on the Namib, unless otherwise noted where cited, are listed in Section III of the Pertinent Publications list.

As previously stated, a portion of the Namib extends northward from South West Africa, along the coastal region of Angola. This desert area of Angola is outlined on Meigs' homoclimatic map (1953, see Pert. Pubs. Sec. I) and is shown on the coastal regions (McGill, 1958, see Pert. Pubs. Sec. I) and geological maps (Portugal, Província de Angola, 1961; Mouta, 1933, 1954) mentioned earlier.

The basic references on this area include the early descriptive reports by Bockemeyer (1890), Vageler (1920), and Jessen (1936), and the work of Beetz on the geology of southwestern Angola (1933) and the Kunene River area (1950). The best modern work has been accomplished by the Portuguese, however. Soares de Carvalho has provided an excellent report on the geology and geography of the Angolan desert (1961) which contains many photographs and detailed maps; it is probably the most authoritative paper that exists on surficial aspects of this region. The same author also presented data on the characteristics of sands in the Moçâmedes area (Soares de Carvalho, 1962). Hydrologic studies have largely been devoted to ground-water resources, problems of salt-water intrusion, and the like, but two useful papers by Ferrão should be cited here (1962, 1964). Both reports contain outline maps and short sections on geomorphology, and both serve as a reference guide to other pertinent Portuguese reports on the water resources of southwestern Angola.

Soares de Carvalho must be considered an authority on the Angolan portion of the Namib desert, on the strength of his comprehensive report (1961), but basic information on research in Angola can be obtained from the Junta de Investigaçoes do Ultramar (Council on Overseas Investigations) in Lisbon, and from *Francisco U. Guimaraes,* Director of the Geological and Mining Survey, and *Jean Pierre Amory,* Director General of Petrofina Petrangel. These two individuals, both in Luanda, should be consulted with respect to mapping, trafficability, and geological studies in Angola.

That part of the Namib which occurs in South West Africa has been the subject of many reports since the mid-1800's. Numerous descriptions of travels or expeditions that were published prior to 1900 exist in the literature and among these are reports or books by Andersson (1855); Baines (1964); Galton (1852); François (1893b, 1899); Dove (1894); Stromer von Reichenbach (1896), who produced an early geologic treatise; and Stapff (1887), who mapped the lower Kuiseb Valley. Many additional works that provide good descriptions of the geology or physiography of all or part of South West Africa have appeared in subsequent years. Foremost among these is the compendium of Kaiser entitled *Die Diamantenwüste* (1927a), to which several authors contributed, but Kaiser also discussed the southern Namib (1925, 1926a), the problem of deserts and their landforms in general (1923a, 1927b, 1928), and landforms and erosion in the Namib (1921, 1923b, 1926b).

Jaeger has also made a major contribution, with respect to morphologic descriptions of the region. He published several works on the Namib (1927a), the surface form of the country (1923, 1921), the morphology of the Windhoek area (1927b), and other subjects through the years. A convenient summary of his several efforts has recently been issued in a single volume (Jaeger, 1965), which treats climate, hydrology, and other topics, as well as surficial morphology. A joint paper by Jaeger and Waibel (1920) on landforms of South West Africa should also be cited here. In addition to the reports on early travels, and the work of Kaiser and Jaeger mentioned above, pertinent information on some aspect of surficial features may be found in other papers.

Schenk (1901) compared South West Africa with southern Africa in general, Cloos provided some observations on desert winds (1911), in addition to his geological work on the Brandberg (1931) and his description of travels in the country (1937), Papparel (1909), Tönnesen (1917), Schneiderhöhn (1931), Rimann (1916), Reuning (1913, 1923),

and Range (1926, 1927, 1937, 1920) have each described the morphology of parts of the arid region, particularly of the southern Namib which contains diamond deposits and can no longer be freely traversed, and Passarge (1908), Moritz (1911), and Gevers (1942a, b, 1947), have also studied desert morphology. Additional general reports which provide much information include Abel's work on geomorphology (1953, 1954, 1955), Logan's review of work that has been done on the central portion of the Namib (1960), reports on the geology of South West Africa by Krenkel (1939), and Martin (1950), Ganssen's treatise on landforms and soils (1960), and descriptions of the Great Escarpment by Born (1933) and by Obst and Kayser (1949) in their comprehensive book on the escarpment and adjacent areas.

The Namib is basically a coastal desert and certain of the reports cited above therefore provide some information on the shoreline proper. The reports of Range (1937, 1920), for example, which treat the geology of the coastal region between Lüderitz and the Kuiseb River, are in this category. Knetsch, however, has specifically discussed sea-level changes (1938) and coastal landforms (1940), Waldron (1901) and Watson (1930) have described aspects of offshore islands, Smith (1961) and Jeppe (1952) have produced theses on the geology along the Swakop and Ugab rivers, respectively, Haughton (1931) has considered the Recent sedimentary deposits along the coast, and Davies (1959) has described the raised beaches of South West Africa. Additional data are obtainable from certain of the hydrological reports to be later cited.

Reports which treat diamond occurrences, other mineral deposits, petrology, and the geology of specific areas have largely been omitted here. The bibliography on South West Africa that has been compiled by the Geological Survey in Windhoek lists all such reports and, as is often the case, relevant information can be derived from these, in addition to geological data. Reuning and Martin (1957), for example, have discussed the Karroo system in South West Africa, but their paper also contains a map and description of the Doros crater.

Other useful reports on the Namib include Mabbutt's treatment of relief forms in granite (1952b) and discussions of climatic change in South West Africa by Korn and Martin (1937), Beetz (1938), and Gevers (1929-1931), and a related paper on Pleistocene glaciation by Martin and Schalk (1957). Gellert (1955) has discussed precipitation fluctuations, but his data were derived from highland areas. Pertinent rainfall data from the Namib proper have been presented in Logan's report (1960). Before turning to hydrology, another paper by Gellert is worthy of note. He has described patterned ground in South West Africa (Gellert, 1961) and presented information on this phenomenon which had not previously been noted.

Useful references on surface-water hydrology of the Namib can be easily assembled. Aside from the early treatment of runoff by Beetz and Kaiser (1919) and papers on miscellaneous matters by Wipplinger (1958, 1961), among others, there are two outstanding published reports by Stengel which adequately summarize the present status of knowledge of this subject in the country. The first of these is a compendium (Stengel, 1963) of the Water Affairs Branch of the South West Africa Administration and the second treats the Kuiseb and Swakop rivers (Stengel, 1964).

The value of the compendium by Stengel (1963) cannot be too greatly stressed. The results of all water resources projects in South West Africa, current work, and future plans are outlined. One section, on the rivers of the country, for example, presents data on the topography, gradients, lengths, catchment areas, and runoff associated with each river, cites springs and waterfalls, shows gaging-station locations, and gives pertinent meteorologic data including lengths of record. Several hydroelectric projects are cited and information is provided on dam locations and specifications, reservoir storage capacity, and estimated storage capacity. The twin problems of water supply and protection measures for the Walvis Bay area are also discussed. The data presented in this regard include the historic floods of the Kuiseb River, which is a major ephemeral river that crosses the Namib, and dune migration near the river's delta. The growth pattern of a sand dune that formed behind an artificial barrier has been documented for the May, 1950 through November, 1961 period, and conclusions have been reached on the rate of dune growth in this coastal area. This study constitutes, perhaps unwittingly, the best quantitative geomorphic study of its kind in the southern African desert.

The second paper cited above (Stengel, 1964) presents a compilation of all available hydrologic information on the Kuiseb and Swakop rivers, both of which are ephemeral, and includes many useful maps, profiles, sections, and photographs, in addition to basic data. Both reports should be considered basic references on surface-water hydrology in South West Africa and on the general problem of flow in the ephemeral channels of a true desert area.

The foregoing discussion of available information on the geomorphology and surface-water hydrology of the Namib should serve to indicate that this desert area is much better known in these respects than is the Kalahari. There is again a relative dearth of large-scale topographic or geologic maps and even the coastal terraces of the northern Namib have not been adequately mapped. Despite these facts, the morphology of the northern Namib is certainly known in the classical sense and the quantitative studies on the Kuiseb River and dune control near its mouth are excellent. Similar studies of other rivers that traverse the northern Namib are lacking for want of sufficient data, however, and no modern, quantitative investigations of the vast dune field in the southern Namib have been undertaken because it is a restricted area. Additionally, as noted in the section of this report entitled "Evaluation and Recommendations," quantitative geomorphic studies of the many inselbergs and other landforms of the northern Namib can profitably be undertaken.

Authorities and Depositories

Authorities on the Namib desert should include *Henno Martin,* University of Göttingen, Germany; *W. L. van Wyk,* Geological Survey, Windhoek; *H. W. Stengel,* Department of Water Affairs, Windhoek; and *R. F. Logan,* University of California, Los Angeles. Information on maps and aerial photographs can be obtained from the Geological Survey or the Surveyor-General Office in Windhoek. Literature on the Namib is scattered through the many German geographical and geological periodicals listed for the citations above and in the South African journals previously noted. Again, the unpublished compilation of reports on South West Africa that is available at the Geological Survey of South West Africa (n.d.) Windhoek, should be noted as a basic source of information. *Soares de Carvalho, F. U. Guimaraes,* and *J. P. Amory* have previously been listed as Angola authorities.

2. The Sahara

The extent of the immense desert that is termed "the Sahara" is well known, despite the ever-present difficulties of defining a desert boundary precisely. The African countries wholly or partially within the arid region can, for the sake of convenience, be classified as southern and northern. The southern countries involved are Sudan, Chad, Niger, Mali, Mauritania, and Spanish Sahara, and the northern tier consists of Egypt, Libya, Tunisia, Algeria, and Morocco. Each of these countries will be accorded some individual treatment with respect to the availability of pertinent information, but it should be noted here that a considerable number of reports treat some region or natural feature that extends across the political boundaries. In such cases, the reference provided will be listed under the single country that seems the more appropriate.

The country-by-country treatment of available information provided below will geographically cross the southern tier of countries mentioned from east to west; the northern countries will then be considered from west to east. The sole exception to this procedure will occur at the outset. Because the Nile flows from Sudan through Egypt on its northerly course, a discussion of information on Egypt will follow that on Sudan.

At the outset, it is appropriate to mention some rather general works on the Sahara and its features that cannot appropriately be assigned to a single country. Among these are the general references on Africa previously noted in this report. Particularly worthy of mention again is the map of North African landforms by Raisz (1952, see Pert. Pubs. Sec. I), which provides excellent general coverage of the entire Sahara, the terrain-analog study of northeastern Africa (U.S. Army Engineer Waterways Experiment Station, 1962), and Furon's book on the geology of Africa (1960, see Pert. Pubs. Sec. II), which provides many references to more detailed reports and to maps. Publications cited in the following text on the Sahara (in general), unless otherwise noted where cited, are listed in Section IV of the Pertinent Publications list.

Among additional works, the early reports of Pomel (1872), Schirmer (1893), and Passarge (1907) are of some value, and Gautier's (1928) excellent book on the Sahara provides much general information. Perret (1935) and Lelubre (1952) have discussed the relief present in the desert and Capot-Rey has considered the limits of a large segment of the Sahara (1952) and has provided an excellent book on the features of this region, the former French Sahara (Capot-Rey, 1953b). Dresch has treated the presumed erosion systems in northern Africa (1953c), Dubief has provided information on the climate (1959), gullying (1953c) and surface-water hydrology (1953a) of the desert, Schwarzbach (1953) has considered the age of the Sahara, Menchikoff (1957) has treated the regional geology, and Büdel (1963) has outlined the evidence for pluvial periods in the Sahara during the Pliocene and Pleistocene. An interesting recent report by Morrison and Chown (1965) on the general geomorphic, geologic, and hydrologic features that can be discerned from satellite photographs of the western Sahara should also be cited as a general reference here. It illustrates one aspect of a modern research approach that is termed "remote sensing."

A considerable number of general reports on

sand dunes in the Sahara are also available. A sampling of these would include reports by Chudeau (1920), Cayeux (1926), who has considered the origin of the sand, and Aufrère (1931, 1932, 1933), who has treated the general wind data in relation to dune morphology and proposed an elaborate classification and system of nomenclature. In addition, Dufour (1936) has studied the dunes of the southern Sahara, Queney (1945) has investigated surface ripples, Capot-Rey and Capot-Rey (1948) have presented a formation-of-dunes theory in accord with Bagnold's observations, and Dubief (1952) and Matschinski (1954) have treated matters of sand transport and dune stability, respectively. The review of theories of origin of longitudinal dunes by Price (1950) and the study of barchan dunes by Capot-Rey (1963) might also be noted within this context.

Authorities on aspects of Saharan geomorphology and important institutes, agencies, and universities, will be cited below by individual countries rather than for the Sahara in its entirety. In recognition of the extensive work done by personnel of the Institut Français d'Afrique Noire, a section on Senegal will be included below, despite the fact that the country is not within the arid zone. A compendium on the Sahara which is in preparation at this writing should be mentioned. This work, entitled *Die Sahara,* to be edited by Professor Schiffers of the University of Cologne, will include reports by various authorities on the geomorphology, geology, flora, fauna, and climate of the Sahara. It will provide far more comprehensive coverage of this desert than can be achieved here and should constitute a most welcome addition to the literature.

Depositories

Leading depositories of information in North Africa are the various agencies and institutions in Dakar, Rabat, and Algiers, where information in addition to that of the world depositories may be found, particularly unpublished material. The depositories are listed below in their countries of location. In addition, the Consejo Superior de Investigaciones Científicas in Madrid should be listed as a depository, in this case for Sahara areas associated in history with Spain. Its subdivisions, Instituto de Investigaciones Geológicas and Instituto de Estudios Africanos, should be contacted when extensive information from the parent depository is required. Also in Madrid, the Instituto Geológico y Minero de España, an agency of the Ministry of Industry, has a specialized library of interest to researchers investigating these areas. A summary of the state of knowledge of the Sahara is provided at the close of the "Sahara" portion of the text.

Sudan

Publications cited in the following text on Sudan, unless otherwise noted where cited, are listed in Section IV, Sahara, of the Pertinent Publications list.

The arid region of Sudan includes approximately the northern half of the country. Several useful reference works, although not restricted in scope to this arid zone alone, serve as guides to additional information. Among these works is the text on regional geography by Barbour (1961), a compendium on agriculture in the Sudan by Tothill (1948), and the *Sudan Almanac*, which is published annually by the Government Press at Khartoum. Barbour's geography presents a general description of the relief, drainage, geology, and climate of the country, as is common in works of this type, and also presents data on the Nile and on aerial photography and mapping coverage. The agriculture compendium includes similarly pertinent information by reason of the contributions of Andrew and others, who will be cited below. Lastly, the *Sudan Almanac* provides an outline of the geomorphology of the country and basic climatic and hydrologic data. Moreover, the availability of maps and reports of the Geological Survey is indicated, through the year prior to publication of this annual report.

In addition to these sources of information on Sudan, numerous reports provide some data of relevance here. Nachtigal's treatise (1879-1881) may be classified as an early-traveler's report but Sandford (1935*a, b*) has provided observations on the seldom-visited northwestern part of Sudan. Andrew (1948*a, b*) has discussed the geomorphology and geology of the country, with particular reference to the vast plainlands, Kassas (1956) has treated the landforms and vegetation in the vicinity of Omdurman, Ruxton (1958), and Ruxton and Berry (1961*a, b*) have produced some fine observations on desert weathering and hillslopes, and Berry has provided reports on the alluvial islands of the Nile (1962*a, b*), the coastal morphology of Sudan (1963*a, b*), the geomorphology of the Khor Eit area (1963*c*) and geographical research in Sudan (1964).

Other papers of related interest to the general subject of geomorphology in the arid regions include Stebbing's discussion of desert encroachment or enlargement (1953), Bhalotra's valuable presentation of data on duststorms (1958) and on the areal variability of rainfall (1960) and other meteorological topics, and several reports on climatic changes in Sudan. On this topic, the valuable contributions by Butzer (1959*a*), and particularly by Arkell (1949*a, b*; 1953) on the archeologic evidence of climatic

changes in Sudan, should be noted. Pleistocene and Recent climates in Sudan have also been discussed by Andrew (1944). Several recent papers of interest that treat geomorphology include Fölster's description of plains (1964), Sestini's comprehensive discussion of the depositional history of the Red Sea coast in the Port Sudan vicinity (1965), a detailed study of the reef complex along this coast by Berry, Whiteman, and Bell (1966), and a report on arid-zone research in Sudan, as of 1962, by Dixey and Aubert (1962). Two reports in preparation that are of particular interest include a geomorphic study of the Red Sea Hills area by L. Berry and an investigation of a large sand area in west-central Sudan by Andrew Warren; these authors are members of the geography departments of the University of Dar es Salaam and the University College of London, respectively.

Hydrologic studies in Sudan have largely centered upon the Nile River and its tributaries. The basic compendium on the Nile consists of a series of volumes entitled "The Nile Basin" which were published in Cairo (Hurst and Phillips, 1931, 1932, 1933*a, b*, 1938; Hurst and Black, 1944; Hurst, Black, and Simaika, 1946; Hurst, 1950) and supplementary reports to this work (Hurst, Simaika, and Black, 1953-57). Pertinent information on the Nile in both Egypt and Sudan is included, but for convenience the series is discussed here, under "Sudan." Additional information on many aspects of hydrology, topography, and ecology in southern Sudan have been published by the Jonglei Investigation Team (n.d., 1952, 1953). This organization has investigated the consequences of proposed controls and storage facilities on the Nile in the equatorial headwater reaches and in Sudan proper. Two other hydrologic reports which similarly treat proposed projects are also of relevance here. The report on Jebel Marra in western Sudan (Sudan, 1960) illustrates the techniques employed to gather basic data in the country today, and *Sudan Irrigation,* a handsome brochure (Sudan, 1957), presents a capsule summary of the hydrologic data for each reach of the Nile between the equatorial source lakes and the Sudan-Egypt border. This report also illustrates irrigable areas in Sudan and the locations of proposed irrigation schemes.

Additional information on the Nile and its valley is available in reports by Lyons (1905), Awad (1930), Wright (1949), Worrall (1958), and Rognon (1960*b*); Oliver (1965) has recently provided a summary of evaporation-precipitation relationships for the northern, arid portion of Sudan which is clearly relevant to the regime of flow in that area. Other aspects of hydrology are presented in the annual reports of the Department of Land Use and

Rural Water Development, Republic of the Sudan, Khartoum. These reports list the water wells, diversion dams and canals, and haffirs (surficial water-storage facilities), that have been constructed or that are under construction each year.

Authorities and Depositories

Sources of information on aspects of geomorphology and hydrology in Sudan include the Department of Geology of the University of Khartoum, the reports of the Arid Zone Research Unit (Whiteman, 1962; Bell, 1964) of the University, the Ministry of Irrigation, Department of Land Use, Geological Survey, and Sudan Survey Department. Authorities on geology and geomorphology in Sudan would include *L. Berry* of the University of Dar es Salaam, *A. J. Whiteman* of the University of Khartoum, and *J. Oliver* of the University College of Swansea, Wales. Among those who have intimate knowledge of current hydrologic investigations in Sudan, *A. M. Ibrahim* of the Ministry of Irrigation should be cited. Available maps can be obtained from the Survey Department or the Geological Survey, but the information on the current status of coverage of Sudan can be obtained from the U. S. AID office in Khartoum. This agency is engaged in a joint cartographic project with the Government of Sudan and is presently establishing a triangulation net for mapping of northeastern Sudan.

Egypt

Publications cited in the following text on Egypt, unless otherwise noted where cited, are listed in Section IV, Sahara, of the Pertinent Publications list.

Information on Egypt of relevance to some aspect of geomorphology is comparatively abundant. In order to avoid a prohibitively extensive list of citations here, it would be best to begin by mentioning certain sources from which further information can be obtained. Among such sources are the bibliography of geology by Keldani (1941) and the more recent bibliography by El Shazly (1957), lists of available publications by the Geological Survey, Cairo, and by the Desert Institute, El Matarîya, Cairo, and the basic works on the geology of the country by Hume (1925-1939) and, more recently, by Said (1962). Hydrologic data are largely supplied by the basic treatise on the Nile Basin (Hurst and Phillips, 1931, 1932, 1933a, b, 1938; Hurst and Black, 1944; Hurst, Black, and Simaika, 1946; Hurst, 1950) and supplements (Hurst, Simaika, and Black, 1953-1957), as previously noted. Additional information can be obtained from the monthly reports on the Hydrological Inspectorate, Nile Control Department, Cairo, Hurst's summary on the Nile (1952), and Simaika's discussion of the regime of flow in relation to the Aswân Dam project (1951) and subsequent studies (1954). In addition to the reports of the agencies noted above, two periodicals should be consulted, the Bulletin of the Royal Geographical Society (*Bulletin Société Royale Géographie d'Egypte*) and the Journal of Geology of the United Arab Republic, published by the Geological Society of the U.A.R.

Topographic mapping of Egypt has been accomplished on scales of 1:250,000 and 1:100,000; maps of larger scale (1:25,000) are available, but the coverage involved essentially pertains to the Nile drainage basin; large desert areas of Egypt are omitted. Mapping information can be obtained from the Geological Survey or the Desert Institute in Cairo, from the Directorate of Overseas Surveys, London, and from the Army Map Service, Washington. Worthy of special mention is the map of terrain analogs of Yuma in the northeast African desert (U.S. Army Engineer Waterways Experiment Station, 1962); no comparable compilation of data is available from other sources.

Because the arid zone of the Sahara completely embraces Egypt, reports on any section of the country are pertinent here. To begin this discussion by citing a few reports that are general in nature, the relatively popular articles on desert landscape by Mitwally (1953) and Hull (1955) might be noted. Additionally, Ascherson's early description of the Sinai peninsula (1887), Hume's physiographic reports (1914, 1921) and Ball's geographic notes (1939) each provide some useful information on the general terrain of the areas treated. Similarly, papers by Peel (1939), Bagnold *et al.* (1939), and Awad (1948) on the Gilf Kebir, King's (1913) description of the Farafra depression, the work of Ball (1933) and Said (1960) on the Qattâra depression, and the physiographic descriptions of the Nile Basin and adjacent areas by Lyons (1906), Attia (1951), and Schmitthenner (1931) may be profitably consulted.

One of the best general geomorphic descriptions of the landforms in southwestern Egypt has been provided by Peel (1941), who stressed the importance of basal sapping of cliffs during more humid periods in the evolution of the present landscape. This argument, which also was presented in his earlier work (Peel, 1939) on the Gilf Kebir, has much merit. Peel's reports also contain scattered data on rainfall, slope angles, and wadi dimensions, as well as several references to earlier work that are not cited here.

Among more recent reports are several valuable works on geomorphology. Dumanowski (1960) has offered few quantitative data on the evolution of slopes in Egypt, but his paper is worthy of note because of his emphasis on the importance of lithology. His assertion to the effect that the presence of certain rock types will result in particular types of hillslopes, under any climatic regime, is essentially correct but is seldom encountered in the Saharan literature. This author has also presented some qualitative observations on Egyptian wadis recently (Dumanowski, 1962). Other papers in this category include the description of physiographic features in the Western Desert by Mitwally (1953a), Awad's (1952) morphologic map of the Sinai peninsula, Mitwally's (1953b) report on the eastern part of this area, Shata's (1954, 1956) fine treatment of the Sinai desert area, and Amin's work on domal features in the Eastern Desert (1955).

Said (1954) has discussed the geomorphology near Helwân, but with the exception of pertinent data on such topics as weathering, dunes, and hydrology, which will be discussed later, the remaining geomorphic observations are largely contained in various geologic reports. Shata's review of the Jurassic rocks of Egypt (1951), structure of the Western Desert (1953), and other geologic studies (1955), Murray's (1952) report on Survey operations in the desert, papers on the geology of the Aswân (Rittman, 1953) and Cairo (Shukri, 1953b) areas, various stratigraphic studies (Farag and Shata, 1954; Mourad, 1954; Farag, 1955), and the petrologic investigations of granites near Aswân by Higazy and Wafsy (1956) each provide some descriptive information on the respective study areas. Additionally, reports on sedimentary mineralogy and petrology are available, and these also provide some useful information on terrain aspects, aside from the basic sedimentary and mineralogical data presented. Among such reports are papers by Shukri (1951) on the mineralogy of sediments from the Nile, Clayton's (1951) discussion of glass sands in the Libyan Desert, and other mineralogical studies by Shukri (1953a) and Shukri and Azer (1952).

Several papers on sand dunes in Egypt are available. Examples include the early description of dunes in the vicinity of the Nile delta by Cornish (1900) and Kamel's (1953) more recent treatment of dunes in the Khârga depression. Oliver (1945, with supplement 1947) has presented some relevant information in an interesting report on the relation of the frequency of dust storms and military activities in Egypt during the Second World War, Sanford (1953) considered dunes in relation to water supply, and Schwegler (1948b) treated coastal dunes of Lower Egypt in connection with a study of subaerial diagenesis. There is no literature available, however, on dune morphology for the country in its entirety.

Many studies of rock weathering have been conducted in Egypt because of the abundance of monuments or archeologic ruins of known age. Reports of such studies commonly provide some descriptive information on topography and geology and are thus pertinent here. As previously mentioned, however, most of the literature in this category will be cited in H. E. Dregne's chapter of this compendium, which treats soils of the arid regions. Walther (1877) offered one of the earliest papers on this subject in a treatment of chalk in the vicinity of the pyramids, and Schweinfurth and Lewin (1898) and Lucas (1905) also discussed aspects of rock weathering in Egypt. Hobbs (1918), Blanck and Passarge (1925), and Barton (1916) provided subsequent reports on weathering in the desert, but one of the first papers of some modern significance is that of Knetsch and Refai (1955). This report concerned microrelief and the weathering of monuments, and Knetsch (1960) has more recently provided a general treatment of rock weathering in Egypt with specific reference to cliffs along the Nile; additional references of interest may be found within his report. One final report in this vein that is worthy of note is Sidorenko's (1959) description of the occurrence of calcareous crusts in the desert areas.

Climatic changes and their consequences in Egypt have not been ignored. Murray (1949, 1951) has discussed desiccation and climate in Egypt today, Kassas and Imam (1957) have treated microclimatic environments in the desert, and Knetsch and Mazhar (1953) have presented deductions of climatic change from a study of subsurface drainage features and their associated water supply. The most excellent reports in this category, however, have been provided by Butzer (1958, 1959b), who discussed the general changes of Saharan landscape during historic time with many specific references to the Egyptian evidence.

Surface-water hydrology in Egypt pertains primarily to the Nile, of course, and the available information on this river has been previously cited. There are, however, additional reports that treat oases or the general hydrology of areas removed from the Nile Basin. Among these are Beadnell's (1909) early treatise, Huntington's (1910) description of the Khârga oasis, general papers on desert hydrology and ground water in Egypt, by Lowy (1954) and Attia (1954), respectively, Mitwally's (1951) discussion of the relation between artesian water supply and oases in the Western Desert and of the physiographic aspects of these oases (1953c), and Kaddah's (1954) outline of irrigation in the desert. In addition, three useful hydrological reconnaissance reports should be recommended here. Paver and Pretorius (1954a, b) have presented pertinent data on the hydrology of the Khârga and Dakhla oases and on the coastal zone of the Western Desert, and Paver and Jordan (1956) have provided similar treatment of the coastal area of northern Sinai. A study by El Gabaly (1954) of soils and agriculture in Sinai and the ecologic report of Tadros (1956) on the coastal area of the Western Desert are also of some relevance here by reason of the hydrologic aspects of these works, but Simaika's review articles (1953, 1962) on hydrologic research and aspects of water use in Egypt should be consulted for additional references.

Authorities

Among the many individuals who qualify as experts on geomorphology in Egypt, *A. Shata* should be cited here. He is an authority by virtue of his own work in the country but is, in addition, cognizant of all current and prospective research efforts because of his position, that of Director of the Desert Institute at El Matarîya. Information on surface-water hydrology in Egypt can also be obtained through his office; one division of the Desert Institute is devoted to this subject. *R. F. Peel* of the University of Bristol should also be cited here by reason of his specialization in Saharan geomorphology in general and his work in south-western Egypt (Peel, 1939, 1941).

As previously noted, the available information on Egypt was considered at this point in order to provide continuity with respect to the area drained by the Nile. To proceed with the country-by-country survey across the southern Saharan area, Chad will next be treated.

Chad

Publications cited in the following text on Chad, unless otherwise noted where cited, are listed in Section IV, Sahara, of the Pertinent Publications list.

The limits of the Sahara in Chad are defined by a zone which trends northeastward from Lake Chad to the Ennedi region. Thus, the northern half of the country is essentially within the arid zone. Little mapping has been undertaken in this area but the geologic map (Gerard, 1958) of the former French Equatorial Africa, on a scale of 1:2,000,000, includes Chad. Information on available aerial photography may be obtained from the Office de la Recherche Scientifique et Technique Outre-Mer, Paris, the Army Map Service, or the Branch of Military Geology of the U. S. Geological Survey, Washington. Information on current progress and future plans for both topographic and geologic mapping can be obtained from the Ministère des Travaux Publics in Fort Lamy.

Geomorphic investigations in Chad have been basically confined to three areas of interest: the Lake Chad region, the Tibesti massif, and the Ennedi plateau. The Tibesti massif, one of the major morphologic features of the central Saharan region, is located in northern Chad and extends into southern Libya. For purposes of convenience, the available literature on the Tibesti area will be summarized here in preference to treating those reports on northern Tibesti in the section of this report that deals with Libya. It would be well to state at the outset that although the rather meagre literature on the arid region of Chad will be reasonably well represented below, some additional references on the country can be obtained from the general African sources previously cited and from a bibliography of geology of the former French Equatorial Africa (Institut Equatorial de Recherches et d'Etudes Géologiques et Minières, 1961).

One of the earliest geographic accounts of the Tibesti area was provided by Tilho (1920), who also explored the Ennedi plateau and the intervening regions. Rottier (1928) visited the region in 1928 and subsequent expeditions by Dalloni (1934-1935), Thesiger (1939), Akester (1958), and Quézel (1958) produced a relatively good general description of various aspects of Tibesti; Quézel's report, for example, treated the flora that occur on the massif and its environs. In addition, Desio (1942b) and, more recently, Kanter (1963) have reported their observations from expeditions of 1942 and 1958, respectively. Lelubre (1946) has outlined the more prominent morphological and structural features of the northern part of the Tibesti massif, and Gèze *et al.* have discussed the Toussidé volcano on the southwest flank of the main massif (1957a) and the general stratigraphic relationships of the Tibesti volcanic rocks (1957b). The best geomorphic treatment of the Tibesti region has been provided by Grove (1960) in a report that includes geological maps, sections, photographs, some quantitative slope measurements, and a description of a flood that occurred during his field study.

Grove's conclusions are in general accord with modern concepts of the role of fluvial processes in the evolution of arid landscapes, but he raises the basic question of the extent to which certain features are relict, or not in adjustment with observable processes. The comments of Savigear, Savage, Peel, and Arkell, which were offered during a discussion of an oral presentation by Grove, are addressed to this point. These comments are included as an appendix to Grove's published report and are cited here because they also constitute a contribution to the available information on the geomorphology of arid regions.

The most recent contribution to general knowledge of the Tibesti region is the guidebook to geology and prehistory by the Petroleum Exploration Society of Libya (1966). In addition to nine papers that treat the geology and archeology of south-central Libya and northern Chad, the guidebook contains road logs and a regional geological map at a scale of 1:2,000,000.

The presence of Lake Chad on the southern fringe of the Sahara constitutes an equally prominent feature and, like the Tibesti massif, the lake and its basin have been the subject of several studies. Freydenburg (1908) provided a general description of the area in 1908; the recent hydrologic report by Bouchardeau (1956) and monograph on Lake Chad by Bouchardeau and Lefevre (1957) are basic works on the area. Pias (1958, 1960) and Pias and Guichard (1957), have made a valuable contribution to knowledge by reason of their reports on sedimentation and stratigraphy in the Chad Basin, and Grove (1959) and Grove and Pullan (1963) have mapped former shorelines in an effort to infer the paleogeography and paleohydrology of the Lake Chad area. These reports present evidence of climatic change in the Sahara in the form of expansion and contraction of the lake, which at its maximum stage may have covered an area of more than 100,000 square miles.

Pullan has recently (1964) provided a review paper on the geomorphic evolution of the south-central Chad Basin which summarizes the stratigraphy, geomorphic units, lake levels, and inferred chronology. This paper also provides some pertinent references to allied studies in northern Nigeria and Cameroon.

Reports on the surficial aspects of the Ennedi plateau area in northeastern Chad are not as abundant. Tilho's early-traveler account (1920) included this region and Dyer provided a popularized description of several canyons and watering locations in the Ennedi (Dyer, 1965, see Pert. Pubs. Sec. XIV). Two of the best hydrological reports on Chad discuss streamflow and runoff from the Ennedi plateau, however. These studies were undertaken in an attempt to gather basic surface-water data in a desert environment (Braquaval, 1957; Roche, 1958).

The remaining reports on the arid region of Chad include such early qualitative accounts as Urvoy's (1933) description of sand dunes in the western part of the country, the geologic outline of northern Chad by Douvillé and Tilho (1933), and the modern but brief consideration of the Bahr el Ghazal (Commission Scientifique du Logone et du Tchad, 1956), a major wadi that extends southwestward from central Chad to Lake Chad. Hydrologic reports that are of relevance here have essentially been cited above. The bulk of the work that has been done treats the Chari and Bahr Salamat drainage systems which occur in the nonarid, southern part of Chad. The aforementioned Ennedi studies of Braquaval and of Roche and the Commission's Bahr el Ghazal studies constitute some of the few happy exceptions to this generalization.

Authorities

Authorities on the geomorphology and surface-water hydrology of Chad should include *A. T. Grove* of Cambridge University and the personnel of ORSTOM and other French research groups that have participated in projects cited above.

Because a few reports which treat northern Nigeria are pertinent to the purposes of this report, these will be next discussed. Nigeria, however, is essentially south of the arid region proper; hence, the discussion that follows will be brief and will be restricted to the papers involved.

Nigeria

Although Nigeria is not within the arid zone, a few reports of studies within the country are of relevance here. Certain of these reports are illustrative of the applicability of aerial photography to geomorphology or the study of landforms. Publications cited in the following text on Nigeria, unless otherwise noted where cited, are listed in Section IV, Sahara, of the Pertinent Publications list.

Grove (1958) has used aerial photographs to study the ancient erg of Hausaland, which is a large area of fixed dune ridges of varying trend in northern Nigeria. His discussion includes similar dune fields which border the southern Sahara between the 150 mm and 1,000 mm isohyets. In addition to description of the sizes, shapes, and distribution of the dunes, Grove discusses the possible relationships between the erg and Quaternary climatic changes.

Dowling and Williams (1964*a, b*) have produced an excellent treatment of the use of aerial photographs in northern Nigeria to classify landforms and have tested the predictability of the method proposed. One may quarrel with the genetic assumptions that are involved in terming a terrain facet a "recently dissected peneplain," for example, but the demonstration of the differentiation of landforms and soils that can be achieved in the area is convincing.

Other reports on Nigeria that are of some interest here include the recent discussion of domes, inselbergs, and similar landforms by Thomas (1965), who argues for an origin of these features by differential weathering, Falconer's early treatment of the geology and geography of northern Nigeria (1911), Grove's discussion of patterned ground (1957), and Clayton's description of sand dunes (1957).

No authorities are cited for Nigeria, but the Dakar authorities listed under "Senegal" should be consulted.

Niger

Publications cited in the following text on Niger, unless otherwise noted where cited, are listed in Section IV, Sahara, of the Pertinent Publications list.

Approximately three-fourths of Niger lies within the arid zone in the south-central Sahara. The general geology of the country is shown on the map of the former French West Africa, discussed by Marvier (1953), and additional general information is provided in the encyclopedia on the Ivory Coast (Anonymous, 1960). Current investigations by the Service des Mines in Niamey are largely nongeomorphic, and a review of the available literature suggests that large areas of the country have not been studied in any detail.

Useful information on various aspects of geology, geomorphology, and surface-water hydrology does exist, however. Urvoy (1936) discussed the structure and surficial forms of the former French Sudan, which partially includes Niger, and also the basins of the Niger River (Urvoy, 1942). The Aïr massif in western Niger has been the subject of several investigations. IFAN (Institut Français d'Afrique Noire, 1950) provided general coverage and subsequently Dresch (1959) and, more recently, Vogt and Black (1963) have discussed the morphology of this prominent surficial feature. In addition, Lefevre (1960) has reported upon some excellent studies of runoff from this area.

Several reports treat some aspect of the features of the Niger Valley area in the extreme western part of the country. This area is semiarid, however, and need not be cited here. Hydrologic studies on the country have not been numerous but in addition to Lefevre's work (1960) and Dubief's general coverage of the Sahara (1953a, c), Rodier's survey of west Africa (1960) and the several ORSTOM reports on small drainage basins (Office de la Recherche Scientifique et Technique Outre-Mer, 1955-1960) provide some pertinent information. Relatively few hydrologic studies have been made within the arid zone proper, however.

Authorities

Hughes Faure, of IFAN, Dakar, has been one of the principal workers in Niger as evidenced by his papers on the structure of Ténéré (Faure, 1959) and the paleogeography (1962) and hydrogeology (1960-1961) of eastern Niger. The latter work is extremely useful, as is Faure's inventory of evaporites in the country (1964). He may be regarded as an authority on Niger for purposes of this report.

Mali

The arid portion of Mali is approximately bounded on the south by latitude 15°N, and most of the remainder of the country may be termed semiarid. Available information on the country is far more extensive than that on Niger, to the east. Publications cited in the following text on Mali, unless otherwise noted where cited, are listed in Section IV, Sahara, of the Pertinent Publications list. Brasseur's general bibliography on Mali (1964) is clearly one of the essential sources of information; it contains 4,902 entries and is, in part, briefly annotated. This bibliography treats source materials, including maps, and contains references to geologic, geomorphic, hydrologic, and geographic studies and to many topics not considered here, such as botany, archeology, history, agriculture, religion, and cultural and economic affairs. Any future investigation of available information on Mali might well begin with a consideration of this valuable work.

Two of the most striking physical features of Mali are the massifs and the marked change in the course of the Niger River. The principal massif is the Adrar des Iforas in northeastern Mali, which has been described by Capot-Rey (1951), among others. One of the much smaller massifs is that near Kita in semiarid western Mali; this area has been studied by Jaeger (1951), and Jaeger and Jarovoy (1952). The change of course of the Niger River in the south-central part of the country, however, has prompted numerous studies of the present and presumed former course of the Niger and of lesser streams as well. Reports on fossil drainage, which contain useful morphologic information, includes Urvoy's work on the basins of the Niger River (1936) previously cited, Chudeau's treatment (1921a) of the Saoura, Niger, Oued Igharghar, and Taffassasset drainages, and the biogeographic consequences of climatic change in the Sahara (1921b), Dars' (1957) discussion of drainage changes of the Baoulé River, northwest of Bamako, and consideration of former tributaries to the Niger in the vicinity of Tombouctou by Clos-Arceduc (1955).

The Niger River proper has been accorded similar treatment by Bélime (1931), Kervran (1959), Tricart (1959), who also discussed the Sénégal River (1955b) in the vicinity of Kayes in the far west of Mali, Palausi (1955), and Hubert (1911), among others. Additionally, Vogt (1962) has studied the Bagoé River, in the semiarid south of Mali.

Geomorphic studies of other subjects which are pertinent here include Daveau's (1959) fine report on the Bandiagara area, a general surficial-features description by Dresch (1953b), the earlier studies by

Chudeau of the Faguibine depression (1918) and hypsometric characteristics of the Tombouctou basin (1916), and descriptions of sand dunes in south-central Mali by Dufour (1936), Grandet (1957), and Prescott and White (1960). Tricart's report on Lake Faguibine (Tricart *et al.*, 1960) is also germane here because it includes a discussion of sand encroachment on the lake. One of the most outstanding works is the compendium by Monod (1958) on the Majâbat Al-Koubrâ, a vast area that extends from latitude 17°N to 22°N and from longitude 3°W to 12°W. Hence, the report treats much of west-central Mali and east-central Mauritania. The physical descriptions provided are good, and the report is replete with sketches of terrain features. It also contains approximately 40 aerial photographs of various types of sand dunes that occur in the region. No comparable work exists on the Majâbat, which Monod has aptly termed the "empty quarter."

With respect to geological investigations, more than 200 references to work in Mali are listed in Brasseur's bibliography (1964), and this compilation is not all-inclusive. As previously stated on several occasions in this report, geologic studies will often encompass certain surficial aspects of a given area and, therefore, should be considered as potential sources of information on the landforms as well as on the bedrock geology. Examples of a few of the more useful works on Mali in this respect include Karpoff's treatment of the Adrar des Iforas (1960a, b), Radier's general coverage of the eastern part of the country (1959), Byramjee's discussion of volcanic rocks (1958, 1959), Blanchot's reports on reconnaissance missions to Taoudenni (1956a) and Tessalit (1956b) in northern Mali, Monod's observations (1952b) between 1935 and 1951 in western Mali, and the annual reports on French West Africa which can be obtained in Dakar.

Certain reports of a hydrologic nature have been cited above, because treatment of the river courses belongs, in part, to this category. Climatic data for most of west Africa are assembled and published by personnel in Dakar, to be discussed, and Dubief's general works (1953a, c) are again of pertinence in considering Mali. The ORSTOM reports on small drainage basins (Office de la Recherche Scientifique et Technique Outre Mer, 1955-1960) include observations on the Tin Adjar and Koumbaki basins in the country and a few additional reports are of some relevance here. Among these are Frowlow's treatment of the lakes of the Niger (1940a) and on the regime, profile, and meteorological conditions that prevail along the course of the Niger in Mali (Frowlow, 1934, 1936, 1940b, 1941). A more recent series of hydrologic reports on the river is also available

(Anonymous, 1953, 1955; Office de la Recherche Scientifique et Technique Outre Mer, 1953; Auvray, Dubreuil, and Lefevre, 1958-1961). Among these works that by Auvray, Dubreuil, and Lefevre (1958-1961) is clearly the most comprehensive with respect to the characteristics and regime of the river.

The availability of information on Mali, and on the southern Sahara in general, may best be indicated by a consideration of sources of information in Dakar. For this reason, as previously stated, a section on Senegal is presented below. Authorities and depositories for Mali are listed there.

Senegal

Publications cited in the following text on Senegal, unless otherwise noted where cited, are listed in Section IV, Sahara, of the Pertinent Publications list.

A veritable wealth of information on the southern and western Sahara exists in Dakar, as might be surmised by consideration of certain references previously cited for Niger (Institut Français d'Afrique Noire, 1950) and Mali (Brasseur, 1964; Monod, 1958). The Institut Fondamental d'Afrique Noire (formerly Institut Français d'Afrique Noire) should unquestionably be considered a major depository for purposes of this report. Publications of relevance that are issued by IFAN include the following:

> *Bulletin de l'IFAN*, Série A, Dakar
> *Mémoires de l'IFAN*, Dakar
> *Mémoires du Comité d'Etudes Historiques et Scientifiques de L'AOF*, Dakar
> *Catalogues et Documents*, Dakar
> *Notes Africaines*, Dakar (quarterly)
> Association Senegalaise pour l'Etude du Quaternaire de l'Ouest Africain, *Bulletin de Liaison*, Dakar

In addition, various reports and maps of the Bureau de Recherches Géologiques et Minières (BRGM) and other organizations are available in Dakar or through the Association des Services Géologiques Africains or BRGM in Paris. These are as follows:

> *Bulletin du Service des Mines de l'AOF,* Dakar
> *Bulletin de la Direction des Mines de l'AOF,* Dakar
> *Bulletin de la Direction Fédérale des Mines et de la Géologie,* Dakar
> *Bulletin du Service de Géologie et de Prospection Minière,* Dakar
> *Rapport Annuel du Service Géologique,* Dakar
> *Rapport Annuel de la Direction Fédérale des Mines et de la Géologie,* Dakar
> *Rapport Annuel de Service de Géologie et de Prospection Minière,* Dakar

Rapport Annuel du Bureau de Recherches Géologiques et Minières, Dakar

BRGM, Notice Explicative et Cartes Géologiques, Dakar

Notes du Service de Géologie et de Prospection Minière, Dakar

Notes du Bureau de Recherches Géologiques et Miniéres, Dakar

The BRGM in Paris also issues bibliographic data on cards, the "Codification des Fischers Bibliographiques, Service d'Information Géologique," which are classified by subject. The subjects are not restricted to work on the Sahara, or on arid regions, but some useful references can be obtained from this source.

Authorities

Several authorities on the southern and western Sahara are resident in Dakar. Among these are *Hughes Faure* and professors *Charles Toupet* and *Henri Hugot* of IFAN. Faure has engaged in geologic mapping in the Sahara and can provide information on the availability of topographic and geologic maps and aerial photography. Toupet has studied Quaternary stratigraphy and geomorphology in Mali and Mauritania and is currently engaged in the mapping of drainage and surficial features from aerial photographs. He is also a participant in an important current project of IFAN, namely the preparation of a climatic atlas for west Africa. Hugot is expert on archeology and prehistory of the entire southern Sahara and has travelled extensively in many regions of interest in this report. Finally, *Theodore Monod,* the founder of the Institute and former director, must be considered an outstanding authority on all aspects of the surficial features of the western Sahara. His work in this region has occupied more than twenty years and his publications are far more numerous than those selected for citation in this report.

This discussion of available information will next treat Mauritania. The activity in that country of personnel based in Dakar will be apparent.

Mauritania

Publications cited in the following text on Mauritania, unless otherwise noted where cited, are listed in Section IV, Sahara, of the Pertinent Publications list.

Mauritania is wholly within the arid zone of the Sahara save for the southernmost part of the country, where a relatively narrow belt is semiarid. The general geology of the country is shown on the map of the former French West Africa (Marvier, 1953), and McGill's map of coastal landforms (1958, see Pert. Pubs. Sec. I) is again of relevance because the Sahara abuts the Atlantic Ocean along the Mauritanian coast. Topographic maps for most of west Africa are available through IFAN or BRGM in Dakar (see Senegal, above). The coverage, on a scale of 1:200,000, is essentially complete for western Mauritania, but only a few scattered sheets represent the eastern half of the country. For this reason, Monod's work on the Majâbat Al Koubrâ (1958), which includes a large part of this unmapped area, is again of significance. A supplement (Monod, 1961) to this work should also be noted here.

Early reports of travels in Mauritania include those of Gruvel and Chudeau (1909) and subsequent geological descriptions by the latter author (Chudeau, 1909, 1911). Papers of more recent years are far more relevant, however. Tricart has provided geomorphic descriptions of the Adrar (1955a) and the erg of Trarza (1960), and with Brochu (Tricart and Brochu, 1955) has produced a more detailed study of this Mauritanian dune field. Vache-Grandet (1959) has also treated the geomorphology of sand dunes, and Vincent-Cuaz (1958) and Coursin *et al.* (1956) have specifically considered barchan dunes. Coursin's study area was near Port Etienne at the northern end of the coast of Mauritania. Additional work on these coastal features was conducted by Guilcher (1954). More recently, Daveau (1963, 1964) has studied the slopes of the Adrar of Mauritania, which are quite sandy and may be mentioned in this context.

Other reports of note include the study of plains and inselbergs by Dresch (1961), several papers on the landform at El Richat (Richard-Molard, 1948, 1952; Cailleux, 1962), outlines of Quaternary stratigraphy by Dubois and Tricart (1954) and Elouard and Michel (1958), and Bense's fine thesis (1961) on the sedimentary rocks of northwestern Mali and southern Mauritania. Monod has outlined the general structural features of western Mauritania (1945) and has provided additional geologic and structural information on the Adrar of Mauritania (Monod, 1949, 1950; 1952a). Each of these reports provides some pertinent information, as do the more standard geologic reports on Mauritania. References to the latter can be obtained from a general bibliography on Mauritania by Toupet (1962). This work, like that on Mali by Brasseur (1964), is extremely useful and should be consulted for further information.

With respect to surface-water hydrology, several references previously provided for the western Sahara are again relevant. Additional work that specifically treats areas in Mauritania includes Thomas' summary of precipitation from 1920-1949 (1954), hydrogeologic studies near the Adrar by Trompette (1961) and Monod (1956), Elouard's work on the Oued Seguelil (1959), and several fine studies, which include maps, by Lelong (1960) and Lermuzeaux

(1958*a, b;* 1960). The ORSTOM reports on small drainage basins that are of specific interest here are on investigations in the Moudjéria region (Office de la Recherche Scientifique et Technique Outre-Mer, 1957; 1960*a, b*) in southcentral Mauritania.

Authorities

Authorities on various aspects of surficial features in Mauritania are, as previously mentioned, mostly resident in Dakar. In addition, *J. Tricart* of the University of Strasbourg and the personnel of the Service Géologique in Nouakchott may profitably be consulted. Depository and source information has been furnished under "Senegal."

Spanish Sahara

Spanish Sahara is wholly within the arid zone and its coastline extends along the Atlantic from Mauritania on the south to the Morocco frontier on the north. Hence, McGill's treatment of coastal landforms of the world (1958, see Pert. Pubs. Sec I) is again germane. Reports that treat Africa or large parts of the Sahara contain little relevant information on Spanish Sahara, however. Furon's compendium on the geology of Africa (1960, see Pert. Pubs. Sec II), for example, does not provide much coverage of the area even though the Canary Islands are included in this work. The African résumé by Dixey (1963, see Pert. Pubs. Sec. II) cites a bibliography on Spanish Guinea and Spanish Sahara that was prepared by Señor Antonio Almela of the Instituto Geológico y Minero de España in Madrid. This would seemingly be one of the better sources of information on the country but the writer has not seen this bibliography and cannot vouch for its content. Publications cited in the following text on Spanish Sahara, unless otherwise noted where cited, are listed in Section IV, Sahara, of the Pertinent Publications list. The best regional survey available is that by Hernández-Pacheco *et al.* (1949), who studied the geology, geography, and flora of Spanish Sahara.

Only a few pertinent references on Spanish Sahara were encountered in the course of the investigation for this report. It is likely that more information exists, however, and it is recommended that users of this report contact the Spanish authorities in Madrid to obtain Almela's bibliography and references to work accomplished during recent years.

An early outline of the geology of the Spanish Sahara was provided by Font y Sague (1911), and Busch-Zantner (1934) and Hernández-Pacheco (1941) subsequently reported on some aspects of the surficial features of the country. Alia Medina (1946, 1952) discussed the geologic structure of Spanish Sahara, Arévalo and Arribas (1960) studied the mineralogy of Quaternary deposits in the southwest part of the country, and Arribas (1960) treated the metamorphic rocks of the area. Each of these papers contain some useful information, but the general geology and structure can best be seen on the geologic map of the Spanish Sahara (Spain, Instituto Geológico y Minero de España, 1958).

The climatic conditions in this part of the Sahara have been reported by Font Tullot (1955) and several hydrologic reports are available. The discussion of wells and ground water by Gómez (1959) is fairly comprehensive, but some information on surface-water conditions has been provided by Alia Medina (1943) and, more recently, by Flores (1951).

Authorities and Depositories

Consejo Superior de Investigaciones Científicas and Instituto Geológico y Minero de España should be considered depositories for this country. No authorities are named, other than those already listed under "Senegal."

Morocco

Most of Morocco can be classified as arid or semi-arid, with the exception of a more equable belt that extends along the coast roughly from Casablanca to Tangier then inland toward the Algerian border. The Atlas Mountains range in elevation to more than 13,000 feet and, as is true of Tibesti and other Saharan massifs, are not truly arid because of orographic controls on precipitation. For the purposes of this report, however, work that has been done in such areas of Morocco will be included in the summary of available information given below. Publications cited in the following text on Morocco, unless otherwise noted where cited, are listed in Section IV, Sahara, of the Pertinent Publications list.

Dixey and Emberger (1962) have reported on some relatively recent work in the arid zone of Morocco, but a review of the literature demonstrates that relevant geomorphic investigations have been conducted since the 1920's. Representative of some of this early work are papers by Joleaud (1926) and Jaranoff (1936) on the geomorphology and historical development of that part of Morocco which borders the Atlantic Ocean and Bourcart's (1927) outline of the Quaternary of Morocco. More recent reports, which treat fairly large parts of the country, have been provided by Kochli (1950), who gave a geographic description of southern Morocco, by Dresch (1952) and Dresch *et al.* (1952), the latter being a comprehensive monograph on the geomorphology of most of the country, and by Awad (1963), who related the geomorphic features to Quaternary climates and climatic change. In addition, Choubert's treatment of the geology of Morocco (Choubert, 1952), with specific reference to the Anti Atlas region, and several reports (Morocco, Service Géologique, 1952*a;* Morin, 1960) on mineral resources in the country also provide useful information on surficial features.

Geomorphic reports on the mountainous areas of Morocco have been provided in recent years by Dresch (1941), Joly (1952*a*, 1962), Birot and Joly (1951), and Mensching (1955), among others, and each of these papers contains some useful data in terms of maps, descriptions, photographs, or measurements of mountain landforms of the Atlas, Anti Atlas, or other ranges of the country. Additional information on slopes and landforms can be obtained from Joly's report on pediments (1949), Beaudet's treatment of slopes and slope evolution in the western Rif (Beaudet, 1962), a discussion of hamadas by Joly (1952*b*), and of plains and other gently sloping surfaces by Gigout (1951), and by Mensching and Raynal (1954). Morphologic descriptions of the Moulouya and Doukkala regions by Raynal (1952*a, b*) and Choubert (1955), respectively, are also of interest in this context. Finally, Ruellan's work on the application of geomorphology to a soil survey in Morocco (Ruellan, 1962) and Wilbert's discussion of calcareous crusts in the country (1962) should be mentioned here, although these topics will be covered in the chapter on soils of the arid regions by H. E. Dregne.

Several useful reports on the surface-water hydrology of Morocco are available in addition to the general hydrologic references for the Sahara and west Africa which have been cited previously in this report. Monographs are available on the hydrogeology of the country (Morocco, Service Géologique, 1952*b*) and on the Wadi Souss (L'Excellent, n.d.), and the Wadi Sebou (Sauvage de Saint-Marc, 1948), Wadi Draa (Robaux, 1951), and Wadi Ouegha (Roederer, 1954) have also been treated by several authors. Many data have been published by Moroccan organizations, to be cited below, but other papers of interest with respect to surface-water hydrology include Joly's treatment of drainage in the Algerian border area (1953), a recent study of the Oumer Rbia river by Loup (1962), and an interesting discussion of the effects of a severe storm in 1963 in the Atlas Mountains by Elk and Mathieu (1963).

Precipitation data for Morocco have been published by the Institut Scientifique Chérifien (1955), Gaussen, Debrach, and Joly (1958), and by Roux (1943). Combined with the information on evaporation rates in the country, provided by Emon (1957) and Mougin (1956), these data are quite pertinent for consideration of potential surface runoff in Morocco.

Depositories

Organizations in Morocco that can supply additional hydrologic information include the Service Météorologique, at Casablanca-Cazés ("Annales"); Service de Physique du Globe et de Météorologie at Casablanca (Statistique Pluviométriques, or Hydrologic statistics); and Travaux Publics du Maroc, at Rabat (*Hydrologie Marocaine,* or Moroccan hydrology).

Geologic maps of Morocco are available at scales of 1:2,000,000 (International Geological Congress, 19th, Algiers, 1952), 1:500,000, and, for certain parts of the country, at 1:200,000. Information on the availability of geologic maps can be obtained in Rabat from the Direction des Mines et de la Géologie, Institut Scientifique Chérifien, or the Université de Rabat. Information on topographic maps can also be obtained from these sources or through the Institut Géographique National, Moroccan Branch, in Paris. Coverage is provided on scales of 1:200,000, 1:100,000, and 1:50,000 and larger. In general, large-scale mapping is available in the vicinity of the coastal region of Morocco and small-scale maps cover the interior of the country.

Other Sources

In addition to the varied sources and periodicals which are represented by the reports cited above, a number of standard publications should be mentioned here. Each provides a source for papers that treat some aspect of physical features. The Société des Sciences Naturelles et Physiques du Maroc, at Rabat, publishes "Bulletins," "Mémoires," and other works of considerable interest; and papers of the Société de Géographie du Maroc, Institut Scientifique Chérifien, Service Géologique du Maroc, and Direction des Mines et de la Géologie, all at Rabat, should all be consulted.

Authorities

Additional information may be obtained from *Hassan Awad* of the Arid Zone Commission of the International Geographical Union, Rabat.

Algeria

Algeria encompasses a large part of the northwestern Sahara; the entire region between the Atlas Mountains and the southern boundaries of the country, near the Adrar des Iforas and Aïr massifs, is within the arid zone. Three vast sandfields occur in the country, namely the Grand Erg Occidental, the Grand Erg Oriental, and Erg Chech, although the latter is shared with Mali to the southwest, and one of the principal Saharan massifs, the Ahaggar. In addition, Algeria exhibits a fair sample of plains, hamadas, inselbergs, and other desert landforms typical of the Sahara. The presence of these features, combined with historical reasons, has served to yield a considerable volume of literature on the arid region of Algeria. It is therefore pertinent to remind the interested reader of this report once again that citations provided here are not intended to be all-inclusive but, rather, to serve as a guide to the work that has been done. Publications cited in the following text on Algeria, unless otherwise noted where cited, are listed in Section IV, Sahara, of the Pertinent Publications list.

Reference should be made to the work cited in Section 2 above of this report (entitled *The Sahara);* many of the works cited there are relevant to Algeria. The forthcoming compendium on the Sahara which will be edited by Professor Schiffers of the University of Cologne should also be consulted. Three additional works of a general nature that are worthy of consideration with respect to Algeria are Smith's report on eolian phenomena in north Africa (1963), the excellent folio report on Yuma analogs in northwest Africa (U. S. Army Engineer Waterways Experiment Station, 1958; Van Lopik, Kolb, and Shamburger, 1965), and Alimen's recent review paper on Quaternary research in the northwestern Sahara (Alimen, 1965).

Among the abundant geomorphic or geographic papers on Algeria, those by Passarge (1909), Bernard (1910), Flamand (1911), and Schirmer (1912) are illustrative of early treatments and Gautier's description of the Ahaggar (1926) may also be considered in this category. The caliber of more recent work can best be discerned by consideration of the publications of the Institut de Recherches Sahariennes. In addition to the reports of this organization that were previously cited, a sampling of pertinent publications should include the morphological descriptions of the western erg (Capot-Rey, 1943) and the Libyan border region (Capot-Rey, 1953a), the Ougarta mountainous area (Dresch, 1953a; Grandet, 1956), and the central Saharan region by Birot, Capot-Rey, and Dresch (1955). In addition, the description of the Arbaa Plateau area by Estorges (1959, 1961) and Rognon's several geomorphic reports (1960a, 1962, 1963, 1964) also appeared in papers of the Institut.

Much geomorphic information can be obtained from other sources, however. Brosset (1939) and Vogt (1952) have discussed the ergs and morphological evolution of the western Sahara in general. Perret (1952), Büdel (1955), and Côte (1957) have treated various aspects of the Ahaggar massif, as did Davies (1955; 1956a, b), who used aerial photographs to aid in determination of geology and

structure. Capot-Rey (1927, 1945), Menchikoff (1930), Despois (1942), Caire (1954, 1963), Perret (1938, 1953), Tinthoin (1948), Cailleux (1949), and Benchetrit (1954) have treated a wide variety of regions and landforms and in each case have provided some pertinent descriptive information.

The problem of wind action, eolian landforms, and the grain-size distributions of dunes and other sand deposits have been treated by several authors. In addition to work in this vein that has been accomplished by Aufrère, Capot-Rey, and others previously cited in the introductory discussion of the Sahara, Dubief (1943, 1953b), Capot-Rey and Grémion (1964), and particularly Alimen et al. (1957) have added to our knowledge of the general relationships between wind and sand in Algeria and of the areal distribution of the several sand bodies. Alimen has also studied the size distribution of dune sand in western Algeria (1953), and with others (Alimen and Fenet, 1954; Alimen, Buron, and Chavaillon, 1958) has extended her investigations in this area. Other pertinent reports in this field of interest include Grandet's description of dune morphology near Beni Abbès (1955), Capot-Rey's discussion of the possible effects of wind erosion (1957), a good paper on the dunes of In Salah by Verlaque (1958), consideration of the hydrologic role of dunes in terms of water supply by Cvijanovich (1953), and Boulaine's description of eolian deposits that occur in conjunction with the Ben Ziane sebkha (1956).

This latter interrelationship, namely the occurrence of sebkhas, saline soils, and eolian deposits, is quite common in the deserts of the world generally and considerable work on several aspects of this association has been undertaken in Algeria. Durand (1954) has provided the fundamental information on soils and their distribution in Algeria and has also treated the problem of the formation of gypsiferous (1949) and calcareous (1951) crusts and their hydrological properties (1953). The formation of crusts has also been discussed by Dalloni (1951) and by Gautier, Laffitte, and Flandrin (1948) among others, but Boulaine's (1953a) treatment of the erosion of saline soils by wind action and the resultant morphology of sebkhas and Gautier's (1953) emphasis on the importance of wind as an evaporative agent that acts on saline lakes are typical of reports within this area of interest.

Many reports of a geological nature that provide general descriptive information on surficial features also exist in the literature. Bütler (1922) and Lelubre (1939, 1940, 1943), for example, have provided information on the Ahaggar massif, Anderson (1936) has treated part of the Atlas range, Boulaine (1953b) has discussed Quaternary rocks in Algeria, and Caire

(1957), and many others, have published geologic reports of individual regions or areas in the country. Becker's (1965) recent note on patterned ground in the Ahaggar area might also be mentioned here. Further information on available geological reports can be obtained in Savornin's (1931) work which covers Algerian geology from 1830 to 1930, in the *Bulletin de l'Algerie* No. 5 of 1954 which includes bibliographies for economic geology and hydrology, from the explanatory notices which accompany geological maps of Algeria, and from BRGM in Paris or the publications of the Service de la Carte Géologique de l'Algérie at Algiers. Each of these organizations has published a geological map of the Sahara (Algeria, Service de la Carte Géologique de l'Algérie, n.d.; France, Bureau de Recherches Géologiques et Minières, 1961). A map of Algeria alone is also available (Algeria, Service . . ., 1952). Basic geological mapping at a scale of 1:50,000 is being pursued, but the work is not yet completed.

Certain available information on surface-water hydrology has been cited previously. Particularly noteworthy are the several reports by Dubief (1959; 1953*a*, *c*) and the ORSTOM investigations of small drainage basins (Office de la Recherche Scientifique et Technique Outre-Mer, 1955-1960). In addition, Drouhin's (1952) discussion of west-African water problems and Rodier's general treatment of hydrologic regimes (1960) are quite pertinent here. Other reports which may profitably be consulted include Schoeller's work on the hydrogeology of the western erg (1945), a subsequent treatment by Cornet (1952), Vanney's (1960) research on precipitation and plant growth relationships, the climatic treatises on Algeria by Dubief and Lauriol (1943) and by Seltzer (1946), and Fournier's (1957) general discussion of soil erosion via surface runoff.

Also available is a map showing the mean annual precipitation for the 1913-1947 period (Gaussen and Bagnouls, 1948), and hydrologic studies of the Wadi Isser (Cardona, 1954-1955), Wadi Saoura (Deleau, 1957), the Mafragh basin (Samie, 1956-1957), and the upper Medjerda region (Samie, 1954). Similar reports can be obtained from the Institut de Météorologie et de Physique du Globe de l'Algérie and the Service des Etudes Scientifiques, both in Algiers. Particularly, the *Annuaire Hydrologique de l'Algérie* should be consulted; many pertinent reports on surface-water hydrology have been published in this journal.

Authorities and Depositories

Among the numerous individuals who qualify as authorities on research efforts in Algeria, *J. Dresch* and *R. Capot-Rey,* of the Institut de Géographie, Paris, and the Université d'Alger, respectively, and *Henriette Alimen,* of the Laboratory for Quaternary Geology, National Scientific Research Center, Bellevue, France, should be cited here. *J. Rodier,* Chef du Service Hydrologique, ORSTOM, is clearly an authority on surface-water hydrology who may profitably be consulted on Algeria or on other countries in the Sahara. The Institut de Recherches Sahariennes (Université d'Alger) is considered the primary local depository for Algeria.

Tunisia

Publications cited in the following text on Tunisia, unless otherwise noted where cited, are listed in Section IV, Sahara, of the Pertinent Publications list.

With the exception of the semiarid to semihumid coastal belt that extends across the northern part of Tunisia, the remainder of the country is within the arid zone of the Sahara. As is true of other countries, one finds that far more work has been done on the nonarid regions and that mapping is generally available at larger scales in these areas. Tunisia is relatively well mapped, however. Topographic maps (on a scale of 1:100,000 and 1:50,000) are available through the Institut Géographique National, Paris, and the basic geological map by Castany (1951, 1953) is available at a scale of 1:500,000. Some additional geological maps at scales of 1:200,000 and 1:50,000 can be obtained through the Service des Mines, Tunis.

Among the reports of physical features in the arid part of Tunisia are several of some interest here. Tixeront and Berkaloff (1954*a*) have described erosion studies and problems, Coque has provided information on the morphology of the large gravel plains (1955*a*) and gypsiferous crusts (1955*b*, *c*) in southern Tunisia, and with Van Campo (Coque and Van Campo, 1960) has more recently given a geomorphic account of an area containing pollen-bearing units. Zimmerman (1963) has also treated the southern gravel areas but Mensching's work (1963, 1964) on Tunisian geomorphology represents the best and most recent outline available. This author has discussed the principal landforms of the southern part of the country, namely the scarps, terraces, wadis, and plains, and has given the usual climatic explanations for these observed features. Additional reports of some relevance are available on the northern part of the country, although they refer to areas that are not entirely within the arid zone. In this category, papers by Jauzein (1959) on alluvial terraces, by Coque on slope evolution (1960) and general morphology (1958, 1962), and by Giessner on the Tunisian ridge (1964) are worthy of examination.

Reports that treat some aspect of surface-water hydrology in Tunisia are fairly abundant and in addition to those cited here, the published papers and statistics of the Service Météorologique and Bureau d'Inventaire des Ressources Hydrauliques (BIRH) in Tunis should be consulted. The hydrologic compilations edited by Berkaloff (1949-1959) and published by BIRH are particularly important.

Tixeront and Berkaloff (1958a) have provided a map of the annual runoff in Tunisia. They have expanded upon the runoff problem (1958b) in the country and also provided an outline of research on the water balance (1954b) in subsequent years. Studies of the hydrology of wadis in Tunisia include the report of the Compagnie des Techniques Hydrauliques Agricoles (1957) on wadis Zeroud and Merguellil, de Montmarin's (1952) treatment of wadis Ellil and Rhezala, and Sogréah reports on wadis Nebana (1957) and Bel Assoud (1959). Although these drainages are not entirely within the arid zone proper, the studies cited have provided either data or principles that are applicable to washes elsewhere in Tunisia.

No local authorities are listed for Tunisia, but those cited for Algeria, above, may be consulted profitably.

Libya

Libya can be treated as entirely arid; the sole exception to this generalization is a small coastal area east of the Gulf of Sirte. With regard to available information, it should be mentioned at the outset that certain Saharan landforms do not coincide with national boundaries and reports that were previously cited on eastern Algeria, the Tibesti massif in Chad, and on western Egypt, should be added to those provided below. Publications cited in the following text on Libya, unless otherwise noted where cited, are listed in Section IV, Sahara, of the Pertinent Publications list.

Topographic maps of Libya are available at several scales, generally 1:200,000 or smaller, from the Army Map Service, Washington; Institut de Recherches Sahariennes, Algiers; and the Military Geography Institute, Florence. The latter can provide maps of larger scale of the cities and coastal areas, but the interior and southern parts of Libya are, in general, not adequately covered. Geologic maps have been provided by Desio (1942c) and the Tripoli Museum (Tripoli, Museo Libico di Storia Naturale, 1939) in Tripoli, among others, but the most recent coverage of the country is given on the map compiled by Conant and Goudarzi (1964) at a scale of 1:2,000,000. This map also lists the sources for the compilation. Maps of local areas at larger

scales are available from the Geological and Mining Services in Tripoli and from geological reports of diverse character. Lastly, maps of a general nature, such as that of northern Africa by Raisz (1952, see Pert. Pubs. Sec. I) and the coastal landform map by McGill (1958, see Pert. Pubs. Sec. I), are also useful with respect to Libya and should be consulted.

Before considering the information on the physical features of Libya that is available through individual papers and reports, two bibliographic sources should be mentioned. The Tripoli Museo Libico di Storia Naturale (1939-1953) issued four volumes that provide a bibliography of work through 1952 in addition to a general discussion of various physical features of Libya. The second Libyan bibliography was compiled by Hill (1959). Both bibliographies are quite useful and contain references to many works that are not cited here.

Papers and reports that provide descriptions of some aspect of the geomorphology or geology of Libya first appeared prior to 1900. Some confusion arises with respect to the areas treated by these early reports and, indeed, by more recent papers as well. In many instances the usages of "Libyan desert," or its German equivalent, "libyschen Wüste," refers to a physiographic feature such as the Great Sand Sea which extends from Libya into the Western Desert of Egypt. Similarly, reports on "the Western Desert" may pertain to some area which is geographically within Libya. Division of citations for purposes of this country-by-country treatment was, necessarily, somewhat arbitrary, but those reports cited here can be assumed to pertain either to Libya proper or to some physiographic feature that is not far removed from the border but which actually occurs in Egypt.

Among the early reports, those considered to provide some useful information include Jordan's work on geography and meteorology (1876), geological papers by von Zittel (1880), Gregory (1911), and Leuchs (1913), and descriptions of landforms in Tripolitani and desert exploration by Witschell (1928) and Kemal el-Dine (1928), respectively. The discussion of desert problems by Ball (1927) and the observations of Sandford (1933) and Crema (1936) are also germane in this context. Desio (1935, 1939, 1942a, 1953) has made several contributions to knowledge of Libyan morphology and geology since 1935 and most recently he has collaborated with others to produce an authoritative work on stratigraphy in Libya (Desio et al., 1963). This latter report also contains information on petrology and physical features. Aside from the work of Desio, papers on structure and morphology by Lipparini (1940), Pfalz (1940), Awad (1945), Knetsch (1950), and Little (1945) are representative of the pertinent literature between 1940 and 1950. The last report, on the geology of Cyrenaica, has been superseded to some extent by the map of Conant and Goudarzi (1964) but is still worth consulting for detailed information on this province.

Since 1950 a number of important reports have been published. Müller-Fuega's (1954) treatise on the geology and hydrology of the Fezzan is a basic reference for this region, and the Saharan Symposium sponsored by the Petroleum Exploration Society of Libya (1963) produced a wealth of useful information. The field trip guide books to Jebel Nefusa and other areas should also be consulted. The research and occasional papers of the Department of Geography, University of Durham, also constitute a valuable source of data on the arid zone of Libya. One example has already been cited, the Libyan bibliography by Hill (1959). Of equal merit in this series is the compilation of field studies in Libya by Willimott and Clarke (1960) and an evaluation of morphometric methods by Clarke and Orrell (1958).

Much basic information on the effects of climatic change in Libya is also available. A text on the prehistory of Cyrenaica (McBurney and Hey, 1955) is a good guide to the literature and further information can be obtained from a series of papers by Hey (1956a, b; 1962, 1963) who has treated the archeologic and physical evidence of climatic changes from studies of shorelines and, most recently, from scree deposits on limestone cliffs in northern Cyrenaica. Within this general context, Moseley's (1965) work on calcrete deposits and cemented dune sands should also be consulted.

One of the best modern geomorphic reports is a paper by Williams and Hall (1965) on the Jebel Arkenu, which is just northwest of 'Uweinat on the Libya-Sudan-Egypt boundaries. Although the Jebel Arkenu is a relatively minute feature in comparison to the Libyan desert as a whole, important quantitative data on the relation of slope angles and lithology are provided. Additionally, drainage and sand features in the area are depicted on maps, wadi dimensions are given, and a chronology of events based on archeologic evidence is discussed. Many useful references on the Arkenu-'Uweinat area, and on Libya and the Sahara in general, are included. In a similar vein, Vita-Finzi has published a number of excellent reports on alluvial chronology in Libya, which particularly treat the evidence of changes since the Roman occupation of medieval time (Vita-Finzi, 1960a, b; 1961a; 1963); his monograph (1961b) on the recent history of the eastern Jebel in Tripolitania should also be consulted.

With respect to dune sand and wind action, areas of Libya, particularly the Great Sand Sea extending into the Western Desert of Egypt, have not been ignored. Reference should again be made to some of the general papers treating these topics in the Sahara but in addition the early work of Beadnell (1910) and Walther (1911), Rathjens' discussion of loess in Tripolitania (1928), Kadar's description of the Great Sand Sea (1934), and Bagnold's early desert observations (1933, 1937) and basic treatise on windblown sand (1941) are all pertinent here. In addition, Leone (1953) has provided an outline of reclamation problems in the dune area of Tripolitania and McKee and Tibbitts (1964) have recently investigated sedimentary structures in Libyan sand dunes. Another work in a similar vein that should be noted is the recent investigation of hamadas, serirs, and ergs in the Fezzan by Fürst (1965), which contains many grain-size analyses of the surficial deposits and photographs of the general features.

The general hydrology of Cyrenaica was discussed by Marchetti (1938) in a report which treated water-table elevations and the discharges of springs in Libya. The numbers of springs and wells in the country are listed in the recent Census of Agriculture (Libya, Ministry of Agriculture, 1962), which is an extremely valuable source of information despite the fact that the margin of error of such estimates may be great. Ground water hydrology is not within the scope of this report, but two papers on this topic are nevertheless germane, namely those by Van Everdingen (1962) and Jones (1964). The pertinence of these papers stems from the fact that both include water-table maps; the report by Jones, in fact, treats this matter exclusively. Some topographic data can be obtained by inference, given knowledge of the depth of subsurface water, and in the vast arid reaches of the country where topographic control is poor such inference may be useful.

Surface-water hydrology proper, however, has been discussed by Bellair (1944), who treated the water resources of the Fezzan, Dagallier (1955), who reported on the hydrologic data obtained on the Wadi Megenin, and Marchand (1957), who considered potential flood danger along Wadi El Hira. In this vein, the recent description of the effects of intense storms on wadis in central Libya by Klitzsch (1966) is quite valuable. Some of the best recent reports on surface waters and drainage in Libya have been issued by the U. S. AID as agriculture reports. Examples of these include Stewart's (1960) treatment of water resources in Tripolitania and a discussion of flood control measures on Wadi Megenin by Tileston and Swanson (1962). The soil survey of the Tauorga region by Willimott et al. (1960) might also be mentioned here because drainage features are included despite preoccupation with the soils of this area. Finally, Sensidoni's discussion of hydrologic problems (1945) in arid regions should be cited among the useful hydrologic reports on Libya.

Authorities for Geomorphology

For purposes of this report, *C. Vita-Finzi* of the University College of London, *R. F. Peel,* University of Bristol, and *W. Meckelein,* University of Stuttgart, may be regarded as authorities on Libyan geomorphology and sources of additional information.

Hydrologic information on Libya can, in part, be obtained from certain of the general Saharan references previously cited, such as Dubief's surface-water treatise (1953*a*). In addition, some basic hydrologic data are published by the Meteorological Service in Tripoli, but individual reports provide the best source materials.

Authorities for Hydrology

Further information on the status of hydrology in Libya can be obtained from *J. R. Jones,* of the Foreign Hydrology Branch of the U. S. Geological Survey, who has wide acquaintance with the available literature and current work. As is true of other countries within the arid regions, however, it is fair to say that basic hydrologic data of all types are woefully sparse. The few reports cited above must be compared to the very large total number of Libyan wadis to gain a proper insight to the status of knowledge of the drainage features and ephemeral-stream discharges in the country.

Summary of State of Knowledge, Sahara

The foregoing country-by-country survey of the available information on the geomorphology and surface-water hydrology of the Sahara permits some broad generalizations to be made here. If one wished to cite specific countries for which the least information is available, in a relative sense, then Chad, Niger, and Spanish Sahara would clearly lead any such list. The volume of work that has been accomplished in Algeria, Morocco, Tunisia, Egypt, and perhaps in Libya and Sudan as well, is certainly greatest. Hence, this would relegate the two remaining Saharan countries, namely Mauritania and Mali, to an intermediate status in any such 3-fold scheme of rank with respect to status of knowledge. This would not, however, be a fair assessment of the status of knowledge nor would it truly indicate the regions within the Sahara about which least is known.

It should be apparent that in most of the Saharan countries there is a decided lack of large-scale topographic and geologic maps. The vast areas involved are, of course, one of the primary reasons for this deficiency. But even in countries where much mapping progress has been made, it is important to note that the deficiency is selective. That is, the dearth of topographic and geologic maps, and of modern geomorphic studies as well, increases decidedly with increasing aridity in any Saharan country. With the exception of the principal Saharan massifs, such as Tibesti, Ahaggar, Aïr, the Adrar des Iforas, and a few smaller features such as Kita, Gilf Kebir, and others, it is the elongate, east-west zone of the central Sahara that is least well known.

The status of knowledge of specific Saharan landforms is basically incorporated in the section of this report entitled "Evaluation and Recommendations." For purposes of generalization at this point, it need only be said that far more information is available on landforms that are dramatic relief features in the Sahara, such as the central massifs, than on the vast surrounding plains which on a percentage basis are actually the most abundant landforms.

With respect to surface-water hydrology, it is clear that the available data and length of record of the Nile suffice to term it one of the best known rivers of the world that occur in an arid environment. Elsewhere in the Sahara, a variety of studies of such rivers as the Niger, Baoulé, and the principal wadis of North Africa have been conducted and there have been some notable investigations of short-term hydrological conditions in small drainage basins in scattered Saharan localities. Despite these efforts, it is fair to say that the hydrologic regimen and physical characteristics of the legion of typical, ephemeral drainage systems of the Sahara are not known today. The truth of this assertion is clear when one considers that precipitation-runoff and sediment-transport relations are not even established for most of the ephemeral drainage systems that are tributary to the Nile proper. The essential climatic data for both hydrologic and geomorphic purposes, as well as streamflow data, are sorely lacking in most instances. These problems will be more fully treated in the evaluation section of this chapter.

3. The Somali-Chalbi

The countries embraced by the Somali-Chalbi include Kenya, Somalia, French Somaliland, and Ethiopia. The arid zone in eastern Africa is not uniformly distributed among these countries. It is essentially a coastal zone, like the Namib in South West Africa. It rims the high interior plateaus, and, because of topographic peculiarities, the width of this zone is highly variable; it is narrowest along the northern coastal plain of Somalia on the Gulf of Aden and widest in the Danakil desert area of Ethiopia and in the southern part of Somalia. The arid zone is a continuous area, however, from the Sudan-Ethiopia border, around the horn of Africa, into easternmost Kenya. Additionally, Meigs' map (1953, see Pert. Pubs. Sec. I) includes the Lake Rudolf area of northwestern Kenya within the arid parts of the region.

The general references cited for Africa at the outset of this discussion of available information on the continent are applicable to eastern Africa, but to provide more specific information here a few pertinent reports will be mentioned by country. Authorities that can be named for this desert are indicated under their individual countries. No local depositories are named, but unpublished information is available at the governmental departments mentioned.

Kenya

Publications cited in the following text on Kenya, unless otherwise noted where cited, are listed in Section V, The Somali-Chalbi, of the Pertinent Publications list.

Several geological maps of Kenya are available, and among those issued as single sheets the map that accompanies the atlas of Kenya (The Survey of Kenya, 1959) is recommended. The geology of the country has been outlined by Cole (1950), and Dixey (1948) reported on the northern portion of Kenya. Fuchs (1939) provided a good treatment of the Lake Rudolf area in the northwest, and Busk (1939) discussed some geologic aspects of the northeast region. The rift valleys of eastern Africa, with which the Lake Rudolf basin is associated, have been most discussed. Gregory (1920), Johnson (1929), Wayland (1929), Willis (1936), Dixey (1946), and Girdler (1958) have each discussed some aspect of the geology or geomorphology of these features.

No specific geomorphic studies of the arid parts of Kenya have been undertaken, but the above reports contain the usual descriptive sections on the areas treated. Similarly, hydrological reports on Kenya tend to exclude the arid region proper because much of the total area of the country is nonarid. Much attention has been devoted to the relationship between land use and its effect upon runoff; an example is provided by Pereira's study (1959).

Hydrologic information on Kenya can be obtained from the East African Meteorological Department and from the Kenya Ministry of Works, Hydraulic Branch. Both agencies are located in Nairobi, as are the Royal College of Kenya and the Mines and Geological Department, both of which can supply additional information on the arid parts of the country.

Somalia

Publications cited in the following text on Somalia, unless otherwise noted where cited, are listed in Section V, The Somali-Chalbi, of the Pertinent Publications list.

Information on the arid zone of Somalia is more abundant than is that for Kenya. Macfadyen's report (1933) on the general geology of the northern part of Somalia is still a basic reference. Included were physiographic descriptions of drainage patterns, terrace heights, raised beaches, and dune locations. The British Military Authority (1945) surveyed this same general area during the Second World War and published a series of similar reports between 1945 and 1949. These contain useful information on topography, meteorology, water supply, and plant ecology, among other topics. Geologic or topographic maps on scale of 1:3,000,000 or 1:2,000,000 are included.

Viney (1947) has provided a 10-page bibliography for this area which lists several geographic and early-traveler-type reports, but the bibliography on geology and mineral resources by Puri (1961) gives much more recent and comprehensive coverage.

Hunt (1951) also has made a general survey; his report includes a map at a scale of 1:1,000,000, but the contour interval is variable and is as great as 1,000 feet. A summary of all the climatic, geologic, and topographic data that were available through 1950 is included, however. Macfadyen's subsequent report (1952) on water supplies also summarizes the available hydrological data for Somalia, and Pallister (1963) has recently contributed one of the few papers on general geomorphology of the northern region.

One of the best sources of information on Somalia is the "Annual Report" of the Geological Survey Department of the Ministry of Industry and Commerce, at Hargeisa. Initial publication was in 1952, all past and current projects are cited, the status of mapping is indicated, and publications issued during the period of a given report are cited. As examples of the useful reports that can be located in this manner, those by Mason and Warder (1956) and by Hunt (1958) might be mentioned here.

The first report, on the geology of the Heis-Mait-Waqderia area, includes some information on drainage patterns and discriminates between ephemeral and intermittent streams; the geology is mapped on a scale of 1:125,000. Similarly, the report by Hunt described the "tugs," as dry washes are designated in the country, and presents the major drainage features on a reasonable map. In the absence of such reports, no information whatever would be available. Hence, although the geological reports leave much to be desired with respect to information on drainage systems in Somalia, they should be consulted for general information.

The subject of vegetation patterns in Somalia has aroused much interest since Macfadyen (1950) described them. Subsequent reports on this phenomenon, so termed because the patterns involved are linear or arcuate, have been provided by Greenwood (1957), and by Boaler and Hodge (1962, 1964). Although the precise reason for the occurrence of vegetation arcs is not obvious, the papers that treat this topic commonly provide basic information on the topography and types of alluvium present, in addition to photographs. Thus, they are relevant to this report as sources of available information.

With respect to hydrology, several of the reports cited above provide much basic information on Somalia. Two additional reports, which also provide convenient summaries of the status of knowledge to their dates of publication, are Brooks' early paper on the meteorology of the area (1920) and Tonini's discussion of water resources (1956). Information on current hydrologic investigations and on unpublished basic data is available through the Department of Public Works in Mogadiscio and Hargeisa, the Food and Agriculture Organization of the U.N. in Mogadiscio, and from *Abdurahman Hassan*, Director General of the Ministry of Agriculture in Mogadiscio.

From the nature of the reports and available information cited above, it should be apparent that neither the geomorphology nor surface-water hydrology of the country can generally be considered to be well known. Large-scale mapping, specific geomorphic investigations, and basic hydrologic data on many more of the ephemeral or intermittent drainage systems in Somalia need to be accomplished in order to alter this assessment.

French Somaliland

French Somaliland is a relatively small country which lies wholly within the arid zone of eastern Africa. Information on the area can be obtained from reports of surveys in the former British Somaliland, which were previously cited under "Somalia," from work in Ethiopia, to be next discussed, and from Italian studies of the former colonies of Eritrea and Italian Somaliland. The French administration has, of course, also contributed to the available information on the country. Publications cited in the following text on French Somaliland, unless otherwise noted where cited, are listed in Section V, The Somali-Chalbi, of the Pertinent Publications list.

Topographic sheets can be obtained from the British Directorate of Overseas Surveys and an out-

line of the geology and geography of French Somaliland was provided by Dreyfuss (1931). This report is still a basic work, but more recent papers are listed in the bibliography of geology (French Somaliland, Service des Travaux Publics, 1960) for the 1930-1959 period. A recent geological map has been provided by Besairie (1946) and Dainelli's work on Italian East Africa is also pertinent (1943).

The best available report on water resources in French Somaliland is that by Moullard and Robaux (1958). Information on any aspect of the status of mapping, water resources, or other pertinent subjects, can best be obtained through the Service des Travaux Publics in Djibouti or from the Paris bureau for French overseas territories.

Ethiopia

Publications cited in the following text on Ethiopia, unless otherwise noted where cited, are listed in Section V, The Somali-Chalbi, of the Pertinent Publications list.

The arid zone in Ethiopia occupies the northern coastal plain and the large, wedge-shaped, Danakil desert area which surrounds French Somaliland. Geologic descriptions of this arid zone are included in works on Ethiopian or east-African geology. Dainelli's report, previously noted (1943), is a basic reference, but a recent treatise on the geology of Ethiopia by Mohr (1964) should also be noted. Included is a good reference list and a geological map of the horn of Africa (scale 1:2,000,000) which is pertinent to all of the east-African area of interest.

Reports of geomorphic interest on the arid zone of Ethiopia are not abundant. Voute (1959) has studied the Assab region and included some descriptions of coastal features, including terrace heights, Tatu (1964) has discussed rainfall in Ethiopia and provided an outline of the general synoptic meteorology as well as basic data, and Murphy (1959) has reported on soils in Ethiopia. In addition, a geophysical report by Gouin and Mohr (1964) presents some detailed structural maps which cover the Danakil desert area.

Hydrologic efforts in the arid region of the country have been limited. One major project that is of relevance here is the Awash Valley scheme. Basic data on water resources have been gathered for approximately 6 years and a land classification based on such factors as surface slope, depth of soil, microrelief, drainage, frequency of flooding, and others, has been established. Information on the Awash Valley project is available through the United Nations Special Project (1964) and Mariam's published account (1964). Unfortunately, only one segment of the area of development lies within the arid zone proper; the Awash Valley is essentially marginal to the arid region.

Some consideration has been given to initiating study of the Shibeli River, which flows into Somalia and crosses the arid coastal plain of that country north of Mogadiscio, but no work has yet begun.

Topographic mapping is commencing in Ethiopia under terms of a joint Ethiopia-U.S. agreement, and aerial photographic coverage will be 1:50,000 and 1:25,000. An outline of the work to be done (Anonymous, 1963; Emmanuel, 1964) is available; the latter citation also provides information on the activities of the Mapping and Geography Institute in Ethiopia.

Unpublished information is available from several sources in Ethiopia. P. A. Mohr has used aerial photographs to map the distribution of volcanic rocks and surficial structure in the desert area. His data can be obtained at the Geophysical Observatory in Addis Ababa. Mobil Petroleum of Ethiopia and Ralph Parsons Company, both headquartered in Asmara, can provide varied information on the surficial features of the northern coastal plain and the Salt Plain area of the Danakil desert, respectively. In the latter case, a point of interest is the fact that cores have penetrated 1,500 meters of salt without reaching the lower limits of the deposit.

The Mines Department, the Geology Department of the University College, and the Mapping and Geography Institute, all in Addis Ababa, also have knowledge of current work and unpublished results in their respective areas of interest. Hydrologic data can best be obtained through the Awash Valley Authority and the Water Resources Institute; the latter agency is largely concerned with construction projects in nonarid areas, however.

Periodicals that report relevant information on Ethiopia include the *Ethiopian Geographical Review*, published since 1963 in Addis Ababa, and the *Bulletin of the Geophysical Observatory*, published since 1959 at the Haile Selassie I University, Addis Ababa. Authorities on trafficability and surficial features in the arid region of Ethiopia include the local managers of the commercial organizations in Asmara previously mentioned and *P. A. Mohr* of the Geophysical Observatory in Addis Ababa.

The available information discussed above serves to indicate that the surficial features and hydrologic conditions of the arid portions of Ethiopia are rather poorly known. This is true because those engaged in various research activities are not primarily concerned with arid-zone geomorphology or, in the case of the several water agencies, because practical needs cause

concentration of effort in semiarid areas. Mapping deficiencies, however, will be overcome in time by work in progress.

C. THE ARABIAN DESERT

For purposes of this report the Arabian Peninsula, Iraq, Syria, Jordan, and Israel are considered to be in the Arabian Desert. The Arabian Peninsula here refers to Saudi Arabia, Kuwait, the neutral territories, Yemen, Aden, Muscat and Oman, the Trucial States, and Qatar. With the exception of Kuwait and the neutral territories, which are north of Saudi Arabia, these states form the southern rim of the Arabian Peninsula proper.

The arid zone of the Arabian Desert embraces the entire area save for two mountain ranges which receive greater precipitation due to orographic effects. These mountain areas are the Asir in southwestern Saudi Arabia and its extension, the Yemen highlands, to the south, and the mountains of Muscat and Oman in the southeastern part of the peninsula. Elsewhere, the southern three-fourths of Iraq, all of Jordan, most of Israel, and the southern part of Syria lie within the arid zone according to Meigs' maps (1953, see Pert. Pubs. Sec. I).

This discussion of the available information on the Arabian Desert departs from the usual order of the other chapters in this series for more effective presentation of the Chapter IV topics. The country-by-country discussion of the Arabian Desert is followed by a summary of the state of knowledge for that part of the world.

Prior to a consideration of the Arabian Peninsula, a few general or regional reports may best be mentioned here. Publications cited in the following text on the Arabian Desert (in general), unless otherwise noted where cited, are listed in Section VI, of the Pertinent Publications list. Several regional geography texts on the Middle East are available and of these Fisher's book (1963) is one of the best. It includes a general treatment of the geology and physical geography of the countries cited above and many maps, diagrams, and data, including climatic information. Few useful references are provided, however. Additional climatic data are provided by the U. S. Army report on analogs of Yuma climate in the Middle East (U. S. Army. Quartermaster Research and Development Command, 1954) and the terrain analogs (U. S. Army Engineer Waterways Experiment Station, 1960) by this same agency; these are a valuable source of information on the geology, geomorphology, soils, and vegetation of the region.

Arabian Peninsula

Publications cited in the following text on the Arabian Peninsula, unless otherwise noted where cited, are listed in Section VI of the Pertinent Publications list.

The Arabian Peninsula is unquestionably one of the best-mapped desert areas of its size in the world. The geologic map (U. S. Geological Survey, 1963), at a scale of 1:2,000,000, is excellent; methods of compilation have been described by Bates (1964). The map covers part of southern Jordan as well as the entire peninsula. More detailed geologic sheets are also available at a scale of 1:500,000 (U. S. Geological Survey, various dates), but coverage of the entire area is not complete. Parts of Yemen, Aden, Muscat and Oman, and the Trucial States are the areas omitted. These geological sheets reveal many physical features such as drainage patterns, sebkhas, and types of sand terrain, but another set of maps, termed "geographic maps" (U. S. Geological Survey, various dates), were produced in order to treat the surficial aspects in detail. These sheets demonstrate the excellent results that can be obtained by plotting features that are revealed on aerial photographs and supplementing such information with field data. It should be noted, however, that the geographic maps provide only general topographic coverage. They are not contour maps, and relief is indicated by hachuring or airbrush shading.

Although the detail of the geographic and geologic maps cited above largely supersedes reports of the early-traveler variety, several such reports are nevertheless worthy of citation here. The desert travels of Philby and the acuteness of his observations are little short of remarkable. Accounts of his journeys are available in three books (1922, 1928, 1933a) and an article (1933b). Descriptive material stemming from similar travels has been provided by Thomas (1932) and, in later years by Thesiger (1946-1947, 1948, 1949, 1950) among others.

The 1950 Thesiger article treats Muscat and Oman and is worthy of note because reports on areas that border Saudi Arabia on the southern margin of the peninsula are not abundant. Carter (1857) provided the earliest information on the southeastern coastal area in 1857 and Lees' later general description of the physical geography (1928b) also treated this region. A more modern work on Muscat and Oman is Morton's (1959) report on the geology, however. Recent papers on Aden and Yemen by Beydoun (1960) and Geukens (1960) are also available, and Evans *et al.* (1964) have provided a good description of the sebkhas and coastal features of the Trucial Coast.

Papers treating structural features or regional tectonics of the Arabian Peninsula include Lees' report on Oman and southeastern Arabia (1928a), Lamare's general report (1936), the work of Picard (1937b), a discussion of tectonics by von Wissman, Rathjens, and Kossmat (1942), a paper on recent uplifts by Lees (1955), and a report on fault patterns in northwestern Arabia by Mitchell (1957).

Additional information on the physical features of the Arabian Peninsula is available from reports that outline petroleum occurrences (Henson, 1951a, b; Kerr, 1953; Steinke, Bramkamp, and Sander, 1958), and such disparate topics as meteorite localities in Arabia (Holm, 1962) and petroglyphs near Mecca (Helal, 1964). The coastal areas of the peninsula are included on McGill's map (1958, see Pert. Pubs. Sec. I) and a number of papers treat aspects of the Red Sea and Persian Gulf, which border the peninsula on the east and west. Among these reports are those by Owen (1938) and, more recently, Swartz and Arden (1960) on the Red Sea, and the work of Pilgrim (1906), Emery (1956), and Sugden (1963a, b) on the Persian Gulf. These reports cover hydrology and sedimentation as well as geology and general coastal features.

Reports on geomorphology proper are not abundant. Little (1925) treated some geomorphic features of southern Arabia, and Käselau (1928) subsequently provided qualitative descriptions of landforms in central and northern Arabia. The geologic and geographic maps previously discussed (U.S. Geological Survey, various dates) provide most of the basic information on landforms of the peninsula, but the best written descriptions of these features are contained in reports by Brown (1960) on western and central Arabia, and by Holm (1960) on the Arabian Peninsula as a whole. These papers treat a variety of topics, including the landforms, rock types, relief, drainage, and presumed historical development of the modern features, but considerable attention is also devoted to the Arabian dunes and the origin and distribution of sand in the Rub'al Khali, Great Nafud, and elsewhere.

The latter is, quite obviously, an important problem in its own right. It is fairly simple, of course, to state that the only three requirements for the occurrence of dunes or sand fields in the desert areas are a source, transport agency, and site of accumulation, but it is less obvious why these sand areas occur in one location in preference to another. This matter will be further discussed in the conclusion of this report, but it is pertinent to cite here some of the available information on sand in Arabia. Phillips (1882) provided one of the earliest descriptions of Arabian sands and noted the reddish hue of some varieties. In more recent years, Bagnold (1951) has discussed sand transport in Arabia and Kerr and Nigra (1952) have provided some excellent works on the basic problems of sand control. Holm (1953) described dome-shaped dunes of the Nedj and in his subsequent work (1960) he also devoted attention to dune classification and the evolution of dune forms. Additional work of considerable value is Finkel's (1961) study of the migration of barchan dunes by use of aerial photographs. Some available information on the al-Hasa area suggests that some encroachment of sand upon cultivated fields may have begun 2,500 years ago, based on extrapolation of a dune migration rate of about 10 meters per year between 1949 and 1961. This rate of migration applies only to dunes in the area, however, which are about 10 meters in height and which can be described by the equality $HD = C$, where H is dune height measured at the slipface, D is distance of migration per year, and C is a constant, equal to approximately 100 at Dhahran and Abqaiq. One of the most recent studies of the size distribution and other characteristics of sands from Arabia, and from the Sahara, has been reported by Hamdan (1965).

In addition to the available information on the Arabian Peninsula which is cited above, a wealth of reports exists in the files of the Arabian American Oil Company in Dhahran. Although the writer was granted the privilege of access to several such reports while in Saudi Arabia and has knowledge of others by reason of a prior period of employment by Aramco, the company has officially requested that individual Aramco file reports not be cited here. Published references to several pertinent Aramco reports, however, can be found in papers by Holm (1960, 1962) and Bates (1964). The last article clearly indicates that the original field observations of surface-mapping parties have been used extensively in compiling the maps of the peninsula (U. S. Geological Survey, 1963 and various dates) but, in addition, it is obvious that these file reports contain much of the currently available information on trafficability and sand-control problems, as well as on the general physical features of the Arabian Desert.

Information on the surface-water hydrology of the Arabian Peninsula is relatively meagre. Although the locations and distribution of drainage features, sebkhas, marsh areas, and the like are shown on the geographic maps (U. S. Geological Survey, various dates) of the region, basic data on many aspects of surface-water hydrology are lacking. The status of hydrologic knowledge was well-summarized by Baumer (1964) in 1964. To use precipitation as an example, Baumer stated in his report that the amount of rainfall is everywhere irregular but that meteoro-

logical information is inadequate and the number of observation stations is ridiculously small.

Because hydrologic events depart significantly from a random distribution in nature, a period of observations should be several times as great as the period for which specification of mean conditions is desired. This is particularly true in arid regions; hence, it is obvious that Baumer's conclusions are valid today. Even if his recommendations had been heeded, a 2-year record of observation in the interior of the peninsula would clearly have been insufficient for generalization. This matter will be further discussed in the conclusion of this report, with specific reference to the validity of the climatic maps of Meigs (1953, see Pert. Pubs. Sec. I) and the climatic analogs of the U. S. Army (1954). It should suffice here to state that none of the observation stations shown on the map of the Water Department, Ministry of Agriculture, in Riyadh are located in the Rub'al Khali, an area of approximately 500,000 square kilometers in southern Arabia. The Arabian American Oil Company maintains observation stations in each of its District headquarters in the eastern part of Arabia, and its field parties also gather data. Although some field parties have operated in the Rub'al Khali, such operations have been intermittent, and nothing approaching a continuous record in this vast sandy desert is available. The point is that it is difficult to justify the production of a boundary delineating arid and extremely arid areas in southern Arabia, or elsewhere in the world, in the absence of any substantial quantitative data. With respect to the availability of information, however, the data that do exist can be obtained from the Arabian American Oil Company in Dhahran, the Ministry of Agriculture in Riyadh, or the U. S. Weather Bureau.

Information on surface-water runoff is also scarce. Burningham (1952) discussed several wadis in southern Arabia which flow to the Red Sea. He used aerial photographs to obtain catchment areas and compiled an isohyetal map from existing data. Tothill (1953) also treated the rainfall data on southern Arabia with reference to the long-term record at Aden, the extrapolation of which is not justified, and de Vajda and Smallwood (1953) used the information in these reports to estimate the mean annual discharge and peak discharge of the Wadi Jiza', which is near the Saudi Arabia border with Yemen.

Simansky (1955) also summarized the meteorologic and hydrologic data on the Wadi Jiza' area, but the most comprehensive treatment is provided in the recent Italconsult report (1964). The difficulties of prediction of runoff events are well-illustrated by the sequence of observations on Wadi Jiza'. Personnel of the FAO made hydrologic measurements during the 1953-1955 period and then left the country. Measurements were partly resumed in 1957-1958, but the results are thought to be unreliable. Finally, the FAO personnel returned in 1962 and attempted to conduct a detailed investigation over an 18-month period, which covered 2 seasons. They estimated a theoretical 200-year flood discharge, but the results are clearly suspect because (1) only surface velocities were obtained, which at once requires estimation to determine the mean velocity of flow, and (2) only 2 years of record were obtained, thus requiring the assumption that these 2 years were indeed representative of long-term, mean conditions.

Considering the fact that the Wadi Jiza' is probably the most thoroughly studied drainage in Arabia, in terms of the hydrologic data that have been gathered, our lack of knowledge is most discouraging. The wadis in this area head in the 'Asir or the Yemen highland and are known to contain some flow nearly every year. Yet, even for these intermittent streams one cannot state with certainty the frequency with which they reach the sea, or their discharge, among other matters. Wadis that head in the Tuwayq escarpment near Riyadh are also known to flow each year during a brief interval of time. Automatic recording equipment will be installed on certain of these drainage systems and, over a period of years, sufficient data will be obtained to enable sound prediction of flow-frequency behavior. But the problems posed by the legion of wadis, many of them major drainages such as the Wadi al Batin in northeastern Arabia, cannot be resolved by such methods. The frequency and magnitude of bankfull discharges in these channels, which are today partially choked by windblown sand, remains enigmatic.

Aside from the studies cited in the Wadi Jiza' area and the plans for data collection from streams near Riyadh, some information is also available in ground-water reports which are concerned with recharge rates. A study of the Wasia aquifer in eastern Saudi Arabia contains a general description of the wadis involved and data on slopes and catchment areas are presented. With respect to actual rates of recharge, this particular report provides an estimate of 50 percent, which is remarkably high for any arid area in which the mean annual precipitation is thought to be about 2.5 inches per year. The basic problem, in Arabia as elsewhere in the arid regions of the world, is lack of the required data; one must estimate such variables as precipitation, evaporation, and infiltration in order to provide an educated guess on recharge rates in most cases. It is therefore unsurprising that estimates ranging from 10 to 90 percent

of runoff have been offered for various Arabian localities.

Lastly, the FAO seminars on irrigation and associated matters in the arid regions also provide a source of information on surface-water hydrology. The seminar held at Lahore, West Pakistan in 1964, for example, includes a report on Kuwait by Banna (1965). This paper includes a useful summary of the general topography, climatic conditions, and soils of this part of the Arabian Peninsula, as well as pertinent data on water resources. Chiefly discussed are the oases, standing bodies of brackish water and their chemical quality, and ground water aquifers.

Authorities and Depositories for Geomorphology

D. A. Holm of Tucson, Arizona and *G. F. Brown,* U. S. Geological Survey, Jiddah, Saudi Arabia, may be listed as expert on the surficial features of the Arabian Desert for purposes of this report. Additionally, *León Ramírez,* of the Ralph Parsons Company, Riyadh, has intimate knowledge of the mapping of the peninsula by reason of his extensive work on this project. For reasons cited above, however, Aramco personnel in Dhahran should also be consulted; residents include several individuals with many years of field experience and wide knowledge of trafficability, sand-control, and hydrologic problems. One man who has authored Aramco file reports treating the latter two matters is no longer resident in Dhahran and may profitably be consulted, namely *W. C. Dimock,* who is at this writing project manager for the U. N. Karamoja ground-water survey in Entebbe, Uganda.

The Ministry of Petroleum and Mineral Resources in Jiddah is another source of information. In the employ of this Ministry are French, Japanese, and American geological field parties which conduct detailed mapping and mineral exploration programs in western and central Saudi Arabia. Examples of useful information in the file reports of this agency include Bogue's reconnaissance of northwestern Arabia (1953), which mentions the elevations of raised beaches or terraces near Tieryim and the weathering of granitic rocks to the east of Umm Lajj, Bhutta's outline of present and future exploration plans (1964), and the recommendations of Herness (1964) which would clearly enlarge our knowledge of coastal features, if followed. The proper contact agency for further information is the Ministry's office in Riyadh.

Authorities and Depositories for Surface-Water Hydrology

Among those individuals who are expert on hydrologic problems and the water resources of the Arabian Peninsula are *Friedrich Vinck,* Senior Hydrologist of the Ministry of Agriculture and Water,

Riyadh, *Robert Painter* of the Arabian American Oil Company, and *W. C. Dimock,* previously cited. The Ministry of Agriculture and Water should be considered a local depository.

Iraq

As previously stated, approximately three-fourths of Iraq is within the arid zone. In this region there are three general physiographic types, namely a continuation of the Arabian plateaus in western and southern Iraq, the floodplain areas of the Tigris and Euphrates rivers, and the Zagros Mountains, which extend northwestward along the border between Iraq and Iran. Publications cited in the following text on Iraq, unless otherwise noted where cited, are listed in Section VI, Arabian Desert, of the Pertinent Publications list. Fisher (1963) provides an adequate description of the general physiography of these areas and also presents some data on climate and on the Tigris-Euphrates drainage system. The U. S. Army's climatic (1954) and terrain (1960) analogs are much more comprehensive, however. Additional reports of interest include a discussion of the development of plains by Lees and Falcon (1952), the description of landforms in western Iraq by Wirth (1958), and Voûte's outline of climatic conditions and morphology in the Zagros Mountains (1960).

A modern geologic map of Iraq is available, but copies are rather rare and this writer has not personally seen one. Information on this map, and on other aspects of the geology and geomorphology of Iraq, can be obtained from the Iraq Petroleum Corporation, British Petroleum Company, and the Arid Zone Research Institute, University of Baghdad. The programs and plans of this Institute through 1967 are available (Arid Zone Research Institute, 1965; Pavel and Kaddouri, 1964), and publication of their first reports has been presented in the "Bulletin" of the Institute (Arid Zone Research Institute, 1964). The type of research that has been and is being conducted is illustrated by papers on clay mineralogy by Kaddouri and Pavel (1964), the sodium content of saline and carbonaceous soils by Al-Rawi and Pavel (1964), and the effects of high water-table elevations on soils by Kaddouri and Barica (1964). Although much of this work is excellent, it is apparent that personnel in Iraq are predominantly concerned with the twin problems of salinity and waterlogging of soils that arise through excessive irrigation practices. Hence, nearly all research is in the field of soil science and, as Knetsch and Gounot indicate in their excellent review of research efforts in Iraq (1963), other subjects are largely ignored. No geomorphic studies, as such, have been undertaken save by a few foreigners.

Sugden (1964), for example, has recently studied the faceting of pebbles in southern Iraq.

In the area of surface-water hydrology, the efforts of Iraqi personnel have been principally devoted to irrigation problems and to approximately 15 projects which involve dam construction and water storage. An outline of these projects has been provided by Gardi (1964), together with a summary of the available hydrologic data on the Tigris and Euphrates rivers. Additional discussions of irrigation and drainage problems, and pertinent hydrological data on Iraq, have been presented by Malaika (1964) and by Kadir (1964). The latter report also provides a few useful references, including one treating the history of flooding at Baghdad.

In general, desert geomorphology and surface hydrology are not well known for the country, with the exceptions noted in the text above.

Authorities and Depositories

Although no individual who has personally conducted much research on the surficial features of Iraq can be cited here, *Nadheema Kaddouri,* Director of the Arid Zone Research Institute, University of Baghdad, is cognizant of all arid-zone research that is conducted in the country. Personnel of the Ministry of Agrarian Reform, Directorate of Irrigation, and of the Iraq Petroleum Corporation should also be conculted. No local depositories are cited for Iraq.

Jordan

Publications cited in the following text on Jordan, unless otherwise noted where cited, are listed in Section VI, Arabian Desert, of the Pertinent Publications list.

Useful information on the geomorphology and surface-water hydrology of Jordan can again be obtained from Fisher's regional geography text (1963), and the U.S. Army's climatic (U.S. Army. Quartermaster Research and Development Command, 1954) and terrain (U. S. Army Engineer Waterways Experiment Station, 1960) analogs. As previously mentioned, the geologic map of the Arabian Peninsula (U. S. Geological Survey, 1963) includes part of southern Jordan. Other maps of the region include Blake's maps of the Trans-Jordan (1939*a*) and of northern Palestine (1939*b*) and Shaw's map of southern Palestine (1947). The most comprehensive source of information on the surficial features and geology of the country has been provided by Burdon (1959) in a handbook designed to accompany Quennell's maps of eastern Jordan. This work includes discussion of the climate, topography, soils, and vegetation, sections on geophysical and hydrologic investigations, and a reference list which contains most of the basic citations on Jordan.

In addition to this most valuable report, there are several papers on aspects of the geomorphology of Jordan that are germane here. Among these are discussions of the structure and geomorphology of the Dead Sea rift by Willis (1928), Auden (1956), Shaw (1956), and Quennell (1959, 1958), among others, Schattner's monograph on fluvial processes and morphology of the lower Jordan Valley (1962), and Vita-Finzi's recent investigation of slope erosion (1964b) by sheetwash. Basic reports from which further reference can be obtained include the bibliography of geologic and ground-water reports by the Jordanian Development Board (Wozab and Kawar, 1960), Moormann's survey of the soils of Jordan (1959), that on geology and mineral resources by Quennell (1951), and a bibliography of land and water-utilization work in the Middle East by Dost (1953). Information on dunes and windblown sands is provided in a general sense in several of the foregoing reports, but Dapples' (1941) paper on surficial deposits in the Syria-Jordan-Iraq region is worthy of citation here.

Surface-water hydrology in Jordan is one responsibility of the Central Water Authority in 'Amman. This agency has issued a number of pertinent technical reports. Among the more basic of these is a paper (Jordan. Central Water Authority, 1964) providing an historical review of rainfall records in Jordan, basic data on the annual rainfall for the country between 1931 and 1960, and for Jerusalem between 1846 and 1964, and which is accompanied by a map at 1:500,000 showing 30-year isohyets and the location of stream gaging stations. Several useful references are contained in this report. Data for years since 1960 have been separately published (Jordan. Central Water Authority, 1965).

Some excellent hydrological reports that summarize existing streamflow data are available. Among these are a report on the Nablus District by Rafe and Raffety (1965), a 1960 evaluation of Jordanian water resources (Wozab, Bradley and Kawar, 1960), MacDonald's report on the east bank of the Jordan River (1965), and an FAO Country Report on Jordan (Food and Agriculture Organization of the United Nations, 1964). One of the most recent reviews of the water resources of Jordan has been provided by Underhill (1965), who cites many of the basic data, the history and locations of surface-water discharge measurements, estimates of the water balance in various parts of Jordan, and several pertinent references. The water balance of the Dead Sea has been calculated by Neumann (1958) and, under

the auspices of the United Nations, an intensive hydrologic study of the Azraq Basin (United Nations, Special Fund, 1965) has recently been completed. The major wadis in Jordan are cited in many of the foregoing reports but, in a different vein, Vita-Finzi has discussed the alluvial terraces that have been produced by surface flows in terms of climatic change (1964a).

Authorities and Depositories

Authorities on the surficial features of Jordan must include *D. J. Burdon* and *A. M. Quennell,* on the basis of their extensive work in the country, and also *C. Vita-Finzi* of University College, London. All aspects of hydrology lie within the province of the Hydrology Division, Central Water Authority, 'Amman, which is to be considered the local depository of information. With respect to sediment transport in Jordanian wadis, *M. I. Ibbitt,* Imperial College, London, is investigating some theoretical aspects of this subject. Specifically, Ibbitt is concerned with the bulking of flows by high sediment concentrations in tributaries to the Jordan River and elsewhere in the country; he is preparing his results for publication at this writing.

Syria and Lebanon

The northernmost area included in the arid zone of the Arabian Desert is that of southern Syria and Lebanon. Publications cited in the following text on Syria and Lebanon, unless otherwise noted where cited, are listed in Section VI, Arabian Desert, of the Pertinent Publications list. Only a small part of Lebanon is actually arid, and because much of the available work on the region has been accomplished in disregard of national boundaries, these two countries are here treated together. Much of the area termed "the Syrian Desert" is similarly unconfined by national boundaries. Wright (1958), for example, has described the general aspects of wadi systems in the northern part of the Arabian plateau, which is included in the Syrian Desert, but the area considered is actually in Iraq. Moreover, there has been considerable cooperative effort between these countries through the years.

With respect to available information on this region, Fisher's regional geography text (1963), and the U. S. Army's climatic (1954) and terrain (1960) analogs must again be cited. In addition, general descriptions of the physical geography and geology are available in the early work of Blanckenhorn (1914), Hourani's text (1954), and the excellent manual by Dubertret and Weulersse (1940). Subsequently, Heybroek (1942) provided a detailed study of the geology of southern Lebanon and Dubertret (1948) treated the physical geography of this same area. A most valuable source of information is Avnimelech's recent bibliography of Levant geology (1965) which contains approximately 4500 references, including those on botany, zoology, and archeology.

A geological map of Syria and Lebanon at a scale of 1:1,000,000 is available (Dubertret, 1945) and Dubertret has provided a more detailed map of Lebanon (1955*a*) at a scale of 1:2,000,000, which is accompanied by a good explanatory handbook (1955*b*). Information on surficial features is contained in Haller's outline of the prehistory of these countries (1945), reports on Quaternary stratigraphy and deposits by Butzer (1958) and Van Liere (1959), de Vaumas' discussion of a presumed polycyclic erosion surface in the Lebanese mountains (1949*a*), and Dubertret's contribution on erosion problems in Lebanon (1954). Additionally, the work of Wirth (1958) and Dapples (1941) on surficial deposits in the region, including sands, should again be cited here.

General terrain descriptions and, often, maps and cross sections on various scales, appear in most of the geologic and geographic papers cited above. Similarly, reports on the structural features of the region, about which there has been much interest through the years, also contain much useful information about the surface. Among such reports are Krenkel's early discussion (1924), Dubertret's description of the structural features of Syria and Palestine (1932), a treatment of the Galilee and Houle depressions by de Vaumas (1949*b*), and two regional-tectonic syntheses by Sanford (1944) and de Vaumas (1950). The volcanic rocks of Syria and Lebanon, which might also be mentioned here, have been briefly discussed by Dubertret (1940).

Basic hydrologic data on Syria and Lebanon were provided by Combier (1933) and Dubertret (1933). More recent information may be obtained from the excellent climatic summary for Lebanon by Rey (1955), which includes a pluviometric map at a scale of 1:200,000 and an explanatory discussion, and Safadi's treatise on the hydrology of volcanic terrain in Syria (1956). The most comprehensive hydrologic report of recent years is that by Abd-El-Al (1953) which treats precipitation-evaporation, surface-water runoff, and springs, as well as the groundwater hydrology of karst terrain in the Syrian-Lebanon border area. Much recent work has also been done in the Yarmuk catchment area and vicinity near the Syrian-Jordan border. Precipitation and other data derived from water projects in this area are contained in File 44A of the Central Water Authority in 'Amman. As indicated in the Country Report on Syria, (Dabbous, 1965), lack of sufficient technical personnel has prevented extensive investigation of drainage systems save where principal streams such as the Euphrates River are involved.

Authorities and Depositories

Authorities on the surficial features and hydrology of the arid regions of Syria and Lebanon cannot be named here by reason of lack of personal acquaintance and information. Further information can be obtained, however, through the Ministry of Public Works in Beirut and from Professor *Nadar Naboulsky* of the Faculty of Science, Damascus University. No local depositories are cited.

Israel

Israel, the last of the countries of the Arabian Desert to be considered, is arid throughout most of its southeastern half; only the northwestern part of the country receives the benefit of maritime conditions. Publications cited in the following text on Israel, unless otherwise noted where cited, are listed in Section VI, Arabian Desert, of the Pertinent Publications list. Although the total area of Israel is negligible in comparison to that of the arid zone of the Middle East, the available literature is disproportionate, largely by reason of the activity of the Geological Survey personnel and various faculty members of the universities and institutes. The following citations represent an attempt at selectivity; much additional information on the arid part of the country is available, as indicated by Avnimelech's bibliography of Levant geology, previously cited (1965).

A geological map of Palestine at a scale of 1:100,000 is available from the Geological Survey of Israel. The sheets of this series also show topographic contours at 25-meter intervals. Sheets of the 1:50,000 and 1:20,000 series are also available through the Geological Survey. Other maps of interest include those of northern (Blake, 1939*b*) and southern (Shaw, 1947) Palestine, but much detailed information has accumulated through the years via geological reports. Hull (1885, 1886) and Lartret (1869) produced regional treatments prior to the turn of the century, but the work of Blake (1928, 1930) on geology and mineral and water resources is a basic reference. Blanckenhorn (1912) and Range (1927) provided early information on geologic aspects of Palestine and, in more recent years, Shaw (1948) and Shalem (1955) have outlined the mineral and water resources of Israel with the benefit of additional exploratory knowledge. In a more specialized vein, Picard (1943) discussed the structural evolution of Palestine, the work of Grader (1958*a, b*) on the Sasa and Heletz-Brur areas is illustrative of many similar reports that treat the geological history of quadrangles or small areas, Bentor discussed the application of aerial photography to geological mapping (1952a) and the tectonic setting of phosphate deposits (1952b) in the country, and Neev (1960) investigated the deposits and drainage development associated with a buried channel system.

Pleistocene geology, which is a subject that generally involves both geology and geomorphology, has been widely studied in Israel. Issar (1961) reported on Pleistocene deposits of the Ashod area, Picard (1952) investigated the peat deposits of Lake Hula, and Avnimelech (1952), Slatkine and Pomerancblum (1958), and Itzhaki, Reiss, and Issar (1961) have studied the Pleistocene deposits and features of the coastal plain of Israel. The work of Slatkine and Pomerancblum cited above includes a study of the heavy mineral distributions present. Vroman (1944) studied the general petrology of sandy sediments in Israel, and Emery and Neev (1960) have recently discussed the Mediterranean beaches which adjoin the coastal plain of the country.

With respect to general geomorphology or physical features, the text by Fisher (1963) and terrain analog map by the U. S. Army (1960) must again be cited as basic references on this Middle Eastern country. Excellent physical descriptions of landforms can be obtained in reports by Kallner (1943) and Picard (1951), which treat the entire country, and by Amiran (1951), de Vaumas (1953), and Sharon (1959), who have each provided reports on the morphology of the Negev. Much information is also available on surficial sediments and dunes. Reifenberg's treatise on the soils of Palestine (1947) is a basic reference and Ravikovitch (1953), Yaalon (1954), and Langozky (1963), among others, have subsequently treated such topics as eolian, lacustrine, and calcareous soils in Israel.

Among some excellent studies on sand dunes in the country, the work of Rim (1948, 1950, 1953, 1958) is outstanding. He has treated the mechanics of dune movement, and his several reports should be considered generally applicable to dune problems rather than pertinent only to local conditions. Other reports that are noteworthy include Reifenberg's (1950) paper on dune encroachment and Striem's description of seif dunes on the Sinai border (1954).

Blake discussed shorelines in Palestine (1937) as early as 1937, and in recent years much study of shorelines as well as other aspects of the Dead Sea, in particular, has been accomplished. Reports on the tectonics of the Dead Sea rift (Willis, 1928; Auden, 1956; Shaw, 1956; Quennell, 1958, 1959) and the water balance (Neumann, 1958) have been previously cited, but pertinent Israeli papers include those of the symposium on the Dead Sea held at Sdom in 1960 (Israel Geological Society, 1960), Bentor's review paper (1961) on geochemical and age aspects of the water, and a discussion of the pH of the brines by Bodenheimer and Neev (1962). These reports suggest that the salinity of the Dead Sea has been produced by evaporation through time, under closed-basin conditions, of waters derived from the Jordan River and from some saline springs in the area.

Useful information on surficial features of the country can also be obtained from papers that treat ancient agriculture in the Negev. The work of Tadmor et al. (1957), Mayerson (1959), and Evenari et al. (1961) is illustrative of reports in this category.

The activities of the Geological Survey of Israel during the 1949-1958 period have been summarized in a report (1959) which indicates the objectives and work of the various divisions. A more recent review (El-Zur, Magnes, and Samueloff, 1961) of arid zone activities in Israel is also available. Further information on the geomorphology or geology of the country can best be obtained through the Geological Survey or from *D. Amiran* of the Arid Zone Commission, Jerusalem.

With respect to hydrology, several basic reports that partially treat the water resources of Israel have been cited above, apart from work on the Dead Sea which also can be so classified. Additionally, Picard's inferences on climatic change (1937a) and a subsequent report on this topic by Shalem (1953) are somewhat related, but a vast array of modern hydrological investigations have been undertaken in the country. The governmental agencies involved in this work include the Hydrological Service of the Ministry of Agriculture, the Hydrogeology Division of the Geological Survey, the Meteorological Service, the Soil Erosion Experiment Station, and Water Planning for Israel, Ltd. Each of these agencies can provide bibliographies of available reports and a list of current projects and personnel. In addition, the departments of geology, geography, botany, and meteorology of Hebrew University, the Hydraulic Engineering Laboratory of Technion, and the Weizmann Institute of Science are all actively engaged in arid zone research and can supply information on all aspects of hydrology.

Authorities and Depositories

The various Israeli government agencies, research organizations, and educational institutions together constitute a network of depositories for the country. Advice on most effective use of library resources and on planning field studies can be obtained from *D. Amiran* (see above), who is named as an authority for Israel.

Summary of State of Knowledge, Arabian Desert

To summarize briefly the status of knowledge of surficial features and surface-water hydrology of the Arabian Desert, it should be noted at the outset that both the topography and geology are much better known, in a relative sense, than are these aspects of the Sahara. This is largely true because of the recently completed mapping program of the Arabian Peninsula, as previously noted, and because early competent surveys in the northern part of the Arabian Desert have led to at least general knowledge of the topography and geology of Jordan, Israel, Lebanon, Syria, and Iraq on a country-wide basis. As stated in the section treating the Arabian Peninsula, however, true topographic maps of moderate to large scale are almost wholly lacking and few quantitative geomorphic studies have been undertaken. The most notable exceptions, with respect to geomorphic work, are the several excellent investigations of wind-blown sand and desert dunes in Saudi Arabia and in Israel. As a generalization for the Arabian Desert in its entirety, it would be fair to say that information on various aspects of physical features is most abundant in these two countries. The gaps in knowledge are greater in Jordan, Iraq, and eastern Syria.

Climatic and hydrologic data of all types are sorely lacking throughout the Arabian Desert. As in other deserts of the world, information is available for principal or perennial drainage systems such as the Tigris / Euphrates or Jordan River / Dead Sea, but the regimen of the vast majority of ephemeral streams is virtually unknown. Current work on irrigation schemes and the like in several of these Middle Eastern countries will provide additional useful information in time, but some of the basic problems, such as the brevity of lengths of records in arid regions, cannot be wholly resolved through such projects.

These problems will be discussed in the concluding section of this report which treats evaluation and recommendations.

D. SOUTHERN ASIA

The countries included in southern Asia for purposes of this report are Iran, Afghanistan, Pakistan, and India. The desert areas that occur in these countries are the Kavir, Lut, and other closed basins in central and eastern Iran; the Dasht-i-Margo which covers the southern part of Afghanistan and blends into the arid portions of Baluchistan, Sind, and much of the Indus plain areas in West Pakistan; and the Thar of northwestern India. The availability of information on geomorphology and surface-water hydrology for each of the arid regions of these four countries will be indicated below, proceeding from west to east.

Publications cited in the following text on Southern Asia (in general), unless otherwise noted where cited, are listed in Section VII, Iranian Desert: Iran and Afghanistan, of the Pertinent Publications list. Among the more general references on this region are Gregory's (1929) work on the structure of Asia, the climatic analogs of south-central Asia by Robison and Dodd (1955), several of the Unesco reports previously included among the general references of this chapter, and the comprehensive terrain-analog study of the U. S. Army (U. S. Army Engineer Waterways Experiment Station, 1962).

The Iranian Desert (Iran)

The Iranian Desert is, in many respects, more similar to the arid area of the western United States than any desert area treated thus far. The basis for this statement is the fact that the Iranian Desert consists of basin-and-range topography, in the broad sense. Because the oil deposits of Iran occur primarily in the western part of the country, in the Zagros Mountain belt which is nonarid, and because much of the agriculture and settlement is either in the west or the north, along the well-watered Elburz Mountain belt, economic interests have not dictated exploration and development of the desert proper. Hence, one finds, with respect to both geomorphology and surface-water hydrology, that a wealth of information is available on the peripheral, nonarid regions of Iran, whereas the desert proper has been largely ignored.

Publications cited in the following text on the Iranian Desert (Iran), unless otherwise noted where cited, are listed in Section VII of the Pertinent Publications list. Among the early work that is available, Blanford's descriptions of the basin deposits (1873) and of the travels of the Boundary Commission (1876) in 1870-1872 are worthy of mention and some information on surficial features can also be obtained from Philippson's work (1918, 1920). Clapp (1940) has described the geology of eastern Iran, Bonnard has similarly treated the northeastern area (1945), and Gansser (1955), Harrison (1943), and Furon (1936, 1941) have each investigated the geology and surficial features of the Iranian Desert. The best geological map available is the map of Iran at a scale of 1:2,500,000 by the National Iranian Oil Company (1959). The explanatory notes that accompany this map include an abundant bibliography of Iranian geology, but few of the references are pertinent to this report. Much detailed information (on the oil-producing areas) can be obtained from the Iranian Oil Company and from the British Petroleum Company (1956).

Additional geological work in Iran is in progress by the Geological Survey, which is responsible for detailed investigations of limited areas, among other matters. The usual scale of mapping is 1:250,000 or 1:100,000, but the reports available and in progress do not treat the arid interior areas. Topographic mapping of Iran at a scale of 1:20,000 is also in progress, but the desert sheets will be the last to be produced. The topographic maps of the Iranian Desert that currently exist are small in scale and show mountains by means of form lines or shading. Information on geologic and topographic maps and reports in progress can be obtained from Mr. David Andrews of the Geological Survey of Iran or from personnel of the Iranian National Oil Company. Announcement of new maps is usually made by the Ministry of Information in addition to the agencies cited.

Geomorphic reports have been provided by Stratil-Sauer (1957), who treated the Dasht-e-Lut, and by Scharlau (1961), who used aerial photographs to interpret morphology. Lackey's (1951) report on environmental factors might also be mentioned here, but essentially it can be said that two men have provided the bulk of the geomorphic literature on the Iranian Desert, namely, Gabriel and Bobek. Gabriel has published a series of papers during a 30-year period on his observations in the central desert basins, particularly the Lut (Gabriel, 1934, 1938, 1942, 1952) and most recently has described the salt pans of central Iran (Gabriel, 1957). Bobek has been similarly engaged through the years and is perhaps best known for his general climatic interpretations (1953-1954) and his monograph on the Dasht-e-Kavir (1959), which is the most comprehensive description available of all the desert landforms of this region. This report includes both ground and aerial photographs and references to some earlier work and travels that are not cited here.

Several water-resources reports provide detailed information and maps of surficial features in the general area of concern. Illustrative of such reports is that of Gibb and Partners (1958) on the Varamin project area to the west of Tehran, and that on soil and water conservation in Iran by Dewan and Rieben (1958). Although both reports are excellent, they do not actually treat areas within the arid zone proper. The latter report, however, does discuss the general problems of wind and water erosion in the country and recommends a study of the slopes, soils, hydrology, and land use of the central Iranian closed basins, of which it is stated that no two are alike in all respects.

An interesting question, with respect to precipitation data and surface-water hydrology, is raised by this statement. There are more than 600 precipitation stations in Iran today, and the establishment of additional stations is planned. At least two-thirds of these stations were not in existence 10 years ago and the data are, in general, referable to relatively short periods of record and are nonhomogeneous. Moreover, the vast preponderance of the precipitation stations is not within the arid region of Iran. One need only glance at the distribution map of hydrologic stations of all types, which is available from the Ministry of Water and Power in Tehran, to recognize that the large areas without stations coincide with the geographic position of the great desert basins, the Dasht-e-Kavir, Dasht-e-Lut, and others. For these reasons, both isohyetal maps and estimates of runoff must be regarded as highly tentative for the desert areas, as emphasized by Ganji in his foreword to a summary of Iranian rainfall data (Independent Irrigation Corporation, various dates). This being true, the merits of climatic analogs and hydrologic summaries for the desert regions in Iran are open to question and, indeed, elsewhere in the arid regions of the world as well because lack of adequate data is a common problem.

Information on the drainage features of Iran, the locations of stream-discharge stations, and data on both water and sediment discharge, is available in the Hydrographic Yearbooks of Iran (Independent Irrigation Corporation, various dates), the country reports presented at various irrigation seminars (The Iranian Delegation, 1960, 1962, 1964), which provide some insight into the status of both general knowledge and of specific water projects in the country, and from summary papers. Among the latter, an excellent review of water resources development in Iran is contained in a survey of multiple-purpose river basin development schemes by the United Nations (1961*b*) and in Ghazinouri's recent paper (1966) presented at a CENTO Symposium.

Although much information on aspects of surface-water hydrology is available, in the form of raw data or in interpretive reports (Hariri, 1966), the study sites invariably rim the central desert basins, and the surface hydrology of the desert is not well known.

In summary, then, despite the excellent work that has been accomplished, the interior basins of central Iran have been largely ignored. There are some notable exceptions, such as the investigations of Bobek and Gabriel, but by any reasonable standards one must conclude that the available information on physical features is largely peripheral to the arid regions proper. The same is clearly true of climatic and hydrologic data in general. Unless future programs are specifically directed toward gathering such data in the arid basins of Iran, our knowledge of surface-water hydrology in these areas must remain meagre indeed.

Information on surface-water hydrology in Iran can be obtained from *Davoud Hariri,* of the hydrological division of the Ministry of Water and Power, and from the current U. S. AID representative in Tehran, *Albert Plummer.* On the basis of his work, *H. Bobek* should be considered an authority on the surficial features of the Iranian desert area. The National Iranian Oil Company is listed as a local depository.

The Iranian Desert (Afghanistan)

The arid zone of Afghanistan occurs in the southwestern part of the country, where the Iranian Desert is termed "Dasht-i-Margo," and also along the northwestern border with the U.S.S.R., where the southeastern fringe of the Kara-Kum extends into Afghanistan. Approximately one-half of the country is arid, and far more work has been done in the nonarid north, particularly in the Hindu Kush Mountain belt. Useful information on the Afghan desert is available, however, and this will be outlined here. Publications cited in the following text on the Iranian Desert (Afghanistan), unless otherwise noted where cited, are listed in Section VII of the Pertinent Publications list.

Early work of some relevance includes descriptive reports by Todd (1844), McMahon (1897), McMahon and McMahon (1897), and Griesbach (1886) prior to 1900, Huntington's (1909) article on the Russian and Persian frontier areas, a book on travels by Fox (1943), and geographic reports by Trinkler (1928), Merzbacher (1925), and Ryshtya (1947). In addition, Sedqi (1952) has discussed the Herat area in northwestern Afghanistan, Zaman (1951) has outlined the desert areas, and Humlum (1959) has provided a fairly recent geography text on Afghanistan which may be considered a basic reference on this subject.

Some geologic information is included in the works cited above but Clapp (1939), Furon (1951), and more recently Desio and Marussi (1960) have specifically treated this subject. The German Geological Mission to Afghanistan has compiled a bibliography of geology of Afghanistan (1964a) which is quite comprehensive. The bulk of the citations, however, either refer to work in the Hindu Kush range and adjacent nonarid areas or are paleontological in nature. The German Geological Mission to Afghanistan has also produced a geological map (1964b) of that portion of Afghanistan which is south of the Hindu Kush divide; the Russian Mission is mapping the northern part of the country. The German map, at a scale of 1:1,000,000, provides an excellent outline of the general geology of the Hindu Kush and

adjacent areas but the Dasht-i-Margo proper has been omitted. The Mission plans to engage a Pleistocene geologist in order to map the deposits of the southern desert, but the work is not currently available.

Hunger (1964) has outlined the status of geological work in Afghanistan through 1964 in a United Nations Technical Assistance Operations (UNTAO) file report and Dahle (1962) has similarly treated topographic mapping. Such UNTAO reports represent a valuable source of information and they can be consulted in Kabul. With respect to topographic mapping, aerial photographs of Afghanistan are available and Dahle indicates that maps of the desert areas will ultimately be produced at a scale of 1:1,000,000. The most comprehensive report available on the southern Afghan desert is that on soil and water resources by International Engineering Company (1959). It includes a description of topography and drainage, a summary of climatic and hydrologic data, and a land-use classification in terms of irrigation, crop potential, and allied matters. It will be referred to below in the treatment of surface-water hydrology.

Information on surface-water hydrology in Afghanistan that is pertinent to arid-zone considerations consists chiefly of data on the Helmand River. The Helmand is one of the world's few major streams, such as the Nile, Tigris-Euphrates, and Indus, which flow through extensive desert areas. Brigham (1964) has presented much of the discharge data obtained through the U. S. AID program in Afghanistan, and additional information on the Helmand River, and on the status of dams and irrigation projects in the country, is presented in country reports (Afghan Delegation, 1962; Roa, 1964; Mahboob, 1965) of 1962-1965. An excellent summary of the status of hydrology in Afghanistan is presented in the United Nations (1961a) river-basin development report and data gathered by the German Hydrologic Mission on northern streams in Afghanistan is available in their yearbook (Deutsche Wasserwirtschaftsgruppe Afghanistan, 1962).

Climatic conditions in Afghanistan have been discussed by Stenz (1947) and the matter has been treated in several of the geographic works previously cited, such as Humlum's text (1959). The Royal Afghan Meteorological Institute in Kabul is responsible for the gathering of climatic data and monthly summaries are available from this organization. Summary papers, such as those by the United Nations (1961a) and the International Engineering Company (1959) present convenient overviews of the available data; the climatic analog study of the U. S. Army (Robison and Dodd, 1955) also includes Afghanistan. The Pakistan Consulate and Morrison-

Knudsen (Afghanistan) also have climatic data but, as is true in most regions, the records are of insufficient duration and the stations too dispersed to place great reliance on isohyetal maps. Morrison-Knudsen reports on the soils and water resources of the Chakhansur area (1955) and on the Arghandab-Tarnak water scheme (1956) are also relevant and should be cited here. The International Engineering Company report previously cited (1959) mentions the areas of lakes and sinks in southern Afghanistan and, in addition to much useful information on climatic conditions, this report includes the Helmand River discharge estimates for the 1872-1901 period that were given in a report of the Persian-Afghan Arbitration Commission in 1905. Thus, through 1957, more than 40 years of record were available. It should be pointed out, however, that the record is not continuous and early estimates are somewhat questionable.

In summary, general knowledge of the Iranian Desert in Afghanistan is available, but as noted above many gaps exist. The geological map of the German Mission to Afghanistan omits the Dasht-i-Margo, large-scale topographic maps are totally lacking, climatic data are widely scattered, and only the hydrologic regimen of the Helmand River and a few principal tributaries can be categorized as moderately well known. As elsewhere in the arid regions, one must conclude that little is known of channel characteristics or streamflow in ephemeral drainage systems and that modern geomorphic studies of both drainage and landforms have not been undertaken.

Authorities

Authorities on the geology and geography of Afghanistan and individuals who can provide more detailed information on the availability of data and source materials include *A. Schreiber,* Chief of the German Geological Mission, *G. H. Benham* of the Asia Foundation, and *R. W. Pike* of the United Nations Mission. The latter two gentlemen are currently engaged in the compilation of all scientific information that is available on Afghanistan. *A. O. Westfall* of the U. S. AID group in Kabul is cognizant of all current surface-water investigations in southern Afghanistan and has access to the records of recent years that are not included in the reports cited above. He should be consulted for further information.

To the agencies and individuals cited above as sources of further information, personnel of appropriate departments at the University of Kabul might be added. At the date of the writer's visit, however, the geology, engineering, and other faculties had no arid-zone research in progress; this was largely due to lack of funds and vehicles for field investigations in the south, in contrast to the proximity of the Hindu Kush range and the economic needs of the non-arid northern area. No local depositories are listed, although the agencies mentioned have useful unpublished information.

The availability of information on geomorphology and surface-water hydrology in southern Asia will next be considered for West Pakistan, which occupies parts of both the Iranian and Thar deserts.

The Iranian-Thar Desert Area (West Pakistan)

The arid region of Pakistan includes the southwestern province of Baluchistan, the central and southern portions of the Indus River valley, and the eastern desert in Sind, which is sometimes referred to as the western Thar desert; each of these areas is in West Pakistan. Parts of both the Iranian and Thar deserts are thus represented in Pakistan. Because West Pakistan was formerly a part of India, the earlier literature, which is fairly extensive, is available in Indian journals and similar sources. Moreover, certain regional references which include information on the arid zone of West Pakistan may mention only India in their titles. This is particularly true if they were written prior to partition or are published in India. Publications cited in the following text on the Iranian-Thar Desert Area (West Pakistan), unless otherwise noted where cited, are listed in Section VIII of the Pertinent Publications list. Among the useful regional references are Spate's (1954) general geography of India and Pakistan, Wadia's (1953) standard work on the geology of India, a physical geography treatise by Chhibber (1945), and a student handbook on India and Pakistan by Mehdiratta (1954).

Early work on West Pakistan is abundant. Aspects of the physical features of Baluchistan, for example, were treated by Masson (1843) and subsequent outlines of the geology or geography of the region were provided by Stiffe (1873), Carter (1861), Cook (1860), Hughes (1877), Tale (1904), Taylor (1882), and Oldham (1892). Stiffe's paper (1873) treats mud volcanoes along the Mekran coast and another early report on the geology and physical features of the Baluchistan coastal area is that by Blanford (1872). Vredenburg's (1901) report on the geology of Baluchistan includes part of Iran but is also pertinent here.

More recent work on this region includes physiographic papers by Zoha (1950-1951) and Pithawalla (1952a), the latter's discussion of soil, water, and vegetation problems in the region (1952b), geological reports by Geb (1946) and Asrarullah (1954), some excellent work by Bakr on the geology (1963a) and physiography (1963b) of the Chagai-Kharan region in western Baluchistan, and Ahmad's (1951) description of volcanoes in Baluchistan. Additional information on Baluchistan has been provided in archeological papers by Raikes (1965), Raikes and Dyson (1961), and Fairservis (1956), and by Farah and Ahmad (1965), who conducted geophysical surveys in the dry lake region of western Baluchistan. In this vein, the gravity survey of the Quetta Valley (Mufti and Siddiqui, 1961) might also be mentioned.

The Indus River valley has received considerable attention because of its economic importance to the country since early times. Excluding reports of a purely hydrological nature at this point, Drew (1873) studied deposits of the Indus basin in 1873, modern investigations of the alluvial sediments have been undertaken by Tahirkheli (1960) and Danilchik and Tahirkheli (1959) in a search for economic mineral deposits, Pithawalla (1936) has provided a geographic description of the lower Indus area and, with Martin-Kaye (Pithawalla and Martin-Kaye, 1946) has published a geologic and geographic outline of the Karachi region. Taylor (1965) has written an informative history of the Indus plain and water development, and Panhwar's (1964) text on ground water in Hyderabad and Khairpur includes an excellent chapter on historical changes in the course of the Indus and the increase of its deltaic area. In addition, three excellent geological reports on the areas between the Indus River and its tributaries, namely the Rechna and Chaj doabs (Kidwai, 1963), the Thal doab (Siddiqi and Kazmi, 1963) and the Bari doab (Kidwai and Alam, 1964), are available. Two works of special significance for the purposes of this report are Fraser's (1958) treatment of landforms, soils, and land use of the entire Indus Plain and a report by a team of Russian geomorphologists to the Oil and Gas Development Corporation (1963-1964) in Karachi.

The Russians used aerial mosaics at a scale of 1:63,360 to plot the positions of such landforms as alluvial fans, floodplains, fixed and migrating dunes, and others. Their final map, showing the relief of uplifted and subsiding areas and landforms is presented on a scale of 1:250,000. Also included in this report is a map showing the principal channels of the Indus River and their varying locations between 1935 and 1960, geophysical maps, and water-table maps. Data on slopes, relief, degree of dissection, and nature and thickness of alluvium are given in the text.

Fraser's work (1958) is most comprehensive and is contained in one volume of the Colombo Plan Project Report by the Canadian Government. He has classified the landforms of the Indus Plain area into 20 types and has grouped these by "province." His distinctions among such features as "active flood plains," "meander flood plains," and "cover flood plains" are somewhat arbitrary, and examination of the aerial photographs employed suggests that it would not be difficult to produce other classifications from the same data. The origin of the 20 landforms discussed follows classical lines and is erroneous in certain instances but, as a whole, this report is a most important contribution; the contained data and interpretations are presented on 25 color maps at a scale of 1:253,440.

Information of a geologic or geographic nature on the arid regions elsewhere in West Pakistan is also contained in both early and modern reports. Blanford (1877, 1879) discussed the geology of Sind as early as 1877, Murray (1880) issued a handbook of the geology, botany, and zoology of Sind in 1880, and Oldham (1903) discussed the sand hills near Karachi in 1903. It should be pointed out that many early reports have intrinsic merit by reason of their vintage alone. If one wishes to study the rates of migration of dunes, changes in river courses or landforms in general, or the changes in vegetation of a given area, then the comparison of previous conditions with the present status can be invaluable.

With respect to eolian sand deposits and wind action, these topics are mentioned in many geological reports on West Pakistan but Naqvi and Tahir (1950), Khan Muhammad (1951), and Smith and Snead (1962) have specifically treated these matters. Other reports worthy of mention here include a discussion of the application of photogeology in Pakistan by Hemphill and Kidwai (1963), Wright's (1964) outline of a possible land classification in the Nagar Parkar area, geological reports on the lower Swat region (Martin, Siddiqi, and King, 1962) and the Sra Khulla damsite (Kazmi, 1962), and basic papers by Anstey (1965) and Khan (1960).

Anstey's work consists of a quantitative investigation of alluvial fans in Pakistan and in the United States, based on map and aerial-photograph measurements, and Khan has provided an outstanding mathematical analysis of the climatic data from West Pakistan in an attempt to determine the recent precipitation trends in the arid areas.

Before turning to the available information on surface-water hydrology, several most important sources of information on West Pakistan and on current work must be cited. The recent geological map of Pakistan by Bakr and Jackson (1964) is excellent, and it presents more detail than might be anticipated from a map at a scale of 1:2,000,000. Kashmir is also included on this map and further information on the region can be obtained from Pithawalla's basic text (1953) on the geology and geography of Kashmir. Thirlaway has provided an outline (1960) of arid-zone research at the Geophysical Institute and Repp (1961) and the Pakistan Food and Agriculture Council (1962) have recently summarized all arid-zone research in West Pakistan. Additional general information is available in Currie's (1956) report on the desert areas and in the Proceedings of the Karachi Symposium on soil erosion (Pakistan Food and Agriculture Council, 1960). The value of this latter report should be emphasized; it contains much basic information on erosion, weathering, and sand-dune migration in all parts of the West Pakistan desert that is not readily available from other sources. Several papers included in these proceedings treat soil and ecological problems as well as summary reports on other countries.

Finally, the bibliographic sources for West Pakistan should be outlined. The Geological Survey of Pakistan has issued a list of the available publications of this agency (1965), Offield has compiled an extensive reference list on the geology of Pakistan (1964), and the efforts of PANSDOC, the Pakistan National Scientific and Technical Documentation Centre, have been outstanding. The latter agency compiles bibliographies on a variety of pertinent subjects for the benefit of all research investigators in Pakistan. This information is presented in the agency's (1965) list of PANSDOC bibliographies. Also compiled is a 1961 list of scientific and technical periodicals in Pakistan and PANSDOC personnel since 1961 have regularly scanned more than 50 journals to obtain references for *Pakistan Science Abstracts*. Most of the PANSDOC bibliographies treat flora, fauna, and agricultural topics, but several are pertinent to surface-water hydrology and these will be cited below.

Basic data that are pertinent to surface-water hydrology in West Pakistan are available from several sources. The Surface Water Circle in Lahore issues annual reports (1962) which provide information on the number and locations of stream gaging stations, water and sediment discharges, and meteorological information. A similar compilation is contained in the joint publication of the Surface Water Circle and Harza Engineering Company (1962). Much useful information on the hydrology of the Indus River and its tributaries is contained in reports on geology and geography previously cited, but in addition, Pithawalla (1943) discussed the problem of flood recurrence, Karpov and Nebolsine (1958) summarized the channel lengths, drainage area, discharge, and precipitation-runoff relations in the Indus River system, and Greenman (1963) and Paver and Scholz (1955) treated hydrology in the Punjab. Andrew's (1958) report on water resources around Quetta and Raikes' (1957) summary of surface-water

hydrology are representative of efforts in Baluchistan, and allied topics such as dry lakes and phreatophytes have been treated by Cotter (1923) and Naqvi and Hamid (1956), respectively.

An excellent summary of water-resources plans in West Pakistan was presented by Parvez (1963) at the Bangkok conference on water-resources development. This paper presents basic data, a map of drainage-basins in West Pakistan, and an outline of water organizations in the country, as well as a discussion of long-term plans for development. The most important hydrologic problem in West Pakistan involves the waterlogging and salinity which accompanies irrigation from the Indus River and its tributaries. Two excellent reports that treat this problem and which provide additional summaries of the general hydrology, geology, geography, soils, and history of land use, are the White House / Interior Panel report (U. S. White House / Department of the Interior Panel on Waterlogging and Salinity in West Pakistan, 1964) and the Pakistan committee report at the FAO Seminar in Lahore (Pakistan Ministry of Agriculture and Works Advisory Committee, 1965).

Additional information on surface-water hydrology in West Pakistan can be obtained from PANSDOC (Pakistan National Scientific and Technical Documentation Centre) bibliographies on flood control (1959), sediment control (1957), dams and reservoirs (1958), and engineering geology (1960), although the contained references are not restricted to work in Pakistan. In summary, one could say that the surface hydrology and geomorphology of the Indus basin are fairly well known, certainly better known than the arid areas to the west.

Authorities and Depositories

Authorities on the physical features and surface-water hydrology of West Pakistan are relatively numerous, and for purposes of this report only a few need be cited here. *S. N. Naqvi*, Director of the Meteorological Department in Karachi, should be consulted on climate-related problems. He has access to all available data and can provide information on a current scheme which involves the establishment of stations at locations for which "forecasts" have been made by extrapolation of existing records. *M. L. Khan*, of Punjab University in Lahore, also can be regarded as expert on meteorological matters, particularly with respect to climatic change and trends.

Personnel of the Surface Water Circle, General Hydrology Circle, and Geohydrology Circle, in Lahore, can provide current information on surface-water hydrology and, in the case of the Geohydrology Circle, on physical features as well. *Abdul Shakur* and *Zamir-uddin Kidwai* are both conversant with the activities of this group. *Thomas Maddock, Jr.,* of the U. S. Geological Survey is particularly knowledgeable on sediment-transport problems in West Pakistan.

Geologic and geographic information on West Pakistan can best be obtained from personnel of the Geological Survey of Pakistan in Quetta; *A. F. M. M. Haque* is Director General and *M. Abu Bakr,* Director of Publications, is particularly worthy of mention by reason of his own work in Baluchistan and on the geological map of Pakistan. Other sources include the Harza Engineering Company and Hunting Group in Lahore, Tipton and Kalmbach, Consulting Engineers, Denver, the Oil and Gas Development Company in Karachi, and the departments of Geology or Geography at the Universities of Karachi, Peshawar, and Punjab. Other local depositories are limited to the agencies mentioned in the text above as working in the field.

The Thar (India)

The arid zone of India includes principally the two northwestern states of Punjab and Rajasthan; the Thar Desert extends westward into Pakistan and merges imperceptibly with the arid region of Sind and the Indus Plain in that country. West of the Aravalli Range in Rajasthan, the primary physiographic characteristic of the Thar Desert is vast sand areas and dune belts. Because encroachment by wind-blown sand occurs in several areas, much literature on the Thar treats the causes and history of deserts and sand tracts in general. Much general physiographic information is available in a variety of works on geology or geography, and a summary of these sources of information is now provided. Publications cited in the following text on the Thar (India), unless otherwise noted where cited, are listed in Section IX of the Pertinent Publications list.

Among the early works still relevant for reasons previously cited, Carter (1857, 1861) discussed the general geology of western India, parts of Pakistan, and other regions as early as 1857. Wynne (1872) contributed to the geology of the Kutch in the southern Thar Desert, Medlicott (1889) outlined the geology of Punjab, which was subsequently treated in greater detail in the Provincial Services compendium (Imperial Gazetter of India, 1908), and La Touche (1902) provided similar material on the western Rajputana.

More modern works that contain pertinent information on the Thar include Pithawalla's (1939) classification of physiographic provinces in India, Ahmad's (1947) discussion of the physiographic features of the Punjab plain, Chhibber's previously-cited geography (1945), and Spate's regional text (1954), also mentioned in the section of this chapter

treating Pakistan. The best geographic descriptions of the Thar Desert are given in reports by Pithawalla (1952) and by Bharadwaj (1961), in an excellent review paper on the arid zone of India and Pakistan. General geologic works on India by Wadia (1953, see Pert. Pubs. Sec. VIII) and Krishnan (1953) and on India and Burma by Krishnan (1960) and Pascoe (1950-1959) will suffice to provide the necessary information on this subject. Additional useful sources, however, are the Geological Survey of India index guides to geologic maps (1943) and to the "Memoirs" and "Records" (1938). Survey personnel should be consulted for more current materials than are included in these index guides.

One of the geomorphic subjects of long-standing interest concerns the past and present drainage features of parts of the desert region. This matter was first discussed by Oldham (1886), and a representative sample of subsequent work includes papers on Punjab river courses by Gulshal (1934), Ahmad (1948), Din (1952), Wadia's (1937), more widely-ranging considerations of drainage changes in the Indo-Gangetic basin, and archeologic reports such as those by Ghosh (1952) and Sankalia (1952), who discuss the evidence suggesting that flow occurred in many of the desert wadis in historic time. Bharadwaj (1961) also discussed this matter, in addition to summarizing the evidence and views on climatic changes in the region.

The most recent reports on the Thar Desert include Raheja's (1962) summary of arid-zone research in India, to which the interested reader is referred for details on personnel, agencies, and current investigations not mentioned here, and a survey of desert development by Kurakova (1964). A review of the literature makes clear, however, the fact that the most important single source of information on many aspects of the Indian desert area is the proceedings of the symposium on the Rajputana desert (National Institute of Sciences of India, 1952), held in New Delhi in 1952. In addition to the several contained papers already cited (Pithawalla, 1952; Ghosh, 1952; Sankalia, 1952), this volume contains reports that treat the evolution of the desert, its geology, topography, meteorology, hydrology, flora, fauna, and soils, and attempts at reclamation. A few of these reports should be discussed here.

The preface to the symposium proceedings volume states that the primary reason for calling a scientific meeting was the widespread "fears . . . that the desert was spreading at an alarming rate." The Planning Commission, in fact, argued that some 50 square miles of fertile land per year were consumed by the desert advance. It is therefore instructive to consider the published evaluations of Krishnamurthy

(1952) and Singh (1952), among others, which were adequately summarized by Hora (1952). It appears that no sequence of adequate topographical surveys have ever proven the case of desert expansion. The Thar expanded in certain areas and retreated in others. The precise boundaries of the Thar and, indeed, of all deserts, cannot be objectively defined and opinions on advance and retreat rely primarily upon the occurrence or absence of windblown sand.

The problem posed by the Thar is duplicated by the southern limit of the Sahara and other deserts as well. First, it is often difficult, if not impossible, to segregate the effects of man from those of nature (von Wissman *et al.,* 1956). It is perhaps equally incorrect to attribute all desert expansion in a given area to overgrazing and other poor agricultural practices of man on the one hand, or to climatic change and natural causes on the other; both causes may well be involved. Secondly, it is equally difficult to extrapolate all changes of desert boundaries, even if such changes are quantitatively established, through long intervals of time. Any desert is undoubtedly an equilibrium body, and its margins will vary through time while occupying some mean position, other factors being equal. The fertile fields that are overrun by sand in one man's lifespan may be naturally regained in the next. This matter is intimately linked with the problems of sand migration and river runoff in the deserts and will be discussed further in the conclusions of this report.

With respect to surface-water hydrology of the Thar Desert, much information on the climatic conditions, saline lakes, catchment areas, and similar matters is contained in a series of symposium papers (National Institute of Sciences of India, 1952) on hydrology and meteorology that will not be individually cited here. In addition, detailed data on the rainfall distribution are available in several reports by Ramdas (1949, 1950) and Govindaswamy (1953). Bhatia (1957) has assessed the water balance of the arid zone in India, and some general surface information is contained in ground-water reports on the eastern Kutch by Taylor and Oza (1954) and Taylor and Pathak (1960).

In summary knowledge of the Thar Desert of India is gradually increasing; particular impetus with respect to both geomorphology and surface-water hydrology was provided by the establishment of a Central Arid Zone Research Institute in Jodhpur about 6 years ago. Geomorphic investigations are patterned on the C.S.I.R.O. land-use scheme and, as will be described more fully in the section of this report on Australia, the maps that are produced provide good descriptions of the geology, topography, vegetation, soils, and other land-use factors on a scale of 1:126,720. In addition, some quantitative data on average slopes in a given area are included. Despite such notable work as that on the Luni River drainage basin in western Rajasthan, it is fair to say that this type of information is available for only a small percentage of the desert area. Although floods occasionally occur in the Thar as in all desert areas, India is primarily a subtropical country and for this reason little effort has been directed toward ascertaining runoff and sediment discharge of streams in the arid area. One of the most comprehensive reports on water-resources development in India is presented in the United Nations (1956) report on Burma, India, and Pakistan. Implicit in the content of this report and in the more recent irrigation progress report as well (Indian Delegation, 1964), is the fact that nearly all data collection and planned water projects in India are or will be conducted in areas outside the Thar. Moreover, investigations of all types, when conducted in the deserts at all, tend to be concentrated upon the desert areas of lesser aridity.

Authorities and Depositories

Information on the several governmental water agencies and personnel in India can be obtained from the U. N. report cited above or from *L. A. Ramdas* of the National Physical Laboratory in New Delhi. The Central Arid Zone Research Institute may be regarded as a depository of information on the Indian desert, and its director, *P. C. Raheja,* as an authority, for purposes of this report. All aspects of current work and future plans in the Thar can be obtained from this source.

E. THE AUSTRALIAN DESERTS

The arid zone of Australia includes approximately three-quarters of the continent, and all states contain some arid regions with perhaps the exception of Victoria, which is marginal. The deserts that occur within the arid zone are the Great Sandy Desert and Gibson Desert in Western Australia, the Great Victoria Desert, which is principally in Western Australia but which extends eastward into South Australia, and the Simpson Desert of the Northern Territory, Queensland, and South Australia. Meigs' map (1953, see Pert. Pubs. Sec. I) also lists the Arunta Desert, but this is a seldom-used name. The Sturts Stony Desert is more commonly referred to in Australia. These desert areas were explored by personnel of several early expeditions, and the descriptive reports of such journeys contain much useful information. As previously indicated, early travel reports often provide an otherwise unobtainable basis for comparative studies of river-channel, sand-dune, vegetation, and, possibly, landform changes through time. Publications cited in the following text on the Australian Deserts, unless otherwise noted where cited, are listed in Section X of the Pertinent Publications list.

Among the reports of early expeditions are Sturt's account (1849) of travels in central Australia between 1844 and 1846, reports of the 1872 Warburton expedition to Western Australia (Warburton, 1875a, b) those of Lindsay (1889, 1893) and Tietkens (1891) of trips from Queensland into central Australia approximately 15 years later, several journals on the Horn expedition to central Australia by Tate and Watt (1896), Winnecke (1896), and Spencer (1896) (the last being the most comprehensive), and accounts of other scientific trips in central and western Australia around the turn of the century by Wells (1902) and Barclay (1916).

Several relatively early works that describe the physical features of parts of the Australian arid zone are available. Gregory (1906) and Taylor (1924) provided such information, Woodward (1912) and Jutson (1914, 1917) treated Western Australia, and the latest edition of the latter's work (Jutson, 1950) is still used as a standard physiography of the region. It summarizes many of Jutson's papers treating Western Australia. Clarke (1926, 1938) also described the physical features of Western Australia, and Clapp (1926) reported on the Great Sandy Desert in the northwestern part of the state. Fenner (1930, 1931) provided the basic descriptions of South Australia and the well-known work of Madigan (1930, 1936b, 1938a, b) is a standard early reference on the features of the Simpson Desert and central Australia in general. For convenience, Madigan's account of sand formation in the Simpson Desert (1946), which was one part of the 1939 expedition report, may also be cited here. Marshall (1948) discussed the total extent of the Australian Desert and Prescott (1936) gave an early account of climatic controls.

Some early reports of a geological nature which also include physical descriptions of the arid regions include the work of Basedow (1905), Talbot (1910), Talbot and Clarke (1917), Jack's (1915) paper on the area in the vicinity of the Musgrave Ranges, and Singleton's review (1939) of the Tertiary geology of Australia. The basic reference on the general geology of Australia is David's (1950) publication, *The Geology of the Commonwealth of Australia.*

A general geography of Australia that would form a companion for David's geologic treatise (1950) does not exist. Jutson has treated Western Australia as noted above (1950), and reports on soils and land use to be subsequently cited contain comparable information on the physical features of parts of Australia. Apart from these, sections of *The Australian Environment* (Australia Commonwealth Scientific and Industrial Research Organization, 1960) on physical geography, climate, and soils, Hills' review paper on geology and geophysics (1957), a similar effort by Christian, Jennings, and Twidale (1957) on geomorphology, and Mabbutt's outline of arid-zone geomorphology (1961a) are useful sources of general information. The availability of maps of all types is indicated in an index published by the Australia Department of National Development (1961) in Canberra. This index covers the 1940-1959 period, and supplementary data can be obtained from this agency. The Australia Department of National Development is currently preparing a revised edition of the *Atlas of Australian Resources* (1962), which is a most important source of general information. The 30 sheets of this map series include geology, physical features, soils, and climatic elements of the continent.

A considerable amount of information on the geomorphology of the Australian arid zone is contained in papers and reports that treat soils and soils problems. The primary reason for this, aside from the personal interest of various investigators, is that the prevalence of paleosols, laterites, duricrust, and other weathered, surficial materials in the Australian arid zone is thought to have an important bearing on problems of rates of erosion, the development of landforms, and the chronology of climatic and erosional events. It is therefore necessary to indicate certain of these soils reports here despite the fact that the soils of the arid regions of the world are treated by H. E. Dregne in another chapter of this compendium. The origin of crusts, and indeed of soils in general, is highly debatable, and the reports cited below contain varying views on this matter. Their inclusion in this report is solely a function of their relevance with respect to the availability of information on the physical features of the arid zone of Australia.

Woolnough (1927) discussed the Australian duricrust in 1927, and other pertinent work prior to 1940 would include reports by Prescott and Hosking (1936), Prescott and Skewes (1938), Piper (1932), Teakle (1936), and others who described soils from various arid parts of the continent. Most of the pertinent literature is of more recent vintage, however. Jessup (1960a, b; 1961a, b; 1962) has treated the stony soils of the southern arid region, as well as chronological problems, Ollier (1961, 1962, 1963) has described the deposits near Coober Pedy in South Australia and weathering phenomena in central Australia, Butler (1950, 1958, 1959, 1961b, 1962) has provided several discussions of the relevance of soils studies to geomorphic problems in addition to information on the prior-streams question in the Riverine Plains, and Hallsworth, Gibbons, and Darley (1951); Hallsworth, Robertson, and Gibbons (1955); Hawkins (1961), Webb (1962), Stephens (1961), Jackson (1957*a, b;* 1960, 1962); Litchfield (1960, 1962), Mulcany (1960), Churchward (1960; 1961*a, b;* 1963*a, b*), Crocker (1946*a, b*), Hays (1962), Mabbutt (1961*b, c*), Taylor (1950), and others have provided much basic information on the general features of the arid zone as well as on the soil types, their possible origins, and their interrelations with geomorphic problems. Finally, the recent paper on duricrust in western New South Wales and Queensland by Langford-Smith and Dury (1965) presents an excellent summary of the interpretive problems of origin, and the field characteristics and distribution of duricrust in these regions.

One of the best sources of information on the physical features of parts of the arid zone of Australia is the Land Research Series of the Commonwealth Scientific and Industrial Research Organization (C.S.I.R.O.). Two reports in this series are particularly relevant, namely that treating the Alice Springs area in Northern Territory (Perry *et al.,* 1962) and the Wiluna-Meekatharra area in Western Australia (Mabbutt *et al.,* 1963). Such reports typify the usual C.S.I.R.O. investigative procedure, which is to assemble teams of experts on geomorphology, geology, soils, vegetation, water resources, and agriculture-animal husbandry in order to produce a comprehensive treatise on each of these aspects of a given area. In addition to the basic information contained in the texts of these reports, maps of the geology, land use, water resources, and land systems, which accompany the reports, are quite valuable. The land-systems maps present a classification scheme used by the C.S.I.R.O. which reflects geology, geomorphology, soils, and vegetation. The Alice Springs map, for example, presents a total of 88 facets or subdivisions, each of which is descriptive of terrain features. Quantitative data, such as the range of slope values within a given subarea, are provided.

Subdivision number 30 of this map is listed as "Hogarth (400 square miles). Sandstone uplands and ridges above dissected limestone plateaus, relief up to 100 ft.; little sandy soil; sparse mulga or gidgee over short grass." The information that is most obviously lacking from such maps is topography; this problem is, in fact, ubiquitous in the Australian arid zone. The topographic sheets that do exist generally show relief by means of form lines, hence mention of the local relief on the land-systems maps of the C.S.I.R.O. and of local gradients in the companion texts often constitutes the only available topographic information for a given area.

Additional information on physical features of the Australian arid zone is, of course, contained in

reports that treat some other aspects of geomorphology. The Murrumbidgee and Murray river systems in New South Wales occupy the region known as the Riverine Plains and several reports treat some geomorphic problems of the area. Butler (1958, 1961*a*) has described the sediments of the plains, as have Hawkins and Walker (1956). Bowler and Harford (1963) have treated the presumed geomorphic sequence of events near Echuca; Pels (1960) has reported on the geology. The existing sand dunes were described by Stannard (1961), and Jessup's proposed soils chronology (1961*b*) is also relevant to this region. Perhaps the most intriguing geomorphic question, that of the prior streams or fossil drainage of the Riverine Plains, has been outlined by Langford-Smith (1960*a*) who has also presented a cogent summary of the essential points at issue in a series of letters to the editor of the *Australian Journal of Science* (Langford-Smith, 1959, 1960*b*, 1962). Schumm has recently attempted to gather quantitative data on the channel morphology and sediment distribution in the ancient (prior) and modern channels in connection with this problem. A project summary of his work is available (Schumm, 1965), but Dury's excellent series of papers on misfit streams in general, and their implications, is the basic reference on the subject (Dury, 1964*a, b;* 1965, see Pert. Pubs. Sec. I).

Other pertinent reports on varied geomorphic topics include the fine papers on slope development and inselbergs by Ollier and Tuddenham (1962, 1961), Ollier's recent discussion (1965) of granite weathering and the resulting forms in Australia, an excellent description of Ayers Rock, the principal inselbergs of central Australia, by Bremer (1965) and of other inselbergs by Twidale (1962, 1964), a description of profile forms in central Australia by Stewart and Litchfield (1957), and a modern investigation of pediments near Broken Hill by Langford-Smith and Dury (1964) that provides quantitative slope data. Mabbutt's (1966) plausible theory of mantle-controlled planation of pediments is also a fine contribution to the literature.

In addition to the above work on slopes, pediments, and inselbergs, Stannard (1961), Madigan (1946, 1936*a*), Carroll (1944), Hills (1939), King (1960), and Webb and Wopfner (1961), among others, have contributed to knowledge of the longitudinal dune fields of Australia and other eolian landforms, Hills has also provided papers on the general surficial features of Australia (1955), a presumed relationship between regional landforms and climate (1953), and a useful summary of arid-zone research in Australia (1961); Mabbutt, in addition to work previously cited (Mabbutt, 1961*a,* *b, c;* Mabbutt *et al.,* 1963), has discussed the degradation of land surfaces (1961*d*) and the problem of inheritance of landform characteristics in the Macdonnell Ranges (1962) and has furnished an excellent description of wanderrie features and their microrelief in Western Australia (1963).

The lakes, pans, and playas in the arid regions of Australia have also been investigated, but equal effort has not been expended on all. These features in Western Australia were described by Woodward (1897), Gregory (1914, 1916), Campbell (1906), and Gibson (1909), each of whom proposed an origin of the lakes; reconstructions, consisting of linking the lakes by hypothetical drainage paths, have been presented by Hills (1953), Clarke, Prider, and Teichert (1944), and most recently Bettenay (1962). The distribution of lakes in Western Australia is also discussed by Jutson (1950), whose physiographic map showing a region of interior drainage in this lake district has been widely reproduced. Floods within historic time (August of 1964) have demonstrated the arbitrary character of such physiographic distinctions, however. Elsewhere in Australia, Lake Eyre in South Australia has received the greatest attention. Bonython (1956) has described the features of this great lake and its salt deposits, as well as the occurrence of the extensive floods of 1949-1950 (1955). In addition, King (1956) has provided an outline of the presumed Quaternary chronology, fossiliferous shoreline deposits, and the present topography of Lake Eyre, and Ludbrook (1961) has presented information on the subsurface stratigraphy based upon deep drilling. The geomorphic history of other lakes in South Australia has been discussed by de Mooy (1959).

Because the arid zone of Australia intersects the coastline in the western and southern parts of the country, McGill's map of coastal landforms of the world (McGill, 1958, see Pert. Pubs. Sec. I) is again of some relevance. Additionally, Bird's (1964) text on coastal landforms provides some pertinent Australian examples. The best source of information on the characteristics of Australian estuaries and on the work that has been done is a summary paper by Jennings and Bird (1964) on this subject; it contains an excellent reference list. Further information on this topic will be presented in a chapter of this compendium by J. F. Schreiber, Jr., treating desert coastal zones.

The general aspects of geomorphology have been comparatively well covered, but only a small proportion of the arid area is known in any detail.

With respect to surface-water hydrology, certain pertinent Australian reports have already been cited, particularly those treating the Riverine Plains area and the lakes of the arid regions. Much additional information exists, however, and its availability will be indicated here.

Climatic data, which are basic for surface-water investigations in any region, are presented in the previously-cited publication, *The Australian Environment.* A tabulation of precipitation data also appears in Anstey's report (1961) on the analogies between climatic conditions in Yuma, Arizona, and in the Australian deserts, and further information on general climatic conditions of the arid zone is contained in the reports from the 1956 Unesco symposium held in Canberra. The best summary of Australian climatic data, however, is presented in the recent *Review of Australia's Water Resources* (Australian Water Resources Council, 1965), which contains an isohyetal map on a scale of 1:12,000,000. The precise position of isohyets on any map of an arid region can be questioned by reason of lack of sufficient data. The map in question here is no exception, but it should be recognized that, by comparison, Meigs' (1953, see Pert. Pubs. Sec. I) arid-zone boundary for Australia includes a considerable area on which precipitation is in excess of 10 inches per year.

The variability of rainfall increases, both in magnitude and areal distribution, with increasing aridity. As mentioned previously in this report, there is a great need for obtaining additional data. One pertinent effort in this direction in Australia is outlined in Chapman's report (1964) on the installation of rain gages and other hydrologic equipment in several experimental watersheds near Alice Springs. Chapman is currently conducting a long-term hydrologic investigation of 18 watersheds in the area.

Chapman has also published a comprehensive study (1962) of all aspects of hydrology at Lorna Glen and Wiluna in central Western Australia. His study includes a modern statistical analysis of the recurrence interval of both precipitation and surface runoff of given magnitudes; the methods employed have also been outlined by Dury (1964). In addition to various reports on the lakes and drainage features of Western Australia previously cited, salinity problems have been investigated by Bettenay, Blackmore, and Hingston (1964) and general reviews of several aspects of water-supply problems in the state have been provided by Langford-Smith (1947) and, more recently, by Western Australia Land Use Study Group (1964), in an advisory report to the Australian government.

The land-research series of reports by the C.S.I.R.O. and, indeed, much of the general geomorphic literature cited above present data on drainage features, but a host of separate agencies in each of the Australian States publish reports on this subject. An example of an excellent report so issued is that on the Cooper's Creek area in southwest Queensland (Whitehouse *et al.,* 1947) which provides much information on flood probability and extent in central Australia. A prohibitive effort would be involved in an attempt to compile all relevant reports published by state agencies, but several general sources of information present the available data. Bauer (1954), for example, has provided a summary of the availability of gaging-station data in Australia which includes drainage-basin characteristics and estimates of annual runoff. The *Water Resources Newsletter* provides current information on research projects, mapping, and basic data collection in hydrology throughout Australia and is an excellent source of information. Finally, the *Review of Australia's Water Resources,* cited above, can be considered the basic reference work on Australian hydrology. In addition to the meteorologic data previously discussed, this comprehensive report includes sections on surface and ground-water hydrology and a list of all Australian agencies responsible for data collection. The surface-water summary presented includes all available information on drainage areas, stream discharge, and variability of discharge. With respect to the arid regions proper, however, this report again serves to indicate the scarcity of hydrologic data.

As of 1963 there were 1439 gaging stations in the country. The river-basin maps that are presented indicate that most of arid Australia is included in two divisions, namely the Western Plateau (1,051,000 square miles) and Lake Eyre (441,600 square miles) basins. None of the Western Plateau is gaged, and only 30 percent of the Lake Eyre drainage is gaged. Some increase in data collection in the arid region of Australia will coincide with the International Hydrologic Decade but vast gaps will nevertheless remain. With respect to sediment discharge of streams, essentially nothing is known of the characteristics of the drainage in the truly arid parts of Australia; lack of water-discharge data alone renders estimates of sediment discharge rather specious.

*Authorities for Geomorphology and
General Surficial Features*

Authorities on the geomorphology and general surficial features of the Australian desert are several, but for purposes of this report three will suffice. *J. A. Mabbutt,* of the School of Geography, University of New South Wales, and *T. Langford-Smith* and *G. H. Dury,* of the Department of Geography, University of Sydney, can each provide further information on available reports and data and current work in progress. The Departments of Geology and Geography of the several Australian universities and the Geological Survey offices of the states contain competent personnel who also can provide such information. The Department of National Development and the C.S.I.R.O., both in Canberra, should be consulted for further bibliographic material and for maps and aerial photographs. In addition to the contained references to various Australian periodicals in this report, the interested reader would also do well to consult the "Annual Reports" of the C.S.I.R.O. and the *Arid Zone Newsletter* (1956-) which is also issued by the C.S.I.R.O. The latter publication presents information on all aspects of current investigations in the country, including those of commercial companies. Reports of the latter that pertain to petroleum exploration are also tabulated in the "Reviews and Recent Publications" section of the *Bulletin of the American Association of Petroleum Geologists.*

Authorities for Surface-Water Hydrology

Further information on the status of hydrologic knowledge in Australia can be obtained from *R. O. Slatyer, G. Fitzpatrick,* and *T. G. Chapman* of the C.S.I.R.O. in Canberra, who are expert on meteorology and surface-water hydrology, from *N. O. Jones* of the Bureau of Mineral Resources in Alice Springs, and from *Eric Bettenay* of the C.S.I.R.O. in Perth. Current studies by *C. Poole,* Resident Engineer of the Northern Territories Department of Works, may remedy the lack of sediment-discharge knowledge in the Alice Springs area. On the strength of his excellent work on sediment yield (Douglas, 1964, 1965) elsewhere in Australia, *Ian Douglas* of Australia National University, Canberra, also can be consulted for advice and information on this subject.

F.   SOUTH AMERICA

The arid zone of South America includes parts of six countries according to Meigs' (1953, see Pert. Pubs. Sec. I) scheme: Peru, Chile, Argentina, Bolivia, Venezuela, and Brazil. The areal extent of the arid zone is greatest in the first three countries. The Atacama-Peruvian occupies northern Chile and southern Peru and extends northward along the Peruvian coast in a relatively narrow belt to the Ecuador border. This northern continuation of the Atacama is sometimes termed "the Sechura Desert." The Monte-Patagonian desert in central and southern Argentine is the other principal arid region of South America. Bolivia will not be discussed separately in this report, but for convenience information on the Altiplano and Puna de Atacama areas in southwestern Bolivia will be included in the discussion of the Atacama-Peruvian Desert. Publications cited in the following text on South America (in general), unless otherwise noted where cited, are listed in Section XI of the Pertinent Publications list.

Discussion of the two minor coastal enclaves of aridity in northern Venezuela and the arid area in northeastern Brazil will essentially be omitted. It might be noted here, however, that Liddle's (1946) text on the geology of Venezuela and Wilhelmy's paper (1954) on aridity in northern South America are pertinent to the coastal enclaves, and King (1956), James (1952), Dresch (1957), and Demangeot (1960) have treated the morphology of northeastern Brazil. The geologic summary by de Oliveira and Leonardos (1943) also contains some useful information on the Brazilian arid area, but the general South American references, to be cited below, should also be consulted. The best hydrologic reports on northeastern Brazil include two administrative reports of the U. S. Geological Survey. The first of these, by Schoff (1962), describes what is termed the "drought polygon" and outlines the past and current hydrological work within the framework of specific project recommendations. A good bibliography is included and, combined with the data presented, this report represents a valuable summary of available information. The second report, by Cederstrom and Assad (1962), presents a more extensive description of the area based on a field reconnaissance and also contains meteorologic, geologic, and hydrologic data. The bibliography of this report should also be consulted. The available data suggest that although northeastern Brazil is indeed an area plagued by low rainfall and periodic drought, it is not a true arid region despite its inclusion on Meigs' (1953*) map.

With respect to South America in general, certain works mentioned at the outset of this report are worthy of repetition here. The global treatments by Machatschek (1955*) and King (1962*) the world atlas of the U.S.S.R. Academy of Sciences (Akademiya nauk S.S.S.R., 1964*), and McGill's map of coastal landforms of the world (1958*) are germane. More specific South American information, however, is available in the geology text by Gerth (1955), Jenks' handbook of geology (1956), a discussion of South American deserts by de Martonne (1947) and Chapman (1960), the regional geography of South America by Shanahan (1959), and early papers on general geography by Rich (1942) and the arid regions by Sorge (1930). The monograph by Rich contains an excellent collection of aerial photographs. Additionally, Smith (1939) has provided a physiographic map of the continent which is still adequate, and Turnbull's (1961) climatic analog of Yuma and South America provides a summary of some basic climatic and physiographic data.

---

*See Pert. Pubs. Sec. I.

Authorities and Depositories

A most important source of general information on arid-zone and other research activities in South America is the Centro de Cooperación Científica de la Unesco para la América Latina, in Montevideo. This organization maintains bibliographies on all South American research, and it reports on arid-zone symposia and similar meetings in a "Boletín." Particularly in South America, depositories of information on desert geomorphology and surface hydrology are the agencies and universities cited below as active in research. Although authorities on surficial features and surface-water hydrology in each of the South American countries will be cited in discussion of those countries, it should be noted here that *Alfonso Wilson* of the U. S. Geological Survey, Tucson, can provide information on all aspects of current surface-water activities and future plans in South America. Hence, for purposes of this report, he should be regarded as a general authority on this topic.

The Monte-Patagonian Desert

The arid zone in Argentina is generally termed the Monte-Patagonian Desert. According to Meigs (1953, see Pert. Pubs. Sec. I) there are two separate arid areas. That in the north is essentially a continuation into northwestern Argentina of the Atacama and Puna de Atacama of Peru, Chile, and Bolivia. The arid area extends southward to approximately 35°S latitude. The second desert area extends from the eastern coast of Argentina to the interior highlands between latitudes 40°S and 50°S; this is the Monte-Patagonian Desert, which covers most of southern Argentina. The precise boundaries of these two areas are difficult if not impossible to determine, but there is no question that the rainfall deficit is not compensated for by the moderate temperatures that occur. The available information on the Argentine deserts will be cited below, but it should be noted at the outset that the general South American references previously provided contain much pertinent material. Publications cited in the following text on the Monte-Patagonian Desert, unless otherwise noted where cited, are listed in Section XII of the Pertinent Publications list.

Among the useful general references on Argentina are the early summaries of physiographic aspects of the country by Kühn (1922) and of geologic aspects by Windhausen (1931), Feruglio's outline of the geology of Patagonia (1950), a review of the climate, geology, geomorphology, hydrology, and flora and fauna of the arid zone by the Argentine Committee for the Study of Arid Regions (Comité Argentina para el Estudio de las Regiones Aridas y

Semiáridas, 1963), and the excellent compendium on the natural resources of the country (Argentina. Consejo Federal de Inversiones, 1962-1963). This latter work consists of nine volumes and provides a modern summary of the status of topographic and geologic mapping, the availability of aerial photography, a list of institutions engaged in geologic and hydrologic investigations, an annotated bibliography of pertinent publications, and a summary of the available surface-water and ground-water data in Argentina. This compendium is one of the most comprehensive summaries of available information on a given country that was encountered in the literature review for this report, and it should be consulted for any future investigations that are concerned with the arid zone of Argentina.

The compendium cited above was published in 1963, and more recent information on the status of topographic and geologic mapping and aerial-photograph coverage is available from the unpublished outline maps of the Dirección Nacional de Geología y Minería (1965a) in Buenos Aires, and from the excellent annotated index to aerial photographic and mapping coverage in Argentina by the Organization of American States (1966). The outline maps showing topographic and geologic work indicate that, as might be expected, the poorest coverage tends to coincide with the locations of the desert areas. The northern desert area has been mapped along its eastern and western fringes and, with the notable exception of the coastal zone and an area between approximately 45°S and 47°S, most of the Patagonian Desert is unmapped. The outline map showing the availability of aerial photographs (Dirección Nacional de Geología y Minería, 1965b) indicates a similar situation. For these reasons, it is necessary here to indicate the geologic and geographic reports that have treated some portions of the Monte-Patagonian Desert in Argentina.

Among the early geographic reports of some value are Penck's (1920, see Pert. Pubs. Sec. XIII) description of climate, topography, and landforms in northwestern Argentina which pertains to the Puna de Atacama, de Martonne's survey of northern Argentina and Chile (1934), and Frenguelli's (1928) investigation of the saline deposits of closed basins in the region. The latter author has subsequently described a closed basin and its sediments in the Patagonian desert (Frenguelli, 1943), and this topic and its climatic implications have been treated by several other workers. Cordini (1947) has discussed the salinas of Mendoza Province and their associated dunes, Zamorano (1950) has emphasized the historic evidence of the migration of fishermen in connection with the desiccation of lakes in this province,

Palese de Torres (1956) has described the Tinogasta Valley and the saline flat that is the outlet for a single perennial stream, and Hueck (1956) has provided information on playas west of Jujuy and Salta in a report that was primarily devoted to the plant ecology of northwestern Argentina.

Additional geographic work relevant to the arid parts of the country includes a climatic study of part of the Patagonian desert by Velasco and Capitanelli (1956), Enjalbert's concept of the evolution of the arid Andes (1957) based on a qualitative study of the Mendoza Valley, and recent descriptions of the physiography of Mendoza Province by Regairez (1962) and Polanski (1963). The latter report is in the classical tradition, but in addition to discussion of several supposed peneplains in the Province, pediments, badlands, volcanic terrain, and the relationship of rock structure and the drainage features are described and discussed. Polanski (1953) has also discussed the occurrence of large isolated blocks on the Mendoza piedmont, the origin of which has been speculated upon since Feruglio's treatment of blocks in Mendoza and Patagonia in 1935. A modern sedimentary study of the finer Patagonian surficial gravels has recently been provided by Cortelezzi and Kilmurray (1965), who concluded that the widespread phenomenon of particle fracture in the area is a consequence of differential solution. A more detailed treatment of the surficial sediments was previously given by Cortelezzi, DeFrancesco, and De Salvo (1963). Lastly, the work of Capitanelli (1955) should be noted here. This author treated aridity in San Luis Province, which is in the northern part of the Monte desert, and his report provides a good summary of the climatic causes of aridity in Argentina in general and references to several useful sources of climatic data that are not cited in this paper.

The remaining literature on Argentina is basically geological, but, as previously stated, general landform descriptions and some geomorphic discussions are included. Within this category of available information on surficial features are Pratt's (1961) description of an intermontane basin in the Puna de Atacama and the effect of mudflows, outlines of physiographic zones in La Rioja and Mendoza Provinces by Fidalgo (1963) and González Díaz (1964), and Arnolds' (1952) discussion of the closed basins, saline pans, and relationship of landforms to geology in the seldom-studied Sierra Grande District of the Patagonian desert. In a similar vein, reports by Yrigoyen (1950), Vilela (1953), Turner (1962), Perrot (1960), and Volkenheimer (1964) treat the geology and geomorphology of areas within the arid zone which are characterized by volcanic terrain. That by Volkenheimer discusses Chubut Province in the southern Patagonian desert, where varied deposits and features occur. Included are pyroclastic, glacial, debris, and fanglomerate deposits, and plains, terraces, and volcanic caldera.

The "Boletines" that give descriptions of the hojas, or Argentine quadrangles, are quite pertinent, and among those on arid areas are reports by Groeber (1933), Vilela (1956), Dessanti (1956), and Polanski (1964*a, b*). Additionally, geologic papers by Frenguelli (1946), Nieniewski and Wieklinski (1950), González Bonorino (1950), Dessanti (1958), and Turner (1958, 1959) include information on a variety of surficial features that range in location from the Puna de Atacama on the Bolivian border to Patagonia.

With respect to surface-water hydrology in Argentina, much of the available information is contained in sources previously cited, such as the summaries of the status of knowledge in the report of the committee for the study of arid regions (Comité Argentina para el Estudio de las Regiones Aridas y Semiáridas, 1963), the compendium on the natural resources of Argentina (Argentina. Consejo Federal de Inversiones, 1963), and the several papers treating climate or river valleys cited above. Additional climatic data can be obtained through *M. Fernández,* of the Dirección Nacional de Meteorología, but several specific hydrologic reports should be mentioned here. Among these are a recent summary of the hydrogeology of Santa Maria Valley by Ruiz Huidobro (1965), hydrologic papers treating various parts of Mendoza Province by Rousseau (1958), Capitanelli (1962), Urien (1965), and Inchauspe (1957), and Bonfils' (1951) analysis of the waters of the Río Lavayen. Also useful are the water-quality data shown on the hydrologic map of Argentina (Argentina, Dirección Nacional de Geología y Minería, 1963*a*), the explanatory text (Argentina, Dirección Nacional de Geología y Minería, 1963*b*) that accompanies the map, and Schoff's (1960) outline of the hydrologic needs of Argentina, which is still pertinent to a large extent.

In summary, as in most countries, data on the magnitude and frequency of runoff in the arid parts of Argentina and details on the channel characteristics of ephemeral streams are largely lacking. Most effort is expended on streams in the nonarid areas. The streams which drain the southern provinces in the Patagonian Desert, however, are gaged in the interior, where some flow exists. These streams seldom flow to the sea save during exceptional events. As mentioned above, the poorest coverage of topographic and geologic mapping is generally in the deserts.

Authorities

Further information on the geology and geomorphology of the Monte-Patagonian desert can be obtained from *Félix González Bonorino* of the University of Buenos Aires and *Juan Turner,* of the Instituto Nacional de Geología y Minería. Additionally, personnel of the Geography Institutes at the Universidad Nacional de Cuyo and the Universidad de Tucumán, of Esso Argentina and Argentina Cities Service companies, and of the Instituto Geográfico Militar are cognizant of the available literature and current research activities in the country. Information on the coastal desert of eastern Patagonia can best be obtained from *Carlos Urien,* of the Servicio Hidrográfico Naval. Information on the current number and distribution of gaging stations and surface-water projects in Argentina can be obtained from *H. Pérez,* Chief of the Division of Hydraulic Resources in Buenos Aires, and from the Dirección Nacional de Geología y Minería, which engages in hydrogeologic investigations.

The Atacama-Peruvian Desert (Peru)

The arid zone of Peru is restricted to a coastal belt west of the Andes which narrows northward, toward the Ecuador border. It is similar in several respects to the Namib in South West Africa, but the presence of the bordering high mountains and the concomitant increase in precipitation with elevation have served to produce fans and pediments along the eastern margin of the desert that are typical of basin-and-range topography. These features, together with the dune field, saline flats, and western coastal terraces, have been described in geologic reports as well as in reports devoted to geomorphology alone. The available information cited here will begin with a consideration of those geologic reports that provide some data on physical features. Publications cited in the following text on the Atacama-Peruvian Desert (Peru), unless otherwise noted where cited, are listed in Section XIII of the Pertinent Publications list.

General geologic references on Peru include Steinmann's text (1929), the geological map of Peru by Bellido, Narváez, and Simons (1956), and the "Boletines" of the Comisión de la Carta Geológica Nacional of Peru. The latter publications commonly contain sections on the geomorphology and general physical features of any area treated. Certain of the specific geological reports cited here stem from this source. In the southern part of Peru, Jenks (1948) has described the Arequipa area and its volcanic terrain and Bellido (1956), Barua (1961), Wilson (1963*b*), and Wilson and García (1962) have provided information on the nature of the topography, drainage, and climate in the course of geological investigations between the Altiplano and the coast. Jaén and Ortiz (1963) have also provided an excellent description of physiographic features in southern Peru, and farther north, in the vicinity of Lima, Newell's geologic reconnaissance (1956) treats part of the Atacama in a similar fashion.

The northern part of Peru is best covered by geologic reports of Bosworth (1922) (which contains excellent early photographs of terraces, alluvial fans, saline flats, and dunes), Iddings and Olsson (1928) who also have provided a basic paper, Benevides Cáceres (1956), Cruzado and Escudero (1959), Wilson (1963a), Wilson and Reyes (1964), and Cossío (1964). In each of these papers the geology of inland or mountainous areas is presented and general descriptive information is included. The early reports of Bosworth (1922) and Iddings and Olsson (1928) might well prove useful for a study of morphologic changes in northern Peru during a 40-year period; the more recent reports are notable chiefly by reason of the contained geologic maps which are based on aerial photography in most cases.

Additional geologic reports on Peru include several that treat primarily the lower desert region rather than the inland and mountainous areas, and which contain information on coastal features. In this category, papers by Rassmus (1931) and Ruegg (1953) on the Pisco area and by Rosenzweig (1953) on the island of San Lorenzo provide pertinent information in the general vicinity of Lima. The physical features of the coastal region from latitude 16°S to the Chilean border have been described in geological quadrangle reports by Bellido and Narváez (1960), Bellido and Guevara (1963), Mendivel and Castillo (1960), and by Narváez (1964). The northern part of the Atacama coastal region has been similarly treated by McDonald (1956) and by Travis (1953), who described the coastal plain, covering dunes, and bordering alluvial fans in a report on the La Brea-Pariñas oil field.

Each of the reports cited above may be profitably consulted, but more specific information on the landforms and features of the Peruvian desert is contained in those reports that are primarily devoted to such topics. In this vein, Bowman's physiographic description of Peru (1949), his earlier geographic reports (1916, 1924), and the general desert observations of Dresch (1961) and Simons and Ericksen (1953) are worthy of note. In addition, several papers treat aspects of climate, climatic change, and presumed morphological differences that are a response to such changes. Brown (1924) discussed the effects of wind and heat in northwestern Peru in one of the early reports on this subject, Nicholson (1942) believed

that climate and morphology were directly linked in southern Peru, Olivieri (1951) has described the cloud bank, which is common to many coastal deserts, and its effect on the desert, Fenner (1948a, b) has treated Pleistocene-Recent climatic change in relation to the dissection of tuff beds in southern Peru, and Smith (1955b), Tricart (1963), and Garner (1959) have discussed various lines of evidence that are suggestive of climatic changes in Peru. The latter paper by Garner (1959) contains a good description of drainage features in northern and southern Peru and some information on precipitation-runoff relationships in these areas. Gonzáles (1955) has also mentioned climatic conditions, with reference to guano deposits along the Peruvian coast.

Other topics treated in the literature include evaporite deposition in northern Peru through infrequent flooding followed by evaporation (Morris and Dicky, 1957a, b), the occurrence and migration of dunes through wind action, and the coastal terraces and beaches. Dunes and dune sand in the Peruvian desert have been described in numerous reports. Smith (1956) emphasized the composite nature of the barchans in northern Peru, Simons (1956) reached much the same conclusion from study of Pur-Pur dune, which is a large barchan associated with numerous smaller dunes that he termed "satellites," Gay (1962) provided a much more comprehensive work on the origin and distribution of various types of dunes in southern Peru, and Broggi (1961), in an interesting paper, offered the view that the migration of dunes in the Atacama is a function of climatic conditions, in the sense that reduced wind velocities and higher humidity coincide with the inland position of the coastal cloud bank. This author had previously discussed sand migration along the Peruvian coast (Broggi, 1952), but Simons and Ericksen (1953) produced some of the few quantitative data on this subject. For the coastal region of north-central Peru they obtained a northward migration rate of approximately 0.45 meters per year. Other studies of dunes and windblown sands that are worthy of note include a general description of coastal dunes by Kinzl (1958) and quantitative observations on dune size, shape, and composition in a study of sand encroachment on farms, roads, and the like by Finkel (1959). On related topics, Amstutz and Chico (1958), Newell and Boyd (1955), and Tricart and Mainguet (1965) have provided some data on the size distribution of eolian sands in Peru, and Smith (1955a, 1963) has discussed a closed basin in northern Peru in terms of the questionable, and classical, deflation-genesis explanation.

Coastal terraces, the last category of surficial features to be considered here, have been described briefly in several of the geological reports previously cited, but in addition Broggi (1946c), Schweigger (1943), and Petersen (1954) have treated the coastal physiography and marine terraces near Ica in southern Peru, Ruegg (1962) has included a section on coastal terraces in his report on the Nasca Ridge area, and Broggi (1946a) has provided a report on the general geomorphology of the Río Tumbes delta in northern Peru. Broggi has published additional reports on coastal features of Peru. One of these papers gives a useful summary of all the marine terraces of the Peruvian coast (1946b) and another treats microterraces, the origin of which is in doubt. Broggi (1957) argues for an origin involving the occurrence of lichens and similar plant-forms in preference to the production of the microterraces by animal movements. It would seem likely, however, that soil creep and slumping are the primary causative factors; the appearance of lichens on the risers is a consequence. Finally, Mabire (1961) has studied some reef deposits between Chala and Atico in southern Peru which suggest an absolute land-sea elevation change of 100 meters or more in the area.

In summary, a considerable number of papers on geomorphic features of arid Peru are available. Perhaps best known are the terraces, dunes, and sandy areas. Taken as a whole, however, the Peruvian Atacama is not known in detail; many geographic gaps exist in the coverage.

With respect to surface-water hydrology in the Atacama desert of Peru, qualitative descriptions of the drainage features are presented in many of the geologic and geomorphic reports cited above. Any data that have been obtained stem from studies of either ground-water conditions along the Peruvian coast or water supply immediately adjacent to the mountain border, which is not truly arid. Studies devoted specifically to the ephemeral washes of the desert proper are not known to the writer. The best recent survey of ground-water activities in Peru has been provided by Taltasse (1963), and an example of the types of hydrologic data that are being obtained is the report of Schoff and Sayan (n.d.) on the Lambayeque Valley in northern Peru. The latter report treats an alluvial-fan aquifer and presents climatic, ground-water, chemical quality, and surficial data for the 1955-1959 period.

Authorities for Geology and Surficial Features

Further information on the geology and surficial features of the Atacama can be obtained from several sources. The Comisión de la Carta Geológica Nacional in Lima is the agency principally charged with mapping in Peru and *E. Bellido,* the Director, or *J. J. Wilson* can provide information on all available

geologic and topographic maps and aerial photography. Aerial photographs and mosaics are also available from the Servicio Aerofotográfico Nacional in Lima, and a most comprehensive index to all maps and aerial photographs of Peru was recently compiled by the Organization of American States (1964b). *J. A. Broggi* of the Instituto Geológico in Lima has conducted many geomorphic investigations in the desert and should be consulted on this subject. Additionally, personnel of the Sociedad Geológica del Perú, the Faculty of Sciences of Universidad Nacional de San Marcos, and the Department of Geology of the Universidad Nacional de San Augustín have information on current desert research in Peru. Finally, such petroleum companies as Empresa Petrolera Fiscal, Cerro de Pasco, Compañía Peruana, International Petroleum Company, Ltd., and the Shell, Mobil, and Gulf Oil companies of Peru each have file reports and some basic information on their respective exploration areas.

Authorities for Surface Hydrology

Information on reports of this type and on other hydrologic studies in Peru can be obtained from the U. S. AID and from the Servicio Cooperativo Interamericano de Irrigación in Lima. The climatic data pertinent to this volume that are available for Peru are available from the Agro de Meteorología, under the Ministry of Agriculture in Lima. Further information on current surface-water hydrology operations and future plans in Peru can be obtained from *Luis de Armero García,* who is president of the Peruvian national committee for the international hydrologic decade in Lima.

The Atacama-Peruvian Desert (Chile)

The Atacama in Chile extends southward from the Peruvian border to approximately 30°S latitude. According to Meigs (1953, see Pert. Pubs. Sec. I), only the terrain in the immediate vicinity of the Chile-Bolivia border is nonarid. As in the Peruvian Atacama, the high Andes form the eastern boundary of the coastal desert, within which varied landforms and geologic rock types occur. The general South American references previously cited are again pertinent, and, as was true of the available information on Peru, most of the geologic reports contain descriptions of the terrain, drainage, and other surficial features, as well as maps and geologic data. Hence, geologic as well as geomorphic reports will be cited below. Publications cited in the following text on the Atacama-Peruvian Desert (Chile), unless otherwise noted where cited, are listed in Section XIII of the Pertinent Publications list.

The Puna de Atacama, which is the high desert country in northeastern Chile, northwestern Argentina, and southwestern Bolivia, has been described in early geographic papers by Penck (1920) and Kantner (1937), and geologic problems of this area have been discussed by Gerth (1921). Wetzel (1928) also cited a number of interpretive problems in northern Chile and discussed the history of the region. Additional early work includes a series of reports prior to 1930 by Mortensen, who provided classical descriptions of northern and central Chile (1927, 1928) and the inselbergs that occur (1929*a*) and set forth his views on the origin of the Atacama (1929*b*). With respect to the Puna de Atacama, however, the available information includes Brüggen's basic geologic and morphologic summaries (1942, 1946) and papers on Quaternary chronology and soils by Vita-Finzi (1959, 1960). The latter has also published a descriptive book, with Aarons, that treats this region (Vita-Finzi and Aarons, 1960).

Some geologic and geographic observations of Wurm (1951, 1952) are useful references for the Atacama of Chile in general, but the best sources of information are the geologic texts on Chile by Brüggen (1950) and Zeil (1964), and similar but briefer treatment by Muñoz Christi (1950, 1956). In addition to information on the geology of the Atacama, these sources contain descriptions of the general drainage, climate, and morphology of the country, and many additional references to pertinent work. This statement particularly applies to the books by Brüggen (1950), and Zeil (1964). Also of great value is the review and general bibliography on the geography of Chile by the Instituto de Geografía of the University of Chile (1960-1964).

Recent papers that specifically treat the geomorphology of the Atacama in Chile include Segerstrom's discussion of a marine terrace that is a sediment source for dunes (1962) and an outline of the Río Copiapó Valley gravels (1965), a good description of salt deposition and the production of microrelief in the Tamarugal Pampa area of northern Chile by Tricart (1966); Cooke's geomorphic reports on the Huasco Valley (1963) and the evidence for sea-level changes (1965), his general outline of Atacama landforms (1964), and a review of the work of University College of London expeditions by Hollingsworth (1964). The latter report provides a summary of such features as terraces, river canyons, and volcanic terrain in northern Chile. In addition, Cooke has in press several pertinent reports not seen by this writer and is participating in the compilation of a bibliography of Chilean geomorphology.

Humberto Fuenzalida *et al.* (1965) have recently provided some of the best summaries of marine terraces and other coastal features of Chile; Cooke's paper (1965), cited above, is one of those included. The remaining works on the Chilean desert that are germane here treat the geology of various regions and contain sections describing the topography and landforms that occur. In this category, Harrington (1961) has discussed parts of the provinces of Antofagasta and Atacama, which include the Pampa del Tamarugal and saline flats treated by Tricart (1966), Castillo Urrutia (1960) has provided further information on this area in the course of a ground-water investigation, and the main geomorphic features of Tarapacá Province are well-outlined in the reports of Cecioni and García (1960), Taylor (1949), and, more recently, by Dingman and Galli Olivier (1965). Geologic reports by Felsch (1933), Fuenzalida Villegas (1937), Muñoz Christi (1942), Galli Olivier (1957), and Klohn (1957) should also be consulted, but the most important sources of information are the quadrangle reports of the Instituto de Investigaciones Geológicas in Santiago, each of which contains a section on the physiography of the quadrangle treated.

The quadrangle-reports on Llampos, Paipote Wash, and Los Loros have been provided by Segerstrom (1959; 1960*a, b*), who has also treated with others the Cerrillos and Chamonate areas (Segerstrom and Parker, 1959; Segerstrom, Valenzuela, and Mahech, 1960) and the Chañarcillo quadrangle (Segerstrom and Moraga, 1964). In addition, Segerstrom has discussed the geology and physiography of a part of Atacama Province (1960*c*). Each of these areas is within the arid zone of Chile. Other pertinent quadrangle-reports have been produced by Dingman (1963, 1965) and Galli Olivier and Dingman (1962).

The Instituto de Investigaciones Geológicas in Santiago conducts a wide range of geological investigations in addition to their basic mapping program, and further information on available reports can be obtained from *C. Ruiz Fuller,* Director or *José Corvalán,* the Vice-Director. A companion organization, the Instituto Geográfico Militar, under *Comandante Cecilio Zeballos,* can also provide much pertinent information, particularly with respect to aerial-photography and topographic-map coverage. This geographic institute is actively engaged in both areas of endeavor and topographic mapping of the Atacama has been accomplished on a scale of 1:250,000; there are some sheets available on a scale of 1:100,000 but very few 1:50,000 or larger scale topographic maps have been produced to date. The best sources of published information on the availability of maps and aerial photographs of Chile are the catalogs of the Instituto Geográfico Militar (1965*a, b*) and the comprehensive annotated index of the Organization of American States for Chile (1964a).

Of other institutes and organizations that can provide information on the surficial features of the Chilean Atacama it should be noted here that the Instituto Hidrográfico de la Armada, in Valparaiso, treats coastal morphology and topography, the Empresa Nacional de Petróleo in Santiago has many file reports and data that are pertinent, and the University of Chile in Antofagasta and Santiago and the University of Concepción have personnel with research experience in the Atacama.

In summary, many geographic gaps exist in the coverage of this coastal desert, and only a relatively small part can be said to be known in detail.

With respect to surface-water hydrology in Chile, the best summary of the status of knowledge is presented in the hydrologic and meteorologic inventory of the United Nations (1960). In certain areas of the country, meteorological data are available for a period of 100 years or longer, as evidenced by Matthews' use of Chilean evaporation data (1931), but in the desert area proper only a few principal stations exist for which long-term data are available. The Department of Meteorology of the Chilean Air Force, Santiago, is the agency that may be contacted for further information. Turnbull's summary (1961, see Pert. Pubs. Sec. XI) for analog purposes is of some value, but few data are given for Chile. Information on the quebradas, or dry washes of the Atacama, are contained in many of the geologic and geographic reports cited above. No systematic hydraulic or other survey of these features has been undertaken, but some details are presented in ground-water reports, such as those by Doyel (1964) and Doyel, Dingman, and Castillo Urrutia (1964). Most of the current surface-water investigations in Chile are undertaken in nonarid areas or are incidental to power-supply or ground-water supply problems.

Authorities for Geomorphology

Professor Hollingsworth is recently deceased and for purposes of this report R. U. Cooke, of the Department of Geology, University College of London, should be regarded as an authority on the Atacama desert of northern Chile. He can provide further information on the continuing research activities of the geologic-geographic group, which is concerned with the interrelations of climate, tectonics, geology, and the landforms of northern Chile through time. K. Segerstrom should also be cited as an authority here on the strength of his excellent work in Chile.

Authorities for Surface Hydrology

Enrique García Merino of the Dirección de Riego in Santiago is an authority on surface water in Chile; he is president of the country's committee for the international hydrologic decade.

G. THE NORTH AMERICAN DESERTS

The deserts of North America lie in an essentially continuous arid area which extends southward from the western United States into Mexico. A summary of pertinent works on geomorphology and surface-water hydrology in these countries is presented below, but it should be emphasized at the outset that some of the most basic geomorphic references on the North American desert were previously discussed in the introductory sections of this report that treat the background of modern geomorphic concepts and may be found in the Pertinent Publications list, Section I. These text and bibliography sections, and the references cited therein, should be consulted by the interested reader of this report in order to gain a better appreciation of the information that is available on the desert area of North America.

United States

The available information on the arid zone of the United States is more abundant than is information on any other desert region. The reasons for this disparity are several, but two reasons are perhaps paramount. First, the arid zone of the United States is small, relative to world deserts in general, and access has always been simpler than is true for many other deserts. Second, funds have always been made available to support academic as well as practical investigations, and such funds have certainly sustained many investigators whose interest in the arid West was solely theoretical. It would be incorrect to assume from these statements that coverage, with respect to geomorphology or hydrology, is either complete or wholly adequate. The intent is solely to suggest that more work has been done on the arid region of the United States than on other deserts, and the available information to be outlined here reflects this fact rather than provincialism. Publications cited in the following text on the United States, unless otherwise noted where cited, are listed in Section XIV of the Pertinent Publications list.

Before essaying a listing of sources of information on the desert region of the United States, it is instructive to consider an analysis of the citations contained in an annotated bibliography issued by the University of Southern California (1959). This compilation was not all-inclusive, but the topics covered were geology, geography, soils, and ecology. Excluding citations that pertain to soils or ecology, this bibliography contained 435 references relevant to this report. Approximately 26 per cent of the total number of references were derived from publications of the U. S. Geological Survey and 20 per cent referred to the Geological Society of America. These were the most frequently cited sources of information. Other percentages are as follows: *Journal of Geology* and the *American Journal of Science,* combined, 10 per cent; state publications, 8 per cent; university publications, 8 per cent; *National Geographic Magazine,* 8 per cent; books, 4 per cent; *Pan American Geologist,* 3 per cent; geographical journals, 3 per cent; publications of other Federal agencies, other geological journals, and miscellaneous, 10 per cent combined.

Although it is clear that the percentages cited would vary as a function of the bias of the authors of any such bibliography, the breakdown of the University of Southern California bibliography given above is nevertheless instructive. It is clear that the publications of the U. S. Geological Survey and the contents of three standard geological journals provided nearly 60 per cent of the total number of references. Moreover, this percentage would be even greater had the qualitative descriptions presented in *National Geographic Magazine* and the somewhat questionable material in the now-defunct *Pan American Geologist* been omitted. Although quantity need not coincide with quality, in the sense that fundamental papers may well be released through other outlets, the foregoing analysis should be borne in mind during consideration of the sources of information outlined below.

Books are often a more useful source of information than would be indicated by the percentage-citation method. In addition to providing a general outline of an arid region, or some aspects thereof, books are commonly sources of further information by reason of their contained bibliographies or citations. Information on the arid regions of the United States has been provided by Fenneman (1931), Lobeck (1939), and Thornbury (1954), and, in sections of books of broader scope, by King (1962) and Machatschek (1955). (The foregoing five books are listed in Pert. Pubs. Sec. I.) The treatise on structural geology by Eardley (1962*b*) contains extensive references to more detailed geological papers, and the recent book on regional geomorphology by Thornbury (1965) can be profitably consulted for information on physiographic provinces and their division in the United States. Two other works previously cited in Pert. Pubs. Sec. I, the compendium on hydrology (Chow, 1964) and the work on fluvial processes (Leopold, Wolman, and Miller, 1964)

complete this listing of pertinent books; both are outstanding and contain a wealth of references.

Scientific periodicals in the United States are numerous. The Geological Society of America publishes a monthly "Bulletin," abstracts of papers that are submitted for national and regional meetings, "Special Papers," and "Memoirs." Relevant information may appear in any of these outlets. The abstracts are valuable in terms of the current work that is reported therein; an example of a significant memoir is the work of Cooper (1958) on coastal sand dunes. Among the special papers that are worthy of note here are the regional studies by Crowell (1962), Silberling and Roberts (1962), and Gilluly (1965); each is a source of further information by reason of references it cites.

Other scientific periodicals that are sources of information for the United States include the *Journal of Geology, American Journal of Science, Bulletin of the American Association of Petroleum Geologists, Journal of Sedimentary Petrology, Journal of Geomorphology, Science, Geographical Review, Annals of the Association of American Geographers, Journal of the Hydraulics Division of the American Society of Civil Engineers, Transactions of the American Geophysical Union,* and *Water Resources Research. Pan American Geologist* is no longer published, but as evidenced by the above discussion of the University of Southern California bibliography, some early papers of relevance are contained in this journal. The same is true of *Journal of Geomorphology.*

To this lengthy list, one might add the *National Geographic Magazine* and *Natural History,* both of which publish articles in a popular vein but present good photographs of some areas visited infrequently. Examples from the former are too well known to be cited; the recent article on wadis in the Ennedi region of the southern Sahara (Dyer, 1965) is illustrative of the general pertinence of *Natural History* to arid regions in general.

It is difficult to assign some qualitative degree of importance to the various periodicals cited because, as previously stated, one cannot actually predict the outlet of any given paper. The most frequent outlets for papers on geomorphology would not include the *Bulletin of the American Association of Petroleum Geologists,* for example, yet many references to surficial geology may appear in articles that are primarily devoted to electric-log correlations, subsurface stratigraphy, or the geological history of sedimentary basins. Examples in the last category include the excellent review articles which appeared in a recent issue on the Oquirrh (Roberts *et al.,* 1965), San Juan (Peterson *et al.,* 1965), and southwestern New Mexico (Kottlowski, 1965) basins. At best, it can be said that articles on hydrology will more commonly appear in the nongeologic or nongeographic journals cited, but if comprehensive coverage is desired then all the periodicals noted here should be consulted.

The U. S. Geological Survey publications are a prime source of information for the United States. These publications include "Professional Papers," "Water-Supply Papers," "Bulletins," "Circulars," topographic and geologic maps, and miscellaneous papers. Of particular importance here is the annually compiled *Bibliography of North American Geology* by this agency, the annual report of water-resources research, and the "Professional Paper" series entitled *Geological Survey Research*. The bibliography of geology is, of course, one of the best for reference purposes, but the reports of water-resources research include summaries of the status of all current research projects in the Water Resources Division for a given year. The articles in *Geological Survey Research* are short papers that commonly present some preliminary conclusions derived from investigations of larger scope; hence, in both cases these publications provide information on work in progress. Also worthy of note is *Manual of Hydrology* and the annotated bibliography on hydrology and sedimentation that have been issued by the U.S.G.S.

Other Federal agencies which have contributed to the available information on the United States include the Agricultural Research Service, Soil Conservation Service, Bureau of Reclamation, Corps of Engineers (notably through the Beach Erosion Board, the U. S. Army Engineer Waterways Experiment Station, and the Environmental Research sections), the Office of Naval Research, and the newly organized Office of Water Resources Research.

The last named agency began publication of a water-resources research catalog in 1965 which, like the Geological Survey compilation, provides information on the status of current projects, but the scope is somewhat broader. Office of Naval Research reports of significance may be found in Pert. Pubs. Sec. I (Miller, 1953; Schumm, 1956; Melton, 1957, 1958; Coates, 1958; Broscoe, 1959; Morisawa, 1959; Maxwell, 1960) and U. S. Army reports will be discussed below. The remaining agencies listed above are primarily concerned with problems of erosion and sedimentation. Examples of their contribution to this subject can be derived by examination of the U. S. Interagency Committee on Water Resources bibliography (1955, see Pert. Pubs. Sec. I) and the extensive reference lists that accompany the recent review articles by Gottschalk (1964) and Einstein (1964) on reservoir and river sedimentation, respectively.

The several states that are concerned with problems of aridity, notably Utah, Nevada, California,

Arizona, New Mexico, and Texas, publish bulletins and reports of water-resources research and issue papers through their state agencies, including state Geological Survey departments, which are clearly important as sources of information. An outstanding example is the report on the geology of southern California (Jahns, 1954) by the California State Division of Mines. This report is probably the best single source of information on the Mojave Desert region, and it serves as an excellent guide to the literature.

The universities that are located within these states must also be listed as information sources. The University of California publishes two excellent periodicals entitled *Publications in Geography* and *Bulletin of the Department of Geological Sciences;* Stanford University publications include a geological science series; the *Bulletin of the University of Utah* has included such notable works as that on the Great Basin (Blackwelder *et al.,* 1948); the University of Arizona has issued the results of arid lands colloquia, a treatise on the interpretation of pollen analyses in the southwest (Martin, 1963), and the *Arizona Bureau of Mines Bulletin* (also appearing in the University series) has provided a bibliography of geological studies in the state. Similar examples could be provided for the remaining states in the region, but it should be stressed that universities in any part of the United States may provide information on the arid region or on related matters.

Consider in this respect the *Quarterly of the Colorado School of Mines*. In 1964 this journal published several articles on trend-surface analysis (Merriam and Lippert, 1964; Harbaugh, 1964a), a topic which can easily be related to geomorphic problems in the arid regions; many publications of the State Geological Survey of Kansas are in a similar category (Harbaugh, 1963, 1964b; Merriam and Harbaugh, 1964). It should be noted in passing that the Kansas Geological Survey and the University of Kansas are among the leaders in the field of computer applications in the earth sciences. The interested reader can obtain many additional references on this subject by written inquiry. Graduate-student theses provide another example; as sources of information the lists of theses submitted to geology or geography departments in any university in the country should be consulted. The study of sand dunes by Eymann (1953), of arroyos by Wertz (1962), and of playa lakes by Stone (1956) were conducted at "arid-zone universities" but Aristarain's (1962) study of the origin of caliche in New Mexico was submitted as a thesis at Harvard.

As a last general source of information on the arid region of the United States, several military reports must be cited. A general bibliography that was prepared under contract with the U. S. Army was previously noted (University of Southern California, 1959) but a second, more specialized work in this vein, is a U. S. Air Force bibliography on playas in the United States (Neal, 1965) which is also worthy of note. The military effort that has been directed toward terrain study and analysis in the United States, however, has been outstanding by reason of the fact that similar types of studies have not generally been accomplished by individuals, agencies, or institutions. Among the many reports in this category, those by Clements *et al.* (1957), Kesseli and Beaty (1959), Shepard *et al.* (1955), Stoerts (1957), Van Lopik and Kolb (1959), Krenkel (1962, 1963), Maxwell (1962), Grabau (1964), Shamburger and Kolb (1961), Shamburger and Duke (1965), Remson *et al.* (1962, see Pert. Pubs. Sec. I) and several others (U. S. Army, Research and Development Division, 1953; U. S. Army Engineer Waterways Experiment Station, 1963; Texas Instruments, 1964; FMC Corporation, 1964) are illustrative of the truth of this claim.

To continue with this treatment of the availability of information on the United States, selected references to the literature on the arid region will be provided here. Those references cited are not of uniform quality and the detail of the data that are presented is by no means equal; the papers selected simply represent a reasonable sampling of the available literature on the American west.

It would be well to consider first those reports which are regional in nature; that is, reports that treat some aspects of the geology or geomorphology of the arid region in its entirety or of several of the states that comprise the arid region. In this category, several early efforts are represented by the work of Gilbert (1874, 1875) and Walther (1892) prior to 1900. During the next 10 years, Spurr (1901), Davis (1903*b*, 1905*a*) and Keyes (1908, 1910*a, b*) produced various papers on the Great Basin, but these efforts were largely speculative. Keyes, for example, argued for the importance of wind erosion in the production of basin-and-range topography, both in the papers cited and in subsequent work (1912, 1915, 1922, 1924). His ideas in this respect were certainly incorrect, but his papers contain some descriptive material on the region and are included as an example of early work.

Davis (1913, 1925, 1932, 1936) elaborated upon his geographic-cycle concept for many years. The citations noted here span the 1913-1936 period and are in addition to his other works that are cited elsewhere in this report. Free (1914) discussed topographic features in 1914 and Fenneman (1916,

1932) devised physiographic provinces or subprovinces, which were later used in his text (Fenneman, 1931; see Pert. Pubs. Sec. I). Gregory (1916, 1917) provided an early treatment of the hydrology and geology of a large portion of the arid region and Blackwelder offered his views on the origin of basin-and-range topography (1928*b*) fault scarps (1928*c*) and the desert surface (1929*a*) some years later. With respect to regional structural and geologic studies of the arid portion of the United States, papers by Gilbert (1928) and Nolan (1943) are excellent. Ambrose (1933) and Longwell (1945) were also concerned with structural problems, and P. B. King (1958) has given the evolution of surficial features in the western states the benefit of more recent thought on the subject.

Aside from previously cited books, such as those by Fenneman and Eardley, the compendium on the Quaternary edited by Wright and Frey (1965*b*, see Pert. Pubs. Sec. I) and regional studies by Gilluly (1965) and others, the remaining works of note include Antevs' (1948) portion of the Great-Basin series of papers, gravity surveys by Mabey (1960), Tuan's (1962) recent description of landforms in New Mexico and Arizona, and some miscellaneous papers such as Taylor's (1937) comparison of the American desert with that of Australia and parts of Jaeger's (1957) popularized account of the North American desert. There are other early papers on basin-and-range morphology or structure, such as those by Louderback (1923, 1924-1926, 1926) for example, but as previously stated, all-inclusive citation is not possible. In addition to the work that is extant, studies in progress, such as that by Lustig (1965) involving a trend-surface analysis of the entire Basin and Range province, should provide some quantitative data of interest that pertain to the entire region.

Nevada

Turning now to consideration of individual states, or subregions of the American desert, a large number of studies are available in the literature. For Nevada, the early monograph by Russell (1885) on Lake Lahontan is still worthy of note, and geologic papers by Spurr (1903), Louderback (1904), and Turner (1909) are representative of publications prior to 1910. Ferguson and Cathcart (1924), Longwell (1926, 1928, 1949), Westgate and Knopf (1932), Jenny (1935), Sharp (1940), Thompson (1952), and Cornwall and Kleinhampl (1959), have all contributed to knowledge of the geology, structure, and geomorphic aspects of parts of Nevada. The paper by Sharp (1940) is the only one among these to concentrate specifically upon geomorphology, however. Within the past few years, Willden and

Mahey (1961) have provided a description of some features of the desert flats, in contrast to the geologic studies that largely center about the mountain ranges, Williams has studied an individual large valley (1962), and Bredehoeft's work on the hydrogeology of the lower Humboldt River basin (1963) is illustrative of a number of modern studies which involve water-resources research. One of the more modern papers noteworthy with respect to the data contained is probably the treatise on Lake Lahontan by Morrison (1964). The various descriptions of earthquakes in Nevada are also worthy of note because information on fault scarps, surficial disruptions, and other associated phenomena are usually provided. Examples of this type include the paper by Gianella and Callaghan (1934), among others. Lastly, in a general vein, Lillard's book (1942) presents a general description of a variety of desert features in Nevada.

New Mexico

The available information on New Mexico is somewhat more extensive and it covers a wider range of topics. Again, early regional coverage was provided by a western survey (Hayden, 1869) prior to the turn of the century, and Dutton (1885) described Mount Taylor and the Zuñi Plateau of this state. Herrick (1898) provided papers on the geology of New Mexico, Herrick and Johnson (1900) studied the Albuquerque area in detail, Johnson published on Mount Taylor (1909), and Darton (1910) presented an early regional reconnaissance of northern New Mexico and Arizona.

Bryan contributed greatly to knowledge of the geology, geomorphology, and Pleistocene history of the Southwest in general. His work in New Mexico included a study of the Albuquerque area in 1909, papers on the Ceja del Río Puerco (Bryan and McCann, 1937, 1938), and the geology of Chaco Canyon (Bryan, 1954). His other works will be cited later, when specific topics are treated.

Ellis (1922), Dake and Nelson (1933), Cabot (1938), Gregory (1938), and Smith (1938) published papers on aspects of the geology and structure of regions within New Mexico between 1922 and 1938. More recently, Horberg (1940) studied the geomorphology of the Carlsbad Caverns, Nichols (1946) considered basalt flows in Valencia County, Kelley and Silver (1952), and Gillerman (1958), have provided thorough geologic studies of the Caballo and Peloncillo Mountains, respectively, and Judson (1953) has demonstrated the interrelationship between archeology, alluvial stratigraphy, and geomorphology at San Jon, in southeastern New Mexico.

Ruhe (1964) has recently described alluvial deposits in southern New Mexico, and Watson and Wright (1963) have treated landslide debris. Wright has considered the origin of lakes (1964, 1965) in this area, with some discussion by Michael (1965). In an earlier study, Wright (1946) has also presented the geology of the lower Río Puerco area. Budding's study of structure in the Jicarilla Mountains (1963) and the survey of caliche in New Mexico by Bretz and Horberg (1949) are also worthy of note, but it should be stressed that several good theses have been written at the universities in New Mexico and these should not be overlooked as sources of information.

Utah

Much information on the geology and structure in the state of Utah has accrued since Gilbert's (1877, see Pert. Pubs. Sec. I) memorable work on the Henry Mountains in 1877. Dutton (1880), Huntington and Goldthwait (1903), Davis (1905b), Loughlin (1913), Hintze (1913), and Dake (1918) all contributed to knowledge of individual structural and topographic features such as the Valley City graben, or to ranges of substantial dimensions, such as the Wasatch, prior to 1920. Pack (1926), Gilluly (1928), and Eaton (1929) published papers in a similar vein, and Gregory and Moore (1931) presented a geomorphological reconnaissance of parts of Utah and Arizona during the next 10 years. More recently, Gregory (1950) has treated the Zion Park area in similar fashion.

Eardley contributed to knowledge of the geology, structure, and physiography of the Wasatch Range area in several papers (1933, 1934, 1944), Bradley furnished information on the Uinta Mountains (1936) and Baker (1936, 1946) has written on the Monument Valley and Green River desert region. Papers by Gardner (1941) and Peterson (1942) are also useful, and that by Hubbs and Miller (1948a) is extremely informative with respect to Pleistocene history in general. Hunt *et al.* (1953) and Hunt, Averitt, and Miller (1953) have provided excellent modern reports on the Lake Bonneville and Henry Mountains regions and have reexamined earlier work on these areas. Both reports contain good reference lists. Felix has studied the Raft River Range (1956), Stokes and Arnold (1958), and Rigby (1958) have treated the geology and physical features of the Stansbury Range, and Rigby (1962) has recently outlined some geomorphic aspects of the Wasatch Mountains. A last geological report of note is a report on sedimentary formations in the Book Cliffs (Fischer, Erdmann, and Reeside, 1960), but Richmond's outstanding treatment (1962) of the Pleistocene and Recent deposits in the La Sal Mountains should be cited here as a general reference on these deposits, on modern soils, and on regional chronologic studies.

Much information can be derived from reports on regional gravity surveys. Several have been made in Utah, primarily in the desert region west of the Wasatch front. Papers by Cook and Berg (1961) and by Stewarts (1958) are representative of efforts in this direction, and the recent work on the entire northern Great Salt Lake area (Cook *et al.,* 1964) should be consulted as a guide to previous work.

A final paper of interest here is that by Bradley (1964) which discusses existing geologic and hydrologic analogies between the Jordan Valley in the Middle East and the Jordan Valley of Utah. Geographic similarities and differences between the two areas are also discussed in this report.

Arizona

In Arizona the earliest reports date from Dutton's monographs on the Grand Canyon region (1880-1881, 1882, see Pert. Pubs. Sec. I). Davis (1903*a*) published a report of his travels and opinions shortly after a trip to this area. Ransome (1904*a, b*) described the Bisbee and Globe areas, Lee (1908) reported on the geology and surficial features of western Arizona, Jenkins and Wilson treated the Tucson and Amole Mountains (1920), and Ross (1923) described the lower Gila River area. All were fine reports, considering their vintage.

Bryan (1926) briefly outlined surficial aspects of the San Pedro Valley in 1926 and Sauer offered a useful treatment of the Chiricahua area in 1930. Davis (1930*a,* 1931) provided information on the Peacock Range and on the Santa Catalina Mountains, accompanied by the usual geographic-cycle interpretations, Wilson (1933) discussed the geology of Yuma County, Williams (1936) treated volcanoes in the Navajo-Hopi area, and papers on the Tombstone district (Butler, Wilson, and Rason, 1938) and the Tucson Mountains (Brown, 1939) appeared prior to Hack's work (1939, 1942*a, b*) on the geology and geomorphology of the Hopi area.

A study of the geomorphology of the Little Colorado River valley by Childs (1948) was followed by McKee's review on sedimentary basins in Arizona (1951). Since that time, some excellent geological studies of parts of Arizona have been given by Peterson (1954), Gilluly (1956), Sabins (1957), Lehner (1958), Davidson (1960), and Heindl (1959, 1960*a, b*), who has also summarized the Cenozoic geology of Arizona (1962) and treated the geology of part of Pinal County (1963). Another fine study is by Longwell (1963), who has recently provided similar information on the Lake Mead / Davis Dam

area. With respect to studies of the geology, geomorphology, or other aspects of restricted areas that are of interest here, an examination of student theses is also pertinent. Theses at the University of Arizona worthy of note include those by Harshman (1939), Ludden (1950), Chew (1952), Plafker (1956), Bennett (1957), Brennan (1957), Van Horn (1957), St. Clair (1957), Heindl (1958), Marlowe (1961), and Smith (1964), among others. As previously mentioned, the theses at any university in the United States may be of relevance. Mears' work on Oak Creek Canyon (1948) is again illustrative of this fact; his thesis was submitted to Columbia University.

Other studies in Arizona that should be cited here include Galbraith's (1959) work on the Pinacate craters, Marlowe's (1960*b*) description of diatremes, Mayo's (1963) discussion of volcanic orogeny in the Tucson Mountains, and the treatment of basin-and-range structure in Arizona by Wilson and Moore (1959). The investigations of earth fissures in alluvium in Arizona are illustrative of structural studies of a different type. These features have been examined since 1929 (Leonard, 1929), and recent papers on this subject (Pashley, 1961; Robinson and Peterson, 1962) have provided information on the areas where fissures are prominent and on the earlier literature.

Many studies of the alluvial sediments in Arizona basins and regional relationships have been accomplished. Several have been cited above, but most pertinent are papers by Cooley (1958), Cooley *et al.* (n.d.), Marlowe (1960*a*), and Van Horn (1962). Cooley has also published a physiographic map of the Little Colorado River area (1960) and a geomorphic study of northeastern Arizona (1962*a*). As indicated by Lance (1959), however, geophysical data are required to develop proper interpretations of basin-and-range relationships and the alluvial deposits. The present gravity program in Arizona has recently been reviewed by Sumner (1965).

Other work that has been done in Arizona will largely be discussed in terms of the literature that exists on the subjects of alluvial fans and pediments. It should be noted in passing, however, that Keyes (1929) and Hoover (1936) have proposed various adjustments of the physiographic boundaries in Arizona and that Lowe (1955) has argued for delimiting the Sonora-desert boundary in the state on faunal grounds.

Texas

The part of the state of Texas that is within the arid region is rather limited, and because the general geology and physiography of this region is covered by reports on both Mexico and New Mexico, only a few references need to be provided here. Eardley

(1962*b*) provides a general description and several references to the area in his text, King's report on the Guadalupe Mountains (1948) is excellent, and a summary of the geology of the Permian basin in west Texas and southeastern New Mexico has been provided by several authors (P. B. King, 1942; R. E. King *et al.*, 1942). The several oil companies which operate in the west-Texas area have a vast amount of surficial data in their files, and additional information on the literature through 1932 is available in a bibliography that accompanies the *University of Texas Bulletin* (Sellards, Adkins, and Plummer, 1932) on the geology of the state.

California

The last state to be considered here is California, and, including the Colorado Delta region, the literature on the arid portions of this state is more extensive than is true of comparable areas elsewhere. The physiography of southern California has been described by Hill (1928), Gale (1933), Reed (1933), Hinds (1952*b*), and others; a physiographic map of the region accompanies a review article by Sharp (1954*a*) on this subject. Abundant references on the geology and geomorphology of southern California can be obtained from the Division of Mines Bulletin previously cited (Jahns, 1954).

A representative sampling of the general literature available includes the early work of Kniffen (1932) and Sykes (1937) on the Colorado Delta area, the description of the area between the head of the Gulf of California and Indio by Blake (1914), studies of the Salton Sea region by Brown (1922, 1923), Buwalda and Santon (1930), and Kelley and Soske (1936). Dibblee's (1954) presentation of the geology of the Imperial Valley region and Longwell's review (1954) of the history of the Lower Colorado River area and Imperial Valley are excellent by reason of the contained information and references to much of the literature that is pertinent to this region in the arid zone.

Baker (1911), Thompson (1929), Hinds (1952*a*), and more recently Hewett (1954), and Wright and Troxell (1954) have contributed data and discussion of regional aspects of the Mojave Desert. Certain specific aspects of the Mojave, such as the occurrence of domes, have been discussed by Davis (1933, 1936). His qualitative observations in this instance have been shown to be incorrect by subsequent work (Sharp, 1954*c*).

General studies that are more limited, in the areal sense, are extremely numerous. Hulin (1925) and Woodford and Harriss (1928) described the geology of the Randsburg quadrangle and Blackhawk Canyon in the 1920's, Russell treated the landforms of San Gorgonio Pass (1932) and Dudley the physiography of part of the Perris block (1936) in the 1930's. Through the years Noble has greatly contributed to knowledge of the geology and structure in the vicinity of the San Andreas rift zone (1927, 1932) and the Death Valley region (Noble, 1941; Noble and Wright, 1954). These areas have been studied more recently by Allen (1957), Drewes (1963), and Hunt and Mabey (1966). The last paper cited is a definitive study of the Death Valley area, but also worthy of note is Nolan's report which includes the region (1943).

Certain specific features in the Death Valley area have been examined in some detail. Turtleback fault surfaces, for example, have been described and discussed by Curry (1938, 1949, 1954) and by Drewes (1959), observations on tilting of the land surface have been made (Greene and Hunt, 1960), and the breccias associated with the Ubehebe craters (Von Engeln, 1932) and the Avawatz Mountains (Jahns and Engel, 1949) in this region are known. Other papers worthy of note include Maxson's paper on the physiography of the Panamint Range (1950*a*), the Salinas Basin report by Simpson (1946), the excellent geological reports by Hazzard (1954), Bowen (1954), and Hewett (1956), which are illustrative of much of the modern work in this field, and the review papers by Putnam (1954), Blackwelder (1954*a*), and Sharp (1954*b*) on aspects of geology and geomorphology, and by Troxell and Hofmann (1954*a*, *b*) on hydrology. The excellent study on drought in the Southwest (Thomas *et al.*, 1963-1964) might also be cited in this vein, although individual chapters pertain to various regions between California and eastern Utah. A paper on aspects of the hydrology of the Lower Colorado River and Salton Sea area (Hely and Peck, 1964) is also available, and the collection of various hydrologic data is still in progress. More recently Hely, Hughes, and Irelan (1966) have provided a comprehensive analysis of the hydrologic regimen of the Salton Sea based upon all available data.

As previously stated, it would be simple to expand greatly any reference list on the general geology and geomorphology of the southern California desert region. Additional citations to this region will be provided within the discussion of information that is available on selected topics, outlined below. But at this point it is again necessary to remind the interested reader that much data can be obtained from student theses of California universities; these should be consulted if comprehensive information on this part of the American desert is desired.

The general topics to be considered, on which information on the American desert is available, include wind action, lakes, fans and pediments, and, last, numerous reports which may best be categorized under the heading of erosion and sedimentation.

Wind Action

Reports on wind action can also be divided by subtopic. To begin with the most common of these, namely, papers that treat some aspect of dunes, the works of Cornish (1897), Hitchcock (1904), Coffey (1909), Holtenberger (1913), and Bailey (1917) are illustrative of many early efforts. A good description of some New Mexico dunes was provided by Bryan and McCann (1943), Smith (1939) treated dunes in Kansas, Wegemann (1939) cited some in Colorado, and Landsberg and Riley (1943) produced some quantitative data on dunes in Michigan. Some of these studies, like those of Hefley and Sidwell (1945), Thorp and Smith (1952), and Cooper (1958), do not refer to parts of the arid region but they provide general descriptive information on dunes and dune characteristics. Within the arid region proper, dunes have been studied by Hack (1941), Roth (1960), Norris and Norris (1961), Evans (1962), Eardley (1962a), and Clements *et al.* (1963). The last report provides some quantitative information on dunes and their movement, but the best studies have been conducted by Sharp (1963, 1964), who studied wind ripples and saltation in California, Horikawa and Shen (1960), Long and Sharp (1964), and Norris (1966). The latter two papers treat the characteristics and migration rates of barchan dunes in Imperial Valley and provide useful quantitative data as well as morphometric parameters that can be applied to barchans generally. Each of the five reports, however, should be regarded as basic for any eolian investigation. Also worthy of note is the proposed dune classification by Melton (1940), and Eymann's study in the Mojave, previously cited (1953).

There are numerous papers that treat the presumed effects of wind action in various ways. The earlier literature abounds in this material, reflecting the influence of such authors as Keyes and Walther, but modern interpretations can also be found. Blake (1885) discussed the polishing of hard rocks by the wind in 1885, Udden (1894) discussed the erosion and transportation achieved by the wind in 1894, Gilbert (1895) considered the origin of certain lake basins to be attributable to wind action, and the work of Cross (1908), Keyes (1910a, b; 1908, 1911, 1912, 1915, 1922, 1924) and Free (1911) serve as examples of this early effort. The paper by Free also contains a bibliography on eolian geology prior to 1911.

Bryan studied the effects of wind action near Lees Ferry, Arizona (1923b), published on ventifacts (1931), and with Nichols interpreted certain shorelines in terms of wind action (Bryan and Nichols, 1939). Blackwelder (1931a, 1934) argued for playa deflation by the wind and for the formation of yardangs by this medium, and Schoewe (1932) presented one of the first experiments that tested the wind-faceting of pebbles. Judson (1950) has offered interpretations of depressions in New Mexico which rely upon the efficacy of wind action, and more recently Shawe (1963) has presented a similar thesis with reference to scarps in Colorado. Among several modern papers probably in error because of disregard of the laws of physics are those of Clements (1952), who thought that the wind moves rocks across playas, and Stokes (1964) who interpreted stream courses of the Colorado Plateau in terms of wind direction. Other examples of undue stress upon the importance of wind action are not difficult to produce, however.

Lastly, some of the many papers that treat loess in the United States might be cited here for their general information content. Among these papers are those by Hilgard (1879), Chamberlain (1897), Call (1882), Campbell (1889), Shimek (1904), Scheidig (1934), Russell (1940), Smith (1942), Leighton and Willman (1950), Fisk (1951), Schultz *et al.* (1945), Swineford and Frye (1951), Ruhe (1954), and Swan (1962).

Lakes and Playas

The lakes and playas of the arid part of the United States have received early, and continuing, treatment by many workers with diverse goals. The purpose of a given investigation may be simple description of the occurrence of a particular playa or group of playas, the interpretation of Pleistocene history, or a consideration of physicochemical relationships between the brines present and the mineral assemblage. In any such case, information about the playas (and often about the surrounding terrain) is provided, and a selected list of such papers will be cited here.

Russell's treatise on Lake Lahontan (1885) and subsequent discussion (1896), combined with Gilbert's monograph on Lake Bonneville (1880-1881; see Pert. Pubs. Sec. I) provide the earliest publications on these subjects in the United States. Both papers are fairly comprehensive, but much additional study has been devoted to these Pleistocene lakes of formerly great extent. Gale (1915a), Jones (1914, 1915, 1925), Stanley (1949), and Morrison (1961, 1964), among others, have contributed to the history and surficial features of the Lake Lahontan area; Lee

(1924), Eardley, Gvosdetsky, and Marsell (1957), Bissell (1963) and Hunt *et al.* (1953) have provided similar information on Lake Bonneville.

Maps showing the locations of playa lakes in the United States have appeared in several reports, but those of Meinzer (1922), Flint (1957, see Pert. Pubs. Sec. I) and, more recently, Feth (1961) are most commonly cited or reproduced. Those reports which treat the lakes or playas of the western states in a regional or general sense are few. Hubbs and Miller (1948*b*) have considered the fish distribution in an effort to interpret the Pleistocene and modern history of the lakes, and Blackwelder (1954*b*) has reviewed the drainage history in the Mojave Desert region. Stone's work (1956) and the Air Force bibliography previously cited (Neal, 1965) can also be included in this context, but the remaining papers are largely hydrologic in content. Langbein (1961) has considered salinity of lakes as an indicator of age, Magin and Randall (1960) have reviewed the literature on evaporation suppression and Meyers (1962) has discussed evaporation in the western United States. The latter two reports contain some relevant material, and in this sense the evaporation maps of Kohler, Nordenson, and Baker (1959) should also be noted. The remaining literature on lakes and playas, with the exception of Hutchinson's general reference work on limnology (1957), pertains to local or more restricted ideas.

Among such studies are several notable papers and California locations predominate. Bailey (1902, 1904) produced the earliest studies of playa lakes in the state, W. T. Lee (1906) and C. H. Lee (1912) followed with fine studies of Owens Valley, Mendenhall (1909) provided the locations of 323 watering places, and MacDougal described and discussed the Salton Sea (MacDougal *et al.*, 1912, 1914; MacDougal, 1917) area prior to 1920. Brown (1923) added considerably to knowledge of the Salton Sea area, and papers by Gale (1915*b*, 1951), Thompson (1921), Foshag (1926), Blackwelder and Ellsworth (1936), Campbell *et al.* (1937), and Blanc and Cleveland (1961) provided information on several aspects of California playas, in the Mojave region and elsewhere. The recent work of Hely, Hughes, and Irelan (1966) on the regimen of the Salton Sea is, as previously noted, the most comprehensive on this subject.

Several papers on the Death Valley playas are available. Among these are Blackwelder's (1933) early discussion of Lake Manly, a description of the archeology and stratigraphy of the salt pan by A. Hunt (1960), and C. B. Hunt's recent paper on the evaporites present (1960). The study of Deep Springs playa by Jones (*in press*) is particularly com-

prehensive, and the work of Smith (1962) on Searles Lake, of Hamilton (1951) on the Rosamond dry lake, of Lombardi (1963) in Saline Valley, and of Droste (1961) in several basins north of the Mojave are illustrative of the diverse literature available on aspects of hydrology, mineralogy, and the geochemistry of the California lakes.

For Nevada, the study of Spring Valley by Snyder and Langbein (1962) and the description of Fish Lake Valley provided by Eakin (1950) are useful and serve to supplement the several references on Lake Bonneville that are noted above. Truesdell, Jones, and Van Denburgh (1965) have provided some descriptive material on saline lakes in Oregon and also in California in the course of a field investigation for the determination of sodium. An earlier survey by Allison and Mason (1947) in Lake County, Oregon, is also available.

The playas and lake basins of western Texas have been described and discussed from several viewpoints in recent years by Reeves. His current review of the subject (Reeves, Jr., 1966) provides an excellent bibliography; among other matters, Reeves summarizes the pluvial history of the area and the possible origin of the varied basin depressions. This latter topic is quite relevant because of the problems posed by pans in the Kalahari and elsewhere in the arid regions. Meinzer (1911) has provided information on Estancia Valley in New Mexico and also on the Tularosa Basin (Meinzer and Hare, 1915) in that state. Bryan's (1938) work on the Río Grande Depression does not deal with playas in the strict sense, nor does Smith's study in Torrance County (1957), but they contain pertinent physical descriptions of areas in which some playa lakes do occur. This statement also pertains to the many reports on the geology and ground-water resources of a given area in the western United States, nearly all of which appear in the "Water-Supply Paper" series of the Geological Survey. These papers should be consulted for additional information and, again, student theses are often the best sources available.

This is true for Arizona, where the much-studied Willcox Playa has provided a subject for theses by Pine (1963), Pipkin (1964), and Robinson (1965), among others. Additional information on this area is available by reference to the work of Martin (1963) and Hevly and Martin (1961) and to the several mimeographed publications issued by the Geochronology Laboratories of the University of Arizona.

Before considering the topic of available information on fans and pediments in the United States, two additional references on playas and lakes should be noted here. Snyder (1962) has provided a classification of valleys in the Great Basin which involves, among other criteria, the water content of a given playa, and Langbein (1962) discussed the hydrology of such arid valleys. The latter paper provides the means by which one can estimate the annual runoff in these basins.

Fans and Pediments

There has been considerable interest in the question of the origin of alluvial fans and pediments in the United States, interest which in large part stems from the basin-and-range type topography exhibited by most of this arid region. Because of this fact, fans and pediments are common and, indeed, few of the general geologic and other reports previously cited fail to note or describe these landforms. Reports which specifically treat fans or pediments, however, are somewhat less numerous, but selective rather than all-inclusive citation is still required here.

The most recent papers on alluvial fans are particularly worthy of note because in addition to the quantitative data that are presented, and the contained references to earlier work, they are illustrative of the variety of conclusions that are possible from consideration of the same basic group of facts. It is for this reason, among others, that a discussion of the different conceptual frameworks of thought was deemed appropriate in the introduction to this report. The particular group of papers involved includes the work of Bull (1964a, 1965) and the following four works listed in Pert. Pubs. Sec. I: Bull (1964) on fans in Fresno County, California, Denny (1965) on alluvial fans in Death Valley, Lustig (1965a) on fans in Deep Springs Valley, California, and Hooke (1965) on fans in Death Valley and elsewhere in the Great Basin.

Earlier papers of interest include that of Trowbridge (1911) on fans in Owens Valley, California, Eckis' (1928) report on fans in southern California, Blackwelder's (1928a) suggestion with respect to the importance of mudflows, Longwell's (1930) description of faulted fans, the report on fan flooding by Chawner (1935), and Buwalda's (1951) discussion of fan channels in terms of sediment transport. In addition, Price (1957) has treated the geomorphology of depositional surfaces, which is a related topic, Voelger (1953) has discussed the deposits along the front of the Santa Catalina Mountains, Croft (1962) has investigated sedimentation along the Wasatch Mountain front. Kesseli and Beaty (1959) have provided descriptions of fans, floods, and drainage basins in the White Mountains, Beaty (1963) has interpreted the genesis of these fans, Arnold (1962) has discussed relict fans in the coastal areas of California, and Troeh (1965, see Pert. Pubs. Sec. I), as previously noted, has applied polynomial

equations to the description of alluvial fans. A recent paper on fans in Lapland by Hoppe and Ekman (1964) must also be cited here because of the pertinence of the observations presented. A few other papers are of some interest, such as those by Blissenbach (1952, 1954), but the contained observations on fans and their particle-size distributions have been superseded by more recent reports by Denny (1965) and Lustig (1965a), both listed in Sec. I of the Pertinent Publications list. The remaining information on fans in the western United States is contained in general or areal reports, in unpublished student theses, and in the papers discussed below, which primarily treat pediments but which often present observations on both fans and pediments.

The available information on pediments in the United States is more abundant than that on fans by reason of the fact that the genesis of pediments would, intuitively, appear to pose the more difficult problem. Although the problem is by no means resolved even today, theories toward its solution have repeatedly been set forth in the literature; hence, descriptive information on a variety of pediment types and their locations is available.

McGee (1897) proposed sheetfloods as a general mechanism for pediment formation in southern Arizona in 1897, and this concept is still widely accepted by the hydraulically unsophisticated. Paige (1912), Lawson (1915), Waibel (1928), and Blackwelder (1929b, 1931b) subsequently provided descriptions of pediments and attendant phenomena elsewhere in the arid region, and Johnson (1931; 1932a, b) published several papers which emphasized the idea of lateral corrasion as an important factor in pediment evolution. Davis wrote many papers on the arid regions, most of which have been previously cited, but his discussion of "rock floors" (1930b) and sheetfloods and streamfloods (1938) pertained specifically to pediments. His claim that Cima Dome in the Mojave Desert (Davis, 1933) represented a pediment-like end product of the arid cycle of erosion and the refutation by Sharp (1957) were noted in the section on available information on California.

Koschmann and Loughlin (1934) reported dissected pediments in New Mexico, and Field (1935) contributed to the general literature on the subject. The work of Bryan, however, was outstanding. His descriptions of landforms in the Papago country of Arizona (Bryan, 1922, 1925b), discussion of San Pedro Valley (1926), thoughts on the formation of pediments (1932, 1935, 1936) and of slope retreat (1940b), and his treatment of the Río Puerco area in New Mexico (Bryan and McCann, 1936) were unexcelled in his time. Similarly, Gilluly's work in the Ajo district of Arizona (1937) is quite praiseworthy. Other contributions to the literature on pediments through 1940 include a discussion of terminology by Maxson and Anderson (1935), the thoughts of Rich (1935) on pediment formation and on multiple surfaces (1938), the work of McCann (1938) and of Church and Hack (1939) in New Mexico, and diverse papers by Bradley (1940) and Meyerhoff (1940).

Subsequent work includes a discussion of pediment-like slopes outside the arid region (Frye and Smith, 1942), Howard's (1942) observations on the extension of pediments into mountain ranges, an early treatment of erosion pavements by Peltier (1951), general remarks on pediments in the Mojave by Lefevre (1952), Tator's presentation of pediment description (1952) and terminology (1953), and some informative papers by Higgins (1953) on miniature pediments in California and on erosional processes in badland terrain by Smith (1958) and Schumm (1962).

Maxson (1950*b*) has added to the burdensome terminology which often encompasses discussion of pediments, Miller (1950) has interpreted pediment-forming processes in terms of earlier opinions, Corbel (1963) and Tuan (1959) have provided notable descriptions of pediments in Arizona, and Mammerickx (1964, see Pert. Pubs. Sec. I) has reported the results of detailed leveling on pediments in Arizona and California. The profiles presented in this report and their interpretation in relation to rock types provide quantitative data that are generally not available in much of the literature on pediments. With respect to quantitative studies in general, the most comprehensive treatments available are those by Melton (1965 and previously cited in Pert. Pubs. Sec. I, 1965*b*), who has presented relationships between drainage-basin variables and the gradients of alluvial deposits and who has shown that no correlation exists between hillslope angle and particle size. The latter point suggests that the boulder-controlled-slope hypothesis of Bryan and others is incorrect, but Rahn (1965) has claimed, essentially, that boulder control can be substantiated. This author has resurrected the lateral-corrasion argument in the same note. Although most of the recent literature on pediments and fans contains some measurements or useful field data in support of the arguments presented, such is not always the case (Warnke and Stone, 1965), and it would be well to avoid equating quality with publication date as a broad generalization. Moreover, such cause-and-effect explanations as freeze-thaw frequencies and boulder production in arid areas are subjects of some dispute (Lustig, 1966).

To conclude this treatment of the available information on fans and pediments a few citations on desert varnish are in order, because varnish is intimately associated with the surficial aspects of both landforms and because relevant information on these aspects is often contained. The literature on this subject is scanty. White (1924) and Laudermilk (1931) provided early descriptions of the phenomenon, Blackwelder (1948) has discussed the historical aspects, as has Hunt (1961). Engel and Sharp (1958) and Lakin *et al.* (1963) have provided information on the chemical constituents of varnish. A good treatment of the interrelationships among varnish, desert-pavement formation, and particle size of the rock fragments involved is presented in Denny's report on Death Valley fans (1965, see Pert. Pubs. Sec. I).

Erosion and Sedimentation

The last group of reports to be treated here with respect to the available information on the United States includes papers on erosion and sedimentation, drainage features, field and theoretical studies of alluvial channels, and a few miscellaneous subjects. These papers, for the most part, have not been previously cited in this report, but the interested reader should be apprised of the fact that the literature that has been previously cited in other contexts in this report is also pertinent to these subjects. Those references cited in the section of this report treating backgrounds of modern geomorphic concepts and which largely pertain to quantitative geomorphology, slope erosion, and fluvial processes, for example, could readily be discussed here were it not for the desirability of avoiding duplication. With respect to erosion and sedimentation in general, those reports which treat alluvial fans and pediments should also be consulted; they are basically germane to this subject but are generally omitted below.

To begin with information on erosion in general, Dole and Stabler (1909) with some exception by Free (1909), provided one of the earliest treatments of denudation rates in the United States, based upon the sediment concentrations that were observed in some of the major rivers. Langbein and Schumm (1958) discussed a method of estimating sediment yield if the effective mean annual precipitation is known, and this paper is significant because it indicates that maximum erosion will occur under semiarid conditions; increased aridity is said to lead to lesser sediment yields. Schumm's argument concerning present rates of orogeny and denudation (1963, see Pert. Pubs. Sec. I) might also be mentioned here because his report summarizes the denudation data obtained from many reservoir studies in the United States and provides a modern adjustment for the conclusions of Dole and Stabler (1909). Other papers of note in a general vein include Bailey's discussion of erosion in the west (1941), that by Thornthwaite, Sharpe, and Dosch (1942) treating climatic factors and accelerated erosion in Arizona, Leopold's thesis on the erosion problem in the Southwest (1950), the review by Gottschalk (1957*a, b*) of problems associated with the sediment yield from watersheds and methods of solution, and a modern restatement of the sediment problem by Sundborg (1964).

Tarr's work in 1890 on erosive agents (1890) is largely of historical interest, but Tolman's early paper (1909) on erosion and deposition in southern Arizona contains some pertinent observations on pavements along flood plains. Reports on natural bridges in the West (Cleland, 1906, 1911; Cummings, 1910; Miser, Trimble, and Paige, 1923) are also useful by reason of the contained descriptions of the areas treated. Rich (1911) offered one of the first reports on channel trenching in New Mexico, Miser considered erosion in San Juan Canyon, Utah (1925), and Bryan (1925*a*, 1927, 1928, 1940*a*) provided a number of basic papers on the general phenomenon of recent erosion in the Southwest. The work of Bryan was, in this instance, again outstanding considering the period of publication involved, and his reports still provide the basis for current discussions of channel cutting in New Mexico and Arizona. More recent reports on arroyos include those by Antevs (1952), Schumm and Hadley (1957), Leighly (1936), and others. Ives (1936) produced some observations of flooding in southern Arizona, but his report is not as incisive as might be desired.

With regard to information on erosion and sedimentation in California, previous discussion and Pert. Pubs. Sec. I contain information on the work of Bull (1964), Denny (1965), Hooke (1965), Anderson (1949), Anderson and Trobitz (1949), and Lustig (1965*a, b*). Also particularly noteworthy are several reports by Anderson (1954, 1955, 1957, see Pert. Pubs. Sec. XIV) (Anderson, Coleman, and Zinke, 1959) and LaMarche (1961). Some excellent field observations of mudflows in California are available (Gleason and Amidon, 1941; Sharp, 1942; Sharp and Nobles, 1953), and Bull (1964*b*) has discussed the history of channel trenching in the Central Valley.

Leopold and Snyder (1951) have provided information on alluvial deposits near Gallup, New Mexico, Stanley (1951) has discussed aspects of the lower Colorado River, for which suspended-sediment data are available (Howard, 1947) and Schumm, in an excellent series of papers, has advanced our knowledge of the shape and characteristics of alluvial channels in relation to several parameters (Schumm, 1960; 1961*a, b;* 1963). Strahler (1956) has dis-

cussed erosion and deposition in channels, but the work of Schumm and that of Hadley (1961, 1963), Cooley (1962*b*), Evans (1963), and Wertz (1964) provides much more specific information on the subject, as well as data on the areas of study in each case. One of the fundamental reports on ephemeral streams is that listed in Pert. Pubs. Sec. I by Leopold and Miller (1956). Miller has also provided a vast amount of quantitative data on alluvial channel characteristics and the particle size of bed material in mountain streams (1958, see Pert. Pubs. Sec. I) and with Wendorf, has treated the chronology of erosion and deposition in a typical New Mexico wash (Miller and Wendorf, 1958). A recent book relevant to changes in surficial features and vegetation during an 85-year period in the southwestern United States has been provided by Hastings and Turner (1965). It provides a reasonable basis for comparative studies of many types, including studies of erosion and sedimentation.

The quantitative work of Melton in Arizona was previously noted (1965 and Pert. Pubs. Sec. I, 1965*b*), but he has also discussed drainage patterns in the state (1960, 1961) and has proposed a hypothesis to explain their origin. With respect to drainage patterns, it should again be stated that the references contained in the introduction to this report and in the sections treating available information by states should be consulted to supplement the papers noted here.

Among the miscellaneous topics that are associated with erosion in the arid region, two are particularly important. First, the problem of piping in alluvial sediments is one that has been largely underrated through the years, save for studies of earth-fill-dam failure where piping is a contributory cause. The best paper on this subject to date is that by Parker (1963) which also provides a reference guide to the meagre literature; however, conclusions on the cause of piping and its development, particularly with respect to the relative importance of clay types, are not yet soundly based. A thesis in progress by N. O. Jones at the University of Arizona will add considerably to our general knowledge of the cause and development of piping in the southwestern United States. The second problem is that of cliff retreat in the arid regions, a process which leads to the formation of pedestal rocks. In addition to earlier treatments by Bryan (1923*a*) and Koons (1955), and the several citations in this report to the quantitative aspects of hillslopes, the recent paper by Schumm and Chorley (1964) provides the most informative and best-documented analysis of this matter. A final miscellaneous topic is the question of the erosion that is produced directly by raindrop impact. The literature on soils and agriculture provides a considerable number of reports on this subject, but as examples of the available information the work of Ellison (1946, 1948, 1950) and the discussion of problems by Elkern (1953) should suffice. Chow and Harbaugh (1964) have recently discussed the artificial production of raindrops of desired diameters for use in laboratory experiments, and some quantitative experimental data on erosion by this mechanism will be forthcoming in the near future.

Although certain of the papers cited above may be considered theoretical studies, they must be differentiated from reports which treat either hydraulic factors of flow in channels or sediment transport in a more fundamental manner. Such reports will be cited below, to conclude this survey of the available information on the United States. Because of their subject content, these reports do not pertain, in all instances, to some specific arid part of the United States or even to what might specifically be termed an arid-region problem. Nevertheless, they represent that information which is available in the literature and which provides the basis for any eventual approach or solution to such problems.

Sediment transportation provides the link between erosion and deposition, in the broad sense. Thus, it is a topic intimately related to geomorphology despite the fact that the literature on sediment transportation seldom contains direct information on landforms as such. Discussions of the basic facets of sediment transportation have been provided by Benedict (1957), Colby (1963), and Einstein (1964), among others, and Ackermann (1957) has outlined some of the needed research on the subject. An early consideration of the energy requirements and dissipation in streams that transport sediment was offered by Rubey (1933), and Laursen and Toch (1954), Dittbrenner (1954), Coldwell (1957), and Colby (1964b) are but a few among many who have discussed scour and fill, or changes in streambed elevation, during high stages of flow. Of these papers, that by Colby (1964b) is the most controversial, but all are worthy of examination. Wolman and Brush (1961) have contributed to knowledge of the factors that influence the size and shape of channels, under specified conditions, and Langbein and Leopold (1964b) have approached the problem of sediment transport in relation to river bars and dunes by application of kinematic-wave theory, or a probabilistic viewpoint, in contrast to the standard fluid-mechanics treatment. Their approach to this difficult problem has much to recommend it.

The actual techniques of measurement of sediment transportation and the computation of that fraction of the total sediment load which is transported as dissolved load, suspended sediment, or bed material, are of themselves truly difficult matters, and much attention has been devoted to the solution of attendant problems. Pierce (1916) has provided an early treatment of sediment measurements in streams, Colby (1964a) has discussed sand discharge in relation to water velocities, Crickmore and Lean (1962) have described the use of radioactive tracers to determine sand transport, Guy and Simons (1963) have outlined the variation in results that may be attributed to different weighting factors combined with the fact that both water velocity and sediment concentration vary nonlinearly with depth of water, and Bagnold (1960a), has contributed to the general topic of sediment discharge in streams.

The use of ultrasonic apparatus, a relatively new method for measuring stream velocities, has been described by Wires (1961); similarly Flammer (1962) has described its application to suspended-sediment concentrations, and the apparatus and methods of measuring the bed load of streams have been described by Hubbell (1963). Although several bed-load functions are available in the literature, that proposed by Einstein (1950) is one of the better-known and often-used relationships, and his report contains references to other papers on this subject. Colby and Hembree (1955) and Colby and Hubbell (1961) have illustrated the procedure for computing the total sediment discharge of a stream by application of Einstein's function to the data on suspended-sediment discharge and the bed-load samples which are obtained. Problems associated with the measurement and computation of sediment discharge are also outlined by Lustig and Busch (1967).

A fine series of papers on sediment transportation in the Río Grande drainage system, and descriptions of attendant features such as the formation of armored mud balls and sediment storage in alluvial islands, has been provided by Nordin and others (Nordin and Dempster, 1963; Nordin and Curtis, 1962; Nordin, 1963, 1964; Nordin and Beverage, 1964); Fahnestock and Maddock (1964) have reported on the bed forms in this river.

The last aspect of sediment transportation germane here is that of experimental, or flume studies. Among many that have been performed, the work of Jopling (1963a, b; 1964a, b), which pertains to the mechanics and characteristics of the formation of bedding, of Simons and his colleagues (Simons, Richardson, and Albertson, 1961; Simons, Richardson, and Haushild, 1963) and of Fahnestock and Haushild (1962) on the transportation of large particles on a sand bed at various stages of flow are illustrative of both the knowledge that has been gained and the inherent limitations of the methods and procedures employed. Several additional experimental studies and abundant references on the subject can be obtained from the excellent collection of papers from the symposium report edited by Middleton (1965). As an interesting example of the difficulty in translating flume results to field conditions, the recent report of Bradley (1965) on vertical density currents demonstrates that the applicability of Stokes' law of settling velocity, which is involved in many expressions of the sediment concentration in streams, is highly questionable under natural conditions.

An exhaustive summary of previous work on sediment transportation has been provided by Maddock (1965). This report not only gives a new sediment-transport function, which is shown to be valid for both low and high velocity-of-flow values, but also discusses the critical matter of the choice and use of dependent and independent variables in transport problems. The limitations of many previous studies are thus made clear, and Maddock's paper should be regarded as authoritative on the general subject of sediment transportation in alluvial channels.

With respect to flow in alluvial channels, adjustment of channel configuration, and the relation of bed forms and erosion and deposition flow characteristics, many of the above papers are relevant. Moreover, a large number of references on these topics was provided in the introduction to this report, and elsewhere. Accordingly, only a few additional papers in a theoretical vein will be cited here, and repetition of citations will be held to a minimum.

Many of the basic aspects of the flow in alluvial channels have been reviewed by Sundborg (1956) in his treatment of processes in the river Klarälven. Kindsvater (1958) and Albertson and Simons (1964) have presented good reviews of fluid mechanics elsewhere, and the basic procedures employed in gathering streamflow data are provided by Corbett *et al.* (1962). The statistical treatment of the data that are obtained is available from many sources. Gumbel (1945, 1954) has treated extreme-value theory and the estimation of floods, Dalrymple (1960) has discussed flood-frequency analysis, and Fiering (1963) has illustrated the use of correlation procedures to improve estimates of mean values. Matalas (1963*a, b, c*) has considered problems of autocorrelation, the probable distribution of low flows, and precipitation-runoff relations, and with Jacobs (Matalas and Jacobs, 1964) has outlined a method for extending hydrologic data for a given period of record, Riggs (1961) and Hunt (1963) have also considered low-flow problems, and Benson (1959, see also Pert. Pubs. Sec. I, 1962, 1964) has discussed some of the factors related to flood frequency and has reviewed the

methods employed in the prediction of flood frequency. Wallis (1964) has recently outlined a comparison of multivariate methods in hydrology. Many other reports on this general topic exist, but the selected references provided above, combined with the vast number contained in the recent *Handbook of Applied Hydrology* (Chow, 1964; see Pert. Pubs. Sec. I), should suffice as a guide to the available literature.

In addition to the statistical work described and basic information on the dynamics of flow, there is much available information on the nature and configuration of alluvial channels and on the theoretical reasons for the observed patterns and geometry of rivers. Most of the papers on this subject have been previously cited in the introduction to this report, within the context of modern work in geomorphology. With a few additions, they will briefly be mentioned here for the sake of completeness and by reason of their basic importance. As a whole, these reports represent one of the major contributions of American thought in the field of geomorphology.

Leopold and Maddock (1953, see Pert. Pubs. Sec. I) presented a treatment of the hydraulic geometry of stream channels that, together with the work of Horton (1945, see Pert. Pubs. Sec. I), provided the impetus for all subsequent work on rivers that is in the category considered here. One of the essential ideas presented, that rivers that flow in adjustable channels rapidly attain a state of quasi-equilibrium, was confirmed by Wolman (1955, see Pert. Pubs. Sec. I), Miller (1958, see Pert. Pubs. Sec. I), Hack (1957, see Pert. Pubs. Sec. I), and many others. Langbein and Leopold (1964*a*, see Pert. Pubs. Sec. XIV) have restated the concept more recently, and Leopold and Langbein (1962, see Pert. Pubs. Sec. I) have attempted to provide a theoretical explanation for the observed facts. Much of the available information on river channel patterns and allied topics is presented in the review paper by Leopold (1962, see Pert. Pubs. Sec. XIV) on rivers and in the excellent text on fluvial processes previously cited (Leopold, Wolman and Miller, 1964, see Pert. Pubs. Sec. I). It should be noted here, however, that Kilpatrick and Barnes (1964, see Pert. Pubs. Sec. XIV) succeeded in demonstrating that the most prominent topographic bench that occurs along channels in semi-humid areas is related to that frequency of stream discharge which is involved in the hydraulic-geometry argument. Dawdy (1963, see Pert. Pubs. Sec. XIV) has also contributed to knowledge of channel-geometry relationships by refinement of practical matters, Simons and Richardson (1962, see Pert. Pubs. Sec. XIV) have discussed the effect of bed roughness, and, in an entirely different vein, Melton (1958, see Pert. Pubs. Sec. XIV) has presented a theoretical consideration of fluvial geometry.

The distinctions among braided, meandering, and straight channels were outlined by Leopold and Wolman (1957, see Pert. Pubs. Sec. I) and Bagnold (1960b, see Pert. Pubs. Sec. XIV), Langbein and Leopold (1966, see Pert. Pubs. Sec. I), and Einstein and Wen Shen (1964, see Pert. Pubs. Sec. XIV) have all provided theoretical discussion of the cause of stream meandering. Wolman and Leopold (1957, see Pert. Pubs. Sec. XIV) have presented an argument concerning the formation of river floodplains. The burden of this report was that such formation can be largely attributed to point-bar deposition and the lateral migration of rivers, rather than to overbank flooding alone. Sigafoos (1964, see Pert. Pubs. Sec. XIV), however, has recently provided abundant evidence for extensive erosion and deposition during overbank flooding in the eastern United States, and the question of the relative importance of each process, for a given stream under any climatic conditions, remains to be answered.

Other reports of this type, which may be germane to the solution of problems in arid regions, include the observations of Schumm and Lichty (1963, see Pert. Pubs. Sec. XIV) on the Cimarron River, the treatment of ephemeral streams in New Mexico by Leopold and Miller (1956, see Pert. Pubs. Sec. I) and Dury's comprehensive consideration of underfit streams in various parts of the world (1964a, b; 1965, see Pert. Pubs. Sec. I). The best available source of information on all aspects of alluvial channels is the "Professional Paper" series of the U. S. Geological Survey, wherein most of the reports cited were published originally.

Authorities

Authorities on aspects of geomorphology or surface-water hydrology in the United States are not rare because of the volume of past and present work within many organizations. Those who may profitably be consulted on these topics include *W. B. Langbein* and *L. B. Leopold* of the U. S. Geological Survey. *B. F. Jones* and *Ivan Barnes* are expert on water quality and playa lakes in the western United States; they also represent this agency. *Thomas Maddock, Jr.* of the U. S. Geological Survey, and *H. A. Einstein* of the University of California are competent in all aspects of sediment transport and the problems surrounding the processes of erosion and sedimentation. Authorities on the geomorphology of the arid region should include *R. P. Sharp* ,California Institute of Technology, *M. A. Melton,* University of British Columbia, and *S. A. Schumm,* U. S. Geological Sur-

vey. *James Gilluly,* U. S. Geological Survey, and *A. J. Eardley,* University of Utah, can provide information on all aspects of the general geology of the western United States. Advice on the application of mathematical methods to geomorphic or other problems can be provided by several individuals previously named, notably *W. B. Langbein* and *M. A. Melton,* but *J. W. Harbaugh* of Stanford University, *W. C. Krumbein* of Northwestern University, *A. N. Strahler* of Columbia University, and *R. L. Miller* of University of Chicago are also competent to render assistance in this respect.

Depositories

For the convenience of the reader, U. S. depositories are relisted here: Harvard University, Yale University, Stanford University, University of Southern California, the University of California system, and the U. S. Geological Survey and Library of Congress collections.

Mexico

The available information relevant to the geomorphology of the Mexican desert areas is sparse relative to that on the United States, and certain sources of information have been mentioned previously. In this respect, the general sources of information, noted in the section of this report so titled, should be consulted. Individual reports and papers that treat some aspect of the Mexican desert will be cited here; they represent a selective sample of a population that is not large. Publications cited in the following text on Mexico, unless otherwise noted where cited, are listed in Section XV of the Pertinent Publications list.

Bibliographic material on Mexico is available in the *Bibliography of North American Geology* and in an annotated bibliography on the Mexican desert prepared by the University of Southern California (1958). Aguilar y Santillán (1898) presented a bibliography that pertains largely to reports on the geology of mining districts through 1898, but which serves as a guide to early work on Mexico in general. Additional lists of useful references can be obtained from certain specific reports. Among these are the chapter on Mexico in Machatschek's *Relief der Erde* (1955, see Pert. Pubs. Sec. I), Jaeger's account of North American deserts (1957, see Pert. Pubs. Sec. XIV), Eardley's treatise on structural geology (1962b, see Pert. Pubs. Sec. XIV), an early work on the physiography of Mexico by Thayer (1916), the more recent treatment of the geography of the country by Vivó (1958), and many of the reports to be cited below. Also worthy of note, in a general vein, are the reports of the International Geological Congress that was held in Mexico (1956, see Pert. Pubs. Sec. I); a number of useful field-trip guidebooks were published, in addition to some reports on the geology, geomorphology or hydrology of the country. The recent report of arid-zone research in Mexico by Fournier d'Albe (1960) and Wallén's discussion of rainfall variability (1956) also should be mentioned here as general references. Finally the review of arid-zone problems by the Instituto Mexicano de Recursos Naturales Renovables (1955) provides a good outline of the arid areas of Mexico in terms of an evapotranspiration map and basic information on water resources, vegetation, and similar subjects.

The best sources of information on mapping in Mexico are provided by King's map and report (1947), the landform map of Mexico by Raisz (1959, see Pert. Pubs. Sec. I), and the folio treating Yuma terrain analogs in the Mexican desert by the U. S. Army (U. S. Army Engineer Waterways Experiment Station, 1959). King's report provides an index to previous mapping in Mexico, accompanied by an appropriate bibliography, and both King and Raisz provide information on the responsible mapping agencies in the country. The terrain folio cited above is unique, and no comparable information on the arid areas of Mexico exists. Most recently, however, an excellent annotated index to all mapping and aerial photographic coverage of Mexico has been provided by the Organization of American States (1966). This comprehensive summary should be consulted for information on the availability of Mexican maps and air photos.

With respect to descriptions of the physiography of various parts of the Mexican desert area, many of the reports to be cited here present such information. In addition to the work of Thayer (1916) and Vivó (1958), Galindo y Villa (1926-1927) has provided a general geographic treatise on Mexico, and Sanders (1921), Ordóñez (1936), and Gonzáles Reyna (1956), among others, have discussed the physiographic provinces of Mexico prior to the publication of the definitive map by Raisz. Staub (1923) has provided an early treatment of the geography of northern Mexico, Porter (1932) has described an area in northeastern Mexico that he termed "the Coahuila physiographic province," Brand (1937) has outlined the major landforms in part of Chihuahua, Pfeifer (1939) has written on the Sinaloan and Sonoran provinces, Dios Bojorquez (1946) has also treated the geography of Sonora, and Blásquez L. (1956) has recently provided an outline of the physiography of western Mexico.

Descriptions of Baja California are also available. Beal (1948) has treated the entire peninsula in connection with an investigation of petroleum

possibilities in the region, Engerrand and Paredes (1913) gave an early description of some of the channels and valleys of north Baja California, Tamayo (1940) has discussed the geography of the southern part of this area, and Hammond (1954) has more recently investigated such geomorphic phenomena as elevated beaches in the Cape Region of Baja California.

Other reports in this descriptive vein include that by Bonillas and Urbina (1913) on the Colorado Delta region. Combined with the later studies of Kniffen (1932, see Pert. Pubs. Sec. XIV), Sykes (1937, see Pert. Pubs. Sec. XIV), and others previously cited, his report contributes to general geographic data on this area.

A larger number of reports on Mexico treat geology primarily but, as in the case of available information on the United States, they also provide some information on the geomorphology or surficial aspects of the regions considered. Within this category are reports on Baja California by Darton (1921), Heim (1922), Woodford and Harriss (1938), and Gálvez (1927). In a similar category are the reports on the geological evolution of the Coahuila Peninsula by Kellum (1936); Kellum, Imlay, and Kane (1936); Kelly (1936); Imlay (1936); and Singewald (1936). Additional papers that appeared during this period and are worthy of note include the treatise on the San Carlos Mountains by Kellum *et al.* (1937) and King's work on southwestern Coahuila (1934) and the northern part of the Sierra Madre Occidental (1939).

Since 1940, geological reports that contain relevant geomorphic data have been published by Kellum (1944) on northern Mexico and the Sonoran desert, Humphrey (1949) on a part of northeastern Mexico, King and Adkins (1946) on the Chihuahua desert region, and López (1947) on northern and eastern Mexico. The latter report was performed in cooperation with the U. S. Geological Survey and contains high quality maps of the region and additional references.

Edwards (1955) has provided an excellent report on some sedimentary rocks of central Mexico, Gianella (1960) and Merriam (1965) have recently reported on faulting in Sonora, and some good studies of volcanic rocks and associated features in the country are available. Among the latter are reports by Heim (1921) and Woodford (1928) on volcanoes in Baja California, by Ives (1956) on the Pinacate area in northern Mexico, and the comprehensive papers on the Paricutín volcanoes by Segerstrom (1950, see Pert. Pubs. Sec. I) and Williams (1950). An additional group of modern reports that treat the geology of parts of Baja California includes papers by Wilson (1948) and Wisser (1954) and Wilson and Rocha (1955). The latter two papers cited are devoted largely to ore deposits but include data on the geography as well as the geology of the region. The treatment of the Peninsular ranges that extend from southern California into Baja California by Jahns (1954) is excellent, and Mina's recent outline of the geology of Baja California (1956, 1957) should also be consulted for pertinent data.

In a different category are those geologic reports which treat some aspect of the Gulf of California or the offshore region to the west of Baja California. Such reports commonly provide some geographic and geologic information on the coastal regions and on the offshore islands. Examples of reports of this type include Anderson's 1950 treatment of the results of the Scripps Oceanographic Institute cruise in the Gulf of California, a consideration of biogeography by Durham and Allison (1960), Hamilton's paper on the origin of the Gulf (1961), and a discussion of sedimentation in coastal lagoons by Phleger and Ewing (1962). Krause (1965) has recently published the results of a geophysical investigation of the continental margin west of Baja California. Bathymetric and tectonic data are presented in addition to the geophysical results, but the paper is useful as background material for this region and contains several pertinent references not cited here.

Reports primarily geomorphic in nature on areas in Mexico are not abundant and are uneven both with respect to the subjects treated and the quality of treatment. Keyes (1908) extended his standard eolian explanations to lake basins in Mexico in 1908 and Hill (1908) provided an early hypothesis on the Mexican Plateau at this time. King (1935) has accorded qualitative treatment to the pediments and inselbergs in Sonora, Ives (1936) has discussed desert floods in a portion of this state, and Shreve (1935)

has compared the abundance of sandy areas in northern Mexico and the southern United States with such areas in other deserts of the world. Several good reports on erosion and sedimentation in the vicinity of Paricutín are available. Among these are papers by Shrock (1945), Lowdermilk (1947), and Segerstrom's excellent 1950 contribution previously cited and listed in Pert. Pubs. Sec. I.

López de Llergo (1953) has invoked a classical explanation to explain changes in drainage characteristics and the presumed increase in the desert area in Mexico, Gálvez (1941) has provided an example of hydrogeological investigations in Mexico, and Arnold (1957) has discussed some landforms in Baja California in relation to Pleistocene and Recent climatic changes and the archeologic record.

In summary, it might be said that coverage of the Mexican desert areas is poor, relative to that of the United States. Baja California and northern Mexico have been most studied but quantitative geomorphic investigations have not been undertaken. This fact, combined with the general absence of large-scale topographic maps of uniform scale, suggests that the available literature on the geography and geology of the country can add few data that are not already incorporated in the terrain folio of the Mexican desert (U. S. Army Engineer Waterways Experiment Station, 1959).

Authorities and Depositories

No authorities are named as knowledgeable about the entire arid zone of Mexico and the past and present research on it. Faculty members at the University of Southern California are knowledgeable about Baja California, and the information collected at that institution is perhaps somewhat stronger on Mexico than that of the other depositories named previously in discussing the U. S.

EVALUATION AND RECOMMENDATIONS

As mentioned at the outset of this report, time limitations precluded the possibility of providing written evaluations of each of the many works cited, and for this reason a general evaluation is offered here. The evaluation consists of an outline of deficiencies of knowledge of the arid regions, outstanding problems that remain, and some recommendations for research to meet the deficiencies cited.

Because this report is intended to meet the needs of a government sponsor, and because the writer is aware that projects such as "The origin of landform X" would seem at first glance to be irrelevant to those needs, a few explanatory remarks are in order here. As indicated in the section of this report entitled "Backgrounds of Modern Geomorphic Concepts," the available papers and reports on geomorphology and aspects of surface-water hydrology present an enormous range of effort. The diversity extends from qualitative geographic descriptions of features or areas, through sophisticated statistical treatments of quantitative data on landforms and hydrologic factors, to theoretical discussions of the applicability of general systems theory and stochastic processes to geomorphic problems. It was also indicated that such diversity of approach largely reflects the differing conceptual frameworks of thought of the authors involved. In relation to the various problems that will be raised in this general evaluation, the point to be made is that given an identical hypothetical problem such as "The origin of landform X," the reports produced by various authors will vary in a predictable manner. Whether the reports are of value for practical governmental purposes will not truly be a function of the phraseology of the problem but rather of the outlook, bias, or conceptual framework of thought of a given investigator.

Let us suppose, for the sake of illustration, that data on the pans, playas, and desert flats of certain arid regions of the world are required for some specific purpose, perhaps for the preparation of terrain analogs. The useful information on such features might well include their size, shape, degree of flatness, surface texture, orientation, distribution with altitude, mineralological composition, and frequency of inundation, among other factors. If such information is not available, then one must obtain it directly or indirectly. The direct method consists of ordering an employee to proceed to the desert flats in question, make the required measurements, and return. The indirect method would involve the support of an academic research project that might well be entitled "The origin of pans in ...." If the chief investigator of such a project is a geographer or geomorphologist of classical bent, who thinks of landform development in terms of erosion cycles and block diagrams, then the likely outcome of the investigation will be a qualitative description of the features involved, a regional interpretation of the landscape based upon questionable assumptions, and an assemblage of "evidence" indicating that deflation by the wind has been a dominant factor in the genesis of the pans. Alternatively, an investigator who considers the problem within the larger context of the questions of relict versus equilibrium features in the desert, the relative importance of wind and water, the magnitude and frequency of forces in arid regions, and the quantitative relationships of landforms and processes, would in all probability gather precisely the data that are desired during the course of the study.

For these reasons, it appears to this writer that few, if any, basic geomorphic questions can be raised that are not of practical as well as academic interest. Qualitative geographic descriptions are no longer satisfactory for either purpose, and it is assumed in the discussion that follows that the investigators who are selected to pursue a given problem will be chosen in such a manner as to insure the gathering of basic, quantitative data on landforms and processes, and that these data will be obtained in accord with modern statistical sampling procedures.

A. DEFICIENCIES OF INFORMATION AND BASIC PROBLEMS

A review of the available literature on the arid regions of the world that has been cited in this report leads to several generalizations concerning deficiencies and basic problems that exist. These can most conveniently be treated in a topical manner, and it is fitting, at the outset, to consider the question of how to define a desert and its boundaries. This discussion will be followed by a consideration of various desert landforms, drainage, mapping problems, and allied matters, but in each instance it will be apparent that a great need for quantitative data of several types exists in order to enlarge our basic understanding of deserts and their landforms and processes. Additional reviews of geomorphic problems in the arid regions are available in two concise but excellent papers by Peel (1960, 1966; see Pert. Pubs. Sec. I).

1. Definition of a Desert

Despite recognition of the fact that all definitions and classifications of natural phenomena are arbitrary and may well vary in utility as a function of some given purpose, it is instructive to consider the question of what a desert is and how its boundaries are determined. This problem is admittedly elementary, but it is by no means trivial. Several basic difficulties are, in fact, intimately associated with the possible range of answers.

In common usage a desert is defined on the basis of a general lack of cultivation and relative absence of inhabitants, but one or more physical characteristics of deserts are, of course, more commonly applied for scientific purposes. Botanists and soils scientists, for example, can delineate deserts on the basis of the types and density of vegetation and "great soils group," respectively, but neither criterion is truly satisfactory because both are dependent variables which reflect climate and source lithologies, among other factors. Moreover, strict application of either these criteria or a dictionary definition leads to inclusion of both polar regions and certain permeable volcanic terrains in humid areas as deserts of a special type. For these reasons, climatic factors are widely used to define desert regions.

With respect to climatic factors, it is clear that the criterion of precipitation alone is also unsatisfactory. One commonly hears that a desert region is one in which the mean annual precipitation does not exceed 10 inches. Again, the polar regions would qualify and for this reason some combination of temperature and precipitation enters into most definitions or classifications. As noted by Landsberg, many classifications have been proposed through the years. Those most widely used are the Köppen system or some modification, which appears in nearly every atlas, Thornthwaite's scheme, and, with specific reference to desert climates, Meigs' system, which provided the basis for treatment in this report.

Any such classification is based upon mean annual values of temperature and precipitation, and

lines of arbitrary location on a 2-variable plot serve to distinguish arid, semiarid, semihumid, and humid regions. Subclassifications are then produced by considering the coldest month, warmest month, and seasonality of the precipitation, which are partly dependent upon hemispheric location and the altitude of a given region. Although it is quite true that the general locations of the desert regions are the same on any map showing world climatic distribution, the boundaries may differ considerably and the following problems emerge:

1) Are the basic climatic data sufficient to delineate the desert regions?
2) Are mean annual values the most meaningful parameters to employ?
3) Are the deserts of the world expanding or contracting today?

These problems will be briefly outlined below.

Basic Climatic Data

The available literature cited in this chapter and the discussion in Chapter II clearly indicates that there is a great lack of basic climatic data on the desert regions of the world. This is particularly true of precipitation data, as was noted in the several climatic-analog reports of the U. S. Army. The insufficiency is of three kinds: the areal distribution of stations, the altitudinal distribution of stations, and the lengths of record that are available.

With respect to the areal distribution of stations, it is obvious that isohyetal maps of desert areas are highly questionable save as general guides. Precipitation data are generally gathered at population centers or at sites of prospective water-resources projects. In both instances, these do not tend to be located in the most arid parts of a given country. The truth of this statement should be apparent from consideration of the locations of capitals of Saharan countries, for example. Capital cities in the northern Sahara are on the coast, whereas in the southern Sahara they tend to occur as close to the semihumid regions as possible. In any event, one finds everywhere that the density of precipitation stations declines markedly with increasing aridity. In the northern Sudan, precipitation stations are clustered along the Nile. East-west trending isohyetal lines, however, are shown on maps to extend across a vast arid area in the northwestern quarter of the country, for which there are essentially no data. In the central and western parts of the Sahara, those charged with the production of a climatic atlas readily admit that the areal distribution of stations leaves much to be desired. In Iran there are perhaps 300 or more hydrologic stations which essentially ring the great arid areas of the Dasht-e-Kavir and Dasht-e-Lut. Only a few scattered stations exist in these areas. In the Rub'al Khali of Saudi Arabia precipitation data are of even greater rarity.

Many other examples could be cited, but the essential point here is that the isohyetal maps of the desert regions of the world are based on extrapolations of data from too few sampling stations. Combined with the fact that the variability of mean annual rainfall increases with increasing aridity, and attains a value of 50 per cent or more for most of the world's deserts, it seems clear that one should not assume that the precipitation is actually known at any given random location within a given desert region. The climatic maps that are available largely reflect the old maxim that one should do the best one can with the data that are available. This adage is not disputed here, but the maps in question should not be assigned a high degree of reliability simply because they exist.

Because the climatic maps serve as the basis for delineation of the desert regions, it is not remarkable that these boundaries vary in accordance with the atlas or author that is consulted. The problem is quite real. One can readily distinguish between central Sumatra and central Arabia, but if one followed any south-to-north transect from central Africa, precisely where would the boundary of the Sahara be encountered: And if one continued northward, precisely where would the boundary between the arid and extremely arid regions defined by Meigs be located?

It is, of course, unlikely that the areal density of precipitation stations in the arid regions will increase many-fold in the near future, but with respect to the desert boundaries, it would be useful to establish lines of climatic stations that extend across the climatic-boundary locations that are depicted on regional maps. Many other types of data could also be obtained at such stations, data that would be pertinent to the problem of the expansion and contraction of deserts. This matter will be treated later, but at this point it would be well to consider the vertical variation of climatic elements in the desert regions and the altitudinal distribution of stations.

It is fair to say that the areal gaps in our knowledge of precipitation in the world's deserts is exceeded by our lack of knowledge of the orographic effects that are associated with many of the principal massifs and mountain ranges of the arid regions. The Tibesti and Ahaggar massifs of the central Sahara and the mountainous regions of central Iran and Baluchistan, the western United States, and elsewhere are most assuredly not truly arid areas despite their incorporation into the desert regions proper on world or regional maps of small scale. Orographic effects are simply assumed or extrapolated in most instances despite the fact that the actual precipitation distribu-

tion, and the distribution of other climatic elements as well, is of great significance in attempted delineation of desert regions and subregions and in hydrologic problems. With respect to the latter, estimates of precipitation-runoff relations, stream discharge, ground-water recharge, and the like must remain highly suspect in the absence of information on altitudinal variation. Even in the United States, which has a relatively high density of hydrologic stations in the arid and semiarid west, mountain data commonly consist of an informed guess. Precipitation in Death Valley, for example, is commonly thought to be on the order of 1.6 inches per year. This is indeed the mean annual value at the Furnace Creek station, but the values in the adjacent high mountains and elsewhere on the basin floor are decidedly different. The experience of this writer suggests that in desert regions of this type, extrapolations based upon values from other stations at considerable distance or upon an assumed precipitation-altitude relationship are apt to be seriously in error. There is no good substitute for basic data in this area of interest, and much useful information could be gained by the establishment of recording instruments at a sequence of elevations on the principal mountains of various deserts. Even where such an effort has been made, the lengths of record are insufficient for generalizations on the precipitation-altitude relationship.

Length of record, which was the third type of deficiency mentioned at the outset of this discussion, is most important in desert regions. Because of the essentially nonrandom character of climatic events, it is well known that a distinction must be made between length of record, in terms of years of observation, and the effective length of record. In nonarid areas it has been shown that the effective length of record is often on the order of 25 per cent of the actual period of observation. This can be translated into terms of reliability, in the sense that a length of record of 100 years will provide predictive information that is only as reliable as would be a 25-year record of randomly distributed events. The reliability factor is probably even less for the arid regions. Hence, it would be most desirable to have the greatest lengths of record for the arid regions as well as the greatest density of stations.

Because of this length-of-record factor and because of general scarcity of climatic data, the classification of the desert regions employed by Meigs is highly suspect. With particular reference to the areas delineated as "extremely arid" on Meigs' maps, there is little statistical justification for the criterion cited, namely that these are areas which on the average receive no rainfall for periods at least as long as one year. The low areal density of precipitation stations within the areas designated as "extremely arid" is, of itself, sufficient reason to question the validity of this unnecessary category. And with respect to length of record, several hundreds of years would be required to support the contention. On the basis of available information, this writer would have no reason to challenge an assertion that rain will fall at least once a year for each of the next five years *somewhere* in the Namib, Atacama, Rub'al Khali, central Sahara, or any other area designated as "extremely arid." In fact, it is conceivable that this occurred during each of the last five years and simply was unnoticed in these large and sparsely populated areas. The primary merit of the "extremely arid" distinction lies in the fact that the concept of the frequency distribution of rainfall is involved. This will be discussed in the following section.

Mean Annual Values

All climatic classifications of the regions of the world are based upon mean annual values of the climatic elements, and from the standpoint of geomorphology and surface-water hydrology this represents a common and important failing. The question to be asked here is whether the mean values of temperature or precipitation are necessarily the most meaningful parameters in distinguishing the climatic, geomorphic, and hydrologic similarities and differences among regions.

With respect to mean annual temperatures, there are several famous examples of Siberian stations for which the mean annual temperature is 0°F whereas the range of extreme values at those same stations is 180°F. Several obvious differences in physical processes might well be anticipated between such regions and those which exhibit identical mean values but a range of only 10°. The same principle applies to desert regions, and it is particularly pertinent if precipitation is considered.

If the mean annual precipitation in a given region is 12 inches, then the region is commonly thought of as occupying the climatic borderland between the semiarid and arid categories. But the most important climatic factor will be the frequency distribution of the 12 inches per year rather than the total amount. If the precipitation is so distributed that, on the average, the region receives 1 inch per month, then the character and density of vegetation, extent of gullying, stream discharge and sediment yield, soil cover, and nearly every physical aspect of the area will be quite different than would be the case if the precipitation occurred in the form of two 6-inch storms per year. This hypothetical contrast is, of course, quite extreme, but the principle is never-

theless valid. If we wish to compare two regions with respect to climatic factors, perhaps for the production of regional desert analogs, then mean annual values should not be used as the basis for comparison. A parameter that more closely reflects the frequency distributions of both temperature and precipitation should be employed.

In this regard, one useful project that might be undertaken is quite apparent. Precipitation and temperature data from the stations that do exist in the arid regions of the world are commonly tabulated as daily or monthly values and are then cumulated and averaged to produce mean annual values. Those workers engaged in climatic analog studies commonly plot the mean annual values and consult the tabulated data in order to add seasonal factors to their classification. It is here recommended that the kurtosis of the daily or monthly climatic factors be computed and that climatic-analog maps be constructed that are based upon the kurtosis values. To the writer's knowledge, no such attempt has ever been made, but from the theoretical viewpoint this parameter, the fourth moment of the normal frequency distribution, should reflect significant climatic similarities and differences more adequately than do mean annual totals. This statement stems from the fact that kurtosis is essentially a ratio between the tails of the frequency distribution and its central portion. As such, it should adequately reflect the climatic variabilities that exist among regions by reason of differing temperature and precipitation distributions.

This same principle can be applied to winds and, to a great extent, it is applied. It is useless to compare regions on the basis of mean annual wind velocities if we are concerned with the movement of sands. For this reason, wind data are commonly tabulated in the form of class-frequency histograms or tables. It seems strange that the desirability of treating temperature and precipitation data in a similar manner is not widely recognized.

With respect to the definition of a desert and subregional distinctions, precipitation variability may well prove to be a better criterion than mean annual values. For this reason it was previously stated that the chief merit of Meigs' "extremely arid" designation lies in its implicit frequency connotation. One cannot, however, apply frequency criteria in the absence of adequate data and, in this instance, in the absence of adequate lengths of record. The geographic locations of the arid-semiarid regional boundaries can be arbitrarily fixed on the basis of frequency criteria, however. Whether such boundaries would prove to be more meaningful and more sharply defined is a question that cannot be answered until some attempt is made to reevaluate the available data in terms of kurtosis or some other parameter that will reflect the frequency distribution of these data.

Expansion and Contraction of Deserts

Several discussions of the expansion and contraction of deserts have appeared in the world literature. The arguments concerning parts of the Thar Desert of India represent one example, but the general problem has been discussed with reference to the southern Sahara and other desert regions as well. It is an extremely difficult question to resolve and, indeed, resolution cannot be accomplished by this review. The discussion here is primarily intended to show the relation between this problem and the basic difficulty of defining a desert.

It has been argued thus far that the definition of a desert is arbitrary, that mean values of climatic factors commonly provide the basis for definition, that these may not be the most meaningful criteria to employ, and that the precise geographic locations of desert boundaries are variable and essentially unknown. This latter point is, quite obviously, crucial to any arguments concerning expansion and contraction of deserts. One cannot determine the precise distance over which a given desert has presumably encroached unless the initial position is known. Aside from this difficulty, most of the "proof" of advancing deserts stems from the complaints of farmers in semi-arid marginal areas, that formerly productive fields have been inundated by windblown sand. As stated previously in this report, such local travail cannot be accepted as evidence for desert expansion.

The reason for this statement is the fact that it is unrealistic to suppose that random climatic perturbations or oscillations will not occur across the vast regions occupied by the margins of the world's deserts through time. Although the precise response of physical processes to any given, finite climatic oscillation remains one of the central problems of geomorphology, the simplest view of the world's deserts is that they are equilibrium bodies. That is, they tend to occupy areas, the boundaries of which fluctuate slightly through time but which remain essentially in the same mean positions in the absence of external constraints. This should not be misconstrued as support for the occasionally encountered misstatement that "once a desert always a desert." Those who support this view ignore the vast body of evidence that suggests that several rather profound climatic changes have occurred through time and, in fact, that the plant, animal, and human communities, as well as the hydrologic regimen of many of the present desert areas, were considerably different only a few thousands of years ago. It is argued here only that the desert areas will tend to fluctuate slightly even in the absence of any demonstrable tendency toward major climatic change. From this point of view the windblown sand that has newly occupied a farmer's tilled field may well be blown back in 50 or 100 years, and its present position is not necessarily an indication of some long-term trend toward desert expansion but merely a reflection of continuous pulsations and adjustments of the mean desert position.

If desert boundaries can vary in the absence of substantial climatic change and can clearly vary if climatic changes in fact occur, then how can the reasons for a given case of encroachment or contraction be discerned? This again raises a problem of considerable importance, namely how to interpret properly measurements of changes in landforms, rates of processes, or positions of boundaries, if the measurements have been made during a relatively short period of time. Suppose for the sake of illustration that the advance of windblown sand upon the hypothetical farmer's field is determined by surveys to have been 500 feet during a 5-year period. Suppose, further, that all of the encroachment can be attributed to major sandstorms that occurred during only 2 of the 5 years. If measurements had been made during only the 2-year period of movement it might have been concluded that the rate of advance was equal to 250 feet per year. If the 5-year period is considered, then the rate of advance becomes 100 feet per year. But the information sought is really the long-term rate and this writer would maintain that it is unsafe to extrapolate the short-term rate measurements. It is entirely conceivable that the 5-year results are merely fluctuations about some long-term mean trend and, in fact, this trend may not even be in the same direction as that of the measured fluctuation.

In addition to this problem of the representativeness of short-term rate samples, this boundary matter is enmeshed in another basic question. How can we distinguish between expansion and contraction of deserts as a result of any natural processes and the dislocations from the effects of man? Poor agricultural practices and overgrazing are rather widespread along the margins, if not within, many of the world's deserts. In the Botswana portion of the Kalahari, for example, drought has been a continuing problem for at least 5 years. The local inhabitants are cattle breeders, and the course of wisdom would seem to dictate that the herds be reduced by shipment to market when dry periods occur. Because the cattle represent wealth to these inhabitants they will not reduce the size of the herds, and the official solution to the problem has been to engage in a drilling program in order to increase water supplies in the Kalahari. As a consequence of this scheme, the cattle have trampled the vegetation around each new well for a distance of many miles, and it appears clear to even the casual observer that when the drought conditions ultimately lift, the character of the vegetation will be quite different from that which formerly prevailed. The desert area will, in fact, have become greater as a sole result of the interference of man. Similar examples can be provided by many countries, including the United States where the Bureau of Land Management has not been able to enforce a reduction of range cattle on the public domain. Gullying and increased sediment yields are but two of the many problems thus created.

The Kalahari tends to be quite flat, and combined with the porous nature of the Kalahari sands that mantle the area, the aforementioned factors tend to inhibit pronounced gullying or erosion. In the topographically high desert regions, such as those of Iran, Afghanistan, West Pakistan, and elsewhere however, the cutting of timber and improper tilling of semiarid marginal areas have led to serious gullying through time and have created man-induced desert areas.

Knowledge of these unfortunate instances is rather widespread today, and many symposia have been held to discuss regional plans and programs designed to improve land usage. Within the context of this report, however, it is clear that desert expansion can be attributed to the effects of man in many instances and that in a given case it may be quite difficult to determine what proportion of the cause of desert expansion should be attributed to man and what proportion to natural events.

The foregoing outline illustrates in a general way the several problems that are associated with the question of the expansion and contraction of deserts and the relationship of this matter to the definition of a desert and its boundaries. The most practical research that might be undertaken in this instance involves the establishment of transects, or zones of sampling stations, that extend from semiarid areas across the desert boundaries and into the arid regions. This establishment was previously mentioned in connection with the gathering of additional climatic data to aid in defining the desert boundaries. It would be quite useful, however, also to obtain data on the precise gradation of soils, vegetation, drainage, landforms, microtopography, and other factors that can be discerned as the arid-boundary area is traversed. Accompanied by measurements of climatic variables at the same stations, such a procedure of repetitive surveys would perhaps permit more quantitative assessments of the changes in processes and characteristics that can be associated with a finite climatic change. The literature is replete with assertions of

the differences that may be anticipated between regions that receive 2 inches of precipitation per year and those which receive 20 inches. No one has yet defined the changes that may result if the precipitation increases from 2 to 3 inches or from 3 to 4 inches, however. Networks of transects, of the sort proposed here, would provide valuable data in this connection as well as on the definition of desert boundaries and their fluctuation through time.

2. Desert Sands

The available literature on desert sands and sand dunes that has been cited in this report reveals that a fairly large number of diverse studies on this subject have been undertaken. Descriptions of sand areas and dunes have been provided for parts of the Sahara, Atacama, Australia, Arabia, and, indeed, for most of the deserts of the world. Much of the early work is qualitative, and a variety of classifications have been offered, most of which rely upon nomenclature and deduction rather than on quantitative data. The work of Bagnold, Sharp, Zim, and others on the dynamics of windblown sand is of another stripe, however. Similarly, empirical data on sand and dune migration, growth rates, maximum heights, and allied matters, have become available in recent years from studies in the Namib, Saudi Arabia, Israel, the United States, and a few other areas.

Additionally, there have been some notable mineralogical studies of desert sands in the Kalahari, parts of the Sahara and Middle East, and in Australia. The remaining papers tend to fall in the category of interpretive studies by those workers concerned with denudation chronology, climatic change, and the like. Differing ages or geneses of sand bodies have been inferred from color distinctions; paleowind directions have been inferred from differing orientations of sand bodies; and the occurrence of sand sheets or dunes that are stabilized by vegetation or occur in nonarid areas today has provided the basis for arguments on climatic change.

In view of the work briefly outlined above it might be supposed that most problems have been resolved. In fact, however, this is far from true. Even the estimates of the areas of the world's deserts that are occupied by sand are probably valid only as a first approximation, for example. No report encountered by this writer clearly explained the methods employed to calculate the area percentages offered, and this suggests that they stem in large part from previous estimates. Moreover, the volumes of desert sands are unknown, and this is related to the area question. Obviously, one would wish to know whether areas that are sand-covered are actually gravel plains with a thin veneer of windblown sand or whether the sand extends to a considerable depth below the surface.

This is the first instance in this evaluation of a general problem that may best be phrased in the form "What is the origin of landform X?" Indeed, what is the origin of the desert sands of the world? The component parts of this general problem are several. It involves first, accurate knowledge of the volumes and areas of sand as mentioned above and the question of why the sands occur in their present distribution. It is insufficient simply to state that a source, transporting agencies, and depositional site are required. What accounts for the present distribution of great ergs and serirs of the Sahara, for example? Have the relative positions of these bodies changed through time? Second, what are the sand source areas of the deserts today and what are the relative rates of sand production, through weathering, of different lithologies under present climatic conditions? Unless knowledge of production rates and volumes of sand is available, interpretations of both sand-body genesis and times of desert formation are quite speculative.

Allied problems include the question of the significance of sand coloration. Can color distinctions be attributed to the ages of various sand bodies and, if so, why should this be true? Even more speculative are the interpretations, based upon present sand distributions, of previous precipitation and wind regimes. With respect to precipitation, it is known that active sand transport is today confined to regions that generally receive less than about 15 inches of annual precipitation. It is incorrect, however, to assume that the occurrence of fixed dunes or sand bodies in a given region necessarily means that the annual precipitation was at some former time less than this value. As pointed out by Flint, but largely ignored by subsequent workers, inactive sand bodies can today be found in such areas as the Congo where the present annual precipitation is on the order of 60 inches. Once again, the frequency distribution of precipitation would appear to be of far greater significance than mean annual values. We do not know the precise relationship between seasonality of precipitation and the movement of sands. In the Congo example, what change would be required to produce active sand transport despite the 60-inch precipitation, in terms of length of the dry season?

The quantitative relationships between the frequency distribution of winds, both with respect to magnitudes and directions, and the movement of sand and dunes also requires much more study. Those fond of classifications and systems of nomenclature inform us that elongate dunes that parallel the predominant wind direction are termed "longitudinal," whereas those elongate dunes that are perpendicular to the predominant wind direction are "transverse" dunes. Few if any authors have been discomfitted by this obvious anomaly; why should two contradictory trends emerge under the same conditions? It would seem apparent to this writer that the conditions must differ and, further, that some specific variation in the magnitude-direction frequency distribution of winds must be involved. The quantitative data obtained to date have been insufficient to resolve this problem.

Finally, with respect to our status of knowledge on desert sands, some mention should be made of wind erosion in the desert. The early workers largely propounded the concept that desert landforms were the result of wind erosion or sandblasting, and even today many authors vastly overrate the efficiency of this process. The winds are efficient in removal of weathered debris, in the transport of surface sands, and in the production of rock polish in certain areas, but with respect to the erosion of resistant bedrock, claims of wind action betray an ignorance of the nature of desert processes and of former hydrologic regimes. Any objective investigator will readily recognize the solution pockets, channels, deep weathering, and attendant phenomena in bedrock of such widely separated regions as the Ennedi of Chad, northwestern Arabia, Ayers Rock in central Australia, and the inselbergs of the Namib in South West Africa as effects of fluvial processes. The question of the precise proportion of work that may be attributed to the effects of water and wind in a given area is difficult to answer, but the vast majority of reports that attribute deep parallel grooves in bedrock or the reduction of resistant surfaces to the work of ancient winds are not based upon facts.

Recommendations for future work can easily be stated in this area of interest. An effective approach to the several problems raised above would involve the use of aerial photographs of the world's deserts to assess accurately the total areas covered by active and fixed sand bodies, and by the several types of dunes. Secondly, both areal and vertical samples of the sands for mineralogical studies are required if source areas and former transport directions are desired. Such studies have, to date, been confined to the uppermost layers of sand alone. The matter of rates of sand production will later be considered in connection with desert weathering in general, but a great need for all related studies is additional data on precipitation and wind frequency distributions. It would be extremely valuable to gather comparable data in areas occupied by each of the several types of sand bodies and along lines of stations that extend from fixed to active sand bodies. The efforts here should be directed toward determining the quantitative relationships between the important climatic factors and the existence and migration of desert sands.

Finally, it is rather surprising to note that sand dunes, as landforms, have been largely ignored from the viewpoint of quantitative description. Empirical relationships have been found among such factors as dune height, angle of slipface, rate of migration, and sand-size distribution, but the dune, as a landform, is invariably discussed in qualitative terms. It would be useful to combine studies of aerial photographs with field work in an attempt to fit lemniscate curves to "tear-drop" dunes, sine functions to "sigmoidal" dunes, parabolic curves to barchans, and, perhaps, tetrahedra to sand mountains or pyramidal dunes. Efforts of this sort might readily be made, and in addition to providing an objective classification of dune forms, such work would serve as a necessary preliminary to elucidation of dune geometry and the relationship of geometrical factors to climatic factors. Arguments concerning dune genesis and the presumed transition between dune types might then be more soundly based than is true at present. Moreover, for the preparation of desert terrain analogs the quantitative description of sand dunes would appear to be essential.

3. Desert Soils and Weathering

Desert soils and weathering are topics that are treated by H. E. Dregne in another chapter of this compendium. The relatively few papers on these subjects that were cited in this report were included either in the interests of completeness of coverage for a given country or because much pertinent information on general physical features was contained. It is impossible to divorce these topics wholly from any treatment of geomorphology, however, and for this reason a few general remarks on outstanding problems will be presented here.

In the previous section on desert sands it was indicated that one aspect of the general problem of the origin of desert sands was the rate of sand production from source areas. This, however, is merely one part of the more general question of rock weathering, in the desert areas or elsewhere, and of the rates of weathering. The earlier literature is replete with claims that mechanical weathering predominates over chemical weathering in desert areas, but in recent years it has become generally recognized that both types are clearly involved and, in fact, that it is undesirable to draw such a distinction. Chemical weathering is operative in all deserts and no instance of weathering solely by mechanical action has ever

been demonstrated. With respect to the status of knowledge of how rocks of different lithology weather and at what rate, it is fair to say that despite many efforts little is truly known.

In a general way we tend to assess rates of weathering in terms of a rule of thumb, namely that the relative solubilities of the common rock-forming minerals are inverse to Bowen's reaction series, which provides their sequence of crystallization from melts at high temperature and pressure. Other things being equal then, basic rocks can be expected to weather at more rapid rates than acidic rocks. Olivine basalts, gabbros, and the like will surely be reduced more rapidly than granitic rocks, and limestones and dolomites will disappear while quartzites remain. But if we ask the precise rate of removal of a unit volume of a given rock type, of given grain size, under specified conditions of temperature, precipitation, and partial pressures of atmospheric constituents, the answer is unknown. Moreover, no quantitative scale of rock weathering is available.

The geochemical approaches to this problem thus far have been based upon the following argument. Any rock is composed of a finite number of phases, and because study of multiphase systems is rendered exceedingly difficult by reason of the vast number of reactions that may take place, it is more profitable to conduct laboratory studies of single-phase systems. It is assumed that once the single-phase relationships are known, the problem of rock weathering will be solved. This argument has led to some fundamental insights to several systems, notably carbonate-water and silica-water, but it is argued here that no quantitative scale of rock weathering will ever emerge from this work.

Lest it be suspected by the reader of this report that there is no practical need for such a scale save to aid in the resolution of academic arguments on the geomorphic history of a given region, the example of sediment-yield problems might be raised at this point. The most sophisticated approach to the problem of prediction of sediment yield of a given basin to date has involved multiple regression analysis of all the suspected variables of importance. These variables include climatic, terrain, soil, and vegetation factors, of course, but they also must include rock types. If one examines such treatments carefully, it will be found that either the rock types were ignored or some arbitrary numerical assignation, such as 1 for sandstones and 2 for shales, was involved.

With respect to recommendations for solution, only two paths are open. The first involves repetitive field surveys over many years to determine actual rates of reduction of a specific rock type under specific climatic conditions. In most instances, the rates obtained will be erosion rates rather than weathering rates, however. The second approach involves laboratory study of rock-water systems rather than single-phase systems. A suite of rocks, chosen to represent the entire range of extrusive and intrusive igneous rocks and the common metamorphic and sedimentary rocks, could be cut with precision to provide cubes of equal size, placed in closed acid systems, and the solutions periodically sampled to obtain curves of ionic concentrations or activity with time. At the conclusion of such an experiment, the time duration of which would be a function of initial pH of solution among other factors, the volume or weight reduction of the various rocks would, of itself, provide greater insight to the relative rate of decay of a given lithology than is presently available.

Under the general heading of weathering, many topics other than rates of rock weathering might be considered. Insolation effects, desert varnish, and allied matters are also important, but in the opinion of the writer, rates of rock weathering pose the most fundamental problem. With respect to soils, one or two basic questions intimately connected with geomorphology are presented below. Duplication of effort is not envisaged.

Nearly any geographic atlas contains a map that depicts the "great soil groups" of the world, and it is apparent that those areas that are classified as arid, on the basis of modern climatic values, contain several species of desert soils. This fact may seem unsurprising, but it is not naive to ask why this should be true. This question again involves the matter of rates and the relationship of climatic factors to observable physical features.

The soils scientists inform us that soils are a function of climate, source material, time, drainage and other factors, and that certain soil properties and profiles are diagnostic for classification purposes. The relative importance of the several factors involved in soil formation is arguable, and no quantitative statement can, in fact, be made at present. With respect to rates of soil formation, the data are too few to generalize. For certain areas of the Earth's surface which were glaciated in the past, we know that the soils present must have formed during the past 8,000 to 10,000 years. On the other hand, soils are known to have formed within time periods on the order of hundreds of years on the rubble of man-made structures, recent and datable volcanic terrain, tombstones, and elsewhere. No reputable soil scientist would be willing to provide an average rate of soil formation in terms of inches per hundred years, however, save in some specific case where absolute dates were available. The point to be made here is that if the climates of the desert regions have undergone fluctuation in the past, and if the desert soils appear to be correlative in most instances with the present arid climates, then either the rate of adjustment of soils to climatic conditions is more rapid than might be supposed or the cumulative effects of climatic change on soils in these regions have been negligible.

Much more work needs to be done before these questions can be answered. Specifically, we need more data on rates of soil formation and on the precise relationship of soils to climatic factors and to parent lithology. With respect to the latter, far too many reports discuss soils on "granitic rocks" in some desert area when the rocks in question may exhibit a great range of mineral and chemical composition as well as different textures and structures. Differences in rates of weathering and soil formation may be anticipated in such instances despite the fact that the rocks may generally be termed "granitic." It would be quite useful to undertake a study of soils on identical rock types across the semiarid-arid boundaries and into the desert interiors — provided that it could be ascertained that the rocks were truly identical. Similarly, a search for specific soil differences on different lithologies under identical climatic conditions would be valuable.

The rather deplorable status of knowledge of soils and weathering in arid regions is perhaps most evident in the abundant literature on silcretes, calcretes, ferricretes and similar deposits which are widespread in many of the desert regions or which occur as cappings on topographic highs. Where these occur in presently semiarid regions it is common to hear the opinion that they represent a more arid former period. In the presently arid regions, however, the same deposits evoke the opinion that more humid conditions were necessary for their formation. Presumably one can conclude only that long time periods are involved and that some unknown climatic conditions prevailed. This problem again illustrates the point that we must know the precise relationships between a given soil type and temperature, precipitation, and lithology if genetic questions are ever to be resolved.

4. Desert Landforms

The locations of the deserts of the world today are in response to several well-known meteorological factors, but for purposes of this report it is important to note that these locations generally accord with the locations of ancient plains and platforms. In fact, it might be said that plains, flats, and depressions, that may partly be covered by sands, are the predominant landforms of the world's deserts. This is clearly true of the Kalahari, Sahara, Arabian, and Australian deserts and, although less obvious, it is also true of the Somali-Chalbi, Namib, Thar, Atacama, and Monte-Patagonian deserts. The deserts of North America are relatively unique because basin-and-range structure prevails. Yet even in this arid region and in those parts of the Iranian Desert that exhibit similar structure, measurements will show that the areas occupied by basins easily exceed those occupied by ranges.

Accordingly, plains and flats represent the first of the important desert landforms. Aside from desert sands, which were previously mentioned, and desert channels, which will be treated separately, the remaining landforms are the massifs and mountain ranges proper, associated features such as pediments and alluvial fans, and the widespread inselbergs, jebels, mesas, and other topographic highs of small areal dimensions.

Before an evaluation of the available literature on desert landforms is essayed, a few general remarks are in order. First, it should be noted that one commonly encounters statements concerning the distinctiveness of desert landforms. This is largely by reason of contrast with the rounded, soil covered, rolling hills of humid regions, and some authors have gone so far as to discuss "morphogenetic regions." This term is intended to convey the notion that broad distinctions of morphology relate to geneses under different climatic conditions. It seems probable to this writer that the concept is substantially in error, despite the fact that marked angularity of form is indeed characteristic of desert regions. Much work in the United States has indicated that a strong relationship exists between slope and particle size, and the recent arguments of Melton (1965, see Pert. Pubs. Sec. XIV) against Bryan's (1925*b,* see Pert. Pubs. Sec. XIV) theory of the "boulder-controlled slope" provide the sole exception. Moreover, the efforts of Williams and Hall (1965, see Pert. Pubs. Sec. IV) in Libya, Ruxton and Berry (1961*a,* see Pert. Pubs. Sec. IV) in the Sudan, Dumanowski (1960, see Pert. Pubs. Sec. IV) in Egypt, several Australian workers, and others, all indicate that the interdependence of slope and particle size is basically related to lithologic differences. The slope-frequency distribution of the Columbia River basalts would not be found to differ significantly from that of the Black Haruj of the Sahara, for example. It is instructive to note the astonishment expressed in a report on slope-frequency distribution in the Fort Knox, Kentucky, area with respect to the finding that the slope distribution was much the same as that at Yuma, Arizona. It was stated in this report that the results seemed to contradict much of the classical literature. Much of the classical

literature is, in fact, in error for the excellent reason that few of the theories propounded were based upon quantitative measurements or accurate maps. The concept of morphogenetic regions, like the early emphasis on wind erosion of bedrock, is of this stripe.

This leads to a second point which, although mentioned previously, cannot be emphasized too strongly. The basic goal of all investigations of desert landforms is the origin of the features observed. The sole exception to this generalization is, perhaps, in the area of terrain analogs, and even these methods have been undertaken for academic purposes by some. Those investigators who have examined desert landforms in terms of block diagrams and presumed cycles of erosion will generally fail to recognize that great deficiencies exist; the origins of desert landforms, like those of other climatic regions, are thought to be well understood from this conceptual viewpoint. The chief failing involved is substitution of classical deductive arguments for measurements of landforms, processes, and rates of processes, and a lack of understanding that modern discussions of entropy, stochastic development of drainage, and the like are indeed related to the question of landforms and their evolution. It can be said that the central problem of arid-lands geomorphology is the extent to which any given landform is a reflection of equilibrium with modern processes, on the one hand, or equilibrium with former processes, on the other. Unless desert landforms are considered within the framework of this problem, an understanding of genesis becomes impossible.

As a final preliminary point, the tendency to extrapolate knowledge gained in the desert areas of the western United States should be mentioned. Several individuals of repute abroad have accused Americans of parochialism in this regard, and the accusation is not entirely without substance. As noted in treating the availability of information on the United States, far more work has been done on the geomorphology of this region than elsewhere. This is largely a consequence of its small size, the relative ease of access, and the adequacy of financing for numerous investigations of diverse types. But it must be borne in mind that the arid region of the United States is quite small relative to the areas of most of the deserts of the world, that it is an area that contains abundant mountain ranges, that the effects of Pleistocene climatic events in the region were relatively profound, and that it contains few areas of desert sands or duricrusts. Considered in the broad sense, it is not typical of the deserts of the world.

The occurrence of basin - and - range types of structure precludes the existence of the plains of considerable dimensions that are in evidence elsewhere, and, beyond this, it provides most of the desert basins with annual sources of runoff because the mountain catchments are not truly arid areas. Orographic effects tend to insure a greater frequency of fluvial processes; hence, rates of erosion and sedimentation and, indeed, of landform formation may be greater than in central Australia or Arabia, for example. This also is of importance with respect to the inferences that can be drawn from certain features in desert channels which will be discussed later. The landforms proper do not differ in kind, however, but only in relative abundance, and it can be argued that if rates of formation are in fact greater then the desert areas of the United States are most worthy of intensive study. This review of the basic problems and deficiencies on desert landforms will begin with a consideration of desert plains, flats, and pans.

Plains

As a specific landform, the desert plain has received relatively little study, and the available literature is far from proportionate to the areal abundance of this feature. There are several reasons for this lack of study. First, of course, the plains are perhaps the least spectacular of the desert landforms. Scarcely a report on the central Sahara, for example, will fail to include some illustration of the Ahaggar, Aïr, Tibesti, or other massifs, depending upon the location treated, but the vast gravel- or sand-covered tracts tend to be monotonous and uninspiring, and, hence, are often excluded. Aside from the personal inclinations of many investigators to devote their attention to topographic highs, it should be noted that it is in many ways far simpler to describe and discuss massifs or mountain slopes than nearly-horizontal plains. Several specific problems of description should be apparent.

If one of the characteristics of these plains is flatness, then obviously a proper description requires slope data; how flat is "nearly billiard-table smoothness," for example? It is one matter to measure slope profiles on a given topographic high but quite another to run many lines of profiles across hundreds of miles of relatively featureless plains. For these reasons, we do not actually have accurate slope data on many of the desert plains of the world. One should qualify such a statement, however, by pointing out that the eye will seldom be deceived by more than perhaps 2 degrees of slope in such cases. That is, if the plain in question appears to be perfectly horizontal, then it is unlikely that the true slope is greater than this amount.

Another characteristic of desert plains that requires adequate description is the nature and size-distribution of the material that occurs at its surface.

Despite some specific studies of desert plains, such as those of Dresch (1961, see Pert. Pubs. Sec. IV) in Mauritania or of Monod (1958, 1961, see Pert. Pubs. Sec. IV) on the Majâbat Al Koubrâ in the empty quarter of Mali, it is fair to say that sampling problems have precluded the possibility of gathering statistically unbiased samples across any given large plain as a whole. By and large, the available literature only provides us with information on surface materials from spot samples. With respect to how these surface materials compare with material at depth, the available information is even more inadequate.

Moreover, there is the question of the actual depth of cover on many of the desert plains of the world, and this, in turn, is linked with the overall problem of the genesis of plains. If the slopes of these surfaces are, in fact, nearly horizontal, then it is difficult to imagine that fluvial processes have created the plains because of the flow distances involved. Clearly, the sedimentary cover has been transported by water, despite the fact that it is subjected to wind transport today. Former flow regimes involving greater discharges can be invoked for this purpose. But when one speaks of the genesis of the plains, it is not only the sedimentary cover or alluvial fill that is involved; the important surface is that of the bedrock beneath. In the absence of borehole information it is unjustified to assume that this underlying surface is of equal horizontality to that of the alluvial cover. If topographic differences do exist, and the alluvial cover has simply filled in the hollows and produced a smoothing effect, then the origin of the plains may well be sought in differential solution and weathering over long time periods. An origin by this means would obviate the inherent difficulties of planation via either the erosion-cycle concept or the cliff-retreat scheme of King. One must engage in a rather desperate search for possible catchment areas to accommodate either hypothesis. Moreover, with the passage of time these theories require the rather contradictory phenomena of increasing lengths of flow while the catchment areas diminish.

The essential point to the above discussion, however, is that all theories of the genesis of desert plains are inadequately based on facts. The characteristics of these landforms as a group are not well known, the depth to bedrock and the nature of this surface is similarly unknown, and no computations of the stream discharges and catchment areas that would be required to support the classical arguments have ever been made. One can only conclude that the desert plains of the world tend to occupy regions of marked stability and that the mechanisms involved in their formation are far from clear.

Topographic Lows

Topographic lows are ubiquitous in the deserts of the world and are quite diverse in character save, perhaps, for topography. Within this category are landforms that have been designated as playas, pans, flats, sinks, sebkhas, deflation basins, and depressions, among other terms. The various names that have been applied only partly reflect differences in local or regional usage. They are intended to reflect the fact that these landforms as a group may have several distinctly different origins. It is therefore curious that certain investigators who are scrupulous in their usage of terminology have produced confusion in the literature. An example of this is the statement of an American investigator who casually equated pans in Africa with the playas of the western United States. One might say that this was akin to equating apples and bananas; the only correct statement that can be made is that both are fruit.

The playas of the western United States are relatively well known, both with respect to surficial features and depositional history. They are essentially dry lakes which have expanded and contracted several times during Pleistocene and, in some instances, Recent time. The numbers of expansions and contractions are roughly correlative with the numbers of glacial and interglacial stages in much of the Great Basin area, but southward, toward the fringe of the position of the Pleistocene storm track and beyond, the evidence for numbers of marked changes in lake level diminishes. Although a rough chronologic correspondence of rise and fall of lake levels has been demonstrated for several playas, this is not necessarily true for all playas. Each of the many closed or semiclosed basins is a separate hydrologic entity, and the rise or fall of lake level in a given basin is a function of the local precipitation-runoff-evaporation balance. This balance varies today because of differences in altitude and relief of the basins, size of catchments, geographic location with respect to storm tracks, soil and vegetation characteristics, permeability of basin sediments and nature of subsurface conditions, and other factors. This variance was not entirely absent in the past, even under the smoothing impress of Pleistocene climatic events.

In any event, the playas of the arid region of the western United States are a product of basin-and-range type topography and the relatively profound climatic changes over much of the area. The high stages of lake level of many of these playas was on the order of several hundreds of feet, and many cores of playa deposits and geophysical surveys demonstrate equivalent thicknesses of a sequence of evaporites, alluvium, muds, and brines. Similar features do, of course, occur elsewhere, particularly in desert areas of South America and in the Iranian Desert, but by and large the American playas differ drastically from the pans of the Kalahari or Australia and the saline or nonsaline marine flats of the coastal Sahara, the Arabian Peninsula, the Namib Desert, and elsewhere. This difference again illustrates the dangers of careless extrapolation of knowledge of the arid region of the United States to other parts of the world.

The features termed "desert pans" in such areas as the Kalahari are flat-floored, shallow depressions that commonly do not contain thick evaporite deposits. The depths to underlying calcretes, silcretes, or bedrock is, in fact, usually only a few tens of feet, and the surrounding terrain commonly consists of desert plains of low relief. The fill in some of these pans may consist largely of silt and clay with relatively little saline material of evaporitic origin; in effect, several different types of pans exist if their contents are considered. The distinctions between pans and playas are therefore great, and with respect to adequacy of knowledge it is the former landforms that require much more study. A few basic problems will be outlined below, and the suggestions that are offered are pertinent to topographic lows of the world's deserts generally.

The basic question, again, is the origin of these depressions. In some instances they may be structural, but it is clear that this cannot be true of most. It is highly suggestive that the distribution of desert pans, as seen on aerial photo mosaics, appears to accord well with ancient drainage paths. Such drainage is often sand-choked today and the frequency of inundation depends largely upon local precipitation and subsequent ponding, but this need not always have been true. Because of the general lack of runoff, and because the winds that blow across the surrounding plains commonly can remove the fine material from the surfaces of the pans, some authors insist upon invoking pan genesis by wind action. Perhaps the winds can prevent the pans from filling with sediment today, or they may even lower the surface of the silt-clay deposits, but wind action certainly could not have carved circular or semicircular depressions in so resistant a material as silcrete. Moreover, the areal distribution of the pans would remain unexplained.

Of the various hypotheses that have been set forth, none seem wholly satisfactory. This writer suspects that the pans originated in most cases from solution effects along the drainage paths of former, intermittent streams, where ponding was produced by windblown sand or by local relief of the subdued topography. The fact that not all pans of a given region are necessarily of the same age would not conflict with such an interpretation, nor would the lack of evaporites, which would be explicable if intermittent through-flow occurred along drainage paths. In order to investigate any such contention, however, certain information that is not currently available must be obtained.

First, it seems obvious that the distribution of pans in a given desert such as the Kalahari should be determined by careful mapping on aerial photographs. Whether the locations of all pans in a given area actually do accord with former drainage systems cannot be stated with certainty. Secondly, a quantitative description of pan morphology on a regional basis would be of value. What are the dimensions of the pans; to what extent do they depart from circular or elliptical configurations; what is their surface gradient; what is the size-distribution of surface materials; what is the magnitude, frequency, and bearing of surface winds; what is the present frequency of inundation or ponding? The available literature on pans indicates in a general way that several varieties can be distinguished on the basis of gross characteristics but no work that has yet been done permits statistical comparison of pan morphology and materials, or permits a search for quantitative relationships among processes and consequences. In this sense, the above questions have not been answered.

Finally, one might add that the present hydrologic balance in topographic lows in general is also not well known, again with the notable exception of certain playas and important water bodies such as the Dead Sea. The present hydrologic balance must be determined if any sound inference on possible former balances is to be made. Similarly, estimates of the possible former discharges of now inactive drainage systems, the relative solubilities of the host materials of the pans, the volumes of water that can be contained in these depressions, and the rates of modern processes in pan areas in general are all factors related to any satisfactory theory of the origin of pans, flats, sinks, and other topographic lows. Like desert plains, it appears to this writer that far more work of a fruitful nature can profitably be undertaken on these desert landforms.

Topographic Highs

The topographic highs of the desert regions of the world include various major features, such as massifs, mountain ranges, plateaus, and the like, and the smaller, but relatively widespread, jebels, inselbergs, pinnacles, and similar features that have been assigned a variety of names in different regions. As previously indicated, the central problem associated with all such desert landforms is their origin, in terms of the extent to which they are in equilibrium with modern processes and the extent to which they are relict.

The answer to such a question requires knowledge of topography, geology, present and former climatic and hydrologic conditions, and, most important, the rates of present processes such as weathering and slope retreat. Previous sections of this report evaluation have indicated deficiencies of knowledge on most of these matters, and mapping will be discussed separately in a subsequent section. One might comment here, in a general way, that although quantitative relationships between form and processes or between slope and rock types have been sought and obtained in several excellent individual reports, most of the topographic highs of the world's deserts are known only in a qualitative way.

Again, the question arises of whether it is fair to extrapolate from the relatively well-studied examples in the arid regions of the United States. To give but one illustration of the dangers involved, inselbergs may be considered. Although this landform is intimately related to pediments, which are treated elsewhere, it should be mentioned here that many topographic surveys in the western United States have indicated that the slopes surrounding inselbergs range from about 2° to 7°. In the absence of tectonic complications these slopes are usually concave upward. Hence, it is not generally known by American workers that elsewhere in the arid regions the slopes surrounding similar features may be perfectly horizontal. Moreover, R. F. Peel (oral communication) has detailed topographic data from the Tibesti area in the Sahara which prove the existence of a depression that entirely surrounds several pinnacle-like landforms.

Such depressions occur in bedrock, beneath a thin alluvial mantle, and exhibit relief on the order of 25 feet. The origin of such features is open to several questions, and these cannot be resolved in the arid region of the United States because comparable landforms do not exist. We do not know the significance of such circular depressions or whether they are related to present or past climatic conditions. It can only be assumed that solution effects and, perhaps, subsurface weathering are involved. In fact, we do not even know the relative abundances of the several varieties of inselbergs in the deserts of the world, or the possible relationships of a given landform variant to rock type and climatic conditions.

In the opinion of this writer, it is impossible to discuss any theory of inselberg development given the present status of knowledge. The importance of precise petrologic data was previously mentioned in connection with weathering and soils, but it is of equal importance here. In South West Africa, for example, four isolated inselbergs occur in the central Namib desert within an area of perhaps 5 square miles. All may casually be designated as granitic, all are of equal height, approximately 100 feet, and it cannot be argued that in one of the most arid regions on Earth different climatic regimes formerly prevailed within the compass of 5 square miles. Nonetheless, each of these inselbergs is decidedly distinctive. One consists entirely of large blocks of rock that are several to perhaps ten feet in diameter. A second is similar in appearance, but upon inspection the blocks may be seen to surround an unbroken bedrock core. The third is relatively smooth and exhibits only scattered patches of coarse sand and fine gravel upon its surface. The last resembles nothing so closely as a glaciated bedrock knob; not a trace of weathered debris can be found. Moreover, this last inselberg contains an extraordinary dendritic network of drainage channels, with smooth, semicircular cross sections, that are incised into bedrock to a depth of 2 to 3 feet and contain small plunge pools along their course. And this, in a region where the mean annual precipitation is presently less than 2 inches. The essential point to this example, however, is that the features described may more readily be attributed to petrologic differences among four different "granitic" rocks than to any other single factor; petrologic data are no less important than are climatic data in problems of this sort, yet they are sorely lacking.

A final point on inselbergs, pinnacles, and the like, concerns their location. This raises a question that is entirely apart from the distribution of particular varieties of such landforms. Where these isolated topographic highs occur in close proximity to some prominent massif or mountain range, the genetic history of the features is not difficult to envision. Separation in such cases can simply be attributed to erosion and subsequent isolation from the parent body. Those isolated landforms that are currently hundreds of miles from the nearest potential parent body, however, are difficult to explain and have led to concepts such as the continent-wide retreat of cliffs or, alternatively, to the opinion that a mountain range formerly occupied the site. The retreat of cliffs over such distances is not plausible on hydrologic grounds, as previously indicated, and the assumed existence of former ranges is in many instances unwarranted. Accordingly, this problem remains open.

In summary, one can only conclude that many problems of genesis remain unresolved and that any soundly-based approach to solution will require the gathering of much additional quantitative data. Projects most worthy of consideration with respect to any of the topographic highs of the arid regions are of two types. First are those directed toward the resolution of local problems by detailed methods, specifically by detailed mapping of surface form and measurement of hydrologic, petrologic, and other variables. Second are regional or desert-wide surveys directed toward quantifying the areal distribution and morphology of topographic highs, segregating specific landform variants by frequency-distribution or similar schemes, and seeking relationships between the morphometric data and any available hydrologic or geologic information. Lack of suitable topographic maps has hindered or reduced the value of the results of several such efforts, but much useful information can be compiled from available aerial photographs of most desert regions.

Alluvial Fans and Pediments

Alluvial fans and pediments have been the most studied of all desert landforms, and a wealth of descriptive papers on these features exists in the literature. This is particularly true for the arid region of the western United States because either or both landforms are present in every desert basin. The areal abundance of fans and pediments would appear to be greatest in regions of basin-and-range structure, of course, and therefore they are most obvious in desert areas such as the Atacama of Peru and Chile, the desert basins of Iran and West Pakistan, and in Mexico and the United States. It should not be thought that they are of negligible areal extent in other world deserts, however, because many, if not all, of the vast desert plains are actually derived from alluvial fans and pediments. One would include here most of the desert-plain area of the Arabian Desert, nearly all of the Namib, and large portions of the Sahara, Thar, and Australian deserts, for example.

There is some confusion in the literature with respect to the meaning of the word "pediment," and it would be best to state here the usage of terms intended by this writer. In the broadest sense possible, an alluvial fan is a sedimentary deposit that is derived and transported from any bedrock source area. The deposit is commonly fan-shaped, but may or may not be consolidated or dissected. In contrast, the term "pediment" in this report connotes any bedrock surface that is relatively flat. The surface may or may not be dissected or covered with a gravel veneer. This usage is accepted by nearly all authors, but in parts of the United States, particularly Arizona, an entirely different distinction has been drawn and this has led to confusion. Some investigators in this area have described unconsolidated sedimentary deposits at the base of topographic highs as pediments simply because the dip of the surface of the deposits differs from the apparent dip of the bedding. Such a feature would be thought of as a fan that has subsequently been modified by surface erosion by most workers. Definitions are arbitrary, but if the term "pediment" is not restricted to bedrock surfaces then the legion of reports on the "pediment problem" lose all significance.

We have learned a great deal about alluvial fans, particularly in recent years, and the available literature indicates that empirical relationships between area of a given fan and the area of its associated drainage basin, slope of a fan and mean particle size, and, as a corollary, slope of a fan and the lithology of the source rocks, are well founded. Moreover, quantitative work has shown that the surfaces of some fans can be described in terms of polynomial equations (Troeh, 1965, see Pert. Pubs. Sec. I). Nearly all of the quantitative data obtained on alluvial fans stem from investigations generally aimed toward gaining a better understanding of the origin of these landforms. The fact that disagreement on this point still exists indicates, first, the importance of the differing conceptual frameworks of thought of various authors, which tend to produce conflicting conclusions from observations of identical evidence, and second, that certain information is still unavailable.

This is well illustrated by work on alluvial fans in the western United States, where Bull (1964, see Pert. Pubs. Sec. I) found evidence that caused him to emphasize the importance of tectonic factors in fan formation, Lustig (1965a, see Pert. Pubs. Sec. I) claimed that the Pleistocene-Recent climatic changes had produced corresponding changes in sediment-transport characteristics and that alternations of processes were involved, Denny (1965, see Pert. Pubs. Sec. I) stressed dynamic equilibrium between form and processes and offered the deduction that the amount of sediment received by a given fan is equal to that removed by erosion, and Hooke (1965, see Pert. Pubs. Sec. I) concurred with Denny by assuming that steady-state conditions do in fact prevail today in order to investigate rates of tilting and other matters.

Reference to these reports was made in the section of this paper entitled "Backgrounds of Modern Geomorphic Concepts." Mention of two recent events may serve to supplement that discussion. First, the paper by Denny (1965, see Pert. Pubs. Sec. I) received the Kirk Bryan Award for the best geomorphic investigation of the year in the United States. This would appear to insure that his conclusions have been approved as valid by the majority of his peers. The second event, however, was the publication of two of the most comprehensive reports on the geology, geomorphology, and hydrology of the Death Valley area ever to appear (Hunt and Mabey, 1966, see Pert. Pubs. Sec. XIV; Hunt *et al.*, 1966, see Pert.

Pubs. Sec. XIV). With respect to precisely the same features discussed by Denny, the first of these papers concludes (p. A97):

The history of erosion and sedimentation in Death Valley evidently is one of changing rates, presumably due to changing processes. Huntington (1907) offered the hypothesis that in arid regions the pluvial periods accelerate weathering and growth of vegetation. During such periods, waste is stored in the mountains. According to him, the transition to an ensuing arid period is the time when most of the waste is transported to the alluvial fans; when the supply of waste becomes exhausted, there is little new material brought from the mountains and the older fill deposits become dissected. The evidence in Death Valley fits well with Huntington's hypothesis.

This quotation is not included as an attempt to belabor much of the excellent work of Denny but simply to indicate that the basic problem of fan formation is not yet resolved. With respect to deficiencies of information, which are partly the cause of this disagreement, it seems apparent that the greatest need is for data on rates of sedimentation and erosion on alluvial fans and rates of bedrock weathering. The critical point of the steady-state argument is the unproven assumption that the rate at which debris is supplied to a fan is equal to the rate at which it is removed by local erosion. If this assumption is true then the fans are indeed in equilibrium with modern processes. If it is not true, then the fans are tending toward equilibrium but nevertheless reflect some former form-process balance, or relict conditions, today.

As previously indicated in this evaluation, the rates of sedimentation and erosion may well be greater in portions of the arid regions of the United States than in some other desert regions. Also, the climatic fluctuations of the past have perhaps left a more visible record in the American Great Basin area. With respect to alluvial fans as desert landforms, however, one *can* safely extrapolate the information gained in this country to other world deserts. This is not always evident in the world literature. A description of landforms on the Indus River Basin, for example, discusses alluvial fans in terms of the old cliche, "deposition occurs at the base of mountains due to a sharp break in slope." Any author who makes such a statement must be unaware of the fact that stream-channel profiles emerge from mountains and cross fan surfaces as smooth exponential curves; the "sharp break in slope" exists at the contact of the fan deposit and the steep mountain front. The stream channel, however, has its origin far within the mountains and does not follow the gradient of the steep slope. Moreover, the distance of flow is governed largely by water-sediment relationships. The vast alluvial fans that exist between the Tuwaiq escarpment and the Persian Gulf in the Arabian Desert, for example, can hardly be said to owe their origin to the change of slope at the mountain front. There is no hydraulic anomaly involved here and this point is of equal relevance in the "pediment problem."

The so-called "pediment problem" does not really differ significantly from any other landform-problem. The central question, again, is one of genesis. The known facts are essentially these: Bedrock surfaces exist around the bases of some mountains in the arid regions or occur as extensive plains elsewhere. There is still dispute over whether good correlation exists between lithology and the slopes of such surfaces but, as mentioned in connection with inselbergs, in mountain regions slopes ranging from 2° to 7° are common whereas in plains areas the slopes may be negligible. The last fact concerning pediments is that, like alluvial fans, there is a marked break in slope along the line of contact between the pediment surface and that of any mountain front that it abuts.

It is rather surprising, given these few facts on pediment configuration, that a vast array of hypotheses have been set forth in the literature, each of which is based upon assumed processes or mechanics of processes that have never been verified. First, it should be made clear that hydraulic anomalies do not exist in the realm of natural phenomena. Those who belabor the matter of the break in slope between pediment and mountain front again must be cited for lack of awareness that the major avenues of runoff emerge from within the mountain mass onto the pediment surface, and that the longitudinal profiles of these channels are essentially smooth exponential curves. Those who speak of changes in flow regime at the break in slope are discussing an unobserved process which may, in fact, be of negligible importance to the problem.

The hypothesis of lateral planation involves a truly absurd physical assumption and yet, even today, one finds authors who believe that it has much merit. In this instance the streams emerging from the mountain mass would, upon occasion, be required to change course by 90°, defy the effects of gravity on a sloping pediment surface, and trim back the resistant bedrock of the mountain front proper. This behavior has certainly never been observed in nature, and one can only remark in opposition that studies of the frequency-distribution of the paths of flow of all streams emerging from mountains demonstrate that the required stream paths seldom, if ever, occur.

Additionally, there are many reports which emphasize sheetflooding on pediment surfaces, despite the fact that no measurements of the hydraulic variables or of the erosive effect on bedrock of such flows have even been obtained. The hypothesis rests essentially upon two classical papers by McGee and Davis and it is from these that many subsequent reports of "walls of water" stem. The fact is that if one examines the classical literature and the "eyewitness accounts" of sheetfloods that are presented, an objective conclusion would be that no extensive sheet of water of a depth of several feet has ever been seen to flow down a pediment surface. Most pediments contain channels, either in the bedrock proper or in the gravel veneer, and when flow occurs it is within such channels. The several accounts of wagons and vehicles that were overtaken by vast sheets of water are true enough but the locations of these disasters are invariably along some trail that parallels the base of the pediment surface. In other words, the "sheets" of water tend to occur in low flats, far from the mountain front, which receive the channelized flow from the pediment surface.

Moreover, as pointed out by Paige as long ago as 1912 and more recently by Peel (1960, see Pert. Pubs. Sec. I) in a fine review, those who advocate sheetfloods as a dominant mechanism in pediment formation confuse cause and effect. If perfectly smooth, ungullied, bedrock surfaces existed in nature, then given the proper precipitation distribution and intensity the runoff might well be in the form of sheetflow. This can only occur, however, after the development of a suitable surface and it certainly does not follow that such hypothetical flows produced the surface in question.

The hypothesis of Mabbutt (1966, see Pert. Pubs. Sec. X), which primarily involved long periods of weathering beneath a mantle of debris, is far more realistic and, in fact, most of the good examples of pediments in the western United States accord with the Australian evidence because they are exhumed features. One must not lose sight of the fact, however, that through time the simple development of drainage systems serves to reduce the mass of any given massif or mountain range. Because a mountain mass cannot be eroded by fluvial processes to depths below the immediate local base level, the production of some bedrock surface must invariably accompany the reduction of mass by erosion; this surface is the pediment. There is really only one question involved in any such instance despite all that has been written on the subject. Is the reduction in mass primarily the consequence of slope retreat by back-weathering or is the development and enlargement of drainage systems of greater importance?

Based upon the available information on the relative rates of these two processes, namely slope retreat and drainage development, it seems clear to this writer that the latter is the principal factor involved. The runoff which occurs on the steeply sloping mountain front is of extremely brief duration and although it can remove some weathered debris, weathering is actually the principal process involved. Much more efficient work is accomplished within the drainage basin proper. It is at the loci of drainage basins that the major reductions of mountain mass occur, and this writer would agree with L. B. Leopold (written communication) that the interfluvial areas, where the steeply sloping mountain front exists, are essentially left behind as residuals during pediment formation. Such residuals will eventually become isolated, at which time they will be termed "inselbergs." Slope retreat by back-weathering can only predominate as a process along mountain fronts that are capped by such resistant material that drainage-basin development is effectively prevented.

In order to evaluate this hypothesis, or indeed, any other on the problem, more work needs to be done. Measurements of rates of sediment production from the mountain front, from drainage basins, and from channels on the pediment proper are clearly needed. Moreover, more field and theoretical work is needed on drainage development as such. The available information suggests that most of the emphasis thus far has been on the enlargement of drainage systems. Consideration has not been given to the ultimate reductions in drainage area and changes in drainage characteristics that must occur. It seems clear to this writer that some optimum drainage area exists for any given mountain mass or massif of finite size, which is a function of that size. To achieve this optimum drainage area, the volume of rock must diminish. Correspondingly, the associated drainage-basin areas must diminish and although Horton's laws and hydraulic theory will still pertain, some mappable, distinctive, drainage types will emerge. Regional morphometric analyses of areas that exhibit an abundance of alluvial fans on the one hand, and of bedrock pediments on the other, would be valuable if such distinctions could be proved on a quantitative basis.

5. Desert Drainage

Desert drainage is intimately involved in all aspects of the physical features of the arid regions. This fact was suggested in connection with the question of pediment formation discussed in the previous section, but all landforms owe a substantial portion of their appearance and characteristics to the fluvial processes that are operative upon them. Moreover, no other single topic shows so clearly the relevance of the central problem of the arid regions. This is, as noted elsewhere in this report, to what extent is any given physical feature in equilibrium with modern processes and to what extent is it a reflection of former processes and, hence, relict.

With respect to stream channels proper, we know a great deal about them from information gained in nonarid regions. Relationships exist among such variables as width, depth, slope, velocity, sediment load, and stream discharge. Moreover, it has been shown in many studies that the frequency of bankfull discharge and the stage of this flow are factors of prime importance in understanding channel properties. In a different vein, we also know that drainage pattern and form, in the absence of constraints, can be attributed to stochastic processes that operate through time in such a manner that stream-channel patterns reflect the least-work principle in a broad sense. In other words, all channels in nonarid regions that are not otherwise constrained by such factors as recent structural deformation can be demonstrated to be near a state of equilibrium with the total hydrologic and geologic conditions that presently prevail.

We also have available a considerable array of empirical relationships on drainage patterns that stem from the work of Horton, Strahler, and many others whose contributions were cited at the outset of this report. Accordingly, we have quantitative procedures that allow the description, classification, and comparison of drainage networks on the basis of stream order, number, drainage density, branching ratios, and so forth. Moreover, subsequent work has provided the means for relating certain of these morphometric parameters to such important variables as stream discharge and sediment yield.

Turning to the arid regions, it should be noted at the outset that one of the guidelines for this study was to indicate the available literature that would provide information on the width, depth, slope, velocity, and water and sediment discharge of desert channels and drainage systems. In effect, this has largely been accomplished by references to the pertinent studies and existent basic data on such major desert rivers as the Nile in Sudan and Egypt, the Kuiseb in South West Africa, the Helmand in Afghanistan, the Indus in West Pakistan, the Tigris-Euphrates system in the Arabian Desert, Coopers Creek in Australia, and a few others. But the problems of arid-region drainage do not actually exist when such rivers are considered. Streamflow is perennial, or nearly so, for most, and although the lengths of record or quality of data may not be uniform, nevertheless the hydraulic factors and channel characteristics exhibit predictable relationships that accord with the outline of the general status of knowledge given above and elsewhere in this report. The typical desert channel, however, and that to which the problem of present equilibrium versus relict applies, is a channel that is dry save for very exceptional events.

In this category we have the legion of Saharan wadis, the "fossil valleys" of Botswana, the intermittently sand-choked washes that cross the Arabian Desert, several notable Australian examples, and others. The ephemeral streams that emerge from mountain areas in the western United States, the Namib, Atacama, the southern rim of Arabia, and parts of the Iranian Desert should be excluded. The highlands involved in these instances do receive some annual precipitation and despite the fact that bankfull flow may not be a very frequent occurrence, these drainage systems are amenable to study. The several ORSTOM reports on small drainage systems in the Sahara, the efforts on Wadi Jiza' in southern Arabia, C.S.I.R.O. work on small catchments in central Australia, and the excellent results in the Namib, all of which have been cited in this report, clearly indicate that efforts to gather basic data on precipitation-runoff relationships, and even flow-frequency information, can be fruitful in such areas.

If we consider a hypothetical channel in a central desert region, however, which typically is of low relief and receives exceedingly infrequent precipitation, what can be predicted about the relationship of channel form to the magnitude and frequency of water discharge and sediment load? Nomads of the region may tell us that no flow has been observed in this channel for 50 years. The denudation chronologist will tell us that this is a Pleistocene relict. The channel obviously cannot be related to some value of mean annual discharge because this may be zero for many successive years. But those who insist that the width-depth relationships observed are related to some value of Pleistocene discharge may also be in error. These dimensions may well reflect some magnitude of discharge that occurs with a frequency of once per hundred or more years. The basic problem is how this can be determined, if true.

There are two means of coping with such a problem. The first is idealistic, in the sense that it requires the establishment of hydrologic recording stations on many such remote drainages around the world. This would not be pointless in the writer's opinion, for events such as the recent flow from an area of supposed interior drainage in Western Australia have occurred, and useful information could be gained. From a practical standpoint, however, no such system is likely. Even the well-studied Nile

indicates this fact, because inquiry about the runoff contributions from wadis in the Eastern Desert area will reveal that these are unknown. Nearly all our existing data on runoff and channel characteristics in the desert regions are derived from studies of perennial or intermittent streams. The few exceptions to this statement were noted above.

The second approach is to attempt to extrapolate the available information on streamflow and channel characteristics to the hypothetical channel considered here. The most notable efforts to date have been those of Dury (1964a, b; 1965, see Pert. Pubs. Sec. I) who attempted to relate stream width, meander wavelength, and other parameters to present and former stream discharges and climatic conditions. It is possible that Dury has not chosen the best parameters for the purpose because the observed maximum width, for example, is not necessarily related to a single frequency of discharge. It is also possible that rather than Pleistocene events, the results accord with the infrequent but catastrophic flows postulated here. Nevertheless, his work provides a good starting point for further efforts in this direction. The problem is of great complexity, however, and it is possible that the actual frequency of occurrence of the channel-forming discharges in arid regions will remain an indeterminate save near highland areas.

Aside from pursuit of Dury's work and the results that could surely accrue by merely gathering basic data on desert drainage and hydrologic regimen near highlands, much additional work could be done on desert drainage patterns. As indicated in the section of this evaluation treating pans, the available aerial photographs have still not been used to map the drainage of many desert areas. Efforts of this sort could aid greatly in enlarging our understanding of the precise similarities and differences of drainage in arid and nonarid regions. Moreover, relationships between streamflow and channel characteristics in the arid regions cannot be deduced in the absence of better information on those characteristics and drainage patterns.

6. Mapping

Mapping is a basic requirement for either geomorphic or hydrologic purposes. The distribution, abundance, and characteristics of a given desert landform throughout the arid regions of the world, for example, cannot be satisfactorily ascertained in the absence of adequate maps. This is rather evident, but the word "adequate" requires some explanation. Any map is merely a pictorial representation of some feature or property of nature. With respect to scale then, what is desired is a map scale that will yield the least distortion and yet remains feasible to produce in terms of time, effort, and financial requirements. For most hydrologic and geomorphic investigations, maps on a scale of approximately 1:25,000 are most desirable, and those on a scale of 1:50,000 are less so but may be termed "adequate." Regional studies may be undertaken on maps that range in scale from 1:100,000 to perhaps 1:250,000 provided that these are accurate. It seems clear from the available information cited in this report that by any reasonable standard there exists a great deficiency of large-scale topographic and geologic maps. Certain desert areas have been relatively well mapped, but it is fair to say that some very extensive desert tracts are known only from small-scale, regional maps of questionable accuracy.

No recommendation can be made in this regard which has not been made before, namely that programs for topographic and geologic mapping should be expanded. But it can be stated that aerial photographs do exist for many unmapped or poorly-mapped regions and much work can profitably be undertaken using these as a base for study. In addition to these more obvious aspects of mapping, several additional types of maps are available and these will be briefly discussed here.

First, the geomorphologic map may be mentioned as an example of special-purpose mapping. These maps generally depict the relief and landforms of a given region on a topographic base and thus render an excellent reproduction of what exists in nature. Few such maps have thus far been produced for areas within the arid zone, with the exception of small zones in Sudan, Senegal-Mauritania, the Atacama, and a few other locations. A review of the literature on geomorphological mapping reveals that no deficiencies in techniques are involved but that those engaged in such mapping are to some extent in conflict. The reason for this is that the mapping is not wholly objective. The goal is not merely to depict the landscape but also to attempt to render the age and origins of the various landforms that occur. Thus, many elaborate schemes for symbols, colors, and various combinations have been offered but the basic difficulty, as abundantly indicated in this report, is that genesis cannot be mapped. It is a subjective quantity that is a function of the beliefs of a given investigator.

Another special-purpose mapping technique is that employed by the C.S.I.R.O. in Australia in the land-systems surveys of that agency. Basically, topography, geology, geomorphology, soils, and vegetation are the major factors considered, and the areas studied are divided into subregions on the basis of classes and combinations of these major factors. As indicated in

discussion of the available information on the Australian deserts, the land-use maps that are produced may exhibit on the order of 100 different subregions which are defined on a semiquantitative basis. Such maps have much to recommend them but, again, they are not widely available. Even the Australian deserts can be said to be largely unmapped by any method.

This leads to a consideration of terrain-analog maps which have been produced by the U. S. Army Waterways Experiment Station to determine the degree of analogy between the desert area around Yuma, Arizona, and the principal arid regions of the world. These maps have been cited where appropriate in the section of this report treating the availability of information. Such citation was usually accompanied by some statement to the effect that the map in question provided the best available composite view of the given region. Although this is generally true, certain aspects of these terrain maps should be discussed here.

The several reports that serve to explain the preparation of the terrain-analog maps outline the terrain factors that were chosen and the reasons for their selection and the purposes and limitations of the folio reports. The purposes of this review do not require detailed reproduction of either methods or arguments, but the general outline of the terrain-analog scheme should be noted.

The factors considered in the preparation of the maps were of three general types, namely geometry, ground, and vegetation factors. Geometry included four subfactors, a characteristic slope, characteristic relief, characteristic plan-profile, and the occurrence of slopes greater than 50 per cent. General terrain factors such as physiography, hypsometry, and landforms proper were not directly employed. The second general type of factor included the soil type, soil consistency, and surface lithology. Accordingly, with inclusion of the vegetation factor, 13 different terrain maps were produced; 9 of these depict each of the geometry and ground subfactors, and the vegetation factor, for a given desert region. The remaining 4 maps are the terrain analogs. These include a geometry, ground, and vegetation analog, and a composite analog, the values of which are determined by superimposing the geometry, ground, and vegetation components and applying integrative procedures. This final map, the composite terrain-analog map, is then used to classify various parts of a given world desert as "highly," "moderately," "slightly," or "inappreciably" analogous to the desert area around Yuma, Arizona.

The first point that is worthy of note with respect to this scheme in the stress of the several investigators on the meaning of "analogous," in contrast to "homologous." The distinction drawn is that homology between two areas would require mapping on identical scales whereas analogy does not. They emphasize, therefore, that it is perfectly proper to designate parts of the world's deserts as analogous to Yuma despite the fact that the regional terrain maps were produced on a scale of 1:5,000,000, whereas the Yuma desert area is mapped on a scale of 1:400,000. Although the several investigators indicated awareness of the limitations imposed by the scale problem, the semantic truism involving homology versus analogy does not obviate the difficulties. There is universal awareness that maps of the same area become increasingly distorted, with respect to the land configurations depicted, as the scales of those maps decreased. Not only do slopes flatten but certain landforms that are of small areal dimensions will tend to "disappear" despite the fact that they may be relatively abundant. Whether the terrain studies are termed "analogs" or "homologs" is immaterial; the fact is that adequate comparisons between two regions can only be achieved if the maps employed are of the same scale or nearly so. In this respect one must conclude that there is a great deficiency of information on the deserts of the world. Moreover, the computation of the several geometry factors is also affected by the scales of the maps involved; a characteristic slope or plan-profile may differ drastically as a function of map scale.

A second matter of some interest with respect to the terrain-analog maps is that the studies of each of the world's deserts produced numerous areas that were mapped as moderately or even highly analogous, whereas physiographic dissimilarity was obvious to the investigators. The converse situation also occurred. In the Arabian Desert, for example, the Wadi Sirhan depression in northern Arabia, the coastal plains in western and southern Arabia, and several areas of sand and gravel plains and undissected plateaus are all mapped as moderately or highly analogous to the Yuma desert terrain and are known to be physiographically dissimilar. The desert plains of southern Iraq and eastern Syria, however, are similar on physiographic grounds but have been mapped as slightly analogous to the Yuma area. Two additional examples of questionable comparisons are the great sand dunes of the Rub'al Khali and the saline flats of this same desert; both features are mapped as analogous.

Similar examples could be drawn from any of the terrain-analog studies, and it is reasonable to inquire about the reasons for such obvious inconsistency. The choice of parameters would not seem to be at fault but, rather, it is the method employed in determining the overall degree of analogy. Given two regions of identical physiographic expression, a difference of either soil type, rock type, or vegetation type and distribution will suffice to render them nonanalogous. Whether this is the most desirable means of determining the degree of analogy is arguable. It is obvious that one is not actually treating independent variables in making the composite summation, because soils and vegetation will be more closely related to the omitted climatic factors and to rock type, whereas physiography or geometry will be most closely related to rock type, and to other variables to a lesser extent. It would appear to this writer to be more desirable to produce one set of analog maps that relate soils, vegetation, and climate, a second set that illustrates geometric factors alone, and a third set involving rock type. This would permit, incidentally, a test of the interrelationships of certain of these variables which have been debated in the literature.

In any event, the terrain-analog folios discussed here are admirable efforts and no comparable work has yet been accomplished. Nevertheless, the maps again represent the old adage that one does the best one can with the information that is available. The available information is far from adequate, and it is to be hoped that the several limitations of these analog maps, which stem primarily from lack of data and lack of adequate maps of uniform scale, will not be ignored: it is hoped that the analog maps will not actually be employed as homologs. With respect to useful projects that would serve to overcome certain of the deficiencies of information, it is obvious that many additional regional studies can and should be undertaken. As previously mentioned in connection with desert sands, topographic lows, and other topics in this review, it is apparent that many individual terrain features can be studied on a quantitative basis by using the available aerial photographs in conjunction with field study. Even in the western United States, for example, it is worthy of note that no regional topographic study of the basin-and-range area has yet been undertaken, despite the general availability of maps. This writer has such a study in progress, and can attest to the possibilities involved. Two of the more useful techniques that should be explored in regional efforts of several types are trend-surface analysis and Fourier analysis of all the parameters chosen for study.

B. SUMMARY

The foregoing discussion of deficiencies of information on the arid regions of the world has centered about two points. First, there is a great deficiency of information on basic climatic, geomorphic, and hydrologic data, in addition to a lack of adequate maps of several kinds. Second, because of these deficiencies of information a legion of unsolved problems exist. It has been argued that the fundamental problem of arid-lands geomorphology is the question of the extent to which any given desert feature is in equilibrium with present processes and the extent to which it is a product of processes operative under some preexisting climatic and hydrologic regime. It has further been argued that this question cannot be answered with respect to desert sands, soils, landforms of all types, drainage features, and, indeed, with respect to desert boundaries and the expansion and contraction of deserts as well.

We need far more data than currently exist on processes and rates of processes, on the relative importance of wind and water, on the magnitude and frequency of winds, precipitation, and runoff, and on the precise relationships between landforms and climatic and geologic factors. Among the recommendations that have been made for improving the status of knowledge and increasing our understanding of these matters are the following:

1) The establishment of basic data stations on transect lines, or zones, that are perpendicular to the presumed boundaries of the arid regions and that extend from semiarid to extremely arid regions. The data gathered at such stations should be climatic, geologic, geomorphic, hydrologic, and pedologic. The chief goal of such a study would be to seek the precise differences in physical characteristics that can be associated with small, finite climatic increments.

2) An attempt to treat the available precipitation data in terms of some parameter such as kurtosis, which relates to the frequency distribution, and to develop climatic classifications in terms of frequency of precipitation rather than mean annual values.

3) The exploration of quantitative descriptive techniques for the treatment of specific landforms on a regional basis. Among the landforms cited in this review of available information, sand dunes of all types, basin-and-range topography, and pans are features that appear to be particularly amenable to such treatment. Any landform can be treated by quantitative methods, however, and where adequate topographic maps are lacking such studies can be undertaken by combining some field work with the information available on aerial photographs.

4) The execution of quantitative studies of limited areal scope that are aimed at the determination of (a) current processes and rates of processes, and (b) the precise relationships between the descriptive parameters of a given landform and these processes.

5) The development of a quantitative scale of rock weathering in terms of specific mineralogical composition and petrologic texture and structure.

6) The initiation of further work of both theoretical and empirical nature on drainage systems and their development. Specifically, a search for some physical characteristics of stream channels that will serve as accurate guides to the probable discharge and frequency of discharge of desert drainage in nonmountainous areas should be undertaken.

Additional, and more specific, recommendations have been offered within the body of the foregoing chapter, particularly in the "Evaluation and Recommendations" section. It has been concluded that there is no essential discord of purpose between academic and practical interests. In the academic sense one speaks of problems in terms of the genesis of landforms in the arid regions, whereas governmental and practical interests require basic data of a quantitative nature. It has been emphasized throughout this report, however, that in the modern academic view classical genetic problems can only be resolved by the gathering of precisely these data, and by their synthesis in terms of the applicability of physical laws of nature and statistical procedure to geomorphic problems. Block diagrams will not provide the answers.

PERTINENT PUBLICATIONS

Each of the 15 sections of this list is alphabetically arranged: sections II through XV include works cited in the portions of the text that treat specific geographical areas; publications cited in the general part of the text are listed in Section I.

The list combines both an annotated bibliography and a more inclusive reference list. Those works which it has been possible to determine are of particular significance or interest to this study within the limitations discussed in the chapter are annotated. Other competent works and best-available works on specific subjects and areas are listed without annotation; lack of annotation should not be construed as *necessarily* indicating a less important publication.

Those works pertinent to the United States that are annotated according to the above criteria are also of general applicability and are listed in Section I rather than in Section XIV.

Where the translation of a title would be identical with the original language (except for articles, prepositions, etc.), the translation is generally omitted. Capitalization of German nouns in titles, though generally still in use, has not been followed here for editorial simplification.

SECTION I

HISTORICAL BACKGROUND AND GENERAL

Includes works cited in the general part of the text prior to the discussions of specific geographical areas.

Abul-Haggag, Y.
1961 A contribution to the physiography of northern Ethiopia. University of London, Athlone Press, London. 153 p.
A standard physiographic treatment of northern Ethiopia that describes the geology, topography, vegetation, and presumed denudation chronology of the area. Numerous maps, cross sections, and photographs are included but most of the area considered is nonarid.

Agassiz, L.
1840 Etudes sur des glaciers. Jenet et Gassmann, Neuchâtel. 346 p.
(Studies of glaciers.)

Akademiya nauk S.S.S.R. i Glavnoye Upravleniye Geodezii i Kartografii G.G.K. S.S.S.R.
1964 Fisiko-geograficheskiy atlas mira. Moscow. 298 p.
(Physico-geographical atlas of the world. Trans-lation of the legend matter and explanatory text, in Soviet Geography, Review and Translation 6(5/6), 1965, 403 p.)
The explanatory material treated here clearly indicates that the maps of this world atlas should be considered an important source for regional data.

Anderson, H. W.
1949 Flood frequencies and sedimentation from forest watersheds. American Geophysical Union, Transactions 30:567-623.
One of the earliest treatments of flood frequencies and their relation to geomorphic variables by multiple-regression methods. Peak discharges in southern California are related to drainage area, precipitation variables, temperature index, antecedent wetness of a basin, and forest density.

Anderson, H. W. and H. K. Trobitz
1949 Influence of some watershed variables on a major flood. Journal of Forestry 47:347-356.

Bakker, J. P.
1960 Dutch applied geomorphological research, notably the research of the Physical-Geographical Laboratory of the Municipal University of Amsterdam. Revue de Géomorphologie Dynamique 10:67-84.

———

1963 Different types of geomorphological maps. *In* Problems of geomorphological mapping. Polish Academy of Sciences, Geographical Studies 46: 13-22.
A general discussion of the principles of geomorphological mapping and a comparison of the similarities and differences among existing maps of various parts of the world.

Bakker, J. P. and A. N. Strahler
1956 Report on quantitative treatment of slope recession problems. Congrès International de Géographie, Rio de Janeiro, Commission pour l'Etude des Versants, Rapport 1:1-12.

Beckett P. H. T. and R. Webster
1962 The storage and collation of information on terrain. Military Engineering Experimental Establishment, Christchurch, England. 39 p.
An outline of the terrain-facet criteria and analysis employed by the Military Engineering Experimental Establishment. Other important reports of this organization are:
M.E.X.E. Report No. 915, 1965, which summarizes previous terrain-classification reports for the 1960-1964 period. These treat description of the terrain facets, collation and storage of data, and determination of analogous areas. The regions treated include Israel, Jordan, Kuwait, and Somali Republic.

M.E.X.E. Report No. 940, 1966, which provides a more detailed description of the terrain-classification methods adopted by this organization, procedures of data compilation, and a discussion of a comprehensive data-storage system.

M.E.X.E. Report No. 972, Preliminary Draft, 1967, which discusses the use of a modified classification scheme, based on that of the C.S.I.R.O., for subdividing the hot deserts of the world into physiographic provinces. The desert areas considered are those delineated by Meigs (1953).

Benson, M. A.
1962   Factors influencing the occurrence of floods in a humid region of diverse terrain. U. S. Geological Survey, Water-Supply Paper 1580-B.
A modern multiple-regression treatment of the relations between storm discharge of a given frequency of occurrence and several geomorphic and hydrologic variables in New England.

———
1964   Factors affecting the occurrence of floods in the Southwest. U. S. Geological Survey, Water-Supply Paper 1580-D.
Application of the principles and methods outlined in the author's previous work (Benson, 1962) to the southwestern United States.

Birot, P.
1959   Précis de géographie physique. Colin, Paris.
(Compendium of physical geography.)

Birot, P. and P. Macar (eds.)
1960   Contributions internationales à la morphologie des versants. Zeitschrift für Geomorphologie, Supplementband 1. 240 p.
(International contributions to the morphology of slopes.)
An excellent summary of research on slope morphology; also a guide to the world literature on this subject by reason of the references provided with each contributor's article.

———
1964   Fortschritte der internationalen handforschung. Zeitschrift für Geomorphologie, Supplementband 5. 238 p.
(International advancement in research on slope morphology.)
A more current companion volume to Birot and Macar (1960) which provides similar information on investigations in many parts of the world.

Broscoe, A. J.
1959   Quantitative analysis of longitudinal stream profiles of small watersheds. U. S. Office of Naval Research, Technical Report 18. Project NR 389-042.

Brown, E. H.
1960   The relief and drainage of Wales. University of Wales Press, Cardiff 186 p

Bull, W. B.
1964   Geomorphology of segmented alluvial fans in western Fresno County, California. U. S. Geological Survey, Professional Paper 352-E.
A detailed discussion of alluvial fan morphology and modern processes. Quantitative data on fan materials and on fan area-catchment area relations are included.

Butzer, K. W.
1961   Climatic changes in arid regions since the Pliocene. *In* A history of land use in arid regions. Unesco, Paris. Arid Zone Research 17:31-56.
A basic reference on climatic changes in the arid regions of the world and the types of data that imply climatic change.

Chebotarëv, A. I.
1955   Gidrologiia sushi i rechnoi stok. 3rd ed. Gidrometeoizdat, Leningrad.
(Continental hydrology and river runoff.)

———
1960   Obshchaia gidrologiia. Gidrometeoizdat, Leningrad.
(General hydrology.)

Chorley, R. J.
1959   The shape of drumlins. Journal of Glaciology 3:339-344.
Drumlin form is examined by analogy with the shapes of airfoils and the eggs of birds, and is quantitatively described by the equation for a lemniscate loop, namely $r = 1 \cos k\, \theta$ in polar coordinates. Comparison of these landforms is based upon the values of r in this equation, where $k = \dfrac{l^2 \pi}{4A}$, l being lemniscate length and A the area of a given loop.

———
1962   Geomorphology and general systems theory. U. S. Geological Survey, Professional Paper 500-B.
This is the best exposition in the literature of open and closed systems, and their relationship to the concepts of the geographic cycle of erosion and dynamic equilibrium of landforms.

Chorley, R. J., A. J. Dunn, and R. P. Beckinsale
1964   The history of the study of landforms. Vol. 1. Methuen and Company, London. 678 p.

Chorley, R. J. and P. Haggett, eds.
1965   Frontiers in geographical teaching. Methuen, London. 379 p.

Chorley, R. J., D. E. G. Malm, and H. A. Pogorzelski
1957   A new standard for estimating drainage basin shape. American Journal of Science 255:138-141.

Chow, V. T. (ed.)
1964   Handbook of applied hydrology. McGraw-Hill, New York. 1418 p.
A fundamental reference work on the status of knowledge, current methods, and available literature on most aspects of hydrology.

Clayton, K. M. (ed.)
1964   A bibliography of British geomorphology. British Morphological Research Group, Occasional Publication 1.

Coates, D. R.
1958   Quantitative geomorphology of small drainage basins of southern Indiana. U. S. Office of Naval Research, Technical Report 10. Project NR 389-042.

Culling, W. E. H.
1963   Soil creep and the development of hillside slopes. Journal of Geology 71:127-161.
A mathematical treatment of soil creep and slope development based upon an equilibrium model. One of the best studies of this type in the literature.

Dausse, M.
1857 Note sur un principe important et nouveau d'hydrologie. Académie des Sciences, Paris, Comptes Rendus 44:756-766.
(Note on a new and important principle of hydrology.)

Davis, W. M.
1889 The rivers and valleys of Pennsylvania. National Geographic Magazine 1:183-253.

———
1954 Geographical essays, edited by D. W. Johnson. Dover Publications, New York. 777 p.

Denny, C. S.
1956 Surficial geology and geomorphology of Potter County, Pennsylvania. U. S. Geological Survey, Professional Paper 288.

———
1965 Alluvial fans in the Death Valley region, California and Nevada. U. S. Geological Survey, Professional Paper 466.
A detailed description of alluvial fans in the Death Valley region, and quantitative data on fan and channel morphology, sizes of sedimentary particles, and fan area-catchment area relations.

Derruau, M.
1965 Précis de géomorphologie. 4th ed. Masson, Paris.
(Compendium of geomorphology.)

Dickson, B. T. (ed.)
1957 Guide book to research data on arid zone development. Unesco, Paris. Arid Zone Research 9.
A somewhat dated but still useful compilation of research pertaining to arid regions.

Dury, G. H.
1964a Principles of underfit streams. U. S. Geological Survey, Professional Paper 452-A.
This part of the overall work (U. S. Geological Survey, Professional Paper 452 A-C) defines underfit streams and presents background information on the general problems that are involved.

———
1964b Subsurface exploration and chronology of underfit streams. U. S. Geological Survey, Professional Paper 452-B.
Presents subsurface data and cross sections of several underfit streams and their associated valleys. The Pleistocene-Recent chronology is discussed in each case, and in general.

———
1965 Theoretical implications of underfit streams. U. S. Geological Survey, Professional Paper 452-C.
This concluding section of Dury's work (1964a, b, 1965) examines the hydrological implications of existing data on underfit streams and is an instructive manual on the general methods of such hydrologic inference.

Dutton, C. E.
1880- The physical geology of the Grand Canyon district.
1881 U. S. Geological Survey, Annual Report 2:47-166.

———
1882 Tertiary history of the Grand Canyon region. U. S. Geological Survey, Monograph 2. 264 p.

Fenneman, N. M.
1931 Physiography of the western United States. McGraw-Hill, New York. 534 p.
Summary of the general physiography of the western United States.

Flint, R. F.
1957 Glacial and Pleistocene geology. John Wiley, New York. 553 p.
This work is still a basic reference on the subject and contains much information peripherally pertinent to arid regions, namely discussions and data on climatic change, pluvial lakes, the terrace problem, and the general effects of Pleistocene climatic conditions in nonglaciated areas.

Gilbert, G. K.
1875 Report on the geology of portions of Nevada, Utah, California, and Arizona (1871-72). *In* Geographical Surveys West of the One Hundredth Meridian, Washington, Report 3:17-187.

———
1877 Report on the geology of the Henry Mountains. U. S. Geographical and Geological Survey of the Rocky Mountain Region, Washington. 160 p.
An outstanding early monograph on the Henry Mountain region and an exposition of the meaning of dynamic equilibrium in terms of the response of landforms to processes.

———
1880- Contributions to the history of Lake Bonneville.
1881 U. S. Geological Survey, Annual Report 2:167-200.

———
1914 The transportation of debris by running water. U. S. Geological Survey, Professional Paper 86.
An excellent study of the competence of flowing water to transport debris. Data are presented in terms of tractive force and velocity of flow.

Gravelius, H.
1914 Flusskunde. Goschensche Verlag, Berlin. 176 p. (Hydrology.)

Hack, J. T.
1957 Studies of longitudinal stream profiles in Virginia and Maryland. U. S. Geological Survey, Professional Paper 294-B.
This report illustrates the methods and procedures involved in examining the question of whether the longitudinal profiles of stream channels reflect equilibrium conditions. The empirical relations, $S = 18 \ (M/A)^{0.6}$, where S is channel slope, M is median size of bed material, and A is drainage area above the reach in question, best describes stream profiles in this region.

———
1960 Interpretation of erosional topography in humid temperate regions. American Journal of Science 258-A: 80-97.

———
1965 Geomorphology of the Shenandoah Valley, Virginia and West Virginia, and the origin of the residual ore deposits. U. S. Geological Survey, Professional Paper 484.
This report contains the author's most recent exposition of the concept of dynamic equilibrium, which, in this instance, is applied to landforms of the Shenandoah Valley and to the formation of certain residual ore deposits.

Hack, J. T. and R. S. Young
1959 Intrenched meanders of the North Fork of the Shenandoah River, Virginia. U. S. Geological Survey, Professional Paper 354-A.
Intrenched meanders in this classic region are shown to be closely related to rock type and to local structural patterns, rather than to superposition from some hypothetical former surface.

Heath, J. A.
1965 Bibliography of reports resulting from U. S. Geological Survey participation in the United States technical assistance program, 1940-65. U. S. Geological Survey Bulletin 1193.

Hooke, R. L.
1965 Quasi steady-state relationships on alluvial fans. Paper presented at the 61st Annual meeting of the Geological Society of America, Fresno, California.

Horton, R. E.
1945 Erosional development of streams and their drainage basins; hydrophysical approach to quantitative morphology. Geological Society of America, Bulletin 56:275-370.

A basic paper on quantitative drainage-basin analysis which sets forth the law of stream order, law of stream number, law of stream slope, and several morphometric variables which have hydrological significance.

Howard, A. D.
1965 Geomorphological systems; equilibrium and dynamics. American Journal of Science 263:302-312.

Hutton, J.
1788 Theory of the earth. Royal Society of Edinburgh, Transactions 1:209-304.

———
1794 An investigation of the principles of knowledge, and of the process of reason, from sense to science and philosophy. Printed for A. Strahan and T. Cadell, London, Edinburgh. 3 vols.

International Association of Scientific Hydrology
1958*a* Land erosion. General Assembly of Toronto, Proceedings 1.

A useful assemblage of papers that treat problems of erosion and sedimentation. The contained references serve as a guide to the world literature on these topics.

———
1958*b* Surface waters. General Assembly of Toronto, Proceedings 3.

The assembled papers treat various aspects of surface-water hydrology and are generally useful for the principles, techniques, and methods that are described. Many references to the world literature are included.

———
1964*a* Symposium: Surface waters. General Assembly of Berkeley. Publication 63. 615 p.

This collection of reports is similar to that cited above (I.A.S.H., 1958*b*) and provides more recent information.

———
1964*b* Land erosion, precipitations, hydrometry, soil moisture. General Assembly of Berkeley. Publication 65. 471 p.

The reports in this volume treat many aspects of surface-water hydrology and problems of erosion and sedimentation. Techniques and methods of instrumentation are also discussed. The included references are quite useful.

International Association of Scientific Hydrology. Surface-Water Commission
1954 Comptes Rendus et Rapports, Assemblée Générale de Rome, 3.

International Geological Congress, 19th, Algiers
1952 Comptes rendus.
The reports of this Congress contain much information on geology and surficial features of Algeria and of North Africa in general. The included maps, cross sections, and photographs render the work as a whole a basic reference on this part of the world.

International Geological Congress, 20th, Mexico 1956.
Session reports.
The reports of this Congress stress geological matters, and relatively few papers treat geomorphology or surface-water hydrology of the arid portion of Mexico. The work as a whole is of moderate reference value and is indicative of the status of knowledge of these subjects in Mexico, as of 1956.

Israel. Research Council
1953 Desert research; proceedings of the International Symposium held in Jerusalem, sponsored by the Research Council of Israel and Unesco. Research Council of Israel, Special Publication 2. 641 p.

A somewhat dated but still useful compilation of papers on many aspects of desert research, largely pertinent to the Middle East.

Jamieson, T. F.
1863 On the parallel roads of Glen Roy, and their place on the history of the glacial period. Geological Society of London, Quarterly Journal 19:235-259.

Kennedy, J. F., P. D. Richardson, and S. P. Sutera
1964 Discussion of "Geometry of river channels." American Society of Civil Engineers, Hydraulics Division, Journal 90:332-341.

King, C. A. M.
1966 Techniques in geomorphology. St. Martin's Press, New York. 342 p.

This book treats techniques that have been employed in quantitative geomorphic investigations, but does so in such a manner that the reader who wishes to employ similar techniques must resort to the original literature. That is, the book describes techniques that have been used by others, and cites results, but it does not fully explain the procedures in any detail. The most recent references that are provided pertain approximately to 1962.

King, L. C.
1950 The study of the world's plainlands; a new approach to geomorphology. Geological Society of London, Quarterly Journal 106:101-127.

———
1953 Canons of landscape evolution. Geological Society of America, Bulletin 64:721-752.

———
1962 Morphology of the earth; a study and synthesis of world scenery. Hafner, New York. 699 p.

This volume is devoted to an exposition of the author's views on the process of pedimentation and on other controversial subjects, such as continental drift. It contains numerous illustrations of the geology and surficial features of all parts of the world, however, and an extensive bibliography, with emphasis on geology and geomorphology.

Langbein, W. B.
1965 Discussion of "Geometry of river channels." American Society of Civil Engineers, Hydraulics Division, Journal 91:297-313.

———
1966 The stochastic geometry of river channels (unpublished manuscript). 19 p.

Langbein, W. B. and L. B. Leopold
1966 River meanders; theory of minimum variance. U. S. Geological Survey, Professional Paper 422-H.

A sine-generated function is presented which is shown to fit the geometry of several natural meandering streams. Field measurements support the theoretically-based argument that meanders are, in effect, a consequence of channel adjustment to accord with the least-work principle. The report therefore provides a basis for future work directed toward prediction of the plan geometry of natural channels.

Langbein, W. B. *et al.*
1947 Topographic characteristics of drainage basins. U. S. Geological Survey, Water-Supply Paper 968-C.

Lartet, L.
1865 Sur la formation du bassin de la Mer Morte ou lac asphaltite, et sur les changements survenus dans le niveau de ce lac. Académie des Sciences, Paris, Comptes Rendus 60:796-800.
(On the formation of the Dead Sea basin and the changes in lake level.)

Leliavsky, S.
1955 An introduction to fluvial hydraulics. Constable, London. 257 p.

Leonardo da Vinci
1906 Leonardo da Vinci's notebooks, arranged with introduction by Edward McCurdy. Duckworth and Company, London. 289 p.

Leopold, L. B.
1962 A national network of hydrologic bench marks. U. S. Geological Survey, Circular 460-B.
This report describes the vigil-network concept and approach, namely to locate a network of bench marks on a regional basis at which hydrologic measurements can be made over long-term periods.

n.d. Trees and streams; the efficiency of branching patterns. U. S. Geological Survey, Professional Paper *(in press)*.

Leopold, L. B. and W. B. Langbein
1962 The concept of entropy in landscape evolution. U. S. Geological Survey, Professional Paper 500-A.
An important theoretical paper which employs the concept of entropy in probabilistic terms. It is argued, on a theoretical basis and by analogy, that stream networks accord with the most probable spatial distribution in the absence of constraints, and hence, are a function of stochastic processes that have operated through time.

Leopold, L. B. and T. Maddock, Jr.
1953 The hydraulic geometry of stream channels and some physiographic implications. U. S. Geological Survey, Professional Paper 252.
A basic guide to nearly all subsequent work on stream-channel morphology. Relations between width, depth, velocity of flow, sediment load, and stream discharge of a given recurrence interval are expressed as simple power functions for a given cross section in a downstream direction.

Leopold, L. B. and J. P. Miller
1956 Ephemeral streams; hydraulic factors and their relation to the drainage net. U. S. Geological Survey, Professional Paper 282-A.
The hydraulic geometry of channels (Leopold and Maddock, 1953) is applied to ephemeral stream channels in New Mexico and is related to certain of Horton's laws (Horton, 1945). A theory of gully formation is also presented.

Leopold, L. B. and M. G. Wolman
1957 River channel patterns; braided, meandering, and straight. U. S. Geological Survey, Professional Paper 282-B.
River-channel patterns are discussed in terms of field observations, simple flume experiments, and the adjustment of variables to be anticipated from knowledge of the hydraulic geometry of channels. It is concluded that no single pattern is representative of an entire stream, from headwaters to mouth. Most streams exhibit braided, meandering, and straight reaches over some portions of their total courses, and of these three patterns, straight reaches are rather rare.

1960 River meanders. Geological Society of America, Bulletin 71:769-794.

Leopold, L. B., M. G. Wolman, and J. P. Miller
1964 Fluvial processes in geomorphology. W. H. Freeman, San Francisco. 522 p.
The best available text on this general subject. It serves as an excellent guide to the pertinent literature because the work is essentially based upon previously published separate reports on fluvial processes.

Lobeck, A. K.
1939 Geomorphology. McGraw-Hill, New York. 731 p.

Lohman, S. W. and C. J. Robinove
1964 Photographic description and appraisal of water resources. Photogrammetria 19(3).

Louis, H.
1960 Allgemeine geomorphologie. Walter de Gruyter, Berlin.
(General geomorphology.)

Lowman, P. D., Jr.
1965 Space photography, a review. Photogrammetric Engineering 31:76-86.

Lustig, L. K.
1965a Clastic sedimentation in Deep Springs Valley, California. U. S. Geological Survey, Professional Paper 352-F.
This report contains a detailed summary of the characteristics of clastic sediments in the basin treated, and sets forth a theory of alluvial-fan formation based upon alternating climatic events.

1965b Sediment yield of the Castaic watershed, western Los Angeles County, California; a quantitative geomorphic approach. U. S. Geological Survey, Professional Paper 422-F.
The long-term sediment yield of the Castaic basin is estimated in the general absence of hydrologic data by means of a comparison of morphometric parameters for this basin and for other basins where the sediment yield is known. Several new parameters, thought to reflect sediment availability, sediment movement, and transport efficiency, are proposed, and these are correlated with known sediment yield.

Lyell, C.
1872 Principles of geology. 11th ed. J. Murray, London. 2 vols.

Machatschek, F.
1955 Das relief der erde. 2. umgearb. aufl. Gebrüder Borntraeger, Berlin. 2 vols.
(Morphology of the earth.)
A useful compendium on the general surficial features of the world.

Mackin, J. H.
 1948   Concept of the graded river. Geological Society of America, Bulletin 59:463-512.

Mammerickx, J.
 1964   Quantitative observations on pediments in the Mohave and Sonoran deserts (southwestern United States). American Journal of Science 262:417-435.
Presents data on pediment profiles and rock type of source areas in southern Arizona and the Mohave. The author concludes that there is a lack of correlation between these variables, but this conclusion is open to question on several grounds.

Maxwell, J. C.
 1960   Quantitative geomorphology of the San Dimas Experimental Forest, California. U. S. Office of Naval Research, Technical Report 19. Project NR 389-042.
An excellent illustration of multiple-regression methods applied to quantitative drainage-basin analysis, and of the relations among morphometric and hydrologic variables.

McGill, J. T.
 1958   Map of coastal landforms of the world. Scale 1:25,000,000. Geographical Review 48:402-405.

Meigs, P.
 1953   World distribution of arid and semiarid homoclimates. *In* Reviews of research on arid zone hydrology. Unesco, Paris. Arid Zone Programme 1:203-210.
This report centers about world maps that show the relatively dry climatic regions. The general locations of semiarid and arid areas do not differ markedly from standard world atlas presentations. The chief innovation is the delineation of "extremely arid" regions, which are classified on the basis of the assumption that precipitation in these areas recurs less frequently than once a year.

Melton, M. A.
 1957   An analysis of the relations among elements of climate, surface properties, and geomorphology.. U. S. Office of Naval Research, Technical Report 11. Project NR 389-042.

———
 1958   List of sample parameters of quantitative properties of landforms; their use in determining the size of geomorphic experiments. U. S. Office of Naval Research, Technical Report 16. Project NR 389-042.

———
 1960   Intravalley variation in slope angles related to microclimate and erosional environment. Geological Society of America, Bulletin 71:133-144.

———
 1965a   The geomorphic and paleoclimatic significance of alluvial deposits in southern Arizona. Journal of Geology 73:1-38.
Presents useful quantitative data on the characteristics of drainage basins and alluvial fans and pediments in southern Arizona, correlations among these characteristics, and an argument concerning differing rates of sedimentation during the Pleistocene and Recent based upon assumed differences in the frequency of occurrence of freeze-thaw cycles, among other factors.

———
 1965b   Debris-covered hillslopes of the southern Arizona desert —consideration of their stability and sediment contribution. Journal of Geology 73:715-729.
Presents quantitative data on the angles of hillslopes of different lithologies and particle size. The author concludes that no statistical correlation exists between slope angle and particle size for the granitic and volcanic terrains studied.

Miller, J. P.
 1958   High mountain streams; effects of geology on channel characteristics and bed material. New Mexico Institute of Mining and Technology, Memoir 4. 53 p.
A detailed analysis of particle size and channel characteristics in the Sangre de Cristo Mountains of New Mexico; the analysis served to demonstrate that streams tend to be graded, or in a state of quasi-equilibrium, even in steep high mountain areas.

Miller, J. P. and L. B. Leopold
 1963   Simple measurements of morphological changes in river channels and hill slopes. *In* Changes of climate. Unesco, Paris. Arid Zone Research 20:421-427.

Miller, V. C.
 1953   A quantitative geomorphic study of drainage basin characteristics in the Clinch Mountain area, Virginia and Tennessee. U. S. Office of Naval Research, Technical Report 3. Project NR 389-042.

Morisawa, M. E.
 1959   Relation of quantitative geomorphology to stream flow in representative watersheds of the Appalachian Plateau province. U. S. Office of Naval Research, Technical Report 20. Project NR 389-042.

Myrick, R. M. and L. B. Leopold
 1963   Hydraulic geometry of a small tidal estuary. U. S. Geological Survey, Professional Paper 422-B.

Peel, R. F.
 1960   Some aspects of desert geomorphology. Geography 45:241-262.
An excellent summary of outstanding geomorphic problems in the deserts of the world, with emphasis on the Sahara.

———
 1966   The landscape in aridity. Institute of British Geographers, Transactions and Papers, Publication 38. 23 p.
This paper contains a good general summary of the characteristics of deserts, their origin and climatic history, and a more current resumé of problems than is afforded by the author's previous work (Peel, 1960).

Penck, W.
 1953   Morphological analysis of landforms; a contribution to physical geology. Translated by Czech and Boswell. Macmillan, London. 429 p.

Playfair, J.
 1802   Illustrations of the Huttonian theory of the earth. Printed for W. Creach, Edinburgh. 528 p.

Polish Academy of Sciences
 1963   Problems of geomorphological mapping. Geographical Studies 46.
This is the best summary paper available on the methods and goals of geomorphological mapping. The individuals and organizations that are engaged in this work in several parts of the world are indicated. The arid areas that are included among the regions treated in individual articles

are parts of Sudan and Morocco. This work contains many references and an appendix which presents the symbols used to depict various types of landforms.

Powell, J. W.
1875 Exploration of the Colorado River of the West and its tributaries. Explored in 1869, 1870, 1871, and 1872, under the direction of the Secretary of the Smithsonian Institution. Government Printing Office, Washington. 291 p.

————— 1876 Report on the geology of the eastern portion of the Uinta Mountains. U. S. Geological and Geographical Survey of the Territories, Washington. 218 p.

————— 1961 The exploration of the Colorado River and its canyons. Dover Publications, New York. 400 p. (First published in 1895 under title: Canyons of the Colorado.)

Raisz, E.
1951 Landforms of the Near East. Author, 107 Washington Avenue, Cambridge 40, Mass.

————— 1952 Landform map of North Africa. Author, 107 Washington Avenue, Cambridge 40, Mass.

————— 1957 Landforms of the United States. Author, 107 Washington Avenue, Cambridge 40, Mass.

————— 1959 Landforms of Mexico. Author, 107 Washington Avenue, Cambridge 40, Mass.

Rapp, A.
1960 Recent developments of mountain slope in Kärkevagge and surroundings, northern Scandinavia. Geografiska Annaler 42 (2-3).

Remson, I. et al.
1962 Some systems for describing, classifying, mapping, and comparing surface-water bodies for military purposes. Annual Report II to U. S. Army Engineer Waterways Experiment Station, Vicksburg, Mississippi.

Richards, H. G. and R. W. Fairbridge
1965 Annotated bibliography of Quaternary shorelines (1945-1964). Academy of Natural Sciences, Philadelphia, Special Publication 6. 280 p.

Robinove, C. J.
1965 Infrared photography and imagery in water resources research. American Water Works Association, Journal 57:834-840.

————— 1966 Remote-sensor applications in hydrology. U. S. Geological Survey, Water Resources Division, Memorandum 66.87.

Roche, M.
1963 Hydrologie de surface. Gauthier-Villars, Paris. (Surface-water hydrology.)

Rodier, J.
1963 Bibliography of African hydrology. Unesco, Paris. 166 p.
An extremely useful bibliography which provides references to most of the important hydrological investigations that have been undertaken in Africa.

Rouse, H. (ed.)
1950 Engineering hydraulics. John Wiley, New York. 1039 p.

Ruxton, B. P.
1958 Weathering and subsurface erosion in granite at the piedmont angle, Balos, Sudan. Geological Magazine 95:353-377.
Presents quantitative data on slope profiles in Sudan which suggest a correlation between slope angle and lithology.

Rzhanitsyn, N. A.
1960 Morphological and hydrological regularities of the structure of the river net. U. S. Agricultural Research Service. 380 p.
Translated by D. B. Krimgold.
This report is illustrative of the application of quantitative drainage analysis to hydrologic problems in the U.S.S.R. It contains an extensive bibliography of allied work that has been reported in the Russian literature.

Savigear, R. A. G.
1956 Technique and terminology in the investigation of slope forms. Congrès International de Géographie, Rio de Janeiro, Commission pour l'Etude des Versants, Rapport 1:66-75.

————— 1965 A technique of morphological mapping. Association of American Geographers, Annals 55:514-538.
Describes a method of morphological mapping that is based upon the recognition of landform facets. The facets selected reflect discontinuities or points of inflection on landform profiles. The techniques of map construction and the utility of various map scales are discussed in detail.

Scheidegger, A. E.
1961a Mathematical models of slope development. Geological Society of America, Bulletin 72:37-50.

————— 1961b Theoretical geomorphology. Springer Verlag, Berlin. 333 p.
This book attempts to treat a wide variety of geomorphic problems by mathematical analysis. In order to set forth a descriptive differential equation, however, in many instances the model employed is based upon simplifying assumptions. These assumptions, in turn, unfortunately involve unwarranted conclusions about processes or process rates.

————— 1964a Lithologic variations in slope development theory. U. S. Geological Survey, Circular 485.

————— 1964b Some implications of statistical mechanics in geomorphology. International Association of Scientific Hydrology, Bulletin 9:12-16.

————— 1966 Stochastic branching processes and the law of stream orders. Water Resources Research 2:199-203.

Schenk, H.
1963 Simulation of the evolution of drainage-basin networks with a digital computer. Journal of Geophysical Research 68:5739-5745.
This paper demonstrates that drainage networks can be stimulated by computer-generated random walks and, therefore, that natural networks may be the product of stochastic processes acting through time.

Schoeller, H.
1959 Arid zone hydrology: recent developments. Unesco, Paris. Arid Zone Research 12.

Schumm, S. A.
1956   Evolution of drainage systems and slopes in badlands at Perth Amboy, New Jersey. Geological Society of America, Bulletin 67:597-646.
A quantitative study of sedimentation and erosion and rates of badland development in New Jersey. Although conducted in a nonarid area, this work is of considerable importance in terms of the principles of terrain changes with time that are presented and the field techniques that are illustrated.

1963   Disparity between present rates of denudation and orogeny. U. S. Geological Survey, Professional Paper 454-H.
The author argues that rates of orogeny greatly exceed rates of denudation on the basis of available sediment-yield data. If accepted, this thesis bears directly upon certain slope-evolution models.

Schumm, S. A. and R. W. Lichty
1965   Time, space, and causality in geomorphology. American Journal of Science 263:110-119.

Segerström, K.
1950   Erosion studies at Paricutín, State of Michoacán, Mexico. U. S. Geological Survey, Bulletin 965-A.
A detailed description of the surficial features of the Paricutín volcano, approximately 320 km west of Mexico City. Rates of formation of the volcano are presented, and processes of erosion and sedimentation are discussed, based upon field observation and some quantitative data. Intense rains induced mudflows in certain instances with specific gravities as great as 2.10.

Sherman, L. K.
1932   The relation of hydrographs of runoff to size and character of drainage basins. American Geophysical Union, Transactions 13:332-339.

Shreve, R. L.
1966   Statistical law of stream numbers. Journal of Geology 74:17-37.
An excellent theoretical paper which utilizes computer techniques to demonstrate the accordance of stochastic principles with certain of Horton's laws (Horton, 1945).

Slaymaker, H. O. and R. J. Chorley
1964   The vigil network system. Journal of Hydrology 2:19-24.

Sokolovskii, D. L.
1959   Rechnoi stok. Gidrometeoizdat, Leningrad.
(River runoff.)

Stamp, L. D. (ed.)
1961   A history of land use in the arid regions. Unesco, Paris. Arid Zone Research 17.

Strahler, A. N.
1950   Equilibrium theory of erosional slopes approached by frequency distribution analysis. American Journal of Science 248:673-696, 800-814.

1952a   Dynamic basis of geomorphology. Geological Society of America, Bulletin 63:923-938.

1952b   Hypsometric (area-altitude) analysis of erosional topography. Geological Society of America, Bulletin 63:1117-1142.
This paper illustrates one of several useful techniques developed by the author for purposes of quantitative drainage basin analysis. In this instance, a hypsometic integral is derived which reflects the volume of material that may have been removed during the formation of a given landmass. In effect, the author has attempted to quantify the terms youth, maturity, and old age with respect to the overall profile of a given landform.

1954   Statistical analysis in geomorphic research. Journal of Geology 62:1-25.

1956   Quantitative slope analysis. Geological Society of America, Bulletin 67:571-596.

1957   Quantitative analysis of watershed geomorphology. American Geophysical Union, Transactions 38:913-920.

1964   Quantitative geomorphology. Sec. 4-II. *In* V. T. Chow, ed., Handbook of applied hydrology. McGraw-Hill, New York.
The best single source or guide to the several excellent papers on quantitative techniques that were published by Strahler or his students during approximately the period from 1950 to 1960.

1965   Introduction to physical geography. John Wiley, New York. 455 p.

Streck, O.
1953   Grundlagen der wasserwirtschaft und gewässerkunde. Springer Verlag, Berlin.
(Fundamentals of water management and hydrology.)

Surell, A.
1841   Etude sur les torrents des Hautes-Alpes. Paris.
(Study of the floods of the high Alps.)

Symposium on Remote Sensing of Environment
1962-   Proceedings. University of Michigan, Institute of
1966   Science and Technology, Ann Arbor, Michigan. U. S. Office of Naval Research Project NR387-028.

Thomas, W. L., Jr. (ed.)
1956   Man's role in changing the face of the earth. University of Chicago Press, Chicago.
An excellent symposium, devoted to examination of the various means by which the natural environment is altered through man's interference. Erosion and sedimentation, and surface-water hydrology in general, are among the topics treated. Specific papers treat such areas of interest as the dry regions of Asia, India, and North America.

Thornbury, W. D.
1954   Principles of geomorphology. John Wiley, New York. 618 p.

Tonini, D.
1959   Elementi di idrografia ed idrologia. Libreria Universitaria, Venice.
(Elements of hydrography and hydrology.)

Tricart, J.
1965   Principes et méthodes de la géomorphologie. Masson, Paris.
(Principles and methods of geomorphology.)

Tricart, J. and A. Cailleux
1955   Introduction à la géomorphologie climatique. *In* Traité de géomorphologie, vol. 1. Société d'Edition d'Enseignment Supérieur, Paris.

Troeh, F. R.
1965 Landform equations fitted to contour maps. American Journal of Science 263:616-627.

Troeh argues that local analysis is in some instances superior to regional analysis with respect to finding functions of best fit for landforms. In this paper he derives an equation for the representation of alluvial fans which is based upon a model of a right circular cone. The equation used is: $Z = P + SR + LR^2$, where Z is the elevation of the surface at any point, P is the elevation of the center of the cone, S is the slope of the sides of the cone at the apex, and R is the radial distance from P to Z. The remaining variable, L, is a function of the rate of change of slope gradient with radial distance along the cone. Examples used in the report are in southern Arizona.

Unesco
1953a Reviews of research on arid zone hydrology. Unesco, Paris. Arid Zone Programme 1.

1953b Proceedings of the Ankara symposium on arid zone hydrology. Unesco, Paris. Arid Zone Programme 2.

1953c Directory of institutions engaged in arid zone research. Unesco, Paris. Arid Zone Programme 3. 110 p.

1962 The problems of the arid zone; proceedings of the Paris Symposium. Unesco, Paris. Arid Zone Research 18.

1963a Changes of climate; proceedings of the Rome Symposium. Unesco, Paris. Arid Zone Research 20. 488 p.

1963b A review of the natural resources of the African continent. Unesco, Paris. Natural Resources Research 1. 437 p.

Union Géographique Internationale
1951 Intérêt des stéréogrammes aériens dans l'enseignement de la géographie physique. Institut Géographique National, Paris.
(Utility of aerial stereo-photographs in the teaching of physical geography.)

Union Géographique Internationale. Commission pour l'Etude des Terrasses Pliocénes et Pléistocènes
1948 Problèmes des terrasses. Louvain, Rapport 6.
(Sixth report of the Commission for the Study of Pliocene and Pleistocene Terraces.)

Union Géographique Internationale. Commission pour l'Etude des Terrasses et Surfaces d'Aplanissment
1952a Rapport 7. Congrès International de Géographie, 17e, Washington.
(Seventh report of the Commission for the Study of Terraces and Erosion Surfaces.)

Union Géographique Internationale. Commission pour l'Utilisation des Photographies Aériennes dan les Etudes Géographiques
1952b Rapport. Congrès International de Géographie, 17e, Washington.
(Report of the Commission for the Utilization of Aerial Photographs in the Study of Physical Geography.)

Union Géographique Internationale. Commission pour l'Etude des Versants
1956 Rapport 1, préparé pour le Congrès International de Géographie, 18e, Rio de Janeiro. Amsterdam. 155 p.
(First report of the Commission for the Study of Slopes.)

United Nations
1951 Flood damage and flood control activities in Asia and the Far East. United Nations Economic Commission for Asia and the Far East, Bureau of Flood Control and Water Resources Development, Flood Control Series 1.

1953 The sediment problem. United Nations Economic Commission for Asia and the Far East, Bureau of Flood Control and Water Resources Development, Flood Control Series 5.

1956 Multiple-purpose river basin development, pt. 2B: Water resources development in Burma, India, and Pakistan. United Nations Economic Commission for Asia and the Far East, Bureau of Flood Control and Water Resources Development, Flood Control Series 11.

1960 Hydrologic networks and methods. United Nations Economic Commission for Asia and the Far East, Bureau of Flood Control and Water Resources Development, Flood Control Series 15.

1961 Multiple-purpose river basin development, pt. 2D: Water resources development in Afghanistan, Iran, Republic of Korea, and Nepal. United Nations Economic Commission for Asia and the Far East, Bureau of Flood Control and Water Resources Development, Flood Control Series 18.

1962a Proceedings of the fourth regional technical conference on water resources development in Asia and the Far East. United Nations Economic Commission for Asia and the Far East, Bureau of Flood Control and Water Resources Development, Flood Control Series 19.

1962b Field methods and equipment used in hydrology and hydrometeorology. United Nations Economic Commission for Asia and the Far East, Bureau of Flood Control and Water Resources Development, Flood Control Series 22.

1963 Proceedings of the fifth regional technical conference on water resources development in Asia and the Far East. United Nations Economic Commission for Asia and the Far East, Bureau of Flood Control and Water Resources Development, Water Resources Series 23.

U. S. Army Map Service
1946- World map series. Scale 1:1,000,000. Washington.

U. S. Coast and Geodetic Survey
19— Aeronautical planning charts. Scale 1:5,000,000. Washington.

19— World aeronautical charts. Scale 1:1,000,000. Washington.

U. S. Interagency Committee on Water Resources
1955   Annotated bibliography on hydrology 1951-54 and sedimentation 1950-54 (United States and Canada), compiled and edited under auspices of Subcommittee on Hydrology and Sedimentation by American Geophysical Union, National Research Council of National Academy of Sciences. Joint Hydrology-Sedimentation Bulletin 7. 207 p.

Von Bertalanffy, L.
1950   The theory of open systems in physics and biology. Science 111:23-29.

———

1951   An outline of general system theory. British Journal for the Philosophy of Science 1:134-165.

———

1952   Problems of life. Watts and Company, London. 216 p.

Warren, A.
1966   Bibliography of literature on sand dunes. University College, London.
A preliminary bibliography, not formally published, which contains many useful entries from various parts of the world. The topics treated are dunes, sand sheets, and windblown sand in general. The author intends to expand this bibliography in the near future and has many additional references in his files at present.

Werner, A. G.
1787   Kurze klassifikation und beschreibung der verschiedenen gebirgsarten. Dresden.
(Short classification and description of the different kinds of rocks.)

White, S. E.
1949   Processes of erosion on the steep slopes of Oahu, Hawaii. American Journal of Science 247:168-186.

Woldenberg, M. J.
1966   Horton's laws justified in terms of allometric growth and steady state in open systems. Geological Society of America, Bulletin 77:431-434.

Woldstedt, P.
1958   Das eiszeitalter. Ferdinand Enke, Stuttgart. 2 vols.
(The Pleistocene.)

Wolman, M. G.
1955   The natural channel of Brandywine Creek, Pennsylvania. U. S. Geological Survey, Professional Paper 271.

Wolman, M. G. and J. P. Miller
1960   Magnitude and frequency of forces in geomorphic processes. Journal of Geology 68:54-74.
An important theoretical paper which examines the question of whether catastrophic events of infrequent return periods, or events of moderate magnitude and relatively frequent occurrence, are of the greater importance in denudation of the Earth's surface. The sediment-transport data that are presented suggest that greater net work is accomplished by events of moderate magnitude and frequent occurrence, but the authors recognize that this may not be true in certain environments, such as the extremely arid areas of the world.

Wright, H. E., Jr. and D. G. Frey (eds.)
1965a   International studies on the Quaternary. Geological Society of America, Special Paper 84.

———

1965b   The Quaternary of the United States. Princeton University Press, Princeton, New Jersey. 922 p.

This volume must be considered a basic reference work on all aspects of the Pleistocene in the United States. Many useful data on surficial features of the western states are contained in the individual reports of the compendium. Emphasis is on alluvial deposits of all types, including soils, and on drainage features, but general geology and other topics of interest are treated. The reference lists that accompany each individual report are also useful as sources of further information.

Wundt, W.
1953   Gewässerkunde. Springer Verlag, Berlin.
(Hydrology.)

Yasso, W. E.
1965   Plan geometry of headland-bay beaches. Journal of Geology 73:702-714.
The author shows that the form, or plan geometry, of beaches that are protected by headlands can be represented by the equation for a logarithmic spiral, namely $r = e^{\theta \cot a}$. Computer methods were employed in order to find the spiral of best fit for beaches in New Jersey and California. The results indicate that the natural beaches accord remarkably well with this function, and the author suggests that South African and other beaches can be described in a similar manner.

SECTION II

AFRICA (IN GENERAL)

Includes works cited in the text discussion of the desert area of Africa in general.

Association of African Geological Surveys
1936-   Carte géologique internationale de l'Afrique. Scale
1952   1:5,000,000. Bureau d'Etudes Géologiques et Minières Coloniales, Paris.
(International geological map of Africa.)

Dixey, F.
1963   Geology, applied geology (mineral resources) and geophysics in Africa. *In* A review of the natural resources of the African continent. Unesco, Paris. Natural Resources Research 1:51-100.
A good summary of the status of geological mapping in Africa and a source of information on active geological organizations on that continent.

Furon, R.
1960   Géologie de l'Afrique. Payot, Paris.
(Geology of Africa.)
A basic guide to the geological literature on Africa, this book provides a resumé of the general geology of all parts of the continent.

Katchevsky, A.
1933   Carte géologique de l'Afrique. Scale 1:8,000,000. Revue de Géographie Physique et de Géologie Dynamique, Paris.
(Geologic map of Africa.)

King, L. C.
1962   Morphology of the earth. Hafner, New York.

Machatschek, F.
1955   Das relief der erde. 2. umgearb. aufl. Gebrüder Borntraeger, Berlin. 2 vols.
(Morphology of the earth.)

Rodier, J.
1963   Hydrology in Africa. *In* A review of the natural resources of the African continent. Unesco, Paris. Natural Resources Research 1:179-220.
An excellent guide to the literature on hydrology, and the organizations and personnel engaged in hydrological investigations in Africa.

Rumeau, A.
1963   Topographic mapping of Africa. *In* A review of the natural resources of the African continent. Unesco, Paris. Natural Resources Research 1: 19-50.
A review paper that summarizes the status and needs of topographic mapping in Africa. Data on the available sheets of various scales, aerial photography, and mapping agencies in Africa are provided.

Unesco
1964   Geological map of Africa. Scale 1:5,000,000. Paris. Natural Resources Research 3.

SECTION III

SOUTHERN AFRICA: THE KALAHARI AND NAMIB

Includes works cited in the text discussions of southern Africa in general, and the Kalahari and Namib.

Abel, H.
1953   Geomorphologische untersuchungen im Kaoko-veld, Südwest Afrika. Deutsches Geographentag, Essen, 29.
(Geomorphic investigations in the Kaokoveld, South West Africa.)

———
1954   Beiträge zur landeskunde des Kaokoveld, Südwest Afrika. Deutsche Geographische Blätter 47.
(Report on the landscape of the Kaokoveld, South West Africa.)

———
1955   Beiträge zur landeskunde des Rehobother westens, Südwest Afrika. Geographische Gesellschaft, Hamburg, Mitteilungen 51:55-97.
(Report on the landscape of the western Rehoboth area, South West Africa.)

Andersson, C. F.
1855   Explorations in South Africa, with route from Walfish Bay to Lake Nagami, and ascent of the Tioge River. Royal Geographical Society, London, Journal 25:79-107.

Baines, T.
1964   Explorations in South West Africa. London.

Bechuanaland. Geological Survey Department
1964   Provisional geological map of Bechuanaland. Scale 1:2,000,000. Lobatsi, Bechuanaland.

Beetz, W.
1933   Geology of southwest Angola, between Cunene and Luanda axis. Geological Society of South Africa, Transactions 36:137-176.

———
1938   Klimaschwankungen und krustenbewegungen in Afrika südlich des äquators von der Kreidezeit bis zum Diluvium. Geographische Gesellschaft, Hannover, Sonderveröffentlich 3.
(Climatic change and crustal movements in Africa south of the equator from the Cretaceous to the Recent.)

———
1950   Die geheimnisse des Kunenelaufes in Südangola und Südwestafrika. Erdkunde 4:43-54.
(The mystery of the course of the Kunene River in southern Angola and South West Africa.)

Beetz, W. and E. Kaiser
1919   Die wassererschliessung in der südlichen Namib. Zeitschrift für Praktische Geologie 27:165-182.
(Flowing water in the southern Namib.)

Bockemeyer, H.
1890   Beschreibung der küste zwischen Mossâmedes und Port Nolloth. Deutsche Kolonialzeitung, Berlin.
(Description of the coast between Mossâmedes and Port Nolloth.)

Boocock, C. and O. J. van Straten
1962   Notes on the geology and hydrogeology of the central Kalahari region, Bechuanaland Protectorate. Geological Society of South Africa, Transactions 65:125-171.
This paper is the best modern source of information on the general geology and hydrology of the central Kalahari region. A discussion of pan characteristics and other surficial features is included, as is a geologic and cultural map of Bechuanaland (now Botswana). The most pertinent references to previous work on the Kalahari are provided.

Born, A.
1933   Das escarpment in Südwestafrika. Centralblatt für Mineralogie, Geologie, und Paläontologie 7:429-431.
(The escarpment in South West Africa.)

Bosazza, V. L., R. J. Adie, and S. Brenner
1946   Man and the great Kalahari desert. Natal University College, Scientific Society, Journal 5:1-9.

Brown, A. E. *et al.*
1961   Musical sand. pt. 1: The singing sands of the seashore. University of Durham Philosophical Society, ser. A, 13:217-230.

Cloos, H.
1911   Geologische beobachtungen in Südafrika. I: Wind und wüste im Deutschen Namalande. Neues Jahrbuch für Mineralogie, Geologie und Paläontologie 32:49-70.
(Geological observations in South Africa. I: Wind and desert in German Namaland.)

———
1931   Der Brandberg. Neues Jahrbuch für Mineralogie 66.

———
1937   Südwestafrika, reiseeindrücke 1936. Geologische Rundschau 28 (3/4):163-187.
(South West Africa, travel impressions of 1936.)

Davies, O.
1959   Pleistocene raised beaches in South West Africa. p. 347-350. *In* Asociación de Servicios Geológicos Africanos, Actas y Trabajos (International Geological Congress, 20th, Mexico, 1956).

Debenham, F.
1948   Report on the water resources of Bechuanaland, Nyasaland, N. Rhodesia, Tanganyika, Uganda, and Kenya. Colonial Resources, London, Publication 2:31-39.

Dixey, F.
1939   Some observations on the physiographical development of Central and South Africa. Geological Society of South Africa, Transactions 41:113-171.

1943   Erosion cycles in Central and South Africa. Geological Society of South Africa, Transactions 45: 151-181.

1956   Some aspects of the geomorphology of Central and Southern Africa. Geological Society of South Africa, du Toit Memorial Lecture 4. 58 p.

Dove, K.
1894   Beiträge zur geographie von Südwestafrika. Petermanns Geographische Mitteilungen.
(Reports of the geography of South West Africa.)

Du Toit, A. L.
1926   Report of the Kalahari reconnaissance of 1925. Government Printer, Pretoria.

1959   The geology of South Africa. 3rd ed. Oliver and Boyd, London.
Contains geological map of South Africa, scale 1:5,000,000.

Fair, T. J. D.
1948   Hillslopes and pediments in the semi-arid Karoo. South African Geographical Journal 30:71-79.

Ferrão, C. A.
1962   A hidrogeologia e o problema do abastecimento de água ao reserva pastoril do Caraculo (Angola). Serviços de Geologia e Minas, Luanda, Boletim 5.
(The hydrogeology and problem of water supply in the Karakul sheep reserve.)

1964   A hidrogeologia e o problema do abastecimento de água ao baixo Cunene (Angola). Laboratório Nacional de Engenharia Civil, Lisbon, Memória 222.
(The hydrogeology and problem of water supply in the inner Cunene area, Angola.)

Flint, R. F.
1959   Pleistocene climates in eastern and southern Africa. Geological Society of America, Bulletin 70:343-374.

François, C.
1892   Bericht über eine reise zwischen Windhoek und Gobabis. Mitteilungen aus den Deutschen Schutzgebieten, Berlin.
(Report on a journey between Windhoek and Gobabis.)

1893*a* Bericht über eine bereisung der Kalahari. Mitteilungen aus den Deutschen Schutzgebieten, Berlin.
(Report on a Kalahari expedition.)

1893*b* Das küstengebiet zwischen Tsoekhaub-Mündung und Cape Cross. Mitteilungen aus den Deutschen Schutzgebieten, Berlin.
(The coastal area between Tsoekhaub-Mündung and Cape Cross.)

1899   Deutsch-Südwestafrika. Berlin.
(German South West Africa.)

Galton, F.
1852   Recent expedition into the interior of South West Africa. Royal Geographical Society, London, Journal 22.

Ganssen, R.
1960   Landschaft und Böden in Südwestafrika. Die Erde 91(2).
(Landscape and soils in South West Africa.)

Gellert, J. F.
1955   Die niederschlagsschwankungen im hochland von Südwestafrika. Deutsche Demokratische Republik, Meteorologische und Hydrologische Dienstes, Abhandlungen 32.
(Precipitation fluctuation in the highland of South West Africa.)

1961   Ein musterboden auf dem schwarzrand in Südwestafrika. Zeitschrift für Geomorphologie 5: 132-137.
(A patterned ground on the dark rim of South West Africa.)

Geological Survey of South West Africa
n.d.   Bibliography of geology of South West Africa. Windhoek. (unpublished)
An unpublished bibliography which contains references to nearly every work on the surficial features of South West Africa. Periodic additions make this bibliography a most useful source of information.

Gevers, T. W.
1929-   Ice ages in South West Africa. South West African
1931   Scientific Society, Journal 5.

1936   The morphology of western Damaraland and the adjoining Namib Desert of South West Africa. South African Geographical Journal 19:61-79.

1942*a* Western Damaraland and the Namib desert. South African Geographical Journal 19.

1942*b* The morphology of western Damaraland. South African Geographical Journal 19.

1947   The morphology of the Windhoek District, South West Africa. South African Geographical Journal 24.

Haughton, S. H.
1931   The late Tertiary and Recent deposits of the west coast of South Africa. Geological Society of South Africa, Transactions 34:19-57.

Hermann, P.
1908   Beiträge zur geologie von Deutsch Südwestafrika. I: Die geologische beschaffenheit des mittleren und nördlichen teils der Deutschen Kalahari. Deutsche Geologische Gesellschaft, Zeitschrift 61: 259-270.
(Contribution to the geology of German South West Africa. I: The geologic nature of the middle and northern part of the German Kalahari.)

Jaeger, F.
1921   Deutsch Südwestafrika. Hettner Festschrift, Breslau.
(German South West Africa.)

1923   Die grundzüge der oberflächengestalt von Südwestafrika. Gesellschaft für Erdkunde zu Berlin, Zeitschrift (1/2):14-24.

1926   Die Etoscha-pfanne. Mitteilungen aus den Deutschen Schutzgebieten, Berlin, 34.
(The Etosha pan.)

Jaeger, F.
1927*a* Die diamentenwüste Südwestafrikas. Geographische Zeitschrift, Leipzig, 33.
(The diamond desert of South West Africa.)

——— 1927*b* Das Windhoeken hochland. Hans Meyer Festschrift. Koloniale Studien, Berlin.
(The Windhoek highland.)

——— 1932 Zur morphologie der Fischflussenke in Südwestafrica. Universität Basel, Geographische Anstalt, Mitteilungen und Arbeiten 100.
(On the morphology of the Fish River depression in South West Africa.)

——— 1936 Kalkpfannen des östlichen Südwestafrikas. International Geological Congress, 16th, Washington, D. C., 1933, Report 2:741-752.
(Lime pans in eastern South West Africa.)

——— 1939 Die trockenseen der erde. Petermanns Geographische Mitteilungen, Ergänzungsheft 236. 159 p.
(Dry lakes of the world.)

——— 1965 Geographische landschaften Südwestafrikas. S. W. A. Wissenschaftliche Gesellschaft, Windhoek.
(Geographic landscapes of South West Africa.)
This recent book summarizes most of the author's previous work in South West Africa and provides a classical descriptive account of the landscape of the country, by regions.

Jaeger, F. and L. Waibel
1920 Beiträge zur landeskunde von Südwestafrika. Mitteilungen aus den Deutschen Schutzgebieten, Berlin, 14.
(Report on the landscape of South West Africa.)

Jennings, C. M. H.
n.d. Note on erosion cycles in the Bechuanaland Protectorate. Bechuanaland Geological Survey, Lobatsi. (unpublished manuscript) 6 p.

Jeppe, N. F. B.
1952 The geology of the area along the Ugab River, west of the Brandberg. Witwatersrand University (unpublished dissertation).

Jessen, O.
1936 Reisen und forschungen in Angola. Berlin.
(Travels and investigations in Angola.)

Kaiser, E.
1921 Morphogenetische ergebnise auf reisen in Südwestafrika. Deutsche Geographische Tages, 20th, Leipzig, Verhandlung.
(Morphogenetic results from trips in South West Africa.)

——— 1923*a* Was ist eine wüste? Geographische Gesellschaft, Munchen, Mitteilungen 16.
(What is a desert?)

——— 1923*b* Abtragung und auflagerung in der Namib, der südwestafrikanischen küstenwüste. Geologische Charakterbilder, Berlin, Teil 27-28.
(Erosion and deposition in the Namib, the southwest African coastal desert.)

——— 1925 Neue topographische und geologische karten der südlichen Namib Südwestafrikas. Deutschen Geographentag, Breslau, 21.
(New topographic and geologic maps of the southern Namib, South West Africa.)

——— 1926*a* Der bau der südlichen Namib. Bayerische Akademie der Wissenschaften, München, Sitzungsberichte.
(The structure of the southern Namib.)

——— 1926*b* Uber wüstenformen, insbesondere in der Namib Südwestafrikas. Düsseldorfer Geographische Vorträge, Breslau, 3.
(On desert landforms, especially in the Namib of South West Africa.)

——— 1927*a* Die diamantenwüste Südwestafrikas (mit beiträgen von W. Beetz, J. Bohn, R. Martin, R. Rauff, M. Storz, E. Stromer, W. Weissärmel, und K. Willmann). Reimer, Berlin. 2 vols.
(The diamond-desert of South West Africa, with reports by . . .)
An early but comprehensive account of the geology and physical features of the Namib.

——— 1927*b* Surface geology in arid climates. Geological Society of South Africa, Transactions 30.

——— 1928 Uber edaphische bedingte geologische vorgänge und erscheinungen. Bayerische Akademie der Wissenschaften, München, Sitzungsberichte.
(On edaphically caused geologic processes and phenomena.)

King, L. C.
1951 South African scenery. 2nd edition. Oliver and Boyd, London.
Contains an "erosion-cycle map" of central and southern Africa, scale 1:7,500,000.

Knetsch, G.
1938 Uber junge meeresspiegelschwankungen und ihre zeugen an der afrikanischen westküste. Deutsche Geologische Gesellschaft, Zeitschrift 90.
(On recent changes of sea level and its effect on the west coast of Africa.)

——— 1940 Zur frage der küstenbildung und der bildung des Oranjetales in Südwestafrika. Geographische Gesellschaft, Hannover, Sonderveröffentlich 3.
(On the question of coastal development and the formation of the Orange River valley in South West Africa.)

Kokut, I. F.
1948 An investigation into the evidence bearing on recent climatic changes over southern Africa. South Africa, Irrigation Department, Memoir.

Korn, H. and H. Martin
1937 Die jüngere geologische und klimatische geschichte Südwestafrikas. Centralblatt für Mineralogie, Geologie, und Paläontologie, Stuttgart, 11:456-473.
(The early geologic and climatic history of South West Africa.)

Krenkel, E.
  1939 Geologie der Deutschen kolonien in Afrika. Born-
       träger, Berlin.
       (Geology of the German colonies in Africa.)

Lewis, A. D.
  1936a Sand dunes of the Kalahari within the borders of
        the Union. South African Geographical Journal
        19:22-32.

———
  1936b Roaring sands of the Kalahari desert. South Afri-
        can Geographical Journal 19:33-49.

Logan, R. F.
  1960 The central Namib desert, South West Africa.
       National Academy of Sciences—National Research
       Council, Publication 758. 162 p. (ONR Foreign
       Field Research Program, Report 9.)
  A recent summary of the available information on the
  central part of the Namib, between Windhoek and Walvis
  Bay, approximately. Data on climate, vegetation, rock
  type, and trafficability are included; photographs of typical
  features supplement the text.

Mabbutt, J. A.
  1952a The evolution of the Middle Ugab Valley, Damara-
        land. Royal Society of South Africa, Transactions
        32:333-365.

———
  1952b A study of granite relief from South West Africa.
        Geological Magazine 89:87-96.

———
  1955a Erosion surfaces in Little Namaqualand and the
        ages of surface deposits in the southwestern Kala-
        hari. Geological Society of South Africa, Trans-
        actions 58:13-30.
  A brief but adequate account of the nature of the landforms in this part of the Kalahari.

———
  1955b Pediment landforms in Little Namaqualand. Geo-
        graphical Journal 121:77-85.
  A comparison paper to the author's (Mabbutt, 1955a)
  previous work in the arid, southwestern Kalahari, with
  emphasis on pediments and hillslopes.

———
  1957 Physiographic evidence for the age of the Kala-
       hari sands of the southwestern Kalahari. In Pan-
       African Congress on Prehistory, 3rd, Livingstone,
       1955, Proceedings p. 123-126.

MacGregor, A. M.
  1930 Geological notes on a circuit of the Great Makari-
       kari Salt Pan, Bechuanaland Protectorate. Geologi-
       cal Society of South Africa, Transactions 33:
       89-102.

Mackenzie, L. A.
  1946 Report on the Kalahari expedition of 1945. Gov-
       ernment Printer, Pretoria.

———
  1949 Surface water, its measurement, control, and use
       in southern Africa. African Regional Science
       Conference, Comm. A(f)a. Johannesburg.

Martin, H.
  1950 Südwestafrika. Geologische Rundschau 38.
       (South West Africa.)
  A good summary paper on the geology and geography of
  South West Africa by a leading authority on the country.

———
  1961 Hydrology and water balance of some regions
       covered by Kalahari sands in South West Africa.
       Commission for Technical Cooperation in Africa,
       Inter African Hydrology Conference, Publication
       66.

Martin, H. and K. Schalk
  1957 Gletscherschliffe an der wand eines U-tales im
       nördlichen Kaokoveld, Südwestafrikas. Geologische
       Rundschau 46.
       (Glacial polish on the walls of U-shaped valleys
       in the northern Kaokoveld, South West Africa.)

McConnell, R. B.
  1959 Notes on the geology and geomorphology of the
       Bechuanaland Protectorate. p. 175-186. In Aso-
       ciación de Servicios Geológicos Africanos, Actas
       y Trabajos de las Reuniones celebradas en México
       en 1956 (International Geological Congress, 20th,
       Mexico), México, D. F.

Menne, T. C.
  1958 Hydrological research in South Africa and its
       importance to the future development of the coun-
       try. South African Institution of Civil Engineers,
       Transactions 8:164-171.

Michaelsen, H.
  1910 Die kalkpfannen des östlichen Damaralandes.
       Mitteilungen aus den Deutschen Schutzgebieten,
       Berlin, 23:111-134.
       (The lime pans of eastern Damaraland.)

Modgley, D. C.
  n.d. A preliminary survey of the surface water resources
       of the Union of South Africa. University of Natal
       (unpublished dissertation).

Moritz, E.
  1911 Reisestudien aus Südwestafrika. Gesellschaft für
       Erdkunde zu Berlin, Zeitschrift 46.
       (Travel studies from South West Africa.)

Mouta, F.
  1933 Carte géologique de l'Angola (1/2,000,000).
       Notice explicative par F. Mouta et H. O'Donnell.
       Ministério das Colônias, Colônia de Angola. 87 p.,
       12 pl., maps.

———
  1954 Notícia explicativa do esbôço geológico de Angola
       (1:2,000,000). Junta de Investigaçoes do
       Ultramar, Lisbon. 151 p.
       (Explanatory text for the geologic map of Angola
       [first published in 1933].)

Obst, E. and K. Kayser
  1949 Die grosse randstufe auf der ostseite Südafrikas
       und ihr vorland. Geographische Gesellschaft, Han-
       nover. 292 p.
       (The great escarpment on the east side of South
       Africa and its bordering area.)

Papparel, O.
  1909 Durch die Namib nach Lüderitzbucht. Deutsches
       Kolonialblatt 20.
       (Through the Namib to Lüderitz Bay.)

Passarge, S.
  1901 Beitrag zur kenntniss der geologie von British
       Bechuanaland. Gesellschaft für Erdkunde zu Ber-
       lin, Zeitschrift 36:20-68.
       (Contribution to the knowledge of British
       Bechuanaland.)

Passarge, S.
1904 Die Kalahari. Reimer, Berlin. 2 vols.
      (The Kalahari.)
A classic work on most aspects of the Kalahari, these volumes contain a wealth of data and must still be considered a basic reference on the region.

_____

1908 Südafrika. Quelle und Meyer, Leipzig.
      (South Africa.)

_____

1943 Kalkpfannen im Hereroland und in her Kalahari. Beiträge zur Kolonialforschung 5.
      (Lime pans in Hereroland and in the Kalahari.)

Pfalz, R.
1944 Hydrogeologie der Deutschen kolonien in Afrika. Berlin.
      (Hydrogeology of the German colonies in Africa.)

Poldervaart, A.
1957 Kalahari sands. *In* Pan-African Congress on Prehistory, 3rd, Livingstone, 1955, Proceedings p. 106-114.

Portugal. Província de Angola
1961 Carta geológica. Notícia explicativa das fôlhas provisórias Iona e Oncocua, escala 1:250,000. Direção Provincial dos Serviços de Geologia e Minas, Luanda.
      (Explanation of the provisional geological map folios of Iona and Oncocua.)

Range, P.
1910 Die deutsche südkalahari. Gesellschaft für Erdkunde zu Berlin, Zeitschrift 46.
      (The German southern Kalahari.)

_____

1912 The topography and geology of the German South Kalahari. Geological Society of South Africa, Transactions 15.

_____

1914 Das artesische becken in der südkalahari. Deutsche Kolonialblatt, Berlin, 8.
      (The artesian basin in the southern Kalahari.)

_____

1920 Geologisches profil von Tsumeb nach Swakopmund. Mitteilungen aus den Deutschen Schutzgebieten, Berlin, 32.
      (Geologic profile from Tsumeb to Swakopmund.)

_____

1926 Geologie der küstenwüste Südwestafrikas zwischen dem Kuiseb und der Lüderitzbuchteisenbahn. International Geological Congress, 14th, Comptes Rendus 3:901-906.
      (Geology of the coastal desert of South West Africa between the Kuiseb River and the Lüderitz Bay railway.)

_____

1927 Die küstenwüste zwischen Lüderitzbucht und Swakopmund in Südwestafrika. Petermanns Geographische Mitteilungen 73.
      (The coastal desert between Lüderitz Bay and Swakopmund in South West Africa.)

_____

1937 Südwestafrika, geologie und bergbau. Deutsche Geologische Gesellschaft, Zeitschrift 89.
      (South West Africa, geology and structure.)

Reuning, E.
1913 Eine reise längs der küste Lüderitzbucht-Swakopmund im Februar-März, 1912; karte, 1:400,000. Mitteilungen aus den Deutschen Schutzgebieten, Berlin, 26.
      (A trip along the coast from Lüderitz Bay to Swakopmund in February-March 1912; map at a scale of 1:400,000 included.)

_____

1923 Geologische ubersichtskarte des mittleron teiles von Südwestafrika, 1:1,000,000. Giessen.
      (Generalized geologic map of the middle part of South West Africa, scale 1:1,000,000.)

Reuning, E. and H. Martin
1957 Die Prä-Karroo-Landschaft, die Karroo-sedimente und Karroo-eruptivgesteine des südlichen Kaokofeldes in Südwestafrika. Neues Jahrbuch für Mineralogie, Abhandlungen 91:193-212.
      (The pre-Karroo landscape, Karroo sediments, and Karroo volcanics of the southern Kaokoveld in South West Africa.)

Rimann, E.
1916 Beitrag zur geologie von Deutsch-Südwestafrika. Deutsche Geologische Gesellschaft, Zeitschrift 68.
      (Report on the geology of German South West Africa.)

Roberts, D. F.
1952 Notes on the relationship between rainfall and runoff. South Africa Institution of Civil Engineers, Transactions 2(11).

_____

1954 Water resources of South Africa: What of the future? South African Institution of Civil Engineers, Transactions 4:119-128.

Rogers, A. W.
1934 The build of the Kalahari. South African Geographical Journal 17:3-12.

_____

1935 The "solid" geology of the Kalahari. Royal Society of South Africa, Transactions 23:165-176.

_____

1936 The surface geology of the Kalahari. Royal Society of South Africa, Transactions 24:57-80.

_____

1940 Pans. South African Geographical Journal 22: 55-60.

Schenk, A.
1901 Deutsch-Südwest-Afrika im vergleich zum übrigen Südafrika. Deutsche Geographische Tages, 8th, Breslau, Verhandlung.
      (German South West Africa compared to the remainder of South Africa.)

Schneiderhöhn, H.
1931 Zwei bilder aus der Namibwüste Südwestafrikas. Naturwissenschaften, Berlin, 61.
      (Two views on the Namib desert of South West Africa.)

Schultze, L.
1907 Aus Namaland und Kalahari. Jena.
      (Through Namaland and the Kalahari.)

Schwartz, E. H. L.
1920 The Kalahari or thirstland redemption. T. Maskew Miller, Cape Town. 163 p.

Schwartz, E. H. L.
1926   The northern Kalahari. South African Geographical Journal 9:27-36.
Simpson, E. S. W. and D. H. Davies
1957   Observations on the Fish River canyon in South West Africa. Royal Society of South Africa, Transactions 35(2).
Smith, D. M.
1961   The geology of the area around the Khan and Swakop rivers in South West Africa. Witwatersrand University (unpublished thesis).
Soares de Carvalho, G.
1961   Geologia do deserto de Moçâmedes (Angola). Junta de Investigaçoes do Ultramar, Lisbon, Memórias 26.
(Geology of the Moçâmedes desert.)
The most authoritative single work on the geology and geography of the Moçâmedes desert area of southern Angola. This report includes many useful maps, cross sections, and other illustrations, in addition to a wealth of data on surficial features. The author's subsequent work (1962) on the characteristics of sands and sand deposits in southern Angola should be regarded as a useful companion work.

1962   O interêsse do estudo sedimentológico das areias da baía de Moçâmedes e das proias do seus arredores (Angola). Garcia de Orta 10:511-526.
(On a sedimentological study of the sands in the Moçâmedes area and its environment.)
South West Africa. Surveyor-General.
1963   Geological map of South West Africa. Scale 1:1,000,000. Windhoek, South West Africa.
Stapff, F. M.
1887   Karte des unteren Kuisebtales. Petermanns Geographische Mitteilungen 33.
(Map of the lower Kuiseb valley.)
Stengel, H. W.
1963   Wasserwirtschaft in Südwestafrika. Afrika-Verlag der Kreis, Windhoek.
(Hydrology in South West Africa.)
The most modern and authoritative summary that exists of all aspects of the hydrology of South West Africa. This volume contains country-wide data on channel and flow characteristics of streams in the Namib, present and proposed sites of gaging stations and dams and reservoirs, an outline of overall water-resources projects and problems in the country, and useful individual reports on other matters such as precipitation and sand control measures.

1964   Die riviere der Namib und ihr zulauf sum Atlantik. I: Kuiseb und Swakop. Namib Desert Research Station, Scientific Paper 22.
(The rivers of the Namib and their discharge into the Atlantic.)
Presents a compilation of data on the flow characteristics of the Kuiseb river; the Kuiseb's channel separates the sands of the southern Namib from the gravel plains to the north. This study is rather unique because there are few streams in truly arid areas that are well-documented through time. Maps and photographs of the Kuiseb drainage area are included.
Stromer von Reichenbach, W.
1896   Die geologie der Deutschen schutzgebiete in Afrika. München und Leipzig.
(The geology of the German protectorates in Africa.)

Taljaard, M. S.
1945   On geomorphic units and geomorphic provinces in South Africa. South African Geographical Journal 27:28-31.
Tönnesen, T.
1917   The South West Africa Protectorate. Geographical Journal 49.
Union of South Africa
1946   Report on the Kalahari expedition of 1945; being a further investigation into the water resources of the Kalahari and their relationship to the climate of South Africa. Government Printer, Pretoria.
Union of South Africa. Desert Encroachment Committee
1959   Report. Government Printer, Pretoria. 27 p.
Vageler, P.
1920   Beobachtungen in südwest-Angola und im Ambolande. Gesellschaft für Erdkunde zu Berlin, Zeitschrift p. 179-193.
(Observations in southwest Angola and in Amboland.)
Van der Walt, C. F. J.
1940   Roaring sands. South African Geographical Journal 22:35-39.
van Straten, O. J.
1955   The geology and groundwaters of the Ghanzi cattle route. Bechuanaland Protectorate Geological Survey, Annual Report, p. 28-39.
Waldron, F. W.
1901   The appearance and disappearance of a mud island at Walvis Bay. South African Philosophical Society, Transactions 11.
Watson, A. C.
1930   The guano islands of South West Africa. Geographical Review 20:631-641.
Wayland, E. J.
1953   More about the Kalahari. Geographical Journal 119:49-56.

1954   Outlines of prehistory and Stone Age climatology in the Bechuanaland Protectorate. Académie Royale des Sciences Coloniales, Brussels, Section des Sciences Naturelles et Médicales, Mémoires 25. 46 p.
Wellington, J. H.
1938   The Kunene River and Etoscha plain. South African Geographical Journal 20:21-32.

1939   The Greater Etoscha basin. South African Geographical Journal 21:47-48.

1955   South Africa, a geographical study. Cambridge University Press. 2 vols.
Wicht, C. L.
1947   Hydrological research in South African forestry. British Empire Forestry Conference, 5th. Department of Forestry, Pretoria.
Wipplinger, O.
1958   The storage of water in sand. South West Africa Administration, Department of Water Affairs, Windhoek.

1961   Deterioration of catchment yields in arid regions, its causes and possible remedial measures. Commission for Technical Cooperation in Africa, Inter African Conference on Hydrology, Nairobi, Publication 66.

SECTION IV
THE SAHARA

Includes works cited in the text discussions on: Sudan, Egypt, Chad, Nigeria, Niger, Mali, Senegal, Mauritania, Spanish Sahara, Morocco, Algeria, Tunisia, and Libya.

Akester, R.
1958   Tibesti, land of the Tebou. Geographical Magazine 21:12-26.

Algeria. Service de la Carte Géologique de l'Algérie
1952   Carte géologique de l'Algérie. Rev.
       (Geological map of Algeria, scale 1:5,000,000.)

———   n.d.   Carte géologique du Sahara.
       (Geological map of the Sahara, scale 1:500,000.)

Alia Medina, M.
1943   Las aguas superficiales y subterráneas en el Sahara español. Africa 24:16-20.
       (The surface and subsurface waters of the Spanish Sahara.)

———   1945   Características morfográficas y geológicas de la zona septentrional del Sáhara español. Consejo Superior de Investigaciones Científicas, Madrid, Instituto de Ciencias Naturales, Trabajos, ser. Geológica 2. 260 p.
       (Morphologic and geologic characteristics of the northern zone of Spanish Sahara.)

———   1946   La posición tectónica del Sáhara español en el conjunto africano. Real Sociedad Geográfica, Boletín 82(1-6):179-196.
       (The tectonic position of Spanish Sahara in relation to Africa.)

———   1949   Contribución al conocimiento geomorfológico de las zonas centrales Sáhara español. Instituto de Estudios Africanos, Madrid. 232 p.
       (Contribution to the geomorphology of the central zones of the Spanish Sahara.)

———   1952   La arquitectura geológica del Sahara español. Instituto de Estudios Africanos, Madrid, Archivos 6.
       (The geologic architecture of the Spanish Sahara.)

Alimen, H.
1953   Variations granulométriques et morphoscopiques du sable le long de profils dunaires au Sahara occidental. Centre National de la Recherche Scientifique, Colloques Internationaux 35:219-235.
       (Granulometric and morphoscopic variations of sand along dune profiles in the western Sahara.)

———   1965   The Quaternary era in the northwest Sahara. Geological Society of America, Special Paper 84: 273-291.
       A review of current Quaternary research in Algeria; includes references to many pertinent works on desert sands.

Alimen, H., M. Buron, and J. Chavaillon
1958   Caractères granulométriques de quelques dunes d'Erg du Sahara nord-occidental. Académie des Sciences, Paris, Comptes Rendus 247:1758-1761.
       (Grand size characteristics of some dunes of the northwest Saharan erg.)

Alimen, H. and D. Fenet
1954   Granulométrie de sables d'erg aux environs de la Saoura (Sahara occidental). Société Géologique de France, Compte Rendu 9-10:183-185.
       (Grain size of erg sand from the vicinity of Saoura, western Sahara.)

Alimen, H. *et al.*
1957   Sables quaternaires du Sahara nord-occidental (Saoura-Ougarta); avec la collaboration de D. Doudoux, J. Ferrer, et M. Caddoux. Service de la Carte Géologique de l'Algérie, Bulletin 15. 207 p.
       (Quaternary sands of the northwestern Sahara (Saoura-Ougarta).)
A comprehensive account of the characteristics of Algerian desert sands and dunes in quantitative terms based upon the author's extensive previous work (Alimen, 1953; Alimen and Fenet, 1954; Alimen, Buron, and Chavaillon, 1958).

Amin, M. S.
1955   Dome regional features of the Precambrian in the central Eastern Desert, Egypt. Desert Institute, Egypt, Bulletin 5(1).

Anderson, R. V. V.
1936   Geology in the coastal Atlas of western Algeria. Geological Society of America, Memoir 4. 450 p.

Andrew, G.
1944   Notes on Quaternary climates in Sudan. Sudan Government, Soil Conservation Report, Appendix 25.

———   1948a   Geology of the Sudan. p. 84-128. *In* J. D. Tothill, ed., Agriculture in the Sudan. Oxford University Press.
A good review of the general geology of Sudan. A companion paper by the author (Andrew, 1948b) on the Sudan Plain and its surficial features should also be consulted.

———   1948b   The development of the Sudan Plain during the Quaternary. *In* J. D. Tothill, ed., Agriculture in the Sudan. Oxford University Press.

Anonymous
1953   Un fleuve d'Afrique occidentale française, le Niger. Cahiers Hebdomadaires de l'Afrique Occidentale Française 32.

———   1955   Un fleuve d'Afrique occidentale française, le Niger. Chronique d'Outre-Mer 18.

———   1960   République du Niger. Rev. Encyclop. Af. Côte-d'Ivoire, suppl. au 3.

Arévalo, P. and A. Arribas
1960   Estudio mineralógico de los sedimentos cuaternarios actuales de la región occidental del Sahara meridional español. Estudios Geológicos 16(4): 163-185.
       (Mineralogical studies of Quaternary sediments of the western region of the southern Spanish Sahara.)

Arkell, A. J.
1949a   The Old Stone Age in the Sudan. Sudan Antiquities Service, Occasional Paper 1.

———   1949b   Early Khartoum. Oxford University Press.

Arkell, A. J.
1953   Shaheinab; an account of the excavation of a Neolithic occupation site carried out for the Sudan Antiquities Service in 1949-50. Oxford University Press.

Arribas, A.
1960   Las formaciones metamórficas del Sahara español y sus relaciones con el precámbrico de otras regiones africanas. International Geological Congress, 21st, Copenhagen, Report 9:51-58.
(The metamorphic rocks of the Spanish Sahara and their relation to the Precambrian of other African regions.)

Ascherson, P.
1887   Die nördliche isthmus-wüste Agyptiens. Gesellschaft für Erdkunde zu Berlin, Zeitschrift 22.
(The northern Egyptian isthmus-desert.)

Attia, M. I.
1951   The Nile Basin, a short account of its topography, geology, and structure. Desert Institute, Egypt, Bulletin 1(1).
A general account of the surficial features of the Nile Basin.

1954   Ground water in Egypt. Desert Institute, Egypt, Bulletin 4(1).

Aufrère, L.
1931   Le cycle morphologique des dunes. Annales Géographie 41:362-385.
(The morphologic cycle of dunes.)

1932   Morphologie dunaire et météorologie saharienne. Association de Géographes Français, Bulletin 56: 34-47.
(Dune morphology and Saharan meteorology.)

1933   Les dunes sahariennes et les vents alizes. Association Française pour l'Avancement des Sciences, Bulletin 62:131-138.
(The Saharan dunes and the trade winds.)

Auvray, C., P. Dubreuil, and R. Lefevre
1958-   Monographie du Niger. Office de la Recherche
1961   Scientifique et Technique Outre-Mer, Paris. 5 vols.
The most comprehensive summary of available information on the hydrology of the Niger River in existence.

Awad, H.
1945   Structure et relief de la Libye méridionale. Annales de Géographie 53-54:192-203.
(Structure and relief of southern Libya.)

1948   Le Gilfel-Kebir et l'Ouenat. Société Royale de Géographie d'Egypte, Bulletin 22(3/4):137-150.
(The Gilf Kebir and 'Uweinat.)

1952   Présentation d'une carte morphologique du Sinai. Desert Institute, Egypt, Bulletin 2(1).
(A morphologic map of Sinai.)

1963   Some aspects of the geomorphology of Morocco related to the Quaternary climate. Geographical Journal 129:129-139.

Awad, M.
1930   Some stages in the evolution of the Nile River. International Geographical Congress, 12th, Cambridge, Proceedings, p. 267-288.

Bagnold, R. A.
1933   A further journey through the Libyan desert. Geographical Journal 82:103-129.

1937   The transport of sand by wind. Geographical Journal 89:409-438.

1941   The physics of blown sand and desert dunes. William Morrow, New York.
This book is still the most authoritative single work available on the dynamics of windblown sand.

Bagnold, R. A. et al.
1939   An expedition to the Gilf Kebir and Uweinat. Geographical Journal 93:281-313.

Ball, J.
1927   Problems of the Libyan desert. Geographical Journal 70:21-38, 105-128, 209-224.

1933   The Qattara depression. Geographical Journal 82: 289-314.

1939   Contributions to the geography of Egypt. Survey and Mines Department, Government Press, Cairo. 308 p.

Barbour, K. M.
1961   The Republic of the Sudan; a regional geography. University of London Press, London. 292 p.

Barton, D. C.
1916   Notes on the disintegration of granite in Egypt. Journal of Geology 24:382-393.

Beadnell, H. J. L.
1909   An Egyptian oasis. Murray, London. 262 p.

1910   The sand dunes of the Libyan Desert; their origin, form, and rate of movement, considered in relation to the geological and meteorological conditions of the region. Geographical Journal 35:379-395.

Beaudet, G.
1962   Types d'évolution actuelle des cersants dans le Rif occidental. Revue de Géographie du Maroc 1-2: 41-46.
(Modes of present slope evolution in the western Rif.)

Becker, C.
1965   Über strukturböden im Hoggar-Massiv. Zeitschrift für Geomorphologie 9:457-460.
(On patterned ground in the Ahaggar massif.)

Bélime, E.
1931   L'hydrographie ancienne du Niger. Union Géodésique et Géophysique Internationale, Conseil International de Recherches, Section Hydrologique Scientifique, Bulletin 17:31-34.

Bell, S. V.
1964   First annual report of the Arid Zone Research Unit for the period August 1962 until July 1964. University of Khartoum, Board for Arid Zone Research and Arid Zone Research Unit. 15 p.

Bellair, P.
1944   Les eaux superficielles et les ressources probables en eaux profondes du Fezzan (Sahara oriental). Académie des Sciences, Paris, Comptes Rendus 219:557-559.
(Surface waters and the probable ground-water resources of the Fezzan.)

Benchetrit, M.
1954 Le problème de l'érosion des sols dans les monts Beni-Chougran. Université de Strasbourg, Laboratoire de Géographie, Travaux. Editions SEDES, Paris.

Bense, C.
1961 Les formations sédimentaires de la Mauritanie méridionale et du Mali nord-occidental (Afrique de l'Ouest). Thèse sciences, Nancy, 271 p.
(The sedimentary formations of southern Mauritania and northwestern Mali, west Africa.)

Berkaloff, E. (ed.)
1949-   Recueil des observations hydrométriques. Bureau
1959   d'Inventaire des Ressources Hydrauliques, Tunis.
(Compilation of hydrometric observations.)

Bernard, A.
1910 Sahara algérien et Sahara soudanais. Annales de Géographie 19:260-270.
(Algerian Sahara and Sudanian Sahara.)

Berry, L.
1962a Large-scale alluvial islands in the White Nile. Revue de Géomorphologie Dynamique 12: 105-109.

1962b The characteristics and mode of formation of Nile islands between Malakal and Sabaloka. Hydrobiological Research Unit, Khartoum, Report 8.

1963a A note on the coastline of the Sudan. University of Khartoum, Geographical Magazine 1.

1963b The coastline of the Sudan. Sudan Notes and Records.

1963c A morphological map of the Khor Eit region, Red Sea coast. International Geographical Union, Sub-Commission on Geomorphic Mapping, Strasbourg.

1964 Geographical research in the Sudan; a review and prospect. Philosophical Society of the Sudan, Khartoum, Annual Conference, Proceedings 12:29-57.

Berry, L., A. J. Whiteman, and S. V. Bell
1966 Some radiocarbon dates and their geomorphological significance, emerged reef complex of the Sudan. Zeitschrift für Geomorphologie 10: 119-143.

Bhalotra, Y. P. R.
1958 Duststorms at Khartoum. Sudan Meteorological Service, Memoir 1. 74 p.

1960 Spatial variability of rainfall in the Jebel Marra region. Sudan Meteorological Service, Special Note 1.

Birot, P., R. Capot-Rey, and J. Dresch
1955 Recherches morphologiques dans le Sahara central. Institut de Recherches Sahariennes, Travaux 13: 13-74.
(Morphological research in the central Sahara.)

Birot, P. and F. Joly
1951 Observations sur la morphologie de l'Anti-Atlas oriental. Société des Sciences Naturelles et Physiques du Maroc, Bulletin 30:209-229.
(Observations on the morphology of the eastern Anti-Atlas.)

Blanchot, A.
1956a Organisation des missions de reconnaissance géologique en régions sahariennes. Chronique des Mines d'Outre-Mer 24:94-98.
(Organization of geologic reconnaissance missions to Saharan regions.)

1956b Rapport de tournée à Tessalit (Soudan). Direction Fédérale des Mines et de la Géologie, Dakar. 9 p.

Blanck, E. and S. Passarge
1925 Die chemische verwitterung in der ägyptischen wüste. Hamburgische Universität, Abhandlungen aus dem Gebeit der Auslandskunde 17.
(Chemical weathering in the Egyptian desert.)

Bouchardeau, A.
1956 Le Lac Tchad. Annuaire Hydrologique de la France d'Outre-Mer. Office de la Recherche Scientifique et Technique Outre-Mer, Paris.
This report and a companion work by Bouchardeau and Lefevre (1957) are basic references on all aspects of the hydrology of Lake Chad.

Bouchardeau, A. and R. Lefevre
1957 Monographie du Lac Tchad. Office de la Recherche Scientifique et Technique Outre-Mer, Paris.

Boulaine, J.
1953a L'érosion éolienne des sols salés et la morphologie superficielle des chotts et des sebkhas. Société d'Histoire Naturelle de l'Afrique du Nord, Algeria.
(Eolian erosion of saline soils and the surface morphology of Algerian salt lagoons and sebkhas.)
Discusses the effect of winds on various pans and flats in Algeria and describes their surface morphology.

1953b Remarques sur les formations quaternaires des plaines de la Mina et du Bas-Chelif. Société de Géographie et d'Archéologie d'Oran, Bulletin.
(Remarks on the Quaternary formations of the plains of Mina and the lower Chelif.)

1956 Les lunettes des basses plaines oranaises; formations éoliennes argileuses liées à l'extension de sols salins; la Sebkha de Ben Ziane, la Dépression de Chantrit. Inqua Congress, 4th, Rome-Pisa, 1953, Résumés des Communication 1:143-151.
(The lunettes of the lower Oranian plains. Eolian formations related to the extension of saline soils of the Sebkha Ben Ziane, the Depression of Chantrit.)

Bourcart, J.
1927 Premiers résultats d'une étude sur le Quaternaire marocain. Société Géologique de France, Bulletin 27:3-33.
(Preliminary results of a study on the Quaternary of Morocco.)

Braquaval, B.
1957 Etudes d'écoulement en régime désertique: Massif de l'Ennedi et region nord du Mortcha. Office de la Recherche Scientifique et Technique Outre-Mer, Paris. 92 p.
(Studies of runoff in a desert environment: the Ennedi Massif.)
This ORSTROM report on the hydrology of small drainage basins in the Sahara, and that by Roche (1958), present the only available data on streamflow in the Ennedi region of Chad.

Brasseur, P.
1964 Bibliographie générale du Mali. Institut Français d'Afrique Noire, Catalogues et Documents 16. 461 p.
A briefly annotated bibliography of Mali with approximately 5,000 entries. The topics covered include geology, geomorphology, hydrology, and others.

Brosset, D.
1939 Essai sur les ergs du Sahara occidental. Institut Français de l'Afrique Noire, Bulletin 1:657-690.
(Essay on the ergs of the western Sahara.)

Büdel, J.
1955 Reliefgeneration und plio-pleistozäner klimawandel im Hoggar-gebirge (Zentral Sahara). Erdkunde 9:100-115.
(Relief production and Plio-Pleistocene climatic change in the Ahaggar highlands, central Sahara.)

——— 1963 Die pliozänen und quartären pluvialzeiten der Sahara. Eiszeitalter und Gegenwart 14.
(The Pliocene and Quaternary pluvial periods in the Sahara.)

Busch-Zantner, R.
1934 Die spanische West-Sahara. Geographische Zeitschrift 40(9):321-332.
(The Spanish West-Sahara.)

Bütler, H.
1922 Contributions à la géologie de l'Ahaggar. International Geological Congress, 13th, Brussels, Comptes Rendus 2:819-848.
(Contributions to the geology of Ahaggar.)

Butzer, K. W.
1958 Studien zum vor- und frühgeschichtlichen landschaftswandel der Sahara. I: Die ursachen, usw. II: Das ökologische problem des neolitischen felsbilder, usw. Akademie der Wissenschaften und der Literatur in Mainz, Mathematik-Naturwissenschaftliche Klasse 1.
(Studies on the pre- and early-historic changes of Saharan landscape. I: The causes, etc. II: The ecological problem of neolithic rock inscriptions, etc.)

——— 1959a Contribution to the Pleistocene geology of the Nile Valley. Erdkunde 13:46-67.

——— 1959b Studien zum vor- und fruhgeschichtlichen landschaftswandel der Sahara. III: Die naturwissenschaft Ägyptiens wahrend der vorgeschichte und der dynastischen zeit. Akademie der Wissenschaften und der Literatur in Mainz. Mathematik-Naturwissenschaftliche Klasse 2:43-122.
(Studies on the pre- and early-historic changes of Saharan landscape. III: The natural science of Egypt during prehistory and dynastic time.)

Byramjee, R.
1958 Sur le complexe éruptif de Denat, Adrar des Iforas (Sahara méridional). Société Géologique de France, Comptes Rendus, p. 233-237.
(On the volcanic complex of Denat, Adrar des Iforas, southern Sahara.)

——— 1959 Le complexe éruptif de l'Adrar des Iforas, Sahara Méridional. Bureau de Recherches Minières de l'Algerie, Bulletin Scientifique et Economique, p. 5-23.
(The volcanic complex of the Adrar des Iforas, southern Sahara.)

Cailleux, A.
1949 Action des écoulements liquides dans la géomorphologie du Sud oranais. Académie des Sciences, Paris, Comptes Rendus 229:669-671.
(The geomorphic process of runoff in southern Oran.)

——— 1962 El Richat: dôme arasé, surbaissé ou cratère bombé. Notes Africanes 93:27-29.
(El Richat: depressed flattened dome or crater.)

Caire, A.
1954 L'Atlas tellien méridional entre la chaîne du Djurdjura et la partie occidentale des monts du Hodna (Algérie). Université de Besançon, Annales Scientifiques 9(6), sér. 2, Géologie 1, p. 35-82.
(The southern Atlas Tell between the Djurdjura range and the western part of the Hodna Hills, Algeria.)

——— 1957 Etude géologie de la région des Biban. Service de la Carte Géologique de l'Algerie, Bulletin n.s. 16. 816 p.

——— 1963 Phénomènes tectoniques de biseautage et de rabotage en Tell Algérien. Revue de Géographie Physique et de Géologie Dynamique 5:299-325.
(The tectonic phenomena of bevelling and planing in the Algerian Tell.)

Capot-Rey, R.
1927 Relief de la Haute Zousfana à l'est de Colomb-Bechar. Annales de Géographie 36:537-539.
(Relief of Upper Zousfana to the east of Colomb-Bechar.)

——— 1943 La morphologie de l'erg occidental. Institut de Recherches Sahariennes, Travaux 2:69-103.
(Morphology of the western erg.)

——— 1945 Dry and humid morphology in the Western Erg. Geographical Review 35:391-407.

——— 1951 Sur quelques formes de relief de l'Adrar des Ifoghas. Institut de Recherches Sahariennes, Travaux 7:195-199.

——— 1952 Les limites du Sahara français. Institut de Recherches Sahariennes, Travaux 8:23-48.
(The limits of the French Sahara.)

——— 1953a Recherches géographiques sur les confins algero-libiens. Institut de Recherches Sahariennes, Travaux 10:33-73.
(Geographical research in Algeria-Libya.)

——— 1953b Le Sahara français. Presses Universitaires de France, Paris. 564 p.
(The French Sahara.)
A good descriptive account of the general surficial features of the former French Sahara. For more general coverage of the entire Sahara the work of Gautier (1928) is still useful.

Capot-Rey, R.
1957 Sur une forme d'érosion éolienne dans le Sahara français. Koninklijk Nederlandsch Aardrijkskundig Genootschap, Tijdschrift 74:242-247.
(On a form of eolian erosion in the French Sahara.)

1963 Contribution à l'étude et à la représentation des barkhanes. Institut de Recherches Sahariennes, Travaux 22:37-59.
(Contribution to the study and occurrence of barchans.)

Capot-Rey, R. and F. Capot-Rey
1948 Le déplacement des sables éoliens et la formation des dunes desertiques d'après R. A. Bagnold. Institut de Recherches Sahariennes, Travaux 5:47-80.
(The transport of eolian sand and the formation of desert dunes, according to R. A. Bagnold.)
The authors apply Bagnold's theory of sand transport to dunes of the Sahara and discuss their mode of formation. The data presented in this report are supplemented by more recent work on Saharan barchan dunes (Capot-Rey, 1963).

Capot-Rey, R. and M. Grémion
1964 Remarques sur quelques sables sahariens. Institut de Recherches Sahariennes, Travaux 23:153-163.
(Remarks on some Saharan sands.)

Cardona, J.
1954- Etude hydrologique de l'oued Isser. Service de la
1955 Colonisation et de l'Hydraulique, Annuaire Hydrologique de l'Algérie, p. 7-37.
(Hydrologic study of the Wadi Isser.)

Carnero Ruiz, I.
1955 Vocabulario geográfico-sahárico. Instituto de Estudios Africanos, Madrid. 287 p.
(Sahara geographic lexicon.)

Castany, G.
1951 Carte géologique de la Tunisie. Direction des Travaux Publics, Service des Mines de l'Industrie et de l'Energie, Tunis. 2 sheets.
(Geologic map of Tunisia, scale 1:500,000.)

1953 Notice explicative de la carte géologique de la Tunisie. Direction des Travaux Publics, Service des Mines de l'Industrie et de l'Energie, Tunis.
(Explanation of the geologic map of Tunisia.)

Cayeux, L.
1926 Origine des sables des dunes sahariennes. Congrès Géologique International, 14th, Madrid, Comptes Rendus 3:783-788.
(Origin of the sand of Saharan dunes.)

Choubert, G.
1952 Géologie du Maroc. Histoire géologique du domaine de l'Anti-Atlas. Service Géologique du Maroc, Rabat, Notes et Mémoires 100.
(Geology of Morocco. Geologic history of the Anti Atlas region.)

1955 Notes sur la géologie des terrains récents des Doukkala. Service Géologique, Rabat, Notes et Mémoires 13:9-46.
(Notes on the geology of the Recent deposits of Doukkala.)

Chudeau, R.
1909 Notes géologiques sur la Mauritanie. Géographie 20:9-24.

1911 Notes sur la géologie de la Mauritanie. Société Géologique de France, Bulletin 11:413-428.

1916 Recherches hypsométriques dans le bassin de Tombouctou. Annales de Géographie 25:190-205.
(Hypsometric investigations in the Tombouctou basin.)

1918 La dépression du Faguibine. Annales de Géographie 27:43-60.

1920 Etudes sur les dunes sahariennes. Annales de Géographie 29:334-351.
(Studies on Saharan dunes).

1921a L'hydrographie ancienne du Sahara. Académie des Sciences, Paris, Comptes Rendus 172:457-460.
(The ancient hydrology of the Sahara.)

1921b L'hydrographie ancienne du Sahara (ses conséquences biogéographiques). Revue Scientifique 8:193-198.
(The ancient hydrology of the Sahara, its biogeographic consequences.)

Clarke, J. I. and K. Orrell
1958 An assessment of some morphometric methods. University of Durham, Department of Geography, Occasional Paper 2.

Clayton, P. A.
1951 The silica glass sand of the Libyan Desert. Desert Institute, Egypt, Bulletin 1(2).

Clayton, W. D.
1957 The swamps, sand and dunes of Hadejia. Nigerian Geographical Journal 1:31.

Clos-Arceduc, A.
1955 Le fleuve fossile de Tombouctou. Tropiques 371:36-41.
(The fossil river of Tombouctou)

Commission Scientifique du Logone et du Tchad
1956 Le Bahr el Ghazala. Office de la Recherche Scientifique et Technique Outre-Mer, Paris. 8 p.

Compagnie des Techniques Hydrauliques Agricoles
1957 Etude hydrologique des oueds Zeroud et Merguellil. Grenoble. Rapport Rct 395.
(Hydrologic study of Wadis Zeroud and Merguellil.)

Conant, L. C. and G. H. Goudarzi
1964 Geologic map of the Kingdom of Libya, at 1:2,000,000 scale. U. S. Geological Survey, Miscellaneous Geologic Investigations, Map I-350A.

Coque, R.
1955a Notes morphologiques sur les grands chotts tunisiens. Association de Géographes Français, Bulletin 253-254:174-185.
(Morphological notes on the vast Tunisian gravel plains.)

1955b Les croûtes gypseuses du Sud tunisien. Société des Sciences Naturelles de Tunisie, Bulletin 8:217-236.
(The gypsiferous crusts of southern Tunisia.)

Coque, R.
1955c Morphologie et croûte dans le Sud-Tunisien. Annales de Géographie 64:359-370.
(Morphology and surficial crust in southern Tunisia.)

1958 Morphologie de la Tunisie présaharienne. Institut de Recherches Sahariennes, Travaux 17:59-81.
(Morphology of Tunisia above the Sahara.)

1960 L'évolution des versants en Tunisie présaharienne. Zeitschrift für Geomorphologie, Supplementband 1:172-177.
(Evolution of slopes in Tunisia above the Sahara.)

1962 La Tunisie présaharienne. Colin, Paris. 488 p.
(Tunisia above the Sahara.)
A basic reference volume on Tunisia with good descriptive accounts of the general surficial features.

Coque, R. and M. Van Campo
1960 Palynologie et géomorphologie dans le Sud tunisien. Pollen et Spores 2:275-284.
(Palynology and geomorphology in southern Tunisia.)

Cornet, A.
1952 Essai sur l'hydrogéologie du Grand Erg Occidental et des régions limitrophes. Institut de Recherches Sahariennes, Travaux 8:71-122.
(Analysis of the hydrogeology of the Grand Erg Occidental and its bordering regions.)

Cornish, V.
1900 On desert sand dunes bordering the Nile delta. Geographical Journal 15:1-32.

Côte, M.
1957 Quelques aspects de la morphologie de l'Ahaggar. Revue de Géographie, Lyon, 32:321-332.
(Some aspects of the morphology of Ahaggar.)

Coubert, G.
1955 Notes sur la géologie des terrains récents des Doukkala. Service Géologique du Maroc, Notes et Mémoires 13:9-46.
(Notes on the geology of the recent deposits of Doukkala.)

Coursin, A. *et al.*
1956 Etude des barkanes à l'est de Port-Etienne. TPOAF Report. Dakar. 17 p.
(Study of barchans east of Port-Etienne.)

Crema, C.
1936 Risalti crestiformi e "seghife," due tipi morfologici proprii delle regioni aride osservati in Libia. International Geological Congress, 16th, Washington, 1933, Report 2:737-740.
(Ribs and "seghife," two morphologic types peculiar to arid regions, observed in Libya.)

Cvijanovich, B. G.
1953 Sur le rôle des dunes en relation avec le système hydrologique de la nappe souterraine du Grand Erg. Institut de Recherches Sahariennes, Travaux 9:131-136.
(On the role of dunes in the hydrologic system of the subterranean sheet of the Grand Erg.)

Dagallier, X.
1955 Oued Megenin. Campagne de mesures hydrologiques 1954-55. Neyrpic, Grenoble.
(Wadi Megenin hydrologic data for 1954-55.)

Dalloni, M.
1934- Mission au Tibesti. Académie des Sciences, Paris,
1935 Mémoires 1-2.

1951 Sur la genèse et l'âge des "terrains a croûte" Nord Africains. Centre National de la Recherche Scientifique, Colloques Internationaux 35:278-285.
(On the genesis and age of the North African "crust terrains.")

Dars, R.
1957 Sur un phénomène de capture observé dans la boucle nord du Baoulé, affluent du Sénégal (Soudan). French West Africa, Direction des Mines et Géologie, Bulletin 20:131-133.
(On the phenomenon of stream capture observed in the northern bend of the Baoulé River, tributary to the Senegal River.)

Daveau, S.
1959 Recherches morphologiques sur la région de Bandiagara. Institut Français d'Afrique Noire, Mémoire 56.
(Morphologic research in the Bandiagara region)

1963 Etude de versants gréseux dans le Sahel mauritanien. Centre Document. Cartogr. Géogr., Mém. Docum. 9(3):3-30.
(Study of sandy slopes in Mauritanian Sahel.)

1964 Façonnement des versants de l'Adrar Mauritanien. Zeitschrift für Geomorphologie, Supplementband 5:118-130.
(Formation of the slopes of the Adrar, Marutiania.)

Davies, R. G.
1955 Report on a preliminary photogeologic interpretation of part of the Hoggar Massif, Algeria. Hunting Aerosurveys, Ltd. 10 p.

1956a Mission to the Hoggar. Hunting Group Review, Autumn issue, p. 9-15.

1956b Report on the photogeological interpretation of two areas in the Ahaggar Massif of the central Sahara. Hunting Aerosurveys, Ltd. 50 p.
Illustrates the use of aerial photographs to map the Ahaggar area. Supplementary information is provided by Perret (1952, 1953), Côte (1957), Büdel (1955), Gautier (1926), and Lelubre (1943) on this major Saharan massif.

Deleau, P.
1957 Le Guir et la Saoura, cours d'eau du Sahara oranaise. La Nature 3122.
(The Guir and Saoura and their course in the Sahara.)

Desio, A.
1935 Studi geologici sulla Cirenaica, sul deserto Libico, sulla Tripolitania e sul Fezzan orientali. Missione scientifica della R. Accademia d'Italia a Cufra (1931), vol. 1. R. Accademia d'Italia, Rome, Viaggi di Studio ed Esplorazioni 3. 466 p.

1937 Geologie e morfologie. Acque superficiali e sotterranee. p. 39-94, 121-138. *In* Reale Società Geografica Italiana, Il Sahara italiano. Part 1: Fezzan e Oasi di Gat. Società Italiana d'Arti Grafiche, Rome.
(Geology and morphology. Surface and ground waters.)

Desio, A.
1939 Studi morphologici sulla Libia orientale. Missione scientifica della R. Accademia d'Italia a Cufra (1931), vol. 2. R. Accademia d'Italia, Rome, Viaggi di Studio ed Esplorazioni. 216 p.
(Morphologic study of eastern Libya)

1940 Osservazioni geologiche sul Tibesti settentrionale, Sahara Centrale. Società Italiana di Science Naturali e del Museo Civico di Storia Naturale, Milano, Atti 79(3):175-192.
(Geologic observations in northern Tibesti, central Sahara.)

1942a Appunti geomorphologici sul Sahara sud occidentale. Museo Libico di Storia Naturale, Tripoli, Annali 3:17-32.
(Geomorphological sketches of the southwestern Sahara.)

1942b Il Tibesti nord-orientale. Reale Società Geografica Italiana. Società Italiana d'Arti Grafiche, Rome. 232 p.

1942c Ubersicht über die geologie Libyens. Geologische Rundschau 33:415-421.
(Outline of the geology of Libya; with map at a scale of 1:5,630,000.)

1953 Brève synthèse de l'évolution morphologique du territoire de Libye. Société de Géographie d'Egypte, Bulletin 25:9-21.
(Brief synthesis of the morphologic evolution of the territory of Libya.)

Desio, A. *et al.*
1963 Stratigraphic studies in the Tripolitanian Jebel (Libya). Rivista Italiana di Paleontologia e Stratigrafia, Memoria 9.
A detailed study of stratigraphy and the general geology in a portion of Tripolitania.

Despois, J.
1942 La bordure saharienne de l'Algérie orientale. Revue Africaine 36:196-219.
(The Saharan border of eastern Algeria.)

Dixey, F. and G. Aubert
1962 Arid zone research in the Sudan. Unesco, Paris. Arid Zone [Newsletter] 16:5-16.

Dixey, F. and L. Emberger
1962 Arid zone research in Morocco. Unesco, Paris. Arid Zone [Newsletter] 17:8-13.

Douvillé, H. and J. Tilho
1933 La géologie de la region au nord du Tchad. Académie des Sciences, Paris, Comptes Rendus 197: 1012-1016.
(The geology of the region to the north of Chad.)

Dowling, J. W. F. and F. H. P. Williams
1964a The use of aerial photographs in materials surveys and classification of landforms. *In* Institution of Civil Engineers, Conference on Civil Engineering Problems Overseas, 9th, 1964, Proceedings.

1964b The classification of landforms in northern Nigeria and their use with aerial photographs in engineering soil surveys. United Kingdom Department of Scientific and Industrial Research, Road Research Laboratory, Paper. 23 p.

Dresch, J.
1941 Recherches sur l'évolution du relief dans le massif central du grand Atlas. Tours, Arrault, Paris. 708 p.
(Research on the evolution of relief in the central massif of the Atlas Mountains.)

1952 Aspects de la géomorphologie du Maroc. Service Géologique du Maroc, Rabat, Notes et Mémoires 96:9-21.
(Aspects of the geomorphology of Morocco.)

1953a Morpholgie de la chaîne d'Ougarte. Institut de Recherches Sahariennes, Travaux 9:25-38.
(Morphology of the Ougarte mountains.)

1953b Plaines soudanaises. Revue de Géomorphologie Dynamique 1:39-44.

1953c Systemes d'érosion en Afrique du Nord. Revue de Géographie, Lyon, 28:253-261.
(Systems of erosion in North Africa.)

1959 Notes sur la géomorphologie de l'Aïr. Association de Géographes Français, Bulletin 280-281:2-30.

1961 Plaines et "eglab" de Mauritanie. Association de Géographes Français, Bulletin 229-300:130-142.
(Plains and inselbergs of Mauritania.)

Dresch, J. *et al.*
1952 Aspects de la géomorphologie du Maroc. Congrès Geologique International, 19th, Algér, Monographie Régionale 3. 182 p.
(Aspects of the geomorphology of Morocco.)
A comprehensive summary of the general geomorphology of the country with many useful illustrations.

Drouhin, G.
1952 Les problèmes de l'eau en Afrique du Nord-Ouest. *In* Compte rendu des recherches effectuées sur l'hydrologie de la zone aride. Unesco, Paris. Programme de la Zone Aride 1:9-41.
(The problem of water resources in north-west Africa.)

Dubief, J.
1943 Les vents de sable dans le Sahara français. Institut de Recherches Sahariennes, Travaux 2:11-35.
(Sandstorms in the French Sahara.)

1952 Le vent et le déplacement du sable au Sahara. Institut de Recherches Sahariennes, Travaux 8: 123-164.
(The wind and the transport of sand in the Sahara.)

1953a Essai sur l'hydrographie superficielle au Sahara, vol. 1. Direction du Service de la Colonisation et de l'Hydraulique, Clairbois-Birmandreis, Algiers.
(Survey of the surface-water hydrology of the Sahara.)

1953b Les vents de sable au Sahara français. Centre National de la Recherche Scientifique, Colloques Internationaux 35:45-70.
(Sandstorms in the French Sahara.)

Dubief, J.
1953c Ruissellement superficielle au Sahara. Centre National de la Recherche Scientifique, Paris, Colloques Internationaux 35:303-315.
(Surface channeling in the Sahara.)

1959 Le climat du Sahara, vol. 1. Institut de Recherches Sahariennes, Mémoires hors Série. 312 p.
(The climate of the Sahara.)
A general summary of climatic data from the Sahara which is still useful as a basic guide. Similar treatments by Dubief of sand transport (1952, 1953b) and surface-water hydrology (1953a, c) also merit general-reference status for the Sahara.

Dubief, J. and J. Lauriol
1943 Moyennes climatologiques du Sahara algérien pour la période 1925-39. Institut de Météorologie et de Physique du Globe de l'Algérie, Travaux, fascicule 4. 69 p.
(Mean climatology of the Algerian Sahara for the 1925-39 period.)

Dubois, J. and J. Tricart
1954 Esquisse de stratigraphie du Quaternaire du Sénégal et de la Mauritanie du Sud. Académie des Sciences, Paris, Comptes Rendus 238:2183-2185.
(Outline of Quaternary stratigraphy of Senegal and Southern Mauritania.)

Dufour, A.
1936 Observations sur les dunes du Sahara méridional. Annales de Géographie 45:276-285.
(Observations on the dunes of the southern Sahara.)

Dumanowski, B.
1960 Notes on the evolution of slopes in an arid climate. Zeitschrift für Geomorphologie, Supplement 1:178-189.
A qualitative description of slopes and lithology in Egypt with several useful photographs and illustrations. A companion work on wadis, of similar nature (Dumanowski, 1962), is also available.

1962 Uwagi o formach wadi w Egipcie. Czasopismo Geograficzne 33:199-214.
(Observations on the Wadi forms in Egypt.)

Durand, J. H.
1949 Formation de la croûte gypseuse du Souf (Sahara). Société Géologique de France, Comptes Rendus 13:303-305.
(Formation of the gypsiferous crust of Souf, Sahara.)

1951 Mode de formation de certaines croûtes calcaires de l'Algérie. Société des Sciences Naturelles de Tunisie, Bulletin 4:27-29.
(Mode of formation of certain calcareous crusts of Algeria.)

1953 Etude géologique, hydrogéologique et pédologique des croûtes en Algérie. Direction du Service de la Colonisation et de l'Hydraulique, Clairbois-Birmandreis. 209 p.
(Geological, hydrogeological and pedological study of crusts in Algeria.)

1954 Les sols d'Algérie. Direction du Service de la Colonisation et de l'Hydraulique, Service des Etudes Scientifiques, Pédalogie 2. 244 p.
An authoritative summary of the distribution and general characteristics of the soils of Algeria; includes theories of the formation of various crusts.

Elk, C. and L. Mathieu
1963 Quelques observations sur les effets des pluies violentes de janvier 1963 dans le Moyen-Atlas et le Prerif (Maroc). Société Royale Belge de Géographie, Brussels, Bulletin 32:281-299.
(Some observations of the effects of violent rains in January 1963 in the middle Atlas and Rif of Morocco.)
A good description of the effects of floods in the Atlas and Rif ranges of Morocco.

Elouard, P.
1959 Underflow d'un oued saharien, l'Oued Seguelil (Mauritanie). Association Internationale des Hydrogéologues, Paris, Mémoire, p. 66-69.
(Underflow of a Saharan wadi, Wadi Seguelil, Mauritania.)

Elouard, P. and P. Michel
1958 Le quaternaire du lac Rkiz et de l'Aftout de Boutilimit (Mauritanie). Société Géologique de France, Comptes Rendus 11:245-248.
(The Quaternary of Lake Rkiz and the Aftout of Boutilimit, Mauritania.)

Emon, J.
1957 L'évaporation au Maroc. Service de Physique du Globe et de Météorologie, Annales 17.
(Evaporation in Morocco.)

Estorges, P.
1959 Morphologie du Plateau Arbaa. Institut de Recherches Sahariennes, Travaux 18:21-56.
(Morphology of the Arbaa Plateau.)

1961 Morphologie du Plateau Arbaa. Institut de Recherches Sahariennes, Travaux 20:29-78.
(Morphology of the Arbaa Plateau.)

L'Excellent
n.d. Monographie de l'oued Souss. Travaux Publics du Maroc, Circonscription de l'Hydraulique et de l'Électricité.
(Monograph on Wadi Souss.)

Falconer, J. D.
1911 The geology and geography of northern Nigeria. Macmillan, London. 295 p.

Farag, I.
1955 Some remarks on the lower Cretaceous exposures of Gebel Maghara dome (northern Sinai). Desert Institute, Egypt, Bulletin 5(1).

Farag, I. and A. Shata
1954 Detailed geological survey of the El Minshera area. Desert Institute, Egypt, Bulletin 4(2).

Faure, H.
1959 Une hypothése sur la structure du Ténéré (Niger). Académie des Sciences, Paris, Comptes Rendus 249:2591-2593.
(A hypothesis on the structure of Ténéré, Niger.)

Faure, H.
1960- Reconnaissance hydrogéologique du Niger
1961   oriental. Bureau de Recherches Géologiques et
       Minières, Dakar. 377 p.
       The most authoritative work in existence on the hydro-
       geology of this central Saharan area. Other reports by this
       author (Faure, 1962, 1964) provide additional maps and
       data on surficial features of eastern Niger.

_____

1962   Esquisse paléogéographique du Niger oriental
       depuis le Crétecé. Académie des Sciences, Paris,
       Comptes Rendus 254:4485-4486.
       (Paleogeographic outline of eastern Niger since
       the Cretaceous.)

_____

1964   Inventaire des évaporites du Niger. Bureau de
       Recherches Géologiques et Minières, Dakar.

Flamand, G. B. M.
1911   Etude géologique et géographique dans le haut
       pays de l'Oranie et le Sahara. Thèse, Lyon. 100 p.
       (Geographical and geological study of the high-
       land of Oran and the Sahara.)

Flores, A.
1951   Hidrografía del Sahara español. Africa 115:
       336-340.

Fölster, H.
1964   Morphogenese der südsudanesischen pediplane.
       Zeitschrift für Geomorphologie 8:393-423.
       (Morphogenesis of the southern Sudan pediplane.)

Font Tullot, I.
1955   El clima del Sahara con especial referencia a la
       zona español. Consejo Superior de Investigaciones
       Científicos, Madrid. 122 p.
       (The climate of the Sahara with special reference
       to the Spanish zone.)

Font y Sague, N.
1911   Les formations géologiques du Río de Oro (Sahara
       occidental). Société Géologique de France, Bul-
       letin 11:212-217.
       (The geologic formations of Río de Oro, western
       Sahara.)

Fournier, F.
1957   L'érosion du sol dans les territoires français d'outre-
       mer. International Association of Scientific Hydrol-
       ogy, General Assembly of Toronto, Proceedings
       1:72-75.
       (Soil erosion in the French overseas territories.)

France. Bureau de Recherches Géologiques et Minières, Paris
1961   Carte géologique du Sahara (massif du Hoggar).
       (Geological map of the Sahara, Ahaggar massif,
       scale 1:500,000.)

France. Direction de la Documentation Française
1959   Sahara occidental espagnol. 80 p.
       (English translation held by U. S. Army Map Service
       Library as HC10, N91, No. 2570.)

Freydenburg, H.
1908   Le Chad et le bassin du Chari. Paris. Thesis.
       (Chad and the Chari basin)

Frowlow, V.
1934   Le Niger moyen. Thèse d'ingénieur-doctor, Fac-
       ulté des Sciences de Paris.
       (Central Niger)

_____

1936   Une monographie du Niger moyen. Annales de
       Géographie 45:206-209.
       (A monograph on Central Niger)

_____

1940a Les lacs du Niger: Horo, Fati, Faguibine. Associa-
       tion de Géographes Français, Bulletin 128-129:
       32-34.
       (The lakes of Niger)

_____

1940b Les pentes du Niger entre Koulikoro et Sama.
       Académie des Sciences, Paris, Comptes Rendus
       211:408-410.
       (The slopes of the Niger between Koulikoro and
       Sama.)

_____

1941   Les pentes du Niger entre Tondifarma et Diré.
       Académie des Sciences, Paris, Comptes Rendus
       212:1041-1043.
       (The slopes of the Niger between Tondifarma and
       Diré.)

Furon, R.
1960   Géologie de l'Afrique. Payot, Paris.
       (Geology of Africa.)

Fürst, M.
1965   Hammada-Serir-Erg. Zeitschrift für Geomorphol-
       ogie n.s. 9:385-421.

El Gabaly, M. M.
1954   The soil, water supply, and agriculture in north-
       eastern Sinai. Desert Institute, Egypt, Bulletin
       4(1).

Gaussen, H. and F. Bagnouls
1948   Carte des précipitations. Moyenne annuelle
       ramenée à la période 1913-47. Echelle 1:500,000,
       Algérie occidentale et orientale. Institut Géog-
       raphique National, Paris.
       (Map of the mean annual precipitation of western
       and eastern Algeria for the 1913-47 period at a
       scale of 1:500,000.)

Gaussen, H., J. Debrach, and F. Joly
1958   Précipitations annuelles. Comité de Géographie
       du Maroc, Atlas du Maroc. Notices explicatives,
       II: Physique du globe et météorologie, Pluvio-
       métrie. Rabat. 36 p.

Gautier, E. F.
1926   The Ahaggar, heart of the Sahara. Geographical
       Review 16:378-394. 2. éd. 232 p.

_____

1928   Le Sahara. Payot, Paris.

Gautier, M.
1953   Les chotts, machines évaporatoires complexes.
       Actions éoliennes phénomènes d'évaporation et
       d'hydrologie superficielle dans les régions arides.
       Centre National de la Recherche Scientifique,
       Paris, Colloques Internationaux 35:317-325.
       (The Algerian salt lagoons, complex evaporating
       mechanisms. Wind-induced phenomena and the
       surface hydrology in arid regions.)

Gautier, M., R. Laffitte, and J. Flandrin
1948   Sur la formation de la croûte calcaire superficielle
       en Algérie. Académie des Sciences, Paris, Comptes
       Rendus 226:416-418.
       (On the formation of calcareous surface-crust in
       Algeria.)

Gérard, G.
1958   Notice explicative de la carte géologique de l'Afrique Equatoriale Française au 1:2,000,000. Direction des Mines et de la Géologie de l'Afrique Equatoriale Française, Brazzaville.
(Exploration of the geologic map of French Equatorial Africa on a scale of 1:2,000,000.)

Gèze, B. *et al.*
1957*a*   Le volcan du Toussidé dans le Tibesti Occidental. Académie des Sciences, Paris, Comptes Rendus 245:813.
(The Toussidé volcano in western Tibesti.)

———   1957*b*   Succession et age probable des formations volcaniques du Tibesti. Académie des Sciences, Paris, Comptes Rendus 245:2328.
(Succession and probable age of the volcanic formations of Tibesti.)

Giessner, K.
1964   Naturgeographische landschaftsanalyse der tunesischen dorsale. Dissertation, Hanover.
(Geographic landform analysis of the Tunisian ridge.)

Gigout, M.
1951   Etudes géologiques sur la meseta marocaine occidentale. Institut Scientifique Chérifien, Travaux 3:200-201.
(Geological studies of the western Moroccan mesa.)

Gómez, M. P.
1959   Pozos del Sahara. Instituto de Estudios Africanos, Madrid. 189 p.
(Wells of the Sahara.)

Grandet, C.
1957   Sur la morphologie dunaire de la rive sud du lac Faguibine. Institut de Recherches Sahariennes, Travaux 16:171-179.
(On the dune morphology along the south shore of Lake Faguibine.)

———   1955   Aspects de la morphologie dunaire dans la région de Beni Abbes. Société Géologique de France, Bulletin 5:135-141.
(Aspects of dune morphology in the Beni Abbes region.)

———   1956   Observations sur la morphologie des dépôts de pente (Région Saoura-Ougarta). Institut de Recherches Sahariennes, Travaux 14:201-212.
(Observations on the morphology of slope deposits in the Saoura-Ougarta region.)

Gregory, J. W.
1911   The geology of Cyrenaica. Geological Society of London, Quarterly Journal 67:572-615.

Grove, A. T.
1957   Patterned ground in northern Nigeria. Geographical Journal 123:271-274.

———   1958   The ancient erg of Hausaland, and similar formations on the south side of the Sahara. Geographical Journal 124:526-633.

———   1959   A note on the former extent of Lake Chad. Geographical Journal 125:465-467.

———   1960   Geomorphology of the Tibesti region with special reference to western Tibesti. Geographical Journal 126:18-31.
A description of the Tibesti region with references to several of the earlier pertinent works of a geologic or geographic nature. Grove's paper includes maps, photographs, sections, some quantitative slope data, and a description of a flood that occurred during his field investigation.

Grove, A. T. and R. A. Pullan
1963   Some aspects of the Pleistocene paleogeography of the Chad basin. In F. C. Howell and F. Bourlière, eds., African ecology and human evolution. Aldine Publishing Company, Chicago. 666 p.

Gruvel, A. and R. Chudeau
1909   A travers la Mauritanie occidentale. Larose, Paris 2 vols.
(Across western Mauritania.)

Guilcher, A.
1954   Dynamique et morphologie des côtes sableuses de l'Afrique atlantique. Information Géographique, Paris, Cahiers 1:57-68.
(Dynamics and morphology of sandy areas of Atlantic-Coastal Africa.)

Hernández-Pacheco, E.
1941   Relieve y geología del norte del Sahara español. Revista Geográfica Española 10:17-23.
(Relief and geology of the northern part of the Spanish Sahara.)

Hernández-Pacheco, E. *et al.*
1949   El Sahara español, estudio geológico, geográfico y botánico. Instituto de Estudios Africanos, Madrid. 808 p.

Hey, R. W.
1956*a*   The Pleistocene shorelines of Cyrenaica. Quaternaria 3:139-144.

———   1956*b*   The geomorphology and tectonics of the Gebel Akhdar (Cyrenaica). Geological Magazine 93:1-14.

———   1962   The Quaternary and paleolithic of northern Libya. Quaternaria 6:435-449.

———   1963   Pleistocene screes in Cyrenaica (Libya). Eiszeitalter und Gegenwart 14:77-84.
Describes the limestone cliffs in northern Cyrenaica and their associated scree deposits with respect to climatic changes.

Higazy, R. A. and H. M. Wafsy
1956   Petrogenesis of granitic rocks in the neighborhood of Aswan, Egypt. Desert Institute, Egypt, Bulletin 6(1).

Hill, R. W.
1959   A bibliography of Libya. University of Durham, Department of Geography, Research Paper 1. 100 p.
A useful bibliography of Libyan studies with emphasis on geographic reports. Other papers in this series include a description of geomorphic field studies in Libya (Willimott and Clarke, 1960).

Hobbs, W. H.
1918 The peculiar weathering process of desert regions with illustrations from Egypt and the Sudan. Michigan Academy of Science, Annual Report 20:93-99.

Hubert, H.
1911 Le relief de la boucle du Niger. Annales de Géographie 20:155-178.

Hull, A. C., Jr.
1955 Egypt, land of contrasts. Desert Institute, Egypt, Bulletin 5(2).

Hume, W. F.
1914 The physiography of arid lands (as illustrated by Desert Egypt). Geological Magazine 1:421-424.

———
1921 The Egyptian wilderness. Geographical Journal 58:249-276.

———
1925- Geology of Egypt. Government Press, Cairo. 4
1939 vols.

Huntington, E.
1910 The Libyan oasis of Kharga. American Geographical Society, Bulletin 42:641-661.

Hurst, H. E.
1950 The Nile Basin. VIII: The hydrology of the Sobat and White Nile and the topography of the Blue Nile and Atbara. Government Press, Cairo.

———
1952 The Nile. Constable, London. 826 p.

Hurst, H. E. and R. P. Black
1944 The Nile Basin. VI: Monthly and annual rainfall totals and number of raining days at stations in and near the Nile Basin. Schindler's Press, Cairo.

Hurst, H. E., R. P. Black, and Y. M. Simaika
1946 The Nile Basin. VII: The future conservation of the Nile. S.O.P. Press, Cairo.

Hurst, H. E. and P. Phillips
1931 The Nile Basin. I: General description of the basin, meteorology and topography of the White Nile Basin. Government Press, Cairo.
This initial report on the Nile Basin and some of the subsequent volumes and allied works (Hurst and Phillips, 1932, 1933a, b, 1938; Hurst and Black, 1944; Hurst, Black, and Simaika, 1946; Hurst, 1950; and Hurst, Simaika, and Black, 1953-1957) should be regarded as the most authoritative source of hydrological data on the Nile.

———
1932 The Nile Basin. II: Measured discharges of the Nile and its tributaries. Government Press, Cairo.

———
1933a The Nile Basin. III: Ten-day mean and monthly mean gauge readings of the Nile and its tributaries. Government Press, Cairo.

———
1933b The Nile Basin. IV: Ten-day mean and monthly discharges of the Nile and its tributaries. Government Press, Cairo.

———
1938 The Nile Basin. V: The hydrology of the Lake Plateau and Bahr El Jebel. Schindler's Press, Cairo.

Hurst, H. E., Y. M. Simaika, and R. P. Black
1953- The Nile Basin. Supplementary reports. Nile Con-
1957 trol Department, Papers.

Institut Equatorial de Recherches et d'Etudes Géologiques et Minières
1961 Bibliographie géologique et minière de l'Afrique Equatoriale Française. Direction des Mines et de la Géologie de l'Afrique Equatoriale Française, Brazzaville.
(Geologic and mining bibliography of French Equatorial Africa.)

Institut Français d'Afrique Noire
1950 Contribution à l'étude de l'Aïr. Mémoire 10. Larose, Paris.

Institut Scientifique Chérifien
1955 Précipitations atmosphériques au Maroc. Valeurs moyennes pour 25 années (1925-1949). Service de Physique du Globe et de Météorologie, Casablanca, Annales 15.
(Atmospheric precipitation in Morocco.)

International Geological Congress, 19th, Algiers
1952 Carte géologique du Maroc (1:2,000,000).

Jaeger, P.
1951 Physiographie du massif de Kita. Revue de Géomorphologie Dynamique 1:1-31.

Jaeger, P. and M. Jarovoy
1952 Les grès de Kita (Soudan occidental). Institut Français d'Afrique Noire, Bulletin 14:1-18.
(The sand of Kita, western Sudan.)

Jaranoff, D.
1936 L'évolution morphologique du Maroc atlantique pendent le Pliocène et le Quaternaire. Revue de Géographie Physique et de Géologie Dynamique 9:301-332.
(Morphological evolution of Atlantic Morocco during the Pliocene and Quaternary.)

Jauzein, A.
1959 Les terrasses alluviales en Tunisie septentrionale. Société Géologique de France, Comptes Rendus Sommaires, p. 31-32.
(The alluvial terraces in northern Tunisia.)

Joleaud, L.
1926 Quelques traits de la géomorphologie du Maroc atlantique. Congrès Géologique International, 14th, Madrid, Comptes Rendus 3:789-798.
(Some aspects of the geomorphology of Atlantic Morocco.)

Joly, F.
1949 Pédiments et glacis d'érosion dans le sud-est du Maroc. International Geographical Congress, 16th, Lisbon, Comptes Rendus 2:110-125.
(Pediments and erosion surfaces in southeastern Morocco.)

———
1952a Le Haut Atlas oriental. Service Géologique du Maroc, Notes et Mémoires 96:71-82.
(The eastern high Atlas.)

———
1952b Le Tafilalt: le problème des Hamada. Service Géologique du Maroc, Notes et Mémoires 96:83-91.
(Tafilalt: the problem of the Hamada.)
A discussion of desert plains in Morocco which, combined with the author's previous work on Moroccan pediments (Joly, 1949) and the observations of Mensching and Raynal (1954), provides much useful information on topographic lows in the country and their surficial character.

Joly, F.
1953   Quelques phénomènes d'écoulement sur la bordure du Sahara, dans les confins algéro-marocains, et leurs conséquences morphologiques. International Geological Congress, 19th, Algiers, Comptes Rendus 7(7):135-143.
(Some phenomena of drainage on the Saharan border in Algeria-Morocco and their morphological consequences.)

1962   Etudes sur le relief du Sud-Est Marocain. Institut Scientifique Chérifien, Travaux, Série Géologie et Géographie Physique 10. 508 p.
(Studies of the relief of southeast Morocco.)

Jones, J. R.
1964   Groundwater maps of the Kingdom of Libya. U. S. Geological Survey, Open File Report. 25 p.

1966   Land mine danger areas in central Libya. U. S. Geological Survey, Water Resources Division, Oral communication.

Jonglei Investigation Team
n.d.   The Equatorial Nile project. Report to the Government of the Sudan. 4 vols.

1952   The Equatorial Nile project. Sudan Notes and Records 33(1).

1953   The Equatorial Nile project and its effects in the Sudan. Geographical Journal 119(1).

Jordan, W.
1876   Physische geographie und meteorologie der libyschen wüste. *In* G. Rohlfs, Expedition zur erforschung der Libyschen wüste . . . im winter 1873-74, bd. 2. Fischer, Cassel. 216 p.
(Physical geography and meteorology of the Libyan desert.)

Kadar, L.
1934   A study of the sand sea of the Libyan desert. Geographical Journal 83:470-478.

Kaddah, M. T.
1954   L'irrigation des Déserts Egyptiens. Desert Institute, Egypt, Bulletin 4(1).
(Irrigation of the Egyptian desert.)

Kamel, K.
1953   Sand dunes in the Kharga depression. Société Royale de Géographie d'Egypte, Bulletin 25:77-80.

Kanter, H.
1963   Eine reise in No-Tibesti (Republic Tschad), 1958. Petermanns Geographische Mitteilungen 107:21-30.
(A journey in northeastern Tibesti, Republic of Chad, 1958.)

Karpoff, R.
1960a   Existence probable d'une tillite au Nord-Ouest de l'Adrar des Iforas. Société Géologique de France, Comptes Rendus, p. 176-177.
(Probable existence of a tillite to the northwest of the Adrar des Iforas.)

1960b   La géologie de l'Adrar des Iforas (Sahara central). Louis-Jean, Paris. Thèse doctorat ès sciences. 273 p.
A detailed study of the general geology of the Adrar des Iforas with maps and other illustrations of this Saharan massif.

Kassas, M.
1956   Land forms and plant cover in the Omdurman desert, Sudan. Société de Géographie d'Egypt, Bulletin 29:43-58.

Kassas, M. and M. Imam
1957   Climate and micro-climate in the Cairo desert. Société de Géographie d'Egypte, Bulletin 30:25-52.

Keldani, E. H.
1941   A bibliography of geology and related sciences concerning Egypt up to the end of 1939. Government Press, Cairo. 428 p.

Kemal el-Dine (S.A.S. Prince Hussein)
1928   L'exploration du désert libyque. La Géographie 50:171-183, 320-336.

Kervran, L.
1959   Le cours fossile du Niger, un élément nouveau. Notre Sahara 10:53-58.
(The fossil course of the Niger, a new concept.)

King, W. J. H.
1913   The Farafra depression. Geographical Journal 42:455-461.

Klitzsch, E.
1966   Bericht über starke niederschläge in der Zentralsahara. Zeitschrift für Geomorphologie 10:161-168.
(Report on intense thunderstorms in the central Sahara.)
Describes in a general way the effects of recent intense storms on Libyan wadis. Some photographs are included.

Knetsch, G.
1950   Beobachtungen in der libyschen Sahara. Geologische Rundschau 38:40-58.
(Observations in the Libyan Sahara.)

1960   Über aride verwitterung unter besonderer berücksichtigung natürlicher und künstlicher wände in Ägyptien. Zeitschrift für Geomorphologie, Supplement 1:190-205.
(On arid weathering with special consideration of natural and man-made walls in Egypt.)
This report provides data on the nature and rates of weathering under the prevailing climatic conditions in Egypt. An earlier report (Knetsch and Refai, 1955) also treats observations of weathering, and decay of both natural outcrops and monuments of some antiquity.

Knetsch, G. and M. A. Mazhar
1953   Traces of subsurface water migration as an indication of former climates. Desert Institute, Egypt, Bulletin 3(2).

Knetsch, G. and E. Refai
1955   Über wüstenverwitterung, wüsten feinrelief und denkmalzerfall in Ägyptien. Neues Jahrbuch für Geologie und Paläontologie 101:227-256.
(On desert weathering, desert microrelief and monument destruction in Egypt.)

Kochli, P.
1950   Südmarokko. Geographica Helvetica 5:92-100.
(Southern Morocco)

Lefevre, R.
1960   Etudes d'écoulement dans le massif de l'Aïr. Office de la Recherche Scientifique et Technique Outre-Mer, Paris. 131 p.
(Studies of runoff in the Aïr massif.)

Lelong, B.
1960   Etude hydrologique du sud et du sud-est de
       l'Affollé. RIM Economie Rurale, Neuilly. Bureau
       de Géologie Appliquée. 80 p.
       (Hydrologic study of the south and southeast
       Affollé.)

Lelubre, M.
1939   Observations géologiques au Hoggar (Sahara Cen-
       tral). Revue de Géographie Physique et de Géol-
       ogie Dynamique 12:346-352.
       (Geological observations in the Ahaggar, central
       Sahara.)

1940   Note sur la géologie de l'Edjereh (Sahara Cen-
       tral). Académie des Sciences, Paris, Comptes
       Rendus 210:338-340.
       (Note on the geology of Edjereh, central Sahara.)

1943   Les grands traits géologiques de l'Ahaggar. Institut
       de Recherches Sahariennes, Travaux 2:55-68.
       (The broad geologic traits of the Ahaggar.)

1946   Le Tibesti septentrional: esquisse morphologique
       et structurale. Académie Royale des Sciences Col-
       oniales, Comptes Rendus 6:337-357.
       (Northern Tibesti, a morphological and structural
       sketch.)

1952   Conditions structurales et formes du relief dans
       le Sahara. Institut de Recherches Sahariennes, Tra-
       vaux 8:189-238.
       (Structural conditions and forms of relief in the
       Sahara.)

Leone, G.
1953   Origin and reclamation of dunes in Tripolitania.
       In Desert Research, proceedings, International
       symposium held in Jerusalem May 7-14, 1952,
       sponsored by the Research Council of Israel and
       Unesco. Research Council of Israel, Special Publi-
       cation 2:401-404.

Lermuzeaux, A.
1958a Hydrologie du Cercle de Guidimaka, Mauritanie.
       Bureau de Géologie Appliquée, Neuilly. 54 p.
       (Hydrology of the environs of Guidimaka, Mauri-
       tania.)
Excellent hydrologic summary of a part of southern
Mauritania; this and the author's allied work (Lermuzeaux, 1958b, 1960) present most of the available surface-
water data for the region.

1958b Hydrologie de la subdivision de Kiffa, Mauritanie.
       Bureau de Géologie Appliquée, Neuilly. 64 p.
       (Hydrology of the subdivision of Kiffa, Mauri-
       tania.)

1960   Etude hydrogéologique de l'Affolé de la région de
       Tamchakett et du nord de la subdivision de Kiffa.
       Bureau de Géologie Appliquée, Neuilly. 49 p.
       (Hydrogeologic study of the Affolé of the Tam-
       chakett region and of the northern part of the
       subdivision of Kiffa.)

Leuchs, K.
1913   Geologisches aus der südlichen Libyschen wüste.
       Gebel Garra, Oase Kurkur, und Gebel Borga.
       Neues Jahrbuch für Mineralogie, Geologie und
       Paläontologie, 22:33-48.
       (Geology of the southern Libyan desert: Jebel
       Garra, Kurkur oasis, and Jebel Borga.)

Libya. Ministry of Agriculture
1962   Census of agriculture, 1960.
       This volume lists the locations of all springs and wells in
       Libya and, despite some inaccuracies, is an extremely
       useful source of information.

Lipparini, T.
1940   Tettonica e geomorfologia della Tripolitania. Soci-
       età Geologica Italiana, Bollettino 59:221-301.
       (Tectonics and geomorphology of Tripolitania.)

Little, O. H.
1945   Geology of Cyrenaica. In Handbook on Cyrenaica,
       Part 1. Middle East Forces, Printing and Stationery
       Services, Cairo (?). 104 p.

Loup, J.
1962   L'Oum-er-Rebia. Revue de Géographie Alpine
       50:519-555.

Lowy, H.
1954   Desert hydrology. Desert Institute, Egypt, Bulletin
       4(1).

Lucas, A.
1905   The blackened rocks of the Nile cataracts and of
       the Egyptian deserts. National Printing Depart-
       ment, Cairo. 58 p.

Lyons, H. G.
1905   On the Nile flood and its variation. Geographical
       Journal 26:395-421.

1906   The physiography of the River Nile and its basin.
       National Printing Department, Cairo. 411 p.

McBurney, C. B. M. and R. W. Hey
1955   Prehistory and Pleistocene geology in Cyrenaican
       Libya. Cambridge University Press. 315 p.

McKee, E. D. and G. C. Tibbitts, Jr.
1964   Primary structures of a seif dune and associated
       deposits in Libya. Journal of Sedimentary Petrol-
       ogy 34:5-17.

Marchand, C.
1957   Wadi El Hira; improvement scheme and general
       examination of the flood problem. Compagnie des
       Techniques Hydrauliques Agricoles, Grenoble.

Marchetti, M.
1938   Idrologia Cirenaica. Instituto Agricolo Coloniale
       Italiano, Firenze. 249 p.
       (Hydrology of Cyrenaica.)

Marvier, L.
1953   Notice explicative de la carte géologique
       d'ensemble de l'Afrique Occidentale Française.
       Direction des Mines de l'Afrique Occidentale
       Française, Bulletin 16.
       (Explanation of the geologic map of French West
       Africa.)

Matschinski, M.
1954   Stabilità delle dune del Sahara. Servizio Geologico
       Italia, Bollettino 55:579-591.
       (Stability of dunes of the Sahara.)

Meckelein, W.
1959   Forschungen in der zentralen Sahara. Bd. 1: Klima-
       geomorphologie. G. Westermann, Braunschweig.
       181 p.
       (Explorations in the central Sahara.)

Menchikoff, N.
1930 Recherches géologiques et morphologiques dan le Nord du Sahara occidental. Revue de Géographie Physique et de Géologie Dynamique 3:103-248. (Geologic and morphologic research in the north-western Sahara)

1957 Les grandes lignes de la géologic Saharienne. Revue de Géographie Physique et de Géologie Dynamique 1:37-45. (The great belts of Saharan geology.)

Mensching, H.
1955 Das Quartär in den gebirgen Marokkos. Petermanns Geographische Mitteilungen, Ergänzungsheft 256. 79 p. (The Quaternary of the Moroccan mountains.)

1963 Morphologie des südtunesischen stufenlandes. Hellenike Geographike Hetaireia, Athens, Deltion 4:152-161. (Morphology of the southern Tunisian borderlands.)

1964 Zur geomorphologie südtunisiens. Zeitschrift für Geomorphologie 8:424-439. (On the geomorphology of southern Tunisia.)
A description of the scarps, terraces, wadis, and plains in southern Tunisia which enlarges upon this author's previous work in the area (Mensching, 1963). The surficial features of this part of Tunisia are well illustrated by this work combined with the earlier studies of surficial morphology and crusts by Coque (1955a, b, c).

Mensching, H. and R. Raynal
1954 Füssflachen in Marokko. Beobachtungen zu ihrer morphogenese an der ostseite des Mittleren Atlas. Petermanns Geographische Mitteilungen 98:171-176. (Basal plains in Morocco. Observations on their morphogenesis on the east side of the Middle Atlas.)

Mitwally, M.
1951 Some new light on the origin of the artesian water of the Egyptian oases of the Libyan desert. Desert Institute, Egypt, Bulletin 1(2).

1953a Physiographic features of the Libyan Desert. Desert Institute, Egypt, Bulletin 3(1).
A general description of the physiography of the Western Desert of Egypt. This author has also treated the Sinai area in similar fashion (Mitwally, 1953b) but more detailed geologic and geomorphic information on the Sinai Peninsula is presented in reports by Shata (1954, 1956).

1953b A scientific expedition to northeastern Sinai. Desert Institute, Egypt, Bulletin 2(2).

1953c Physiographic features of the oases of the Libyan desert. Desert Institute, Egypt, Bulletin 3(2).

1954 The call of the desert. Desert Institute, Egypt, Bulletin 4(2).

Monod, T.
1945 La structure du Sahara atlantique. Institut de Recherches Sahariennes, Travaux 3:27-55.

1949 Observations nouvelles sur l'Adrar mauritanien. Société Géologique de France, Bulletin 19:409-414. (Recent observations on the Adrar of Mauritania.)

1950 Sur la structure de l'Adrar mauritanien occidental. Académie des Sciences, Paris, Comptes Rendus 231:202-205. (On the structure of the Adrar of western Mauritania.)

1952a L'Adrar mauritanien (Sahara occidental); esquisse géologique. Afrique Occidental Française, Direction des Mines, Bulletin 15, vol. 1. 284 p. (Geologic outline of the Adrar of Mauritania, western Sahara.)
A major contribution to knowledge of the geology of this portion of Mauritania; includes some description of geographic features in addition to geologic maps and data.

1952b Notes géologiques sur le Sahara occidental. Afrique Occidentale Française, Direction des Mines. 2 vols. (Geologic notes on the western Sahara)

1956 Sur une eau minérale de l'Adrar mauritanien (Sahara occidental). Institut d'Hydrologie et de Climatologie, Annales 27:142-146. (On a mineral water of the Adrar of Mauritania, western Sahara.)

1958 Majâbat Al Koubrâ, contribution à l'étude l'"Empty Quarter" Ouest-Saharien. Institut Française d'Afrique Noire, Mémoire 52. (The Majâbat Al-Koubrâ, contribution to the study of the "empty quarter" of the western Sahara.)
An excellent summary of surficial conditions in a seldom-studied area in west-central Mali and east-central Mauritania. Numerous aerial photographs are included as an appendix to this monograph. A supplement to this report (Monod, 1961) should also be consulted.

1961 Majâbat Al Koubrâ (supplément). Institut Français d'Afrique Noire, Bulletin 23:591-637.

Montmarin, A. de
1952 Etude hydrologique de l'oued Ellil et de l'oued Rhezala. Service des Etudes et Grands Travaux, Tunis. (Hydrologic study of Wadi Ellil and Wadi Rhezala.)

Morin, P.
1960 Le Maroc central; un aperçu de ses ressources minières. Mines et Géologie 9. (Central Morocco; an outline of its mineral resources.)

Morocco. Service Géologique, Rabat
1952a Géologie des gîtes minéraux marocains. Notes et Mémoires 87. (Geology of Moroccan mineral deposits.)

1952b Hydrogéologie du Maroc. Notes et Mémoires 97. (Hydrogeology of Morocco.)

Morrison, A. and M. C. Chown
1965 Photographs of the western Sahara from the Mercury MA-4 satellite. Photogrammetric Engineering 31:350-362.
An illustration of the general geologic, geomorphic, and hydrologic features that can be discerned from satellite photographs. The area covered is the northwestern Sahara.

Moseley, F.
1965 Plateau calcrete, calcreted gravels, cemented dunes and related deposits of the Maallegh-Bomba region of Libya. Zeitschrift für Geomorphologie 9: 166-185.

Mougin, G.
1956 Evaporation des surfaces libres au Maroc; bilan de la compagne 1953-1955 de mesures en bacs type Colorado. Ministère des Travaux Publics, Circonscription de l'Hydraulique et de l'Electricité, Rapport Technique. Rabat.
(Free-surface evaporation in Morocco)

Mourad, I.
1954 Stratigraphy of the Gebel Oweina Section, near Esna, Upper Egypt. Desert Institute, Egypt, Bulletin 4(2).

Muller-Fuega, R.
1954 Contribution à l'étude de la géologie, de la pétrographie, et des ressources hydrauliques et minérales du Fezzan. Direction des Travaux Publics, Tunis, Annales des Mines et de la Géologie 12. 354 p.
(Contribution to the study of the geology, petrography, and hydrologic and mineral resources of the Fezzan.)

Murray, G. W.
1949 Desiccation in Egypt. Société Royale de Géographie d'Egypte, Bulletin 23:19-34.

──── 1951 The Egyptian climate; an historical outline. Geographical Journal 117:422-434.

──── 1952 The work in the desert of the Survey of Egypt. Desert Institute, Egypt, Bulletin 2(2).

Nachtigal, G.
1879- Sahara and Sudan. Weidmann, Berlin. 2 vols.
1881

Office de la Recherche Scientifique et Technique Outre Mer
1953 L'hydrologie et la navigation sur le Niger de Koulikoro à Mopti. Annuaire Hydrologique, 1951.
(The hydrology and navigation of the Niger from Koulikoro to Mopti.)

──── 1955- Etudes hydrologiques des petits bassins d'Afrique
1960 occidentale. Paris. 9 vols.
(Hydrologic studies of small basins in west Africa.)
This 9-volume compendium is the most valuable report available on hydrologic investigations in the Sahara. Emphasis is placed on small drainage basins in various locations which have been studied during runoff periods. Also see Rodier (1960) for a summary of west African surface-water data.

──── 1957 Observations effectuées sur le bassin de Séloumbo (région de Moudjeria, Mauritanie), p. 1-25. *In* Etudes hydrologiques des petits bassins versants d'AOF, vol. 2, chapter 7. Paris.
(Observations on the Séloumbo basin, Moudjeria region, Mauritania. *In* Hydrologic studies of small drainage basins of French West Africa.)

──── 1960a Observations effectuées sur les bassins versants de l'Oued Séloumbo (Mauritanie), p. 1-18. *In* Etudes hydrologiques des petits bassins versants d'AOF, vol. 2, chapter 8. Paris.
(Observations on the drainages of the Wadi Séloumbo, Mauritania. *In* Hydrologic studies of small drainage basins of French West Africa.)

──── 1960b Observations effectuées sur les bassins de l'Oued Séloumbo (région de Moudjeria, Mauritanie), p. 1-21. *In* Etudes hydrologiques des petits bassins versants d'AOF, vol. 2, chapter 6. Paris.
(Observations on the basins of the Wadi Séloumbo, Moudjeria region, Mauritania. See 1960a, above.)

Oliver, F. W.
1945, Dust-storms in Egypt and their relation to the war
1947 period, as noted in Maryut, 1939-45. Dust storms in Egypt as noted in Maryut, a supplement. Geographical Journal 106:26-49; 108:221-226.

Oliver, J.
1965 Evaporation losses and rainfall regime in central and northern Sudan. Weather 20:58-64.

Palausi, G.
1955 Au sujet du Niger fossile dans la région de Tombouctou. Revue de Géomorphologie Dynamique 6:217-218.
(On the fossil Niger in the Tombouctou region.)

Passarge, S.
1907 Geomorphologische probleme aus der Sahara. Gesellschaft für Erdkunde zu Berlin, Zeitschrift 42.
(Geomorphic problems from the Sahara.)

──── 1909 Verwitterung und abtragung in den steppen und wüsten Algeriens. Geographische Zeitschrift 15: 493-510.
(Weathering and transportation in the Algerian steppes and deserts.)

Paver, G. L. and D. A. Pretorius
1954a Report on hydrogeological investigations in Kharga and Dakhla oases. Desert Institute, Egypt, Publication 4.

──── 1954b Report on reconnaissance hydrogeological investigations in the Western Desert coastal zone. Desert Institute, Egypt, Publication 5.

Paver, G. L. and J. N. Jordan
1956 On reconnaissance hydrological and geophysical observations in the north Sinai coastal area of Egypt. Report of the Ministry of Public Works. Desert Institute, Egypt, Publication 7.

Peel, R. F.
1939 The Gilf Kebir. Geographical Journal 93:295-307.

──── 1941 Denudational landforms of the central Libyan Desert. Journal of Geomorphology 5:3-23.

Perret, R.
1935 Le relief du Sahara. Revue de Géographie Physique et de Géologie Dynamique 8:211-256, 363-410.
(The relief of the Sahara.)

──── 1938 Les "côtes" du Sahara français. Annales de Géographie 47:602-616.
(The "hills" of the French Sahara.)

Perret, R.
1952 Le relief des granits de l'Ahaggar. Association de Géographes Français, Bulletin 226-228:82-88.
(The relief of granitic rocks in the Ahaggar.)

1953 Morphologie de quelques îlots granitiques du Sahara français. Société Royale de Géographie d'Egypte, Bulletin 25:49-56.
(Morphology of some granitic islands of the French Sahara.)

Petroleum Exploration Society of Libya
1963 Premier Symposium Saharien. Tripoli.
(First Saharan symposium.)
An extremely useful and modern account of geology and morphology in northern Libya; includes maps, road logs, and other illustrations.

1966 South central Libya and northern Chad. A guidebook to the geology and prehistory. Petroleum Exploration Society of Libya, 8th Annual Field Conference Guidebook, Tripoli.
A modern guidebook on the geology and archeology of south-central Libya and northern Chad; it includes a regional geologic map at a scale of 1:2,000,000.

Pfalz, R.
1940 Geomorphologisches probleme in Italisch-Libyen. Gesellschaft für Erdkunde zu Berlin, Zeitschrift 75.
(Geomorphological problems in Italian Libya.)

Pias, J.
1958 Transgressions et régressions du Lac Tchad à la fin du Tertiaire et au Quaternaire. Académie des Sciences, Paris, Comptes Rendus 246:800-803.
(Transgressions and regressions of Lake Chad from the end of the Tertiary to the Quaternary.)
This short note, and that of Grove (1959), indicate the extent of fluctuation of the level of Lake Chad through time and the abandoned strandlines that attest to this fact.

1960 Sedimentation dans l'Est de la cuvette tchadienne. Académie des Sciences, Paris, Comptes Rendus 250:1514-1516.
(Sedimentation in the eastern part of the Chad basin.)

Pias, J. and E. Guichard
1957 Origines et conséquences de l'existence d'un cordon sableux dans la partie sud-ouest de la cuvette tchadienne. Académie des Sciences, Paris, Comptes Rendus 244:791-793.
(Origins and consequences of the existence of a sandy border in the southeastern part of the Chad basin.)

Pomel, A.
1872 Le Sahara; observation de géologie et de géographie physique et biologique. Société Climatologie Algérie, Bulletin 8:3-165.
(The Sahara; observations of the geology and physical and biological geography.)

Prescott, J. R. V. and H. P. White
1960 Sand formations in the Niger valley between Niamey and Bourem. Geographical Journal 126:200-203.

Price, W. A.
1950 Sahara sand dunes and the origin of the longitudinal dune: a review. Geographical Review 40:462-465.

Pullan, R. A.
1964 The recent geomorphological evolution of the south-central part of the Chad basin. West African Science Association, Journal 9:115-139.

Queney, P.
1945 Observations sur les rides formées par le vent à la surface du sable dans les ergs sahariennes. Annales de Géophysique 1:5-8.
(Observations on the ripples formed by the wind on the surface of the sand in the Saharan ergs.)

Quézel, P.
1958 Mission botanique au Tibesti. Institut de Recherches Sahariennes, Mémoire 4.
(Botanical expedition to Tibesti.)

Radier, H.
1959 Contribution à l'étude géologique du Sudan Oriental. Service de Géologie et de Prospection Miniére, Dakar, Bulletin 26. 2 vols.
(Contribution to the geologic study of the eastern Sudan.)

Raisz, E. J.
1952 Landform map of North Africa. Cambridge, Mass.

Rathjens, C.
1928 Löss in Tripolitanien. Gesellschaft für Erdkunde zu Berlin, Zeitschrift 63:211-228.
(Loess in Tripolitania.)

Raynal, R.
1952a Notes de stratigraphie et de morphologie en moyenne Moulouya; quelques données nouvelles sur le tertiaire continental. Service Géologique du Maroc, Rabat, Notes et Mémoires 95:51-66.
(Morphologic and stratigraphic notes on the middle Mouloya.)

1952b La région de la Haute Moulouya. Service Géologique du Maroc, Notes et Mémoires 96:53-69.
(The upper Mouloya region.)

Richard-Molard, J.
1948 La boutonnière du Richat en Adrar mauritanien. Académie des Sciences, Paris, Comptes Rendus 227:142-143.
(The buttonhole-form of Richat in the Mauritanian Adrar.)

1952 La pseudo-boutonnière du Richat. Afrique Occidentale Française Direction des Mines, Bulletin 15:391-401.
(The pseudo-buttonhole-form of Richat.)

Rittman, A.
1953 Some remarks on the geology of Aswan. Desert Institute, Egypt, Bulletin 3(2).

Robaux, A.
1951 Essai de détermination du bilan hydraulique d'un oued de type saharien: l'Oued Draa. Centre National de la Recherche Scientifique, Colloques Internationaux 35.
(Essay on the determination of the hydraulic regime of a wadi of the Saharan type: the Wadi Draa.)

Roche, M.
1958 Etudes d'écoulement en régime désertique: Massif de l'Ennedi. Office de la Recherche Scientifique et Technique Outre-Mer, Paris. 80 p.
(Studies of runoff in a desert environment: the Ennedi Massif.)

Rodier, J.
  1960   Régimes hydrologiques de l'Afrique de l'Ouest. Office de la Recherche Scientifique et Technique Outre-Mer, Paris. 116 p.
         (Hydrologic regimes in west Africa.)

Roederer, M.
  1954   Etude du régime de l'oued Ouegha. Société Hydrotechnique de France, IIIes Journées de Hydraulique, 12-14 avril, Question A. La Houille Blanche, Grenoble.
         (Study of the flow region of Wadi Ouegha.)

Rognon, P.
  1960a L'évolution morphologique des vallées de l'Atakor. Institut de Recherches Sahariennes, Travaux 19: 25-49.
         (Morphological evolution of the valleys of Atakor.)

  1960b L'évolution de la vallée du Nil d'après des études récentes. Institut de Recherches Sahariennes, Travaux 19:151-156.
         (Evolution of the Nile Valley in light of recent studies.)

  1962   Observations nouvelles sur le Quaternaire du Hoggar. Institut de Recherches Sahariennes, Travaux 21:57-80.
         (Recent observations on the Quaternary of Ahaggar.)

  1963   L'évolution actuelle des formes du relief dans l'Atkor. Institut de Recherches Sahariennes, Travaux 22:61-78.
         (Present evolution of relief forms in Atakor.)

  1964   L'Atakor septentrional au 1:200,000^e, esquisse de carte géomorphologique saharienne. Institut de Recherches Sahariennes, Travaux 23:31-44.
         (Northern Atakor at a scale of 1:200,000; a Saharan geomorphic outline map.)
  A relatively detailed map based upon the author's previous geomorphic investigations in Algeria (Rognon, 1960a, 1962, 1963).

Rottier, R.
  1928   Une mission au Tibesti, l'Afrique Française. Commission de l'Afrique Française, Bulletin, Renseignements Coloniaux 7.
         (A mission to Tibesti, French Africa.)

Roux, G.
  1943   Notice sur la carte de la moyenne annuelle des précipitations (années 1926-1940). Archives Scientifiques du Protectorat Français. Variétés Scientifiques Recueillies par la Société des Sciences Naturelles du Maroc, 6. 19 p.
         (Explanation of the mean annual precipitation map for the 1926-1940 period)

Ruellan, A.
  1962   Utilisation de la géomorphologie pour l'étude pédologique au 1/20,000 de la plaine du Zebra (Basse Moulouya). Revue de Géographie du Maroc 1-2:23-29.
         (Use of geomorphology for the soil survey of the Zebra Plain, Lower Mouloya, at a scale of 1:20,000.)

Ruxton, B. P.
  1958   Weathering and subsurface erosion in granite at the piedmont angle, Balos, Sudan. Geological Magazine 95:353-377.

Ruxton, B. P. and L. Berry
  1961a Notes on faceted slopes, rock fans and domes on granite in the east central Sudan. American Journal of Science 259:194-205.
  This report and a companion work by the same authors (Ruxton and Berry, 1961b) provide some of the few quantitative data on hillslope profiles in relation to rock type in the Sudan.

  1961b Weathering profiles and geomorphic position on granites. Revue de Géomorphologie Dynamique 12:16-31.

Said, Rushdi
  1954   Remarks on the geomorphology of the area east of Helwan, Egypt. Société Royale de Géographie d'Egypte, Bulletin 27:93-103.

  1960   New light on the origin of the Qattara depression. Société Royale de Géographie d'Egypte, Bulletin 33:37-44.

  1962   The geology of Egypt. Elsevier Publishing Company, Amsterdam. 377 p.
  A modern and comprehensive survey of the geology of Egypt which provides more current data than the original compendium by Hume (1925-1939).

Samie, C.
  1954   Etude hydrologique de la Haute-Medjerdah. Société Hydrotechnique de France, Compte rendu des IIIes, Journées de l'Hydraulique, Alger, 12-14 avril 1954. "Pluie, évaporation, filtration, et d'écoulement," Question A, 106-16.
         (Hydrologic study of the upper Medjerdah.)

  1956- Monographie du bassin de la Mafragh. Service de
  1957   la Colonisation et de l'Hydraulique, Annuaire Hydrologique de l'Algérie, p. 1-67.
         (Monograph on the Mafragh basin.)

Sandford, K. S.
  1933   Geology and geomorphology of the southern Libyan desert. Geographical Journal 82:213-219.

  1935a Geological observations on the northwest frontiers of the Anglo-Egyptian Sudan and the adjoining part of the southern Libya Desert. Royal Geological Society of London, Quarterly Journal 91:323-381.

  1935b Sources of water in the northwestern Sudan. Geographical Journal 85:412-431.

  1953   Notes on sand dunes and artesian water in Egypt and the Sudan. Geographical Journal 119:363-366.

Sauvage de Saint-Marc, G.
  1948   Le problémé de l'oued Sebou. Neyrpic, Grenoble.
         (The problem of Wadi Sebou.)

Savornin, J.
  1931   Géologie algérienne et nord-africaine depuis 1830. Service de la Carte Géologique de l'Algérie.

Schirmer, H.
  1893   Le Sahara. Hachette, Paris.

Schirmer, H.
1912　Le Haut-Pays Oranais et le Sahara. Annales de Géographie 21:159-168.
(The Oranian highland and the Sahara.)

Schmitthenner, H.
1931　Die stufenlandschaft am Nil und in der libyschen wüste. Geographische Zeitschrift 37(9):526-540.
(The terrace landscape of the Nile and in the Libyan desert.)

Schoeller, H.
1945　L'hydrogéologie d'une partie de la vallée de la Saoura et du Grand Erg Occidental. Société Géologique de France, Bulletin 15:563-585.
(The hydrogeology of a part of the Saoura Valley and the Grand Erg Occidental.)

Schwarzbach, M.
1953　Das alter der wüste Sahara. Neues Jahrbuch für Geologie und Paläontologie, Monatshefte 4: 157-174.
(The age of the Sahara Desert)

Schwegler, E.
1948a　Die boden nordestrafrikanischer wüsten und halbwüsten. Neues Jahrbuch für Minerologie, Geologie, und Paläontologie, Abhandlungen, Abt. B, Geologie-Paläontologie 89(3):349-406.
(The soils of the deserts and semideserts of northeast Africa.)

——　1948b　Vorgange subaerischer diagenese in küstendünensanden des Ägyptischen Mittelmeer-gebietes. Neues Jahrbuch für Mineralogie, Geologie, und Paläontologie 82:9-16.
(Reactions of subaerial diagenesis in coastal dune sands of the Egyptian Mediterranean region.)

Schweinfurth, G. and L. Lewin
1898　Topographie und geochemie des ägyptischen Natron-Tals. Gesellschaft für Erdkunde zu Berlin, Zeitschrift 33.
(Topography and geochemistry of the Egyptian Soda Valley.)

Seltzer, P.
1946　Le climat de l'Algérie. Institut de Météorologie et de Physique du Globe de l'Algérie, Travaux, Hors série. 219 p.

Sensidoni, F.
1945　Contributo al problema idrico delle regioni costiere a clima arido. Giornale del Genio Civile, Rome, fascicule 1.
(Contribution on a hydrologic problem of a coastal region in an arid climate.)

Sestini, J.
1965　Cenozoic stratigraphy and depositional history, Red Sea coast, Sudan. American Association of Petroleum Geologists, Bulletin 49:1453-1472.

Shata, A.
1951　The Jurassic of Egypt. Desert Institute, Egypt, Bulletin 1(2).

——　1953　New light on the structural development of the Western Desert. Desert Institute, Egypt, Bulletin 3(1).

——　1954　Geomorphological aspects of the west Sinai foreshore province. Desert Institute, Egypt, Bulletin 5(1).

——　1955　An introductory note on the geology of the northern portion of the Western Desert of Egypt. Desert Institute, Egypt, Bulletin 5(2).

——　1956　Structural development of the Sinai peninsula, Egypt. Desert Institute, Egypt, Bulletin 6(2).

El Shazly, E. M.
1957　Review of Egyptian geology. In Egyptian reviews of science, vol. 1. Science Council, Cairo. 91 p.

Shukri, N. M.
1951　Mineral analysis of some Nile sediments. Desert Institute, Egypt, Bulletin 1(2).

——　1953a　The mineralogy of Egyptian sediments. Desert Institute, Egypt, Bulletin 3(1).

——　1953b　The geology of the desert east of Cairo. Desert Institute, Egypt, Bulletin 3(2).

Shukri, N. M. and N. Azer
1952　The mineralogy of Pliocene and more recent sediments in the Faiyum. Desert Institute, Egypt, Bulletin 2(1).

Sidorenko, A. V.
1959　Izvestkovye pustynnye kory Egipta. Akademii nauk S.S.S.R. Doklady 128(4):812-814.
(Calcareous desert crusts of Egypt. Academy of Sciences of the U.S.S.R., Earth Sciences Section, Doklady 128:926-928. Translation.)

Simaika, Y. M.
1951　The regime of the Nile and the use of forecasts — preservation of the Aswan reservoir. United Nations Scientific Conference on Conservation and Utilization of Resources, Proceedings, vol. 4.

——　1953　Research in hydrology and fluid mechanics and development of underground water in the arid regions of northeast Africa. In Reviews of research on arid zone hydrology. Unesco, Paris. Arid Zone Programme 1:42-57.

——　1954　The hydrology of the Sudd-El-Aali project. International Association of Scientific Hydrology, General Assembly, Rome, Publication 38.

——　1962　Alternative uses of limited water supplies in the Egyptian region of the United Arab Republic. In The Problems of the arid zone. Unesco, Paris. Arid Zone Research 18:381-393.
A review of water-resources problems and development in Egypt. An earlier report by this author (Simaika, 1953) emphasizes groundwater research and development in the country.

Smith, H. T. U.
1963　Eolian geomorphology, wind direction and climatic change in North Africa. U. S. Air Force, Cambridge Research Laboratories, Contract Report AF 19(628)-298. 28 p. (Also cited as AD-405 144.)

Sogréah
1957　Aménagement de l'oued Nebana. Etude hydrologique. Rapport Sogréah, Grenoble.
(Control of Wadi Nebana. Hydrologic study.)

Sogréah
1959   Etude hydrologique de l'oued Bel Assoud. Rapport Sogréah, Grenoble.
(Hydrologic study of Wadi Bel Assoud.)

Spain. Instituto Geológico y Minero de España
1958   Mapa geológico del Sahara Español y zonas limítrofes, por J. de la Viña y C. Muñoz Cabezón. Dirección General de Minas, Madrid.
(Geologic map of Spanish Sahara and environs at 1/1,500,000.)

Stebbing, E. P.
1953   The creeping desert in the Sudan and elsewhere in Africa. McCorquodale, Sudan, Ltd. 165 p.

Stewart, J. H.
1960   Land and water resources of Tripolitania. U. S. AID Agriculture Report.
One of the best modern summaries of the water resources of Tripolitania; this report contains all the available data through date of publication.

Sudan. Ministry of Irrigation and Hydro-Electric Power
1957   Sudan irrigation. Khartoum.

Sudan. Survey Department
1960   National report on scientific hydrology to 1960, submitted to the Association of Scientific Hydrology at Helsinki. Khartoum.

Tadros, T. M.
1956   An ecologic survey of the semiarid coastal strip of the Western Desert of Egypt. Desert Institute, Egypt, Bulletin 6(2).

Thesiger, W.
1939   A camel journey to Tibesti. Geographical Journal 94:433-446.

Thomas, J.
1954   Pluviométrie 1920-49 (Mauritanie). Afrique Occidentale Française Service Météorologique Fédéral. 25 p.
Presents a 30-year record of precipitation in Mauritania based upon data from available stations.

Thomas, M. F.
1965   Some aspects of the geomorphology of domes and tors in Nigeria. Zeitschrift für Geomorphologie 9:63-81.

Tileston, F. M. and L. E. Swanson
1962   Water and soil development flood control on Wadi Megenin, Libya. U. S. AID Agriculture Report.

Tilho, J.
1920   The exploration of Tibesti, Erdi, Borkou, and Ennedi in 1912-17. Geographical Journal 56:81-99, 161-183, 241-263.

Tinthoin, R.
1948   Les aspects physiques du Tell Oranais. Fouque, Oran.
(Physical aspects of the Oranian Tell.)

Tixeront, J. and E. Berkaloff
1954a Méthode d'étude et d'évaluation de l'érosion en Tunisie. Association Internationale d'Hydrologie Scientifique, Rome, Compte Rendu 1:172-177.
(Method of study and estimate of erosion in Tunisia.)

1954b Recherches sur le bilan d'eau en Tunisie. Association Internationale d'Hydrologie Scientifique, Congrès U.G.G.I. (International Union of Geodesy and Geophysics), Rome, Compte Rendu 3.
(Research on the water balance in Tunisia.)

1958a Carte au 1:500,000 due ruissellement annuel moyen en Tunisie. Bureau d'Inventaire des Ressources Hydrauliques, Tunis.
(Map of mean annual runoff in Tunisia at a scale of 1:500,000.)
This map and the authors' associated discussion (Tixeront and Berkaloff, 1958b) summarize recorded runoff in Tunisia, presenting all available data to the date of publication.

1958b Le ruissellement en Tunisie. La Tunisie Agricole, mars.
(Runoff in Tunisia.)
This work complements the authors' map (Tixeront and Berkaloff, 1958a) and expands upon the problem of runoff in Tunisia.

Tothill, J. D.
1948   Agriculture in the Sudan. Oxford University Press.

Toupet, C.
1962   Orientation bibliographique sur la Mauritanie. Institut Français d'Arique Noire, Bulletin, sér. B, 24:594-613.
An extremely useful bibliography of work in Mauritania; includes pertinent references on geology and geography.

Tricart, J.
1955a Notes géomorphologiques sur les environs d'Atar (Mauritanie). Institut Français d'Afrique Noire, Bulletin, sér. A, 17:325-337.
(Geomorphic notes on the Atar region)

1955b Types de fleuves et systèmes morphogénétiques en Afrique Occidentale. Comité de Travaux Historiques et Scientifiques, Lille, Section Géographique, Bulletin 78:303-315.
(Types of rivers and morphogenetic systems in west Africa.)

1959   Géomorphologie dynamique de la moyenne vallée du Niger. Annales de Géographie 68:333-343.
(Dynamic geomorphology of the central Niger valley)

1960   A propos de l'erg Trarza. Institut de Recherches Sahariennes, Travaux 19:199-200.
(On the erg of Trarza)

Tricart, J. and M. Brochu
1955   Le grand erg ancien du Trarza et du Cayor (sud-ouest de la Mauritanie et nord du Sénégal). Revue de Géomorphologie Dynamique 4:145-176.
(The great ancient dune field of Trarza and Cayor, southwestern Mauritanie and northern Senegal.)

Tricart, J. *et al.*
1960   Etud géomorphologique du projet d'aménagement du las Faguibine (République du Mali). Sols Africains 5:207-289.
(Geomorphic study of the control project on Lake Faguibine, Republic of Mali.)

Tripoli. Museo Libico di Storia Naturale
1939   Carta geologica della Libia. Scale 1/3,000,000. Accompanying "Le nostre conoscenze geologiche sulla Libia sino al 1938." Annali 1:13-54.
(Geologic map of Libya)

Tripoli. Museo Libico di Storia Naturale
1939- Annali 1-4.
1953
These volumes provide a good bibliography of work in Libya through 1952 and a general description of surficial features in the country.

Trompette, R.
1961   Etude géologique et hydrogéologique de la bordure occidentale de l'Adrar de Mauritanie. Direction des Travaux Publics, R.I.M., Rapport.
(Geologic and hydrogeologic survey of the western border of the Adrar of Mauritania.)

U. S. Army Engineer Waterways Experiment Station
1958   Analogs of Yuma terrain in the Northwest African desert. Vicksburg, Mississippi. Technical Report 3-630.

1962   Analogs of Yuma terrain in the northeast African desert. Rev. ed., folio. Technical Report 3-630, Report 1.

Urvoy, Y.
1933   Les formes dunaires à l'Ouest du Tchad. Annales de Géographie 43:506-515.
(Dune forms in western Chad.)

1936   Structure et modelé du Soudan Français (Colonie du Niger). Annales de Géographie, année 45, 253:19-49.
(Structure and forms of the French Sudan.)

1942   Les bassins du Niger. Institut Français d'Afrique Noire, Dakar, Mémoire 4.
(The Niger basins)

Vache-Grandet, C.
1959   L'erg du Trarza. Notes de géomorphologie dunaire. Institut de Recherches Sahariennes, Travaux 18: 161-171.
(The erg of Trarza. Notes on dune geomorphology.)

Van Everdingen, R. O.
1962   The deeper ground water in Libya. International Association of Scientific Hydrology, Bulletin 7: 33-39.

Van Lopik, J. R., C. R. Kolb, and J. H. Shamburger
1965   Analogs of Yuma terrain in the northwest African desert. Rev. U. S. Army Engineer Waterways Experiment Station, Vicksburg, Mississippi, Technical Report 3-630, Report 6. 2 vols.

Vanney, J. R.
1960   Pluie et crue dans le Sahara nord-occidental. Institut de Recherche Sahariennes, Monographie Régionale 4. 118 p.
(Precipitation and growth in the northwestern Sahara.)

Verlaque, C.
1958   Les dunes d'In Salah. Institut de Recherches Sahariennes, Travaux 17:12-58.

Vincent-Cuaz, L.
1958   Les barkanes de la Mauritanie ont-elles toujours existé? Bulletin Liaison Sahariennes 30:141-146.
(Have the barchans of Mauritania always existed?)

Vita-Finzi, C.
1960a Post-Roman changes in the Wadi Lebda. *In* S. G. Willimott and J. I. Clarke, eds., Field studies in Libya. University of Durham, Department of Geography, Research Paper 4:46-51.

1960b Post-Roman erosion and deposition in the wadis of Tripolitania. International Association of Scientific Hydrology, Publication 53:61-64.

1961a Roman dams of Tripolitania. Antiquity 35:14-20.

1961b Recent alluvial history of the eastern Gebel, Tripolitania. Cambridge University (unpublished Ph.D. thesis).
A comprehensive discussion of erosion and deposition in Libyan wadis, based upon field studies and archeologic evidence. See Vita-Finzi (1960a, b. 1961a, 1963) for allied published information on this topic.

1963   Carbon-14 dating of medieval alluvium in Libya. Nature 198:880.

Vogt, J.
1952   Aspects de l'évolution morphologique de l'Ouest Africain. Annales de Géographie 61:193-206.
(Aspects of the morphological evolution of west Africa.)

1962   Un vallée soudanaise: la moyenne Bagoé. Revue de Géomorphologie Dynamique 13:2-9.
(A Sudanese valley: the central Bagoé)

Vogt, J. and R. Black
1963   Remarques sur la géomorphologie de l'Aïr. Bureau de Recherches Géologiques et Minières, Paris. Bulletin 1:1-29.
(Remarks on the geomorphology of Aïr massif)
This most recent description of the surficial features of the Aïr Massif is a useful addition to earlier work (Institut Français d'Afrique Noire, 1950). Data on runoff from some Aïr catchments has been provided by Lefevre (1960).

Walther, J.
1877   L'apparition de la craie aux environs des pyramides. Institut Egyptien, Cairo, Bulletin.
(The occurrence of chalk in the environment of the pyramids.)

1911   Windkanter in der libyschen wüste. Deutsche Geologische Gesellschaft, Zeitschrift 7.
(Wind-formed stones in the Libyan desert.)

Whiteman, A. J.
1962   Report on arid zone research in the University of Khartoum ending July 1962. University of Khartoum, Department of Geology. 20 p.
This report on arid-zone research activities at the University of Khartoum, and that of Bell (1964), which covers the 1962-1964 period, give a useful summary of the projects that are underway, personnel that are involved, and preliminary results.

Wilbert, J.
1962   Croûtes et encroûtements calcaires au Maroc. Al Awamia 3:175-192.
(Calcareous crusts and encrustations in Morocco.)

Williams, M. A. J. and D. N. Hall
1965   Recent expeditions to Libya from the Royal Military Academy, Sandhurst. Geographical Journal 131:482-501.
Presents quantitative data on the relations of slopes and rock type in the Jebel Arkenu area, and a map showing drainage features, sand areas, and the general geology. Many useful references on southeastern Libya are included.

Willimott, S. G. and J. I. Clarke (eds.)
1960 Field studies in Libya. University of Durham, Department of Geography, Research Paper 4.

Willimott, S. G. *et al*
1960 Water and soil development soil survey of the Tauorga Region, Libya. U. S. AID Agriculture Report.

Witschell, L.
1928 Klima und landschaft in Tripolitanien. Universität Königsberg, Geographisches Institut, Veröffentlichungen 10.
(Climate and landforms in Tripolitania.)

Worrall, G. A.
1958 Deposition of silt by the irrigation waters of the Nile at Khartoum. Geographical Journal 124: 219-222.

Wright, J. W.
1949 The White Nile flood plain and the effect of proposed control schemes. Geographical Journal 114: 173-190.

Zimmerman, H.
1963 Zur kenntnis des Quartärs der südtunesischen schottregion. Naturforschende Gesellschaft in Zürich, Vierteljahrsschrift 2.
(On knowledge of the Quaternary in the southern Tunisia gravel plains area.)

Zittel, K. von
1880 Über den geologischen bau der libyischen wüste. Königliche Akademie, München. 47 p.
(On the geologic structure of the Libyan desert.)

SECTION V

THE SOMALI-CHALBI

Includes works cited in the text discussions on: Kenya, Somalia, French Somaliland, and Ethiopia.

Anonymous
1963 Aerial and ground survey of Ethiopia. Ethiopian Geographical Review 1(1).

Besairie, H.
1946 Notice explicative; carte géologique de la côte française des Somalis (1:400,000). Imprimerie Nationale, Paris.
(Explanation of the geologic map of French Somalia, scale 1:400,000.)

Boaler, S. B. and C. A. H. Hodge
1962 Vegetation stripes in Somaliland. Journal of Ecology 50:465-474.

_____
1964 Observations on vegetation arcs in the northern region, Somali Republic. Journal of Ecology 52: 511-544.

British Military Authority
1945 Report on general survey of British Somaliland. Government Press, Mogadishu.
The first of a series of reports between 1945 and 1949 which treat topography, meteorology, water supply, and vegetation. These reports provide excellent summaries of available information on these topics.

Brooks, C. E. P.
1920 The meteorology of British Somaliland. Royal Meteorological Society, Quarterly Journal 46: 434-438.

Busk, H. G.
1939 Notes on the geology of the northeastern extremity of the Northern Frontier Province, Kenya Colony. Geological Magazine 76:215-221.

Cole, S. M.
1950 An outline of the geology of Kenya. Pitman, London.
One of the best available summaries of the general geology of Kenya with some information on surficial features. A more recent geological map of the country is available through the Survey of Kenya (1959), under Kenya below.

Dainelli, G.
1943 Geologia dell'Africa orientale. Reale Accademia d'Italia, Rome. 3 vols.
(Geology of east Africa, with map at scale of 1:2,000,000.)

Dixey, F.
1946 Erosion and tectonics in the East African rift system. Geological Society of London, Quarterly Journal 102:339-379.

_____
1948 Geology of northern Kenya. Geological Survey, Kenya, Report 15.

Dreyfuss, M.
1931 Etude de géologie et de géographie physique sur la côte française des Somalis. Revue de Géographie Physique et de Géologie Dynamique 4(4).
(Study of the geology and physical geography of French Somalia; includes map at scale of 1:5,000,000.)
This work must still be considered a basic reference on the geology and surficial features of French Somaliland. See text for more recent works on these subjects and consult Moullard and Robaux (1958) for a summary of available hydrologic data.

Emmanuel, H. W.
1964 The Imperial Ethiopian Mapping and Geography Institute, a review. Ethiopian Geographical Review 2(2).

French Somaliland. Service des Travaux Publics
1960 Bibliographie géologique et miniére (1930-59). Djibouti.
(Geologic and mining bibliography.)

Fuchs, V. E.
1939 The geological history of the Lake Rudolf basin, Kenya Colony. Royal Society of London, Philosophical Transactions ser. B(560), 229:219-274.

Girdler, R. W.
1958 The relationship of the Red Sea to the East African rift system. Geological Society of London, Quarterly Journal 114:79-106.

Gouin, P. and P. A. Mohr
1964 Gravity traverses in Ethiopia. University College of Addis Ababa, Geophysical Observatory, Bulletin 3(3).

Greenwood, J. E. G. W.
1957 The development of vegetation patterns in Somaliland Protectorate. Geographical Journal 123: 465-473.

Gregory, J. W.
1920 The African rift valleys. Geographical Journal 56: 13-47.

Hunt, J. A.
1951 A general survey of the Somaliland Protectorate, 1944-50. Crown Agents for the Colonies, London.

Hunt, J. A.
1958   Report on the geology of the Adadleh area. Somaliland Protectorate, Geological Survey, Report 2.

Johnson, D. W.
1929   Geomorphologic aspects of rift valleys. International Geological Congress, 15th, Pretoria, Compte Rendu 2:354-373.

Kenya. Survey of Kenya
1959   Atlas of Kenya. Geological map of Kenya, scale 1:3,000,000.

Macfadyen, W. A.
1933   The geology of British Somaliland. Crown Agents, London.
A basic reference on the geology of northern Somalia with descriptions and illustrations of such surficial features as drainage patterns, terraces, and dunes.

_____
1950   Vegetation patterns in the semi-desert plains of British Somaliland. Geographical Journal 116: 199-211.

_____
1952   Water supply and geology of parts of British Somaliland. Crown Agents for the Colonies, London.

Mariam, M. W.
1964   The Awash Valley. Ethiopian Geographical Review 2(1):18-27.

Mason, J. E. and A. J. Warder
1956   The geology of the Heis-Mait-Waqderia area. Somaliland Protectorate, Geological Survey, Report 1.

Mohr, P. A.
1964   The geology of Ethiopia. University College of Addis Ababa Press.
A modern and authoritative summary of the general geology of Ethiopia, accompanied by a map of the "horn" of east Africa at a scale of 1:2,000,000. A good list of references is provided. See Dainelli (1943) for earlier but more extensive treatment of geology and Tatu (1964) for a summary of precipitation data for Ethiopia.

Moullard, L. and A. Robaux
1958   Inventaire des ressources en eau de la côte française des Somalis. Bureau Central pour les Equipements d'Outre-mer, Paris. 3 parts.

Murphy, H. F.
1959   A report on the fertility status of some soils of Ethiopia. Imperial Ethiopian College of Agriculture and Mechanic Arts, Experiment Station, Bulletin 1.

Pallister, J. W.
1963   Notes on the geomorphology of the northern region, Somali Republic. Geographical Journal 129:184-187.

Pereira, H. C.
1959   Study of the stream flow effects of land use changes in catchment areas. *In* Conference of the British East and Central African Territories on Hydrology and Water Resources, 3rd, Kampala, 1958, Proceedings. Government Printer, Nairobi.

Puri, R. K.
1961   Bibliography relating to geology, mineral resources, paleontology, etc., of the Somali Republic. Somali Republic, Survey Report RKP/1, Hargeisa.
A good bibliography on Somalia through the date of publication. For current information on mapping, geological studies, and allied topics, the "Annual Reports" of the Geological Survey Department of the Ministry of Industry and Commerce, at Hargeisa, should be consulted. These reports list all current projects and their completion status, and all publications issued during the year involved.

Tatu, K.
1964   Rainfall in Ethiopia. Ethiopian Geographical Review 2(2):28-36.

Tonini, D.
1956   Criteri per l'utilizzazione delle risorse idrauliche nell'Africa orientale italiana. Società Italiana per il Progresso delle Scienze, Atti della 25 Reunione. (Criteria for the utilization of water resources in Italian east Africa.)

United Nations, Special Project
1964   Survey of the Awash River basin, preliminary report to the Imperial Ethiopian Government. Addis Ababa. 17 p.

Viney, N. M.
1947   A bibliography of British Somaliland. War Office, London.

Voûte, C.
1959   The Assab region, its geology and history during the Quaternary period. University College of Addis Ababa, Geophysical Observatory, Bulletin 1:73-101.

Wayland, E. J.
1929   Rift valleys and Lake Victoria. International Geological Congress, 15th, Pretoria, Compte Rendu 2:323-353.

Willis, B.
1936   East African plateaus and rift valleys. Carnegie Institution of Washington, Publication 470.

SECTION VI

ARABIAN DESERT

Includes works cited in the text discussions on: the Arabian Peninsula, Iraq, Jordan, Syria and Lebanon, and Israel.

Abd-El-Al, I.
1953   Statics and dynamics of water in the Syro-Lebanese limestone massifs. *In* Proceedings of the Ankara Symposium on Arid Zone Hydrology. Unesco, Paris. Arid Zone Programme 2:60-76.
This report treats precipitation, surface-water runoff, springs, and ground-water hydrology in the Syria-Lebanon border area. Basic hydrological data for both countries were summarized by Combier (1933) and Dubertret (1933), and relatively recent precipitation data for Lebanon have been published by Rey (1955).

Amiran, D. H. K.
1951   Geomorphology of the central Negev highlands. Israel Exploration Journal 1:107-114.

Arid Zone Research Institute, Abu-Ghraib
1964   Reports and research papers accomplished during 1963. Annual Bulletin 1.

_____
1965   Research plan, 1964-1967. University of Baghdad. 37 p.

Auden, J. B.
1956 Discussion on the structural and geomorphic evolution of the Dead Sea Rift. Geological Society of London, Proceedings 1544.

Avnimelech, M.
1952 Late Quaternary sediments of the coastal plain of Israel. Research Council of Israel, Bulletin 2:51-57.

———
1965 Bibliography of Levant geology. Davey, New York. A valuable bibliography with many references to reports treating surficial features in this portion of the Arabian Desert.

Bagnold, R. A.
1951 Sand formations in southern Arabia. Geographical Journal 117:78-86.

Banna, S. I.
1965 Country report of Kuwait. *In* Seminar on water logging in relation to irrigation and salinity problems, Lahore, November 1964. FAO, Rome, EPTA Report 1932:74-77.

Bates, B. A.
1964 A peninsula in profile. Aramo World Nov./Dec.: 2-9.

Baumer, M.
1964 Scientific research aimed at developing the arid zone of Saudi Arabia. Unesco, Paris. Arid Zone [Newsletter] 24:4-12.

Bentor, Y. K.
1952a Air photographs and geological mapping, with special reference to the geological conditions in the Negev. Research Council of Israel, Bulletin 2:157-169.

———
1952b Relations entre la tectonique et les dépôts de phosphates dans le Néguev iraélien. International Geological Congress, 19th, Algiers, Comptes Rendus, section 11:93-101.
(Relations between tectonics and phosphate deposits in the Negev.)

———
1961 Some aspects of the Dead Sea and the question of its age. Geochimica et Cosmochimica Acta 25: 239-260.

Beydoun, Z. R.
1960 Synopsis of the geology of east Aden Protectorate. International Geological Congress, 21st, Copenhagen, Report 21:131-149.
A good outline of the general geology of Aden which serves to supplement the excellent map of the Arabian peninsula by the U. S. Geological Survey (1963). A more detailed report on the geology of this area is now available in U. S. Geological Survey Professional Paper 560-H by Beydoun, 1966.

Bhutta, M. A.
1964 Other minerals. Directorate of Mineral Resources, Jeddah, Geology Department, Report 3/x/1558.

Blake, G. S.
1928 Geology and water resources of Palestine, Jerusalem. 51 p.

———
1930 The mineral resources of Palestine and Transjordan. Geological Adviser in Palestine, Publication 2.

———
1937 Old shore lines of Palestine. Geological Magazine 74:68-78.

———
1939a Reconnaissance geological map of Trans-Jordan, scale 1:1,000,000. *In* M. G. Ionides and G. S. Blake, Report on the water resources of Transjordan and their development. Crown Agents for the Colonies, London. 372 p.

———
1939b Geological map of northern Palestine. Scale 1:250,000. Survey of Palestine, Jaffa.

Blanckenhorn, M.
1912 Kurzer abriss der geologie palästinas. Deutscher Palästina-Vereins, Zeitschrift, p. 119-139.
(Short outline of the geology of Palestine)

———
1914 Syrien, Arabien, und Mesopotamien. Handbuch der Regionalen Geologie 4(17).

Bodenheimer, W. and D. Neev
1962 On the change of pH in Dead Sea brine on dilution with distilled water. Research Council of Israel, Bulletin 11G.

Bogue, R. G.
1953 Report on geologic reconnaissance in northwestern Saudi Arabia. Technical Cooperation Administration, Jeddah, Natural Resources Division, (unpublished) Report.

Brown, G. F.
1960 Geomorphology of western and central Saudi Arabia. International Geological Congress, 21st, Copenhagen, Report 21:150-159.
A brief outline of the principal geomorphic features of western and central Saudi Arabia.

Burdon, D. J.
1959 Handbook of the geology of Jordan. Government of the Hashemite Kingdom of Jordan.
The most comprehensive recent summary of the general geology of Jordan, with pertinent sections on topography, soils, hydrology, and vegetation. Many references to earlier works on Jordan are provided.

Burningham, C. W.
1952 Report to the Government of Saudi Arabia on land and water resources. FAO, Rome, EPTA Report 40.

Butzer, K. W.
1958 Quaternary stratigraphy and climate in the Near East. Bonn.

Carter, H. J.
1857 Memorandum on geology of the southeastern coast of Arabia. p. 33-34, 94-95. *In* Geological papers on Western India, including Cutch, Sinde, and south-east coast of Arabia; to which is appended a summary of the geology of India generally. Edited for the Government by H. J. Carter.

Combier, C.
1933 La climatologie de la Syrie et du Liban. Revue de Géographie Physique et de Géologie Dynamique 6(4):319-346.

Dabbous, B.
1965 Country report of Syria. *In* Seminar on water logging in relation to irrigation and salinity problems, Lahore, November 1964. FAP, Rome, EPTA Report 1932.

Dapples, E. C.
    1941   Surficial deposits of the deserts of Syria, Trans-
            jordan, and Iraq. Journal of Sedimentary Petrology
            11:124-141.

Dost, H.
    1953   Bibliography on land and water utilization in the
            Middle East. Wageningen Agricultural University
            College, Wageningen, Netherlands. 115 p.

Dubertret, L.
    1932   Les formes structurales de la Syrie et de la Pales-
            tine, leur origine. Académie des Sciences, Paris,
            Comptes Rendus 195:66-68.
            (Structural forms of Syria and Palestine, their
            origin.)

    1933   L'hydrologie et aperçu sur l'hydrographie de la
            Syrie et du Liban. Revue de Géographie Physique
            et de Géologie Dynamique 6:347-452.
            (Hydrology and outline of hydrography of Syria
            and Lebanon.)

    1940   Sur l'âge du volcanisme en Syrie et au Liban.
            Societe Géologique de France, Comptes Rendus
            Sommaires, p. 55-57.
            (On the age of vulcanism in Syria and Lebanon.)

    1945   Carte géologique au millionième de la Syrie et du
            Liban. Beyrouth.
            (Geologic map of Syria and Lebanon at
            1:1,000,000.)

    1948   Aperçu de géographie physique sur le Liban,
            l'Anti-Leban et la Damascène. Etudes Géologiques
            et Géographiques sur le Liban, la Syrie et le
            Moyen-Orient, Beyrouth, Notes et Mémoires 4:
            191-226.
            (Outline of the physical geography of Lebanon,
            Anti-Lebanon, and Damascus.)

    1954   Formes d'érosion au Liban. p. 130-133. *In* Colloque
            sur la protection et la conservation de la nature
            dans le Proche-Orient, Beyrouth, 3-8 juin 1954.
            Centre de Cooperation Scientifique de l'Unesco
            pour le Moyen-Orient. 173 p.
            (Erosion forms of Lebanon.)

    1955a   Carte géologique du Liban au 1:200,000. Minis-
            tère des Travaux Publics, Beyrouth.
            (Geological map of Lebanon at a scale of
            1:200,000.)

    1955b   Notice explicative du carte géologique du Liban.
            Ministère des Travaux Publics, Beyrouth. 74 p.
            (Explanatory notes on the geological map of
            Lebanon.)

Dubertret, L. and J. Weulersse
    1940   Manuel de géographie de la Syrie et de la Proche
            Orient. Imprimerie Catholique, Beirut.
            (Manual of geography of Syria and the Near
            East.)
An excellent summary of the physical features of this
region, which is still useful despite the subsequent information that has become available. See Hourani (1954)
for more recent data and Dubertret (1948, 1954).

Emery, K. O.
    1956   Sediments and water of the Persian Gulf. Ameri-
            can Association of Petroleum Geologists, Bulletin
            40:2354-2383.

Emery, K. O. and D. Neev
    1960   Mediterranean beaches of Israel. Geological Sur-
            vey of Israel, Bulletin 26. 23 p.

Evans, G. *et al.*
    1964   Origin of the coastal flats, the sabkha, of the Tru-
            cial Coast, Persian Gulf. Nature 202:759-761.

Evenari, M. *et al.*
    1961   Ancient agriculture in the Negev. Science 133:
            979-996

Finkel, H. J.
    1961   Movement of barchan dunes measured by aerial
            photogrammetry. Photogrammetric Engineering
            27: 439-444.

Fisher, W. B.
    1963   The Middle East. 5th ed. Methuen, London.
One of the more useful geographic works that treat the
Arabian desert area. This volume outlines the general
geology, surficial features, and climatic conditions in the
region.

Food and Agriculture Organization of the United Nations
    1964   FAO Mediterranean Development Project, Coun-
            try Report: Jordan. Rome.

Gardi, O. R.
    1964   Country progress report on Iraq. p. 71-80. *In* Irri-
            gation practices seminar, 5th, New Delhi. Gov-
            ernment of India and U. S. AID, New Delhi.

Geological Survey of Israel
    1959   Summary of activities, 1949-1958. Israel Ministry
            of Development. 27 p.

Geukens, F.
    1960   Contribution à la géologie du Yémen. Université
            de Louvain, Institut Géologique, Mémoires 21:
            117-180.
A major report on the geology of Yemen which serves to
supplement other sources of information on this part of
the Arabian peninsula (U. S. Army Engineer Waterways
Experiment Station, 1960; U. S. Geological Survey, 1963).

Grader, P.
    1958a   Geological outline of the Sasa region, Galilee.
            Geological Survey of Israel, Bulletin 20.

    1958b   Geological history of the Heletz-Brur area, Israel.
            Geological Survey of Israel, Bulletin 22.

Haller, J.
    1945   Aperçu sur la préhistoire de la Syrie et du Liban
            en 1945. Délégation Générale de France au Levant,
            Beyrouth, Section Géologique, Notes et Mémoires
            4:49-58.
            (Outline of the prehistory of Syria and Lebanon.)

Hamdan, A. A.
    1965   The size and shape characteristics of some modern
            desert sands. University of Sheffield (unpublished
            Ph.D. dissertation).
A detailed comparison of the characteristics of sands from
Saudi Arabia and the Sahara.

Helal, A. H.
    1964   Die bedeutung eines ägyptischen felsbildes bei
            Mekka für die frage nach dem alter von block-
            meerbildungen und desquamationen in
            Saudi-Arabien. Zeitschrift für Geomorphologie 8:
            367-369.
            (The significance of Egyptian petroglyphs at
            Mecca on the question of the age of block-field
            formation and exfoliation in Saudi Arabia.)

Henson, F. R. S.
1951*a* Observations on the geology and petroleum occurrences of the Middle East. World Petroleum Congress, 3rd, The Hague, Proceedings 1:118-140.

——— 1951*b* Oil occurrences in relation to regional geology of the Middle East. Tulsa Geological Society, Digest 19:72-81.

Herness, K. S.
1964 Placer gold deposits on the Red Sea drainage shelf. Directorate of Mineral Resources, Jeddah, Geology Department, Report 3/204/4172.

Heybroek, F.
1942 La géologie d'une partie du Liban Sud. Leidsche Geologische Mededelingen 12:251-470.
(The geology of a part of southern Lebanon.)

Holm, D. A.
1953 Dome-shaped dunes of central Nejd, Saudi Arabia. International Geological Congress, 19th, Algiers, Comptes Rendus 7:107-112.

——— 1960 Desert geomorphology in the Arabian peninsula. Science 132:1369-1379.
A brief outline of the general geomorphic features of Saudi Arabia with discussion of desert problems. Based upon the author's previous work which is described in an Arabian American Oil Company file report, this latter report contains much useful information on Arabian sand areas and other aspects of surficial features.

——— 1962 New meteorite localities in the Rub' al Khali, Saudi Arabia. American Journal of Science 260:303-309.

Hourani, A. H.
1954 Syria and Lebanon. London.

Hull, E.
1885 Mount Seir, Sinai, and western Palestine. Published for the Committee of the Palestine Exploration Fund by R. Bentley and Son, London. 227 p.

——— 1886 Memoir on the geology and geography of Arabia Petraea, Palestine, and adjoining districts, with special reference to the mode of formation of the Jordan-Arabah depression and the Dead Sea. Published for the Committee of the Palestine Exploration Fund by R. Bentley and Son, London.

Ibbitt, M. I.
n.d. The effect of sediment on streamflow and gauging. Imperial College, London (in preparation).

Israel Geological Society
1960 Symposium on the Dead Sea and Sdom region, Proceedings. Research Council of Israel, Bulletin 9G:165-173.
An excellent assemblage of papers on the Dead Sea. See Bentor (1961) and Bodenheimer and Neev (1962) for data on the water quality of the Dead Sea.

Issar, A.
1961 The Plio-Pleistocene geology of the Ashdod area. Research Council of Israel, Bulletin 10G:173-182.

Italconsult
1964 Land and water surveys on the Wadi Jizan. Vol. 2: Hydrogeological report. UN Special Fund Project, FAO, Rome.
A summary and analysis of all available hydrologic data on the Wadi Jiza', which heads in the 'Asir and flows to the Red Sea, north of the Yemen border.

Itzhaki, Y., Z. Reiss, and A. Issar
1961 Contributions to the study of the Pleistocene in the coastal plain of Israel. Geological Survey of Israel, Bulletin 32.

Jordan. Central Water Authority
1964 Technical Paper 34 (1-2), and accompanying map. Amman.
Provides an historical review of rainfall records in Jordan, data on mean annual precipitation for the 1931-1960 period, and for Jerusalem between 1846 and 1964. This report includes a map at a scale of 1:5,000,000, showing 30-year isohyets and the locations of stream gaging stations. Country-wide data for the 1960-1964 period are also available (Jordan Central Water Authority, 1965).

——— 1965 Rainfall in Jordan in the water year 1963/64. Amman. Technical Paper 35.

Kaddouri, N. and J. Barica
1964 High ground water table and its effect on soils in arid areas. Al-Ma'aref Press, Baghdad. 21 p.

Kaddouri, N. and L. Pavel
1964 Mineralogical composition of two clays from Iraq. Al-Ma'aref Press, Baghdad. 11 p.

Kadir, N. A.
1964 Drainage development and problems in Iraq. p. 229-238. *In* Irrigation practices seminar, 5th, New Delhi. Government of India and U. S. AID, New Delhi.

Kallner, H.
1943 Outlines of the geomorphology of Judea. Société Royale de Géographie d'Egypte, Bulletin 21.

Käselau, A.
1928 Die natürlichen landschaften nord- und zentralarabiens. Petermanns Geographische Mitteilungen 74:341-342.
(The natural landscapes of northern and middle Arabia.)

Kerr, R. C.
1953 The Arabian peninsula. Science of Petroleum 6:93-98.

Kerr, R. C. and J. O. Nigra
1952 Analysis of eolian sand control. American Association of Petroleum Geologists, Bulletin 36:1541-1573.
An excellent description of sand-control measures undertaken in eastern Saudi Arabia.

Knetsch, G. and P. Gounot
1963 Arid zone research in Iraq. Unesco, Paris. Arid Zone [Newsletter] 22:9-18.

Krenkel, E.
1924 Der Syrische bogen. Centralblatt für Mineralogie, Geologie und Paläontologie, p. 274-281, 301-313.
(The Syrian Arc)

Lamare, P.
1936 Structure géologique de l'Arabie. Charles Beranger, Paris.
(Geologic structure of Arabia.)

Langozky, Y.
1963 High-level lacustrine sediments in the Rift Valley at Sdom. Israel Journal of Earth-Sciences 12:17-25.

Lartet, L.
1869 La géologie de la Palestine. Annales des Sciences Géologiques, Paris, 1(1).
(The geology of Palestine.)

Lees, G. M.
1928a The geology and tectonics of Oman and parts of southeastern Arabia. Geological Society of London, Quarterly Journal 84:585-670.

———

1928b The physical geography of south-eastern Arabia. Geographical Journal 71:441-470.

———

1955 Recent earth movements in the Middle East. Geologische Rundschau 43:221-226.

Lees, G. M. and N. L. Falcon
1952 The geographical history of the Mesopotamian plains. Geographical Journal 118:24-39.

Little, O. H.
1925 The geography and geology of Makalla, South Arabia. Geological Survey of Egypt, Cairo. 250 p.

MacDonald, M. and Partners
1965 East bank Jordan, water resources. Report to the Hashemite Kingdom of Jordan.

Malaika, J.
1964 Irrigation conditions and problems in Iraq. p. 119-125. *In* Irrigation practices seminar, 5th, New Delhi. Government of India and U. S. AID, New Delhi.

Mayerson, P.
1959 Ancient agricultural remains in the central Negev, the Tleilat-el-'Enab. American Schools of Oriental Research, Bulletin 153:19-31.

Mitchell, R. C.
1957 Fault patterns of northwestern Hejaz, Saudi Arabia. Eclogae Geologicae Helvetiae 50:257-270.

Moormann, F.
1959 Report to the Government of Jordan on the soils of east Jordan. FAO, Rome, EPTA Report 1132. 64 p.

Morton, D. M.
1959 The geology of Oman. World Petroleum Congress, 5th, New York, Proceedings, Section 1:277-294.

Neev, D.
1960 A pre-Neogene erosion channel in the southern coastal plain of Israel. Geological Survey of Israel, Bulletin 25.

Neumann, J.
1958 Tentative energy and water balances for the Dead Sea. Research Council of Israel, Bulletin 7G(2/3).

Owen, L.
1938 Origin of the Red Sea depression. American Association of Petroleum Geologists, Bulletin 22:1217-1223.

Pavel, L. and N. Kaddouri
1964 Present problems and plan of development of the Arid Zone Research Institute at Abu-Ghraib. Memorandum to the President of the University of Baghdad. Tal-Tamaddun Press, Baghdad.

Philby, H. S.
1922 The heart of Arabia. Constable, London. 2 vols.

———

1928 Arabia of the Wahhabis. Constable, London. 422 p.

———

1933a The Empty Quarter. Constable, London. 433 p.

———

1933b Rub' al Khali. Geographical Journal 81:1-26.

Phillips, J. A.
1882 The red sands of the Arabian desert. Geological Society of London, Quarterly Journal 38:110-113.

Picard, L.
1937a Inferences on the problem of the Pleistocene climate of Palestine and Syria, drawn from flora, fauna, and stratigraphy. Prehistory Society, Cambridge, Proceedings 5:58-70.

———

1937b On the structure of the Arabian peninsula. Hebrew University, Jerusalem, Geology Department, ser. 1, Bulletin 3. 12 p. Also published, in Russian, *in:* International Geological Congress, 17th, Moscow, 1937, Comptes Rendus 2:433-442.

———

1943 Structure and evolution of Palestine, with comparative notes on neighboring countries. Hebrew University, Jerusalem, Geology Department, Bulletin 4(2/4).

———

1951 Geomorphogeny of Israel. Part 1: The Negev. Geological Survey of Israel, Publication 1:5-31. A good summary of the landforms and general geomorphology of the Negev. Amiran's (1951) account of this area is also useful, as is Kallner's (1943) earlier work and the morphological descriptions of de Vaumas (1953).

———

1952 The Pleistocene peat of Lake Hula. Research Council of Israel, Bulletin 2:147-156.

Pilgrim, G. E.
1906 The geology of the Persian Gulf and adjoining portions of Persia and Arabia. Geological Survey of India, Memoir 34 (4).

Quennell, A. M.
1951 The geology and mineral resources of (former) Trans-Jordan. Colonial Geology and Mineral Resources, London, 2(2):85-115.

———

1958 The structural and geomorphic evolution of the Dead Sea rift. Geological Society of London, Quarterly Journal 114:1-24.

———

1959 Tectonics of the Dead Sea rift. p. 385-405. *In* Asociación de Servicios Geológicos Africanos, Actas y Trabajos de las Reuniones celebradas en México en 1956 (International Geological Congress, 20th, Mexico), México, D. F.

Rafe and Raffety
1965 Nablus District, water resources survey, report to Central Water Authority, Amman, Jordan.

Range, P.
1927 Neuere forschungen zur geologie und geographie Palästinas. Gesellschaft für Erdkunde zu Berlin, Zeitschrift 62.
(New research on the geology and geography of Palestine.)

Ravikovitch, S.
1953 The aeolian soils of the northern Negev. *In* Desert research, proceedings of the international symposium held in Jerusalem, May 7-14, 1952, sponsored by the Research Council of Israel and Unesco. Research Council of Israel, Special Publication 2:404-433.

Al-Rawi, A. H. and L. Pavel
1964   Exchangeable sodium percentage in Iraqi saline and carbonaceous soils and determined on the basis of the Donnan Equilibrium equation. Al-Ma'aref Press, Baghdad. 9 p.

Reifenberg, A.
1947   The soils of Palestine. 2nd ed. Munby, London.

———
1950   Man-made dune encroachment on Israel's coast. International Congress of Soil Science, 4th, Amsterdam, Transactions 1:325-327.

Rey, J.
1955   Carte pluviométrique du Liban au 1:200,000 avec aperçu sur les facteurs du climat. Ministère des Travaux Publics, Ksara, Liban. 26 p.
(Pluviometric map of Lebanon on a scale of 1:200,000, with an outline of the climatic factors)

Rim, M.
1948   The movement of dunes and the origin of red sand in Palestine from a physical point of view. Hebrew University (unpublished thesis).

———
1950   Sand and soil in the coastal plain of Israel. Israel Exploration Journal 1(1).

———
1953   Le classement des minéraux du sable par les agents naturels sur les dunes côtières. Centre National de la Recherche Scientifique, Colloques Internationaux 35:261-276.

———
1958   Simulation, by dynamical model, of sand tract morphologies occurring in Israel. Research Council of Israel, Bulletin 7G(2/3).
One of the best reports on sand transport in Israel, employing model technique. The earlier reports of this author (Rim, 1948, 1950, 1953) adequately describe the characteristics of sands in the country and also treat problems of sand transport. See Reifenberg (1950) and Striem (1954) for related papers on dunes.

Safadi, C.
1956   Hydrogéologie des terrains volcaniques de la Syrie méridionale. Nancy, thèse.
(Hydrogeology of the volcanic terrain of southern Syria.)

Sandford, K. S.
1944   Structure and evolution of the Levant and northern Africa. Nature 154:569-571.

Schattner, I.
1962   The Lower Jordan Valley; a study in the fluviomorphology of an arid region. Hebrew University, Jerusalem, Scripta Hierosolymitana 11. 123 p.
A good description of geomorphology and fluvial processes of this portion of the Jordan Valley.

Shalem, N.
1953   La stabilité du climat en Palestine. Research Council of Israel, Special Publication 2:153-175.
(Stability of climate in Palestine.)

———
1955   The mineral and water resources of Israel. Israel Economic Forum 6(3).

Sharon, D.
1959   Physiographic aspects of the Tleilat-el-'Enab in the Negev (translated title). Israel Exploration Society, Bulletin 23:194-202.
In Hebrew.

Shaw, S. H.
1947   Geological map of southern Palestine. Scale 1:250,000. Public Works Department, Jerusalem.

———
1948   The geology and mineral resources of Palestine. Imperial Institute, London, Bulletin 46:87-103.
A good summary of the geology of Israel, which provides some revision of the basic reference works by Blake (1928, 1930) on the geology and water resources of the general area. See Shalem (1955) for a more recent outline of water resources in Israel.

———
1956   Discussion on the structural and geomorphic evolution of the Dead Sea rift. Geological Society of London, Proceedings 1544.

Simansky, N.
1955   Report to the Government of Saudi Arabia on the preliminary project for land and water use development in Wadi Jizan. FAO, Rome, EPTA Report 410.

Slatkine, A. and M. Pomerancblum
1958   Contribution to the study of the Pleistocene in the coastal plain of Israel. Geological Survey of Israel, Bulletin 19.

Steineke, M., R. A. Bramkamp, and N. J. Sander
1958   Stratigraphic relations of Arabian Jurassic oil. p. 1294-1329. *In* Habitat of oil, American Association of Petroleum Geologists, Tulsa, Oklahoma.

Striem, H. L.
1954   The seifs on the Israel-Sinai border and the correlation of their alignment. Research Council of Israel, Bulletin 4:195-198.

Sugden, W.
1963*a* The hydrology of the Persian Gulf and its significance in respect to evaporite deposition. American Journal of Science 261:741-755.

———
1963*b* Some aspects of sedimentation in the Persian Gulf. Journal of Sedimentary Petrology 33:355-364.

———
1964   Origin of faceted pebbles in some recent desert sediments of southern Iraq. Sedimentology 3:65-74.

Swartz, D. H. and D. D. Arden, Jr.
1960   Geologic history of the Red Sea area. American Association of Petroleum Geologists, Bulletin 44:1621-1637.

Tadmor, N. H. *et al.*
1958   The ancient agriculture in the Negev, gravel mounds and gravel strips near Shivta. Ktavim 8:127-151.

Thesiger, W.
1946-   A new journey in southern Arabia. Geographical
1947   Journal 108:129-145; 110:188-200.

———
1948   Across the Empty Quarter. Geographical Journal 111:1-21.

———
1949   A further journey across the Empty Quarter. Geographical Journal 113:21-46.

———
1950   Desert borderlands of Oman. Geographical Journal 116:137-171.

Thomas, B.
1932 Arabia Felix; across the "empty quarter." c. Scribner's Sons, N.Y. 397 p.

Tothill, J. D.
1953 Report to the Government of the Kingdom of Saudi Arabia on agricultural development. FAO, Rome, EPTA Report 76.

Underhill, H. W.
1965 Report to the Government of Jordan on the establishment of the National Hydrologic Service. FAO, Rome, EPTA Report 1998. 31 p.
One of the most recent reviews of water resources in Jordan. This report contains many basic hydrologic data, including gaging station locations, and provides water-balance estimates for the country. Many pertinent references to earlier work are included.

United Nations, Special Fund
1965 Azrac Basin, water resources. Report. N. Y.

U. S. Army Engineer Waterways Experiment Station
1960 Analogs of Yuma terrain in the Middle Eastern Desert. Technical Report 3-630, Report 4. Also cited as AD-478 848.
The most comprehensive summary of the geology, soils, vegetation, and geomorphic characteristics of the Arabian desert that is available. For detailed information on the geology and surficial features of the Arabian peninsula see the U. S. Geological Survey Professional Paper series entitled "Geology of the Arabian Peninsula," number 560, chapters A-, which constitutes the text to accompany the map of the peninsula (U. S. Geological Survey 1963).

U. S. Army. Quartermaster Research and Development Command. Environmental Protection Division
1954 Analogs of Yuma climate in the Middle East. Research Study Report RER-1.

U. S. Geological Survey
v.d. Geologic maps of quadrangles, Kingdom of Saudi Arabia. Scale 1:500,000. Miscellaneous Geologic Investigation, Maps I 200-A to I 220-A, inclusive.

——— v.d. Geographic maps of quadrangles, Kingdom of Saudi Arabia. Scale 1:500,000. Miscellaneous Geologic Investigation, Maps I 200-B to I 220-B, inclusive. 21 sheets.

——— 1963 Geologic map of the Arabian peninsula, scale 1:2,000,000. Miscellaneous Geologic Investigation, Map I 270-A.

Vajda, A. de and T. O. Smallwood
1953 Proposal for the Wadi Jizan irrigation development scheme, Saudi Arabia. FAO, Rome, EPTA Report 81.

Van Liere, W. J.
1959 Summary of observations on the Quaternary of the Syrian Steppe. Quaternaria 3.

Vaumas, E. de
1949a Sur la surface d'érosion polycyclique de l'Anti-Liban et de l'Hermon. Académie des Sciences, Paris, Comptes Rendus 228:326-328.
(On the polycyclic erosion surface of the Anti-Lebanon and Hermon ranges.)

——— 1949b Sur la structure de la Galilée Libanaise et de la dépression du Houlé. Académie des Sciences, Paris, Comptes Rendus 229:943-946.

(On the structure of Lebanese Galilee and the Houlé depression.)

——— 1950 La structure du Proche-Orient; essai de synthèse. Société Royale de Géographie d'Egypte, Bulletin 33:265-320.

——— 1953 Le Negeb, ètude morphologique. Société de Géographie d'Egypte, Bulletin 26:119-163.
(The Negev, morphologic study.)

Vita-Finzi, C.
1964a Observations on the late Quaternary of Jordan. Palestine Exploration Quarterly 8:19-33.

——— 1964b Slope downwearing by discontinuous sheetwash in Jordan. Israel Journal of Earth Sciences 13:88-91.

Voûte, C.
1960 Climate and landscape in the Zagros mountains (Iraq). International Geological Congress, 21st, Copenhagen, Report 4:81-87.

Vroman, J.
1944 The petrology of the sandy sediments of Palestine. Hebrew University, Jerusalem, Geology Department, Bulletin 5(1).

Willis, B.
1928 Dead Sea problem: rift valley or ramp valley. Geological Society of America, Bulletin 39:490-542.

Wirth, E.
1958 Morphologische und bodenkundliche beobachtung in der syrisch-irakischen wüste. Erdkunde 12:26-42.
(Morphological and soil-science observations in the Syrian-Iraqi Desert.)

Wissman, H. von, C. Rathjens, and F. Kossmat
1942 Beiträge zur tektonic arabiens. Geologische Rundschau 33:221-353.
(Contribution to the tectonics of Arabia.)

Wozab, D. H., E. Bradley, and K. A. Kawar
1960 Summary and evaluation of hydrogeologic data in Jordan. Central Water Authority, Amman.

Wozab, D. H. and K. A. Kawar
1960 Bibliography of geologic and groundwater reports. Jordanian Development Board, Amman. Circular 1.

Wright, H. E., Jr.
1958 An extinct wadi system in the Syrian Desert. Research Council of Israel, Bulletin 7G:53-59.

Yaalon, D. H.
1954 Calcareous soils of Israel. Israel Exploration Journal 4:278-285.

El-Zur, A., J. Magnes, and S. Samueloff
1961 Arid zone research in Israel. Unesco, Paris. Arid Zone [Newsletter] 14:10-16.

SECTION VII

IRANIAN DESERT: IRAN AND AFGHANISTAN

Includes works cited in the text discussions of Southern Asia (in general) and the parts of the Iranian Desert in Iran and in Afghanistan.

Afghan Delegation
1962 Afghanistan. p. 30-33. *In* Irrigation Practices Seminar, 4th, Ankara.

Blanford, W. T.
1873 On the nature and probable origin of the superficial deposits in the valleys and deserts of central Persia. Geological Society of London, Quarterly Journal 29:495-501.

_____ 1876 Geology. *In* Eastern Persia, an account of the journeys of the Persian Boundary Commission, 1870-72, vol. 2. London, Oxford. 2 vols.

Bobek, H.
1953- Klima und landschaft Irans in vor- und frühge-
1954 schichtlicher zeit. Geographischer Jahresbericht aus Osterreich 25:1-42.
(Climate and landscape of Iran in pre- and early historic time.)

_____ 1959 Features and formation of the Great Kawir and Masileh. University of Tehran, Arid Zone Research Centre, Publication 2. 63 p., 16 pl., map.
The best description of the surficial features of the Dasht-e-Kavir that is available. Aerial and ground photographs supplement the text. The author discusses the salt pans from the viewpoint of climatic changes in Iran; in this regard, and for additional general information, his earlier work (Bobek, 1953-1954) should be consulted.

Bonnard, E. G.
1945 Contribution à la connaissance géologique du nord-est de l'Iran (environs de Méched). Eclogae Geologicae Helvetiae, Basel, 37(2):331-354.
(Contribution to the geologic knowledge of northeastern Iran, vicinity of Mashad.)

Brigham, R. H.
1964 Compilation of hydrologic data, Helmand River Valley, Afghanistan, through September 1960. U. S. Geological Survey, Helmand Valley Authority, and U. S. AID Mission to Afghanistan. Kabul. 236 p.

British Petroleum Company, Ltd.
1956 Geologic maps and sections of southwest Persia. International Geological Congress, 20th, Mexico, Proceedings.

Clapp, F. G.
1939 Geology of Afghanistan. Geological Society of America, Bulletin 50:1904.

_____ 1940 Geology of eastern Iran. Geological Society of America, Bulletin 51(1):1-101.

Dahle, E. O.
1962 A review of topographic mapping in Afghanistan, 1957-1961. UNTAO file report. Kabul. 35 p.

Desio, A. and A. Marussi
1960 Ricogniziono geologiche nell'Afghanistan. Società Geologica Italiana, Bollettino 79(3). 81 p.
(Geologic outline of Afghanistan.)

Deutsche Wasserwirtschaftsgruppe Afghanistan
1962 Gewasserkundliches jahrbuch, Kabul gebiet, abflussjahr 1960. Report for Royal Afghan Ministry of Mines and Industry. 35 p.
(Hydrologic yearbook, Kabul area, water year 1960.)

Dewan, M. L. and H. Rieben
1958 Soil and water conservation in Iran. Report to the Government of Iran. FAO, Rome. 51 p.
This report discusses the general problems of wind and

water erosion in Iran, and sets forth recommendations for study of slopes, soils, and hydrology in the central closed basins. Like the report of Gibb and Partners (1958), the water-resources information provided has been obtained from semiarid areas and not from the central basins.

Fox, E. F.
1943 Travels in Afghanistan. Macmillan, New York.

Furon, R.
1936 Premiers résultats d'une exploration géologique du grand désert Iranien. Académie des Sciences, Paris, Comptes Rendus 203(9):494-496.
(Preliminary results of a geological exploration of the great Iranian desert.)

_____ 1941 Géologie du plateau iranien (Perse, Afghanistan, Béloutchistan). Muséum National d'Histoire Naturelle, Paris, Mémoires 7(2):177-411.
(Geology of the Iranian plateau: Persia, Afghanistan, Baluchistan.)

_____ 1951 L'Iran, Perse, et Afghanistan. Paris.
(Iran, Persia, and Afghanistan.)

Gabriel, A.
1934 Beobachtungen in Wüstengürtel Innerpersiens 1933. Geographische Gesellschaft, Wien, Mitteilungen 77(1-6):53-77.
(Observations in the desert belt of Inner Persia.)

_____ 1938 The southern Lut and Iranian Baluchistan. Geographical Journal 92:193-210.

_____ 1942 Die Lut and ihre wege. Zeitschrift für Erdkunde 19:423-442.
(The Lut desert and its roads.)

_____ 1952 Die erforschung Persiens. Vienna.
(The exploration of Persia.)

_____ 1957 Zur oberflächengestaltung der pfannen in den trockenräumen zentralpersiens. Geographische Gesellschaft, Wien, Mitteilungen 99(2-3):146-160.
(On the surface form of the pans in the dry regions of central Persia.)
A good descriptive account of pans and saline flats in the central desert basins of Iran. This author's earlier works (Gabriel, 1934, 1938, 1942, 1952) should be consulted for pertinent descriptions of the Dasht-e-Lut in general.

Gansser, A.
1955 New aspects of the geology in central Iran. World Petroleum Congress, 4th, Rome, Proceedings, Sec. 1:279-300.

German Geological Mission to Afghanistan
1964a Bibliography of the geology of Afghanistan up to 1964. Kabul. 18 p.

_____ 1964b Geological map of Afghanistan, central and southern part, scale 1:1,000,000. Kabul.

Ghazinouri, M.
1966 Hydrology of surface water in Iran. CENTO Symposium on Hydrology and Water Resources, Ankara, Proceedings.

Gibb and Partners
1958 Water resources survey, Tehran region. Imperial Government, Iran Plan Organization, Tehran. 190 p.

Gregory, J. W.
1929   The structure of Asia. Methuen, London.

Griesbach, C. L.
1886   Afghan and Persian field notes. Geological Society of India, Records 19:48-65.

Hariri, D.
1966   A study of interrelationship between surface water and ground water in Karaj River basin. CENTO Symposium on Hydrology and Water Resources, Ankara, Proceedings.

Harrison, J. V.
1943   The Jaz Murian depression, Persian Baluchistan. Geographical Journal 101:206-225.

Humlum, J.
1959   La géographie de l'Afghanistan. Scandinavian University Books, Oslo. 421 p.
(The geography of Afghanistan.)
A fairly good standard geography of Afghanistan which provides a summary of the physiography, climate, and allied topics.

Hunger, J. P.
1964   Geological survey in Afghanistan. United Nations Technical Assistance Operations file report. Kabul. 47 p.

Huntington, E.
1909   The Afghan borderland. Part I: The Russian frontier. Part II: The Persian frontier. National Geographic Magazine 20:788-799, 866-876.

Independent Irrigation Corporation
n.d.   Hydrographic yearbook. Hydrographic Service of Iran, Tehran.
A basic source of information on the available hydrologic data in Iran, including station locations.

International Engineering Company
1959   Report on soil and water resources of southwest Afghanistan. San Francisco. 2 vols.
A comprehensive summary of the topography, soils, drainage features, and hydrologic data in the southwestern desert area of Afghanistan.

Iran. Ministry of Information
n.d.   Realités sur l'Iran. Tehran.
(Information on Iran.)

Iranian Delegation
1960   Iran. p. 45-49. *In* Regional Irrigation Practices Leadership Seminar, 3rd, Lahore.

_____
1962   Iran. p. 53-56. *In* Irrigation Practices Seminar, 4th, Ankara.

_____
1964   Iran. p. 68-70. *In* Irrigation Practices Seminar, 5th, New Delhi.

Lackey, E. E.
1951   Iran: environmental conditions affecting logistics. U. S. Army, Quartermaster General, Research and Development Branch, Environmental Protection Section, Report 179. 36 p.

Mahboob, A.
1965   Country report of Afghanistan. *In* Seminar on waterlogging in relation to irrigation and salinity problems. FAO, Rome, EPTA Report 1932:69-71.

McMahon, A. H.
1897   The southern borderlands of Afghanistan. Geographical Journal 10:393-415.

McMahon, A. H. and C. A. McMahon
1897   Note on some volcanic and other rocks which occur near the Baluchistan-Afghan frontier. Royal Geological Society of London, Quarterly Journal 53:289-309.

Merzbacher, G.
1925   Afghanistan. Geographische Zeitschrift 31: 289-293.

Morrison-Knudsen (Afghanistan)
1955   Reconnaissance soils and drainage survey and land and water development potentials. Chakhansur area. Report to the Royal Afghan Government.

_____
1956   A study of Arghandab-Tarnak water allocations. Report to the Royal Afghan Government.

National Iranian Oil Company
1959   Geological map of Iran, scale 1:2,500,000, with explanatory notes. Tehran.
The best available geologic map of Iran. The explanatory notes that accompany the map include an extensive bibliography of Iranian geology.

Philippson, A.
1918   Kleinasien. Handbuch der Regional Geologie 5. 187 p.
(Asia Minor.)

_____
1920   Zur morphologischen karte des westlichen Kleinasiens. Petermanns Geographische Mitteilungen 66:197-202.
(On a morphological map of western Asia Minor.)

Roa, M. M. A.
1964   Country progress reports, Afghanistan. p. 50-52. *In* Irrigation Practices Seminar, 5th, New Delhi.

Robison, W. C. and A. V. Dodd
1955   Analogs of Yuma climate in south-central Asia. U. S. Quartermaster Research and Development Center, Natick, Mass., Environmental Protection Division, Research Study Report RER series 4. 24 p., figures, tables.

Ryshtya, S. Q.
1947   L'Afghanistan au point de vue géographique. Afghanistan 2(1):16-22.
(Afghanistan from geographic consideration.)

Scharlau, K.
1961   Klimamorphologie und luftbildauswertung im hochland von Iran. Zeitschrift für Geomorphologie 5:141-144.
(Climatic morphology and aerial photo interpretation in the highlands of Iran.)

Sedqi, M. O.
1952   La plaine de Herat. Afghanistan 7(4):54-55.
(The plain of Herat.)

Stenz, E.
1947   The climate of Afghanistan. Geographical Review 37:672.
A good review paper on the climatic conditions in Afghanistan but somewhat dated. See text for sources of information on climatic conditions and data.

Stratil-Sauer, G.
1957   Die pleistozänen ablagerungen im innern der wüste Lut. Geographische Gesellschaft, Wien, Festschrift Hundertjahrfeser, p. 460-484.
(The Pleistocene deposits of the inner Lut desert.)

Todd, N.
1844 Report from a journey from Herat to Simla via Candahar and Kabul. Asiatic Society of Bengal, Calcutta, Journal 13:339.

Trinkler, E.
1928 Afghanistan. Petermanns Geographische Mitteilungen, Ergänzungsheft 196. 80 p.

United Nations. Bureau of Flood Control and Water Resources Development
1961a Afghanistan. *In* Multiple-purpose river basin development, part IId. Flood Control Series 18: 1-18.
Presents an outline of the status of hydrological investigations and projects in Afghanistan, including the locations of reservoirs and dams, irrigation areas, and gaging stations.

1961b Iran. *In* Multiple-purpose river basin development, part IId. Flood Control Series 18:19-40.

U. S. Army Engineer Waterways Experiment Station
1962 Analogs of Yuma terrain in the south central Asian desert. Rev. Technical Report 3-630, Report 2 (folio vol.). Vicksburg, Miss.
A comprehensive summary of available information on geology, rock, vegetation, and surface geometry, presented in folio format.

Zaman, M.
1951 The regions of drybelts in Afghanistan. Afghanistan 6(2):63-68.

SECTION VIII

IRANIAN-THAR DESERT AREA: WEST PAKISTAN

Includes works cited in the text discussion of the Iranian-Thar desert area of West Pakistan.

Ahmad. K. S.
1951 Climatic regions of West Pakistan. Pakistan Geographical Review 6(1):1-35.

Ahmad, M. I.
1951 Volcanoes and sulphur of western Baluchistan. Geological Survey of Pakistan, Records 4(3).

Ahmad, N.
1958 An economic geography of East Pakistan. Oxford University Press, London. 361 p.

Andrew, G.
1958 Report to the government of Pakistan on water resources investigations in the Quetta-Kalat Division. FAO, Rome, EPTA Report 855. 73 p.

Anstey, R. L.
1965 Physical characteristics of alluvial fans. U. S. Army Natick Laboratories, Natick, Mass., Technical Report ES-20.
This report provides quantitative data on slopes, relief, area, and other characteristics of alluvial fans in West Pakistan. No similar information is available elsewhere. Some aerial photographs are included.

Asghar, A. G.
1950 The soils of Pakistan. International Congress of Soil Science, 4th, Transactions 3, Sectional papers p. 134-141.

Asghar, A. G. and H. S. Zaidi
n.d. Soil survey, Rechna Doab, West Pakistan. Water and Power Development Authority, Lahore, Water and Soils Investigation Division, Bulletin 2. 22 p.

Asghar, A. G. and H. S. Zaidi
n.d. Soil survey manual for the former Punjab Province area. Water and Power Development Authority, West Pakistan, Water and Soils Investigation Division, Bulletin 1. 18 p.

Asrarullah
1954 Geology of southwest Makran, Baluchistan. Pakistan Journal of Science 6:5-21.

Bakr, M. A.
1963a Geology of the western Ras Koh Range, Chagai and Kharan Districts, Quetta and Kalat Divisions, West Pakistan. Geological Survey of Pakistan, Records 10(2-A).
An excellent and detailed geological report on this arid area. For a description of the general physiography see Bakr (1963b) and for regional geological coverage of West Pakistan see Bakr and Jackson (1964).

1963b Physiography of the Chagai-Kharan region. Pakistan Geographical Review 18(2).

Bakr, M. A. and R. O. Jackson
1964 Geological map of Pakistan, scale 1:2,000,000. Geological Survey of Pakistan.

Bhatti, M. A.
1949 Orography and drainage of the Potwar Plateau. Pakistan Geographical Review 4(1):1-16; (2): 46-55.

Blanford, W. T.
1872 Note on geological formations seen along the coasts of Baluchistan and Persia from Kerachi to the head of Persian Gulf, and some gulf islands. Geological Survey of India, Records 5(2).

1877 Geological notes on the great desert between Sind and Rajputana. Geological Survey of India, Records 10(1):10-21.

1879 The geology of western Sind. Geological Survey of India, Memoirs 17(1):1-210.

Carter, H. J.
1861 On contributions to the geology of western India including Sind and Baloochistan. Asiatic Society of Bombay, Journal 6:161-206.

Chaterjee, A. B.
n.d. Some geographical features of the Thar Desert. Library of Congress catalogue no. GB618.71, C49.

Chhibber, H. L.
1945 India. Part I: Physical basis of the geography of India. Nand Kishore, Benares. 282 p.

Cook, H.
1860 Topographical and geological sketch of the province of Sarawan, or northern portion of the tableland of Beloochistan. Medical and Physical Society of Bombay, Transactions 6:1-44.

Cotter, G. de P.
1923 The alkaline lakes and the soda industry of Sind. Geological Survey of India, Memoirs 47(2): 202-297.

1933 The geology of the part of the Attock District west of the longitude 72°45′E. Geological Survey of India, Memoirs 55(2):63-161.

Coulson, A. L.
1938 The water supply of the Isa Khel and Mianwali Tahsils of the Mianwali District, Punjab. Geological Survey of India, Records 72(4):440-466.

Coulson, A. L.
1939   The underground water supply of the Peshawar and Mardan Districts of the North-West Frontier Province, with an appendix on the Kobat Valley. Geological Survey of India, Records 74(2): 229-259.

Currie, D. M.
1956   Report to the Government of Pakistan on desert areas of West Pakistan. FAO, Rome, EPTA Report 564

Danilchik, W. and R. A. K. Tahirkheli
1959   Investigation of alluvial sands for uranium and minerals of economic importance. The Indus, Gilgit, Nagat, and Hunza rivers, Gilgit Agency, West Pakistan. Geological Survey of Pakistan, Information Release 11.

Drew, F.
1873   Alluvial and lacustrine deposits and glacial records of the upper Indus basin. Part I: Alluvial deposits. Geological Society of London, Quarterly Journal 29:441-471.

Fairservis, W. A., Jr.
1956   Excavations in the Quetta Valley, West Pakistan. American Museum of Natural History, Anthropological Papers 45(2).

Farah, A. and A. Ahmed
1965   Seismic refraction survey in the dry lakes of Chagai District, Quetta Division, West Pakistan. Geological Survey of Pakistan, Information Release 22.

Fraser, I. S.
1958   Report on a reconnaissance survey of the landforms, soils and present land use of the Indus Plains, West Pakistan: a survey conducted by the Resources Survey Division, Photographic Survey Corporation, Ltd., Toronto, Canada, in cooperation with the Central Soil Conservation Organization, Ministry of Food and Agriculture, Government of Pakistan (a Colombo Plan Co-operative Project). 401 p.
The most valuable single reference on the landforms and general features of the entire Indus River basin. The landforms are classified into 20 types on the basis of aerial photographs, which are included, and the data and interpretations are presented on 25 color maps at a scale of 1:253,440.

Geb, E. R.
1946   Problems of Baluchistan geology. Indian Science Congress, Proceedings 38.

Geological Survey of India
n.d.   Map of India, showing areas of maps published by the Geological Survey of India, scale 1:3,168,000, 4 sheets.

Geological Survey of Pakistan
n.d.   Geological map of West Pakistan, scale 1:2,000,000.

_____
1958   Geologic map of Pakistan (preliminary), scale 1:5,000,000.

_____
1965   List of reports issued (as of 31st January 1965). Quetta. 8 p.
A basic source of information on all reports published by the Geological Survey. See Offield (1964) for a general bibliography of geology of Pakistan and the PANSDOC

reference lists (Pakistan National Scientific and Technical Documentation Center, 1957, 1958, 1959, 1960, 1961, 1965) on nongeologic subjects.

Greenman, D. W.
1963   Hydrology and scientific reclamation in the Punjab, West Pakistan. p. 332-342. United Nations Conference on the application of science and technology for the benefit of the less developed areas, Geneva, vol. 1, Natural Resources.

Harrison, J. V.
1944   Mud volcanoes on the Makran Coast. Geographical Journal 103:180-181.

Hemphill, W. R. and A. H. Kidwai
1963   The application of photogeology and photogrammetry to geological surveys of natural resources in Pakistan. p. 194-206. *In* United Nations Conference on the application of science and technology for the benefit of the less developed areas, Geneva, vol. 2: Natural Resources.

Hughes, A. W.
1877   The country of Baluchistan, its geography, topography, ethnology, and history. London. 294 p.

Islam, A.
1961   Soil and land classification activities in East Pakistan. *In* J. T. Maletic, Report on the Central Treaty Organization Land Classification Seminar, Ankara, Turkey. U. S. Department of the Interior, Bureau of Reclamation, Division of Project Investigations, Land Resources Branch, Denver, Colorado, Annex F, 5 p.

Karpov, A. V. and R. Nebolsine
1958   Indus River Valley — past, present, future. Hydrotechnic Corporation, New York, Report.

Kazmi, A. H.
n.d.   The water supply of Baluchistan. Geological Survey of Pakistan, Records 3(1). 105 p.

_____
1962   Geological and hydrological appraisal of the proposed Sra Khula damsite, Quetta-Pishin District. Geological Survey of Pakistan, Engineering Geology Site Evaluation Report 8.

Khan, M. I.
1955   Flood control on the Indus River system. Pakistan Journal of Science 7(1):3-14.

Khan, M. L.
1960   Recent pluviometric changes in the arid and semi-arid zones of West Pakistan. Pakistan Geographical Review 15:1-24.
A mathematical analysis of all available rainfall data in an attempt to project precipitation trends in the arid areas of West Pakistan.

Kidwai, Z.
1963   Geology of Rechna and Chaj doabs. Water and Power Development Authority, Lahore, Water and Soils Investigation Division, Bulletin 5.

Kidwai, Z. and S. Alam
1964   The geology of Bari doab, West Pakistan. Water and Power Development Authority, Lahore, Water and Soils Investigation Division, Bulletin 8.

Kirmani, S. S.
1956   The phenomena of losses and gains in the Indus River System. Pakistan, Ministry of Industries, Pakistan Water Delegation, Washington, D. C. 220 p.

Martin, N. R., S. F. A. Siddiqi, and B. H. King
1962   A geological reconnaissance of the region between the lower Swat and Indus Rivers of Pakistan. Punjab University, Geological Bulletin 2:1-14.

Masson, C.
1843   Narrative of a journey to Kalat, including an account of the insurrection at that place in 1840; and a memoir on eastern Baluchistan. London. 463 p.

Mehdiratta, R. C.
1954   Geology of India and Pakistan for intermediate and degree students of Indian universities. Atma Ram, Delhi.

———
1962   Geology of India, Pakistan and Burma. Atma Ram and Sons, Delhi. 203 p.

Morgan, J. P. and W. G. McIntire
1959   Quaternary geology of the Bengal Basin, East Pakistan and India. Geological Society of America, Bulletin 70:319-342.

Mufti, I. and F. A. Siddiqui
1961   A gravity survey of Quetta and Mastung Valleys. Pakistan Journal of Scientific and Industrial Research 4:15-20.

Muhammad, Khan
1951   A note on wind erosion in Thal, its causes, effects, and possible control measures. Punjab Forestry Conference, Proceedings, p. 144-147.

Murray, J. A.
1880   A handbook to the geology, botany, and zoology of Sind. Karachi. 310 p.

Naqvi, S. N.
1949   Coefficient of variability of monsoon rainfall in India and Pakistan. Pakistan Geographical Review 4(2):7-17.

Naqvi, S. N. and Q. Hamid
1956   Water requirements of plants. West Pakistan Meteorological Department, Publication.

Naqvi, S. N. and M. Rahamatullah
1962   Weather and climate of Pakistan. Pakistan Geographical Review 17(1):1-18.

Naqvi, S. N. and J. Tahir
1950   Wind data for the Thal desert in the northwest Punjab. Pakistan Science Conference, Proceedings 2(3).

Offield, T. W.
1964   Preliminary bibliography and index of the geology of Pakistan. Geological Survey of Pakistan, Records 12(1).

Oil and Gas Development Corporation
1963-   Geomorphology and recent tectonics of Sind
1964   Plain, West Pakistan. Geological Party, File Report. Karachi.
This report by a team of Russian geomorphologists shows alluvial fans, dunes of various types, floodplains, and other such landforms on a map at a scale of 1:250,000. Data on slopes, relief, and degree of dissection are provided, and a series of maps portraying the locations of the channels of the Indus River between 1935 and 1960 is included. For additional data on the history and migrations of the Indus River see Panhwar (1964), which also contains data on the changes of the Indus delta region with time.

Oldham, R. D.
1892   Subrecent and recent deposits of the valley plains of Quetta, Pishin, and the Dasht-i-Bedaolat; with appendices on the Chamans of Quetta and Pishin. Geological Survey of India, Records 25:36-53.

———
1903   A note on the sandhills of Clifton near Karachi. Geological Survey of India, Memoirs 34(3): 133-157.

Pakistan. Food and Agriculture Council
1960   Soil erosion and its control in arid and semiarid zones, Proceedings of the Karachi Symposium, November 1957, held under the joint auspices of the Council and Unesco. Karachi. 400 p.
An excellent assemblage of reports that treat soil erosion problems, dune migration, weathering, and other topics, and that present basic data on these subjects that are not otherwise available.

———
1962   Arid zone research and development in West Pakistan. Government of Pakistan Press, Karachi. 212 p.

Pakistan. Ministry of Agriculture and Works Advisory Committee
1965   Country report on Pakistan. *In* Seminar on waterlogging in relation to irrigation and salinity problems. FAO, Rome, EPTA Report 1932:18-68.

Pakistan National Scientific and Technical Documentation Centre
1957   Sediment control in rivers, canals, and reservoirs. Karachi. Bibliography 18.

———
1958   Dams and reservoirs. Karachi. Bibliography 75.

———
1959   Flood control, a select bibliography (1900-1958). Karachi. Bibliography 101. 116 p.

———
1960   Engineering geology. Karachi. Bibliography 212.

———
1961   Scientific and technical periodicals of Pakistan. Bibliography 303. 12 p.

———
1965   List of PANSDOC bibliographies. Karachi. 27 p.

Panhwar, M. H.
1964   Ground water in Hyderabad and Khairpur divisions. Director of Agriculture, Hyderabad Region, West Pakistan. 217 p.

Parvez, J. A.
1963   Formulation of a planning programme for water resources development in West Pakistan. *In* Proceedings of the 5th regional conference on water resources development in Asia and the Far East. U. N. Bureau of Flood Control and Water Resources Development, Water Resources Series 23:164-173.
A good summary of water-resources plans for West Pakistan; it includes basic hydrologic data, a map of drainage basins, and an outline of organizations that are involved in water resources investigations of all types.

Paver, G. L. and H. C. Scholz
1955   Preliminary hydrological and geophysical ground water investigation in the Punjab and Baluchistan; report to the Government of Pakistan. FAO, Rome, EPTA Report 348. 24 p.

Photographic Survey Corporation, Ltd., Toronto, Canada
1956a Landforms and soils, West Pakistan, scale 1:253,440, 25 sheets. Photographic Survey Corporation, Ltd., Toronto, Canada in cooperation with Central Soil Conservation Organization, Ministry of Food and Agriculture, Pakistan.

────── 1956b Present land use, West Pakistan, scale 1:253,440, 25 sheets. Photographic Survey Corporation, Ltd., Toronto, Canada, in cooperation with Central Soil Conservation Organization, Ministry of Food and Agriculture, Pakistan.

────── 1958 Reconnaissance geology maps, West Pakistan, scale 1:253,440, 29 sheets (and 2 sheets of explanatory notes). Photographic Survey Corporation, Ltd., Toronto, Canada, in cooperation with Geological Survey of Pakistan.

Pithawalla, M. B.
n.d. Pakistan, its resources and potentialities. Revised by A. R. Khan. The Publishers United Ltd., Lahore. 149 p.

────── 1936 A geographical analysis of the lower Indus Basin (Sind). National Academy of Science, India, Proceedings, Section B, 4:283-355.

────── 1943 The physics of the Indus River and its relation to recurrence of floods in Sind. Science and Culture, Calcutta, 9:62-68.

────── 1952a Physiographic sub-divisions of the Baluchistan Plateau. Indian Geographical Society, Silver Jubilee Souvenir and N. Subrahmanyam Memorial Volume, p. 217-223.

────── 1952b The problem of Baluchistan; development and conservation of water resources, soils, and natural vegetation. Pakistan Ministry of Economic Affairs, Karachi. 162 p.
A good review paper on the soils and water resources of this region with data on drainage features and soil erosion. See Pithawalla (1952a) for a description of the physiographic subdivisions that have been devised for the area and the criteria involved.

────── 1953 An introduction to Kashmir, its geology and geography. Kashmir Publications, Muzaffarabad.

────── 1959 A physical and economic geography of Sind (the Lower Indus Basin). Aage Kadam Printery, Karachi. 389 p.

Pithawalla, M. B. and P. Martin-Kaye
1946 Geology and geography of Karachi and its neighborhood. Karachi. 227 p.

Platt, R. R.
1961 Pakistan, a compendium. American Geographical Society, New York, N. Y. 383 p.

Raikes, R. L.
1957 Surface water development in Baluchistan; report to the Government of Pakistan. FAO, Rome, EPTA Report 762. 31 p.

────── 1965 The ancient gabarbands of Baluchistan. East and West, Rome, 15:3-12.

Raikes, R. L. and R. H. Dyson, Jr.
1961 The prehistoric climate of Baluchistan and the Indus Valley. American Anthropologist 63:265-281.

Repp, G.
1961 Arid zone research in Pakistan. Unesco, Paris, Arid Zone [Newsletter] 12:6-9.

Rizavi, A. A.
1950 Natural regions of East Pakistan. Pakistan Geographical Review 5(1):32-51.

Robison, W. C. and A. V. Dodd
1955 Analogs of Yuma climate in south-central Asia. U. S. Quartermaster Research and Development Center, Natick, Mass., Environmental Protection Division, Research Study Report RER Series 4. 24 p., figures, tables.

Salam, K. and I. B. Kadri
1963 Geologic appraisal of the Potwar-Kohat-Bannu region and adjacent areas, Upper Indus Basin, Punjab, West Pakistan. Tidewater Oil Company, International Exploration Department, Karachi. 52 p.

Siddiqi, M. R. and S. A. T. Kazmi
1963 The geology of Thal doab, West Pakistan. Water and Power Development Authority, Lahore, Water and Soils Investigation Division, Bulletin 7.

Smith, D. D. and R. E. Snead
1962 Thick eolian sand prism of probable Middle to Late Pleistocene age near Karachi, West Pakistan. Geological Society of America, Special Paper 68:274.

Spate, O. H. K.
1954 India and Pakistan. A general and regional geography. Methuen, London.
A standard geography text which provides a good summary of the general surficial features of the arid areas in India and West Pakistan.

Stiffe, A. W.
1873 On the mud craters and geological structure of the Mekran coast. Geological Society of London, Quarterly Journal 30:50-53.

Surface Water Circle
1962 Annual report of river and climatological data of West Pakistan. Water and Power Development Authority, Lahore.
Presents basic data on the locations of stream gaging stations, water and sediment discharges, and meteorology in West Pakistan. See Surface Water Circle and Harza Engineering Company (1962) for supplementary data on these topics.

Surface Water Circle and Harza Engineering Company (International)
1962 Annual report of river and climatological data of West Pakistan. Water and Power Development Authority, Lahore. 642 p.

Tahirkheli, R. A. K.
1960 Investigations of gold and other placer minerals in Indus alluvium. Geological Survey of Pakistan, Information Release 14.

Tale, G. P.
1904 Sketch of the Baluchistan desert and part of eastern Persia. Geological Survey of India, Memoirs 21(2).

Taylor, A.
1882   Unexplored Baluchistan, a survey with observations astronomical, geographical, botanical, etc. London.

Taylor, G. C., Jr.
1965   Water, history, and the Indus plain. Natural History 74:40-49.

Thirlaway, H. I. S.
1960   The results of arid zone research at the Geophysical Institute, Quetta. Pakistan Geographical Review 15:32-49.

Tipton, R. J.
1959   Irrigation and drainage in West Pakistan. American Society of Civil Engineers, Annual Convention, October 1959. 28 p.

United Nations, Water Control Mission to Pakistan
1959   Water and power development in East Pakistan. New York, United Nations. 162 p.

U. S. Army Engineer Waterways Experiment Station
1957- Limited reconnaissance for pavement evaluation
1958   and soil-type aerial photograph ties: Report No. 123: RPAF Station Mauripur, Karachi, 1957. Report No. 125: PAF Station Peshawar, Peshawar, 1958. Report No. 126: PAF Station Drigh-Road, Karachi, 1957.

———
1962   Analogs of Yuma terrain in the south central Asian desert. Rev. Technical Report 3-630, Report 2 (folio vol.). Vicksburg, Miss.

U. S. Army Map Service, Corps of Engineers
n.d.   India and Pakistan (topographic maps), scale 1:250,000, 76 sheets, Series U 502.

———
n.d.   Survey of India Series (topographic maps), scale 1:253,440, 24 sheets, Series U 501.

U. S. White House — Department of the Interior Panel on Waterlogging and Salinity in West Pakistan
1964   Report on land and water development in the Indus Plain. The White House, Washington, D. C. 453 p.
Excellent summaries of the general hydrology, geology, geography, soils, and land use of West Pakistan are presented by a panel of authorities, in connection with a general investigation of the problems of salinity and waterlogging in the country.

Vredenburg, E. W.
1901   A geological sketch of the Baluchistan desert and part of eastern Persia. Geological Survey of India, Memoirs 31:179-302.

Wadia, D. N.
1953   Geology of India. 3rd ed. Macmillan, London.
The standard geological reference work on the Indian subcontinent.

Wright, R. L.
1964   Land system survey of the Nagarparkar peninsula, Pakistan. Unesco, Paris. Arid Zone [Newsletter] 25:5-13.

Zoha, S.
1950- Physiographical personality of Baluchistan. Paki-
1951   stan Geographical Review 5(2):1-15; 6(1).

SECTION IX

THE THAR: INDIA

Includes works cited in the text discussion of the part of the Thar in India.

Ahmad, A.
1948   Drainage of the Punjab. Punjab Geographical Review 3:39-47.

Ahmad, K. S.
1947   Physiography of the Punjab plain. Punjab Geographical Review 2:2-7.

Bharadwaj, O. P.
1961   The arid zone of India and Pakistan. *In* L. D. Stamp, ed., A history of land use in arid regions. Unesco, Paris. Arid Zone Research 17:143-174.
A good review paper on land use and historical data on the arid zones of India and West Pakistan; also describes the general physical features of these areas. The author also discusses drainage in the arid areas and the subject of climatic changes.

Bhatia, S. S.
1957   Arid zone of India and Pakistan, a study in its water balance and delimitation. Indian Journal of Meteorology and Geophysics 8(2).

Carter, H. J.
1857   Geological papers on western India, including Cutch, Sinde, and the southeast coast of Arabia; to which is appended a summary of the geology of India generally. Bombay. 808 p.

———
1861   On contributions to the geology of western India, including Sind and Baluchistan. Royal Asiatic Society, Bengal, Journal 6:161-206.

Chhibber, H. L.
1945   India. Part I: Physical basis of the geography of India. Nand Kishore, Benares.

Din, M. A.
1952   Drainage in the Punjab. Pakistan Science Conference, Proceedings 4:13-22.

Geological Survey of India
1938   Geographical index to the Memoirs, v. 1-54; and Records, v. 1-65, of the Geological Survey of India. 576 p.

———
1943   Catalogue of publications and index of geological maps of the Geological Survey of India up to June 1941. Memoirs 77. 114 p.

Ghosh, A.
1952   The Rajputana desert — its archeological aspect. *In* Symposium on the Rajputana Desert, Proceedings. National Institute of Sciences, India, Bulletin 1:43-50.

Govindaswamy, T. S.
1953   Rainfall abnormalities, week by week, in India during 1908 to 1950. Irrigation and Power Journal 10:15-38.

Gulshal, R.
1934   Ancient courses of the Punjab rivers. Punjab University Historical Society, Journal 3:81-84.

Hora, S. L.
1952   The Rajputana desert; its value in India's national economy. *In* Symposium on the Rajputana desert, proceedings. National Institute of Sciences, India, Bulletin 1:1-11.

Imperial Gazetteer of India
1908   The Punjab. Provincial Services, Calcutta. 2 vols.

Indian Delegation
1964   Country progress report on India. p. 55-67. *In* Irrigation Practices Seminar, 5th, New Delhi.

Krishnamurthy, K. V.
1952   The creep of the desert. *In* Symposium on the Rajputana Desert, Proceedings. National Institute of Sciences, India, Bulletin 1:131-136.

Krishnan, M. S.
1953   The structural and tectonic history of India. Geological Survey of India, Memoirs 81. 109 p.

——
1960   Geology of India and Burma. Higgenbothams, Ltd., Madras.

Kurakova, L. I.
1964   Development of the Rajasthan desert (India). Vestnik Moskovskogo Universiteta, seriya geografiya 3:44-50.

La Touche, T. D.
1902   Geology of western Rajputana. Geological Survey of India, Memoirs 35.

Medlicott, H. B.
1889   Sketch of the geology of the Punjab. p. 22-79. *In* Punjab Gazetteer, Provincial Volume, Chapter 2. Calcutta.

National Institute of Sciences, India
1952   Symposium on the Rajputana desert, proceedings. Bulletin 1. 302 p.
The most useful single report on the Thar desert area, this volume contains separate papers on the geology, topography, meteorology, hydrology, soils, and flora and fauna of the Thar. The supposed evolution of the Indian desert is also discussed, as is the question of possible desert expansion during recent years.

Oldham, R. D.
1886   On probable changes in the geography of the Punjab and its rivers; a historico-geographical study. Asiatic Society, Bengal, Journal 55:322-343.

Pascoe, E. H.
1950-   A manual of the geology of India and Burma. 3rd
1959   ed. Government of India Press, Calcutta. 2 vols.

Pithawalla, M. B.
1939   Physiographic divisions of India. Madras Geographical Association, Journal 14:423-434.

——
1952   The great Indian desert, a geographic study. *In* Symposium on the Rajputana Desert, Proceedings. National Institute of Sciences, India, Bulletin 1: 137-150.

Raheja, P. C.
1962   Research and development in the Indian arid zone. Unesco, Paris. Arid Zone [Newsletter] 15:7-12.

Ramdas, L. A.
1949   Rainfall of India, a brief review. Indian Journal of Agricultural Science 19(1):1-19.
A good summary of precipitation data for India, with isohyetal maps and long-term means. See also Ramdas (1950).

1950   Rainfall and agriculture. Indian Journal of Meteorology and Geophysics 1:262-274.

Sankalia, H. D.
1952   The condition of Rajputana in the past as deduced from archeological evidence. *In* Symposium on the Rajputana Desert, Proceedings. National Institute of Sciences, India, Bulletin 1:43-50.

Singh, G.
1952   The Rajputana Desert: geography. *In* Symposium on the Rajputana Desert, proceedings. National Institute of Sciences, India, Bulletin 1:151-152.

Spate, O. H. K.
1954   India and Pakistan. A general and regional geography. Methuen, London.
A standard geography of India and Pakistan, useful as a supplement to the data presented in symposium papers on the Thar (National Institute of Sciences, India, 1952).

Taylor, G. C., Jr. and M. M. Oza
1954   Geology and ground water of the Dudhai area, eastern Kutch (India). Geological Survey of India, Bulletin, series B, 5.

Taylor, G. C., Jr. and B. D. Pathak
1960   Geology and ground water resources of the Anjar Khedoi region, eastern Kutch (India), with particular reference to the Kandla Port water supply. Geological Survey of India, Bulletin, series B, 9.

United Nations. Bureau of Flood Control and Water Resources Development
1956   India. *In* Multiple-purpose river basin development, part IIb. Flood Control Series 11:49-77.

Wadia, D. N.
1937   Recent geologic changes in northern India and their effect upon the drainage of the Indo-Gangetic basin. Science and Culture, Calcutta, 2:384-387.

Wissmann, H. von *et al.*
1956   On the role of nature and man in changing the face of the dry belt of Asia. p. 278-303. *In* W. L. Thomas, ed., Man's role in changing the face of the earth. University of Chicago Press.

Wynne, A. N.
1872   Geology of Kutch. Geological Survey of India, Memoirs 9(1):1-293.

SECTION X

AUSTRALIAN DESERTS

Includes works cited in the text discussion of the deserts of Australia.

Anstey, R. L.
1961   Analogs of Yuma climate in Australia. U. S. Army, Quartermaster Research and Engineering Command, Natick, Mass., Earth Sciences Division, Research Study Report RER-36. 23 p., 13 figs.

Arid Zone Newsletter
1956-   vol. 1 (annual) - to date. C.S.I.R.O., Canberra.

Australia. Commonwealth Scientific and Industrial Research Organization
1960   The Australian environment. 3rd ed. Melbourne. 151 p.

Australia. Department of National Development
1961   Index to Australian resources maps of 1940-59. Government Printer, Canberra.
This index lists the available maps on Australian natural resources of all types for the 1940-1959 period. A supplement, entitled "Index to Australian Resources Maps: Supplement for 1960-64," was published in 1966 by this same agency. The listed categories of interest include landforms, geology, soils, vegetation, land classification, water resources, and others.

Australia. Department of National Development
1962   Atlas of Australian resources, 2nd ser. Canberra. 30 sheets.
The 30 sheets of the original atlas include the geology, physical features, soils, and climate of Australia. A revised edition is currently in preparation by this agency. These sheets constitute an important source of information for the country as a whole.

Australian Water Resources Council
1965   Review of Australia's water resources, 1963. Department of National Development, Canberra.
The best single report on the water resources of Australia. This comprehensive volume presents a compilation of all available data on precipitation, drainage, stream discharge, and ground water, as of 1963. The locations of the 1439 stream gaging stations also are given.

Barclay, H. V.
1916   Report on exploration of a portion of Central Australia by the Barclay-Macpherson expedition, 1904-1905. Royal Geographical Society of Australasia, South Australian Branch, Proceedings 16: 106-130.

Basedow, H.
1905   Geological report on the country traversed by the South Australian Government North-West Prospecting Expedition, 1903. Royal Society of South Australia, Transactions and Proceedings 29:57-102.

Bauer, A. F. T.
1954   Availability of stream gauging information in Australia. Water Research Conference, Cooma, New South Wales. 82 p.

Bettenay, E.
1962   The salt lake systems and their associated aeolian features in the semi-arid regions of Western Australia. Journal of Soil Science 13:10-17.
A good review paper on the dry lakes of Western Australia and the surrounding terrain. Several pertinent references to earlier work are included, most of which suggest that the lakes were formerly part of a vast drainage system.

Bettenay, E., A. V. Blackmore and F. J. Hingston
1964   Aspects of the hydrologic cycle and related salinity in the Belka Valley, Western Australia. Australian Journal of Soil Research 2:187-210.

Bird, E. C. F.
1965   Coastal landforms. Australian National University, Canberra.

Bonython, C. W.
1955   Lake Eyre, South Australia; the great flooding of 1949-50. Royal Geographical Society of Australasia, South Australia Branch, Lake Eyre Command, Adelaide.
An excellent account of the flooding of Lake Eyre, in South Australia, during a catastrophic (?) climatic event. See Bonython (1956) and King (1956) for data on the water quality and subsurface deposits of the lake.

———   1956   The salt of Lake Eyre, its occurrence in Madigan Gulf and its possible origin. Royal Society of South Australia, Transactions 9:66-92.

Bowler, J. M. and L. B. Harford
1963   Geomorphic sequence of the Riverine Plain near Echuca. Australian Journal of Science 26:88.

Bremer, H.
1965   Ayers Rock, ein beispiel für klimagenetische morphologie. Zeitschrift für Geomorphologie 9: 249-284.
(Ayers Rock, an example of climatic-genetic morphology.)
An excellent description of one of the principle inselbergs of the Australian desert. Photographs and data support the contention that solution effects were of importance during previous climatic regimes. See Ollier and Tuddenham (1961) and Twidale (1962, 1964) for additional information on Australian inselbergs, and Langford-Smith and Dury (1964) and Stewart and Litchfield (1957) for data on pediment slopes.

Butler, B. E.
1950   A theory of prior streams as a causal factor of soil occurrence in the Riverine Plain of southeast Australia. Australian Journal of Agricultural Research 1:231-252.

———   1958   Depositional systems of the Riverine Plain of southeastern Australia in relation to soils. C.S.I.R.O., Soils Publication 10.

———   1959   Periodic phenomena in landscapes as a basis for soil studies. C.S.I.R.O., Soils Publication 14.

———   1961a   Groundsurfaces and the history of the Riverine plain. Australian Journal of Science 24:39-40.

———   1961b   The study of soil development in relation to geomorphology. Australian Soil Science Conference, 3rd, Canberra, Proceedings.

———   1962   The place of soils in studies of Quaternary chronology. Symposium on geochronology and land surfaces in relation to soils in Australia. Australian Academy of Science — C.S.I.R.O., Adelaide, 1961.

Campbell, W. D.
1906   The geology and mineral resources of the Norseman District. Geological Survey of Western Australia, Bulletin 21.

Carroll, D.
1944   The Simpson Desert expedition: desert sands. Royal Society of South Australia, Transactions 68: 49-59.

Chapman, T. G.
1962   Hydrology survey at Lorna Glen and Wiluna, W. A. C.S.I.R.O., Division of Land Research and Regional Survey, Technical Paper 18.
Discusses all aspects of the hydrology of this area in the central part of Western Australia and presents a statistical analysis of precipitation and runoff data to obtain recurrence intervals. See also Dury (1964) for similar analyses and Chapman (1964) for methods of data collection in selected watersheds in central Australia.

———   1964   Design and initial instrumentation of a rainfall-run-off experiment in the Alice Springs area. C.S.I.R.O., Technical Memorandum 64/5.

Christian, C. S., J. N. Jennings, and C. R. Twidale
1957   Geomorphology. In Guidebook to research data for arid-zone development. Unesco, Paris. Arid Zone Research 9:51-65.

Churchward, H. M.

1960   Complex soil and ground surface development in an aeolian landscape; a study of soils near Swan Hill. University of Sydney (M.Sc. thesis).

——— 1961a   Ground surfaces as a guide to landscape events. Australian Soil Science Conference, 3rd, Canberra, Proceedings.

——— 1961b   Soil studies at Swan Hill. I: Soil layering. Journal of Soil Science 12:73.

——— 1963a   Soil studies at Swan Hill. II: Dune moulding and parna formation. Australian Journal of Soil Research 1.

——— 1963b   Soil studies at Swan Hill, Victoria, Australia. III: Some aspects of soil development on aeolian material. Australian Journal of Soil Research 1.

Clapp, F. G.

1926   In the northwest of the Australian desert. Geographical Review 16:206-231.

Clarke, E. de C.

1926   Natural regions of Western Australia. Royal Society of Western Australia, Journal 12.

——— 1938   Middle and West Australia: vol. I, Ch. 7. *In* Regionale Geologie der Erde, Leipzig.

Clarke, E. de C., R. T. Prider, and C. Teichert

1944   Elements of geology for Western Australian students. 2nd ed. University of Western Australia, Perth.

Crocker, R. L.

1946a   Post-Miocene climatic and geologic history and its significance in relation to the genesis of the major soil types of South Australia. Australian Council of Scientific and Industrial Research, Bulletin 193.

——— 1946b   The Simpson Desert expedition, 1939 scientific reports. Number 8: The soils and vegetation of the Simpson Desert and its borders. Royal Society of South Australia, Transactions 70: 235-258.

David, T. W. E.

1950   The geology of the Commonwealth of Australia. E. Arnold, London. 3 vol.
The standard reference work on the general geology of Australia.

Douglas, I.

1964   Intensity and periodicity in denudation processes with special reference to the removal of material in solution by rivers. Zeitschrift für Geomorphologie 8:453-473.

——— 1965   Sediment yield in relation to land characteristics and land use in selected catchments in northeast Queensland. Australian and New Zealand Associations for the Advancement of Science, 38th, Congress, Hobart.

Dury, G. H.

1964   Some results of a magnitude-frequency analysis of precipitation. Australian Geographical Studies 2: 21-34.

Fenner, C. E.

1930   The major structural and physiographic features of South Australia. Royal Society of South Australia, Transactions and Proceedings 54:1-36.

——— 1931   South Australia. Whitcombe Tombs, Ltd., Melbourne. 352 p.

Gibson, C. C.

1909   The geological features of the country lying along the route of the proposed transcontinental railway in Western Australia. Geological Survey of Western Australia, Bulletin 37.

Gregory, J. W.

1906   The dead heart of Australia. J. Murray, London. 384 p.

——— 1914   The lake system of Westralia. Geographical Journal 43:656-662.

——— 1916   The central lakes of Westralia and the Westralian peneplain. Geographical Journal 48:326-331.

Hallsworth, E. G., F. R. Gibbons, and W. E. Darley

1951   Desert soil formations of Australia. Australian Journal of Science 13:110-111.

Hallsworth, E. G., G. K. Robertson, and F. R. Gibbons

1955   Studies in pedogenesis in New South Wales, VII: The "gilgai" soils. Journal of Soil Science 6:1-31.

Hawkins, C. A.

1961   Periodicity in landscapes and soil evolution. Australian Soil Science Conference, 3rd, Canberra, Proceedings.

Hawkins, C. A. and P. H. Walker

1956   A study of layered sedimentary materials in the Riverine Plain. Royal Society of New South Wales, Journal and Proceedings 90:110-123.

Hays, J.

1962   Laterite and land surface in the Northern Territory of Australia, north of the McDonnell Ranges. Symposium on geochronology and land surfaces in relation to soils in Australia. Australian Academy of Science — C.S.I.R.O., Adelaide, 1961.

Hills, E. S.

1939   The lunette, a new land-form of aeolian origin. Australian Geographer 3:15-21.

——— 1953   Regional geomorphic patterns in relation to climatic types in dry areas of Australia. *In* Desert research, proceedings of the international symposium held in Jerusalem, May 7-14, 1952, sponsored by the Research Council of Israel and Unesco. Research Council of Israel, Special Publication 2:355-364.

——— 1955   Die Landoberfläche Australiens. Die Erde 3-4: 195-205.
(The Australian land surfaces.)

——— 1957   Geology and geophysics. *In* Guidebook to research data for arid-zone development. Unesco, Paris. Arid Zone Research 9:44-50.

——— 1961   Australian arid zone research. Arid Zone [Newsletter] 13:12-14.

Jack, R. L.

1915   The geology and prospects of the region to the south of the Musgrave Ranges. Geological Society of South Australia, Bulletin 5.

Jackson, E. A.

1957a   Soil features in arid regions with particular reference to Australia. Australian Institute of Agricultural Science, Journal 23:196-208.

Jackson, E. A.
1957*b* Some facts and fallacies concerning the soils of Australia's arid regions. Australian Soil Science Conference, 2nd, Melbourne, Proceedings.

1960 A study of soils in a portion of central Australia. C.S.I.R.O., Soils Publication 19.

1962 Soils studies in central Australia: Alice Springs-Hermansburg-Rodinga areas. C.S.I.R.O., Soils Publication 19.
A good description of the types and distribution of soils in central Australia. A vast literature on Australian soils exists, however, and the following reports from this bibliography should be consulted: Woolnough (1927), Prescott and Skewes (1938), Teakle (1936), Jessup (1960*a, b,* 1961*a, b,* 1962), Ollier (1961, 1962, 1963), Butler (1959, 1961*b,* 1962), Hallsworth *et al.* (1951, 1955), Hawkins (1961), Webb (1962), Stephens (1961), Litchfield (1960, 1962), Mulcany (1960), Churchward (1960, 1961*a, b,* 1963*a, b*), Crocker (1946*a, b*), Hays (1962), Taylor (1950), Langford-Smith and Dury (1965), and some additional work by Jackson (1957*a, b,* 1960), among others. See also chapter V of this compendium, by H. E. Dregne, which treats soils of the arid environments.

Jennings, J. N. and E. C. F. Bird
1964 Regional geomorphological characteristics of some Australian estuaries. Mimeographed copy of conference paper. Australian National University, Canberra.

Jessup, R. W.
1960*a* Identification and significance of the buried soils of Quaternary age in the southeastern portion of the Australian arid zone. Journal of Soil Science 11:197-205.

1960*b* The stony tableland soils of the southeastern portion of the Australian arid zone and their evolutionary history. Journal of Soil Science 11:197-205.

1961*a* Evolution of the two youngest (Quaternary) soil layers in the southeastern portion on the Australian arid zone. Journal of Soil Science 12:52-72.

1961*b* A Tertiary-Quaternary pedological chronology for the southeastern portion on the Australian arid zone. Journal of Soil Science 12:199-213.

1962 Stony tableland soils on inland Australia. Australian Journal of Science 24:456-457.

Jutson, J. T.
1914 Physiographical geology of Western Australia. Geological Survey of Western Australia, Bulletin 61.

1917 Erosion and the resulting landforms of West Australia. Geographical Journal 50:418-437.

1950 The physiography of Western Australia. 3rd ed. Geological Survey of Western Australia, Bulletin 95.
A standard reference work on Western Australia, which describes the landforms, climate, and drainage, and provides references to earlier work in this state.

King, D.
1956 The Quaternary stratigraphic record at Lake Eyre North and the evolution of existing topographic forms. Royal Society of South Australia, Transactions 79:93-103.

1960 The sand ridge deserts of South Australia and related aeolian land forms of the Quaternary arid cycles. Royal Society of South Australia, Transactions 83:99-108.

Langford-Smith, T.
1947 Water supply in the agricultural areas of Western Australia. Australian Geographer 5:115-156.

1959 Deposition on the Riverine Plain of southeastern Australia. Australian Journal of Science 21:73-74.

1960*a* The dead river systems of the Murrumbidgee. Geographical Review 50:368-389.
A detailed discussion of "fossil drainage" as reflected by the Murrumbidgee area, with many data that are pertinent to the problem. For additional information on the prior streams and the various interpretations of causes that have been offered see Langford-Smith (1959, 1960*b,* 1962), Butler (1961*a*), and Schumm (1965). Pertinent data on the characteristics of sedimentary deposits (Hawkins and Walker, 1956) and sand dunes (Stannard, 1961) in the general area are also available.

1960*b* Reply to Mr. Butler. Australian Journal of Science 22:452-453.

1962 Riverine Plains chronology. Australian Journal of Science 25:96-97.

Langford-Smith, T. and G. H. Dury
1964 A pediment survey at Middle Pinnacle, near Broken Hill, New South Wales. Geological Society of Australia, Journal 11:79-88.

1965 Distribution, character, and attitude of the duricrust in the northwest of New South Wales and the adjacent areas of Queensland. American Journal of Science 263:170-190.

Lindsay, D.
1889 An expedition across Australia from south to north, between the telegraph line and the Queensland boundary. Royal Geographical Society, Proceedings 11:650-671.

1893 Journal of the Elder scientific exploring expedition 1891-2. Government Printer, Adelaide. 207 p.

Litchfield, W. H.
1960 Soil research in central Australia. Arid Zone Technical Conference, Adelaide, v. 1.

1962 Soils of the Alice Springs area. C.S.I.R.O., Land Research Series 6(8).

Ludbrook, N. H.
1961 The stratigraphic sequence intersected in deep drilling in Lake Eyre. C.S.I.R.O. file report.

Mabbutt, J. A.
1961a The geomorphology of the Australian arid zone. C.S.I.R.O., Technical Memorandum 61/23.
This paper presents an outline of the principal characteristics of the Australian arid area and should be consulted together with the several additional excellent accounts of surficial features that have been provided by the same author. Of particular interest are his papers treating general degradation in the arid regions (Mabbutt, 1961b, d, 1962), a description of the extensive weathering that has occurred (Mabbutt, 1961c) and its possible relationship to the formation of pediments (Mabbutt, 1966), and his Western Australian studies (Mabbutt, 1963; Mabbutt et al., 1963). The last two reports provide data on microrelief features, and on land-use classifications based on geomorphology, geology, soils, and vegetation, in portions of the state. Maps, photographs, or other useful illustrations accompany these reports.

1961b Degradation of land surfaces in arid Australia. Arid Zone Technical Conference, Victoria, Proceedings.

1961c The deeply weathered land surface in central Australia. Arid Zone Technical Conference, Victoria, Proceedings.

1961d Degradation of land surfaces in arid Australia. C.S.I.R.O., Technical Memorandum 61/8.

1962 Periodicity and inheritance in land-form development in the western MacDonnell Ranges, Northern Territory. Symposium on geochronology and land surfaces in relation to soils in Australia: Australian Academy of Science — C.S.I.R.O., Adelaide, 1961.

1963 Wanderrie banks; microrelief patterns in semiarid western Australia. Geological Society of America, Bulletin 74:529-540.

1966 Mantle-controlled planation of pediments. American Journal of Science 264:78-91.

Mabbutt, J. A. et al.
1963 General report on lands of the Wiluna-Meekatharra area, Western Australia, 1958. C.S.I.R.O., Land Research Ser. 7.

Madigan, C. T.
1930 An aerial reconnaissance into the southeastern portion of Central Australia. Royal Geographical Society of Australasia, South Australian Branch, Proceedings 30:83-108.

1936a The Australian sand-ridge deserts. Geographical Review 26:205-227.

1936b Central Australia. Oxford University Press. 267 p. This work by one of the early explorers of the region provides a good descriptive account of the surficial features of the central Australian desert. See Madigan (1930, 1936a, 1938a, b, 1946) for additional information of this nature, Crocker (1946b) for data on soils and vegetation that were obtained during the same general period, and Carroll (1944) for information on the distribution and characteristics of sands in central Australia.

1938a Desiccation in Australia. Australian Journal of Science 1:26

1938b The Simpson Desert and its borders. Royal Society of New South Wales, Journal and Proceedings 71:503.

1946 The sand formations. The Simpson Desert Expedition, 1939, Scientific Report 6. Royal Society of South Australia, Transactions 70:45-63.

Marshall, A.
1948 The size of the Australian Desert. Australian Geographer 5:168-175.

Mooy, C. J. de
1959 Notes on the geomorphic history of the area surrounding Lakes Alexandrina and Albert, South Australia. Royal Society of South Australia, Transactions 82:99-118.

Mulcany, M. J.
1960 Laterites and lateritic soils in southwestern Australia. Journal of Soil Science 11:206-225.

Ollier, C. D.
1961 Lag deposits at Coober Pedy, South Australia. Australian Journal of Science 24:84-85.

1962 Stony tableland soils at Coober Pedy, South Australia. Australian Journal of Science 25:10-21..

1963 Insolation weathering; examples from central Australia. American Journal of Science 261:376-381.

1965 Some features of granite weathering in Australia. Zeitschrift für Geomorphologie 9:285-304.

Ollier, C. D. and W. G. Tuddenham
1961 Inselbergs of central Australia. Zeitshrift für Geomorphologie 5:257-276.

1962 Slope developments at Coober Pedy, South Australia. Geological Society of Australia, Journal 9:91-105.

Pels, S.
1960 The geology of the Murrumbidgee irrigation area and surrounding districts. New South Wales, Department of Conservation, Water Conservation and Irrigation Commission, Bulletin 5.

Perry, R. A. et al.
1962 General report on lands of the Alice Springs area, Northern Territory, 1956-67. C.S.I.R.O., Land Research Ser. 6.
A typical example of the C.S.I.R.O. team reports. The Alice Springs area in central Australia is analyzed in detail, with respect to the geology, geomorphology, soils, and vegetation. The terrain in this case was represented by 88 different facets, which are shown on the accompanying map, and the quantitative and qualitative characteristics of these subdivisions are discussed in the text.

Piper, C. S.
1932 The soils of the South Australian Mallee. Royal Society of South Australia, Transactions 56:118-147.

Prescott, J. A.
1936 The climatic control of the Australian deserts. Royal Society of South Australia, Transactions 60:93-95.

Prescott, J. A. and J. S. Hosking
1936   Some red basaltic soils from South Australia. Royal Society of South Australia, Transactions 60:35-45.

Prescott, J. A. and H. R. Skewes
1938   An examination of some soils from the more arid regions of Australia. Royal Society of South Australia, Transactions 62:320-341.

Schumm, S. A.
1965   Project summary: geomorphology of the prior rivers of the Murrumbidgee River system. *In* Report of water resources research, July 1964-June 30, 1965. U. S. Geological Survey.

Singleton, F. A.
1939   The Tertiary geology of Australia. Royal Society of Victoria, Proceedings 53:1-70.

Spencer, B. (ed.)
1896   Report on the work of the Horn Scientific Expedition to Central Australia. London and Melbourne, 4 vols.

Stannard, M. E.
1961   Sand dunes of the Riverina Plain, New South Wales. Australian Soil and Science Conference, 3rd, Canberra, Proceedings.

Stephens, C. G.
1961   The soil landscapes of Australia. C.S.I.R.O., Soils Publication 18.

Stewart, G. A. and W. H. Litchfield
1957   Major profile forms of the central arid zone. Australian Soil Science Conference, 2nd, Melbourne, Proceedings.

Sturt, C.
1849   Narrative of an expedition into Central Australia, during the years 1844, 1845 and 1846. Boone, London. 2 vols.

Talbot, H. W. B.
1910   Geological observations in the country between Wiluna, Hall's Creek, and Tanami. Geological Survey of Western Australia, Bulletin 39.

Talbot, H. W. B. and E. de C. Clarke
1917   A geological reconnaissance of the country between Laverton and the South Australia border (near South Latitude 26°). Geological Survey of Western Australia, Bulletin 75.

Tate, R. and J. A. Watt
1896   Geology and botany. *In* B. Spencer, ed., Report on the work of the Horn Scientific Expedition to Central Australia, III. Dulau and Company, London.

Taylor, G.
1924   Uninhabited Australia; and the reasons therefor. Pan-Pacific Science Congress, 2nd, Australia, Proceedings 1:659-664.

Taylor, J. K.
1950   Soils of Australia. p. 35-48. *In* The Australian environment; handbook prepared for the British Commonwealth Specialist Agricultural Conference on Plant and Animal Nutrition in relation to Soil and Climatic factors held in Australia, August 1949. 2nd ed. C.S.I.R.O., Melbourne. 151 p.

Teakle, L. J. H.
1936   The red and brown hard-pan soils of the Acacia semi-desert scrub of Western Australia. Journal of Agriculture of Western Australia, 2d Ser., 13:480-499.

Tietkens, W. H.
1891   Journal of the Central Australia Exploration Expedition, 1889. Government Printer, Adelaide. 84 p.

Twidale, C. R.
1962   Steepened margins of inselbergs from northwestern Eyre Peninsula, South Australia. Zeitschrift für Geomorphologie 6:52-69.

————
1964   Domed inselbergs. Institute of British Geographers, Transactions and Papers 34:91-113.

Unesco
1956   Australia symposium on arid zone climatology with special reference to microclimatology. Canberra. Arid Zone Research 11.

Warburton, P. E.
1875a Colonel Warburton's explorations, 1872-3; diary of Colonel Warburton's exploring expedition to Western Australia in 1872-3. South Australia, Parliamentary Paper 28.

————
1875b Journey across the western interior of Australia. Ed. by H. W. Bates. S. Low, Marston, Low and Searle, London. 307 p.

Webb, B. P.
1962   The age and relationship of the siliceous duricrust in South Australia. Symposium on geochronology and land surfaces in relation to soils in Australia. Australian Academy of Science — C.S.I.R.O., Adelaide, 1961.

Webb, B. P. and H. Wopfner
1961   Plio-Pleistocene dunes northwest of Lake Torrens, South Australia, and their influence on erosional pattern. Australian Journal of Science 23:379-380.

Wells, L. A.
1902   Journal of the Calvert scientific exploring expedition 1896-7. Western Australia, Parliamentary Paper 46.

Western Australia Land Use Study Group
1964   Report of Special Advisory Committee. N. Y. 54 p.

Whitehouse, F. W. *et al.*
1947   The channel country of southwest Queensland with special reference to Cooper's Creek. Queensland Department of Public Lands, Bureau of Investigation, Technical Bulletin 1. 158 p.

A comprehensive report on the drainage system of Cooper's Creek in east-central Australia and the probability of flooding. Many useful photographs and field observations of the channels and surrounding terrain are presented.

Winnecke, C.
1896   Journal of the Horn Scientific Expedition to Central Australia, 1894. South Australia, Parliamentary Paper 19.

Woodward, H. P.
1897   The dry lakes of western Australia. Geological Magazine, p. 363.

————
1912   A general description of the northern portion of the Yilgarn goldfield and the southern portion of the north Coolgardie goldfield. Geological Survey of Western Australia, Bulletin 46.

Woolnough, W. G.
1927   The duricrust of Australia. Royal Society of New South Wales, Journal and Proceedings 61:24-53.

SECTION XI

SOUTH AMERICA (IN GENERAL)

Includes works cited in the text discussion of the South American desert areas in general.

Cederstrom, D. J. and J. C. Assad
1962 Observations on the hydrology of northeastern Brazil. U. S. Geological Survey, Administrative Report. Rio de Janeiro.

Chapman, V. J.
1960 Salt marshes and salt deserts of the world. Leonard Hill, London.

Demangeot, J.
1960 Essai sur le relief du nord-est Brésilien. Annales de Géographie 69:157-176.
(On the relief of northeast Brazil.)

Dresch, J.
1957 Les problèmes morphologiques du nord-est Brésilien. Association de Géographes Français, Bulletin 263:48-60.
(Morphologic problems of northeast Brazil.)

Gerth, H.
1955 Geologie von Südamerika. Gebrüder Borntraeger, Berlin.
(Geology of South America.)
A good summary of the geology of the continent with maps and cross sections. See Jenks (1956) for additional geological information.

James, P. E.
1942 Latin America. Lothrop, Lee, and Shepard, New York. 908 p.
A standard geographic text on South America which presents the regional physiography and much general information on surficial features. See Shanahan (1959) for more recent similar data, and also Chapman (1960) and de Martonne (1947).

———
1952 Observations on the physical geography of northeast Brazil. Association of American Geographers, Annals 42:153-176.

Jenks, W. F. (ed.)
1956 Handbook of South American geology. Geological Society of America, Memoir 65.

King, L. C.
1956 A geomorfologia do Brasil oriental. Revista Brasileira de Geografia 18(2):147-265.
(Geomorphology of eastern Brazil)

Liddle, R. A.
1946 The geology of Venezuela and Trinidad. 2nd ed. New York.

Martonne, E. de
1947 Les déserts de l'Amérique du Sud. Société Royale de Géographie d'Egypte, Bulletin 22:1-19.
(The deserts of South America.)

Oliveira, A. I. de, and O. H. Leonardos
1943 Geologia do Brasil. 2nd ed. Serviço de Informação Agrícola, Rio de Janeiro.
(Geology of Brazil.)

Rich, J. L.
1942 The face of South America. American Geographical Society, Special Publication 26:180-208.

Schoff, S. L.
1962 Hydrologic investigations for northeastern Brazil. U. S. Geological Survey, Administrative Report. Recife.

Shanahan, E. W.
1959 South America. Methuen, London, 318 p.

Smith, G.-H.
1939 Physiographic diagram of South America. Columbia University Press, New York.

Sorge, E.
1930 Die trockengrenze Südamerikas. Gesellschaft für Erdkunde zu Berlin, Zeitschrift 65:277-287.
(The arid boundary of South America.)

Turnbull, T. G.
1961 Analogs of Yuma climate in South America. U. S. Army, Quartermaster Research and Engineering Center, Natick, Mass., Earth Sciences Division, Research Study Report RER-34.

Unesco
n.d. Boletín del Centro de Cooperación Científica Montevideo.
(Bulletin of the Scientific Cooperation Center.)
This bulletin presents information on arid-zone research meetings and symposia in South America and is an excellent source of data.

Wilhelmy, H.
1954 Die klimamorphologische entwicklung des trockengebietes am nordrand Südamerikas seit dem Pleistozän. Die Erde 85:244-273.
(The climatic-morphologic development of the dry regions on the northern margin of South America since the Pleistocene.)

SECTION XII

MONTE-PATAGONIAN DESERT

Includes works cited in the text discussion of the Monte-Patagonian Desert.

Argentina. Consejo Federal de Inversiones
1962- Evaluación de los recursos naturales de la Argen-
1963   tina. 9 vols. Kraft, Ltd., Buenos Aires.
(Evaluation of the natural resources of Argentina.)
Summarizes the status of geologic and topographic mapping in Argentina, indicates the availability of aerial photographs, presents information on the institutions engaged in geologic or hydrologic investigations in the country, and provides a good summary of available data on water resources.

Argentina. Dirección Nacional de Geología y Minería
1963a Mapa hidrogeológico de la República Argentina. Buenos Aires.
(Hydrogeologic map of the Republic of Argentina, scale 1:5,000,000.)

———
1963b Texto explicativo del mapa hidrogeológico de la República Argentina. Buenos Aires.
(Explanatory text for the hydrogeologic map of the Republic of Argentina.)

———
1965a Index map of topographic and geologic coverage in Argentina. (unpublished)

———
1965b Index map of aerial-photography coverage in Argentina. (unpublished)

Arnolds, A.
1952   Aspectos generales de la geología y geomorfología del distrito Sierra Grande (Territorio de Río Negro). Asociación Geológica Argentina, Revista 7:131-142.
(General aspects of the geology and geomorphology of the Sierra Grande district, Rio Negro.)

Bonfils, C. G.
1951   Estudio agrohidrológico en el Valle del Río Lavayen. Argentina, Instituto Suelos y Agrotécnica, Publicación 18. 60 p.
(Agro-hydrologic study of the Lavayen River Valley.)

Capitanelli, R. G.
1955   Régimen de aridez de la Provincia de San Luis. Universidad Nacional de Cuyo, Boletín de Estudios Geográficos 2:291-317.
(Arid regime of San Luis Province.)

————
1962   Balance hídrico del piedmonte Mendocino. Universidad Nacional de Cuyo, Boletín de Estudios Geográficos 9:1-38.
(Hydrologic balance of the Mendocino piedmont area.)

Comité Argentina para el Estudio de las Regiones Aridas y Semiáridas
1963   Conferencia latinoamericana para el estudio de las regiones áridas. Instituto Nacional de Tecnología Agropecuaria, Buenos Aires.
(Latin American conference on the study of arid regions.)

Cordini, I. R.
1947   Contribución al conocimiento de los cuerpos salinos de La Argentina. Asociación Geológica Argentina, Revista 3:145-200.
(Contribution to understanding of the saline bodies of Argentina.)

Cortelezzi, C. R., F. DeFrancesco, and O. De Salvo
1963   Estudio de las gravas tehuelches de la región comprendida entre el Río Colorado y el Río Negro. An. Jour. Geol. Argentinas-Saltas 2.
(Study of the "tehuelches" gravels of the little-known region between the Colorado and Negro rivers.)

Cortelezzi, C. R. and J. O. Kilmurray
1965   Surface properties and epigenetic fractures of gravels from Patagonia, Argentina. Journal of Sedimentary Petrology 35:976-980.

Dessanti, R. N.
1956   Descripción geológica de la Hoja 27c. Dirección Nacional de Geología y Minería, Buenos Aires, Boletin 85.
(Geologic description of quadrangle 27c.)

————
1958   Geologic outline of natural regions of Mendoza, Argentina. American Association of Petroleum Geologists, Bulletin 42:2670-2691.

Enjalbert, H.
1957   La vallée du Río Mendoza; essai sur l'évolution du modelé des Andes sèches. Association de Géographes Français, Bulletin 267-268:40-46.
(The valley of the Mendoza River; essay on the evolution of the relief of the arid Andes.)

Feruglio, E.
1935   Sobre la presencia de grandes rodados en las mesetas de la región del Golfo de Jorge (Patagonia) y en las Guayquerias de Tunuyán (Mendoza). Gaea 4:189-208.
(On the occurrence of large tracks on the plateaus in the Golfo de Jorge region of Patagonia and in the badlands of Tunuyán, Mendoza.)

————
1950   Descripción geológica de la Patagonia. Vol. 3. Yacimientos Petrolíferos Fiscales, Buenos Aires. 3 vols.

Fidalgo, F.
1963   Algunos rasgos tectónicos y geomorfológicos de la Sierra de Sanogasto-Vilgo (Provincia de La Rioja). Asociación Geológica Argentina, Revista 18:139-153.
(Some tectonic and geomorphic characteristics of the Sierra de Sanogasto-Vilgo, La Rioja Province.)
Discusses geomorphic zones in this province and the occurrence of alkali flats and playas, pediments, and dunes. See Frenguelli (1928, 1943), Hueck (1956), and Arnolds (1952) for descriptive information on closed basins, saline deposits, and allied topics elsewhere in the Argentine desert.

Frenguelli, J.
1928   Acerca del origen de los salares de los desiertos de la Puna de Atacama. Gaea 3:167-186.
(On the origin of the saline flats in the deserts of the Puna de Atacama.)

————
1943   Vestigios de una fase lacustre reciente en la cuenca de Salina Chica en península Valdez (Chubut). Gaea 7:65-71.
(Evidence of a recent lacustrine phase in the Salina Chica basin in the Valdez peninsula, Chubut Province.)

————
1946   Consideraciones sobre la "Serie de Paganzo" en las provincias de San Juan y La Rioja. Museo de La Plata, Revista 2:107-116.
(Reflections on the Paganza series of San Juan and La Rioja Provinces.)

Gonzáles Bonorino, F.
1950   Geologic cross section of the Cordillera de los Andes at about parallel 33°S (Argentina-Chile). Geological Society of America, Bulletin 61:17-26.

Gonzáles Díaz, E. F.
1964   Rasgos geológicos y evolución geomorfológica de la Hoja 27d ,San Rafael) y zona occidental vecina (Provincia Mendoza). Asociación Geológica Argentina, Revista 19:151-188.
(Geologic characteristics and geomorphic evolution of the San Rafael Quadrangle, Sheet 27d, and the neighboring western zone in Mendoza Province.)

Groeber, P.
1933   Confluencia de los Ríos Grande y Barrancas (Mendoza y Neuquen). Descripción de la hoja 31c del mapa geológica general de la República Argentina. Dirección de Minas y Geología, Buenos Aires, Boletín 38. 72 p.
(Confluence of the Grande and Barrancas rivers, Mendoza and Neuquen Provinces. Description of quadrangle 31c of the general geologic map of Argentina.)

Hueck, K.
1956   Mapas fitogeográficos de la República Argentina. Universidad Nacional de Cuyo, Boletín de Estudios Geográficos 3:87-100.
(Phytogeographic maps of Argentina.)

Inchauspe, O.
1957   La cuenca superior y media del Río Tunuyán. Universidad Nacional de Cuyo, Boletín de Estudios Geográficos 4:131-145.
(The upper and middle basin of the Tunuyan River.)

Kühn, F.
1922   Fundamentos de fisiografía argentina. Talleres Gráficos P. Preusche, Buenos Aires. 217 p.

Martonne, E. de
1934   Les régions arides de nord de l'Argentine et de Chili. Association de Géographes Français, Bulletin 79.
(The arid regions of northern Argentina and Chile.)

Nieniewski, A. and E. Wieklinski
1950   Contribución al conocimiento del anticlinal de Zalpa (Provincia de Jujuy). Asociación Geológica Argentina, Revista 5:169-203.
(Contribution to knowledge of the Zalpa anticline, Jujuy Province.)

Organization of American States
1966   Annotated index of aerial photographic coverage and mapping of topography and natural resources: Argentina; Brazil; Mexico. Pan American Union, Washington.

Palese de Torres, A.
1956   El Valle de Tinogasta. Universidad Nacional de Cuyo, Boletín de Estudios Geográficos 3:187-227.
(Tinogasta Valley.)

Perrot, C. J.
1960   Estudio geológico de las inmediaciones del Paraje "El Molle" (Departamento Tehuelches, Provincia de Chubut). Asociación Geológica Argentina, Revista 15:53-80.
(Geologic study of the "El Molle" area, Tehuelches Department, Chubut Province.)

Polanski, J.
1953   Supuestos englazimientos en la llanura pedemontana de Mendoza. Asociación Geológica Argentina, Revista 8:195-213.
(Supposed glacially-derived rocks on the extensive plain of Mendoza.)

———
1963   Estratigrafía, neotectónica, y geomorfología del Pleistoceno pedemontano entre los Ríos Diamante y Mendoza. Asociación Geológica Argentina, Revista 17:127-349.
(Stratigraphy, recent tectonics, and geomorphology of the Pleistocene piedmont between the Diamante and Mendoza rivers.)
A description of surficial features in Mendoza Province and a classification of the region by physiographic types on a classical basis. Pediments, badlands, drainage, and lithology are discussed and described. See Polanski (1964a, b) for additional geologic and geomorphic descriptions, and Dessanti (1956, 1958) and Gonzáles Díaz (1964) for similar treatment of adjacent areas.

———
1964a Descripción geológica de la Hoja 25a-Volcán San José. Dirección Nacional de Geología y Minería, Buenos Aires, Boletín 98.
(Geologic description of quadrangle 25a-San Jose volcano.)

———
1964b Descripción geológica de la Hoja 26c-La Tosca. Dirección Nacional de Geología y Minería, Buenos Aires, Boletín 101.
(Geologic description of quadrangle 26c-La Tosca.)

Pratt, W. P.
1961   Local evidence of Pleistocene to Recent orogeny in the Argentine Andes. Geological Society of America, Bulletin 72:1551-1560.
A good description of desert topography in the Puna de Atacama area with a discussion of gullying and mudflows.

Regairez, C. A.
1962   Importancia de algunos rasgos geomorfológicos del presente y del pasado en Mendoza y su vinculación con recursos naturales energéticos. Universidad Nacional de Cuyo, Boletín de Estudios Geográficos 9:151-159.
(Importance of certain geomorphic features of the past and present in Mendoza and their relation to natural energy resources.)

Rousseau, S. A.
1958   Estudio hidrogeológico de la zona Media Agua, Departamento de Sarmiento, Provincia de San Juan. Asociación Geológica Argentina, Revista 13.
(Hydrogeologic study of the Media Agua zone of Sarmiento, San Juan Province.)

Ruiz Huidobro, O.
1965   Hidrogeología del Valle de Santa María (Provincia de Catamarca). Asociación Geológica Argentina, Revista 20:29-66.
(Hydrology of Santa Maria Valley, Catamarca Province.)
A recent description of surficial deposits and the known hydrogeology in a region receiving about 6 inches of precipitation per year. See Urien (1965) and Rousseau (1958) for descriptions of landforms, valley deposits, and flow characteristics elsewhere in Mendoza Province, and Capitanelli (1962) for an outline of the hydrologic balance of the province.

Schoff, S. L.
1960   A hydrologic investigation program for Argentina. U. S. Geological Survey, Administrative Report.

Turner, J. C. M.
1958   Estratigrafía de la Sierra de Narváez (Catamarca). Asociación Geológica Argentina, Revista 12:18-60.
(Stratigraphy of the Sierra de Narvaez, Catamarca Province.)

———
1959   Estratigrafía del Cordón de Escaya y de la Sierra de Rinconada (Jujuy). Asociación Geológica Argentina, Revista 13:15-40.
(Stratigraphy of the Escaya Range and the Sierra de Rinconada, Jujuy Province.)

———
1962   Estratigrafía de la región al naciente de la Laguna Blanca (Catamarca). Asociación Geológica Argentina, Revista 17:11-45.
(Stratigraphy of the region to the east of Laguna Blanca, Catamarca.)

Urien, C. M.
1965 Hidrogeología del Valle de Toba. Asociación Geológica Argentina, Revista 20:241-262.
(Hydrogeology of the Toba Valley.)

Velasco, M. I. and R. G. Capitanelli
1956 Somero estudio climático de los valles de los ríos Neuquen, Limay, y Negro. Universidad Nacional de Cuyo, Boletín de Estudios Geográficos 3:19-51.
(Climatic summary of the Neuquen, Limay, and Negro river valleys.)

Vilela, C. R.
1953 Los períodos eruptivos en la Puna de Atacama. Asociación Geológica Argentina, Revista 8:5-36.
(Volcanic episodes in the Puna de Atacama.)

1956 Descripción geológica de la Hoja 7d, Rosario de Lerma, Provincia de Salta. Dirección Nacional de Geología y Minería, Buenos Aires, Boletín 84.
(Geologic description of quadrangle 7d, Rosario de Lerma, Salta Province.)

Volkenheimer, W.
1964 Estratigrafía de la zona Extra Andina del Departamento de Cushamen (Chubut) entre los paralelos 42° y 42°30′ y los medidianos 70° y 71°. Asociación Geológica Argentina, Revista 19:85-107.
(Stratigraphy of the Extra-Andina zone, Cushamen Department, Chubut Province, between latitudes 42°S and 42°30′S and longitudes 70°W and 71°W.)
Provides a discussion of lava plains, pyroclastic deposits, terraces, and landslide phenomena, among other topics, in the Andean foothills area near Chubut.

Windhausen, A.
1931 Geología Argentina. Talleres s. a. Casa J. Peuser, Ltda., Buenos Aires.
(Geology of Argentina.)

Yrigoyen, M. R.
1950 Algunas observaciones sobre los basaltos cuaternarios del sur de la provincia de Mendoza. Asociación Geológica Argentina, Revista 5.
(Some observations on the Quaternary basalts of Mendoza Province.)

Zamorano, M.
1950 Las desaparecidas balsas de Guanacache. Universidad Nacional de Cuyo, Boletín de Estudios Geográficos 2:165-184.
(The vanished fishing rafts of Guanacache.)

SECTION XIII

ATACAMA-PERUVIAN DESERT: PERU AND CHILE

Includes works cited in the text discussions of the parts of the Atacama-Peruvian Desert in Peru and in Chile.

Abercromby, R.
1889 Nitrate of soda and the nitrate country. Nature 40:186-188, 308-310.

Amstutz, G. C. and R. Chico
1958 Sand size fractions of south-Peruvian barchans and a brief review of the genetic grain shape function. Vereinigung Schweizerischen Petroleum-Geologen und-Ingenieure, Bulletin 24(67):47-52.

Barclay, W. S.
1917 Sand dunes in the Peruvian desert. Geographical Journal 11:53-56.

Barua, V. R.
1961 Reconocimiento geológico-zona de Tacna y Moquegua. Sociedad Geológica del Perú, Boletín 36:35-59.
(Geologic reconnaissance of the Tacna and Moquegua area.)

Bellido, E.
1956 Geología del curso medio del Río Huaytará, Huancavelica. Sociedad Geológica del Perú, Boletín 30:33-47.
(Geology of the middle reach of the Huaytará River.)

Bellido, E. and C. Guevara
1963 Geología de los Cuadrángulos de Punta de Bombón y Clemesi. Comisión de la Carta Geológica Nacional, Lima, Boletín 2(5).
(Geology of the Punta de Bombón and Clemesi Quadrangles.)

Bellido, E. and S. Narváez
1960 Geología del Cuadrángulo Atico. Comisión de la Carta Geológica Nacional, Lima, Boletín 1(2).
(Geology of the Atico Quadrangle.)

Bellido, E., S. Narváez, and F. S. Simons
1956 Mapa Geológico del Perú, scale 1:2,000,000. Sociedad Geológica del Peru.

Benevides Cáceres, V.
1956 Geológia de las región de Cajamarca. Sociedad Geológica del Peru, Boletín 30:49-72.
(Geology of the Cajamarca region.)

Bosworth, T. O.
1922 Geology and paleontology of northwest Peru. Macmillan, London.

Bowman, I.
1916 The Andes of southern Peru. Henry Holt, New York.

1924 Desert trails of Atacama. American Geographical Society, Special Publication 5. 362 p.

1949 Fisiografía peruana. Sociedad Geológica del Peru, Boletín Jubilar 2.
(Peruvian physiography.)

Broggi, J. A.
1946a Geomorfología del delta del Río Tumbes. Sociedad Geográfica de Lima, Boletín 63.
(Geomorphology of the Río Tumbes delta.)

1946b Las terrazas (ensayo geomorfológico). Sociedad Geológica del Peru, Boletín 19:5-20.
(Terraces; a geomorphic essay.)

1946c Las terrazas marinas de la Bahía de San Juan en Ica. Sociedad Geológica del Peru, Boletín 19:21-33.
(The marine terraces of San Juan Bay at Ica.)

1952 Migración de arenas a lo largo de la costa. Sociedad Geológica del Peru, Boletín 24.
(Migration of sand along the coast.)

1954 Pasamayo y la geología. Escuela Nacional de Ingenieros, Lima, Boletín 27:28-59.
(Pasamayo and its geology.)

Broggi, J. A.
1957   Las terracitas fitogénicas de las lomas de la costa del Perú. Sociedad Geológica del Peru, Boletín 32:51-64.
(Phytogenetic microterraces in the coastal hills of Peru.)

1961   Las ciclópeas dunas compuestas de la costa peruana, su origen y significación climática. Sociedad Geológica del Peru, Boletín 36:61-66.
(The giant composite dunes of the Peruvian coast, their origin and climatic significance.)

Brown, C. B.
1924   On some effects of wind and sun in the desert of Tumbez, northwest Peru. Geological Magazine 8: 337-339.

Brüggen, J.
1929   Zur glazialgeologie der chilenischen Anden. Geologische Rundschau 20:5.
(On the glacial geology of the Chilean Andes.)

1942   Geologia de la Puna de San Pedro de Atacama y sus formaciones de areniscas y arcillas rojas. Congreso Panamericano de Ingeniería de Minas y Geología, 1st, Santiago de Chile, Anales 2(1): 342-367.
(Geology of the Puna de San Pedro de Atacama and its red sandstone and shale formations.)

1946   Geología y morfología de la Puna de Atacama. Imprenta Universitaria, Santiago. 132 p.

1950   Fundamentos de la geología de Chile. Instituto Geográphico Militar, Santiago. 374 p.
(Elements of Chilean geology.)
A basic text on the geology of Chile including regional descriptions of drainage, climate, and surficial features. See Muñoz Christi (1950, 1956) and Zeil (1964) for supplementary information, and Harrington (1961) for treatment of northern Chile.

Castillo Urrutia, O.
1960   El agua subterránea en el norte de la Pampa del Tamarugal. Instituto de Investigaciones Geológicas, Santiago, Boletín 5. 89 p.
(Ground water north of the Tamarugal Pampa.)

Catalano, L. R.
1926   Geología económica de los yacimientos de boratos y materiales de las cuencas Salar Cauchari. Dirección General de Minas, Geología e Hidrología, Buenos Aires, Publication 23. 110 p.

Cecioni, G. O. and A. F. García
1960   Stratigraphy of the Coastal Range in Tarapaca Province, Chile. American Association of Petroleum Geologists, Bulletin 44:1609-1620.

Chamberlin, R. T.
1912   The physical setting of the Chilean borate deposits. Journal of Geology 20:763-768.

Chile. Universidad. Instituto de Geografía
1960-   Informaciones geográficas.
1964   Vol. 1, 1951.   Santiago de Chile.
A general bibliography of reports treating Chilean geography; includes many useful references.

Clarke, F. W.
1924   The data of geochemistry. U. S. Geological Survey, Bulletin 770. 841 p.

Cooke, R. U.
1963   Landforms of the Huasco Valley, northern Chile. University of London. (unpublished M.Sc. thesis.)

1964   Landforms in the southern Atacama desert. British Association for Advancement of Science, Annual Meeting, Proceedings E:101-102.

1965   Evidence of changing sea level between latitudes 28° and 30°S during Quaternary time. In H. Fuenzalida Villegas, High stands of Quaternary sea level along the Chilean Coast, part 3. Geological Society of South America, Special Paper 84: 482-489.
Discusses the morphology of the Chilean coastal region between latitudes 28°S and 30°S. See also Fuenzalida Villegas *et al.* (1965) and Segerstrom (1962, 1964, 1965) for treatment of Quaternary features and interpretations.

Corporación de Fomento de la Producción
1950   Geografía Económica de Chile, Tomo 1. Santiago de Chile. 428 p.

Cossío, N. A.
1964   Geología de los Cuadrángulos de Santiago de Chuco y Santa Rosa. Comisión de la Carta Geológica Nacional, Lima, Boletín 8.
(Geology of the Santiago de Chuco and Santa Rosa Quadrangles.)

Cruzado, J. and J. Escudero
1959   Geología del área comprendida entre los Ríos Santa y Cabana. Sociedad Geológica del Peru, Boletín 34.
(Geology of the area between the Santos and Cabana rivers.)

Darwin, C.
1846   Geological observations on the volcanic islands and parts of South America visited during the voyage of the H.M.S. *Beagle;* reprinted 1915 by D. Appleton and Co., New York. p. 302-312.

Dingman, R. J.
1962   Tertiary salt dunes near San Pedro de Atacama, Chile. U. S. Geological Survey, Professional Paper 450-D:92-94.

1963   Cuadrángulo Tulor. Instituto de Investigaciones Geológicas, Carta Geológica de Chile 11.
(Tulor quadrangle.)

1965   Cuadrángulo San Pedro de Atacama, Provincia de Antofagasta. Instituto de Investigaciones Geológicas, Carta Geológica de Chile 14.
(San Pedro de Atacama quadrangle, Antofagasta Province.)

Dingman, R. J. and C. Galli Olivier
1965   Geology and ground-water resources of the Pica area, Tarapaca Province, Chile. U. S. Geological Survey, Bulletin 1189.
This report describes the canyons, plateaus, drainage, and other surficial features of a part of Tarapacá province. See Cecioni and García (1960), Taylor (1949), and Tricart (1966) for additional information on this general area. See geological quadrangle reports by Segerstrom (1959, 1960a, b), Segerstrom and Parker (1959), Segerstrom and Moraga A. (1964), Segerstrom, Valenzuela B., and Mahech (1960), Dingman (1963, 1965), and Galli Olivier and Dingman (1962) for descriptions of climate, topography, and drainage in each of the areas treated.

Donoso, L.
1959 Premier examen de la fraction argileuse de quelques sols du Chili. Société Française de Minéralogie et de Cristallographie, Paris, Bulletin 82(10-12): 361-363.

Doyel, W. W.
1964 Ground water in the Arica area, Chile. U. S. Geological Survey, Professional Paper 475-D:213-215.

Doyel, W. W., R. J. Dingman, and O. Castillo Urrutia
1964 Hydrogeology of the Santiago area, Chile. U. S. Geological Survey, Professional Paper 475-D: 209-212.

Dresch, J.
1961 Observations sur le désert cotier du Pérou. Annales de Géographie 70:179-184.
(Observations on the coastal desert of Peru.)

Ericksen, G. E.
1961 Rhyolite tuff, a source of the salts of northern Chile. U. S. Geological Survey, Professional Paper 424:C224-225.

——— 1963 Geology of the salt deposits and the salt industry of northern Chile. U. S. Geological Survey, Open File Report 698. 164 p.

Felsch, J.
1933 Informe preliminar sobre los reconocimientos geológicos de los yacimientos petroleros en la cordillera de la provincia de Antofagasta. Boletín de Minas y Petróleo (Santiago de Chile) 3(29):411-422.
(Preliminary report on a geologic reconnaissance of oil fields in the cordillera of Antofagasta Province.)

Fenner, C. N.
1948a Pleistocene climate and topography of the Arequipa region, Peru. Geological Society of America, Bulletin 59:895-917.

——— 1948b Incandescent tuff flows in southern Peru. Geological Society of America, Bulletin 59:879-894.

Finkel, H. J.
1959 The barchans of southern Peru. Journal of Geology 67:614-647.

Fuenzalida Villegas, H.
1937 El Rético en la costa de Chile central. Dep'to. Minas y Petrol., Min. Fomento.
(The Rhaetic of the coast of central Chile.)

Fuenzalida Villegas, H. *et al.*
1965 High stands of Quaternary sea level along the Chilean coast. Geological Society of America, Special Paper 84:473-496.

Gale, H. S.
1918 Potash in the Pintados Salar, Tarapaca, Chile. Engineering and Mining Journal 105:674-677.

Galli Olivier, C.
1957 Las formaciónes geológicas en el borde occidental de la Puna de Atacama, sector de Pica, Tarapaca. Instituto de Ingenieros de Minas de Chile, Santiago, Revista 12:14-26.
(The geologic formations on the western border of the Puna de Atacama, Pica sector, Tarapaca.)

Galli Olivier, C. and R. J. Dingman
1962 Cuadrángulos Pica, Alca, Matilla, y Chacarilla. Instituto de Investigaciones Geológicas, Carta Geológica de Chile 3(2-5).
(Pica, Alca, Matilla, and Chacarilla quadrangles.)

Garner, H. F.
1959 Stratigraphic-sedimentary significance of climate and relief in four regions of the Andes Mountains. Geological Society of America, Bulletin 70: 1327-1368.
A good description of surficial features, including drainage, in a paper that bears upon the evidences for climatic change in Peru. See Fenner (1948a), Tricart (1963), Nicholson (1942), Smith (1955b), and Olivieri (1951) for allied discussions of climate and climatic change in relation to desert morphology in Peru.

Gay, P., Jr.
1962 Origen, distribución y movimiento de las arenas eólicas en el área de Yauca a Palpa. Sociedad Geológica del Peru, Boletín 37:37-58.
(Origin, distribution, and movement of eolian sand in the Uauca-Palpa area.)

Gerth, H.
1921 Die bedeutung der geologischen enforschung des südrandes der Puna de Atacama. Geologische Rundschau 12:320-340.
(Significance of geological research in the southern margin of the Puna de Atacama.)

Gonzáles, O. B.
1955 Los terrenos áridos de la costa peruana. Compañía Administradora del Guano, Lima, Boletín 31(5).
(The arid lands of the Peruvian coast.)

Harbour, J.
1963 Investigations of the relationships between topographically closed basins and their playa characteristics. U. S. Geological Survey, Branch Military Geology, for Air Force Cambridge Research Laboratories, 28 p. (unpublished ms.)

Harding, J. E.
1926a The Andean salares. Engineering and Mining Journal 121:797-800.

——— 1926b Genesis of Chilean nitrate. Engineering and Mining Journal 121:885-888.

Harrington, H. J.
1961 Geology of parts of Antofagasta and Atacama Provinces, northern Chile. American Association of Petroleum Geologists, Bulletin 45:169-197.

Hollingsworth, S. E.
1964 Dating the uplift of the Andes of northern Chile. Nature 201:17-20.

Iddings, A. and A. A. Olsson
1928 Geology of northwest Peru. Geological Society of America, Bulletin 12:1-40.

Instituto de investigaciones Geológicas
1960 Mapa Geológica de Chile, scale 1:1,000,000.

Instituto Geográfico Militar
1954 Carta Preliminar, scale 1:250,000, 104 sheets.

——— 1958-1963 Topographic maps, scale 1:100,000, ca. 50 sheets.

——— 1965a Catálogo de mapas y cartas. Santiago. 23 p.
(Catalog of maps and charts.)
A good catalog of available maps of Chile. See also Organization of American States (1964a).

Instituto Geográfico Militar
1965*b* Catálago de fotografías aéreas. Santiago. 15 p.
(Catalog of aerial photographs.)
A catalog of available aerial photographs for Chile. See also Organization of American States (1964*a*).

Jaén, H. and G. Ortiz
1963   Geología de los cuadrángulos de La Larada y Tacna. Comisión de la Carta Geológica Nacional, Lima, Boletín 6:1-54.
(Geology of the Yarada and Tacna quadrangles.)

Jenks, W. F.
1948   Geology of the Arequipa quadrangle of the Carta Nacional del Perú. Instituto Geológico del Peru, Boletín 9.

Johnson, G. R.
1930   Peru from the air. American Geographical Society, Special Publication 12.

Johnston, I. M.
1929   Papers on the flora of northern Chile. Harvard University, Gary Herbarium, Contributions 85. 172 p.

Kanter, H.
1937   Probleme aus der Puna de Atacama. Petermanns Geographische Mitteilungen 83:10-15, 42-46.
(Problems from the Puna de Atacama.)

Kinzl, H.
1958   Die dünen in der küsten landschaft von Peru. Geographische Gesellschaft, Wien, Mitteilungen 100(1/2):5-17.
(Dunes of the Peruvian coastal landscape.)

Klohn, C.
1957   Estado actual del estudio geológico de la "Formación Porfirítica." Instituto de Ingenieros de Minas de Chile, Santiago, Minerales 11:49-60.

Korotkevich, G. V.
1964   Dynamics of karsting in the halite deposits of dry salinas (translated title). Akademiia nauk S.S.S.R., Doklady 157:866-869.

Lachenbruch, A. H.
1962   Mechanics of thermal contraction cracks and ice-wedge polygons in permafrost. Geological Society of America, Special Paper 70, 69 p.

Lamb, M. R.
1910   History and review of the niter industry of Chile. Engineering and Mining Journal 90:18-22.

Langbein, W. B.
1961   Salinity and hydrology of closed lakes. U. S. Geological Survey, Professional Paper 412. 20 p.

Mabire, B.
1961   Fondo emergido entre Chala y Atico. Sociedad Geológica del Peru, Boletín 36:147-149.
(Emergent beaches between Chala and Atico.)

MacCoy, F.
1917   "Caliche" deposits of Atacama Desert, Chile. Engineering and Mining Journal 103:1059-1060.

Manriquez, F.
1958   Las Salinas de Cahuil. Universidad de Chile. Instituto de Geográfia, Informaciones Geográficas 5:23-42.

Matthews, H. A.
1931   Köppen's climatic formulae and Chilean evaporation data. Scottish Geographical Magazine 47:159-163.

McDonald, G. H.
1956   Miocene of the Sechura desert, Peru. Sociedad Geológica del Peru, Boletín 30:225-242.

Mendivel, S. and W. Castillo
1960   Geología del cuadrángulo de Ocoña. Comisión de la Carta Geológica Nacional, Lima, Boletín 1(3).
(Geology of the Ocoña quadrangle.)

Miller, B. L. and J. T. Singewald, Jr.
1919   The mineral deposits of South America. McGraw-Hill, New York. 598 p.

Morris, R. C. and P. A. Dickey
1957*a*   Modern evaporite deposition in Peru. American Association of Petroleum Geologists, Bulletin 41:2467-2474.

——— 1957*b*   Deposición de evaporitas en un estuario de Peru. Sociedad Geológica del Peru, Boletín 32:249.
(Deposition of evaporites in a Peruvian estuary.)

Mortensen, H.
1927   Der formen schatz der nord-Chilenischen wüste. Gesellschaft der Wissenschaften, Göttingen, Abhandlungen 12 (1).
(Varied desert forms of northern Chile.)

——— 1928   Die landschaft mittelchiles. Deutscher Geographentag 22:113-129.
(The landscape of central Chile.)

——— 1929*a*   Inselberglandschaften in nordchile. Zeitschrift für Geomorphologie 4.
(Inselberg-landscape in northern Chile.)

——— 1929*b*   Über Vorzeilbildungen in der nordchilenischen wüste. Geographische Gesellschaft, Hamburg, Mitteilungen 40.
(Ancient development of the desert of northern Chile.)

Mueller, G.
1960   The theory of formation of north Chilean nitrate deposits through "capillary concentration." International Geological Congress, 21st, Copenhagen, Report 1:76-86.

Muñoz Christi, J.
1942   Rasgos generales de la constitución geológica de la cordillera de la costa, especialmente en la Provincia de Coquimbo. Congreso Panamericano de Ingeniería de Minas y Geología, 1st, Santiago de Chile, Anales 2:285-318.
(General characteristics of the geologic framework of the coastal cordillera, particularly in Coquimbo Province.)

——— 1950   Geología. *In* Geografía económica de Chile, vol. 1. Corporación de Fomento de la Producción, Santiago de Chile.

——— 1956   Chile. *In* W. F. Jenks, ed., Handbook of South American geology. Geological Society of America, Memoir 65:187-214.

Narváez, S.
1964)   Geología de los cuadrángulos de Ilo y Lacumba. Comisión de la Carta Geológica Nacional, Lima, Boletín 7.
(Geology of the Ilo and Lacumba quadrangles.)

Neal, J. T.
  1965 Giant desiccation polygons of Great Basin playas. Air Force Cambridge Research Laboratories, Environmental Research Papers 123. 30 p.

Newell, N. D.
  1956 Reconocimiento geológico de la región Pisco-Nazca. Sociedad Geológica del Peru, Boletín 30: 261-295.
        (Geologic reconnaissance of the Pisco-Nazca region.)

Newell, N. D. and D. W. Boyd
  1955 Extraordinarily coarse eolian sand of the Ica desert, Peru. Journal of Sedimentary Petrology 25: 226-228.

Nicholson, C.
  1942 Nota acerca de la influencia del clima en la morfología de los alrededores de Arequipa. Congreso Panamericano de Ingeniería de Minas y Geología, 1st, Santiago de Chile, Anales 2:760-765.
        (Note on the influence of climate on morphology in the vicinity of Arequipa.)

Ogilvie, A. G.
  1922 Geography of the central Andes; a handbook to accompany the La Paz sheet of the Map of Hispanic America on the millionth scale. American Geographical Society of New York, Special Publication 1. 240 p.

Olivieri, A.
  1951 Neblinas y desiertos. Sociedad de Ingenieros del Perú, Lima, Memorias 52.
        (Clouds and deserts.)

Organization of American States
  1964a Annotated index of aerial photographic coverage and mapping of topography and natural resources: Chile. Pan American Union, Washington. 20 p.
        The best single source of information on the status of mapping and the availability of aerial photographs in Chile.

  ———
  1964b Annotated index of aerial photographic coverage and mapping of topography and natural resources: Peru. Pan American Union, Washington. 26 p.
        The best single source of information on the status of mapping and the availability of aerial photographs in Peru.

Penck, W.
  1920 Der südrand der Puna de Atacama. Akademie der Wissenschaften, Leipzig, Mathematische-Physische Klasse, Abhandlungen 37(1). 420 p.
        (The southern border of the Puna de Atacama.)

Penrose, R. A. F., Jr.
  1910 The nitrate deposits of Chile. Journal of Geology 18:1-32.

Petersen, G.
  1954 Informe preliminar sobre la geología de la faja costanera del Departamento de Ica. Empresa Petrolera Fiscal, Boletín Técnico 1:33-77.
        (Preliminary report on the geology of the coastal belt of the Province of Ica.)

Rassmus, J. E.
  1931 Geología de Pisco. Sociedad Geológica del Peru, Boletín 4.
        (Geology of Pisco.)

Rich, J. L.
  1941 The nitrate district of Tarapaca, Chile. Geographical Review 31:1-22.

  ———
  1942 Physiographic setting of the nitrate deposits of Tarapaca, Chile; its bearing on the problem of origin and concentration. Economic Geology 37: 188-214.

Rogers, A. H. and H. R. Van Wagenen
  1918 The Chilean nitrate industry. American Institute of Mining Engineers, Bulletin 134:505-522.

Rosenzweig, A.
  1953 Geología de la Isla de San Lorenzo. Instituto Nacional de Investigación y Fomento Mineros, Lima, Boletín 7.
        (Geology of San Lorenzo Island.)

Rudolph, W. E.
  1927 The Rio Loa of northern Chile. Geographical Review 17:553-585.

Ruegg, W.
  1953 Geología de la Bahía de Pisco, hundimiento y acenso del litoral y la posición tectónico de la cordillera de la costa. Sociedad Geológica del Peru, Boletín 26:191-228.
        (Geology of the Bay of Pisco, subsidence and upwarp of the shore and tectonic movements of the mountains relative to the coast.)

  ———
  1962 Rasgos morfológicos-geológicos intramarinos y sus contrapartes en el suelo continental peruano. Sociedad Geológica del Peru, Boletín 38:97-142.
        (Morphologic and geologic outline of offshore structure and its continental counterpart in Peru.)
        This report treats structural features along the Peruvian coast between latitudes 14° 50′ S and 17° 00′ S, and their offshore counterparts. Also includes a fairly good description of coastal terraces in this area. See Mabire (1961) and Broggi (1946b, c, 1957) for additional data on Peruvian terraces and coastal features.

St. Amand, P. and C. R. Allen
  1960 Strike-slip faulting in northern Chile. Geological Society of America, Bulletin 71:1965.

Salcedo, S.
  1915 Potash deposits in Chile. Engineering and Mining Journal 100:218.

Schoff, S. L. and J. L. Sayán.
  n.d. Hydrologic data for the Lambayeque Valley, northern Peru. U. S. Geological Survey, Openfile Report, 52 p.

Schweigger, E.
  1943 La Bahía de Pisco. Sociedad Geológica del Peru, Boletín 13.
        (The Bay of Pisco.)

Segerstrom, K.
  1959 Geología del cuadrángulo Los Loros. Instituto de Investigaciones Geológicas, Carta Geológica de Chile 1(1).
        (Geology of Los Loros quadrangle.)

  ———
  1960a Cuadrángulo Llampos, Provincia de Atacama. Instituto de Investigaciones Geológicas, Carta Geológica de Chile 2 (2).
        (Llampos quadrangle, Atacama Province.)

Segerstrom, K.
1960b Cuadrángulo Quebrada Paipote, Provincia de Atacama. Instituto de Investigaciones Geológicas, Carta Geológica de Chile 2(1).
(Paipote Wash quadrangle, Atacama Province.)

——— 1960c Structural geology of an area east of Copiapó, Atacama Province, Chile. International Geological Congress, 21st, Copenhagen, Report 18:14-20.

✓ ——— 1962 Deflated marine terrace as a source of dune chains, Atacama Province, Chile. U. S. Geological Survey, Professional Paper 450-C:91-93.

——— 1963 Matureland of northern Chile and its relationship to ore deposits. Geological Society of America, Bulletin 74:513-518.

✓ ——— 1964 Quaternary geology of Chile; brief outline. Geological Society of America, Bulletin 75: 157-170.

✓ ——— 1965 Dissected gravels of the Río Copiapó Valley and adjacent coastal area, Chile. U. S. Geological Survey, Professional Paper 525-B:117-121.

Segerstrom, K. and B. Moraga A.
1964 Cuadrángulo Chanarcillo, Provincia de Atacama. Instituto de Investigaciones Geológicas, Carta Geológica de Chile 13.
(Chanarcillo quadrangle, Atacama Province.)

Segerstrom, K. and R. L. Parker
1959 Cuadrángulo Cerrillos, Provincia de Atacama. Instituto de Investigaciones Geológicas, Carta Geológica de Chile 1(2).
(Cerrillos quadrangle, Atacama Province.)

Segerstrom, K., L. Valenzuela B., and S. Mahech
1960 Cuadrángulo Chamonate, Provincia de Atacama. Instituto de Investigaciones Geológicas, Cartas Geológica de Chile 2(3).
(Chamonate quadrangle, Atacama Province.)

Simons, F. S.
1956 A note on Pur-Pur Dune, Virú Valley, Peru. Journal of Geology 64:517-521.

Simons, F. S. and G. E. Ericksen
1953 Some desert features of northwest central Peru. Sociedad Geológica del Peru, Boletín 26:229-246.
A study of sand transport along the Peruvian coast between Huarmey (Huarmay) and Chimbote, where a northward migration rate of 0.45 meters per year was observed. See Broggi (1954) for sand migration north of Lima; Newell and Boyd (1955), Amstutz and Chico (1958), and Tricart and Mainguet (1965) for data on the size distribution and characteristics of Peruvian sands; and Finkel (1959), Simons (1956), Smith (1955a, 1956, 1963), Broggi (1961), Kinzl (1958), and Gay (1962) for treatments of the stability and characteristics of specific dunes and associated aeolian features.

Singewald, J. T., Jr.
1942 Origin of Chilean nitrate deposits. Economic Geology 37:627-639.

Singewald, J. T., Jr. and B. L. Miller
1916 A unique salt industry in Chile. Pan American Union, Bulletin 42:52-60.

Smith, H. T. U.
1955a Deflation basin in the Sechura desert of northern Peru. Geological Society of America, Bulletin 66: 1618. (Abstr.)

——— 1955b Geomorphic evidences of recent climatic fluctuations in the Peruvian coastal desert. Science 122: 418-419.

——— 1956 Giant composite barchans of the northern Peruvian deserts. Geological Society of America, Bulletin 67. (Abstr.)

——— 1963 Deflation basin in the coastal area of the Sechura desert, northern Peru. U. S. Office of Naval Research, Geography Branch, Technical Report 3-A. 16 p.

Steinman, G.
1929 Geologie von Peru. Carl Winters, Heidelberg.
A basic guide to the geology of Peru. See Bellido, Narváez, and Simons (1956) for a recent geological map, at a scale of 1:2,000,000, and Harrington (1961) for a useful discussion of paleogeography. The various "Boletines" cited in the text of this report should be consulted for more detailed geological information on specific areas and for descriptions of surficial features within these areas.

Storie, R. E. and C. Mathews
1946 Preliminary study of Chilean soils. Soil Science Society of America, Proceedings 10:351-355.

Taltasse, P.
1963 Groundwater resources of the Peruvian coastal desert. Arid Zone [Newsletter] 20:8-13.

Taylor, G. C., Jr.
1947a Ground water studies in the Province of Antofagasta, Chile. U. S. Geological Survey, Water Research Division. 29 p. (unpublished ms.)

——— 1947b Ground water studies in Tarapaca Province, Chile. U. S. Geological Survey, Water Research Division. 87 p. (unpublished ms.)

——— 1948 Ground water in northern Chile—a summary. U. S. Geological Survey, Water Research Division. 15 p. (unpublished ms.)

——— 1949 Geology and groundwater of Azapa Valley, Province of Tarapacá, Chile. Economic Geology 44: 40-62.

Travis, R. B.
1953 LaBrea-Pariñas oil field, northwestern Peru. American Association of Petroleum Geologists, Bulletin 37:2093-2118.

Tricart, J.
1963 Oscillations et modifications de caractère de la zone aride en Afrique et en Amerique latine lors des périodes glaciaires des hautes latitudes. *In* Changes of climate, proceedings of the Rome Symposium. Unesco, Paris. Arid Zone Research 20: 415-419.
(Fluctuations and modifications of the arid zone of Africa and Latin America during the glacial periods of the northern latitudes.)

Tricart, J.
1966 Un chott lans le désert chilien; la pampa del Tamarugal. Revue de Géomorphologie Dynamique 16:12-22.
(A saline pan in the Chilean desert: the Tamarugal Pampa.)
A good description of the surficial features of the Tamarugal area in northern Chile, including a prominent saline pan.

Tricart, J. and M. Mainguet
1965 Caractéristiques granulometríques de quelques sables éoliens du désert péruvien; aspects de la dynamique des barkanes. Revue de Géomorphologie Dynamique 15:110-121.
(Grain-size characteristics of some Peruvian desert sands; aspects of barchan dynamics).

United Nations
1960 Los recursos hidráulicos de Chile. Mexico City. 190 p.
(The hydraulic resources of Chile.)

Vita-Finzi, C.
1959 A pluvial age in the Puna de Atacama. Geographical Journal 125:401-403.

1960 Sols polygonaux dans la Puna bolivienne. Revue de Géomorphologie Dynamique 11:61.
(Polygonal soils of the Bolivian Puna de Atacama.)

Vita-Finzi, C. and J. Aarons
1960 The useless land. Robert Hale, London.

Wells, R. C.
1918 Extraction of potassium salts from the Pintados Salar. Engineering and Mining Journal 105:678-679.

Wetzel, W.
1928 Geologische und geographische probleme des nördlichen Chile. Gesellschaft für Erdkunde zu Berlin, Zeitschrift 63.
(Geologic and geographic problems of northern Chile.)

Whitehead, W. L.
1920 The Chilean nitrate deposits. Economic Geology 15:187-224.

Wilson, J. J.
1963a Cretaceous stratigraphy of Central Andes of Peru. American Association of Petroleum Geologists, Bulletin 47:1-34.

1963b Geología del cudráangulo de Huaylillas. Comisión de la Carta Geológica Nacional, Lima, Boletín 6:55-59.
(Geology of the Huaylillas quadrangle.)

Wilson, J. J. and W. García
1962 Geología de los cuadrángulos de Pachía y Palca. Comisión de la Carta Geológica Nacional, Lima, Boletín 2(4).
(Geology of the Pachia and Palco quadrangles.)

Wilson, J. J. and L. R. Reyes
1964 Geología del cuadrángulo de Pataz. Comisión de la Carta Geológica Nacional, Lima, Boletín 9.
(Geology of the Pataz quadrangle.)

Wurm, A.
1939 Salzpfannen in der nordchilenischen kordillere. Natur und Volk 69:573-578.
(Salt pans in the cordillera of northern Chile.)

1940 Beobachtungen in den salzpfannen (salaren) der nordchilenischen kordillere. Deutsche Geologische Gesellschaft, Zeitschrift 92:159-164.
(Observations on salt pans in the cordillera of northern Chile.)

1951 Beobachtungen in der wüste nordchiles. Natur und Volk 81:239-245.
(Observations in the desert of northern Chile.)

1952 Geologische beobachtungen in der wüste von nord-Chile. Neues Jahrbuch für Geologie und Paläontologie, Abhandlungen 95(2):293-301.
(Geological observations in the desert of northern Chile.)

Zeil, W.
1964 Geologie von Chile. Gebrüder Borntraeger, Berlin. 233 p.
(Geology of Chile.)

SECTION XIV
NORTH AMERICAN DESERTS: UNITED STATES

Includes works cited in the text discussion of the desert areas of the United States.

Ackermann, W. C.
1957 Needed research in sedimentation. American Geophysical Union, Transactions 38:925-927.

Albertson, M. L. and D. B. Simons
1964 Fluid mechanics. Section 7:1-49. *In* V. T. Chow, ed., Handbook of applied hydrology. McGraw-Hill, New York.

Allen, C. R.
1957 San Andreas fault zone in the San Gorgonio Pass, southern California. Geological Society of America, Bulletin 68:315-350.

Allison, I. S. and R. S. Mason
1947 Sodium salts of Lake County, Oregon. Oregon Department of Geology and Mineral Industry, Short Paper 17.

Ambrose, J. W.
1933 A discussion of the movement of fault blocks. American Journal of Science 26:552-563.

Anderson, H. W.
1954 Suspended sediment discharge as related to streamflow, topography, soil, and land use. American Geophysical Union, Transactions 35:268-281.

1955 Detecting hydrologic effects of changes in watershed conditions by double-mass analysis. American Geophysical Union, Transactions 36:119-125.

1957 Relating sediment yield to watershed variables. American Geophysical Union, Transactions, 38:921-924.

Anderson, H. W., G. B. Coleman, and P. J. Zinke
1959 Summer slides and winter scour — dry-wet erosion in southern California mountains. U. S. Forest Service, Pacific Southwest Forest and Range Experiment Station, Berkeley, California, Technical Paper 36. 12 p.

Antevs, E.
1948   The Great Basin, with emphasis on glacial and post glacial times, part 3. University of Utah, Bulletin 38:168-191.

———
1952   Arroyo cutting and filling. Journal of Geology 60:375-385.

Aristarain, L.
1962   Origin of caliche. Harvard University (unpublished dissertation).

Arnold, B.
1962   Proposed relics of coastal alluvial fans in southern California. California Geographer 3:123-130.

Bagnold, R. A.
1960a   Sediment discharge and stream power; a preliminary announcement. U. S. Geological Survey, Circular 421.

———
1960b   Some aspects of the shape of river meanders. U. S. Geological Survey, Professional Paper 282-E.

Bailey, E. S.
1917   The sand dunes of Indiana. Chicago. 165 p.

Bailey, G. E.
1902   The saline deposits of California. California State Bureau of Mines, Bulletin 24. 216 p.

———
1904   The desert dry lakes of California. California State Bureau of Mines, Bulletin 25. 200 p.

Bailey, R. W.
1941   Land erosion, normal and accelerated, in the semiarid West. American Geophysical Union, Transactions 22:240-250.

Baker, A. A.
1936   Geology of the Monument Valley - Navajo Mountain region, San Juan County, Utah. U. S. Geological Survey, Bulletin 865.

———
1946   Geology of the Green River Desert - Cataract Canyon region, Emery, Wayne, and Garfield counties, Utah. U. S. Geological Survey, Bulletin 951.

Baker, C. L.
1911   Notes on the Cenozoic history of the Mohave Desert region in southern California. University of California, Department of Geological Science, Publication, Bulletin 6:333-383.

Beaty, C. B.
1963   Origin of alluvial fans, White Mountains, California and Nevada. Association of American Geographers, Annals 53:516-535.

Benedict, P. C.
1957   Fluvial sediment transportation. American Geophysical Union, Transactions 38:897-902.

Bennet, P. J.
1957   The geology and mineralization of the Sedimentary Hills area, Pima County, Arizona. University of Arizona (unpublished M.S. thesis).

Benson, M. A.
1959   Channel slope factor in flood frequency analysis. American Society of Civil Engineers, Hydraulics Division, Journal 85:1-9.

Bissell, H. J.
1963   Lake Bonneville; geology of southern Utah Valley, Utah. U. S. Geological Survey, Professional Paper 257-B:101-130.

Blackwelder, E.
1928a   Mudflow as a geological agent in semiarid mountains. Geological Society of America, Bulletin 39: 465-484.

———
1928b   Origin of desert basins of the southwest United States. Geological Society of America, Bulletin 39:262-263.

———
1928c   The recognition of fault scarps. Journal of Geology 36:289-311.

———
1929a   Cavernous rock surfaces of the desert. American Journal of Science 217:393-399.

———
1929b   Origin of piedmont plains of the Great Basin. Geological Society of America, Bulletin 40: 168-169.

———
1931a   The lowering of playas by deflation. American Journal of Science 221:140-144.

———
1931b   Rock-cut surfaces in desert ranges. Journal of Geology 20:442-450.

———
1933   Lake Manly, an extinct lake of Death Valley. Geographical Review 23:464-471.

———
1934   Yardlangs. Geological Society of America, Bulletin 45:159-166.

———
1948   Historical significance of desert lacquer. Geological Society of America, Bulletin 59:1367. (Abstr.)

———
1954a   Geomorphic processes in the desert. California Division of Mines, Bulletin 170, Chapter 5, p. 11-20.

———
1954b   Pleistocene lakes and drainage in the Mohave region, southern California. California Division of Mines, Bulletin 170, Chapter 5, p. 35-40.

Blackwelder, E. and E. W. Ellsworth
1936   Pleistocene lakes of the Afton Basin, California. American Journal of Science 31:453-463.

Blackwelder, E. *et al.*
1948   The Great Basin with emphasis on the glacial and postglacial time. University of Utah, Bulletin 38.

Blake, W. P.
1885   On the grooving and polishing of hard rocks and minerals by dry sand. American Journal of Science 20:178-181.

———
1914   The Cahuilla basin and desert of Colorado in the Salton Sea, a study of the geography, geology, floristics, and ecology of a desert basin. Carnegie Institution of Washington, Publication 193.

Blanc. R. P. and G. B. Cleveland
1961   Pleistocene lakes of southeastern California. California Division of Mines and Geology, Mineral Information Service 14 (4):1-8, (5):1-6.

Blissenbach, E.
1952   Relation of surface angle distribution on alluvial fans. Journal of Sedimentary Petrology 22:25-28.

Blissenbach, E.
1954 Geology of alluvial fans in semiarid regions. Geological Society of America, Bulletin 65:175-190.

Bowen, O. E.
1954 Geology and mineral deposits of Barstow quadrangle, San Bernardino County, California. California Division of Mines, Bulletin 165.

Bradley, E.
1964 Geohydrologic analogies between the Jordan Valleys of Utah and the Holy Land. International Association of Scientific Hydrology, Bulletin 9(3): 12-23.

Bradley, W. H.
1936 Geomorphology of the north flank of the Uinta Mountains. U. S. Geological Survey, Professional Paper 185-I.

1940 Pediments and pedestals in miniature. Journal of Geomorphology 3:244-255.

1965 Vertical density currents. Science 150:1423-1428.

Bredehoeft, J. D.
1963 Hydrogeology of the lower Humboldt river basin, Nevada. Nevada Department of Conservation and Natural Resources, Water Resources Bulletin 21.

Brennan, D. J.
1957 Geologic reconnaissance of Cienega Gap,, Pima County, Arizona. University of Arizona (unpublished dissertation).

Bretz, J. H. and L. Horberg
1949 Caliche in southwestern New Mexico. Journal of Geology 57:491-511.

Brown, J. S.
1922 Fault features of Salton Basin, California. Journal of Geology 30:217-226.

1923 The Salton Sea region, California. U. S. Geological Survey, Water-Supply Paper 497.

Brown, W. H.
1939 Tucson Mountains, an Arizona basin range type. Geological Society of America, Bulletin 50: 697-760.

Bryan, K.
1909 Geology of the vicinity of Albuquerque, New Mexico. University of New Mexico Bulletin, Geology Series 3:1-24.

1922 Erosion and sedimentation in the Papago country, Arizona. U. S. Geological Survey, Bulletin 730: 19-90.

1923a Pedestal rocks in the arid Southwest. U. S. Geological Survey, Bulletin 760-A:1-11.

1923b Wind erosion near Lee's Ferry, Arizona. American Journal of Science 206:291-307.

1925a Date of channel entrenching (arroyo-cutting) in the arid Southwest. Science 62:338-344.

1925b The Papago country. U. S. Geological Survey, Water-Supply Paper 499. 436 p.

1926 The San Pedro Valley, Arizona, and the geographical cycle. Geological Society of America, Bulletin 37:169-170 (Abstr.).

1927 Channel erosion of the Rio Salado, Socorro County, New Mexico. *In* Contributions to the geography of the U. S., 1926. U. S. Geological Survey, Bulletin 790:17-19.

1928 Historic evidence on changes in the channel of the Rio Puerco, a tributary of the Rio Grande in New Mexico. Journal of Geology 36:265-282.

1931 Wind-worn stones or ventifacts. National Research Council, Reprint and Circular Series 98:29-50.

1932 Pediments developed in basins with through drainage. Geological Society of America, Bulletin 43: 128-129.

1935 The formation of pediments. International Geological Congress, 16th, Washington, Report 2: 765-775.

1936 Processes of formation of pediments at Granite Gap, New Mexico. Zeitschrift für Geomorphologie 9:125-135.

1938 Geology and groundwater conditions of the Rio Grande depression in Colorado and New Mexico. p. 197-225. *In* Regional Planning, Part 6: Rio Grande Joint Investigation in upper Rio Grande basin in Colorado, New Mexico, and Texas, 1936-1937, Vol. 1. U. S. National Resources Committee, Washington, D. C.

1940a Erosion in the valleys of the Southwest. New Mexico Quarterly 10:227-232.

1940b The retreat of slopes. Association of American Geographers, Annals 30:254-268.

1954 The geology of Chaco Canyon, New Mexico. Smithsonian Institution, Miscellaneous Collection 122. 65 p.

Bryan, K. and F. T. McCann
1936 Successive pediments of the Upper Rio Puerco in New Mexico. Journal of Geology 44:145-172.

1937 The Ceja del Rio Puerco; a border feature of the basin and range province in New Mexico. Part 1: Stratigraphy and structure. Journal of Geology 45:801-828.

1938 The Ceja del Rio Puerco; a border feature of the basin and range province in New Mexico. Part 2: Geomorphology. Journal of Geology 46:1-16.

1943 Sand dunes and alluvium near Grants, New Mexico. American Antiquity 8:281-295.

Bryan, K. and R. L. Nichols
1939 Wind-deposition shorelines. Discussion. Journal of Geology 47:431-435.

Budding, A. J.
1963   Origin and age of superficial structures, Jicarilla Mountains, central New Mexico. Geological Society of America, Bulletin 74:203-208.

Bull, W. B.
1964a   Alluvial fans and near-surface subsidence in western Fresno County, California. U. S. Geological Survey, Professional Paper 437-A:1-71.

———   1964b   History and causes of channel trenching in western Fresno County, California. American Journal of Science 262:249-258.

———   1965   The alluvial fans of western Fresno County, California. Geological Society of America, Cordilleran Section, Annual Meeting, Field Trip Guidebook.

Butler, B. S., E. D. Wilson, and C. A. Rason
1938   Geology and ore deposits of the Tombstone district, Arizona. Arizona Bureau of Mines, Bulletin 143.

Buwalda, J. P.
1951   Transportation of coarse material on alluvial fans. Geological Society of America, Bulletin 62:1497 (Abstr.)

Buwalda, J. P. and W. L. Santon
1930   Geological events in the history of the Indio Hills and the Salton Basin. Science 71:104-106.

Cabot, E. C.
1938   Fault border of the Sangre de Cristo Mountains. Journal of Geology 46:88-105.

Call, R. E.
1882   The loess of North America. American Naturalist 16:369-381, 542-549.

Campbell, E. W. C. et al
1937   The archeology of Pleistocene Lake Mohave. Southwest Museum, Los Angeles, Papers 11.

Campbell, J. T.
1889   Origin of the loess. American Naturalist 23:785-792.

Chamberlain, T. C.
1897   Supplementary hypothesis respecting the origin of the loess of the Mississippi valley. Journal of Geology 5:795-802.

Chawner, W. D.
1935   Alluvial fan flooding, the Montrose, California flood of 1934. Geographical Review 25:255-263.

Chew, R. T., III
1952   The geology of the Mineta Ridge area, Pima and Cochise counties, Arizona. University of Arizona (unpublished M.S. thesis).

Childs, O. E.
1948   Geomorphology of the valley of the Little Colorado River, Arizona. Geological Society of America, Bulletin 59:353-388.

Chow, V. T. and T. E. Harbaugh
1964   Artificial raindrops for laboratory watershed experimentation. American Geophysical Union, Transactions 45:611 (Abstr.)

Church, F. S. and J. T. Hack
1939   An exhumed erosion surface in the Jemez Mountains, New Mexico. Journal of Geology 47:613-629.

Cleland, H. F.
1906   The formation of natural bridges. American Journal of Science 20:119-124.

———   1911   The formation of North American natural bridges. Geological Society of America, Bulletin 21:313-338.

Clements, T.
1952   Wind-blown rocks and tails on Little Bonnie Claire Playa, Nye County, Nevada. Journal of Sedimentary Petrology 22:182-186.

Clements, T. et al.
1957   A study of desert surface conditions. U. S. Army, Quartermaster Research and Development Center, Natick, Massachusetts, Environmental Protection Research Division, Technical Report EP-53. 110 p.

———   1963   A study of wind-borne sand and dust in desert areas. U. S. Army Natick Laboratories, Earth Sciences Division, Technical Report ES-8. 61 p.

Coffey, G. N.
1909   Clay dunes. Journal of Geology 17:754-755.

Colby, B. R.
1963   Fluvial sediments, a summary of source, transportation, deposition and measurement of sediment discharge. U. S. Geological Survey, Bulletin 1181-A.

———   1964a   Discharge of sands and mean-velocity relationships in sand-bed streams. U. S. Geological Survey, Professional Paper 462-A.

———   1964b   Scour and fill in sand-bed streams. U. S. Geological Survey, Professional Paper 462-D.

Colby, B. R. and C. H. Hembree
1955   Computations of total sediment discharge, Niobrara River near Cody, Nebraska. U. S. Geological Survey, Water-Supply Paper 1357.

Colby, B. R. and D. W. Hubbell
1961   Simplified methods for computing total sediment discharge with the modified Einstein procedure. U. S. Geological Survey, Water-Supply Paper 1593.

Coldwell, A. E.
1957   Importance of channel erosion as a source of sediment. American Geophysical Union, Transactions 38:908-912.

Cook, K. L. and J. W. Berg, Jr.
1961   Regional gravity survey along the central and southern Wasatch front, Utah. U. S. Geological Survey, Professional Paper 316-E.

Cook, K. L. et al.
1964   Regional gravity survey of the northern Great Salt Lake Desert and adjacent areas in Utah, Nevada, and Idaho. Geological Society of America, Bulletin 75:715-740.

Cooley, M. E.
1958   Physiography of the Black Mesa Basin area, Arizona. New Mexico Geological Society, Guidebook of Black Mesa Basin 146-149.

———   1960   Physiographic map of the San Francisco plateau, Little Colorado River area. University of Arizona, Geochronology Laboratory, Report.

Cooley, M. E.
1962*a* Geomorphology and the age of volcanic rocks in northeastern Arizona. Arizona Geological Society, Digest 5:97-115.

——— 1962*b* Late Pleistocene and Recent erosion and alluviation in parts of the Colorado River System, Arizona and Utah. U. S. Geological Survey, Professional Paper 450-B:48-50.

Cooley, M. E. *et al.*
n.d. Introduction and regional hydrogeology of the Navajo and Hopi country, Arizona, New Mexico, and Utah. U. S. Geological Survey, Professional Paper 521-A *(in press)*.

Cooper, W. S.
1958 Coastal sand dunes of Oregon and Washington. Geological Society of America, Memoir 72.

Corbel, J.
1963 Pédiments d'Arizona. Centre National de Recherche Scientifique, Paris, Centre Documents Cartographique, Mémoires et Documents 9:31-95. (Pediments of Arizona.)

Corbett, D. M. *et al.*
1962 Stream-gaging procedure. U. S. Geological Survey, Water-Supply Paper 888.

Cornish, V.
1897 On the formation of sand dunes. Geographical Journal 9:278-309.

Cornwall, H. R. and F. J. Kleinhampl
1959 Stratigraphy and structure of Bare Mountain, Nevada. Geological Society of America, Bulletin 70:1714. (Abstr.)

Crickmore, M. J. and G. H. Lean
1962 The measurement of sand transport by the time-integration method with radioactive traces. Royal Society of London, Proceedings, ser. A, 270:27-47.

Croft, A. R.
1962 Some sedimentation phenomena along the Wasatch mountain front. Journal of Geophysical Research 67:1511-1524.

Cross, C. W.
1908 Wind erosion in the plateau country. Geological Society of America, Bulletin 19:53-62.

Crowell, J. C.
1962 Displacement along the San Andreas fault, California. Geological Society of America, Special Paper 71.

Cummings, B.
1910 The great natural bridges of Utah. National Geographic Magazine 21:157-167.

Curry, H. D.
1938 Turtleback fault surfaces in Death Valley, California. Geological Society of America, Bulletin 59:1875. (Abstr.)

——— 1949 Turtlebacks of central Black Mountains, Death Valley, California. Geological Society of America, Bulletin 60:1882. (Abstr.)

——— 1954 Turtlebacks in the central Black Mountains, Death Valley, California. California Division of Mines, Bulletin 170, Chapter 4, p. 53-59.

Dake, C. L.
1918 Valley City graben, Utah. Journal of Geology 26: 569-573.

Dake, C. L. and L. A. Nelson
1933 Postbolson faulting in New Mexico. Science 78: 168-169.

Dalrymple, T.
1960 Flood-frequency analyses. U. S. Geological Survey, Water-Supply Paper 1543-A.

Darton, N. H.
1910 A reconnaissance of parts of northwestern New Mexico and northern Arizona. U. S. Geological Survey, Bulletin 425.

Davidson, E. S.
1960 Geology of the eastern part of the Safford Basin, Graham County, Arizona; a preliminary report. Arizona Geological Society, Digest 3:123-126.

Davis, W. M.
1903*a* An excursion to the Grand Canyon of the Colorado. Harvard Museum of Comparative Zoology, Bulletin 42:1-40.

——— 1903*b* Mountain ranges of the Great Basin. Harvard Museum of Comparative Zoology, Bulletin 42: 129-177.

——— 1905*a* The geographical cycle in an arid climate. Journal of Geology 13:381-407.

——— 1905*b* The Wasatch, Canyon, and House Ranges, Utah. Harvard Museum of Comparative Zoology, Bulletin 49:17-56.

——— 1913 Nomenclature of surface forms on faulted structures. Geological Society of America, Bulletin 24: 187-216.

——— 1925 The Basin Range problem. National Academy of Sciences, Proceedings 11:387-392.

——— 1930*a* The Peacock Range, Arizona. Geological Society of America, Bulletin 41:293-313.

——— 1930*b* Rock floors in arid and humid climates. Journal of Geology 38:1-27, 136-158.

——— 1931 The Santa Catalina Mountains, Arizona. American Journal of Science 130:289-317.

——— 1932 Basin range types. Science 76:241-245.

——— 1933 Granite domes of the Mohave Desert, California. San Diego Society of Natural History, Transactions 7:211-258.

——— 1936 Geomorphology of mountainous deserts. *In* Geomorphogenic processes in arid regions and their resulting forms and products. International Geological Congress, 16th, Washington, D. C., 1933, Report 2:703-714.

——— 1938 Sheetfloods and streamfloods. Geological Society of America, Bulletin 49:1337-1416.

Dawdy, D. R.
1963   Channel geometry and hydraulics. U. S. Geological Survey, Water Resources Division, Bulletin, November:32-33.

Dibblee, T. W., Jr.
1954   Geology of the Imperial Valley region, California. California Division of Mines, Bulletin 170, Chapter 2, p. 21-28.

Dittbrenner, E. F.
1954   Discussion of river bed scour during floods. American Society of Civil Engineers, Proceedings 80: 13-17.

Dole, R. B. and H. Stabler
1909   Denudation. U. S. Geological Survey, Water-Supply Paper 234:78-93.

Drewes, H.
1959   Turtleback faults of Death Valley, California; a reinterpretation. Geological Society of America, Bulletin 70:1497-1508.

──────
1963   Geology of the Funeral Peak quadrangle, California, in the east flank of Death Valley. U. S. Geological Survey, Professional Paper 413.

Droste, J. B.
1961   Clay minerals in sediments of Owens, China, Searles, Panamint, Bristol, Cadiz, and Danby Lake basins, California. Geological Society of America, Bulletin 72:1713-1722.

Dudley, P. H.
1936   Physiographic history of a portion of the Perris block, southern California. Journal of Geology 44:358-378.

Dutton, C. E.
1880   Geology of the high plateaus of Utah. U. S. Geological and Geographical Survey, Rocky Mountain region 69-81.

──────
1885   Mount Taylor and the Zuñi Plateau. U. S. Geological Survey, Annual Report 6:113-198.

Dyer, W. G.
1965   Guelta of the bleak Sahara. Natural History 74: 36-39.

Eakin, T. E.
1950   Preliminary report on ground water in Fish Lake Valley, Nevada and California. Nevada Department of Conservation and Natural Resources, Water Resources Bulletin 11.

Eardley, A. J.
1933   Strong relief before block-faulting in the vicinity of the Wasatch Mountains. Journal of Geology 41:243-267.

──────
1934   Structure and physiography of the southern Wasatch Mountains, Utah. Michigan Academy of Science, Papers 19:377-400.

──────
1944   Geology of the north-central Wasatch Mountains, Utah. Geological Society of America, Bulletin 55: 819-895.

──────
1962a Gypsum dunes and evaporate history of the Great Salt Lake desert. Utah Geological and Mineralogical Survey, Special Studies 2. 27 p.

──────
1962b Structural geology of North America. 2nd ed. Harper and Row, New York.

Eardley, A. J., V. Gvosdetsky, and R. E. Marsell
1957   Hydrology of Lake Bonneville and sediments and soils of its basin. Geological Society of America, Bulletin 68:1141-1201.

Eaton, H. N.
1929   Structural features of Long Ridge and West Mountain, Central Utah. American Journal of Science 18:71-79.

Eckis, R.
1928   Alluvial fans of the Cucamonga district, southern California. Journal of Geology 36:224-247.

Einstein, H. A.
1950   The bed-load function for sediment transportation in open channel flows. U. S. Department of Agriculture, Technical Bulletin 1026.

──────
1964   River sedimentation: Section 17-II:35-67. *In* V. T. Chow, ed., Handbook of applied hydrology. McGraw-Hill, New York.

Einstein, H. A. and H. Wen Shen
1964   A study on meandering in straight alluvial channels. Journal of Geophysical Research 69: 5239-5247.

Elkern, P. C.
1953   Problems of raindrop impact erosion. Agricultural Engineering 34:23-25.

Ellis, R. W.
1922   Geology of the Sandia Mountains, New Mexico. University of New Mexico, Bulletin 108.

Ellison, W. D.
1946   The raindrop and erosion. American Forests 52: 360-363.

──────
1948   Erosion by raindrop. Scientific American 179: 40-45.

──────
1950   Soil erosion by rainstorms. Science 133:245-249.

Engel, C. G. and R. P. Sharp
1958   Chemical data on desert varnish. Geological Society of America, Bulletin 69:487-518.

Evans, G. C.
1963   Geology and sedimentation along the lower Rio Salado in New Mexico. New Mexico Geological Society, Guidebook of the Socorro Region, Socorro, New Mexico, p. 209-216.

Evans, J. R.
1962   Falling and climbing sand dunes in the Cronese ("cat") mountain area, San Bernardino County, California. Journal of Geology 70:107-113.

Eymann, J. L.
1953   A study of sand dunes in the Colorado and Mohave deserts. University of Southern California (unpublished M.S. thesis).

Fahnestock, R. K. and W. L. Haushild
1962   Flume studies of the transport of pebbles and cobbles on a sand bed. Geological Society of America, Bulletin 73:1431-1436.

Fahnestock, R. K. and T. Maddock, Jr.
1964   Preliminary report on bed forms and flow phenomena in the Rio Grande. U. S. Geological Survey, Professional Paper 501-B:140-142.

Felix, C. E.
1956 Geology of the eastern part of the Raft River Range, Box Elder County, Utah. Utah Geological Society, Guidebook to the Geology of Utah 11: 76-97.

Fenneman, N. M.
1916 Physiographic divisions of the United States. Association of American Geographers, Annals 6:19-98.

_____
1932 Physiographic history of the Great Basin. Pan American Geologist 57:131-142.

Ferguson, H. G. and S. H. Cathcart
1924 Major structural features of some western Nevada ranges. Washington Academy of Science, Journal 14:376-379.

Feth, J. H.
1961 A new map of the western conterminous United States showing the maximum known or inferred extent of Pleistocene lakes. U. S. Geological Survey, Professional Paper 424-B:110-112.

Field, R.
1935 Stream carved slopes and plains in desert mountains. American Journal of Science 29:313-322.

Fiering, M. B.
1963 Use of correlation to improve estimates of the mean and variance. U. S. Geological Survey, Professional Paper 434-C.

Fischer, D. J., C. E. Erdmann, and J. B. Reeside, Jr.
1960 Cretaceous and Tertiary formations of the Book Cliffs, Carbon, Emery, and Grand counties, Utah, and Garfield and Mesa counties, Colorado. U. S. Geological Survey, Professional Paper 332.

Fisk, H. N.
1951 Loess and Quaternary geology of the lower Mississippi valley. Journal of Geology 59:333-356.

Flammer, G. H.
1962 Ultrasonic measurement of suspended sediment. U. S. Geological Survey, Bulletin 1141-A.

FMC Corporation
1964 A research study concerning the application of a Fourier series description to terrain geometries associated with ground mobility and ride dynamics. Phase I: Terrain and vehicle models. U. S. Army Engineer Waterways Experiment Station, Contract Report.

Foshag, W. F.
1926 Saline lakes of the Mojave desert. Economic Geology 21:56-64.

Free, E. E.
1909 A possible error in the estimates of the rate of geologic denudation. Science 29:423-424.

_____
1911 The movement of soil material by wind, with a bibliography of eolian geology by S. C. Stuntz and E. E. Free. U. S. Department of Agriculture, Bureau of Soils, Bulletin 68:1-173.

_____
1914 Topographic features of the desert basins of the United States. United States Department of Agriculture, Bulletin 54.

Frye, J. C. and H. T. U. Smith
1942 Preliminary observations on pediment-like slopes in the central High Plains. Journal of Geomorphology 5:215-221.

Galbraith, F. W.
1959 Craters of the Pinacates, Arizona. Arizona Geological Society, Southern Arizona Guidebook 2: 162-163.

Gale, H. S.
1915a Geologic history of Lake Lahontan. Science 41: 209-211.

_____
1915b Salines in Owens, Searles, and Panamint basins, southeastern California. U. S. Geological Survey, Bulletin 580:251-323.

_____
1933 Geology of southern California. International Geological Congress, 16th, Washington, Guidebook 15:1-10.

_____
1951 Geology of the saline deposits of Bristol dry lake, California. California Division of Mines, Special Report 13.

Gardner, L. S.
1941 The Hurricane fault in southwestern Utah and northwestern Arizona. American Journal of Science 239:241-260.

Gianella, V. P. and E. Callaghan
1934 The earthquake of December 20, 1932 at Cedar Mountain, Nevada, and its bearing on the genesis of basin range structure. Journal of Geology 42: 1-22.

Gilbert, G. K.
1874 Preliminary geologic report, expedition of 1872. U. S. Geological and Geographical Surveys West of the 100th Meridian, Report, p. 48-52.

_____
1875 Surveys west of the 100th meridian. U. S. Geological and Geographical Survey of the Territories, Part 1.

_____
1895 Lake basins created by wind erosion. Journal of Geology 3:47-49.

_____
1928 Studies of basin range structure. U. S. Geological Survey, Professional Paper 153.

Gillerman, E.
1958 Geology of the central Peloncillo Mountains, Hidalgo County, New Mexico, and Cochise County, Arizona. New Mexico Bureau of Mines, Bulletin 57.

Gilluly, J.
1928 Basin range faulting along the Oquirrh Range, Utah. Geological Society of America, Bulletin 39: 1103-1130.

_____
1937 The physiography of the Ajo region, Arizona. Geological Society of America, Bulletin 48:323-347.

_____
1956 General geology of central Cochise County, Arizona. U. S. Geological Survey, Professional Paper 281.

_____
1965 Volcanism, tectonism, and plutonism in the western United States. Geological Society of America, Special Paper 80.

Gleason, C. H. and R. E. Amidon
1941   Landslide and mudflow, Wrightwood, California. U. S. Forest Service, California Forest and Range Experiment Station, unpublished report, p. 1-7.

Gottschalk, L. C.
1957a   Problems of predicting sediment yields from watersheds. American Geophysical Union, Transactions 38:885-888.

1957b   Symposium on watershed erosion and sediment yields. American Geophysical Union, Transactions 38:885-927.

1964   Reservoir sedimentation: Section 17-I. *In* V. T. Chow, ed., Handbook of applied hydrology. McGraw-Hill, New York.

Grabau, W. E.
1964   A comparison of quantitative versus nonquantitative terrain description systems for mobility analysis. U. S. Army Engineer Waterways Experiment Station, Miscellaneous Paper 4-652.

Greene, G. W. and C. B. Hunt
1960   Observations on current tilting of the earth's surface in Death Valley, California. U. S. Geological Survey, Annual Report 1959-60.

Gregory, H. E.
1916   The Navajo country; a geographic and hydrographic reconnaissance of parts of Arizona, New Mexico, and Utah. U. S. Geological Survey, Water Supply Paper 380.

1917   Geology of the Navajo country. U. S. Geological Survey, Professional Paper 93.

1938   The San Juan country. U. S. Geological Survey, Professional Paper 188.

1950   Geology and geography of the Zion Park region, Utah and Arizona. U. S. Geological Survey, Professional Paper 220.

Gregory, H. E. and R. C. Moore
1931   The Kaiparowits region; a geographic and geologic reconnaissance in parts of Utah and Arizona. U. S. Geological Survey, Professional Paper 164.

Gumbel, E. J.
1945   Floods estimated by probability methods. Engineering News-Record 134:97-101.

1954   Statistical theory of extreme values and some practical applications. U. S. National Bureau of Standards, Applied Mathematics Series 33. 51 p.

Guy, H. P. and D. B. Simons
1963   Dissimilarity between spatial and velocity-weighted sediment concentrations. U. S. Geological Survey, Professional Paper 475-D:134-137.

Hack, J. T.
1939   The later Quaternary history of several valleys of northern Arizona. Museum of Northern Arizona, Notes 11.

1941   Dunes of the western Navajo country. Geographical Review 31:240-263.

1942a   The changing physical environment of the Hopi Indians. Peabody Museum of Natural History, Papers 35.

1942b   Sedimentation and vulcanism in the Hopi Buttes, Arizona. Geological Society of America, Bulletin 53:335-372.

Hadley, R. F.
1961   Influence of riparian vegetation on channel shape, northeastern Arizona. U. S. Geological Survey, Professional Paper 424-C:30-31.

1963   Characteristics of sediment deposits above channel structures, Polacca Wash, Arizona: 2nd Federal Inter-Agency Sedimentation Conference. U. S. Department of Agriculture, Miscellaneous Series.

Hamilton, W. B.
1951   Playa sediments of Rosamond dry lake, California. Journal of Sedimentary Petrology 21:147-150.

Harbaugh, J. W.
1963   Balgol program for trend-surface mapping using an IBM 7090 computer. Kansas Geological Survey, Special Distribution Publication 3.

1964a   Trend-surface mapping of hydrodynamic oil traps with the IBM 7090/94 computer. Colorado School of Mines, Quarterly 59:557-578.

1964b   A computer method for four-variable trend analysis illustrated by study of oil gravity variations in southeastern Kansas. Kansas Geological Survey, Bulletin 171.

Harshman, E. N.
1939   Geology of the Belmont-Queen Creek area, Superior, Arizona. University of Arizona (unpublished dissertation).

Hastings, J. R. and R. M. Turner
1965   The changing mile. University of Arizona Press.

Hayden, F. V.
1869   Preliminary field report of the U. S. Geological Survey of Colorado and New Mexico. U. S. Geological and Geographical Survey of the Territories, Annual Report 3:66-67.

Hazzard, J. C.
1954   Rocks and structures of the northern Providence Mountains, San Bernardino County, California. California Division of Mines, Bulletin 170, Chapter 4, p. 27-35.

Hefley, H. M. and R. Sidwell
1945   Geological and ecological observations of some High Plains dunes. American Journal of Science 234:361-376.

Heindl, L. A.
1958   Cenozoic alluvial deposits of the upper Gila River area, New Mexico and Arizona. University of Arizona (unpublished dissertation).

1959   Geology of the San Xavier Indian Reservation, Arizona. Arizona Geological Society, Southern Arizona Guidebook 2:152-159.

1960a   Cenozoic geology of the Papago Indian Reservation, Pima, Maricopa, and Pinal counties, Arizona; a preliminary report. Arizona Geological Society, Digest 3:31-34.

Heindl, L. A.
1960*b* Geology of the lower Bonita Creek area; a preliminary report. Arizona Geological Society, Digest 3:35-39.

_____ 1962 Cenozoic geology of Arizona; a 1960 resume. Arizona Geological Society, Digest 5:9-23.

_____ 1963 Cenozoic geology in the Mammoth area, Pinal County, Arizona. U. S. Geological Survey, Bulletin 1141-E.

Hely, A. G., G. H. Hughes, and B. Irelan
1966 Hydrologic regimen of Salton Sea, California. U. S. Geological Survey, Professional Paper 486-C.

Hely, A. G. and E. L. Peck
1964 Precipitation, runoff, and water loss in the lower Colorado River - Salton Sea area. U. S. Geological Survey, Professional Paper 486-B.

Herrick, C. L.
1898 Papers on the geology of New Mexico. University of New Mexico Bulletin, Geology Series 1:94-98.

Herrick, C. L. and D. W. Johnson
1900 The geology of the Albuquerque sheet. University of New Mexico Bulletin, Geology Series 2:3-8.

Hevly, R. H. and P. S. Martin
1961 Geochronology of pluvial Lake Cochise, southern Arizona. I: Pollen analysis of shore deposits. Arizona Academy of Science, Journal 2:24-31.

Hewett, D. F.
1954 General geology of the Mohave Desert region, California. California Division of Mines, Bulletin 170, Chapter 2, p. 5-20.

_____ 1956 Geology and mineral resources of the Ivanpah quadrangle, California and Nevada. U. S. Geological Survey, Professional Paper 275.

Higgins, C. G.
1953 Miniature pediments near Calistogo, California. Journal of Geology 61:461-465.

Hilgard, E.
1879 The loess of the Mississippi valley. American Journal of Science 18:106-112.

Hill, R. T.
1928 Southern California geology and Los Angeles earthquakes. Southern California Academy of Science, Los Angeles. 232 p.

Hinds, N. E. A.
1952*a* Basin range, Mohave Desert, Colorado Desert, and Modoc Plateau. California Division of Mines, Bulletin 158:61-108.

_____ 1952*b* Evolution of the California landscape. California Division of Mines, Bulletin 158.

Hintze, F. F., Jr.
1913 A contribution to the geology of the Wasatch Mountains, Utah. New York Academy of Sciences, Annals 23:133.

Hitchcock, A. S.
1904 Controlling sand dunes in the United States and Europe. National Geographic Magazine 15:43-47.

Holtenberger, M.
1913 On a genetic system of sand dunes. American Geographical Society, Bulletin 45:513-515.

Hoover, J. W.
1936 Physiography of Arizona. Pan American Geologist 65:321-338.

Hoppe, G. and S.-R. Ekman
1964 A note on the alluvial fans of Ladtjovagge, Swedish Lapland. Geografiska Annaler 46:338-342.

Horberg, L.
1940 Geomorphic problems of the Carlsbad Caverns area, New Mexico. Journal of Geology 48:464-476.

Horikawa, K. and H. W. Shen
1960 Sand movement by wind action: on the characteristics of sand traps. U. S. Army, Corps of Engineers, Beach Erosion Board, Technical Memorandum 119. 51 p.

Howard, A. D.
1942 Pediment passes and the pediment problem. Journal of Geomorphology 5:1-31, 95-136.

Howard, C. S.
1947 Suspended sediment in the Colorado River, 1925-41. U. S. Geological Survey, Water-Supply Paper 998. 165 p.

Hubbell, D. W.
1963 Apparatus and techniques for measuring bedload. U. S. Geological Survey, Water-Supply Paper 1748.

Hubbs, C. L. and R. R. Miller
1948*a* The Great Basin with emphasis on glacial and post-glacial times. University of Utah, Bulletin 38(20):18-166.

_____ 1948*b* The Great Basin. Part II: The zoological evidence. University of Utah, Bulletin 38:103-113.

Hulin, C. D.
1925 Geology and ore deposits of the Randsberg quadrangle, California. California State Bureau of Mines, Bulletin 95.

Hunt, A.
1960 Archeology of the Death Valley salt pan, California. University of Utah, Anthropological Paper 47.

Hunt, C. B.
1960 The Death Valley salt pan, a study of evaporite. U. S. Geological Survey, Professional Paper 400-B:456-457.

_____ 1961 Stratigraphy of desert varnish. U. S. Geological Survey, Professional Paper 424-B:194-195.

Hunt, C. B., P. Averitt, and R. L. Miller
1953 Geology and geography of the Henry Mountains region, Utah. U. S. Geological Survey, Professional Paper 228.

Hunt, C. B. and D. R. Mabey
1966 Stratigraphy and structure, Death Valley, California. U. S. Geological Survey, Professional Paper 494-A.

Hunt, C. B. *et al.*
1953 Lake Bonneville; Geology of Northern Utah Valley. U. S. Geological Survey, Professional Paper 257-A.

_____ 1966 Hydrologic basin, Death Valley, California. U. S. Geological Survey, Professional Paper 494-B.

Hunt, O. P.
1963 Use of low-flow measurements to estimate flow-duration curves. U. S. Geological Survey, Professional Paper 475-C:196-197.

Huntington, E. and J. W. Goldthwait
1903 The Hurricane fault in the Toquerville district, Utah. Harvard Museum of Comparative Zoology, Bulletin 42:226-245.

Hutchinson, G. E.
1957 A treatise on limnology. John Wiley, New York.

Ives, R. L.
1936 Desert floods in the Sonoyta Valley. American Journal of Science 32:349-360.

Jaeger, E. C.
1957 The North American deserts. Stanford University Press, Palo Alto.

Jahns, R. H. (ed.)
1954 Geology of southern California. California Division of Mines, Bulletin 170.

Jahns, R. H. and A. E. J. Engel
1949 Pliocene breccias in the Avawatz Mountains, San Bernardino County, California. Geological Society of America, Bulletin 60:1940. (Abstr.)

Jenkins, O. P. and E. D. Wilson
1920 A geological reconnaissance of the Tucson and Amole mountains. Arizona Bureau of Mines, Bulletin 106.

Jenney, C. P.
1935 Geology of the central Humboldt Range, Nevada. University of Nevada, Bulletin 29(6).

Johnson, D. W.
1909 Volcanic necks of the Mount Taylor region, New Mexico. Journal of Geology 18:303-324.

Johnson, W. D.
1931 Planes of lateral corrasion. Science 73:174-177.

_____ 1932a Rock planes of arid regions. Geographic Review 22:656-665.

_____ 1932b Rock fans of arid regions. American Journal of Science 223:389-416.

Jones, B. F.
The hydrology and mineralogy of Deep Springs Lake, Inyo County, California. U. S. Geological Survey, Professional Paper 502-A (*in press*).

Jones, J. C.
1914 The geologic history of Lake Lahontan. Science 40:827-830.

_____ 1915 Origin of the tufas of Lake Lahontan. Geological Society of America, Bulletin 26:392.

_____ 1925 The geologic history of Lake Lahontan. *In* Quaternary climates. Carnegie Institution of Washington, Publication 352:1-50.

Jopling, A. V.
1963a Effect of base-level changes on bedding development in a laboratory flume. U. S. Geological Survey, Professional Paper 475-B:203-204.

_____ 1963b Hydraulic studies on the origin of bedding. Sedimentology 2:115-121.

_____ 1964a Laboratory study of sorting processes related to flow separation. Journal of Geophysical Research 69:3403-3418.

_____ 1964b Interpreting the concept of the sedimentation unit. Journal of Sedimentary Petrology 34:165-172.

Judson, S.
1950 Depressions of the northern portion of the southern high plains of eastern New Mexico. Geological Society of America, Bulletin 61:253-273.

_____ 1953 Geologic antiquity of the San Jon site, eastern New Mexico. Smithsonian Institution, Miscellaneout Collections 121(1):1-70. Publication 4098.

Kelley, V. C. and C. Silver
1952 Geology of the Caballo Mountains. University of New Mexico, Publications in Geology 5. 120 p.

Kelley, V. C. and J. L. Soske
1936 Origin of the Salton volcanic domes, Salton Sea, California. Journal of Geology 44:496-509.

Kesseli, J. E. and C. B. Beaty
1959 Desert flood conditions in the White Mountains of California and Nevada. U. S. Army, Quartermaster Research and Engineering Command, Natick, Mass., Environmental Protection Research Division, Technical Report EP-108. 107 p.

Keyes, C. R.
1908 Rock floors of intermontane plains of the arid regions. Geological Society of America, Bulletin 19:63-92.

_____ 1910a Deflation and the relative efficiencies of erosional processes under conditions of aridity. Geological Society of America, Bulletin 21:565-598.

_____ 1910b Relations of present profiles and geologic structures in desert ranges. Geological Society of America, Bulletin 21:543-564.

_____ 1911 Mid-continental eolation. Geological Society of America, Bulletin 22:687-714.

_____ 1912 Deflative scheme of the geographic cycle in an arid climate. Geological Society of America, Bulletin 23:537-562.

_____ 1915 False fault-scarps of desert ranges. Geological Society of America, Bulletin 26:65. (Abstr.)

_____ 1922 Physiographic paradox of the desert. Pan American Geologist 38:161-176.

_____ 1924 Mastery of winds in land sculpture. Pan American Geologist 41:321-334.

_____ 1929 Physiographic provinces in deserts. Pan American Geologist 52:129-150.

Kilpatrick, F. A. and H. H. Barnes, Jr.
1964 Channel geometry of piedmont streams as related to frequency of floods. U. S. Geological Survey, Professional Paper 422-E.

Kindsvater, C. E.
1958   Selected topics of fluid mechanics. U. S. Geological Survey, Water-Supply Paper 1369-A.

King, P. B.
1942   Permian of west Texas and southeastern New Mexico. American Association of Petroleum Geologists, Bulletin 26:535-763.

———
1948   Geology of the southern Guadalupe Mountains, Texas. U. S. Geological Survey, Professional Paper 215.

———
1958   Evolution of modern surface features of western North America. *In* C. L. Hubbs (ed.), Zoogeography. American Association for the Advancement of Science, Publication 51:3-60.

King, R. E. *et al.*
1942   Resume of the geology of the south Permian basin, Texas and New Mexico. Geological Society of America, Bulletin 53:539-560.

Kniffen, F. B.
1932   The natural landscape of the Colorado Delta. University of California, Publications in Geography 5:149-244.

Kohler, M. A., T. J. Nordenson, and D. R. Baker
1959   Evaporation maps for the United States. U. S. Weather Bureau, Technical Paper 37.

Koons, D.
1955   Cliff retreat in the southwestern United States. American Journal of Science 253:44-52.

Koschmann, A. H. and G. F. Loughlin
1934   Dissected pediments in the Magdalena district, New Mexico. Geological Society of America, Bulletin 45:463-478.

Kottlowski, F. E.
1965   Sedimentary basins of south-central and southwestern New Mexico. American Association of Petroleum Geologists, Bulletin 49:2120-2139.

Krenkel, P. A.
1962   Application of terrain descriptive techniques to Fort Knox, Kentucky. Vanderbilt University, Department of Civil Engineering, Contract Report.

———
1963   A technique for macrogeometry terrain analysis. Vanderbilt University, Department of Civil Engineering, Contract Report.

Lakin, H. W. *et al.*
1963   Variation in minor-element content of desert varnish. U. S. Geological Survey, Professional Paper 475-B:28-31.

LaMarche, V.
1961   Rate of slope erosion in the White Mountains, California. Geological Society of America, Bulletin 72:1579-1580.

Lance, J. F.
1959   Geologic framework of arid basins in Arizona. Geological Society of America, Bulletin 70:1729-1730. (Abstr.)

Landsberg, H. and N. A. Riley
1943   Wind influences on the transportation of sand over a Michigan sand dune. University of Iowa Studies in Engineering, Bulletin 27:342-352.

Langbein, W. B.
1961   Salinity and hydrology of closed lakes. U. S. Geological Survey, Professional Paper 412. 20 p.

———
1962   The water supply of arid valleys in intermountain regions in relation to climate. International Association of Scientific Hydrology, Bulletin 7(1):34-39.

Langbein, W. B. and L. B. Leopold
1964a   Quasi-equilibrium states in channel morphology. American Journal of Science 262:782-794.

———
1964b   River channel bars and dunes: theory of kinematic waves. U. S. Geological Survey (unpublished manuscript).

Langbein, W. B. and S. A. Schumm
1958   Yield of sediment in relation to mean annual precipitation. American Geophysical Union, Transactions 39:1076-1084.

Laudermilk, J. D.
1931   On the origin of desert varnish. American Journal of Science, ser. 5, 21:51-66.

Laursen, E. M. and A. Toch
1954   Discussion of river-bed scour during floods. American Society of Civil Engineers, Proceedings 80:17-20.

Lawson, A. C.
1915   The epigene profiles of the desert. University of California, Publications, Geology Department, Bulletin 9:23-48.

Lee, C. H.
1912   An intensive study of the water resources of a part of Owens Valley, California. U. S. Geological Survey, Water-Supply Paper 294.

Lee, W. T.
1906   Geology and water resources of Owens Valley, California. U. S. Geological Survey, Water-Supply Paper 181.

———
1908   Geological reconnaissance of a part of western Arizona, with notes on igneous rocks by Albert Johannsen. U. S. Geological Survey, Bulletin 352.

———
1924   Geography, geology and physiography of the Great Salt Lake basin. U. S. Geological Survey, Water-Supply Paper 517:3-9.

Lefevre, M.
1952   Note sur les pédiments du désert Mojave (Californie). Société Belge d'Etudes Géographiques, Brussels, Bulletin 21:259-268.
(Note on the pediments of the Mojave Desert, California.)

Lehner, R. E.
1958   Geology of the Clarkdale quadrangle, Arizona. U. S. Geological Survey, Bulletin 1021-N.

Leighly, J. B.
1936   Meandering arroyos of the dry Southwest. Geographical Review 26:270-282.

Leighton, M. M. and H. B. Willman
1950   Loess formations of the Mississippi valley. Journal of Geology 58:599-623.

Leonard, R. J.
1929   An earth fissure in southern Arizona. Journal of Geology 37:765-774.

Leopold, L. B.
1950 The erosion problem in southwestern United States. Harvard University (unpublished Ph.D. dissertation).

——— 1962 Rivers. American Scientist 50:511-537.

Leopold, L. B. and C. T. Snyder
1951 Alluvial fills near Gallup, New Mexico. U. S. Geological Survey, Water-Supply Paper 1110-A. 19 p.

Lillard, R. C.
1942 Desert challenge; an interpretation of Nevada. Alfred Knopf, New York.

Lombardi, O. W.
1963 Observations on the distribution of chemical elements in the terrestrial saline deposits of Saline Valley. U. S. Naval Ordnance Test Station, Technical Publication 2916.

Long, J. T. and R. P. Sharp
1964 Barchan-dune movement in Imperial Valley, California. Geological Society of America, Bulletin 75:149-156.

Longwell, C. R.
1926 Structural studies in southern Nevada and Western Arizona. Geological Society of America, Bulletin 37:551-583.

——— 1928 Geology of the Muddy Mountains, Nevada. U. S. Geological Survey, Bulletin 798.

——— 1930 Faulted fans west of the Sheep Range, southern Nevada. American Journal of Science 220:1-13.

——— 1945 Low-angle normal faults in the Basin-and-Range province. American Geophysical Union, Transactions 26:107-118.

——— 1949 Structure of the northern Muddy Mountain area, Nevada. Geological Society of America, Bulletin 60:923-968.

——— 1954 History of the lower Colorado River and the Imperial depression. California Division of Mines, Bulletin 170, Chapter 5, p. 53-56.

——— 1963 Reconnaissance geology between Lake Mead and Davis Dam, Arizona-Nevada. U. S. Geological Survey, Professional Paper 374-E.

Louderback, G. D.
1904 Basin Range structure of the Humboldt region. Geological Society of America, Bulletin 15:289-346.

——— 1923 Basin Range structure in the Great Basin. University of California, Department of Geological Sciences, Bulletin 14:324-376.

——— 1924-1926 Period of scarp production in the Great Basin. University of California, Publications in Geological Sciences 15:1-38.

——— 1926 Morphological features of the Basin Range displacements in the Great Basin. University of California, Department of Geological Sciences, Bulletin 16.

Loughlin, G. F.
1913 Reconnaissance in the southern Wasatch Mountains, Utah. Journal of Geology 21:436-452.

Lowe, C. H.
1955 Eastern limit of Sonoran desert in the United States. Ecology 36:343-345.

Ludden, R. W., Jr.
1950 Geology of the Campo Bonito area, Oracle, Arizona. University of Arizona (unpublished M.S. thesis).

Lustig, L. K.
1965 A topographic analysis of the basin and range province. Geological Society of America, Annual Meeting Program p. 98. (Abstr.)

——— 1966 The geomorphic and paleoclimatic significance of alluvial deposits in southern Arizona: A discussion. Journal of Geology 74:95-102.

Lustig, L. K. and R. B. Busch
1967 Sediment transport in Cache Creek drainage basin in the Coast Ranges west of Sacramento, California. U. S. Geological Survey, Professional Paper 562-A.

Mabey, D. R.
1960 Regional gravity survey of part of the Basin and Range province. In U. S. Geological Survey, Professional Paper 400-B:283-285.

MacDougal, D. T.
1917 A decade of the Salton Sea. Geographical Review 3:457-473.

MacDougal, D. T. et al.
1914 The Salton Sea; a study of the geography, geology, floristics and ecology of a desert basin. Carnegie Institution of Washington, Publication 193.

Maddock, T., Jr.
1965 The behavior of straight open channels with movable beds. U. S. Geological Survey (unpublished manuscript).

Magin, G. B., Jr. and I. E. Randall
1960 Review of literature on evaporation suppression. U. S. Geological Survey, Professional Paper 272-C.

Marlowe, J. I.
1960a Late Cenozoic geology of the lower Safford Valley; a preliminary report. Arizona Geological Society, Digest 3:127-129.

——— 1960b Diatremes and a ring intrusion on the San Carlos Indian Reservation. Arizona Geological Society, Digest 3:151-154.

——— 1961 Late Cenozoic geology of the lower Safford basin on the San Carlos Indian reservation, Arizona. University of Arizona (unpublished dissertation).

Martin, P. S.
1963 The last 10,000 years. University of Arizona Press.

Matalas, N. C.
1963a Probability distribution of low flows. U. S. Geological Survey, Professional Paper 434-A.

——— 1963b Autocorrelation of rainfall and streamflow minimums. U. S. Geological Survey, Professional Paper 434-B.

Matalas, N. C.
1963c Statistics of a runoff-precipitation relation. U. S. Geological Survey, Professional Paper 434-D.

Matalas, N. C. and B. Jacobs
1964 A correlation procedure for augmenting hydrologic data. U. S. Geological Survey, Professional Paper 434-E.

Maxson, J. H. and G. H. Anderson
1935 Terminology of surface forms of the erosion cycle. Journal of Geology 43:88-96.

Maxson, J. H.
1950a Physiographic features of the Panamint Range, California. Geological Society of America, Bulletin 61:99-114.

———
1950b Pediments and pediplains. Geological Society of America, Bulletin 61:1556-1557.

Maxwell, J. C.
1962 Test of quantitative terrain description systems at Fort Leonard Wood, Missouri. Missouri School of Mines and Metallurgy, Contract Report.

Mayo, E. B.
1963 Volcanic orogeny of the Tucson Mountains; a preliminary report. Arizona Geological Society, Digest 6:61-82.

McCann, F. T.
1938 Ancient erosion surface in the Gallup-Zuñi area, New Mexico. American Journal of Science, Ser. 5, 36:260-278.

McGee, W. J.
1897 Sheetflood erosion. Geological Society of America, Bulletin 8:87-112.

McKee, E. D.
1951 Sedimentary basins in Arizona and adjoining areas. Geological Society of America, Bulletin 62:481-506.

Mears, B. J.
1948 Cenozoic faults, gravels, and volcanics of Oak Creek Canyon, Arizona. Columbia University (unpublished dissertation).

Meinzer, O. E.
1911 Geology and water resources of Estancia Valley, New Mexico. U. S. Geological Survey, Water-Supply Paper 275.

———
1922 Map of the Pleistocene lakes of the Basin-and-Range province and its significance. Geological Society of America, Bulletin 33:541-552.

Meinzer, O. E. and R. F. Hare
1915 Geology and water resources of Tularosa Basin, New Mexico. U. S. Geological Survey, Water-Supply Paper 343.

Melton, F. A.
1940 A tentative classification of sand dunes; its application to dune history in the southern high plains. Journal of Geology 48:113-174.

Melton, M. A.
1958 Geometric properties of mature drainage systems and their representation in an E₄ phase space. Journal of Geology 66:35-54.

———
1960 Origin of the drainage of southeastern Arizona. Arizona Geological Society, Digest 3:113-122.

———
1961 Origin of the drainage and geomorphic history of southeastern Arizona. University of Arizona, Tucson, Arid Lands Colloquia 1959/60-1960/61:8-16.

———
1965 Debris-covered hillslopes of the southern Arizona desert—consideration of their stability and sediment contribution. Journal of Geology 73:715-729.

Mendenhall, W. C.
1909 Some desert watering places in southeastern California and southwestern Nevada. U. S. Geological Survey, Water-Supply Paper 224.

Merriam, D. F. and J. W. Harbaugh
1964 Trend-surface analysis of regional and residual components of geologic structure in Kansas. Kansas Geological Survey, Special Distribution Publication 2.

Merriam, D. F. and R. H. Lippert
1964 Pattern recognition studies of geology structure using trend-surface analysis. Colorado School of Mines, Quarterly 59:237-245.

Meyerhoff, H. A.
1940 Migration of erosional surfaces. Association of American Geographers, Annals 30:247-254.

Meyers, J. S.
1962 Evaporation from the 17 western states. U. S. Geological Survey, Professional Paper 272-D:71-100.

Michael, E. D.
1965 Origin of the lakes in the Chuska Mountains, northwestern New Mexico; discussion. Geological Society of America, Bulletin 76:267-268.

Middleton, G. V. (ed.)
1965 Primary sedimentary structures and their hydrodynamic interpretation. Society of Economic Paleontologists and Mineralogists, Special Publication 12.

Miller, J. P. and F. Wendorf
1958 Alluvial chronology of the Tesuque Valley, New Mexico. Journal of Geology 66:177-194.

Miller, V. C.
1950 Pediments and pediment-forming processes near House Rock, Arizona. Journal of Geology 58:634-635.

Miser, H. D.
1925 Erosion in San Juan Canyon, Utah. Geological Society of America, Bulletin 36:365-377.

Miser, H. D., K. W. Trimble, and S. Paige
1923 The Rainbow Bridge, Utah. Geographical Review 13:518-531.

Morrison, R. B.
1961 Lake Lahontan stratigraphy and history in the Carson desert (Fallon) area, Nevada. U. S. Geological Survey, Professional Paper 424-D:111-114.

———
1964 Lake Lahontan; geology of southern Carson desert, Nevada. U. S. Geological Survey, Professional Paper 401.

Neal, J. T.
1965 Geology, mineralogy, and hydrology of U. S. playas. U.S. Air Force Cambridge Research Laboratories, Environmental Research Paper 96. 176 p.

Nichols, R. L.
1946   McCarty's basalt flow, Valencia County, New Mexico. Geological Society of America, Bulletin 57:1049-1086.

Noble, L. F.
1927   The San Andreas rift and some other active faults in the desert region of southeastern California. Seismological Society of America, Bulletin 17:25-39.

——— 1932   The San Andreas rift in the desert region of southern California. Carnegie Institution of Washington, Yearbook 31:355-372.

——— 1941   Structural features of the Virgin Spring area, Death Valley, California. Geological Society of America, Bulletin 52:941-999.

Noble, L. F. and L. A. Wright
1954   Geology of the central and southern Death Valley region, California. California Division of Mines, Bulletin 170, Chapter 2, p. 143-160.

Nolan, T. B.
1943   The Basin and Range province in Utah, Nevada, and California. U. S. Geological Survey, Professional Paper 197-D.

Nordin, C. F., Jr.
1963   A preliminary study of sediment transport parameters, Rio Puerco near Bernardo, New Mexico. U. S. Geological Survey, Professional Paper 462-C.

——— 1964   Aspects of flow resistance and sediment transport, Rio Grande near Bernalillo, New Mexico. U. S. Geological Survey, Water-Supply Paper 1498-H.

Nordin, C. F., Jr., and J. P. Beverage
1964   Temporary storage of fine sediments in islands and bars of alluvial channels of the Rio Grande, New Mexico and Texas. U. S. Geological Survey, Professional Paper 475-D:138-140.

Nordin, C. F., Jr. and W. F. Curtis
1962   Formation and deposition of clay balls, Rio Puerco, New Mexico. U. S. Geological Survey, Professional Paper 450-B:37-40.

Nordin, C. F., Jr. and G. R. Dempster, Jr.
1963   Vertical distribution of velocity and suspended sediment, Middle Rio Grande, New Mexico. U. S. Geological Survey, Professional Paper 452-B.

Norris, R. M.
1966   Barchan-dunes of Imperial Valley, California. Journal of Geology 74:292-306.

Norris, R. M. and K. S. Norris
1961   Algodones Dunes of southeastern California. Geological Society of America, Bulletin 72:605-620.

Pack, J. F.
1926   New discoveries relating to the Wasatch fault. American Journal of Science 11:399-410.

Paige, Sidney
1912   Rock-cut surfaces in the desert ranges. Journal of Geology 20:442-450.

Parker, G. G.
1963   Piping, a geomorphic agent in landform development of the drylands. International Association of Scientific Hydrology, Publication 65:103-113.

Pashley, E. F., Jr.
1961   Subsidence cracks in alluvium near Casa Grande, Arizona. Arizona Geological Society, Digest 4:95-101.

Peltier, L. C.
1951   Discussion of "Erosion pavement, its formation and significance." American Geophysical Union, Transactions 32:466-467.

Peterson, J. A. *et al.*
1965   Sedimentary history and economic geology of San Juan basin. American Association of Petroleum Geologists, Bulletin 49:2076-2119.

Peterson, N. P.
1954   Geology of the Globe quadrangle, Arizona. U. S. Geological Survey, Geological Quadrangle 41.

Peterson, V. E.
1942   Geology and ore deposits of the Ashbrook silver mining district, Utah. Economic Geology 37:466-502.

Pierce, R. C.
1916   The measurement of silt-laden streams. U. S. Geological Survey, Water-Supply Paper 400-C.

Pine, G. L.
1963   Sedimentation studies in the vicinity of Willcox Playa, Cochise County, Arizona. University of Arizona (unpublished M.S. thesis). 38 p.

Pipkin, B. W.
1964   Clay mineralogy of the Willcox Playa and its drainage basin. University of Arizona (Ph.D. dissertation). 160 p.

Plafker, L.
1956   Geologic reconnaissance of the Cenozoic Walnut Grove basin, Yavapai County, Arizona. University of Arizona (unpublished M.S. thesis). 62 p.

Price, W. A.
1957   Geomorphology of depositional surfaces. American Association of Petroleum Geologists, Bulletin 31:1784-1800.

Putnam, W. C.
1954   Marine terraces of the Ventura region and the Santa Monica Mountains, California. California Division of Mines, Bulletin 170, Chapter 5, p. 45-58.

Rahn, P. H.
1965   Inselbergs of southwestern Arizona. Geological Society of America. Annual Meeting, Program, p. 130-131. (Abstr.)

Ransome, F. L.
1904a   Geology and ore deposits of the Bisbee quadrangle, Arizona. U. S. Geological Survey, Professional Paper 21.

——— 1904b   Description of the Globe quadrangle. U. S. Geological Survey, Folio 111.

Reed, R. D.
1933   Geology of California. American Association of Petroleum Geologists, Tulsa. 355 p.

Reeves, C. C., Jr.
1966   Pluvial lake basins of west Texas. Journal of Geology 74:269-291.

Rich, J. L.
1911   Recent stream trenching in semi-arid New Mexico, a result of removal of vegetation cover. American Journal of Science 32:237-245.

Rich, J. L.
1935 Origin and evolution of rock fans and pediments. Geological Society of America, Bulletin 46: 999-1024.

_____ 1938 Recognition and significance of multiple erosion surfaces. Geological Society of America, Bulletin 49:1695-1722.

Richmond, G. M.
1962 Quaternary stratigraphy of the La Sal Mountains, Utah. U. S. Geological Survey, Professional Paper 324.

Rigby, J. K.
1958 Geology of the Stansbury Mountains, eastern Tooele County, Utah. Geological Society of Utah, Guidebook to the Geology of Utah 13:1-134.

_____ 1962 Some geomorphic features of the South Wasatch Mountains and adjacent areas. Brigham Young University, Geological Studies 9:80-84.

Riggs, H. C.
1961 Regional low flow frequency analysis. U. S. Geological Survey, Professional Paper 424-B:21-23.

Roberts, R. J. *et al.*
1965 Pennsylvanian and Permian basins in northwestern Utah, northeastern Nevada, and south-central Idaho. American Association of Petroleum Geologists, Bulletin 49:1926-1956.

Robinson, G. M. and D. E. Peterson
1962 Notes on earth fissures in southern Arizona. U. S. Geological Survey, Circular 466.

Robinson, R. C.
1965 Sedimentology of beach ridge and nearshore deposits, pluvial Lake Cochise, southeastern Arizona. University of Arizona (unpublished M.S. thesis). 111 p.

Ross, C. P.
1923 The lower Gila region, a geographic, geologic, and hydrologic reconnaissance. U. S. Geological Survey, Water-Supply Paper 498.

Roth, E. S.
1960 The silt-clay dunes at Clark dry lake, California. Compass 38:18-27.

Rubey, W. W.
1933 Equilibrium conditions in debris-laden streams. American Geophysical Union, Transactions 14: 497-505.

Ruhe, R. V.
1954 Relations of the properties of Wisconsin loess to topography in western Iowa. American Journal of Science 252:663-672.

_____ 1964 Landscape morphology and alluvial deposits in southern New Mexico. Association of American Geographers, Annals 54:147-159.

Russell, I. C.
1885 Geological history of Lake Lahontan. U. S. Geological Survey, Monograph 11.

_____ 1896 Present and extinct lakes of Nevada. p. 101-138. *In* National Geographic Society, The physiography of the U.S., American Book Co., New York.

Russell, R. J.
1932 Landforms of San Gorgonio Pass, California. University of California, Publications in Geography 6:23-121.

_____ 1940 Lower Mississippi valley loess. Geological Society of America, Bulletin 55:1-40.

Sabins, F. F., Jr.
1957 Geology of the Cochise Head and western part of the Vanar quadrangle, Arizona. Geological Society of America, Bulletin 68:1315-1342.

St. Clair, C. S.
1957 Geologic reconnaissance of the Agua Fria River area, central Arizona. University of Arizona (unpublished M.S. thesis). 76 p.

Sauer, C.
1930 Basin and range forms in the Chiricahua area (Arizona and New Mexico). University of California, Publications in Geography 3:339-414.

Scheidig, A.
1934 Der Löss und seine geotechnische eigenschaften. Dresden. 233 p.

Schoewe, W. H.
1932 Experiments on the formation of wind-faceted pebbles. American Journal of Science 24:111-134.

Schultz, C. B. *et al.*
1945 Symposium on loess. American Journal of Science 243:225-304.

Schumm, S. A.
1960 The shape of alluvial channels in relation to sediment type; erosion and sedimentation in a semi-arid environment. U. S. Geological Survey, Professional Paper 352-B.

_____ 1961a Effect of sediment characteristics on erosion and deposition in ephemeral stream channels. U. S. Geological Survey, Professional Paper 352-C.

_____ 1961b Dimensions of some stable alluvial channels. U.S. Geological Survey, Professional Paper 424-B: 26-27.

_____ 1962 Erosion on miniature pediments in Badlands National Monument, South Dakota. Geological Society of America, Bulletin 73:719-724.

_____ 1963 A tentative classification of alluvial river channels. U. S. Geological Survey, Circular 477.

Schumm, S. A. and R. J. Chorley
1964 The fall of Threatening Rock. American Journal of Science 262:1041-1054.

Schumm, S. A. and R. F. Hadley
1957 Arroyos and the semiarid cycle of erosion. American Journal of Science 255:161-174.

Schumm, S. A. and R. W. Lichty
1963 Channel widening and flood-plain construction along Cimarron River in southwestern Kansas. U. S. Geological Survey, Professional Paper 352-D.

Sellards, E. H., W. S. Adkins, and F. B. Plummer
1932 The geology of Texas. Vol. I: Stratigraphy. University of Texas, Bulletin 3232.

Shamburger, J. H. and L. M. Duke
1965 Project OTTER; terrain evaluation research test report. U. S. Army Engineer Waterways Experiment Station, Technical Report 3-588, Part 2.

Shamburger, J. H. and C. R. Kolb
  1961   Project OTTER; terrain evaluation research pre-test report. U. S. Army Engineer Waterways Experiment Station, Technical Report 3-588, Part 1.

Sharp, R. P.
  1940   Geomorphology of the Ruby - East Humboldt Range, Nevada. Geological Society of America, Bulletin 51:337-371.

_____
  1942   Mudflow levees. Journal of Geomorphology 5: 222-227.

_____
  1954a   Some physiographic aspects of southern California. California Division of Mines, Bulletin 170, Chapter 5, p. 5-10.

_____
  1954b   Physiographic features of faulting in southern California. California Division of Mines, Bulletin 170, Chapter 5, p. 21-28.

_____
  1954c   The nature of Cima Dome. California Division of Mines, Bulletin 170, Chapter 5, p. 49-52.

_____
  1957   Geomorphology of Cima Dome, Mohave Desert, California. Geological Society of America, Bulletin 68:273-289.

_____
  1963   Wind ripples. Journal of Geology 71:617-636.

_____
  1964   Wind-driven sand in Coachella Valley, California. Geological Society of America, Bulletin 75: 785-803.

Sharp, R. P. and L. H. Nobles
  1953   Mudflows of 1941 at Wrightwood, southern California. Geological Society of America, Bulletin 64: 547-560.

Shawe, D. R.
  1963   Possible wind-erosion origin of linear scarps on the Sage Plain, southwestern Colorado. U. S. Geological Survey, Professional Paper 475-C:138-141.

Shepard, J. R. *et al.*
  1955   Terrain study of the Yuma test station area, Arizona. Joint Highway Research Project, Purdue University, Engineering Experiment Station, Contract Report.

Shimek, B.
  1904   Papers on the loess. Iowa State University, Laboratory of Natural History, Bulletin 5:298-381.

Sigafoos, R. S.
  1964   Botanical evidence of floods and flood-plain deposition. U. S. Geological Survey, Professional Paper 485-A.

Silberling, N. J. and R. J. Roberts
  1962   Pre-Tertiary stratigraphy and structure of northwestern Nevada. Geological Society of America, Special Paper 72.

Simons, D. B. and E. V. Richardson
  1962   The effect of bed roughness on depth-discharge relations in alluvial channels. U. S. Geological Survey, Water-Supply Paper 1498-E.

Simons, D. B., E. V. Richardson, and M. L. Albertson
  1961   Flume studies using medium sand (0.45 mm). U. S. Geological Survey, Water-Supply Paper 1498-A.

Simons, D. B., E. V. Richardson, and W. L. Haushild
  1963   Some effects of fine sediment on flow phenomena. U. S. Geological Survey, Water-Supply Paper 1498-G.

Simpson, T. R.
  1946   Salinas Basin investigation. California Division of Water Reserve, Bulletin 52.

Smith, D. G.
  1964   Pleistocene geology and geomorphology of an area of the San Pedro Valley, Cochise County, Arizona. University of Arizona (unpublished M.S. thesis).

Smith, G. D.
  1942   Illinois loess; variations in its properties and distribution; a pedological interpretation. Illinois Agricultural Experiment Station, Bulletin 490. 184 p.

Smith, G. I.
  1962   Subsurface stratigraphy of Late Quaternary deposits, Searles Lake, California; a summary. U.S. Geological Survey, Professional Paper 450-C: 65-69.

Smith, H. T. U.
  1938   Tertiary geology of the Abiquiu quadrangle, New Mexico. Journal of Geology 46:933-965.

_____
  1939   Sand dune cycle in western Kansas. Geological Society of America, Bulletin 50:1934-1935.

Smith, K. G.
  1958   Erosional processes and landforms in Badlands National Monument, South Dakota. Geological Society of America, Bulletin 69:975-1008.

Smith, R. E.
  1957   Geology and groundwater resources of Torrance County, New Mexico. New Mexico Bureau of Mines and Mineral Resources, Groundwater Report 5.

Snyder, C. T.
  1962   A hydrologic classification of valleys in the Great Basin, western United States. International Association of Scientific Hydrology, Bulletin 7(3): 53-59.

Snyder, C. T. and W. B. Langbein
  1962   The Pleistocene lake in Spring Valley, Nevada, and its climatic implications. Journal of Geophysical Research 67:2385-2394.

Spurr, J. E.
  1901   Origin and structure of the basin ranges. Geological Society of America, Bulletin 12:218-270.

_____
  1903   Descriptive geology of Nevada south of the 40th parallel and adjacent portions of California. U. S. Geological Survey, Bulletin 208.

Stanley, G. M.
  1949   Elevations of some Lake Lahontan shorelines. Geological Society of America, Bulletin 60:1945. (Abstr.)

Stanley, J. W.
  1951   Retrogression on the lower Colorado River after 1935. American Society of Civil Engineers, Transactions 116:943-957.

Stewarts, S. W.
  1958   Gravity survey of Ogden Valley in the Wasatch Mountains, north central Utah. American Geophysical Union, Transaction 39:1151-1157.

Stoerts, G. E.
  1957   Techniques for determination of terrain analogs. U. S. Army Engineer Waterways Experiment Station, Vicksburg, Mississippi.

Stokes, W. L.
  1964   Incised, wind-aligned stream patterns of the Colorado Plateau. American Journal of Science 262: 808-816.

Stokes, W. L. and D. E. Arnold
  1958   Northern Stansbury Range and the Stansbury formation. Utah Geological Society, Guidebook to the Geology of Utah 13:135-149.

Stone, R. O.
  1956   A geological investigation of playa lakes. University of Southern California (unpublished dissertation).

Strahler, A. N.
  1956   The nature of induced erosion and aggradation: p. 621-638. *In* W. L. Thomas, Jr., ed., Man's role in changing the face of the earth. University of Chicago Press, Chicago.

Sumner, J. S.
  1965   The gravity program in Arizona. American Geophysical Union, Transactions 46:560-563.

Sundborg, A.
  1956   The River Klarälven; a study of fluvial processes. Geografiska Annaler 38:125-316.

  _____
  1964   The importance of the sediment problem in the technical and economic development of river basins. Annales Academiae Regiae Scientiarum Upsaliensis, K. Vetenskapssamhällets i Uppsala, Arsbok 8:33-52.

Swan, L. W.
  1962   Eolian zone. Science 140:77-79.

Swineford, A. and J. C. Frye
  1951   Petrography of the Peoria loess in Kansas. Journal of Geology 59:306-322.

Sykes, G.
  1937   The Colorado Delta. American Geographical Society, Special Publication 19.

Tarr, R. S.
  1890   Erosive agents in the arid regions. American Naturalist 24:455-459.

Tator, B. A.
  1952   Pediment characteristics and terminology. Part I: Pediment characteristics. Association of American Geographers, Annals 42:295-317.

  _____
  1953   Pediment characteristics and terminology: Part II: Terminology. Association of American Geographers, Annals 43:47-53.

Taylor, G.
  1937   Comparison of the American and Australian deserts. Economic Geography 13:260-268.

Texas Instruments, Dallas
  1964   Final report, terrain analysis Gamma, Project WESTAG. U. S. Army Engineer Waterways Experiment Station, Contract Report.

Thomas, H. E. *et al.*
  1963- Drought in the Southwest. U. S. Geological Survey,
  1964   Professional Paper 372, Chapters A-H.

Thompson, D. G.
  1921   Pleistocene lakes along the Mohave River, California. Washington Academy of Science, Journal 11:423-424. (Abstr.)

  _____
  1929   The Mohave Desert region, California. U. S. Geological Survey, Water-Supply Paper 578.

Thompson, G. A.
  1952   Basin and range structure south of Reno, Nevada. Geological Society of America, Bulletin 63: 1303-1304.

Thornbury, W. D.
  1965   Regional geomorphology of the United States. John Wiley and Sons, New York.

Thornthwaite, C. W., C. F. S. Sharpe, and E. F. Dosch
  1942   Climate and accelerated erosion in the arid and semi-arid southwest with special reference to the Polacca Wash drainage basin, Arizona. U. S. Department of Agriculture, Technical Bulletin 808. 134 p.

Thorp, J. and H. T. U. Smith
  1952   Pleistocene eolian deposits of the United States, Alaska, and parts of Canada. National Research Council, Washington, D. C.

Tolman, C. F.
  1909   Erosion and deposition in the southern Arizona bolson region. Journal of Geology 17:136-163.

Trowbridge, A. C.
  1911   The terrestrial deposits of Owens Valley, California. Journal of Geology 19:706-747.

Troxell, H. C. and W. Hofmann
  1954*a* Hydrology of the Los Angeles region. California Division of Mines, Bulletin 170, Chapter 6, p. 5-12.

  _____
  1954*b* Hydrology of the Mohave Desert. California Division of Mines, Bulletin 170, Chapter 6, p. 13-18.

Truesdell, A. H., B. F. Jones, and A. S. Van Denburgh
  1965   Glass electrode determination of sodium in closed basin waters. Geochimica et Cosmochimica Acta 29:725-736.

Tuan, Y.-F.
  1959   Pediments in southeastern Arizona. University of California, Publications in Geography 13:1-163.

  _____
  1962   Structure, climate, and basin landforms in Arizona and New Mexico. Association of American Geographers, Annals 52:51-68.

Turner, H. W.
  1909   Contribution to the geology of the Silver Peak quadrangle, Nevada. Geological Society of America, Bulletin 20:223-264.

Udden, J. A.
  1894   Erosion, transportation, and sedimentation performed by the atmosphere. Journal of Geology 2:318-331.

U. S. Army, Research and Development Division, Environmental Protection Branch, Natick, Mass.
  1953   Handbook of Yuma environment. Research Report 200.

U. S. Army Engineer Waterways Experiment Station
  1963   Analogs of Yuma terrain in the southwest United States desert. Technical Report 3-630, Report number 5. 2 vols.

University of Southern California
1959   An annotated bibliography for the desert areas of the United States. Prepared under contract for the U. S. Army Engineer Waterways Experiment Station. Vicksburg, Mississippi. 387 p.

Van Horn, W. L.
1957   Late Cenozoic beds in the upper Safford Valley, Graham County, Arizona. University of Arizona (unpublished M.S. thesis).

———
1962   Late Cenozoic alluvial deposits of the upper Safford Valley, Graham County, Arizona. Arizona Geological Society, Digest 5:89-96.

Van Lopik, J. R. and C. R. Kolb
1959   A technique for preparing desert terrain analogs. U. S. Army, Corps of Engineers, Technical Report 3-506.

Ver Planck, W. E.
1958   Salt in California. California Division of Mines, Bulletin 175. 168 p.

Voelger, K.
1953   Cenozoic deposits in the southern foothills of the Santa Catalina Mountains near Tucson, Arizona. University of Arizona (unpublished M.S. thesis).

Von Engeln, O. D.
1932   The Ubehebe craters and explosion breccias in Death Valley, California. Journal of Geology 40: 726-734.

Waibel, L.
1928   Die Inselberglandschaft von Arizona und Sonora. Gesellschaft für Erdkunde zu Berlin, Festschrift, Sonderbund zur Hundertijahrferer, p. 68-91.
    (The inselberg landscape of Arizona and Sonora.)

Wallis, J. R.
1964   A comparison of some of the multivariate statistical methods of hydrology using data of known functional relationship. American Geophysical Union, Transactions 45:612. (Abstr.)

Walther, J.
1892   Die nordamerikanischen wüste. Gesellschaft für Erdkunde zu Berlin, Verhandlungen 1:1-14.
    (The North American deserts.)

Warnke, D. A. and R. O. Stone
1965   Determinants of pediment evolution in the central Mohave Desert, California. Geological Society of America, Annual Meeting, Program, p. 179. (Abstr.)

Watson, R. A. and H. E. Wright, Jr.
1963   Landslides on the east side of the Chuska Mountains, Arizona-New Mexico. American Journal of Science 261:525-548.

Wegemann, C. H.
1939   Great sand dunes of Colorado. Mines Magazine 29:445-448, 592.

Wertz, J. B.
1962   Mechanism of erosion and deposition along channelways. University of Arizona (unpublished dissertation).

———
1964   Les phénomènes d'érosion et de depôt dans les vallées habituellement seches du Sud-Ouest des Etats-Unis. Zeitschrift für Geomorphologie 8: 71-104.

(The processes of erosion and deposition in ephemeral valleys of the southwestern United States.)

Westgate, L. G. and A. Knopf
1932   Geology and ore deposits of the Pioche district, Nevada. U. S. Geological Survey, Professional Paper 171.

White, C. H.
1924   Desert varnish. American Journal of Science 7: 413-420.

Willden, R. and D. R. Mahey
1961   Giant desiccation features on the Black Rock and Smoke Creek deserts, Nevada. Science 133: 1359-1360.

Williams, H.
1936   Pliocene volcanoes of the Navajo-Hopi country. Geological Society of America, Bulletin 47: 111-172.

Williams, J. S.
1962   Lake Bonneville; geology of southern Cache Valley, Utah. U. S. Geological Survey, Professional Paper 257-C.

Wilson, E. D.
1933   Geology and mineral deposits of southern Yuma County, Arizona. Arizona Bureau of Mines, Bulletin 134.

Wilson, E. D. and R. T. Moore
1959   Structure of the basin and range province in Arizona. Arizona Geological Society, Southern Arizona Guidebook 2:89-105.

Wires, H. O.
1961   Development of an ultrasonic method for measuring stream velocities. U. S. Geological Survey, Professional Paper 424-B:58-60.

Wolman, M. G. and L. M. Brush, Jr.
1961   Factors controlling the size and shape of stream channels in coarse noncohesive sands. U. S. Geological Survey, Professional Paper 282-G.

Wolman, M. G. and L. B. Leopold
1957   River flood plains; some observations on their formation. U. S. Geological Survey, Professional Paper 282-C.

Woodford, A. O. and T. F. Harriss
1928   Geology of Blackhawk Canyon, San Bernardino Mountains, California. University of California, Department of Geological Sciences, Bulletin 17: 265-304.

Wright, H. E., Jr.
1946   Tertiary and Quaternary geology of the lower Rio Puerco area, New Mexico. Geological Society of America, Bulletin 57:383-456.

———
1964   Origin of the lakes in the Chuska Mountains, northwestern New Mexico. Geological Society of America, Bulletin 75:589-598.

———
1965   Origin of the lakes in the Chuska Mountains, northwestern New Mexico; reply. Geological Society of America, Bulletin 76:269-270.

Wright, L. A. and B. W. Troxell
1954   Western Mohave Desert and Death Valley region; Geologic Guide 1: California Division of Mines, Bulletin 170.

SECTION XV

NORTH AMERICAN DESERTS: MEXICO

Includes works cited in the text discussion of the desert areas of Mexico.

Aguilar y Santillán, R.
1898   Bibliografía geológica y minera de la República Mexicana. Oficina Tipográfica de la Secretaría de Fomento, México. 148 p.
(Bibliography of geology and mines of the Republic of Mexico.)

Anderson, C. A.
1950   E. W. Scripps 1940 cruise to the Gulf of California. Part 1: Geology of islands and neighboring land areas. Geological Society of America, Memoir 43.

Arnold, B. A.
1957   Late Pleistocene and Recent changes in land forms, climate and archaeology in Central Baja California. University of California, Publications in Geography 10:201-318.

Beal, C. H.
1948   Reconnaissance of the geology and oil possibilities of Baja California, Mexico. Geological Society of America, Memoir 31.

Blásquez L., L.
1956   Bosquejo fisiográfico y vulcanológico del occidente de México. Congreso Geológico Internacional, 20th, México. Excursión A-15: 9-17.
(Outline of the physiography and volcanology of western Mexico.)

Bonillas, Y. S. and F. Urbina
1913   Informe acerca de los recursos naturales de la parte norte de la Baja California, especialmente del Delta de Río Colorado. Instituto de Geología de México, Parergones 4:162-235.
(Report on the natural resources of northern Baja California, particularly the Colorado River Delta.)

Brand, D. D.
1937   The natural landscape of northwestern Chihuahua, Mexico. University of New Mexico Bulletin, Geological Series 5(2). 74 p.

Darton, N. H.
1921   Geological reconnaissance in Baja California. Journal of Geology 29:720-748.

Dios Bojorquez, J. de
1946   Descripción de Sonora. Sociedad Mexicana de Geografía y Estadística, Boletín 61:11-35.

Durham, J. W. and E. C. Allison
1960   Symposium: The biogeography of Baja California and adjacent seas. Part I: Geologic history. Systematic Zoology 9:47-91.

Edwards, J. D.
1955   Studies of some Early Tertiary red conglomerates of central Mexico. U. S. Geological Survey, Professional Paper 264-H.

Engerrand, J. and T. Paredes
1913   Informe relativo a la parte occidental de la región norte de la Baja California. Instituto de Geología de México, Parergones 4:278-306.
(Report on the western part of northern Baja California.)

Fournier d'Albe, E. M.
1960   Arid zone research in Mexico. Arid Zone [Newsletter] 8:11-16.

Galindo y Villa, J.
1926-   Geografía de la República Mexicana. 2 vols. Socie-
1927   dad de Edición y Librería Franco Americana, México.
(Geography of the Republic of Mexico.)

Gálvez, V.
1927   Algunas exploraciones en el distrito sur de la península de Baja California. Instituto de Geología de México, Anales 2:217-275.
(Some explorations in the southern district of the Baja California peninsula.)

Gálvez, V. *et al.*
1941   Estudios hidrogeológicos practicados en el estado de San Luis Potosí. Instituto de Geología de México, Anales 7.
(Practical hydrogeological studies in the state of San Luis Potosí.)

Gianella, V. P.
1960   Faulting in noreastern Sonora, Mexico, in 1887. Geological Society of America, Bulletin 71:2061.
(Abstr.)

Gonzáles Reyna, J.
1956   Aspectos fisiográficos de México. *In* Riqueza Minera y Yacimientos Minerales de México. Congreso Geológico Internacional, 20th, México, p. 19-29.
(Physiographic aspects of Mexico.)

Hamilton, W.
1961   Origin of the Gulf of California. Geological Society of America, Bulletin 72:1307-1318.

Hammond, E. H.
1954   A geomorphic study of the Cape Region of Baja California. University of California, Publications in Geography 10:45-112.

Heim, A.
1921   Vulkane in der umgebung der oase La Purísima auf der halbinsel Niederkalifornien. Zeitschrift für Vulkanologie 6:15-21.
(Volcanoes in the area of the La Purisima oasis on the Baja California Peninsula.)

1922   Notes on the Tertiary of southern Lower California. Geological Magazine 59:529-547.

Hill, R. T.
1908   Growth and decay of the Mexican plateau. Engineering and Mining Journal 85:681-686.

Humphrey, W. E.
1949   Geology of the Sierra de los Muertos area, Mexico. Geological Society of America, Bulletin 60:89-176.

Imlay, R. W.
1936   Evolution of the Coahuila Peninsula, Mexico. Part IV: Geology of the western part of the Sierra de Parras. Geological Society of America, Bulletin 47:1091-1152.

Instituto Mexicano de Recursos Naturales Renovables
1955   Problems de las zonas áridas de México. Biblioteca Central de la Ciudad Universitaria. 262 p.
This review of arid-zone problems in Mexico provides a good outline of the arid areas in terms of an evapotranspiration map and basic data on water resources.

Ives, R. L.
1936   Desert floods in the Sonoyta Valley (Sonora, Mexico). American Journal of Science 232:349-360.

————
1956   Age of Cerro Colorado crater, Pinacate, Sonora, Mexico. American Geophysical Union, Transactions 37:221-223.

Jahns, R. H.
1954   Geology of the Peninsular Range province, southern California and Baja California. California Division of Mines, Bulletin 170, Chapter 2, p. 29-52.

Kellum, L. B.
1936   Evolution of the Coahuila Peninsula, Mexico. Part III: Geology of the mountains west of the Laguna district. Geological Society of America, Bulletin 47:1039-1090.

————
1944   Geological history of northern Mexico and its bearing on petroleum exploration. American Association of Petroleum Geologists, Bulletin 28: 301-325.

Kellum, L. B., R. W. Imlay, and W. G. Kane
1936   Evolution of the Coahuila Peninsula, Mexico. Part I: Relation of structure, stratigraphy, and igneous activity to an early continental margin. Geological Society of America, Bulletin 47.935-1009.

Kellum, L. B. *et al.*
1937   The geology and biology of the San Carlos Mountains, Tamaulipas, Mexico. University of Michigan Studies, Scientific Series 12.

Kelly, W. A.
1936   Evolution of the Coahuila Peninsula, Mexico. Part II: Geology of the mountains bordering the valleys of Acatita and Las Delicias. Geological Society of America, Bulletin 47:1024-1038.

Keyes, C. R.
1908   Eolian origin of certain lake basins of the Mexican tableland. Iowa Academy of Science, Proceedings 15:137-141.

King, P. B.
1947   Carta geológica de la parte septentrional de la República Mexicana. Cartas Geológicas y Mineras de la República Mexicana, no. 3. 24 p.
        (Geologic map of the northern part of the Republic of Mexico.)
This map and report on the northern part of Mexico provides an index to previous geological mapping in the country, a useful bibliography, and information on mapping agencies.

King, R. E.
1934   The Permian of southwestern Coahuila, Mexico. American Journal of Science 27:98-112.

————
1935   Geological reconnaissance of central Sonora. American Journal of Science 28:81-101.

————
1939   Geological reconnaissance in northern Sierra Madre Occidental of Mexico. Geological Society of America, Bulletin 50:1625-1722.

King, R. E. and W. S. Adkins
1946   Geology of a part of the lower Conchos Valley, Chihuahua, Mexico. Geological Society of America, Bulletin 57:275-294.

Krause, D. C.
1965   Tectonics, bathymetry, and geomagnetism of the southern continental borderland west of Baja California, Mexico. Geological Society of America, Bulletin 76:617-650.

López, R. M.
1947   Carta geológica de la parte septentrional de la República Mexicana. Universidad Nacional Autónoma de México, Instituto de Geología, Geofísica, y Geodesia no. 3.
        (Geologic map of the northern part of the Republic of Mexico.)

López de Llergo, R.
1963   The importance of the phenomenon of capture in changes in the character of hydrological basins and in the growth of deserts and semi-desert areas. *In* Proceedings of the Ankara symposium on arid zone hydrology. Unesco, Paris. Arid Zone Programme 2:151-157.

Lowdermilk, W. C.
1947   Erosional phenomena associated with volcanic eruption of Paricutín, Mexico. American Geophysical Union, Transactions 28:269-270.

Merriam, R.
1965   San Jacinto fault in northwestern Sonora, Mexico. Geological Society of America, Bulletin 76: 1051-1054.

Mina, U. F.
1956   Bosquejo geológico de la parte sur de la península de Baja California. International Geological Congress, 20th, Mexico, Excursion A-7:1-79.
        (Geologic sketch of the southern part of the peninsula of Baja California)

————
1957   Bosquejo geológico del Territorio de la Baja California. Asociación Mexicana Geológica y Petroleo, Boletín 9:141-269.
        (Geologic sketch of the Territory of Baja California.)

Ordóñez, E.
1936   Principal physiographic provinces of Mexico. American Association of Petroleum Geologists, Bulletin 20:1277-1307.

Organization of American States
1966   Annotated index of aerial photographic coverage and mapping of topography and natural resources: Argentina; Brazil; Mexico. Pan American Union, Washington.
An excellent index that summarizes all available information on mapping and aerial photographic coverage of Mexico.

Pfeifer, G.
1939   Sinaloa und Sonora. Geographische Gesellschaft in Hamburg, Mitteilungen 41.

Phleger, F. B. and G. C. Ewing
1962   Sedimentology and oceanography of coastal lagoons in Baja California. Geological Society of America, Bulletin 73:145-182.

Porter, W. W.
1932   The Coahuila piedmont, a physiographic province in northeastern Mexico. Journal of Geology 40: 338-352.

Sanders, E. M.
1921 The natural regions of Mexico. Geographical Review 11:212-226.

Shreve, F.
1935 Sandy areas of North American deserts. Association of Pacific Coast Geographers, Yearbook 4: 11-14.

Shrock, R. R.
1945 Sedimentation and wind action around Volcán Paricutín, Mexico. Indiana Academy of Sciences, Proceedings 55:120.

Singewald, Q. D.
1936 Evolution of the Coahuila Peninsula, Mexico. Part V: Igneous phenomena and geologic structures near Mapimí. Geological Society of America, Bulletin 47:1153-1176.

Staub, W.
1923 Beiträge zur landeskunde des nördlichen Mexiko. Gesellschaft für Erdkunde zu Berlin, Zeitschrift 64.
(Contributions to the geography of northern Mexico.)

Stoertz, G. E.
1965 Studies in applied geomorphology, Mexico. U. S. Geological Survey, Branch Military Geology, for Air Force Cambridge Research Laboratories, Terrestrial Sciences Laboratory. 239 p. (unpublished M.S.)

Tamayo, J. L.
1940 Datos para la geografía de la Baja California, particularmente del Distrito Sur. Revista Mexicana de Geografía 1:117-140.
(Data on the geography of Baja California, particularly the southern part.)

Thayer, W. N.
1916 The physiography of Mexico. Journal of Geology 24:61-94.

U. S. Army Engineer Waterways Experiment Station
1959 Analogs of Yuma terrain in the Mexican desert. Technical Report 3-630, Report 3.
The most comprehensive assemblage of information on the surficial features of the Mexican desert areas that is available.

University of Southern California
1958 An annotated bibliography for the Mexican desert. Prepared under contract for the U. S. Army Engineer Waterways Experiment Station, Vicksburg, Mississippi.
One of the most useful available bibliographies of geologic and geographic reports treating the Mexican desert areas.

Vivó, J. A.
1958 Geografía de México. 4th ed. Fondo de Cultura Ecónomica. 349 p.
A standard geographic treatment of the country including a useful outline of the surficial features.

Wallén, C. C.
1956 Fluctuations and variability in Mexican rainfall. *In* G. F. White, ed., The future of arid lands. American Association for the Advancement of Science, Publication 43:141-155.

Williams, H.
1950 Volcanoes of the Paricutín region. U. S. Geological Survey, Bulletin 965-B.

Wilson, I. F.
1948 Buried topography, initial structures, and sedimentation in Santa Rosalia area, Baja California, Mexico. American Association of Petroleum Geologists, Bulletin 32:1762-1807.

Wilson, I. F. and V. S. Rocha
1955 Geology and mineral deposits of the Boleo copper district, Baja California, Mexico. U. S. Geological Survey, Professional Paper 273.

Wisser, E.
1954 Geology and ore deposits of Baja California, Mexico. Economic Geology 49:44-76.

Woodford, A. O.
1928 The San Quintín volcanic field, Lower California. American Journal of Science 15.

Woodford, A. O. and T. F. Harriss
1938 Geological reconnaissance across Sierra San Pedro Mártir, Baja California. Geological Society of America, Bulletin 49:1297-1336.

SURFACE MATERIALS
OF DESERT ENVIRONMENTS

HAROLD E. DREGNE
Department of Agronomy
New Mexico State University

INTRODUCTION

"Surface material," as the term is used in this chapter, refers to the organic and inorganic portion of the Earth's crust that lies within about five feet of the surface. It is not always synonymous with "soil" because some surface materials may not be altered significantly from what they were when originally deposited or exposed. Soil is a physically, chemically, and biologically weathered product of the total environment, including time.

Despite those instances when the terms "soil" and "surface material" would not be considered synonymous, they are used interchangeably in this chapter. Lithosols and regosols, the former typified by broken rocks overlying bedrock within a few inches of the surface and the latter by sand dunes, constitute the prime instances where disagreement on terminology might arise. While recognizing that legitimate reasons may be given for separating some soils from some surface materials, the distinction in terminology is not made here. This chapter, then, attempts to review, appraise, and recommend research on the solid phase of the outer portion of the Earth's crust, and the objective is to treat material relevant to the arid zone.

No attempt has been made to define the arid zone. The criteria described in the introductory chapter of this compendium have been followed in deciding upon the area coverage to be made for soils. It should be noted that Meigs' extremely arid zones are the center of attention, but considerable reference is made to the semiarid zone because there is no sharp line separating the semiarid from the arid. As will become apparent to the reader, the semiarid zone has been studied by investigators far more intensively than the arid zone. It sometimes is necessary, then, to attempt to extrapolate from the dry fringe—the semiarid zone—to the truly arid zone in order to develop concepts of the latter zone in some parts of the world. Cold arid zones are not included in this review.

One potential source of confusion for the reader is the difference between the extent of the desert to which reference is made in the text and the reader's concept of the areal extent of that desert. The Arabian and Iranian deserts are good examples of the problem. The areal extent of both deserts, as covered in this chapter, is that shown on the map in the introductory chapter. Readers who have not consulted that map may believe, as some reviewers of this chapter did, that the two deserts include only the arid zone of the Arabian Peninsula and of Iran. This is not the case. Also, it is well to remember that not everyone refers to parts of the various deserts in the way it has been done here. Few, if any, Pakistanis would consider that southwestern West Pakistan lies in the "Iranian" Desert, even though the compendium map so indicates.

In citing references, only a few of those that have been reviewed have been chosen for citation. The selection does not mean that those references necessarily are superior in quality of research to uncited ones; rather, the choice was made on the basis of comprehensiveness of the work, apparent relevance to broad areas, clarity of presentation of data and results, and geographic representation. No references have been cited that have been judged to be unreliable, except in those rare instances where the cited work is the only one pertaining to the subject discussed. In those cases, that fact is noted. Several works in the Pertinent Publications list of particular significance or interest to this study are annotated.

Two quite different methods of approach have been used in the preparation of this chapter. Section II, describing the soils of the individual deserts and citing soil-survey publications, represents a synthesis of information culled from a variety of sources, many of them accounts of travels made by persons who were not soil specialists. The synthesis approach was necessitated by the meager amount of research data published for some deserts or for part of the desert. Gautier's book *Le Sahara*, for example, is an account by an informed geographer of his travels into the arid and extremely arid part of the Sahara. While it does not contain technical descriptions of surface materials, it does describe several important landforms and their genesis and contains informative pictures. Coupled with technical discussions by other authors, the book helps to bring the distribution and kind of surface materials in the Sahara into clearer focus. Sections IV - VII are reviews of research in the more conventional sense of citing and interpreting the more useful and reliable scientific papers, and these sections cover fields of research rather than research done in specific deserts. Work reviewed in these sections is judged more likely to have general arid-zone validity. For specific arid areas, information more detailed than could be presented in this chapter may be obtained by contacting the authorities listed in Section III, Authorities and Depositories.

Research on the soils of the arid zones began to be important in the early part of the 20th century when interest in the potential of the soils for irrigation agriculture developed in the Soviet Union, the United States, the Nile Valley, and the Indus Valley. In later years, a similar interest was generated in Africa and Australia, as well as in southwest Asia. Today, with the increased demand for producing food and for developing sparsely settled arid zones, every nation having such zones within its borders has evinced interest in inventorying its soil resource in those zones. While the agriculturally important characteristics have been emphasized, some research has been done on the engineering properties. Both are reviewed in this chapter.

Early soil research was directed toward *(1)* describing the physical characteristics of soils, *(2)* indicating their depth over rock strata, and *(3)* making total analyses of soil particles. As science in general developed, techniques were devised to make meaningful studies of such things as processes of soil development, measurement of physical, chemical, and biological properties, and the relationship of these properties to plant growth and engineering uses. Present-day emphasis in soil research is on water relations and chemical properties, among agricultural soil scientists, and on mechanical properties and water relations, among soil engineers. Soil biology has been and remains an orphan seeking recognition as a significant field of research.

Two other chapters of this compendium contain information that will be of special interest to readers of this chapter. They are the chapter on weather and climate, by C. H. Reitan and C. R. Green, and the chapter on geomorphology and surface hydrology, by L. K. Lustig.

Listed below are some terms used in various parts of the world that appear in reports dealing with surface materials. Although some of these terms have the same or similar meanings, they frequently are not defined when used in reports, and they are therefore presented here by way of introduction to the works and the discussion in this chapter.

Type of Surface	*Terms*
Extensive plains of fine-textured material, with or without sand dunes	1) clay desert 2) clay plain
Extensive sand dunes, usually 30 or more feet high, with few nonsandy interdune areas	1) dune field 2) erg 3) sand sea
Extensive saline depressions, usually fine-textured	1) salt flat 2) salina 3) sebkha 4) chott 5) kavir
Fine-textured depressions, large or small, usually moderately saline	1) playa 2) takyr 3) pan 4) clay flats
Stony or gravelly surfaces *Note:* the first 5 terms may or may not apply to plain surfaces; the others are plain surfaces.	1) desert pavement 2) stone pavement 3) gibber 4) billy gibber 5) grey billy 6) stony tableland 7) stony plain 8) reg 9) serir (sarir) 10) hamada 11) gobi
Steep-sided watercourses in arid zones	1) arroyo 2) wadi 3) nullah 4) quebrado

ACKNOWLEDGMENTS

It is a distinct pleasure to acknowledge gratefully the invaluable assistance rendered by several colleagues in the preparation of this manuscript. A. C. Orvedal of the U. S. Soil Conservation Service; G. V. Jacks of the Commonwealth Bureau of Soils; M. Batisse of the Natural Resources Division of Unesco; G. Aubert of the Office de la Recherche Scientifique et Technique Outre-Mer; R. E. Carlyle, M. L. Dewan, and Luis Bramao of the Food and Agriculture Organization; and P. Buringh of the Agricultural University of Wageningen graciously made available published and unpublished information in the files of their organizations.

Portions of the manuscript were reviewed by R. Dudal of the Food and Agriculture Organization, C. R. van der Merwe of the South African Soil Institute, and A. J. Prego and P. H. Etchevehere of the Instituto de Suelos y Agrotecnia in Argentina. Their comments did much to improve the manuscript.

Special thanks are due G. Aubert of the Office de la Recherche Scientifique et Technique Outre-Mer for painstakingly reviewing the entire manuscript and making numerous helpful suggestions for improving it.

Finally, deep appreciation is extended to B. J. Goldman and Patricia Paylore of the Office of Arid Lands Studies for their generous and patient assistance during the entire project and to my wife for her invaluable help in organizing and handling many phases of the project.

DISCUSSION OF STATE OF KNOWLEDGE:
PRINCIPAL SOILS AND SOIL SURVEYS

A. KALAHARI - NAMIB

Information on the soils of the Kalahari- Namib Desert area and adjoining territories is very scarce for the South West Africa and Botswana portions. Generalized soil maps have been prepared for the fringe areas of the desert in South Africa, Rhodesia, and Angola. A few localized studies have been made of the flora and fauna, and some soils information has been gleaned from them as well as from geographers' comments.

1. Principal Soils Synthesis

In South West Africa, Ganssen (1960) made a study from which he concluded that desert soils occur in the west and south of the country, semidesert soils in the south and middle (at the higher elevations), and dry forest soils in the north. This distribution follows the rainfall pattern, which increases from southwest to northeast. The Namib Desert (Koch, 1962; Giess, 1962) is said to have three types of surficial materials: littoral sands in a narrow strip along the coast where ephemeral streams empty into the ocean, barchan dune fields (ergs) south of the Kuiseb River, and stony and gravelly plains (regs) north of the Kuiseb River on the Namib flats. Inland from the Namib Desert along the coast is a series of generally barren mountains of lithosols with scattered inclusions of weakly developed semidesert brown soils where moisture conditions favor some chemical weathering. East of the mountains is the vast plain, the Kalahari Desert, consisting dominantly of coarse textured materials, with calcrete exposed or covered by a fairly thin layer of sand on the desert outskirts in the west, south, and southwest. *The Soil Map of Africa* (Hoore, 1964) places the Kalahari in two broad soil groups. In most of the desert, the soils are classed as brown to reddish brown on sandy materials. The other group, in the north, is ferruginous tropical soils on sandy parent materials, reflecting the greater precipitation that occurs there. Soil development in the Kalahari, where siliceous layers occur in some of the soils (Debenham, 1952), seems to be similar to that of arid Australia (Ganssen and Moll, 1961), where the soils have developed on geologically old

materials. Indurated calcareous (calcrete) and siliceous (silcrete) layers appear to be widespread (van der Merwe, 1941; Debenham, 1952). Calcrete is found at or near the surface whereas silcrete is deeper in the soil profile. Debenham says that farmers in the Kalahari place their wells on the top of low hills because water can be found beneath the indurated but porous calcrete.

One of the distinctive features of the Kalahari, according to both Debenham and Ganssen, is the presence of "pans" (playas). Pan soils are deep, fine-textured alluvium that is nonsaline and high in organic matter in the wetter north, but is saline in the south, with much less organic matter. Some of the pans are many miles in diameter.

In the Kalahari Desert, deep sands, on a plain topography seamed with low ridges and grass-covered fossil dunes, occupy much of the upland areas. Clays are found in the level depressions (Ganssen, 1960). Much wind erosion occurs, as a result of overgrazing that has denuded the landscape (Debenham, 1952). The Namib Desert is bare of vegetation, with the major exception of the wide flood plain of the Kuiseb River; extensive wind erosion is restricted to the sand dunes in the south. The surface gravel in the north of the coastal plains serves to protect the underlying finer material from removal by wind. Erosion of watercourses occurs readily after the infrequent rains.

In the northwestern Cape Province of South Africa, a characteristic feature of the arid-zone soils is desert pavement consisting of rock materials ranging from white quartz fragments to almost black waterworn pebbles and stones (van der Merwe, 1954a). The same author notes that some of the soils in the semiarid region of the eastern Cape Province have also a calcareous crust, while others in the central regions are saline.

The surficial material known as "Kalahari sand," which is extensive in the Kalahari Desert, is believed to be of eolian origin, laid down during an arid period of Miocene or earlier time (van der Merwe, 1954b). It is not restricted to the desert but also occurs in Rhodesia, Zambia, and the Congo, where rainfall amounts to as much as 60 inches. Sand pH changes from slightly alkaline in the arid south to moderately acid in the wetter north, and more fine-textured particles are found in sands of the drier region, presumably because there is less clay cementation with iron oxides.

In the Kalahari-Namib Desert area, soils are weakly developed if at all. Except for the mountains inland from the Namib coast, and the calcrete tract to the east thereof, the entire region is a plain, broken by shifting sand dunes extensive in the southern part of the Namib Desert and scattered, but fossilized throughout the Kalahari Desert. Soils are slightly alkaline to slightly acid, generally. Colors range from white to red, with reddish brown dominant. Deep soils are the rule but calcrete is present at shallow depths, generally, on the outskirts of the Kalahari sands, particularly in the west, south, and southeast. Saline soils are found in depressions in the south. Organic matter in upland areas ranges from about 0.5 per cent in the south to somewhat more in the north, with much higher levels in the northern swamplands. Dominant soil textures are sand, sandy loam, gravelly sandy loam, and clay or clay loam (Ganssen, 1960; Hoore, 1964).

2. Soil Surveys

Only three published soil maps are known for the Kalahari-Namib Desert area (Botelho da Costa and Azevedo, 1960; Hoore, 1964; van der Merwe, 1941), and none of them is more than a rough approximation. All are small-scale maps. They are fair to good for showing general soil conditions but are inadequate for providing information on soils of any specific area.

B. SAHARA

Soil studies in the Sahara have been restricted largely to the semiarid peripheral areas or to irrigated oases such as the Nile Valley in the Sudan and Egypt. Major contributions to the better understanding of soil conditions in the extreme arid part of the Sahara have been made by scientists from Algeria and Egypt, in particular.

1. Principal Soils Synthesis

Several small-scale maps of Africa have been prepared, the most recent and best being that of Hoore (1964). The latter map, with accompanying text, was the result of a cooperative effort under the auspices of the Commission for Technical Cooperation in Africa. The mapping legend for the identified soil units is a combination of French and Belgian soil survey terminology, in the main.

Sahara soils, according to Hoore, consist of rock debris, desert detritus, and weakly developed soil. In the extremely arid parts of the Sahara, it probably is more proper to refer to surficial deposits than to soils, because the surface rocks and sediments have been little altered by the soil-forming factors of vegetation and climate. In fact, Hoore cites a surface-material map by Dutil as his primary source of information on the soils of the arid Sahara (Dutil, 1962). Map reliability is variable: fairly good in Algeria, Morocco, Tunisia, and on the southern semiarid fringe of the Sahara, but only approximate in much of the vast strip, about 800 miles wide and 2,500 miles long, that represents the extremely arid part of the Sahara.

Rock debris includes exposed rocks (principally igneous) and calcareous crusts. Exposed rocks occur throughout the mountains, such as the Ahaggar and Tibesti, of the central Sahara and western Libya. Calcareous crusts (compact or indurated layers) of calcium carbonate and calcium sulfate are secondary formations, with the hardened layers occurring at or near the surface. They are found extensively in northern Africa; the carbonate crusts in the semiarid areas and the gypsiferous (calcium sulfate) crusts in the more arid areas. A detailed study of Algerian crusts, in this case referring to crusts found at the surface or in the subsoil, was made by Durand (1959), who classified them into types and described their use in agriculture and for building materials. Durand recognized calcareous, gypsiferous, and saline crusts. Most of the known calcareous crusts occurring in Morocco, northern Algeria, and Tunisa are paleoclimatic remains. Siliceous crusts have been described only from the semiarid southern part of the Sahara.

Desert detritus, the second of the extensive groups of surface materials in the arid Sahara, is comprised of sands, stony deserts and clay plains. The geomorphic surface known as erg consists of extensive areas of high, connected sand dunes. The soil that occurs on erg surfaces is referred to as desert ablation soil in recognition of the mode of deposition of the parent material. Ergs are widespread in southern Algeria and Tunisia, northern Mali, Mauritania, and the Libyan Desert. They consist of loose, coarse-textured materials, bare of vegetation, without profile development; they are easily erodible by wind.

Stony deserts have gravel and rock fragments on the surface; when they occupy plain surfaces, they are called regs in northwest Africa and serirs in northeast Africa. They are similar to the gobi of China and the stony plains of Australia. Reg surfaces are of two types: residual and transported (Dutil, 1962). Residual regs are dissected plateaus and plains having stony surfaces which result when the finer material formed by weathering is blown or washed away. Frequently, in the southern Sahara, the stones of residual regs are due to weathering of surface horizons of paleosols formed in a previous, more humid, tropical climate, followed by wind erosion and, probably, some water erosion to remove fine particles. In the Middle East and some parts of north Africa, regs are called hamadas when they occur as plateaus. They are extensive in central and western Sahara and are scattered throughout the eastern Sahara. Transported regs represent gravelly and rocky plain surfaces in which running water is responsible for the presence of the stony material. They occupy alluvial fan and broad floodplain positions, commonly along the flanks of desert mountains and the Atlas Mountains.

Clay plains, probably the result of lacustrine deposits, are extensive in Mauritania, Mali, Niger, Chad and Sudan. They consist of deep, fine-textured materials, weakly developed, on a smooth topography; they are frequently quite saline if the subsoil is impermeable enough (Worrall, 1957). Some are crossed with sand dunes encroaching upon the clay plains from surrounding higher and more coarse-textured lands or that are remnants of a dune landscape that has been partially covered by fine sediments during later inundations (Dieleman and de Ridder, 1964).

Weakly developed soils (semidesert or subdesert soils) occur in the higher mountains and on the periphery of the Sahara (in southern Tunisia and southern Mauritania, for example), where the climate is less arid than in the main body of the Sahara (Hoore, 1964). Coarse textures predominate, and the degree of soil development, as shown by a weak differentiation of soil horizons, is only slightly greater than is found in desert detritus. There usually is a weak accumulation of calcium carbonate or soluble salts somewhere in the profile, generally within 12 inches of the surface and very often on the surface. These soils are transitional between the practically abiotic desert detritus and the well-developed brown or sierozem soils of wetter areas. Oasis soils are a particular type of weakly developed soils, high in organic matter but often saline, that have been strongly affected by human occupation.

Halomorphic (salt-affected) soils are widespread but occupy a small part of the total area of the Sahara, and usually they are confined to depressions, valleys, and coastal regions. The Qattâra Depression is the largest single body of saline soils. Sebkhas (sebkras) and chotts, which are depressions that become flooded after rains, have fine-textured, very saline soils that are bare of vegetation. Customarily, a salt crust forms on the surface; the crust may be broken and eroded away by wind action. In other halomorphic soils, the excess salts in the upper layer result from the upward movement of saline water from a shallow water table.

This is the most common source of the salt under both natural and irrigated conditions.

For the Sahara as a whole, sandy and stony materials are dominant, vegetation cover is very sparse, susceptibility to wind erosion is high, water infiltration rates are good, soils of depressions are saline, water erosion is locally severe near mountainous areas, stony desert plains (regs) and dune chains (ergs) are widespread, compact and indurated layers (crusts) are largely restricted to the northwest section of the desert in association with calcareous bedrock, fine-textured material is rare outside depressions, and soil development is weak. Ergs and regs are neutral to slightly alkaline in pH, soils of the depressions are moderately to strongly alkaline, and grey is the dominant soil color although in some places, mostly in the south, soils have a reddish color.

2. Soil Surveys

Detailed soil surveys of the extremely arid part of the Sahara are few and are confined to small areas west of the Nile Valley in Egypt (Abdel-Samie, 1959, 1961; Anwar, 1959). Soil profile descriptions and mechanical analyses of these soils show that stony deserts and loose sands occupy most of the upland areas, while desert oases are finer textured and frequently saline as the result of irrigation. Soil development is very weak and coarse textures are dominant. These large-scale maps are good sources of soils data because they are based on profile studies and laboratory analyses. A useful but less accurate map is available for a coastal area west of Alexandria (Hume, 1921). Hume's map is a land type map rather than a soil map, showing the distribution of the regs, sand dunes, and coarse-textured wadis of the area.

A good reconnaissance soil map of the New Valley in the western desert of Egypt has been made (Roberts, 1962) for the purpose of determining irrigation potentialities. One small scale map of northwest Egypt shows soil and soil-rock associations and compares the terrain with that of Yuma, Arizona (U.S. Army Engineer Waterways Experiment Station, 1959).

Generalized soil maps of some of the Saharan countries have been made, and they are of use as guides to the development planning for the particular country. Their accuracy is generally a direct function of the map scale but varies depending upon whether the maps are based upon climate, geology, physiography, soil observations, or a blend of all four coupled with personal experience. The ones cited here are of moderate to good reliability, with the inclusion of areas where reliability is poor because of their remoteness from settled populations. These generalized maps include the Sudan (Worrall, 1961), Tunisia (Agafonoff and Yenkovitch, 1935-1936; Roederer, 1959), Morocco (Cavallar, 1950) and the United Arab Republic (Gordonov, 1953; Veenenbos, 1963).

In the arid and semiarid perimeter of the Sahara, several soil surveys have been made, some detailed and some reconnaissance, in Algeria (Durand, 1953*a*, 1954, 1959), Chad (Pias, 1964*a, b;* Pias and Guichard, 1956), Libya (Caswell, 1953; Stewart, 1962), Mauritania (Audry, 1961; Audry and Rossetti, 1962), Niger (Bocquier and Gavaud, 1962; Dabin and Perraud, 1960*a, b;* Office de la Recherche Scientifique et Technique Outre-Mer, 1962), Sudan (Barbour, 1961; Hunting Technical Services, Ltd., 1963; Sudan Geological Survey, 1958-1959), Tunisia (Tunis. Ecole Supérieure d'Agriculture, Laboratoire Agronomique, 1955), and Egypt (United Nations Special Fund, 1961*a*). Most of these maps were made for the purpose of assessing the agricultural development possibilities of the regions studied. Soil properties receiving primary consideration are texture, depth to a root-limiting layer, permeability, salinity, type of parent rock, slope, rockiness, lime, pH, susceptibility to wind erosion, and fertility status. Along with discussions and classifications of soils, the reports usually contain brief descriptions of climate, vegetation, hydrology, topography, geology, and geomorphology of the area. The recently initiated series of publications on soils ("Notices Explicatives") by ORSTOM (Office de la Recherche Scientifique et Technique Outre-Mer, Bondy [Seine], France) is an excellent source of information on the former French territories in Africa, particularly for the southern edge of the Sahara from Chad to Mauritania. A brief description, without maps, of the soils of the Sudan is given in an issue of the *Arid Zone* Newsletter (Dixey and Aubert, 1962). A soil survey of a section of the northwest coast of Egypt is now underway for the purpose of estimating the suitability of soils and groundwater for irrigation and dry land agriculture. It is under the direction of A. M. Balba and M. M. El-Gabaly of the Soil Science Department of the University of Alexandria (*see* Balba and El-Gabaly, 1964).

Soil maps for the periphery of the Sahara are good, although their areal extent usually is limited, but those for the central Sahara are of limited reliability.

C. SOMALI - CHALBI

Soils information for the Somali-Chalbi desert area is extremely fragmentary. A few analyses of soils have been made, but the only published maps aside from the highly generalized *Soil Map of Africa* (Hoore, 1964) is one for the Lower Giuba (Juba) River (U. S. Agency for International Development, 1961) and the *Soil Map of Kenya* (Gethin-Jones and Scott, 1958). The Lower Giuba soil survey was at a reconnaissance level and gives descriptions of the alluvial soils that are mapped by associations and complexes. The generalized maps of Kenya and Africa are only approximate in their accuracy, due to the lack of reliable information. The best description, although admittedly sketchy, of the soils and surface materials of the area is given in Volume VI of the Unesco "Arid Zone Research" series (Pichi-Sermolli, 1955).

From the little information available, the soils of the Somali-Chalbi seem to be largely skeletal, with some moderate development in the reddish colored soils of the Kenya-Somalia border region. Deep soils of clay plains are said to occur on the upland areas in the vicinity of the Giuba and Scebeli rivers. Alluvial soils on the flood plains of those two rivers, especially the Scebeli, are deep, calcareous, medium to fine textured, moderately alkaline and sometimes saline.

While crystalline and calcareous rock detritus are common in the vicinity of French Somaliland, calcareous and gypsiferous materials are most extensive in Somalia. The latter materials, which occupy much of the Somalia peninsula between the Indian Ocean and the Gulf of Aden, lead to skeletal soils that frequently are quite saline, as are many of the coastal plains soils, and may contain hardened gypsiferous layers. Sand dunes appear to be restricted in the main to the coastal areas, especially along the Indian Ocean.

Stony plains are found in and around French Somaliland and probably occur on the footslopes of the desert mountains and elsewhere. Subdesert or semidesert soils are extensive in the French Somaliland plain and along the Indian Ocean coast, particularly on the lower valley of the Scebeli River.

Excess salt accumulation occurs in the large Danakil salt pan west of the Danakil Mountains and in the coastal, gypsiferous, and irrigated soils, as well as on miscellaneous soils throughout French Somaliland.

There are no good soil maps for this desert.

D. ARABIAN DESERT

Most of the Arabian Desert area is unknown, insofar as soils information is concerned. Detailed soil studies largely are confined to Israel, eastern Iraq and southwestern Iran. Characteristics of soils in the remainder of the desert must be inferred from a few samplings or from the local geologic, geomorphic, and climatic conditions.

1. Principal Soils Synthesis

Erosion, by wind and water, has played a major role in shaping the surface of the Arabian Desert. Loose sands blown into dunes occupy most of the extremely arid Rub' al Khali (Empty Quarter), are widespread in northern Saudi Arabia, and are fairly common in Israel. The remainder of the desert consists mainly of regs (stony desert, hamadas), rocky escarpments, mountains, wadis (watercourses), clay footslopes, and broad, flat plains that frequently are saline. All of these soils show little or no development. Where moderate development occurs, either the climate is semiarid or the soils probably are relicts (paleosols) of a wetter period. Soils showing some development frequently are calcareous, whereas undeveloped soils may or may not be calcareous, depending upon the nature of the parent rock from which they are derived (Dan *et al.*, 1962; Buringh, 1960; Moormann, 1959; Dewan and Famouri, 1964; Liere, 1954).

Residual regs (hamadas) and transported regs, having a surface of what sometimes is called desert pavement, occur on broad plains and tablelands in the northern part of the desert (Dan *et al.*, 1962; Buringh, 1960; Moormann, 1959; Liere, 1954). They are calcareous and may also be gypsiferous. The underlying material in upland areas may be fragmented limestone or dolomite, or it may be calcareous and/or gypsiferous sedimentary deposits that contain flint or limestone gravel. In the valleys and plains, hamada surface and subsoil material is coarse-textured alluvium. The same is true for transported regs of the wadis. Gravel plains called "hibakah" are deltaic in origin. Regs of the southern desert generally are calcareous whereas those of the western desert may or may not be. There are no large areas of regs in the east, where sand dunes are extensive. Calcareous and gypsiferous desert soils, with and without surface concretions, occur in the north, and are similar to upland hamadas in showing little development. A range survey in the central Negev of Israel (Seligman, Tadmor, and Raz, 1962) showed that rocky slopes occupied 42 per cent of the area, dunes and plains 22 per cent, loessial plains 12 per cent, sandy plains 10 per cent, and gravel plains (hamadas) 8 per cent. The remainder consisted of wadis, etc.

Medium- to fine-textured soils are found at the mouths of the large wadis, on alluvial plains of intermittent and ephemeral streams as well as of permanent rivers (such as the Tigris, Euphrates, and Jordan), in depressions, in many interdune areas, and on footslopes of hills (Buringh, 1960; Holm, 1953). These are the best soils for irrigation unless soil salinity becomes excessive, as it frequently does.

Deposits of loess (medium-textured windborne material) on some of the coarse-textured valley bottoms have increased the water- and nutrient-holding capacity of these soils.

Halomorphic soils in which the salts are naturally present are common along coastal areas, in interior depressions where there is no surface outlet for flood waters, around the shores of the Dead Sea, and on gypsiferous deposits such as those near Palmyra in Syria. Man-made halomorphic soils resulting from irrigation comprise a large part of the stratified lower Mesopotamian alluvial plain in eastern Iraq (Buringh, 1960). They also are common around oases throughout the desert.

Marshlands are found in the delta of the Tigris and Euphrates rivers, which extends many miles inland from the Persian Gulf. They are flooded seasonally and have accumulated considerable fine-textured river sediment over the centuries. The topography is uneven, due to local differences in deposition or erosion (Buringh, 1960).

Calcareous and gypsiferous plains with smooth to undulating topography having many depressions of fine-textured and saline material are extensive in northwestern Iraq and southeastern Syria. Lava beds are significant in eastern Jordan and in parts of western Saudi Arabia. A long, narrow, level to gently undulating plain (the Tihamah) lies between the mountains of southwestern Arabia and the Red Sea. Next to the sea is a flat, barren, saline belt varying in width from several hundred feet up to about 2 miles. Sand dunes have formed over the saline flats in some places, while in others coral beds are exposed. Inland from the coastal belt is a sandy and featureless alluvial plain with small hummocks of sand on the surface, usually around shrubs (Ferris, 1953).

Arabian Desert soils commonly are light-brown to yellowish-white in color, with red colors prevalent in the interior dunes. In the less arid fringes of the desert, where precipitation amounts to 10 to 12 inches annually, sierozem or even isohumic brown soils occur on the sandy or loessial deposits of the plains and plateaus. They show a slight movement of lime and organic matter from the surface into the subsoil. As a whole, surficial deposits of the Arabian Desert consist of sandy and stony materials, with fine-textured (largely silt), saline sediments occurring extensively in the lower Mesopotamian plain and in the plains of central Saudi Arabia. Sand dunes of the erg type occur in a broad arc extending from southern Jordan through northeastern and eastern Saudi Arabia to the vast expanse of the Rub' al Khali (Holm, 1953). Stony and gravelly plains cut by wadis, along with barren and rocky desert mountains, form another arc beginning in western Iraq and circling around through Jordan, the Negev in Israel, Sinai, western Saudi Arabia, Yemen, and South Arabia. Calcrete is locally important in the Dahna' and Summan areas of Saudi Arabia.

2. Soil Surveys

Information on soils of the Arabian Peninsula is rare, and general soil conditions must be inferred from reports such as those on sand dunes (Thesiger, 1951; Holm, 1953) and those of FAO experts reporting on the agricultural potential of a section of the peninsula (Simansky, 1955). A soil map of Wadi Jizan, on the Red Sea coast near Yemen, is in FAO files in Rome (Finielz, 1954), as is a small-scale map of the Tihamah (Ferris, 1953). The report by Finielz describes the soils of Wadi Jizan in detail, and the Ferris report discusses soil-plant associations in a broad way.

A first draft of a generalized soil map of the Near East has been prepared by Dudal for the World Soil Resources Office of FAO in Rome (Dudal, 1962). It is the most authoritative map for the region as a whole. Larger-scale maps have been prepared for northeast Sinai (el-Gabaly, 1954), Israel (Dan *et al.,* 1962) eastern Jordan (Moormann, 1959), Syria (Liere, 1954), Iraq (Buringh, 1960) and Iran (Dewan and Famouri, 1964). All of these maps are reasonably good for the cultivated areas and the nearby uncultivated areas but are of varying reliability for the desert proper except in Israel, the lower Mesopotamian plan in Iraq, and the Khuzestan Plains in Iran, where the reliability is good.

Some detailed soil surveys of the arid portions of the Arabian Desert countries have been made. In Israel they are prepared by the Soil Conservation Department of the Ministry of Agriculture, but they do not appear to have been published. Many surveys of kibbutzim have been completed and used as a basis for soil and water management. Iraq and Iran are the two countries in the Arabian Desert for which there are several published detailed surveys of selected areas. In Iraq, most of the survey areas are in irrigated or potentially irrigated lands north and south of Baghdad on the Tigris and its tributaries, and south of Baghdad on the Euphrates (Buringh and Edelman, 1955; Hunting Aerosurveys, Ltd., 1956a, b; Kloes, 1956; Schilstra, 1961; West, 1955). The Hunting and West surveys show soil series that are, in reality, associations of soil series. The other three maps show individual soils in greater detail and are more accurate in their soil descriptions. The best description of the soils of Iraq, and in particular the Mesopotamian plain, is that found in the book by Buringh (Buringh, 1960). In Iran, the Arabian Desert is an extension of the Mesopotamian plain east of Baghdad and is

know as the Khuzestan Plain in the vicinity of the Persian Gulf. The Khuzestan Plain consists of alluvial deposits, principally of the Karun and Karkheh rivers, that are coarse to medium in texture near the Zagros Mountains but become fine-textured on the low-lying plains. As in Iraq, the soils are stratified and frequently saline. Numerous detailed, semi-detailed, and reconnaissance soil surveys have been made of the Khuzestan Plain, where large irrigation developments are being attempted. A complete listing of those surveys with notations on area and map scale may be found, starting on page 302, in the book *The Soils of Iran* (Dewan and Famouri, 1964). Most of them are recent and of good quality. Only one semidetailed survey has been found for a part of the Sinai Peninsula (Abdel-Salam, 1961). It gives a general grouping of soils by surface texture and stoniness.

The Ralph M. Parsons Company of Los Angeles, California was engaged in 1965-66 in a water and agricultural development program in Saudi Arabia that included soil studies of four irrigated areas. The results of this work, which were not accessible to this reviewer, should be instructive for understanding soil conditions in some inland areas.

There are no reliable surface-material maps for large parts of the Arabian Desert, particularly for the Arabian Peninsula and the north central area.

E. IRANIAN DESERT

While considerable good information is available on the soils of the Iranian Desert area in Iran, little is known about the soils of Pakistan and Afghanistan. The Food and Agriculture Organization of the United Nations can claim most of the credit for collecting what information there is for the three countries. A soil-survey program is well underway in Iran but is weak in Afghanistan and Pakistan. Primary emphasis in all of them is on the irrigation potentials of the land.

1. Principal Soils Synthesis

Stony deserts (regs, hamadas), grey desert soils, sierozems, and saline soils constitute the majority of the surface materials of the Iranian Desert area. Grey is the dominant soil color and nearly all the soils are calcareous at the surface or in the subsoil. Some development is evident in the sierozems and in soils of depressions where runoff water collects regularly, but development is absent in most of the upland desert soils. Sand dunes occur along the Persian Gulf and the Arabian Sea, and they constitute important areas in eastern Iran (the Dasht-e-Lut) and southern Afghanistan (Registan). Recent alluvium on river flood plains makes the best irrigated soils.

Except for parts of northern Afghanistan and Iran, the Iranian Desert is a repeating mixture of desert mountains and low hills, alluvial fans on the edges of the mountains, and level to nearly level plains between them, all of it cut by watercourses that usually are intermittent or ephemeral. The exceptions in Afghanistan and Iran are the sand dunes mentioned earlier and the extensive salt desert of northern Iran (the Dasht-e-Kavir) where the soil is covered by a salt crust over large areas.

On the desert mountains and hills, stony soils that are shallow over bedrock are typical. They show little or no profile development and, because vegetation is sparse, have little organic matter. Whatever fine material may form at the surface by weathering processes is blown away by the wind or washed away by water running down the steep slopes. The landscape is highly dissected by watercourses (Dewan and Famouri, 1964).

Alluvial fans have coarse-textured soils on the upper side, with finer-textured materials lower down on the slope. A little profile development can be observed in the form of lime accumulation as concretions or as gravel coatings and some cementation by lime of gravels and finer material. Where the mountain slopes level off, grey desert soils and sierozems (grey soils) occur. In places where there is slightly more development, soils resembling isohumic brown soils can be observed.

Sierozems also are found on the smooth to gently undulating loessial deposits forming an east-west belt in Afghanistan between the Hindu Kush mountains west of Kabul and the U. S. S. R. border. Whether on fan bottoms or on loess, sierozems are very low in organic matter, highly calcareous, alkaline, and generally not saline in the upper soil but sometimes saline in the lower subsoil; they are commonly found on level to moderately sloping land. They are widespread in northern Afghanistan, scarce in Pakistan, and occupy a semicircle on the west, north, and east of the Dasht-e-Kavir and Dasht-e-Lut in Iran. Surface soil textures seem to be finer (silt loam to loam) in the loessial materials than in the fans (Dewan and Famouri, 1964; Rozanov, 1945).

Grey desert soils have practically no development, are calcareous throughout the profile, and usually have a carbonate layer close to the surface. They are alkaline, frequently saline, and covered with small angular stones that form a desert pavement. Underlying materials are usually coarse textured, with coarse gravel in the subsoil. Slopes are nearly level or gently undulating. Grey desert soils and coarse-textured alluvial fans constitute reg surfaces, in north African terminology.

Saline (halomorphic) soils are present along the coast of the Persian Gulf, the Gulf of Oman, and the Arabian Sea; they are also found in small playas of Afghanistan, and Iran, in the very large Dasht-e-Kavir, and in the large depression in eastern Iran into which the Helmand River flows from Afghanistan (Dewan and Famouri, 1964) The Dasht-e-Kavir and the delta of the Helmand River are called "salt marshes" by Dewan and Famouri because they are wet throughout most of the year. Soil textures in the saline depressions are fine and the soils are deep. Some saline soils occur on upland areas where the underlying material is gypsiferous and saline marls. This type of sedimentary material is present around the Dasht-e-Kavir and presumably accounts for the salty character of that desert.

A unique type of surface formation in Iran is the salt plug (Dewan and Famouri, 1964). It appears to result from the uplift of gypsiferous and saline marlstones and siltstones, forming low to medium hills. The hills are highly dissected by water erosion, and runoff causes strongly saline soils to develop around the base of the hills. They are most common west of the Dasht-e-Kavir and in southern Iran near the mouth of the Persian Gulf.

Sand dunes of local character may be found in any of the smooth parts of the Iranian Desert area, including the coast. Two major dune areas are in the south of the Dasht-e-Lut of central Iran and in Registan in southern Afghanistan along the Pakistan border (Dewan and Famouri, 1964; Rozanov, 1945). These extensive dune fields are similar to the ergs of north Africa but have many more interdune areas where finer-textured material occurs at the surface or under a shallow cover of loose sand. The dune sands are loose and ready to move whenever the wind blows. The interdune areas sometimes are saline, highly alkaline, and very hard when dry.

Recent alluvium along the larger streams represents some of the best irrigated land because it is medium- to fine-textured and lies on level or gentle slopes of the river flood plains. Sometimes it is saline but frequently it is not, at least until salts accumulate as the result of irrigation (Dewan and Famouri, 1964; Fly, 1950-1956).

In summary, soils of the Iranian Desert generally are coarse textured except in topographic depressions, calcareous throughout the profile, deep except on rough broken land, alkaline, very low in organic matter, saline in depressions, grey in color, undeveloped, and frequently covered with desert pavement.

2. Soil Surveys

The best general information about the soils of the desert regions of Iran is found in the book, *The Soils of Iran* (Dewan and Famouri, 1964).

Dewan has himself participated in most of the soil surveys made in that country in recent years and he has traveled extensively in Iran. The only known published map, with report, on the soils of Afghanistan is that by Rozanov (Rozanov, 1945). The latter work was based upon deductions from climate, vegetation, geology, and geomorphology data and can be considered only approximate, especially for the southern part of the country. For Pakistan, a very small-scale map has been published for the entire country (United Nations, 1949), but it is of doubtful reliability. The Indus Plain has been mapped on a reconnaissance basis (Hunting Survey Corporation, Ltd., 1958) showing broad groupings of soils with little specific information on soil characteristics.

Many good detailed, semidetailed, and reconnaissance soil surveys have been made in Iran (*see* Dewan and Famouri, 1964, p. 302), most of them for the Khuzestan Plain of southwestern Iran and for northwestern Iran. The Soil Institute of the Iranian Ministry of Agriculture is responsible for the soil survey program. A few surveys have been made in Afghanistan, primarily in the Helmand Valley in the southern part of the country (Fly, 1950-1956; International Engineering Company, 1955; United Nations Special Fund, 1961*b;* Youngs, 1948). They are in potentially irrigated areas and emphasize the irrigability of the soils. No detailed published surveys are known for significant areas of the Iranian Desert in West Pakistan. Some interesting wind erosion and soil conservation studies have been made in Baluchistan south of Quetta, and were reported at the 1957 Unesco conference on soil conservation in the arid zones. The conference was held in Karachi, Pakistan. Little concern has been evidenced about the soils outside the Indus Plain in Pakistan, since irrigation development, as in Afghanistan, has been the overriding consideration except around Quetta in Baluchistan where climatic conditions are more favorable for plant growth without irrigation.

Soils information for Iran is far superior to that for Afghanistan and Pakistan, and the detailed surveys for Iran are fairly reliable.

F. THAR

Research on uncultivated soils of the Thar (also known as the Indian, Rajputana, or Rajasthan Desert) of India and Pakistan was meager prior to the establishment in 1959 of the Central Arid Zone Research Institute at Jodhpur, India. Since then a start has been made on understanding the physical, animal, and human resources of Rajasthan Desert and the other arid areas of India. In Pakistan the irrigated land of the Indus Valley has received primary attention,

to the exclusion of the uncultivated lands east of the irrigated plains.

1. Principal Soils Synthesis

Four kinds of soils appear to be most prevalent in the Thar Desert: *(1)* deep, saline, fine-textured alluvium on the extensive flats of the seasonally inundated Rann of Kutch, with coarser-textured alluvium on the higher slopes of the Rann, *(2)* sand-dune fields (ergs) of the Tharparkar area north of the Rann, *(3)* sand dunes and sandy soils interspersed with medium-textured saline alluvium north and east of the Tharparkar region, and *(4)* the medium-textured, frequently silty, recent alluvium of the Indus Plain on the west (Wright, 1964; Hunting Survey Corporation, Ltd., 1958). The entire desert, from the Aravalli hills in India on the east to the western edge of the Indus Plain in Pakistan, is a level to gently sloping plain broken by sand dunes and low barren hills on which the soils are lithosols.

Wright's (1964) excellent report on the soils of the southern part of the Thar Desert is the only known paper on soils of this area. The saline coastal plains of the Rann of Kutch are barren sandy clays having about 0.2 per cent slope, with some low mounds of coarser-textured soils scattered throughout the area. Most of the soils have a salt crust; the disintegration and removal by wind of this crust is believed by some people to be the source of the salt occurring in the soils of the interior of the desert. On the higher margins of the Rann, coastal plains of sandy and gravelly material lying on nearly level slopes are cut by drainage channels with some cliffs of up to 15 feet in height. Some salt crusts can be found on the soil surface in lower-lying spots.

Between the Rann of Kutch and the Tharparkar sand dunes are some rocky granite hills having gravelly footslopes. Wide smooth plains of sandy or clayey alluvium separate the hills of the region. The finer-textured depressions of the area have hummocks scattered over them. Sandy plains commonly have hummocks and occasionally are broken by dunes. Gravel appears to underlie the sandy plains in the vicinity of the granite hills and the Rann of Kutch.

Loose sands constitute the extensive Tharparkar dunes, which begin abruptly near the eastern edge of the irrigated Indus Plain and extend eastward. Sand dunes caused by overgrazing of sandy plains are widespread in western Rajasthan, and the moving dunes pose a threat to nearby cultivated areas on the east. North and east of the Tharparkar dune fields, it appears that mixed sand dunes, sandy plains, and fine-textured plains of Quaternary alluvium are most common (Tamhane, 1952). The fine-textured plains usually are saline, probably due to the upward rise of water from a shallow water table and to evaporation of runoff water collecting on the surface. The topography is smooth except in the occasional watercourses that traverse the northern, eastern, and southern part of the desert. Salt lakes occur in depressions of the center and north into which intermittent streams flow.

Soils of the Indus Plain are, except for the sandy Thal area on the east side of the Indus River in the Punjab, medium-textured, moderately to slowly permeable, deep, high in silt, alkaline, calcareous, low in organic matter, level, grey in color, and frequently saline where soil drainage is poor (Hunting Survey Corporation, Ltd., 1958). In the Thal area, sandy soils and sand dunes are widespread, interspersed with medium-textured soils that are said to occur in strips between sand dunes, with the dunes and the medium-textured strips oriented parallel with the dominant wind direction, which is from the southwest. Both the sandy and medium-textured soils are deep and are similar in chemical characteristics to other Indus Plain soils. Waterlogging and salinity are the major soil problems in the Indus Plain.

For the Thar Desert as a whole, interspersed sandy and medium- to fine-textured surface materials are dominant. Gravelly and skeletal soils are restricted to mountains, hills, footslopes, and watercourses, none of which is extensive. Soil salinity is high in the uncultivated fine-textured soils and in much of the irrigated land. Sand dunes in the Indus Plain are restricted to the Thal area but may occur nearly anywhere outside the Indus Plain.

2. Soil Surveys

Detailed soil surveys of small sections of the Thar Desert have been made by personnel of the Central Arid Zone Research Institute in Jodhpur, India, and by the Water and Soils Investigation Division of the West Pakistan Water and Power Development Authority in Lahore. The maps and reports are in the offices of the surveying groups. In both countries, the impetus for making soil surveys has been provided by the need for soils information as an aid to agricultural development. In all likelihood, whatever detailed soil surveys may be available in Ministry of Agriculture or Central Arid Zone Research Institute files in Rajasthan will be for the proposed large irrigation project in northern Rajasthan or for the semiarid region of eastern Rajasthan. In Pakistan, the soil survey program of the Ministry of Agriculture of West Pakistan has been largely ineffective. Those surveys that have been conducted have been made by the West Pakistan Water and

Power Development Authority in Sind and in the Punjab (e.g., Asghar and Zaidi, 1960). Some information on soils should be in the files of the West Pakistan Soil Conservation Department, but it has not been possible to determine the quality or quantity of it. A few reports on Pakistan soils were presented at the Unesco meeting on soil conservation in the arid zones that was held in Karachi in 1957.

General soil maps for the desert have been made. Those for India appear to be fairly reliable whereas those of Pakistan are of variable reliability. Soil surveys have been completed, on a reconnaissance scale, under the All India Soil Survey Scheme, for the entire country (Indian Council of Agricultural Research, 1953; Indian Agricultural Research Institute, 1961; Raychaudhuri, 1963), Rajasthan (National Council of Applied Economic Research, 1963a), Gujarat (National Council of Applied Economic Research, 1963b), and Bombay (Poona College of Agriculture, 1955). In Pakistan, the two small-scale maps (Khan and Arshad, 1947; Pithawalla, 1951) are of low reliability. The larger-scale maps prepared under a Colombo Plan Cooperative Project (Hunting Survey Corporation, Ltd., 1958) are good where soil materials can be identified easily from aerial photographs but poor where soil conditions are not obvious.

G. TURKESTAN

A wealth of information has been accumulated on the soils of Soviet Turkestan during the past 50 years. The present leading organization in the field of soils is the V. V. Dokuchaev Soil Institute of the U.S.S.R. Academy of Sciences in Moscow. The Dokuchaev Institute operates throughout the Soviet Union and functions somewhat like a research coordinating agency, in addition to carrying on research by its own staff. There are soil institutes in each of the academies of sciences of the Central Asian republics, where field and laboratory studies are conducted on local soils. Soil mapping has been an important phase of the U.S.S.R. soil program for several decades. Since virtually all of the publications on soils for the past 30 years have been in Russian, it was not until the advent of the comprehensive U. S. foreign-language translation program after World War II that the details of Soviet work became widely known in the United States. Soil maps at a useful scale still are difficult to obtain, with the exception of the small-scale (1/25,000,000) general soil map of Asia, which has just been published under Professor V. Kovda's and Professor I. P. Gerasimov's leadership and worked out by Professor V. Kovda, Dr. E. Lobova and Professor N. Rozov (no publication information available).

1. Principal Soils Synthesis

Most of the information on the soils of Soviet Turkestan reported here comes from a book by Rozanov (Rozanov, 1951), a report and personal observation made on a tour of the area (Bower *et al.,* 1962), a paper delivered at the 1960 Congress of the International Society of Soil Science (Ivanova and Rozov, 1960), and the most recent soil map of Central Asia (Dokuchaev Soil Institute, 1956).

Central Asia is bordered by high mountains on the south (the Kopet-Dag) and east (the Pamirs, Hindu Kush, and Tien Shan). There are no marked topographic barriers on the north, where the Turkestan Desert area gradually merges into the semiarid and prairie regions of Siberia and the European part of the U. S. S. R. On the west are the Caucasus Mountains. The desert is an immense expanse of low alluvial plains, sand dunes, and denuded low plateaus. Included within it are two large sandy deserts, the Kara-Kum (black sands) and the Kyzyl-Kum (red sands).

Relatively minor areas of stony and gravelly soils occur within the arid region of Central Asia. They are confined to the footslopes of the mountains on the south and east and on the plateaus, such as the Ustyurt, in the northwest of the desert area. The extensive soils are either sand dunes, loessial and alluvial plains, fine-textured depressions, or river terraces and flood plains. Except for the sand dunes of the Kara-Kum and Kyzyl-Kum, silt is widespread, with soil textures of fine sandy loam to silt loam being dominant (Bower *et al.,* 1962).

Water and wind are responsible for most of the kinds of soil that are found in Turkestan. During a geologically earlier period, streams descending from northern glaciers and the mountains deposited tremendous amounts of sediment in the low-lying Turanian plain. Subsequently, wind action formed sand dunes and the loessial plains of eastern Soviet Turkestan. Continued deposition of alluvium by large rivers such as the Amu-Dar'ya and the Syr-Dar'ya caused the formation of extensive fine-textured flood plains along the rivers and deltas around the Aral Sea. Lowering of the Caspian Sea in recent centuries has brought to the surface saline materials that are prevalent in the Kura-Araks lowland in Azerbaijan, in the Volga and Ural deltas, and on the east side of the Caspian Sea (Bower *et al.,* 1962).

The Kara-Kum and Kyzyl-Kum deserts are not continuous sand dunes but are interspersed with medium- to fine-textured depressions where takyrs (saline and sodium-effected soils) and solonchaks (saline soils) occur. They also are cut by the dry channels of former rivers, where a mixture of surface soil textures may be found. Gravel appears to under-

lie much of Turkestan, although this may not be true in the central and western parts which were farther from the sources of the ancient rivers. In any event, gravel is not important on the present plain surface (Rozanov, 1951).

The sandy deserts, with their finer-textured depressions, are surrounded by medium- to fine-textured soils, often of the loess type. On the north, east, and south are fairly typical grey-colored sierozems that show only weak development, are medium textured, calcareous throughout the profile, low in organic matter, deep, on level to gently undulating slopes, fertile, and have a good plant cover. On the west of the sands, along the Caspian Sea, are saline, fine-textured, barren coastal plains that are several miles in width.

All parent rocks of the sierozem soils in Turkestan belong to the calcite-quartz-feldspar group, mineralogically. Soils are rich in bases and mineral plant nutrients as a result of little chemical weathering of the parent rock. Gypsum deposits can be found in some areas, and both takyrs and solonchaks commonly have gypsum crystals in the profile at a depth of about 24 inches or more (Rozanov, 1951).

A mesa-and-valley type of landscape is found northeast of the Aral Sea, in western and southeastern Kara-Kum, and in southeastern Kyzyl-Kum. The flat-topped buttes (kyrs or turkuls) consist of shallow, frequently stony, horizontal beds of clays, sandstones, marls, limestone, and conglomerates. Between them are depressions, which may be deep and small or shallow and extensive. Sand ridges (over finer-textured material), takyrs, gravelly or stony plains, solonchaks, or salt lakes may be found in the depressions. Footslopes of the mesas are gravelly or stony. The Ustyurt plateau between the Aral and Caspian seas is a large tableland rising above the surrounding Turanian lowland. It consists of horizontally bedded limestones and marls underlain by thick layers of gypsum-bearing clays. Solonchaks occupy the many depressions in the tableland. Surface materials are medium to fine textured, shallow, calcareous, and weakly developed, and often are covered with pebbles and stones.

The deltas of the Amu-Dar'ya and Syr-Dar'ya on the shore of the Aral Sea are very flat lowlands with many channels crossing them. The depressions between the channels are occupied by swamps and lakes inundated periodically with sediment-laden flood waters. Fine textures predominate, and some solonchaks occur in the deltas.

Extensive areas of takyrs are located in southern Turkmenistan, along the Syr-Dar'ya, and east and south of the Aral Sea. They are as level as a floor and appear to be ideal for irrigation, but their high salinity and very low permeability make them difficult to farm successfully. Surface textures are fine sandy loam to silty clay loam, exchangeable sodium is high, the soils are badly dispersed, and they usually are devoid of vegetation. The widespread occurrence of takyrs points to the presence of an earlier pluvial period when alluvial deposition was much greater than it is now, as does the fact that ancient alluvial plains greatly exceed recent alluvial plains in area within the desert (Rozanov, 1951; Dokuchaev Soil Institute, 1956).

Solonchak soils, resulting from deposition of salt in ancient alluvial basins or by prolonged irrigation with inadequate leaching, may be found throughout the Turkestan Desert area. Many irrigated oases, particularly in Turkmenistan, contain extensive areas of soils that have been abandoned as the result of excessive salt accumulation. The flatness of the land frequently makes it difficult to provide adequate drainage for the irrigated soils or for the land on the ancient flood plain of the Syr-Dar'ya and Amu-Dar'ya. Turkestan soils consist, by and large, of medium-textured sierozems, sand dunes, shallow plateau soils, and medium- to fine-textured takyrs and solonchaks. Salinity is a problem in the takyrs, solonchaks, irrigated oases, river deltas, and Caspian coastal plains (Rozanov, 1951; Lobova, 1960).

2. Soil Surveys

A good generalized soil map of the U.S.S.R. was printed in 1956 (Dokuchaev Soil Institute, 1956). An earlier map of.the European part of the U.S.S.R., which is of good quality, is the latest accessible at a larger scale (Lobova and Rozov, 1947). Some medium-scale maps have been published (Anonymous, 1959 and 1960) but the large-scale maps prepared by various soil institutes for farms are not accessible to foreigners (Bower *et al.*, 1962). A small-scale map on the 1956 U.S.S.R. map shows that detailed surveys have not been made in most of the Kara-Kum and Kyzyl-Kum deserts but have been made in the remainder of Central Asia, particularly along the rivers. A soil manual for the U.S.S.R. has been translated into English and is useful for interpreting Soviet soil maps (Tyurin *et al.*, 1959).

A generalized soil map of Asia has been prepared by V. A. Kovda, E. Lobova, and N. Rozov of the Dokuchaev Soil Institute at a scale of 1/25,000,000.

The generalized maps for the Turkestan Desert area in the Soviet Union are reliable. Presumably, the detailed maps also are reliable but no opportunity has arisen to evaluate them.

H.   TAKLA - MAKAN

Little attention has been given to the soils of the Takla-Makan Desert by either Chinese or foreign scientists, presumably because the remoteness and aridity of the desert made knowledge of it relatively unimportant to the economic development of China. The little scientific work done there seems to have been conducted on a rapid-reconnaissance basis. There appears to be no doubt that data on the characteristics of the desert soils in China were scarce prior to the establishment of the Communist government. Two Americans, C. F. Shaw and James Thorp, probably knew as much about Chinese soils as anyone, and they had little knowledge of the desert areas.

The Communist government seems to have stepped up the study of soil conditions, in the arid as well as the humid regions. Several prominent Soviet soil scientists, among them V. A. Kovda, E. Lobova, and I. P. Gerasimov, have made studies of Chinese soils in recent years. It seems probable that the scope of the soil-survey program has been increased at the same time, but that is only conjecture. The translation problem is more acute at present than it was under the Nationalist government, and a good part of what is known about Chinese soils is found in Russian publications that are translated into English. Under the Nationalists, many publications, such as those of the National Geological Survey in which soils reports appeared, were written in English.

Soil surveys are made under the Communist government by the Soils Division of the Chinese Geological Survey and the Soil Institute of the Chinese Academy.

Any comments on Takla-Makan soils must be considered as of dubious reliability when it comes to specifics, but general observations based on published reports and checked against what might be expected in view of climatic, topographic, and geologic conditions there may be instructive. The best source of usable information on the Takla-Makan Desert is one of a series of three translations of a study begun by a Chinese Academy Sand Control Group in 1957 (Academia Sinica, Sand Control Group, 1962).

1.   Principal Soils Synthesis

The Takla-Makan Desert, in the central portion, is an extensive expanse of shifting sands that have been moving southward for several centuries. Several large rivers flow into the desert from the Tien Shan and Kunlun Shan (mountains) on the north, northwest, and southwest borders of the desert. Soils vary, in general, from coarse-textured sand and gravelly material with surface stones (gobi) on the footslopes of the mountains, to sandy to medium-textured alluvial fans and plains, then to fine-textured material in the river flood plains, and, finally, to the loose sand dunes in the center. Among the variations from this sequence are some clay soils in places near the Tien Shan, small to large sand dunes on the alluvial plains, soils of depressions, and gravelly and sandy deposits along the stream beds of the rivers that flow for some distance into the central Takla-Makan before their water disappears into the porous river beds. A similar variety of soils occurs in the Dzungaria Desert of northern Sinkiang.

While the coarse- and medium-textured soils at the base of the mountain footslopes, where practically all of the present-day farming is done, are nonsaline or low in soluble salts, soil salinity becomes greater toward the desert and within the desert. The salts are said to have their source in the rocks of the mountains and are carried down into the desert by surface streams and underground water. Saline ground waters seem to be the normal condition on the periphery of the desert and in the center. Oases taking water from rivers have been productive because the water is low in salts, but sand-dune encroachment is said to have destroyed many of them and to be a constant threat to others.

Sand dunes dominate the Takla-Makan landscape, with some of them said to be over 300 feet high, although more commonly they seem to be 30 to 50 feet high. Stabilization of the dunes to protect communities must be a very difficult task, judging from the reports of the Sand Control Group. Mechanical devices, such as fences, have been proposed for protecting important roads, but the only permanent solution of the problem is considered to lie in revegetation of the dunes (Chang and Hsu, 1962). In view of the aridity of the climate and the pastoral pressure on the sparse vegetation, prospects for success appear to be poor.

In the eastern Takla-Makan, south of the Bogdo Ula Mountains, broad areas of sierozem soils are said to occur (Kovda and Kondorskaya, 1957) on a level to gently undulating topography. Large depressions such as the Turfan Depression and Lop Nor are fairly common, and marshy, fine-textured soils occur. Many of them are very saline as the result of evaporation of water that collects in the depressions in spring.

The apparent paucity of published soils information does not permit a reliable description to be made of the surface materials; however, reports indicate that the soils are deep everywhere except near the mountains. They are uniformly low in organic matter, especially in the sand dunes. Gravelly, medium-textured, and fine-textured soils probably are calcareous to the surface and alkaline in reaction. Sand-dune soils would be expected to be noncalcareous

or only slightly calcareous, and may be slightly acid on the surface. No mention was found of sodium-affected soils, although it would seem likely that they do occur in at least some of the saline, fine-textured flood-plain and depression soils on the fringe of the desert. Soil salinity is definitely a widespread problem throughout the desert.

2. Soil Surveys

None but generalized soil maps have been found for northwestern China, and they certainly are not reliable for any part of the arid regions. Maps that have been used as guides to soil conditions in the Takla-Makan Desert are all small-scale maps, and the impression they give is that the persons who prepared the maps were doing so on very sketchy information (Anonymous, 1962; Hou, Chen, and Wang, 1957; Ma, 1947, 1957; Ma and Wen, 1958; Thorp and Hou, 1935). The entire Takla-Makan and Gobi deserts, for example, are placed in two soil groups, that of desert soils of level ground (Takla-Makan) and of desert soils of semimountain areas (Gobi), in Ma and Wen's 1958 map. To compound the difficulty of using the map, there are several errors in designation of soil areas. The English translation of a paper by two Russians entitled "A New Soil Map of China" (Kovda and Kondorskaya, 1957), does not include a copy of the map. The descriptive matter in the paper is so general as to be of little use. The Kovda-Lobova-Rozov soil map of Asia published by the Dokuchaev Soil Institute at a scale of 1/25,000,000 probably is as good as or better than any other map of the Takla-Makan Desert.

I. GOBI

A little more is known of the soils of the Gobi Desert than of the Takla-Makan Desert, thanks to translations of a Russian report on the soils of Outer Mongolia (Bespalov, 1951) and of two reports of the Chinese Academy Sand Control Group (Academia Sinica, Sand Control Team, 1958). Other reports may have been prepared by Chinese soil scientists in recent years but, if so, they are not known in the United States by persons compiling information on world soils. Prior to 1960, soil scientists of the Soviet Union participated in the classification of Chinese soils and they reported on their studies in the Russian publications. Since then the Chinese have apparently been working alone.

1. Principal Soils Synthesis

The Gobi Desert is a repeating sequence of mountains, gravelly and stony footslopes, plains, and gentle slopes and depressions, giving a mountain-and-basin landscape in which some basins are up to 5-20 miles across. Sand dunes are extensive in some parts of the desert and may be found nearly anywhere on the plains. They are not, however, anywhere near as extensive as those in the Takla-Makan Desert.

Judging from Bespalov's map, skeletal mountain soils occupy about 25 per cent of the Gobi Desert in Outer Mongolia, brown gobi soils about 40 per cent, salt- and sodium-affected soils of depressions about 25 per cent, and sand dunes about 5 per cent. The skeletal mountain soils are primarily loams with admixtures of gravel and stone, with parent rock material of granite, limestone, and metamorphic rocks. Slopes are steep, soils are shallow, and lime accumulations can be found near the soil surface.

Brown gobi soils are the most extensive soils in the Gobi Desert of Outer Mongolia and, apparently, in Inner Mongolia as well (although sand dunes are widespread in the Chinese part of the Gobi). The term "gobi" is ambiguous (Academia Sinica, Sand Control Group, 1962). Originally, its meaning in Mongolian and Manchu languages was that of a "vast and flat area of the Mongolian plateau where the ground is covered with coarse substances and population is scarce." At present, the term frequently is used as a synonym for desert. The characteristics of a gobi are those of aridity, a flat and stony ground surface, and a vegetative cover of less than 30 per cent and usually less than 1 per cent. The stony surface is the most important characteristic in classifying gobis, of which there are many, depending upon the kind of parent material represented by the surface stones or gravels. The typical brown gobi soil of Bespalov is nonsaline, nongypsiferous, coarse-textured, deep, calcareous to the surface, and brown in color with lime accumulation layers in the subsoil. It is found on level-to-gentle slopes and has stones or gravel on the surface and in the subsoil. The soil resembles the isohumic brown and sierozem soils in many characteristics. A variation of the brown gobi soil occurs on steeper mountain footslopes where the stone content of the soil is greater. Surface stones of gobis protect the finer underlying soil to a considerable degree, but the strong winds of the desert manage to pick up large amounts of soil in spite of the stone cover (Bespalov, 1951).

Saline (solonchak) soils occur not only in closed depressions of the Gobi plains but also in the rolling plains of brown gobi soils and in depressions within the mountains. Soil textures are medium to fine and salt crusts are common. There is a very large number of small to large closed basins in the Gobi Desert where salts, mainly chloride and sulfate, accumulate. During periods of high winds, thick clouds of saline dust rise from the surface of the depressions, sometimes removing crusts of 2 or 3 centimeters in thickness (Bespalov, 1951). Such movement of salt by wind undoubtedly contributes to the salinization of soils in places where the parent rock is low in soluble materials. Takyrs, which are sodium-saline soils of the depressions, do not have a salt crust on the surface but are highly saline in the subsoil.

Sodium-affected (solonetz) soils are common on the slopes of large depressions above the saline soils of the bottoms, and they are found also on rolling plains. Surface soils are coarse to medium textured, and subsoils are finer textured, with a columnar or prismatic structure. Most solonetz are calcareous below the upper B horizon and contain gypsum in the lower subsoil (Bespalov, 1951).

Hummocky sandy soils and sand dunes occupy plains, gentle slopes, river valleys, and lake basins and usually are bare of vegetation due to heavy grazing pressure. While Bespalov estimated that only 5 per cent of the Gobi Desert in Outer Mongolia was composed of surface sands, the Sand Control Group surveying the Gobi and adjoining deserts in Inner Mongolia estimated that shifting sands occupied about 20 per cent of the area, with gobi soils covering some 34 per cent of the desert, low hilly land about 21 per cent, and marshy solonchaks most of the remainder. Extensive sand-dune fields (ergs) probably are found in some sections, but most of the dunes, which range from high to low in size, seem to be separated by gravelly and medium-textured materials. Sometimes the dunes form long lines across the landscape.

2. Soil Surveys

As is the case for the Takla-Makan Desert, only generalized small-scale maps are accessible for the Gobi Desert. The best is that of Bespalov for Outer Mongolia (Bespalov, 1951). The reports of the Sand Control Group (Academia Sinica, Sand Control Team, 1958) include some small-scale maps showing surface materials, but the reproduction (or the original maps) is too indistinct to be of much use. Other maps are only very general guides to the soils (Hou, Chen and Wang, 1957; Ma, 1947, 1957; Ma and Wen, 1958; Thorp and Hou, 1935).

J.   DESERTS OF AUSTRALIA

Australian soil scientists probably know the soils of the extremely arid part of their continent as well as or better than soil scientists in other countries know their own desert soils. As elsewhere, however, attention has been centered on the desert fringe where prospects for agricultural development are better than for the more arid interior.

1. Principal Soils Synthesis

A comparison of the 1944 map of Prescott (1944) and the 1959 map of Stephens (1960) displays the difference that 15 years has made in the knowledge of Australian arid-land soils. In addition to the change in terminology made at the great-soil-group level, soil boundaries also are quite different. Jackson (1957), who has worked extensively and intensively in the arid interior of Australia, has pointed out the change in thinking about soil conditions that have occurred since Prescott's map was published.

The variety of soils found in Australia is similar to those of other arid regions, with the exception that loose, eroding sand dunes appear to be limited in extent. Rather, the sand dunes, which are common, are fixed by a fairly dense vegetation cover. Among the more important soils are stony tablelands, sand plains having ironstone gravel, coarse-textured and deep brown soils, red and brown hardpan soils, deep red earths of medium to fine texture, and saline- and sodium-affected soils.

The similarity in variety of soils is not matched by a similarity in characteristics, if we exclude the salt and sodium soils which are much the same everywhere in the world. Australian arid-region soils, like those of a part of the Sahara, have characteristics indicative of soils having developed under a moister environment than the present. They are among the older soils in the world, and seem to resemble more nearly the soils of the Kalahari Desert and some of the southern Sahara soils than any others. The solution, movement, and dehydration of silicates has led to extensive occurrence of indurated siliceous (silcrete) layers, many of which now are exposed as surface crusts or as disintegrated crusts that constitute the stony surfaces. Calcareous soils are found on the less arid fringes of the desert more than in the interior. The reason for this somewhat anomalous situation is in dispute. Some scientists believe that the lime is the result of upward movement of water from weathered parent material, whereas others contend that it is the result of leaching of eolian deposits of calcareous materials from places such as the Nullarbor Plain or the seacoast (Jackson, 1957). In any event, data show that soils of the interior usually are acid, whether coarse or fine textured. This characteristic is in contrast to soils of the northern hemisphere deserts, in which the sandy soils may be slightly acid near the surface but the remainder commonly are alkaline throughout the profile and typically are calcareous at some depth. Whether this contrast is due to differences in age, kind of parent material, or groundwater conditions is an unresolved question.

Stony tableland soils resemble the reg and hamada soils of north Africa and southwest Asia, but, whereas regs and hamadas consist of stony surfaces of native rocks and gravels, the surfaces of the Australian stony deserts are covered with broken silcrete or silicified stones (Jackson, 1962). The exposed silcrete has an intense desert varnish or patina. The tableland designation arises from the occurrence of small, flat-topped mounds capped with silcrete, much like miniature sandstone-capped mesas of the United States. Underlying materials are medium to fine textured and deep unless more silcrete layers are present. Stony tableland soils commonly are calcareous, gypsiferous, or saline at some depth, probably as the result of former salt accumulation in depressions between the mounds, which now may be only a few feet high. Surface stones are called "gibber," billy gibber," or "grey billy," and they sometimes consist of native rocks coated with a siliceous crust (Jessup, 1951).

Sand plains are extensive in central and northern Australia, and, as the name indicates, they occupy level to gently undulating slopes. One of their distinctive features is the fossil lateritic ironstone gravels that they contain. Frequently, gently rolling fixed sand dunes are found on the plains, but wind erosion does not seem to be a major problem unless the sand dunes are disturbed. Sand plain soils have inclusions of what are called "clayey sands" because of the presence of significant amounts of clay. As with so many arid-region soils in Australia, they give evidence of being developed under a higher rainfall than the present one or of developing now on old, strongly weathered materials (Stephens, 1960). Sand dunes cover large areas near the flood plains of intermittent streams, from which coarse material has been blown out to form the dunes.

Coarse-textured brown soils are scattered throughout the semiarid regions, principally in southern Australia but also at the higher elevations near Alice Springs in the Northern Territory. They occupy a moderately rolling topography, are freely drained, deep, generally alkaline, and calcareous in the substratum.

Red and brown hardpan soils are confined, almost entirely, to the high plateau of Western Australia. The hardpan is an indurated siliceous layer that usually is within one or two feet of the soil surface and that may have a calcareous layer beneath it. Textures are coarse and stone pavements are widespread. The topograhy is smooth and slopes are moderate (Stephens, 1960).

Red earths are deep, coarse- to medium-textured soils having a porous structure unless underlain by alkaline clay subsoils, in which case they are called "texture-contrast" soils. Surface soils are acid, but lime may accumulate at some depth in the soils. The topography is gently rolling or level. Texture-contrast soils are saline above the clay subsoil, and internal drainage is restricted. They are referred to as solonetzic because of the fine texture, columnar or prismatic structure, and alkaline reaction of the subsoil.

Grey and brown fine-textured soils containing lime and sometimes gypsum in the subsoil are found in the northeastern arid and semiarid zones and in far southwestern Australia (Christian *et al.,* 1954; Perry *et al.,* 1962; Mabbutt *et al.,* 1963). They appear to be somewhat similar to sierozems and subtropical or semiarid isohumic brown soils but are finer textured than most sierozems of the northern hemisphere. The topography is level in some cases, and they show a surface microrelief called "gilgai," which consists of mounds a foot or more high and several feet across (Jessup, 1951).

Medium-textured calcareous soils of the arid regions are prevalent in the central, south, and west-coast sections. They may be derived from old calcareous alluvium, from limestone, or from calcareous material blown out of the salt lakes and deposited on leeward surfaces. Again, the topography is level to gently undulating, in the main. Surface soils may be noncalcareous, but subsoils are calcareous and may be gypsiferous as well (Stephens, 1960).

Salt- and sodium-affected soils are common components of the Australian landscape, in the semiarid and subhumid zones as well as in the arid zone. Saline soils occupy the numerous closed basins and intermittent lakes that are distinctive features of the dry part of the continent. The very extensive occurrence of saline subsoils, deep beds of gypsum, and saline groundwater indicates that salt accumulation has been going on for a very long time, in every section of the semiarid to arid zones. Stephens (1960) contends that the salts must be windborne oceanic salts, since the amount of chlorides on the continent cannot be accounted for by solution of the low-chloride minerals in the native rock. Analyses of rainwater from Perth, on the coast of Western Australia, to nearly 100 miles inland showed that the salt concentration decreased with distance from the coast (Hingston, 1958). Cyclic salts also could account for the high exchangeable sodium in the solonetz soils of the continent (Downes, 1954).

The landscape of arid Australia appears to be a vast plain interrupted by occasional desert mountains, large and small tablelands, and sand dunes, having many saline depressions and flood plains of intermittent streams. The dominant soil colors are red and reddish brown. Surface soil textures range from coarse to fine; surface-soil pH frequently is on the acid side of neutrality; calcareous, saline, and gypsiferous subsoils are common; organic matter content is very low; the red-earth soils are more highly leached and show much more development than would be expected under present climatic conditions; siliceous hardpans and silicified surface stones occur extensively in the interior; sand dunes and sandy soils in general are stabilized in position unless the surface is disturbed; arroyos and wadis are less common than in North America, North Africa, and the Middle East; and the soils are rather infertile.

2. Soil Surveys

Numerous soil surveys have been made by the Division of Soils of the Commonwealth Scientific and Industrial Research Organization (C. S. I. R. O.), which is headquartered at the Waite Institute near Adelaide, South Australia (FAO/Unesco Project, Soil Map of the World, 1965). The great majority of the surveys were conducted in the agricultural or potentially agricultural sections of southeastern, eastern, and southwestern Australia. Soil mapping was done on the basis of series and type, as used in the United States, and the mapping scale varied from 1/16,000 up to 1/64,000, in general, with soil-association maps at scales of 1/126,000 to 1/1,000,000. In recent years the C.S.I.R.O. Division of Land Research and Regional Survey has initiated a Land Research Series of publications which attempts to integrate the geology, geomorphology, climate, soils, vegetation, and hydrology of a large region into one comprehensive report that will show the resources of the region. Instead of mapping soils in the conventional way used by the Division of Soils, the Land Research Series maps show land systems. Land systems were defined by Christian and Stewart as "an area or group of areas throughout which there is a recurring pattern of topography, soils, and vegetation" (Christian and Stewart, 1953). Division teams survey large areas in relatively short periods, and much of the work depends on the interpretation of aerial photographs. In 1965 four teams were engaged in land-resource surveys, two on the mainland and two in Papua / New Guinea. Each team consists primarily of a geomorphologist, a pedologist (soil surveyor), and an ecologist, supplemented when needed by hydrologists, climatologists, and plant taxonomists.

The generalized soil map described at the 1960 International Congress of Soil Science (Stephens, 1960) is the latest and best for the entire continent. Several reconnaissance maps have been produced for parts of the arid zone, but, by and large, southwestern Queensland, northwest New South Wales, northern South Australia, and most of Western

Australia outside the extreme north and the agricultural southwest are little known. The most informative soil surveys that have been published for the arid zones include some in South Australia (Jackson, 1958; Jessup, 1951), Queensland (Christian *et al.*, 1954; Holland and Moore, 1962; Hubble and Beckmann, 1956; Sleeman, 1963), Northern Territory (Jackson, 1962; Perry *et al.*, 1962; Stewart, 1956), and Western Australia (Bettenay, 1961; Burvill and Teakle, 1938; Churchward and Bettenay, 1962; Mabbutt *et al.*, 1963; Speck *et al.*, 1960, 1964; Teakle, 1938).

Informative descriptions of soils in other sections of the arid regions, without soil maps, have been made for a small area in New South Wales (Sleeman and Butler, 1956), the township of Alice Springs in the Northern Territory (Wright, 1959), pasture lands in the Northern Territory (Perry, 1960), the Avon Valley in Western Australia (Wright, 1962), and for the arid regions in general (Jackson and Wright, 1960).

In 1960, the C. S. I. R. O. Division of Soils began to compile an atlas of Australian soils, with maps at a scale of 1/2,000,000, that will be the most accurate source of information on arid-zone soils, as well as for the remainder of the continent. The first of 10 projected sheets, for the Port Augusta/ Adelaide/Hamilton section of South Australia, has been completed. A revision of C. G. Stephens' (1962) "Manual of Australian Soils" will be published by C. S. I. R. O. in 1968.

All soil maps of Australia appear to be reliable and of high quality except that of Prescott (1944), which necessarily was based upon fragmentary information.

K. MONTE - PATAGONIAN DESERT

A few detailed soil surveys have been made in small and widely scattered parts of Argentina, and several generalized maps of the entire country have been prepared. These have associated with them numerous vegetation, geographic, land-use, and erosion maps containing information of interest to soil scientists, as well as many studies that have been conducted on soil-plant relations. The National University of Cuyo, in Mendoza, is the principal center for soils research located in the arid zones, but several other institutions conduct research in the semiarid areas to the east and north. The Instituto de Suelos y Agrotecnia in Buenos Aires has responsibility for nationwide research on soils.

1. Principal Soils Synthesis

Arid Argentina is located in the shadow of the Andes Mountains and, in the north, is an area of mountains, valleys, and extensive depressions occupied by saline deposits. In the south, the Patagonian Desert consists of low tablelands dissected by stream valleys. The mountain-and-valley appearance of arid western Argentina (north of Patagonia) merges on the east with the semiarid pampa and the semiarid chaqueña region (the Chaco). Both the pampa and the chaqueña are plains, the former covered with grass and the latter with shrubs and xerophytic trees. The semiarid pampa occupies the south, from Córdoba to Patagonia, while the chaqueña occupies the north, from Córdoba into Paraguay. South of the pampa is Patagonia. The puna and prepuna region of extreme northwestern Argentina is similar to the high altitude deserts of the Atacama-Peruvian deserts.

Mountain and hill soils in and near the Andes are lithosols. Wind and water erosion has removed the small amount of fine material that accumulates from weathering processes, leaving a shallow, stony soil. Slopes vary from steep to moderate, and there are many hills that have well-rounded tops, as well as some mesa-like mountains with steep escarpments.

Footslopes grade from coarse to medium in texture as one proceeds down the slope, and soils of the red desert group (north) or desert (south) may occur on the broad plains of the lower portion of the footslope. In most cases, the underlying material is calcareous. Some few sand dunes are present on the plains, but in areas where sandy surface material predominates it is more common to find small hummocks of sand around bushes than to see sand dunes.

Soils of the valleys are of variable texture, usually sandy or gravelly, occupying terraces and river flood plains. They are likely to be underlain by gravel in those cases where the surface deposit was medium- to fine-textured material. Soils are alkaline and normally calcareous to or near the surface, with some lime concretions and cementing of gravel in the subsoil. Salinity sometimes is a problem on the low-lying flood plains but usually is not a problem on the terrace soils (Miaczynski and Etchevehere, 1962).

Saline (halomorphic) soils occupy the small and large closed basins of the arid and semiarid north, the largest being the Salinas Grandes, which is about 150 miles long and nearly 30 miles across at its widest point. Soils of the salinas are deep, fine-textured, calcareous, low in organic matter, and frequently barren, and they have the polygonal surface-cracking pattern of takyrs. Salt crusts may or may not be present on the flat surface of the depressions (Papadakis, 1963).

Soils of the Patagonian plain are in some respects quite different from their arid counterparts around Mendoza. They are desert soils, developed on cemented gravels deposited by glacial rivers on what are now referred to as tablelands (Papadakis, 1963). Surface soils are medium textured, underlain by a textural B horizon higher in clay, which overlies the lime-cemented gravels. The surface and subsoil are very slightly to moderately acid down to the gravel layer. Organic matter is relatively high and, while strong winds blow continuously, wind erosion is not a serious problem because of the gravelly surface and the aggregation of soil particles by organic matter. Recent alluvial and saline soils are found along rivers and in depressions. Low-lying soils tend to be marshy and remain wet throughout most of the year.

Soil development is weak in the semiarid pampa and chaqueña areas, becoming greater as precipitation increases toward the east, where isohumic brown soils may be found as the subhumid pampa is approached. Shallow cemented calcium carbonate layers, called "tosca" in Argentina, are common in the brown soils adjoining the arid areas, but many deep alluvial soils are found there as well. Soil salinity is a problem wherever irrigation is practiced, apparently due to the presence of a high water table that results from heavy applications of water to the permeable soils.

2. Soil Surveys

The most authoritative maps of the soils of Argentina are the ones prepared by staff members of the Instituto de Suelos y Agrotecnia of the Instituto Nacional de Tecnología Agropecuaria (INTA) (Miaczynski and Etchevehere, 1962; Papadakis, Calcagno and Etchevehere, 1960). A brief description of Argentine soils in terms of the United States 7th Approximation Classification (Papadakis, 1963) is of interest but gives little information on the profile characteristics of the soils. Dr. P. H. Etchevehere of the Instituto de Suelos y Agrotecnia translated the English edition of the 7th Approximation of the U. S. D. A. Soil Classification into Spanish (U. S. Department of Agriculture, Soil Conservation Service, Soil Survey Staff, 1962).

A few reconnaissance and generalized maps have been published for parts of western and southern Argentina (Cappannini, 1952; Mikenberg, 1957; Papadakis, 1956), but they represent only a very small part of the arid regions and the soils descriptions are quite general. All in all, while many reports on some aspects of the soils of Argentina have been published, information on the characteristics and distribution of the important soils of the arid regions is severely limited (Comité Argentino . . ., 1963). The Instituto de Suelos y Agrotecnia, under the leadership of D. Cappannini and P. H. Etchevehere, is collaborating with P. Arens of FAO on the Argentina section of the FAO-Unesco Soil Map of the World Project.

Comprehensive descriptions of Argentine soils will be included in that publication.

L. ATACAMA - PERUVIAN

Studies of the soils of the extremely arid, arid, and semiarid regions of the Atacama and Peruvian deserts largely have been confined to the irrigated or potentially irrigable valleys along the Pacific Coast and in the Altiplano. A few detailed surveys have been made and a number of reports have been written on the characteristics of cultivated soils, but only general descriptions have been made of the non-irrigated soils other than in far-northern Chile.

1. Principal Soils Synthesis

In the arid regions of northern Chile only three kinds of soils are of any significance: skeletal soils of the mountains and plains, recent alluvial soils of the river valleys, and old lacustrine soils (Wright, 1961). A typical cross section of the country from the high Andes Mountains on the east to the Pacific Ocean on the west shows north-south bands of lithosols and barren rocks on the steep-sided mountains, followed by colluvial slopes of rock debris and gravel, which give way to the smoothly undulating plains of what Chileans call the "Meseta Central" and then to lower plains. West of the interior plains is the Cordillera de la Costa, with elevations up to about 6,000 feet in places, and between the mountains and the coast is a narrow, highly dissected marine terrace that becomes fairly wide in the extreme north of Chile and in Peru. Deep canyons with a sizable river floodplain in the bottom cut across the landscape from east to west and are the places where practically all the agriculture is located (Comité Chileno para el Estudio de las Zonas Aridas, 1963). The parent material of the plains west of the Andes is marine and continental sediments of sands, gravels, conglomerates, silts, and clays.

The central plains have very little vegetation and the predominant soils are very weakly developed coarse-textured and stony deposits. The plains of the Meseta Central are cut by alluvial formations and covered in places on the east by extensive coarse-textured colluvial deposits from the Andes, some of which have a salt crust on the surface. In the west of the Meseta Central, between latitude 20° and 25°S, are indurated nitrate beds that are a rich source of sodium and potassium nitrate plus other salts. There are no soils, only soft or indurated salt deposits of considerable thickness on smooth to gently undulating slopes.

In the Cordillera de la Costa, the soils are skeletal lithosols and regosols, without development, derived from indurated marine sediments and igneous rocks. North of about latitude 20°S one usually encounters saline soil materials, and there are extensive beds of gypsum. South of that latitude the soils are saline only in minor areas. The marine terraces between the coastal range and the ocean may be either coarse textured or medium textured, and they show a little tendency toward development of a textural B horizon of reddish color, presumably because of the high humidity caused by the heavy fogs along the coast. They are cut by river valleys and arroyos (quebrados) in which stratified soils occur, generally saline and sometimes slowly permeable. Sand dunes and broad sandy alluvial fans are found at the mouths of the streams (Comité Chileno para el Estudio de las Zonas Aridas, 1963).

The Meseta Central ends in the semiarid area of the Province of Coquimbo, where numerous low mountains and valleys cross the country between the Andes and the coastal range. Again, skeletal soils are encountered almost exclusively except in the valley bottoms. Soil materials of the low mountains are deep marine sediments of coarse to medium texture with clay layers sometimes found beneath the surface. The valley bottoms are coarse to medium textured, also, and frequently are underlain by gravel that may be cemented with lime (Díaz Vial *et al.*, 1958*a, b*; Díaz Vial and Meléndez Aguirre, 1958). The upland soils are calcareous, and the valley soils usually are calcareous within a foot or so of the surface.

A peculiarity of the desert landscape in Chile is the absence of sand dunes in a region such as in the central plain where soils are sandy and low in organic matter and where fairly strong winds blow regularly. The explanation for the resistance of the sands to wind movement appears to lie in the stabilizing effect of a thin crust of salt that forms at the soil surface (Wright, 1961). The salt comes from the original soil material or is brought in on the winds, and crust formation becomes less with increased distance from the coast.

Although solonchaks seldom are mentioned in discussions of coastal soils of Peru and Chile, it seems likely that many if not most of them would be at least slightly to moderately saline as the result of the deposition and accumulations of cyclic salt.

The coastal arid region of Peru is a continuation of the marine terrace found along the coast of Chile, where it is much narrower, for the most part, than in Peru. East of the coastal plain and in a few places within the plain are low barren mountains of lithosols that grade into the high mountains of the Cordillera de los Andes (Drosdoff, Queredo, and Zamora, 1960). About 52 rivers, half of which are perennial, have cut valleys across the marine terrace on their way from the Andes to the Pacific Ocean. All soils of the south and central part of the coastal plain are undeveloped; some of the northern soils, where precipitation is greater, show moderate development. About 5 per cent of the arid coastal region consists of alluvial soils, 65 per cent of lithosols, 25 per cent of regosols, and 5 per cent of red desert and black clay soils (Comité Peruano de Zonas Aridas, 1963).

Soils of the marine terrace are regosols that occur on a level to undulating topography and are derived from unconsolidated marine sediments of Quaternary age and from material deposited by wind. The marine sediments are stratified sands, gravels, and clays, with frequent inclusions of strata of gypsum, lime, and indurated salts (Comité Peruano de Zonas Aridas, 1963). Sand dunes are common and in many cases occupy relatively large expanses of land. The terrace soils are the best of the extensive potentially irrigable soils of western Peru.

Alluvial soils of the transverse valleys of the coastal plain are found in long, narrow strips along the rivers. They are stratified and vary in texture and depth from shallow, coarse-textured soils near the mountains to deep, fine-textured soils near the sea. The soils are neutral to alkaline and frequently contain an abundance of soluble salts, gypsum, and calcium carbonate. As agricultural soils, they have high potential if soil drainage is adequate to control salt accumulation.

In the northern zone of the Peruvian coastal plain where the precipitation averages about 10 to 12 inches per year, soils display some development in contrast to the central and southern soils. Red desert soils generally are fine textured, deep, moderately well drained, and contain lime concretions or indurated lime layers in the lower subsoil. Dark grey soils are the second of the two important soils of the north. They are deep, plastic clays having a high pH and a low permeability. Salinity does not appear to be a problem in most of the northern coastal soils, but there are areas of saline soils in the dark grey soils (Flores Cosio, 1954).

The semiarid altiplano of Peru and Bolivia is a level to gently undulating plain with low hills. The soils are (*a*) shallow loams to silt loams, with a stony or gravelly surface, (*b*) deep loams to silt loams with good drainage, and (*c*) deep, black, poorly drained, medium- to fine-textured soils in depressions and near Lake Titicaca (Storie, 1963). They are derived from alluvial or lacustrine deposits and are neutral to slightly acid, indicating that a moderate degree of leaching has occurred. Organic matter content is less than 2 per cent except in the black soils. The latter probably are quite similar to vertisols.

On the 12,000-foot altiplano of Chile where frosts may occur any day of the year, many of the soils are derived mainly from coalescent fan alluvium and colluvium of volcanic origin and of various ages. There are inclusions of sierozems, bog soils known as "bofedales," some alluvial soils, and saline depressions. Soil development is weak, and the sequence of surface materials goes from stony shallow soils on the sides and slopes of mountain peaks and volcanos to deep medium-textured soils in the valleys and depressions. Organic matter is high in the bog soils, which form near springs on the altiplano (Wright, 1961).

2. Soil Surveys

Generalized soil maps have been made for Chile (Roberts, 1958), Peru (Drosdoff, Queredo, and Zamora, 1960; Drosdoff and Zamora, 1959), and Bolivia (Storie, 1953). The map and accompanying report for Chile is the only single source of information on the distribution of great soil groups in northern Chile, but descriptions of arid-zone soils in it are much less complete than those of Wright and others (Díaz Vial *et al.*, 1958*a, b*; Díaz Vial and Meléndez Aguirre, 1958; Meléndez Aguirre and Wright, 1962, 1963*a, b*; Wright, 1961). Peruvian soil reports are most accurate for the coastal region where irrigation developments have ben planned and for an area on the west and north of Lake Titicaca (Zamora, 1958*a, b, c, d*; 1961; Zavaleta, 1960), again where irrigation is planned.

Detailed surveys have been made of several irrigated valleys of northern Chile by the Ministry of Agriculture, but the maps have not been published and there does not appear to be any intent to do so. Similarly, unpublished maps are in the files of the Servicio Cooperativo Interamericano de Producción de Alimentos (SCIPA) in Lima, Peru. None is known for the arid regions of Bolivia.

M. DESERTS OF NORTH AMERICA

The United States soil-survey program was started in 1899 for the purpose of determining the suitability of soils for farming. In the arid western states, this determination consisted of analyzing suitability for irrigation agriculture along the rivers and for dry-land farming in the Great Plains and the northwest. Maps showing the areas covered by soil surveys in the western states make it apparent that emphasis on agricultural land has continued and that knowledge of nonirrigated arid region soils is rather limited.

In Mexico an active soil-survey program has not developed, with the consequence that information is scarce on the soil resources of that country. The federal government has centered its attention in the arid regions on soil fertility, salinity, and drainage problems.

1. Principal Soils Synthesis

Soils of the arid regions of North America belong, for the most part, to the red desert, desert (grey desert), sierozem, calcisol, solonchak, solonetz, lithosol, regosol, and alluvial great soil groups, with sierozem, lithosol, red desert, regosol, and alluvial groups being most extensive, in approximately that order (Western Regional Soil Survey Work Group, 1964).

The major great soil groups of the semiarid fringe of the arid regions are brown, reddish brown, chestnut, and reddish chestnut. The greatest expanse of such soils is in the Great Plains and in the Intermountain Basin.

Mountains and basins of the basin-and-range province of Nevada, western Utah, southeastern California, southwestern Arizona, and western Sonora represent the largest part of the arid regions. The Colorado Plateau, with its highly dissected landscape, is another major unit, as is the so-called Chihuahuan Desert of New Mexico and all of Mexico north of the city of San Luis Potosí between the Sierra Madre Oriental and the Sierra Madre Occidental. Smaller units include substantial parts of Baja California, the Central Valley of California, the Wyoming Basin, the Snake River Plain, and the Columbia Basin.

In the mountain and basin country, the sequence of soils typically follows a repeating pattern of lithosols on mountains, medium- to coarse-textured red desert, desert, or sierozem soils on alluvial fans and terraces, and alluvial, solonchak, or solonetz soils in the bottoms (Western Regional Soil Survey Work Group, 1964). Salt-affected (solonchak) and sodium-affected (solonetz) soils commonly occur in the playas that occupy the bottoms of the closed basins, as do nonsolonetz sodium soils. The basins, whether closed or with surface drainage, usually are several miles wide, and a cross section of the surface from mountain to mountain resembles a flattened bowl. In the sequence of soils, the only ones showing significant amounts of development are the red desert, desert, sierozem, and solonetz soils. Red desert soils occur in the hotter parts of the arid regions, in the north of Chihuahua, Sonora, and Baja California, and in the southern parts of (U. S.) California, Nevada, Utah, Arizona, and New Mexico. Sierozems are found in the cooler areas and desert soils in the transitional zone between red desert and sierozem. Regosols of the arid regions are formed on eolian sands, in the main, and occur as dunes or hummocks on alluvial fans, terraces, and plains.

Lithosols are shallow, stony, or rocky soils that have a thin surface horizon and show weak development due to erosion and the downslope movement of weathered rocks. They may be found on ridges, plateaus, or mesas, as well as on the colluvial slopes beneath them. Some organic matter accumulates in the surface, and calcium carbonate commonly is precipitated on the fractured rocks of the parent material.

Regosols, like lithosols, have only a thin surface horizon and little or no evidence of development, although there may be some slight accumulation of lime under the surface. Regosols of arid North America are wind-worked soils, principally of granite alluvium or weathered sandstone. Sand dunes and hummocks are small compared to those of North Africa and the Arabian Desert area, and there are no large fields of barren, shifting dunes like the ergs of North Africa except for the sand-dune fields near Yuma (Ives, 1959). Localized dunes, both barren and stabilized, are common in the red desert area.

Red desert soils have sandy loam to silt loam A horizons that usually are less than 6 inches thick, reddish brown in color, and platy; they have a pronounced vesicular character in the top 1 or 2 inches. The underlying B horizon is thicker, redder, and a little finer textured than the surface layer. Calcium carbonate layers are found in the lower B horizon, and they are sometimes cemented, particularly if the soil is underlain by gravels. Not much is known about silica movement and precipitation in red desert soils, but it appears that silica hardpans, consisting of a mixture of silica and lime, are fairly common and that silica may contribute significantly to the cementation of carbonate layers. Internal drainage is good and red desert soils are nonsaline in the upper horizons. They may or may not be calcareous and alkaline in the A-horizon. A gravelly surface (desert pavement), probably due largely to removal of fine materials by wind and water erosion, is characteristic of these soils, and it contributes to the stability of the surface and its resistance to further wind and water erosion (Springer, 1958; Denny, 1965). The topography on which red desert soils occur is gently undulating to smooth with long slopes, and the landform may be alluvial fans and terraces, colluvial slopes, plateaus, or mesas.

Sierozem soils are found in the less-arid part of the arid region. Although some soils in the area have a grey or greyish-brown surface color and a little more organic matter in the surface horizon they are included in the sierozems because they have similar profile characteristics. Sierozems occupy desert basins, valleys, plateaus, and mesas.

Desert soils are transitional between red desert and sierozem in all characteristics, the principal distinguishing feature being a browner color than the other two.

Calcisols are highly calcareous soils having a pale brown to dark brown color, weak development, and, frequently, high concentrations of gypsum in the subsoil. A soft or indurated accumulation of calcium carbonate occurs within a foot or so of the soil surface, and the layer may be several feet thick. Calcisols are found on fans, terraces, plateaus, and mesas, where the topography is smooth to gently undulating.

Solonchaks are highly saline and medium to fine textured in most cases. Usually found in low-lying areas (Hunt, 1960), they also occur on upland areas where the parent material is saline sediments. The soils commonly show little or no development. They may or may not have salt crust on the surface and be high in exchangeable sodium. Playa soils having low amounts of salt in the surface soil and high amounts in the subsoil, with moderate to high exchangeable sodium percentages in the surface and subsoil, are similar to Russian takyrs. The surface is smooth, crusted, and hard when dry; it has polygonal cracks. Such playas are barren or only sparsely vegetated.

Solonetz soils typically have a distinctive prismatic or columnar subsoil structure overlain by a thin surface horizon having a platy structure. The surface soil usually is alkaline and the subsoil strongly alkaline and slowly permeable. Textures of the surface soil vary from fine sandy loam to silt loam, with the subsoil finer textured. Solonetz soils may be calcareous throughout the profile or there may be an accumulation of calcium carbonate, and sometimes gypsum and soluble salts, in the lower subsoil. Exchangeable sodium usually is high in the prismatic horizon, which leads to the typical poor permeability of that horizon. Solonetz soils usually are found in desert basins.

Recent alluvial soils are important for irrigated agriculture in the mountain and basin region but are restricted to stream fans (Denny, 1965) and to rather narrow flood plains along stream bottoms except for the large sections of alluvium in the Central Valley and Imperial Valley of California (Storie and Harradine, 1958) and the Mexicali area in Baja California. Alluvial soils commonly are stratified, have textures that run the gamut from gravel to clay, and often are underlain by sand or gravel. Usually they are calcareous to the surface and contain moderate to low amounts of salt. Little or no development is apparent in them although they may contain moderate amounts of organic matter in the surface.

In the Chihuahuan Desert on the east of the North American arid zone, the same variety of soils occurs as is found in the mountain and basin area previously described. The principal difference seems to be that in Mexico there are fewer and lower desert mountains and the landscape is more dissected by dry stream beds (Comité Mexicano de Zonas Aridas, 1963).

In southwestern New Mexico, southeastern Arizona, and northern Chihuahua, the topography is similar to that of the mountain and basin area and the same sequence of soils is found. The Pecos Valley of New Mexico and Texas is distinguished by the large area of calcisols that is found there (Baldwin, Kellogg and Thorp, 1938). In Mexico, the arid area between the Sierra Madre Oriental and the Sierra Madre Occidental is referred to as the "Altiplanicie Mexicana" because elevations are over 3,000 feet and the topography is that of a plain broken by low mountains, hills, and erosion channels (Comité Mexicano de Zonas Aridas, 1963). The dominant rock of the mountains is calcareous sedimentary material, which accounts for the calcareous nature of the great majority of the soils. The closed basins range from small to very large in size, and the soils are deep, silty desert soils, sometimes saline but generally not sodium-affected prior to irrigation. There are limited areas of red desert soils in the uplands of northern Chihuahua, but most of the upland soils in the Altiplanicie Mexicana are called sierozems. Sandy soils are not mentioned in the meager number of reports on Mexican arid-zone soils, so it is probable that they are not extensive or that sand dunes are not obvious features of the landscape even though sandy soils may occupy significantly large areas.

Personal observations in Chihuahua and the character of the landscape indicate that gravelly and stony surfaces should be a common feature of the alluvial and colluvial fans and of the mesas. Extrapolating from similar conditions in the United States and elsewhere, the underlying material should be coarse-textured sands and gravels or shallow soils over bedrock.

Sierozems are said to be the principal soils of Baja California and the area along the Gulf of California in Sonora and Sinaloa (Comité Mexicano de Zonas Aridas, 1963). There probably are significant areas of lithosols and alluvial soils, too.

Turning to the northwestern states of the U. S., the Snake River Plains of southern Idaho and eastern Oregon and the Columbia Basin in Washington and Oregon have extensive areas of typical sierozem soils (Marbut, 1935). The underlying material may be basalt, which is widespread in both regions, or gravelly glacial outwash. Eolian sand and loessial deposits cover large areas. As a consequence, sandy loam and silt loam are the common textures of surface soils in both regions. Calcisol, lithosol, solonetz and alluvial soils are much less extensive than sierozems, and only small areas of regosols and solonchak soils are present.

The highly dissected Colorado Plateau of Colorado, Utah, Arizona, and New Mexico has sierozem soils on the tops of the individual plateaus and lithosol, regosol, reddish brown, and red desert soils on the edges. Desert and sierozem soils are extensive in the rolling plains of the Wyoming Basin, with only small areas of lithosol found there.

Alluvial soils consisting of recent deposits on alluvial fans, terraces and floodplains cover most of the Central Valley of California (Storie and Harradine, 1958). In the San Joaquin Valley, south of the Sacramento delta, there also are large areas of solonchak and solonetz soils, some of them formed as a result of high water tables caused by irrigation.

2. Soil Surveys

A few detailed soil surveys and some reconnaissance surveys were made in Mexico by the Comisión Nacional de Irrigación 20 to 30 years ago in areas where irrigation was practiced or where irrigation development was anticipated. These maps, with a brief description of the soils and the results of simple chemical analyses, are in the files of the Ministry of Hydraulic Resources in Mexico City. According to one estimate (Fernández de Lara, 1953), reconnaissance soil surveys completed before 1958 covered 30 million acres of land, most of it in the arid regions.

A generalized soil map based upon climate and the geographic features of the country has been prepared for Mexico (Brambila and Ortiz Monasterio, 1956) and is the official soil map of the nation. It indicates the kind of zonal soils that should be formed under the climatic conditions of Mexico, rather than what actually is present. A series of maps showing erosion status, surface texture, etc., of the soils of Mexico also has been published (Ortiz Monasterio, 1956).

About 100 soil-survey reports of U. S. arid regions, with maps, have been published by the U. S. Department of Agriculture since the survey program was begun in 1899 (U. S. Department of Agriculture, Soil Conservation Service, 1963). Prior to 1957, the usual map scale was 1 inch equals 1 mile (1/62,500 or 1/63,360) for detailed maps and up to 1/400,000 for reconnaissance maps. Since 1957, most detailed maps have been published at scales from 1/20,000 to 1/7,920. Earlier published maps were on a planimetric base, whereas maps printed since the 1950's commonly have been on a photomosaic base. The University of Arizona Office of Arid Lands

Studies has a card index file on United States soil-survey reports for the arid regions, and requests for information can be directed there, to the agricultural experiment stations of the various state universities, or to the Information Division of Soil Conservation Service in Washington, D. C. Three publications, one for Texas (Carter, 1931) and two for California (Storie and Weir, 1951; Storie and Harradine, 1958) discuss the soils of those two states in some detail and are good sources of information.

Numerous unpublished soil surveys were made by the Soil Conservation Service in the late 1930's and 1940's. In general, the surveys are of limited value because of the difficulty of correlation of soil series, and the fact that series concepts have changed since the surveys were made. The present soil-survey program of the Federal Soil Conservation Service is an active one, but publication of maps and reports lags far behind the field-survey work. No western state publishes detailed soil-survey reports. U.S. Forest Service soil surveys are published by the Soil Conservation Service.

In some areas, the United States Bureau of Reclamation conducts a land-classification survey to determine the suitability of soils for irrigation. Bureau maps of the final land classification provide no soils information, but fairly complete data on the physical and chemical properties of the soils can be obtained by referring to the office records of the Bureau soil scientists.

The most reliable generalized soil map for the United States was prepared in 1964 (U. S. Department Agriculture, Soil Conservation Service, 1964). It is an experimental map using 7th Approximation terminology along with approximate equivalents in great soil groups.

Soil surveys conducted in the United States prior to about 1920 are of historical interest, in the main. In later years, with improved techniques and understanding of soil formation, quality has improved. Surveys made during the past 20 years usually are reliable. No significant soil surveys of the arid regions of Mexico have been seen by this reviewer.

AUTHORITIES AND DEPOSITORIES

Outstanding experts on aspects of surface materials of the world's deserts are listed in Table I by area and subject of specialization. Table II lists the world's libraries and other depositories of desert-soils information by country of location of the institution; notes are made of holdings transcending the borders of the nation of depository location.

Table I
Part A. Geographic Table of Soil Authorities

Arabic numbers are explained in the list of authorities constituting part B of this table.

Desert	Country	General	Chemistry	Physics	Biology	Classification
Kalahari-Namib	South West Africa	1				1, 2, 3, 4
	South Africa	2, 3		5, 6		2, 3, 7
Sahara		8	9			4, 8, 9, 10
	Algeria	11, 13		11	12	11, 13
	Chad	10	10			10
	Mauritania	14			14	14
	Niger					15
	Sudan		16		17	18
	Egypt (U.A.R.)	19	19, 20, 21		22	23
	Morocco	24			25	24
Somali-Chalbi		4				4, 26
Arabian						26,
	Iran	27, 28				27, 28
	Iraq	29, 30	30, 31			29
	Israel	32, 34	33, 34, 35	36	37	32, 34
	Jordan					26
	Saudi Arabia					38
	Syria					39
Iranian	Afghanistan					40
	Iran	27, 38				27, 28
	Pakistan	41	41			41, 42
Thar	India	44, 45	44, 45, 47	48	49	44, 46
	Pakistan	41, 42	41			41, 42, 43
Turkestan	U. S. S. R.	50, 51	54, 55, 51 52, 53	56, 57, 58, 59	60, 61	62, 63, 64, 65
Takla-Makan	China	66, 67, 68				66, 67, 68
Gobi	China	66, 67, 68				66, 67, 68
	Outer Mongolia	67, 69				67, 69
Australian	Australia	70, 71	96, 97,	75, 76, 77	79	70, 72, 80 81, 82
Monte-Patagonian	Argentina	83	98, 99			85, 86
Atacama-Peruvian	Chile	87				87
	Peru	89, 90, 91	72, 73, 74			89, 90
North American	Mexico	92				92
	U. S. A.	93, 94, 95	84 88	100, 101, 102, 103,	104, 105, 106	93, 94, 38, 107

Table I (Continued)
Part B. List of Soil Authorities
Arabic numbers are used to represent these authorities in part A of this table.

1. R. Ganssen
   Institut für Bodenkunde der
   Universität
   Bertoldstrasse 17
   78 Freiburg/Breisgau
   German Federal Republic
2. C. R. van der Merwe
   Soils Research Institute
   Private Bag 79
   Pretoria, South Africa
3. R. F. L. Loxton
   Soils Research Institute
   Private Bag 79
   Pretoria, South Africa
4. J. L. d'Hoore
   Centre for Tropical Soil Science
   92 Avenue Cardinal Mercier
   Hererlee-Lenven, Belgium
5. S. H. Kuhn
   National Institue for
     Road Research, C. S. I.R.
   Pretoria, South Africa
6. P. J. Rigden
   National Institute for
     Road Research, C. S. I. R.
   Pretoria, South Africa
7. J. M. de Villiers
   Soil Science Department
   University of Natal
   Private Bag 9021
   Pietermaritzburg (Natal),
     South Africa
8. Georges Aubert
   Office de la Recherche Scientifique
     et Technique Outre-Mer
   24, rue Bayard
   Paris 8ᵉ, France
9. B. Dabin
   Office de la Recherche Scientifique
     et Technique Outre-Mer
   70 - 74, Route d'Aulnay
   Bondy (Seine), France
10. J. Pias
    Office de la Recherche Scientifique
      et Technique Outre-Mer
    70 - 74, Route d'Aulnay
    Bondy (Seine), France
11. J. H. Durand
    Service Pédologique
    Division des Sols de l' I. R. A. T.
    45 Avenue de la Belle Gabrielle
    Nogent-sur-Marne (Seine), France
12. Charles Killian (deceased)
    Laboratoire de Biologie
      Saharienne
    Beni-Ounif, Algeria
13. J. Boulaine
    Ecole Nationale Supérieure
      Agronomique
    Grignon, France

14. P. Audry
    Office de la Recherche Scientifique
      et Technique Outre-Mer
    70 - 74, Route d'Aulnay
    Bondy (Seine), France
15. G. Bocquier
    Centre de Recherche Pédologie,
    O. R. S. T. O. M.
    B. P. No. 138
    Dakar, Senegal
16. K. D. Rai
    Soil Section,
      Gezira Research Station
    P. O. Box 126
    Wad Medani, Sudan
17. G. Jagnow
    Soil Section,
      Gezira Research Station
    P. O. Box 126
    Wad Medani, Sudan
18. L. H. J. Ochtman
    Soil Survey Division,
      Gezira Research Station
    P. O. Box 126
    Wad Medani, Sudan
19. M. Elgabaly
    Faculty of Agriculture
    University of Alexandria
    Alexandria, United Arab Republic
20. M. A. Abdel Salam
    Desert Institute
    Mataria
    Cairo, United Arab Republic
21. Malek T. Kaddah
    Soil Salinity Laboratory
    Bacos
    Alexandria, United Arab Republic
22. S. Eldin Taha
    Department of Soil Microbiology
    Faculty of Agriculture
    Ain Shams University
    Cairo, United Arab Republic
23. A. G. Abdel Samie
    National Research Center
    Dokki
    Cairo, United Arab Republic
24. A. Ruellan
    Office National des Irrigations
    B. P. 97
    Berkane, Morocco
25. A. Sasson
    Laboratoire de Microbiologie
    Faculté des Sciences
    Rabat, Morocco
26. R. Dudal
    World Soil Resources Office,
      F.A.O.
    Viale delle Terme di Caracalla
    Rome, Italy

27. M. L. Dewan
    F.A.O.
    Viale delle Terme di Caracalla
    Rome, Italy
28. Jalal Famouri
    Soils Institute
    Amirabad
    Tehran, Iran
29. P. Buringh
    Division of Tropical Soils
    State Agricultural University
    Wageningen, The Netherlands
30. L. T. Kadry
    Division of Soils and Agricultural
      Chemistry
    Directorate General of
      Agricultural Research
    Abu-Ghraib, Iraq
31. L. Pavel
    Arid Zone Research Institute
    University of Baghdad
    Abu-Ghraib, Iraq
32. Joel Dan
    Agricultural Research Station
    Beit Dagan
    Rehovot, Israel
33. D. H. Yaalon
    Department of Geology
    Hebrew University
    Jerusalem, Israel
34. S. Ravikovitch
    Faculty of Agriculture
    Hebrew University
    Rehovot, Israel
35. M. Ben-Yair
    The Standards Institute of Israel
    Bney Yisrael Street
    Ramat Aviv
    Tel Aviv, Israel
36. D. Hillel
    Agricultural Research Station
    Beit Dagan
    Rehovot, Israel
37. Shira Borut
    Department of Microbiology
    Hebrew University
    Jerusalem, Israel
38. LeMoyne Wilson
    Department of Soils
      and Meterology
    Utah State University
    Logan, Utah, U. S. A.
39. W. J. van Liere
    World Soil Resources Office,
      F. A. O.
    Viale delle Terme di Caracalla
    Rome, Italy
40. Claude L. Fly
    1604 Prospect Lane
    Fort Collins, Colorado, U. S. A.

Table I (Continued)

41. Abdul Wahhab Khan
    Director of Agriculture
    Peshawar District
    Peshawar, West Pakistan
42. R. A. Gardner
    G. P. O. Box 48
    Lahore, West Pakistan
43. A. G. Asghar
    Water and Soils Investigation
        Division
    Water and Power Development
        Authority
    Lahore, West Pakistan
44. S. P. Raychaudhuri
    Planning Commission, Government
        of India
    Vojna Bhavan, Parliament Street
    New Delhi - 1, India
45. R. V. Tamhane
    Soil Conservation Department
    Ministry of Food and Agriculture
    New Delhi - 1, India
46. S. P. Seth
    Indian Agricultural Research
        Institute
    New Delhi - 12, India
47. J. S. Kanwar
    Indian Council of
        Agricultural Research,
    New Delhi, India
48. C. T. Abichandani
    Central Arid Zone Research
        Institute
    Jodhpur, Rajasthan, India
49. W. V. B. Sundara Rao
    Indian Agricultural Research
        Institute
    New Delhi - 12, India
50. I. P. Gerassimov
    Geography Institute
    U.S.S.R. Academy of Sciences
    Staromonetni 29,
    Moscow - 17, U.S.S.R.
51. V. A. Kovda
    Dokuchaev Soil Institute
    Pyjevski - 7, Moscow - 17, U.S.S.R.
52. V. Egorov
    Dokuchaev Soil Institute
    Pyjevski 7, Moscow - 17, U.S.S.R.
53. I. M. Lipkind
    Institute of Soil Science
    Tadzhik Academy of Sciences
    Dushanbe, Tadzhik S.S.R.,
        U.S.S.R.
54. Academician I. S. Rabochev
    Institute of Soil Sciences
    Ashkhabad, Turkmen S.S.R.,
        U.S.S.R.
55. N. I. Gorbunov
    Dokuchaev Soil Institute
    Pyjevski - 7, Moscow - 17, U.S.S.R.
56. N. V. Ornatsky
    Department of Geology
    Moscow State University
    Moscow, U.S.S.R.

57. R. A. Tokar
    Institute of Foundation
        Engineering Research
    Academy of Construction and
        Architecture
    Moscow, U.S.S.R.
58. A. A. Rode
    Dokuchaev Soil Institute
    Pyjevski - 7, Moscow - 17, U.S.S.R.
59. A. V. Nikolaev
    Institute of Soil Science
    Tadzhik Academy of Sciences
    Dushanbe, Tadzhik S.S.R.,
        U.S.S.R.
60. Yu. O. Darzniyek
    Institute of Soil Science
    Turkmen Academy of Sciences
    Ashkhabad, Turkmen S.S.R.,
        U.S.S.R.
61. M. M. Kononova
    Dukuchaev Soil Institute
    Pyjevski 7, Moscow - 17, U.S.S.R.
62. E. Lobova
    Dokuchaev Soil Institute
    Pyjevski 7, Moscow - 17, U.S.S.R.
63. Academician V. R. Volobuyev
    Institute of Soil Science and
        Agrochemistry
    Azerbaidjan Academy of Sciences
    Baku, Azerbaidjan S.S.R., U.S.S.R.
64. P. A. Kerzum
    Institute of Soil Science
    Tadzhik Academy of Sciences
    Dushanbe, Tadzhik S.S.R.,
        U.S.S.R.
65. M. A. Pankov
    Institute of Soil Science
    Uzbek Academy of Agricultural
        Sciences
    Tashkent, Uzbek S.S.R., U.S.S.R.
66. Ma Yung-chin
    Institute of Soil Science
    Chinese Academy
    Nanking, China
67. V. A. Kovda
    Dokuchaev Soil Institute
    Pyjevski 7, Moscow - 17, U.S.S.R.
68. James Thorp
    Department of Geology
    Earlham College
    Richmond, Indiana, U.S.A.
69. N. D. Bespalov
    Dokuchaev Soil Institute
    Pyjevski 7, Moscow - 17, U.S.S.R.
70. C. G. Stephens
    Division of Soils, C. S. I. R. O.
    Waite Institute, Private Bag No. 1
    Adelaide, South Australia, Australia
71. G. A. Stewart
    Division of Land Research,
        C.S.I.R.O.
    P. O. Box 109
    Canberra City, A. C .T., Australia

72. E. G. Hallsworth
    Division of Soils, C. S. I. R. O.
    Waite Institute, Private Bag No. 1
    Adelaide, South Australia, Australia
73. J. P. Quirk
    Department of Soil Science and
        Plant Nutrition
    University of Western Australia
    Nedlands, Western Australia,
    Australia
74. J. K. Powrie
    Waite Institute, Private Bag No. 1
    Adelaide, South Australia, Australia
75. R. O. Slatyer
    Australian National University
    P.O. Box 475
    Canberra City, A. C. T., Australia
76. A. M. Posner
    Department of Soil Science and
        Plant Nutrition
    University of Western Australia
    Nedlands, Western Australia,
    Australia
77. R. J. Millington
    Department of Agronomy
    University of Illinois,
    Urbana, Illinois, U.S.A.
78. G. D. Aitchison
    Soil Mechanics Section, C. S. I. R. O.
    Coleman Pde.
    Syndal, Victoria, Australia
79. C. M. Sims
    Department of Biology
    University of Adelaide
    Adelaide, South Australia,
    Australia
80. E. A. Jackson
    Agricultural Research Liaison
        Section, C. S. I. R. O.
    372 Albert Street
    East Melbourne, C2, Victoria,
    Australia
81. W. H. Litchfield
    Division of Land Research,
        C.S.I.R.O.
    P. O. Box 109
    Canberra City, A. C. T., Australia
82. R. Brewer
    Soil Micropedology Section
    Division of Soils, C.S.I.R.O.
    Canberra City, A.C.T., Australia
83. A. J. Prego
    Instituto de Suelos y Agrotecnia,
        I. N. T. A.
    Castelar - F. C. Sarmiento
    Provincia de Buenos Aires,
    Argentina
84. L. Nijensohn
    Instituto Investigaciones de Suelo
        y Riego
    Facultad de Ciencias Agrarias
    Chacras de Coria
    Mendoza, Argentina

Table I (Continued)

85. P. H. Etchevehere
Instituto de Suelos y Agrotecnia,
I. N. T. A.
Castelar - F. C. Sarmiento
Provincia de Buenos Aires,
Argentina

86. Juan Papadakis
Instituto de Suelos y Agrotecnia
I. N. T. A.
Castelar - F. C. Sarmiento
Provincia de Buenos Aires,
Argentina

87. Eduardo Melendez
Departamento de Conservación y
Asistencia Técnica
Ministerio de Agricultura
Arica, Chile

88. Elias Letelier A.
Sociedad Nacional de Agricultura
Tenderini 187
Santiago, Chile

89. Carlos Zamora
Ministerio de Agricultura,
S. C. I. P. A.
Lima, Peru

90. A. G. Zavaleta
Estación Agricola La Molina
Apartado 2791
Lima, Peru

91. Matthew Drosdoff
International Agricultural
Development Service
U. S. Department of Agriculture
Washington, D. C. 20025, U. S. A.

92. Rafael Ortiz Monasterio
Ministerio de Recursos Hidráulicos
Mexico, D. F., Mexico

93. W. G. Harper
c/o U. S. Salinity Laboratory
P. O. Box 672
Riverside, California, U. S. A.

94. W. M. Johnson
Soil Conservation Service,
U. S. D. A.
P. O. Box 520
Berkeley, California, U. S. A.

95. H. E. Dregne
Department of Agronomy
New Mexico State University
Las Cruces, New Mexico, U. S. A.

96. C. A. Bower
U. S. Salinity Laboratory
P. O. Box 672
Riverside, California, U. S. A.

97. Roy Overstreet
Department of Soils and Plant
Nutrition
University of California
Berkeley, California, U. S. A.

98. R. S. Whitney
Department of Agronomy
Colorado State University
Fort Collins, Colorado, U. S. A.

99. L. D. Whittig
Department of Soils and Plant
Nutrition
University of California
Davis, California, U. S. A.

100. W. D. Kemper
Department of Agronomy
Colorado State University
Fort Collins, Colorado, U. S. A.

101. W. H. Gardner
Department of Agronomy
Washington State University
Pullman, Washington, U. S. A.

102. D. D. Evans
Department of Agricultural
Chemistry and Soils
University of Arizona
Tucson, Arizona, U. S. A.

103. C. H. M. van Bavel
Department of Biology
Texas A & M University
College Station, Texas, U.S.A.

104. F. E. Broadbent
Department of Soils and
Plant Nutrition
University of California
Davis, California, U. S. A.

105. R. E. Cameron
Jet Propulsion Laboratory
California Institute of Technology
Pasadena, California, U. S. A.

106. W. H. Fuller
Department of Agricultural
Chemistry and Soils
University of Arizona
Tucson, Arizona, U. S. A.

107. A. A. Aandahl
Soil Conservation Service,
U. S. D. A.
134 South 12th Street
Lincoln, Nebraska, U. S. A.

Table II
DEPOSITORIES OF SOILS INFORMATION

Afghanistan: Ministry of Agriculture
                Kabul, Afghanistan

Algeria: Institut de Recherches Sahariennes
                Université d'Alger
                Alger, Algeria

Angola: Geological and Mining Survey
                Luanda, Angola

Argentina: (1) Instituto Nacional de Tecnología
                    Agropecuaria
                    Castelar (Provincia de Buenos
                    Aires), Argentina

                (2) Facultad de Ciencias Agrarias
                    Universidad de Cuyo
                    Mendoza, Argentina

Australia: (1) Waite Institute
                    Private Mail Bag
                    Adelaide, South Australia, Australia

                (2) Division of Land Research and
                    Regional Survey
                    C. S. I. R. O.
                    Canberra, A. C. T., Australia

                (3) Library
                    University of Western Australia
                    Nedlands, Western Australia,
                    Australia

China: (1) Soils Division
                    Chinese Geological Survey
                    Nanking, China

                (2) Soil Institute
                    Academia Sinica
                    Nanking, China

Chile: Instituto de Suelos
                Ministerio de Agricultura
                Santiago, Chile

India: Central Arid Zone Research
                    Institute
                Jodhpur, Rajasthan, India

Iran: Soil Institute
                Amirabad
                Teheran, Iran

Iraq: Arid Zone Research Institute
                College of Agriculture
                Abu-Ghraib, Iraq

Israel: (1) Library
                    Hebrew University
                    Rehovot, Israel

                (2) Negev Institute for Arid Zone
                    Research
                    Beersheba, Israel

Jordan: Deir Alla Research Station
                Agricultural Research Service
                Amman, Jordan

Mali: Office du Niger
                Section de Documentation
                Segou, République de Mali

Mexico: Instituto de Investigación de
                    Zonas Desérticas
                Universidad Autónoma de
                    San Luis Potosí
                San Luis Potosí, Mexico

Morocco: Faculté des Sciences
                Service Bibliotheque
                Rabat, Morocco

Pakistan: (1) Library
                    West Pakistan Agricultural
                        University
                    Lyallpur, West Pakistan

                (2) Water and Soils Investigation
                        Division
                    Water and Power Development
                    Lahore, West Pakistan

Peru: Facultad des Sciences Agrarias
                Universidad Agraria "La Molina"
                Lima, Peru

Senegal: Centre de Recherches
  (for   Pédologiques
  Mauritania)   ORSTOM
                Dakar, Senegal

South Africa: (1) Soils Research Institute
                    Private Bag 79
                    Pretoria, South Africa

                (2) Namib Desert Research Association
                    c/o Transvaal Museum
                    Pretoria, South Africa

                (3) Council for Scientific and
                        Industrial Research
                    Pretoria, South Africa

Sudan: Library
                Gezira Research Station
                Wad Medani, Sudan

Syria: Steppe Department
                Ministry of Agriculture
                Damascus, Syria

Tunisia: Service Pédologique
                Secretariat de l'Etat a
                    l'Agriculture
                Avenue de la République
                Tunis - Port, Tunisia

Table II (Continued)

U.S.S.R.:

V. V. Dokuchaev Soil Institute
U.S.S.R. Academy of Sciences
Moscow, U.S.S.R.
(Most important. Has
soil reports for China
and other Asian countries.)

United Arab
Republic:
(Egypt)

(1) Desert Institute
Mataria, Mathaf-el-Mataria Street
Cairo, U. A. R.

(No. 1 and 2
are more
important
than 3 and 4)

(2) Faculty of Agriculture
University of Alexandria
Alexandria, U. A. R.

(3) Faculty of Agriculture
Ain Shams University
Cairo, U. A. R.

(4) National Research Center
Dokki
Cairo, U. A. R.

U.S.A.

(1) National Agricultural Library
U. S. Department of Agriculture
Washington, D. C.
(First source in U. S. A.
for all U. S. and foreign
material.)

(2) Library
University of Arizona
Tucson, Arizona 85721

(3) Library
University of California
Berkeley, California

(4) Library of Congress
Washington, D. C.

France:

(1) Service de Documentation
Office de la Recherche Scientifique
et Technique Outre-Mer
70 - 74 Route d'Aulnay
Bondy (Seine), France
(Has information on former
French colonies)

(2) Natural Resources Division
Unesco
7 Place de Fontenoy
Paris 7e, France
(Has information on soils
of deserts in underdeveloped
countries)

Italy:

Library
FAO
Via delle Terme di Caracalla
Rome, Italy
(Has information on soils
of deserts in underdeveloped
countries)

England:

Library
Rothamsted Experimental Station
Harpenden, England
(Bulk of information is on
soils of deserts in former
British colonies; has other
English language reports)

BIOLOGICAL PROPERTIES

The microbial population of arid-zone soils is, as one would expect from the harsh environmental conditions, lower than that of soils found in more favorable surroundings. Small though their numbers may be, microorganisms are by no means absent even in places like the Sahara and Mojave deserts (Killian, 1940; Killian and Fehér, 1936; Cameron and Blank, 1965; Thornton, 1953). Cameron and Blank ranked the microbial population of the Mohave Desert in decreasing order: aerobes plus actinomycetes, anaerobes, facultative anaerobes, algae, and fungi. Only the algae were (at times) present in greater numbers than are found in fertile agricultural soils; all the others were less populous. Soil samples taken from the periphery of the Atacama Desert in Chile were notable for the very low abundance of common groups of microflora (Cameron *et al.,* 1965). Microaerophiles, however, were as abundant as the authors had found in other desert soils, indicating that specialized groups of microorganisms were present. In the Sahara, microbial numbers were directly related to the amount of carbon and nitrogen in the soils rather than to any other soil factors (Killian, 1940). Arid-zone soils in Mauritania have microflora that seem to be well adapted to temperatures between 40° and 60° C (Audry and Rossetti, 1962).

A. MICROBIAL ACTIVITY

In the less-arid sierozem area, noncultivated soils in Central Asia show reduced microbiological activity, especially in nitrification (Volobuev, 1963), although an earlier study (Samsonov, Samsonova, and Chernova, 1930) claimed that sierozems were especially rich in nitrifying organisms and in Azotobacter. Sandy soils and takyrs had fewer microorganisms, according to the latter authors, except for a high population of blue-green algae on the surface of takyrs. Volobuev's contention that nitrifying organisms were less active in sierozems, where the pH is moderately alkaline, is supported by studies in Arizona on the relation of pH to nitrification (Caster, Martin, and Buehrer, 1942). Caster and his associates concluded that the threshold pH for nitrification was 7.7 ± 0.1. Above that pH, com-

plete oxidation of ammonia did not occur. Protozoa, which are important in organic matter transformations in soils, are abundant in sierozem, sandy, and takyr soils to a depth of 20 to 30 centimeters (Brodskii and Yankovskaya, 1930). Iraq alluvial soils that had been cultivated for over 4,000 years without any known application of organic matter had very low levels of bacteria and molds when dry, but the levels increased to values comparable to moderately fertile humid-region soils after incubation (Chandra, Bollen, and Kadry, 1962). Azotobacter also were present. It was noted that ammonifying, nitrifying, and sulfur oxidizing capacities of the soils were moderately good but that decomposition of native and added organic matter was slow. The soils were alkaline, and one was strongly saline.

The effect of a desert plant on the microbial population of a Sahara soil was demonstrated by the high numbers of bacteria in the rhizosphere as compared to low numbers in the adjacent soil (Vargues, 1953). Similar results were obtained in an Egyptian desert study (Elwan and Mahmoud, 1950) in which Azotobacter and Clostridium species were isolated from the rhizosphere but not from the surrounding soil. In the arid zones of Morocco, aerobic cellulolytic bacteria were present, but no Azotobacter (Sasson, 1960). Under extreme-arid Saharan conditions, no Azotobacter, Clostridia, or nitrifying organisms were found in the surface 10 centimeters of soils, and the activity of ammonifying, denitrifying, cellulolytic, and amylolytic organisms was very low (Pochon, de Barjas, and Lajudis, 1957). The latter effect was attributed to extremely high diurnal temperature variations and very low soil moisture. The small number of thermophilic microflora presumably was due to low soil organic matter. Bacterial activity was low in central Tunisia soils when irrigation was initiated on previously uncultivated soils.

Different results were obtained in an Australian comparison of ammonia-oxidizing bacteria in desert and subhumid region soils (Sims and Collins, 1960). In this study, there was little difference between the number and type of nitrifying bacteria present in the desert soils of the Northern Territory compared with soils of the more temperate areas of South Australia.

Studies conducted on soils of the arid and semiarid parts of West Africa demonstrated that certain microbial groups, at least, can function at soil moisture contents considerably below the wilting point (Dommergues, 1962). Audry and Rossetti classified microbial groups found in Mauritania soils as hyperxerophylic if they grew at a soil moisture pF greater than 4.9, xerophylic if they grew at a pF between 4.2 and 4.9, and hygrophylic if they required a pF of less than 4.2 (Audry and Rossetti, 1962).

B.   AZOTOBACTER

Several studies have been centered on the distribution and activity of Azotobacter in arid-zone soils, in addition to those previously cited. In Arizona (Martin, 1940), range soils generally were lacking in Azotobacter, with only 23 per cent of the sampled soils having any, and they usually were inactive. On the other hand, 87 per cent of cultivated soils contained Azotobacter. When the soluble sodium or calcium content of the soils exceeded 3,000 parts per million, Azotobacter were absent; conversely, Azotobacter were found in some samples of Utah semiarid-zone soils that had 2 per cent salt and were maintained in an air dry condition for 20 years (Greaves and Jones, 1941). Ammonifying bacteria survived the long dehydration, but nitrite- and nitrate-producing bacteria did not.

In a Washington State University investigation of semiarid soils, Azotobacter were common in irrigated soils where the average annual precipitation was less than 10 inches but were rare in similar non-irrigated soils. Under a 15 to 20 inch rainfall, Azotobacter frequently were found in non-irrigated soils (Vandecaveye and Moodie, 1942). The inhibition of Azotobacter population in non-irrigated soils of Central Asia has been attributed to low moisture in summer and low temperatures in winter (Darzniyek, 1961).

Azotobacter number and activity in Nile Valley soils were greater when large amounts of plant residue were added to the soil (Abdel-Malek and Isham, 1962) and when the soils were fine textured rather than sandy. Irrigation water enriched the soils with Azotobacter, and the terminal canals had more in the water than did the main canals or the Nile itself. Soils of the Central Niger Delta had very small quantities of Azotobacter (Dabin, 1953), and the addition of phosphorus, alone, was not enough to bring about increased growth.

C.   FUNGI

The fungal population is described as "rich" for soils of the arid northern Negev (Borut, 1960), with 82 species isolated. Aspergillus and Penicillium are represented by a great number of species. Some of the 82 species were found in all soils whereas others were in certain soils only. Loessial soils had the most, hamadas next, and sands least, in proportion to the amount of organic matter they contained. Total number of fungi and actinomycetes was less in uncultivated soils than in cultivated ones. Another study (Rayss and Borut, 1958) found 102 species in the Judaean desert and the northern Negev, 11 of which seemed to be new.

In central Iraq soils, 150 species and 41 genera were reported (al-Doory, Talba, and al-Ani, 1959), the majority belonging to the Fungi Imperfecti. The order of dominance, which was Hormodendrum, Aspergillus, Fusarium, Alternaria, and Penicillium, varied in individual soils but could not be related to soil or climatic factors. North Africa desert sands also have a diverse and adaptable fungal population (Nicot, 1955), as do Sudan soils (Nour, 1956), those of the Nevada (U. S.) atomic test site (Durrell and Shields, 1960), soils in Egypt (Sabet, 1939), and soils of Mauritania (Audry and Rossetti, 1962).

Schiffman noted the predominance in Negev loess soils of symbiotic bacteria that were ineffective nodulators of alfalfa (Schiffman, 1958). He concluded that innoculation of alfalfa with efficient strains of Rhizobium could increase yields greatly without fertilizer. Similar results have been reported for the Senegal Valley of west Africa. A Nebraska survey found that only 40 per cent of the soils contained *Rhizobium meliloti,* while 93 per cent contained Azotobacter (Peterson and Goodding, 1941). Azotobacter population was not related to soil pH or soluble phosphorus. Ninety-five per cent of the carbonate-containing soils had both Azotobacter and Rhizobium. Azotobacter were least in sandy soils.

D.   ALGAE

Algae have attracted considerable interest because of their pronounced ability to fix atmospheric nitrogen and because of the crusts they form on soil surfaces in arid regions. Data from the Soviet Union (Bolyshev, 1964) showed that algae are the principal components of the soil crust of takyrs, solonetz, and some other soils of the desert and semidesert zones of Central Asia. Such crusts attain a thickness of 2 to 3 millimeters and are sufficiently tough to permit their removal from the surface as a film. Some observers of the effect of algal crusts believe that they may cause considerable water runoff by sealing soil surfaces (Rozanov, 1951). They also serve to stabilize the surface of cohesionless materials as do lichens, in addition to adding considerable quantities of nitrogen to the soil through their nitrogen-fixing ability

(Shields, Mitchell, and Drouet, 1957). Sierozem soils in Tadzhikistan (U.S.S.R.) were found to contain 217 algal species, more than half of them blue-green algae (Melnikova, 1962). There were more algae, both in numbers and species, in alfalfa fields than in cotton fields under irrigation. Seasonal variations appeared in the quantity and kinds of algae during the year in Uzbekistan (Troitskaya, 1961), with maximum algal growth in the spring of the year. Blue-green algae were most abundant in summer, while green and diatomaceous algae were prominant in fall.

Algal growth on the soil surface seems to be more common on sodium-affected fine-textured soils occupying basins in the arid regions than on other arid region soils, probably due to the presence of sodium required by algae for normal metabolism, as well as the low soil permeability to water. Algal crusts have been noted in southern Morocco on alkali isohumic brown soils as well as other basin alkali soils.

Algal and lichen crusts have been found to contain 4 to 8 times as much nitrogen as the underlying soil (Cameron, 1961; Fuller, Cameron, and Raica, 1960; Shields, 1957; Sims and Dregne, 1962). Water extracts from cultures of field crusts did not contain nitrite or nitrate, and only traces of ammonia (Mayland and McIntosh, 1963). This finding supports earlier data (Shields, Mitchell, and Drouet, 1957) where the alga-stabilized crusts were high in amino nitrogen but very low in nitrite and nitrate nitrogen.

E.   TERMITES

Termites apparently are fairly common in soils of arid zones, if not of the extremely arid portions. Litchfield, in the Alice Springs report (Perry *et al.,* 1962), says that little is known about the effect of the termite population on the organic cycle and circulation of plant nutrients in arid-zone and northern Australia soils. He notes that termites seem to consume a significant proportion of the available plant debris, and their population is appreciable even on spinifex sand plains. Paleosols near Beni-Abbès in Saharan Algeria appear to have been influenced by termites at the time of their formation (Conrad, 1959).

F.   RESEARCH STATUS AND NEEDS

Research on soil microbiology has been rather neglected in the United States as well as in most other countries outside Europe. The amount of information on microbial numbers and species in arid-zone soils is very small, and the research, as in many other cases, has raised more questions than it has answered. Aside from the need for survey data on just what is present in the soil under varying conditions of salinity, carbonate content, organic matter, pH, texture, nutrient conditions, maximum and minimum temperatures, and moisture content, the reasons for whatever differences may occur should be determined. The question of whether extremely arid soils actually are abiotic or only so outside the rhizosphere needs to be answered. Whether algal and lichen crusts are significant factors in soil stabilization, particularly of sand dunes, in upland soils is unresolved, as is the effect of such crusts on water penetration and runoff, to say nothing of their effect on soil development. Another question relates to the function of termites, which are distributed worldwide in the arid zones, in affecting the soil environment. Just why ammonifying organisms are prevalent and active in arid-zone soils whereas nitrite- and nitrate-producing organisms frequently are inactive is a question with many practical implications.

PHYSICAL PROPERTIES

A voluminous amount of literature on water movement and retention in soils has been reviewed in a publication of the Unesco Arid Zone Research series (Milthorpe, 1960; Gardner, 1960) and in a symposium (National Research Council, Highway Research Board, 1958). While the reviews pertain to climatic conditions in general, several of the points discussed are especially pertinent to the arid zones. Among them is the observation that infiltration of rain water is greatly retarded if the soil surface is hard and dry or if a crust, however thin, is present. Both of these conditions are common in the arid zones where plants are spaced far apart and the organic matter content of the surface soil is low. The rapid decrease noted in infiltration into a bare soil is accompanied by a decrease in surface-soil porosity resulting from swelling of clay particles and the compacting effect of raindrops. Since the compacting action is a function of the size and terminal velocity of the rain drops, the intense, heavy rains characteristic of many arid regions have an especially severe effect on packing the surface soil. Additionally, arid-zone soils frequently have a thin surface film of readily dispersible clay colloids that swell to the extent of forming an almost impervious barrier to the entry of water, even when the water remains ponded on the surface. Soils containing appreciable amounts of exchangeable sodium in the surface have even greater dispersion and sealing effects. One of the desirable attributes of desert pavement is to break the force of the raindrops striking the soil, thereby reducing surface compaction.

A. MOISTURE LOSS

Soil moisture loss from a bare soil depends upon, among other things, the evaporation potential and the capacity for liquid flow in the soil. Under conditions of high temperature, low humidity, and strong wind movement, evaporation from arid-zone soils tends to be rapid (Fritschen and van Bavel, 1962; van Bavel, Fritschen, and Reginato, 1963). If the soil is sandy and has a low coefficient of conductivity when dry (Taylor, 1960), upward movement of water into the dry surface may be quite slow. This fact presumably accounts for the observation that sandy soils near Suez in Egypt remain permanently wet below 50 centimeters (Abdel-Rahman and El Hadidy, 1958), the moisture being retained from years of heavy rainfall. Fine-textured soils having a higher conductivity when dry will continue to lose water from a considerable depth, even when the evaporation potential is high. In both sandy and fine-textured soils of whatever water conductivity, the greatest conservation of subsurface moisture will occur where the initial rate of evaporation is most rapid; surface tillage helps this conservation. A greater loss of water occurs from saline than non-saline soils because a high salt concentration in the surface causes a reduction in the initial rate of water loss due to the reduction in vapor pressure. Lower rates of loss are maintained for a longer period and liquid flow to the surface is greater.

B. MOISTURE MEASUREMENT

Moisture - measuring devices suitable for dry soils include neutron scattering, gamma-ray attenuation, thermal conductivity, resistance blocks, and the standard for all measurements: gravimetric determination of moisture (Holmes, 1958). Tensiometers operate only over the wet range. Of the methods that are useful, the gravimetric, neutron-scattering, and thermal-conductivity methods, which measure moisture volume, are the most accurate. Accuracy in measurement, however, does not mean accuracy in evaluation of the soil moisture status, because soil variability is a common but usually unknown factor that may significantly affect the validity of the data. Soil variability is a particularly important factor in the undeveloped, transported soils of the arid regions.

In its application to field work, the neutron method has the advantage of being constructed of durable materials, and recent models are considerably lighter and less unwieldy than the heavy and cumbersome early models. When moisture tensions, as contrasted to moisture volume, are to be determined, the best tool for doing so in dry soils is the gypsum block, despite the limitations of the block. Nylon and fiberglass blocks are less reliable than gypsum blocks in situations where the salt concentration of the soil solution changes appreciably with moisture changes, as frequently is true for arid region soils. Gypsum blocks are buffered by the saturated gypsum solution that surrounds the block (Fadda, 1960). Large errors are introduced when calculations of moisture volume are made from measurements of moisture tension, or vice versa. Such conversions should be made only when approximate estimates are adequate (Taylor, Evans, and Kemper, 1961).

C. UNSATURATED MOISTURE FLOW

Unsaturated moisture flow is more usual than saturated flow in arid-zone soils and, as with saturated flow, the volume of flow, or flux density, is proportional to the potential gradient in homogeneous soils under isothermal conditions. With some modifications, the Darcy equation for saturated flow has been extended to unsaturated flow. Whether or not this is warranted is a matter of dispute. The dispute arises from the difficulty of measuring capillary conductivity and soil moisture diffusivity in unsaturated systems when transient conditions prevail.

D. MOISTURE AVAILABILITY TO PLANTS

The amount of soil moisture available to plants cannot presently be calculated from soil properties but must be determined by actual measurement of the moisture-retention curve. Neither soil texture nor structure is related to available moisture in any consistent manner, although estimates of available moisture commonly are made from considerations of texture. Improved soil aggregation may decrease both water-holding capacity and available water. Infiltration and permeability, on the other hand, may be increased, permitting more water to be stored at a depth where it is less susceptible to evaporation loss. Under the high temperatures characteristic of arid zones, water is more readily available to plants, at any one soil moisture content, because soil suction is strongly temperature-dependent, particularly at the higher suctions found in arid areas. In addition, high temperature affects the rate of movement of water by lowering its viscosity, which could increase the depth of water penetration (Taylor, 1962).

E. EVAPOTRANSPIRATION

Techniques for measuring and estimating evapotranspiration have been reviewed in Arid Zone Research publications (Deacon, Priestley, and Swinbank, 1958; Eckhardt, 1960). Meteorological methods for measuring water consumption of the plant cover are used widely and, while not precise, are capable of providing useful information. Estimates of transpiration over a large area, by measuring changes in water content of selected plants and extrapolating to the larger area, appear promising in arid regions despite their inadequacy in humid regions. The reasons for their better utility in arid regions are the open character of the vegetation cover, which exposes all transpiring organs to similar meteorological conditions, the greater uniformity of radiation intensity from day to day, and the greater homogeneity of the vegetation. A field investigation of water balance in the Negev (Hillel and Tadmor, 1962) under natural vegetation showed that loessial plains with deep saline soils had the least amount of water available to plants annually, with rocky slopes having somewhat more, sands a little more than rocky slopes, and wadis the most, by far. The reader is referred to chapter II of this compendium (Reitan and Green, 1967) for further discussion of evapotranspiration.

F. THERMAL PROPERTIES

The thermal properties of soils are dependent upon mineral composition, dry density, and moisture content (de Vries, 1958). Assuming soil moisture to be at the wilting point in arid zones and at field capacity in humid zones, de Vries calculated that the annual difference in variation of the heat flux into the soil was rather small between arid and humid conditions in Australia at a latitude of 30° S. The difference was greater in the Sahara and parts of Asia and was larger at 50° N latitude in Central Asia. Differences in diurnal variation in Australia were about 20 times greater that the annual variation. The amount of heat stored in the soil during the daytime and released at night is usually considerably larger in the arid than in the humid part of Australia. In Arizona, it was noted that convection accounts for as much as half of the heat transfer from soil to air at night (Guild, 1950). Irrigation influenced air and soil temperatures and relative humidity in a downwind direction on the Riverine Plain of Australia but had little effect in the upwind direction (de Vries and Birch, 1961). Comparison of a station in the center of an irrigated area with a station downwind and outside the irrigated area showed that irrigation lowered the soil temperature at 5 and 30 centimeters by approximately 10° C and the air temperature at 4 feet by 1 to 2°. The relative humidity of the atmosphere was slightly higher under irrigation. At Davis, California, when the air temperature about 2 feet above the ground was 47° C, the soil temperature at ½ inch below the surface was 62° C. At 3 inches it was 42 °C, and at 24 inches it was 29° C (Smith, 1929). The range in air temperature during one year was 48° C, while the soil temperature range at ½ inch depth was 63° C but only 17° C at 36 inches. The soil was a loam. Similar or greater variations were found in Arizona (Sinclair, 1922), western

Australia (Mason, 1959-1960), and other places (Buxton, 1924).

G. SOIL AGGREGATION

The principles of soil aggregation are discussed at length in a standard textbook on soil physics (Baver, 1956) and in a recent textbook on soil mechanics (Means and Parcher, 1963). Some of the differences in aggregation that can be found in arid and semiarid zone soils are given in a report on Israel soils (Ravikovitch and Hagin, 1957). The authors noted that terra rossa and rendzina soils had a very high degree of stable aggregates, with terra rossa colluvium, alluvial soils of Mediterranean red earth origin, and grey calcareous soils intermediate in aggregation. Loessial soils had less, and loess-like and brownish red sandy soils had negligible aggregation. A positive correlation was found between organic matter content and stable aggregation in the upper horizons. A high percentage of calcium carbonate (40-60 per cent) favored aggregation. Cultivation reduced it. Flooding alluvial soils of the arid part of the Senegal Valley for an extended period is reported to have a very deleterious effect on soil aggregation. Punjab soils had a statistically significant negative correlation of stability index with pH and dispersion coeffecient (Dhawan and Sharma, 1950). A vesicular structure just below the soil surface has been noted in arid-zone soils and appears to be characteristic of such soils (Jackson, 1957; Lapham, 1932). The surface over it consists of a thin, platy layer that may be soft or hard when dry. The platy structure seems to result from the beating effect of rain on the dispersed fine soil particles, and the vesicular structure from air bubbles formed under alternate wetting and drying conditions (Miller, 1966; Springer, 1958). An apparatus to measure the strength of surface crusts has been devised (Richards, 1953). Microbial activity is important in aggregation of humid area soils but becomes less significant with increasing aridity and lesser microbial activity.

H. HARDPANS

Hardpans of various kinds are common in arid-zone soils. Classifications of calcium carbonate hardpans (Gile, 1961) and other soil concretions (Durand, 1959) have been made and the sequence of formation of a calcium carbonate horizon has been described (Gile, Peterson, and Grossman, 1966). In New Mexico, carbonate horizons occur on a variety of sediments and geomorphic surfaces (Gile, 1961). In gravelly materials, the sequence of formation begins with carbonate coating on pebbles, then proceeds to filling of spaces between the pebbles, and ends with cementation and formation of a laminar layer

characteristic of indurated calcium carbonate layers (calcrete). The source of the calcium carbonate is a subject of conjecture in areas where the original rock material is low in calcium. In the absence of better explanations, recourse is made to the postulate that carbonate is brought in by wind movement of calcareous material from somewhere else. This seems to be the source of soil carbonate in western Australia, on the leeward side of calcareous saline depressions (Stephens, 1960).

In Morocco, calcareous crusts of the kind that are extensive in North Africa appear to have been formed as the result of lateral leaching of calcium carbonate from higher parts of the landscape. (Ruellan, 1965).

Another kind of hardpan that is extensive in Australia, the Kalahari Desert and the southern Sahara, and which probably is present in many other deserts, is the silicified hardpan called silcrete. In Australia it is associated with the laterization soil-forming process and silicification is continuing in present-day alluvium (Litchfield and Mabbutt, 1962; Teakle, 1950). A comprehensive review of silica in soils (McKeague and Cline, 1963; Millot, 1960) demonstrates the widespread occurrence of soluble silica. Indurated or partially indurated horizons of precipitated silica and calcium carbonate are believed to be common in arid regions although analytical data to prove it are scarce (Price, 1933; Stuart, Fosberg, and Lewis, 1961; Nikiforoff, 1937).

I. SOIL DISPERSION

While carbonate and silica act to increase soil aggregation, exchangeable sodium promotes dispersion (U.S. Salinity Laboratory, 1954). The dispersing action is greatest when the exchangeable sodium is a high percentage of the soil cation exchange capacity, when soil salinity is low, and when soils are high in clay. These conditions frequently are present in playas and clay plains of arid regions (Dabin, 1951). Exchangeable potassium, which is closely related to sodium in chemical properties does not, according to Reeve *et al.* (1954), markedly affect soil permeability or, by inference, dispersion. Exchangeable magnesium has been suspected as also causing soil dispersion and poor permeability, but this effect was not present in an Arizona experiment (Smith, Buehrer, and Wickstrom, 1949).

J. DESERT PAVEMENT

Desert pavement of many kinds has been reported in all of the arid parts of the world. It has been described (Marbut, 1935) as consisting of "a layer of gravel and small stone, lying practically bare of fine material by the wind, which usually forms a rather firm crust capable of bearing some weight but in most places not sufficiently strong to bear the weight of a man." Marbut goes on to say that underneath the gravel is a grey, almost white, fine-grained material which usually is extremely porous and vesicular. This material is not always present, however. An excellent study of desert pavement in the Lahontan Basin of Nevada (Springer, 1958), indicates that upward displacement of stones and gravel under the effect of soil shrinking contributes to the formation of desert pavement, as does the removal of finer material by wind or water.

Springer, too, notes the vesicular structure of the soil immediately beneath the pavement. Upward movement during alternate wetting and drying appears to be one cause of surface stones in stony tableland soils of Australia (Jessup, 1962). Hamadas and regs, by definition, have a desert pavement, and the surface stones serve to protect the underlying soil from erosion (Karschon, 1953; Dapples, 1941). Removal of fine material by wind is responsible for the high concentration of stones and gravel on the surface of one kind of reg in North Africa (Durand, 1953b), of the gibber plains of Australia (Teakle, 1950), gobi in China (Chao, 1962), and desert pavement in Iran (Dewan and Famouri, 1964). A desert pavement of stones and gravel ranging from white quartz fragments to black waterworn pebbles and stones is said to be a characteristic feature of the arid-zone soils of South Africa (van der Merwe, 1954a). Stony surfaces in some Australian arid-zone soils are the results not of upward movement of stones but of the weathering of remnants of an exposed siliceous B horizon developed under an old surface (Crocker, 1946). An interesting explanation for a carbonate-rock desert pavement in the Caucasus is that the pea-sized lime concretions were formed by the mortaring action of individual rain drops on limestone. The soft nodules so formed then were rolled and rounded by the wind before they hardened (Kulik, 1959).

The stones and gravels of desert pavement frequently have a hard, colored coating on the exposed side that is called "desert varnish." The dark stains are believed to be iron and manganese oxides, but few analyses have been made to confirm this. According to one theory, the oxides were deposited in arid regions 2,000 or more years ago, during plutonic periods (Hunt, 1961). Many soil scientists are of the opinion that desert varnish results from alternate wetting and drying of the surface of stones and pebbles and is more characteristic of a semiarid climate than an arid one. In a study of alluvial fans in Death Valley, California, desert varnish was noted on the surface materials of extensive abandoned washes (Denny, 1965). Desert pavements on these

fans are described as being smooth, gently sloping surfaces composed of closely packed angular fragments of rock. The surfaces are crossed by meandering gullies less than an inch high which form when the underlying silt becomes saturated with water and flows downslope.

K. PIPING

A peculiar feature of certain arid-zone soils is the phenomenon of "piping" or "tunnel erosion." Piping is a type of erosion in which the subsoil erodes out from under the surface (Fletcher and Carroll, 1948). Three types of piping were studied by these authors: the first results from the lateral flow along a subsoil into an open stream-bank, the second results from surface water running into cracks, and the third occurs when dispersed surface soil is washed into the pore spaces of coarse, poorly graded upper subsoil, causing sinking and caving of the soil. Piping is to be anticipated in alluvial soils with highly dispersed subsoils (Carroll, 1949) and where pH, soluble salts, and exchangeable sodium are high (Fletcher and Carroll, 1948).

Animal burrows, deep root casts, lowered water table due to entrenching of streams, deep cracking of soil, and dense underlying strata contribute to piping. The conditions required in order that piping may occur are (1) there must be a source of water, (2) the surface infiltration rate must exceed the permeability rate of some subsurface layers, (3) there must be an erodible layer immediately above the retarding layer, (4) the water above the retarding layer must be under a hydraulic gradient, and (5) there must be an outlet for the lateral flow (Fletcher et al., 1954). Piping has been observed in Australia on sodium-affected soils and saline soils, and where runoff water accumulates in depressions in which the surface structure and permeability are good (Downes, 1956). The phenomenon is a threat in Central Asia on loessial soils (Glukhov, 1956), where the recommended control measure is to wet the soil thoroughly before cropping in order to compact it. Piping has been observed in the Niger Valley of Mali and in the semiarid parts of the Chad-Logone Valley.

L. SAND

Movement of sand always is an important factor in arid zones. Two sources of detailed information on the physics of sand movement and on methods of control are recommended (Bagnold, 1943; Chepil and Woodruff, 1963). Chepil has devised a wind-erosion equation based upon five factors: soil erodibility, soil ridge roughness, climate, field length, and vegetative cover (Woodruff and Siddoway, 1965). Dry soil particles less than 0.84 mm in diameter are considered to be the most erodible. The 5 factors are, in turn, combinations of 11 primary variables that govern wind erodibility. The United Nations Food and Agriculture Organization has prepared recommendations for control of wind erosion (Food and Agriculture Organization, Agricultural Engineering Branch, 1960) and it is a continuing subject of research in the Soviet Union (Yakubov, 1959) and China (Academia Sinica, Sand Control Group, 1962; Kao, 1963), as it is in Pakistan and India.

The composition of dune material varies although all dunes usually are called sand dunes. The White Sands dunes of southern New Mexico and the kopi dunes of South Australia are composed of nearly pure gypsum (Bettanay, 1962). Quartz sand is a common dune mineral, but the sand dunes near Yuma, Arizona are rock fragments of variable composition (Ives, 1959). In Sonora, the continuation of the Yuma dunes has a composition largely of shell fragments derived from recently elevated bottom marls. Saline clay dunes have been studied (Price, 1963; Boulaine, 1961); the factors besides wind action that are critical in their formation are changes in cohesiveness and volume with changes in moisture content of the clay. Drying crusts of saline clay flats of arid lands break down under deflation into sand-sized pellets by disruption of efflorescent evaporite crystals, collapse of crust blisters, or rolling of sun-cracked crusts of polygons. Configuration and grain size of climbing and falling dunes of the Mojave Desert of California have been studied (Evans, 1962). Climbing dunes have sorting coefficients ranging from 1.5 to 1.9, whereas falling dunes have coefficients of 1.2 or 1.3. Variations in the amplitude and wavelength of surface ripples on sand dunes is a function of wind velocity and grain size and of location on the dune (Wilcoxon, 1962). The effect of meteorological conditions on surface-sand movement has been discussed by Bagnold (1953). A formula for calculating the yearly horizontal displacement of barchan dunes in southern Peru has been developed (Finkel, 1959). The lower the dune height, the greater is the movement. In a Libyan study of a seif dune, an interdune area, and a nearby soil containing a range in textures, indications were that there were sufficiently marked differences in texture and structure of the different materials to assist in recognition of such deposits when they are preserved in the geologic record (McKee and Tibbitts, 1964). An interesting account has been made of the history and formation of sand dunes in Kordofan Province of the Sudan in relation to climatic fluctuations, and the form, size distribution pattern, and sorting and shape characteristics have been described (Warren, 1964).

A U. S. S. R. study (Romanova, 1960) of the photometric properties of a 350,000-square-kilometer area of sands south of the Aral Sea indicated that the petrographic composition of the sands can be estimated from their photometric properties. The wavelength of the spectrograph used was in the range of 490-650 millimicrons. Quartz and rutile increased spectral brightness in all regions of the spectrum, zircon increased it in the blue-green region, and effusives, granites, and monoclinic pyroxenes lowered it in the long wavelengths.

M. WIND EFFECTS

The use of lateritic gravel pavements to cover sand subgrade material was proved effective in Australia when the pavement thickness was 6 inches (Beattie, 1964). This thickness was optimum irrespective of moisture content and density. A thorough study of the subject showed that severe sand and dust storms occur at a rate of less than two per year in the southwestern United States (Clements *et al.,* 1963). Wind-driven sand is carried, mostly, within 2 feet of the ground surface, with 6 feet as a maximum height in all but extremely high winds. The critical pickup velocity of wind varies with the type of desert surface and the grain size and coherence of the surface materials, and depends also upon whether the surface was disturbed artificially. In dune areas, winds of 10 to 15 miles per hour will initiate movement, whereas on other sandy areas a velocity of 20 miles per hour is required. Fine material on desert flats will be set in motion at 20 to 25 miles per hour and on alluvial fans at 30 to 35. No windblown materials will be moved from desert pavement unless the surface has been broken. Disturbing the surface, in all cases, lowers the critical pickup velocity by as much as 5 miles per hour. The reader is also referred to the chapter by Reitan and Green (1967) in this compendium series.

N. SOIL STABILITY

Bituminous suspensions have been used for many years in constructing roads on sands, such as in the Fayoum Desert of Egypt (Noakes, 1932). Techniques for applying cutback bitumen in the stabilization of road base courses have been developed for South Africa sands (Marx and Faure, 1964). Research in Israel demonstrated that bitumen reduces permeability of sand-asphalt mixtures by reducing voids content. Bitumen was about twice as effective in doing so as dust filler (Shklarsky and Kimchi, 1962). The use of various soil stabilizers for South Africa conditions has been summarized in a recent paper (Fossberg and Gregg, 1963).

Determining the suitability of arid-zone soils for foundations requires thorough sampling and testing, even though the soils may appear firm and nonplastic when observed under dry field conditions. An Arizona study of valley fills having a mixture of sand, salt, and clay demonstrated this fact (Warne and Sergent, 1962). Many soils had wide variations in density and porosity and had a high degree of plasticity when wet. An attempt to forecast trafficability of most soils from analysis and interpretation of aerial photographs has given promising results (U.S. Army Engineer Waterways Experiment Station, 1963).

O. RESEARCH STATUS AND NEEDS

An understanding of the factors that determine the physical properties of soils is essential if the study of soils is to be more than an empirical one, as it largely is now. On the subject of soil aggregation, one of the most important characteristics that affects the movement of air and water through soil and its suitability as construction material, little progress has been made in understanding the causes of aggregation and how it can be modified. Scientists understand fairly well the role of organic fibers, microbial gums, carbonates, silica, and iron and aluminum oxides and hydroxides in forming a solid or highly viscous matrix within which soil particles are trapped to form aggregates. What is not understood is the part played by the positive and negative charges of the mineral, organic, and dissolved particles in causing aggregation or dispersion. Even the measurement of the state of aggregation of a soil cannot be agreed upon, some investigators maintaining that dry sieving is satisfactory while others vigorously contending that wet sieving must be performed if meaningful data are to be obtained. Relating laboratory evaluation of aggregation to field performance of soils is difficult and, consequently, aggregate analyses of any kind generally are considered to be unworthy of the time required to make them, except in the special case of dry sieving for erodibility estimation. There probably is more said about soil aggregation and less known about it than any single property of soils.

There is widespread dissatisfaction with the measurement of two other soil properties: texture and permeability to water. Textural analysis involves one of two kinds of treatment prior to the analysis: removal of organic matter, carbonates, soluble salts, and cementing agents like iron oxides, or removal of organic matter only. Subsequent to the pretreatment, various dispersing agents are added to produce particle separation. In the former procedure, only individual mineral units of clay, silt, or sand size are expected to be present in the soil-water suspension after pretreatment. In the latter procedure, the particles may consist of soil lime as well as of clay, silt, or sand that is cemented together into large particles. One procedure is supposed to give the amount of sand, silt, and clay present in a soil irrespective of the presence of anything else, whereas the second is supposed to give a textural analysis that more nearly represents field conditions. In most cases, a pipet is used for the first method and a hydrometer for the second. Aside from the disagreement about which method is more meaningful, there is no agreement about how much the pretreatment and dispersion in either method alters the composition of the mineral fraction by solution of components or by disruption of lattice frameworks that are stable in the field (Anderson, 1963).

Soil permeability to water is something that soil engineers and soil scientists want to know about because a large number of other characteristics of the soil hinge upon permeability. Like aggregation, everyone talks about it, but predicting it is a hazardous pastime without a number of tests on which to base one's conclusions. Numerous claims have been made for the validity of measurements of disturbed soil permeability, undisturbed permeability, and field measurements with double-ring permeameters. To date, any close relations that have been obtained appear to be either fortuitous or the result of many previous correlations between tests and field performance on the same soil. The source of the prediction difficulty is easy to identify: the factors that control permeability (surface tension, electrostatic forces, flow characteristics, etc.) are not well enough understood in relation to permeability to permit valid deductions to be made. The problem of unsaturated flow in a nonhomogeneous system like a soil, operating under transient conditions instead of a steady state, is another area of research that needs much work if we are to understand what happens in the great majority of soil-water conditions that exist in nature.

An area of research that applies equally to the physical, chemical, and biological status of the soil is the very promising one of remote sensing of environment. The use of photographic film sensitive to different wavelengths of light has already been demonstrated to be of value in identifying wet soils and diseased, insect-infected, or otherwise unhealthy plants. Visual inspection of aerial photographs can be rewarding to persons having a high degree of familiarity with surface soil characteristics, but it is a rather crude approach when one considers the many possibilities for obtaining quantitative data from remote sensing devices. Remote thermal, magnetic, electric, and spectral measurements may well revolutionize the study of soils.

Research also should be increased on the recurring question of whether the so-called solonetz type of subsoil structure is caused by exchangeable sodium or by some other process of soil development. At present, the prismatic structure typical of solonetz soils is believed, for the most part, to be due to the dispersing effect of exchangeable sodium. Sometimes exchangeable magnesium is implicated in the development of prismatic horizons, but no one knows whether either cation is responsible, especially since there are many soils containing excessive exchangeable sodium that do not have the solonetz structure. High exchangeable sodium soils are common features of arid lands throughout the world.

The uncertainty about the source of the calcareous material in most northern hemisphere arid-zone soils has been noted. Similarly, the absence of carbonate in many soils of the extremely arid part of Australia has been mentioned as a major difference between the soils of arid Australia and those of other arid lands. Present hypotheses are that the lime could be due to evaporation of water from a shallow water table, solution of calcium from the parent material during soil formation and the precipitation of calcium carbonate at the average depth of water penetration, deposition of wind-blown calcareous material, or deposition of calcareous alluvium. An understanding of soil properties peculiar to arid lands will be facilitated once it is known which explanations are correct. Since calcareous material seems to have its own inherent particle size distribution in arid-zone soils, determination of the latter may furnish information on the properties of the parent material, leaching, and soil development processes in these soils.

CHEMICAL PROPERTIES

An abundance of soluble salts is commonly found in the surface of low-lying alluvial soils of the arid zones. High salt concentrations also are present in many chloride-containing gypsiferous materials and in saline shales. While some of the salt deposits, such as the nitrate beds of Chile and the borax deposits in California, are the source of important commercial salts, most of them represent a problem to the economic development of the areas in which they occur.

A. SOURCE OF SALTS

The earliest explanation for the presence of salts in solid form or as highly saline waters was that they were the accumulation of weathering products that, due to the low rainfall and high evaporative rate, were not leached from the soil. Later it was found that the amount of chloride, a common constituent of the soluble salts in the soil, could not be accounted for by weathering, any more than the insoluble calcium carbonate could. That led to the marine invasion explanation of the high chloride concentration, with proof of the prior marine inundations available from the paleontological evidence in the geologic strata of the area. The saline shales of the Colorado Plateau of the United States offer an example of the type of material that would come within the marine inundation theory of salt origin. Qualitatively, this latter explanation appears quite satisfactory, but there is no way to establish a quantitative evaluation of how much salt would be deposited by a marine inundation, so it is not an intellectually satisfying explanation, however reasonable it may be. A third theory of salt accumulation, that of atmospheric transport of sea salts into arid regions, can be checked quantitatively and has many proponents (Eriksson, 1958). The weakness in this theory lies in the scarcity of data on the salt concentration and ion composition of rainwater falling in various parts of the arid regions, as contrasted to the considerable amount of data from northern Europe, and the low value for the sodium-calcium ratio of the rainwaters that have been analyzed (Hutton, 1958). According to Hutton, since the sodium-calcium ratio of sea water is 22 and that of

rainwater is much lower, particularly as distance from the seacoast increases, some source other than the ocean must be contributing to the salts dissolved in rainwater. That other source may be terrestrial or cosmic, and it is much more likely to be terrestrial. While the source of the terrestrial contribution cannot be determined without ambiguity, the logical source is the soil surface. Salt efflorescences are common in the playas, salinas, and sebkhas of the arid regions, and salt particles are carried into the air when strong winds break the salt crust. However, because the number of salt particles found in the air during dust storms is lower than that found in maritime air masses, Eriksson concluded that there is no substantial evidence to support the theory of terrestrial salt transport in arid regions. For calculation of the contribution sea salt makes to soil salinity, Eriksson estimated that air moving from the sea into continental regions in the tropics and subtropics has a vertical concentration of about 20 milligrams of salt per square meter of surface area. For temperate regions, the estimate is a minimum of 10 milligrams of salt per square meter. If rain completely removed all atmospheric salt, the amount deposited would be, then, from about 10 to 20 milligrams per square meter of soil surface per rain.

The transport of insoluble mineral matter from arid into humid zones is well documented by the presence of extensive areas of loess in China, the Soviet Union, the United States, Israel, and elsewhere. Since loess is calcareous, it appears reasonable to believe that calcium carbonate, an insoluble salt, can be carried long distances by movement of terrestrial dust, while soluble salts are not. Some workers in Australia are of the opinion (Hutton, 1958; Stephens, 1960) that many calcareous soils in that country have developed from eolian carbonate deposition and that the low sodium-calcium ratio of at least some rain waters is due to the mixture of cyclic salt and calcareous dust.

An Algerian study showed that rain waters along the coast contained an average of 22 grams of sodium chloride per cubic meter of water and that the annual total of salt deposited was 40 to 50 kilograms per hectare of land (Chevalier, 1951). The contribution of sea salts to the salinity of U. S. S. R. soils is believed to be considerable (Borovskii, 1961), and the statement is made unequivocally in an Israel investigation (Yaalon, 1963) that the contribution of weathering to the process of soil salinization is small, whereas airborne salts add an estimated 100,000 tons of sodium chloride annually to Israel soils. Sandy coastal plain soils that do not accumulate soluble salt are nevertheless affected by cyclic salt deposition, as is shown by increasing exchangeable sodium. Fossil salt accumulations (marine inundations) are of local or regional importance only. Rock weathering certainly is a source of considerable soil salt, and may be especially important as a source of sodium salts in arid-zone soils occupying interior basins (Bocquier, 1964).

B. SALT FORMATION IN SOILS

Salt deposition in desert valleys, irrespective of the source of the salt, appears to follow a definite order of compounds, depending upon their solubilities. In Death Valley salt pans, chlorides, which are the most soluble, are in the center of the pan or at places on the surface where groundwater evaporates. Sulfates surround the chloride zone and, where groundwater is evaporating, form a layer beneath the chloride crust. Carbonates surround the sulfates and underlie the sulfates and chlorides (Hunt, 1960; Kovda, 1954).

The origin of gypsum sand dunes, which has perplexed many geologists, is explained for the Great Salt Lake desert as being the result of upward movement of sulfate ions by capillary movement of water during evaporation from plastic surface clays (Eardley, 1962). A similar explanation was given for the formation of gypsum crusts in Tunisia, near Gabès (Bureau and Roederer, 1961). Gypsum-producing bacteria also may have been operative. In any event, sand-sized gypsum crystals grew and are still growing in the top 3/4 inch of the clay. After further drying of the clay, the crystals are released to the wind and drift into dunes. A marine source of the gypsum beds in the Rajasthan desert is denied because sodium chloride is completely absent (Shastri, 1962). Investigations in the Belka Valley of Western Australia have demonstrated that clearing native shrub-type vegetation has upset the natural hydrologic balance sufficiently to allow saline groundwater to reach the surface (Bettenay, Blackmore, and Hingston, 1962). It was estimated in 1951 that over 100,000 acres of land in the Western Australia wheat belt had been destroyed by salt caused by

valley waterlogging following clearing (Pennefather, 1951). It had gone up to 180,000 by 1956 (Burvill, 1956).

C. SOIL SALINITY AND PLANT GROWTH

A comprehensive review of soil-plant relations on saline and sodium soils is given in the Paris *Symposium on The Problems of the Arid Zone* (Bernstein, 1962), and several papers on the subject are in the Teheran symposium on salinity problems in the arid zones (Unesco, 1961). A good, concise summary of the problems of salt- and sodium-affected soils of the arid lands is given in a report on French Somaliland (Tkatchenko, 1951). The problem there is described as one of high exchangeable sodium and magnesium in the soil and saline irrigation water. The harmful effect on vegetable crops is the result of (*1*) a deficiency of organic matter, (*2*) nonavailability of nutrients, (*3*) poor physical condition of the soil, (*4*) inadequate quantity of irrigation water, and (*5*) high osmotic pressure of the soil solution. Under these conditions, the author recommends abandoning the production of sensitive vegetable crops and turning to tolerant date palms. In Israel, four types of native plants are recognized in the Negev: (*1*) chloride-absorbing xerohalophytes, (*2*) chloride-absorbing hydrohalophytes, (*3*) xerohalophytes absorbing salts other than chlorides, and (*4*) nonhalophytic xerophytes (Tadmor, Orshan, and Rawitz, 1962). The osmotic potentials of the first two are high; the third has medium and the fourth low potential. It appears that the salt character of the soil is the principal factor determining the chemical composition of the plants growing on the soil, at least insofar as chloride and sulfate uptake is concerned (Akzhigitova, 1959). There was a good correlation between soil and plant chloride and sulfate, using aqueous soil extracts.

The effect of saline and sodium soils on plant growth was presented clearly in the first issue of *Advances in Agronomy* (Hayward and Wadleigh, 1949) and their chemical and physical properties have been described for the United States (Richards, 1950), Asia with particular reference to India (Raychaudhuri and Biswas, 1954), Pakistan (Ahmad, 1961), Iran (Antipov-Karataev and Kizilova, 1962), and Peru (Flores Cosio, 1954), among others. The development and principles of reclamation of saline and sodium soils is fully described in several books (Bonnet, 1960; Kelly, 1951; Kovda, 1946-1947; U. S. Salinity Laboratory, 1954; Greene, 1948), and the latest information has been brought together by FAO / Unesco in a book entitled *International Sourcebook on Irrigation and*

Drainage in Relation to Salinity and Alkalinity (Kovda, Hagan, and van den Berg [eds.], 1967, *in press*).

D. TERMINOLOGY

Confusion in terminology about saline and sodium soils has hampered an understanding of their characteristics. In early work on saline soils, it was recognized that the salts had different effects upon soils and plants, depending upon whether the cations were or were not sodium and whether the anions were carbonates or not. Kelley (1951) called all saline and sodium soils "alkali" soils; the U. S. Salinity Laboratory (1954) differentiated between salt-affected (saline) and exchangeable-sodium-affected soils (alkali). To confound matters more, Sigmond (1938) in Hungary had earlier labelled saline soils "salty soils" and those high in exchangeable sodium as "alkali" or "sodium" soils. The term "alkali" has so many connotations (alkali metals, caustic salt, alkaline, sodium carbonate, exchangeable sodium, sodium plus potassium, etc.) that it should be dropped from the literature. Either "sodic" or "sodium" seems much more acceptable because these terms denote only sodium, in one form or another. "Sodic" sometimes is confused with soda; "sodium" is the favored term here because it refers only to the chemical element.

E. EXCHANGEABLE SODIUM

Excess salts exert their harmful effects on the physiologic or metabolic activities of plants. The only change they make in soil characteristics is to improve soil permeability temporarily. Exchangeable sodium, on the other hand, has some effect on physiologic and metabolic activities of the plant but acts primarily upon the physical properties of the soil, in the presence or absence of plants. Several investigators have measured the effect of varying amounts of exchangeable sodium on soil properties (Eaton and Horton, 1940; Gardner, 1945; Whitney and Peech, 1952). As exchangeable sodium increases, dissociation and hydrolysis of clays generally increased, but reduced soil permeability is not always closely correlated with exchangeable sodium per cent because of variations in salt concentration of the soil water and the amount of puddling that has been done. Exchangeable sodium causes soil moisture to be less available to plants, as measured by the moisture equivalent and wilting point of high- and low-sodium soils (Eaton and Horton, 1940), and the increase in moisture equivalent, in particular, acts to reduce soil aeration with consequent adverse effects on plants. The very low permeability of takyrs and other fine-textured sodium soils prevents plant growth by, among other things, reducing the amount of soil air and its circulation when the soil is wet (Kuznetzova, 1958; Yegorov, 1961).

Since desert soils frequently are saline, they tend to be quite corrosive to metals. The great difficulty that can be encountered when trying to protect pipes has been described in a paper on buried pipeline corrosion in Syria and Iraq (Whalley, 1961).

F. SOIL ANALYSES

Soil analyses to determine the salinity and exchangeable sodium content are made in different ways by different investigators. Salinity is measured by determining the amount of salt in a soil wetted to saturation or to an arbitrary soil-water ratio such as 1/1, 1/2, 1/5, or 1/10. In the U. S. S. R. a soil-water ratio of 1/5 is used, the suspension is filtered, and the amount of salt in the filtrate is obtained by evaporating a sample to dryness and weighing the residue (Tyurin *et al.,* eds., 1959). The usual method in the United States is to saturate the soil with water, extract part of the soil solution by pressure or vacuum, and determine the electrical conductivity of the extract (U. S. Salinity Laboratory, 1954). Soviet scientists are interested in knowing not only the quantity of salt but what kind of anions are present (chlorides, sulfates, or carbonates) because they classify saline soils on the basis of the anion distribution. They do not ordinarily determine cations. U. S. soil scientists, like those of many other countries, consider conductivity to be a measure of salt activity and therefore a better indicator of the salt hazard than would be obtained from a weight determination. The kinds of salts present are considered, generally, to be of little consequence unless they are carbonates or borates. Scientists in other countries, as well as in the United States, use various soil-water ratios; therefore in interpreting data it is essential to know what ratio was used, just as it is in interpreting pH figures for soils, because results may differ widely on the same soil when different soil-water ratios are used. In fact, they differ even when the saturated paste, alone, is used (Little, 1963). Exchangeable sodium percentage figures also are subject to considerable error when the soil is capable of fixing the ammonium ion (Overstreet, Martin, and King, 1951), and no one has yet figured out a reliable method for determining exchangeable calcium and magnesium in calcareous soils or exchangeable sodium in highly saline soils. The barium chloride-triethanolamine method appears to give more accurate figures for exchangeable calcium and magnesium in calcareous soils than do other commonly used methods.

G. RECLAMATION

While reclamation of saline soils is attempted wherever an adequate water supply is available and it is economic to do so, some attempts have been and are being made to grow crops under irrigation with water that is generally considered unsatisfactory for use (Asghar, 1961). Some success has been achieved in Israel under the special conditions of a good supply, salt-tolerant plants, frequent heavy irrigation and a highly permeable soil (Boyko and Boyko, 1964). Sahara experiments using saline water have been successful if green manuring is done to maintain soil fertility (Simonneau, 1959; Simonneau and Aubert, 1963). Mostly, however, removal of salts and exchangeable sodium is tried in the time-tested methods of leaching salts and replacing exchangeable sodium with calcium, then leaching out the resultant sodium salt (Abell and Gelderman, 1964; Amemiya and Robinson, 1958; Antipov-Karataev, 1956, 1960; Ayazi, 1961; Boumans *et al.,* 1963; Bower and Goertzen, 1958; Delver, 1962; Dhawan, Bhatnager, and Ghai, 1958; Dzhalilov, 1957; Eaton, 1954; Evans, 1960; Gardner and Brooks, 1957; Laktionov, 1962; Panin, 1962; Talati, Mehta, and Mathur, 1959; U. S. Department of Agriculture, 1962). The report by Boumans *et al.* is an especially valuable account of the approach to the salinity problem and measures taken to reduce it in Iraq.

H. IRRIGATION WATER QUALITY

Adsorption of sodium from irrigation waters by soils is a matter of prime interest because exchangeable sodium has a pronounced effect on the physical properties of soils, including plasticity, strength, permeability to air and water, and others. The sodium-adsorption-ratio has been developed to provide an indication of the likelihood that sodium will or will not be adsorbed from a particular soil solution or irrigation water (U. S. Salinity Laboratory, 1954). To use the ratio, sodium and calcium-plus-magnesium in the solution must be known. Some scientists consider the sodium / calcium ratio to be the important one. For high-carbonate waters, another criterion, the residual-sodium-carbonate, has been devised (Eaton, 1950). It is based upon the expectation that, as a soil dries out after wetting with a high-carbonate water, all the calcium and magnesium will precipitate as their carbonate salts if carbonates exceed calcium plus magnesium. The result, of such precipitation would be, in effect, to raise the per cent of sodium in the soil solution, since sodium carbonate would remain in solution. The extent to which calcium and magnesium carbonates do precipitate in soils is a question upon which conflicting data are available.

An Israeli study indicates that the anions associated with sodium in irrigation water influence the amount of sodium adsorbed by the soil (Bidner-Barhava and Ravikovitch, 1952). Sodium was adsorbed more when the anion was sulfate than when it was chloride or nitrate. Several classification systems have been published as guides to the agricultural use of saline and sodium waters, with that of Wilcox (Wilcox, 1955), probably the most widely used, although there is little agreement about which system is best. Whether any classification system based on the composition of water alone can be more than a very general guide is questionable because soil, plant, and climatic conditions are important in moderating the use of a water (Longenecker and Lyerly, 1959). The salt-balance concept (Wilcox and Resch, 1963) is useful, in certain limited physiographic areas, as an indicator of whether salts are being accumulated in or removed from the soils of an irrigated area. A comprehensive experiment on the use of saline water for irrigation is in progress in Tunisia under the auspices of Unesco, the French Office de la Recherche Scientifique et Technique Outre-Mer, and the Tunisian Soil Department.

I. SOIL MINERALOGY

The mineralogical composition of arid-zone soils should be representative of the original minerals from which the soils are derived, since chemical weathering presumably is low (Jackson, 1959). Illite, quartz, feldspar, ferromagnesium minerals, carbonates, and gypsum, accordingly, should be most abundant in clays of the deserts. Secondary layer silicates such as vermiculite, secondary chlorite, montmorillonite, kaolinite, and halloysite are most abundant in clays of moderately weathered parent materials. Secondary sesquioxide minerals such as hematite, goethite, allophane, gibbsite, and anatase, and residual resistant primary minerals such as limonite and magnetite, predominate in the more highly weathered parent materials, according to Jackson. The clay minerals present in colloids of the Kalahari sand and solonetzic soils of arid South Africa are about as would be expected since the clay minerals of the parent material have not decomposed under the low rainfall (van der Merwe and Heystek, 1955). Illite and montmorillonite also are the clay minerals dominant in arid Chile (Donoso, 1959). Montmorillonite is the dominant clay mineral in arid-zone soils in Israel, with illite, kaolin, quartz, and sometimes attapulgite present (Ravikovitch, Pines, and Ben-Yair, 1958; Ben-Yair, 1959).

In the central and northern part of the western Sahara (Atar to Beni-Abbes), Conrad is studying the clay minerals of arid- and semiarid-zone soils. He has found that relict kaolinite is present in iron crusts of the central part, while illite seems to be a stable component of the mineral fraction. South of Beni-Abbès, attapulgite was detected in some deposits of Villafranchian or older periods containing dolomitic sediments, particularly on the Hamada Plateau of Algeria and Libya lying north of the Ahaggar (Hoggar). The attapulgite appears to be undergoing decomposition as the result of present pedological processes in the semiarid areas.

Various results have been obtained in Egypt, where Nile alluvium is said by one author to consist mainly of illite, with some montmorillonite and kaolinite present, and with an indication of attapulgite in one sample (Khadr, 1963). An earlier paper reported that the clay of Nile sediment was formed mainly of amorphous aluminum silicates of the allophane group, along with muscovite mica (Hamdi and Mega, 1950). Soils of the Khârga desert oases west of the Nile valley may be dominantly kaolinite (Khârga and Ginâh [Ganah] oases) or montmorillonite (Bûlâq [Boulaq] and Bârîs [Beris] oases), while the Nile alluvium is rich in montmorillonite (El-Gabaly and Khadr, 1962). Attapulgite was the dominant clay mineral in two grey sandy soils of the U. A. R. western desert (El-Gabaly, 1962). The attapulgite may have formed from montmorillonite under saline submerged conditions. Kaolinite was the principal clay mineral of a soil from the Sinai Peninsula (Farag and Guirgis, 1960). Weathering of the illite in fresh sediment of the Nile is said to convert it into montmorillonite and boehmite under irrigation (Hamdi and Epprecht, 1955; Hamdi, 1959; Hamdi and Barrada, 1960) as the result of leaching with carbon dioxide and magnesium chloride.

Spanish Morocco montmorillonite seems to be the product of weathering of andesite in the presence of magnesium in the soil water (Gutiérrez Ríos and González García, 1950). Lower Mesopotamian alluvium in Iraq is composed largely of montmorillonitic clay minerals, with small quantities of illite (Buringh, 1960; Kaddouri, 1960). Both salted and normal soils of the Punjab plain in India had illite as the principal clay mineral, with some chlorite present (Kanwar, 1961), and salinization did not affect significantly the clay mineralogy of the soils. Sierozems of Central Asia have clay minerals that are dominantly of the montmorillonite group, with mica and quartz and, in some cases, hydrous mica and kaolinite present (Rozanov, 1951). In a solonetz soil, beidellite was the main secondary mineral in the silt fraction (Sharoskhina, 1960). Using a combination of several methods, a study of some United States and one West Pakistan arid-zone soils showed that mica and montmorillonite were dominant in the less-than-2-micron fraction of a majority of the soils

(McNeal and Sansoterra, 1964). There were moderate amounts of chlorite and quartz-plus-feldspar, and small amounts of kaolinite, vermiculite, and amorphous materials. The presence or absence of attapulgite could not be determined by the method that was used. By a similar method, the main clay mineral in cultivated Arizona soils was found to be montmorillonite, followed by illite, with some kaolinite and hydrous mica (Buehrer, Robinson, and Deming, 1949). Clay minerals in the surface of the Mojave soil of Arizona, on the other hand, were dominantly kaolinite and illite (Buol and Yesilsoy, 1964). Playas of the Mojave desert had a similar distribution of clay minerals: montmorillonite, illite, chlorite, and kaolinite (Mathews, 1960). These four playa minerals were traceable to the source areas surrounding the basin, and there was no evidence that they are unstable in the sodium or calcium lake environment (Droste, 1959). Mica, quartz, feldspar, calcite, and halite were the dominant nonclay minerals in the playas (Mathews, 1960). About 75 per cent of the colloids of Mojave desert alluvial fans and granitic soils were hydrous mica and montmorillonite, the remainder being kaolinite (Brown and Drosdoff, 1940).

A different distribution of clay minerals was noted in red-brown earths of the Australian arid zone, where the dominant clay minerals in the south were illite and kaolinite and in the north kaolinite. Soils developed on alluvial materials contained more illite than kaolinite, whereas those on igneous rocks were mainly kaolinite (Rudoslovich, 1958). In the higher-rainfall areas, poorly crystalline kaolinite was the principal clay mineral, with some gibbsite (Simonett and Bauleke, 1963). Weatherable minerals such as feldspars and ferromagnesium minerals are scarce in sand-size particles of arid New South Wales (Carroll, 1952).

J. CALCAREOUS SOILS

A summary of the chemical characteristics of Negev Desert soils (Pines, 1957) depicts quite well the conditions that may be expected to be found in calcareous arid-zone soils. All Negev soils are said to contain calcium carbonate; they have a pH of 7.0 to 8.5, and all except the sandy soils are saline. The main salts are gypsum and the chlorides of sodium, calcium, and magnesium. Few soils contain much organic matter or nitrogen, all are rich in phosphorus, and some are rich in potassium. Microbial populations are fairly well developed in loess and loess-like soils but are poor in the hamadas, texture and soil depth usually are suitable for cultivation, and the lowering of the groundwater table is necessary in some cases. Variations in these characteristics, particularly carbonate content, pH, and the phosphorus and potassium status, are common, but the general relations hold widely (Abdel-Salam and Allison, 1958; Calzada, 1951; Ferguson, 1951; Jewitt, 1955; Mitkees, 1959; Yaalon, 1954).

An interesting study of the relation of soil color to chemical composition in Australia (Beck, 1939) showed that calcium carbonate darkens certain soils due to the increase in humus associated with it. Grey, black, and white soils have very low free iron oxide, while in normal brown and red soils ferric oxide and humus are the predominating coloring materials. In certain red soils of basaltic origin, the color seems to be due in part to the presence of a brown complex iron silicate.

K.   SOIL FERTILITY

Countless experiments conducted in all parts of the world's arid zones have demonstrated conclusively that the plant nutrient element most likely to be deficient under intensified cropping is nitrogen. This absence is documented for the calcareous soils of the United States (Thorne and Peterson, 1950), which are representative of North American, South American, and Asian deserts, and for the red and brown soils of Australia (Norman and Wetselaar, 1960; Wetselaar and Norman, 1960; and Stephens and Donald, 1958), which have characteristics similar to those of red and brown soils of arid Africa. Phosphorus is the next element most likely to be deficient for legumes and some other crops in the desert and sierozem soils, and for all crops in the red desert soils. After phosphorus, the next deficiency to be expected varies with the soil and crop. Iron deficiencies are widespread in calcareous soils (Noy, 1959) and zinc deficiencies apparently are common in many of the same soils (Viets, 1961). In the highly leached red soils, sulfur deficiencies can be expected, along with potassium deficiencies in some cases (McLachlan, 1953; Stephens and Donald, 1958). Molybdenum deficiency in the northern territory of Australia has been found on red and on granitic soils (McLachlan, 1953). The phosphorus level of some Northern Territory soils is so low that sorghum and cotton respond to nitrogen only in the presence of adequate phosphorus (Arndt and Phillips, 1961).

Fine-textured, grey, alluvial soils of the Gezira in the Sudan are deficient in nitrogen but contain adequate phosphorus for nonleguminous crops (Crowther, 1941; Jewitt, 1955). Gezira soils are benefitted by fallowing, even under irrigation, presumably because the severe drying under the intense heat of the central Sudan improves the physical condition of the soil, as well as helping to control weed growth (Crowther and Cochran, 1942). The benefit ascribed to fallowing may be the result of the deep cracks that are formed upon dehydration of the soil, which permits water and applied fertilizer to penetrate into the cracks to a considerable depth. Fallowing also appears to be beneficial on the deep, fine-textured alkaline clays of Villaggio on the Scebeli River in Somalia (Rainey, 1949).

In a classic investigation of the effect of moisture content on the dissolved and exchangeable ions of arid-zone soils (Reitemeier, 1946), the necessity for controlling soil-water ratios is clearly demonstrated. Exchangeable sodium, for example, decreased by 58 per cent as the soil-water ratio was changed from saturation to 1 to 5. Ammonia, carbonates plus bicarbonates, and phosphate increased with dilution, but exchangeable calcium and magnesium behaved differently in different soils. Chlorides and nitrates were reduced upon dilution.

A comparison of several widely used methods for determining the amount of phosphorus in calcareous soils that is in a form that plants can utilize (Li, 1963) placed the 0.5 per cent sodium bicarbonate (Olsen) method first in correlation with pot and azotobacter fertilizer tests, followed by 1 per cent ammonium carbonate, 3.5 per cent sodium citrate (Radet), lactate (Egner-Riche), and 0.2N ammonium oxalate (Joret-Hubert).

L.   SOIL ORGANIC MATTER

Soil organic matter is a complex mixture of chemical compounds that have been studied in considerable detail for decades, in recognition of the importance of organic matter in affecting the chemical, physical and biological properties of soils. Two treatises on the subject of organic matter (Waksman, 1936; Kononova, 1961) demonstrate the complexity of the material and the difficulty of characterizing it in a way that will explain how it affects soil properties. The mineralization of organic nitrogen in soils has been reviewed, but with little reference to arid lands (Harmsen and Schreven, 1955). One of the few papers on organic matter in arid-zone soils (Oberholzer, 1936) notes that resistant fractions like lignin do not accumulate in these soils as much as in humid-zone soils, and that the rate of organic matter decomposition is greater in arid lands. Furthermore, decomposition has no significant effect on either the soil pH or phosphorus availability in calcareous soils, apparently because the carbon dioxide evolved is lost rapidly to the atmosphere. The conclusion is drawn that it is difficult, if not impossible, because of the rapid decomposition processes, to increase the supply of soil organic matter under arid conditions. This statement does not mean, however, that soil organic matter cannot be increased when arid-zone soils are irrigated and given good soil management (Dabin, 1951).

M. NITROGEN

A review of the effect of arid- and semiarid-zone calcareous soils on the reactions and movement of nitrogen fertilizers indicated that there are losses of gaseous nitrogen from soils due to chemical or bacterial reactions (Fuller, 1963). The loss of surface-applied ammonia increased as the pH increased above 7, and nitrates form readily in calcareous soils at a pH up to 9 if ammonia concentrations are favorable. Ammonia in rainwater in Israel depends markedly upon ground temperature, in upwind areas; the mean concentrations during the warm spring was four times as much as in the cool winter (Yaalon, 1964). Total seasonal washout of ammonia by rain was from about 4 to over 20 kilograms per hectare, for an average of 40 grams per hectare per millimeter of rain.

Among the limited tests of fertilizer use on arid-zone range plants, one in Arizona gave what appears to be fairly typical results (Freeman and Humphrey, 1956). There was a growth response to nitrogen and an effect of both nitrogen and phosphorus on the chemical composition of the range grasses.

N. MOISTURE - FERTILITY RELATIONS

Under irrigated conditions, raising the soil moisture content increased the uptake of radio-phosphorus in corn and barley when grown on a north Sinai soil, but in barley only at high moisture levels (Abdel-Salam and Hashish, 1962). While only a small portion of phosphorus fertilizer applied to calcareous Arizona soils was held against prolonged extraction by water, microbial fixation was important in soils low in available phosphorus (Fuller and McGeorge, 1950). Neutral salts decreased phosphorus solubility in calcareous soils by increasing the soluble calcium content of the soil solution (Olsen, Watanabe, and Cole, 1960). A study of phosphorus movement by tracer technique demonstrated the insignificant amount of movement that occurs under irrigation even when water-soluble phosphates are applied (Stanberry *et al.*, 1963).

O. TRACE ELEMENTS

Boron is not an element ordinarily deficient in arid-zone soils. On the contrary, its excess in soils and irrigation waters presents a problem to irrigated agriculture (Eaton, 1935; Mathur, Mogne, and Talati, 1964). Boron frequently is found in saline soils, where salinity effects on plants generally exceed boron toxicity effects until the soils are leached. Since boron compounds are more strongly adsorbed by soil particles than chlorides and sulfates, boron compounds are more difficult to remove by leaching (Hatcher and Bower, 1958; Reeve, Pillsbury, and Wilcox, 1955).

Trace elements in soils have been measured in various countries (Donald, Passey, and Swaby, 1952; Dobrovol'skii, 1961; Iyer and Satyanarayan, 1959; McKenzie, 1960; Riceman, 1953; Rish *et al.*, 1962; Robinson and Alexander, 1953) for the purpose of geochemical prospecting, studying soil development, or identifying plant nutrient deficiencies or toxicities. Selenium, a common constituent of arid zone soils, may be harmful to livestock if it occurs in big concentrations in forage plants (Ravikovitch and Margolis, 1957). Total analyses of soils to determine their trace-element content is of little value in estimating the possibility of a deficiency occurring when plants are grown on the soils. The solubility of the trace-element carrier compounds usually is variable, but low, and deficiencies result from a combination of environmental factors, such as pH, aeration, moisture content, other ions in the soil solution, plant species, etc. (not alone from the amount of trace element present). Some correlation was found between ore provinces and the trace-elements composition of desert varnish (the colored coating on surface stones) in Death Valley, California, and northeastern Nevada, but it was concluded that desert varnish may not be a meaningful indicator of mineralized soil zones (Lakin *et al.*, 1963).

Total analyses of soils provide information on the kind and extent of shallow ore bodies and on the degree of weathering of parent rock that has occurred. They do not, however, tell anything about the nature of the compounds that comprise the soil, and it is the interaction of mineral and organic compounds that determines soil properties.

P. RESEARCH STATUS AND NEEDS

Much disagreement exists with respect to methods of extracting soils preparatory to making analyses, and the disagreement is a measure of the uncertainty about what is being measured and what the analytical data mean. This situation is especially apparent in two areas of soil research: salinity and fertility. In salinity evaluation, soil-water ratios in common use vary from low to high, and the analyses made may be for all eight common cations and anions (sodium, potassium, calcium, magnesium, carbonate, bicarbonate, chloride, and sulfate); for these eight plus others; for only sodium, calcium, and magnesium; or for only chlorides, sulfates, and carbonates. The choice of analyses may be based upon correlation studies with soil properties and plant growth or upon someone's idea of what is needed. There still is no satisfactory method for determining exchangeable calcium or magnesium in calcareous soils. The extent to which sodium fixation occurs in arid-zone soils is unknown, and little is known about the factors that determine what exchangeable sodium percentage or exchangeable sodium amount will significantly affect the physical properties of soils or plant reactions.

In fertility studies, there is no chemical test to tell approximately how much of the organic nitrogen will be mineralized during the plant growing season, so estimates commonly are made on the basis of total nitrogen, irrespective of the kind of organic matter present. Some progress has been made on developing chemical tests for mineralizable nitrogen, based on the difference in ease of oxidation of organic compounds in the soil. This approach appears promising.

The concept of "availability" of plant nutrients is fraught with problems, which is why there are so many methods to measure it, none of them wholly satisfactory. In the final analysis, interpretation of the available nutrient data is based upon some knowledge of the testing method and upon experience with the soil and the crop being grown. Obviously, this is not a very satisfactory situation.

Except in a very general way, the significance of the presence or absence of a particular clay mineral in soils, insofar as it reflects upon soil properties, is not well understood. Differences between montmorillonitic swelling clays and kaolinitic nonswelling clays are apparent when these particular clays are dominant in the soil. Soils of the arid lands, however, frequently are an intimate mixture of several minerals, and how they interact to affect ion fixation and cation exchange reactions, for example, is not clear. Nor is it clear how organic matter and clay minerals react with one another. In fact, the chemistry of organic matter in arid-zone soils is largely unknown, just as is the microbiology that so strongly affects organic matter content and form.

SOIL CLASSIFICATION

Recognition that soils are natural bodies and not simply finely divided geologic material is generally credited to V. V. Dokuchaev in Russia and E. W. Hilgard in the United States. These scientists independently concluded in the latter part of the 19th century that climate was a dominant factor in soil development, although not always the most important one. Other factors were topography, vegetation, geologic material, and time. In the development of a particular soil, any one or a combination of these soil-forming factors could play a dominant role. The principles of soil development enunciated by Dokuchaev, in particular, have had a strong impact.

A number of systems for classifying soils of the world are in use today, including a recent one, the Seventh Approximation of the United States Soil Conservation Service, that was put into effect in 1965. Systems used most widely in the arid regions are the Russian, French, Dutch, and "Marbut" U. S. For purposes of this discussion, the Marbut system refers to the classification used in the United States prior to 1965, which undoubtedly will continue to be used by many soil scientists both in the United States and overseas.

A. RUSSIAN SYSTEM

The Russian soil classification system (Tyurin *et al.,* 1959; Rozov and Ivanova, 1966) is a genetic system, based upon what are known as "types" in the U.S.S.R. and "great soil groups" in the United States (Podzol, Chernozem, Sierozem, etc.). The relation of soil-forming factors to the development of any particular soil is stressed. The basic classification category is the type, which is divided into subtypes, genera, species, subspecies, variety, rank, and phase. Field mapping units, usually at the species level for detailed maps, are adjectival forms of type names. For example, a soil might be mapped as a "weakly solonchakous" soil, meaning that it had the general characteristics of a solonchak. Since all species (mapping unit) names are forms of type names, there never is any doubt of the general soil group (type) to which a specific soil belongs. This has the real merit of encouraging the soil surveyor to think of the relation

of one soil to another during the course of the survey instead of considering each soil to be an isolated entity.

In addition to maps showing the distribution of soils, Soviet soil scientists prepare single-factor maps for use in soil management. These maps show such information as the amount of available phosphorus, depth to water table, and other conditions that are locally important for proper management of the soils. Map scale for single-factor maps may be as large as 1/2,000. Soil maps usually are at a scale of 1/10,000 or smaller.

B. FRENCH SYSTEM

French soil scientists have developed a classification system that has some elements of the Russian system. It is a morphological-genetic classification and recently has been revised (Aubert, 1963, 1965). The categorical order is: class, subclass, group, subgroup, facies, family, and series, with phases sometimes added to further differentiate soils on the basis of properties important for management purposes. The mapping unit for small-scale maps usually is the group or subgroup. For large-scale maps, the mapping unit is the family (1/100,000 and 1/200,000) or series (1/20,000 or larger). There are 10 classes, in which the effect of time and environmental conditions are emphasized but classification is dependent upon soil properties. Arid-zone soils may belong in as many as six of the 10 classes. Soil groups are at the level of great soil groups or great groups (U.S.) or types (U.S.S.R.), and several of the group names are taken from the Russian. Terms used for mapping units are usually, but not always, variations of class names, and the class to which the mapping unit belongs is readily apparent from the mapping legend. Insert maps showing soil associations and sequences frequently are included with the published map.

Some variation on the foregoing mapping system has been and is used in overseas surveys. Prior to 1959, a special soil classification based upon climatic and soil chemical data was in use in Algeria. French scientists working in Lebanon have developed a "land system" classification similar to that employed in Australian regional surveys. Detailed land-utilization maps showing agricultural capabilities of lands also are prepared, especially in Tunisia. Lastly, single-factor soil maps of texture, permeability, etc., sometimes are used to supply basic data required for regional development plans.

Reconnaissance soil maps, which are the most common ones published for tropical and north Africa by the Office de la Recherche Scientifique et Technique Outre-Mer (ORSTOM), have a map scale of 1/50,000 to 1/200,000. Detailed soil maps are at a scale of 1/5,000 or 1/10,000, usually.

C. DUTCH SYSTEM

A markedly different soil classification system is used by the Dutch, who conduct soil surveys in many parts of the world. While there is considerable flexibility in the nomenclature applied to a particular survey in the different countries, presumably due to local wishes and previous experiences, the preferred first level of soil separation is on a physiographic basis (Vink, 1963). The intent is to identify the physiographic systems that have been or are predominant in the formation of the area. Sometimes these systems are of a geologic nature; other times sedimentary and erosional processes may be more significant. Examples from central Iraq, where soils are built up on a levee-and-basin pattern, are river levee, high river basin and low river basin. The second category of map units is based on type of parent material, color, lime content, etc. The third, and lowest, level is based on slope, stoniness, texture, depth, and similar special features of the soil. In some surveys, soil series, as defined in the Marbut U. S. system, are used for mapping, with great soil groups being the higher category rather than physiographic systems. Use of physiographic systems permits virtually limitless flexibility in selection of mapping units but leaves each survey unrelated to surveys in different areas. The same criticism applies to the use of soil series unless the series are placed within the great soil groups of which they are representative.

Mapping scales vary, depending upon the use to which they are put. Detailed published maps usually have a scale of 1/20,000 or smaller, whereas more general maps are at a scale of 1/100,000 or smaller.

D. UNITED STATES SYSTEMS

In the United States a new soil classification system known as the 7th Approximation (U. S. Department of Agriculture, Soil Conservation Service, Soil Survey Staff, 1960), has been developed by the Soil Conservation Service of the U. S. Department of Agriculture. Since 1965, the new system has become the required system for S. C. S. soil scientists. It replaces the system that had been used for nearly 40 years, since C. F. Marbut introduced the Russian type (great soil group) concept to the United States in 1927 with the translation of K. D. Glinka's *Die Typen der Bodenbildung.*

Soil mapping in the United States began at the end of the 19th century, when geologic concepts of soil were in force. The first soil surveys published by the U. S. Department of Agriculture, the leading soil-survey agency in the United States, in 1899 were based upon identification of soil series and types. There were no higher categories. Numerous soil surveys were completed in the first 35 years of the 20th century, all using series and types as the map unit, without reference on the maps or in the reports to higher categories. Ever since the term "series" was introduced, it has been criticized widely because the name used, such as Pullman, has absolutely no connection with soil characteristics. A person wanting to know what kind of soil belongs to the Pullman series would have to refer to an official description in order to have even a vague idea of its characteristics.

A number of lectures by Marbut in 1928 brought out his ideas on soil genesis and classification and changed the thinking of American soil scientists from that time forward (Marbut, 1951). The *Atlas of American Agriculture* (Marbut, 1935) carried the first comprehensive discussion of the application of great soil groups to the U. S. soil survey. A revision of Marbut's classification was presented in *Soils and Men,* the 1938 Yearbook of Agriculture (Baldwin, Kellogg, and Thorp, 1938).

Very few soil-survey reports were published by the U. S. Department of Agriculture in the 1940's, but the number increased greatly in the 1950's and then decreased again in the early 1960's. Reports published in the last ten years have carried some information on the great soil groups to which the soil series belonged. There seems to have been little effort, however, to do more than give very general descriptions of what morphological, chemical, or physical limits were to be applied to individual great soil groups. The result was to place virtually all soil classification emphasis on soil series and to pay little attention to whether a series actually belonged to one great soil group or another. An inevitable consequence of the concentration upon the series as the significant soil unit was to emphasize soil properties that were important in agriculture and to minimize the natural character of the soil as a distinct entity in the earthly environment. This emphasis continues today in the United States and in many other countries.

Soil surveys conducted by the U. S. Department of Agriculture and the land-grant colleges are agricultural soil surveys, primarily, which delineate soil series and types. Soil surveys conducted by the U. S. Bureau of Reclamation are land-classification surveys designed to determine the suitability of soils for irrigation. Land elevation, slope, drainage, and soil permeability are the important considerations in the latter type of survey. State highway departments and others concerned with the use of soil as a building material make still another type of soil study. They are interested in such things as the bearing strength, grain size distribution, plasticity, permeability, cohesion, and consolidation of soils. Several engineering soil classification systems, based upon accepted tests of physical properties, are in use, with the Unified Soil Classification (U. S. Army Engineer Waterways Experiment Station, 1960) being most widely used.

E. DUPLICATION IN CLASSIFICATION

A common tendency among soil-survey groups in the United States is to consider that no type of soil classification other than the one each is using is suitable for its needs. Thus, different groups may survey and classify the same soil area several times, each obtaining separate bits of information and usually duplicating at least part of the work previously done. Some of the apparent duplication is not, in fact, real, because different methods of analysis may be used or terms such as sand, silt, and clay may refer to different size limits. This situation holds particularly for soil surveys for agricultural and engineering purposes. It is open to question, however, whether some of the distinctions are meaningful rather than merely habitual.

Attempts have been made to translate the information in agricultural soil surveys into a form that soil engineers can use (Maytin and Gilkeson, 1962). The success of such efforts depends upon the extent to which soil scientists and engineers understand each other's language. Regrettably, few do, so each side generally goes its own way. United States experience in this respect seems to be duplicated around the world, although this statement may be less true where the Dutch operate under their physiographic system of soil classification, because it more nearly approximates the engineering approach.

F. A UNIFIED NOMENCLATURE

No soil classification system in present use adequately classifies all soils of the world. It is doubtful that any system will do so in the foreseeable future, because many large sections of the Earth's surface have not been studied in sufficient detail to permit classification of the soils. Arid areas are, next to the polar and high mountain regions, the least-known parts of the world.

A limitation found in all agricultural soil classification systems results from the fact that the developers of the particular system tend to have a restricted view of soils that are absent from or are not widespread in their own country or in associated territories. Furthermore, the classification system may be unbalanced because one type of soil either has received more attention than others or is of greater economic importance. An example of the former is the emphasis placed by the French (in Africa) and Australians upon soils derived from very old surficial geological materials. Such materials are absent or unimportant in the Soviet Union and the United States, so they receive little attention. Conversely, sierozems are widespread and important in the latter two countries but are not significant in Africa and Australia.

These differences in importance of and experience with particular soils have led to confusion in nomenclature. Few soil scientists would be so bold as to say, without seeing the soils or reading a detailed account of profile characteristics, whether a grey soil, a sierozem, and a grey desert soil were one and the same or were two or three different soils. And the situation probably is even more uncertain when it comes to defining a "desert" soil.

A single soil classification system for use throughout the world may be undesirable, for many reasons; however, there is little excuse for applying the same name to different soils or for having several names for the same soil at the group (French), type (Soviet Union), or great soil group (U. S.) level. Soil science needs an international body to arbitrate its disputes over definitions, names, and priorities. Botany, zoology, and microbiology have such international bodies. The busiest is the International Commission on Zoological Nomenclature. In all biological nomenclature disputes, the basic criterion employed in resolving them is the law of priority: the oldest published name, supported by substantiating descriptions, is the valid name. Provision is made for receiving objections from individual biologists anywhere in the world.

An "International Commission on Soil Classification Nomenclature" would have the arduous and time-consuming tasks of arbitrating disputes over definitions, names, and priorities. Unless an effort of this kind is made, an ever greater multiplicity of artificially created or incomprehensible local dialect names will be introduced to the literature. The opportunity is at hand through international collaboration on the FAO / Unesco Soil Map of the World Project, but prospects of reaching agreement on a common soil nomenclature seem remote, largely for political rather than scientific reasons. The International Society of Soil Science is the logical organization to take the leadership in establishing a nomenclature commission. An effort to develop an international soil classification system was begun in 1909 at the First International Conference of Pedologists in Budapest (Prasolov, 1937), but nothing came of it. After nearly 60 years, the fear of Prasolov that there would arise a multiplicity of duplicating and confusing terms if international collaboration were not achieved has been proven true.

G. KINDS OF SOILS

A good description of the kinds of soils that occur in arid and semiarid regions has been given by Aubert (1962). He recognizes soils of the extremely arid regions (severely blown soil, deposited soil, unshifted soil), the arid regions (desert steppe soils, sierozem), and the subarid regions (brown). The extremely arid soil groups are weakly developed or undeveloped raw mineral soils such as regs, sand dunes, skeletal soils, and soluble salt pans. Desert steppe soils include the gray and red desert groups. Sierozem subgroups include the gray sierozem (the typical sierozem), red sierozem, tropical sierozem, and hydromorphic sierozem. Brown soils have several subgroups: typical brown steppe, reddish brown, brown tropical, brown incrusted, brown pseudogley, saline brown, and alkali or solonetzic brown. Soil development increases from the raw mineral soils to desert steppe to sierozem to brown. The most comprehensive discussion of any of these groups is that of Rozanov for sierozems of the Soviet Union (Rozanov, 1951).

Great-soil-group terminology developed by the Russians and slightly modified by the Americans has not been considered adequate for classification of the soils of Africa and Australia. In Australia, for example, great soil groups of the semiarid region are called brown soils of light texture, grey and brown soils of heavy texture, solonized brown soils, mallee sandhills, and solonetz. Arid-zone soils are desert loams, stony desert, desert sandhills, desert sandplain, grey-brown calcareous desert soils, and red calcareous desert soils (Stephens, 1949). Among the differences in Australian and North American arid-zone soils is the much brighter red of Australian soils, from 5YR and 7.5YR in the U. S. to 2.5 YR and 10R in Australia on the Munsell color chart.

The variety of soils found in arid zones is a reflection of the dominance of physical weathering, topographic differences, scarcity of vegetative cover, severity of water and wind erosion, variety of parent materials, differences in age of soils, locally wet conditions in depressions, and retention of windblown salt. Another factor is the change in climate from wetter to drier that has occurred in some areas. This

appears to be the case in Spanish Sahara (Albareda and Alvira, 1950), north Africa (Durand, 1953b; Dutil, Martinez, and Quézel, 1959), Australia (Carroll and Wolf, 1951; Christian et al., 1954; Stephens, 1949), and the Arabian Peninsula (Holm, 1960), among others. As in other climatic zones, sequences of soils (catenas) can be recognized. The most common sequence starts with bare rock and skeletal soils on desert mountains, then goes to coarse alluvial fans on the upper slopes, fine alluvium on the lower slopes and in the broad valleys, and saline soils in the depressions, with sand dunes likely to be found in the broad valleys (Beckett, 1958; Ganssen, 1960). The Israeli soil classification system (Dan, Koyumdjisky, and Yaalon, 1962) has soils of the arid zones placed in four orders, climatogenic, lithogenic, fluviogenic and eolian, and hydrogenic soils, showing a diversity of formation that is duplicated in other arid zones.

H. SOIL - PLANT RELATIONS

Because arid-zone soils, like any others, are a product of their environment, aerial photographic interpretation techniques have been devised that assist materially in the mapping of extensive tracts of uninhabited or sparsely inhabited land (Liang, 1964). It sometimes is overlooked, however, that this method of identifying soil features always requires a systematic field check (Vink, 1963). It is a powerful tool, but like any tool, it must be used with discretion. Some air photo interpreters stress soil-vegetation relations (Gunn, 1955), while others emphasize soil-vegetation-landform relations (U. S. Army Engineer Waterways Experiment Station, 1959; Vinogradov, 1961). Killian, checking indicator value of plants in a chott (saline depression) in Algeria, expressed the belief of many ecologists when he concluded that soil-plant relations are too complicated to permit formulation of lists of plants indicating certain soil conditions (Killian, 1953). One source of the difference of opinion of the indicator value of plants in the arid lands is that some investigators study individual species distribution whereas others study plant communities. Individual species may not be closely dependent upon restricted soil properties (Duverger, 1960; Fireman and Hayward, 1952; Gates, Stoddart, and Cook, 1956; Kassas, 1952; Nechaeva, 1961; Valentine and Norris, 1964), although the growth of a plant called mallee, which is a dwarf eucalyptus, is used to identify solonized brown soils of Australia (Beare, 1959; Prescott, 1931; Stephens, 1949), and spinifex grass is an indicator of sandy desert soils (Prescott, 1931). Plant communities do bear a close relation to soils, and they are the best basis for predicting soil conditions from vegetative cover (Dabin, 1959; Davis, 1953; Kassas and Iman, 1954; Kassas, 1957; Marks, 1950; Smith, 1954). A Moroccan study of the value of psammophilic species as indicators of the depth of sand and the percentage of sand in the soil demonstrated that the relation was not a close one and that soil moisture was the main controlling factor (Ionesco, 1958). An Arizona study concluded that the soil properties characterize, and are intimately associated with, distinctly different and major climax vegetation types existing under the same macroclimate (Yang and Lowe, 1956). Available soil moisture was the main determinant of vegetation differences.

Patterns of vegetation that show up in aerial photographs but may be difficult to discern on the ground have been related to soil conditions. A peculiar arcuate form of vegetation bands was noted in Somalia and found to be due to the deposition of organic litter and sandy or silty materials around local obstacles (Greenwood, 1955). The deposited material provided better water relations than the underlying impermeable clays. Greenwood suggested that vegetation arcs of mesquite (*Prosopis* spp.) might be established on the sandy soils to reduce wind erosion. Alternating bare and grassed areas in the Butana region of the Sudan, where there were no measurable differences in elevation between the bands, was attributed to differences in the presence or absence of surface soil cracks and to water supply (Worrall,

1959). Lines of vegetation that aroused curiosity when they were noticed on aerial photographs appear to be related to the ancient dune sand patterns of a mid-Pleistocene period in the Kalahari Desert (King, 1952).

That plants play an important role in soil development is a cardinal principle of soil science. In arid lands their effect frequently is more apparent than in the humid regions, because plants tend to be widely spaced and differences between soil influenced or not influenced by plants is easier to see. So called "mineral roots" in arid-zone soils are examples. Distinctive formations develop in sandy soils of the Kara-Kum desert of Central Asia upon decomposition of roots of bushes (Tolchel'nikov, 1960), filling the former root spaces with gypsum, calcium carbonate, and chlorides, with some organic residue remaining, and preserving the appearance of roots. The effect of vegetation, particularly perennial crops, on soil development on shifting sands along the Mediterranean coast of Israel becomes readily apparent after several years (Ravikovitch and Ramati, 1957). The sequence of development of sandy soils in the arid U.S.S.R. has been described, and the desirability of hastening plant action on soil formation is noted (Yakubov and Bespalova, 1961). Under a cover of *Anabasis salsa*, grey-brown desert soils of Central Asia are said to acquire solonetz properties (Karayeva, 1963).

CONCLUSIONS AND RECOMMENDATIONS

Sections IV through VII above contain sub-sections entitled "Research Status and Needs." The reader is referred to those sections for recommendations, and to the indications of little-known aspects of surface materials of particular geographic areas discussed in section II, which are also implied recommendations for research. The recommendations in the present section, then, include summarization of earlier recommendations and additional material appropriate to this concluding statement.

Soils of the hot arid zones are quite variable in their physical, chemical, and biological properties despite the uniformly low precipitation and the high potential evaporation. These differences in properties, which make it impossible to describe *a* desert soil, are due to variations in age of the surficial materials, mineral composition, physiographic position, amount of wind and water erosion to which they have been exposed, past climate conditions, seasonal rainfall distribution, and other factors. Fine-textured saline soils of depressions are as typical of arid zones as are upland gravelly surfaces. Because the depressions will receive considerably more water as runoff from higher land than is represented by the average annual precipitation, depressions and upland soils will differ substantially in several important respects, but both are typical despite their differences. The presence on the land surface or at a shallow depth of remnants of paleosols developed under different climatic conditions further complicates the identification of a typical arid-zone soil. While paleosols are common throughout the world, they have left an indelible mark on contemporary surfaces in Africa and Australia, especially.

The most common characteristics of upland arid-zone soils are a low level of organic matter in comparison to humid zone soils, a slightly acid to moderately alkaline pH, the presence of calcium carbonate throughout the upper 5 feet or an accumulation of it at some depth in the profile, weak profile development, coarse to medium texture, and low biological activity. Other characteristics that distinguish many arid-zone soils are stony and gravelly surfaces overlying a wide variety of materials, and accumulations of sand as hummocks around clumps of vegetation or as large sand dunes which may be fixed or moving.

A common, but by no means universal, topographic sequence of arid-zone soils is: rock outcrops on desert mountains and hills; coarse-textured, dissected alluvial fans on the upper slopes; finer-textured lower fans and plains, with or without sand dunes; and fine-textured saline and/or gypsiferous depressions or variably textured water courses and flood plains in the bottomlands.

A. AVAILABILITY OF DATA

There is a large amount of information on arid-zone soils for the world as a whole but only a minimal amount for the central Sahara, the Somali-Chalbi, the Kalahari-Namib, the Arabian Desert excluding Israel and Iraq, the Takla-Makan and the Gobi deserts, the Thar, and the Iranian Desert excluding Iran. Research data are available from the responsible organizations in most countries, with the principal exception of detailed soil survey maps of the Soviet Union, China, and parts of southwest Asia, for security reasons. Publications other than those having soil-survey maps are limited in accessibility by translation problems in Russian, Chinese, and Arabic, although there has been a considerable improvement in availability of Russian publications in translation in the United States. It is doubtful whether there are many soil research papers written only in Arabic, and the amount of good information accumulated by the Chinese is an unknown quantity although it is probably considerable.

B. SOURCES OF DATA

Countries having active and extensive programs of soil research in the arid zones are Australia, France, Israel, the Soviet Union, and the United States. Of these, France is the only one conducting major programs outside its national boundaries. The Office de la Recherche Scientifique et Technique Outre-Mer (ORSTOM) has a wealth of information on the arid zones of the French-speaking nations of north and tropical Africa. In Australia, the principal source of research information is the Commonwealth Scientific and Industrial Research Organization, in its Division of Soils and Division of Land Research and Regional Survey. Israel soil surveys are made by the Soil Conservation Department of the Ministry of Agriculture, and much soil research is done by staff members of Hebrew University. The premier soil research establishment in the Soviet Union is the V. V. Dokuchaev Soil Institute of the U. S. S. R. Academy of Sciences. In the United States, a great majority of soil surveys conducted in the country are done by the Soil Conservation Service of the U. S. Department of Agriculture. Other soil research is handled by agricultural and engineering experiment stations of universities and by the research arms of the federal government, in the main.

Among international agencies supporting arid-zone research in soils is the Food and Agriculture Organization of the United Nations in Rome, and Unesco in Paris. These two specialized agencies of the United Nations are collaborating in the preparation of a world soil map at a scale of 1/5,000,000. The South American sheet has been completed.

The reader is also referred to section III, Authorities and Depositories.

C. ADEQUACY OF DATA

Overall, the information on arid-zone soil properties is inadequate to permit a comprehensive understanding of the processes involved in soil development and in the reactions of soils to natural and man-made forces. Much excellent work has been done by researchers on all continents, and the caliber of research in general is improving, but the world-wide coverage is spotty. A major reason for this spottiness undoubtedly lies in the inhospitable environment of the extremely arid and arid zones, as contrasted with the semiarid and humid zones. Where intensive studies have been conducted, they are usually in arid areas where agricultural development is or will be attempted. One glance at the map showing the areas where soil surveys have been made in the United States gives a striking demonstration of this fact: whereas some humid-area states have been covered completely by standard soil surveys, the arid western states have been surveyed almost exclusively in those places where dry-land or irrigation agriculture is practiced.

Relatively little basic research has been done or is underway on arid-zone soils. The primary emphasis is on applied studies to determine the suitability of soils for man's use. This statement may be more true for the United States than for the Soviet Union, France, and Australia. The absolute magnitude of research, both basic and applied, in the United States and the Soviet Union appears to exceed that of any other country. Worldwide, soil classification

and studies of the chemical properties of soils are receiving much more emphasis than research on physical properties, with biological research receiving the least emphasis.

D. PRINCIPAL DEFICIENCIES IN INFORMATION

A look at research data from arid zones throughout the world makes it apparent that several significant questions remain unanswered.

Soils Reflecting Arid Environment

We still must determine what kinds of soils develop under arid and extremely arid conditions. It is standard operating procedure to say that upland arid-zone soils showing more than moderate-to-weak development must be the product of an earlier, more moist environment. The Australian, Kalahari, and Sahara deserts, notably, contain soils quite different from those found in the Northern and Western hemispheres. By and large, they are redder than their counterparts and have finer-textured surface and subsoil horizons. Resembling as they do, in some details, soils presently found in the subhumid tropics, there is reason to believe that they, too, must have formed under more humid conditions. Red soils also are found along the arid Arabian coast, and on the southern fringe of the Sahara where 200 mm or more of rain may fall in a period of 60 to 90 days, leaving the remainder of the year virtually rainless. Red colors are noted in soils of the United States and Soviet Union, too, but they are much weaker reds than those in Australia. Differences in iron-oxide content of the surfaces of soil particles would appear to be the logical explanation for the color differences, but why they occur and why organic matter does not obscure the color equally when present in the same amount is not apparent. Apart from questions of color, however, the basic question is unanswered: what kind of soil truly reflects an arid environment?

Color

Confusion among terms used to classify arid-zone soils is another major deficiency. Color already has been mentioned from one standpoint; it also presents a problem when used as it is to identify soils of great soil groups. The term "red desert" soil is used in the United States to mean color that is several shades less red, in the Munsell system, than the "red" soils of Australia. The term "grey" is subject to similar different interpretations, although less extreme than the aforementioned case of red colors. If color is to have interpretive value, then obviously the terms used to describe it must be consistent. The solution comes down to the use of the Munsell or some similar notation system for color descriptions to avoid the difficulty encountered in this review, where color designations found in the original papers were used without knowing what the true color was.

Nomenclature

Resolving differences in color terms should be easy; it will be much more difficult to resolve another, more important deficiency: the use of different great soil group, great group, type, or group names to refer to the same soil at the same categorical level. The nomenclature problem is illustrated by the common reference to "desert" soils, despite the ambiguity of the term, not only on a worldwide basis but within individual arid zones. It appears that everyone knows what a desert soil is but no one can define it. Other points of nomenclature confusion include (1) the use of the terms "grey desert soil," "grey soil," and "sierozem" (which means grey soil) to refer to soils that may or may not be similar, (2) calling soils "semidesert," "subdesert," or "semiarid," without indicating what properties distinquish those soils, (3) not knowing what is meant by the term "brown" in Soviet, French, Australian, and American usage, and (4) uncertainty as to whether exchangeable sodium is or is not an essential constituent of solonetz soils. Many other nomenclature problems could be cited. We need urgently to resolve ambiguities in terms so that publications from throughout the world can be understood by the serious reader.

Soil-Water Ratio

A very real deficiency results from failure of authors to indicate the soil-water dilution used in measuring pH and soluble salts, in particular. The dependence of pH and salt solubility data upon the soil-water ratio is well documented, yet many authors fail to indicate which of the variety of ratios in common use was employed in their own studies. It becomes impossible, then, to make reliable comparisons of pH or soil salinity data among authors.

Physical and Chemical Properties

The deficiencies in physical and chemical methods of soil analysis have been noted at some length in their respective research review sections. The most important deficiencies in determination of physical properties are those for soil texture and soil aggregation. Among chemical methods needing much improvement are those for determination of exchangeable calcium and magnesium in calcareous soils and for exchangeable sodium in highly saline soils.

While the effects of exchangeable sodium, potassium, and magnesium on soils usually is considered in the United Sates to be well known (exchangeable sodium has unique effects on physical properties of soils), it is, in fact, not. Scientists in other countries believe that exchangeable potassium behaves similarly to sodium, or that exchangeable magnesium, at least under some conditions, affects soils in a manner similar to exchangeable sodium. This fundamental question should be answered by appropriate basic research.

Trafficability

An area of research that appears to have been almost completely ignored except by military organizations is that of soil trafficability. Trafficability refers to the capacity of soils to support moving vehicles, men, or beasts of burden. Most evaluations of trafficability found in the nonmilitary literature are based upon common sense: loose sand dunes offer poor trafficability, dry clay plains provide good traveling surfaces. Field tests to measure trafficability consist of measuring the cone index, remolding index, and slope. An estimate of slipperiness is attempted, and the trafficability is calculated from a comparison of these tests with the vehicle cone index for the vehicle in question, in addition to subjective evaluation of obstacles such as forests, ditches, and rivers. The work involved in actually measuring trafficability has led to procedures for estimating it from soil maps. Since organizations primarily interested in trafficability are engineering organizations, the soil maps they want to use are engineering soil maps. These are scarce for the humid zones and nearly nonexistent for the arid zones, but agricultural soil maps are available for many parts of the arid zones. Unfortunately, few engineers are able to interpret agricultural soil maps (and few agriculturists can interpret engineering soil maps).

The subject of trafficability appears to be one that should be amenable to a fairly good degree of predictability from detailed agricultural soil maps and, to a lesser degree, from semidetailed and reconnaissance maps. The persons capable of making predictions would be those thoroughly familiar with soil classification procedures and techniques who also are familiar with engineering soil terminology and the factors of importance in determining trafficability. The latter are not difficult to learn. The more difficult task will be to determine the relation between factors influencing trafficability and the soil characteristics that are identified on soil maps. To accomplish that determination, a comprehensive research study must be undertaken that will relate trafficability to kinds of soils occurring throughout the arid zones and the way they react to varying moisture conditions. In making the study, chemical properties of soils must be considered, as well as physical properties and surface conditions, since the soil layer critical to trafficability may extend to as much as 15 inches, or thereabouts, beneath the surface. Pending the initiation of a research project that would improve predictions of trafficability, it should be possible to make more meaningful predictions than we have at present by making use of the large amount of soil-survey information available now.

Cooperation between Soil Engineers and Soil Scientists

None of the present national soil-survey programs discussed in this chapter provide information in the form that the field of soil mechanics requires. Suitability of soils for brickmaking, oil-well mud, ceramics, road construction, and building construction is difficult to determine from soil-survey reports unless an individual is thoroughly familiar with agricultural and engineering terminology and with the criteria employed in evaluating soil properties. Soil scientists are inclined to look at soils only from the standpoint of their plant growth potential, which calls for as much or more emphasis upon chemical and biological properties as upon physical properties. Soil engineers, on the other hand, are inclined to ignore chemical and biological properties while centering their attention upon tests of physical properties.

Engineers are faced with the necessity of meeting specifications for road construction, as an example, that are established by the contracting agency. While judgment must be exercised by engineers in interpreting data and local conditions, there is less obvious need for it in agricultural soil investigations. Part of this variation stems from the difference between intensive (engineering) and extensive (agricultural) surveys. Another source is the greater agreement among engineers about the soil-testing methods they should employ. Whatever the reason, soil scientists tend to be subjective in evaluating soil conditions while soil engineers tend to be objective. Opinions differ about whether soil scientists can be more explicit in evaluating soil conditions with respect to their effects on the use to which the soil will be put. There are so many unknown factors involved in the plant-soil-water-climate relation that precise interpretation of the soil factor is usually not justified. On the other hand, the present state of knowledge about soil mechanics does not appear adequate to permit more than a fairly reliable estimate to be made of the engineering characteristics of soils. In both areas, judgment must be exercised, and there is no substitute for experience.

Distinctions between soil engineers and soil scientists have become sharpened as the field of soil mechanics has developed. At present, soil scientists are almost wholly oriented toward the study of soils from the viewpoint of their ability to grow plants (Buckman and Brady, 1960). Soil engineers have the completely different purpose of learning how soils behave as building material (Means and Parcher, 1963). In the United States, soil science has, with few exceptions, become agricultural soil science. This condition is regrettable because it has led to isolation of the two dominant groups, Despite some attempts to bridge the gap, little progress is apparent even in the area of soil physics, which should be closely associated with soil mechanics. A more serious defect arising from the separation into specialized fields of scientists studying and using soils is the restricted exchange of knowledge. Plasticity, compressibility, and grain size distribution are significant in the development of tillage pans and poor soil structure in agricultural soils, but many agricultural soil scientists are not aware of their significance. Few of them have even heard of the Unified Soil Classification, to say nothing about knowing what it is. Soil engineers are equally uninformed about the significance of agricultural soils studies and data. Soil chemistry, especially, is a largely unknown field to them even though exchangeable sodium, for example, can influence greatly the physical properties of soils. The nearest thing to a common ground for soil engineers and scientists is mineralogy, a knowledge of which is basic to the understanding of physical and chemical properties of soils.

What may be a regrettably representative view of the difficulty encountered in removing the barrier between soil scientists and soil engineers was expressed in a report on engineering soil surveys in New Jersey (Holman *et al.*, 1957). The authors of the report say that agricultural soil maps are useful but are only one of many aids in the preparation of engineering soil maps, because soil scientists are primarily concerned with the top 3 feet of soil. They mention that an engineer trained in certain phases of soil science, pedology, geomorphology, geology, and agriculture could interpret an agricultural soil map and prepare an engineering soil map without any more surveying. Individuals with that kind of training are rare, however, so Holman and his colleagues conclude that engineering soil surveys should be made specifically for the engineer, using terms with which he is familiar. That conclusion, only substituting "agricultural" for "engineering," is exactly the same as would be drawn by a typical agricultural soil scientist, and the preceding statements, too, would be echoed.

The unfortunate result of such thinking is that little attempt is made to find grounds of common interest and to promote cooperation instead of conflict. It is unlikely that either soil scientists or soil engineers will profit from following increasingly diverging paths. Recognition of the legitimate needs of all users of soils information must be given, followed by understanding of how those needs can be met by unified effort instead of wasteful duplication and the erection of a false barrier.

One heartening step has been taken toward improving coordination among engineers, geologists, and soil scientists. It took the form of a conference on particle size distribution held at the 1965 Columbus meeting of the Soil Science Society of America, with E. P. Whiteside, Department of Soil Science, Michigan State University, presiding. It was sponsored by the Joint A. S. C. E. / A. S. T. M. Committee on Nomenclature in Soil Mechanics and Foundations, the Society of Economic Paleontologists and Mineralogists, the Highway Research Board and the Building Research Advisory Board of NAS-NRC, and the Soil Science Society of America. Its objective was "to exchange views on the desirability and possibility of coordinating the size class limits currently used by engineers, geologists, and soil scientists in characterizing earthy materials." During the conference, it was pointed out that there are no common grain (particles) size limits among either engineers or soil scientists, so the opportunity for coordination is both intradisciplinary and interdisciplinary. The conference agreed to invite participation by other interested groups in future deliberations and for each group to prepare position papers on particle size classes (by 1 June 1966). Perhaps the start that has been made in particle size limit uniformity can be carried over into other areas, such as soil surveys, in which many disciplines have a common interest.

PERTINENT PUBLICATIONS

This bibliography combines in one alphabetical sequence for simplicity both an annotated bibliography and a more inclusive reference list. Those works which it has been possible to determine are of particular significance or interest to this study within the limitations discussed in the chapter are annotated. Other competent works and best-available works on specific subjects are listed without annotation; lack of annotation should not be construed as necessarily indicating a less important publication. CA numbers identify abstracts in *Chemical Abstracts* pertaining to the publications.

Abdel-Malek, Y. and Y. C. Isham
1962 Abundance of *Azotobacter* in Egyptian soils. International Congress for Microbiology, 8th, Montreal, Abstracts, B 14.6. 57 p.
Changes in the density of *Azotobacter* and N_2 fixing clostridia in a cultivated clay loam were followed monthly for 4 successive years. In the part of the land receiving only mineral fertilizer, the *Azotobacter* counts ranged from 10^4 - 10^7 per gram, while in the part receiving in addition big amounts of plant residues they kept between 10^6 and 10^8 per gram throughout. Clostridial spore counts were at all times higher than *Azotobacter* counts.

Abdel-Rahman, A. A. and E. M. N. Hadidy
1958 Observations on the water output of the desert vegetation along Suez Road. Egyptian Journal of Botany 1:19-38.
Total rainfall for 1955 - 1956 was 23.4 mm and it moistened the sandy soil to 25 cm. Below 50 cm the soil was permanently wet, moisture being retained from years of heavy rainfall.

Abdel-Salam, M. A.
1961 Soils of the Wadi Arish area. Société de Géographie d'Egypte, Bulletin 34.
Scale: 1/75,000. In English and Arabic. 9 soils classed by texture. Area on Sinai Peninsula.

Abdel-Salam, M. A. and L. E. Allison
1958 Chemical and physical properties of extension area soils in Egypt. Institut du Désert d'Egypte, Bulletin 8:109-121.
The soils were poor in organic matter, low in permeability, rich in lime, and varied in texture from sandy loam to heavy clay. Addition of $CaSO_4$ for replacement of exchangeable Na should be considered.

Abdel-Salam, M. A. and S. Hashish
1962 Effect of varying moisture levels in desert soils on phosphorous uptake by plants. p. 351-361. *In* Symposium on the use of radioisotopes in soil-plant nutrition studies, Bombay, Proceedings series. International Atomic Energy Agency, Vienna.
Increases in soil moisture to 28% caused remarkable increases in P32 uptake for both corn and barley plants, accompanied by a corresponding increase in the P content and vegetative growth.

Abdel-Samie, A. G.
1959 The soil survey and classification of the Fuka-Ras El-Hekma area. Institut du Désert d'Egypte, Publication 12. 70 p.
Scale: 1/45,000. Areas in western coastal desert of U.A.R.

——— 1961 The distribution of various soil profile types around the Deep Wells, El Kharga Oasis. Société de Géographie d'Egypte, Bulletin 34.
Scale: 1/25,000. New Valley, Southern Egypt. Soils classed by texture; coded profile types show rocky soils, dunes, temporary saline lakes, and permanent saline lakes.

Abell, L. F. and W. J. Gelderman
1964 Annotated bibliography on reclamation and improvement of saline and alkali soils (1957-1964). International Institute for Land Reclamation and Improvement, Wageningen, Bibliography 4. 59 p.

Academia Sinica, Sand Control Team
1958 Reports on the coordinated research on the desert region, 1-2. Scientific Publications Society, Peiping. (Issued in translation by Joint Publications Research Service, 1963, as JPRS 18,658 and 18,178. Also cited as OTS 63-21563 and 63-21341).
Covers parts of Kansu and Shensi provinces and the Ninghsia plains, in the area of the midsection of the Yellow River in north China.

——— 1962 Research on sand control. Peiping. 508 p. (Issued in translation by Joint Publications Research Service, 1963, as JPRS 18,993. Also cited as OTS 63-31183).
Covers parts of Sinkiang, Chinghai, Kansu, Ninghsia, and Shensi provinces of Northwest China.

Agafonoff, V. and L. Yenkovitch
1935- Sols types de Tunisie. Service Botanique et
1936 Agronomique de Tunisie, Annales 12-13.
(Soil types of Tunisia)
Scale: 1/800,000.

Ahmad, N.
1961 Soil salinity in West Pakistan and means to deal with it. *In* Salinity problems in the arid zones, Proceedings of the Teheran symposium. Unesco, Paris. Arid Zone Research 14:117-125.
The subject is discussed under the headings: subsoil water-table conditions; causes of the rapid rise of the water table in the canal regions; salts in subsoil water;

salts in river waters, removal of salts by leaching; difficulties of successful leaching in West Pakistan; open drains; tile drains, drainage by pumping; hydraulics of tube wells.

Akzhigitova, N. I.
1959 The relationship between the chemical composition of plants and the salinization of soils (translated title). Uzbekskii Biologicheskii Zhurnal 6:76-82.
From the analyses of soil horizons and plants it appeared that the salt character of soil was the principal factor determining the chemical composition of the plants. CA 54 (12452).

Albareda, J. M. and T. Alvira
1950 Mediterranean soils of the Spanish Levant and North Africa. International Congress of Soil Science, 4th, Amsterdam, Transactions 2:185-186.
The low value of the $SiO_2: Al_2O_3$ ratio, which is approximately 2, and the presence of kaolinite in the clays suggest that red soils from south and east Spain and northern Morocco were formed under humid conditions and later suffered a change to arid conditions with simultaneous deforestation.

Amemiya, M. and C. W. Robinson
1958 The use of undisturbed soil cores to investigate the reclamation of saline and alkali soil. Soil Science Society of America, Proceedings 22: 76-78.
In view of the similarity of results obtained from undisturbed cores in the laboratory and field plots, it appears that soil cores, properly encased, can be used to predict with reasonable accuracy the reclaimability of saline and alkali soils.

Anderson, J. U.
1963 Effects of pretreatment on soil dispersion. New Mexico Agricultural Experiment Station, Research Report 78.
Pretreatment at high pH disrupts crystal species.

Anonymous
1959 Pochvennaya karta Azerbaydzhanskoy S.S.R. Agrolimaticheskoy Spravochnik pa Azerbaydzhan S.S.R. Leningrad.
(Soil map of the Azerbaydzhan S.S.R.)
Scale: 1/1,500,000.

Anonymous
1960 Skhematickeskaya pochvennaya karta vostochno-Kazakhstanskoy Oblast. Glavnoe Upravleniye Gidrometeorologicheskoy Sluzhby, Agroklimaticheskoy Spravochnik pa Vostochno-Kazakhskoy Oblast. Leningrad.
(Schematic soil map of East Kazakhstan Oblast)
Scale: 1/1,500,000. Note: Many schematic soil maps for other oblasts were published in 1960 by the Glavnoe Upravleniye Gidrometeorologicheskoy Sluzhby under titles roughly similar to the above (e.g., Agroklimaticheskoy spravochnik pa Buryatskoy A.S.S.R.).

Anonymous
1962 Pedogeographic map of Uighur Autonomous Region of Sinkiang Province (translated title). Acta Pedologica Sinica 10:324a.
Scale: 1/6,000,000. Poor map. Text gives description of main soil groups.

Antipov-Karataev, I. N.
1956 L'amélioration des solonetz en U.R.S.S. International Congress of Soil Science, 6th, Paris, Rapport D, p. 531-536.
(Amelioration of solonetz in U.S.S.R.)
The process of interaction of the solonetz horizon with gypsum and calcium carbonate is very slow; therefore agricultural measures have been devised aiming to create a fertile upper layer on top of the solonetz horizon. These measures are: spreading additional earth on top of the solonetz when the top layer overlying the solonetz horizon is insufficiently thick, or subsoiling the solonetz with special plows.

——— 1960 Physikalisch-chemische untersuchungen im zusammenhang mit der melioration der alkaliböden. International Congress of Soil Science, 7th, Madison, Transactions 1:571-576.
(Physico-chemical investigations on the reclamation of alkali soils)
The utilization of the "inner reserves" of solonetz soils, such as $CaSO_4$ and $CaCO_3$ at available depths and presence of soils colloids, for the "self-amelioration" of the vast tracts of solonetz soils in the Soviet Union is being studied with a view to dispensing with huge amounts of $CaSO_4$ so far required for reclamation.

Antipov-Karataev, I. N. and A. A. Kizilova
1962 Certain types of soil salinization in irrigated zones of Iran. Soviet Soil Science 1962(3):302-310.
Salinity in the soils of the Garmsar and Dasht-i-Kavir Desert is of the chloride-sulphate type. In the Gezelhezar the salinity is of the soda-sulphate type and solonetzic-solonchakous processes are the predominant soil-forming processes.

Anwar, R. M.
1959 Soil and land classification of Baris Plain in El Kharga Oasis. Institut du Désert d'Egypte, Publication 12. p. 50.
Scale: 1/200,000. 8 soil classes, mechanical analysis of 374 profiles.

Arndt, W. and L. J. Phillips
1961 Fertilizer responses of annual crops at Katherine, N.T. C.S.I.R.O. Division of Land Research and Regional Survey, Technical Paper 15.
On clay-loam soil, groundnuts, cotton and sorghum responded up to 3 cwt/acre super, and the residual effect of P was high, that of rock phosphate being higher than super. Legumes tolerate lower P levels than do sorghum and cotton. Sorghum and cotton respond to N only in the presence of added P. There was no clear response to other nutrients.

Asghar, A. G.
1961 Use of saline water for irrigation with special references to saline soils. *In* Salinity problems in the arid zones, Proceedings of the Teheran symposium, Unesco, Paris. Arid Zone Research 14: 259-266.
An account of experiments conducted in Pakistan is given and the choice of suitable species for cultivation and the management techniques which will lead to satisfactory yields (despite strongly mineralized irrigation waters) are discussed.

Asghar, A. G. and H. S. Zaidi
1960 Soil Survey, Rechna Doab, West Pakistan. West Pakistan Water and Power Development Authority, Water and Soils Investigation Divison, Bulletin 2(1, 2, 3).
Covers Chukarkana, Jaranwala, and Haveli areas.

Aubert, G.
1962   Arid zone soils, a study of their formation, characteristics, utilization and conservation. *In* The Problems of the arid zone, Proceedings of the Paris symposium. Unesco, Paris. Arid Zone Research 18:115-137.

———
1963   La classification des sols: la classification pédologique française 1962. Cahiers de Pédologie ORSTOM 3:1-7.
The 1962 soil classification system was built upon the earlier system of Demolon and Oudin. It is a genetic classification, having classes, subclasses, groups, subgroups, series, and phases. The highest category (class) has 10 members: Raw Mineral Soils, Weakly Developed Soils, Vertisols and Paravertisols, Calcomagnesimorphic, Steppe Soils, Development Humus Soils, High Humus Soils, Sesquioxide Soils, Halomorphic, and Hydromorphic. The mapping unit usually is the group or subgroup.

———
1965   La classification des sols: tableaux des classes, sous-classes, groupes, et sous-groupes des sols. Cahiers de Pédologie ORSTOM 3:269-288.
Latest scheme of soil classification used by French soil scientists for soil classes, subclasses, groups, and subgroups. Brings 1962 report up to date.

Audry, P.
1961   Etude pédologique du Cercle du Guidimaka. Office de la Recherche Scientifique et Technique Outre-Mer, Centre de Recherches Pédologiques de Hann-Dakar et Convention Agriculture, République Islamique du Mauritanie. 4 vols.
(Soil study of Guidimaka Circle)
Scale: 1/200,000. 5 groups of soils. Area of 10,000 km.
Map in vol. 4; analytical data in vol. 3. Comprehensive.

Audry, P. and C. Rossetti
1962   Observations sur les sols et la végétation en Mauritanie du sud-est et sur la bordure adjacente du Mali (1959 et 1961). U. N. Special Fund Project: Prospection Ecologique, Etudes en Africa Occidentale. FAO, Rome, in collaboration with ORSTOM. UNSF/DL/ES/3. 267 p.
Observations on the soils and vegetation of southeast Mauritania and adjacent area in Mali)
Scale: 1/200,000. Shows land types only. Analytical data for numerous soil profiles in report.

Ayazi, M.
1961   Drainage and reclamation problems in the Garmsar area. *In* Salinity problems in the arid zones, Proceedings of the Teheran symposium. Unesco, Paris, Arid Zone Research 14:285-290.
Report of the research by the Ministry of Agriculture on methods of reclaiming saline and alkali soils of the Garmsar district, in northern Iran.

Bagnold, R. A.
1943   Physics of blown sand and desert dunes. William Morrow and Co., New York. 265 p.
Book is concerned with phenomena produced by action of wind on sand; wind-tunnel experiments on mechanism of sand transport; small-scale surface phenomena such as ripples and problems of size grading of grains; growth and movement of dunes in general and peculiar characteristics of two main types.

———
1953   The surface movement of blown sand in relation to meteorology. *In* Desert research, Proceedings, International Symposium held in Jerusalem May 7-14, 1952, sponsored by the Research Council of Israel and Unesco. Research Council of Israel, Special Publication 2:89-96.

Balba, A. M. and M. M. El-Gabaly
1964   Soil and ground water survey for agricultural purpose in the NW coast of Egypt, U. A. R. International Congress of Soil Science, 8th, Abstracts of Papers 5:226-228.
Purpose of survey is to estimate suitability of soils and ground water for agricultural use-irrigated and dry land. Area extends 600 km from Alexandria west to El Sallum.

Baldwin, M., E. Kellogg, and J. Thorp
1938   Soil classification, p. 979-1001. *In* Soils and Men. U. S. Department of Agriculture, Yearbook.
A revision of Marbut's classification of soils, with introduction of Sibertsev's zonal, intrazonal terms into system, at highest level. Some rearrangement of great soil groups into pedocal and pedalfer divisions. Additional great soil groups have been named.

Barbour, K. M.
1961   Soils of the Upper Nile Basin, the Republic of the Sudan. University of London Press.
Scale: 1/5,000,000. Covers eastern Sudan north of Khartoum.

Baver, L. D.
1956   Soil physics. 3rd ed. John Wiley and Sons, New York.

Beare, J. A.
1959   Soils of South Australia. Department of Agriculture of South Australia, Journal 63:43-48.
They respond to super and are deficient in Ca and Cu. Sandy mallee soils form a characteristic pattern of alternating sand ridges and flats. They are deficient in P and N, and with irrigation Zn, M, and Cu deficiencies appear on fruit trees and vines.

Beattie, R. B.
1964   Flexible pavement built on sand subgrades in Perth area, Western Australia. Australian Road Research 1(10):30-48.
Laboratory study of laterite gravel pavements overlying sand subgrade. These results gave optimum pavement thickness of 6" independent of all variables except sequence of construction; field study confirmed results obtained by laboratory method.

Beck, A. B.
1939   The relation between colour and chemical composition in soils. Australia, Council of Scientific and Industrial Research, Journal 12(2):128-136.
Calcium carbonate darkens certain soils due to humus. The yellow color of some podzolic subsoils appears to be intrinsic to the mineral colloid of the soil. In grey, black, and white soils the free iron oxide is probably very low, while in normal brown and red soils free ferric oxide and humus are the predominating coloring materials. In certain red soils of basaltic origin, the color seems to be due in part to the presence of a brown complex iron silicate.

Beckett, P. H. T.
1958   The soils of Kerman, South Persia. Journal of Soil Science 9:20-32.
The catenary sequence shows bare rock and skeletal soils, derived from Cretaceous limestone, or shales, grits and brown limestone or gravel conglomerate; soils on fine outwash alluvium; loose sand and moving sand-dunes, and saline soils.

Ben Yair, M.
1959 Studies on the mineralogy of Israel soils. Research Council of Israel, Bulletin 8G:156.
In well drained rainy areas the dominant clay mineral in terra rossa is kaolinite; in poorly drained areas with little rain it is montmorillonite. In other soils montmorillonite with various amounts of illite, kaolin, calcite, etc.

Bernstein, L.
1962 Salt-affected soils and plants. *In* The Problems of the arid zone, Proceedings of the Paris symposium. Unesco, Paris. Arid Zone Research 18:139-174.
A review.

Bespalov, N. D.
1951 Pochvy Mongol'skoi Narodnoi Respubilik. Izdatel'stov Akademii Nauk S. S. S. R., Moscow. (Soils of Outer Mongolia. Issued in translation by Israel Program for Scientific Translations, Jerusalem, 1964, 328 p. Also cited as OTS 64-11073)
Soil map scale equal 1/5,000,000.

Bettenay, E.
1961 The soils and land use of the Merredin area, Western Australia. C.S.I.R.O Division of Soils, Soils and Land Use Series 41.
Scale: 1/126,720. 9 soil associations. Text has soil descriptions and lab analyses and climate, topography, and vegetation. Covers area along Great Eastern RR, 160 miles east of Perth.

———
1962 The salt lake systems. Journal of Soil Science 13:10-17.
Gypsum dunes occur in western Australia next to salt lakes, with lunettes of clay, silt, and sand occurring next to gypsum dunes. Gypsum dunes and lunettes are common in southern Australia. Salt lakes are gypsum and halite. Parna is eolian clay material.

Bettenay, E., A. V. Blackmore, and F. J. Hingston
1962 Salinity investigations in the Belka Valley, Western Australia. C.S.I.R.O. Divison of Soils, Adelaide, Divisional Report 10-62.
Removing shrubs raises water table and increases salinity by removing deep-rooted plants that keep water table low.

Bidner-Barhava, N. and S. Ravikovitch
1952 Adsorption of sodium by soils from solutions of sodium salts. Ktavim 2-3:5-9.
Na_2SO_4 yielded on the whole the largest amounts of exchange Na, while in most concentrations there was little difference in adsorption from $NaNO_3$ and NaC1. Lime had only slight effect, confined to low salt concentration, in impeding Na adsorption. Gypsum reduced Na adsorption very considerably, even from highly concentrated solutions.

Bocquier, G.
1964 The presence of tropical solothized solonetz features in the Chad basin. International Congress of Soil Science, 8th, Abstracts of Papers 5:103-106.

Bocquier, G. and M. Gavaud
1962 Carte pédologique de reconnaissance de la République du Niger. Office de la Recherche Scientifique et Technique Outre-Mer, Centre de Recherche Pédologique de Hann-Dakar, Senegal. (Reconnaissance soil map of the Republic of Niger)

Two sheets completed in south. Soils classed by genetic type and grouped by maturity of profile and parent material.

Bolyshev, N. N.
1964 Role of algae in soil formation. Soviet Soil Science 1964 (6):630-635.
Algae are the principal vegetation of the soil crust of the takyr, solonetz, and some other soils of desert and semidesert zones.

Bonnet, J. A.
1960 Edafología de los suelos salinos y sódicos. Universidad de Puerto Rico, Estación Experimental Agrícola, Río Piedras. 337 p. (Edaphology of saline and sodic soils)

Borovskii, V. M.
1961 Salt exchange between the sea and the land, and long-term dynamics of soil processes. Soviet Soil Science 1961(3):237-244.
A review with 36 references.

Borut, S.
1960 An ecological and physiological study on soil fungi of the northern Negev (Israel). Research Council of Israel, Bulletin 8D:65-80.
A comprehensive study was made of 82 species of fungi isolated from the arid soils in the Northern Negev (Israel). The genera *Aspergillus* and *Penicillium* are represented by a great number of species. Some species of fungi were found in all kinds of soils investigated; others appeared in peculiar soils only. Loess soils were found to be the richest, both in the number of fungi per gram earth and in the number of species. Hamada soils are less rich and sand soils are the poorest. These data stand in correlation with the quantity of organic matter in these soils and not with their humidity.

Botelho da Costa, J. A. and L. Azevedo
1960 Generalized soil map of Angola. International Congress of Soil Science, 7th, Madison, Transactions 4:56-62.
Map not reproduced in printed Transactions. Available from Junta de Investigaçoes de Ultramar, Lisboa, Portugal. Scale: 1/3,000,000. Soils of arid regions are: Xerolithosols, Desert Pebbles, Desert Crusts, Desert Dunes, Gray Brown and Reddish Brown Arid Soils. Soils usually calcareous.

Boulaine, J.
1961 Sur le rôle de la végétation dans la formation des carapaces calcaires Méditerranéennes. Académie des Sciences, Paris, Comptes Rendus 253:2568-2570.
Formation of calcareous crusts beneath soil surface due to pedologic and vegetation effects. Plant roots deposit appreciable Ca upon decomposition.

Boumans, J. H. *et al.*
1963 Reclamation of salt affected soils in Iraq. Soil hydrological and agricultural studies. International Institute of Land Reclamation and Improvement, Publication 11. 175 p.
The saline soils of Iraq are described, results of leaching of salt-affected soils (including the alkalinity aspects of the process) are reported, and crop yields, consumptive use, irrigation and drainage on reclaimed soils are discussed.

Bower, C. A. and J. O. Goertzen
1958   Replacement of adsorbed sodium in soils by hydrolysis of calcium carbonate. Soil Science Society of America, Proceedings 22:33-35.
A reaction has been studied from the standpoint of describing the replacement of adsorbed Na in calcareous soils subjected to leaching by rainfall.

Bower, C. A. *et al.*
1962   Soil salinity and irrigation in the Soviet Union. U. S. D. A., Agricultural Research Service, Report of a Technical Study Group.
Observations on soils, salinity and irrigation in the U.S.S.R. made in 1960.

Boyko, H. and E. Boyko
1964   Principles and experiments regarding direct irrigation with highly saline and sea water without desalination. New York Academy of Sciences, Transactions, ser. 2, 26:1087-1102.

Brambila, M. and R. Ortiz Monasterio
1956   [Soil map of Mexico.] *In* R. Ortiz Monasterio, Los recursos agrológicos de la República Mexicana. Ingeniería Hidráulica en México 10(4):71-84.
Latest official map of soils of Mexico.

Brodskii, A. L. and A. Yankovskaya
1930   Materialy k poznaniyu pochvennoi fauny Srednei Azii. Pochvovedenie 1/2.
(Data on the soil fauna of Central Asia)
Sierozem, sandy, and takyr soils have high population of all classes of Protozoa, which are important in organic matter transformation.

Brown, I. C. and M. Drosdoff
1940   Chemical and physical properties of soils and of their colloids developed from granitic materials in the Mojave Desert. Journal of Agricultural Research 61(5):335-352.
Colloids are saturated with bases, chiefly Ca and Mg. About 25% of the Fe present is free iron oxide. X-ray data indicate that the composition of about 75% of the colloids is a mixed-layer mineral of hydrous mica and montmorillonite and that of about 25% is kaolinite (halloysite).

Buckman, H. O. and N. C. Brady
1960   The nature and properties of soils. Macmillan Company, New York. 567 p.
An introductory textbook of edaphology.

Buehrer, T. F., D. O. Robinson, and J. M. Deming
1949   The mineral composition of the colloidal fraction of some southwestern soils in relation to field behavior. Soil Science Society of America, Proceedings 13:157-165.
The main minerals are montmorillonite, which in several profiles tended to increase with depth, and illite, with some kaolinite and hydrous oxide.

Buol, S. W. and M. S. Yesilsoy
1964.   A genesis study of the Mojave sandy loam profile. Soil Science Society of America, Proceedings 28:254-256.
Only a weak and relatively recent carbonate accumulation is pedogenically associated with the present soil surface. Kaolinite and illite are the predominant clay minerals in the upper layer. Thin sections reveal few clay skins developed in the profile.

Bureau, P. and P. Roederer
1961   Sols gypseux au sud de Tunisie. Association Française pour l'Etude du Sol, Bulletin, Notice Spéciale, pp. 150-176.
The importance of gypsum in the pedogenesis of these soils appears to justify their inclusion as a subclass of calcimorphic soils, as proposed by Aubert (1960).

Buringh, P.
1960   Soils and soil conditions in Iraq. Ministry of Agriculture, Directorate General of Agricultural Research and Projects, Baghdad. 322 p.
Map scale: 1/1,000,000. Book has detailed descriptions of soils and physical and chemical analysis. Comprehensive coverage. Greatest detail on Mesopotamian plain.

Buringh, P. and C. H. Edelman
1955   Some remarks about the soils of alluvial plain south of Baghdad. Netherlands Journal of Agricultural Science 3(1):40-49.
Scale: 1/250,000 and 1/50,000. 7 map units: strip of land 6 x 40 miles, south from Baghdad. The Mussayib Project and El Sabbaghiyah.

Burvill, G. H.
1956   Salt land survey, 1955. Department of Agriculture of Western Australia, Journal 3d ser., 5:113-119.

Burvill, G. H. and L. J. H. Teakle
1938   The occurrence of solonetz (structural alkali) soils in Western Australia. Department of Agriculture of Western Australia, Journal 2nd ser., 15(1):100.

Butzer, K. W.
1961   Climatic changes in arid regions since the Pliocene. *In* L. D. Stamp, ed., A history of land use in arid regions. Unesco, Paris. Arid Zone Research 17:31-56.

Buxton, P. A.
1924   The temperature of the surface of deserts. Journal of Ecology 12:127-134.
Temperature fluctuations much greater in soil than air.

Calzada, J. B.
1951   Análisis de las tierras cultivadas de la costa y sierra. Agronomía (Peru) 16(68):53-64.
(Analysis of cultivated soil at the coast and in the sierra)
Data are presented on sand, Ca, colloids, N, P, K, organic matter and pH of Peruvian soils.

Cameron, R. E.
1961   Algae of the Sonoran Desert in Arizona. University of Arizona (Ph.D. dissertation).118 p.

Cameron, R. E. and G. B. Blank
1965   A. Soil studies—microflora of desert regions. VIII: Distribution and abundance of desert microflora. California Institute of Technology, Pasadena, Jet Propulsion Laboratory, Space Programs Summary 37-34, vol. 4:193-202.
There were significant numbers of microflora present in 34 California desert soils examined at 6 sites in the Colorado, Mojave, and the Great Basin to depths of 3-4 feet. Order of population was aerobes plus actinomycetes, anaerobes, facultative anaerobes, algae, fungi. Only algae at times greater than in agricultural soils.

Cameron, R. E. *et al.*
1965   C. Soil studies — desert microflora. X: Soil properties of samples from the Chile Atacama Desert. California Institute of Technology, Pasadena, Jet Propulsion Laboratory, Space Programs Summary 37-35, vol. 9.

Cappannini, D. A.
1952   Rio Salado: mapa de suelos. Instituto de Suelos y Agrotecnia, Sección Geoedafología, Buenos Aires, Publicación 25.
(Rio Salado: soils map)
Map scale: 1/100,000. 5 soils series related to landforms.

Carroll, D.
1952   Mineralogy of some Australian desert soils. Journal of Sedimentary Petrology 22:153-161.
20 soil profiles (73 samples) from the arid western part of New South Wales on the southeastern edge of the Simpson Desert were examined for sand-grade minerals and mechanical composition. Weatherable minerals such as feldspars and ferromagnesiums were scarce.

Carroll, D. and M. Wolf
1951   Laterite developed on basalt at Inverell, New South Wales. Soil Science 72:87-99.
The profile described is a fossil laterite development on Tertiary basalt. The present distribution of constituents of the profile is probably due to leaching under acid conditions and deposition during drier periods.

Carroll, P. H.
1949   Soil piping in southeastern Arizona. U. S. Department of Agriculture, Soil Conservation Service, Regulation 6, Bulletin 110. 21 p.
It occurs in alluvial soils with highly dispersed subsoil. Factors contributing to piping are animal burrows, deep root casts, lowered water table due to entrenching of streams, deep cracking of soil, and dense underlying strata that cause lateral movement of water until it reaches an entrenched stream channel.

Carter, W. T.
1931   The soils of Texas. General characteristics and capabilities of Texas soils. Texas Agricultural Experiment Station, Bulletin 431. 192 p., map.

Caster, A. B., W. P. Martin, and T. F. Buehrer
1942   The microbiological oxidation of ammonia in desert soils. I: Threshold pH value for nitrification. Arizona Agricultural Experiment Station, Technical Bulletin 96.
A threshold pH of 7.7±0.1 was found, above which complete oxidation of ammonia did not occur.

Caswell, A. E.
1953   Land classification and soil survey maps of Tripolitania and Cyrenaica. U. S. Foreign Operations Administration, Natural Resources Division, I. A. T. A. S., Land Classification and Soil Survey Report.
Scale: not uniform, 1/30,000. Soils and land class denoted by fractional code showing texture, topography, and drainage, United States Bureau of Reclamation mapping system.

Cavallar, W.
1950   Esquisse préliminaire de la carte des sols du Maroc. Société des Sciences Naturelles du Maroc, Section de Pédologie, Travaux 1:19-43.
(Preliminary sketch of the soil map of Morocco)
Scale: 1/1,500,000. 40 units described briefly. Soils classed by color, genesis, and texture.

Chandra, P., W. B. Bollen, and L. T. Kadry
1962   Microbial studies of two Iraqi soils representative of an ancient site. Soil Science 94:251-257.
The numbers of bacteria and molds were very low in dry samples, but after 5 days incubation at 50% moisture capacity and 26° C increased to values comparable to those in moderately fertile humid soils. *Azotobacter* were present. The fungi consisted entirely of *Aspergillus niger* or a similar species. The ammonifying, nitrifying, and S-oxidizing capacities were moderately good, but decomposition of native and added organic matter was slow, especially in the Annanah soil.

Chang, H. W. and K. H. Hsu
1962   Microbiological properties of the sand dunes in Tengkeli desert of Ninghsia Hio autonomous region (translated title). Acta Pedologica Sinica 10:227-234.
Fixed dunes differ from mobile dunes in composition of microflora number and activity in fixed dunes, particularly in rhizosphere. Number greater in surface than subsoil.

Chao Sung-ch'iao
1962   A preliminary discussion on the types of gobi in the northwestern part of Ho-hsi Tsou-lang and its reclamation and utilization. p. 189-224. *In* Academia Sinica, Sand Control Group, ed., Research on sand control. Peiping. (Issued in translation by Joint Publications Research Service as JPRS 19,993. Also cited as OTS 63-31183)
Gobi ground surface composed of coarse conglomerate or bedrock. Fine material blown away.

Chepil, W. S. and N. P. Woodruff
1963   The physics of wind erosion and its control. Advances in Agronomy 15:211-302.
Kinds of wind erosion and factors controlling them.

Chevalier, G.
1951   Pluies à Alger au cours de la campagne 1949-1950 et apports salins aux sols. Institut Agricole et des Services de Recherches d'Experimentation Agricole de l'Algérie, Annales 6(3):3-9.
(Rains in Algiers during the season 1949-1950 and their salt supply to soils)
Pluviometric studies showed that rainwater of the littoral regions contained an average of $22g/m^3$ of NaCl. Rains supplied an average of 40-54 kg/ha of Na annually.

Christian, C. S. and G. A. Stewart
1953   General report on survey of the Katherine-Darwin region, 1946. C. S. I. R. O. Land Research Series 1.
These reports all show landforms, soils and vegetation. Definition of land system: "an area or groups of areas throughout which there is a recurring pattern of topography, soils, and vegetation."

Christian, C. S. *et al.*
1954   Survey of Barkly region, in Queensland and Northern Territory along Gulf of Carpentaria. 1947-48. C. S. I. R. O. Land Research Series 3.
Map scale: 1/1,100,000. Describes climate, geology, geomorphology, hydrology, soils, vegetation, land systems, land-use groups, agricultural and pastoral potentials. 120,000 square miles. Has map of land systems, not soils.

Churchward, H. M. and E. Bettenay
1962   The soils of a portion of the Fitzroy River Valley at Liveringa Station, Western Australia, C.S.I.R.O. Division of Soils, Soils and Land Use Series 42. 31 p.
The chief feature of the 400 square miles surveyed was the alluvial river plain; soil distribution was related to a sequence of 4 depositional layers which form the soil parent materials. Suitability for flood irrigation and the presence of extensive areas of soils which would probably

be fairly impermeable gave good prospects for rice growing. P content of the soils was moderate to good, N content was poor and K level was adequate.

Clements, T. *et al.*
1963 A study of windborne sand and dust in desert areas. U. S. Army, Natick Laboratories, Earth Sciences Division, Technical Report ES-8. 61 p.
Severe sand and dust storms occur at a rate of less than 2 per year on the average in desert areas of southwestern U. S. Critical pickup velocities of winds vary according to the type of desert surface, the grain size and coherency of the surface materials, and whether or not the surface has been disturbed artificially. In dune areas, winds of 10-15 mph will initiate movement, and on other sandy terrain winds of 20 mph will be necessary for this. Fine material on desert flats will be set in motion at 20-25 mph, and alluvial fans and playas at 30-35 mph. No windblown materials will be derived from desert pavements unless the surface has been broken, and on all other above-mentioned types, disturbing the surface will lower critical pickup velocities by as much as 5 mph.

Comité Argentino para el Estudio de las Regiones Aridas y Semiáridas
1963 Las tierras áridas y semiáridas de la República Argentina, informe nacional. Conferencia Latino-americana para el Estudio de las Regions Aridas, Buenos Aires. 54 p.
(Arid and semiarid lands of the Argentine Republic, national report)
Soil map at scale of 1/15,000,000.

Comité Chileno para el Estudio de las Zonas Aridas
1963 Informe nacional sobre las zonas áridas de Chile. Conferencia Latinoamericana para el Estudio de las Regiones Aridas. Santiago. 99, [1] p.
(National report on the arid zones of Chile)

Comité Mexicano de Zonas Aridas
1963 Informe nacional México. Conferencia Latino-americana para el Estudio de las Zonas Aridas, México, D. F. 52 p.
(Mexican national report)
Climate, geology, geomorphology, soils, hydrology, vegetation, fauna, economics, industry, and population of the Mexican arid regions.

Comité Peruano de Zonas Aridas
1963 Informe nacional sobre 'las zonas áridas. Conferencia Latinoamericana para el Estudio de las Regiones Aridas, Lima.
(National report on the arid zones)
Climate, geology, geomorphology, soils, hydrology, vegetation, fauna, economics, industry, and population of Peruvian arid regions.

Conrad, G.
1959 Importance et rôle des termites dans les formations pédologiques fossiles du Quaternaire de la région Beni-Abbes. Académie d'Agriculture de France, Comptes Rendus Hebdomadaires des Séances 249:2089-2091.
(The importance and role of termites in the Quaternary fossil-soil formations in the Beni-Abbes region.)
Paleosols in the northwest Sahara indicate an active role of termites in the physical modification (crusting, concretions) and chemistry (migration and precipitation of Fe) of the soil in the Quaternary period.

Crocker, R. L.
1946 The soils and vegetation of the Simpson Desert and its borders. Simpson Desert Expedition, 1939, Scientific Report 8. Royal Society of South Australia, Transactions 70:235-258.
Gibbers (stones) on surface are in part fossil remnants of B horizons of the laterite or lateritic profile developed over the Pliocene peneplain.

Crowther, F.
1941 Form and date of nitrogenous manuring of cotton in the Sudar ᴜezira. Empire Journal of Experimental Agriculture 9:125-136.
It is suggested that the greater efficiency of N fertilizers applied before or after the rains is due to the more extensive cracking of the soils and the better penetration of nitrate. Calcium nitrate gives a greater yield-increase than does ammonium sulphate, especially if small dressings are compared.

Crowther, F. and W. G. Cochran
1942 Rotation experiments with cotton in the Sudan Gezira. Journal of Agricultural Science 32:390-405.
Under the intense heat of the Central Sudan fallow improves the physical structure of the soil and is of importance for the control of weed growth, through cessation of irrigation. Frequent fallows are of prime importance for cotton in the Sudan Gezira, the longer the fallow, the greater the benefit.

Dabin, B.
1951 Influence du rapport Na/Ca sur les propriétés physiques de certains sols argileux du Delta Central Nigerien. Office de la Recherche Scientifique et Technique Outre-Mer, Office du Niger, Côte de Classement 1339.
(Influence of the Na/Ca on the physical properties of certain clay soils of the delta of Central Niger)
Some poorly permeable soils. Problem is exchangeable Na. Soils with low Na/Ca have increased permeability and decreased dispersion.

———— 1953 Premiéres notions sur la flore microbienne utile dans les sols du Delta Central Nigerien. Office de la Recherche Scientifique et Technique Outre-Mer, Office du Niger, Côte de Classement 1250.
(First concepts on the useful microbial flora in the soils of the Central Niger Delta)
Azotobacter occur in soil in very small quantity. The addition of P, alone, is not sufficient to bring about spontaneous proliferation.

———— 1959 Mission pédologique au Niger Central. Institut d'Enseignements et de Recherches Tropicales, Adiopodoume, Niger, Rapport 4533.
Sahelien vegetation on dunes in north of area; *Guiera senegalensis, Bauhinia reticulata, Boscia senegalensis, Zizyphus jujuba Commiphora africana.* Clay soils (sols bruns argileux) occupied by *Acacia arabica* in wetter areas and *Acacia seyal* in the dry zones. Dune soils are "sols beiges sableux."

Dabin, B. and A. Perraud
1960a Carte pédologique: Plaine de Koulou. Office de la Recherche Scientifique et Technique Outre-

Mer, Centre de Recherche Pédologique de Hann-Dakar, Senegal.

Scale: 1/10,000. In French. 10 soils classed by texture and depth and grouped in legend on genetic types.

—————

1960b Carte pédologique: Plaine de Say. Office de la Recherche Scientifique et Technique Outre-Mer, Centre de Recherche Pédologique de Hann-Dakar, Senegal.

Scale: 1/5,000. 2 sheets. 8 soils classed mainly by texture and grouped mainly by genetic types. Covers area north of Vers Niarne.

Dan, J., H. Koyumdjisky, and D. H. Yaalon
1962 Principles of a proposed classification for the soils of Israel. International Soil Conference, New Zealand. p. 410-421.

Soils are classed into orders, suborders, great soil groups, subgroups, families and types. The 4 soil orders include climatogenic soils, lithogenic soils, fluviogenic and eolian soils, and hydrogenic soils.

Dan. J. *et al.*
1962 The soils and soil associations map of Israel. Ministry of Agriculture and the University of Jerusalem.

Scale: 1/1,000,000. 17 soil associations.

Dapples, E. C.
1941 Surficial deposits of the desert of Syria, Trans-Jordan, Iraq, and western Iran. Journal of Sedimentary Petrology 11:124-141.

Soil under desert pavement disintegrates in water or when moved by wind, suggesting that present surface is stabilized by the pavement.

Darzniyek, Y. O.
1961 Causes of the suppression of *Azotobacter* in the non-irrigated soils of Central Asia. Soviet Soil Science 1961(7):738-743.

In summer, late spring and early autumm, when temperature conditions are favorable, *Azotobacter* cannot develop because of the low moisture content of the soil. In winter, when the moisture content is sufficient, they cannot develop because soil temperature is too low.

Davis, P. H.
1953 The vegetation of the deserts near Cairo. Journal of Ecology 41(1):157-173.

A preliminary account is given of the main plant communities of the Eastern and Western deserts of Egypt, chiefly in the neighborhood of Cairo. The communities are closely related to the particular geological formations and topography of the area. The presence or absence of blown sand is very important in determining the type of community that develops.

Deacon, E. L., C. H. B. Priestley, and W. C. Swinbank
1958 Evaporation and the water balance. *In* Climatology, reviews of research. Unesco, Paris. Arid Zone Research 10:9-34.

Discusses micrometeorological analysis.

Debenham, F.
1952 The Kalahari today. Geographical Journal 118:12-23.

Sand is distributed as in true desert in ridges and dunes, seaming land in rough pattern easily visible from air but not obvious on ground. Almost everywhere covered by fine yellowish calcareous sand 5-500' thick. Rain has caused cementing of lower layers to produce 2 kinds of rock: calcrete and silcrete, which grade into one another. Calcrete is useful; silcrete is useless. Calcrete is ragged and porous limestone found at or near surface in more arid Kalahari. Easy to sink wells through. Silcrete usually at lower level, hard, intractable. Farmers say wells should be placed on top of hills, where water can be found just below the calcrete. Rainfall increases from 5" in SW to 27" in NE, approximately.

Delver, P.
1962 Properties of saline soils in Iraq. Netherlands Journal of Agricultural Science 10(3):194-210.

Gypsum contents seem to be high enough to insure adequate replacement of Na by Ca during the leaching process, but some temporary decline in the permeability in early stages of leaching is to be expected.

Denny, C. S.
1965 Alluvial fans in the Death Valley region, California and Nevada. U. S. Geological Survey, Professional Paper 466. 62 p.

Desert pavements are smooth, gently sloping surfaces composed of closely packed angular fragments of rock and traversed by meandering gullies less than an inch high.

de Vries, D. A.
1958 The thermal behaviour of soils. *In* Climatology and microclimatology, Proceedings of the Canberra Symposium. Unesco, Paris. Arid Zone Research 11:109-113.

Annual heat flux into soil nearly same in arid and humid Australia, greater in Sahara, and greatest at 50° N latitude in Central Asia. Diurnal flux differences much greater in arid Australia.

de Vries, D. A. and J. W. Birch
1961 The modification of climate near the ground by irrigation for pastures on the Riverine Plain. Australian Journal of Agricultural Research 12:260-272.

In summer at an irrigation rate of approximately 0.3 cm/day the observed differences between the dry-land station and a station in the center of the irrigation area were 1-2°C for air temp at screen height (125cm), approx 10°C for soil temp, 5-10% for relative humidity at screen height, and 0.5-1.5 mm Hg vapor pressures at screen height.

Dewan, M. L. and J. Famouri
1964 The soils of Iran. Food and Agriculture Organization, Rome. 319 pp.

Map scale: 1/2,500,000. Has detailed profile descriptions and physical and chemical analyses.

Dhawan, C. L., B. B. L. Bhatnagar, and P. D. Ghai
1958 Role of green manuring in reclamation. National Academy of Science of India, Proceedings 27A: 168-176.

Jantar (*Sesbania aculeata*), guara (*Cyamopsis psoralioides*) and san (*Crotalaria juncea*) all contained sufficient Ca for replacing Na from alkali soils. The most effective was jantar, which has the highest Ca content and the most acid juice.

Dhawan, C. L. and R. N. Sharma
1950 Structure of the Punjab soils. Indian Journal of Agricultural Science 20:461-478.

Statistical analysis of data on samples collected from areas with different vegetation showed that the correlation of stability index with pH and dispersion coefficient, and that of probable permeability with pH and degree of alkalinization were negative and significant.

Díaz Vial, C. and E. Meléndez Aguirre
1958   Reconocimiento de suelos de la quebrada de Camarones. Agricultura Técnica (Santiago, Chile) 18(2):78-109.
(Soil reconnaissance of the Camarones quebrada)
Has detailed soil descriptions.

Diaz Vial, C. *et al.*
1958*a*   Estudio agrológico y de riego del Valle del Río Huasco. Agricultura Técnica (Santiago, Chile) 18(2):355-411.
(Agronomic and irrigation study of the Río Huasco Valley)

————
1958*b*   Reconocimiento de suelos del Valle del Río Lluta. Agricultura Técnica (Santiago, Chile) 18(2): 305-354.
(Soil reconnaissance of the Río Lluta Valley)

Dieleman, P. J. and N. A. de Ridder
1964   Studies of salt and water movement in the Bol Guini Polder, Chad Republic. Journal of Hydrology 1:311-343. Reprinted by International Institute for Land Reclamation and Improvement, Wageningen, as *its* Bulletin 5.

Dixey, F. and G. Aubert
1962   Arid zone research in the Sudan. Unesco, Arid Zone [Newsletter] 16:5-16.
A brief description of the soil resources of the Sudan.

Dobrovol'skii, V. V.
1961   Migration of small elements in gray-brown soils of trans-Caspian deserts (translated title). Rol' Mikroelementov v Sel'skom Khozyaistre, Mezhdynarognyi Soveshchanne po Mikroelementan, 2-go, Trudy, p. 5-8.
Soil samples were taken between the Caspian and Aral Seas. Figures for 20 trace elements occur in table form. Plant activity was the main factor in migration of these microelements.

Dokuchaev Soil Institute
1956   Soil map of U.S.S.R. Academy of Sciences, U.S.S.R., Moscow.
Scale: 1/4,000,000. In color. 2 sheets for southern part of U.S.S.R. including Central Asia and Caucasus in files of H. E. Dregne, New Mexico State University.

Dommergues, Y.
1962   Contribution à l'étude de la dynamique microbienne des sols en zone semi-aride et en zone tropicale seche. Annales Agronomiques 13(4):265-466.
A thesis submitted to University of Paris for the Doctor of Science degree. Comprehensive laboratory study. pF4.2 is not threshold value for stopping microbial activity. Some organisms tolerate pF more than 4.9 (hyperxerophilous).

Donald, G., B. I. Passey, and R. J. Swaby
1952   Bioassay of available trace metals from Australian soils. Australian Journal of Agricultural Research 3:305-325.
From a large number of samples, seven soil groups (red-loam, acid humic, podzol, rendzina and terra rossa, chernozem, red-brown earth, desert soil) showed more deficiencies than all the other groups. The commonest deficiency was that of Zn, followed by Cu and Mo, and occasionally Fe and Mn.

Donoso, L.
1959   Clay fraction of some soils of Chile. Société Française de Minéralogie et de Cristallographie, Bulletin 82:361-363.
Illite and montmorillonite are characteristic of clay formed in arid conditions; pseudosandy soils form under humid climate conditions.

al-Doory, Y., M. K. Tolba, and H. al-Ani
1959   On the fungal flora of Iraqi soils. II: Central Iraq. Mycologia 51:429-439.
Altogether order of dominance varied but could not be related to soil or climatic factors; for the 5 soils it was: *Hormodendrum, Aspergillus, Fusarium, Alternaria, Penicillium, Humicola, Mucor, Pythium.*

Downes, R. G.
1954   Cyclic salt as a dominant factor in the genesis of soils in south-eastern Australia. Australian Journal of Agricultural Research 5(3):448-464.
A theory is presented suggesting that during the Recent Arid Period the rainfall was approximately half that of the present day and enabled cyclic salt to be accumulated in areas in southeastern Australia, where it does not accumulate at present. The salinization and subsequent desalinization during the wetter conditions since the Arid Period have operated with varying degrees of intensity to produce solods, solodic, and solonized soils over larger areas. However irrespective of the degree of intensity, some of the pre-Arid soils because of their chemical or physical properties have been able to resist these processes and remain unaffected. Five pedogenetic zones have been defined according to the degrees of intensity with which the salinization and desalinization processes are thought to have operated, and it is found that soil distribution and morphology is correlated with these defined zones. The zone in which the effect has been most intense has an average annual rainfall at present of between 20 and 30 in., and the most widespread soils, those formerly called red and yellow podzolics, are solodic soils and solods. The theory provides a reasonable explanation for the anomalous distribution of soils within the "podzol" zones where those showing the greater degree of horizon differentiation (solods and solodic soils) occur in the driest parts. In addition the postulated processes for the formation of the soils provide a reason why Mo deficiency is so common on these soils in zone 3.

————
1956   Conservation problems on solodic soils in the State of Victoria (Australia). Journal of Soil and Water Conservation 11:228-232.
Tunnel erosion on solodic and saline soils.

Drosdoff, M., F. Queredo, and C. Zamora
1960   Suelos del Perú, serie 1. Servicio Cooperativo Interamericano de Producción de Altimentos (SCIPA), Lima.
Map scale: 1/4,000,000.

Drosdoff, M. and C. Zamora
1959   Soils of southern Peru. U. S. International Cooperation Administration, Report PS/A/Z, Lima Peru.
Map scale: 1/1,300,000.

Droste, J. B.
1959   Clay minerals in playas of the Mojave Desert, California. Science 130 (3367):100.
Montmorillonite, illite, chloride, and kaolinite in the playas of southern California are traceable directly to the source areas surrounding the basins.

Dudal, R.
1962 Soil map of the Near East. *In* C. C. Wallén and G. Perrin de Brichambaut, eds. A study of agroclimatology in semiarid and arid zones of the Near East. FAO/Unesco/WMO Interagency Project on Agroclimatology, Technical Report.
Scale: 1/5,000,000. Jordan, Iran, Iraq, Syria, Israel, Lebanon, and eastern Turkey.

Durand, J. H.
1953a Carte schematique des sols des environs de Beni Ounif. *In* Desert research, proceedings, International Symposium held in Jerusalem, May 7-14, 1952, sponsored by the Research Council of Israel and Unesco. Research Council of Israel, Special Publication 2:440.
(Schematic soil map of the environs of Beni Ounif)
Scale: 1/200,000.

1953b La vent et sa consequence, l'erosion eolienne, facteur de formation des sols au Sahara. *In* Desert research, proceedings, International Symposium held in Jerusalem, May 7-14, 1952, sponsored by the Research Council of Israel and Unesco. Research Council of Israel, Special Publication 2:434-437.
(Wind and its effects; wind erosion, a soil formation factor in the Sahara)
Residual regs are autochthonous regs; transported regs are allochthonous regs. Wind blows out fine material, leaving stones and gravel.

1954 Notice explicative général de la carte des sols d'Algérie au 1/200,000 et au 1/500,000. Service de la Colonisation et de l'Hydraulique, Alger, Section de Pédologie.
(General explanatory report on the soil map of Algeria)
Sheets for Alger, Biskra, Constantine, Mascara, Oran, Orléansville, Tébessa at 1/500,000; sheet for Nemours, Mostaganem, and Bône at 1/200,000.

1959 Les sols rouges et les croûtes en Algérie. Direction de l'Hydraulique et de l'Equipement Rural, Clairbois-Birmandreis, Etude Général 7. 188 p.
(The red soils and crusts in Algeria)
Profile descriptions and chemical and physical analysis are given of red soils (terra rossa, red rendzina, red loam, reddish soils) and of various crusts (powdery limestone indurated calcareous horizons and crusts, concretionary nodules); their age, mode of formation, and distribution in Algeria and Mediterranean countries (shown on maps) are described, and utility in agriculture and for building purposes is briefly discussed. 166 references.

Durrell, L. W. and L. M. Shields
1960 Fungi isolated in culture from soils of the Nevada Test Site. Mycologia 52:636-641.
In culture on rose-bengal agar containing streptomycin, 41 fungal taxa were isolated from surface and 3-6 inch samples of arid soils. Four taxa developed in 40 to less than 80% of the samples accultured in different series: *Stemphylium ilicis, Fusarium* sp., *Phoma* sp. and *Penicillium exalicum.*

Dutil, P.
1962 Carte des matériaux superficiels du Sahara. Commission for Technical Cooperation in Africa, Lagos, Nigeria.
(Map of surface materials of the Sahara)
Scale: 1/2,000,000. Manuscript map.

Dutil, P., C. Martinez, and P. Quézel
1959 Etude pédologique et palynologique d'un profil de formations Quaternaires de la désert de M'Rara. Société d'Histoire Naturelle de l'Afrique du Nord, Bulletin 50(5/6):196-203.
(A pedologic and palynologic study of a cross section of Quaternary formations of the M'Rara desert)
A study of this northern Saharan basin to discover its suitability for agriculture through analysis of sediments and fossil pollens reveals a history of humid climate followed by aridity at 2,000 and 5,000 years B. C., similar to other such studies of the Central Sahara.

Duverger, E.
1960 Etude des sols à pâturages du Hodh (Mauritanie). Office de la Recherche Scientifique et Technique Outre-Mer, Centre de Pédologie de Hann-Dakar.
(Study of pasture soils of Hodh)
Soils:
1. Sols steppiques (these are the climatic soils)
   A. Sols brun-rouge cover practically all the dunes zones and the well-drained sandy accumulation.
   B. Sols bruns limited to interdune depressions, at border of cuvettes.
2. Sols hydromorphes.
Present land utilization is pasturage for nomads.

Dzhalilov, K. M.
1957 The Golodnaya Steppe and prospects for its reclamation (translated title). Izdatel'stvo Akademii Nauk Uzbekskoi S. S. R. 32 p. (Issued in translation by Israel Program for Scientific Translations. Also cited as OTS 60-21133)
Discusses plans for developing irrigation, principally for cotton, on Golodnaya Steppe; natural and climatic conditions on the steppe; history of reclamation, experience of kolkhozes and sovkhozes; prospects for developing the steppe; small-scale map (1 inch equals 12 miles, approx.) of the Golodnaya Steppe and proposed development.

Eardley, A. J.
1962 Gypsum dunes and evaporite history of the Great Salt Lake Desert. Utah Geology and Minerology Survey, Special Studies 2.
Evaporation at the surface of the plastic clays resulted in a capillary draw-up of moisture, bringing with it sulfate ions. Probably associated with the capillary advance of the clay water were gypsum-producing bacteria, and myriads of sand-size gypsum crystals grew and are still growing in the top 3/4 inch or so of the clays. By further drying of the clay, these crystals are released and drift into dunes. It has previously been supposed that the gypsum was an early precipitate of a lake that finally dried up where the salt crust is now.

Eaton, F. M.
1935 Boron in soils and irrigation waters and its effects on plants with particular reference to the San Joaquin Valley of California. U. S. Department of Agriculture, Technical Bulletin 448:1-131.
A survey of boron content of waters used for irrigation in the western U. S. Boron adsorption and movement in soils is discussed. A table of crop tolerance for boron is presented. Boron deficiency symptoms are given as are boron toxicity symptoms. There is a marked tendency toward more boron in more saline waters.

Eaton, F. M.
1950   Significance of carbonates in irrigation waters. Soil Science 69:123-134.
Black alkali soils occur frequently in the Nile Valley of Egypt. Analyses show that Nile water consistently contains residual sodium carbonate (more HCO_3 plus CO_3 than Ca plus Mg.) No black alkali has been found in Iraq soils irrigated with water from the Tigris or Euphrates, which do not contain residual sodium carbonate. Percentage sodium found in irrigation water and percentage sodium possible, should be calculated, as well as residual sodium carbonate.

———
1954   Formulas for estimating leaching and gypsum requirements of irrigation waters. Texas Agricultural Experiment Station, Miscellaneous Publication 11.
Formulas are presented and discussed for characterizing and interpreting analyses of irrigation waters in the following terms: 1) the percentage of applied irrigation water which should pass through the root zone as drainage to insure reasonable yields (70 to 80 percent of yields on nonsaline land) of rotation crops of intermediate salt tolerance in a semiarid climate. 2) the amount of calcium which should be added to irrigation waters to insure that the soil water leaving the root zone will not contain more than about 70 percent of sodium.

Eaton, F. M. and C. R. Horton
1940   Effect of exchange sodium on the moisture equivalent and wilting coefficient of soils. Journal of Agricultural Research 61:401-425.
Moisture equivalents of soils partially saturated with Na were substantially higher than those of the same soils treated with Ca, provided most of the soluble electrolytes were removed. Adsorbed Na caused soil moisture to be less available to plants. The Ca and Na averages of 9 soils were: at the moisture equivalent, 17.5 and 29.5; at the wilting coefficient, 8.4 and 11.3; at the ultimate wilting point, 7.8 and 9.2 respectively. A close parallelism was found for 10 soils between the effect of Na on the moisture equivalent and the percentage of clay, the exchange capacity, and the quantity of adsorbed Na. K, Ca, and Mg had similar effects on the moisture equivalent.

Eckardt, F. E.
1960   Eco-physiological measuring techniques applied to research on water relations of plants in arid and semi-arid regions. *In* Plant-water relationships in arid and semi-arid conditions. Reviews of research. Unesco, Paris, Arid Zone Research 15:139-171.
Transpiration measurements, water balance, and laboratory and field devices.

Elwan, S. H. and S. A. Z. Mahmoud
1950   Note on the bacterial flora of the Egyptian desert in summer. Archiv für Mikrobiologie 36:360-364.
Total bacterial counts were much higher in the rhizosphere than in the adjacent soil, and *Azotobacter* and *Clostridium* species were isolated from the rhizosphere but not from the soil.

Eriksson, E.
1958   The chemical climate and saline soils in the arid zone. *In* Climatology, reviews of research. Unesco, Paris. Arid Zone Research 10:147-188.

Evans, J. R.
1962   Falling and climbing sand dunes in the Cronese ("Cat") Mountain area, San Bernardino County, California. Journal of Geology 70(1):107-113.
6 sand dunes, 3 climbing and 3 falling, were studied in detail. The climbing dunes, composed mostly of medium-grained sand, have sorting coefficients that range from 1.5 to 1.9, whereas the falling dunes, composed mostly of fine-grained sand, have sorting coefficients of 1.2 or 1.3.

Evans, N. A.
1960   Reclamation and drainage of saline-sodic soils in the Upper Colorado River Basin. Congress on Irrigation and Drainage, 4th, Madrid, Transactions 5:13. 113-130.
Soils in the Upper Colorado River Basin can be reclaimed by simple leaching, provided good drainage exists. Six feet of water will reclaim to a four-foot depth. Gypsum at a rate of four tons per acre is of no benefit to the reclamation process.

FAO/Unesco Project, Soil Map of the World
1965   Catalogue of maps. 3rd ed. FAO, Rome. 165 p.

Fadda, N. R.
1960   The use of electrical resistance units for the study of soil moisture changes and irrigation requirements in the Sudan Gezira. Empire Cotton Growing Review 37:118-130.
The plain nylon units were most affected by salt content; the jacketed units gave results comparable with those from Bouyoucos blocks.

Farag, M. S. and K. A. Guirgis
1960   A study of some Egyptian clay minerals. Journal of Chemistry of the U. A. R. 3:23-34.
Differential thermal analysis showed the presence of fireclay, a mixture of kaolinite and dickite, and kaolinite, respectively, in 2 Aswan and 1 Sinai samples.

Ferguson, H. S.
1951   Sugar cane trials on the flood plains of the Bahr el Jebel in the Anglo-Egyptian Sudan. Sudan Ministry of Agriculture, Bulletin 6. p. 51.
Data for the soils of the area include pH, and contents of clay, N, exchangeable Ca, and exchangeable Mg. Results indicated their suitability for sugar cane.

Fernández de Lara, G. A.
1953   Hydrology and utilization of hydraulic resources in the arid and semi-arid areas of Latin America. *In* Reviews of Research on Arid Zone Hydrology. Unesco, Paris. Arid Zone Programme 1:153-178.
Extent of the arid and semi-arid zones, groundwater resources, fluctuations in the water-table, occurrence of saline waters and underground waters are discussed for Mexico and each of the countries of South America. 170 references.

Ferris, H. J.
1953   Report to the Government of Saudi Arabia on reconnaissance soil and land classification of the south Asir Tihama. FAO, Rome, EPTA Report 69. 36 p.
Land type map at 1/400,000. Area is along the Red Sea, northwest of Yemen. Alluvial plain (sandy, smooth) between mountains and tidal flats.

Finielz, H.
1954   Rapport au Gouvernement de l'Arabie Saoudité sur l'étude des sols, leur classification et l'utilisa-

tion des terrains en fonction de l'irrigation dans
de périmètre de l'Oued Jizan. FAO (Rome),
EPTA Report.
(Report to the Government of Saudi Arabia on
the soils, their classification and the utilization
of land for irrigation in Wadi Jizan)
Soil map: 1/50,000.

Finkel, H. J.
1959   The barchans of southern Peru. Journal of Geology
67:614-647.
These crescentic sand dunes occur extensively along the
desert coast; quantitative measurements of seventy-five
of them showed a rather longer west horn on most.
There was an increase in proportion of fine materials in
samples taken further downwind (northwards) from the
Pampa de Clemesi: bulk specific gravity varied with
dune height and also decreased with distance from
Clemesi; the proportion of volcanic fibrous glass increased
downwind. An expression is derived for calculating the
yearly horizontal displacement of the dunes; displacement
of dunes measuring 1, 2, 3, 4, 5, 6, and 7 m, respectively,
in height averaged 32.3, 22.0, 16.8, 14.5, 12.2, 11.5, and
9.2 m.

Fireman, M. and H. E. Hayward
1952   Indicator significance of some shrubs in the
Escalante Desert, Utah. Botanical Gazette 14(1):
143-155.
There is a general relation between plant species and
pH, ESP, and soluble salt. Desert shrubs occurring
in the Escalante Desert, Utah, and generally recognized
as indicators of the agricultural possibilities of new
lands, were studied.

Fletcher, J. E. and P. H. Carroll
1948   Some properties of soils associated with piping
in southern Arizona. Soil Science Society of
America, Proceedings 13:545-547.
3 types of "piping" erosion were studied. The first is
the result of lateral flow along a subsoil to an open
bank, the second is the result of surface water running into
cracks, and third is the dispersed surface soil being
washed into the pores of the coarse, poorly graded
upper subsoil, causing sinking and caving. The soil
properties which correlated with this phenomenon are
pH, soluble salts, and exchangeable Na.

Fletcher, J. E. *et al.*
1954   Piping. American Geophysical Union, Transactions 35:258-263.
5 conditions required for piping: water, high infiltration
rate, erodible layer, water under pressure in soil, and
outlet for "pipes."

Flores Cosio, D.
1954   Salinidad y alcalinidad en los suelos de la costa.
Estación de la Experimental Agrícola de la Molina,
Lima, Informe 91. 70 p.
(Salinity and alkalinity of coastal soils)
In soils of the Peruvian coast, commonly regarded as
alkaline, Na_2CO_3 is not the predominant salt; most
commonly, a mixture of NaCl, $CaSO_4$, and $MgSO_4$
occurs as dominant feature.

Fly, C. L.
1950-   Reports and soil maps of Kandahar and other
1956   parts of Afghanistan. Land Development Division,
Morrison-Knudsen Afghanistan, Inc., Boise, Idaho.

Food and Agriculture Organization, Agricultural
Engineering Branch
1960   Soil erosion by wind and measures for its control.
Institution of Agricultural Engineers, London,
Journal and Proceedings 16(1):2-17.
Erosion of soil by wind is due to depletion or destruction
of natural vegetation cover. Whenever possible, this
cover should be restored. A thorough understanding of
the processes of soil denudation, erosion, and stabilization
is a prerequisite for developing effective methods of
control.

Fossberg, P. E. and J. S. Gregg
1963   Soil stabilization in road construction in South
Africa. Civil Engineer in South Africa 8:217-227.
Outline of test procedures, design criteria, road construc-
tion methods, and soil stabilization research in South
Africa.

Freeman, B. N. and R. R. Humphrey
1956   The effects of nitrates and phosphates upon forage
production of a southern Arizona desert grassland
range. Journal of Range Management 9(4):176-
180.
Nitrogen increased yields; nitrogen and phosphorus
affected chemical composition of plants.

Fritschen, L. J. and C. H. M. van Bavel
1962   Energy balance components of evaporating surfaces in arid lands. Journal of Geophysical
Research 67:5179-5185.
Indicated that the daily totals of sensible heat flux to
the air were generally negative, that is, away from the
surface. The rate of evaporation was larger from a wet
soil surface than from a free water surface. On days of
similar solar radiation, the evaporative flux tended to be
correlated with wind speed.

Fuller, W. H.
1963   Reactions of nitrogenous fertilizers in calcareous
soils. Journal of Agricultural and Food Chemistry
11:188-193.
Loss of surface-applied NH_4 increases as the pH increases
above neutral. Nitrates form readily in calcareous soils
up to pH of 9.0 if NH_4 concentration is favorable.
Nitrites accumulate at almost any pH value above neutral
depending on the concentration of NH_4. There are
gaseous losses of NO_3 and NO_2 as oxides of N, or as
N gas formed by chemical reaction or bacterial nitrification. 38 references.

Fuller, W. H., R. E. Cameron, and N. Raica, Jr.
1960   Fixation of nitrogen in desert soils by algae.
International Congress of Soil Science, 7th,
Madison, Transactions 2:617-624.
Algal and lichen crusts were found to be 4-5 times as
high in N as the soils below. Both algal crusts and algae
in pure and mixed cultures were found to fix N.

Fuller, W. H. and W. T. McGeorge
1950   Phosphates in calcareous Arizona soils. I:
Solubilities of native phosphates and fixation of
added phosphates. Soil Science 70(6):441-460.
Only a small portion of the P added to some calcareous
soils was securely fixed against extraction with water.
Fixation by microorganisms depends upon the amount
of available C present in the soil and the activity of the
microorganisms under certain farming circumstances.
In soils low in "available" P, this form of fixation seriously limits crop production.

el-Gabaly, M. M.
1954 Soil map of northeast Sinai. Institut du Désert d'Egypte, Bulletin 4(1):124-52.
Scale: 1/500,000. Soils classed by texture and kind of transportation of parent material (little residual material.)

1962 The presence of attapulgite in some soils of the western desert of Egypt. Soil Science 93:387-390.
The mineral composition of two gray sandy soils northwest of Cairo indicated the dominance of attapulgite. The soils were supposedly formed from calcareous argillaceous material in a saline lagoon.

el-Gabaly, M. M. and M. Khadr
1962 Clay mineral studies of some Egyptian desert and Nile alluvial soils. Journal of Soil Science 13:333-342.
In the soils of Khârga and Ginâh the clay minerals are dominantly kaolinite; the soils of Khârga are low in lime content and those of Ginâh are rich in lime. In the soils of Bûlâq and Bârîs montmorillonite is dominant. The soils of the Nile alluvium have less kaolinite.

Ganssen, R.
1960 Böden und landschaft in Südwestafrika. International Congress of Soil Science, 7th, Madison, Transactions 4:49-55.
(Soil and landscape in South West Africa)
Desert soils in west and south, semidesert soils in south and middle, and dry forest soils in north. Depressions have clay soils high in organic matter in the north and high in salts in the south, with some takyr-like soils in the south. Soil catenary sequence similar in highland-valley areas throughout South West Africa. Much wind and water erosion. Overgrazing has denuded the landscape.

Ganssen, R. and W. Moll
1961 Beiträge zur kenntnis der böden warm-arider gebiete, dargestellt am beispiel Südwestafrika. Zeitschrift für Pflanzenernährung, Dungung, Bodenkunde 94(1):9-25.
(Contributions to the knowledge of soils in warm arid regions, represented by examples in South West Africa)
Trends of soil formation in South West Africa are similar to those in other arid regions, producing well defined soil complexes according to topography, regular occurrence of catenas in a downslope direction, and accumulation of soluble salts and $CaCO_3$ in the top soil. The soils resemble those in the arid regions of Australia and greatly differ from Central-European soils especially in respect of their saturation with metallic cations and high contents of soluble salts; they comprise desert soils, dry-forest soils, solonchaks, takyr-like soils and calcareous soils. Characteristics of the semi-arid and arid soils investigated are compared in tabular form with soils of Central Europe formed from the same parent rocks and under similar conditions of topography and water supply. Data on pH, humus level, N and Ca content, exchange capacity, and chemical composition of HCl and aqueous extracts of the different soils are reported, and the problems of secondary salinization and black-alkali formation by irrigation are discussed.

Gardner, R.
1945 Some soil properties related to the sodium salt problem in irrigated soils. U. S. Department of Agriculture, Technical Bulletin 902.
The poor physical condition of many saline soils is modified by so many other factors that it is not always directly correlated with either the percentage of replaceable sodium or the concentration of salts found in the soil. Puddling and salt concentration of applied water are some of the contributing factors.

Gardner, W. R.
1960 Soil water relations in arid and semi-arid conditions. *In* Plant-water relationships in arid and semi-arid conditions, Reviews of research. Unesco, Paris. Arid Zone Research 15:37-62.
A review of soil moisture research, without restriction to arid areas.

Gardner, W. R. and R. H. Brooks
1957 A descriptive theory of leaching. Soil Science 83:295-304.
Equations are derived to describe the leaching of soluble salts from soils. The flow process itself, rather than diffusion, is assumed to be responsible both for the diffuse boundary between the soil solution and the leaching water and for the subsequent removal of the bypassed salt. Agreement between theory and experiment was found to be satisfactory.

Gates, D. H., L. A. Stoddart, and C. W. Cook
1956 Soil as a factor influencing plant distribution on salt-deserts of Utah. Ecological Monographs 26(2):155-175.
Significant differences between vegetation types were found for only 5 factors, namely: total soluble salt, saturation extract conductivity, exchangeable sodium, 1/3 atmosphere percentage, and soluble sodium.

Gethin-Jones, H. G. and R. M. Scott
1958 Soil map of Kenya. *In* Atlas of Kenya, Survey of Kenya, Nairobi.
Scale: 1/3,000,000. 36 soils and 2 miscellaneous land types.

Giess, W.
1962 Some notes on the vegetation of Namib desert with a list of plants collected in the area visited by the Cape-Transvaal Museum expedition during May 1959. Cimbebasia 2:1-35.
The area under study has been divided into 4 ecological regions: the red sand dunes, the river beds, the Namib flats, and the mountains, with the vegetation of each region discussed individually. A list of plants collected in the area is given. Included in the list is a gymnosperm family (Welwitschiaceae), 4 monocot families (Typhaceae, Gramineae, Cyperaceae, and Liliaceae), and 30 dicot families with a total of 126 species. Each species is discussed briefly with respect to habit and habitat.

Gile, L. H.
1961 A classification of Ca horizons in soils of a desert region, Dona Ana County, New Mexico. Soil Science Society of America, Proceedings 25(1):52-61.
Field study in Dona Ana County, New Mexico, shows that Ca horizons occur in soils on a variety of sediments and geomorphic surfaces.

Gile, L. H., F. F. Peterson, and R. B. Grossman
1966 Morphological and genetic sequences of carbonate accumulation in desert soils. Soil Science 101:347-360.
Carbonate horizons formed in gravelly sediments display different morphological sequence than in nongravelly sediments. Sequence is (1) carbonate coating on pebble, (2) filling interstices, (3) cementing and forming laminar layer.

Glukhov, I. G.
1956   Seepage of water from canals in loess formations and subsidence phenomena in irrigated areas (translated title). Gidrotekhnika i Melioratsiya 8(10):9-18. (Issued in translation by Israel Program for Scientific Translations, Jerusalem. Also cited as OTS 60-21152)
Subsidence and piping of irrigated soils is a threat in Central Asian loess soils. Solution is a thoroughly wet soil before beginning cropping, in order to compact the soil.

Gordonov, L. S.
1953   Egipet, ocherk ekonomicheskoy geografii. Gosudarstvennoe Izdatelstvo Geograficheskoy Literaturi, Moskva.
Shown in Nuttonson, M. Y., 1961, The Physical environment and agriculture of Libya and Egypt with special references to their regions containing areas climatically and latitudinally analogous to Israel. p. 272. American Institute of Crop Ecology, Washington, D. C. Scale: 1/7,000,000. Text gives brief soil descriptions.

Greaves, J. E. and L. W. Jones
1941   The survival of microorganisms in alkali soils. Soil Science 52:359-364.
Alkali soils with 2% salt were kept 20 years under air-dry conditions. *Azotobacter chroococcum* was found in some soils. Ammonifying organisms survived, but nitrite and nitrate producing bacteria did not. Soils were from semiarid regions.

Greene, H.
1948   Using salty lands. FAO Agricultural Studies 3. 49 p.
An account of soil reclamation of salty lands in Egypt, Sudan Gezira, north China, San Joaquin Valley, north India, U. S. S. R., and Hungary, and of marine reclamation in New Zealand, Germany, Netherlands, and Belgium.

Greenwood, J. E. G. W.
1955   The development of vegetation patterns in Somaliland Protectorate. Geographical Journal 123:465-473.
The arcuate form of vegetation bands is due to deposition of organic litter, and sandy or silty materials around local obstacles.

Guild, W. R.
1950   Note on heat transfer at the soil surface. Journal of Meteorology 7:140-144.
Heat balance and eddy diffusion are determined for nocturnal cooling in desert regions of Arizona. Convection accounts for as much as half of the transfer.

Gunn, R. H.
1955   The use of aerial photography in soil survey and mapping in the Sudan. Soils and Fertilizers 18:104-106.
Aerial photography was used in the White and Blue Nile areas for selecting and mapping areas suitable for pumped and gravity irrigation. The method used is described. Aerial photography was combined with soil sampling. Relationships between soils and vegetation are essential for interpreting the photographs.

Gutiérrez Ríos, E. and F. González García
1950   Genesis of the bentonite from Tidinit (Spanish Morocco). International Congress of Soil Science, 4th, Amsterdam, Transactions 1:29-96.
Samples showing increasing transformation into bentonite from the original reddish andesite with beach inclusions of biotite were subjected to chemical and thermal analysis.

Hamid, H.
1959   Alterations in the clay fraction of Egyptian soils. Zeitschrift für Pflanzenernährung, Düngung und Bodenkunde 84:204-211.
Data of x-ray and differential thermal analyses and electron-microscope observations indicate that submerged conditions and severe leaching with CO_2-saturated water in the Nile delta caused illitic clay to transform into boehmite and a montmorillonite-type clay of expanding lattice.

Hamdi, H. and Y. Barrada
1960   Transformation of the clay fraction of the alluvial soils of Egypt. Annals of Agricultural Science (Cairo) 5(2):135-139.
Weathering sequence in the transformation of the alluvial clay of Egypt is suggested as: eruptive rocks of the Ethiopian plateau, to illite, then to montmorillonite through the agency of CO_2 or $MgCl_2$.

Hamdi, H. and W. Epprecht
1955   Der einfluss der chemischen verwitterung auf die alluvialentone von Ägypten. Zeitschrift für Pflanzenernährung, Düngung und Bodenkunde 70:1-9.
(The effect of chemical weathering on the alluvial clays of Egypt)
The illite of the fresh mud tends to be converted by irrigation water into montmorillonite, which increases with depth. This conversion occured when fresh mud was treated in the laboratory with CO_2-containing water. With increasing weathering, chlorite or vermiculite is formed and possibly boehmite.

Hamdi, H. and M. Mega
1950   Chemical and mineralogical investigation on Egyptian soils. Schweizerische Mineralogische und Petrographische Mitteilungen 29:537-540.
Most of the minerals are formed from the suspended matter of the Nile. The clay particles consist mainly of AlFe silicates. X-ray analysis shows that all the soils are formed mainly of amorphous Al silicates of the allophane clay group besides fine particles of the mica group (muscovite). CA44(9880).

Harmsen, G. W. and D. A. van Schreven
1955   Mineralization of organic nitrogen in soils. Advances in Agronomy 7:299-398.
A review. Several hundred references.

Hatcher, J. T. and C. A. Bower
1958   Equilibria and dynamics of boron adsorption by soils. Soil Science 85(6):319-323.
It has been found that, over limited concentration ranges, the equilibrium between dissolved and adsorbed boron in soils can be expressed approximately by Langmuir's adsorption equation. Three soils and two boron concentrations were studied and satisfactory agreement was obtained between experimental results and calculations using the Thomas, Hiester, and Vermeulen equation.

Hayward, H. E. and C. H. Wadleigh
1949   Plant growth on saline and alkali soils. Advances in Agronomy 1:1-38.
A review.

Hillel, D. and N. Tadmor
1962   Water regime and vegetation in the central Negev highlands of Israel. Ecology 43(1):33-41.
Moisture conditions governing growth of natural vegetation in the Negev desert (average rainfall 100 mm) were investigated. Data were collected on rainfall and runoff; soil moisture storage, availability and use; and plant phenology in relation to the moisture region.

Hingston, F. J.
1958   The major ions in Western Australia rainwaters. C.S.I.R.O. Division of Soils, Adelaide, Divisional Report 1/58.
Perth rainwater, 4 miles from coast, had 330 microequivalents of Cl per liter; 15 miles inland, Cl was 250; 25 miles, 270; 65 miles, 130; and 95 miles, 120.

Holland, A. A. and C. W. E. Moore
1962   The vegetation and soils of the Bollon District in South-Western Queensland. C.S.I.R.O. Division of Plant Industry, Technical Paper 17.
8 soil associations. Map scale: 1/360,000.

Holm, D. A.
1953   Dome-shaped dunes of Central Hejd, Saudi Arabia. International Geological Congress, 19th, Algiers, 1952. Comptes Rendus 7:102-112.
Scale: 1/2,350,000.

———

1960   Desert geomorphology in the Arabian Peninsula. Science 132(3437):1369-1379.
About 30% of the 1,060,000 sq. mi. is covered by sand. The sand occupies areas of low relief. The area has a complex wind regime; thus, the dunes show a great diversity of shape and size. Gravel plains are very extensive; these were, in fact, deposited in wetter Pleistocene times. Sabakhas (sebkhas, saline flats) are often disguised by a thin cover of sand or silt; they are a hazard for vehicles.

Holman, W. W. *et al.*
1957   Practical application of engineering soils maps. Engineering Soil Survey of New Jersey, Report 22. Rutgers University, New Brunswick, Engineering Research Bulletin 36.
Describes the New Jersey survey system.

Holmes, J. W.
1958   Aspects of soil moisture measurement with reference to arid soils. *In* Climatology and microclimatology, Proceedings of the Canberra Symposium. Unesco, Paris. Arid Zone Research 11:295-300.
Neutron scattering and thermal conductivity give results within 1% of actual. Gypsum blocks only means for measuring tension in dry soils, but has several faults.

Hoore, J. L. d'
1964   Soil map of Africa. Commission for Technical Cooperation in Africa, Lagos, Nigeria. Publication 93.
Scale: 1/5,000,000. Describes geology, landforms, climate, vegetation, and soils. Soils grouped by parent material, development, and moisture relations, using French and Belgian systems.

Hou, H. Y., C. T. Chen, and H. P. Wang
1957   The vegetation of China with special reference to the main soil types (translated title). Acta Pedologica Sinica 5(1):19-49.
Scale: 1/10,000,000. 12 units are combination of vegetation type and associated soils. Text has general descriptions of soils and vegetation characteristic of each map unit. English summary.

Hubble, G. D. and G. G. Beckman
1956   Soil map of Millungera Estate, Dalgonally Estate, and Kamileroi. C.S.I.R.O. Division of Soils, Divisional Report 6/56.
Scale: 1/250,000. Text has soil description and lab analyses.

Hume, W. F.
1921   The soil and water supply of the Maryut District west of Alexandria. Ministry of Finance, Survey of Egpyt.
Scale: 1/50,000. Shows land types.

Hunt, C. B.
1960   The Death Valley salt pan, study of evaporites. U. S. Geological Survey, Professional Paper 400-B:456-458.
Salts in the Death Valley salt pan are in orderly zones and layers reflecting their different solubilities. Chlorides are in center and on top, sulfates around or below chlorides, carbonates around or below sulfates.

———

1961   Stratigraphy of desert varnish. U. S. Geological Survey, Professional Paper 424-B:194-195.
The origin of this dark natural strain of Fe and Mn oxides is uncertain. It was deposited in arid regions of the world, 2,000 or more years ago, during plutonic periods.

Hunting Aerosurveys, Ltd.
1956a Makhmour area, Iraq: Irrigation, soil survey, land classification and agricultural reports. Report to the Development Board, Government of Iraq.
Scale: 1/50,000.

———

1956b Soil survey and land classification, Nahrwan, Adhaim, and Ishaqi areas. Report to the Development Board, Government of Iraq.
Scale: 1/50,000 (Nahrwan and Adhaim). 1/250,000 (Ishaqi).

Hunting Survey Corporation, Ltd.
1958   Landforms, soils and land use of the Indus Plains, West Pakistan. A Colombo Plan Cooperative Project.
Map scale: 1/40,000. Report available from the Director of Agriculture, Government of West Pakistan, Lahore, Pakistan. Maps available from the Surveyor General of Pakistan, P. O. Box 3906, Karachi, West Pakistan.

Hunting Technical Services, Ltd.
1963   Land and water use survey in Kordofan Province of the Republic of the Sudan, Interim Ed. United Nations Special Fund and Food and Agriculture Organization.
Soil map scale: 1/250,000. A survey of geology, geomorphology and soils, vegetation, and present land use. Two soil zones: sand dunes in north, red developed soils in south.

Hutton, J. T.
1958   The chemistry of rainwater with particular reference to conditions in southeastern Australia. *In* Climatology and microclimatology, Proceedings of the Canberra Symposium. Unesco, Paris. Arid Zone Research 11:285-294.
Na/Ca of rainwater varies from 7 at coast to 0.5 200 miles inland, whereas Na/Ca of sea water is 22. Some other source of salt must be contributing.

Indian Agricultural Research Institute
1961   Study on wastelands, including saline, alkali, and waterlogged lands and their reclamation measures. Indian Planning Commission, New Delhi, Committee on Natural Resources.
Map scale: 1/9,500,000. 28 soils. Text has descriptions of soils ill-suited to agriculture.

Indian Council of Agricultural Research
1953   India soil survey scheme, Final report. New Delhi.
Scale: 1/13,500,000. Map, based on soil surveys and field investigation, is fairly reliable.

International Engineering Company
1955   Chakhansur reconnaissance; drainage survey. Report on reclamation on the Chakhansur prepared for the Land Development Division of Morrison-Knudsen (Afghanistan), Inc., Boise, Idaho.
Scale: 1/225,000. Nine soils delineated on map. Text has general soil descriptions. In Lower Helmand River Valley on aerial photo background.

Ionesco, T.
1958   Essai d'estimation de la valeur indicatrice des espèces psammophiles en pays semi-aride (Doukkala, Maroc). Service de la Carte Phytogéographique, Bulletin, sér. B, 3(1):7-68. (Study on the estimation of the index value of psammophilic species in a semi-arid country)
It was demonstrated that the index value of psammophilic species is not the same, according to the soil in which they are found, and that the index value is related to all characteristics of the soil. Among these water is the most important factor.

Ivanova, E. N. and N. N. Rozov
1960   Classification of soils and the soil map of the U.S.S.R. International Congress of Soil Science, 7th, Madison, Transactions 4:77-87.
Scale: 1/10,000,000.

Ives, R. L.
1959   Shell dunes of the Sonoran shore. American Journal of Science 257(6):449-457.
To the north the dunes are composed largely of rock fragments and are in part reworked Colorado River sediments; to the south they are composed largely of shell fragments, derived from recently elevated bottom marls, geologically, and probably archeologically, recent.

Iyer, J. G. and Y. Satyanarayan
1959   Distribution of trace elements in some soils profiles of the arid and semi-arid regions of India. Journal of Biological Sciences 2(2):110-115.
The distribution of total Co, Cu, B, Mo, Mn, and Zn in 3 profiles from Rajasthan, Gujarat, and the Deccan, respresenting the arid and semi-arid regions of India, was studied. While in the Rajasthan profile there is uniform distribution of the trace elements, in the profiles from Gujarat and the Deccan surface accumulation of most of the trace elements has been observed.

Jackson, E. A
1957   Soil features in arid regions with particular reference to Australia. Australian Institute of Agricultural Science, Journal 25:196-208.

1958   A study of the soils and some aspects of the hydrology at Yudnapinna station, South Australia.

C. S. I. R. O., Division of Soils, Soils and Land Use, Melbourne, Survey Series 24.
Scale: 1/200,000. 12 soils associations. Text has soil descriptions and lab analyses and detailed maps of small areas.

1962   Soil studies in Central Australia: Alice Springs-Hermannsburg-Rodinga areas. C. S. I. R. O., Division of Soils, Soil Publication 19:5-18.
Soil map at scale of 1/650,000 by E. A. Jackson and M. J. Wright. Soil studies in Central Australia: Alice Springs. This study embraces 18,000 square miles in the Alice Springs district of Central Australia. The area extends north and south of the Tropic of Capricorn and includes country on either side of the Macdonnell Ranges, together with the northwestern margin of the Simpson Desert. The largest plain area is the Burt plain and it is suggested that the detritus of this area was deposited by a system of prior streams. The Macdonnell Ranges, which dominate the landscape, provide the source materials for many of the soils. Apart from their northwestern slopes the entire region is drained by rivers of the Lake Eyre basin. The climate is arid; mean rainfall varies from about 7-11 inches in different parts of the area, and increases from south to north. Temperatures are moderate to high for most of the year. The 34 soil families recognized are described in general terms and detailed descriptions of typical profiles are given in Appendix I. Data are presented on selection of soils to indicate their water retention characteristics, density, infiltration rates, and probable depth of water penetration.

Jackson, E. A. and M. J. Wright
1960   Some reconnaissance soil inspections in arid Australia. C.S.I.R.O., Division of Soils, Divisional Report 5-60.

Jackson, M. L.
1959   Frequency distribution of clay minerals in major great soil groups as related to the factors of soil formation. *In* A. Swindford, ed., Clays and clay minerals. National Conference on Clays and Clay Minerals, 6th, Berkeley, California, 1957, Proceedings p. 133-143.
Inherited minerals such as illite, quartz, feldspars, ferromagnesium minerals, carbonates and gypsum are most abundant in clays of little-weathered parent materials. Secondary layer silicate minerals such as vermiculite, secondary chlorite, montmorillonite, kaolinite and halloysite are most abundant in clays of moderately weathered parent materials. Secondary sesquioxide minerals such as hematite, goethite, allophane, gibbsite, and anatase, and residual resistant primary minerals such as limonite and magnetite predominate in the more highly weathered parent materials.

Jessup, R. W.
1951   The soils, geology, and vegetation of northwestern South Australia. Royal Society of South Australia, Transactions 74:189-273.
Scale: 1/750,000. Has detailed descriptions and discussion of soils, geology, vegetation.

1962   Stony tableland soils of inland Australia. Australian Journal of Science 24:456-457.
Stony surface appears to be due to alternate wetting and drying causing upward movement of stones.

Jewitt, T. N.
1955   Gezira soil. Republic of the Sudan, Ministry of Agriculture, Bulletin 12.
Soils are fine textured, slowly permeable, saline, sodium affected, and respond to N.

Kaddou, N. S. (Kaddouri, N. S.)
1960   Clay mineraology of some alluvial soils of Iraq and Dubuque silt loam and underlying Dolomitic limestone of Wisconsin. University of Wisconsin, Ph. D. dissertation. 129 p. Abstr. *in* Dissertation Abstracts 21(3):392.

Kanwar, J. S.
1961   Clay minerals in saline alkali soils of the Punjab. Indian Society of Soil Science, Journal 9:35-40.
The dominant clay mineral in the soils was illite with some chlorite. There was little difference in the clay-mineral composition of saline-alkali and normal soils of the same tract.

Kao Shang-tun
1963   Issledovanie peschanoi pustyni i gebi v Sintszyana. (In Chinese with Russian summary.) Scientia Silvae 8(1):42-67.
        (Investigation of the sand desert and gobi in Sinkiang)
These deserts occur widely in the Sinkiang territory. Dunes with psammophilic shrubs occurred primarily in the Dzungarian basin, and in the Tarim basin bare drifting barchan dunes occupied a large area.

Karayeva, Z. S.
1963   Ash composition of some plants in the Bet-Pak-Dala Desert. Soviet Soil Science 1963(3):273-280.
It was shown that the mineralization of the litter in connection with an active accumulation of Ca and Na by the studied plants is accompanied by an increase in carbonate content in the upper soil horizons, and under the *Artemisia salsa* the soil acquires solonetz properties.

Karschon, R.
1953   The hammada in Wadi Araba, its properties and possibilities of afforestation. Ilanoth 2:19-45.
A desert pavement of dark brown or black pebbles protects the underlying sandy saline soils.

Kassas, M.
1952   On the distribution of *Alhagi maurorum* in Egypt. Egyptian Academy of Science, Proceedings 8:149-151.
This is a wild plant of wide distribution, not only in Egypt, but in Nubia, Tripoli, Libya, Palestine, Syria, Iraq, Iran, Arabia, South Balkan, and Cyprus. The plant obtains its water from underground sources that are deep under the desert and more shallow along the coast. It is intolerant of high salinity.

1957   On the ecology of the Red Sea coastal land. Journal of Ecology 45(1):187-203.
The plant cover and soil are studied in 2 main ecosystems: salt marsh and maritime desert plain. Within the former, 8 plant communities are recognized; within the desert plain, 6 plant communities are recognized.

Kassas, M. and M. Iman
1954   Habitat and plant communities in the Egyptian desert. III: The wadi bed ecosystem. Journal of Ecology 43(2):424-441.
The gradual modification of the plant cover proceeds with the gradual accumulation of alluvial sediments, a process

dependent on the physical factors of topography and the hydrological regime of the wadi.

Kelley, W. P.
1951   Alkali soils. Reinhold Publishing Corporation, New York, N. Y. 176 p.

Khadr, M.
1963   The clay mineral composition of some soils of the UAR. Journal of Soil Science of the UAR 1:141-155.
The Nile sediment consists mainly of illite; montmorillonite and kaolinite are also present. A sample from one area contained attapulgite.

Khan, F. and A. Arshad
1947   West Pakistan in maps and statistics. Ferroz Printing Works, Lahore. 63 p.
Map scale: 1/10,000,000. Four kinds of soils. Very general. Low reliability. Covers less than half of West Pakistan.

Killian, C.
1940   Etudes comparatives de la biologie des sols du nord et du centre saharien. Annales Agronomiques 10(1):56-100.
        (Comparative studies of the biology of soils of the north and central Sahara)
Soil of the Ahaggar region in the central Sahara was compared with soil from the region of Beni-Ounif, in the northern Sahara. For the soil of both regions the biology is governed by the limited soil factors, C and N.

1953   La végétation autour du Chott Hodna, indicatrice des conditions culturales et son milieu edaphique. *In* Desert Research, proceedings, International Symposium held in Jerusalem, May 7-14, 1952, sponsored by the Research Council of Israel and Unesco. Research Council of Israel, Special Publication 2:241-256.
        (Vegetation around Chott Hodna, indicator of cultivation and the edaphic environment)
Soil-plant relations are too complicated to permit formulation of lists of plants indicating certain soil conditions. Further research is needed to determine ranges of edaphic requirements and salt tolerance.

Killian, C. and D. Fehér
1936   La fertilité des sols du Sahara. Génie Civil 108 (2790):114-124.
        (The fertility of the soils of the Sahara)
Results of chemical and bacteriological studies of soils of Sahara Desert. Shows a wide variety of microflora.

King, L.
1952   Vegetation patterns revealing former Kalahari dunesands in Southern Rhodesia. South African Journal of Science 43(10):374-375.
Certain curious lines of vegetation shown in air photographs of Southern Rhodesia are regarded as related to ancient dunesand patterns of a late-Kalahari phase (mid-Pleistocene).

Kloes, L. J. J. van der
1956   Soil survey of the Naifa project near Samarra, Iraq. Government of Iraq, Ministry of Agriculture.
Scale: 1/50,000.

Koch, C.
1962   The Tenebrionidae of southern Africa. XXXI: Comprehensive notes on the Tenebrionid fauna of the Namib Desert. Namib Desert Research Station, Scientific Papers no. 5, X. 38 p.

Three ecological regions are identified: (1) littoral sands, (2) barchan dunes in the inland south, and (3) sandy to gravelly plains in the inland north.

Kononova, M. M.
1961 Soil organic matter, its nature, its role in soil formation and in soil fertility. Translated from the Russian by T. Z. Nowakowski and G. A. Greenwood. Pergamon Press, Oxford, New York. 450 p.

Kovda, V. A.
1946- Proiskhozhdenie i rezhim zasolennykh pochv.
1947 Akademiya Nauk S.S.S.R., Moskva. 2 vols. (Origin and management of saline soils)

———
1954 La géochemie des déserts de l'U.R.S.S.. Akademiya nauk S. S. R., Moscow.

Kovda, V. A., R. Hagan, and C. van den Berg, eds.
1967 International sourcebook on irrigation and drainage in relation to salinity and alkalinity. FAO/Unesco. (*in press*)

Kovda, V. A. and N. I. Kondorskaya
1957 Novaya pochvennaya karta Kitaya. Pochvovedenie 12:45-51. (A new soil map of China. Issued in translation by Israel Program for Scientific Translations, Jerusalem. Also cited as OTS 60-21140)
No soil map in translated paper.

Kulik, N.
1959 Lime concretions in semidesert soils. Soviet Soil Science 1959(1):126.
Lime concretions as large as peas in desert pavement areas of the Caucasus were formed by the mortaring action of individual rain drops on naturally calcined limestone and rolled into nodules by wind before hardening.

Kuznetzova, T. V.
1958 Some properties of takyrs of the Kizyl-Arvat Plain in the southwestern part of the Turkmenian SSR. Soviet Soil Science 1958 (5)497-504.
Development of the takyrs of the Kizyl-Arvat piedmont plain takes place under conditions of sharply varying water-salt relations. The soil forming profile in takyrs is limited to a thickness of 20-25 cm; that is, to the depth to which wetting by atmospheric precipitation takes place. Solodization is characteristic only of takyrs in this area.

Lakin, H. W., *et al.*
1963 Variation in minor-element content of desert varnish. U. S. Geological Survey, Professional Paper 475-B:28-31.
The Co content of desert varnish from Death Valley and northeastern Nevada shows a close correlation with the Mn content of the desert varnish, and Ba, La, Mo, Ni, Pb, and Y show a general correlation. Thus the content of these elements in desert varnish may not be meaningful as an indicator of mineralized zones.

Laktionov, B. I.
1962 Nature of the high dispersity of solonetzic soils and methods for their chemical melioration. Soviet Soil Science 1962(6):635-642.
The degree of dispersion of the soil mass is determined not by the concentration of absorbed Na in the soil but by the content of peptized highly dispersed particles, which are determined by microaggregate analysis. $FeSO_4$ improved the physical properties of a crusty solonetz, increased yields of winter wheat and sugar beet and the sugar content of the beet.

Lapham, M. H.
1932 Genesis and morphology of desert soils. American Soil Survey Association, Report of 12th annual meeting, Bulletin 13:34-52.
Asks if it is not possible that Tubac soils (Nogales, Arizona) which are solonetzic may represent the end product of weathering, which is but partially developed in Mojave soils. Most grey desert soils, such as Portneuf of Idaho, have little if any evidence of illuviation in B horizon. Some grey desert soils developed on uneroded remnants of old surfaces are redder and have more clay in B horizon. Suggests that weathering is rapid in southern red deserts because of high temperatures (Marbut's idea).

Li Yao-hui
1963 A comparative study of several methods for determining available phosphorous in calcareous soils (translated title). Acta Pedologica Sinica 11:215-219.
Correlation of the various methods tested with results of pot experiments and *Azotobacter* tests showed the following decreasing efficiency in P determination: 0.5 M $Na HCO_3$ (Olsen), 1% $(NH_4)_2 CO_3$ (Michigan) 3.5% Na-citrate (Radet) lactate method (Egner-Riehm) plus 0.2n $(NH_4)_2 C_2O_4$ (Joret-Hubert).

Liang, Ta
1964 Tropical soils, characteristics and airphoto interpretation. Air Force Cambridge Research Laboratories, Bedford, Massachusetts, AFCRL 64-937 Final Report 164, 20 p., 90 figs. (Also cited as AD-613 555)
To facilitate engineering studies of tropical soils, and particularly their airphoto interpretation, a classification system is proposed which covers major groups of soil peculiar to the tropics, soils common in both tropical and subtropical regions, and soils common in all climates. A method of airphoto interpretation by direct recognition of soil features, and by inference gained from observation of soil forming factors and circumstances is presented. Supplementary use of other remote sensing devices is suggested. Illustrations from the Americas, Africa, Asia, and Australia are given.

Liere, W. J. van
1954 Etude générale des grandes groupes des sols de la Syrie. Preliminary Report. FAO, World Soil Resources Office, Rome.
(General study of great soil groups of Syria)
Map scale: 1/2,000,000. Other unpublished soil maps of Syria by Liere in World Soil Resources Office are 1956 map at 1/1,000,000. and 1963 map (5 sheets) at 1/5,000,000. These are the best on Syria.

Litchfield, W. H. and J. A. Mabbutt
1962 Hardpan in soils of semi-arid Western Australia. Journal of Soil Science 13:148-159.
Strongly cemented hardpan is widespread on gentle alluvial slopes formed by partial destruction of a lateritized Tertiary land surface. It also occurs in sand plains on remnants of this surface, but it is found only locally in saline alluvial plains in the low lying areas of interior drainage. Hardpan results from cementation with silica and deposition of clay.

Little, I. P.
1963 The preparation and use of saturated soil pastes. C. S. I. R. O. Division of Soils, Divisional Report 3/63.
The saturation extracts from 7 soils were analyzed.

Evidence is presented to show that for one soil at least, the SAR varied progressively during extraction.

Lobova, E. V.
1960 Pochvy pustynnoi zony S.S.S.R. Akademiia Nauk S.S.S.R., Pochvennyi Institut im. V. V. Dokuchaeva. 362 p. (Translated 1967 by Israel Program for Scientific Translations, Jerusalem, as "Soils of the desert zone of the U.S.S.R." 405 p. Also cited as TT 67-51279.)
Bibliography (original), p. 351-363; (translation), p. 373-403.

Lobova, E. V. and N. N. Rozov
1947 Pochvennaya karta Europeisko chastu S.S.S.R. Akademii Nauk S.S.S.R., Pochvenni Institut im V. V. Dokuchaev.
(Soil maps of the European part of the U.S.S.R.)
Scale: 1/2,500,000. 84 separations of great soil groups and variations. Copy on file at World Soil Resources Office, FAO, Rome. 4 sheets.

Longenecker, D. E. and P. J. Lyerly
1959 Some relations among irrigation water quality, soil characteristics and management practices in the Trans-Pecos area. Texas Agricultural Experiment Station, Miscellaneous Publication 373.
The study indicates strongly that knowledge of the nature and quantity of salts in the water is not sufficient to evaluate the water properly for irrigation purposes. Other important factors that should be considered are the texture and permeability characteristics of the soil and the management practices followed.

Ma, Y. C.
1947 Soil geography of Bogdo-Ula, Sinkiang. Soils Quarterly 6(3).
Scale: 1/1,500,000. Soils grouped as Desert soils, Brown Chestnut, etc. Note: Soil Institute, Chinese Academy, is institute for soil survey.

———
1957 General principles of geographical distribution of Chinese soils (translated title). Acta Pedologica Sinica 5(1):1-18.
Scale: 1/20,000,000. Text has general soil and landscape descriptions. Russian summary.

Ma Yung-tzu and Chen-wang Wen
1958 The principle of soil classification, the basis of agricultural development. Acta Pedologica Sinica 6(3):157-176.
Soil map scale: 1/15,000,000.

Mabbutt, J. A. *et al.*
1963 General report on lands of the Wiluna-Meekatharra Area, Western Australia, 1958. C.S.I.R.O. Land Research Series 7.
Land system map scale: 1/550,000. 48 land systems, 7 soil associations. Text has brief soil descriptions. Describes climate, geology, geomorphology, soils, vegetation, water supply, and pastures.

Marbut, C. F.
1935 Soils of the United States. *In* Atlas of American Agriculture, Part III, Advance Sheets no. 8. 98 p. U. S. Department of Agriculture, Washington, D. C.
Profile descriptions, laboratory physical and chemical analyses, discussion of great soil groups in relation to U. S. soils, colored illustrations of soil profiles typical of great soil groups.

———
1951 Soils, their genesis and classification. Soil Science Society of America, Madison, Wisconsin.
This is the stenographic record of a series of lectures Marbut gave at the Graduate School of the U. S. Dept. of Agriculture in 1928. It presents his concepts of soil, soil forming processes, soil development, climatic soil groups, and the processes of podzolization, lateritization, and calcification, as well as his introduction of the terms pedalfer and pedocal.

Marks, J. B.
1950 Vegetation and soil relations in the lower Colorado Desert. Ecology 31:176-193.
Plant communities are listed according to salt content; salt tolerance of plants and change in salt content in the soil profile are discussed.

Martin, W. P.
1940 Distribution and activity of *Azotobacter* in the range and cultivated soils of Arizona. Arizona Agricultural Experiment Station, Technical Bulletin 83:332-369.
Range soils generally lacking in *Azotobacter*. Only 22.7% had any and they usually were inactive. 87% of cultivated soils had them. Soluble calcium and sodium above 3,000 ppm caused absence of *Azotobacter*.

Marx, H. and P. D. Faure
1964 Stabilization of desert sand using cut-back bitumen. Civil Engineer in South Africa 6(11):199-208.
Practical approach in use of bitumen in stabilization of road base courses in South Africa is described; development of cutback bitumens in stabilizing and application of techniques are described, and grading curves of various sands are presented.

Mason, B.
1959- Soil temperatures, Giles, Western Australia.
1960 Australian Meteorological Magazine 24:10-20; 28:43-45.
Monthly mean soil temperatures at various depths up to 40 inches at a desert station are given. Diurnal variation, direction of heat flow, and thermal diffusivity of the soil are discussed.

Mathews, D. L.
1960 The clay mineralogy of some Mojave Desert playas. Compass 38(1):28-38.
Montmorillonite is the most abundant clay mineral, illite ranks 2nd, and chlorite and/or kaolinite are present in minor amounts. Mica, quartz, feldspar, calcite, and halite are the dominant nonclay minerals present.

Mathur, C. M., V. B. Mogne, and N. R. Talati
1964 Distribution of boron in soils of western Rajasthan irrigated with high boron waters. Indian Society of Soil Science, Journal 13:319-324.
In irrigated soils total and available boron contents were much more than in the unirrigated soil. No relation was found between total and available boron.

Mayland, H. F. and T. H. McIntosh
1963 Nitrogen fixation by desert algal crust organisms. Agronomy Abstracts 1963:33.
Continuously moist subsamples of field crusts fixed up to 0.3 mg nitrogen/cm^2 in 30 days under laboratory conditions. Continuous light (600 footcandles); temperature of 25° C; and an induced atmosphere of 75% N2 (5% N^{15} excess), 20% O_2, 5% CO_2. Water extracts

from these cultures did not contain NO_2 or NO_3 and yielded only traces of NH_4.

Maytin, I. L. and R. Gilkeson
1962 State of Washington engineering soils manual: Soils of Spokane County. Washington State Institute of Technology, Division of Industrial Research, Bulletin 262.
A manual written primarily for the engineer, presenting detailed information on the soils of Spokane County and their engineering characteristics.

McKeague, J. A. and M. G. Cline
1963 Silica in soils. Advances in Agronomy 15:339-396.
A comprehensive review.

McKee, E. D. and G. C. Tibbitts, Jr.
1964 Primary structures of a seif dune and associated deposits in Libya. Journal of Sedimentary Petrology 34(1):5-17.
Examination of a seif dune, an interdune area, and an adjoining serir near Sebba Oasis in Libya indicates marked differences in texture and structure that should assist in the recognition of such deposits where they are preserved in the geologic record.

McKenzie, R. M.
1960 Trace elements in some soils from the Todd River area, Central Australia, C.S.I.R.O. Division of Soils, Divisional Report 6/60:17.
Analytical results are given for Co, Cu, Mn, Mo, and Zn, in loam solonetz, brown soils of light texture, brown soils of heavy texture, skeletal soils, eolian sands, calcareous red earths, and red earths.

McLachlan, K. D.
1953 Phosphorous, sulfur and molybdenum deficiencies on some soils of the Northern Territory. Australian Institute of Agricultural Science, Journal 19(3): 197-199.
The treatments were: nil, P-S-Mo, P-S, P-Mo, and S-Mo, applied in solution as sodium phosphate, sodium sulphate, and sodium molybdate. Signficant responses to P were obtained on all 4 soils; to S, on 3 (all except Granitic) and to Mo, on Red and Granitic.

McNeal, B. L. and T. Sansoterra
1964 Mineralogical examination of arid-land soils. Soil Science 97(6):367-375.
Mica and montmorillonite predominate in a majority of samples from typical arid-land soils. Moderate amounts of chloride and quartz-plus-feldspar and small amounts of kaolinite, vermiculite, and amorphous materials also occur.

Means, R. E. and J. V. Parcher
1963 Physical properties of soils. Charles E. Merrill Books, Inc., Columbus, Ohio. 464 p.
Soil mechanics and soil engineering textbook; stresses basic understanding of soil properties. An introductory book.

Meléndez Aguirre, E. and A. C. S. Wright
1962 Estudio de los suelos del Valle del Río Azapa. Ministry of Agriculture, Santiago, Chile. (unpublished)
(Study of the soils of the Río Azapa Valley)

——— 1963a Los suelos de la región central del Valle del Río Loa, y su desarrollo agrícola potencial. Archives of the Ministry of Agriculture, Santiago, Chile.
(Study of soils of the central region of the Río Loa Valley, and their potential for crop production)

——— 1963b Estudio de suelos de la parte inferior del Valle de Lluta. Ministry of Agriculture, Santiago, Chile. (unpublished)
(Study of soils of the lower part of the Lluta Valley)

Melnikova, V. V.
1962 Vodorosli poyasa serozemnykh pochv. Akademii nauk Tadzhikskoi S. S. R., Instituta Botaniki, Trudy 8:286-313. Referativnyi Zhurnal, Biologiya, 1963, no. 16V17.
(The algae of the Tadzhik sierozem belt)
217 algal species have been discovered in the sierozem (gray desert soil) belt. More than half of these belong to the blue-green type. Plots of land with *Medicago sativa* have a larger quantitative and qualitative distribution of algae than plots with cotton.

Miaczynski, C. and P. H. Etchevehere
1962 Mapa de asociaciones de suelos, República Argentina. Instituto de Suelos y Agrotecnia, Castelar, Argentina.
(Map of soil association, Argentine Republic)
Map scale: 1/5,000,000.

Mikenberg, N.
1957 Bosquejo de distribución de los suelos de Tucumán y capacidad de uso actual. Instituto de Suelos y Agrotecnia, Castelar, Argentina, Publicación 53.
(Outline of the distribution of the soils of Tucumán and land capability)
Soil map scale: 1/1,000,000.

Miller, D. E.
1966 "Bubble" structure under irrigation furrows in silt loam soils. Western Society of Soil Science, Annual Meeting, 1966, Seattle, Program and Abstracts.
Says bubbles can be formed in lab by repeated wetting and drying (4 to 8 cycles). Thickness of vesicular layer in field about 2 inches.

Millot, G.
1960 Silice, silex, silicifications et croissance des cristaux. Alsace-Lorraine, Service de Géologie, Bulletin 13:129-146.

Milthorpe, F. L.
1960 The income and loss of water in arid and semi-arid zones. *In* Plant-water relationships in arid and semi-arid conditions, reviews of research. Unesco, Paris. Arid Zone Research 15:9-36.
A review of soil-plant-water research, not restricted to arid regions.

Mitkees, A. G.
1959 Some chemical studies on soils of Baris plain, Kharga oasis. Agricultural Research Review (Cairo) 37:177-182.
Tabulated data are reported on soluble Ca and Mg, exchangeable cations, saturation capacity, Na saturation, and Ca SO_4 requirement of these mainly saline soils.

Moormann, F.
1959 Report to the Government of Jordan on the soils of east Jordan. FAO, Rome, EPTA Report 1132. 64 p.
Scale: 1/1,750,000. 23 soils, based on genetic type. Text contains soil descriptions and review of physical geography of area. East of 38° longitude.

National Council of Applied Economic Research
1963a Techno-economic survey of Rajasthan. New Delhi. Map scale: 1/3,150,000. 8 soils classified mainly by color. Gives only general information.

1963b Techno-economic survey of Gujarat. New Delhi. Map scale: 1/2,250,000. Shows saline soils, sandy coastal soils, etc. Fairly reliable.

National Research Council, Highway Research Board
1958 Water and its conduction in soils, an international symposium. Special Report 40. 338 p.

Nechaeva, N. T.
1961 Vidovii sostav i rasprostraneni pustynnykh osok podrela Vignea p yugo-vostochno Turkmenu. Akademii Nauk Turkmenskoi S. S. R., seriya Biologicheskaya Nauk, Izvestiya 3:3-12. Referativnyi Zhurnal, Biologiya, 1962, no. 10V141.
(The species composition and distribution of desert sedges of the subgenus *Vignea* in southeastern Turkmenia)
The article stresses that *Carex subphysodes* is a morphologically and ecologically well specialized species. In the deserts of Central Asia it grows on the poorly broken up sandy loam sierozem of the foothills, on shallow layers of sand with a desert substrate, and on loose mottled and sandy-gravel soils.

Nicot, J.
1955 Remarques sur les peuplements de micromycetès des sables désertiques. Académie des Sciences, Paris, Comptes Rendus 240:2082-2084.
(Notes on the population of micromycetes in desert sands)
The microfungal population of sands and superficial soils is very diverse and adaptable. It consists of short-lived species (Micorinae) which complete their life-cycle more rapidly when conditions become favorable, and species which are morphologically adapted to excessive sunlight, temperature, and dryness. Their mycelia and spores are strongly pigmented.

Nikiforoff, C. C.
1937 General trends of the desert types of soil formation. Soil Science 43:105-125.
Desert crusts (lime, gypsum, silica) form from upward movement of salts from ground water. One of the principal zonal characterists of desert types of soil formation is claypans developed by weathering in place in B horizons. Hilgard considers kaolinization to be typical of weathering in hot, grey regions. Nikiforoff agrees. Desert soils do not belong to Pedocals or Pedalfers. Lime accumulation occurs in some soils, not in others.

Noakes, F. C. T.
1932 Desert roads. Royal Engineers Journal 46:515-521. Materials and construction methods used in making mixed-in-place roads by Shell Oil Co. of Egypt in Fayoum desert; method consisted of spraying bituminous suspension and mixing it into sand by means of grader pulled by caterpillar tractor.

Norman, M. J. T. and R. Wetselaar
1960 Losses of nitrogen on burning native pasture at Katherine, N. T. Australian Institute of Agricultural Science, Journal 26:272-273.
In a native pasture composed mainly of *Sorghum plumosum, Themeda australis* and *Chrysopogon fallax,* the average N content of grass was 0.37% before burning and 0.17% after burning.

Nour, M. A.
1956 A preliminary survey of fungi in some Sudan soils. British Mycological Society, Transactions 39:357-360
35 species of fungi are listed. There are little differences in the kinds of fungi isolated from different soils.

Noy, J.
1959 The activity of calcium carbonate in the soil as a function of its particle size. Research Council of Israel, Bulletin 8G:159.
No correlation between total $CaCO_3$ and plant chlorosis. $CaCO_3$ activity slight in particles over 200 microns in diameter and strong in those under 20 microns. "Active limestone" refers to under 50-micron size.

Oberholzer, P. C. J.
1936 The decomposition of organic matter in relation to soil fertility in arid and semiarid regions. Soil Science 42:359-379.

Office de la Recherche Scientifique et Technique Outre-Mer
1962 Carte pédologique du périmètre d'irrigation de: Taboye, Keita, d'Adouna, République Niger. Centre de Recherche Pédologique de Hann-Dakar.
(Soil map of irrigated areas of Taboge, Keita, Adouna, Republic of Niger)
Scale: 1/5,000. Soils classed by texture and grouped in legend by parent material, depth, and soil profile characteristics.

Olsen, S. R., F. S. Watanabe, and C. V. Cole
1960 Phosphates in calcareous soils as affected by neutral salts. International Congress of Soil Science, 7th, Madison, Transactions 2:397-403.
The effect of neutral salts on P solubility in calcareous soils, as compared with being in a mixture of $CaHPO_4$ with calcite, is due to the increase in Ca concentration arising from the exchangeable Ca by ion exchange with the cation of the salt.

Ortiz Monasterio, R.
1956 Características general de la erosión en los suelos. Mapa[s] de: textura, reacción, nitrógeno, fósforo, potasio, de los suelos de la República Mexicana. Ingeniera Hidráulica 10(1-2).
(General characteristics of soil erosion. Maps of texture, reaction, nitrogen, phosphorus, potassium, in Mexican soils)
Scale: 1/8,500,000.

Overstreet, R., J. C. Martin, and H. M. King
1951 Gypsum, sulfur, and sulfuric acid for reclaiming an alkali soil of the Fresno series. Hilgardia 21(5):113-127.

Panin, P. I.
1962 Salt discharge from soils and determination of leaching norms. Soviet Soil Science 1962(7):703-709.
Uses monoliths $0.4m^2$ in cross section and 0.5 to 2 m high enclosed in metal casing. Presumably undisturbed soils are used. Relation between leaching norm determined with monolith and field leaching norm was not tested.

Papadakis, J.
1956 Informe ecológico sobre le Provincia de Córdoba. Instituto de Suelos y Agrotecnia, Castelar, Publicación 48.
(Ecologic report on the Province of Córdoba)
Soil map scale: 1/7,500,000.

Papadakis, J.
1963   Soils of Argentina. Soil Science 95:356-366.
Map scale: 1:29,000,000. Argentine soils are outlined and some questions concerning their formation and classification are discussed in terms of the following areas: the grassland, the midlatitude thorny woodland, the subtropical dry woodland and parkland, the subtropical forest, the desert, the temperate forest of certain mountains, the subantarctic cool-summer grassland, the antarctic subglacial desert. Soils are described in terms of great soil groups and the 7th approximation.

Papadakis, J., J. E. Calcagno, and P. H. Etchevehere
1960   Regiones de suelos de la República Argentina. Mapa esquemático. Instituto de Suelos y Agrotecnia, Castelar.
(Soil regions of the Argentine Republic. Schematic map)
Mimeographed map at scale of 1/5,000,000.

Pennefather, R. R.
1951   The salinity problem in Western Australia. Western Mail 66(3759):59-61.

Perry, R. A.
1960   Pasture lands of the Northern Territory. C.S.I.R.O. Land Research Series 5.
No soil map. Short description of physiography, soils, climate, vegetation, animals.

Perry, R. A. *et al.*
1962   General report on lands of the Alice Springs Area, Northern Territory, 1956-57. C. S. I. R. O. Land Research Series 6.
Scale: 1/1,000,000. 88 land systems, by topography and geology, with soil features of each system. Has maps of land systems, pasture lands, geology, and ground water provinces and piezometric form-lines of Alice Springs area.

Peterson, H. B. and T. H. Goodding
1941   The geographic distribution of *Azotobacter* and *Rhizobium meliloti* in Nebraska soils in relation to certain environmental factors. Nebraska Agricultural Experiment Station. Research Bulletin 121.
40% of the soils had *Rhizobium meliloti*. 92.6% had *Azotobacter*. 20 of 23 samples without *Azotobacter* were from sandy soils. *Azotobacter* population not associated with pH or soluble phorphorus. *Rhizobium* less on acid soils. 95% of carbonate soils had *Azotobacter* and *Rhizobium*.

Pias, J.
1964a Notice explicative sur les cartes pédologiques de reconnaissance au 1/200,000. Feuilles d'Abéché, Biltine, Oum-Hadjer. Office de la Recherche Scientifique et Technique Outre-Mer, Centre de Fort-Lamy, République de Tchad.
(Explanatory Report. Reconnaissance soil map at 1/200,000. Abéché, Biltine, Oum Hadjer sheets)

————
1964b Notice explicative sur les cartes pédologiques de reconnaissance au 1/200,000. Feuilles de Fort-Lamy, Massenya, Mougroum. Office de la Recherche Scientifique et Technique Outre-Mer, Centre de Fort-Lamy, République du Tchad.
(Explanatory Report. Reconnaissance soil map at 1/200,000. Fort-Lamy, Massenya, Mougroum sheets)
Subdesert.

Pias, J. and E. Guichard
1956   Carte pédologique de: la dépression du Bahr el Chazal de Massakory à Moussoro; rives sud-est et nord du Lac Tchad de Tourba à Bol. Office de la Recherche Scientifique et Technique Outre-Mer, Centre de Fort-Lamy, République du Tchad.
(Soil map of: the depression of Bahr el Ghazal from Massahoury to Moussoro; the southeast and north shores of Lake Chad, from Tourba to Bol)
Scale: 1/100,000. 5 sheets. 13 soils and complexes classed by color and lime.

Pichi-Sermolli, R. E.
1955   Tropical East Africa (Ethiopia, Somaliland, Kenya, Tanganyika). *In* Plant ecology, reviews of research. Unesco, Paris. Arid Zone Research 6:302-360.
Described the soils and vegetation of east Africa. Estimates of soils based largely on geology.

Pines, F.
1957   Chemical composition of the desert soils in Central and Southern Negev. Research Council of Israel, Bulletin B6:269. (Abstr.)
All contain $CaCO_3$ and are of pH 7.0-8.5; all except the sandy soils are saline, the chlorides of Na, Ca, and Mg and gypsum being important; few contain much organic matter or N; all are rich in P; some are rich in K. Microbial populations are fairly developed in the loess and loess-like soils, but in the hamadas are poor. Texture and depth are, in most cases, suitable for cultivation but excess soluble salts would need removing, and lowering of groundwater level would be necessary in some cases.

Pithawalla, M. B.
1951   An introduction to Sind; its wealth and welfare. Karachi.
Map scale: 1/500,000. Little detail. Low reliability.

Pochon, J., H. de Barjar, and J. Lajudie
1957   Recherches sur la microflore des sols Sahariens. Institut Pasteur, Paris, Annales 92:833-836.
(Studies on the microflora of Sahara soils)
In soil samples from a depth of 10 cm *Azotobacter, Clostridium,* and nitrifying organisms were absent. The activity of ammonifying, denitrifying, cellulose decomposing and amylolytic organisms was very low.

Poona College of Agriculture
1955   Soil map of the Bombay State. College of Agriculture, Poona, Agricultural Chemistry Section.
Scale: 1/3,200,000. Shows 9 soils (coastal alluvium, salt lands, alkaline soils, etc.). Includes present state of Maharashstra.

Prasolov, L. I.
1937   A unified nomenclature and the principles of a genetic classification of soils (translated title). Pochvovedenie 6:77'-782. (Issued in translation by Israel Program for Scientific Translations. Also cited as TT 65-50081)
Establishment of a general nomenclature should aim primarily at defining the general genetic groups and the regularity of soil processes instead of a quality grading of soils.

Prescott, J. A.
1931   The soils of Australia in relation to vegetation and climate. C. S. I. R. O. Bulletin 52.

Prescott identified major great soil groups:
1. Desert soils (spinifex sand hills)
2. Soils of the semi-desert and desert steppe (Mulga-myall and bluebrush and saltbush associations). Dwarf eucalyptus
3. Mallee soils (lime soils in subsoil, with illuvial clay horizon, presumably result of solonization, not podzolization)
4. The red-brown earths (open savannah-best wheat soils)
5. The black earths (heavy soils—Rendzina-like)
6. Grey and brown soils (heavy soils under deficient rainfall)
7. Podzolized soils
8. Red loams (north strip across eastern Australia)
9. High moor and mountain soils
10. The Western Australian Sand Plains

_____

1944   Soil map of Australia. C.S.I.R.O. Bulletin 177. Scale: 1/9,500,000. Shows great soil groups. Out of date.

Price, W. A.
1933   Reynosa problem of south Texas and the origins of caliche. American Association of Petroleum Geologists, Bulletin 17:488-522.
Silicates cement caliche.

_____

1963   Physicochemical and environmental factors in clay dune genesis. Journal of Sedimentary Petrology 33:776-778.
Critical factors in clay dune genesis are wind action and changes in cohesiveness and volume with gain or loss of moisture from atmosphere. Drying crusts of saline flats of dry climates break down into sand-sized pellets.

Rainey, R. C.
1949   Cotton in Ethiopia and the Somalilands. Empire Cotton Growing Review 26:186-195.
The importance of light irrigation and of fallow is indicated. The heavy, deep, alkaline clays of Villaggio Duca degli Abruzzi and Gezira produced good yields, the latter benefiting from Blue Nile water.

Ravikovitch, S. and J. Hagin
1957   The state of aggregation in various soil types in Israel. Ktavim 7(2/3):107-122.
The terra rossa and rendzina soils were found to excel in their very high degree of stable aggregation. An intermediate degree of stable aggregation typifies the colluvium of terra rossa, the alluvial soils of Mediterranean red-earth origin, and the grey calcareous soils. The loessial soils possess a limited degree of stable aggregation. Loess-like and brown-red sandy soils have but negligible aggregation.

Ravikovitch, S. and M. Margolis
1957   Selenium in soils and plants. Ktavim 7(2/3): 41-62.
A case of selenium poisoning of cattle in a region of selenium-infected soils was found in the country. The selenium was found in alluvial soils which originated mainly from limestone. In particular, alfalfa must be pointed out as possessing a large capacity for selenium uptake.

Ravikovitch, S., F. Pines, and M. Ben-Yair
1958   Composition of colloids in the soils of Israel. Ktavim 9:69-82.
Composition of colloids of arid region soils dominated by montmorillonite, with lesser amounts of illite, kaolin, quartz, and sometimes attapulgite.

Ravikovitch, S. and B. Ramati
1957   The formation of brown-red sandy soils from shifting sands along the Mediterranean coast of Israel. Ktavim 7(2/3):79-82.
There is evidence that vegetation, particularly perennial crops, on shifting sand is providing a colloidal coating to the sand grains by means of the mineral compounds and organic residues supplied by the sand and plants, respectively.

Raychaudhuri, S. P.
1963   Soil map of India. Indian Planning Commission, New Delhi, Committee on Natural Resources.
Scale: 1/8,870,000. Similar to soil map prepared by All Indian Soil Survey Scheme in 1953.

Raychaudhuri, S. P. and N. R. D. Biswas
1954   Saline and alkali soils of Asia with particular reference to India. International Congress of Soil Science, 5th, Leopoldville, Transactions 1:191-207.
The distribution and nature of saline and alkali soils in China, Java, Palestine, Afghanistan, Pakistan, and India are discussed, together with ameliorative measures applied for successful crop growth.

Rayss, T. and S. Borut
1958   Contribution to the knowledge of soil fungi in Israel. Mycopathologia 10:142-174.
A list with descriptive notes is given of 107 species of soil fungi isolated from arid soils of the Judaean Desert and the northern Negev. 11 of the species seem to be new to soils; 3 new forms are described; 23 species are common to Israel and Egypt. 40 references.

Reeve, R. C., A. F. Pillsbury, and L. V. Wilcox
1955   Reclamation of a saline and high boron soil in the Coachella Valley of California. Hilgardia 24(4):69-91.
Boron more difficult to remove by leaching than soluble salts.

Reeve, R. C. et al.
1954   A comparison of the effects of exchangeable sodium and potassium upon the physical condition of soils. Soil Science Society of America, Proceedings 18:130-132.
Exchangeable sodium affected markedly the permeability ratio and modulus of rupture. Exchangeable potassium did not.

Reitan, C. H. and C. R. Green
1967   Inventory of research on weather and climate of desert environments. Chap. 2 of An Inventory of geographical research on desert environments. University of Arizona, Office of Arid Lands Research, Tucson. 72 p.

Reitemeier, R. F.
1946   Effect of moisture content on the dissolved and exchangeable ions of soils of arid regions. Soil Science 61(3):195-214.
In soils with appreciable contents of mixed salts, the exchangeable base status applies only at the moisture content at which the soluble salts are determined. It is concluded that the mobile soil solution cannot be homogeneous throughout its volume and generally is less concentrated near the surface of the soil colloids.

Riceman, D. S.
1953 Minor element deficiencies and their correction. International Grassland Congress, 6th, 1952, Proceedings 1:710-717.
A review of 49 references to trace-element deficiencies in Australia, with special reference to the extreme Zn and Cu deficiencies occurring in crops in the Coonamble Downs desert region.

Richards, L. A.
1950 Chemical and physical characteristics of saline and alkali soils of Western United States. Internatonal Congress of Soil Science, 4th, Amsterdam, Transactions 1:378-382.

Richards, L. A.
1953 Modulus of rupture as an index of surface crusting of soil. Soil Science Society of America, Proceedings 17:321.
Apparatus and procedure are described for measuring the modulus of rupture of soil. Data are correlated with ability of bean seedlings to emerge.

Rish, M. A. *et al.*
1962 Soderzhanie mikroelementov v pochvakh i rasteniyakh peschanoi pustyni. Instituta Karakulevodstva Uzbekskoi Akademii Sel' skokhozyaistvennykh Nauk, Samarkand, Trudy 12:209-231. Referativnyi Zhurnal, Biologiya, 1963, no. 19V149.
(Trace-element content in soils and plants of sandy desert)
The content of Fe and 6 important trace elements was determined in the plants of the preserve of the Repetek Sandy Desert Experimental Station (northeastern part of the Kara-Kum desert). The plants contained sufficient quantities of Co (0.7 mg/kg), I (0.5 mg/kg), Mo (1-2 mg/kg), Mn (71.0 mg/kg), and a somewhat decreased content of Zn (15.3 mg/kg). In the summer an obvious deficiency of Ca (3.7 mg/kg) developed in the plants because of burning-out.

Roberts, R. C.
1958 Great soil groups and their relationship to natural land and water resources. Food and Agriculture Organization, Santiago, Chile (typewritten manuscript).
Map scale: 1/10,000,000. 19 soils and groups of soils. Coverage of arid regions incomplete.

———
1962 New Valley-Western Desert, Egypt, UAR Reconnaissance Soil Survey. U. S. AID and Egyptian General Desert Development Organization.
Scale: 1/100,000. 145 soils and groups of soils. Text has detailed soil descriptions and analyses.

Robinson, W. O. and L. T. Alexander
1953 Molybdenum content of soils. Soil Science 75:287-291.
A review of Mo content of soils from several countries and some analyses of French and Hawaiian soils.

Roederer, P.
1959 Etude préliminaire d'une carte pédologique de Tunisie. Secretaire d'Etat à l'Agriculture, Tunis, Section Spéciale d'Etudes de Pédologie et d'Hydrologie.
(Preliminary study of a soil map of Tunisia)
Scale: 1/1,000,000. 15 genetic soil types. In French with English translation.

Romanova, M. A.
1960 O fotometricheskikh svoystvakh peskov pustyn Karakum i Kyzlkum. Akademii Nauk S.S.S.R., Doklady 132(3):681-684.
(Photometric properties of sand of the Kara-Kum and Kyzyl-Kum deserts. Akademii Nauk S.S.S.R., Doklady, Earth Sciences Section 132 (1/6):636-639. Translation)
The spectral brightness (rho lambda) of sands in a 350,000 square km area south of the Aral Sea (U.S.S.R.) was measured from the air using a light R-ShCh-1 einespectrograph in the range 490-650 mμ. The photometric properties of the sands are dependent upon their petrographic composition.

Rozanov, A. N.
1945 Pochvy Afganistana. Pochvovedenie 3/4:199-208.
(The soils of Afghanistan. Issued in translation by Israel Program for Scientific Translations, Jerusalem. Also cited as OTS 60-21114)
Map scale: 1/7,000,000. Based on climate, vegetation, geology, and geomorphology data. No personal observations.

———
1951 Serozemy Srednei Azii.
(Serozems of Central Asia. Issued in translation by Israel Program for Scientific Translations, Jerusalem, 1961, 550 p. Also cited as OTS 60-21834)
A comprehensive discussion of the soils of Central Asia, with extensive chemical and physical analyses.

Rozov, N. N. and E. N. Ivanova
1966 Soil classification and nomenclature used in Soviet pedology. Lomonosov State University, Moscow, Soil Biology Faculty. 31 p.

Rudoslovich, E. W.
1958 Clay mineralogy of some Australian red-brown earths. Journal of Soil Science 9:242-251.
The dominant minerals in southern Australia are illite and kaolin, and in Queensland predominantly kaolin. Red-brown earths developed on alluvial and similar materials contained more illite than kaolin; those developed on igneous rock, mainly kaolin.

Ruellan, A.
1965 Le rôle des climates et des roches sur la répartition des sols dans les plaines de la basse Moulouya. Académie des Sciences, Paris, Comptes Rendus 261:2379-2382.
Isohumic subtropical soils of the plains of Quaternary accumulation of lower Moulouya around Triffa and Zebra result from: deep distribution of organic matter; leaching of lime, with more or less intense accumulation at depth of various forms (granules, nodules, crusts, hardened layers); deep accumulation of clay.

Sabet, Y. S.
1939 On some fungi isolated from soil in Egypt. Fouad I University, Faculty of Science, Bulletin 19:59-112.
The distribution is recorded, with illustrations and short descriptions of the cultural features and diagnostic characteristics, of about 90 species from 9 different soils of pH8.1-8.5.

Samsonov, P. F., M. F. Samsonova, and T. A. Chernova
1930 Mikrobiologicheskaya kharakteristika pochv Srednei Azii. Pochvovedenie 1/2.
(Microbiological characteristics of Central Asia soils)
All main groups of microrganisms appear to be present in sierozems. Nitrifying organisms and *Azotobacter* are especially abundant. Takyrs have less, as do sandy soils.

Sasson, A.
1960 Premiére contribution à la connaissance de la microbiologie des sols de régions arides du Maroc. Société des Sciences Naturelles et Physiques du Maroc, Bulletin 40(2):97-120.
(First contribution to the study of the microbiology of the soils of the arid regions of Morocco)
The absence of *Azotobacter* is noted. Aerobic cellulolytic bacteria are present. The humidity of the soil and organic matter present are the predominant factors regulating the presence of the cellulolytic microflora.

Schiffman, J.
1958 Ineffectiveness of alfalfa nodule bacteria (*Rhizobium meliloti*) in Negev soils and improvement by soil inoculation. Ktavim 9:57-67.
Failures with lucerne in certain Negev loess soils are due to the predominance of ineffective symbiotic bacteria. Inoculations with highly efficient bacteria improved growth of potted lucerne and in practice could greatly increase yields without necessitating further fertilizing.

Schiffman, J.
1961 Soil survey report of the Hussainiyah Beni Hassan Drainage Project. Republic of Iraq Ministry of Agriculture, Division of Soils and Agricultural Chemistry, Technical Bulletin 2.
Semidetailed soil survey of 1/100,000 made in 1958. Soil salinity map at 1/100,000 made in 1958.

Seligman, N. G., N. H. Tadmor, and Z. Raz
1962 Range survey of the central Negev. The National and University Institute of Agriculture, Rehovot, Department of Field Crops, Bulletin 67.
Habitat types: rocky slopes (41.9% of area), dunes and plains (21.7%), loessial plains (12.5%), sandy plains (9.6%), others. 2,300,000 dunams (582,500 acres).

Sharoskhina, N. B.
1960 Mineralogical characteristics of the silt fraction of solonetz soils (translated title). Akademii Nauk Kazakhskoi S.S.R., Seriya Botaniki i Pochvovedeniya, Izvestiya 2(8):46-54. Referativnyi Zhurnal, Biologiya, 1961, no. 5G226.
Beidellite was the predominant secondary mineral.

Shastri, G. G. K.
1962 Origin of the desert gypsum in Rajasthan. Geological Survey of India, Records 87:781-786.
The gypsum beds occur near the surface in depressions surrounded by sand dunes. Anhydrite and NaCl are completely absent. The origin of the gypsum is discussed; evaporation of marine waters is excluded.

Shields, L. M.
1957 Algal and lichen floras in relation to nitrogen content of certain volcanic and arid range soils. Ecology 38(4):661-663.
Surface nitrogen much higher than in underlying soil when algae and lichen crusts present.

Shields, L. M., C. Mitchell, and F. Drouet
1957 Alga- and lichen-stabilized surface crusts as soil nitrogen sources. American Journal of Botany 44:489-498.
Blue-green algae occur in surface crusts from the basin floor surrounding the gypsum sand; amino N of crusts from the basin floor surrounding the gypsum sand averaged 1031 ppm for algal crusts and 1553 ppm for lichen crusts.

Shklarsky, E. and A. Kimchi
1962 Influence of voids, bitumen and filler contents on permeability of sand-asphalt mixtures. Highway Research Board, Bulletin 358:1-11.
The bitumen and filler contents of the sand-asphalt mixture tested affect the coefficient of permeability indirectly, through their influence on the voids content. For a given mixture, an increase in bitumen content by 1% decreases the voids content by almost the same amount as an increase of 2% in dust filler.

Sigmond, A. J. de
1938 The principles of soil science. Translated from the Hungarian by Arthur B. Yolland, edited in English by G. V. Jacks. Thomas Murby and Co., London. 362 p.

Simansky, N.
1955 Report to the Government of Saudi Arabia on the Preliminary Project for Land and Water Use Development in Wadi Jizan. FAO, Rome, EPTA Report 410. 38 p.
Wadi soil association consists mainly of fine textured soils, silt loams dominant. Saline soils mostly near wadi mouth. Water table 0.3 to 1.0 meter below wadi bed.

Simonett, D. S. and M. P. Bauleke
1963 Mineralogy of soils on basalt in north Queensland. Soil Science Society of America, Proceedings 27:205-212.
Poorly crystalline kaolinite is the chief mineral (52-79%). Halloysite may be present in high-rainfall areas. Total Fe content increased 12-20% with increasing rainfall. Gibbsite content was 0.19%. Haematite, goethite and magnetite were the main forms of iron oxide.

Simonneau, P.
1959 Essais et études de la campagne 1957-1958. Centre d'Etude Irrigation du Sahara Occidental, Birmandreis, Sections Pédologie et Agrologie, Travaux, Bulletin 5. 51 p.
(Field experiments and studies in 1957-1958)
Irrigation of solonchaks with saline water has permitted cultivation of wheat, barley, and vegetables in very arid regions of the Sahara. Organic or green manuring is necessary to maintain fertility.

Simonneau, P. and G. Aubert
1963 Utilisation des eaux salées dans le Sahara. Annales Agronomiques 14:859-872.

Sims, C. M. and F. M. Collins
1960 The numbers and distribution of ammonia-oxidizing bacteria in some Northern Territory and South Australian soils. Australian Journal of Agricultural Research 2:505-512.
There was little difference between the number and type of nitrifying bacteria present in the desert soils compared with those from more temperate areas, nor did the average annual rainfall have any appreciable effect.

Sims, J. R. and H. E. Dregne
1962 Fertilizer response on a sodium soil. New Mexico Agricultural Experiment Station, Research Report 63.
There was no response by barley to nitrogen or calcium but there were significant responses to NP and NPK combinations. KCl was better than K_2SO_4. Explanations for the results obtained are based upon the nitrogen-fixing capabilities of blue-green algae and upon the concept of ion antagonism.

Sinclair, J. G.
1922 Temperatures of the soil and air in a desert. Monthly Weather Review 50 (3):142-144.

Sleeman, J. R.
1963 Soils of the Leichhardt-Gilbert area, Northwestern Queensland. Morphology and laboratory data. C.S.I.R.O. Division of Land Research and Regional Survey, Divisional Report 63/1.

Sleeman, J. R. and B. E. Butler
1956 Soils and land use of portion of Brenda station north-west N.S.W., with special reference to irrigation problems. C.S.I.R.O. Soils Division, Report 5. 24 p.

Smith, A.
1929 Diurnal, average, and seasonal soil temperature changes at Davis, California. Soil Science 28: 457-568.

Smith, H. V., T. F. Buehrer, and G. A. Wickstrom
1949 Effect of exchangeable magnesium on the chemical and physical properties of some Arizona soils. Soil Science 68 (6):451-462.
From the standpoint of structure, Mg saturated soils behaved more nearly like those saturated with Ca than those saturated with Na.

Smith, R.
1954 Plants and soils of the semi-arid zone of southwestern Australia. p. 111-124. *In* Symposium on Scientific Problems of Land Use in Arid Regions, 1953, Cairo, held under joint auspices of the Egyptian Desert Institute and Unesco.
The soils are highly impoverished clays, often calcareous and saline. There are no permanent surface waters and the groundwater in salt pans is often more salty than the sea. The vegetation is sclerophyllus woodland with eucalyptus dominant.

Speck, N. H. *et al.*
1960 The lands and pastoral resources of the North Kimberly Area, W. A. C.S.I.R.O. Land Research Series 4.
Land system map scale: 1/1,000,000. 9 land systems. Text has soil descriptions. Area covered is 34,000 square miles.

_____
1964 General report on lands of the West Kimberley area, W. A. C.S.I.R.O. Land Research Series 9.
Scale of soil map: 1/1,125,000. As with other land research division surveys, scientists representing several descriptions (hydrology, geology, climatology, pedology, and ecology) work in close collaboration. "Land systems" are composite mapping units developed and defined by Christian and Stewart.

Springer, M. E.
1958 Desert pavement and vesicular layer of some soils of the desert and of the Lahontan basin, Nevada. Soil Science Society of America, Proceedings 22:63-66.
Upward displacement of stones and gravel under the effect of soil-shrinking contribute to the formation of desert pavement, in addition to removal of finer material by wind or water.

Stanberry, C. O. *et al.*
1963 Vertical movement of phosphorous in some calcareous soils of Arizona. Agronomy Abstracts 1962:17.
From a practical standpoint the vertical depth of P movement was almost insignificant. The water-soluble phosphates moved only about ½ inch farther than the non-water-soluble phosphates, 1.43 inches vs 0.92 inches.

Stephens, C. G.
1949 Comparative morphology and genetic relationships of certain Australian, North American, and European soils. Journal of Soil Science 1:123-149.
Subdivisions of great soil groups have been made to show relation of calcimorphic, and ferrimorphic, hydromorphic, halomorphic, and chronomorphic soils to the automorphic (zonal) soils.

_____
1960 The Australian soil landscape. International Congress of Soil Science, 7th, Madison, Transactions 3:20-26.
Has a small-scale generalized version of the 1/5,000,000 map in the "Manual of Australian Soils," a C.S.I.R.O. Division of Soils Publication.

_____
1962 A manual of Australian soils. 3rd ed. C.S.I.R.O., Melbourne.

Stephens, C. G. and C. M. Donald
1958 Australian soils and their responses to fertilizers. Advances in Agronomy 10:167-256.
Discusses climate and land use, the relationship of genetic factors to soil fertility, soil classification, the soil map of Australia, fertilizer use, and deficiencies of N, P, K, S, and other elements. Tabulated data show responses to fertilizers on different soils and content of those elements in Australian soils. 130 references.

Stewart, G. A.
1956 The soils of the Katherine-Darwin Region, Northern Territory. C.S.I.R.O. Soil Publication 6.
Map scale: 1/500,000. 19 soil associations. Text contains soil descriptions and chemical and physical analyses.

Stewart, J. H.
1962 Land classification of the agricultural zone. *In* Land and water resources of Tripolitania. U.S. AID, Tripoli.
Scale: 1/100,000. 19 sheets, 6 soils and land types. Very general. Covers coastal zone of Tripolitania.

Storie, R. E.
1953 Preliminary study of Bolivian soils. Soil Science Society of America, Proceedings 17(2):128-131.
Scale: 1/9,000,000. 11 soil regions. Very general descriptions.

Storie, R. E. and F. Harradine
1958 Soils of California. Soil Science 85(4):207-227.
Discusses the principal soil formers of California, namely climate, parent material, time, physiography, and vegetation; has maps of rainfall zones, soil parent materials, physiography, vegetation types, broad soil zones, and soil regions of the state. Includes profile descriptions of 50

dominant soil types listed in the 12 soil regions of California.

Storie, R. E. and W. W. Weir
1953 Generalized soil map of California. University of California, College of Agriculture, Agricultural Experiment Station, Manual 6. 47 p.
Scale: 1/1,200,000. Map shows 4 major topographic divisions and 18 mapping categories.

Stuart, D. M., M. A. Fosberg, and G. C. Lewis
1961 Caliche in southwestern Idaho. Soil Science Society of America, Proceedings 25:132-135.
Silicates help cement caliche.

Sudan Geological Survey, Khartoum
1958- Soil Map of Talodi   1958
1959 Soil Map of Rashad   1958
       Soil Map of Er Rahad   1959
       Soil Map of Umm Ruwaba   1959
Scale 1/100,000 (1959 series), 1/250,000 (1958 series). Mainly geologic relations.

Tadmor, N. H., G. Orshan, and E. Rawitz
1962 Habitat analysis in the Negev Desert of Israel. Research Council of Israel, Bulletin, Section D, Botany, 11(3):148-173.
Osmotic types were distinguished: *(A)* chloride absorbing xerohalophytes. *(B)* chloride absorbing hydrohalophytes, *(C)* xerohalophytes absorbing other salts than chlorides, *(D)* nonhalophytic xerophytes.

Talati, N. R., K. M. Mehta, and C. M. Mathur
1959 Importance of soil tests in developing canal irrigation with special reference to commanded area of Rajasthan. Indian Society of Soil Science, Journal 7:177-186.
Percolation rate determined on packed soil in the laboratory was fairly indicative of drainage conditions in the field. In the absence of high amounts of soluble salts, exchangeable Na was correlated with soil texture. The rate of percolation in saline soils (pH greater than 8.5) was markedly reduced where exchangeable Na exceeded 9% of the cation-exchange capacity.

Tamhane, V. A.
1952 Soils of the Rajputana and Sind deserts. National Institute of Sciences of India, Bulletin 1:254-259, 266-268.
One soil from central Rajputana contained about 96% sand and 2.4% clay; the other about 46% sand and 30.7% clay. Three soils from Sind contained 19.7, 86.8, and 19.7 of sand, and 6.0, 10.6, and 24.2% clay respectively. A further soil from Sind contained 2.4% soluble salts comprising 0.96% Na_2SO_4, 0.62% $CaSO_4$, 0.43% NaCl, 0.33% mg SO_4, 0.03% $CaCO_3$, and 0.01% Na_2CO_3.

Taylor, S. A.
1960 Principles of dry land crop management in arid and semi-arid zones. *In* Plant-water relationships in arid and semi-arid conditions, Reviews of research. Unesco, Paris. Arid Zone Research 15:192-204.
Principles of plant-soil water relationships.

1962 The influence of temperature upon the transfer of water in soil systems. Landbouwhogeschool en de Opzoekingsstations van de Staat te Gent, Mededelingen 27(2):535-551.
Temperature can now be included in the water flow equation.

Taylor, S. A., D. D. Evans, and W. D. Kemper
1961 Evaluating soil water. Utah Agricultural Experiment Station, Bulletin 426.
Concentration of water in soil or soil moisture tension should be estimated from measurement of the other only when approximate estimates are adequate. The errors are large.

Teakle, L. J. H.
1938 Soil salinity in Western Australia. Department of Agriculture of Western Australia, Journal, 2nd ser., 15(4):434-452.
Soil map scale of 1/2,217,600. Area southwest of Perth.

1950 Red and brown hardpan soils of Western Australia. Australian Institute of Agricultural Science, Journal 16(1):15-17.
The hypothesis is presented that the red and brown hardpan soils of Western Australia, found at depths of 6 inches to 3 feet, in layers 30-40 feet thick, are forming on the "billy" or silicified layer, exposed by the truncation of a laterite profile. The hypothesis was suggested by two observations: the character of the soils is not in keeping with present arid climatic factors, and the soils have certain features in common with soils in the mulga (*Acacia aneura*) country of southwest Queensland, where the upper portions of the old laterite formation have been removed. The hardpan coloring is due to iron oxides.

Thesiger, W.
1951 Map to accompany Bagnold's article (q.v.): Sand formations in southern Arabia. Geographical Journal 117:78-86.
Scale: 1/250,000. Shows dunes. Area between 51° 45'-60° 00' E and 19° 30' - 25° 30' N.

Thorne, D. W. and H. B. Peterson
1950 Irrigated soils, their fertility and management. The Blakiston Co., Inc. New York. 288 p.
A textbook.

Thornton, H. G.
1953 Some problems presented by the microbiology of arid soils. *In* Desert Research, Proceedings, International symposium held in Jerusalem, May 7-14, 1952, sponsored by the Research Council of Israel and Unesco. Research Council of Israel, Special Publication 2:295-301.
The technical difficulties of estimating the number of microorganisms in arid soils are briefly discussed and the need for the study of their distribution and adaptation under adverse conditions is stressed. Some contradictory finds on the effects of saline and alkali conditions on the microflora are briefly dealt with.

Thorp, J. and K. C. Hou
1935 Generalized soil map of parts of northern and northwestern China. National Geological Survey of China, Soil Bulletin 2.
Scale: 1/2,500,000. Shows genetic soil groups.

Tkatchenko, B.
1951 Les sol solontchakoïdes de la Somalie française. Agronomie Tropicale 6:341-369.
(Solonchak-like soils of French Somaliland)
In these soils both Na and Mg are in excess in exchangeable form. Obstacles to their utilization for market-garden crops include deficiency of organic matter, nonavailability of nutrients, poor physical conditions and high mineral

content of available irrigation water as well as its insufficient quantity. Cultivation of date palms is suggested as a practicable alternative.

Tolchel'nikov, Yu. S.
1960 "Mineral' nye Korni" v pochvakh pustyn'. Priroda 10:84-85. Referativny Zhurnal, Biologiya, 1961, no. 11G160.
("Mineral roots" in desert soils)
Distinctive new formations are formed in the upper layers of sandy soils in the Kara-Kum desert (Turkmeniya SSR). The new formations develop in place of the roots of bushes. The basic material of "mineral roots" consists of gypsum, calcium carbonate, and chlorides. The organic remnants of the roots make up only 25%.

Troitskaya, E. N.
1961 Sesonnye izmeneniya vodoroslei nekotorkh pustynnykh rastitel' nykh formatsii. p. 53-56. *In* Voprosy biologii i kravoi meditsiny. Tashkent. Referativnyi Zhurnal, Biologiva, 1963, no. 13V8.
(Seasonal changes in algae of some desert formations)
Blue-green algae were more significant in summer, and green algae were less significant. There were almost no diatomaceous algae. In fall most of the cells were green algae. Quantitative determination of algae was made by the Winogradskii method, as modified by Stein. Quantitative composition in water cultures was determined in a Danilov medium with overgrowth sprouting on glass. Seasonal periodicity of quantitative and qualitative composition appeared during the development of the algae. Maximum algal development occurred in spring. Green and diatomaceous algae were basic types and blue-green algae were rarely found in spring.

Tunis. Ecole Supérieure d'Agriculture, Laboratoire Agronomique
1955 Carte pédologique: Gabesi-Sidi-Chemmakh (d'après J. Gelpe). Service Botanique et Agronomique de Tunisie, Annales 28.
(Soil map: Gabesi-Sidi-Chemmakh [after J. Gelpe])
Scale: 1/1,000,000. Shows saline alkali soils, gypsum soils, caliche soils, etc.

Tyurin, I. V. *et al.,* eds.
1959 Soil survey, a guide to field investigations and mapping of soils (translated title). Akademiya Nauk S.S.S.R., Pochvennyi Institut im. V. V. Dokuchaeva. (Issued in translation, 1965, by Israel Program for Scientific Translation)
The book was designed as a scientific and methodological manual generalizing the principles, rational forms, and working techniques of soils mapping that have been developed in the U.S.S.R. Part one deals with the general methods and techniques of soil mapping, while part two discusses features and methods of mapping for special purposes.

Unesco
1961 Salinity problems in the arid zones, Proceedings of the Teheran symposium. Unesco, Paris. Arid Zone Research 14. 395 p.

United Nations
1949 Pakistan: soils. United Nations Presentation #1250.
Scale: 1/10,000,000. 8 soils based on position/color, texture, and genesis.

United Nations Special Fund
1961a Soil maps of the non-cultivated lands. UAR High Dam Soil Survey Project, United Nations Special Fund, New York.
Scale: 1/50,000. Sheets for Ismaeliya-Salhiya, Suez-Ismaeliya, Salhiya-Port Said, Rosetta East, El Amiriya, Qarra-Damietta, Hamid-Baltim. A semidetailed survey for irrigation potential.

1961b Soil map of Farah Valley. FAO/UNSF Cooperative Project, Ministry of Agriculture, Government of Afghanistan.
Scale: 1/800,000. Map on file in World Soil Resources Office, FAO, Rome.

U. S. Agency for International Development
1961 Soil survey reconnaissance map: Lower Giuba River. Inter-River Economic Exploration of the Somali Republic. 14 p.
Scale not given but small. 6 land classes, 11 soils by associations and complexes. Text has detailed soil description and sections on climate and vegetation.

U. S. Army Engineer Waterways Experiment Station
1959 A technique for preparing desert terrain analogs. Handbook. Technical Report 3-506.
Scale: 1/4,700,000. Egyptian section of the northeast African desert. Soil types: 4 soil-rock associations and 8 soil associations. Contains map of soil consistency. Compares area to Yuma, Arizona.

1960 The unified soil classification system. Rev. Technical Memorandum 3-357. Vol. 1. Vicksburg, Mississippi.

1963 Forecasting trafficability of soils. Technical Memorandum 3-331, Report 6(1), 219 p.; (2), 121 p.
Development of techniques for analyzing and interpreting vertical aerial photographs for trafficability purposes based on data collected over several years from 33 humid climate and 2 arid-climate states.

U. S. Department of Agriculture
1962 A bibliography of publications in the field of saline and sodic soils through 1961. Agricultural Research 41-80, 47 p.
Papers are grouped under the following main headings: the occurrence, development, and properties of salt-affected soils; the effects of salt and sodium on plants; tolerance of crops to salts and to sodic soils; evaluating soils for crop production with reference to salinity and sodium; management practices for saline and sodic soils; reclamation of saline and sodic soils; and water quality.

U. S. Department of Agriculture, Soil Conservation Service
1963 List of soil survey reports. Washington, D. C.
Lists soil survey reports by state, county or area, and year. No author, title, or scale.

1964 General soil map of the United States (Coterminous 48 states.) Experimental, based on 7th Approximation. Hyattsville, Maryland.
Scale: 1/20,000,000. Shows soil orders of the new classification along with approximate equivalents in Great Soil Groups. Generalized by D. K. Gallup from unpublished experimental soil map of June, 1964, at a scale of 1/5,000,000.

U. S. Department of Agriculture, Soil Conservation Service, Soil Survey Staff
1960 Soil classification, comprehensive system, 7th approximation. 265 p.

——— 1962 Un sistema comprensible de clasificación de suelos, 7ª approximación. Translated from the English by P. H. Etchevehere. Instituto Nacional de Tecnología Agropecuaria, República Argentina.

U. S. Salinity Laboratory
1954 Diagnosis and improvement of saline and alkali soils. U. S. Department of Agriculture, Handbook 60.

Valentine, K. A. and J. J. Norris
1964 A comparative study of soils of selected creosote bush sites in southern New Mexico. Journal of Range Management 17(1):23-32.
The physical and chemical properties of soils from 4 sites and subsites were determined along with black grama seedling emergence from pot tests of the soils. The soils generally were similar, with one exception, and are capable of supporting establishment and growth of climax dominant grasses.

van Bavel, C. H., L. J. Fritschen, and R. J. Reginato
1963 Surface energy balance in arid lands agriculture 1960-1961. U. S. Department of Agriculture, Production Research Report 76. 46 p.
Evaporation, moisture, and drying of soil.

Vandecaveye, S. C. and C. D. Moodie
1942 Occurrence and activity of *Azotobacter* in semi-arid soils in Washington. Soil Science Society of America, Proceedings 7:229-236.
Azotobacter were dominant in irrigated soils with rainfall less than 10 inches annually, frequent in nonirrigated soils with rainfall 15 to 20 inches, and rare in non-irrigated soils with less than 10 inches of rainfall.

van der Merwe, C. R.
1941 Soil groups and sub-groups of South Africa. South Africa Department of Agriculture, Science Bulletin 231 (Chemical Series 165). 316 p. Accompanied by Soil map of South Africa, scale 1/5,000,000.
Representative profiles are described in detail and data from mechanical analyses and from chemical analyses of the whole soil and of the colloid are presented for each horizon. Soils that dominate extensive areas include: *(1)* Typical Desert soils, *(2)* Sandy Soils of the Kalahari Desert, both with and without an indurated "limestone" horizon, *(3)* Solonetzic or Solonetz-like soils, *(4)* Gley-like Podzolic Soils, *(5)* Podzolic Soils, commonly truncated, of the winter-rainfall areas, *(6)* Unleached Subtropical Soils, including Brown Forest Soils and Subtropical Black Clays that resemble the Indian "Regur" Soils, *(7)* both Red and Yellow Lateritic Soils, *(8)* Ferruginous Lateritic Soils, both grey and brown, having ferruginous hardpans suggestive of Ground-Water Lateritic Soils, *(9)* Lithological Types, including black clays from basic igneous rocks, and sandy littoral and eolian deposits. Map shows zonal, intrazonal, and azonal soils.

——— 1954a The soils of the desert and arid regions of South Africa. Interafrican Soil Conference, 2nd, Leopold-ville, Proceedings 2:827-834.
The region consists of the major part of the Cape Province, except for narrow coastal fringes. The soil parent materials, surface relief, and rainfall vary considerably; but the active soil-forming factors are fairly uniform, because the limited amount of rain in the summer is minimized by the extremely high evaporation and the growth of the vegetation is adversely affected thereby. The soils are therefore deficient in organic matter and chemical decomposition plays a secondary part in their formation. They are poorly developed and of a skeletal nature. The clay minerals also indicate a low degree of weathering. The chief soil-forming factor is the diurnal fluctuation in temperature. A very peculiar feature characterizing the great diversity of the soils in this region is the "desert pavement" ranging from white quartz fragments to almost black water-worn pebbles and stones. All the soils have a crust. Solonchak and solonetzic soils in this region are intrazonal.

——— 1954b Kalahari and Sahara sandy soils. International Congress of Soil Science, 5th, Leopoldville, Transactions 4:117-122.
A review with 7 references of these desert soils developed under fairly constant temperatures with rainfall ranging from 6 to 60 inches. With increasing rainfall there is a gradual change in soil color from brick-red through yellow and grey to an ultimate white, accompanied by a decrease in pH and colloidal material. General belief that soil is of windblown origin, laid down during arid period. Kalahari soils are reddish brown to brick-red friable sand, fairly well fixed by grass and brush roots. Little development, neutral to alkaline. Northern Kalahari soils (humid tropics) are arid. Soils are deep.

van der Merwe, C. R. and H. Heystek
1955 Clay minerals of South African soil groups. III: Soils of the desert and adjoining semiarid regions. Soil Science 80:497-494.
Clay minerals of Kalahari sand on limestone and solonetzic soils are mainly illite and montmorillonite. The soils were developed mainly from sedimentary rocks under a summer rainfall of 5.2 inches a year and the clay minerals of the parent material have not decomposed.

Vargues, H.
1963 Etude microbiologique de quelques sols sahariens en relation avec la présence d' *Anabasis aretioides* Coss. et Moq. *In* Desert Research, Proceedings of the international symposium held in Jerusalem, May 7-14, 1952, sponsored by the Research Council of Israel and Unesco. Research Council of Israel, Special Publication 2:318-324.
(Microbiological study of some soils in the Sahara with respect to the presence of *Anabasis aretioides* Coss. and Moq.)
Anabasis is a desert plant capable of accumulating large amounts of sand in its vegetative organs. Microbiological tests showed that the soil taken from the rhizosphere of the plant contained much higher bacterial numbers and exhibited stronger N fixation and nitrification than adjacent desert soils.

Veenenbos, J. S.
1963 Soil associations map of United Arab Republic-Egypt. (First and Second Drafts.) FAO, Rome. Scale: 1/2,000,000. Broad groups of soils.

Viets, F. G., Jr.
1961 Zinc deficiency of field and vegetable crops in the west. U. S. Department of Agriculture, Leaflet 495.
Describes deficiency symptoms and methods of control. Zn deficiency in lima beans, soybeans, field beans, hops, onions, corn, potatoes, and castorbeans shown.

Vink, A. P. A.
 1963 Planning of soil surveys in land development. International Institute for Land Reclamation and Development, Wageningen, Publication 10.
Principles involved in planning and executing soil surveys are discussed. Various aspects of the use of aerial photographs in soil surveys are presented. Advantages and disadvantages of different kinds of surveys, scale, and base maps are noted, and the interpretation of soil surveys for practical purposes is described.

Vinogradov, B. V.
 1961 Vegetation as an indicator in the interpretation of aerial photographs of desert landscapes in western Turkmenia (translated title). Izvyestiya Vsesoyuznogo Geografocheskogo Obshchestva. (Issued in translation by Israel Program for Scientific Translations, Jerusalem. Also cited as TT 65-50064)
The method described is called "botanico-geographical interpretation." An aerial photograph of a stony-sandy desert of western Turkmenia, fringed by solonchak, is used as a sample. Initially, one interprets the vegetation, then, with the help of direct or indirect indexes provided by plant indicators, one interprets the soils and hydro-geological conditions. By comparison of soil-geobotanical complexes, it is possible to interpret the direction of flow and the areas of upwelling of the ground water as well as the most recent tectonic ruptures and the character of the rocks in contact.

Volobuev, V. R.
 1963 Ekologiya pochv. Akademii Nauk Azerbaidzhan-skoi S.S.R., Baku. (Ecology of soils. Issued in translation by Israel Program for Scientific Translations, Jerusalem, 1964, 264 p.)
Noncultivated soils of sierozem zone have reduced microbiological activity, especially in nitrification.

Waksman, S. A.
 1936 Humus, origin, chemical composition and importance in nature. Williams and Wilkins Co., Baltimore, Maryland.

Warne, J. E., Jr. and B. D. Sergent
 1962 Application of soil mechanics theory to foundations investigations in the arid Southwest. *In* Symposium on geology as applied to highway engineering, 13th, Phoenix, Proceedings p. 26-53.
Many arid region soils appear firm and nonplastic when dry, but show wide variation in density and porosity, and a high degree of plasticity when wet.

Warren, A
 1964 The dunes of Kordofan. Hunting Group Reviews 3:5-9.
An account of the history and formation of the dunes in relation to climatic fluctuations during various geological periods. Their forms, size-distribution pattern, and the sorting and shape characteristics of the sand are described.

West, B.
 1955 Report of the soil survey and land classification, Dujaila Project. Government of Iraq, Ministry of Agriculture.
Scale: 1/20,000.

Western Regional Soil Survey Work Group
 1964 Soils of the western United States. Washington State University, Agricultural Experiment Station.
Map scale: 1/25,000,000.

Wetselaar, R. and M. J. T. Norman
 1960 Soil and crop nitrogen at Katherine, N. T. C.S.I.R.O. Division Land Research and Regional Survey, Technical Paper 10.
Results of four years of study are summarized.

Whalley, W. C. R.
 1961 Cathodic protection in desert soils. Corrosion 17(12):75-81.
Special conditions contributing to severe corrosion of buried pipe lines in arid desert soils of Syria and Iraq. In unfavorable conditions general polarization of pipe surfaces may be very difficult unless pipe has first-class coating surrounded by substantial thickness of soil.

Whitney, R. S. and M. Peech
 1952 Ion activities of sodium clay suspensions. Soil Science Society of America, Proceedings 16:117-122.
A study was made of dissociation and hydrolysis of sodium clay as a function of the degree of sodium saturation of the clay and the concentration of NaCl in the clay suspension.

Wilcox, L. V.
 1955 Classification and use of irrigation waters. U. S. Department of Agriculture, Circular 969.
A system for evaluating the salt, sodium, and boron hazard of irrigation water when applied to soils.

Wilcox, L. V. and W. F. Resch
 1963 Salt balance and leaching requirement in irrigated lands. U. S. Department of Agriculture, Agricultural Research Service, Technical Bulletin 1920.
A comparison of methods for calculating leaching requirement, using data for the Rio Grande in New Mexico.

Wilcoxon, J. A.
 1962 The relationship between sand ripples and wind velocity in a dune area. Compass 39(2):65-76.

Woodruff, N. P. and F. H. Siddoway
 1965 A wind erosion equation. Soil Science Society of America, Proceedings 29:602-608.
Aggregates less than 0.84 mm in diameter are more erodible. 5 factors in equation by Chepil: soil erodibility, soil range roughness, climate, field length, and vegetative cover.

Worrall, G. A.
 1957 Features of some semi-arid soils in the district of Khartoum, Sudan. I: The high-level dark clays. II: The red sand-ironstone soils. Journal of Soil Science 8:193-217.
I. Soil is strongly alkaline. Bicarbonate salts in surface, with sulfates and chlorides at 2 or 3 feet. Contains calcareous concretions and gypsum "curves." Proposes name of "Solonized Sub-tropical Black Earths."
II. Soils are related to Goz sands of western Sudan.

 1959 The Butana grass patterns. Journal of Soil Science 10:35-53.
Repeating bands of vegetation in the Butana region of the Sudan consist entirely of grasses and herbs and lie on gentle slopes of about 1 in 200; there is no measureable difference in elevation between the grasses and bare areas. Slopes of less than 1 in 500 have no pattern. There are differences in soil surface, the bare areas being smooth and the grassed areas broken by cracks and potholes. The origin of the patterns appears to be related to water supply, topography, and soil, but not to wind.

Worrall, G. A.

1961   A brief account of the soils of the Sudan. African Soils 6(1):82.
Scale: 1/5,500,000. 24 soils. Text has general soil descriptions.

Wright, C. S.

1961   Informe trimestral del asesor en suelos, Enero—Febrero—Marzo, 1961. Food and Agriculture Organization, Santiago, Chile.
(Quarterly report of the soils expert, January, February, March, 1961)
Soils and vegetation of Tarapaca Province. 3 ecological zones: coastal and plain, precordilleran, and altiplano.

Wright, M. J.

1959   A soil survey of the township area of Alice Springs, N. T. C.S.I.R.O. Division of Soils, Divisional Report 2/59. 21 p.

Wright, R. L.

1962   Land forms and soils in the Avon valley, near York, Western Australia. Royal Society of Western Australia, Journal 45:51-64.
The relationships between soil and erosional and depositional surfaces are complex. Most of the soils are the result of geomorphologically relatively recent episodes. Young soils can occur on geomorphologically old sites that have been stripped of an earlier soil. Sites inherited from the same stage of landscape evolution may have different soils and similar soils may occur on sites relating to different geomorphological stages.

1964   Land systems survey of the Nagarparkar peninsula, Pakistan. Arid Zone [Newsletter] 25:5-13.
The erosional and nine depositional land systems are defined. Granite skeletal soils, gravelly slopes, and sandy and clayey plains occupy most of the area.

Yaalon, D. H.

1954   Physico-chemical relationships of $CaCO_3$, pH, and CO_2 in calcareous soils. International Congress of Soil Science, 5th, Leopoldville, Transactions 2:356-363.
Arid soils are characterized by a high content of calcareous material. The physico-chemical equilibria governing the solubility of $Ca CO_3$ in water in pure systems, and in the presence of neutral salts, CO_3 and Ca ions, and $CaSO_4$ are described. These equilibria are directly applicable to the soil-$CaCO_3$ system. The possible extreme values of pH in calcareous soils are shown graphically.

1963   On the origin and accumulation of salts in groundwater and in soils of Israel. Research Council of Israel, Bulletin, Jerusalem ser., 11G(3):105-131.
The contribution of weathering to the process of salinization is small, and the fossil salt accumulations is local; oceanogenic airborne salts are the main source of soluble salts in coastal areas. The annual accession of airborne salts for the whole country is estimated at 100,000 tons NaCl.

1964   The concentration of ammonia and nitrate in rain water over Israel in relation to environmental factors. Tellus 16:200-204.
The concentration of NH_4 in monthly composite rainwater samples from seven stations in Israel depended markedly on soil temperature. The mean concentration during the cool winter months was 0.17 e. p. m. while in spring it rose at least four times higher. Total seasonal washout by rain ranged from 4 to over 20 kg/ha NH_4-N according to rainfall, i. e. an average of 40 g/ha NH_4-N for each mm of rain.

Yakubov, T. F.

1959   New contributions to the study and control of wind erosion of soils. I: Mechanism and dynamics of wind erosion. Soviet Soil Science 1959 (7): 792-800.
Factors governing initiation and intensity of wind erosion.

Yakubov, T. F. and R. Ye. Bespalova

1961   Soil-formation processes during the invasion of sands by plants in the northern deserts of the Caspian region. Soviet Soil Science 1961 (6): 651-658.
As the sands become invaded by plants, the content of fines in the soils increases, especially that of silt and clay particles, and the humus content increases. As the sands become invaded and soil formation processes develop, their water-physical properties also change.

Yang Tien-wei and C. H. Lowe, Jr.

1956   Correlation of major vegetation climaxes with soil characteristics in the Sonoran desert. Science 123(3196):542.
From analysis of pertinent soil characteristics and their correlation with climax vegetation types of the Sonoran Desert, it is concluded that here specifically different soil attributes characterize, and are intimately associated with, distinctly different and major climax vegetation types existing under the same macroclimate. Available soil moisture is the main determinant.

Yegorov, V. V.

1961   Sodium carbonate salinization of soils in southern Sin'tszyan (Sinkiang). Soviet Soil Science 1961 (5):479-487.
Discusses soils, water, and geology (very generally) of southern Sinkiang on edge of Takla-Makan Desert, particularly the Tarimskiy Basin, with emphasis on mode of accumulation and reclamation of saline soils in irrigated oases of the area.

Youngs, F. O.

1948   Reconnaissance land classification on the Arghandab Valley. FAO, Rome.
Scale: 1/126,720. Shows land types classified by suitability for agriculture. Text has general soil description. Area is near Kandahar.

Zamora, C.

1958a   Informe del estudio de los suelos de la zona de Sicuani y Yanaoca-Langui. Servicio Cooperativo Interamericano de Producción de Alimentos, Lima, Peru.
(Report of soil studies of Sicuani and Yanaoca-Langui)
Southern Cuzco Province.

1958b   Informe del estudio de los suelos de Ilave (Puno). Servicio Cooperativo Interamericano de Producción de Alimentos. Lima, Peru.
(Report of soil studies on the Ilave zone (Puno)
Area is in Puno Province.

1958c   Informe del estudio de los suelos de la zona de Nuñoa. Servicio Cooperativo Interamericano de Producción de Alimentos, Lima, Peru.
(Report on soil studies on the Nuñoa zone)
Area is in Puno Province.

Zamora, C.
 1958*d* Informe del estudio de los suelos del Valle de Moquegua. Servicio Cooperativo Interamericano de Producción de Alimentos. Lima, Peru.
 (Report of soil studies on the Moquegua Valley)
 Area is in Moquegua Province.

———

 1961 Informe del estudio de suelos de la sección Tambo Grande de la irrigación del Quiróz, Piura. Servicio Cooperativo Interamericano de Producción de Altimentos, Lima, Peru.

(Report on soils studies of the Tambo Grande section of the irrigated area of Quiroz, Piura)
Area is in Piura Province.

Zavaleta, A. G.
 1960 Estudio de suelos Viña Vieja—San José—La Estrella—San Regis, del Valle de Chincha. Universidad Agraria, Lima, Peru, Archives.
 (Study of soils of Viña Vieja—San José—La Estrella—San Regis, of the Chincha Valley)
 Area is in Puno Province.

VEGETATION
OF DESERT ENVIRONMENTS

WILLIAM G. McGINNIES
Office of Arid Lands Studies,
University of Arizona

INTRODUCTION

1. Objective

The objective of this chapter is to review and evaluate existing information and research on the vegetation of the deserts of the world, to ascertain notable deficiencies, and to propose possible future research and improvements to the general body of knowledge of desert vegetation.

I hope that this effort will suggest to scientists and students some advantageous avenues for future work, and that it will encourage the efforts of foundations and agencies to sponsor research. In this way, perhaps the chapter can serve to improve our knowledge of the vegetation of arid lands and the physical and natural processes affecting that vegetation.

2. Scope

In the present discussion, all major deserts classified *E* (extremely arid) and *A* (arid) on Meigs' 1952 homoclimatic maps are considered, but time did not permit treatment of the small, isolated desert areas such as that in eastern Brazil, arid Madagascar, and the Venezuelan coast and neighboring islands.

Items considered to be of major importance for the purposes of this inventory are: *(1)* physiognomy of major species; *(2)* relative abundance of trees, shrubs, succulents, herbs, grasses; *(3)* seasonal variation in composition, including year-long or seasonal duration of all elements of the vegetation; *(4)* seasonal aspects, including changes in structure (e.g., dropping leaves) or color; *(5)* effect of plants on the habitat (e.g., stabilization of sand); *(6)* resistance to unfavorable conditions such as drought, fire, pests, and herbicides; *(7)* economic uses, such as for food, fiber, forage, fuel, and medicines. All of this information was not available or accessible for every area, but the subjects were investigated insofar as information could be obtained.

For each desert area an attempt is first made to describe the overall plant community context. These general descriptions *(1)* permit the publications (especially those on specific aspects of vegetation or on important species) to be cited and discussed against a coherent conceptual context, even for those desert areas for which the literature cited is minimal or spotty, *(2)* permit readers with specific interests and some knowledge of arid areas to appraise more readily the relevance of the works to their own tasks without having to examine the publications themselves, and *(3)* briefly disclose some similarities and differences between the habitats and flora of various desert areas, facilitating selection of related works for interim use in some instances where gaps in research and literature exist.

Readers may further establish their possible interest in works on various species named herein by referring to p. 473, Species Summary, which gives additional data on the species and names publications that discuss them further.

The general descriptions of plant communities that introduce the discussions of the state of knowledge for each desert area in part have been adapted from, and in cases compare and synthesize, the best available descriptions of the vegetation of the areas.

The treatment of vegetation has largely been restricted to its structural characteristics. Complete plant descriptions have not been made, but an attempt has been made to sketch general conditions and identify the important types of vegetation. Consideration of taxonomy has been limited to those phases essential for plant identification. Works on economic uses of plants have been considered as they involve native plants, but the subjects of grazing use or the practice of forestry have not been treated except as incidental to investigating the production or destruction of native plants.

Research not relating to form, structure, or distribution of plants has not been treated in this chapter. Work on such physiological processes as photosynthesis, assimilation, transpiration, flowering, fruiting, and water requirements, which have an important bearing on the life history of plants, has been discussed only insofar as it relates directly to growth, survival, and distribution of plants.

Especially in the discussions of individual desert areas, references have been made to works appearing in the Pertinent Publications list at the end of the chapter, which combines in one alphabetical sequence both an annotated bibliography and a more inclusive reference list. Those works which it has been possible to determine are of special importance, interest, or relevance to this study are annotated. Many other competent and best-available works are listed without annotation; lack of annotation should not be construed as necessarily indicating a less important publication.

Of the numerous works initially considered many were dismissed as unimportant, between 2000 and 2500 were checked further for possible use, and approximately 1050 are included in the final Pertinent Publications list.

3. Relation to Other Chapters

It is difficult to divorce a discussion of vegetation entirely from climate because major patterns of vegetation are to a great extent a response to climate, but an attempt has been made in this chapter to concentrate on investigations of vegetation itself, leaving the consideration of climate to the chapter by C. H. Reitan and C. R. Green. It should be noted, however, that information on such items as precipitation, temperature, and evapotranspiration is essential to understanding the distribution of plants; the chapter on weather and climate should be consulted by readers interested in vegetation.

Consideration of soils is also pertinent to an understanding of plant growth and distribution; therefore discussions of soils and plants cannot be completely divorced. Soil conditions influence the local distribution of species and are interrelated with plant distribution over wider areas. Not only do soil conditions influence vegetation, but vegetation of the past has been a factor in determining the type of soil developed from the parent material. Soils and soil management affect plants in other ways; such efforts as the control of drifting sands, stabilization of watercourses, reclamation of saline areas, and production of forage, food, and fiber involve plant-soil relationships. In some cases the toxicity of plants is determined by soil conditions, and certain plants reflect and can be used as indicators of various soil conditions. The reader is referred to the chapter on surface materials by H. E. Dregne for further information.

4. Acknowledgments

A great many people have given substantial assistance during the preparation of this manuscript. To all of them I wish to express my hearty thanks and to absolve them all of responsibility for any errors, omissions, or misstatements; I assume full accountability for these categories. Among those who deserve particular credit are Hugo Boyko, President, World Academy of Art and Science; Arturo Burkart, Director, Instituto de Botánica Darwinion; Clifford S. Christian, Member of the Executive, and Ray A. Perry, both of C.S.I.R.O., Australia; Louis Emberger, Director, Centre d'Etudes Phytosociologiques et Ecologiques, Montpellier; Antonio J. Prego, Instituto Nacional de Tecnología Agropecuaria, Argentina; all of whom served as consultants. Full use has been made of the comments by these consultants, who have reviewed parts of this manuscript treating their specialties. In some cases their comments have been subsumed in the text, and in other cases statements have been credited to the consultant. To save unnecessary repetition and awkwardness, the statements are credited by name ("Consultant X informs me...") without stating that the information was furnished in a personal communication.

I also want to thank Mr. Kirby B. Payne of the National Agricultural Library and his staff, who were exceptionally helpful in finding obscure reference material, and those members of the library staff of the University of Arizona who were so cooperative in making the facilities of the library available. Special thanks are due to Charles T. Mason, Professor of Botany and Curator of the Herbarium at the University of Arizona, for his cheerful help with many problems relating to plant nomenclature.

I also would like to recognize the help provided by the staff of U. S. Army Natick Laboratories, particularly that of Dr. Lester W. Trueblood and Dr. William C. Robison. Dr. Peveril Meigs, formerly of that organization, also provided valuable information and encouragement. Dr. Wesley Keller of the Agricultural Research Service, U.S.D.A., graciously loaned useful Russian maps and obtained special reports from the National Archives.

It is impossible to express adequately my thanks to those who worked with me in generating this manuscript: to Patricia Paylore who was untiring in her efforts to obtain references and verify citations; to Bram Goldman for his extensive editorial assistance; to James Meadows, Jr., for his help in writing the text; and to members of the secretarial staff of the Office of Arid Lands Studies, who spent long hours struggling with unfamiliar terms, checking scientific names, and typing and retyping the text. Among these, special mention should go to Raymond W. Christian (graduate assistant, 1964-1965) and to Mrs. Elizabeth J. Wall, both of whom assisted with bibliographical tasks.

DISCUSSION OF STATE OF KNOWLEDGE

A. SOURCES OF INFORMATION

Voluminous information on the vegetation of the deserts of the world is available in several forms and from myriad sources. Forms include published and unpublished papers and reports, plant specimens themselves in herbaria and botanical gardens, data collected for past projects and ongoing research, and oral communication of experience by living scientists and students. The present chapter lists, by name, important authorities, libraries, and herbaria.

The material used in this chapter was obtained from a variety of sources. I had accumulated a great deal of pertinent reference material, especially for the Americas, prior to the initiation of this study. Lists of additional references were obtained from Unesco publications and published bibliographies. The second step was to review material in major pertinent abstracting journals such as *Biological Abstracts, Herbage Abstracts,* and *Weed Abstracts.* As titles were accumulated the more promising ones were checked by reference to the original, so far as this was possible. Many of these works were available at the University of Arizona, others were obtained by means of library loans, and microfilm and Xerox copies. Two weeks were spent in further review at the Library of Congress and the National Agricultural Library.

The rough draft text prepared from this material was submitted to knowledgeable consultants for review, and their comments and suggestions were used in preparation of the final text.

Spelling of plant names is in accordance with the *Index Kewensis* (1895-). Synonomy was also checked against the *Index Kewensis* and by various consultants. Capitalization was eliminated for all species epithets in accordance with the procedure approved under International Rules of Botanical Nomenclature.

The outstanding single source of published information on the vegetation of the deserts of the world is Unesco's Arid Zone Research series. Many of the 28 numbers (published by mid-1967) included important information about desert flora. The more significant of these are listed below by Unesco number:

I. *Arid Zone Hydrology* contains description and maps by Peveril Meigs (1953) showing the world distribution of arid and semiarid homoclimates.

II. *Proceedings of the Ankara Symposium on Arid Zone Hydrology* includes a contribution by H. Boyko (1953), "Ecological Solutions of Some Hydrological and Hydro-Engineering Problems."

IV. *Utilization of Saline Water* reviews excellently the knowledge of plant growth under saline conditions, by H. E. Hayward (1956).

V. *Plant Ecology, Proceedings of the Montpellier Symposium* (1955a), as the title implies, is oriented entirely toward vegetation. Several of the papers in this number have been cited separately in the present chapter. The symposium included structural and physiological features of vegetation; climatic, ecoclimatic, and hydrologic influences on vegetation; soil and vegetation; and other factors.

VI. *Plant Ecology, Reviews of Research* (1955b) is devoted to a discussion of the research on plant ecology pertaining to arid and semiarid regions, and is based upon available published literature and other information accessible to Unesco. The ten regions covered by the various reports include most of the deserts of the world outside the Soviet Union and China. The papers in this number have also been cited separately in the present chapter.

IX. *Arid Zone Research, Guide Book to Research Data for Arid Zone Development* includes a discussion of physical, biological and human factors. The chapter on vegetation (McGinnies, 1957) is most directly applicable to the present chapter, but the other discussions of factors related to vegetation are also applicable to a lesser extent.

XI. *Climatology and Microclimatology, Proceedings of the Canberra Symposium* (1958) includes an article by L. Emberger on North Africa and "Mediterranean" Australia.

XIII. *Medicinal Plants of the Arid Zones* (1960*a*) includes two parts, the first oriented particularly to botanical aspects and the second to pharmacological aspects; it is a very well documented treatment giving a great deal of information on the plants and their chemical and medicinal characteristics.

XIV. *Salinity Problems in the Arid Zones, Proceedings of the Teheran Symposium* (1961*b*) devotes approximately 71 pages to the physiology of plants and animals (mostly plants) in relation to the consumption of saline water. Its scope includes the adaptation of plants to saline soils, physiology of plants consuming saline water, salt tolerance of plants, and physiological problems concerning crop production under saline conditions.

XV. *Plant-Water Relationships in Arid and Semi-Arid Conditions, Reviews of Research* (1960*b*) includes a comprehensive review of the subject. Each of the nine papers by authorities in the various fields presents a review of knowledge of the assigned topic and an extensive bibliography.

XVI. *Plant-Water Relationships in Arid and Semi-Arid Conditions, Proceedings of the Madrid Symposium* (1961*a*) covers five general topics: methodology of water relation study of plants, water sources for plants, water balance of plants under arid and semiarid conditions, drought and heat resistance of plants, and practical applications to agronomy. Under each topic specialists present several papers, referred to individually in the present text.

XVIII. *The Problems of the Arid Zone, Proceedings of the Paris Symposium* (1962) includes general information on the state of scientific knowledge of the arid lands. Three papers emphasize vegetation: "Salt Affected Soils and Plants" (Bernstein, 1962), "Plant Physiology and Arid Zone Research" (Evenari, 1962), and "Plant Ecology" (Emberger and Lemée, 1962).

XXI. *Bioclimatic Map of the Mediterranean Zone, Explanatory Notes* (1963) is a map with notes prepared by a joint committee of Unesco and the Food and Agriculture Organization. The map portion includes two larger sheets (scale 1:5,000,000) covering the Mediterranean region and western Asia, and three small sheets (scale 1:10,000,000) covering the western part of the United States, the west coast and southernmost part of South America, and the southern two-thirds of Australia. The classification of bioclimates worked out by the committee is used to compare aridity in these areas. The methodology is discussed in more detail in the present compendium, in the chapter on weather and climate by Reitan and Green.

XXV. *Methodology of Plant Eco-Physiology, Proceedings of the Montpellier Symposium* (1965) contains 526 pages of basic material relating to ecophysiology, and extensive bibliographies. The first part is devoted to the measurements of environmental factors, the second part to the physiology of plants considered individually, and the third part to the physiology of the plant cover.

XXVIII. *The Geography of Coastal Deserts* is a monographic treatment of the subject by Peveril Meigs (1966), with a good bibliography. The location and extent of coastal deserts are shown on a series of maps; while vegetation is not discussed extensively, what information is presented proves to be of considerable value.

The many FAO publications related to arid zones are also of great value. Some of these have been cited in the discussions of individual deserts later in this chapter, but the FAO releases cover such a wide field that it was not possible to list every one that might include some portion that would fall within the scope of this chapter.

Also, the following bibliographies which appeared in *Excerpta Botanica* during the period 1961-1966 were found to be particularly useful: on the ecology of the arid and semiarid regions of India, Gupta (1966); and on the phytosociology of Iraq, Hadac (1966) and Kreeb (1961), China, Hanelt (1964), Chile, Oberdorfer (1961), North Africa, Roussine and Sauvage (1961), and the Palestine area, Zohary (1959, 1961).

The general subject of desert vegetation has received attention from many scholarly and popular writers. Schimper (1898) included a 50-page chapter on the deserts. This classical work in German, the first systematic classification and map of the world vegetation, and the English translation published in 1903 are both still of interest. The third edition by Schimper and Faber (1935) was published in two volumes, and the chapter on the deserts was expanded to 165 pages. A different approach to the classification of desert plant communities was outlined by Warming (1909). Another general German publication covering desert vegetation is that of Rübel (1930) on the plant communities. This work includes an excellent colored map and well illustrated discussion of the deserts.

Outstanding also is the recent comprehensive treatment of tropical and subtropical vegetation by Walter (1964). In eight different chapters the author deals with the arid zones in general (chapter 7) and the different deserts in America, Africa, Asia, and Australia (chapters 8-14).

Among the publications dealing with deserts in general, several are worthy of mention here because of their discussions of vegetation. Pickwell's *Deserts* (1939) includes pictures and a discussion of desert vegetation. Ramaley's unpublished special report, *World Deserts,* (1952) has had limited distribution, but it should be noted because of excellent treatment of deserts in general. Cuny's *Les Deserts dans le Monde* (1961), and *La Vie dans les Deserts,* the French translation by Monod after Kachkarov and Korovine (1942), are both excellent sources of general information on desert vegetation. Two recent popular publications also include some useful background information. These are Brown (1963) *World of the Desert,* and Pond (1965) *Deserts—Silent Lands of the World.* Cloudsley-Thompson and Chadwick's *Life in Deserts* (1964) includes a good discussion of vegetation and its means of survival under desert conditions.

The characteristics of desert climates have been considered by Emberger (1942), who dealt with the philosophy of classification and prepared a map showing what he considered to be true deserts. Leighly (1952) reviewed the nature and distribution of dry climates on a broader basis, including past changes in climate. Bagnouls and Gaussen (1953, 1957) suggested a basis for classification of climates which was superseded later by the classification of the joint FAO-Unesco committee (Unesco, 1963).

The relation of vegetation to saline conditions has been reviewed both on a general basis and with reference to specific regional or local conditions. Hayward and Wadleigh (1949) and Hayward (1956) discussed plants growing under saline and alkaline soil conditions, and Bernstein (1962) brought information on the subject up to date in a review presented at the 1960 Unesco symposium on arid-zone problems. Chapman (1942, 1954)

reviewed the studies concerning plants growing under saline conditions, noted the effects of salt on terrestrial halophytes, and discussed the halophyte vegetation of the world. Later, he published a 392-page book on salt marshes and salt deserts of the world (Chapman, 1960).

The most recent work dealing with these problems is the book *Salinity and Aridity—New Approaches to Old Problems* (Boyko, 1966a), which appeared in 1966 as Vol. XVI in the series "Monographiae Biologicae"; it is mainly dedicated to the principles and successful experiments of plantgrowing in the presence of particularly high salt concentrations. This work, sponsored by the World Academy of Art and Science and partly also by Unesco, led to the Unesco/W. A. A. S. symposium in Rome, Italy, September 5-9, 1965. The proceedings of this international symposium are now in press as Vol. IV of the W. A. A. S. publication series.

B. DELINEATION OF DESERTS

The establishment of desert boundaries on the basis of climate is difficult, as is brought out in Reitan and Green's chapter (in this series) on weather and climate. Delineation on the basis of vegetation is equally difficult, because vegetation is influenced by local environmental conditions such as geology, topography, drainage, soil moisture and nutrition, protection, and shade. Other conditions that reduce climatic growth potentials by inhibition are instability, salinity, and lack of moisture. Successively advanced vegetation may be eliminated as a result of grazing, lumbering, burning, and other destructive influences commonly associated with man. In spite of these difficulties, local desert boundaries are usually based upon vegetation because of the lack of climatic data for much of the world.

From the standpoint of botany, the problem of delineating the desert has two parts. First we must decide what criteria should be used to define the limits of the desert; then we must express the limit in quantitative and qualitative terms.

If we decide that the boundary should be drawn where physical conditions permit no vascular plant growth, the task of defining the limits might be relatively easy, but if we accept a line below which conditions make plant growth very difficult, we are faced with a harder task because of differences of opinion as to what degree of difficulty should govern. It is this latter concept with which we are concerned in this assignment.

The characteristics of plant distribution do not allow us to use the presence or absence of certain species to mark the desert boundary. Most students of desert vegetation agree that species do not stop growing at the boundary line, but are rather more abundant and possibly more robust under more favorable conditions. Again, under a given set of climatic conditions, there may be a very great variety of local growing conditions because of differences in local landscape features, such as slight depressions, shade provided by rocks, exposure to humid winds, slopes that offer less exposure to direct light, and favorable soils that provide maximum reception and delivery of moisture to plants. All these and many other conditions influence growth (Kassas, 1953, 1955; Davis, 1953; Boyko, 1949b).

Consultant Emberger has commented that the great variety of ecological conditions owing to microgeographic differences is very important, and that the desert is in effect a mosaic of microbiotopes.

Scientists have long sought an empirical method of establishing boundary lines for vegetation communities or types: some measurement of physical conditions that could mark limits of arid, semiarid, subhumid, and humid domains (Hanson, 1949). All methods have fallen short of the goal because of the apparent impossibility of integrating all factors operating locally to determine plant growth.

Historically the methods have gone from the relatively simple to the more complex. Lines have been drawn solely on the basis of precipitation, with varying success. This method has been improved by taking temperature or evaporation or both into account, and more complicated calculations have been made involving such factors as net radiation and turbidity of the atmosphere. Also, because total precipitation does not present a complete picture, investigators have looked into the possibilities of expressing moisture conditions in terms of favorable and unfavorable seasons. All these considerations, important in the life and distribution of plants, are discussed in the chapter on weather and climate (by C. H. Reitan and C. R. Green), rather than in the present chapter.

One basic problem in drawing boundaries clearly is the difference of opinion among scientists on the criteria for terming an area "desert." The extent of the difference is evident in *Plant Ecology, Reviews of Research* (Unesco, 1955b), which reviews ecological conditions for most of the semiarid and arid portions of the world; no two contributors use the same criteria for establishing the boundaries of the desert. Bharucha (1955) sets the upper limit at 10 inches of precipitation in Afghanistan, India, and Pakistan. Boyko (1955a) defines a dry desert as an area with a waterless surface as a result of poor and erratic precipitation. Cabrera (1955b) accepts the 500-mm isohyet as the boundary between arid and semiarid in Latin America. Davies (1955) states that in Australia the desert formations ("desert sclerophyll grassland

and desert steppe") occupy areas where the mean rainfall is less than 8 inches. Delbes (1955) set the 300-mm isohyet as the lower boundary of the humid zone and the 100-mm isohyet as the upper boundary of the arid zone, "properly speaking," in the Middle East. Drar (1955) accepts Köppen's climatic zones, with the upper boundary of the semiarid zone at 500 mm, but he does not clearly indicate the boundary of the desert in northeast Africa. For South Africa Dyer (1955) follows Köppen's and Thornthwaite's classification and establishes the 20-inch isohyet as the upper boundary of the semiarid. By inference based upon Köppen's classification, the boundary between arid and semiarid would be the 10-inch isohyet. Emberger (1955) considers the true desert to be restricted to a climate characterized by precipitation without seasonal rhythm and periods of more than a year without precipitation. Pichi-Sermolli (1955b) accepts a limit corresponding to a value of 10 on de Martonne's aridity index and minus 40 on Thornthwaite's moisture index, which approximates the isohyet of 350 mm.

Some of these differences are understandably related to the geographical locations of the desert areas discussed, as noted by Meigs (1966, p. 12): "As a rough guide it can be stated that the terminus (−40 moisture index) of the coldest type of coastal desert, that of Patagonia, is marked at the cold end by a precipitation of approximately 8 to 10 inches; the Mediterranean type of desert, with winter rain, by 12 to 14 inches; and the hot tropical deserts by about 16 to 20 inches, or even more in the most equatorward of these deserts in southern Somaliland." No consistent agreement is found among botanists as to what constitutes a desert. In each locality there may be general agreement among the various botanists, but often even this is not true. Some botanists have depended upon the climatologist to furnish guidelines to the upper-rainfall-limit boundary of the desert, but then upon the basis of their practical experience with vegetation the botanists have selected some of the boundaries proposed and rejected others. In every case they have had some doubts as to the applicability of the climatic projections as a basis for delineating deserts.

Consultant Christian has pointed out that while deserts are in part a product of present climate, past climate has also had a significant role in determining the landscape features with which present climate interacts. If this concept is accepted, the difficulty of defining deserts according to any single criterion such as climate becomes obvious. Each desert becomes a product of a unique genesis. There will be broad relationships to present climate but they will be only broad relationships.

C. GENERAL CHARACTERISTICS OF DESERT VEGETATION

Certain characteristics are held in common, to a degree, by the vegetation of all deserts of the world. The most obvious characteristic is scarcity. The vegetal cover varies from nothing to an open stand; even under the most favorable conditions a closed canopy is rarely achieved. The second major characteristic, seasonality of the vegetation, varies from one desert area to another depending upon the amount and seasonal distribution of precipitation and the particular plants found locally.

The vegetation usually includes two general classes: *(1)* perennial plants, which may be succulent or (often) dwarfed and woody, and *(2)* annuals or ephemerals, which appear after rains and complete their growth cycle during a short season. Ephemerals may form a fairly dense stand, providing a short season of forage and becoming a fire hazard when dry. Often these two classes are interdependent, as pointed out by Muller (1953); sometimes they are antagonistic, as reported by Bonner (1950). At the upper precipitation limit (250 mm), trees and shrubs are commonly found with the low-growing ephemerals and perennials (Shreve, 1951).

Many of the perennial plants are spiny, of a harsh texture, and leafless during the drier part of the year. Some are leafless or almost leafless at all times; the photosynthetic processes are then assumed by the green stems of the plant (Oppenheimer, 1951*a*).

Although some desert plants produce edible grains and fruits, none is considered an important food source for indigenous people; they can be useful supplements, however. Some offer survival nourishment; for others, it would take more energy to gather the food than would be derived from eating it. In the western Gran Chaco, with very long dry seasons, some tubers are consumed for their water content, e. g., the Coriaceous subshrub *Facaratia hassleriana*.

Except for the vegetation in wadis, basins, and along drainage courses, extreme deserts have little wood for fuel or construction purposes. The primitive shelters of desert dwellers are usually of skin or cloth, and desert people often use dried manure as their main source of fuel.

1. Types of Desert Vegetation

The vegetation of desert areas may be divided into three general categories:

1) Vegetation dependent upon local precipitation only,

2) Vegetation dependent upon the accumulation in drainage courses and depressions of rain that falls within the local area,

3) Vegetation dependent upon moisture from sources outside the desert itself, such as rivers or lakes fed partly from without the area.

The first and second categories include what is usually considered to be true desert vegetation, the drought-escaping, drought-evading, drought-enduring, and drought-resisting species described by Shantz (1927).

Vegetation in the first category may be entirely lacking under extreme conditions, but even then the recently discovered phenomenon of subterranean dew may in many cases furnish sufficient moisture for a sparse vegetation of adapted species, particularly on sand, with its high heat capacity, and in areas with great differences between day and night temperatures (Boyko, 1966*b*). The second category consists of vegetation growing under favorable conditions of topography, which may not be as xerophytic in character as vegetation of the first category (Zohary, 1962). As pointed out by Kassas (1953, 1955), physiography is an important factor in controlling local water resources. The lowest portions of desert areas receive water (and soil) from more-or-less extensive drainage, and, consequently, the moisture available for plant growth is several times the actual rainfall. Slopes and higher areas retain the least amount of water. Local differences, although small, will favor one area at the expense of another. Under minimum precipitation only the lower areas may support vegetation; under larger amounts of precipitation the lower areas will show quantitative and qualitative differences in vegetation compared to higher ground. The distinctions are especially noticeable in the wadis (oueds) of the Sahara and other very dry deserts.

In the rainless belt between Wadi Halfa and Qena in Egypt, according to Kassas (1955), a rainfall on the order of 10 mm occurs once every 10 years or more. The rainwater runs off the plateaus and collects in wadis and depressions, some thousands of kilometers long and often 300 meters below the general plateau level. In the depressions are oases where small areas are cultivated. The floors of the depressions have deep alluvial deposits that support a patched cover of vegetation in the years when moisture is available.

Monod (1931) has pointed out that in the central Sahara the vegetation is contained exclusively in wadis. He refers to this as "mode contracté," compared to scattered vegetation growing under more favorable moisture conditions, which he terms "mode diffus."

Davis (1953) has reported similar influences with special references to the vegetation of sandy areas. A compact rock surface affords little possibility for plant growth; a rocky surface veneered with rocks (a hamada desert) provides no surface for seedlings except in pockets of soft materials among the fragments. A rocky surface covered with duricrust is usually sterile; a gravel surface may be so closely strewn as to be impenetrable to plant roots.

Kassas (1955) has classified desert habitats into the following ecosystems: desert plateau, desert wadis, desert mountains, erosion surfaces, erosion pavements, gravel desert, desert plains and playas, and desert sand drifts and dunes; each of these evolves through several phases of development.

The depth and physical texture of the soil are also very important, especially as they influence the amount, availability, and continuity of the water supply. It requires only the accumulation of sand a few centimeters in depth to create ecological differences. A shallow soil is subject to desiccation during the long rainless season; a deep soil may allow the storage of some water in a deep-seated layer. The shallow soil may support only ephemerals; the deep soil may provide suitable moisture conditions for perennials.

Another aspect of topography is exposure to the sun; the contrast in vegetation between north-facing and south-facing slopes is often great (Boyko, 1947*a*). A great vegetational difference is sometimes to be distinguished even on parts of the same slope but with different angles of inclination, according to the different amount of direct sun radiation they receive.

In addition to wadis and similar drainage features, the deserts have internal basins ranging in size from small shallow depressions to great "dry lakes," which may have a water cover following rains. The larger depressions are usually saline, because they have no surface or subsurface drainage and lose their moisture through evaporation. (Saline accumulation and other soil variations are discussed in other chapters of this series, especially that on surface materials by Harold E. Dregne.) These desert basins should not be confused with basins supplied with water from outside the desert that may have a more-or-less permanent shallow water table. Such areas may support a type of vegetation in the third category (dependent upon outside moisture). Included also in the third category is vegetation along stream banks and the shores of ponds and lakes, including many phreatophytes and "oasis" types of plant communities. The hydrological and soils aspects of these basins are discussed in other chapters, especially those on surface materials by Harold E. Dregne and on geomorphology and surface hydrology by Lawrence K. Lustig.

In mentioning favorable desert conditions, the types of vegetation produced near cloudy coasts as in Mauritania and the western coast of South America should not be overlooked. It might be said that this type of vegetation is dependent upon sources of moisture from outside the desert itself; the moisture is provided by clouds generated within the neighboring maritime environment rather than by rainfall within the desert area. Such vegetation is often rich in epiphytes and lichens.

2. Effects of Man

The question of possible deterioration of vegetation cover in dry climates as a result of the actions of man is another upon which there is not a full agreement, particularly in the United States. Some scientists believe the changes are largely due to changes in climate, and others believe that the activities of man have been important influences, either independent of climatic changes or combined with climatic changes. In the portions of the world where human settlements are of greater age, there seems to be greater agreement that man has had an important influence in extending the arid environment or in locally increasing the degree of aridity. It is important to find out, not only in general but in specific cases, if increase in aridity of the environment results from man's activities, so that the potentialities of the specific areas can be properly assessed.

Changes in the composition of vegetation over periods of time are especially noticeable along the boundaries of deserts. Opinions differ sharply as to the causes of these changes and as to whether they are cyclic or long time trends (Chevalier, 1934); some observers believe that the changes are results of climatic changes and some that they result from the influences of man. According to Hare (1961), arid climates are dependent upon deep-seated features of the Earth's general atmospheric circulation and do not rise from man-made circumstances. Others believe that the activities of man have caused local changes in vegetation (Calder, 1951). The following typical investigations in the North American deserts may be cited as representing the various approaches to the problem of vegetation change, but it should be noted that similar changes have been pointed out for all the desert regions of the world. Buffington and Herbel (1965) studied the vegetational changes in a semi-desert area in southern New Mexico during a period extending from 1858 to 1963. They found that mesquite increased tenfold and was a principal invader on sandy soils. Creosotebush, which was present on the shallow soils in 1858, became dominant on more than 12,000 acres in 1963, an increase of 20 times. They believed that livestock grazing was the main factor in the spread of mesquite. The reduction of grass cover during periodic droughts aided the establishment of these woody plants. In a similar study over a shorter period, extending from 1915 to

1946, Branscomb (1958) found that there was a 28 per cent loss of original grassland type; he believed that this loss was a result of general changes over the past 90 years in accordance with a natural cyclic climatic pattern, but that grazing pressure was also a major factor. Ellison (1960) summarized the various publications relating to the effect of grazing on plant succession of rangelands, including the northern and southern desert shrub regions. His analysis included a comprehensive literature review. Hastings (1963), and Hastings and Turner (1965a) reviewed the history of changes in the vegetation of the desert region of Arizona and Sonora. They concluded that natural trends toward decreased rainfall and increased temperature have been largely responsible for these changes, and that these climatic causes may have been reinforced by cultural factors. A similar conclusion was reached by Collier and Dundas (1937) in Nigeria, where they found that the extent of the desert fluctuated with oscillations of world climate. Contrasted with this are comments of consultants Emberger for Africa and Christian and Perry for Australia, in which they point out major changes in vegetation which are believed to be the result of the activities of man. As stated by Perry, "Under low and erratic rainfall, vegetation is in a delicate balance with the environment, and the influence of grazing can be dramatic."

3. Distribution

Information regarding the worldwide distribution of many species of desert flora is included in the species summary at the end of the chapter.

Literature describing the local distribution of plants in individual areas is discussed below in the sections covering in turn the individual desert areas of the Earth.

D. BASIS FOR DESCRIPTION OF DESERT VEGETATION

The task of describing desert vegetation has been approached in several ways. The most generally used approaches can be summarized under the following headings:

1) Floristic enumerations
2) Phytosociological studies
3) Vegetation type descriptions
4) Life-form compilations
5) Autecological observations

These may be used singly or in combination; in some cases all may be used in the same study.

Early works on desert vegetation were almost entirely taxonomic enumerations devoted to identification, classification, and description of the various species found. As geographically wider information on occurrence of plants became available, consideration of plant distribution and affinities increased. And as knowledge of plant communities increased, emphasis grew on studies such as phytosociology. Phytosociology, in a strict sense, according to Carpenter (1956), is a branch of ecology devoted to the consideration of vegetation rather than habitat factors. Autecology is defined by Carpenter (1956) as the conditions of environment and of adaptation of individual plant species, the relation of individual plants to their habitats, the ecology of the individual organism.

1. Phytosociological Methods

The phytosociological approach to vegetation studies, under the original leadership of Braun-Blanquet (1932) and the more recent leadership of Emberger (1950, 1951), director of the ecological work at the Centre d'Etudes Phytosociologiques et Ecologiques (hereafter cited as C. E. P. E.), Montpellier, France, has gained considerable support throughout much of the world. This system of studying vegetation is adaptable to various types of mapping and can be used to good advantage with aerial surveys. The systems and methodology of vegetation analysis were reviewed and evaluated by Cain and Castro (1959), but they gave very little attention to desert conditions.

Although full agreement has not been reached on methods of sampling and on how some items are to be evaluated, there seems to be a converging of ideas toward greater uniformity. McGinnies (1957) summarized the items considered by the phytosociologist on the quantitative and qualitative characteristics of vegetation. For example, the relative abundance of various species is usually the first thing to be studied and may be expressed on a relative basis such as "very rare," "rare," "infrequent," "abundant," or "very abundant." Whenever an adequate sample can be obtained and the number of individuals counted, abundance can be expressed on a unit area basis; when this is accomplished, the numerical expression is termed "density." Specifically, density is the average number of individuals per area sampled. In this respect it differs from "frequency," which is used to express the percentage of sample plots on which a species occurs. These two factors are very important in considering the structure of a plant community, as they show not only how well the species is represented numerically but also how the individuals are distributed. Studies of representative areas throughout the world have shown that there is a tendency toward a normal distribution of species by frequency classes and that a departure from this distribution indicates abnormality in the vegetation, probably due to some disturbance (McGinnies, 1934).

Density and frequency determinations give some information on the distribution of plants in a stand, but it is often desirable to record additional information regarding the dispersion of individuals. Phytosociologists have used the term "sociability" to indicate the degree to which individuals of a species are grouped or how they are distributed in a stand: whether they occur singly, in patches, colonies, mats, or pure stands. Consultant Emberger has stated that the correct application of this concept is often impossible because of the difficulty of defining an individual, and that certain phytosociological ecologists, viz. the C. E. P. E. group at Montpellier, prefer to substitute "distribution" for "sociability." The statistical phytosociologist uses the term "dispersion" to express differences in distribution. A normal dispersion implies a randomization to be expected by chance. If individuals are crowded in some areas and absent in others, the term "hyperdispersion" is used. If distribution is more regular than would be expected by chance, it is called "hypodispersion." Some ecologists use the term "contagious distribution" rather than "hyperdispersion" and "regular distribution" as an alternative for "hypodispersion."

Although density and frequency indicate numbers and distribution, they do not indicate size, volume of space occupied, or amount of ground covered or shaded. These characteristics are needed to fill in the picture, because they are closely related to dominance and are necessary wherever total volume information is needed, as in range surveys where it is important to estimate available forage.

The portion of the total area occupied by a given species is not easily measured and for this reason is usually estimated. Ecologists frequently make their estimates on the basis of assigning each species to one of five cover classes. The problem is complicated by kinds of cover, e. g. basal cover, foliage cover, and canopy cover.

The problems of relating one stand of vegetation to another and of determining whether both are parts of the same large community or whether they belong to different communities necessitate observations at various points to determine which species are common to all stands, and which are uncommon or rare. The degree of regularity with which a species is present in the observed stands is expressed as "presence" and is commonly shown on a 5-degree scale denoting degrees from "rare" (1-20 per cent) to "constantly present" (81-100 per cent).

Another important factor to determine in comparing communities is which species are characteristic of the community and which are not. To do this, species are classified according to their "fidelity," indicating the degree of which they are restricted to a particular community. On this basis, species are grouped into five fidelity classes: (1) "strangers," appearing accidentally, (2) "indifferents," without pronounced affinity for any community, (3) "preferents," present in several communities but predominantly in one of them, (4) "selectives," found especially in one community but met with occasionally in others, and (5) "exclusives," found completely or almost so, in only one community. The differences that have developed between the phytosociologists of Europe and of America have been outlined by Poore (1955).

In the course of their most recent research, the ecologists at Montpellier have set up floristic-ecological methods for study of vegetation, reducing to a minimum the subjectivity of field research and permitting a precise sampling that allows an exact statistical elaboration of the observations. Floristics and ecology check each other. The group has worked out a code (in press) in order to be able to utilize modern mechano-graphical means for the interpretation of materials resulting from the observations.

The most characteristic features of the method used at present at the C. E. P. E. may be summarized as follows:

1) Experience having shown that results obtained from a study depend to a considerable degree on the way in which the plots of the inventory have been located within each part of the area under study, the Centre staff attaches very great importance to the methods of sampling, attempting in a diversified region to make a truly representative sampling, allowing a valid statistical elaboration of the plot data. Routinely before each field study, the staff members collect and consolidate their data about the area under consideration, in such forms as climatic, edaphic, and geologic maps, and physiognomic maps of vegetation. Thus, more-or-less distinct zones become evident. They next locate the plots at random in each of the delimited zones, so that the statistical conditions can be calculated from the observed parameters.

2) The study of the environment is carried on simultaneously with the study of the vegetation and the flora of an area; indeed, more attention may be given to the description of the environment than to that of the vegetation, for the aim is not only to study vegetation, but also to establish the relationships between the vegetation and the environment.

To standardize the observations of different observers for the same area, the C. E. P. E. staff has perfected after several years of tests a manual of plot codification of an ecological inventory of vegetation (in press). Particular care has been given to codifying those ecological factors that the staff believe to be the most outstanding, even though codification is sometimes difficult.

3) The floristic plots are made about the smallest area of grouping which it seems of interest to study, supplemented by a concentric extension around it, first double, then quadruple the area.

When the homogeneity or heterogeneity of a locality requires closer study, a device utilizing grids of squares, linear segments, or even points is set up and interpreted with the aid of many tests (number of series, frequency curves, interspecific relationships and so forth).

4) The fourth main feature is the importance given to statistical interpretation of the data. Several methods are used, including:

> *a)* The differential analysis of Czekanowski and the similar methods used in numerical classification.
>
> *b)* "Ecological profiles": An ecological profile is a cross section showing the frequency distribution of a species in each class of the ecological factor considered. These profiles characterize the reaction of a species to various factors of the environment.

5) The test of independence and application of X^2.

6) Multivariance analysis.

The results yielded by these methods are sometimes difficult to interpret, but this inconvenience is compensated for by their objectivity compared to those obtained by classical methods.

The endeavor undertaken for more than ten years by the C. E. P. E. could be characterized as a search for rational objectivity and to decrease to a minimum the role of subjectivity in all processes.

In connection with phytosociological surveys, consultant Emberger has suggested the following references: Duvigneaud (1946, 1953), Carles (1948), Emberger (1950), Ionesco (1956a), and Gounot (1961).

In commenting on phytosociological surveys, consultant Christian expressed his ideas about such subjects as vegetation distribution and communities. If they have the chance, that is are present, species will grow where the environment suits them. The environment will be determined mainly by climate and landscape features, and will also be influenced by phytosociological community factors.

The extent of a community will depend on the geographical extent of a suitable environment, often determined by geomorphic features. If a community happens to be large it will appear important.

Many communities are landscape type. Environmental factors will vary, to a large or small extent, within the community. The composition of the broad community of plants will be determined as much by this variability as by sociability. Thus phytosociological units are often expressions of the specific variability of the physical factors as much as of sociological relationships. In some cases the two sources of variability (physical and sociological) can be recognized, but in most cases they cannot. To a degree, then, vegetation classification systems cannot be universal, since the distribution of species and community groupings will be a product of physical factors which are unique for each locality. More emphasis on description based upon geomorphic subdivisions of the landscape is preferable.

2. Phytogeographical Descriptions and Maps

The term "vegetative type description" is used to cover a wide variety of descriptive terminology, sometimes very loosely used and sometimes very precisely and carefully defined. Descriptions may range from the general remarks of the casual traveler to the rather exactly defined usage of Clements (1916), Tansley (1913, 1920), Nichols (1923), and Shelford (1932). Although useful accuracy and precision is attained in these descriptions, the terminology often has local connotations that make it difficult to compare one vegetal unit with another (Küchler 1947b, 1949a, 1951), or the classification of one author with that of another in the same general area. (See Table IV, a 1932 comparison by Monod of various classifications.) Küchler (1949a) has suggested a system for the physiognomic classification of vegetation that might apply universally. His method, with some additional refinements, has been used in the preparation of world maps of natural vegetation in *Goode's World Atlas* (Espenshade, 1964). He has recently (1966) added further refinements; his revised classification is shown in Table I. His method (together with many others) is discussed in a recently published book entitled *Vegetation Mapping* (Küchler, 1967).

Christian and Perry (1953) developed a field method for the rapid and systematic description of plant communities in terms of appearance, structure, height, density, and floristic composition. The method took form during a series of potentiality surveys of very large undeveloped regions of Northern Australia by the Land Research and Regional Survey Section of the Commonwealth Scientific and Industrial Research Organization. The aim of this continuing series of surveys, which began in 1946, is to describe and map the inherent land characteristics of the regions and from these to assess the possibilities and likely forms of economic development.

The approach is based upon the concept of "land units" and "land systems." The concept recognizes

Table I

PHYSIOGNOMIC CATEGORIES OF KÜCHLER

LIFE FORM CATEGORIES

Basic Life Forms		Special Life Forms	
Woody Plants:		Climbers (Lianas)	C
Broadleaf evergreen	B	Stem succulents	K
Broadleaf deciduous	D	Tuft plants	T
Needleleaf evergreen	E	Bamboos	V
Needleleaf deciduous	N	Epiphytes	X
Aphyllous	O		
Semideciduous $(B + D)$	S	*Leaf Characteristics:*	
Mixed $(D + E)$	M	Hard (sclerophyll)	h
		Soft	w
Herbaceous Plants:		Succulent	k
Graminoids	G	Large (>400 cm²)	l
Forbs	H	Small (<4 cm²)	s
Lichens, mosses	L		

STRUCTURAL CATEGORIES

Stratification		Coverage	
Class	*Height (meters)*	Class	*Coverage*
8	>35	c	Continuous ($>75\%$)
7	20 -35	i	Interrupted (50-75%)
6	10 -20	p	Parklike, in patches (25-50%)
5	5 -10	r	Rare (6-25%)
4	2 - 5	b	Barely present, sporadic (1-5%)
3	0.5- 2	a	Almost absent, extremely scarce ($<1\%$)
2	0.1- 0.5		
1	<0.1		

that the landforms that comprise the landscape of an area are the products of geological parent material and geomorphological processes operating upon it. Associated with these landforms, which have necessarily been influenced by the past and present climate of the region, there have been developed a specific array of soils and microenvironments that support characteristic vegetation communities. Each landscape type is formed by a recurring pattern of a limited number of landforms with their associated characteristics. These landforms, and the patterns which they make, change where there is a major change in geological material or geomorphological process. A landscape pattern that can be defined, described, and associated with the genetic factors of landscape origin is termed a "land system." The boundaries of land systems can be seen on aerial photographs. These are first examined and a field itinerary is then planned so as to sample all land systems within the survey area adequately. A "land unit" is a unit of sampling, and it may represent a whole landform or character-

istic part of it. The landforms and land units within each land system are identified and described. The description of the vegetation of the surveyed region is based upon the individual vegetation descriptions for each of the land units sampled. From these data community classifications can be made, but the essential feature is the description of the communities associated with specific environmental factors.

Plant communities can be described either by species and associations (requiring numerous and lengthy observations) or by visible structure (a more rapid means, enabling general characteristics and differences to be noted and related to environment, irrespective of the species present). For the rapid survey of the vast undeveloped regions, Christian and Perry developed a method of concise description of visible structure. The descriptive notations are made in the form of a formula of figures and letters which represent three vegetation stories (tree, shrub, and ground), their component layers, and the density and heights of each of these in the community. Floristic composition and dominant species are also indicated.

More particularly, according to Christian and Perry, the tree story is indicated by the letter *A,* the shrub story by *B,* and the ground story by *C;* the recording of some or all of these letters immediately imparts some information about the appearance and structure of a community. Further information can be given by designating the layers present within each of these stories. Three layers (low, midheight, and tall) within each story have proved adequate to describe the vegetation in northern Australia. Three layers are not always present; frequently a story is composed of only one or two layers. These layers are indicated by the subscripts $_1$, $_2$, $_3$, following the applicable letters, *A, B,* and *C.* Thus A_1 denotes low trees, A_2 trees of medium heights, and A_3 tall trees. Similarly B_1, B_2, and B_3, and C_1, C_2, and C_3, denote low, midheight, and tall shrubs (*B*) and herbs (*C*), respectively.

The average height of each layer in meters is estimated and is shown by writing this figure as a superscript index to the letter used to indicate the layer. Thus A_3^{15} would represent a tall tree layer 15 meters high. In practice it has been found desirable not to set down rigid height limits for each story or layer. Frequently, comparable layers occur at similar heights in different localities, but the heights of comparable layers may vary between localities. Thus one may describe a fairly low community containing three layers by the formula A_3^{10}, A_2^{6}, A_1^{3}, in which the tall trees are 10 meters, midheight trees 6 meters, and low trees 3 meters high. Another community in which three comparable layers are equally distinctive, but with heights of 20, 12, and 6 meters, would be described by a similar formula differing only in the height indexes.

The general height ranges (in meters) for the various stories and layers in different communities in northern Australia are:

A_3:	10-25 m		B_1:	0.3-1 m
A_2:	5-15 m		C_3:	1-3 m
A_1:	3- 8 m		C_2:	0.3-1.3 m
B_3:	2- 5 m		C_1:	0-0.5 m
B_2:	1- 3 m			

It will be observed that the heights of corresponding layers in different communities can vary considerably and the the heights of different layers in different communities can overlap.

Where a single tree layer occurs, the symbol applied to it is the one appropriate to the general height class; however, these height classes are significant only within defined regions. The A_2 layer height-range for many Northern Australian communities (5-15 meters), for example, may be the normal height range for an A_1 layer in a tall forest community elsewhere. Thus, it would not be practicable to adopt a fixed universal series of height classes.

The floristic composition of a community is shown by writing the species names (or abbreviations for commonly recurring plants) under the appropriate layer symbol in the formula. The dominants in each layer are preferably listed first and underlined. The relative density of each species is indicated by the symbol *xx* (very dense), *x, y, z,* or *zz* (very sparse) preceding the species name.

Where time permits more precise records can be applied to the formula in terms of measured heights and counted densities, etc.

3. Life Forms

At various times attempts have been made to classify plants in relation to their ability to withstand climatic conditions. One of the broadest classifications divides the plants into the three major groups: hydrophytes, mesophytes, and xerophytes. In the desert environment we are primarily concerned with xerophytes as far as perennial plants are concerned, but examples of the other two categories are to be found under especially favorable conditions. Maximov (1929, 1931) has done much to explain the xerophytic relationships, and the physiological and morphological responses of plants to dry conditions.

It should be pointed out that ephemerals which complete their life cycle when moisture conditions are favorable are not xerophytes in a structural sense, but are often an important component in xeric habitats.

Life form is the characteristic vegetation form of a plant species, such as tree, shrub, herb, forb, or grass. Raunkiaer (1905, 1934, 1937) was more specific in his characterization of life form. He believed the characterization must be essential and represent something fundamental in the plant's relationship to climate; that it must be fairly easy to see; and that it must represent a single aspect of the plant, thus making possible a comparative statistical treatment of the vegetation of different regions.

The classification is that of Raunkiaer (1937), based upon the degree of protection afforded the perennating buds. Although this was originally oriented toward protection in relation to winter killing, the classification has been widely used to categorize plants making up plant communities under conditions of both temperature and moisture stress. The principal classes used in the Raunkiaer classification are shown in table II.

Table II
PRINCIPAL CATEGORIES OF RAUNKIAER CLASSIFICATION

Group	Symbol	Characteristics
Megaphanerophytes	Mg } MM	Trees over 30 m
Mesophanerophytes	Ms	Trees 8-30 m
Microphanerophytes	Mi	Shrubs or trees 2-8 m
Nanophanerophytes	N	Shrubs under 2 m
Chamaephytes	Ch	Buds just above or at surface of ground
Helo- and Hydrophytes	HH	Marsh and water plants
Hemicryptophytes	H	Buds in the surface
Geophytes	G	Bulbs, rhizomes, tubers
Therophytes	Th	Annuals
Stem Succulents	S	Plants with aboveground water storage

Shreve (see discussion of North American Deserts and table VII) adopted a modified life forms description, which provides more detailed information and indicates the plant characteristics related to survival under desert conditions. Adamson (1939) and Cain (1950) made comparisons of the life forms of desert locations in Transcaspia; Aden; El Golea in the Central Sahara; the Oudjda and Ghardaia areas, the Libyan Desert, and Tombouctou in North Africa; Death Valley and Salton Sink in California; Tucson, Arizona; Ooldea, Australia; and Whitehill, South Africa. They found few vegetational characteristics generally common among the deserts, except the presence of a relatively large number of annuals. Some of their findings are presented in table III (after Cain).

Consultant Emberger informs me that he has in press a critique of the biological spectrum in which it is shown as a spectrum of floristic diversity within each biological type, and not the expression of the ecology of the site. He has indicated the rules accord-

Table III
SOME LIFE-FORM SPECTRA FOR DRY CLIMATES COMPARED WITH KÖPPEN TYPES (after Cain)

Locality	Köppen class	No. of spp.	S	MM	N	Ch	H	G	HH	Th
Hot desert climate:										
Death Valley, Calif.	BWh	294	3	2	21	7	18	2	5	42
Salton Sink, Calif.	BWh	81	0	0	33	6	(14)		0	47
El Golea, Central Sahara	BWh	169	0	0	9	13	15	5	2	56
Ghardaia, North Africa	BWh	300	0.3	0	3	16	20	3	0	58
Libyan Desert, North Africa	BWh	194	0	3	9	21	20	4	1	42
Oudjda desert, North Africa	BWh	49	0	0	0	4	17	6	0	73
Oudjda semidesert	BWh	32	0	0	0	59	14	0	0	27
Aden	BWh	176	0	7	26	27	19	3	0	17
Ooldea, Australia	BWh	188	4	19	23	14	4	1	0	35
Cool desert climate:										
Transcaspian lowlands	BWh	768	0	0	11	7	27	9	5	41
Hot steppe climate:										
Tucson, Arizona	BS	266	0	0	18	11	(24)		0	47
Whitehill, South Africa	BSh	428	1	1	8	42	2	18	0	23
Tombouctou, Mali	BSh	138	1	11	12	36	9	3	3	25

*See table II for explanation of symbols

ing to which a spectrum should be established in order to have ecological validity, bearing in mind the stratification and the degree of coverage of each biological type present.

E. SPECIFIC QUALITIES AND USES

1. Cover

Very little information is oriented directly toward vegetation as cover. The best examples of attempts to classify plant cover are the terrain analog studies (U. S. Army Engineer Waterways Experiment Station, 1959; 1960; 1962*a,b;* 1963; 1965) comparing desert conditions around Yuma, Arizona, with desert conditions in other parts of the world (including northwest Africa, northeast Africa, south central Asia, the Middle East, Mexico, and the southwest United States). The Geology Branch, Soils Division of the U. S. Engineers Waterways Experiment Station, Corps of Engineers, Vicksburg, Mississippi, has prepared the analogs, based upon secondary information, using selected factors for comparison including vegetation factors. The vegetation categories include:

1) Barren
2) Sparse shrub and grass
3) Scattered shrub and grass
4) Scattered shrub and/or scrubby trees
　　4a) with scattered third-story trees
5) Dense shrub and/or scrubby trees
　　5a) with scattered third-story trees
　　5b) with grain-herb cultivation
6) Palms with or without grain-herb cultivation
7) Steppe
8) Steppe savanna
9) Grain-herb cultivation
10) Marsh

The descriptive system developed by Küchler (1949*a*) also provides some indications of the general characteristics of plant cover, and the system developed by Christian and Perry (1953) in Australia furnishes a great deal of useful information regarding the nature of the plant cover. For the Sahara, there is much interesting information in the recent publication of Quézel (1965).

Life-form spectra, such as those developed by Raunkiaer (1937), can be used as a basis of interpretation of cover, and similarly the phytosociological studies under the general leadership of Emberger (1951) provide a basis for broad information on cover characteristics.

2. Other Uses

Agricultural plants and production are beyond the scope of this chapter, but mention should be made of the availability of material pertaining to the characteristics and uses of native plants. The list of publications included here is not exhaustive, but rather is representative of the rather scattered literature. One of the best sources of information in brief descriptions is the *Dictionary of Economic Plants* (Uphof, 1959). Sanders (1934) collected a great deal of information on native plants of the United States, including food plants, beverage plants, plant substitutes for soap, medicinal plants, fiber plants, and oil- and wax-producing plants; many desert plants appear, including the mesquite, agaves, yuccas, and cacti. Trabut (1935) catalogued the useful plants of northern Africa including the native names of both wild and cultivated plants. Martínez (1936, 1959) compiled information on the useful plants of Mexico with a bibliography for each of the more important plants; he included information on useful plants, their cultivation, chemical composition, industrial application, and food and medicinal values. Martínez (1945) also contributed some additional notes on the principal plants of Baja California. In a more specific way, Duisberg (1952, 1963) discussed the utilization of various desert plants, including mescal, lechuguilla, creosotebush, canaigre, yucca, guayule, jojoba, gourds, devils-claw, mesquite, and cactus. Grossweiler (1948-1950) compiled a 3-part treatise on Angola, which is partly desert, including the origin, distribution, and economic importance of more than 800 plant species. Burgess (1965) summarized existing ethnobotanical knowledge of the southwestern U. S. A. under the headings of food uses, drink plants, building material, and miscellaneous uses. Earlier ethnobotanical discussions include those on drink plants of the North American Indian by Havard (1896), the ethnobotany of the Hopi by Whiting (1939), Pima and Papago Indian agriculture by Castetter and Bell (1942), and the wild, emergency foods of Australian and Tasmanian aborigines by Irvine (1957), who noted that the main food of the natives is vegetable.

Fiber plants have been given special attention by a number of authors. Campbell and Keller (1932) studied the rate of growth of *Yucca elata,* the utilization of its flower stalks by cattle, and the general characteristics of yucca fiber. Muench (1943) discussed four yuccas in California, noting the use of the fibers for cordage, the roots for detergents, and the porous, pliable wood for splints. Botkin, Shires, and Smith (1943) and Botkin and Shires (1944) discussed the distribution and yields of various yuccas and compared the fibers with other fiber plants. Webber (1953) provided in a monograph information on yucca ecology, uses, taxonomy, growth rates, and culture of yucca plants. Gómez-Pompa (1963) discussed the genus *Agave* and its importance in Mexico; he emphasized the identification of various species of this genus.

Native rubber plants have received some consideration. The earliest general review was that of Hall and Goodspeed in 1919 reporting on a rubber plant survey of western North America; they found a high-grade rubber source in rabbitbush (*Chrysothamnus*), but later investigation showed that these plants did not have as much promise as guayule (*Parthenium argentatum*). In 1943, Geraldine Whiting completed a summary of the literature on milkweeds and their utilization; she found that some milkweeds of arid zones offered promise for rubber production of low quality and that milkweeds are valuable for fiber and oils. Buehrer and Benson (1945) reported on a survey of the rubber content of 93 native plant genera of the Southwest desert; they found that most had very small rubber source content and that milkweeds appeared to be the most promising. Taylor (1951) reviewed the historical development of guayule as a source of rubber; it has proved the most valuable of all the native rubber plants and is probably still being grown in parts of the world for rubber production, although its culture in the United States has been abandoned. Mirov (1952) studied the jojoba (*Simmondsia californica*); he suggested that the wax produced from the seeds, having properties similar to sperm oil, might be used in salad dressing, high-temperature lubricants, and candles.

In the arid parts of Argentina, the pods of several species of *Prosopis* (*P. alba, P. nigra, P. caldenia, P. algorobilla, P. chilensis, P. flexuosa*) are important as concentrated forage and sometimes even as food; it is well known that their fructification is more abundant in dry years, when grass is scarce. There are some other desert trees which give feed in the form of pods: *Acacia aroma*, the "tusca," *Geoffroea decorticans*, the "chañar," *Zizyphus mistol*, the "mistol," etc. Unfortunately, some of them are "increasers" under overgrazing conditions (the tusca by seed germinating after having passed the digestive tract of the animals; the chañar more often by rootsprouts). Several *Prosopis* species deserve attention for reforestation in arid zones, especially *P. alba, P. chilensis, P. nigra* and *P. flexuosa,* because of the good quality of their timber (Burkart, 1952; Ragonese and Martínez Crovetto, 1947).

3. Undesirable Plants

Important publications covering undesirable plants are discussed below. Additional information, noting individual species that are toxic or structurally dangerous, is presented in the species summary table page 473.

Various undesirable plants, especially those imported from other areas, have received attention in the United States from time to time. Wooton (1895) discussed the Russian thistle (*Salsola*), which at that time had a very limited distribution in the United States. Stevens (1943) noted its additional spread, and gave information on the anatomy, germination, growth periods, flowering, and seeding of this undesirable plant.

Halogeton, another undesirable import, has received considerable attention: a noteworthy contribution is that of Major (1953), a translation from the Russian on the description, geographical distribution, and soil preferences of the three Asian members of the genus *Halogeton.* Tisdale and Zappettini (1953) noted the rapid spread of *Halogeton* in the previous 15 years and discussed its ecology and possibilities of control through management.

Several weeds have received consideration. Piemeisel (1932) described the weedy plants in various desert areas. Parker (1958) described the most common farm and garden weeds of Arizona. The rayless goldenrod or burroweed (*Aplopappus fructicosus*) has been recognized as a range pest for many years; Marsh, Roe, and Clawson (1926) discussed it as a poisonous plant. Tschirley and Martin (1961) made a comprehensive review of burroweed in the arid and semiarid Southwest. Parodi (1950) published a very comprehensive study on the grasses poisonous to livestock in Argentina. He noted that species of *Stipa, Festuca,* and *Cynodon* may be poisonous to livestock.

Most of the studies on harmful plants of Africa have considered toxic rather than structural features; important works include Foley and Musso (1925), Kirk (1946), and Sandberg *et al.* (1957-1960). Medicinal and poisonous plants of the Somali-Chalbi were described by Negri (1948); the weeds of Lebanon were discussed by Edgecombe (1964).

4. Control

The most reliable means of control of woody plants is through the use of chemicals. Hull and Vaughn (1951) experimented with various chemicals under varying conditions (in several concentrations, at different times of the year, and by both ground- and air-spraying); they found that up to 90 per cent kill could be obtained. Robertson and Cords (1957) found that complete eradication of rabbitbrush could be obtained by spraying with the chemical compound 2, 4-D eleven months after burning.

Reynolds and Tschirley (1956) experimented with chemical control of mesquite and reported that good control could be obtained by the proper application of the right chemicals. Similar results were obtained by Valentine and Norris (1960) with the chemical compound 2, 4, 5-T in southern New Mexico. Hoffman (1961) cited examples of the economic advantage of chemical weed control in range improvement in Texas.

Schmutz (1963) found that the susceptibility of creosotebush to 2, 4, 5-T varied widely from year to year and from season to season, with seasonal temperatures and relative humidity playing an important role through their effects on plant growth.

The methods of control of brush in tropical and subtropical grassland have been reviewed by Little and Ivens (1965), and the various means and methods of control of undesirable plants in general has been summarized by the Range Seeding Equipment Committee of the U. S. Department of Agriculture/Department of the Interior (1959) and released in the form of a handbook on the chemical control of range weeds.

One of the factors keeping woody plants in check has been fire; controversy exists regarding the incidence of fire in the past compared to the present, and whether the importance of other factors equals or surpasses that of fire as a cause of invasion by shrubs. Pechanec and Stewart (1944) summarized the effects of the burning of sagebrush in the Great Basin area, including the portion that is commonly considered desert. They found that from an economic viewpoint burning could be either good or bad depending upon the ecological conditions, which strongly influence the results obtained from burning. Reynolds and Bohning (1956) studied the effects of burning upon the desert grass shrub range in southern Arizona; they found that fire reduced burroweed by about nine-tenths, cholla by about one-half, prickly pear by about one-fourth, and mesquite by about one-tenth; it also reduced the density of perennial grasses.

5. Radioecology

Radioecology has emerged as a new division of science in the atomic age. Representative studies in this field include: Rickard (1963); Rickard and Shields (1963); Shields, Wells, and Rickard (1963); and Shields and Wells (1963); all of these pertain to the recovery of vegetation near the Nevada atomic test site.

6. Plants as Indicators

Important publications covering the valuable indicator aspect of plants are discussed below. Additional information, noting some individual species which are indicators, is presented in the species summary table at the end of this chapter.

Where rainfall is scanty and irregular, differences in habitat exert strong influences on growth and survival of vegetation (Sampson, 1939). Because each species reacts differently to various combinations of conditions, it is possible to use plants as indicators of such life elements as moisture, soil type, and salinity (Shantz, 1938; Meinzer, 1926, 1927; Killian, 1941, 1950; Chikishev and Vikmorov, 1963). It should be kept in mind, however, that the same plant may indicate different conditions in different areas. For example, at its lower moisture limits, a species may indicate the most favorable soil conditions; at its upper moisture limits, it may indicate poor soil conditions (being unable to compete with other species on the better soils). For this reason, Boyko (1962) introduced the concept "climatic soil coefficient" and presented a scale of these coefficients for the Negev as an example. On the other hand, just as certain plants always indicate saline conditions so do other nontolerant plants indicate the absence of accumulated salts in the soil.

Plant-soil relations of selenium poisoning were reviewed by Trelease and Martin (1936). The most comprehensive studies on selenium poisoning and seleniferous soils have been made by Beath and his associates at the Wyoming Experiment Station. An early paper by Beath, Eppson, and Gilbert (1935) pointed out the existence of selenium and other toxic materials in soils and vegetation; later publications include Beath, Gilbert, and Eppson (1941) on indicator plants and Beath (1943), which lists geologic formation where toxic vegetation is commonly found. Consultant Emberger has suggested the following references as contributing to the subject of plant indicators: Ionesco (1956*b*, 1958) and Gounot (1958, 1961).

7. Important Species and Their Qualities

For each of the major desert areas, the text treatment includes a description of the vegetation and more important species adapted or synthesized from the most reliable sources. The reader's attention is directed to the Species Summary (page 473). By referring to this summary in connection with each plant name mentioned in the vegetation description portions of the text, the reader may pursue such subjects as whether the species has indicator significance, has uses of interest, is spinous or poisonous, and what authors to consult for further information on these species.

F. DESERT AREAS OF THE EARTH

Because the total desert area is so great and because the amount of information varies so widely among deserts, individual desert areas will be considered in turn, beginning with Africa, then Asia, Australia, South America, and finally North America. The Kalahari-Namib of southern Africa will be considered first. Then, as there is a relationship between the North African and Asian desert, these will be considered beginning with the Sahara and Somali-Chalbi, proceeding north and east to the Arabian, Iranian, and Thar deserts, and then, farther north in Asia, to the Turkestan, Takla-Makan, and Gobi areas (which include both steppe and desert). Next we will consider the deserts of Australia, then the Patagonia, Monte, and Atacama-Peruvian deserts of South America, and finally the North American deserts.

For each desert area an attempt is first made to provide a general description of the overall plant community context: to identify and describe components of the vegetation and note important species present. This general description permits the publications cited (especially the works on specific aspects of vegetation, including important species) to be discussed against a coherent conceptual context, even for those desert areas for which the relevant literature is minimal or spotty. This vegetation and species context also permits those readers with specific interests and with some knowledge of arid areas to appraise more readily the relevance of works cited in this chapter (including works on specific species and specific plant communities) to their own tasks without having to seek out and examine the cited works. (Readers may further establish their possible interest in works on species named herein by referring to "Species Summary," a section which gives additional data for the species listed and cites publications that discuss the species further.) These introductory discussions of the overall plant community for each desert also briefly disclose some similarities and differences among the habitats and flora desert to desert, and thereby can point toward related works for interim limited use in some instances where gaps in research and literature exist.

Substantial studies and works on the vegetation of each area will be considered under two broad headings:

1) Taxonomic and floristic works, and

2) Ecological works (including phytogeography, phytosociology, physiognomy, and environmental relationships).

The references cited have been selected from a much larger collection of titles that has been evaluated and screened to select those of greatest value in providing information on the flora and ecological structure and relationships for each desert. Where appropriate an evaluation has been included, but where this is lacking it should be understood that the inclusion of the material indicates that it has been judged as making an important contribution.

1. Southern Africa: The Kalahari-Namib

General Descriptions of Plant Communities

Southern and southwestern Africa have extensive areas with semiarid and arid climates. South West Africa, Botswana (formerly Bechuanaland), about two-thirds of the Republic of South Africa, and the southern portion and a coastal strip of Angola are arid or semiarid.

The Namib Desert extends along the western coast of Africa from the vicinity of Moçâmedes, Angola, across South West Africa into the Cape Province of South Africa, to the vicinity of Port Nolloth; its width from the coast line to the Great Western Escarpment is about 100 miles at most places. Extreme desert conditions extend inland for 50-70 miles, giving way to less severe conditions near the Great Western Escarpment and to semiarid conditions eastward of the edge of the plateau. In southern South West Africa, the Namib merges with the Kalahari.

The Kalahari, in popular concept, occupies Botswana and eastern South West Africa, from the Okavango River in the north to the northern border of the Republic of South Africa in the south. The northern part, however, has neither the climate nor the vegetation of true desert; referred to locally as "thirstland" and lacking surface water because of deep layers of subsurface sand, it supports a year-round stand of trees and grass, and luxuriant growths of ephemerals following the December-to-March rains.

But from 22° south latitude southward to the Orange River, the Kalahari is more truly desert, receiving only little and unreliable rainfall in the summer, and supporting scattered small trees, bushes, and, in occasional wet years, summer grasses. South of the Orange River the Karroo subdesert receives both summer and winter rains and supports scattered low succulent shrubs.

In the Kalahari area, gourds are prominent, particularly *Citrullus vulgaris.** In southern Africa succulent plants make up a large portion of the vegetation. These include representatives from several genera including *Crassula, Cotyledon, Aloë, Euphorbia, Stapelia* and *Mesembryanthemum.* Many of the shrublets belong to the family Compositae.

The Namib Desert receives an average of less than 2 inches of rainfall but benefits from sea fogs and dews, and in areas it supports a scanty vegetation. The essential characteristic of the climate is its cloudiness, which results from a cold ocean current.

---

* Species Summary, p. 473, gives additional data for the species listed throughout this chapter and cites publications that discuss the species further.

The fog deposits dew amounting to 40-50 mm of moisture per year, which penetrates 1 to 3.5 cm into the soil.

According to information supplied by consultant Emberger, the Namib can be divided into three general areas: the southern Namib between the Orange River and Lüderitz Bay, the middle Namib between Lüderitz Bay and Cape Cross, and the northern Namib to the north of Cape Cross. The last area is little known. Consultant Logan, in a personal communication and in Logan (1960), points out that by considering Walvis Bay and the Kuiseb River as the boundary between middle and northern Namib, we can thereby distinguish the dunes from the nondune country.

The following ecological habitats can be distinguished according to Emberger:

1) The external Namib next to the sea, rocky and sandy between the cliffs. It supports *Mesembryanthemum salicorniodes, Aïzoön dinteri, Zygophyllum simplex,* some ephemerals and halophytes.

2) Interior Namib, characterized by no halophytes but some *Aristida.*

3) Rocks of various mineralogical composition, which support numerous stem succulents such as *Trichocaulon, Euphorbia, Pelargonium, Kleinia;* leaf succulents such as *Lithops, Aloë, Cotyledon;* tree succulents such as *Cissus, Pachypodium;* and ferns such as *Notochlaena.*

4) Arroyos, characterized by *Tamarix, Lycium, Suaeda fruticosa, Arthrocnemum glaucum, Phragmites communis, Cyperus laevigatus,* and also *Welwitschia* in the middle Namib, Hope Mine area, and southern Angola.

The plants do not show any visible adaptation to fogs; only the lichens on the rocks in the fog zone are nephelophytes. The vegetation can without doubt absorb the water that penetrates the soil at night or that penetrates joints in the rocks; in many parts of the Namib the rock outcrops are the habitats of the largest plants.

To the south of Kuiseb River in the northern part of the middle Namib, the land is practically without vegetation.

Pole Evans (1937) has divided the area from the western slopes of the escarpment to the coast into five distinguishable zones: the western slopes of the escarpment, the gravel plains, the sand dunes, the rocky hills, and the seashore. The plants that characterize the western slopes are *Aloë dichotoma, Euphorbia virosa, Euphorbia dregeana,* and *Sarcocaulon burmanni.* He has stated that the gravel plains may be devoid of obvious plants for miles, but sometimes they bear a scanty growth of *Eragrostis spinosa, Aristida brevifolia, Augea capensis,* and several species of *Sarcocaulon.* In the neighborhood of Walvis Bay, the *Welwitschia bainesii* occurs. With it is commonly associated *Zygophyllum stapfii.* Little vegetation is found on the sand dunes, but occasionally *Eragrostis cyperoides* and *Eragrostis spinosa* are found in widely isolated tufts. Along the seashore are found succulents belonging to the genera *Salicornia* and *Salsola.* Several tree species occur along the river valleys; these include the *Acacia giraffae, Acacia albida, Euclea pseudebenus, Tamarix articulata,* and *Combretum primigenum.* In the low-lying valleys, large, spreading bushes of *Euphorbia gregaria* are found, and where the river mouths become buried in the sand dunes, *Acanthosicyos horrida,* a leafless cucurbitaceous plant, occurs. The rocky mountains that flank the Orange River support a variety of vegetation, including *Pachypodium namaquanum,* a tall cylindrical-stem succulent that attains a height of 12 to 15 feet and bears at its crown a few small leaves and flowers. It has the remarkable habit of always pointing northwards, a useful item of information for travelers. Other stem succulents present include *Ceraria namaquensis, Aloë dichotoma, Euphorbia virosa,* and several species of *Cotyledon, Sarcocaulon,* and *Commiphora.*

Pole Evans (1937) stated that a desert shrub vegetation covers a broad belt extending from the Namibian South West Africa and the northern Cape Province eastward across the plateau of South Africa almost to the Indian Ocean back of Port Elizabeth and Port Alfred. The rainfall varies from 5 to 15 inches, the greatest in the southeastern portion. Although the plant associations have many distinct compositions, the general appearance of the vegetation throughout the area is remarkably uniform; desert shrubs and shrublets characterize the whole area except in the extreme south where succulents dominate. The widely spaced plants may be either woody or fleshy, and generally they appear to be of uniform height; the leaves in most cases are small. Trees are not a conspicuous feature except in the southern portion, where the common trees are *Acacia karroo, Pappea capensis, Euclea undulata,* and *Boscia albitrunca.*

Characteristic bushes and shrubs include *Rhigozum trichotomum, Phaeoptilum spinosum, Lycium arenicolum, Nymania capensis, Melianthus comosus;* shrublets include *Pentzia virgata, P. incana, P. globosa, Chrysocoma tenuifolia, Euryops multifidus, Salsola aphylla,* and *S. zeyheri.* The common succulents include *Galenia africana, Euphorbia mauritanica, Cotyledon jascicularia,* and *Mesembryanthemum spinosum.*

Taxonomic and Floristic Works

The flora of southern Africa has been studied, classified, and described in detail, because of its special botanical interest. Important taxonomic works are: W. H. Harvey and O. W. Sonder, *Flora Capensis,* in 7 volumes, 1859-1925; and R. Marloth, *The Flora of South Africa,* in 4 volumes beautifully illustrated, 1913-1932. A basic and useful series of publications entitled *Flowering Plants of South Africa* (1920- ; in Pertinent Publications list under "Flowering") was initiated under the editorship of I. B. Pole Evans (from 1920 through 1939). Each number described and illustrated ten species with hand-colored plates. This series was continued under the editorship of E. P. Phillips (from 1940 through 1944) and of R. A. Dyer (from 1945 on) under the title *The Flowering Plants of Africa.* More recently, Dyer, Codd, and Rycroft (1963) have started a projected 33-volume series entitled *Flora of Southern Africa.* In addition to these publications of a broad nature, some of more local coverage should be noted, such as the publications of Exell and Mendonça on the flora of Angola (1937-1962) and Codd (1951) on the trees and shrubs of Kruger National Park. Among the more specialized publications are Heumann and Winkler (1931) on characteristic plants from southwest Africa, Palmer and Pitman (1961) on trees of South Africa, Meeuse (1962) on Cucurbitaceae, Pilger (1954) on Gramineae, Reynolds (1950) on aloes, Torre (1962) on Leguminosae, Verdoorn (1956) on Oleaceae, and White, Dyer, and Sloane (1941) on Euphorbiaceae. Githens (1949) listed the drug plants of Africa and Watt and Breyer-Brandwijk (1962) have prepared what appears to be the most complete list of poisonous and medicinal plants of southern Africa. The well-illustrated *Families of Flowering Plants of Southern Africa* (Riley, 1963) includes 114 color plates and a discussion of many aspects of the flora including economic uses and phytogeography. Another popular publication worth consulting is *Wild Flowers of the Transvaal* by Dyer, Verdoorn, and Codd (1962), with colored plates by C. Letty.

Ecological Works

The vegetation of southern Africa has been very well mapped. The major maps to consult include those of Pole Evans (1936), a colored map of South Africa; the Portuguese overseas atlas (Portugal, 1948), which includes a phytogeographic map on Angola and Moçambique; Keay (1959), a vegetation map of Africa south of the Tropic of Cancer; Rattray (1960), the grass cover of Africa; and Domke (1963), a revised vegetation map of Africa. The C.C.T.A. / C.S.A. (Commission for Technical Co-operation in Africa / Scientific Council for Africa) produces regular reports on vegetation mapping completed and in progress and urges the use of common scales and comparable principles in mapmaking.

Various reliable plant community studies that cover the arid area in general are noted in this paragraph. Such studies include Adamson's (1938) work on the Kamiesberg area, a region that received 5 to 13 inches of rainfall, and Bews' (1916, 1920) coverage of the chief vegetal types, a work that considered plant distribution and succession. Compton (1929*a,b*) discussed Karroo vegetation, including dry and transitional types, and Miller (1946) the Kalahari. Dyer (1955) reviewed the vegetation in South West Africa, Bechuanaland (now Botswana), and South Africa. Edwards (1951) reported on vegetation in relation to soil and water conservation in low-rainfall areas. Important publications on the Namib include Walter (1936*a*, 1964), Logan (1960), and Giess (1962). Phillips (1959) presented in a 424-page book a comprehensive study of agriculture and ecology in Africa. (He divides the continent into bioclimatic regions based upon rainfall, vegetation, humidity, and temperature. These divisions form the basis for a discussion of agricultural uses and potentialities; a map of the regions is included.) Pole Evans (1929) prepared a chapter on the vegetation of South Africa which was included in a handbook on South Africa and science. Editions of the official yearbook on the Union of South Africa appearing in 1937 and earlier also contained chapters by Pole Evans on vegetation. Shantz (1940-1943) discussed the agricultural regions of Africa on an ecological basis. Shantz and Marbut (1923) mapped and discussed the vegetation and soils of Africa, and Shantz and Turner (1958) documented vegetation changes photographically over a third of a century. Muir (1929) described the Klein Karroo in the Cape province.

Walter (1936*b*) described the peculiar meteorological conditions of the Namib and their effect upon the soil and vegetation. Shaw (1947) published a paper on the vegetation of Angola.

The vegetation of Madagascar has been described by Perrier de la Bathie (1921, 1936) and Battistini (1964). Phillips (1956) reviewed the ecology of Great Nama Land desert, Karroo and Kalahari, and the dry regions of southern and eastern Africa. Rodin (1953) reported on the distribution of *Welwitschia mirabilis,* and Bullock (1952) listed the poisonous plants of South Africa. Bews' (1925) book on plant forms and their evolution in South Africa is outstanding for its discussion, under the heading of physiognomy, of size and growth characteristics of desert plants.

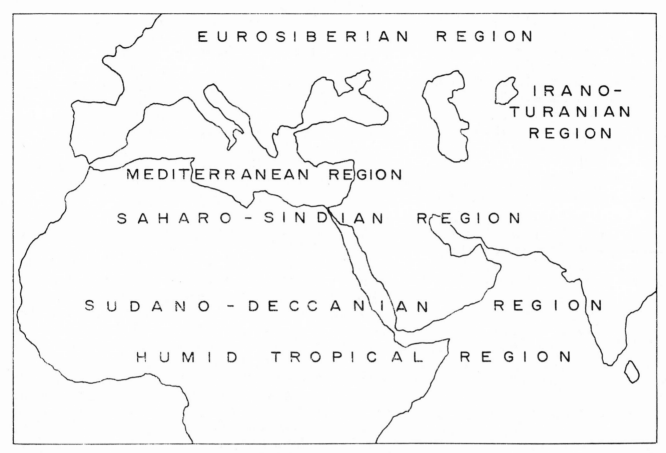

FIGURE 1. Floristic Regions of Afro-Asia (after Ozenda)

The published literature on the Kalahari-Namib desert area is adequate in all respects. Most of the publications are accessible in major scientific libraries. The coverage for the Namib is less extensive than that on the Kalahari, but, considering the paucity of vegetation, it is adequate. Current ecological research activities for both deserts is centered at the Botanical Research Institute, Pretoria.

2. Afro-Asian Deserts

Some desert areas of Asia and those of Africa have much in common; certain conditions of climate, terrain, and soils occur in the deserts of both continents. Ozenda (1958) noted the relative positions of different floristic regions of Afro-Asia; the Saharo-Sindian Region extends from the western Sahara in Africa far eastward into India (see Figure 1). Under Köppen's classification the desert areas of northern Africa, Arabia, and the southern part of Asia are BWh (desert, average annual temperature over 18°C); eastward from the Caspian Sea and northward from the Himalayas the desert becomes BWk (desert, average annual temperature under 18°C). Meigs (1960) shows these same areas as extremely arid or arid, and ranging from hot areas to warm areas with cold winters. Consultant Emberger has

commented that he believes the map of Meigs is the better of these two.

The recent Unesco-FAO map (Unesco, 1963), which is the most accurate of all bioclimatic maps, shows *true desert* regions surrounded by *desert* regions in both the Sahara and in the Arabian Peninsula, and in the Iranian Desert areas shows *desert* regions interrupted and surrounded by regions of lesser aridity. The map also shows a *desert* region in Pakistan and India separated from the Iranian *desert* regions by an area with more favorable moisture conditions.

The physical features of the Afro-Asian desert, including physiography and soils, have much in common. They all have relatively small sandy areas (10 per cent or less of total area), some mountainous areas, and large expanses of relatively flat land. The desert flora is sufficiently uniform from the Atlantic coast of North Africa through the Sahara, the Sinai Peninsula, extratropical Arabia, Southern Iraq, and Iranian Baluchistan to Sind to be considered as a single floral region, although some subdivisions have been recognized. Because of the similarity of vegetation and physical conditions, many studies have wide application outside of the specific area in which the work was done. For example, research in Algeria applies in some degree to the desert area from Morocco to Egypt; likewise, research in Egypt applies in some degree to Tunisia, the Sinai Peninsula, and Sudan. Israel serves as a scientific center for the region from the Sinai Peninsula to Turkestan, and from the Mediterranean to Afghanistan. Similarly, the work at the Central Arid Zone Research Institute at Jodhpur, India, applies widely throughout the eastern portions of the Afro-Asian desert area.

The Sahara

General Descriptions of Plant Communities

The Sahara, although the largest desert in the world, has great uniformity from west to east; the north-to-south differences are similar in the west, the center, and the east. Consultant Emberger points out, however, that the Atlantic Sahara is quite unique because of its relatively warmer winters and pronounced cloud cover. Capot-Rey's (1953) comprehensive book contains a great amount of basic information on the Sahara with special emphasis on the French Sahara. This standard reference is, unfortunately, out of print and not readily available in the United States.

Emberger has made many excellent studies in the Saharan area and has supervised the mapping of vegetation over a large part of the desert. He reported (1939) that even the driest places in Morocco receive small amounts of precipitation each year during the winter. Even outside the valleys there is a permanent although very scanty vegetation, partly dominated by *Acacia* species (*A. raddiana, A. seyal,* and *A. gummifera*)* on sandy soils, partly by smaller bushes or dwarfbushes like *Anabasis aretioides* on rocky soils. The sand dunes are colonized by *Aristida pungens.* Consultant Emberger supplemented the description with the following comments on the vegetation of Morocco. In eastern Morocco, almost the entire valley of the Moulouya River is extremely arid with a mean annual precipitation of 100 mm. In the main part of the valley the vegetation is a steppe of *Stipa tenacissima* or *Artemisia herba-alba* without trees except along the water course where there is *Populus alba, P. euphratica, Salix purpurea, Zizyphus* and *Retama.* In the lower valley *Pistacia atlantica* and the halophytes (*Anabasis,* etc.) *Zizyphus* and *Lycium intricatum* are frequent. In very arid western Morocco the vegetation consists of *Pistacia atlantica, Zizyphus, Atriplex halimus, Asparagus stipularis,* and annuals. In the south *Argania spinosa* is important because of its economic value. It is associated with the previously mentioned species and with cactiform species

of *Euphorbia: Euphorbia beaumierana* and *E. echinus.*

Tits (1926) divided the area south of the Atlas Mountains in the western Sahara into four vegetation districts:

1) "Dayas Sud-Oranaises," a semidesert steppe, is a transition between the Sahara and the steppe of the plateau. It is covered in part by an association including *Pistacia atlantica, Olea europaea,* and *Zizyphus lotus* and used as sheep pasturage by nomads.

2) "Hammada du Guir-Saoura" is an immense plateau of rocks characterized by *Acacia tortilis.*

3) "Grand Erg Occidental" is the large western sand desert. The dunes were categorized as low, medium, and high; and the vegetation on each was described by Tits.

4) "La Saoura," alluvial soil along the river, irrigated and planted with date palms.

The recently published book by Pierre Quézel (1965), *Vegetation du Sahara,* gives a great deal of very useful information on the western portion of the Sahara. The territory covered is bounded on the west by the Atlantic Ocean and on the north by the Atlas Mountains; the eastern boundary is roughly represented by a line between Tunis and the east side of the Tibesti massif; the southern boundary extends roughly from the middle of Chad on the east to the southern boundary of Mauritania on the Atlantic coast. Quézel, with some reservations, defines the limits of the Sahara on the north by the isohyet of 100 mm and on the south by the isohyet of 150 mm.

After a preliminary consideration of the environmental factors, Quézel presents detailed information on the vegetation of this portion of the Sahara. He first considers the vegetation on saline and sandy areas, then discusses the vegetation by geographical areas in the following order: the northern Sahara with three subdivisions, the northwest Sahara, the oceanic Sahara, the central Sahara, the western Sahara, the high mountains within the Sahara, and finally the southern Sahara. The characteristics of these various areas and their vegetation are summarized in 93 tables and the accompanying text discussion. All in all, Quézel provides a very complete and thorough coverage of the vegetation of this portion of the Sahara.

Quézel indicates that about one-fourth of the total area of the Sahara has a precipitation of less than 20 mm per year and that in these areas vegetation is practically lacking. When the precipitation is increased to between 20 and 50 mm per year the plant cover remains generally poor, but in favorable locations that receive runoff such as depressions and dayas, the beds of wadis, and some rocky slopes, the vegetation is richer. This statement holds particularly true in the northern and northwestern Sahara and

---

* Species Summary, p. 473, gives additional data for the species listed throughout this chapter and cites publications that discuss the species further.

part of the western Sahara. In the mountains of central Sahara, the beds of the wadis are generally occupied by a relatively very rich vegetation, whereas the rocks and the surrounding slopes remain almost barren. Above 50 mm of rainfall the vegetation cover is generally complete, but extremely variable. Quézel recognized three general bioclimatic areas to which he applied the terms "érémitique moyen," "érémitique inférieur," and "érémitique supérieur," the last being ordinarily totally barren.

In commenting on the foregoing discussions on the Sahara, consultant Emberger has stated that special mention should be made of the east central Sahara. He mentions that Leredde (1957) has described the remains of the forests of *Cupressus dupreziana* in the Tassili n' Ajjer in the middle of the Sahara. It is not a forest in the usual sense but an extremely scattered population of one hundred individuals, some with a circumference of 10-12 meters. The maximum density is about 16 trees per 2 kilometers of travel. The trees are regenerating but with difficulty. No characteristic species accompanies these trees, so it seems certain that the group should properly be classified as a relict forest.

Chipp (1930*b*) presented an easily readable discussion of the vegetation observed along a 1500-mile motor trip to Tamanrasset, including the western Ahaggar. He mentioned that southward from Algiers beyond the Atlas Mountains, the only permanent vegetation was confined to dry watercourses and drainage systems (oueds). He noted also that, apart from the vegetation of the oueds, ephemeral vegetation of grass-herbs springs into life for a few days after the very infrequent rainstorms.

Chipp (1930*a*), in describing the Nubian Desert, stated: "The rainfall of this region is very small and the country is a desert of sand, pebbles, and rock. There is a general absence of vegetation except the isolated *Acacia* bushes, tufted grasses, and hard desert herbs, which occur along the drainage lines in wadis, or curiously enough on small exposed escarpments. This is the type of country which stretches westward through the Libyan Desert, right across the Sahara, interrupted here and there by areas which are entirely devoid of all plant life."

Chevalier (1932, 1933) placed the upper limit of the desert at 200 mm precipitation in the north and agreed with Maire on 250 mm as the limit in the south, constituting the boundary with the Sahélienne area. The Sahélienne is a band of vegetation found where precipitation is from 250 to 500 mm, between the Sahara zone and the Soudanaise area. He noted that the northern Sahara has winter rains, the central Sahara irregular rains, and the southern Sahara summer rains. Monod (1954) gave a rather vivid description of the differences of vegetation related to terrain, substratum, and climate. He applied the term "contracté" (constricted) to the vegetation limited by general conditions of low rainfall to growing only in the wadis and used the term "diffus" for vegetation more generally distributed over the terrain where precipitation is not less than 30-50 mm in the north and 50-100 mm in the south. Monod also (1932) compared various classifications of vegetation made by different workers in the field and summarized his results in tabular form (see Table IV). See also his excellent work (1957) in which he dealt with the plant geographical subdivisions of Africa from various points of view, comparing again the more recent relevant works of many authors.

Cannon (1913) provided an excellent description of the vegetation of the Algerian Sahara. He described the topography and vegetation, beginning at an elevation of about 2,400 feet, which marks the northern edge of the region of the dayas. This region has poorly developed surface drainage; frequent depressions collect the runoff of surrounding small areas. These dayas differ from the undrained areas of the chotts in that they do not contain an excess of salt, probably because of efficient subsurface drainage. From this region the surface falls away, to the south and southeast, to a region of low and flat-topped mountains so irregularly disposed as to have given rise to the name "chebka," which means "net." The southern limit of the chebka is at an elevation of about 1,600 feet; below this are undulating stony plains (hamada) and large salty areas (chotts); below this, at an elevation of about 200 feet, is the reg desert. Each of these landscape types has its distinct vegetation. Scattered throughout this area are several important oueds. Cannon noted that an unexpectedly small amount of sand was observed in this area, but that a large portion of southern Algeria is covered by sand.

At the upper end of the desert in the vicinity of Laghouat, Cannon noted that one's first glance over the arid plain with its covering of small stones and pebbles gives the impression of total barrenness, but a closer examination of the plains, dunes, and mountains reveals the presence of either living plants or the dried remnants of plants from the preceding moist season. The most prominent plants in this area were *Acanthyllis tragacanthoides*, *Zollikoferia spinosa*, *Haloxylon articulatum*, and *Aristida pungens*. *Acanthyllis tragacanthoides* is a rather stout grayish-green shrub not over 47 cm high consisting of a group of unbranched or little-branched stems and provided with long, stout spines. *Haloxylon articulatum* is a shrub or halfshrub very common in the Sahara. It is spineless, and is browsed by all herbivorous animals. Cannon found that in this area the most

Table IV

COMPARISON OF ARID CLASSIFICATIONS (after Monod)

Pluies (hypothetique)	Monod (1932)	A. Engler (1910, 1925)	H. L. Shantz and C. F. Marbut (1923)	A. Chevalier (1927)
>500 mm >500 mm	(Berbérie)	*Mediterrangebiet*		*Région méditerranéenne* — Domaine mauritano-méditerraneen
150-500 mm 150-200 mm	PROVINCE STEPPIQUE NORD-AFRICAINE		Desert Shrub - Desert Grass (*Dg* on the map)	
0-150 mm	I. PROVINCE SAHARO-MÉDITERRANÉENNE ou SAHARO-SEPTENTRIONALE "Sahara algérien" "Sahara arabe" "Sahara septentrional"	"mediterrane Wüste"		*Région désertique intertropicale de l'ancien monde* — Domaine du Sahara occidental — Secteur algérien
150 mm	II. PROVINCE SAHARO-AFRICAINE ou SAHARO-CENTRALE "Sahara soudanais" des auteurs *pro parte* "Sahara touareg" "Sahara central" (parties hautes des massifs exclues)	Provinz der grossen oder zentralen Sahara	Desert-Shrub (*Db* on the map)	Secteur soudanais
150-500 mm	III. PROVINCE SAHARO-SAHÉLIENNE ou SAHARO-MÉRIDIONALE Sous-province sahélo-désertique Sous-province sahélo-soudanaise "Sahara soudanais" des auteurs *pro parte* "Sahel" ou "Zone sahélienne" "Sahara méridional" des auteurs *pro parte* "Zone subdésertique du Nord-Africain tropical" (H. Jumelle 1928)	Übergangsprovinz	Desert Shrub - Desert Grass (*Dg* on the map) Acacia - Desert Grass Savana (*a* on the map)	*Région intertropicale africaine* — Domaine sahélien
500 mm				
500-1500 mm	PROVINCE SOUDANAISE	Sudanische Parksteppenprovinz	Acacia - Tall Grass Savana (*s* on the map)	Domaine soudanais
1,500 mm			High Grass - Low Tree Savana (*ss* on the map)	Domaine guinéen
>1,500 mm	PROVINCE GUINÉO-FORESTIERE "Forêt dense équatoriale" "Forêt vierge"	Westafrikanische oder guineensische Waldprovinz	Tropical Rain Forest (*ff* on the map)	Domaine de la forêt dense équatoriale

Region bands (Monod): *Région méditerranéenne* / *Région désertique et subdésertique interrtopicale de l'ancien monde* / *Région intertropicale africaine*.
Engler bands: *Mediterrangebiet* / *Nordafrikanisch-indische Wüstengebiet* / *Afrikanische Wald und Steppengebiet*.
Shantz and Marbut bands: *Deserts* / *Grasslands* / *Forests*.

characteristic plant of the dunes is *Aristida pungens,* a grass common to a large area in the Sahara, locally called "drinn." In the nearby mountains he found *Acanthyllis tragacanthoides, Asparagus spinosa, Deverra scoparia,* and *Zollikoferia spinosa* (the most abundant plant in the area). Farther into the desert, Cannon observed a striking decrease in the general amount of vegetation, both by dwarfing and by decrease in number of individuals. Farther south, he noted that small perennials, 20-30 cm high, were widely scattered on the higher portions of the plain, but that the bare ground gave the general character to the landscape. Chief among these small perennials were species of *Aristida, Stipa, Anabasis,* and *Haloxylon,* with dwarf specimens of *Zizyphus lotus* in the washes near the dayas. In spite of heavy browsing by sheep and goats, *Haloxylon articulatum* was sometimes present in surprising numbers.

Cannon was also much surprised at the vegetation he found on the dayas. The principal tree is the betoum *(Pistacia atlantica),* which may attain both a height and a spread of 15 meters or more. Most individuals have their branches removed up to a height of about 10 feet, the reach limit of the browsing camel. The betoum is heavily browsed and owes its existence to protection by *Zizyphus* plants when it is young. *Zizyphus,* a spreading shrub reaching a height of 10 to 12 feet, has branches well-armed with stout spines and is rarely eaten by animals.

In the northern portion of the chebka region are scattered specimens of the jujube and betoum, as well as *Zilla macroptera, Retama sphaerocarpa,* and *Coronilla juncea.*

The habitat preferences of the plants of southern Algeria are marked, as would be expected from the striking differences in the habitats. On the dunes, for example, drinn *(Aristida pungens)* is possibly the most commonly occurring and most widely distributed sand-plant. On sand areas one finds also *Tamarix* species, *Euphorbia guyoniana, Ephedra* species, *Retama raetam, Limoniastrum guyonianum,* and other forms in smaller numbers. On the wadi banks are *Tamarix* and *Nerium oleander,* and near the oases are date palm and other introduced plants. On the floodplains a large number of species flourish, among the most typical of which are *Peganum harmala, Retama raetam,* and various species of *Ephedra, Genista,* and *Haloxylon.* The typical plants of the dayas are *Pistacia atlantica* and *Zizyphus lotus,* the latter occurring both on floodplains and on the reg. On the chotts are found mainly halophytes, such as *Anabasis articulata, Halocnemon strobilaceum, Salsola* species, and *Limoniastrum guyonianum.* The flora of the reg is essentially like that of the floodplains, which would be expected from the relation of the two habitats. South of Biskra, however, where the reg is probably not of fluvial origin, is a forest of *Zizyphus lotus,* which also includes a striking representation of *Ephedra* species.

On the hamada are to be found the fewest species and smallest individuals. Probably most perennials of the hamada are under 30 cm in height. Among the characteristic plants of the hamada are species of *Artemisia, Teucrium, Deverra, Centaurea, Acanthyllis,* Thymelaeaceae, *Echinops, Henophyton,* and *Haloxylon. Haloxylon* is probably the most widely distributed, occurring in other habitats as well.

In comparing the characteristic vegetation of the Algerian Sahara and of the desert of the southwestern United States, Cannon found little in common and many differences. In the Sahara, passing southward from the Sahara Atlas, he noted a great variety of topography, of which plains are the most extensive. The plains included three well differentiated regions: the dayas, the chebka, and the hamada. The topography is further differentiated by wadis and their floodplains and by low flat-topped mountains. In the northern portion of the plains, the sparse population of low perennials becomes continuously poorer until finally there appears to be none. The hamadas and the low mountains are almost entirely barren, but the floodplains and the wadis support a luxuriant population of perennials.

In contrast, the wide-stretching plains (bajadas) of southern Arizona are well covered with perennials of good size. The watercourses are fringed with trees, and often open forests are encountered on the floodplains. The mountains have a fairly dense plant population including trees and shrubs.

In the plains of southern Algeria, a region may appear barren, and only close inspection will show that plants are present. Cannon believes that the reason large numbers of plants can grow in certain areas is their small size, and that it probably would be difficult to find an equal number if the individuals were large. The perennials are inconspicuous, partly because they are small and partly because leaves are either absent or greatly reduced. Cannon does not believe that the plants of the northern Sahara are as spiny as those of Arizona.

Ozenda (1958) described seven biological habitats in the northern and central Sahara:

1) Ergs and other sandy soils
2) Regs with clay or rocky soils
3) Hamadas and rocky soils
4) Nonsaline depressions not inundated
5) Saline soils
6) Aquatic habitat
7) Oasis habitat

The vegetation of the ergs and of sandy soils is characterized by the dominance of drinn, *Aristida pungens*. When the vegetation of the erg is well developed, it includes (in addition to drinn) a woody vegetation including *Ephedra alata, Retama raetam, Genista saharae*, and *Calligonum azel*; and herbaceous plants of which *Cyperus conglomeratus* and *Moltkia ciliata* are the most abundant. In the central Sahara the ergs are generally bare.

On the rocky regs and the gravelly zones of the northern Sahara, a very diffuse community is dominated by *Haloxylon scoparium*. Where the reg has a superficial cover of sand, it develops a more luxuriant cover. The vegetation of the level or slightly sloping plateaus is characterized by *Fagonia glutinosa* and *Fredolia aretioides*. In the dry season these appear to be the only permanent vegetation, but after rains a cover of annual plants develops, including *Erodium, Lifago, Convolvulus supinus*, and others. In sloping soils occur *Haloxylon scoparium* communities. The rocky plateaus and the regs of the central Sahara are absolutely bare. The vegetation of the slopes and cliffs is relatively rich, with a large proportion of rare and endemic species.

The vegetation of the dayas (nonsaline depressions) is dominated by *Pistacia atlantica* and *Zizyphus lotus*. The beds of wadis and valleys support a vegetation dominated by woody species. In a dry valley with a lime or rocky surface a "formation" with *Acacia* and *Panicum turgidum* is likely; in the northern Sahara the predominant *Acacia* species are *A. raddiana* and *A. tortilis*; in the central Sahara this "formation" becomes much richer floristically, including several species of *Acacia, Cassia obovata, Zizyphus lotus*, and *Z. mauritiana*.

Where moisture is available for a longer season, the association is characterized by *Tamarix articulata*. In the central Sahara this community includes *Atriplex halimus, Salsola foetida* and *Calligonum comosum*. Towards the south there is an increase in the number of tropical species such as *Calotropis procera, Aerva persica*, and *Ipomoea* species.

On those saline soils that are not extremely dry is found a plant community characterized by *Zygophyllum album* and perennial chenopods: *Salsola foetida, Traganum nudatum*, and *Salsola sieberi*. Where the ground is more moist the community gives way to *Tamarix*, and where the salt content is less, to *Atriplex halimus*. In the south, saline formations are rare and are accompanied by phreatophytic vegetation.

The following description of the vegetation regions of the Libyan Sahara was furnished by consultant Emberger. The Libyan portion of the Sahara, considering that area which receives less than 100 mm of precipitation annually, covers an area of 1,600,000 square kilometers or approximately 92 per cent of the territory of Libya. On the basis of ecological conditions and flora this immense area can be divided into several natural regions. The Hamada El Homra, in southern Tripolitania province, is an immense denuded plateau in which the depressions are occupied by a white sagebrush vegetation, *Artemisia herba-alba, Zilla spinosa*, various annuals, and often some clumps of jujube *(Zizyphus)*. It is a Mediterranean Saharan zone.

Fezzan, distinctly more arid than the Hamada El Homra, is the country of ergs and dunes with the valleys enriched from groundwater sources (phreatic). The regs are entirely bare, except in the depressions where a vegetation with *Salsola foetida* and *Hyoscyamus muticus* is developed. The dunes are generally bare, but sometimes support in the protected zones a vegetation including *Calligonum comosum, C. azel, Cornulaca monacantha* and *Aristida pungens*. The region of Ghat is entirely distinct; tropical influences are very clearly evident with a vegetation of such species as *Cassia lanceolata, Solenostemma argel*. One of the principal characteristics is the relative abundance of *Acacia raddiana* and *Maerua crassifolia*, which colonize not only the depressions but often the slopes of Nubian sandstone. The Sirte Desert is inland opposite the Gulf of Sirte. It is a gypseous desert interspersed with ergs and sebkhas. The reg is generally bare, but the depressions are occupied by communities where *Anabasis articulata, Zygophyllum album, Z. simplex*, and *Arthrophytum schmittianum* dominate physiognomically.

The Sirte mountains, between the Sirte Desert and Fezzan, include the elevated hills of the Jebels Uaddan (Ouaddans), Harvj (Harovj), and Sauda, which reach an altitude of 800 meters. The rains are more frequent than in the desert environments, and accordingly the wadis and talwegs are covered with a relatively rich vegetation of such species as *Acacia raddiana, Maerua crassifolia, Panicum turgidum* and *Rottboellia hirsuta*. The Libyan Desert, properly speaking, covers more than 900,000 square kilometers or 53 per cent of the area of Libya. It is desert with gypseous and clay regs in the north on Tertiary terrain, in the depressions of which develops a vegetation dominated by *Anabasis articulata* and *Salsola foetida*; further south it is characterized by gravelly regs and ergs (absolute desert). The Libyan Desert rejoins the Fezzan to the south of the Sirte mountains. It is devoid of perennial plants outside of the zones with permanent underground water tables. Rains are exceptional; as of 1965, there had not been more than 0.2 mm per year at Kufra for 12 years. The Jebel Uweinat (Auenat) and the outer hills of Tibesti in the south (south of the Tropic of Cancer) present a vegetation of Sudanese affinities, including such plants as *Acacia raddiana, Maerua, Aerva, Panicum turgidum, Cleome droserifolia, C. chrysantha,* etc.

Kassas and El-Abyad, who studied the vegetation of Egypt extensively, divided (1962-1963) the vegetation into fourteen community types, each with its particular dominance as follows:

1) Desert grassland, dominated by the tussock-forming and sand-binding plant, *Panicum turgidum* (a favorite fodder plant subject to destruction by grazing). This community includes other perennials and some small shrubs. It is found in the lower courses of the main channels of the drainage systems where the ground is covered with continuous sheets of sands of negligible salinity.

2) Open desert scrub, dominated by the succulent chenopod *Haloxylon salicornicum* and others. (This type is also found in the channels of the drainage systems where the ground surface is covered with coarse materials.) This community also includes other shrubby plants and *Panicum turgidum.*

3) A transitional community type occurring within the drainage channels, codominated by *Haloxylon salicornicum* and *Panicum turgidum.*

4) A community found in the main channels of drainage systems, particularly in limestone areas. Stream beds are often covered with mixed rock detritus. The community is dominated by *Zygophyllum coccineum* and a large number of other species varying from grasses to shrubs.

5) A transitional community between types and dominated by *Zygophyllum coccineum* and *Panicum turgidum.*

6) A community type codominated by *Zygophyllum coccineum* and *Launaea spinosa;* it is confined to the eastern edges of the Cairo-Suez desert and widespread in the wadis of the limestone country in that area.

7) An open scrubland, codominated by *Retama raetam* and *Panicum turgidum.* This community type is present in limited stretches of downstream parts of the main wadis, where the soil is mixed sand and silt, mostly waterborne.

8) A scrubland, characterized by great abundance of *Anabasis articulata* and codominated by *Retama raetam.* This community is abundant in the channels of the upstream parts of wadis.

9) A community type dominated by *Anabasis*

articulata and found on both limestone desert and gravel desert.

10) A community type dominated by *Ephedra alata,* covering limited parts of the major channels of the main drainage systems.

11) A community type dominated by *Artemisia monosperma,* abounding within a few distantly isolated drainage systems. *A. monosperma* is the most abundant species although subject to destruction by cutting.

12) A community type dominated by *Zygophyllum decumbens* and restricted to the smaller tributaries of the drainage systems. It includes some species that are not recorded elsewhere within the area.

13) A desert grassland community dominated by *Lasiurus hirsutus,* occurring in the smaller or upper parts of runnels where the surface veneer of sand is thin and discontinuous; it differs in this from the grassland type (*1,* above) dominated by *Panicum turgidum,* which is well developed only in the main channels where there is a continuous cover of sand.

14) A scrubland type of vegetation dominated by *Acacia tortilis* and found in a limited area of the northeastern corner of the Cairo-Suez desert.

Kassas pointed out that the Egyptian desert is a mosaic of numerous microbiotopes. This very important factor explains the distribution of the species in these hyperarid regions. It is probable that Kassas' remarks may be extended to a degree to all deserts, according to consultant Emberger.

Hassib's (1951) system in general agrees with that of Kassas, but it describes the vegetation of Egypt a little differently. He divides the desert area into what he calls "plant associations." The more important of these are as follows:

1) The *Panicum turgidum* association is the most important because of wide distribution; it is found on sandy plains and broad shallow valleys; mixed grasses, herbs, and shrubs occur with it.

2) The *Zilla spinosa* association has wide distribution on deep sandy soils.

3) The *Pithuranthos tortuosus* association covers large areas of sand in the Libyan Desert, often with *Zilla spinosa.*

4) The *Zygophyllum coccineum* association is common on rocky desert plateaus and shallow depressions on the margins of deep valleys; *Reaumuria hirtilla* is often associated with it.

5) The *Haloxylon salicornicum* association is common and widely distributed on the sandy floors of shallow wadis and on small sandy dunes.

6) The *Capparis spinosa* association is found on rocks and the high cliffs of deep wadis.

7) The *Odontospermum pygmaeum* association is abundant on loose stony areas or banks of wadis.

8) The *Cornulaca manacantha / Convolvulus lanatus* association is found on sandy soil with the drifting sand collecting around the plants.

9) The *Reaumuria hirtilla* association is widely distributed in depressions on exposed plateaus; this species forms pure associations and is also common on rocky ground in deep wadis associated with *Zygophyllum coccineum*.

10) The *Salsola foetida* association is abundant in the sandy ground of broad shallow wadis.

11) The *Cleome droserifolia* association is found in broad shallow wadis.

12) The *Aristida coerulescens / Danthonia forskalii* association accumulates sand, forming small dunes in drifting sand areas.

Hassib (1951) also stated that of the 755 species listed for the Egyptian desert, 46 per cent are annuals, 7.2 per cent small trees and shrubs, 0.1 per cent succulents, and most of the remainder are low-growing perennial plants.

Taxonomic and Floristic Works

Basic catalogs and lists of names in various languages include the works of Issa (1930), Latin, French, English, and Arabic names; Emberger and Maire (1941), catalog of plants of Morocco; Trabut (1935), cultivated and useful plants; and Long (1963), glossary of herbage terms.

Sahara vegetation is well known and is adequately covered in major publications such as: Maire (1921 - 1945, 1952-); Sauvage and Vindt (1952-1954) and Jahandiez and Maire (1931-1934) on Morocco; Monteil (1949-1953, with Sauvage) on the western Sahara; Hutchinson and Dalziel (1927-1936) on West Africa; Tits (1926) on the western Sahara; Monod (1938) on the eastern Sahara and Afro-Asian deserts in general; Maire (1921-1945, 1926, 1933-1940, 1938, 1943, 1952-) with various associates, on Algeria, Libya, and the northern Sahara in general; Täckholm (1956) and Täckholm and Drar (1941-1954) on Egypt and the Sudan; Muschler (1912), a very useful 2-volume flora of Egypt; Broun and Massey (1929) and Andrews (1950-1956) on the Sudan (three volumes); and Quézel (1954, 1954-1961) and Quézel and Simonneau (1960) on northern Africa. Corti (1942) compiled a comprehensive catalog of the flora with a statistical analysis and biological spectrum for the central Sahara. The most recent flora of Algeria and the southern Sahara is that of Quézel and Santa (1962-1963).

Many localized or specialized studies cover small areas or groups of plants. Among the best are studies of: cucurbits by Hassib (1938); *Anabasis aretioides* by Killian (1939*b*); acacias by Chevalier (1928) and Roberty (1948); ferns by Macleay (1951); lichens by Faurel, Ozenda, and Schotter (1953); and the ferns, gymnosperms, and monocotyledons of Tunisia by Cuénod (1954). Here again the monumental work of Täckholm and Drar (1941-1954) must be mentioned, since many genera and species are dealt with in monographic form. Although not readily accessible, the works of Battandier (1888-1890) and Battandier and Trabut (1895) provide excellent coverage for Algeria.

Ecological Works

Many generalized vegetation maps have been published covering all or major portions of the Sahara. Noteworthy are those of Aubréville (1949), whose map extends south of the Sahara; Emberger (1957); Unesco (1963) (bioclimatic map); Shantz and Marbut (1923); and Monod (1957). Maps covering portions of the Sahara are those of Maire (1926) of Algeria and Tunisia; Barbour (1961) of the Sudan; Harrison and Jackson (1955) of the Sudan; Jaeger (1936) of Algeria and Ionesco (1964*a*) of Morocco.

Numerous studies of plant distribution and plant sociology cover a major portion of the Sahara. The lightest coverage is in the center, where the vegetation is scarcest. Most of the reports on vegetation of the interior are based upon observations by botanists traveling through or spending very little time there; therefore long-time records are largely lacking. Studies are also very limited along the southern border. Even after all but the most important are eliminated, more than a hundred remaining vegetation studies have made significant contributions to the knowledge of the Sahara. A selection of these appears in the Pertinent Publications list, and many are cited below in the remainder of this section.

A sample of the various good descriptions of the vegetation and ecological relationships includes Osborn (1939) comparing Morocco and Australia; Guinea (Hernández-Pacheco *et al.*, 1949, vol. 4) on the Spanish Sahara; Chevalier (1933) on northwestern tropical Africa; Nègre (1959) on western Morocco; Hagerup (1930) on Tombouctou; Humbert (1928) on the western Atlas area; Quézel (1957) on the high mountains of the northern Sahara; Zolotarewsky and Murat (1938) on the southern Sahara; Maire (1938, 1933-1940, 1943, and many other publications) on the Sahara; Monod (1932) and Ozenda (1958) on the northern and central Sahara; Emberger (1939) on Morocco; Emberger (1955) on northwest Africa; Cannon (1913) on Algeria; Thomas (1921) on the Libyan Desert; Guinochet (1951), Long (1954), and Burollet (1927) on Tunisia; Hassib (1951) on Egypt; Kassas (1952c, 1953, 1955, 1961), Kassas and Girgis (1964), and Kassas and Imam (1957) on Egypt and the northeast Sahara; Halwagy (1961) and Chipp (1930a) on the Sudan.

These studies are all in general agreement that the vegetation changes from moister Mediterranean types in the north to tropical savanna types in the south. The vegetation is strongly influenced by winter rainfall in the north, irregular and very scarce rainfall in the center, and predominantly tropical summer rainfall in the south; the amount of rainfall varies from 300 mm at the north and south boundaries down to less than 10 mm in a great part of the desert area. In some areas a large decrease in annual rainfall is found as one considers locations quite close to one another. The amount and character of the vegetation varies in general with the rainfall, from communities of trees, shrubs, and herbaceous plants to scanty stands of small shrubs and herbs, and finally to totally barren land.

Useful detailed ecological studies have been made in many local areas, covering the general relationships of plants to an arid environment and sometimes special conditions such as salinity, sand, cultivation, human occupation, grazing, and burning. For example, Stocker (1926, 1927) treated the area northwest of Cairo, and Halwagy (1963) described the vegetation of islands in the Nile near Khartoum. Lavauden (1927) described forests, Boudy (1949) the North African forests, and Crossa-Raynaud (1960) fruit orchards. Some of these studies also dealt with individual plants rather than groups of plants. These include such plants as *Acacia*: Aubréville, (1937), Boulhol (1940), and Quézel and Simonneau (1963); *Alhagi*: Kassas (1953); *Haloxylon*: Haines (1951a); *Bromus*: Killian (1942); *Frankenia*: Killian (1951); *Fagonia*: Montasir and Shafey (1951); *Kochia*: Drar (1952), Foury (1952), and Thoday (1956); Mangrove: Ascherson (1903); *Zilla*: Montasir (1951); *Zygophyllum*: Montasir and Abd el Rahman (1951); Zygophyllaceae: Ozenda and Quézel (1956).

The interrelationships of plants in sand dunes have been studied at various locations by such ecologists as Drar (1948), Capot-Rey (1953), Monod (1955), Ionesco (1958), Aufrère (1932, 1935), and Brosset (1939).

Saline soils and halophytes have been studied at various areas; among the important studies are those of Berger-Landefeldt (1959), Burollet (1925), Dubuis and Simonneau (1955, 1957, 1960), Killian (1931, 1935; 1951), Killian and Lemée (1948-1949), Novikoff (1958, 1964), Quézel and Simonneau (1960), Simonneau (1953a, b; 1954a, b), Tadros (1953), and Tadros and Atta (1958). Finally, the climatic map of the Sinai peninsula by Boyko and Boyko (1957) may be mentioned in this connection since it is based entirely on plant-ecological studies and serves as an example of the new line of research, "Ecological Climatography."

Studies of useful plants include Renaud and Colin (1934) on medicinal plants, Busson *et al.* (1965) on forage plants. Most of the studies on harmful plants have considered toxic rather than structural features. Important contributions have been made by Foley and Musso (1925), Kirk (1946), and Sandberg *et al.* (1957-1960).

Summary of State of Knowledge

The coverage for the Sahara is adequate in all botanical categories in the eastern, northern, and western portions, but is weak in the central and southern areas. The taxonomy of plants has been covered very well, but the information in general is not in form easily accessible for ordinary use. Many of the manuals are in several volumes with publication over a period of years, such as the work of Maire and his associates (1921-1945). The ecological coverage, including phytogeography and phytosociology, is very good, but most of the publications are in French only, and some are in serials not available in most libraries. It is unfortunate that Capot-Rey's (1953) valuable work on the French Sahara is presently out of print, although it is available in many libraries.

There appears to be a general slowdown in the research program due to several causes, possibly the most important of which is the withdrawal of European scientists. Botanical research is, however, being done to a limited extent in Algeria, Egypt, Libya, Mauritania, Morocco, Senegal, and Sudan (Paylore, 1967).

The Somali-Chalbi
General Descriptions of Plant Communities

In delineating the extent of the Somali-Chalbi, the work of Trewartha (1954), Meigs (1966), and Pichi-Sermolli (1955a) should be reviewed. Chapter I of this series presents a map of the desert area used in the present study.

Pichi-Sermolli (1955a, b) has provided the most comprehensive discussion of the overall Somali-

Chalbi desert area, and the following account is based on his publications. He divided the arid zones into eight principal types: maritime vegetation, desert vegetation, subdesert shrub and grass, subdesert shrub with trees, subdesert scrub, subdesert bush and thicket, xerophilous open woodland, and vegetation of sites where water is present.

1) Maritime Vegetation: This type is important because it extends from approximately 15° N to 2° N (approximately 3,000 square kilometers) and includes the driest portion of the Somali-Chalbi desert area. Along the coast of the Red Sea, the Gulf of Aden, and the northern part of the Indian Ocean, the annual precipitation varies from approximately 25 to 125 mm, with a dry season of 8 months and mean annual temperature of 30° C. In part of this area dews are abundant. Most of the beaches have a substratum derived from recent coral rocks. The vegetation is largely made up of salt-tolerant plants, including herbs, shrubs, and some small trees. This vegetation is not too well known by botanists, but has been studied to some extent by Pichi-Sermolli (1955a), Beguinot (1915, 1918) (mangrove communities), Ciferri (1939a), Gilliland (1952), and Meigs (1966).

2) Desert Vegetation: Extensive areas of absolute desert, devoid of vegetation, are not found in the Somali-Chalbi area, but in some parts the vegetation is very scanty, consisting of a few widely-spaced herbs, grasses, undershrubs, dwarf shrubs, and occasional solitary stunted trees. Throughout much of the year patches of ground are devoid of any vegetation, but when rains occur an ephemeral flora appears. Climatic conditions are severe with an annual rainfall of less than 100 mm and mean annual temperature near or above 30° C. In many localities, however, the desert vegetation is a result of edaphic aridity rather than climatic deficiencies.

The desert vegetation has not been the subject of intensive studies, and most of our knowledge has been gained from the reports of traveling scientists. Among those who have contributed are: Chiovenda (1929-1936), Edwards (1940), Gilliland (1952), and Popov (1957) on the Socotra area.

According to Pichi-Sermolli (1955a, b), desert vegetation is made up of nearly the same species as subdesert vegetation with a gradual transition between the types, the principal difference between the two being the different degree of cover of the soil surface.

3) Subdesert Shrub and Grass: Included here are plant communities in which more than half the soil surface is bare of vegetation. Occasional solitary dwarfed trees sometimes occur. On deep homogeneous soils a tussock grass and widely spaced woody plants may be found. The typical sites for this type

are plains and gentle slopes with homogeneous soil surfaces.

Comparing with categories of other scientists, this type includes the "desert shrub/desert grass," the "salt desert shrub," and in part the "acacia/desert grass savannah" of Shantz and Marbut (1923); the "subdesert" of Gillett (1941); the "subdesert association" and in part the "gypsum-tolerant vegetation" of Gilliland (1952); and the "acacia/desert grass savannah," the "open grassland" (desert grass), the "desert shrub/desert grass," the "shrub desert," and in part the "shrub acacia/desert shrub" of Edwards (1940). It also includes in part the "steppe" of German authors and the "steppa" of some Italian botanists.

The climate in which the subdesert shrub and grass is found is hot and dry, with mean annual rainfall below 180 mm (Pichi-Sermolli, 1955a) and a dry season of 6 months or more. The mean annual temperature is near or above 30° C. Information on this type is well summarized by Pichi-Sermolli (1955a). He believes on the basis of available information that the type covers large areas: in French Somliland, in areas flanking French Somaliland to the northwest (Dankalia, now part of Ethiopia) and to the southeast (former British Somaliland, now part of Somalia), and in northern and eastern Kenya. The type is also present in Socotra.

4) Subdesert Shrub with Trees: This type of vegetation consists of a very open stand of shrubs and shrublets with scattered trees. The shrubs are 1 to 2 meters in height, solitary or in small groups. The shrublets are solitary or associated with shrubs to form small colonies. Succulents of various sizes are common. Some scattered perennial grasses and herbs occur. The scattered solitary trees, either deciduous or succulent, rarely exceed 6 to 7 meters in height. This vegetation occurs in a very severe climate, with annual rainfall less than 150 mm and annual mean temperature near or above 30° C.

The subdesert shrub with trees type is characteristic of slopes and escarpments of hills, plateaus, and mountains where the substratum is rocky and stony with a discontinuous or broken soil surface. It is found on the slopes of the Danakil Alps, the Ethiopian plateau, the mountains of northern Somalia, and Socotra, where the type attains its greatest growth and covers a large part of the hill slopes.

5) Subdesert Scrub: The plant communities included in this type of vegetation consist of an open assemblage of dwarf trees, usually less than 3 meters in height, stunted shrubs, shrublets, succulents, and ephemeral grasses and forbs. The absence of perennial grasses and scarcity of trees are important features of this type vegetation, which includes the "desert shrub" of Shantz and Marbut (1923); part of the "Buschsteppe," the "Dornbuschsteppe," and the "Gebüsch" of Engler (1910, 1925); and part of the "boscaglia" and "spineto" of Italian writers.

The climate in which this type develops has a rainfall of 150 to 270 mm with mean annual temperatures from a little below to a little above 30° C. The substratum is similar to that for subdesert shrub and grass, but more open and with less water-retaining capacity near the surface, hence providing more favorable conditions for deep-rooted woody plants.

The type is found in the Danakil-Dancalla region, in the territories formerly known as Italian and Ethiopian Somaliland, and in part of French Somaliland. It extends into Kenya southeastward from Lake Rudolph nearly to Garissa. Some limited areas have also been reported in Tanganyika by Gillman (1949).

6) Desert Bush and Thicket: This type of vegetation consists of an open community of woody plants with grasses and forbs. The dominant deciduous, woody plants branch from near the ground or have short trunks, and rarely exceed 4 meters in height. Solitary bushes about 1 meter high are scattered among tufts of perennial grasses with ephemerals growing in the bare spaces following rains. The solitary bushes or thickets are well separated, so that it is easy to walk among them.

Included in this type are the *"Commiphora* bush/*Acacia* open deciduous scrubs" of Gillett (1941), in part the "mixed deciduous woodland and thicket" of Gilliland (1952), a small part of the "shrub acacia/desert shrub" and the "desert grass/bush (dry bush with trees)" of Edwards (1940), and in part the "boscaglia" of Italian writers and the "Dornbuschsteppe" of Engler (1904).

Climatic conditions fostering this type are similar to those for subdesert scrub, with an annual rainfall of 150 to 220 mm and mean annual temperatures of 28° to 29° C. Soils have a high proportion of sand, varying in color from red to light gray. Limestone and noncalcareous substrata occur. This vegetation type is well represented in the northern part of the Somali-Chalbi area but is not present in its typical constitution in the southern part.

7) Xerophilous Open Woodland: Pichi Sermolli (1955a) pointed out that this type overlaps the arid and semiarid zones as commonly outlined, as for example by Thornthwaite's and de Martonne's classifications. It is found under rainfall of 250 to 360 mm and mean annual temperatures of 28° to 31° C.

He described this type as an open assemblage of woody plants, grasses, and herbs among which large bushes and perennial grasses are dominant. The large, deciduous, and thorny shrubs are 3 to 5 meters in height and either branching from near the ground or short-boled. The bushes occasionally form thickets, but are generally widely spaced, with scattered trees characterizing the type. Climbers are common. Grasses, forbs, and low shrubs form a discontinuous ground cover, with ephemerals filling in the spaces following rains. The physiognomy of this type is characterized chiefly by trees and shrubs, frequently with flat, umbrella-like crowns, and grassy ground vegetation.

The xerophilous open woodland corresponds to the "desert grass/bush (dry bush with trees)" of Edwards (1951), to the "tree acacia open woodland" of Gillett (1941), to the *"Acacia bussei*[*] woodland" and the *"Acacia etbaica* woodland" of Gilliland (1952), to the "boscaglia xerofila" of Italian authors, to the "laubwerfende Dornbuschsteppe" and "Dornbuschgehölze" of Engler (1904; 1910, 1925), to the "thorn forest" and in part to the *"Acacia*/desert-grass savannah" of Shantz and Marbut (1923), in part to the "tropical thornland" of Burtt-Davy (1938), in part to the "bushland, thickets and scrub" ("deciduous bushland"; "tall deciduous thickets, thorny"; "dry scrub with trees") of Greenway (1943), in part to the "bushland and thicket" of Gilliland (1952), in part to the "deciduous scrub formation" of Phillips (1930).

This type of vegetation covers a great part of the arid zone. It is present in the Danakil-Dancalla region, throughout Somalia, and extends into Kenya, where it covers all the areas of the arid zone not occupied by types of vegetation described above.

8) Vegetation of sites where water is present: These sites are represented by pools, wells, rivers without permanent running water (wadi or tug), drainage basins with no outlet (bogh and bulleh), inland deltas (doho), banks of rivers, shores of lakes, and swamps.

In areas of desert vegetation, these more favorable sites may support a few scattered trees of which species of *Acacia* are the most common. In some places they are accompanied by a few scattered palms (*Hyphaene* and *Phoenix*). In subdesert areas where moisture may be available for longer periods or all year, phreatophytes become dominant. These include species of palms, *Acacia, Zizyphus, Ficus, Tamarix,* and others, together with smaller plants including sand-binding grasses. The constituents of this type and the conditions under which they grow are briefly but comprehensively summarized by Pichi-Sermolli (1955a).

---

[*] Species Summary, p. 473, gives additional data for the species listed throughout this chapter and cites publications that discuss the species further.

Taxonomic Works

The taxonomic coverage for the Somali-Chalbi is light in terms of numbers of published flora and is spotty in geographic coverage. Ethiopia has been well covered by the publications of Cufodontis (1953-1965). Somalia, especially the part formerly called Italian Somaliland, has been covered by Chiovenda (1929-1936) and Chiovenda and Corni (1929). Medicinal and poisonous plants have been described by Negri (1948). The works of Githens (1949) and Watt and Breyer-Brandwijk (1962) have been cited previously.

Ecological Works

The phytogeography of this area has been briefly but comprehensively reviewed by Pichi-Sermolli (1955a), and the principal publications previous to that date are listed in the extensive bibliography of that review. This is the only readily available description of the vegetation of the area as a whole, and one of the few descriptions of the Chalbi in the vicinity of Lake Rudolph. Among the phytogeographical discussions of more limited areas are those of Collenette (1931) for the northeastern part of the former British Somaliland, the rather general treatise of Drake-Brockman (1912) on the same area, the discussion of plant formations of western British Somaliland by Gillett (1941), the vegetation of eastern British Somaliland by Gilliland (1952) and French Somaliland by Chevalier (1939), the vegetation map and discussion of Kenya by Edwards (1940), the vegetation of Socotra by Popov (1957), and several papers relating to the vegetation of the former Italian Somaliland by Ciferri (1939b), Negri (1940), and Scortecci (1932). The 1904 publication of Engler included a discussion of vegetation relationships in the Somalilands.

Summary of State of Knowledge

Very little literature discusses phytosociological relationships for the Somali-Chalbi. Most of the ecological papers are phytogeographic descriptions and cover some information on physiognomy, but no extensive listing of life forms or similar plant characteristics was found.

The taxonomic coverage for the Somali-Chalbi is not extensive and is generally spotty. There is no compact manual of the flora. Many of the publications are in Italian. The Somali-Chalbi is in need of further study, especially the area around Lake Rudolf and the southern borders where it merges into savanna and other semiarid types.

The Arabian Desert

This desert, for the purposes of the present study, is defined to include the Syrian, Saudi, Aden, and Tihama deserts and the very dry Rub 'al Khali. It lies within the Arabian peninsula and Iran, Iraq, Israel, and Syria, and is roughly a rectangle, with its longer axis extending from southeast to northwest through the Arabian Peninsula to the Mediterranean Sea. The Arabian desert area has been classified in slightly differing ways by Meigs (1957) and Unesco (1963).

General Descriptions of Plant Communities

The vegetation of this area has been most thoroughly studied in Palestine. The earlier studies of Eig have been further amplified by the Department of Botany, Hebrew University of Jerusalem, headed by M. Zohary, whose *Plant Life of Palestine* (1962) offers an excellent foundation for anyone desiring to obtain a general knowledge of the phytogeography and ecology of the Arabian Desert area. There are also many FAO reports containing information of value. Palestine, as considered by Zohary, includes Israel, Jordan, and the Gaza strip, and in his opinion has flora and vegetation problems shared by neighboring lands.

The arid vegetation of this area as outlined by Eig (1931-1932) belongs to three phytogeographic regions: Saharo-Sindian, Irano-Turanian, and Sudanian. Consultant Emberger has pointed out that these subdivisions are classic, but it should not be forgotten that they deal principally with plant species and not with ecological relationships. The Saharo-Sindian Region extends from the Atlantic Coast of North Africa, through the Sahara, the Sinai Peninsula, extratropical Arabia, southern Iraq, Iran, Baluchistan, and into India, to Sind.

The Irano-Turanian Region includes the steppes and deserts extending from the lowermost part of the Danube in the west to the tributaries of the 'Amur on the east. (There are also some areas with Irano-Turanian flora in Africa.) The Sudanian Region occupies part of tropical Africa north of the equatorial forest region, the southwestern corner of Arabia, southern Iran, and Baluchistan.

The following comments on the Eig classification result from correspondence with consultant Boyko.

In general the plant geographical subdivision of Eig, described in his great 2-volume work (1931-1932) containing 120 pages of distribution tables, has been used by Zohary and his collaborators, but it refers mainly to the macrodistribution, i.e., the general distribution of the single species. This feature has an advantage in that the work is easily used by nonecologists or for superficial studies. The disadvantage of the arrangement is that it disregards for the most part the actual ecological interrelationships of plant species and plant communities. It is therefore in many cases misleading.

The more recent plant geographical subdivision of Boyko (1954) is based upon a combination of the general (macro-) distribution and the ecological amplitude of plant species. This combination seems to be particularly necessary in those regions where not only all woody plants including all dwarfy half-shrubs, but even certain annuals like *Centaurea hyalolepis* and others, are used for fuel and where this use, together with overgrazing, shifting agriculture in the flatlands, and terracing in the wadis, has distorted the natural distribution over a period of several thousand years.

The new plant geographical subdivision combines the old subdivision of Eig with the new ecological points of view, recognizing for the steppe and desert region a number of zonation belts applicable in horizontal as well as in vertical direction (that is, both by geography and by altitude). (The steppe belt is subdivided into the Anatolian steppe-belt, Irano-Turano steppe-belt, and Mauretano-Irano steppe-belt; in the desert belt, the Central Asiatic or Irano-Turano desert types are distinguished from the Saharo-Sindic desert types, with both meeting in Israel.) This plant geographical-ecological subdivision applies according to Boyko (1954) and Monod (1957) to the whole of Southwest Asia and partly to North Africa, as well.

Consultant Boyko points out that Palestine is the meeting place of the principal Africo-Asian plant-geographical belts including: the Mediterranean Forest Belt, the Arid Border-Forest Belt, the Steppe Belt, the Desert Belt, and the Sudano-Deccanean Belt.

The large global desert belt on both sides of the equator is subdivided according to the respective plant geographical regions. Two of these regions overlap in Israel. They are the Central Asiatic or Turanian Desert Region and the Saharo-Sindic Desert Region. The first is characterized by *Haloxylon persicum,* the second by the thermophilous *Haloxylon salicornicum.* Both these desert regions, apart from their high aridity, have few climatic features in common, but both characteristic species meet in the areas of the Wadi 'Araba that are at the higher altitudes and have the most continental conditions.

Quite generally the arid factor is more decisive in Palestine than the thermal factor for the distribution of many floristic elements of these two regions, and it is, therefore, difficult to define the two plant geographical regions as separate areas.

Pure Saharo-Sindic desert types are found only in the southern part of Wadi 'Araba and in the lower parts of the Dead Sea depression.

A particularly characteristic feature of the Saharo-Sindic Desert Region in contrast to the Central Asiatic Desert Region, is the occurrence of the date palm, *Phoenix dactylifera* in the oases. The south-ernmost oases in Israel (Dafieh and Sabcha of Eilat) are already the northernmost habitats of *Hyphaena thebaica,* growing there about 1½ meters higher above the groundwater level than does the date palm.

Zohary (1962) recognizes "steppe" as a timberless landscape with an open but more-or-less continuous vegetation of xerophilous shrubs, semishrubs, and herbs, with an upper precipitation limit of 350 mm. Deserts under certain conditions may have the same type of vegetation as steppe, but with lower and intermittent coverage.

Zohary recognizes three types of deserts: *(1)* "rain deserts," in which vegetation is patchy and very sparse, but still maintained by rainfall, *(2)* "runoff deserts," in which the amount of precipitation is insufficient to support any kind of vegetation except in depressions and low-lying places where ground water or runoff moisture accumulates, and *(3)* "absolute desert," in which there is no sign of vegetation.

In addition to categorizing vegetation by climatic determinants, he also categorizes them by edaphic determinants, notably the vegetation of the light soils belt along the coastal plain, the vegetation of swamps along the coastal plain, and the vegetation of saline areas. All of these may occur within the desert area but are not limited to it.

The Saharo-Sindian Region includes rain deserts, runoff deserts, and absolute deserts, using Zohary's terminology. He believes, however, that from the ecologic point of view, plants growing in temporary waterways, depressions, and runnels within desert surroundings can hardly be regarded as desert plants because such sites receive a considerable amount of runoff moisture in addition to rainfall. Plants growing under these conditions may differ largely in ecologic behavior from desert plants which subsist on the small amount of rainfall alone. He believes that, strictly speaking, there are no true desert plants in "runoff deserts."

Boyko differs from this opinion. In his review of the present manuscript he expressed the opinion that most of the species in the erosion channels, i.e., temporary waterways of the southern part of the Negev, are true desert plants from all points of view: morphologically, physiologically, plant geographically, and (not least) ecologically. Runoff water occurs there very rarely and in some years not at all. When it does occur it is usually connected with a sudden local rainfall of only a few minutes' duration; after a few hours the soil is again as dry as before. The amount of water rushing quickly through these erosion channels may be relatively high, but the effect on the root systems is in general very small.

A difference does exist, however, between these erosion channels and the surrounding area. Because the easily soluble chlorides are washed out in the soil beneath them, germination and establishment is easier there for most plants; the higher amount of water at disposal from time to time is an additional factor. Extensive studies have been carried out on salt conditions in erosion channels by Karschon (1956). In the southern Negev, as in all hot deserts with less than 50 mm yearly average rainfall, the slopes outside these erosion channels are almost completely bare of any vegetation but a few lichens, except in the shadows of big stones or on steep slopes with very low insolation.

Characteristic features of the Saharo-Sindian territory affecting vegetation include large expanses of hamadas, saline areas, and sand dunes, and almost complete lack of cultivation. Zohary (1962), from whom the ensuing discussion is adapted, divides the vegetation into four classes of plant communities: the first occupies coastal dunes and sand fields, the second consists of the halophytic vegetation, the third consists mainly of hamada vegetation, and the fourth is characteristic of interior sand dunes and sandy soils. To this consultant Boyko would add the vast areas of rock deserts, on which the vegetation varies with the type of surface material (e.g., igneous rocks, hard limestone, soft limestone, or marl). These variations are caused by mineral (chemical) composition as well as by physical characteristics (e.g., weathering and cracking differences, and even variations in color and heat capacity).

In the northern and central Negev, the *Zygophyllum* plant community is the most important; the key plant in this community is *Zygophyllum dumosum.** The community inhabits hamada and hamada-like gravel or stony hills and hillsides interrupted by plains and wadis (annual rainfall, 75 to 100 mm). The community supports a large number of winter annuals and some succulent perennials, many shedding their leaves during the dry season. In the case of *Zygophyllum*, this shedding results in a reduction of exposed plant surface that may amount to 87 per cent.

On soft gypseous soils are found dwarf shrubs with small succulent leaves and shallow root systems: *Chenolea arabica* or *Suaeda asphaltica* dominate in these areas.

Haloxylon salicornicum is a leafless, succulent, articulate dwarf shrub very similar to *Anabasis;* it flowers in late autumn and fruits in early winter. It is very widespread in the Middle East, covering vast stretches in the eastern part of the Saharo-Sindian areas of North Africa, and in Sinai, Arabia, southern Iraq, and Iran. In Palestine, the community dominated by this species is confined to sandy soils or sandy hamadas derived from the Nubian sandstone and igneous rocks; it never occurs on coastal dunes.

In the Arava and lower Jordan valleys and near the shores of the Dead Sea, certain tropical species are often found associated with Saharo-Sindian vegetation (largely confined to wadis having permanent or ephemeral watercourses). The most common of these tropical plants are *Acacia raddiana, Zizyphus spina-christi, Salvadora persica, Moringa aptera, Balanites aegyptiaca,* and *Calotropis procera.* The last is a highly salt tolerant Saharo-Sindian phreatophyte penetrating into the drier parts of Sudan, East Africa, and northwestern India.

Emberger thinks these areas should not be classed as having a tropical climate, but rather as having a Mediterranean climate, with rather warm winters (the average minimum of the coldest month, January, is about $10°$ C) but with the norm of rainfall being typically Mediterranean.

The salt desert communities of the Saharo-Sindian territory in the vicinity of the Dead Sea include such plants as *Suaeda monoica, S. forskalii, S. palestina, S. vermiculata, Salsola rosmarinus, S. tetrandra, Atriplex* spp., *Nitraria retusa, Tamarix* spp., and *Tetradiclis salsa.*

The *Anabasis articulata/Retama raetam* plant community is prevalent on the sandy plains of the central Negev. The dominant plant, *Anabasis articulata,* is deeply-rooting, articulate, leafless, and succulent. *Retama* is an evergreen shrub with a deep root system; it sheds its leaves at the end of the rainy season. In the sandy areas of the lower Jordan area an *Anabasis articulata/Zilla spinosa* association is very common.

A richer flora is found in the wadis, runnels, and depressions that cut across the sterile hamadas of the southern Negev, Edom, and Sinai, where moisture conditions are more favorable, including *Anabasis articulata, Zilla spinosa, Gymnocarpos fruticosum,* and others. In the deeper and broader wadis are often found *Tamarix* or *Acacia* trees along with *Retama* bushes.

According to Zohary (1962), in the interior sandy desert of dunes and sandy plains is found a community dominated by *Haloxylon persicum.* In Edom and the Arava Valley it forms a peculiar type of forest or scrub that is also present in the Aralo-Caspian sand deserts (the "saxaul" forests), in eastern Persia, and in the An Nafud region of northern Arabia. This is the southernmost area of distribution of *Haloxylon persicum,* which is a rather succulent, spartoid, articulate, many-branched shrub or tree (up to 4 meters high) with very deep roots. It flowers in

---

* Species Summary, p. 473, gives additional data for the species listed throughout this chapter and cites publications that discuss the species further.

spring and is well known as the ghada tree of the Arabs, which travelers to Arabia have mentioned as useful for camel fodder and charcoal. In this connection consultant Boyko makes the comment that ecological investigations and the distribution map of this true desert tree and its plant community (Boyko, 1949a) show its extremely wide ecological amplitude with regard to maximum and minimum temperatures and at the same time its extremely narrow amplitude with regard to soil. It occurs exclusively on sand, from sand deserts east of the Aral Sea with their extremely low winter temperatures (January isotherm minus 10° C) to the An Nafud desert with its extremely hot summers (July isotherm 35° C). Profiles through its root systems revealed one dense network beneath the sand surface using subterranean dew and every possible raindrop, and a very deep second system reaching 20-25 meters down to any permanent or seasonal groundwater level (Boyko, 1951). It is probably this *Haloxylon* "forest" that supplied the necessary charcoal fuel for the adjacent copper mines of King Solomon. Other plants noted along with *Haloxylon persicum* include: *Calligonum comosum, Salsola foetida, Zilla spinosa, Farsetia aegyptiaca, Pennisetum ciliare, Eremobium lineare,* and *Retama raetam.*

Zohary states that the Irano-Turanian vegetation is found on gray steppe soil and loess, mostly with very shallow A-C or C profiles (see chapter on surface materials by Harold E. Dregne). At times it occurs on hamada-like plains. The leading plants of the majority of the communities are dwarf shrubs, and only a few are trees. The most characteristic plants in Palestine are: *Pistacia atlantica, Zizyphus lotus, Retama raetam* var. *raetam, Phlomis brachyodon, Rhus tripartita, Artemisia herba-alba, Noaea mucronata, Anabasis haussknechti, Haloxylon articulatum,* and *Achillea santolina.* Related communities are widely distributed in the steppe belt of North Africa, the Syrian Desert, and Iraq.

According to Ashbel (1949), dew is a major factor in the water balance of the vegetation of Palestine, a subtropical country with rainless summers. He distinguishes between fog and dew, the former being a cloud that settles on the ground. Dewdrops differ in size and number, and hence the quantity that condenses upon the surface of objects varies. Measurements on the leaves and plants of different genera show different quantities of dew. The bulb, cereal, and rose families condense large quantities of dew, while conifers collect relatively little.

Some areas in Palestine have more than 200 dewy nights in a year, with a total accumulation of dew of more than 100 mm. The amount of dew formed on plants may be three times or more than that formed on a horizontal surface. Under favorable climatic conditions large amounts of dew can be deposited, and consequently, under certain circumstances, dew can be a major source of moisture for desert plants. In his recent work (1966b, pages 158-165) Boyko dealt with the condensation of "subterranean dew" in desert regions. He calculated a supply of 2 liters for one single cool morning on the feeder roots of a *Juncus arabicus* individual with a basal area of 30 cm diameter, i. e. of approximately 1/10 square meter. Indeed, in the western Negev plants may get more moisture from dew than from rainfall.

Vesey-Fitzgerald (1955, 1957a, b) studied the west coast and interior. He described the vegetation of the Red Sea coastal area as Sudano-Deccanian, and the interior largely Saharo-Sindian. A large part of the vegetation is composed of mesophytic herbs that grow only following rains. Perennials include many halophytes but almost no true succulents. The rainfall is light and irregular with the average below 5 inches. North of the Tropic of Cancer the Mediterranean Sea influences the climate and hence the vegetation strongly; below the Tropic, Vesey-Fitzgerald found the influence of the tropical monsoons predominant. The interior is dominated by great sand areas, notably An Nafud, the Ad Dahna', and the Rub' al Khali; much sand is also found along the coast. The sands are red or white, and the vegetation varies with the color of the sand. Consultant Boyko comments that here, too, the main color-related differences in the vegetation result principally from either differences in soil temperature (which varies with color) or differences in reflex radiation (reflected from the sand with intensity varying according to the sand color). Reflex radiation from the white sands adds to the radiation the plants receive directly from the sun, especially in the case of certain plant species morphologically more exposed to the reflex radiation. These color-related factors play a particularly important role in desert regions with the low cloudiness of the Arabian Desert and southwestern Asiatic deserts in general.

In an unpublished report on the Arabian Peninsular, Popov and Zeller (1963) noted that precipitation was higher on the mountain slopes facing the sea and that aridity increased progressively as one went inland. In the south they found rainfall more reliable in the summer and in the north more reliable in the winter. They noted that the western half of the Rub' al Khali is occupied by well-defined ridge dunes oriented west-southwest to east-northeast, sometimes reaching heights of 100 meters but usually lower. In the eastern Rub' al Khali the dunes may reach a height of 250 meters. This work of Popov and Zeller includes clear photographs of many different habitats and their accompanying vegetation. Adjacent text describes in detail each habitat shown and lists important species present in each.

Little vegetation grows on the deep sands, but no part of them is completely devoid of vegetation. The principal shrub is *Calligonum comosum*. *Cornulaca monacantha* is more local, being most common toward the east. Following rains many other varieties of plants appear.

According to Popov and Zeller (1963), a sparse vegetation exists in most of the interior of Arabia, even in the Rub' al Khali, which apparently receives under 50 mm of rainfall. Here grow deeply-rooted plants such as *Calligonum comosum* and *C. torophytes* together with species of *Aristida, Tribulus*, and *Fagonia*. They noted the total absence of vegetation on some gravel ergs and on mud and salt flats both within and outside the Rub' al Khali, and ascribed this absence to soil aridity rather than to climatic conditions. They define "subdesert vegetation" as that which occurs in areas receiving less than 100 mm of rainfall; this is the condition over most of the Arabian Peninsula, notably on the plains and the sands of Najd and Al Hasa and the drier hills of Hijaz. In central and eastern Arabia much of the vegetation is halophytic, especially on the plains, where such genera as *Haloxylon, Seidlitzia, Salsola*, and *Suaeda* predominate. Consultant Emberger mentions that he has seen specimens of *Juniperus phoenicea* from this region. In northeastern Arabia, aromatic bushes such as *Rhanterium epapposum* and species of *Artemisia* occur. In the foothills are found species of *Acacia and Lycium*; these shrubs form associations with tussock grasses such as *Panicum turgidum* and *Cymbopogon schoenanthus*, especially in the wadis. In the sands of the An Nefud and the Ad Dahna', the vegetation is more abundant and richer floristically than in the Rub' al Khali and includes such species as *Calligonum comosum, Haloxylon persicum, Ephedra alata, Artemisia monosperma*, and *Rhanterium epapposum* (the last largely confined to the gaps between the dunes).

Concerning Iraq, Zohary (1946) stated that the vegetation had been inadequately studied, but more recent work (Springfield, 1954; Guest, 1966) has improved this situation. Zohary recognized three types of vegetation: desert, steppe, and woodland. He considered the critical limit for desert vegetation to be 150 mm of rain per year in Iraq, compared to 100 mm in Transjordan and even less in the western Negev of Palestine and northern Egypt. Iraq includes Saharo-Sindian and considerable areas of Irano-Turanian territory (*sensu* Eig), notably the Western

Desert. From west to east and from south to north the vegetation changes rapidly from typical desert to steppe.

Zohary (1940*a*) outlined the Syrian Desert as a triangular area with its base on the 30th parallel and apex in the environs of Aleppo (Haleb). It is bounded on the east by the Euphrates River and on the west by a line drawn from Aqaba along the Wadi 'Araba, the Jordan Valley, the eastern slopes of Mt. Herman, Anti-Lebanon, and from Homs to Aleppo. It is a plateau with an average elevation of 700 meters sloping toward the east and southeast. It has a Mediterranean climate with a rainfall of less than 350 mm. The floristic elements of the Syrian Desert are: Mediterranean, Irano-Turanian, Saharo-Sindian, Eurosibero-Boreoamerican, and Sudano-Deccanian.

Taxonomic and Floristic Works

Few complete floras cover all vascular plants of the Arabian Desert, but a great number of limited studies have been made of small groups of plants (families and orders) and within local areas. The basic flora manual for this and other Asian areas is Boissier's *Flora Orientalis* (1867-1888). Also among the general floras are R. Blatter's *Flora of Aden* (1914-1916), Dickson's *The Wild Flowers of Kuwait and Bahrain* (1955), E. Blatter's *Flora Arabica* (1919-1936), Post's *Flora of Syria, Palestine and Sinai* (1932-1933), Bouloumoy's *Flore du Liban et de la Syrie* (1930), the *Florula Cisjordanica* (1940) and *Florula Transjordanica* (1930) of Oppenheimer and Evenari, Thiébaut's *Flore Libano-Syrienne* (1936-1940), Mouterde's (1966) *Flora of Liban and Syria*, and Eig, Zohary, and Feinbrun's (1948) *Analytical Flora of Palestine*. One of the best floras is Rechinger's (1964) *Flora of Lowland Iraq*. The key, descriptions, and other notes on the flora of Iraq compiled by Blakelock are less convenient to use, scattered as they are through issues of the *Kew Bulletin* from 1948 to 1949. A valuable handbook for those interested in plant names is the *Dictionary of Assyrian Botany* by Thompson (1949). More limited publications include Burret (1943) on arabian palms, Edgecombe's (1964) *Weeds of Lebanon*, Eig (1955) on the genus *Astragalus*, Zohary (1956) on the genus *Tamarix*, and Bilewski (1965) on the moss flora of Israel. Al-Rawi and Chakravarty (1964) discussed the distribution, constituents, and uses of medicinal plants of Iraq, and Al-Rawi (1964) the wild plants of Iraq.

Ecological Works

A great many phytogeographical and phytosociological studies have been made in the Arabian

Desert, two-thirds or more concerned with Israel. Practically all of these and most similar studies in adjacent areas have been made by Israeli scientists. A number of studies have been made by Zohary, who followed the pioneering studies of Eig (1926, 1931-1932, 1933, 1938, 1939, 1946).

Zohary has published important papers on the area (1945, 1947*a, b*, 1950, 1962), as senior author with Orshan (Orshansky) (1949, 1954, 1956, 1959), and with Feinbrun (1951), and as junior author with Feinbrun (1955) and with Orshan (1963). D. Zohary (1953) has published a vegetation map of the central and southern Negev, and Boyko, Bugoslav and Tadmor (1957) have described vegetation in the central Negev.

Eig, in addition to providing a great deal of taxonomic information on the flora of this region, established the phytosociological foundation for studies throughout the Afro-Asian area. He was the first to point out the close relationships between floristic populations found throughout this area. Zohary and his associates expanded on the studies of Eig. They and other Israeli scholars filled in the gaps; consequently, the phytogeography of Israel and adjacent areas has been more completely covered than any other desert area in the Old World. To this phytosociological base Boyko (1946, 1949*a*, 1952, 1954, 1955*a, b*) has added a great amount of sociological and ecological information that has helped to complete the broad plant ecological picture. Other useful contributions to the phytogeography of Israel have been made by Aaronson (1913), Evenari and Richter (1937), Oppenheimer (1940), Whyte (1950), and Gruenberg-Fertig (1954).

Zohary has also been one of the major contributors to the phytogeography of desert areas outside of Israel, including the Syrian Desert (1940*a*), Sinai (1944), and Iraq (1946). Other contributors include Boyko (1955*b*), Delbes (1955), Guest (1953), Guenther (1930), Schwartz (1934), and Regel (1954, 1956*a, b*). Guest's 1966 work on the flora of Iraq is the best concise description available on the subject

The vegetation of the Arabian Desert exclusive of the Arabian Peninsula has been thoroughly studied because of its central position in plant migration routes. Phytogeographical relations have been treated with special thoroughness. Israel has offered an excellent opportunity to study floristic relationships of the Eurosibero-Boreoamerican Region, the Mediterranean Region, the Saharo-Sindian Region, the Irano-Turanian Region, and the Sudanian Region (Zohary, 1962). Zohary discussed these phytogeographic categories using the terminology of Braun-Blanquet

(1932), which is based upon the names of dominant plants with a series of suffixes denoting: class (suffix "-etea"), order (suffix "-etalia"), alliance (suffix "-ion"), and association (suffix "-etum").

A great amount of research has been completed in this area upon relationships of the vegetation to desert environment. Again the majority of the studies have been in Israel, but all countries ouside the Arabian Peninsula have been included. These ecological investigations can be divided roughly into four groups: *(1)* general studies, *(2)* climatic relationships, *(3)* soil relationships, and *(4)* special studies limited in scope. Representative samples of these publications are discussed below.

Boyko (1949*a*) provided an overall discussion of climax vegetation of the Negev. Eig (1931-1932, 1933) covered broad phytogeographic relationships and included remarks on the ecological conditions under which they occur. Rikli (1942-1948) discussed the vegetation of the countries bordering the Mediterranean Sea. Feinbrun and Zohary (1955) reported on a geobotanical survey of (former) Transjordan, including a map showing the relation of the desert to other vegetation types. Zohary published an outline of the vegetation of Wadi 'Araba (1945), a geobotanical analysis of the Syrian Desert (1940*a*), a comprehensive review covering plant life of Palestine (1962), and, with G. Orshan, a second paper on Wadi 'Araba (1956).

Evenari (1962), in an excellent review of plant physiology and arid vegetation, classified plants according to their means of adjusting to dry periods, as follows:

1) Herbaceous whole shoot shedders (winter annuals, hemicryptophytes, and geophytes)
2) Phanerophytic summer leaf shedders (e. g., *Lycium arabicum*)
3) Petiolate leaflet shedders (leaflets are shed and petioles remain, later petioles also are partly discarded, e. g., *Zygophyllum dumosum*)
4) Aphyllous leaf and branch shedders (e. g., *Retama, Calligonum*, which shed their few leaves in winter and discard part of the previous year's branches in summer)
5) Aphyllous branch shedders (e. g., *Ephedra*, which has no leaves and sheds branches like *4*)
6) Basiphyllous leaf shedders (e. g., *Artemisia*, which sheds the large winter leaves situated at the bases of its branches at the beginning of the dry season, while the small upper summer leaves remain)
7) Brachyblastic leaf shedders (e. g., *Reaumuria*; the winter leaves are shed, and only

the small leaves and the brachyblasts, borne in the axils of the winter leaves, remain in summer)

8) Aesticladous leaf shedders (e. g., *Noaea mucronata*; the brachyblasts, each consisting of a spiny axis carrying minute leaflets, develop in summer, and the brachyblasts and leaves die at the end of the dry season)

9) Articulate shoot splitters (should be called "Articulate cortex shedders"); the green cortex of the previous year's shoots dries out during summer and is shed (e. g., *Anabasis*)

10) Articulate branch splitters and shedders (e. g., *Haloxylon persicum,* like 9, but in addition part of the previous year's branches are shed).

Several publications on climate apply to ecological studies. Among these are Ashbel's (1939) rainfall map of Palestine, (former) Transjordan, southern Syria, and southern Lebanon, and his 1941 rainfall map of Palestine. He also published a discussion of the frequency and distribution of dew in Palestine (1949). The general climate of Arabia was outlined by Brooks in 1932, of Syria and Lebanon by Combier in 1945. The agroclimatology and crop ecology of Palestine and Transjordan and climatic analogs in the U. S. A. were lucidly covered by Nuttonson (1946).

Climate in relation to vegetation has been extensively studied by Boyko (1947*a*, 1949*b*, 1952), resulting in statements on the geoecological law of distribution for plants and on climatic extremes as decisive factors for plant distribution. On the basis of his "aridity scales" with plant species as indicators, he worked out together with his wife Dr. Elisabeth Boyko a climatic map of the Sinai Peninsula (Boyko and Boyko, 1957). Hillel and Tadmor (1962) and Oppenheimer (1951*a, b*, 1961) reported on plant-water relations and water balance in desert plants.

Soil relations have received considerable attention, both in general terms and by certain specific aspects, especially sandy and saline conditions. Among the general studies are those of Harris (1960), and Zohary (1942, 1947*a*), and the most recent work on *Salinity and Aridity* by Boyko (1966*a*). Studies on saline soils include Boyko (1931), Orshan and Zohary (1955), and Tadmor, Orshan, and Rawitz (1962). Studies on light-textured soils include Eig (1939); Boyko, Boyko, and Tsuriel (1957); and Sharma (1966). Zohary and Orshan (1951) also studied plants growing on rocks (lithophytes). One of the most interesting papers is that of E. Boyko (1952), in which she describes the

development of a desert garden using saline water.

Many detailed studies of local areas and individual plants make important contributions to the overall knowledge of desert vegetation. Among these are Evenari's study of root conditions (1938*a*), and his work on plant anatomy (1938*b*). Negbi and Evenari summed up the survival means of desert summer annuals (1961) and studied hydroeconomy in desert plants.

Summary of State of Knowledge

Great contrasts are found in the adequacy of coverage in the Arabian Desert. The Palestine portion has been intensively studied, but the vegetation of the Arabian Peninsula has been studied only superficially. Most studies have been restricted to the peripheral areas, with only sketchy investigations being made of the flora of the central parts. Until recently the only knowledge of that peninsula was that gained by hardy travelers, but more recently oil explorations have provided more detailed information. A great amount of detailed research that has been conducted in Palestine applies to most of the Arabian Desert and beyond.

The principal deficiencies are in the phytogeographical descriptions of the more remote areas, but thanks to modern transportation methods it appears that these will become better known. One great contribution to knowledge is that made by locust surveys, in which the surveyors were interested in vegetation types as related to egg-laying (Popov and Zeller, 1963). Israel is the center for research at present, and, despite the handicaps of international political problems, that nation will probably remain in a leading role.

The Iranian Desert
General Descriptions of Plant Communities

The Iranian Desert, which includes parts of Iran, Afghanistan, and Pakistan (Baluchistan), is one of the smaller desert areas and one of the least known botanically. Meigs classed this desert as *Ac*13 and *Ac*14 (arid with cool winters, winter precipitation, and warm [3] or hot [4] summers). Consultant Emberger points out that these climates are thus Mediterranean, but with very cold winters. It includes five major units: The Dasht-e-Kavir ("kavir" meaning salt swamp) in the northwest, the Kavir-i-Namak in the north, the Dasht-e-Lut in the southwest, the Dasht-i-Naomid in the east, and the Dasht-i-Margo in the southeast.

Pabot (1964) recognized arid regions as those having precipitation of less than 100 mm, semiarid having 100 to 250 mm, and dry subhumic having more than 250 mm; his arid and semiarid fall within our usual classification of desert. The area described as arid includes the Dasht-e-Kavir and the Dasht-e-Lut, and it covers 13 per cent of Iran. In consequence of the fact that large areas of Iran have no outlet to the sea, we encounter there the most extended salt desert of the globe, the Great Salt Desert. It is the largest absolutely vegetationless desert with the exception of the snow and ice deserts of Antarctica and of Greenland. It is covered by a thick layer of crystallized salt with salty mud beneath. It is most dangerous for travelling and, therefore, one of the least known areas of the globe. Altogether the desert areas of Iran cover about 150,000 square miles (Boyko, 1966a, pp. 1-22).

The semiarid region includes a large part of the coastal area of the Persian Gulf and the Gulf of Oman, the Khurasan and Azerbaijan, and central Iran. It is mostly between 1,000 and 2,000 meters in elevation and represents about 61 per cent of the land surface of Iran. On the basis of vegetation, the drier areas of Iran were categorized into desert, subdesert, steppe, substeppe, and xerophilous forest zones. In Iran, as in the whole of Southwest Asia, we can well recognize the belt pattern of the vegetation around the most arid desert centers. This pattern is best described by Boyko (1954) and also by Monod (1957, 1964). Another paper by Boyko (1955b) contains a plant geographical map of Iran. The pattern of belts is, however, strongly influenced in Iran by its orographical features surrounding the central parts and by the relatively high altitude of the inner plateau.

The interior of the southern units of the Iranian Desert belongs to the hottest-summer regions of the globe with summer temperatures over 130° F (54.5° C). This climatic feature combined with the frequent and very strong winds and the scanty rainfall makes plant life as well as animal life very difficult there. Human habitation is almost impossible in extensive areas.

According to Pabot (1964) the Baluchi region has an annual precipitation under 300 mm and plant affinities with the Saharo-Sindian and subtropical regions. Although this zone appears extremely arid and sometimes desertlike, it does include in Persian Baluchistan a large number of tree and shrub species that are rare in the rest of Iran. The date palm is probably indigenous and *Zizyphus* and *Acacia* occur frequently. Among the trees and shrubs of this region are *Prosopis spicigera,** *Dalbergia sissoo, Diospyros tomentosa, Tamarindus indica,* and many shrubby or herbaceous Leguminosae, including such genera as

Indigofera, Tephrosia, Caragana, Crotalaria, Rhynchosia, Cajanus, Cassia, and *Taverniera.* The grasses are nearly all hot-region species belonging to the genera *Pennisetum, Cenchrus, Panicum, Sporobolus,* and *Eragrostis.*

The Irano-Turanian region of Iran has rainfall which varies up to 500 mm, but with a summer drought of at least three months throughout; the winters are usually cold. The subdesert zone has an annual precipitation under 100 mm; the steppe zone has cold winters and an annual precipitation between 100 and 250 mm.

The Irano-Turanian flora is characterized by many species of *Astragalus* (at least 600), *Cousinia* (more than 200 species), *Silene* (nearly 100 species), *Allium* (90 species), *Nepeta* (80 species), *Euphorbia* (80 species), *Acantholimon* (70 species), *Salvia* (about 70 species), *Onobrychis* (60 species), and *Centaurea* (60 species). Among the genera with fewer species, but still well represented in the Irano-Turanian zone, are *Acanthophyllum, Artemisia, Stipa, Aristida, Salsola, Phlomis, Stachys, Achillea, Bromus, Poa, Agropyron, Hordeum, Schrophularia, Eremurus, Echinops,* and *Ephedra.* The arborescent vegetation includes species of *Amygdalus, Prunus, Crataegus, Pyrus, Rhamnus,* and *Ficus.* The principal trees are *Quercus persica, Pistacia atlantica, Juniperus excelsa,* various *Tamarix* species, and *Populus euphratica.* Deteriorated pasture lands support a stand of *Poa bulbosa* and *Carex stenophylla.* Cultivated land weeds include *Alhagi maurorum, A. camelorum, Glycyrrhiza glandulifera, G. glabra,* and *Prosopis stephaniana.* Two spiny species, *Noaea mucronata* and *Lactuca orientalis,* are usually extremely widespread in grassland and wasteland areas which receive more than 150 mm of rain.

In the central deserts of Iran the vegetation is sparse and includes many halophytes.

The steppe flora in the vegetation zone with cold winters is dominantly an *Artemisia herba-alba* community. *Noaea mucronata* is widespread and *Poa bulbosa* is abundant on noneroded soils along with *Carex stenophylla. Aristida plumosa* is the dominant grass on sandy soils. Woody and spiny species of *Astragalus, Acantholimon,* and *Acanthophyllum* are generally quite common, especially above 1,000 meters. On slightly saline soils, *Anabasis, Haloxylon, Salsola,* and *Seidlitzia* are common. Legumes are not common, but occasionally *Onobrychis* and *Trigonella* can be seen, and the herbaceous *Astragulus* and *Cousinia* are fairly common. Annual species are often abundant in spring but are stunted and dry up very quicky. The sand dunes have their peculiar vegetation, which nearly always includes *Aristida* and *Calligonum* species, *Pennisetum dichotomum,* and

---

* Species Summary, p. 473, gives additional data for the species listed throughout this chapter and cites publications that discuss the species further.

Cyperus conglomeratus. There are a few trees in the steppe zone, including *Pistacia atlantica* on rocky slopes, *Amygdalus scoparia,* and other bushy shrubs including *Pteropyrum, Ephedra,* and *Lycium. Tamarix stricta* and *Haloxylon ammodendron* grow as trees on sand dunes. Other species of *Tamarix* are restricted to shrub form appearing on moist depressions, on salty land, and sometimes on very arid soils. In the latter case it is mainly *T. articulata,* indicating a deep-lying water source. *Populus euphratica* can be found in valley bottoms and *Zizyphus spina-christi* may penetrate into the southern steppes.

Linchevsky and Prozorovsky (1949), in a paper translated by Shaw, have provided the best available information on Afghanistan. These authors noted that the only weather station at the time of their study was located in Kabul; therefore they had to determine climatic conditions by inference. Desert areas are located in the southeast and southwest of the country. This Afghano-Iranian desert province has a rainfall of approximately 200 mm annually, mostly falling in the spring with droughts developing in summer. Winter mean temperatures are above 0° C, but the area is subject to occasional frosts. The vegetation is characterized by drought-resistant semi-shrublets, shrublets, semishrubs, and shrubs, with a few arborescent plants. Sometimes there is a fairly copious development of ephemeral and perennial bulbous and rhizomotous plants, which may form a continuous turf between bushes after rain. Shaw notes that the vegetation is similar to that of the Great Basin Desert in the United States. Volk (1954) classifies the vegetation as Irano-Turanian, with *Artemisia herba-alba* the characteristic species of the southwestern desert.

Taxonomic Works

There are few taxonomic publications covering the Iranian Desert, but the flora is fairly well known; *Flora Orientalis* of Boissier (1867-1888) is the basic manual. Blatter, Halberg, and McCann (1919-1920) have contributed to the knowledge of the flora of Baluchistan, and Rechinger's (1963-) 3-volume *Flora Iranica* is a basic flora providing good coverage for the western portion of the Iranian Desert. Aitchison (1881-1882) provided local coverage for the Kurram Valley in Afghanistan.

Ecological Works

Phytogeographical publications for the area are even fewer than taxonomic, and ecological investigations are rare. Blanchard (1929) discussed the geography, including climate and vegetation for an area extending from the Mediterranean Sea to the Indus River; a colored map shows the vegetation

types. The reviews by Boyko (1955b) on Iran, Israel, and Turkey, and of Bharucha (1955) on Afghanistan, India, and Pakistan give only very sketchy information about the ecological features of Iran, but Boyko's paper presents a plant geographical map in an attached folder and contains a very rich bibliography. According to Rechinger (1951), the dry northern portion of Iran has the Irano-Turanian type of vegetation that would be expected from its geographic location and temperature conditions. In the south of Iran are Saharo-Sindian elements, and there is evidence that these extend into the Baluchistan area. Zohary (1963) has given a description of the geobotanical structure of Iran with information on the flora and its affinities, based almost entirely on the work of Eig and particularly on Eig's (1931-1932) plant geographical distribution tables. These tables contain the plant geographical affinities of about 1,000 species from the Iranian flora alone and several hundred from the flora of Baluchistan and Afghanistan. A main source, geographically as well as ecologically, is also Bobek's (1951) climatic-ecological subdivision of Iran and the excellent accompanying map.

Summary of State of Knowledge

Compared to the deserts previously discussed, very little is known of the flora and ecology of the Iranian Desert. The flora of the more accessible parts is perhaps adequately covered, but floristic relationships are not well known. The ecology can be interpreted from studies in adjacent areas, but there is need for additional research to adapt knowledge gained elsewhere to the specific conditions in the Iranian Desert.

A limited amount of botanical research is being carried out at the University of Teheran, where the relatively large private herbarium of Professor E. Khabiri (with its several thousand species) complements the official herbarium of the University.

Another center of botanical research, particularly regarding the woody plants, is the Iranian Department of Forests. Beyond these efforts there is little organized activity designed to fill the gaps where information is lacking.

The Thar

General Descriptions of Plant Communities

The Thar, sometimes called the Indian Desert, includes the arid portions of western India and eastern West Pakistan. Some authors extend the arid area to include the area eastward to the Aravalli Range and southward into Sind. There is some question, however, as to how much of this area is naturally arid and how much has resulted from the activities of man (Carter, 1954; Mulay, 1961; Raychaudhuri, 1964).

Bharucha (1955), in an overall review, uses the 10-inch isohyet for the limit of the desert. He locates the Rajasthan Desert mostly north and west of the Aravalli Hills, notes that two-fifths of Rajasthan is sandy and has precarious rainfall, and states that taxonomic coverage is good but few ecological studies have been accomplished, especially in Baluchistan, Sind, the Punjab, and Wazirstan.

Biswas and Rao (1953) divide the vegetation of this area into three broad categories: the true desert, the arid zone, and the semiarid zone, and provide a rather complete list of all the principal species in tabular form. They point out that there are both climatic and edaphic influences and discuss the vegetation of three main community types: sand, gravel, and rock communities.

In the sand communities, the most common plant is *Crotalaria burhia*,* which follows the pioneer vegetation. The pioneer plants include *Calotropis procera, Indigofera argentea, Leptadenia aerva,* and species of *Panicum. Calligonum polygonoides* is found on crests of dunes.

In gravel communities, *Boerhaavia diffusa* and *Cleome papillosa* are most common plants, but other plants adapted to the same environment are present. Trees and shrubs of the gravel communities are *Zizyphus rotundifolia, Capparis decidua,* and species of *Prosopis, Salvadora,* and *Gymnosporia. Calligonum polygonoides* becomes a climber in the gravel.

In the rock communities, the lithophyte *Euphorbia nereifolia* is the most common plant and forms dense shrub thickets that support climbers and twiners.

Taxonomic Works

The taxonomic information for this area is fairly complete. Some of the earlier studies were made by Boissier (1867-1888), and Aitchison (1869); collections and descriptions have been brought up to date by Blatter and Halberg (1918*a, b*); Blatter, McCann, and Sabnis (1927-1929); Blatter and Fernandez (1933-1935); Bamber (1916); Sabnis (1923, 1940-1941); and Stewart (1957-1958).

Many publications cover local areas or specific plant groups. Among these are a 2-volume monograph on the grasses of West Pakistan by Ahmad and Stewart (1958, 1959) and two publications on the vegetation of Pilani and its neighborhood, the first by Bakshi (1954) and the second by Nair and

Nathawat (1956). Jafri (1958) contributed a list of additions to the flora of Karachi; Naqvi (1961) published a list of the common plants of the arid regions of Baluchistan; and Razi (1957) furnished a list of parasitic flowering plants.

Ecological Works

Although phytogeographic coverage for the area is not as comprehensive as the taxonomic coverage, it does provide adequate information on the characteristics of the vegetation.

Sabnis (1919) studied the physiological anatomy of plants in the Indian Desert after a very heavy rainfall (40 inches) in 1917. He followed this with an article (1929) in which he gave detailed information on the ecology of the flora of the Sind. He described this area as a desert continuous with the great desert of northwest India, compared it with the western Saharo-Sindian desert, and noted the floristic relationships. Puri (1952) discussed the present position of plant ecology. These and other studies are noted by Misra (1955) in a publication on the progress of ecological studies in India, but this review for the entire country gives little detailed information applicable to the desert. Bhandari (1954) discussed *Ephedra* species, which are often found on gravel soils and sand dunes and may occur as climbers. Raizada and Chatterji (1954) described the various species of introduced mesquite (*Prosopis*) and their culture and economic importance. The progress made in studying distribution patterns in Rajasthan was reviewed by Mulay (1961). Rutter and Sheikh (1962) have described the vegetation of the wastelands in the vicinity of Lahore in relation to physical and chemical conditions, and Raheja surveyed salinity and land use (1966). Sarup (1951) and Rolla and Kanodia (1962-1963) listed species and families of plants found in the vicinity of Jodhpur, with annotations relative to habitat and location, and Sen (1966) classified the associations according to the Braun-Blanquet system. Satyanarayan (1963) has divided the vegetation into five formations and described the physiognomy and structure of each. He described the arid zone of western Rajasthan as an area of 80,000 square miles with rain falling from June to September only, decreasing from 500 mm in the south and southeast to 250 mm in the northwest.

Summary of State of Knowledge

The Thar is fairly well known botanically and sufficient information is available on the flora and ecology for general purposes. More detailed information is needed for local areas.

---

* Species Summary, p. 473, gives additional data for the species listed throughout this chapter and cites publications that discuss the species further.

Several agencies are actively conducting research, especially in the applied fields of forestry and range management. Among the more important are the Central Arid Zone Research Institute at Jodhpur, the Pakistan Forest Institute at Peshawar, and the West Pakistan Range Improvement Scheme at Lahore. Paylore (1967) lists additional agencies.

3. Central Asia

Petrov (1966-1967) establishes four physical-geographic regions in the Asian continent: the Irano-Turan, the Dzungaro-Kazakhstan, the "Central Asiatic" or Mongolian, and the Tibetan. The last includes the high-elevation cold deserts of Pamir and Tibet, which are not discussed in detail by Petrov. The description given in the present section 3 follows his system and terminology, except that we will use "Mongolian" whenever possible. Types of vegetation and basic species for the first three regions are presented in table IV*a*.

Table IV*a*

TYPES OF DESERTS OF ASIA (after Petrov, 1966-1967)

Climatic type of desert	Dzungaro-Kazakhstan	Irano-Turan	Mongolian (Central Asiatic)

EDAPHIC TYPE:

1. TYPICAL SANDY DESERTS ON THE DESERT-SANDY SEROZEM AND GRAY-BROWN SOILS OF THE PALEOALLUVIAL AND COASTAL PLAINS

Type of vegetation and basic species:	Brush psychroxerophyte psammophyte: *Calligonum* sec. *Pterococcus, Ammodendron karelinii, Ephedra lomatolepis, Salix caspica, S. rubra, Elaeagnus angustifolia, Haloxylon persicum, H. aphyllum*	Brush xerophyte psammophite: *Calligonum* sec. *Eucalligonum, Ammodendron conollyi, Haloxylon persicum, H. aphyllum, Ephedra strobilacea, Salsola richteri, S. paletzkiana, Astragalus* sec. *ammodendron.*	Brush mesoxerphyte psammophyte: *Caragana microphylla, C. bungei, C. korshinskii, Hedysarum scoparium, H. mongolicum, Atraphaxis frutescens, Salix flavida, Nitraria schoberi, Oxytropis aciphylla, Haloxylon ammodendron.*
	Psammophyte grasses and subshrubs: *Elymus giganteus, Aristida pennata, Agropyron sibiricum, Artemisia arenaria, A. santolina, Agriophyllum arenarium, Horaninovia ulicina.*	Psammophyte grasses and subshrubs: *Aristida pennata, A. karelini, Carex physodes, Artemisia eriocarpa, Agriophyllum minus, A. latifolium, Horaninovia ulicina.*	Psammophyte grasses and subshrubs: *Psammochloa villosa, Artemisia ordosica, A. sphaerocephala, Pugionium cornutum, Agriophyllum gobicum.*

2. SANDY-PEBBLY DESERTS (GOBIS) ON GYPSUMED GRAY-BROWN SOILS OF TERTIARY AND CRETACEOUS PLATEAUS

Type of vegetation and basic species:	Lowbrush and sublowbrush gypsophyte: *Reaumuria soongarica, Salsola arbuscula, S. rigida, S. laricifolia, Iljinia regelii, Nanophyton erinaceum, Ephedra procera, Anabasis salsa, A. aphylla, A. truncata, A. eriopoda, Atriplex cana, Artemisia terrae-albae, A. pauciflora maikara, Sympegma regelii, Convolvulus tragacanthoides, C. gortschakovii, C. fruticosus.*	Lowbrush and sublowbrush gypsophyte: *Reaumuria fruticosa, Salsola arbuscula, S. rigida, S. gemmascens, S. laricifolia, Anabasis salsa, A. truncata, Astragalus* sec. *ammodendron, Calligonum molle,* etc., *Convolvulus erinaceus, Artemisia sieberi.*	Lowbrush and sublowbrush gypsophyte: *Zygophyllum xanthoxylon, Z. kaschgaricum, Potaninia mongolica, Ephedra przewalskii, Nitraria sphaerocarpa, Sympegma regelii, Iljinia regelii, Reaumuria soongarica, Calligonum mongolicum, Anabasis brevifolia, Salsola arbuscula, S. passerina, Caragana pygmaea, Convolvulus tragacanthoides, C. gortschakovii, C. fruticosus, Eurotia ceratoides, Asterthamnus,* sp. sp., *Artemisia xerophytica, Potaninia mongolica, Ammopiptanthus mongolicus, Stipa glareosa, S. gobica.*

3. GRAVELLY GYPSUMED DESERTS ON GRAY-BROWN SOILS OF TERTIARY PLATEAUS

Type of vegetation and basic species:	Lowbrush and sublowbrush gypsophyte: *Iljinia regelii, Salsola laricifolia, Anabasis salsa, Artemisia pauciflora, A. terrae-albae, Convolvulus fruticosus.*	Sublowbrush and lowbrush gypsophyte: *Artemisia sieberi, Anabasis brachiata, Salsola rigida, S. arbuscula, S. gemmascens, Convolvulus fruticosus.*	Very rare.

Table IV*a* (Continued)

TYPES OF DESERTS OF ASIA (after Petrov 1966-1967)

Climatic type of desert	Dzungaro-Kazakhstan	Irano-Turan	Mongolian (Central Asiatic)

4. STONY AND GRAVELLY DESERTS ON HILLOCKY AND LOW-MOUNTAIN AREAS

| Type of vegetation and basic species: | Lowbrush and sublowbrush gypsophyte: *Iljinia regelii, Ephedra procera, Eurotia ceratoides, Salsola laricifolia.* | Lowbrush and sublowbrush gypsophyte: *Anabasis brachiata, Convolvulus fruticosus, Salsola laricifolia.* | Lowbrush and sublowbrush gypsophyte: *Nitraria sphaerocarpa, Ephedra przewalskii, Iljinia regelii, Sympegma regelii, Gymnocarpos przewalskii, Zygophyllum xanthoxylon, Anabasis brevifolia, Tetraena mongolica, Ammopiptanthus mongolicus, Salsola laricifolia, S. arbuscula.* |

5. LOAMY DESERT ON SLIGHTLY CARBONATE GRAY-BROWN SOILS OF STRATIFIED PLAINS AND PLATEAUS OF NORTHERN DESERTS

| Type of vegetation and basic species: | Sublowbrush sage - Russian thistle: *Artemisia pauciflora maikara, A. terrae-albae, A. lercheana, Kochia prostrata, Eurotia eversmanniana, Camphorosma monspeliacum.* | Not encountered. | Not encountered. |

6. CLAY-LOESS DESERT ON SEROZEMS OF PIEDMONT PLAINS

| Type of vegetation and basic species: | Grassy ephemeroid with participation of Northern Turan wormwood: *Artemisia kaschgarica, A. terrae-albae, A. boratalensis, Poa bulbosa, Carex pachystylis, C. stenophylloides, Allium,* sp. sp., *Tulipa* sp. sp. | Grassy ephemeroid with participation of Southern Turan wormwood: *Artemisia sieberi, Poa bulbosa, Carex pachystylis, Psoralea drupacea, Phlomis thapsoides, Cousinia* sp. sp., *Allium* sp. sp., *Tulipa* sp. sp., *Gagea* sp. sp. | Not encountered. |

7. TAKYR DESERT ON PIEDMONT PLAINS AND IN ANCIENT RIVER DELTAS

| Type of vegetation and basic species: | Large brush vegetation of the takyred ancient deltas: *Haloxylon aphyllum, Tamarix ramosissima, Anabasis aphylla.* | Thallophyte psychroxerophyte algae, lichen and annual Russian thistle vegetation of the takyrs. Large shrub vegetation of the takyred ancient deltas: *Haloxylon aphyllum, Tamarix ramosissima, Salsola rigida, Anabasis ramosissima.* | Annual Russian thistle shrub vegetation of ancient deltas: *Haloxylon ammodendron, Tamarix chinensis.* |

8. BADLANDS

| Type of vegetation and basic species: | Annual lush Russian thistle, very sparse. | Annual lush Russian thistle, very sparse. | Annual lush Russian thistle, very sparse. |

9. SOLONCHAK DESERTS OF SALINED DEPRESSIONS OF LAKE AND SEACOASTS

| Type of vegetation and basic species: | Lowbrush and sublowbrush halophyte: *Halocnemon strobilaceum, Halostachys belangeriana, Kalidium foliatum, K. schrenkianum, Nitraria sibirica, Tamarix laxa, T. hispida.* | Lowbrush and sublowbrush halophyte: *Halocnemon strobilaceum, Seidlitzia rosmarinus, Halostachys belangeriana, Kalidium caspicum, Nitraria schoberi, Tamarix laxa, T. hispida, Salsola dendroides.* | Lowbrush and sublowbrush halophyte: *Halocnemon strobilaceum, Halostachys belangeriana, Kalidium gracile, K. foliatum, K. cuspidatum, Tamarix laxa, T. hispida, Nitraria sibirica.* |

In particular, in the Irano-Turan region includes Southern Turan and the Iranian Uplands; the Dzungaro-Kazakhstan encompasses Dzungaria and Southern Kazakhstan; the Mongolian contains Mongolia, Kashgaria, and Tsaidam; and the Tibetan region components are Tibet, Tsing-hai, and Pamir.

Irano-Turan Region

The climate of the Irano-Turan regions is subtropical, continental and arid. The precipitation is related to the influx of the Mediterranean cyclone and the total annual precipitation is 100-200 mm with the maximum season being March-April. The spring is humid and warm.

The soils are deserty and light serozems or heavily carbonate gray-brown, solonchak and takyrs. The vegetation growth shows a clear spring maximum and a summer depression period. Ephemerals and ephemeroids grow over much of the region.

The vegetation is characterized by the wide spread of psammophyte shrub formations (*Calligonum, Haloxylon, Salsola*) on sands, gypsophytes (*Salsola, Anabasis*) on the Tertiary plateaus, and the ephemeroid-ephemeral herbaceous plants on the piedmont plains (*Carex, Poa, Gagea, Tulipa*).

Dzungaro-Kazakhstan Region

The climate of the Dzungaro-Kazakhstan region is moderately continental and moderately arid. Precipitation is caused by the action of cyclones originating in the northern Atlantic; the total annual precipitation is 80-150 mm with a spring-summer maximum (April-August). Spring is cool and wet.

The soils are gray-brown, slightly carbonate, and solonets, takyr, and solonchak. Vegetation growth shows a slight summer depression. Fewer ephemerals and ephemeroids grow in this region than in the Irano-Turan. Wormwood and wormwood-Russian thistle formation predominate in the vegetation cover (*Artemisia, Salsola, Anabasis*). There are many species in common with the Irano-Turan and Mongolian regions.

Mongolian Region

The climate of the Mongolian region is temperate, extra arid, and sharply continental. The precipitation season is related to the arrival of the eastern Chinese monsoon; the annual total is 10-100 mm and the maximum precipitation falls in the summer (August-September). The spring is dry, cold and windy.

The soils are gray-brown, slightly carbonate in the north, and heavily carbonate in the south. The vegetation growth in the south clearly decreases in the spring and does so less sharply in the summer; in the northern deserts of this region only the spring decrease takes place.

The plant forms in the Mongolian region are diverse—these are predominantly brush and low-brush, subbrush, and sublowbrush. The grassy vegetation is little developed, and ephemerals are almost completely absent. The ephemeroids are more common, but they have a summer vegetation maximum and in this differ from the ephemeroids of the Dzungaro-Kazakhstan and Irano-Turan regions.

The Turkestan Desert

General Descriptions of Plant Communities

The vegetation of the Turkestan Desert, an immense undrained basin with parts below sea level, must depend upon average precipitation varying from 3 to 8 inches and falling in late spring and early autumn, leaving the summer and winter months without precipitation, at least in the northern portion. The temperature range is great; summer high temperatures reach 115° F and winter lows may drop to minus 40° F. Consultant Emberger comments that this range is typical of the northern Turkestan Desert, but the southern Turkestan Desert has winter rains and hence a Mediterranean climate. The soil base includes two great sandy expanses: the Kara-Kum (meaning black sands) covers about 86 million acres, and the Kyzyl-Kum (or Kizil-Kum, meaning red sands) covers about 49 million acres. The desert is crossed by two main rivers, the Amu-Dar'ya and the Syr-Dar'ya, which support extensive stream-bank vegetation (tugai). To some extent other vegetation is supported by underground water, especially in salt flats.

In his report on the vegetation of the Transcaspian lowlands, Paulsen (1912) covered an area extending from the Caspian Sea to Lake Balkhash, and from the mountains of northern Persia in the south to the Kirgiz Step' in the north. He viewed the area as composed of five plant communities: salt-desert, clay-desert, stone-desert, sand-desert, and riverside thickets. Of these the clay-desert is driest, and the riverside thickets and salt-desert areas have the most soil moisture. The average precipitation in this area varies from about 90 mm to 370 mm.

The vegetation is extremely scanty in the salt-desert areas, which have shallow water tables and salts crystallizing on the surface. The dominant plant is the *Halostachys caspica** bush, widely spaced and accompanied by a few summer annuals. The clay-

---

* Species Summary, p. 473, gives additional data for the species listed throughout this chapter and cites publications that discuss the species further.

deserts are very dry, have very little salt, and consist largely of loess soils. *Poa bulbosa* is the dominant spring plant; the community also includes other grasses and herbs, and some bulb and tuberous plants. The stone-desert areas are rock and gravel with stones common at the bases of the mountains; they are unfavorable for plant growth and support a sparse stand of *Atraphaxis compacta, Salsola arbuscula, S. rigida, Capparis spinosa, Artemisia* species, and *Alhagi camelorum.* The sand-deserts consist largely of quartz sand upon which *Aristida pennata* is the first invader. *Ammodendron conollyi* is an early tree invader, followed by *Calligonum, Salsola arbuscula,* saxaul (*Haloxylon ammodendron*) and sometimes *Ephedra alata.*

The other important species of the area described by Paulsen (1912) include *Reaumuria fruticosa,* a strongly-branched shrub with the branches thick and light in color; *Tamarix* (with 15 species of this genus in the Turkestan area), which is very abundant on river banks, which indicates that water is not far off or presumably not very far down, which can hold its own in the sand-desert to some extent, and which under favorable conditions appears as trees with thick foliage but under unfavorable conditions appears as shrubs; *Capparis spinosa,* a decumbent undershrub found on clay soils and especially on stony soil, with long branches bearing large, bright green leaves that carry two spinous stipules at the base; *Haplophyllum obtusifolium,* a strongly-branched and typical undershrub occurring especially on stationary sand; *Stellaria lessertii,* an undershrub 20-50 cm in height occurring in the clay-desert, much-branched and with numerous dead branches; *Alhagi camelorum,* one of the most common plants in the Transcaspian area, looking like a stumpy shrub with green branches, with aerial parts that commonly die back to the ground; *Heliotropium dasycarpum,* an undershrub occurring in the clay-desert, having leaves 1 to 2 cm long, coated with stiff hairs; *Frankenia hirsuta,* occurring in comparatively moist localities and usually on saline soil, having decumbent, lignified branches; *Convolvulus eremophilus,* an undershrub growing on clay or stationary sand; *Convolvulus fruticosus,* an undershrub with stiff, spiny branches; *Acanthophyllum elatius,* a plant of stony and clay soils, having a woody base that gives rise to numerous straight unbranched twigs about half a meter long, with white bark and bearing opposing stiff, prickly leaves; *Noaea spinosissima,* a much-branched thick, spiny, globular undershrub that prefers stony soils; *Anabasis salsa,* occurring on clay or stony and saline soil, an undershrub chenopod with slightly branched annual shoots which die off yearly almost to the surface of the ground; *Anabasis*

aphylla, a salt plant; *Arthrophytum subulifolium,* an undershrub growing on firm soils and not exceeding a height of 30 cm; *Anabasis eriopoda,* with shoots measuring 30 cm or more in length and rising from a white, wooly cushion that lies in the uppermost crust of the soil, bearing leaves reduced to small opposite scales which on older branches terminate in rather long slender spines; *Heliotropium sogdianum,* forming long, horizontal subterranean shoots from which aerial shoots rise, sometimes widely apart; *Aristida pennata,* a sand-binding grass of thick, shrubby growth, forming lateral shoots that extend existing tufts and form new tufts when buried by the sand (the most valuable of all sand-binders).

Taxonomic Works

The extensive literature for the Turkestan area covers taxonomy, phytogeography, ecology, and plant utilization. Practically all is in Russian, but a few publications have been translated into English in their entirety and many have English summaries or abstracts.

The most important taxonomic work is the *Flora U. R. S. S.* (Akademiia Nauk S. S. S. R., Botanicheskii Institut, 1934-   ); this comprehensive work, published in Russian, includes 30 volumes[*] by many authors; to date three volumes have been translated into English. A useful guide to geographical and other abbreviations is provided by Stearn (1947) in a work that enables one to obtain plant distribution information from *Flora U. R. S. S.* with only a minimal knowledge of Russian. Publications also cover specific areas and special plant groups; among these are works on desert flora by Gvozdeva (1960), the flora of Uzbekistan by Bondarenko *et al.* (1962), and the trees and shrubs of Tadzhikistan by Zapriagaev (1938).

Ecological Works

A particularly illuminating source of knowledge of all arid and semiarid parts of the U. S. S. R. is contained in the *Geobotanicheskaia Karta S. S. S. R.,* (Akademiia Nauk S. S. S. R., Botanicheskii Institut, 1955). This important work was executed by a great number of plant geographers and ecologists under the editorial supervision of E. M. Lavrenko and V. B. Sochava. In addition to the very instructive colored maps at a scale of 1:4,000,000, we find in the two accompanying volumes (Akademiia Nauk S. S. S. R., Botanicheskii Institut, 1956) descriptions of all plant communities and many photographs, distribution maps of single species, and other instructive material. A great part of it is dedicated to the desert and semi-desert areas of Turkestan. The whole work is in

Russian, but a legend (p. 1-15) is in English and, of course, the Latin names of plant species are easily recognizable. An English translation of the two volumes would be very useful.

Many publications describe local vegetation. Some of these emphasize floristic and geographic relations ,Akademiia Nauk Kazakhskoi S. S. R., 1962, 1963), others cover the structure and physiognomy of local plant communities, others describe environmental relationships, and a few discuss utilization. Some of the more important are listed below (all these are in Russian with English abstracts except as noted). Abolin (1929) divided central Asia into eight zones according to summer temperature and into districts with different seasonal distributions of precipitation: the Turkestan district has a relatively wet winter and spring with abundant ephemeral vegetation. Bazilevskaia (1927) described the vegetation of the southeastern part of the Kara-Kum in regions adjacent to the Amu-Dar'ya and noted sand-binding species near Repetek. Dubianskii (1928) considered the sand desert in the same area with particular attention to agricultural possibilities, and Petrov (1935) discussed the vegetation of the Repetek Preserve. Borisova *et al.* (1961) listed in tabular form a large number of basic plants of northern Kazakhstan according to life forms and ecological groups. Bykov (1959) reviewed the history of geobotanical studies in Kazakhstan with a bibliography of 114 references, and (Bykov, 1960) characterized the vegetation of stone-deserts in the basin of the Ili River with detailed descriptions of the vegetation of various sites. Golovkova (1961) described the flora of central Tyan-Shan', noting that deserts and steppes have a poor flora. Granitov (1961) analyzed the flora of the Kyzyl-Kum (some 900 species), noting habitats, ecological forms, and other features. Karamysheva and Rachkovskaya (1963) described the distribution patterns of vegetation in central Kazakhstan and noted the vegetal relationships with other regions including the Sahara and Gobi. Korovin discussed the vegetation of the Kara-Kum (1927) and its subdivisions (1928); the history and development of vegetation in middle Asia (based on vegetation around Bet-Pak-Dala, characterized by *Artemisia* and *Salsola)* (Korovin, 1935); the water requirements of vegetative species of the arid zone (Korovin, 1958); and the phytogeographical types of vegetation in central Asia (Korovin, 1961*a*) and their use in agriculture (1961*b*, 1961-1962).

Kachkarov and Korovin (1942) wrote one of the most comprehensive publications on deserts, which was translated into French by Theodore Monod and published as *La Vie Dans les Deserts*. Kurochkina

(1962*a, b*) studied *Calligonum* societies on the sands of Kazakhstan and noted the important species in what he considered a center of their development; he also described stage mosaic patterns in formations of white *Haloxylon* and *Calligonum* stands in sand desert areas of the Kyzyl-Kum. Lavrenko and Nikol'skaya (1963) noted the distribution of desert area plants, with special attention to middle Asia (Turan) and central Asia (Gobi) elements. Momotov (1961) described the vegetation of the Kyzyl-Kum station of the Uzbek S. S. R. Academy of Science; Pavlov (1961) made a survey of patterns of flora and vegetation of Kazakhstan and noted their great heterogeneity. Arifkhanova (1961) described the tugai vegetation of the Ferghana Valley; Petrov has compared the tugai vegetation of the Amu-Dar'ya and Tarim rivers and noted their great floristic and ecological similarities. Vernik and Momotov described (1959) the tugai halophytic and psammophytic flora of the Amu-Dar'ya delta. Rotov (1962) described the plant groupings and floristic composition of the vegetation of the southwestern part of the Muyunkum desert and listed the species by life forms. Rustamov studied the vegetation of the western Uzboy area (1961) and discussed in detail the vegetation of the Uzboy River streambed (1962). Seifriz (1931-1932) described the vegetation of some southern provinces of the U. S. S. R. in two journal articles; he included a description of vegetation and climate in the vicinity of Repetek.

Smirnov (1935) made a detailed geobotanical investigation of the west Kazakhstan region and, based upon the results of his study, made recommendations regarding possible agricultural utilization of the area. Popov *et al.* (1929) described many fruit-bearing trees and shrubs of Central Asia, including *Juglans, Ficus, Ribes, Prunus, Amygdalus, Pyrus Malus, Pistacia, Vitis,* and *Elaeagnus*. The genus *Tamarix* is represented by more than 20 species in the U. S. S. R.; some are wild and others are cultivated for their sand-binding qualities and other purposes (Gorschkova, 1957). Thistles, largely pests, are represented by 63 species and distributed from high mountains to low desert areas.

A number of special studies deal with soil indicators, plants of sandy soils, plants of saline soils, and river-valley and lake-shore plants. Some studies that deserve special attention are discussed in the remainder of this paragraph. Vostokova, Shavyrina, and Laricheva (1962) contributed a handbook on plant indicators of groundwater and soil types of the southern deserts of the U. S. S. R. Orlov (1928) studied moisture conditions in the Kara-Kum and found alternating horizons of moisture concentration down to a depth of 200 cm resulting from water vapors in the soil. Petrov (1933) studied the root systems of 450 plants in the Kara-Kum and correlated root systems with drought resistance. Bazilevskaia and Suslova (1933) studied root systems in the Kara-Kum sands and observed the formation of adventitious roots in moist layers; they also wrote about dune reclamation. Rivière (1931) recommended the *Haloxylon ammodendron* (saxaul or sacsaoul) as a plant suitable for binding desert sands; it is also valuable for wood, food, and shade for animals. Vostokova and Vyshivkin (1961) found that black saxaul thickets *(Haloxylon aphyllum)* indicate fresh or brackish water at depths of 24 to 40 meters, and Nunnayev and Veyisov (1965) found that stands declined because of logging and increases in mineralization. Petrov (1936) studied both black saxaul and sandy saxaul and noted that the former formed thickets in northern Kazakhstan and the latter was found singly in the central Kara-Kum and Kyzyl-Kum.

Sandy deserts are extensive in Central Asia, and continual research is under way to make these areas more useful to humans. Petrov (1960) summarized the results of some scientific investigations in sandy deserts of Central Asia; the investigations were of conditions in the areas, methods of sand stabilization by plant and other means, and possibilities of reclamation. More recently (Petrov, 1966-1967) he has authored two volumes (in Russian) with more detailed information on the Ordos, Ala Shan, Bei Shan (Peishan), Tsaidam, and Tarim Basin deserts.

Petrov recognized three categories of sand conditions: *(1)* sand areas with precipitation of over 250 mm (which permits the growth of natural cover of mesophytic psammophytes), *(2)* sand areas with precipitation of 100 to 150 mm (which permits the natural growth of cover of xerophilous bushes and grasses), and *(3)* sand areas of arid deserts with insufficient atmospheric moisture and precipitation of less than 100 mm (which does not permit the growth of plant cover on the sands).

The scientists selected plants (trees, shrubs, underbrush, and grasses) for use in sand stabilization under various local conditions in eastern and western Central Asia; table V lists these plants, and also plants in corresponding use in the sand deserts of Soviet Asia and Kazakhstan.

Summary of State of Knowledge

The Turkestan Desert has been fairly well covered, a considerable amount of general information has been collected, and some intensive studies have been made, notably those at Repetek. This information is unfortunately not accessible to those unable to read Russian, and it is not generally found in American libraries.

In the Turkmeniya S. S. R. a very active research program is underway to establish methods of combating shifting sands and to develop forest and crop production through studies in ecology, physiology, and morphology. Studies are also being made to determine medicinal, industrial, and other economic uses of native plants.

The Takla-Makan and Gobi

Petrov (1960) and Richardson (1966) may be consulted for descriptions of the extensive arid and semiarid lands of China and Outer Mongolia. The Gobi, the largest desert in Asia, lies in Outer Mongolia and Chinese Inner Mongolia. To the southwest of the Gobi lies the Takla-Makan, and east of it and south of the Gobi lie other desert areas, including notably the Tsaidam, Ala Shan (Ala-chan), and Ordos.

Vegetation in the Central Asian deserts, which are surrounded on nearly all sides by mountains, grows at altitudes ranging from 300 meters below sea level in the Turfan Depression to about 2,000 meters in the high desert. (Average elevation varies from 1,300 meters in the north and the east to 800 meters in the Tarim Basin and to 280 meters in Dzungaria.) The area lacks external drainage and the vegetation receives very little rainfall; mean annual precipitation seldom exceeds 100 mm and may be as low as 50 mm. In the Turfan and Hami depressions, both below sea level, the summers are hotter than in the tropics and the frost-free season is 240 days; elsewhere the vegetation must contend with extremely low winter temperatures (January means from 6° C to minus 19° C) and warm summers (July average of 24° C to 26° C).

Petrov (1962) has recognized the following widely-varying types of desert conditions in Central Asia:

1) Deserts with rugged angular debris at the base of rock mountains. The sparse vegetation, shrubby and semishrubby, inhabits the lower inselbergs and the little sopkas throughout the deserts of Central Asia as well as the lower ridges. These desert soils are formed from pre-Tertiary crystalline rocks or from metamorphic sedimentary rocks.

2) The badland deserts of the lower mountains of the southern Tyan-Shan' (Tien-Shan, Tian-Chan) range and the northern Tsaidam desert. These deserts, nearly devoid of vegetation, are formed mainly by Tertiary deposits (marls, clays, sandstone, and conglomerates).

Table V

SAND-STABILIZING PLANTS OF THE DESERTS AND SEMIDESERTS
OF THE U.S.S.R. AND CHINA (after Petrov, 1960)

Sand Deserts of Soviet Asia and Kazakhstan	Sand Deserts of Central Asia	
	Eastern Part	Western Part
Trees:		
Populus nigra	*Populus simonii*	—
Elaeagnus angustifolia	*Elaeagnus moorcroftii*	*Elaeagnus angustifolia*
Shrubs:		
Haloxylon aphyllum	*Haloxylon ammodendron*	*Haloxylon ammodendron*
Haloxylon persicum	—	*Haloxylon persicum*
Tamarix ramosissima	*Tamarix ramosissima*	*Tamarix ramosissima*
Tamarix laxa	*Tamarix laxa*	*Tamarix laxa*
Salix caspica	*Salix flavida*	—
Salix rubra	*Salix mongolica*	—
Calligonum arborescens	*Calligonum mongolicum*	*Calligonum zaidamense*
Calligonum caput-medusae	—	*Calligonum aphyllum*
Calligonum aphyllum	*Hedysarum scoparium*	—
Salsola richteri	*Caragana microphylla*	—
Salsola paletzkiana	*Caragana korshinskii*	—
Underbrush:		
Artemisia arenaria	*Artemisia sphaerocephala*	—
—	*Artemisia ordosica*	*Artemisia ordosica*
—	*Artemisia halodendron*	
Perennial Grasses:		
Aristida karelini	—	*Aristida pennata*
Aristida pennata	—	—
Elymus giganteus	—	—
Annuals:		
Agriophyllum arenarium	*Agriophyllium arenarium*	*Agriophyllium arenarium*
Agriophyllum latifolium	*Pugionium cornutum*	—
Horaninovia ulicina	*Stilpnolepis centiflora*	—
Salsola turcomanica	*Salsola praecox*	*Salsola praecox*
Salsola praecox	—	*Horaninowia ulicina*

3) Deserts with boulders and with rugged debris, found on high foothills of all the mountain systems in Central Asia, with a sparse shrubby and semishrubby vegetation, especially abundant along the channels of permanent or temporary streams.

4) Deserts with boulders and with rugged debris found on low foothills (the young gobi) with a short, very sparse, shrubby and semishrubby vegetation which is a little more abundant along even dry stream beds. Such deserts are widely distributed everywhere in the area of transition between foothills, plains, and high plains, either alluvial or structural.

5) Sandy deserts with gravel, and gravel deserts with sand, found on the high plains of Cretaceous or Tertiary deposits (old, typical gobi), with advanced wind erosion and poor vegetation of short xerophilous shrub; deserts of this type are widely distributed on the high plains of Ordos, Ala Shan, Gachoun Gobi, Gobi Mongol, and western Tsaidam.

6) Sandy deserts with shifting sand dunes and ridges of sand, almost devoid of vegetation (mainly old alluvial, lacustrian plains) found throughout the Central Asian deserts. The particularly large sand massifs are located in the Tarim depression (Takla-Makan) and in Ala Shan (the sands of Tengueri, of Badan-Tchjarengh, and others).

7) Sandy deserts with ridges of fixed sand or ridges of sand with pans, where the natural colonization of the sand by plants is made possible by sufficient atmospheric precipitation. Such are the settle sands of the eastern part of the desert region (Ordos), the eastern end of the Ala Shan desert, and the northwest part of Dzungaria.

8) Sandy deserts with rounded, settled, sand dunes, small and large, upon which colonization by plants is supported by underground water relatively close to the surface; this type of terrain is widespread on the periphery of old and present river valleys, on deltas, and in lacustrian depressions.

9) Clay deserts, with a fairly abundant, halophilous, shrubby and herbaceous vegetation of the eastern Kazakhstan type, found on the northern plains of the eastern Tyan-Shan' (Tien-Shan, Tian-Chan) foothills.

10) Takyr deserts with clay, where shrubby vegetation (such as saxaul and tamarisk) is abundant, in the old deltas of streams of the Tarim depression and in Dzungaria.

11) Saline deserts, with a sparse, halophilous, shrubby and herbaceous vegetation; these deserts occur in contour depressions wherever brackish underground water is near the surface, in dry lakes, old valleys and river deltas. The most important salt deserts are found in the Tsaidam depressions of the Lop Nor area and of the Gachoun-Nor area, in Dzungaria, and in the Ala Shan (Ala-Chan) desert.

Other areas contrast remarkably with the desert areas, such as present river valleys and deltas with lush forestal (tugai) vegetation, meadows, and oases. Also contrasting with the surrounding desert are the areas of steppe and woods found on inselbergs such as the Kholan-chan.

Table V, above, presents a list of selected plants in use for sand stabilization. The Takla-Makan Desert is discussed in the following section; the other areas mentioned above, which are contiguous with or part of the Gobi, are included in the subsequent section on the Gobi.

The Takla-Makan

General Descriptions of Plant Communities

Vegetation of the Takla-Makan receives very little rainfall, what there is coming mostly in June, July, and August. Climatic data are scarce or inaccessible, but some available records show annual precipitation under 100 mm in the Kashgar delta and 36 mm at Mingfen. The Tarim basin includes

lush tugai vegetation (in small areas along river valleys), transitional stony clay formations, and predominant large sandy areas (including barchan or mammelonné dunes) unstabilized with little or no vegetation or stabilized with some vegetation.

According to Petrov (1962), the Tarim depression includes the following types of desert:

1) Deserts of rocky debris at the base of mountains at the edge of the Tarim depression

2) Badland desert in the northwest part of the depression

3) Gobi with gravel

4) Gobi of sand with gravel on the piedmont plains

5) Sand deserts, which occupy the largest part of the depression, the Takla-Makan

6) Alkali deserts of takyrs in the ancient valleys and river deltas

7) Salt deserts, widespread in the depression of Lop Nor.

Of these the most widespread in the Tarim depression are deserts of sand with gravel, deserts of sand, and salt deserts.

The principal plants of the gobi areas are still xerophytic shrubs. *Ephedra przewalskii,** *Zygophyllum xanthoxylon, Z. kaschgaricum, Gymnocarpos przewalskii, Anabasis aphylla,* and occasionally in local areas *Calligonum roborobski* and *Nitraria sphaerocarpa* are principal plants.

The psammophytic vegetation of the sand deserts is represented by two groups:

1) Herbaceous vegetation, found on the barchans of the Takla-Makan and on other large sand bodies where the atmospheric moisture is very low (including *Aristida pennata, Agriophyllum arenarium,* and *Corispermum* species)

2) Woody vegetation found on the large mammelonnés at the periphery of the deserts of sand in the old valleys and deltas of rivers (dominant species is *Tamarix ramosissima*).

The halophytic vegetation is distributed largely in the old valleys and on river deltas and lake depressions; it includes:

1) The annual vegetation of the alkali takyrs (including *Halogeton glomeratus* and species of *Salsola* and *Suaeda*).

2) Small woody vegetation of the salt grounds and small mammelonnés (including *Kalidium cuspidatum, Halocnemon strobilaceum,* and *Nitraria sibirica*).

3) The taller halophytic woody vegetation of

---

* Species Summary, p. 473, gives additional data for the species listed throughout this chapter and cites publications that discuss the species further.

the higher parts of the saline deserts (including *Tamarix laxa, Halostachys caspica, Nitraria schoberi,* and *Lycium turcomannicum*).

To sum up from Petrov, the Tarim basin is occupied principally by the Takla-Makan sand-desert, in which psammophytic vegetation is dominated by species of *Calligonum, Tamarix,* and *Aristida.*

Richardson (1966) is also an important source on aspects of the vegetation of the Tarim basin. Immediately surrounding the salt lake (Lop Nor) in the Takla-Makan is a vegetation community consisting of two psammophytes, *Agriophyllum arenarium* and *Corispermum hyssopifolium.* Surrounding the sand plain are concentric belts of gravel becoming the foothills of the surrounding mountains. Within these gravel belts are found numerous oases which carry remnants of a relatively luxuriant vegetation including such trees as *Populus euphratica, P. pruinosa, P. alba, P. nigra, Salix* species, *Ulmus pumila, Tamarix chinensis, T. hispida, T. juniperina, Myrciaria germanica, Morus alba, Elaeagnus angustifolia,* and *Lycium turcomannicum.* The vegetation of the desert area includes many species of *Stipa,* species of *Cleistogenes* and *Allium,* and a scrub growth of *Artemisia frigida, A. caespitosa, A. xerophytica, A. incana, Tanacetum achilleoides, T. fruticulosum, T. trifidum, Salsola passerina, Caragana pygmaea, C. bungei, Potaninia mongolica,* and *Sympegma regelii.*

On the drier soils the vegetation cover is composed of several species of halophytes, including: *Tanacetum achilleoides, Anabasis brevifolia, Salsola passerina, S. ruthenica, S. collina, Sympegma regelii, Eurotia ceratoides, Agriophyllum gobicum, Echinopsilon divarticatum,* and *Kalidium gracile,* together with *Salsola arbuscula, Peganum nigellastrum, Nanophyton erinaceum, Haloxylon ammodendron, Calligonum mongolicum, Nitraria sphaerocarpa, N. sibirica, Zygophyllum xanthoxylon, Ephedra przewalskii, Alhagi camelorum,* and *Caragana leucophyloea.*

Summary of State of Knowledge

The literature covering the Takla-Makan is quite scanty; taxonomic publications are few in number. Fortunately the flora consists largely of eastern and western elements; therefore, taxonomic manuals of adjacent areas can be used for identification of plants of the Tarim basin.

Very few phytogeographical studies have been made and the results are not readily accessible. Some conclusions can be deduced from studies in adjacent areas, but there still are major gaps. There is no indication of any vigorous program aimed toward closing these gaps. The information in this chapter

was obtained from scientists living far from the Takla-Makan.

The Gobi
General Descriptions of Plant Communities

The vegetation of the Gobi lives under a combination of steppe and desert conditions; sand dunes are comparatively rare. The vegetation receives rainfall varying from 50 to 80 mm in the western Gobi to 170 mm in the east; 80 per cent of the rainfall occurs in summer, mostly in July and August. Temperatures affecting the plants range from minus 25° C to 44° C with strong diurnal and yearly variations; the growing season is 150 to 180 days, many of them having strong winds.

According to Armand *et al.* (1956), the word "gobi" is a Mongolian common name used to designate landscapes of either flat desert steppes or semi-deserts without rivers, with water found only in wells or springs, and with rocky, clayey, sandy, and (in spots) saline soils. According to the report of a group of Chinese scientists* participating in a project of research on sand control (Academia Sinica, Sand Control Team, 1958, 1962), the term "gobi" is more ambiguous or complicated. The original application of the word was to a vast, flat area of the Mongolian plateau where the ground is covered with coarse substance and population is sparse. The characteristics of a gobi are listed as:

1) The climate is arid and continental.
2) Water is generally scarce, and the level of underground water is low.
3) The ground surface is generally even and flat.
4) The ground surface is composed of coarse conglomerate or bedrock.
5) The soil is mostly brown desert soil, gray-brown desert soil, or brown calcium soil with very low fertility.
6) The vegetative cover is sparse, generally less than 30 per cent and in most places less than 1 per cent.

The report of the sand control research group includes information useful to students of the vegetation of the Dzungarian area in the western Gobi. That vegetation receives rainfall of 70 to 150 mm, coming mostly in spring and fall. The area has low winter temperatures and high summer temperatures,

---

*Some technical reports, as is the case with other publications originating in mainland China, may include somewhat overstated phrases of accomplishment due to political and administrative conditions in that area; however, the basic scientific work reported in the publications on desert vegetation seems in general to be careful and competent and to provide some of the best available information for the areas covered.

* Species Summary, p. 473, gives additional data for the species listed throughout this chapter and cites publications that discuss the species further.

and the western part is drier than the eastern. The vegetation of this basin consists of plants affiliated with the vegetation systems of Mongolia and central Asia, the central Asian species dominating. Principal plants include *Haloxylon persicum,† Artemisia santolina, A. terrae-albae, Carex physodes,* and *Agropyron sibiricum.* The Mongolian type of vegetation is found mostly on the southern and eastern edges and in the northern part of the desert and includes *Haloxylon ammodendron, Ephedra distachya,* and *Hedysarum.*

The Chinese sand control research group (Academia Sinica, Sand Control Team, 1962) listed and characterized several plants suitable for sand stabilization; most are native species:

1)	*Eremosparton* species	Excellent wind erosion tolerance, suitable for purpose of quick stabilization
2)	*Aristida* species	Good wind tolerance, but not very good sand tolerance
3)	*Allium polyrhizum*	Excellent tolerance of wind and sand
4)	*Calligonum mongolicum*	Good sand tolerance, also a good producer of firewood
5)	*Haloxylon przewalskii*	Very popular for large, semistabilized sand dunes, but not suitable for spaces between sand dunes; also produces firewood
6)	*Haloxylon* species	Suitable only for the spaces between dunes and for low dunes where underground water condition is fair; also produces firewood
7)	*Cobresia*	Suitable only for areas where the underground water is not very deep; may be used along the edges of dunes to transform the area into pasturage
8)	*Ephedra przewalskii*	May be used for further stabilization of semistabilized dunes; its economic value is not yet determined
9)	*Carex*	A short-lived plant; may be used on semistabilized dunes and low places between the dunes

Because high mountain ranges provide a rain-shadow effect in the Tsaidam area, Tsinghai province, the desert in places extends upward to above 5,000 meters. The vegetation is semidesert or desert and includes such plants as: *Lasiagrostis splendens, Salsola nitraria, Haloxylon ammodendron, Kalidium,* and *Calligonum mongolicum.*

In the gobi area of western Inner Mongolia (around the Ala Shan northward to the Mongolian border), the precipitation averages 50 to 60 mm a year, 80 per cent of which comes in summer. The daily and yearly variation in temperatures is very great, and winds are strong. Vegetation varies with the characteristics of the soil; the major plants are *Potaninia mongolica, Salsola passerina, Reaumuria soongarica,* and *Oxytropis aciphylla.* Toward the west, *Potaninia mongolica, Salsola passerina,* and *Oxytropis* are no longer found; the vegetative cover is reduced to below 5 per cent consisting largely of *Nitraria sphaerocarpa* and *Reaumuria soongarica.* Where the underground water level is shallow, the cover vegetation is increased; principal plants are *Haloxylon ammodendron, Reaumuria soongarica, Nitraria sphaerocarpa, Calligonum mongolicum* and *Zygophyllum xanthoxylum.* Along the banks of rivers are found *Populus diversifolia, Elaeagnus moorcroftii, Tamarix* species, and *Lycium ruthenicum.* This area boasts the only natural forest of the gobi of western Inner Mongolia.

In the dune areas of western Inner Mongolia the vegetation is mostly thorny, drought- and sand-tolerant shrubs and semishrubs. Movable dunes over 10 meters high have no vegetative cover; below 10 meters there may be a few plants, mostly on the lower slopes to the lee of the wind. Vegetation also grows on the low areas between the dunes. The plants include *Artemisia sphaerocephala, Psammochloa villosa, Calligonum mongolicum, Hedysarum scoparium, Peucedanum rigidum,* and *Apocynum hendersonii.*

On the stabilized dunes, the vegetative cover depends upon the degree of stabilization and the depth of the water table. On stabilized sand areas drought-tolerant shrubs and semishrubs are dominant. The plants include *Ammopiptanthus mongolicus, Reaumuria soongarica, Eurotia ceratoides, Caryopteris mongholica, Artemisia ordosica, Stipa glareosa,* and *Allium mongolicum.*

Indicating areas with deep underground water are *Thermopsis lanceolata, Iris ensata, Oxytropis aciphylla, Caragana microphylla, Psammochloa villosa, Hedysarum scoparium,* and *Calligonum mongolicum.*

In the (Ordos) area east and south of the Yellow River (Hwang Ho), the vegetation varies from grassland on the east to desert on the west.

Among the important species are: *Caragana steno-phylla, Caragana tibetica, Reaumuria soongarica, Potentilla mongolica, Tetraena mongolica, Eurotia ceratoides, Salsola laricifolia, Salsola passerina, Stipa gobica, Stipa glareosa,* and *Allium monogolicum.*

Petrov (1962), in his publication on the type of deserts of Central Asia, also discusses the vegetation found in the Ordos and Ala Shan (Ala-Chan). Discussing specifically the local sand deserts of Ordos, Petrov gives as the principal plants the psammophtic shrubs *Caragana korshinskii, C. microphylla, Hedysarum scoparium* and the half-shrubs *Artemisia ordosica* and *A. sphaerocephala.* In the western region the plants are more xeromorphic; the shrubs are small shrubs or half-shrubs which are gypsophilic or halophilic, including *Nitraria sphaerocarpa, Reaumuria soongarica, Kalidium cuspidatum, K. foliatum, Anabasis brevifolia, Salsola arbuscula, S. passerina,* and *Sympegma regelii.*

According to Petrov, the vegetation in the Ala Shan is varied but poorer than in the Ordos, because the precipitation is less. He distinguishes the following types of deserts: the deserts of rock with angular gravel, the sand-desert with gravel (gobi), the sand-deserts with barchans (mobile dunes), and the salt-deserts. The sand-deserts are most widespread, especially those with barchans. Along the rivers there is tugai vegetation including *Ulmus pumila, Populus diversifolia, Haloxylon ammodendron.* On the rock-deserts, one finds *Amygdalus mongolica, Sympegma regelii, Salsola laricifolia, Caragana stenophylla, Zygophyllum xanthoxylon,* and the grasses *Stipa bungeana* and *S. glareosa.*

The vegetation of the gobi plains (sand with gravel) is characterized by shrubs and semishrubs, including *Reaumuria soongarica, Nitraria sphaero-carpa, Convolvulus tragacanthoides, C. gortschakovii, Zygophyllum xanthoxylon, Salsola passerina,* and the small shrubs *Potaninia mongolica* and *Gymnocarpos przewalskii.*

The vegetation of the moving dunes resembles that of the Ordos; one finds the widely spaced shrubs *Caragana korshinskii, C. microphylla, Hedysarum scoparium* and *Atraphaxis frutescens,* the perennial grass *Psammochloa villosa,* and the annual *Agriophyllum arenarium.* On sands, where the moisture layer is closer to the surface, grow *Nitraria schoberi* or *Tamarix ramosissima* and sometimes *Artemisia ordosica* and *A. sphaerocephala* (Petrov, 1962).

Taxonomic Works

The bibliography of the taxonomy of Chinese plants by Liu (1930) provides a great deal of information on early studies on the flora, and the bibliog-graphy of eastern Asiatic botany by Merrill and Walker (1938) lists many valuable references.

Walker (1944) reviewed the history of botany in China and pointed out the general lack of knowledge of the flora. Grubov and Unatov (1952) noted that investigations of the Mongolian flora were initiated by Russia in the eighteenth century and that the flora of 16 floral districts had been described by species. There are other lists of plant collections, but none appear to be complete and most do not include descriptions of species.

Ecological Works

Petrov's reviews (1959, 1962, 1966-1967) of central Asian deserts give a great amount of general information on the Gobi. The vegetation of the Gobi was described in relation to other vegetation types by Handel-Mazzetti (1931); he noted that the Gobi is "contiguous" with western Asiatic and African deserts, that it has many species distributed throughout its entire breadth, and that it has few endemics. Nuttonson (1947) compared crop geography of China with agroclimatic analogs in North America. Vinogradov and Petrov (1962) compared the vegetation of central Asia with that of the Algerian Sahara by means of aerial photography. Ivanov (1962) described the major sand-plants found in Inner Mongolia and northwestern China, and Kao (1963) discussed the vegetation of the sandy and clay deserts in the Dzhungarian and Tarim basins.

Summary of State of Knowledge

Floristically speaking, the information relating to the Gobi is the least reliable of all deserts. Early descriptions were largely made by travelers untrained in botany. Prior to the present Chinese regime there was little interest in this area by the Chinese. Some of the earlier explorations were made by Russians, and the most reliable and accessible recent information comes from Russian sources. It is known that many studies are underway to improve the utilization of this large area and to develop methods of sand stabilization; details are largely lacking, however.

4. The Australian Deserts

General Descriptions of Plant Communities

The vegetation of more than half of Australia (56 per cent) must contend with arid conditions (Davies, 1955): less than 10 inches of rainfall per year. One fifth of the continent receives less than 5 inches. Although the deserts of Australia do not reach the dry extremes of some others, they are nevertheless sizeable and important.

R. A. Perry, one of our consultants for Australia, states that so little is known of actual climatic conditions in the center of the Australian desert that there is no certain answer to the question of maximum degree of aridity. He also points out that in northern Australia, desert conditions may extend up to 25 inches of precipitation because of the high temperatures and because of the predominance of summer precipitation, which has a very low efficiency in the production of vegetation.

In fact, the effect of a certain amount of rainfall on plant growth depends on season of fall, temporal distribution, intensity of fall, runoff or runon, and permeability and other physical characteristics of the soil. Thus in Australia, from the point of view of plant growth and production, the 10-inch isohyet in the south (winter incidence) is regarded as being roughly equivalent to the 25-inch isohyet in the north (summer incidence). It is soil-plant moisture and length of periods of adequate soil moisture for plant growth which are important rather than precipitation.

In consultant Emberger's opinion there apparently are no true climatic deserts in Australia comparable to those of the Sahara. Furthermore some of the Australian "deserts" have a Mediterranean tendency, others a tropical tendency (Emberger, 1958). Between the two, for example, the region of Broken Hill is intermediate in the sense that in certain years the climate is of Mediterranean tendency, while during others of tropical tendency.

The literature pertaining to the vegetation of Australia is extensive, it is wide in its coverage (from taxonomy to use), and it includes many publications on phytogeography, physiognomy, ecological relations, and basic research in the fields of physiology and genetics. In spite of the great number and variety of publications, relatively little is known about conditions in the interior desert as has been mentioned, and it is only during and since the last half of the 19th century that explorations have penetrated to some parts of the interior. Indeed, Brown (1963) has reported that the Arunta (Simpson) Desert was first crossed in 1934.

Wood (1950) and Davies (1955) have contributed extensive categorizations of Australian vegetation. Wood's system of plant formations of Australia and their characteristics is presented in table VI.

Davies (1955) defined several categories of plant formations in Australia. His desert and arid vegetation formations, with corresponding mean annual rainfall, are as follows:

Desert formations:	Rainfall (inches):
Sclerophyllous grassland	8 or less
Desert steppe	8 or less

Arid formations:	
Sclerophyllous grass steppe	------
Mulga scrub	5—8
Shrub steppe	5—8
Arid scrub	8—10

Consultants Christian and Perry comment that these figures apply to southern Australia and that the precipitation amounts would be much higher in northern Australia.

According to Wood (1950) and Davies (1955), deserts are extensive in Australia, occurring where the mean annual rainfall is less than 8 inches and where evaporation is greater (Davies says substantially greater) than the rainfall during each month of the year. They consist of (1) sandy deserts and (2) stony deserts. In the three large sandy deserts —the Great Sandy, the Great Victoria, and the Simpson— which consist of parallel sand ridges sometimes more than 100 miles long, vegetation grows both on the dunes (20 to 100 feet high, often unstable at the crests) and in the interdunal corridors (300 to 600 yards wide). The dominant perennial plants of the sandy deserts caused Davies to call these areas "desert sclerophyllous grassland." The most widespread is *Triodia basedowii** (spinifex), which grows in dense scattered tussocks; the individual plants are much branched and have hard, spiny leaves. It occurs on the lower ridge slopes, the sand areas between the dunes, and the sandplains of all these deserts. Davies mentions other *Triodia* species. In the Simpson desert, *Spinifex paradoxus* (canegrass) with rigid, much-branched stems grows on the crests of the dunes (Wood) or on the lower slopes of stabilized dunes (Davies). Occasional small shrubs of *Hakea, Grevillea, Eremophila,* and *Crotalaria* occur with the spinifex in the sandy hollows and interdune corridors of the Simpson desert; after rains a wealth of ephemerals springs up, chiefly composites and grasses. Also in the Simpson desert, according to Davies (1955), extensive floodplains carry a characteristic community of *Eucalyptus coolabah* (coolibah) and *Atriplex nummularia* (old man saltbush).

Consultants Christian and Perry have pointed out the confusion resulting from changes in scientific and common names over the years, and they are the source of the following:

The word "spinifex" has two uses in Australia. It is utilized as the common name applied to all species of the genera *Triodia* and *Plectrachne*, which are perennial evergreen tussock grasses, very harsh and spiny,

_____
* Species Summary, p. 473, gives additional data for the species listed throughout this chapter and cites publications that discuss the species further.

Table VI

PLANT FORMATIONS OF AUSTRALIA AND
THEIR CHARACTERISTICS (after Wood, 1950)

Formation	Characteristics
Desert	Sparse tussocks of sclerophyllous grass seasonal herbage after rains or chenopodiaceous plants; marked
Savanna	Grass with herbs and few subfruticose shrubs; trees rare or absent
Shrub steppe	Small perennial shrubs, chiefly Chenopodiaceae, not forming continuous cover; trees rare or absent
Scrub	Small trees with dense or scattered shrubs; few herbs
Savanna woodland	Trees of woodland form, mainly spaced in parklike manner; shrubs rare; undergrowth herbaceous
Sclerophyll forest	Trees of forest form, in close community; dense undergrowth of hard-leaved shrubs; grass rare
Rain forest	Dense assemblage of trees, canopy continuous; woody climbers present
High moor	Tussocks of grasses or sedges at high altitudes

and it is applied as a generic name to a totally unrelated grass genus which is now more correctly referred to as *Zygochloa*. In arid Australia there are many *Triodia* and *Plectrachne* species, all commonly called spinifex. In desert areas, only one is referable to the old genus *Spinifex, i. e. Spinifex paradoxus,* which should now be referred to as *Zygochloa paradoxa.* The genus *Triodia* is entirely restricted to Australia. A small grass from Arizona has been referred to the genus, but incorrectly. (It is now referred to the genus *Tridens.*)

The plant earlier referred to by Davies and others as *Eucalyptus coolabah* with the common name of coolabah is more correctly identified as *E. microtheca* with the common name of coolibah. Also the name of *Casuarina lepidophloia* has been changed to *Casuarina cristata.*

According to Wood, desert steppe conditions are found in three large stony deserts: The Gibson desert in Western Australia, the desert area to the west of Lake Eyre in South Australia, and the area (sometimes called the Sturt desert) in the northeast

corner of South Australia, extending into Queensland. The soils are brown, heavy textured, and relatively saline. The Gibson desert is dominated by *Triodia basedowii.* West of Lake Eyre a mixed steppe of *Kochia* and *Atriplex* is characteristic (Wood), with a ground flora of grasses; according to Davies, in the South Australian desert areas occurs a well-marked association of grasses and small chenopodiaceous shrubs forming a mixed steppe. In the northern parts of the deserts (both sources) and in the Queensland portion of the Sturt desert (Davies) the dominant grasses are *Astrebla* species (Mitchell grasses); further south *Agrostis** species are dominant (both sources). The shrubs are species of *Kochia* (bluebushes) and *Atriplex* (saltbushes). After rains the annual saltbushes and *Bassia* species are prominent. The Gibson desert is little known, but the dominant grass is *Triodia.*

Fringing the deserts are arid formations with perennial grass prominent in the northern area with summer rainfall (the dominant plant is *Triodia pungens*) and chenopodiaceous shrubs prominent in the southern area with winter rainfall. In the south,

* According to consultant Perry, *Eragrostis* is the genus occurring on more arid areas.

the community merges with mulga scrub (an open scrub with *Acacia aneura* dominant among various other species of *Acacia*) which is found along the southern and eastern boundaries of the desert.

The mulga scrub is one of the most widespread and important arid formations in Australia; the treatment here is adapted from Davies. Mulga grows on an extensive zone in the Eremean province of Western Australia, reaching to the coastal zone south of the Hammersly ranges. It forms an almost continuous belt across the center of South Australia into northwest New South Wales and southwest Queensland, where it is strongly developed. In southwest Queensland, it alternates with savanna woodland. The dominant plant of mulga scrub is *Acacia aneura* (which may vary from a shrubby form less than a meter high to a relatively tall woodland form in closed communities). Other *Acacia* species found with *A. aneura* are *A. cyperophylla* (red mulga) and *A. brachystachya,* and species of *Eremophila, Dodonaea,* and *Cassia* also coexist with it.

An arid shrub that occurs on desert loams is closely associated with the mulga scrub. This type formation includes the *Acacia cambagei* (gidgee) scrubs, the *Acacia harpophylla* (brigalow) scrub of Queensland, the open boree *Acacia pendula* scrub of New South Wales, the *Casuarina cristata* (black oak or belah), the *Myoporum platycarpum* (false sandalwood), and the *Acacia sowdenii* (South Australian myall) (Davies, 1955).

In southern Australia on heavy soils, the shrub steppe is found (Wood). This type is dominated by *Atriplex vesicaria, Kochia sedifolia,* and *Kochia planifolia.* It also includes annuals belonging to Chenopodiaceae, Compositae, Gramineae, and others.

Taxonomic Works

The most widely used taxonomic reference for arid Australia is J. M. Black's handbook, *Flora of South Australia* (1943-1957). A useful supplement to this is Chippendale's (1959) *Check List of Central Australian Plants.*

The first comprehensive work on the flora of Australia was the *Fragmenta Phytographiae Australiae* written by Ferdinand von Mueller (published in 11 volumes and part of a 12th) during the period 1858 to 1882. The 7-volume *Flora Australiensis* compiled by George Bentham was published in London between 1863 and 1878. In more recent years, Gardner (1952a) authored a *Flora of Western Australia.* Galbraith published a series of articles on Australian wattles (*Acacia* species) in the *Victorian Naturalist* beginning in 1959 (1959-1962). Anderson (1930) studied the genus *Atriplex* and Burbidge (1953, 1960a) the genus *Triodia.* A very useful

book, especially for amateur botanists, is that on wildflowers by Blackall (1954); its botanical keys are all illustrated with line drawings.

Ecological Works

According to consultants Christian and Perry, the best, most detailed, and most up-to-date publications on the distribution of Australia's arid plant communities are Blake (1938) on the plant communities of western Queensland, Beadle (1948) on the vegetation and pastures of western New South Wales, Jessup (1951) on the soils, geology, and vegetation of north western South Australia, and a series of publications from the C. S. I. R. O. Division of Land Research. These together provide a broad-scale coverage for about half the area of arid Australia. The latter include Perry (1960) on the pasture lands of the Northern Territory and (1962) on the Alice Springs area; Perry and Christian (1954) on the Barkly region, Perry *et al.* (1964) on the Leichhardt-Gilbert area; Speck (1963) and Wilcox and Speck (1963) on the Wiluna-Meekatharra area; and Speck, Fitzgerald, and Perry (1963) and Speck and Lazarides (1963) on the west Kimberley area.

Other publications on these areas include: Christian and Donald's (1950) pasture map of Australia; Holland and Moore (1962) on the Bollon district; Osborn, Wood and Paltridge (1935), Wood (1936), and Hall, Specht, and Eardley (1964) on the Koonamore vegetation reserve; Burbidge (1945) on the De Grey/Coongan and (1944b) on Eighty Mile Beach; and Crocker (1946a) on the Eyre Peninsula and (1946b) on the Simpson Desert.

A major reference for the desert vegetation of Australia is that portion of Walter's (1964) *Die Vegetation der Erde* devoted to the Australian desert.

One of the earliest descriptions of the arid portions of Australia was that written by Diels in 1906 and included in Engler and Drude, *Die Vegetation der Erde;* the area covered was Western Australia south of the Tropic. In 1921, Cannon, an American botanist who had for some time been associated with the Carnegie Desert Laboratory, reported on plant habits and habitats as a part of a worldwide study. Taylor (1926) described the various ecological regions of Australia with reference to their agricultural use. Prescott (1929) prepared maps to show the native vegetation of South Australia prior to settlement. Gardner (1942) prepared a comprehensive report on the vegetation of Western Australia, depicting its origins, relations to other areas, and ecology of various communities; and Davies (1955) summarized arid-zone conditions in Australia, providing a good overall picture of conditions, vegetation, use, and the progress of research.

A map of the vegetation regions was compiled by Williams (1955). Gardner (1959) contributed an article on the vegetation of Western Australia to a compendium edited by Keast, Crocker, and Christian (1959) entitled *Biogeography and Ecology in Australia*. Burbidge (1960b) reported comprehensively on the phytogeography of the Australian region; this work brings together in one volume a complete discussion of the floristic distribution of various plant elements and their worldwide affinities.

An interesting article by G. Taylor (1937), an Australian geographer, compared American and Australian deserts. He noted that many of the landforms in the two areas were similar, but that the American desert supported more varied vegetation and a greater amount of animal life. His comparison was with the Tucson-Phoenix area (in Arizona), which has a more favorable climate than much of the American desert.

Many studies have been made of the vegetation of local areas. They range from those with a strong phytogeographic emphasis to those relating vegetation to environmental conditions.

Some of the more important descriptions include those of Adamson and Osborn (1922) on the ecology of the Ooldea District; Collins (1923, 1924) on the vegetation in two localities in New South Wales; and Murray (1931) on the results of observations and collections made from 1927 to 1930 in the Lake Torrens plateau of South Australia.

Burbidge (1959) reported on the Abydos-Woodstock area in Western Australia; her study included habitat studies of various communities and a phytogeographical analysis. Chippendale (1958, 1963) reported on the vegetation of an area west of Alice Springs in central Australia; detailed lists of species and ecological conditions, including fire and grazing, were included in the two reports. Perry and Lazarides (1962) also reported on the vegetation of the Alice Springs area; their interests were largely floristic.

A study on the floristics and ecology of mallee (largely *Eucalyptus*) scrub on the desert edge by Wood (1929) is of interest because this type often borders desert areas, especially in the south where the 8-inch isohyet may mark the boundary between desert and mallee.

Everist (1949) outlined the climate, topography, and soils of the Queensland mulga belt; this belt, occurring mainly between the 8- and 20-inch isohyets, was mapped and its fodder value and management discussed. A number of publications emphasizing climate but of special note for students of vegetation should be mentioned. Davidson (1935-1937) suggested a climatic classification based upon precipitation and saturation deficit and prepared a map showing the bioclimatic zones of Australia with special reference to climate and soils. Gentilli (1948) compared the climatic classifications of Köppen and Thornthwaite and their relations to vegetational regions. Fenton (1949) used the same classifications in a study of the climate of the Lake Victoria Plateau, and Marshall (1948) analyzed various systems for determining the size of the Australian desert.

Relationships of vegetation to soils have also received considerable notice. Attention has been given to saline soils, including the study of Osborn and Wood in arid South Australia (1923), the studies of Ashby and Beadle (1957), and that of Charley (1959). The sand formations of the Simpson Desert and the spinifex cover were discussed by Madigan (1946); he saw no evidence of greater aridity in the past and did not believe natural expansion was possible.

The degeneration of arid lands has long been recognized. Osborn (1929) reviewed the climatic and edaphic influences in arid Australia and the regressive results from grazing. Crocker and Skewes (1941) discussed soil and vegetation relationships at the Yudnapinna Station, established for soil deterioration and regeneration studies in northwest South Australia in the 7.5-inch rainfall belt.

The advantageous and disadvantageous effects of burning have been considered in various localities. Burbidge (1944a) studied the effects of burning on *Triodia pungens* in northwestern Australia; she found that the tussocks might be destroyed or might regenerate from the base and that permanent change in vegetation resulted in some places. In Western Australia, Gardner (1957) found that fire has affected plants for a long time, presumably since prehistoric times; burning favored a species of *Eucalyptus* and absolute protection from fire has a detrimental effect upon the vegetation. The effects of grazing and burning have received a comprehensive literature review by Moore (1960).

Prickly pear introduced from the United States became a pest in Australia, and biological control measures were initiated many years ago; these measures were described by Dodd (1927).

The toxic plants of Western Australia were described, their habitats noted, and toxic characteristic discussed in a series of papers by Gardner (1952-1958), and Gardner and Bennetts (1956). The poisonous plants of the Northern Territory were listed by the Animal Industry Branch (1956-1959) and for New South Wales by Hurst (1942). Royce (1952) prepared maps showing the distribution of 75 poisonous plants in southwestern Australia.

Summary of State of Knowledge

The flora of the desert regions is well known, and ecological studies, especially those that relate to use of native vegetation, have been made in several localities; however there is a recognized need for detailed surveys and more intensive ecological investigations, particularly in relation to the grazing industries. Work of these classes is presently being carried out by C. S. I. R. O., the Soil Conservation Service, university scientists, and other professionals. There is an apparent need for consolidating taxonomic studies into manuals for more convenient use of technicians and travelers. Much less is known of the interior of the Australian desert area than of the outer areas.

5.   South America

General Descriptions of Plant Communities of South American Deserts

By way of introduction to the discussion of desert vegetation for South America, material adapted from Cabrera's (1955*b*) authoritative review of the vegetation of the arid and semiarid regions of Latin America is included.

The following categorization of vegetation is essentially according to Cabrera, with some modifications and additions by consultant Burkart:

1) Desert: Vegetation absolutely or practically nonexistent; climate extremely dry (e. g., Peruvian coast and northern Chile).

2) Scrub steppe: Vegetation of bushy or tussocky shrubs sparsely distributed and interspaced by bare soil during the dry season; climate very dry, continental and windy. Many Compositae such as *Chuquiraga* species; also *Verbena, Mulinum,* etc. (the prevailing type of vegetation in the Puna and Patagonia).

3) Cactus scrub (cardonal): Vegetation of ceriform or candelabrum Cactaceae and low shrubs; climate very dry and hot (e. g., the cactus scrub of Peru and the Ante-Puna, Argentina). Mostly species of *Trichocereus, Cereus, Oreocereus,* etc.

4) Monte: Vegetation of taller and thicker growing shrubs, often resinous; climate dry, hot temperature (e. g., Monte province, Argentina).

5) Thorn forest (espinal): Vegetation of tall bushes and low spiny trees with leaves or folioles of reduced size; climate dry (e. g., the mesquite woods of central Chile). Consultant Burkart adds here the "espino," "tusca," and "espinillo" (*Acacia caven*) in Argentina; and the "algarrobales" and "caldenales" (*Prosopis nigra, P. alba, P. caldenia*) in central Argentina, western Gran Chaco, and Bosque Pampeano.

6) Sclerophyllous scrub: Vegetation dominated by shrubs and small trees with coriaceous leaves; climate less dry than (5) (e. g., the vegetation of central Chile).

7) Grassy steppe: Vegetation dominated by clumps of xerophytic hard bunch grasses, mostly *Stipa, Festuca, Calamagrostis,* and *Poa* species, fairly widely spaced; climate temperate, slightly more humid than (6) (e. g., steppes of western Patagonia).

Cabrera's classification of life forms of the arid zones is based on that of Du Rietz in a 1931 work and Raunkiaer (1937). Cabrera recognizes:

1) Holoxiles

Woody plants with persistent stem and boughs. In all cases the stem develops secondary structures from the second year of the plant's life.

a) Arboriform. With a main trunk either plain or ramified some distance above ground level.

(1)   Trees. Ramified trunk. The commonest types in arid zones are the Microphanerophytes or trees growing to a height of from 1 to 8 m. There are species which are deciduous during the dry season such as the *Prosopis* and a few permanently in leaf (e. g. *Zizyphus joazeiro** in Brazil). An interesting type is the very thick-trunked waterstoring tree such as the *Cavanillesia arborea* of northeastern Brazil. (Consultant Burkart comments that the same thing occurs in northwestern Argentina, in the western Gran Chaco, with *Chorisia insignis.*)

(2)   Rosulates. Stem with no, or few, ramifications, the stem proper or the ramification terminating in rosettes of leaves which may be either entire and ensiform as in the various species of *Yucca* or divided as in the palms.

(3)   Cereiform. Tall plants with thick, leafless trunk and branches. They contain stores of water and in most cases are very spiny. Examples: *Trichocereus, Browningia, Neoraimondia* and other similar cactaceae. (Consultant Burkart includes *Cereus* as well.)

b) Arbustiform (Nanophanerophytes). Woody plants with ramification starting at root level. This is one of the plant types most typical of the arid zones.

(1)   Upright shrubs. This is the commonest type. In arid zones the leaves are usually small in size and are lost in the dry sea-

---

* Species Summary, p. 473, gives additional data for the species listed throughout this chapter and cites publications that discuss the species further.

son, whether winter or summer; at the slightest increase in humidity they bud quickly. In the desert of northern Chile shrubs lose their leaves during the summer . . . , whereas in the Puna this occurs with many species in the winter, which is the dry season there. Such deciduous plants are much less well protected against drought than evergreens such as *Chuquiraga, Nassauvia,* etc. . . . The leaves of most of the evergreens are coriaceous, narrow-bladed *(Chuquiraga)* or even spiniform. They frequently exhibit heteroblastic characteristics. . . , combining thick stems (macroblasts), with usually spiniform foliage, and short stems or branches (brachyblasts) with a dense foliage of small leaves set in glomeruli or rosettes; the latter type of development is found in many species of the Puna and Patagonia, e. g. *Verbena tridens, Nassauvia glomerulosa, Nassauvia axillaris, Verbena seriphioides, Fabiana bryoides,* etc. An extreme form is that of the leafless shrubs, with diminutive foliage which falls almost at once. It is common in all arid zones, examples being *Cassia aphylla, Cassia crassiramea, Ramorinoa girolae, Fabiana patagonica, Psila (Pseudobaccharis) spartioides, Aphyllocladus spartioides, Neosparton ephedroides,* etc.

(2) Creeping shrubs. Stem and branches hugging the soil. Not numerous in arid zones; commoner in Alpine areas.

(3) Cushion shrubs. Woody plants with very short branches closely interwoven to form an extremely thick pillow- or cushion-shaped mass, sometimes almost rock-like in appearance. This is an example of adaptation to drought and even more to wind, and is highly typical of the highest mountain levels and also of the arid zones of Patagonia and the Puna. In arid zones without strong winds, this plant form is nonexistent; on the other hand specialized variants of it . . . are found in the humid "paramos" of Colombia and Ecuador . . . . (Forty-six species of pulviform plants have been found in Chile, and in Patagonia more than) sixty of various families, mostly Caryophyllaceae, Cruciferae, Frankeniaceae, Umbellifers, Verbenaceae, Solanaceae, Valerianaceae

and composites. . . . In the Andean and Patagonian regions there are probably not less than 170 different pulviform species, mostly Caryophyllaceae, Cruciferae, and composites. However, these species vary widely in texture from the loose soft structure of some species of *Mulinum* to the stiff dense mass of *Azorella compacta.* In other instances the plants are less like cushions than like woody plaques lying almost flat to the soil. . . . (Three types have been distinguished): *(a)* convex cushions consisting of a great number of rosettes— e. g. *Azorella gilliesii;* *(b)* convex cushions of short highly ramified exposed stems—e. g. *Adesmia hemisphaerica, Adesmia horrida,* etc.; *(c)* subterranean shrubs with twigs forming a compact mat on the surface of the soil—e. g. *Adesmia subterranea, Oxalis bryoides, Verbena uniflora,* etc. In all these pulviform varieties, the leaves are diminutive, thick and either evergreen or remain on the plant when dead. . . . Many varieties exude resins which serve to bind the "cushion," while in others earth accumulates among the twigs. The close growth of twigs and leaves, with water vapour filling the interstices, affords these plants a notable degree of protection against excessive transpiration. . . .

(4) Thick-stemmed shrubs. Branches are thick and practically leafless, e. g. many varieties of shrub-Cactaceae and Chenopodiaceae such as *Allenrolfea, Salicornia, Heterostachys,* etc.

2) *"Hemixiles"* (Suffrutices)
Plants in which the lower part of the stem is woody and perennial and the upper herbaceous and dying off yearly. They appear to be rare in arid zones.

3) *Herbs*
Plants without a woody stem above ground.

a) *Hemicryptophytes.* Plants in which the annual resting buds are at soil level.

(1) Graminiform. Plants with long, narrow, "lineate" leaves concentrated in the lower part of the stem. The best known types are the thickstemmed grasses, which are very common on the grassy steppes. During the dead season stems and leaves dry up, leaving only the resting buds at soil level.

(2) Rosular. Herbs with a rosette of leaves at ground level from the centre of which the stalks or shoots spring. This type is relatively common in arid zones because it is protected from wind by its foliage which is on the ground. . . . *Calycera crenata,* and several species of *Nototriche, Oxalis,* etc. (have been recorded) in Puna.

(3) Caulifoliates. Hemicryptophytes without rosettes and with leaves growing direct from the stem.

(4) Creepers. Hemicryptophytes with creeper stems. This is a frequent plant form in arid zones.

b) *Geophytes* (=Cryptophytes). Herbs with subterranean resting buds, so that in the "dead" season no part of the plant is visible above ground. A very common plant form in dry areas.

(1) Rhizomata. The resting buds form on rhizomes. Many species of this type are found in the arid zones, rhizomes not merely serving to accumulate food reserves and produce new growth, but also being alimentary organs which can reach moist horizons. They also constitute a strong network which prevents the uprooting of plants growing in very light soil. Little work has been done on the rhizomes of arid-zone species. In northwestern Argentina *Sporobolus rigens* is a grass widely distributed in the dunes of the Monte province. Its rhizomes may attain a length of over 15 m and lie between 25 and 35 cm below the surface. The ends are furnished with very hard bud-sheaths acting almost as drill heads to penetrate the soil. The rhizome may extend up to 6 m per year, with aerial shoots every 18 to 20 cm. The roots are about 40 cm long and may reach a depth of 70 to 80 cm below the surface. When the plant is buried by sand, the rhizome throws out vertical sprouts which emerge above ground. This variety also seeds extensively.

(2) Tubers. The resting buds form on underground tubers. This is another form very common in arid and semi-arid zones, the tubers developing to a remarkable size (up to a volume of several cubic feet) and being rich in starch and other nutriment. The plant can thus resist extended periods of drought, and the buds open when there is sufficient moisture or even by drawing exclusively on the plant's own resources. The tubers are often at considerable depths below soil level and are difficult to extract.

The group includes several species of *Solanum, Ipomoea minuta, Portulaca rotundifolia, Oxalis elegans,* etc. . . . One of the most unusual of the tuberiferous geophytes is *Juelia subterranea,* a Balanoforaceous parasite of a number of shrubs of the Bolivian and north Chilean plateau (Consultant Burkart adds the northwestern Argentinian plateau). The flowers spring from the tubers but never reach the surface, and fertilization takes place underground.

(3) Bulb geophytes. The resting buds are protected by thick bud-sheaths forming bulbs. Biologically this form is analogous to that above, with the difference that the reserves are stored in the bud-sheath. Many arid zone liliflorales belong to this type.

(4) Radicigemadas. The resting buds form on the roots. A biological form which has been little studied or has on occasion been confused with rhizomed geophytes.

c) *Therophytes.* Annuals without resting buds. On the conclusion of its short vegetative cycle the whole plant dies and the species only survives in the form of seed during the "dormant" period. This biological type is of frequent occurrence in arid and semi-arid zones and under certain extreme climatic conditions is the only one capable of survival. The vegetative cycle of the desert zone therophytes (ephemerophytes) is very short and in many cases four or five weeks are enough to cover germination, growth, flowering, seeding and death. A short wet period every few years is all that such species need to survive in a given region . . . A peculiarity of desert herbaceous flora is the early stage of growth at which plants flower, sometimes when they are barely 2 cm in height, continuing, if they live so long, until they have reached their full growth of anything from 60 to 90 cm. In the arid zones of Mexico, the physical conditions operative in controlling the life cycle of the ephemerophyte are very different from those affecting the perennials, the development of the first being dependent on the state of humidity of the top soil. . . . Both the size of the plant and the stage at which the first flowers appear may vary within very wide limits: a seedling with little moisture available may be no more than 2 to 5 cm high with a single flower, whereas another individual of the same species, with more moisture, may ramify, reach a height of 30 to 50 cm and bear hundreds of flowers. Thus the short-lived annuals counter the adverse conditions of the dormant season and adapt themselves to the amount of water available. . . . Some 35 species of the Argentine Puna belong to this group. As they only sprout when the conditions of humidity are favourable, they have few defences against drought and need no special adaptations—morphological or anatomical.

The Monte-Patagonian Desert
General Descriptions of Plant Communities and Ecological Works: The Monte

According to Morello (1958), the Monte phytographical province extends from 24° 35′ S to 44° 20′ S in the center of Patagonia and from 65° 54′ W on the Atlantic coast to 69° 50′ W inland. It is located in the pre-Andean region occupying intermountain bolsones (flat and short valleys), where the moist air currents rarely penetrate. Precipitation is generally less than 200 mm; no permanent streams reach the ocean, except, in Northern Patagonia, the ríos Colorado, Negro, and Chubut.

Much of the Monte has a cover of resinous bushes, with Zygophyllaceae (*Larrea*) bushes being dominant. Many species are totally or partially aphyllous. Trees, if present at all, are found on river borders, where they form gallery forests. Perennial grasses are limited to moist places.

Monte develops on extensive semiarid plains or "mesetas," and also in depressions, typically flat-bottomed and circular or elliptical and often limited by very high mountain ranges. Main habitats are muddy depressions (barriales), salt pans, dunes, slopes, badlands, downward slopes, permanent rivers, mountain torrents, brackish soils, alluvial cones, and tablelands.

Life forms include plants with all parts perennial, plants that shed leaves in the dry season, plants that shed branches, plants that shed whole aerial body, and ephemerals. According to Morello, the main plant communities include subdesert scrub (e. g., *Larrea, Prosopis, Bulnesia, Plectrocarpa,* and *Monttea*), cactus scrub (succulent scrub, *Trichocereus,* and *Cereus*), xerophilous open woodland (*Prosopis, Celtis, Acacia,* and *Geoffroea*), and also rock associations (*Abromeitiella Dyckia,* and *Deuterocohnia*), psammophilous associations, gypsophilous associations, and halophilous associations.

The surrounding phytogeographical provinces include: Chaco province (deciduous forests of *Schinopsis, Aspidosperma, Prosopis, Chorisia, Bulnesia,* etc. in central Argentina), Patagonia province (bush province of extra-Andean Patagonia), and Puna province (low bush steppe of the high mountains above 3,000 meters in northwestern Argentina). Cabrera (1958) published a popular and well illustrated article on the plant geography of Argentina.

Cabrera (1955*a, b*) described the Monte as a phytogeographical province extending from Catamarca and La Rioja to the extreme north of the Chubut territory, and including depressions, plains, and tables with gravel or sandy soils, usually deep and permeable. He noted the same type of vegetation as Morello, and mentioned halophile and psammophile communities. Both of these authors referred to the plant communities as "steppe," but the area falls in Meigs' *A* (arid) classification; its rainfall of less than 200 mm categorizes it as desert under our present classification. Other publications include those of Monticelli (1938) on the province La Pampa; Ragonese (1951) on the "Salinas Grandes" (an enormous salt field); and Ragonese (1955) on the poisonous plants of Argentina.

General Descriptions of Plant Communities and Ecological Works: the Patagonian Desert

Meigs (1953) states that the Patagonian desert, the only high latitude east-coast desert, has no counterpart among the world's deserts. It owes its dryness to the Andes Mountains, a barrier to the rain-bearing air masses from the west, and the cold Falkland current off the east coast. According to comment by consultant Burkart, Mesozoic remains in Patagonia of *Araucaria* and *Araucarioseylon,* sometimes forming fossil forests, are proof of the influence that the raising of the Cordillera had in drying out the Patagonian mesetas.

Parodi (1945) described the vegetation of the area from the Straits of Magellan to the mouth of the Chubut River as low scrub with a few grasses, with its western limit meeting the Monte area. The climate is cold temperate, very dry, and windy. The vegetation receives rainfall that varies from 150 to 300 mm, with the maximum during the warm season. The soils are dry or rocky on the mesetas and moist in the lowlands, where broad meadows may be found. The grasses and grasslike plants include species of *Poa,*

Festuca, Agrostis, Deschampsia, Carex, Juncus, etc. The low shrubs, often cushionlike, include species of *Berberis, Azorella, Verbena, Nardophyllum, Adesmia,* etc. The xerophytic grasses include species of *Stipa, Poa, Hordeum, Agropyron, Bromus, Trisetum,* etc.

Soriano's (1956*a*) up-to-date map should be consulted by those interested in the different vegetational districts of the Patagonian Province (in Cabrera's sense, 1955*a*). Soriano's study covered the Argentine Patagonian territory south of parallel 42° S, disregarding the portion of Patagonian vegetation to the northwest, mainly in the political provinces Neuquén and Mendoza, which the author could not explore. The districts mentioned are:

1) D. Occidental (Western district)
2) D. Central (Central district)
      a) Subd. chubutense
      b) Subd. santacrucense
3) D. del Golfo San Jorge (Gulf of St. George district)
4) D. Subandino (Subandine district)
5) D. Fueguino (Fuegian district)

Their main characteristics are:

1) *Distrito Occidental.* Dominance of branch grasses of the harsh type, *Stipa speciosa, S. humilis, S. chrysophylla,* some *Bromus, Poa, Festuca* species, and a number of dicotyledons such as *Senecio filaginoides, Mulinum spinosum,* and *Adesmia campestris.* This district goes down from Mendoza along the Cordillera to northern Santa Cruz, extending from the lower slopes of the Cordillera outward across the plains some 100-150 kilometers. Due to the abundance of grass (though coarse), this is one of the better sections of Patagonia for sheep.

2) *Distrito Central.* The largest within Patagonia, very desertic. The vegetation is low and covers not more than 35 per cent of the surface. Mesetas and low sierras are distinguished. The mean annual temperature varies between 8 and 13° C; the rain and snowfall total only 100-150 mm per year. Winds are very strong and persistent. The soils are poor in organic material.

The dominant subshrub is the spiny colapiche, *Nassauvia glomerulosa,* a composite (considered a fairly good sheep feed), another composite, *Chuquiraga avellanedae,* and scattered low shrubs of different species, the grass flora being scanty. Consultant Burkart has commented that the best years for vegetation are those with much snow in winter; this moisture has time enough to enter the soil and provide for all the spring and summer growth; the occasional rains in spring and summer are mostly ineffective because of the winds and high temperatures, with consequent excessive evaporation.

The chubutense subdistrict has much territory with quilenbai *(Chuquiraga avellanedae).* This subshrub is nearly absent in the santacrucense subdistrict, which is the larger portion of the whole district and has otherwise a very similar vegetation. In place of the quilenbai, "mata negra" *(Verbena tridens)* forms extensive communities in the santacrucense subdistrict.

3) *Distrito del Golfo San Jorge.* A coastal mesetas strip around St. George's Gulf, approximately 44° 30' S to 48° S, from Cabo Raso in Chubut to Puerto Deseado (the Port Desire of Darwin's route on the *Beagle,* in the 1830's). This district is a little less desertic than *(2)*; vegetation covers 56-60 per cent of the surface and sometimes even more, the mesetas being covered with bunch grass *(Stipa speciosa, S. humilis)* and many low shrubs; the hillsides are densely shrubby *(Trevoa patagonica* and *Colliguaya integerrima* being dominant).

4) *Distrito Subandino.* This narrow strip along the Cordillera in Chubut probably continues in parts of the Chilean territory and appears again more to the south, in Santa Cruz, from parallel 51° S southward, reaching there the Atlantic coast on both sides of the Río Gallegos.

This strip is steppe where the grasses *Festuca pallescens* and *F. argentina* dominate markedly, the first being a fair pasture grass, the second being poisonous. Many other herbs and shrubs grow there.

In southern Santa Cruz, this district mixes with Distrito Central. The mean annual rainfall is 290 mm.

5) *Distrito Fueguino.* This district covers the northern portion of the main island of Tierra del Fuego, ending at the 54° S, where the sub-Antarctic forest and grassland vegetation begins.

The main grass vegetation is dominated by *Festuca gracillima,* with many other herbs and grasses; locally abundant are the low shrubs *Empetrum rubrum* and *Chiliotrichum diffusum.* In the more humid valleys or vegas *Hordeum comosum* dominates. The soil is sandy, rich in humus; average yearly temperature is about 5° C and average yearly precipitation is about 396 mm.

Beetle (1943) compared Patagonia to the Great Basin in western North America. He described the shrubby vegetation noting that size decreases from north to south, with the shrubs becoming prostrate in the south. He noted that the rapidly eroding large streams support a poor vegetation and that the land drops cliff-like into the sea, with marshes and sand dunes and their consequent vegetation being rare.

Taxonomic Works

The basic publication on the flora is J. D. Hooker's *Flora Antarctica,* in 2 volumes (1844-

1847). Applicable taxonomic studies are few; some have a rather wide coverage (Descole, 1943-1956), and others are restricted to a segment of the flora. G. Macloskie's *Flora Patagonica, Flowering Plants* (Reports of the Princeton University Expeditions to Patagonia, 1896-1899, vol. 8, pts. 1-2, 1903-1906) was rather a failure, and, owing to its many mistakes, it is not to be recommended.

Summary of State of Knowledge

The Patagonian Desert has not been very thoroughly covered by botanists. Some excellent local studies have been carried out, such as those of Soriano (1949*a, b;* 1956*a*), but the area as a whole needs more study to fill in the floristic and ecological gaps. Some of the ongoing work by Soriano and others should be of help.

Several contributions on the flora of Patagonia by Carlos Spegazzini are very important (1897*a, b;* 1898-1902); he described many of the characteristic endemic plant species. Hauman gave two interesting accounts of the southern Monte (1913) and the Patagonian (1926) desert vegetation, including some good illustrations. Later Soriano (1949*a, b;* 1950; 1952; 1956*a, b*) made careful studies of the vegetation of Chubut in central Patagonia and Boelcke (1957) studied the pre-Andean vegetation in the northwestern sector.

On the whole, the Patagonian Desert needs more study to fill in the floristic and ecological gaps still existing. The taxonomy of its flora is now better known but is scattered in many systematic monographs of different genera and species groups.

At present, a regional flora of Patagonia is being prepared by a group of Argentine botanists under the guidance of Dra. Maevia N. Correa, sponsored by the Instituto Nacional de Investigaciones Agropecuarias (INTA). This flora will contribute greatly to ease of access to information about Patagonian plants. The first volume will probably appear at the end of 1967.

Information on the flora and ecology of the Monte is high in quality but deficient in quantity. Most of the information has been the result of studies of two scientists, Cabrera and Morello. Considering future use of this area, more intensive research is needed. The Puna desert has received attention by Fries (1905) and Cabrera (1947, 1957) and the high northwestern part of Argentina by Hunziker (1952) and Czajka and Vervoorst (1956). A great deal of information on the vegetation of these areas and related resources can be expected in the future, through the very active scientific organization in Argentina, Comité Argentino para el Estudio de las Regiones Aridas y Semiáridas (CAPERAS).

The Atacama-Peruvian Desert

General Descriptions of Plant Communities

A recent Unesco publication (Meigs, 1966) on the geography of coastal deserts summarizes a great amount of information on the deserts of this area. Meigs describes the Atacama as the driest coastal desert in the world; for example, the vegetation must contend with an annual rainfall at Arica and Iquique of less than 0.04 inches. At the southern limit of the Atacama, near the town of Copiapó, the annual rainfall is 2.52 inches.

Cabrera (1955*b*) divides the west coastal strip into three districts: the desert district, the cardonal district, and the xerophilous woodland district. The desert district extends along the coast from 6° S to about 31°S, and it is almost without vegetation except along streams. On slopes moistened by mist or drizzle during the winter, a sparse stand of *Tillandsia* may exist with a few lichens in association.

The lomas, barren mist-bathed slopes with ephemeral vegetation, occur between 150 and 1,500 meters above sea level. The vegetation of the lomas has been described by Vargas (1940), Knuchel (1947), and Velarde Nuñez (1949).

According to Cabrera (1955*b*), the commonest annual herbs of the lomas are *Stipa annua,** *Festuca australis, Urtica urens, Crassula cosmantha, Tropaeolum minus,* and *Bowlesia palmata.* Geophytes frequently found are *Alstroemeria recumbens, Commelina fasciculata, Begonia octopetala, Dioscorea chancayensis, Oxalis solarensis,* and others. Semicryptophyte perennial herbs also grow, and a few suffrutices and shrubs.

In the Tacna area of Peru, the winter flora of humid years consists of various species of *Cristaria, Hoffmanseggia, Helosciadium, Tetragonia, Plantago, Gilia,* and others. Along the coast of Tarapaca, Antofagasta, and Atacama, mists from the ocean (known locally as camanchacas) permit the development of vegetation at altitudes between 300 and 800 meters.

The valleys crossing the desert coastal belt have vegetation of trees and shrubs along the banks of the rivers. They are the oases of the zone and the only areas in which human habitation and agriculture seem possible at present. The commonest trees there include *Salix humboldtiana* (willow), *Acacia macrantha, Prosopis limensis, Prosopis chilensis* (algarrobo), *Caesalpinia tinctoria, Inga feuillei,* and *Schinus molle.*

A halophytic association is found on saline soils in the valleys and near the sea; the dominant species

---

* Species Summary, p. 473, gives additional data for the species listed throughout this chapter and cites publications that discuss the species further.

is *Distichlis spicata,* usually in conjunction with *Sporobolus virginicus, Sesuvium portulacastrum, Cressa truxillensis, Spilanthes urens, Heliotropium curassavicum,* and other herbaceous halophytic species.

Above the lomas is the cardonal district, characterized by succulent columnar cacti, some thick-stemmed Bromeliaceae, and xerophilous shrubs or stunted trees. During the rainy season an herbaceous vegetation grows with the cacti. The columnar cacti range in height from 1 to 7 meters.

In the extreme south of Peru and in northern Chile are coastwise woodlands consisting of small trees, shrubs, and columnar cacti. These include many genera common to both Americas including *Capparis, Acacia, Prosopis, Bursera, Cercidium, Salix, Baccharis,* and *Atriplex.*

Taxonomic Works

Early basic studies include those of Philippi (1860, 1891), which described endemic plants and gave information on plant distribution. Johnston contributed papers on the flora of northern Chile (1929), the guano islands of Peru (1931), and San Felix Island (1935). Macbride (1936-1961) prepared a series of papers on the flora of Peru published by the Field Museum of Natural History. McVaugh (1958) prepared the section on Myrtaceae for the same series. The unfinished work on the flora of Peru and Chile by Ruiz and Pavón (1953-1959) was published 150 years after its preparation. Soukup (1959-1961) covered the flora of Peru; he has since (1962-1964) published a vocabulary of common names of the Peruvian flora. Reiche (1934-1937) covered the flora of Chile in a 2-volume publication. Tryon (1964) recently completed a monograph on the ferns of Peru.

Ecological Works

The phytogeography of Chile has not been covered as well in literature as has the phytogeography of Peru; this statement is particularly true for desert areas. Follmann (1961*b*) reviewed the most important plant associations of Chile and their economic significance. Goodspeed (1945) presented a discussion on the vegetation and plant resources. Johnston (1929) included phytogeographic information in his *Papers on the Flora of Northern Chile.* Mann (1960) discussed the biogeographic regions of Chile, including climate, vegetation, and animal life. Ricardi (1957) presented a local study of the phytogeography of the coast of the department of Taltal in northern Chile. Follmann (1960, 1961*a*) described the lichen communities on the thorns of succulent plants in the coastal desert area receiving moisture from mists and dew.

An ecological description of the coastal deserts of Chile as well as of Peru is to be found in Walter's (1964) great synthesizing work on the vegetation of our globe. Walter (p. 422) also gives a schematic profile (after Ellenberg, 1958) through the coastal loma of Peru up to an altitude of 800 meters, and furnishes instructive data on frequency and amount of dewfall. In some places there is enough dew to allow trees to grow, e. g., an indigenous *Eugenia* species; in another area small afforestation experiments succeeded with *Eucalyptus globulus* and *Casuarina.*

Smith and Johnston (1945) covered the phytogeography of Peru. Knuchel (1947) and Velarde Nuñez (1949) described the loma vegetation of Peru. Weberbauer (1936) reviewed phytogeography in *Flora of Peru,* published by the Field Museum. Later, Weberbauer, who for more than 30 years studied the Andean vegetation of Peru, published a comprehensive book on it (1945). Svenson (1946) compared the vegetation of the coast of Ecuador and Peru with that of the Galápagos Islands. Vargas C. (1940) described the plant communities of the department of Arequipa, Peru; Velarde Nuñez (1949) described the vegetation of the lomas in the same vicinity.

Summary of State of Knowledge

The taxonomy of the vegetation of this coastal desert area has been fairly well documented, but there is little information available on phytogeography and environmental relationships.

The phytosociology of the desert areas of Chile and Peru has been treated in a general way, but not thoroughly. Much of the published material covers the less arid zones as well; few papers apply exclusively to the desert.

6. The North American Deserts
General Descriptions of Plant Communities

The delineation of the North American deserts by Shreve (1942*a*) agrees very well with Meigs (1960), except that the latter carries the arid area across the southern part of Arizona and New Mexico, extends the desert farther up the Rio Grande and Pecos River, and includes some additional areas in Wyoming and Colorado. Meigs also includes a portion of the San Joaquin valley as arid and a small area around the mouth of the Colorado River as extremely arid.

The map of Unesco (1963) classifies an area roughly approximating the Sonoran and Chihuahuan deserts as "desert" but does not show any areas as "true deserts." The highest xerothermic indexes shown are 340 near Yuma and 350 in Death Valley ("true desert" has a xerothermic index of 355 or more).

Küchler (1964) applies the term "desert" to

areas where the vegetation is either absent or at least very sparse. Less arid categories that others have termed "desert" he divides into several shrub types; the upper rainfall limits of his categories agree fairly well with the categories of other scientists, although his map goes into more detail than those of other geographers.

Earlier plant geographers classified much the same areas as arid (for example the early general map of Schimper, 1903; McGinnies, 1955). Shreve's map of the vegetation of the United States (1917) and that of Shantz and Zon (1924) are in general agreement, except that the latter extends the northern desert farther to the east and northwest and extends the creosotebush desert farther southward into the Rio Grande plains and adjacent Mexico. Jaeger (1957) agrees fairly well with Shreve on the overall extent of the desert, but divides the desert area into more individual deserts.

Accurate maps of the vegetation of Mexico are scarce, because of lack of information and the physiographic diversity of the area; Shreve's map (1942a), although general, gives a fairly good overall picture of the distribution of desert vegetation in Mexico.

Taxonomic Works

The taxonomy of the North American deserts has been well covered; notable publications and their subjects include those of the University of Southern California (1958, 1959), and floras of Arizona by Kearney and Peebles (1960), of California by Jepson (1925) and Munz and Keck (1959), of the Pacific States (four volumes) by Abrams (1940-1960), of Utah and Nevada by Tidestrom (1925), of New Mexico by Wooton and Standley (1915), of Colorado by Harrington (1964), and of the Rocky Mountain area by Coulter (1909). The Sonoran desert has been well covered by Shreve and Wiggins (1964) in their two volumes on vegetation and flora. A useful addition is the checklist of Río Mayo plants by Gentry (1942). The flora of the Chihuahuan desert has been covered in part by Johnston (1943-1944); and the woody flora of Mexico has been covered by Standley (1920-1926) in *Trees and Shrubs of Mexico*. All of these references and many more are listed by Langman (1964).

Many local floras are helpful in identifying plants of local areas; among these are *Flora of the Charleston Mountains in Nevada* by Clokey (1951), *Botany of the Death Valley Expedition* by Coville (1893), a volume of illustrated descriptions of plants in lower California by Goldman (1916), Jaeger's (1941) second edition of *Desert Wild Flowers* (very useful in California, Nevada, and Arizona), *Plants*

of the Big Bend National Park in Texas by McDougall and Sperry (1951), notes on plants in southern Baja California (in Spanish) by Martínez (1945), and descriptions of plant life on islands off the coast of Baja California by Moran (1950, 1951) and Moran and Lindsay (1950, 1951).

Some very useful publications cover specific groups of plants. The cactus family has been particularly well covered by various authors, including *How to Know the Cacti* by Dawson (1963), *The Cacti of Arizona* by Benson (1940, 1950), *The Cactaceae of Southern Utah* by Clover (1938), two papers on the Opuntiae of the Big Bend by Anthony (1949, 1956), Schulz (1930) on Texas cacti, and Sánchez-Mejorada (1961) on the Cactaceae of Sinaloa (in Spanish). For overall coverage Britton and Rose (1919-1923) is still the standard reference work.

References for other plant groups are spotty, but the more important groups are adequately covered. Hitchcock's (1950) *Manual of Grasses of the United States* is the standard reference work for grasses. Saltbushes have been covered by Bidwell and Wooton (1925), range plants and browse plants by Dayton (1931), and Dayton et al. (1937), mesquites and screwbeans by Benson (1941), the legumes of Texas by Turner (1959), and trees and shrubs of the southwest by Little (1950) and by Benson and Darrow (1954).

The species of *Zizyphus* in the United States have been described by Johnston (1963), the North American species of *Ephedra* by Cutler (1939), and the Zygophyllaceae by Porter (1963); according to Porter, the Zygophyllaceae family, which includes the creosotebush, is represented by six genera in Baja California and also has important representatives in other deserts. The *Yucca* species of the southwestern United States have been described by McKelvey (1938-1947) and their ecology and utilization discussed by Webber (1953) and Muench (1943). The *Agaves* in the southwestern United States have been described by Breitung (1959-1963) and their economic importance in Mexico by Gómez-Pompa (1963).

Ecological Works

Climate and vegetal-climatic relationships have been treated from many points of view. Clements (1936) discussed the origin of the desert climax and climate. Contreras Arias (1942) prepared a climatic map of Mexico based upon Thornthwaite's 1931 classification. Ives (1949) discussed the climate of the Sonoran desert region. Three broad climatic studies with even more direct applicability to desert vegetation are a study of climatic areas as related to plant growth by Livingston (1913), a comprehensive publication on the distribution of vegetation in the United States as related to climatic conditions by Livingston and Shreve (1921), and an analysis of rainfall, runoff, and soil moisture by Shreve (1934a). The maps of Meigs (1953, 1960) have been mentioned elsewhere. Muller (1937) studied plants as indicators of climate in northeast Mexico and the relationships of vegetation and climatic types in Nuevo León (1939). Russell (1932) discussed the frequency of dry and desert years in the western United States and wrote about the climate of Texas using a modification of Köppen's classification (1954). Shreve (1944) reported on the rainfall of northern Mexico summarizing Sykes' (1931) investigation and the analysis of rainfall in the Sonoran desert and adjacent territory by Turnage and Mallery (1941); a large amount of the information was obtained from long-period rain gauges developed by Sykes.

Several papers of wide geographic coverage include substantial reference to the deserts of Mexico (e. g., University of Southern California, 1958). Two publications of Ochoterena (1937, 1945) outline the characteristics of the vegetation of Mexico and include substantial information on the desert regions. Shreve (1942b) discussed the grassland and related vegetation in Mexico and concluded that the *Hilaria* llanos desert areas are determined by soil conditions rather than by climate. Goldman and Moore (1946) outlined the biotic provinces of Mexico, and Goldman (1951) reported on the biological exploration by E. W. Nelson and E. A. Goldman from 1892 to 1906 and discussed the biotic relations of the ten thousand plants they collected. Miranda and Hernández (1963) recognized 32 different types of vegetation categorized largely by physiognomy and by relation to the climatic types of Köppen.

Bonillas and Urbina (1913) described conditions in northern Baja California, including the delta of the Colorado River. Shreve (1926, 1934b) described the vegetation of the area north of San Felipe Bay and east of the Sierra San Pedro Mártir in Baja California, and also the mainland area extending down to the Río Mayo, noting that this area includes some of the most arid conditions in North America. Nelson (1921) described lower Baja California and its natural resources.

Brand (1936) prepared a detailed map and discussed the vegetation of northwest Mexico, including portions of the Sonoran and Chihuahuan deserts. Shreve (1939) recognized five physiographic types in Chihuahua and noted that the larger plant communities of vegetation are distributed in close accord with the physiographic regions. Lesueur (1945) mapped and discussed the vegetation types north of

28° N latitude in relation to physiography and climate. Beltrán (1953) reviewed plant and animal life along the Pan-American Highway. Sanders' (1921) paper on natural regions of Mexico also includes a brief discussion of vegetation.

Some general descriptions of the vegetation of the United States and the North American continent provide a background for considering desert vegetation in relation to that of moister areas; the following are especially noteworthy in that regard: Clements (1920), Clements and Shelford (1939), Dice (1943), Harshberger (1911), Shantz and Zon (1924), Shelford (1963), and Shreve (1917).

MacDougal (1908) discussed the features of the North American deserts. This effort was followed by Shreve's (1942a) thorough literature review and description of the desert vegetation of North America. Shreve's work included a comprehensive categorization of life forms of the vegetation of the North American desert area; his categorization is summarized in table VII. Aldous and Shantz (1924) discussed the types of vegetation of the semiarid portions of the United States and their economic significance. Other general treatises include those by Townsend (1897) on the biogeography of Mexico and the southwestern United States, Dice (1939) on the Sonoran biotic province, and both the brief discussion by Shreve (1936) and his comprehensive publication (1951) on the vegetation of the Sonoran desert. This last has recently been combined in a 2-volume work by Shreve and Wiggins (1964) which also includes the taxonomy of the Sonoran desert.

Ecologists (Hall and Grinnell, 1919; Kendeigh, 1932) have questioned the validity of Merriam's (1890; 1893a, b, c; 1898) observations of the effect of temperatures upon the distribution of plants; nevertheless Merriam's "life zones" do provide a convenient division of vegetation on an elevation basis (Muesebeck and Krombein, 1952). Life-zone descriptions, including desert areas, have been made for Arizona by Merriam (1890), for California by Hall and Grinnell (1919), for Colorado by Cary (1911), for New Mexico by Cockerell (1900) and Bailey (1913), for Oregon by Bailey (1936), for Texas by Bailey (1905), and for Wyoming by Cary (1917).

The Great Basin desert has been described by Billings (1951), Passey and Hugie (1962) (the Idaho portion), Hironaka (1963), and Hironaka and Tisdale (1963). Utah has been the locale of many studies, including those by Dixon (1935), Evans (1926), Fautin (1946), Flowers (1934), Graham (1937), Shantz and Piemeisel (1940), and Vest (1962). The detailed ecological study of Flowers and Evans (1966) on the flora and fauna of the

Great Salt Lake region shows the adaptation possibilities of numerous species to the extremely saline conditions in and around this almost saturated brine. Shantz (1925) also described the plant communities in Utah and Nevada. The Red desert in Wyoming, which is an extension of the Great Basin desert, was described by Nelson in 1898. Ramaley (1929) reported on the San Luis Valley (high altitude, low precipitation) in Colorado, and Flowers (1961) on the Navajo reservoir basin in Colorado and New Mexico.

The vegetation of the state of Arizona has been described by Nichol (1937, 1952), Shreve (1942c), and Lowe (1964), and the vegetation of northeastern Arizona by Hanson (1924). The mountains of Arizona have been the subject of several publications by botanists such as those on the Chiricahua Mountains by Blumer (1909), on the desert mountains near Tucson by Blumer (1912), on the Santa Catalina Mountains and others by Shreve (1915, 1922), and on the Huachuca Mountains by Wallmo (1955); each of these studies included material pertinent to desert vegetation. Niering, Whittaker, and Lowe (1963) studied the saguaro cactus (*Cereus giganteus**) throughout its vertical range, including investigations at lower mountain elevations.

In New Mexico, Gardner (1951) covered the creosotebush area of the Rio Grande, and Shields and Crispin (1956) studied the diversity and distribution of vegetation on a recent volcanic flow.

The diversity of California vegetation is reflected by the literature. The mapping of the vegetation of the state was described by Jensen (1947). Munz and Keck (1949, 1950) classified its plant communities, including those of the desert. Shreve (1925) discussed the ecological aspects of the deserts of California, and Cockerell (1945) prepared an accurate but more popular description of the Colorado desert of California. Eymann (1953) studied the sand dunes of the Colorado and Mojave deserts. Glendinning (1949) outlined the desert contrasts in the Coachella Valley, making brief references to the vegetation.

Bray (1901), who outlined the ecological relations of the vegetation of western Texas, later (1906) discussed the distribution and adaptation of vegetation throughout the state. Gould (1962) made an ecological summary, including a checklist of all vascular plants. The vegetation of mountain slopes in southwest Texas was the subject of a study by Cottle (1932), and the ecology of the Big Bend National Park received similar attention from Gahlbach

---

* Species Summary, p. 473, gives additional data for the species listed throughout this chapter and cites publications that discuss the species further.

(1963). Many of the publications mentioned above are listed in an annotated bibliography prepared by the University of Southern California (1959).

Many descriptions have been made of vegetation of specific areas, and many of these include ecological discussion; examples of such publications are Billings (1945) on the Carson desert region in western Nevada; Billings (1949) on the shadscale vegetation of Nevada and eastern California; Brand (1937) on the northwestern Chihuahua; Emerson (1935) and Murbarger (1950) on the Great White Sands in New Mexico; Fosberg (1940) on Mesilla Valley, New Mexico; Jaeger (1965) on the California deserts; Muller (1947) on Coahuila in Mexico; Palmer (1929) on the Davis Mountains in Texas; Rzedowski (1957) on San Luis Potosí and Zacatecas in Mexico; Waterfall (1946) on the gypsum area of southwestern Texas and adjacent New Mexico, and Sykes (1937) on the Colorado River delta.

Many important desert plants have received individual study, such as the studies on sagebrush (*Artemisia tridentata*) by Diettert (1938) and Goodwin (1956); creosotebush (*Larrea tridentata*) by Runyon (1934), by García, Soto, and Miranda (1960), and by Dalton (1962); and yuccas (*Yucca* species) by Trelease (1902), Braunton (1926), Campbell and Keller (1932), and Muench (1943).

Some of these special studies have led to the identification of plants as indicators of environmental conditions. Kearney *et al.* (1914) outlined the indicator significance of vegetation in Tooele Valley, Utah, and Daubenmire (1940) in the Big Bend area of Washington. Fireman and Hayward (1952) executed a similar study in the Escalante desert of Utah, and Daubenmire (1940) in the Big Bend area precipitation, and vegetation for the southwestern desert region; and Shantz (1938) summarized his many observations on plants as soil indicators. Meinzer (1926, 1927) used the term "phreatophyte" to designate plants that obtain their water from a zone of saturation and listed and described many plant indicators of groundwater. In a specialized study, Beath, Gilbert, and Eppson (1939) correlated the presence of selenium in plants with the geographical formations upon which the plants grew.

Much work of wide applicability has been done on local problems. For example, Spalding (1909) investigated the factors of major importance in determining local distribution of plants; he found that soil water was the most important, but aeration and alkali were also important. He also found that some plants were very sensitive to differences in edaphic condition, but that creosotebush showed a high capacity for adjustment. Went and Westergaard (1949) attributed differences in floristic composition

Table VII
LIFE FORMS OF THE NORTH AMERICAN DESERT (after Shreve, 1942a)

Ephemerals
Strictly seasonal
    Winter ephemerals .... 1. *Daucus, Plantago*
    Summer ephemerals .... 2. *Pectis, Tidestromia*
Facultative perennials .... 3. *Verbesina, Baileya*

Perennials
Underground parts perennial
    Perennial roots .... 4. *Penstemon, Anemone*
    Perennial bulbs .... 5. *Allium, Hesperocallis*
Shoot base and crown perennial .... 6. *Hilaria, Aristida*

Shoots perennial
Shoot reduced (a caudex)
  Caudex short, all or mainly leafy
    Leaves succulent .... 7. *Agave, Hechtia*
    Leaves nonsucculent .... 8. *Nolina, Dasylirion*

  Caudex long, leafy at top
    Leaves simple, semisucculent .... 9. *Yucca*
    Leaves branched, nonsucculent .... 10. *Inodes, Washingtonia*

Shoot elongated
Plant succulent (soft)
  Leafless, stem succulent
    Shoot unbranched .... 11. *Ferocactus, Thelocactus*
    Shoot branched

      Shoot poorly branched
        Plant erect and tall .... 12. *Pachycereus, Carnegiea*
        Plant erect and low or
        semiprocumbent and low .... 13. *Pedilanthus, Mammillaria*

      Shoot richly branched
        Stem segments cylindrical .... 14. *Cylindropuntia*
        Stem segments flattened .... 15. *Platyopuntia*
  Leafy, stem not succulent .... 16. *Talinum, Sedum*

Plant nonsucculent (woody)
Shoots without leaves, stems green .... 17. *Canotia, Holacantha*

Shoots with leaves
  Low bushes, wood soft .... 18. *Encelia, Franseria*
  Shrubs and trees, wood hard
    Leaves perennial .... 19. *Larrea, Mortonia*
    Leaves deciduous

      Leaves drought deciduous
        Stems specialized
          Stems indurated on surface .... 20. *Fouquieria*
          Stems enlarged at base .... 21. *Bursera, Idria*

        Stems normal
          Stems not green .... 22. *Jatropha, Plumeria*
          Stems green .... 23. *Cercidium, Euphorbia*

      Leaves winter deciduous
        Leaves large .... 24. *Populus, Ipomoea*
        Leaves small or compound .... 25. *Olneya, Prosopis*

to salinity, altitude, and other factors; they also observed that the temperatures following rains determine the germination of seeds of various plants: some germinated only under warm temperatures and others only under cool temperatures. Gates, Stoddart, and Cook (1956) studied pure stands of sagebush, winterfat, shadscale, saltbush, and greasewood; they found no reliability in these as indicators of specific soil characteristics, but in some instances the plants were found to determine upper limits.

Shreve and Mallery (1933) found that caliche in soil influenced strongly the character of vegetation, especially creosotebush. In pot tests they determined that creosotebush grew best with caliche mixed in the soil. Yang (1957) found creosotebush associated with relatively fine-textured soil and a relatively low proportion of water available for plant use and, in contrast, found paloverde associated with coarser-textured soil and a relatively higher proportion of water available for plant use.

Many ecological studies have been made on specific desert plants and on specific phases of plant adaptation to desert conditions. Cannon (1911) described the variety of form of the roots of desert plants. He found that root systems were of three general types and that these were correlated with types of aerial growth. For example, cacti have (1) spreading roots very close to the surface; some plants such as the *Ephedra* have (2) deep roots; and those of the third general type have (3) a combination of both deep and shallow roots. Cannon (1916), in a later study of cacti, noted that the wide, very shallow root system is able to collect moisture from even light rainfall; he also stated that cacti usually occur where rains fall in the warm season.

Robison (1958) reviewed comprehensively the phreatophytes of the arid and semiarid portions of the United States. The report lists the distribution and characteristics of the more common phreatophytes, their relation to depth of water table, water quality tolerance, and use of water in acre feet per acre of groundwater. Substratum conditions receive considerable attention, both in general terms and in terms of specific relationships to vegetation. Shreve (1938) summarized the information on the sandy areas of the North American deserts. He noted that sandy areas are not common and cover a much smaller portion of the total area than in the Saharan and Asian deserts; he also listed types of plants found on the sandy areas of the North American deserts. Rempel (1936) investigated the unstable crescentic dunes near Kane Springs, California, and concluded that

the sparse vegetation is not capable of stabilizing these dunes. Bryan (1928) noted a change of vegetation along the Santa Cruz and San Pedro Rivers in Arizona from bulrushes to mesquite, following a lowering of the water table because of a drier climate and arroyo cutting. He indicated that the condition was accentuated by overgrazing during the past 40 to 50 years. McDonough (1964) measured the reduction in solar energy by desert shrub cover and found that even defoliated shrubs and plants with very few branches reduce the solar energy arriving at ground level (as measured with a pyrheliograph); for example, creosotebush with leaves reduced the energy by 57 per cent, blue paloverde by 49, smokebush by 31, creosotebush without leaves by 18, and ocotillo by ten.

The rise and fall of the population of the giant cactus has been given considerable study. Shreve (1911) noted the influence of low temperatures on the distribution of the giant cacti, and found that a single day without thawing (failure of the plant to warm to above freezing) results in death to the saguaro (*Cereus giganteus*), although other species of cacti can withstand many hours of freezing. Shreve (1910) also noted that saguaro plants less than 1 decimeter high are extremely hard to find and grow very slowly; the saguaro takes 30 years to grow to 1 meter in height and 60 years to reach 5 meters. Tschirley (1963) studied the "jumping" cholla, *Opuntia fulgida,* and found that the life span is about 40 years, that reproduction is largely by vegetative means, and that the plant has a high invasion potential and is a menace to man and beast.

Summary of State of Knowledge

The North American deserts are better known, both taxonomically and ecologically, than any other deserts in the world. This is especially the case for the portion of the North American deserts within the United States. The Mexican portion is not quite so well known; it is covered rather well taxonomically but less so ecologically. Fortunately, much of the ecological information available for desert areas in the United States is also applicable, to varying degrees, to the desert areas of Mexico.

No major gaps exist in either taxonomic or ecological knowledge of the desert areas within the United States, although room remains for a great deal of additional specific research, especially to obtain more detailed coverage of various plant communities and individual plants.

CONCLUSIONS

To the North American familiar with his western deserts, limited in area and interspersed with nondesert vegetation, the expanse of the Afro-Asiatic desert belt is astounding. He could travel from a point at the western coast of Africa to the western part of India and be in desert almost all the way. Throughout this trip he would encounter similar vegetation, with many genera of plants represented across the entire area. If he traveled further to the north in Asia, he would find desert conditions with a few interruptions extending through Turkmeniya S. S. R. on into Outer Mongolia and China to within a few hundred miles of the Yellow Sea. Along the southern route he would recognize many of the plant families familiar from the southwestern deserts of North America, and on the northern route he would find many of the plant families of the Great Basin represented.

In the Sahara he might be surprised to find few succulents such as are found in the United States Southwest, and those he would find would belong to a different family from our familiar cacti. In southern Africa he would find many succulents of great variety, largely belonging to the family Euphorbiaceae, which has few succulent members in the United States, and also Aïzoaceae and even succulent Compositae (*Kleinia* species) related to the genus *Senecio*.

In Australia the traveler would find greater differences. He would be surprised at the lack of spiny plants, and that the species of *Acacia* present are different in appearance from their relatives elsewhere. He would also find the principal grass of the desert (*Triodia basedowii*) substituted for the common shrubs of other deserts.

Between the deserts of North and South America a traveler would find a great deal in common, even to the same species in some cases. Perhaps the greatest noticeable difference would be the much greater development of the cushion type of growth in some of the arid areas of South America.

The fact that these desert areas have a great deal in common gives support to the concept that they can be considered as a unit, although a large one, with common characteristics when only major conditions are considered.

It is evident that there are some real differences, but it should be emphasized that some of the differences reported in the literature are differences in the concepts of the researchers rather than differences in the vegetation. The most outstanding of these differences is in the definition of the desert environment. Consultant Emberger has emphasized the importance of this problem, especially as it concerns international understanding among botanists. A researcher in Africa may set the limit of the "desert" at 100 mm and another in the United States at 300 mm. A comparison of vegetation between these two areas would show differences, but likewise a comparison between the vegetation at the isohyets of 100 and 300 mm in the United States would show great differences. On the other hand, a comparison of vegetation at the 200 mm isohyet in Africa, the Palestine area, India, South America, and North America would show great physiognomic similarity, and many of the same families of plants would be found to be important in all the areas. Consultant Boyko comments that to a certain degree Australia may be considered to serve as an exception. Even tree growth can there be found penetrating much deeper into the actual desert. The reason may be the isolation of this continent for many millions of years and the much longer adaptation possibility of its whole vegetation to a dry climate. Consultant Christian points out that there is a great variation in efficiency of precipitation; for example, 500 mm of precipitation occurring during summer in a hot climate may have no more effect than would 250 mm of precipitation occurring during winter in a cooler climate. Consultant Christian also believes that there are great differences in soil factors of desert and their relationship to climate, e. g. higher phosphate level of Rajasthan soils permit dominant grasses such as *Cenchrus*. The low phosphate level of Australian desert soils cannot support these, but carry *Triodia* species, a very different plant form both in physiognomy and in physiology.

On the basis of this review of the vegetation of the world's arid regions it seems to me that from the viewpoint of the scientist the two major problems are as follows:

1) Inadequacy of communications among scientists
2) Lack of agreement as to what constitutes a desert.

These two are related in the sense that there would be more agreement as to what constitutes a desert if there were better communications.

From the standpoint of information for practical, but nonagricultural, use, the main deficiencies are *(1)* insufficient information on the amount or the degree of cover, *(2)* insufficient information on the life forms and characteristics of the vegetation, *(3)* insufficient information on noxious and poisonous characteristics of plants, *(4)* insufficient information on economic possibilities of the vegetation and possible uses for food, fiber, fuel, and other industrial purposes (e. g., waxes, essential oils, drugs). Consultant Emberger has indicated that he believes these deficiencies are very important and has suggested another item to be added here: *(5)* insufficient knowledge of the indicator value of plant species.

1. Communications

Basically, the weakness in communications stems from the extent of desert environments. They occupy at least an eighth of the world's land surface (another eighth is semiarid) in 50 different nations on all continents. In addition to the geographical and political problems resulting from this spread, one must remember the difficulty of language and the multiplicity of publication outlets. The principal language of works covering the flora of the Sahara is French, but important contributions are also published in German, Spanish, English and Italian. For the Latin American deserts, where Spanish is the dominant language, major publications also appear in German, French, Portuguese, and English. In the central and eastern Asian deserts, Russian is the predominant language, but available translations may be in German, French, or English.

Much useful information is published only in local journals, bulletins, and books of very limited distribution, and it is therefore very difficult or impossible of access (as in the case of political barriers); in some cases it is a struggle even to learn of the existence of the information.

Throughout the world, scientists are seeking and developing knowledge by which arid areas may be made more hospitable and useful for man, but it is at present expensive for each to try, and effectively impossible to learn of, evaluate, and obtain all information relevant to the program at hand. The consequent inefficiencies of time, money, and energy are considerable. There is a great need to facilitate more general distribution, communication, and accessibility of information on arid lands.

2. Community of Knowledge

Improved distribution, communication, and accessibility of information among numerous scientists and others the world over engaged in the study of desert environments would help to create a more coherent community of knowledge, serving to better connect and integrate the many related, but geographically far-flung accomplishments. This would help to standardize and clarify terms. But beyond this, students may then be more widely trained, theories may be developed, and research may be designed on the advantageous base of more complete pertinent information; each new local contribution of research and knowledge would be both *(1)* of greater value to all because of clarified complementary relationships, and *(2)* of readier and wider accessibility to scientists engaged in related research throughout the world.

3. Problems of Defining Desert

The term "desert" (like many other terms, especially those of wide and previously popular use) is often used so differently by different authors in different areas as to hinder rather than further communication. Why is this the case? What might be done to remove this barrier to effective communication?

Terminology

Historically, peoples have called the dry areas within their experience by the name "desert," or by a name in another language which is translated into English as "desert." This practice has continued despite the fact that the many areas that happened to receive the same loose name were in fact often greatly different. But even though ancient men and contemporary common English call all dry places "desert," perhaps scientists of today need not seek among the many for any one "correct" or "best" definition of "desert." Rather it may be useful to define distinctly different types of dry places by using distinctly different terms.

Environmental and Vegetal Criteria

One reason that there is no uniform basis for delineating deserts and areas of arid and semiarid conditions is that no easily recognized natural division points exist in desert environmental conditions. The range of conditions is a continuum from those extremely dry, under which no vegetation can grow, to the environment where climate and soils no longer limit, but rather plants compete among themselves. Any attempt to mark absolute dividing points along the complex continuum of conditions is in a sense arbitrary, because there are no natural boundary points along the line.

Perhaps one of the most useful ways to describe arid relationships would be in terms of the vegetation, for example, in terms of the following observably distinct natural categories:

1) Extremely dry, no vascular plants at all (extreme desert)

2) Marginal, plants occur in only the most favorable sites of the terrain (desert)

3) Sparse cover with great variability (semi-arid)

4) General distribution of plants throughout the environment (i. e., mesophytic grassland and forest)

5) Plant competition only; slope, exposure, etc., exert little influence upon the distribution of component species (i. e., rain forest).

There would also be other intermediate changes in plant growth that could be easily recognized; these would be both qualitative (the kind of plants present) and quantitative (the relative vigor, size, and density of growth).

In commenting on this subject, consultant Christian gave his definition of a desert as an area of low rainfall where vegetation is absent, sparse, or ephemeral. He doubts if one can be more specific in a universal sense. The rainfall limits will vary according to other factors and there will often be transitional zones except perhaps where there is a sudden geomorphic change such as increase in elevation.

Table VIII

ADEQUACY OF STATE OF KNOWLEDGE
Area and Subject

Desert	Part	Taxonomy	Phyto-geography	Phyto-sociology and Local Studies	Ecology	Harmful Effects	Uses and General Agriculture	Adequacy:
Kalahari-Namib		3	3	2	1	3	3	4 - Adequate 3 - Good 2 - Fair 1 - Poor 0 - Insig-nificant
Sahara		3	4	4	3	2	2	
Somali-Chalbi		2	2	2	0	0	1	
Arabian	Palestine	3	4	4	3	3	3	
	Remainder	2	2	2	1	1	1	
Iranian		2	2	0	0	0	0	
Thar		3	3	2	2	2	2	
Turkestan		3	3	3	2	1	2	
Takla-Makan Gobi		1	2	1	0	0	1	
Australian		3	3	3	3	2	3	
Monte-Patagonian		2	3	2	2	2	3	
Atacama-Peruvian		3	3	2	1	0	0	
North American	U. S.	4	4	4	4	3	3	
	Mexico	3	3	2	2	1	3	

Multiple Definition

The climatic, edaphic, and anthropeic (cultural) factors that result in "desert" areas are multiple and interrelated, and no delineation of desert areas on the basis of any one factor alone will adequately serve man's complex interest in the subject. For example, some areas are now more desertlike than climate restrictions alone would require, because of past destruction of vegetal cover by men and domestic animals or due to other factors; such "contingent" desert areas would be excluded by a delineation of deserts in terms of climate alone. Conversely, scaled by the criterion of present vegetation alone, areas otherwise different (such as climate-determined desert versus a better area reduced to desert by man) would be very wrongly considered equivalent, and contingent deserts of superior vegetational recovery potential would be grouped with natural deserts of much less vegetational potential.

4. State of Knowledge

The coverage for each desert has been discussed by subjects, subareas, and individual works in the preceding treatments of individual desert areas of the Earth, and additional information is provided in the annotated bibliography (Pertinent Publications list) following this chapter.

The state of knowledge of various subjects pertaining to each of the several major desert areas of the world is summarized in table VIII. The table estimates the comprehensiveness of coverage based on a review of the material in the Pertinent Publications list and discussed in this chapter. In this table "taxonomy" includes regional and local floras, plant lists, scientific and common names in English and local languages. "Phytogeography" includes general discussions of climate, soils, and/or vegetation, and these discussions usually cover a large area of two or more plant communities. "Phytosociology" includes studies centered in local areas, usually with consideration of the structure of the vegetation and successional relationships. In practice phytogeography and phytosociology merge, and it is impossible to draw a sharp line between them; usually the former stresses geography and the latter ecology. "Ecology" includes material mostly autecological in nature, but also covers some basic material not fitting into other categories. "Harmful effects" includes discussion of weeds, plants with noxious characteristics, poisons, bitter or odoriferous juices, cutting edges, or spines. It also includes methods of control. "Uses" includes useful plants, range and forest use, plant indicators, and other items of value to man in the desert.

If we use the United States as a basis for comparison, the relative information coverage can be assigned values as shown in table VIII ranging from *4* (adequate coverage quantitatively and qualitatively) to *0* (insignificant).

In southern Africa the coverage for the Namib and Kalalari is about equal when consideration is given to the relative size and complexity of each. The coverage for taxonomy and general plant descriptions is good, but detailed sociological and ecological studies are rated fair to poor. The coverage on harmful effects and use is rated as good.

A large amount of the voluminous botanical literature for the Sahara is of very high quality. The coverage for the western Sahara is much better than that for the eastern portion, where there have been fewer workers interested in the desert vegetation. The completion of taxonomic studies now underway should bring the base level up to adequate, but there will still be a lack of simple flora manuals such as are needed by ecologists and agriculturists. In the fields of phytogeography and phytosociology the coverage is adequate in the western portion of the Sahara and qualitatively good in the eastern part, but the total number of publications is much smaller. There are good ecological studies throughout, especially those relating to saline conditions. Information on harmful effects of plants and native plant uses is at a lower level. The coverage for the Somali-Chalbi area is at a much lower level throughout than that for the Sahara. The Italians have done some excellent work, but in general the coverage is spotty and inadequate.

The coverage for the Arabian Desert shows extreme contrasts, with Palestine having adequate coverage in nearly every respect while the Arabian Peninsula shows the other extreme of poor to negligible coverage. This same low level extends through the Iranian Desert.

The Thar shows good to fair coverage throughout, with better coverage generally in India than in Pakistan.

A great deal of information has been accumulated by the Russians in the Turkestan Desert. A large amount of this is not readily accessible, but it appears that the work that has been done provides good coverage in spite of the size and remoteness of the area.

East of the Turkestan Desert the level of coverage falls rapidly. Very little information is accessible on the Takla-Makan, and the large Gobi area is only slightly better. Much of the information that is available comes from Russian sources.

M. Petrov, Leningrad State University, Department of Geography, Leningrad, U.S.S.R., who has seen a preliminary copy of the present work, has written me that more has been written about the vegetation of Asia than is indicated here in the

Table IX
WORKSHEET FOR ADEQUACY OF STATE OF KNOWLEDGE
(Number of prime citations considered for Table VIII)

Desert	Taxonomy	Phyto-geography	Phyto-sociology and local studies	Ecology	Harmful Effects	Uses and Agriculture in General	Total
Kalahari-Namib	18	15	14	1	4	3	55
Sahara	31	59	62	20	3	15	190
Somali-Chalbi	6	14	8	—	—	4	32
Arabian	20	36	22	12	2	12	104
Iranian	3	10	—	—	—	—	13
Thar	15	7	8	4	1	3	38
Turkestan	5	26	12	5	1	8	57
Takla-Makan	2	2	—	—	—	—	4
Gobi	3	5	—	—	—	6	14
Australian	10	29	23	5	9	10	86
Monte-Patagonian	8	16	3	3	2	4	36
Atacama-Peruvian	11	13	7	—	—	—	31
North American	40	89	42	43	23	41	278
General	6	45	12	23	4	5	95
Unclassified	—	—	—	—	—	—	18
Subtotal by Subject	178	366	213	116	49	111	—
Total	—	—	—	—	—	—	1051

Pertinent Publications list and text. It is believed that this is true; many more works are published than are readily accessible to the Western reader.

The coverage in Australia is good for the outer portions of desert areas, but in the interior portions with low economic use the coverage drops to fair or poor.

The taxonomic coverage for the Monte-Pataganian Desert area is poor, but the phytogeographical coverage is good, especially qualitatively. Phytosociology and ecology drop to fair, although there have been some good studies related to range use. The taxonomic and phytogeographical coverage for the Atacama-Peruvian Desert is good to excellent, but few phytosociological and ecological studies have been conducted.

The taxonomic coverage for the desert areas of Mexico is nearly as good as that for the United States, which has been covered adequately. Phytogeographical knowledge of Mexico is also almost as good as the adequate coverage in the United States, but in phytosociology and ecology the ranking drops to fair and in harmful effects to poor. The rating for uses is good in Mexico, largely because of the studies of Martínez (1936), but also because much of the information obtained in the United States applies equally to Mexico.

For those interested in the genesis of table VIII, the number of *prime citations* considered for each category is shown on a worksheet as table IX. Number alone is clearly not a true measure, as the quality and comprehensiveness of the individual items cited vary greatly and the number of items was arbitrarily selected. There probably is some relation, however, between the number selected and the total available, but if this is an uncontrolled variable it probably favors the areas with the fewest citations, as there was a tendency to include as a "prime citation" almost everything available in those instances, while there was a great deal of screening when many items were available.

RECOMMENDATIONS

For all the deserts of the world it can be said that there is need for additional research on all items related to vegetation, its growth and development, its characteristics, and the use and abuse of vegetation as a hindrance or help in the social, political, and economic welfare of man.

As a top priority I would place the comprehensive collection, synthesis, analysis, and dissemination of pertinent information related to desert vegetation. It would follow that there would be greater understanding among scientists and others of the geographic, climatic, and biological parameters; at the same time such action would make available the information needed for local "problem analyses" as a logical basis for the determination of research objectives, to make possible the greatest progress with the least amount of unnecessary duplication. Some specific suggestions for further research are listed below.

1. Regional Syntheses

Regional vegetation syntheses are needed. Most of the publications cover relatively small areas and have very little correlation with other studies in adjacent areas. In particular, there should be a synthesis or amalgamation of information covering the Afro-Asian deserts in the Saharo-Sindian group, a synthesis of the information related to the Irano-Turanian regions, and a synthesis of information covering the Transcaspian-Chinese-Mongolian desert areas. There also appears to be a need for a synthesis of information relating to the entire desert area of Australia. In North America there should be a more comprehensive coverage of the cool desert, or sagebush area, and also of the complete warm desert area, possibly divided between east and west.

2. Ecological Studies

Further studies of ecological structure should be conducted covering both the autecology of characteristic component plants and the phytosociology of plant communities (including the density and relative abundance of various life forms.) In this connection, however, it should be kept in mind, as consultant Emberger points out, that on the desert there is very little synecology involved, as the plants are so widely spaced. Under very dry conditions, the distribution is more a matter of autecological relations than it is of phytosociological relationships.

3. Regional Coverage

Desirable additional research would include more comprehensive coverage of many of the areas not at present adequately described. These would include: The Arabian Peninsula, Iran, Afghanistan, the Thar, the Somali-Chalbi, the deserts of east-central Asia, the Patagonian Desert, the Monte, and the Mexican deserts other than the Sonoran. Subject needs for these areas may readily be adduced from table XIII and the section entitled "Desert Areas of the Earth."

4. Vegetation Comparisons and Analogs

It is most important that the methods used to compare the vegetation of one area with that of another be improved, and such improvement is today feasible. The systems of climatic analogs and terrain analogs used by the U. S. Army have some merit, but a combination of the two, if possible, would be more useful, because it would help disclose the interacting influences of soils and climate upon growth of vegetation. One weakness of the analog system is that it starts out with a base area and compares other areas only with this particular base.

We need more of the analog type of comparison between more local climatic types, for example, Tucson, Las Cruces, Salt Lake City, Chihuahua City, Guaymas, and their counterparts throughout the world. An addition or alternative might be preparation of climatological tables such as those compiled by Meigs (1966) for coastal deserts.

The methods of agroclimatic comparisons reviewed by Hanson (1949) and used by Nuttonson (1946, 1947) and the ecological crop geography methods described by Klages (1942) have considerable merit, but here again there is a great deal of room for improvement.

5. Phytocartography

One deficiency of most present methods of mapping vegetation is that only categories of cover and not species are indicated. The classifications used by plant geographers interested in describing the general elements of the vegetation, such as Küchler (1966) and Christian and Perry (1953), are useful for general mapping of the vegetation, but fall short of giving sufficient information on its characteristics. Some general ideas concerning the vegetation can be derived from a study of the data from a given area, but often the specific characteristics of the plants themselves remain unknown: whether they are spiny or smooth, weak-stemmed or strong, with many branches or few, the color of leaves and bark, duration of leaves, characteristic of roots. Many other essential features are missed in the effort to provide simple descriptions of the main features of the vegetation.

For certain purposes it is enough to know simply whether an area is barren or has "scattered shrubs and grass," but for other purposes it makes a further great difference which species are present. For example, if one of the scattered shrub species present is spinescent or grows thickly by watercourses, it could make passage through the area much more difficult than would other "scattered shrubs." And the very general vegetation information indicated on most maps is inadequate for many scientific considerations unless augmented by taxonomic texts that tell the species present.

6. Inconsistent Use of Terms

The terms "desert" and "steppe" are used so inconsistently by different authors that their descriptions are difficult to interpret. Such inconsistencies arise from local common uses and individual preferences and are fostered by the lack of clear and adequate definitions. "Steppe," in particular, is a term that has led to a great deal of confusion. Some writers restrict the use of the term "steppe' to semiarid grasslands, while others include brushlands also in the steppe category. There is also a large variation in terminology in the descriptions of woody vegetation with such terms as "shrubby," "half-shrub," "xerophilous woodland," and "savanna." Inconsistent use of terms makes it difficult to compare one desert area with another. This is one of the widely prevalent matters that should be considered at the forthcoming International Arid Lands Conference at the University of Arizona in 1969.

7. Climatic Factors

For many of the large desert areas of the world, no climatic data are available except around the edges. The data that are available are often of doubtful accuracy, sometimes because of the brief duration of the period of observation, sometimes because the observations were not properly made. In most cases only data on temperature and precipitation are available, and from the latter the number of days without rain can be deducted. So climatologists and botanists have attempted to outline desert boundaries using the data that are at hand: temperature, precipitation, and number of rainless days. They have also considered the season of precipitation: whether the rains occur in the warm season or the cool.

Even where there is sufficient data so that isolines can be drawn, many unanswered questions remain. For example, what quantitative value should determine the boundary of the desert, 100 mm of rain, or 500 mm of rain? What is to be done with the fog deserts such as the Atacama and Namib?

Both long-term climatic trends and shorter-term climatic cycles also affect conditions in desert areas, and the validity of scientific studies depends upon the recognition and proper interpretation of these factors. There are very few desert areas with sufficient data to determine trends (as Reitan and Green state in their chapter on weather and climate in this compendium). Additional data should be obtained wherever possible.

Some promise is offered by the studies of Boyko (1947*a*, 1949*b*, 1951, 1955*a*, 1962, 1966*a*) on ecological climatography, in which he uses the vegetation for determining the climate as related to aridity scales and the overlapping of amplitudes of the various species. He uses also a scale of "climatic soil coefficients" (C. S. C.) to correlate the influence of soil factors on the climatically-determined distribution of plant species. Application of this new line of research on an international basis has begun, but has still to be developed on a broader scale.

Parallel efforts to determine the climate by plants are carried out in the Laboratory of Tree-Ring Research of the University of Arizona, using the annual rings of trees as indicators of climatic fluctuations. These two research lines should be expanded and integrated by a cooperative international research program with one or two main centers.

8. Soil Factors

Another weakness of most attempts to define the limits of the desert is that soils are not considered. Perhaps there is not enough information available on soils to provide a measurable basis for establishing boundary lines, but nevertheless soil types and conditions cannot be ignored. This is also pointed out in the chapter on surface materials by Harold E. Dregne.

9. Life Forms

The information available on the life forms of plants, also, is only partly adequate. Here again, there is not full agreement as to methods. The system of life forms proposed by Raunkiaer has been most widely used, but it is only partly adequate for the classification of desert vegetation; it falls short in many ways. It has been used by some and condemned by others, but all agree that some scheme for the expression of plant forms as related to environmental conditions is desirable. Further study in this field is recommended in order to set up a system of easily recognized and universal characteristics that will aid in the classification and categorization of plants in relation to environment.

10. Translations

The most important works on all aspects of the flora and vegetation of the world's deserts already available in one language should be translated into other major languages, permitting their use by additional broad segments of the world scientific community. Also, some important and still useful works now out of print and generally unavailable should be reprinted.

An example of the type of work that should be translated and made much more accessible is Monod (1957).

AUTHORITIES

In table X are listed those individuals who are regarded, upon the basis of available information, as primary authorities or eminent specialists on desert vegetation.

The first authorities listed are those considered knowledgeable on the subject worldwide. The other authorities listed are grouped according to major desert areas of experience and knowledge.

For each authority listed, the following information is given, if known, in the appropriate columns: name, institution and location, subject specialties, and area specialties.

Table X
AUTHORITIES

Desert	Institution and Location of Institution	Subject Specialties	Area Specialties
WORLDWIDE			
Boyko, Hugo	World Academy of Art and Science Rehovot Israel	pure and applied desert ecology, salinity problems	worldwide (sand-deserts, salt-deserts)
Emberger, L.	Centre d'Etude Phytosociologiques et Ecologiques Université de Montpellier Montpellier (Hérault) France	phytosociological mapping, ecology, plant geography, bioclimatology, taxonomy for northern Africa	Mediterranean
Meigs, Peveril	(Retired, resides at:) Wayland, Massachusetts U. S. A.	bioclimatology, coastal deserts	worldwide
Nuttonson, M. Y.	American Institute of Crop Ecology Silver Springs, Maryland U. S. A.	agroclimatic relations	worldwide
Troll, Carl	Geographical Institute Bonn University Bonn Federal Republic of Germany	geography, bioclimatology, life forms	worldwide
Walter, Heinrich	Botanisches Institut u. Botanischer Garten Landwirtschaftliche Hochschule Hohenheim Stuttgart-Hohenheim Federal Republic of Germany	ecology, bioclimatology, water balance	worldwide
KALAHARI-NAMIB			
Dyer, R. A.	National Herbarium Division of Botany and Plant Pathology Pretoria South Africa	flora of southern Africa	Kalahari-Namib
Logan, R. F.	University of California at Los Angeles Los Angeles, California U. S. A.	geography	Kalahari-Namib
Merxmüller, H.	Botanische Staatssammlung Munich Federal Republic of Germany	taxonomy, flora of southern Africa	deserts of South West Africa

Table X (Continued)
AUTHORITIES

Desert	Institution and Location of Institution	Subject Specialties	Area Specialties
SAHARA			
Capot-Rey, R.	Université d' Alger Algiers Algeria	geography	Sahara
Faurel, L.	Université d'Alger Algiers Algeria	lichens	Sahara
Guinea, E.	Consejo Superior de Investigaciones Científicas Madrid Spain	phytogeography	Spanish Sahara
Hassib, M.	Desert Institute El Matarîya Cairo, Egypt (U. A. R.); Cairo University Giza, Egypt (U. A. R.)	Egyptian flora	eastern Sahara
Ionesco, T.	Université de Montpellier Centre d'Etude Phytosociologiques et Ecologiques Montpellier (Hérault) France	ecology, phytosociology, flora	Morocco
Kassas, M. A.	University of Khartoum Khartoum Sudan	botany	Egypt, Sudan
Le Houérou, H.	Université de Montpellier Centre d'Etude Phytosociologiques et Ecologiques Montpellier (Hérault) France	ecology	Tunisia
Lemée, G.	Université de Paris à La Sorbonne Paris France	plant ecology	
Migahid, A. M.	Cairo University Botany Department Giza, Egypt (U. A. R.)	ecophysiology	Egypt
Monod, Théodore	Muséum National d'Histoire Naturelle Paris France	taxonomy, ecology	northern Africa, southwestern Asia
Montasir, A. H.	Ain Shams University Botany Department Cairo Egypt (U. A. R.)	plant ecology, general botany	Egypt
Nègre, R.	Faculté de Science St. Jérôme Marseilles France	taxonomy	northern Africa

Table X (Continued)
AUTHORITIES

Desert	Institution and Location of Institution	Subject Specialties	Area Specialties
SAHARA continued Novikoff, G.	Centre de Recherches pour l'Utilisation de l'Eau Salée en Irrigation Ariana Tunisia	structure of vegetation, halophytes	Tunisia
Ozenda, P.	Université de Grenoble Faculté des Sciences Grenoble France	flora of the Sahara, phytogeography	Sahara
Quézel, P.	Faculté de Science St. Jérôme Marseilles France	phytogeography	western Sahara
El-Shishiny, E. D. H.	University of Alexandria Department of Botany Alexandria Egypt (U.A.R.)	plant ecology	Egypt
Täckholm, V.	Cairo University Giza Egypt (U.A.R.)	taxonomy	eastern Sahara
Tadros, M.	University of Alexandria Department of Botany Alexandria Egypt (U.A.R.)	systematic Mediterranean flora	Egypt
SOMALI-CHALBI Pichi-Sermolli, R. E. G.	Università Degli Studi di Genova Genoa Italy	flora of Ethiopia and Somalia, ecology of Somali-Chalbi desert	northeastern Africa
ARABIAN DESERT Evenari, M.	Hebrew University Department of Botany Jerusalem Israel	plant physiology	Palestine
Feinbrun, N.	Hebrew University Department of Botany Jerusalem Israel	plant geography, flora of Palestine	Palestine
Mouterde, P.	Université St. Joseph Beirut Lebanon	taxonomy	Syria and Lebanon
Orshan, G.	Hebrew University Department of Botany Jerusalem Israel	plant geography, ecology	Palestine
Zohary, M.	Hebrew University Department of Botany Jerusalem Israel	plant geography, ecology, flora of Palestine and Middle East	Middle East

Table X (Continued)
AUTHORITIES

Desert	Institution and Location of Institution	Subject Specialties	Area Specialties
IRANIAN DESERT			
Bharucha, F. R.	Institute of Science Bombay India	plant ecology	southern Asia
Khabiri, E.	University of Tehran Department of Botany Tehran Iran	taxonomy	Iran
Mobayen, S.	University of Tehran Faculty of Sciences Tehran Iran	botany	Iran
Pabot, H.	Food and Agriculture Organization Tehran Iran	plant ecology, taxonomy	Near East
Rechinger, K. H.	Naturhistorisches Museum Vienna Austria	taxonomy	Iraq, Iran
Zohary, M.	Hebrew University Department of Botany Jerusalem Israel	plant geography, ecology, flora of Palestine	Middle East
THE THAR			
Bharucha, F. R.	Institute of Science Bombay India	plant ecology	southern Asia
Biswas, K.	Central Drugs Laboratory Calcutta India	taxonomy, medicinal plants	India
Raheja, P. C.	Central Arid Zone Research Institute Jodhpur, Rajasthan India	soil and salinity problems, reclamation for agriculture	Rajasthan desert
TURKESTAN DESERT			
Kovda, V. A.	Dokuchaev Soil Institute Moscow U.S.S.R.	salinity and irrigation problems, reclamation for agriculture	Aralo-Caspian area
Petrov, M. P.	Leningrad State University Department of Geography Leningrad U.S.S.R.	geographer, botanist, problems of shifting sands, reclamation for agriculture	deserts of Asia

Table X (Continued)
AUTHORITIES

Desert	Institution and Location of Institution	Subject Specialties	Area Specialties
TAKLA-MAKAN			
Petrov, M. P.	Leningrad State University Department of Geography Leningrad U.S.S.R.	geographer, botanist, problems of shifting sands, reclamation for agriculture	deserts of Asia
AUSTRALIAN DESERTS			
Beadle, N. C. W.	University of New England Armidale, New South Wales Australia	plant ecology	western New South Wales
Burbidge, N. T.	Commonwealth Scientific and Industrial Research Organization Canberra, A.C.T. Australia	taxonomy and plant distribution, systematic botany	Australia
Chippendale, G. M.	Commonwealth Scientific and Industrial Research Organization Alice Springs, Northern Territory Australia	botany	
Christian, C. S.	Member of Executive Commonwealth Scientific and Industrial Research Organization Canberra, A.C.T. Australia	plant ecology	Australia
Condon, R. W.	Soil Conservation Service of New South Wales Sydney, New South Wales Australia	applied ecology	New South Wales
Everist, S. L.	Department of Primary Industries Brisbane, Queensland Australia	plant taxonomy, climatology	Queensland
Gardner, C. A.	(Retired, resides at:) Mt. Yokine Western Australia	taxonomy, poisonous plants	Western Australia
Perry, R. A.	Research School of Biological Sciences Australian National University Canberra City, A.C.T. Australia	ecology	Australia
Slatyer, R. O.	Research School of Biological Sciences Australian National University Canberra City, A.C.T. Australia	plant physiology	Australia
Specht, R. L.	University of Queensland Brisbane, Queensland Australia	plant ecology	South Australia

Table X (Continued)
AUTHORITIES

Desert	Institution and Location of Institution	Subject Specialties	Area Specialties
MONTE-PATAGONIAN DESERT			
Cabrera, A. L.	Universidad Nacional de La Plata La Plata, Prov. Buenos Aires Argentina	plant ecology, taxonomy of South American Compositae	Argentina
Covas, G.	Estación Experimental Agropecuria de Anguil (INTA) Anguil, La Pampa Argentina	taxonomy and ecology of southern Monte	south-central Argentina
Hunziker, A. T.	Universidad Nacional de Córdoba Facultad de Ciencias Exactas, Físicas y Naturales Museo Botánico Córdoba Argentina	taxonomy and ecology, flora of central Argentina	central Argentina
Luti, Ricardo	Universidad Nacional de Córdoba Facultad de Ciencias Exactas, Físicas y Naturales Museo Botánico Córdoba Argentina	ecology	Argentina
Morello, J. H.	Estación Experimental (INTA) Colonia Benítez Chaco Argentina	plant ecology	Monte, Gran Chaco
Prego, A. J.	Instituto de Suelos y Agrotecnia (INTA) Castelar, Prov. Buenos Aires Argentina	edaphology, soils, erosion control	Argentina
Ragonese, A. E.	Estación Experimental (INTA) Castelar, Prov. Buenos Aires Argentina	plant geography, plant resources, forage plants	Argentina
Ruiz Leal, A.	Universidad Nacional de Cuyo Facultad de Ciencias Agrarias Chacras de Coria, Mendoza Argentina	taxonomy and ecology of the flora of Mendoza (central Monte)	western and central Argentina
Soriano, A.	Universidad de Buenos Aires Facultad de Agronomía y Veterinaria Laboratorio de Fisiología Vegetal Buenos Aires Argentina	plant ecology	Argentina
ATACAMA-PERUVIAN DESERT			
Armesto, J. M.	Universidad de Chile Santiago Chile	plant ecology	Atacama

Table X (Continued)
AUTHORITIES

Desert	Institution and Location of Institution	Subject Specialties	Area Specialties
ATACAMA-PERUVIAN DESERT continued			
Cabrera, A. L.	Universidad Nacional da La Plata Museo de Ciencias Naturales La Plata, Prov. Buenos Aires Argentina	plant ecology, taxonomy of South American Compositae	—
Cárdenas, M.	Universidad Mayor de "San Simon" de Cochabamba Cochabamba Bolivia	taxonomy and ecology especially Cactaceae and tuber-bearing *Solanum* species	—
Ellenberg, H.	Georg-August-Universitat zu Göttingen Göttingen Federal Republic of Germany	pure and applied ecology	—
Ferreyra, R.	Universidad Mayor de San Marcos Museo de Historia Natural "Javier Prado" Lima Peru	flora and plant distribution	Peru
NORTH AMERICAN DESERTS			
Beltrán, E.	Instituto Mexicano de Recursos Naturales Renovables Mexico, D. F. Mexico	natural resources	Mexico
Benson, L.	Pomona College Claremont, California U. S. A.	North American desert vegetation, Cactaceae	—
Billings, W. D.	Duke University Department of Botany Durham, North Carolina U. S. A.	plant ecology	Great Basin desert
Cottam, W. P.	University of Utah Salt Lake City, Utah U. S. A.	flora and ecology of Great Basin desert	Great Basin desert
Gardner, J. L.	U. S. D. A. Agricultural Research Service Tucson, Arizona U. S. A.	ecology	Sonoran and Chihuahuan deserts
Hernández Xolocotzi, E.	Instituto Mexicano de Recursos Naturales Renovables Mexico, D. F. Mexico	botany	Mexico
Holmgren, A. H.	Utah State University Logan, Utah U. S. A.	flora of inter-mountain region	Great Basin desert

Table X (Continued)

AUTHORITIES

Desert	Institution and Location of Institution	Subject Specialties	Area Specialties
NORTH AMERICAN DESERTS continued			
Jaeger, E. C.	(Retired, resides at:) Riverside, California U.S.A.	ecology, natural history	North American deserts
Lowe, C. H.	University of Arizona Tucson, Arizona U.S.A.	animal and plant ecology	Sonoran desert
Lundell, C. L.	Texas Research Foundation Renner, Texas U.S.A.	flora of Texas and Mexico	Chihuahuan desert
Pechanec, J.	Intermountain Forest and Range Experiment Station Ogden, Utah U.S.A.	plant ecology	Great Basin
Shelford, V. E.	(Retired, resides at:) Urbana, Illinois U.S.A.	ecology	North America
Went, F.	University of Nevada Desert Research Institute Reno, Nevada U.S.A.	plant ecology	California-Nevada
Wiggins, I.	(Retired) Stanford University Stanford, California U.S.A.	taxonomy	Sonoran desert

DEPOSITORIES: LIBRARIES

On the following pages are listed in table XI those libraries regarded, upon the basis of available information, as outstanding depositories for literature covering some aspect of desert flora. Where available, the number of volumes related to vegetation is listed, but where this information was not available the total holdings are listed.

Table XI
DEPOSITORIES: LIBRARIES

Name	Number of Volumes	Specialties	Remarks
AFRICA			
Botanical Research Institute Pretoria, South Africa	—	southern Africa	excellent library
Desert Institute El Matarîya, Cairo, Egypt (U.A.R.)	—	desert publications	good library
Institut Fondamental d'Afrique Noire Université de Dakar Dakar, Senegal	50,000	African	
University of Khartoum Khartoum, Sudan	140,000	northern Africa, Unesco depository	
ASIA			
Herbarium Boyko Rehovot, Israel	—	arid zones	about 15,000 publication reprints mainly on arid zone ecology
Hebrew University Jerusalem, Israel	20,000		botany subjects only
Negev Institute for Arid Zone Research Beersheba, Israel	—	arid zones	
AUSTRALIA			
Barr-Smith Library University of Adelaide Adelaide, South Australia	375,000	—	
C.S.I.R.O. Library East Melbourne, Victoria, Australia	—	—	head office library; system includes 2 regional libraries and 50 divisional and sectional libraries

Table XI (Continued)
DEPOSITORIES: LIBRARIES

Name	Number of Volumes	Specialties	Remarks
AUSTRALIA continued			
Mitchell Library Sydney, Australia	—	—	
National Library of Australia Canberra, A.C.T., Australia	820,000 vol. 125,000 maps	Australiana	copyright depository; publishes "Australian National Bibliography" and other bibliographic tools
EUROPE			
Biblioteca Nacional Madrid, Spain	2,173,000	worldwide, very early publications	
British Museum (Natural History) Library London, England	300,000	—	natural history items
Central Scientific Agriculture Library Moscow, U.S.S.R.	2,500,000	worldwide	
Food and Agriculture Organization David Lubin Memorial library Rome, Italy	600,000	worldwide, collection of publication reprints; cartographic archives	comprehensive documentation and information services
Muséum National d'Histoire Naturelle Paris, France	8,000,000	worldwide, early publications	includes large holdings on scientific subjects
Science Library London, England	383,000	worldwide	science subjects only
Universidad de Madrid Madrid, Spain	632,605	worldwide, very early publications	
Université de Montpellier Montpellier, France	100,000	ecology, phytogeography, taxonomy	
LATIN AMERICA			
Centro Nacional de Investigaciones Agropecuarias Castelar, Argentina	—	—	
Instituto de Botánica Darwinion San Isidro, Prov. Buenos Aires, Argentina	60,000	botany, particularly South American, taxonomy, plant geography	

Table XI (Continued)
DEPOSITORIES: LIBRARIES

Name	Number of Volumes	Specialties	Remarks
LATIN AMERICA continued			
Universidad de Buenos Aires Facultad de Agronomía y Veterinaria Buenos Aires, Argentina	100,000	agronomy and veterinary sciences	
Universidad de Chile Santiago, Chile	1,000,000	—	
Universidad Nacional Autónoma de México Biblioteca Nacional de México México, D. F.	600,000	Latin America	best in Latin America
Universidad Nacional de Tucumán Tucumán, Argentina	85,000	—	
NORTH AMERICA			
Biology Library University of California Berkeley, California, U.S.A.	129,000	biology	biology holdings only
Boyce Thompson Institute of Plant Research Yonkers, New York, U.S.A.	—	seed catalogs and seed exchange lists	
Duke University Biology-Forestry Library Durham, North Carolina, U.S.A.	71,652	forestry and biology	
Harvard University Arnold Arboretum Gray Herbarium Cambridge, Massachusetts, U.S.A.	79,209	botany, worldwide	botany holdings only
John Crerar Library Chicago, Illinois, U.S.A.	1,000,000	general science	scientific holdings only
Library of Congress Washington, D.C., U.S.A.	45,000,000	—	
Missouri Botanical Garden St. Louis, Missouri, U.S.A.	25,000	taxonomy and plant geography	
New York Botanical Garden Library New York City, New York, U.S.A.	65,000	botany, worldwide	
United States Department of Agriculture National Agricultural Library Washington, D.C., U.S.A.	1,300,000	worldwide in field of agriculture	publishes "Bibliography of Agriculture"

DEPOSITORIES: HERBARIA

In table XII are listed those herbaria regarded, upon the basis of available information, as outstanding collectors of specimens of desert flora.

The first herbaria listed are those whose collections are considered outstanding on desert flora worldwide. The other herbaria listed are grouped by major desert areas of outstanding competence.

For each herbarium listed, the following information is given, if known: name, institution and location, number of specimens, and subject specialties.

Table XII

DEPOSITORIES: HERBARIA

Name	Number of Specimens	Specialties
WORLDWIDE		
Arnold Arboretum Harvard University Cambridge, Massachusetts, U.S.A.	700,000	worldwide
L. H. Bailey Hortorium New York State College of Agriculture Ithaca, New York, U.S.A.	315,000	cultivated plants and wild counterparts of the world
Botanical Institute Barcelona Spain	400,000	worldwide, Ibero- Mauritania
Botany Department University of California, Davis Davis, California, U.S.A.	33,000	weedy species of world regions having Mediterranean- type climate
Gray Herbarium Harvard University Cambridge, Massachusetts, U.S.A.	1,485,000	worldwide
Komorov Botanical Institute Leningrad U.S.S.R.	5,000,000	worldwide
New York Botanical Garden New York City, New York U.S.A.	3,000,000	worldwide
Muséum National d'Histoire Naturelle Paris France	5,000,000 seed plants 1,200,000 nonflowering	seed plant collection, worldwide
Royal Botanic Gardens Kew, Richmond England	6,500,000	worldwide

Table XII (Continued)
DEPOSITORIES: HERBARIA

Name	Number of Specimens	Specialties
WORLD WIDE continued		
Smithsonian Institution Washington, D.C. U.S.A.	3,000,000	worldwide
AFRICA—EAST		
East African Herbarium Nairobi Kenya	300,000	East Africa
Istituto Botanico Hanbury Università di Genova Genoa, Italy	70,000	Ethiopa, Somalia
Università di Firenze Florence Italy	3,500,000	Libya, Ethiopia, Somalia, and other areas
AFRICA—NORTH		
Consejo Superior de Investigaciones Científicas Madrid Spain	450,000	Mediterranean region
Department of Botany Cairo University Giza, Egypt (U.A.R.)	—	Sahara
Desert Institute El Matarîya Cairo, Egypt (U.A.R.)	16,000	arid and semiarid regions of Nile basin
Institut Botanique Université de Montpellier Montpellier, France	3,150,000	mainly Mediterranean
Institut Fondamental d'Afrique Noire Université de Dakar Dakar, Senegal	100,000	Sahara
Institut de Scientifique Chérifien Rabat Morocco	100,000	Sahara
Laboratoire de Botanique Université de Montpellier Montpellier, France	350,000	Sahara
AFRICA—SOUTH		
Botanische Staats-Sammlung München Germany	1,500,000	South West Africa
Herbarium University of Zürich Zürich, Switzerland	1,500,000	southern Africa and South America

Table XII (Continued)
DEPOSITORIES: HERBARIA

Name	Number of Specimens	Specialties
AFRICA-SOUTH continued		
Overseas Ministry Lisbon Portugal	80,000	Portugal, West Africa, Moçambique
National Herbarium Pretoria South Africa	420,000	southern Africa, Mediterranean
ASIA—ARABIAN		
Department of Botany Hebrew University Jerusalem, Israel	350,000	Eig collection, Arabian Desert
Herbarium Aaronsohn Zikhron-Ya'aqov Israel	20,000	mainly Cisjordania and Transjordania
National Herbarium of Iraq Baghdad Iraq	25,000	mainly Iraq
Naturhistorisches Museum Vienna Austria	2,500,000	Near and Middle East
ASIA—IRANIAN		
University of Tehran Tehran Iran	100,000	Iran
ASIA—THAR		
Botanical Survey of India Calcutta India	1,000,000	India, West Pakistan, Afghanistan
Botanical Survey of India Western Circle Poona, India	85,000	western India
ASIA—TURKESTAN		
Botanical Institute Academy of Sciences Kazakhstan Alma-Ata, U.S.S.R.	60,000	Kazakhstan
Botanical Institute Academy of Sciences Turkmenskaya S.S.R. Ashkhabad, U.S.S.R.	60,000	Turkmenistan
Herbarium of Cultivated Plants Institute of Plant Industry Leningrad, U.S.S.R.	92,000	

Table XII (Continued)
DEPOSITORIES: HERBARIA

Name	Number of Specimens	Specialties
ASIA-TURKESTAN continued		
University Herbarium of Middle Asia Tashkent U.S.S.R.	500,000	Middle Asia
ASIA—GOBI AND TAKLA-MAKAN Academia Sinica Peking China	750,000	China
AUSTRALIA Adelaide State Herbarium and Botany Department University of Adelaide Adelaide, South Australia	150,000	mostly South Australia
Animal Industry Branch Alice Springs, Northern Territory Australia	15,000	Northern Territory plants
Commonwealth Scientific and Industrial Research Organization Canberra, A.C.T., Australia	25,000	—
National Herbarium Sydney, New South Wales Australia	750,000	New South Wales
Queensland Botanic Museum and Herbarium Brisbane, Queensland Australia	500,000	Australia and worldwide
Western Australia Herbarium Perth Western Australia	66,000	Western Australia
SOUTH AMERICA—ATACAMA-PERUVIAN INTA, Instituto de Botánica Castelar Prov. Buenos Aires, Argentina	140,000	Argentina
Museo Botánico Facultad de Ciencias Exactas y Naturales Córdoba, Argentina	135,000	Argentina
Museo de La Plata La Plata, Argentina	220,000	Argentina
Instituto Central de Biología Universidad de Concepción Concepción, Chile	30,000	Chilean plants
C. Jiles Ovalle Prov. Coquimbo, Chile	5,000	Chilean plants
G. Looser Casilla 5542 Santiago 6, Chile	20,000	Chilean plants

Table XII (Continued)

DEPOSITORIES: HERBARIA

Name	Number of Specimens	Specialties
SOUTH AMERICA - ATACAMA - PERUVIAN continued		
Museo Nacional de Historia Natural Santiago Chile	30,000	Chilean plants
Museo de Historia Natural "Javier Prado" Universidad Mayor de San Marcos Lima Peru	60,000	Peru
NORTH AMERICA		
Intermountain Herbarium Utah State University Logan, Utah, U.S.A.	100,000	Intermountain region
Pomona College Claremont, California U.S.A.	325,000	western North America and southwestern U.S.
Texas Research Foundation Renner, Texas U.S.A.	65,000	Grasses of world, plants of Texas and Mexico
University of Arizona Tucson, Arizona U.S.A.	150,000	southwestern United States, Sonoran Desert
University of California, Berkeley Berkeley, California U.S.A.	1,225,000	North and South America
University of Colorado Boulder, Colorado U.S.A.	175,000	Rocky Mountains, American deserts
University of Texas Austin, Texas U.S.A.	230,000 (35,000 Mexican)	Mexico and southwestern United States
University of Utah Salt Lake City, Utah U.S.A.	62,000	northern desert

In table XIII are listed the main desert plant species mentioned in publications that were reviewed for this chapter.

The plants are listed by scientific names, alphabetically, by genus and by species. Certain information pertaining to each species is indicated, if known (upon the basis of search of available literature), in the columns to the right of the plant names; the meaning of entries in these columns is as follows:

General: Multiple entries separated by commas (e. g. 14, 2, 9) are of equal importance; where multiple entries are separated by slant-lines subsequent entries are of lesser importance than the first (e. g., 14/2/9 means primarily 14, also 2 to a lesser extent, and also 9 to an even lesser extent).

Authors: The primary research publications containing discussions of the species are cited by author and date. To save space, the following abbreviated author-year notations are used:

Ac58	: Academia Sinica (1958)	Hu52	: Hunziker (1952)
Ac62	: Academia Sinica (1962)	Ki39	: Killian (1939a)
		Lo60	: Logan (1960)
BR53	: Biswas and Rao (1953)	M58	: Morello (1958)
		Mu12	: Muschler (1912)
Bo57	: Boelcke (1957)	Oz58	: Ozenda (1958)
Bk54	: Boyko (1954)	P64	: Pabot (1964)
Bk67	: Boyko (1967)*	Pa12	: Paulsen (1912)
B53	: Burbidge (1953)	Pe36	: Petrov (1936)
B60	: Burbidge (1960a)	Pe60	: Petrov (1960)
Bu52	: Burkart (1952)	Pe62	: Petrov (1962)
Bu67	: Burkart (1967)*	PE37	: Pole Evans (1937)
C55	: Cabrera (1955a)	Po29	: Popov (1929)
C57	: Cabrera (1957)	Pr67	: Perry (1967)*
Ca13	: Cannon (1913)	Pi55	: Pichi-Sermolli (1955a)
D55	: Davies (1955)	PZ63	: Popov-Zeller (1963)
DF64	: Dewan and Famouri (1964)	Q65	: Quézel (1965)
E62	: Evenari (1962)	Re64	: Rechinger (1964)
Em39	: Emberger (1939)	R66	: Richardson (1966)
Em67	: Emberger (1967)*	Ri31	: Rivière (1931)
Ha51	: Hassib (1951)	Ro53	: Rodin (1953)
		Sh42	: Shreve (1942a)

So50	: Soriano (1950)
So52	: Soriano (1952)
So56	: Soriano (1956a)
Ti26	: Tits (1926)
VV61	: Vostokova and Vyshivkin (1961)
Wa64	: Walter (1964)
We45	: Weberbauer (1945)
WE34	: Westover-Enlow (1934)
Wo50	: Wood (1950)
Zo62	: Zohary (1962)

Family: Names of families into which the plants fall, according to Willis (1966), are given in the second column.

Deserts Where Found: The deserts within which each species is known to occur are indicated by the following numbers:

1	North American Desert	7	Turkestan Desert
2	Atacama-Peruvian Desert	8	Thar Desert
		9	Iranian Desert
3	Monte-Patagonian Desert	10	Arabian Desert
		11	Somali-Chalbi Desert
4	Australian Desert	12	Sahara Desert
5	Gobi Desert	13	Kalahari-Namib Desert
6	Takla-Makan Desert	13-N	Namib Desert

Common Habitats: Notable habitat conditions under which the species is most often found are indicated by the following symbols:

Terrain Features:

P	Plains
H	Hills: (t) tops, (s) sides, (b) between
D	Dunes: (t) tops, (s) sides, (b) between
PC	Protected cleft
WE	Watercourse, ephemeral (s) sides, (bo) bottom
B	Small nondraining basin
RO	Rocky outcropping
E	Erg
R	Reg
WP	Watercourse, permanent (e) edge, (n) nearby

Surface Textures:

c	clayey
h	hamada

s	sandy
r	rocky

Chemistry:

Ak	Alkaline
Sa	Saline

*Personal communication

Other
FB   fog belt

Growth Forms: The general growth forms of the species are indicated in terms of the following categories and abbreviations:

TR   tree
SH   shrub
HSH   half-shrub
PR   perennial (other than grasses)
SC   succulent
GR   grass
AN   annual

Life Forms: The life forms of the species are indicated by the following symbols, which indicate the corresponding group categories of Raunkiaer:

Symbol	Group Name
Mg \} MM	Megaphanerophytes (Trees over 30 meters)
Ms	Mesophanerophytes (Trees 8-30 meters) meters)
Mi	Microphanerophytes (Shrubs or trees 2-8
N	Nanophanerophytes (Shrubs under 2 meters)
Ch	Chamaephytes (Buds just above or at surface of ground)
H	Hemicryptophytes (Buds just in the surface)
G	Geophytes (Bulbs, rhizomes, tubers)
Th	Therophytes (Annuals)
S	Stem Succulents (Plants with aboveground water storage)

Toxic or Structurally Dangerous: Plants known to be toxic, containing materials either poisonous if ingested or strongly irritating if touched, are noted by the letter "T." Plants known to be structually dangerous, by possessing spines, thorns, cutting edges, and the like, are noted by the letter "S."

Indications: If the plant is known to be a significant indicator of a certain condition, that condition is indicated by one of the following notations:

Sal   saline conditions
Phr   phreatophytic condition
Dis   disturbance—overgrazing

Uses: Known uses of the species are indicated, in terms of the following categories and abbreviations:

Con   construction material
D   dye
Fib   fiber
G   gum
M   medicine
Nh   nourishment (food) for humans (u) fruit, (e) seeds, (o) foliage
Na   nourishment (food) for herbivorous animals (u) fruit, (e) seeds, (o) foliage
Sb   sand binding
Sh   shade
T   tannin
Wd   firewood

Table XIII

SPECIES SUMMARY

Genus and Species	Authors	Family	Deserts Where Found	Common Habitats	Growth Forms	Life Forms	Noxious	Indicator	Uses
Abromeitiella lorentziana	M58	Bromeliaceae	3	RO	—	Ch	S	—	—
Acacia albida	PE37, Mu12	Leguminosae	10, 12, 13	—	TR	Ms	S	—	Na(o)
Acacia aneura	Wo50, D55	Leguminosae	4	P, s, c	TR	Mi	—	—	Na, Wd
Acacia aroma	Bu67	Leguminosae	3	—	—	—	—	—	Na(u)
Acacia brachystachya	Wo50	Leguminosae	4	P, s, c	TR	Mi	—	—	Na
Acacia bussei	Pi55	Leguminosae	11	—	—	—	—	—	—
Acacia cambagei	D55	Leguminosae	4	P, s, c	TR	Mi	—	—	—
Acacia caven	Bu67	Leguminosae	3	—	—	—	—	—	—
Acacia constricta	Sh42	Leguminosae	1	P, WE	SH, T	N	S	—	—
Acacia cyperophylla	Wo50	Leguminosae	4	P, s, WE	TR	Mi	—	—	—
Acacia etbaica	Pi55	Leguminosae	11	—	—	—	—	—	—

Table XIII (Continued)
SPECIES SUMMARY

Genus and Species	Authors	Family	Deserts Where Found	Common Habitats	Growth Forms	Life Forms	Noxious	Indicator	Uses
Acacia furcatispina	M58, Bu52	Leguminosae	3	P	—	Mi	S	—	Wd
Acacia georginae	Pr67	Leguminosae	4	P, c	TR, SH	Mi	T	—	Na(o), Wd
Acacia giraffae	PE37	Leguminosae	13	—	TR, SH	—	—	—	T, Na(e)
Acacia greggii	Sh42	Leguminosae	1	P, H, WE	TR, SH	Mi	S	—	Wd
Acacia gummifera	Em39	Leguminosae	12	s	TR	Mi	—	—	T, G
Acacia harpophylla	D55	Leguminosae	4	P, c	TR	Mi, Ms	—	—	D, Con, Wd
Acacia kempeana	Pr67	Leguminosae	4	P, s, Ak	SH	N	—	—	Na(o)
Acacia karroo	PE37	Leguminosae	13	—	TR	—	S	—	—
Acacia macracantha	C55, Bu52	Leguminosae	2	P	TR	Mi	S	—	Na(u)
Acacia paucispina	Sh42	Leguminosae	1	P, WE	SH, T	N	S	—	—
Acacia pendula	D55	Leguminosae	4	PC	TR	Mi, Ms	—	—	Na (o), Con
Acacia raddiana	Oz58, Q65, Zo62, Em39	Leguminosae	10, 12	s, WE, WP	—	—	S	—	—
Acacia seyal	Em39, Q65, Mu12, Bk54	Leguminosae	10, 12	s, h	TR	Mi	S	—	T, G
Acacia sowdenii	D55	Leguminosae	4	P, c	TR	Mi	—	—	Na(o)
Acacia tortilis Syn. *A. raddiana*	Oz58, PZ63, Zo62, Ti26, Ka62	Leguminosae	10, 12	R, H, WE, s	TR, SH	Mi	S	—	—
Acanthophyllum elatius	Pa12	Caryophyllaceae	7, 9	c, s	HSH	Ch	S	—	—
Acanthosicyos horrida	PE37	Cucurbitaceae	13	D	SH	S	—	—	Nh(o)
Acanthyllis tragacanthoides	Ca13	Leguminosae	12	P, s	SH	N	S	—	—
Achillea santolina	Zo62, Mu12, Bk54	Compositae	10, 12	P	PR	Ch	—	—	M
Adesmia campestris	So56, Bu52	Leguminosae	3	P	—	N	—	—	—
Adesmia hemisphaerica	C55	Leguminosae	3	—	SH	N	—	—	—
Adesmia horrida	C55	Leguminosae	3	—	SH	N	—	—	—
Adesmia subterranea	C55	Leguminosae	3	—	SH	N	—	—	—
Aegilops kotschyi	Zo62	Gramineae	10	H, h, P, s	GR	H	—	—	—

Table XIII (Continued)
SPECIES SUMMARY

Genus and Species	Authors	Family	Deserts Where Found	Common Habitats	Growth Forms	Life Forms	Noxious	Indicator	Uses
Aerva persica	Oz58, Q65	Amaranthaceae	12	—	PR	—	—	—	—
Aerva tomentosa Syn. *A. javanica*	Zo62, Mu12, Pi55	Amaranthaceae	8, 10, 11, 12	Hs, P, WE	SH	N	—	—	M
Agriophyllum arenarium	Ac58, R66, Pa12, Pe62	Chenopodiaceae	5, 6, 7	D (s) (b)	AN	Th	—	—	Sb, Na
Agriophyllum gobicum	Pe62, R66	Chenopodiaceae	6	Sa	—	—	—	—	Nh, Na
Agriophyllum latifolium	Pa12, Pe60	Chenopodiaceae	7	s	AN	Th	S	—	Sb
Agropyron sibiricum	WE34, Ac62	Gramineae	5, 7	—	GR	G	—	—	Na
Agropyron spicatum	Sh42	Gramineae	1	P	GR	G	—	—	Na
Aïzoön dinteri	Bu67	Aïzoaceae	—	—	—	—	—	—	—
Alhagi camelorum	R66, Pa12, Pe62, P64, DF64	Leguminosae	6, 7, 9, 10	P, widespread	HSH	Ch	—	—	M
Alhagi maurorum	P64, Mu12	Leguminosae	9, 10, 12	s	HSH	N	S	Phr	Na(o), Nh
Allenrolfea occidentalis	Sh42	Chenopodiaceae	1	P, Sa	HSH	Ch	—	Sal	—
Allium mongolicum	Ac58, Ac62	Liliaceae	5, 6	D	PR	G	—	—	Na
Allium polyrhizum	Ac62	Liliaceae	5, 6	—	—	—	—	—	Sb
Aloë dichotoma	PE37	Liliaceae	13-N	H, r	TR, SC	S	—	—	M
Alstroemeria recumbens	C55	Alstroemeriaceae	2	FB	PR	G	—	—	—
Ammodendron conollyi	Pa12	Leguminosae	7	s	TR	Mi	S	—	—
Ammopiptanthus mongolicus	Ac62	—	5, 7	D	—	—	—	—	—
Amygdalus mongolica	Pe62, Ac58	Rosaceae	5	H, r, WE	SH	N	S	—	—
Amygdalus scoparia	P64	Rosaceae	9	H, r	SH	Mi	—	—	—
Anabasis aphylla	Pa12, Pe62	Chenopodiaceae	6, 7	s, Sa	HSH	Ch	—	—	—
Anabasis aretioides Syn. *Fredolia aretioides*	Em39, Ti26, Ki39	Chenopodiaceae	12	r	HSH	Ch	—	—	—
Anabasis articulata	Zo62, Mu12, Cal3, Ka62	Chenopodiaceae	10, 12	Sa, WE, P, s	SC, SH	Ch	—	—	Na (o), M
Anabasis brevifolia	R66, Pa12, Pe62	Chenopodiaceae	5, 6, 7	Sa	HSH	Ch	—	—	—
Anabasis eriopoda	Pa12	Chenopodiaceae	7	—	HSH	Ch	S	—	—

Table XIII (Continued)
SPECIES SUMMARY

Genus and Species	Authors	Family	Deserts Where Found	Common Habitats	Growth Forms	Life Forms	Noxious	Indicator	Uses
Anabasis haussknechti	Zo62	Chenopodiaceae	10	H	S	—	—	—	—
Anabasis salsa	Pa12	Chenopodiaceae	7	r, s, Sa	HSH	Ch	—	—	—
Aphyllocladus spartioides	C55	Compositae	3	—	SH	N	—	—	—
Aplopappus fructicosus	Sh42	Compositae	1	—	SH	N	T	Dis	—
Aplopappus heterophyllus	Sh42	Compositae	1	P	HSH	Ch	P	—	—
Apocynum hendersonii	Ac58, Ac62	Apocynaceae	5, 7	P, s, Sa	PR	Ch	—	Sal	Sb, Fib
Argania spinosa	Em67	Sapotaceae	12	—	TR	MM	S	—	Na (u) (o)
Aristida adscensionis	M58, Ac58	Gramineae	1, 2, 3, 5, 12	P, D	GR	Th	S	—	Na
Aristida brevifolia	PE37	Gramineae	13-N	P	GR	—	—	—	—
Aristida browniana	Pr67	Gramineae	4	P, s	GR	Ch	—	—	Na(o, e)
Aristida californica Syn *A. adscensionis*	Sh42	Gramineae	1	P	GR	H	S	—	Na (o)
Aristida coerulescens	Ha51	Gramineae	10, 12	D, s	PR, GR	—	—	—	—
Aristida contorta	Pr67	Gramineae	4	P, s	GR	Ch	—	—	Na(o, e)
Aristida humilis	—	Gramineae	3	—	GR	H	—	—	—
Aristida inaequiglumis	Pr67	Gramineae	4	P, s	GR	Ch	—	—	Na(o, e)
Aristida karelini	Pe60	Gramineae	7	—	—	—	—	—	Sb
Aristida latifolia	Pr67	Gramineae	4	P, c	GR	Ch	—	—	Na(o, e)
Aristida obtusa	Zo62, Mu12, Bk54	Gramineae	10, 12	P, s, H	GR	H	S	—	Sb
Aristida pennata	Pa12, WE34, Pe62	Gramineae	6, 7	s	GR	G	S	—	Sb, Na
Aristida plumosa	P64, Mu12, Bk54	Gramineae	9, 10, 12	P, s	GR	H	S	—	Na (o)
Aristida pungens	Em39, Ca13, Oz58, Mu12	Gramineae	10, 12	D, E, s	PR, GR	G	S	—	Na(e)
Arjona patagonica	So56	Santalaceae	3	P	—	G	—	—	Nh
Artemisia arenaria	Pe60	Compositae	7	—	—	—	—	—	Sb
Artemisia caespitosa	Pe62, R66	Compositae	6	s	—	—	—	—	—
Artemisia filifolia	Sh42	Compositae	1	P, D, s	SH	N	—	—	Sb
Artemisia frigida	Sh42, Ac58, Pe62, R66	Compositae	1, 5, 6	P, s, D	HSH	Ch	—	—	Na

Table XIII (Continued)
SPECIES SUMMARY

Genus and Species	Authors	Family	Deserts Where Found	Common Habitats	Growth Forms	Life Forms	Noxious	Indicator	Uses
Artemisia halodendron	Pe60, Ac58	Compositae	5, 7	D, s	HSH	Ch	—	—	Sb
Artemisia herba-alba	Zo62, P64, Mu12, Bk54	Compositae	9, 10, 12	wide spread	SH	N	—	—	M, Na(o)
Artemisia incana	Pe62, R66	Compositae	6	s	—	—	—	—	—
Artemisia monosperma	Ka62, Zo62, Mu12	Compositae	10, 12	D(s), P, s	PR, SH	N	—	—	Sb
Artemisia ordosica	Ac58, Ac62, Pe60, Pe62	Compositae	5, 7	D, s	HSH	Ch	—	Phr	Sb, Wd
Artemisia santolina	Ac62	Compositae	5	—	—	—	—	—	—
Artemisia sphaerocephala	Ac58, Ac62, Pe60, Pe62	Compositae	5, 7	s	HSH	Ch	—	Phr	Sb
Artemisia tridentata	Sh42	Compositae	1	P, H	SH	N	—	—	Na
Artemisia xerophytica	Pe62, R66	Compositae	6	s	—	—	—	—	—
Arthrophytum subulifolium	Pa12	Chenopodiaceae	7	—	HSH	Ch	—	—	—
Arthrocnemum glaucum	Em67	Chenopodiaceae	10, 12	WE	SH	N	—	Sal	Nh
Arthrocnemum indicum	—	Chenopodiaceae	—	—	SH	N	—	—	Nh
Asparagus spinosa	Ca13	Liliaceae	12	—	HSH	Ch	S	—	—
Asparagus stipularis	Em67	Liliaceae	12	—	—	—	S	—	—
Asteriscus pygmaeus	Zo62, Mu12	Compositae	10, 12	P	PR	H	—	—	—
Astragalus arequipensis	Bu52	Leguminosae	2	H(s)	PR	H	T	—	—
Astragalus bergii	Bu52	Leguminosae	2	P	PR	H	T	—	—
Astragalus garbancillo	Bu52, C57	Leguminosae	2	H(s), Puna	PR	H	T	—	—
Astragalus spinosus	Zo62, Re64	Leguminosae	10	H(s)	SH	N	S	—	—
Astragalus tribuloides	Zo62, Pa12, Mu12	Leguminosae	7, 8, 10, 12	H, h	AN	Th	—	—	—
Astrebla elymoides	Pr67	Gramineae	4	P, c	GR	Ch	—	—	Na(o,)
Astrebla lappacea	Pr67	Gramineae	4	P, c	GR	Ch	—	—	Na(o, e)
Astrebla pectinata	Pr67	Gramineae	4	P, c	GR	Ch	—	—	Na(o, e)
Astrebla squarrosa	Pr67	Gramineae	4	P, c	GR	Ch	—	—	Na(o, e)
Atalaya hemiglauca	Pr67	Sapindaceae	4	P, c, s	TR, SH	Mi, N	T	—	Na(o)
Atractylis serratuloides	Zo62	Compositae	10, 12	—	AN	Th	S	—	—
Atraphaxis compacta	Pa12	Polygonaceae	7	r	—	—	—	—	—

Table XIII (Continued)
SPECIES SUMMARY

Genus and Species	Authors	Family	Deserts Where Found	Common Habitats	Growth Forms	Life Forms	Noxious	Indicator	Uses
Atraphaxis frutescens	Pe62, Ac58	Polygonaceae	5	D, P, WE	SH	N	—	—	Na, Sb
Atriplex canescens	Sh42	Chenopodiaceae	1	P	SH	N	—	—	Na
Atriplex confertifolia	Sh42	Chenopodiaceae	1	P	SH	N	—	—	Na
Atriplex halimus	Oz58, Mu12	Chenopodiaceae	10, 12	WP, WE	SH	Mi, N	—	—	Na(o)
Atriplex nummularia	W50	Chenopodiaceae	4	P, c	SH	N	—	—	Na(o)
Atriplex polycarpa	Sh42	Chenopodiaceae	1	P	SH	N	—	—	Na
Atriplex vesicaria	W50	Chenopodiaceae	4	P, c, s	SH	N	—	—	Na(o)
Augea capensis	Lo60, PE37	Chenopodiaceae	13	D, P	HSH	Ch	—	—	—
Azorella compacta	Bu67 C55	Umbelliferae	2, 3	Cordillera High	HSH	N	—	—	—
Azorella gilliesii	C55	Umbelliferae	3	—	SH	N	—	—	—
Azorella monantha	C55, So50	Umbelliferae	3	P	SH	N	—	—	—
Balanites aegyptiaca	Zo62, Mu12	Balanitaceae	10, 12	WP, WE	SH	N	S	—	Nh(o), Con
Bassia spp.	Pr67	Chenopodiaceae	4	P, c, s	PR, AN	Ch, Th	S	—	Na
Begonia octopetala	Ca55	Begoniaceae	3	FB	—	G	—	—	—
Berberis cuneata	So50, So56	Berberidaceae	3	P	SH	N	S	—	—
Boerhaavia diffusa	BR53, Mu12	Nyctaginaceae	4, 8, 12	P, c, s	AN	Th	—	Dis	—
Boscia albitrunca	PE37	Malvaceae	13	—	TR	—	—	—	—
Bouteloua aristidoides	Sh42	Gramineae	1	P	AN, GR	Th	S	—	—
Bouteloua lophostachya	M58	Gramineae	3	—	GR	H	—	—	Na
Bouteloua rothrockii	Sh42	Gramineae	1	P	GR	H	—	—	Na
Bouteloua simplex	C57	Gramineae	1, 2	P	GR	Th	—	—	Na
Bowlesia palmata	C55	Umbelliferae	2	FB	AN	Th	—	—	Sb
Bromus brevis	So50	Gramineae	3	P	GR	H	—	—	Na, D
Bromus macranthes	So56	Gramineae	3	P	GR	H	—	—	Na, D
Bursera microphylla	Sh42	Burseraceae	1	H	TR	Mi	—	—	—
Caesalpinia tinctoria	C55	Leguminosae	2	—	—	—	—	—	—
Calandrinia balonensis	Pr67	Portulacaceae	4	P, s, D (s)	SC, AN	Th	—	—	Na(o)
Calligonum aphyllum	Pe60	Polygonaceae	6, 7	—	—	—	—	—	Sb
Calligonum arborescens	Ac58, Pe60, Pa12	Polygonaceae	5, 7	D (t) (s)	SH	Mi	—	—	Sb
Calligonum azel	Oz58	Polygonaceae	12	E	SH	N	—	—	—

Table XIII (Continued)
SPECIES SUMMARY

Genus and Species	Authors	Family	Deserts Where Found	Common Habitats	Growth Forms	Life Forms	Noxious	Indicator	Uses
Calligonum caput-medusae	Ac58, Pe60, Pa12	Polygonaceae	5, 7	P, D, s	SH	Mi	S	—	Sb
Calligonum comosum	Oz58, Zo62, Bk54	Polygonaceae	7, 9, 10, 12	P, D, s	SH	N, Mi	—	—	Sb, Na (o)
Calligonum mongolicum	Ac58, Pe60, Ac62, Pe62, R66	Polygonaceae	5, 6	D, s	SH	N	—	Phr	Sb, Na
Calligonum polygonoides	BR53	Polygonaceae	8	D	TR	Mi	—	—	—
Calligonum roborobski	Pe62	Polygonaceae	6	s	—	—	—	—	—
Calligonum torophytes	PZ63	Polygonaceae	10	P, s	—	—	—	—	—
Calligonum zaidamense	Pe60	Polygonaceae	6	—	—	—	—	—	Sb
Calliguaya integerrima	So56	—	3	P, s, c	—	—	—	—	—
Callitris spp.	Pr67	Cupressaceae	4	P, s	TR	Ms, Mi	—	—	Con
Calotis hispidula	Pr67	Compositae	4	P, s	AN	Th	—	—	—
Calotropis procera	Mu12, Oz58, Zo62, PZ63, BR53, Pi55	Asclepiadaceae	8, 10, 11, 12	c, WP, WE	SH	S	—	Phr	Fib, M
Calycera crenata	C55	Calyceraceae	3	—	PR	H	—	—	—
Calycera pulvinata	C55, C57	Calyceraceae	2	Puna	—	H	—	—	—
Capparis decidua	Mu12	Capparidaceae	7, 8, 9, 10, 12	WE	TR, SH	Mi	S	—	—
Capparis spinosa	Mu12, Pa12, Ha51	Capparidaceae	7, 12	c, r	HSH, SH	Mi	S	—	Nh(u, e)
Caragana bungei	Pe62, R66	Leguminosae	6	s	—	Ch, N	—	—	—
Caragana korshinskii	Pe60, Pe62	Leguminosae	5, 7	s, D	SH	—	—	—	Sb
Caragana leucophyloea	Pe62, R66	Leguminosae	6	—	—	—	—	—	—
Caragana microphylla	Ac58, Ac62, Pe60, Pe62	Leguminosae	5, 7	s, D	SH	N	—	Phr	Na, Sb, Wd
Caragana pygmaea	Pe62, R66	Leguminosae	6	s	—	—	—	—	—
Caragana stenophylla	Ac58, Ac62, Pe62	Leguminosae	5, 7	r, H, P	SH	N	—	—	Na
Caragana tibetica	Ac58, Ac62	Leguminosae	5	P	SH	N	—	—	Na
Carex andina	So56	Cyperaceae	3	W	GR	G	—	—	—

Table XIII (Continued)
SPECIES SUMMARY

Genus and Species	Authors	Family	Deserts Where Found	Common Habitats	Growth Forms	Life Forms	Noxious	Indicator	Uses
Carex physodes	WE34, Ac62	Cyperaceae	5, 7	—	GR	H	—	—	—
Carex stenophylla	P64, Mu12	Cyperaceae	6, 7, 9, 10, 12	P, s	GR	G, H	—	—	—
Carrichtera annua	Zo62, Mu12	Cruciferae	10, 12	H, h	AN	Th	—	—	—
Caryopteris mongholica	Ac58, Ac62	Verbenaceae	5	D, P	—	—	—	—	Sb
Cassia aphylla	C55	Leguminosae	3	—	SH	N	—	—	Fib
Cassia crassiramea	C55	Leguminosae	3	—	SH	N	—	—	Fib
Cassia eremophila	Pr67	Leguminosae	4	P, s	SH	N	—	—	—
Cassia lanceolata	Em67	Leguminosae	12	—	—	—	—	—	—
Cassia obovata	Oz58, Mu12	Leguminosae	8, 10, 11, 12	—	SH	N	—	—	M
Casuarina cristata	Pr67, D55	Casuarinaceae	4	P, s	TR	Mi	—	—	—
Casuarina decaisneana	Pr67	Casuarinaceae	4	D(t,s,b), P, s	TR	Ms	—	—	Con
Casuarina lepidophloia Syn. *C. cristata*	D55	Casuarinaceae	4	P	—	—	—	—	—
Cavanillesia arborea	C55	Malvaceae	Brazil	—	TR	Mi	—	—	—
Celtis pallida	Sh42	Ulmaceae	1	—	SH	N	S	—	—
Cenchrus ciliaris Syn. *Pennisetum ciliare*	Q65	Gramineae	8, 9, 12	—	GR	H	—	—	—
Centaurea hyalolepis	Bk54	Compositae	10	—	AN	Th	—	—	—
Ceraria namaquensis	PE37	Portulacaceae	13	—	SC	S	—	—	—
Cercidium australe	C55	Leguminosae	3	P	TR	Mi	S	—	G
Cercidium floridum	Sh42	Leguminosae	1	WE	TR	Mi	S	—	Wd
Cercidium microphyllum	Sh42	Leguminosae	1	P, H	TR	Mi	—	—	Wd
Cercidium praecose	M58	Leguminosae	2	P	TR	Mi	S	—	G
Cercidium sonorae	Sh42	Leguminosae	1	P, H	TR	Mi	S	—	Wd
Cereus candelaris	We45	Cactaceae	2	H	SC	S	S	—	—
Cereus giganteus	Sh42	Cactaceae	1	H, P	SC	(MM)S	S	—	Nh(u)
Cereus macrostibas	We45	Cactaceae	2	H(s)	SC	S	—	—	—
Chenolea arabica	Zo62, Mu12	Chenopodiaceae	10, 12	Sa(gyp)	SH, PR	Ch	—	—	—
Chenopodium auricomum	Pr67	Chenopodiaceae	4	P, B	SH	N	—	—	Na(o)
Chenopodium guinoa	C57	Chenopodiaceae	2	Puna	—	Th	—	Dis	Nh(e)
Chenopodium pellidicaule	C57	Chenopodiaceae	2	Puna	—	Th	—	Dis	Nh(e)

Table XIII (Continued)
SPECIES SUMMARY

Genus and Species	Authors	Family	Deserts Where Found	Common Habitats	Growth Forms	Life Forms	Noxious	Indicator	Uses
Chiliotrichum diffusum	So56	—	3	—	—	—	—	—	—
Chloris acicularis	Pr67	Gramineae	4	WE, s	GR	Ch	—	—	Na(o)
Chrysocoma tenuifolia	PE37	Compositae	13	—	SH	—	—	—	—
Chuquiraga avellanedae	So52, So56	Compositae	3	P	—	N	S	—	—
Citrullus colocynthis	Zo62	Cucurbitaceae	8, 9, 10, 12	H, s	AN	H	T	—	M
Citrullus vulgaris	Mu12	Cucurbitaceae	12, 13	—	SH	AN, PR	—	—	Nh(u)
Cleome droserifolia	Ha41, Mu12	Capparidaceae	10, 12	Sa, WE	SH	N	—	—	—
Cleome chrysantha	Em67	Capparidaceae	10, 12	H	PR	H	—	—	—
Cleome papillosa	BR53	Capparidaceae	7, 8	—	—	—	—	—	M
Coleogyne ramosissima	Sh42	Rosaceae	1	P	SH	N	—	—	Na
Combretum primigenum	PE37	Combretaceae	13	—	SH	—	—	—	—
Commelina fasciculata	C55	Commelinaceae	2	FB	PR	G	—	—	—
Condalia lycioides	Sh42	Rhamnaceae	1	P	SH	N	—	—	Na
Condalia microphylla	Bu67	Rhamnaceae	3	P	—	Mi	S	—	Nh(u)
Convolvulus eremophilus	Pa12	Convolvulaceae	7	c, s	HSH	Ch	—	—	—
Convolvulus fruticosus	Pa12, Ac58	Convolvulaceae	5, 7	P, s	HSH	Ch	S	—	Sb
Convolvulus gortschakovii	Pe62	Convolvulaceae	5	P	—	—	—	—	—
Convolvulus lanatus	Ha51, Mu12	Convolvulaceae	10, 12	s	SH	N	—	—	Na (o)
Convolvulus supinus	Oz58, Q65	Convolvulaceae	12	—	—	Ch, H	—	—	—
Convolvulus tragacanthoides	Pe62	Convolvulaceae	5, 7	P	—	—	—	—	—
Corispermum hyssopifolium	Pa12, R66	Chenopodiaceae	6, 7	—	AN	Th	—	—	—
Coronilla juncea	Q65, Ca13	Leguminosae	12	WE	—	N	—	—	—
Cornulaca monacantha	Ha51, Mu12	Chenopodiaceae	12	P, D (s), s	SH	N	—	—	N (o)
Cotyledon jascicularia	PE37	Crassulaceae	13	—	SC	S	—	—	—
Crassula cosmantha	C55	Crassulaceae	2	FB	AN	Th	—	—	—
Cressa truxillensis	C55	Convolvulaceae	2	Sa	—	G	—	—	—
Crotalaria aegyptiaca	Zo62, Mu12	Leguminosae	10, 12	P, H, s	SH	N	—	—	—
Crotalaria burhia	BR53	Leguminosae	8	s	PR	—	—	—	Fib
Cupressus dupreziana	Em67	Cupressaceae	12	H, P	TR	MM	—	—	Sh, Wd

Table XIII (Continued)
SPECIES SUMMARY

Genus and Species	Authors	Family	Deserts Where Found	Common Habitats	Growth Forms	Life Forms	Noxious	Indicator	Uses
Cymbopogon schoenanthus	PZ63	Gramineae	8, 9, 10, 11, 12	WE, P	GR	—	—	—	M
Cyperus conglomeratus	Oz58, P64, Mu12, Pi55	Cyperaceae	9, 10, 11, 12, 13	W, D (s), E	PR	H	—	—	—
Cyperus laevigatus	Em67	Cyperaceae	10, 12, 13	WE	PR	—	—	—	—
Dactyloctenium radulans	Pr67	Gramineae	4	P, c, s	GR	Th	—	Dis	Na(o)
Dalbergia sissoo	P64	Leguminosae	8, 9	—	TR	MM	—	—	Con
Dalea scoparia	Sh42	Leguminosae	1	—	SH	N	—	—	—
Dalea spinosa	Sh42	Leguminosae	1	WE	TR	Mi	S	—	—
Danthonia forskalii	Mu12	Gramineae	7, 9, 10, 12	P, s	GR	H	—	—	Na (o)
Danthonia picta	So56	Gramineae	3 (Patag.)	P, H	GR	H	—	—	—
Deverra scoparia	Ca13	Umbelliferae	12	—	SH	N	—	—	Na (o)
Deyeuxia fulva	C57	Gramineae	2	WE, P	—	G	—	—	Na
Dioscorea chancayensis	C55	Dioscoreaceae	2	FB	PR	G	—	—	Na
Diospyros tomentosa	P64	Ebenaceae	9	—	TR	MM	—	—	—
Diplotaxis harra	Zo62	Cruciferae	9, 10, 12	h, s	PR	H, Th	—	—	—
Distichlis scoparia	So56	Gramineae	13	Sa	GR	G	—	—	Na
Distichlis spicata	Sh42, Ca56	Gramineae	1	P, Sa	GR	G	S	Sal	Na
Dodonaea viscosa	Sh42	Sapindaceae	1, 4	WP, H	SH	N	—	—	M
Duboisia hopwoodii	Pr67	Solanaceae	4	P, s	SH	N	T	—	—
Echinocereus fendleri	Sh42	Cactaceae	1	P	SC	S	S	—	—
Echinopsilon diuarticatum	Pe62, R66	Chenopodiaceae	6	Sa	—	—	—	—	—
Elaeagnus angustifolia	R66, Ac58, Mu12, Pe60	Elaeagnaceae	5, 6, 7, 10, 12	H (t) (s), P, s, WP	TR	Mi	—	Phr	Sb, Con, Nh (u), Na
Elaeagnus moorcroftii	Pe60, Ac62	Elaeagnaceae	5	P, s	TR	Mi	—	—	Sb, Con, Na (o)
Elymus giganteus	WE34, Pe60	Gramineae	7	s, c	GR	G	—	—	Na, Sb
Elymus patagonicus	So56	Gramineae	3	P, H	GR	H	—	—	Na(o)
Empetrum rubrum	So56	Empetraceae	3	—	—	—	—	—	—
Encelia farinosa	Sh42	Compositae	1	H	SH	N	—	—	—
Enneapogon avenaceus	Pr67	Gramineae	4	P, s, c	GR	Th	—	—	Na(o)
Enneapogon polyphyllus	Pr67	Gramineae	4	P, s, c	GR	Th	—	—	Na(o)

Table XIII (Continued)
SPECIES SUMMARY

Genus and Species	Authors	Family	Deserts Where Found	Common Habitats	Growth Forms	Life Forms	Noxious	Indicator	Uses
Ephedra alata	Oz58, Ka62, Pa12, PZ63, Mu12, Q65	Ephedraceae	7, 10, 12	E, P, D (s), r, s	SH	N, Mi	T	—	—
Ephedra americana	C57	Ephedraceae	2	Puna	—	N	—	—	M
Ephedra breana	C57	Ephedraceae	2	Puna	—	N	—	—	M
Ephedra distachya Syn. *E. alte*	Ac62	Ephedraceae	5, 7, 10	—	—	Ch	—	—	—
Ephedra multiflora	Bu67	Ephedraceae	2	Puna	—	Mi	T	—	M
Ephedra nevadensis	Sh42	Ephedraceae	1	P, H	SH	N	—	—	M, Na
Ephedra przewalskii	Ac58, Ac62, Pe62, R66	Ephedraceae	5, 6	P, c	SH	N	—	Sal	Sb, M
Eragrostis binnata	Bk54	Gramineae	9, 10, 12	B	GR	—	—	Phr	Fib
Eragrostis cyperoides	PE37	Gramineae	13	D	GR	—	—	—	—
Eragrostis eriopoda	Pr67	Gramineae	4	P, s	GR	Ch	—	—	Na (o)
Eragrostis setifolia	Pr67	Gramineae	4	P, c	GR	Ch	—	—	Na (o)
Eragrostis spinosa	PE37	Gramineae	13-N	D	GR	—	—	—	—
Eremobium lineare	Zo62	Cruciferae	10, 12	P, s	AN	Th	—	—	Na (o)
Eremophila maculata	Pr67	Myoporaceae	4	P, s, Ak	SH	N	—	—	—
Eremosparton appyllum	Pa12	Leguminosae	7	s, P	SH	Mi	—	—	—
Eriachne aristidea	Pr67	Gramineae	4	P, s	GR	Ch	—	—	Na
Eriachne helmsii	Pr67	Gramineae	4	P, s	GR	Ch	—	—	Na
Eriogonum wrightii	Sh42	Polygonaceae	1	P	HSH	Ch	—	—	Na
Erodium hirtum	Zo62, Mu12	Geraniaceae	10, 12	H (s), WE	SH, PR	G, N	—	—	Na (o), Nh
Erodium laciniatum	Zo62	Geraniaceae	10	H, h	AN	Th	—	—	Na (o)
Eschscholtzia mexicana	Sh42	Papaveraceae	1	P	AN	Th	—	—	—
Eucalyptus camaldulensis	Pr67	Myrtaceae	4	WE, s	TR	Ms	—	Phr	Con
Eucalyptus globulus	Wa64	Myrtaceae	2	FB	TR	MM	—	—	—
Eucalyptus largiflorens	Pr67	Myrtaceae	4	E (e, n), WE, s, WP	TR	Mi	—	Phr	Con
Eucalyptus microtheca Syn. *E. coolabah*	Pr67	Myrtaceae	4	WE (s), B	TR	Mi	—	—	—
Euclea pseudebenus	PE37	Ebenaceae	13	—	TR	MM, Mi	—	—	Con
Euclea undulata	PE37	Ebenaceae	13	—	TR	—	—	—	—
Eulalia fulva	Pr67	Gramineae	4	P, c, s, WE, WP (e, n)	GR	Ch	—	—	Na (o)

Table XIII (Continued)

SPECIES SUMMARY

Genus and Species	Authors	Family	Deserts Where Found	Common Habitats	Growth Forms	Life Forms	Noxious	Indicator	Uses
Euphorbia antisiphylitica	Em67	Euphorbiaceae	13	—	SC	S	T	—	G (wax)
Euphorbia beaumierana	Sh42	Euphorbiaceae	1	P, H	PR	G	T	—	Na (o)
Euphorbia echinus	Em67	Euphorbiaceae	13	—	SC	S	—	—	—
Euphorbia dregeana	PE37	Euphorbiaceae	13-N	—	SC	S	—	—	—
Euphorbia gregaria	PE37	Euphorbiaceae	13	—	—	—	—	—	—
Euphorbia guyoniana	Ca13, Q65	Euphorbiaceae	12	s, WE	HSH	H	—	—	—
Euphorbia mauritanica	PE37, Mu12	Euphorbiaceae	11, 12, 13	s, c	SH, SC	N	—	—	—
Euphorbia nereifolia	BR53	Euphorbiaceae	8	r	TR	Mi	P	—	M
Euphorbia portulacoides	So50	Euphorbiaceae	3	P	—	H	T	—	—
Euphorbia virosa	PE37	Euphorbiaceae	13-N	H, r	SC	S	—	—	—
Eurotia ceratoides	R66, Ac58, Ac62, Pe62, Mu12	Chenopodiaceae	5, 6, 12	Sa, D	HSH	Ch	—	—	Na, Sb
Eurotia lanata	Sh42	Chenopodiaceae	1	P	HSH	Ch	—	—	Na
Euryops multifidus	PE37	Compositae	13	—	SH	—	—	—	—
Fabiana bryoides	C55	Solanaceae	2, 3	—	SH	N	—	—	—
Fabiana patagonica	C55	Solanaceae	3	—	SH	N	—	—	—
Fagonia bruguieri	Zo62, Re64, Mu12	Zygophyllaceae	8, 9, 10, 12	h, s	HSH	Ch	S	—	—
Fagonia glutinosa	Oz58, Re64, Mu12	Zygophyllaceae	10, 12	s	PR	H	S	—	—
Farsetia aegyptiaca	Zo62	Cruciferae	8, 10, 12	—	PR	H	—	—	—
Ferocactus acanthodes	Sh42	Cactaceae	1	H, WE	SC	S	S	—	—
Ferocactus wislizeni	Sh42	Cactaceae	1	H, P	SC	S	S	—	—
Festuca argentina	So52, So56	Gramineae	3 (Patag.)	P	GR	H	S, T	—	—
Festuca australis	C55	Gramineae	2	FB	AN, GR	Th	—	—	—
Festuca gracillima	So56	Gramineae	3	—	—	—	—	—	—
Festuca pallescens	So52, So56	Gramineae	3 (Patag.)	P	GR	H	—	—	Na (o)
Flourensia cernua	Sh42	Compositae	1	P	SH	N	—	—	M
Flourensia suffrutescens	C57	Compositae	2	Puna	—	N	—	—	—
Fouquieria splendens	Sh42	Fouquieriaceae	1	H, P	SH	Mi	S	—	—
Frankenia hirsuta	Pa12, Mu12	Frankeniaceae	6, 7, 9, 10, 12	Sa	HSH	Ch	—	—	—
Franseria deltoidea	Sh42	Compositae	1	P, H	SH	N	—	—	—

Table XIII (Continued)
SPECIES SUMMARY

Genus and Species	Authors	Family	Deserts Where Found	Common Habitats	Growth Forms	Life Forms	Noxious	Indicator	Uses
Franseria dumosa	Sh42	Compositae	1	P, H	SH	N	—	—	—
Franseria fruticosa	We45	Compositae	2 (Peru)	P	—	N	—	—	—
Fredolia aretioides Syn. *Anabasis aretioides*	Oz58	Chenopodiaceae	12	—	HSH	Ch	—	—	—
Galenia africana	PE37	Aïzoaceae	13	—	SC	S			
Genista saharae	Oz58	Leguminosae	12	E	SH	N	—	—	Na
Geoffroea decorticans	Bu52, M58	Leguminosae	2, 3	P	—	G	—	—	Na(u)
Glycyrrhiza astragaline	Bu52	Leguminosae	3	P, D	—	G	—	—	—
Glycyrrhiza glabra	Re64, P64, Pa12	Leguminosae	7, 9, 10, 12	H(s)	PR	H	—	—	Nh
Glycyrrhiza glandulifera	P64	Leguminosae	9	—	PR	—	—	—	M, Nh
Grayia spinosa	Sh42	Chenopodiaceae	1	P	SH	N	S	—	Na
Grevillea juncifolia	Pr67	Proteaceae	4	P, s, D(s, t)	SH	N	—	—	—
Grevillea striata	Pr67	Proteaceae	4	P, c, s	TR	Mi	—	—	—
Grindelia chiloënsis	C55	Compositae	3 (Monte)	D, P	N	—	—	—	—
Gymnarrhena micrantha	Zo62, Re64, Mu12	Compositae	9, 10, 12	H, h	AN	Th	—	—	—
Gymnocarpos fruticosum	Zo62, Mu12	Caryophyllaceae	8, 9, 10, 11, 12	H, s, WE	SH	N	—	—	—
Gymnocarpos przewalskii	Pe62, Ac58	Caryophyllaceae	5, 6	P, s	SH	N	—	—	Na
Hakea intermedia Syn. *H. divaricata*	Pr67	Proteaceae	4	P, s	SH	N, Mi	—	—	—
Hakea leucoptera	Pr67	Proteaceae	4	P, s, c, Ak	SH	N, Mi	—	—	—
Halocnemon strobilaceum	Pa12, Mu12, Pe62, Ca13	Chenopodiaceae	6, 7, 10, 12	c, Sa, s	SH	N, Mi	—	Sal	—
Halogeton alopecuroides	Zo62, Re64	Chenopodiaceae	10, 12	Sa (gyp)	SH	N	—	—	—
Halogeton glomeratus	Pa12, Pe62	Chenopodiaceae	6, 7	Ak	AN	Th	T	—	—
Halophytum ameghinoi	Hu52	Halophytaceae	3	H(s)	AN	Th	—	—	—
Halostachys caspica	Pa12, Pe62	Chenopodiaceae	6, 7	c, Sa	SH	N	—	—	—

Table XIII (Continued)

SPECIES SUMMARY

Genus and Species	Authors	Family	Deserts Where Found	Common Habitats	Growth Forms	Life Forms	Noxious	Indicator	Uses
Haloxylon ammodendron	Ac58, Ac62, Pa12, Ri31, Pe62, R66	Chenopodiaceae	5, 6, 7	s, P	SH, TR	Mi, MM	—	Phr	Sb, Wd, Na
Haloxylon aphyllum	Pe36, Ac58, VV61, Pe60	Chenopodiaceae	5, 7	P, c	SH	N	—	Phr	Na, Wd, Sb
Haloxylon articulatum	Ca13, Zo62, E62	Chenopodiaceae	9, 10, 12	P, H, WE	SH	N	—	—	Na
Haloxylon persicum	Pe60, Ac58, Ac62, Zo62, PZ63, Bk54	Chenopodiaceae	5, 6, 7, 8, 9, 10	s, D, P	SH, TR	Mi	—	Phr	Sb, Na(o), Wd
Haloxylon salicornicum	Bk54, Zo62, PZ63	Chenopodiaceae	10	s, P, R	SC	S	—	—	Na
Haloxylon scoparium	Oz58	Chenopodiaceae	12	R, r	PR	H	—	—	—
Haplophyllum obtusifolium	Pa12	Rutaceae	7	s	—	Ch	—	—	—
Hedysarum scoparium	Ac62, Pe60, Pe62	Leguminosae	5, 7	s, D	SH	—	—	Phr	Nh (e), Wd, Sb, Na
Helianthemum kahiricum	Zo62, Mu12	Cistaceae	10, 12	Sa (gyp)	SH	Ch	—	—	—
Heliotropium curassavicum	C55	Boraginaceae	2	Sa	PR	—	—	—	—
Heliotropium dasycarpum	Pa12	Boraginaceae	7, 8	c	SH	N	—	—	—
Heliotropium sogdianum	Pa12	Boraginaceae	7	—	—	G	—	—	—
Helipterum floribundum	Pr67	Compositae	4	P, s, c	AN	Th	—	—	—
Herniaria hemistemon	Mu12	Caryophyllaceae	9, 10, 12	s	PR	H	—	—	—
Heterodendron oleifolium	Pr67	Sapindaceae	4	P, s	TR	Mi	—	—	Na(o)
Heteropogon contortus	Sh42	Gramineae	1	P	GR	H	S	—	Na
Hilaria jamesii	Sh42	Gramineae	1	P	GR	G	—	—	Na
Hilaria mutica	Sh42	Gramineae	1	P	GR	G	—	—	Na
Hilaria rigida	Sh42	Gramineae	1	P, H	GR	Ch	—	—	Na
Horaninovia ulicina	Pa12, Pe60	Chenopodiaceae	6, 7	s	AN	Th	S	—	Sb

Table XIII (Continued)
SPECIES SUMMARY

Genus and Species	Authors	Family	Deserts Where Found	Common Habitats	Growth Forms	Life Forms	Noxious	Indicator	Uses
Hordeum comosum	So56	Gramineae	3	P	GR	H	—	—	Na(o)
Hyalis argentea	Bu67	Compositae	3 (Monte)	P, D(t,s)	—	G	—	—	Sb, Nh(u)
Hymenoclea monogyra	Sh42	Compositae	1	WE	SH	N	—	—	—
Hyoscyamus muticus	Em67	Solanaceae	8, 10, 12	R	—	—	T	—	M
Hypheane thebaica	Bk54	Palmae	10	WP	TR	MM	—	Phr	Fib
Idria columnaria	Sh42	Fouquieriaceae	1	H, P	TR	MM	S	—	—
Indigofera argentea	BR53, Mu12	Leguminosae	8, 12	—	SH	N	—	—	—
Indigofera enneaphylla Syn. *I. linnaei*	Pr67	Leguminosae	4	P, s	AN	Th	T	—	Na(o)
Inga feuillei	C55	Leguminosae	2	—	—	—	—	—	—
Ipomoea arborescens	Sh42	Convolvulaceae	1	H	TR	MM	—	—	—
Ipomoea minuta	C55	Convolvulaceae	3	—	—	G	—	—	—
Iris ensata	Ac58, Ac62, Pa12	Iridaceae	5, 7	P, Sa	PR	G	—	Phr	Sb
Iseilema vaginiflorum	Pr67	Gramineae	4	Pc	GR	Th	—	—	Na(o)
Isomeris arborea	Sh42	Capparidaceae	1	H	SH	N	—	—	—
Jatropha cordata	Sh42	Euphorbiaceae	1	H	SH, TR	Mi	—	—	—
Jatropha spathulata	Sh42	Euphorbiaceae	1	P	SH	N	—	—	—
Juelia subterranea	C55	Balanophoraceae	3	—	PR	G	—	—	—
Juniperus excelsa	P64	Cupressaceae	9	—	TR	Mi	—	—	M, Con
Juniperus utahensis	Sh42	Cupressaceae	1	H, P	TR	Mi	—	—	Wd, Con
Kalidium caspicum	Pe62	Chenopodiaceae	6	Sa	HSH	Ch	—	—	—
Kalidium cuspidatum	Pe62	Chenopodiaceae	5, 6	Sa	HSH	Ch	—	—	—
Kalidium foliatum	Pe62, Ac58	Chenopodiaceae	5	Sa	HSH	Ch	—	—	Na (o), Nh (e)
Kalidium gracile	Pe62, R66	Chenopodiaceae	6	Sa	—	—	—	—	—
Karwinskia humboldtiana	Sh42	Rhamnaceae	1	WE	TR	Mi	—	—	—
Kochia aphylla	Pr67	Chenopodiaceae	4	Pc	SH	N	—	—	Na(o)
Kochia planifolia	W50	Chenopodiaceae	4	P, s, Ak	SH	N	—	—	Na(o)
Kochia pyramidata	Pr67	Chenopodiaceae	4	P, s, Ak	SH	N	—	—	Na(o)
Kochia sedifolia	W50	Chenopodiaceae	4	P, s, Ak	SH	N	—	—	Na(o)
Kochia vestita	Sh42	Chenopodiaceae	1	P	PR	Ch	—	—	—
Koeberlinia spinosa	Sh42	Capparidaceae	1	WE, P, H	SH, TR	Mi	S	—	—
Krameria illuca	C57	Leguminosae	3	Puna	—	Ch	—	—	M
Lactuca orientalis	Mu12, P64, Re64	Compositae	9, 10, 12	P	SH	N	S	—	—
Lactuca ruthenicum	DF64	Compositae	9	—	—	—	—	—	—

Table XIII (Continued)
SPECIES SUMMARY

Genus and Species	Authors	Family	Deserts Where Found	Common Habitats	Growth Forms	Life Forms	Noxious	Indicator	Uses
Lactuca turcomanicum	DF64	Compositae	9	H	—	—	—	—	—
Larrea ameghinoi	So56, So50, M58	Zygophyllaceae	3 (Patag.)	P	—	N	—	—	—
Larrea cuneifolia	M58	Zygophyllaceae	3 (Monte)	—	SH	N	—	—	—
Larrea divaricata	M58, C55, So50	Zygophyllaceae	1, 3	P	SH	Mi	—	—	Wd
Larrea nitida	M58, So50	Zygophyllaceae	3 (Monte)	—	SH	N	—	—	—
Larrea tridentata	Sh42	Zygophyllaceae	1, 3	P	SH	N	—	—	—
Lasiagrostis splendens	Ac62	Gramineae	5, 7	—	GR	H	—	—	—
Lasiurus hirsutus	Ka62	Gramineae	10, 11, 12	s	PR, GR	G	—	—	Na (o)
Launaea spinosa	Ka62, Mu12	Compositae	10, 12	WE	SH	N	S	—	—
Lemaireocereus thurberi	Sh42	Cactaceae	1	H, P	SC	Mi, S	S	—	—
Leptadenia aerva	BR53	Asclepiadaceae	8	—	—	—	—	—	—
Limoniastrum guyonianum	Ca13	Plumbaginaceae	12	Sa, s	SH	N	—	—	—
Lopohocereus schottii	Sh42	Cactaceae	1	H, P	SC	Mi, S	S	—	—
Lycium arenicolum	PE37	Solanaceae	13	—	SH	—	—	—	—
Lycium arabicum	E62, Mu12	Solanaceae	8, 9, 10, 12	WE, s	SH	Mi	S	—	Nh
Lycium brevipes	Sh42	Solanaceae	1	WE, H, P	SH	Mi	S	—	—
Lycium californicum	Sh42	Solanaceae	1	Sa	SH	N	S	—	—
Lycium chilense	So52	Solanaceae	3	P	—	N	—	—	Na(o)
Lycium intricatum	Em67	Solanaceae	12	Sa	—	—	—	Sal	
Lycium ruthenicum	Pa12, Ac62	Solanaceae	5, 8, 12	WE, s	SH	Mi	S	—	—
Lycium turcomannicum	R66, Pa12, Pe62	Solanaceae	5, 6, 7	Sa, WP	TR	—	—	—	—
Machaerocereus gummosus	Sh42	Cactaceae	1	H, P	SC	S	S	—	—
Maerua crassifolia	Em67	Capparidaceae	10, 12	—	SH	N	—	—	—
Melianthus comosus	PE37	Melianthaceae	13	—	SH	—	—	—	M
Mesembryanthemum spinosum	PE37	Aïzoaceae	13	—	SC	S	—	—	—
Moltkia ciliata	Oz58	Boraginaceae	12	E	—	—	—	—	—
Monsonia nivea	Zo62, Mu12, Re62	Geraniaceae	10, 12	H(s)	PR, AN	H, Th	—	—	—
Monttea aphylla	M58	Scrophulariaceae	3	P	SH	N	—	—	Wd
Moringa aptera	Zo62, Mu12	Moringaceae	10, 12	WE	TR	Mi	—	—	—

Table XIII (Continued)
SPECIES SUMMARY

Genus and Species	Authors	Family	Deserts Where Found	Common Habitats	Growth Forms	Life Forms	Noxious	Indicator	Uses
Mortonia scabrella	Sh42	Celastraceae	1	H	SH	N	—	—	—
Morus alba	R66	Moraceae	5	WP	TR	MM	—	—	—
Muehlenbeckia cunninghamii	Pr67	Polygonaceae	4	WP (e,n), B, WE, s	SH	N	—	—	—
Muhlenbergia fastigiata	C57	Gramineae	2	WP	GR	G	—	—	—
Muhlenbergia porteri	Sh42	Gramineae	1	P	GR	H	—	—	Na
Mulinum spinosum	Bo57, So52	Umbelliferae	3	P	HSH	Ch	S	—	Na(o)
Munroa mendocina	Hu52	Gramineae	3	P	AN	Th	—	—	—
Myoporum platycarpum	D55	Myoporaceae	4	P, s	TR	Mi	—	—	Na(o)
Myrciaria germanica	Pe62, R66	Myrtaceae	5, 6	WP	TR	—	—	—	—
Nanophyton erinaceum	R66, Pe62, Pa12	Chenopodiaceae	6, 7	—	HSH	Ch			
Nardophyllum obtusifolium	So56	Compositae	3	P	SH	N	—	—	—
Nassauvia axillaris	C55, So50	Compositae	3	P, H(s)	SH	N	—	—	—
Nassauvia glomerulosa	C55, So50, So56	Compositae	3	P	SH	N	—	—	Na(o)
Neocracca heterantha	C57, Bu52	Leguminosae	3	Puna	AN	TH	—	—	Nh
Neosparton ephedroides	C55	Verbenaceae	3	—	SH	N	—	—	—
Nerium oleander	Ca13, Mu12	Apocynaceae	10, 12	WP, WE, r	SH	N	T	—	M
Nitraria retusa	Zo62, Re64	Zygophyllaceae	10	Sa	SH	N	S	—	—
Nitraria schoberi	Pa12, Pe62	Zygophyllaceae	5, 6, 7	c, Sa	SH	Mi	S	Phr	Nh (u)
Nitraria sibirica	Ac58, R66, Pe62	Zygophyllaceae	5, 6	Sa, P	SH	N	—	—	Nh (u), Sb
Nitraria sphaerocarpa	Ac58, Ac62, Pe62, R66	Zygophyllaceae	5, 6	WE, s, Sa, P	SH	N	—	Sal	Sb
Noaea mucronata Syn. *N. spinosissima*	P64, Re64	Chenopodiaceae	9, 10, 12	P	SH	N	S	—	—
Noaea spinosissima	Zo62, E62, Pa12	Chenopodiaceae	6, 7, 10, 12	H (s), r, s	SH	N	S	—	—
Nymania capensis	PE37	Melianthaceae	13	—	SH	N	—	—	—
Odontospermum pygmaeum Syn. *Asteriscus pygmaeus*	Ha51, Mu12	Compositae	10, 12	P	PR	H	—	—	—

Table XIII (Continued)
SPECIES SUMMARY

Genus and Species	Authors	Family	Deserts Where Found	Common Habitats	Growth Forms	Life Forms	Noxious	Indicator	Uses
Olea europaea	Ti26, Mu12	Oleaceae	10, 12	—	TR, SH	N	—	—	Nh(u), Con, Na
Olneya tesota	Sh42	Leguminosae	1	WE	TR	Mi	S	—	Wd, Con
Opuntia cholla	Sh42	Cactaceae	1	P, H	SC	S, Mi	S	—	—
Opuntia engelmanni	Sh42	Cactaceae	1	P, H	SC	S, N	S	—	—
Opuntia fulgida	Sh42	Cactaceae	1	P, H	SC	S, N	S	—	—
Opuntia glomerata	Hu52	Cactaceae	3	P	SC	S	S	—	—
Opuntia nigrispina	C57	Cactaceae	2	H(s)	SC	S, Ch	S	—	—
Opuntia pampeana	Bu67	Cactaceae	3 (Monte)	P, H	SC	S	S	—	—
Opuntia soehrensii	Hu52, C57	Cactaceae	2	P, H	SC	S	S	—	M, D
Opuntia spinosior	Sh42	Cactaceae	1	P, H	SC	S, N	S	—	—
Opuntia versicolor	Sh42	Cactaceae	1	P, H	SC	S, N	S	—	—
Oreocereus celsianus	C57	Cactaceae	2	Puna	SC	Mi, S	S	—	—
Oreocereus trollii	C57	Cactaceae	2	Puna	SC	Ch, S	S	—	—
Oxalis bryoides	C55	Oxalidaceae	3	—	SH	N	—	—	—
Oxalis elegans	C55	Oxalidaceae	3	—	PR	G	—	—	—
Oxalis solarensis	C55	Oxalidaceae	2	FB	PR	G	—	—	—
Oxytropis aciphylla	Ac58, Ac62	Leguminosae	5	H, r, s	PR	Ch	—	—	Na
Pachycereus pringlei	Sh42	Cactaceae	1	H, P	SC	S, Mi	S	—	—
Pachypodium namaquanum	PE37	Cruciferae	13	H, r	SC	S	S	—	—
Panicum obtusum	Sh42	Gramineae	1	P	GR	H	—	—	Na
Panicum turgidum	PZ63, Zo62, Mu12, Oz58, Ka62, Ha51	Gramineae	9, 10, 11, 12	r, s, WE, P, h	GR, PR	G, Ch	—	—	Na (o), Nh (e)
Panicum urvilleanum	C55	Gramineae	3 (Monte)	D	GR	G	—	—	Sb
Panicum virgatum	Sh42	Gramineae	1	—	G	G	—	—	Na
Pappea capensis	PE37	Sapindaceae	13	—	TR	—	—	—	oil
Parkinsonia aculeata	Sh42	Leguminosae	1	P	TR	Mi	—	—	Wd
Parthenium argentatum	Sh42	Compositae	1	P, H	SH	N	—	—	rubber
Peganum harmala	Mu12, Pa12, Ca13	Zygophyllaceae	12	E, s, WE	SH	—	—	—	oil, T, M
Peganum nigellastrum	Ac58, R66, Pe62	Zygophyllaceae	5, 6	—	—	—	—	—	—
Pennisetum chinense	C55	Gramineae	2	D, B, Puna	G, GR	—	—	—	Sb, Na

Table XIII (Continued)
SPECIES SUMMARY

Genus and Species	Authors	Family	Deserts Where Found	Common Habitats	Growth Forms	Life Forms	Noxious	Indicator	Uses
Pennisetum ciliare	Zo62	Gramineae	—	—	GR	—	—	—	—
Pennisetum dichotomum	P64	Gramineae	9	—	GR	—	—	—	—
Pentzia globosa	PE37	Compositae	13	—	SH	N	—	—	—
Pentzia incana	PE37	Compositae	13	—	SH	N	—	—	—
Pentzia virgata	PE37	Compositae	13	—	SH	N	—	—	Na
Peucedanum rigidum	Ac58, Ac62	Umbelliferae	5	S, WP	PR	H	—	—	Na
Phacelia magellanica	So50	Hydrophyllaceae	3	P	—	H	—	—	—
Phacelia pinnatifida	C57, Hu52	Hydrophyllaceae	2, 3	Monte, Puna	PR	H	—	—	—
Phaeoptilum spinosum	PE37	Nyctaginaceae	13	—	SH	N	—	—	—
Phlomis brachyodon	Zo62	Labiatae	10	H(s), r	—	—	—	—	—
Phoenix dactylifera	Bk54	Palmae	9, 10, 11, 12	B	TR	MM	—	Phr	Nh (u), Fib
Phragmites communis	Em67	Gramineae	13	WE	GR, G	—	—	Phr	Na (o), Fib
Pinus cembroides	Sh42	Pinaceae	1	H	TR	Mi	—	—	Wd, Nh(e)
Pinus monophylla	Sh42	Pinaceae	1	H	TR	Mi	—	—	Wd, Nh(e)
Pistacia atlantica	Ti26, Ca13, Oz58, P64, Zo62	Pistaciaceae	9, 10, 12	H, r, P	TR	Mi, MM	—	—	Wd, Con, Nh(u)
Pithuranthos tortuosus	Ha51, Mu12	Umbelliferae	10, 12	P(s), E	AN	H	—	—	Na, M
Pittosporum phillyraeoides	Pr67	Pittosporaceae	4	P, s	TR	Mi	—	—	Na(o)
Plantago monticola	Ca57	Plantaginaceae	2	Puna	PR	H	—	—	—
Plantago ovata	PZ63, Re64, Mu12	Plantaginaceae	8, 9, 10, 12	D(s), E	AN	Th	—	—	Na, M
Plectrachne schinzii	Pr67	Gramineae	4	P, s	GR	Ch	—	—	Na(o)
Plectrocarpa tetracantha	M58	Zygophyllaceae	3	P	SH	Mi	—	—	Sb
Poa bulbosa	Pa12, P64	Gramineae	7, 9, 10	H, c	PR, GR	Ch	—	—	Na (u)
Poa ligularis	So52, So56	Gramineae	3	Sa	GR	H	—	—	Na (o)
Poliomintha incana	Sh42	Labiatae	1	P, s	SH	N	—	—	Nh(o), Sb
Populus alba	Ac58, R66, Re64	Salicaceae	7, 9, 10, 12	WP, Sa	TR	MM	—	—	Con

Table XIII (Continued)
SPECIES SUMMARY

Genus and Species	Authors	Family	Deserts Where Found	Common Habitats	Growth Forms	Life Forms	Noxious	Indicator	Uses
Populus diversifolia	Ac58, Ac62, Pe62	Salicaceae	5, 6, 7	WP	TR	Mi	—	Sal	Con, Sb
Populus euphratica	P64, Mu12, Pa12	Salicaceae	7, 9, 10, 12	WP	TR	Mi	—	—	Wd, Con
Populus nigra	R66, Pe60, Pa12	Salicaceae	6, 7	WP	TR	MM	—	—	Con
Populus pruinosa	Pa12, R66	Salicaceae	6, 7	WP	TR	—	—	—	—
Populus simonii	Ac58, Pe60, Pa12	Salicaceae	5, 6	P, s	TR	MM	—	Phr	Sb, Con
Portulaca rotundifolia	C55	Portulacaceae	3	—	PR	G	—	—	—
Potaninia mongolica	Ac58, Ac62, Pe62, R66	Rosaceae	5, 6	P, s	SH	N	—	—	Na
Potentilla mongolica	Ac62	Rosaceae	5	—	—	—	—	—	—
Prosopidastrum globosum	Bu64, So52	Leguminosae	3	P	SH	Mi	S	—	Na(o)
Prosopis alba	M58, Bu67	Leguminosae	3	P	TR	Ms	S	—	Nh(u), Na, Con
Prosopis alpataco	Bu67	Leguminosae	3	P	SH	Mi	S	—	Na(u,o)
Prosopis algorobilla	Bu67	Leguminosae	3	—	—	—	—	—	Na(u)
Prosopis argentina	Hu52, Bu52	Leguminosae	3	D	SH	Mi	S	—	Sb
Prosopis caldenia	Bu67	Leguminosae	3	—	—	—	—	—	—
Prosopis chilensis	C55	Leguminosae	1, 2, 3	P, WE	TR	Mi	S	—	Wd, Na(o)
Prosopis denudans	So50, Bu52	Leguminosae	3 (Patag.)	P	SH	Mi	S	—	—
Prosopis ferox	C57	Leguminosae	2	P, H(s)	TR	Mi	S	—	Con
Prosopis flexuosa	M58	Leguminosae	3	P	TR	MM	—	—	—
Prosopis limensis	C55	Leguminosae	2	—	—	—	—	—	—
Prosopis nigra	Bu67	Leguminosae	3	—	—	—	—	—	Na(u)
Prosopis spicigera	P64	Leguminosae	8, 9	—	TR	MM	—	—	—
Prosopis stephaniana	Pa12, Mu12, Re64, DF64, P64	Leguminosae	7, 9, 10, 12	P, s, c, H	SH	N	S	Phr	—
Prosopis strombulifera	M58	Leguminosae	3	P	SH	G	S	—	M, Sb
Prosopis torquata	C55	Leguminosae	3 (Monte)	P, H(s)	TR	Mi	S	—	Na(u)
Prunus amygdalus	Po29	Rosaceae	7, 9, 10, 12	H, RO	TR	Mi, N	—	—	Nh(u)
Psammochloa villosa	Pe62, Ac58, Ac62	Gramineae	5, 6, 7	D, s	GR	—	—	Phr	Fib, Sb, Na

Table XIII (Continued)
SPECIES SUMMARY

Genus and Species	Authors	Family	Deserts Where Found	Common Habitats	Growth Forms	Life Forms	Noxious	Indicator	Uses
Psila (Pseudobaccharis) spartioides	C55	Compositae	3	—	SH	N	—	—	—
Pterocactus tuberosus	M58	Cactaceae	3	P, D	—	G, SC	S	—	—
Ptilotus polystachyus	Pr67	Amaranthaceae	4	D(t,s,b), AN P, s		Th	—	—	—
Pugionium cornutum	Pe60, Ac58	Cruciferae	5, 6	D(b)	AN, PR	Th	—	—	Na, oil, Nh, Sb
Purshia tridentata	Sh42	Rosaceae	1	H	SH	N	—	—	Na(o)
Puya tuberosa	M58	Bromeliaceae	2	Puna	—	Ch	—	—	—
Puya raimondii	We45	Bromeliaceae	2	Puna	SC	S, Ch	—	—	—
Quercus persica	P64	Fagaceae	9	H	TR	Mi	—	—	Na (u), Nh(u)
Ramorinoa girolae	C55	Leguminosae	3	H	SH	N	—	—	Nh(o)
Reaumuria fruticosa	Pa12	Tamaricaceae	7	s	SH	N	—	—	—
Reaumuria hirtilla	Ha51, Mu12	Tamaricaceae	10, 12	r	SH	N	—	—	—
Reaumuria palaestina	Zo62	Tamaricaceae	10	H(s)	—	—	—	—	—
Reaumuria soongarica	Pe62, Ac62	Tamaricaceae	5	D, Sa, P	—	—	—	—	—
Reboudia pinnata	Zo62	Cruciferae	10	H, h	AN	Th	—	—	—
Retama raetam	Mu12, Zo62, E62, Ka62, Q65, Ca13, Oz58	Leguminosae	10, 12	E, WE, s	SH	N	—	—	Sb
Retama sphaerocarpa	Ca13	Leguminosae	12	—	SH	Mi	—	—	—
Rhanterium epapposum	PZ63, Re64	Compositae	10	RO, P, D (b)	SH	N	S	—	—
Rhigozum trichotomum	PE37	Bignoniaceae	13	—	SH	N	—	—	—
Rhus microphylla	Sh42	Anacardiaceae	1	H	SH	N	T	—	—
Rhus tripartita Syn. R. oxyacantha	Zo62	Anacardiaceae	10, 12	RO	SH	N	S	—	—
Robbairea prostrata	Zo62, Mu12	Caryophyllaceae	10	h, s	PR	H	—	—	—
Rottboellia hirsuta	Em67	Gramineae	12	WE	GR	—	—	—	—
Rumex roseus	Zo62	Polygonaceae	10, 12	H, h	AN	Th	—	—	Nh (o), Na (o)
Salazaria mexicana	Sh42	Labiatae	1	H, WE	SH	N	—	—	—
Salicornia ambigua	So56	Chenopodiaceae	3 (Patag.)	Sa	—	—	—	—	—
Salicornia pulvinata	C57	Chenopodiaceae	2	Sa, Puna	—	Ch	—	—	—
Salicornia rubra	Sh42	Chenopodiaceae	1	—	AN	Th	—	—	—

Table XIII (Continued)
SPECIES SUMMARY

Genus and Species	Authors	Family	Deserts Where Found	Common Habitats	Growth Forms	Life Forms	Noxious	Indicator	Uses
Salix caspica	Pe60	Salicaceae	7	—	—	—	—	—	Sb
Salix flavida	Pe60, Ac58	Salicaceae	5	D, s	SH	N	—	Phr	Sb, Fib
Salix humboldtiana	C55	Salicaceae	2, 3	WP, E	TR	Mi	—	—	Fib, Con
Salix mongolica	Pe60	Salicaceae	5	—	—	—	—	—	Sb
Salix purpurea	Em67	Salicaceae	12	WP	TR	—	—	—	—
Salix rubra	Pe60	Salicaceae	7	—	—	—	—	—	Sb
Salsola aphylla	PE37	Chenopodiaceae	13	—	SH	N	—	—	Na
Salsola arbuscula	R66, Pa12, Pe62	Chenopodiaceae	5, 6, 7	Sa	SH, T	—	—	—	Sb
Salsola collina	R66, Ac58, Pa12, Pe36	Chenopodiaceae	5, 6, 7	Sa	AN	N, Mi	—	—	Na, Sb
Salsola foetida	Zo62, Q65, Oz58, Re64, Ha51, Mu12	Chenopodiaceae	8, 9, 10 11, 12	D (s), H (s), Sa, s, P	SH	Ch	—	—	Na
Salsola inermis	Re64, Mu12	Chenopodiaceae	9, 10, 12	Ph	AN	Th	—	—	—
Salsola laricifolia	Pe62, Ac62	Chenopodiaceae	5, 6, 7	r	—	—	—	—	—
Salsola nitraria	Ac62	Chenopodiaceae	5	—	—	—	—	—	—
Salsola paletzkiana	Pe60, Ac58	Chenopodiaceae	5, 6, 7	P, s	SH	N	—	—	Sb
Salsola passerina	Ac58, Ac62, Pe62, R66	Chenopodiaceae	5, 6	Sa, s, P	—	—	—	—	—
Salsola praecox	Pe60	Chenopodiaceae	5, 6, 7	—	—	—	—	—	Sb
Salsola richteri	Ac58, Ac62, WE34	Chenopodiaceae	7	D, s	SH	N	—	—	Na, Sb
Salsola rigida	Mu12, Pa12	Chenopodiaceae	7, 10, 12	c	SH	Ch	—	—	—
Salsola rosmarinus	Zo62	Chenopodiaceae	10	—	—	—	—	—	—
Salsola ruthenica	R66, Pe62, Re64	Chenopodiaceae	6	Sa	AN	Th	—	—	—
Salsola sieberi	Oz58	Chenopodiaceae	12	Sa	PR	—	—	—	—
Salsola tetrandra	Zo62, Mu12	Chenopodiaceae	10, 12	Sa	PR	Ch	—	—	—
Salsola turcomanica	Pe60	Chenopodiaceae	7	—	AN	Th	—	—	Sb
Salsola zeyheri	PE37	Chenopodiaceae	13	Sa	SH	N	—	—	Na

Table XIII (Continued)
SPECIES SUMMARY

Genus and Species	Authors	Family	Deserts Where Found	Common Habitats	Growth Forms	Life Forms	Noxious	Indicator	Uses
Salvadora persica	Zo62, Mu12	Salvadoraceae	8, 10, 11, 12	WP, WE	SH, TR	Mi	—	—	Con, M, Nh(o)
Salvia aegyptiaca	Re64, Mu12, Zo62	Labiatae	8, 9, 10, 12	WE, H (s)	SH	Ch	S	—	—
Sapium (Stillingia) patagonicum	So56	Euphorbiaceae	3	P	SH	N	—	—	—
Sarcobatus vermiculatus	Sh42	Chenopodiaceae	1	P, Sa	SH	N	S	Phr, Sal	Na(o)
Sarcocaulon burmanni	PE37	Geraniaceae	13-N	—	HSH	—	—	—	—
Scabiosa aucheri	Zo62, Mu12, Re64	Dipsacaceae	10, 12	H, h	AN	Th	—	—	—
Schinus molle	C55	Anacardiaceae	2	H	TR	MM	—	—	G, M, Nh
Schinus polygamus	So50	Anacardiaceae	3	P	SH	N	S	—	—
Schismus barbatus	Zo62, Re64	Gramineae	7, 9, 10, 12	h, s	AN	Th	—	—	Na (o)
Sclerocaryopsis spinicarpos	Zo62	Boraginaceae	10	H, h	AN	Th	—	—	—
Scorzonera judaica	Zo62	Compositae	10	H, h	AN, PR	G	—	—	Nh, roots
Seidlitzia rosmarinus	Mu12	Chenopodiaceae	9, 12	—	SH	N	—	—	—
Senecio filaginoides	So50, So56	Compositae	3	P, s	SH	N	—	—	—
Senecio gregorii	Pr67	Compositae	4	P, s	AN	Th	—	—	—
Sesuvium portulacastrum	C55	Aïzoaceae	2	Sa	PR	—	—	—	—
Simmondsia californica	Sh42	Simmondsiaceae	1	H	SH	N	—	—	—
Simmondsia chinensis	Sh42	Simmondsiaceae	1	H	SH	Mi	—	—	Na, Nh (e) wax
Solanum acaule	C57	Solanaceae	2	RO, Puna	PR	G	—	—	Wild potato
Solanum veruli	C57	Solanaceae	2	RO, Puna	PR	G	—	—	Wild potato
Solenostemma argel	Em67	Asclepiadaceae	12	—	PR	Ch	—	—	—
Spilanthes urens	C55	Compositae	2	Sa	PR	—	—	—	—
Spinifex paradoxus Syn. *Zygochloa paradoxa*	Pr67, W50, D55	Gramineae	4	D(t, s)	GR	Ch	—	—	—
Sporobolus airoides	Sh42	Gramineae	1	P	GR	H	—	—	Na
Sporobolus cryptandrus	Sh42	Gramineae	1	P	GR	H	—	—	Na
Sporobolus pyramidalis	M58	Gramineae	3	Sa	GR	H	—	—	—

Table XIII (Continued)
SPECIES SUMMARY

Genus and Species	Authors	Family	Deserts Where Found	Common Habitats	Growth Forms	Life Forms	Noxious	Indicator	Uses
Sporobolus rigens	C55	Gramineae	3	s	GR	G, H	—	—	—
Sporobolus virginicus	C55	Gramineae	2	Sa	GR	—	—	—	—
Stellaria lessertii	Pa12	Caryophyllaceae	7	C	SH	N	—	—	—
Stenopetalum nutans	Pr67	Cruciferae	4	P, s, c	AN	Th	—	—	—
Stipa annua	C55	Gramineae	2	FB	AN, GR	Th	—	—	—
Stipa bungeana	Pe62	Gramineae	5, 6	r	GR	—	—	—	—
Stipa chrysophylla	So56, Hu52	Gramineae	2, 3	—	GR	H	—	—	—
Stipa glareosa	Pe62, Ac58, Ac62	Gramineae	5, 6	D, r	GR, AN	Th	—	—	Na, Sb
Stipa gobica	Ac58, Ac62	Gramineae	5, 6	P, c	GR, AN	Th	—	—	Na, Sb
Stipa humilis	So56	Gramineae	3 (Patag.)	P	GR	H	—	—	—
Stipa hypogona	So52	Gramineae	3	P	GR	H	—	—	Na(o)
Stipa ibari	So56	Gramineae	3 (Patag.)	P	GR	H	—	—	Na(o)
Stipa leptostachya	C57	Gramineae	2	H (s), Puna	GR	H	T	—	—
Stipa speciosa	So56, Hu52	Gramineae	3	H (s), Puna	GR	H	—	—	—
Stipa tenacissima	Em67	Gramineae	12	—	GR	—	—	—	Fib, Na (o)
Stipa tortilis	PZ63, Re64, Bk54	Gramineae	7, 9, 10, 12	WE	AN, GR	Th	—	—	Na (o)
Stilpnolepis centiflora	Pe60, Ac58	Compositae	6, 7	D(b), s	AN, PR	Th	—	—	Sb
Suaeda asphaltica	Zo62	Chenopodiaceae	10	Sa (gyp)	SH	N	—	—	—
Suaeda divaricata	So56, Hu52	Chenopodiaceae	3	Sa, D	SH	N	—	—	—
Suaeda fruticosa	Em67	Chenopodiaceae	8, 9, 10, 11, 12, 13	WE	SH	N	—	Sal	Na (o)
Suaeda forskalii	Zo62	Chenopodiaceae	10	Sa	—	—	—	—	—
Suaeda monoica	Zo62, Mu12	Chenopodiaceae	10, 11, 12	Sa	SH	Mi	—	—	—
Suaeda palaestina	Zo62	Chenopodiaceae	10	Sa	SH	N	—	—	—
Suaeda patagonica	So56	Chenopodiaceae	3	Sa	SH	N	—	—	—
Suaeda vermiculata	Mu12, Zo62, Re64	Chenopodiaceae	10, 12	Sa	SH	N	S	—	Na (o)
Sympegma regelii	Pe62, R66	Chenopodiaceae	5, 6	Sa, s, r	—	—	—	—	—
Tamarindus indica	P64	Leguminosae	8, 9	Cult	TR	MM	—	—	Nh(u), M

Table XIII (Continued)

SPECIES SUMMARY

Genus and Species	Authors	Family	Deserts Where Found	Common Habitats	Growth Forms	Life Forms	Noxious	Indicator	Uses
Tamarix articulata	Oz58, Mu12, PE37	Tamaricaceae	8, 9, 10, 11, 12, 13	Sa, s	SH, TR	Mi	—	Phr	Con, T, M
Tamarix chinensis	Pa12, R66	Tamaricaceae	6	P, WP	TR	—	—	—	—
Tamarix hispida	R66	Tamaricaceae	6, 7	WP	TR	—	—	—	—
Tamarix juniperina	R66	Tamaricaceae	6, 7	WP	TR	—	—	—	—
Tamarix laxa	Pe60, Pe62	Tamaricaceae	6, 7	Sa	—	—	—	—	Sb
Tamarix ramosissima	Pe60, Re64, Pe62, Ac58	Tamaricaceae	5, 6, 7, 10	s, P, Sa	SH	N	—	Sal, Phr	Sb, Con
Tamarix stricta	P64	Tamaricaceae	9	D	TR	—	—	—	—
Tanacetum achilleoides	Pe62, R66	Compositae	6	s, Sa	—	—	—	—	M
Tanacetum fruticulosum	Pe62, R66	Compositae	6	s	—	—	—	—	—
Tanacetum trifidum	Pe62, R66	Compositae	6	s	—	—	—	—	—
Tecoma garrocha	Hu52	Bignoniaceae	3	W	—	Mi	—	—	—
Tetradiclis salsa	Zo62, Mu12	Zygophyllaceae	10, 12	Sa, s	AN	Th	—	—	—
Tetradymia spinosa	Sh42	Compositae	1	P	SH	N	—	—	—
Tetraena mongolica	Ac58, Ac62	Zygophyllaceae	5	P, s	SH	N	—	—	Wd, Sb
Themeda australis	Pr67	Gramineae	4	P, s	GR	Ch	—	—	Na(o)
Thermopsis lanceolata	Ac62	Leguminosae	5, 7	—	—	—	—	Phr	—
Tillandsia recurvata	Sh42	Bromeliaceae	1	—	Epi-phyte	—	—	—	—
Tillandsia xiphioides	M58	Bromeliaceae	3	—	Epi-phyte	—	—	—	—
Traganum nudatum	Mu12, Oz58, Re64, Q65, Zo62	Chenopodiaceae	10, 12	Sa, h, H (s)	SH	Ch	S	—	—
Trevoa patagonica	So52, So56	Rhamnaceae	3	H(s)	SH	Mi	S	—	—
Tribulus terrestris	Pr67	Zygophyllaceae	4, 11	P, s, c	AN	Th	S	—	—
Trichocereus pasacana	M58, Wa64	Cactaceae	2 (Atacama)	H(s)	SC	MM-S	S	—	Con
Trichocereus terschechii	M58	Cactaceae	2	H(s)	SC	MM-S	S	—	Con
Trigonella stellata	Re64, Mu12	Leguminosae	10, 12	s	AN	Th	—	—	—

Table XIII (Continued)
SPECIES SUMMARY

Genus and Species	Authors	Family	Deserts Where Found	Common Habitats	Growth Forms	Life Forms	Noxious	Indicator	Uses
Triodia basedowii	B53, B60, Wo50, D55	Gramineae	4	P, s, D (b) (s)	GR	Ch	—	—	—
Triodia pungens	B53, B60, Wo50	Gramineae	4	P, s	GR	Ch	—	—	—
Tropaeolum minus	C55	Tropaeolaceae	2	FB	AN	Th	—	—	—
Ulmus pumila	Ac58, R66, Pe62	Ulmaceae	5, 6	P, WP	TR	MM	—	—	Na(u), Nh, Con, Sb
Urtica urens	C55	Urticaceae	2, 10	FB	AN	Th	—	—	Nh(o), **M**
Ventilago viminalis	Pr67	Rhamnaceae	4	P, s	TR	Mi	—	—	Na(o)
Verbena aphylla	C55, So56	Verbenaceae	3	P	SH	N	—	—	—
Verbena ligustrina	So52	Verbenaceae	3	P	SH	N	—	—	Na(o)
Verbena seriphioides	C55	Verbenaceae	3	H(s)	SH	N	—	—	—
Verbena tridens	C55, So56	Verbenaceae	3	—	SH	N	—	—	—
Verbena uniflora	C55	Verbenaceae	3	—	SH	N	—	—	—
Washingtonia filifera	Sh42	Palmae	1	WE, PC	TR	Mi	—	—	—
Welwitschia bainesii	PE37	Welwitschiaceae	13-N	—	—	N	—	—	—
Welwitschia mirabilis Syn. *W. bainesii*	Ro53	Welwitschiaceae	13-N	—	—	N	—	—	—
Yucca brevifolia	Sh42	Liliaceae	1	P	TR	Mi	—	—	—
Yucca elata	Sh42	Liliaceae	1	P	TR	Mi	—	—	Fib
Yucca valida	Sh42	Liliaceae	1	P	TR	Mi	—	—	—
Zilla macroptera	Ca13	Cruciferae	12	—	PR	—	—	—	—
Zilla spinosa	Ha51, Q65, Zo62, Mu12, Bk54	Cruciferae	10, 12	D(s), s, WE, P	AN	Th	S	—	—
Zizyphus joazeiro	C55	Rhamnaceae	Brazil	—	TR	Mi	—	—	Na
Zizyphus lotus	Ti26, Oz58, Q65, Ca13, Zo62	Rhamnaceae	10, 12	R, P	SH	N, Mi	S	—	Nh (u), Wd
Zizyphus mauritiana	Oz58, Q65	Rhamnaceae	12	—	—	Mi	—	—	—
Zizyphus mistol	M58	Rhamnaceae	3 (Monte)	—	—	Mi	—	—	Nh(u)
Zizyphus rotundifolia	BR53	Rhamnaceae	8	—	—	—	—	—	—
Zizyphus spina-christi	DF64, Mu12, Zo62, PZ63	Rhamnaceae	9, 10, 12	WP, WE, c, Sa	SH, TR	Mi, Ms	S	—	Nh (u)
Zollikoferia spinosa Syn. *Launaea spinosa*	Ca13, Mu12	Compositae	10, 12	H(s), r	SH	N	S	—	—

Table XIII (Continued)
SPECIES SUMMARY

Genus and Species	Authors	Family	Deserts Where Found	Common Habitats	Growth Forms	Life Forms	Noxious	Indicator	Uses
Zygochloa paradoxa	Pr67	Gramineae	4	D(t)	GR	Ch	—	—	—
Zygophyllum album	Oz58, Mu12	Zygophyllaceae	10, 12	Sa, s	SH	N	—	—	M
Zygophyllum coccineum	Ka62, Ha51, Mu12	Zygophyllaceae	8, 9, 10, 12	r, s	SH	N	—	—	—
Zygophyllum decumbens	Ka62, Mu12	Zygophyllaceae	12	—	HSH	N	—	—	—
Zygophyllum dumosum	Zo62, Mu12, E62	Zygophyllaceae	10, 12	r, s, H	HSH	N	—	—	—
Zygophyllum kaschgaricum	Pe62	Zygophyllaceae	6	s	SH	N	—	—	—
Zygophyllum simplex	Em67	Zygophyllaceae	8, 10, 11, 13	P, r, s	AN	Th	—	—	Na (o)
Zygophyllum stapfii	PE37	Zygophyllaceae	13	P	SH	N	—	—	—
Zygophyllum xanthoxylon	Ac58, Ac62, Pe62, R66	Zygophyllaceae	5, 6	s, r	SH	N	T	—	Wd

PERTINENT PUBLICATIONS

This bibliography combines in one alphabetical sequence for simplicity both an annotated biliography and a more inclusive reference list. Those works which it has been possible to determine are of particular significance or interest to this study within the limitations discussed in the chapter are annotated. Other competent works and best-available works on specific subjects and areas are listed without annotation; lack of annotation should not be construed as *necessarily* indicating a less important publication. The abbreviation BA indicates that an abstract of the listed publication can be found in *Biological Abstracts*.

Aaronson, A
1913 Notules de phyto-géographie palestinienne. 1 et 2. Société Botanique de France, Bulletin 60: 493-503, 585-592.

Abolin, R. I.
1929 Osnovy yestestvenno-istoriueskogo rayonirovaniya Sovetskoy Sredney Azii. Sredne-Asiatskogo Gosudarstvennogo Universiteta, Tashkent, Trudy, seriya 12-a, 2:5-73.
Sets up a regional division of Soviet Central Asia, dividing the area into 8 zones corresponding to degrees of mean summer temperature and into 6 districts with different seasonal distribution of precipitation. BA 5(1)249.

Abrams, L.
1940- Illustrated flora of the Pacific states: Washington,
1960 Oregon, and California. Vol. 4 with R. S. Ferris. Stanford University Press, Stanford, California. 4 vols.
Gives keys, descriptions, synonyms. Species are illustrated by line drawings. Habitat, general distribution, life zones, flowering times, and often phytogeographic notes. Vol. IV includes a key to the families described in volumes I to IV and an index of common and scientific names. BA 15(3) 5352, BA 18(10)22479, BA 26(3)6772, and BA 35(11) 29989.

Academia Sinica, Sand Control Team
1958 Reports on the coordinated research on the desert region, 1-2. Scientific Publications Society, Peiping. (Issued in translation by Joint Publications Research Service, 1963, as JPRS 18,658 and 18,-178. Also cited as OTS 63-21563 and 63-21341.)

1962 Research on sand control. Peiping. 508 p. (Issued in translation by Joint Publications Research Service, 1963, as JPRS 19,993. Also cited as OTS 63-31183.)

Adamson, R. S.
1938 Notes on the vegetation of the Kamiesberg. Botanical Survey of South Africa, Memoir 18:1-25.
Precipitation in this area ranges from about 5 to 13 inches, depending upon elevation. Desert shrub vegetation prevails at the lower altitudes.

1939 The classification of life-forms of plants. Botanical Review 5:546-561.
Reviews various systems, compares life-forms spectra for 5 desert areas, and finds very little in common except for high percentage of therophytes (annuals).

Adamson, R. S. and T. G. B. Osborn
1922 On the ecology of the Ooldea District. Royal Society of South Australia, Transactions 46: 539-564.
An excellent discussion of conditions, including climate, edaphic conditions, and flora, of this desert area centered at Ooldea, 427 miles west of Port Augusta and 374 feet above sea level.

Addor, E. E.
1963 Vegetation description for military purposes. *In* Military evaluation of geographic areas; report on activities to April 1963. U. S. Army Engineer Waterways Experiment Station, Vicksburg, Miss., Miscellaneous Paper 3-610:98-128.

Aellen, P. and C. Sauvage
1953 Une nouvelle espèce d'Atriplex au Maroc oriental, *Atriplex malvana* sp. nov. Société des Sciences Naturelles du Maroc, Comptes Rendus 3:45-46.

Agnew, A. D. Q.
1961 Studies on the plant ecology of the Jazira of Central Iraq, II. College of Science, Baghdad, Bulletin 6:42-60.
Considers the capacity of *Haloxylon salicornicum to* accumulate mounds of wind-borne debris and the association of other species with these mounds. These changes may lead by succession to the ultimate growth of *Zizyphus nummularia* and a more advanced community structure.

Agnew, A. D. Q. and R. W. Haines
1960 Studies on the plant ecology of the Jezira of Central Iraq, I. College of Science, Baghdad, Bulletin 5:41-60.
Notes that associations between perennials and annuals are commonly positive. The exclusion of annuals by perennials is much rarer. Deposition of wind-borne material is largely responsible for association of annuals and perennials. For example, mounds forming around the perennial *Astragalus spinosus* are fixed by annuals which add further organic matter, resulting in more efficient utilization of available rainfall by the vegetation of the mound.

Ahmad, S. and R. R. Stewart
1958 Grasses of West Pakistan. I: Subfamily Panicoideae. Biological Society of Pakistan, Monograph 3:1-151
Gives description and distribution information for this important subgroup in West Pakistan. Much of the area is desert and most is arid. Representatives of these grasses are found in all environments and at all altitudes from sea level to the alpine pastures of the Himalayas. BA 35(6)16805.

——— 1959 Grasses of West Pakistan. Subfamily Pooideae. Biological Society of Pakistan, Monograph 3:154-388.
Some members of this group are important in the desert area. BA 35(14)39101.

Aitchison, J. E. T.
1869 A catalogue of the plants of the Punjab and Sindh. Taylor and Francis, London. 204 p.

——— 1881- On the flora of the Kuram Valley, Afghanistan.
1882 Linnean Society of London, Botany, Journal 18:1-113; 19:139-200.
These items are particularly valuable because of the scarcity of botanical descriptions for Afghanistan. Contain hand-drawn illustrations and descriptions of vegetation and plants in a local area of the Kuram Valley, but include few desert plants.

Akademiia Nauk S. S. S. R., Botanicheskii Institut
1934- Flora U. R. S. S. Vol. 1-   (30 vols., of which Vols. 2, 3, and 12 have been translated into English, published to 1966).

——— 1955 Geobotanicheskaia karta S.S.S.R. (Geobotanical maps of the U. S. S. R.). E. M. Lavrenko, V. B. Sochava, eds.
Scale 1:4,000,000. Colored map 162 x 239 cm on 8 sheets 90 x 67 cm.

——— 1956 Rastitel' nyi pokrov S.S.S.R. E. M. Lavrenko, V. B. Sochava, eds. 2 vols.
To accompany Akademiia Nauk S. S. S. R., Botanicheskii Institut (1955). Added title-page in Latin. Bibliography vol 2, p. 869-917.

Akademiia Nauk Kazakhskoi S. S. R.
1962 Materialy k flore i rastitel'nosti Kazakhstana. Instituta Botanika, Trudy 13. 285 p. Referativnyi Zhurnal, Biologiya, 1963, no. 19V8K.
(Data on the flora and vegetation of Kazakhstan. Proceedings of the Institute of Botany of the Academy of Sciences of Kazakh S. S. R., 13.)
BA 45(11)48029.

——— 1963 Materialy k flore i rastitel' nosti Kazakhstana. Instituta Botanika, Trudy 15. 261 p. Referativnyi Zhurnal, Biologiya, 1963, no. 19V9K.
(Data on the flora and vegetation of Kazakhstan. Proceedings of the Institute of Botany of the Academy of Sciences of Kazakh S. S. R., 15.)
BA 45(11)48030.

Aldous, A. E. and H. L. Shantz
1924 Types of vegetation in the semi-arid portion of the United States and their economic significance. Journal of Agricultural Research 28:99-127.
A comprehensive discussion. Covers 102 mostly semiarid and arid types. Valuable for information on soil textures but includes nothing on precipitation or temperature.

Anderson, R. H.
1930 Notes on the Australian species of the genus *Atriplex*. Linnean Society of New South Wales, Proceedings 55:493-505.
A comprehensive taxonomic study.

Andreanszky, G. v.
1932 Beiträge zur pflanzengeographie nordafrikas. Index Horti Bot. Univ. Budapestinensis 1:61-147.
Hungarian with German summary.

Andrews, F. W.
1950- The flowering plants of the Anglo-Egyptian Sudan.
1956 Arbroath, Scotland, 3 vols.
This valuable contribution includes descriptions of families, genera, and species, illustrations of important species, and keys to families and larger genera.

Andrews, J. and W. H. Maze
1933 Some climatological aspects of aridity and their application to Australia. Linnean Society of New South Wales, Proceedings 58:105-120.

Anthony, M. S.
1949 An ecologic and systematic analysis of the genus *Opuntia miller* in the Big Bend Region of Texas. University of Michigan (Ph. D. dissertation)
As a physiographic entity the Big Bend Region of southwestern Texas includes igneous and sedimentary rocks; shallow and deep soils; clay soils to sands; sub-humid to semi-arid and arid climates; xerophytic to mesophytic habitats; desert, arid grassland, encinal and montane belts of distinctive vegetation, and Rio Grande Flood Plain plant associations. It is a meeting ground for faunal and floral forms of four adjacent biotic provinces.

——— 1956 The Opuntiae of the Big Bend region of Texas. American Midland Naturalist 55:225-256.
Lists 31 species and hybrids with a key for their identification. Distinguishing characteristics include growth habit, form and color of spines, presence or absence of bristles, types of fruit, and length of individual spines. BA 31(7) 22128.

Argentine Republic. Consejo Federal de Inversiones
1963 Suelo y flora. Vol. 3 of *its* Evaluación de los recursos naturales de la Argentina. Kraft, Ltd., Buenos Aires. 9 vols.
(Evaluation of the natural resources of Argentina)
A general discussion of soils and flora with particular reference to forestry. Includes an excellent bibliography.

Arifkhanova, M. M.
1961 Tugai Ferganskoi doliny. Tashkent University, Trudy 187:77-80. Referantivnyi Zhurnal, Biologiya, 1962, no. 12V183.
(The tugais of the Fergan Valley)
Discusses the origin, classification, and ecology of tugais. BA 41(3)8988.

Armand, D. L. *et al.*
1956 Zarubezhnaya Azuya. p. 190-300, 378-425. State Textbook and Pedagogic Publishing House, Moscow.
(Asia beyond the border: physical geography. Issued in partial translation by Joint Publications Research Service, 1961, as JPRS 4473)
An excellent source for physical and geographical information on Central Asia deserts.

Ascherson, P.
1903 Der nordlichste fundort der mangroven in Egypten. Botanische Zeitung 61(2):235-238.
(The most northern locality of the mangroves in Egypt.)

Ashbel, D
1939 Rainfall map; Palestine, Transjordan, southern Syria, southern Lebanon. Average for the period 1859-1938 in mm. 3rd corr. ed. Hebrew University Press, Jerusalem.
This map based on topography shows rainfall by 100-mm intervals. Local contrasts of rainfall dependent on topography are brought out as accurately as the data permit. A small insert map shows the number of rainy days a year. BA 14(5)8051.

——— 1941 Map of rainfall in Palestine. Hebrew University Press, Jerusalem.

——— 1949 Frequency and distribution of dew in Palestine. Geographical Review 39:291-297.
Discusses instruments for measuring dew, dew formation, and dew distribution in Palestine. Notes that up to 214 dewy nights may occur per year, that the amount of dew may be 0.3 to 0.5 mm per night for large dew formations, that the total dew during the year may equal precipitation (100 to 250 mm), and that dew forms during the hot months and hence is especially valuable for plant growth. A well-written publication also suitable for a person with little or no knowledge of dew.

Ashby, W. C. and N. C. W. Beadle
1957 Studies in halophytes. III: Salinity factors in the growth of Australian saltbushes. Ecology 38:344-352.
Plants were grown in nutrient solutions in which sodium was substituted for the calcium or potassium. The saltbushes did not grow when this substitution was made. BA 31(9).

Aubréville, A.
1937 Remarques écologiques sur la distribution géographique de quelques espèces d'acacia en Afrique Occidentale. Revue de Botanique Appliquée et d'Agriculture Tropicale 17(195):796-804.
This article of ecological notes concerns the geographical distribution of some species of *Acacia* in West Africa and relates distribution of various species to climate. The distribution is shown on a map.

——— 1949 Climats, forêts et désertification de l'Afrique tropicales. Société d'Editions Géographiques, Maritimes et Coloniales, Paris.
Detailed analysis of vegetation and climate groupings for Africa between the Sahara and Union of South Africa. Includes a series of original maps, scale 1:40,000,000, showing climatic regions described according to a number of climatic elements.

Aufrère, L.
1932 Morphologie dunaire et météorologie saharienne. Association de Géographes Français, Bulletin 56:34-38.

——— 1935 Essai sur les dunes du Sahara Algerien. Geografiska Annaler 17A:481-498.

Aufrère, L. *et al.*
1938 La vie dans la région désertique nord-tropicale de l'ancien monde. *In* Société de Biogéographie, Mémoire 6:351-406.
This discussion of life in the north-tropical desert region of the Old World is a fundamental work on north Africa and Asiatic deserts, and on the character of deserts generally.

Bagnouls, F. and H. Gaussen
1953 Saison sèche et indice xérothermique. Société d'Historie Naturelle de Toulouse, Bulletin 88:193-239.

——— 1957 Les climats biologiques et leur classification. Annales de Géographie 64(355):193-220.
(The biological climates and their classification)

Bailey, V.
1905 Biological survey of Texas. North American Fauna 25:1-222.
One of a series of surveys based on Merriam's life zones; includes material on the vegetation of the lower Sonoran zone of western Texas.

——— 1913 Life zones and crop zones of New Mexico. North American Fauna 35:1-100.
Another in the series of surveys based on Merriam's life zones.

——— 1936 The mammals and life zones of Oregon. North American Fauna 55:1-416.
Includes worthwhile material on the vegetation and environmental conditions of the state, although primarily zoological. Shows upper Sonoran zone in the southeast and east central north boundary along the Columbia River. States that the western arid division covers most of the Columbia and Snake River Valley of eastern Oregon and about half the higher sagebrush plains area of the state east of the Cascade Range.

Bakshi, T. S.
1954 The vegetation of Pilani and its neighborhood. Bombay Natural History Society, Journal 52 (2/3):484-514.
An annotated list of plants collected in the vicinity of Pilani, including some desert types of vegetation. BA 30(10)29492.

Bamber, C. J.
1916 Plants of the Punjab. Superintendent of Government Printing, Lahore, 652 p.
Reprinted from Bombay Natural History Society, Journal vol. 18-22, 1908-1913.

Barbour, K. M.
1961 The Republic of the Sudan. A regional geography. University of London Press. 292 p.
A very usable book with complete information on climate, soils, and vegetation, including maps. The annual rainfall maps provide a good basis for the discussion of vegetation. In his discussion Barbour makes use of a publication by J. Smith on the distribution of tree species which shows relationship of site, rainfall, soil texture and tree species. On this basis he outlines the distribution of *Acacia* from low rainfall to high rainfall, and on sands and clays under different amounts of rainfall.

Battandier, J. A.
1888- Flore de l'Algérie. II(1): Dicotylédones. A.
1890 Jourdan, Alger. 825 p.
The outstanding manual of flora of Algeria, but very rare.

Battandier, J. A. and L. Trabut
1895   Flore de l'Algérie. I(1): Monocotylédones. A. Jourdam, Alger. 256 p.
Outstanding manual of flora for Algeria, but very rare.

Battistini, R.
1964   L' Extrême-sud de Madagascar. Vol. I: Le relief de l'intérieur. Université de Madagascar, Laboratoire de Géographie, Etudes Malgaches 10.
Includes information on physiography, climate, and vegetation of the extreme south of Madagascar. A climatic map shows a thin strip along the south and southwest that might qualify as arid and a fairly large area of semiarid. Battistini uses de Martonne's index of aridity, also Thornthwaite's. Includes a 1-page black-and-white map of vegetation with description of types and many aerial and other photographs showing types of vegetation.

Baumer, M.
1960   Quelques noms vernaculaires du Soudan Nilotique utiles en écologie. Journal d'Agriculture Tropicale et de Botanique Appliquée 7(6/7/8): 299-315.
A useful compilation of common terms of the Sudan used in ecology in referring to soils, vegetation types, natural regions, geographical forms, and so forth. BA 37(3)8335.

Bazilevskaia, N. A.
1927   Ocherki rastitel' nosti yugo-vostochnykh Karakumo. Glavnogo Botanicheskogo, Sada, S.S.S.R., Izvestiya 26(2):139-153.
Includes a geobotanical outline of vegetation of the southeastern part of the Kara-Kum desert in the regions adjacent to Amu-Dar'ya and a description of natural sand-binding processes by psammophytes. English summary. BA 3(4-6)4810.

Bazilevskaia, N. A. and M. I. Suslova
1933   Izuchenie morfologii i biologii psammofitov v sviazi s vyborom naibolee prigodnykh vidov dlia zakrepleniia peskov. Trudy po Prikladnoi Botanike, Genetike i Selektsii, Seriia 1, 1:89-110. (Study of the morphology and biology of psammophytes for the purpose of choosing the fittest to bind the sands. In Russian with English summary.)
A study of plants growing in the sands of the Kara-Kum desert to determine their reaction to varying degrees of exposure resulting from changes in the drifting sands. BA 10(9)20360.

Beadle, N. C. W.
1948   The vegetation and pastures of western New South Wales, with special reference to soil erosion. New South Wales Soil Conservation Service, Sydney. 280 p.

Beath, O. A.
1943   Toxic vegetation growing on the Salt Wash sandstone member of the Morrison formation. American Journal of Botany 30(9):698-707.
Beath found that native vegetation growing on the Salt Wash members of the Morrison formation in southeastern Utah was generally seleniferous; hence forages are hazardous to livestock in these areas. The occurrence of selenium-indicator plants on other formations was also noted. BA 18(3)4106.

Beath, O. A., H. F. Eppson, and C. S. Gilbert
1935   Selenium and other toxic materials in soils and vegetation. Wyoming Agricultural Experiment Station, Bulletin 205. 56 p.

One of a series of reports on selenium and other toxic materials in soils and vegetation.

Beath, O. A., C. S. Gilbert, and H. F. Eppson
1939   The use of indicator plants in locating seleniferous areas in western United States. II: Correlation studies by states. American Journal of Botany 26(5):296-315.

———
1941   The use of indicator plants in locating seleniferous areas in western United States. IV: Progress report. American Journal of Botany 28(10):887-900.
The selenium content of 407 native and cultivated plants was determined. Seleniferous plants have been found in the Chinle, Wingate, Kayenta, Sundance, and Paradox formations in Arizona, New Mexico, Utah and Wyoming. BA 16(4)8916.

Bedevian, A. K.
1936   Illustrated polyglottic dictionary of plant names. Argus and Papazian Press, Cairo. 644 p.

Beetle, A. A.
1943   Phytogeography of Patagonia. Botanical Review 9:667-679.
A brief review of the phytogeography of Patagonia. One of the few descriptions of the area as a whole. Includes a useful bibliography.

Beguinot, A.
1915   Missione scientifica Stefanini-Paoli nella Somalia meridionale (1913). Frutti e semi della formazione delle Mangrovie raccolti lungo la costa somala. Reale Società Geografica Italiana, Bollettino, ser. 5, 4(1):7-30.

———
1918   Sulla costituzione dei boschi di mangrovie nella Somalia Italiana. Reale Società Geografica Italiana, Bollettino, ser. 5, 7 (3-4).

Beltrán, E.
1953   Vida silvestre y recursos naturales a lo largo de la carretera panamericana. Instituto Mexicano de Recursos Naturales Renovables, A. C., México, D. F. 228 p.

Benson, L.
1940   The cacti of Arizona. University of Arizona, Biological Science Bulletin 11:1-134.
A very readable description of the native cacti of Arizona, which includes plant descriptions, habitat, general range, altitudinal and geographic distribution within Arizona. Illustrations of 56 species, and distribution maps for 60 species. BA 15(8)19191.

———
1941   The mesquites and screw-beans of the United States. American Journal of Botany 28(9):748-754.
Benson, an authority on the mesquites and screw-beans of the United States, provides a taxonomic study aimed towards eliminating the confusion in nomenclature for this group. BA 16(3)7767.

———
1950   The cacti of Arizona. 2d ed. University of New Mexico Press, Albuquerque. 135 p.
A popular discussion of the cacti of Arizona including notes on the structure of cacti, the differences between juvenile and adult forms, the identification and geographical distribution of cacti that occur in Arizona. Includes excellent photographs and maps showing occurrence and ecological areas. BA 25(10)31743.

Benson, L. and R. A. Darrow
1954 The trees and shrubs of the Southwestern deserts. University of Arizona Press and University of New Mexico Press. Tucson and Albuquerque. 437 p.
The first part of this book discusses desert climates and physiography, and includes an idealized profile through a desert mountain range and basin showing the vegetational types and soil conditions. The discussion includes the Mojave, Sonoran, and Chihuahuan deserts, and the nature of the vegetation in each. Includes small maps showing the distribution of major species and color photographs of important species.

Bentham, G.
1863- Flora australiensis. London. 7 vols.
1878

Berg, L. S.
1950 Natural regions of the U.S.S.R. Translated by Olga Titelbaum. Edited by John Morrison and C. C. Nikiforoff. Macmillan, New York. 436 p.

Berger-Landefeldt, U.
1959 Beitrage zur oekologie der pflanzen nordafrikanischer salzpfannen. IV: Vegetation. Vegetatio 9(1/2):1-47.
Part IV of a contribution on the ecology of plants of North African saline depressions. Discusses morphology, anatomy, and transpiration of major species. Points out that the vegetation of the salt pans is relatively lush compared to that of the surrounding desert, and that grazing in the areas is possible, but not permanent irrigated agriculture.

Bernstein, L.
1962 Salt-affected soils and plants. *In* The problems of the arid zone, proceedings of the Paris Symposium. Unesco, Paris. Arid Zone Research 18: 139-174.
A comprehensive review of recent research related to salt-affected soils and plants. Discusses the occurrence, properties, and management of salt-affected soils, fertilizer requirements, indicator plants, and the tolerance of various plants to saline conditions.

Bews, J. W.
1916 An account of the chief types of vegetation in South Africa, with notes on the plant succession. Journal of Ecology 4:129-159.

———
1920 Plant succession and plant distribution in South Africa. Annals of Botany 34:288-297.

———
1925 Plant forms and their evolution in South Africa. Longmans, Green and Co., London. 199 p.
Describes the vegetation of the Karroo, with precipitation from 14 down to 5 inches. Includes extensive information on characteristics of desert plants, a 1-page black-and-white map, and many line drawings.

Bezanger-Beauquesne, L.
1955 Contribution des plantes à la défense de leurs semblables. Société Botanique de France, Bulletin 102:548-575.
(Contribution of plants to their self-defense.)
Includes a review of literature pertaining to the means by which plants protect themselves against plant and animal enemies. BA 31(10)30277.

Bhandari, M. M.
1954 On the occurrence of *Ephedra* in the Indian desert. Bombay Natural History Society, Journal 52: 10-13.
Lists in tabular form the localities, habitats, and conditions of substratum common to this important desert plant. Notes that *Ephedra* is often a climber, is found on gravel soil or sand dunes, and provides browse for camels. BA 30(10)29412.

Bharucha, F. R.
1955 Afghanistan, India and Pakistan. *In* Plant ecology, reviews of research. Unesco, Paris. Arid Zone Research 6:19-34.
A description of arid and semiarid portions of Afghanistan, India, and Pakistan. The area north and west of the Aravalli hills receives precipitation of less than 10 inches and is considered desert. Bharucha points out that there is good taxonomic coverage but very little ecological coverage of this area, discusses erosion problems, and makes suggestions for afforestation and windbreaks.

Bidwell, G. L. and E. O. Wooton
1925 Saltbushes and their allies in the United States. U. S. Department of Agriculture, Bulletin 1345: 1-40.
Discusses this group of plants very important in the northern desert shrub vegetation of North America. Gives descriptions, distribution, habitat, chemical analyses, forage value, and common names of many Chenopodiaceae. Includes good illustrations of desert vegetation and of individual species.

Bilewski, F.
1965 Moss-flora of Israel. Nova Hedwigia 9(1/4): 335-434.
An excellent and up to now the only descriptive moss flora of the eastern Mediterranean and southwest Asian region. Apart from a technical glossary and a taxonomic key for the genera, the paper contains a detailed descriptive text and excellent drawings of all characteristic parts of 137 species, for easy determination.

Billings, W. D.
1945 The plant associations of the Carson Desert region, western Nevada. Butler University, Botanical Studies 7:89-123.

———
1949 The shadscale vegetation zone of Nevada and eastern California in relation to climate and soils. American Midland Naturalist 42:87-109.

———
1951 Vegetational zonation in the Great Basin of western North America. International Union of Biological Sciences, Ser. B, 9:101-122.
A detailed discussion of the vegetation of the Great Basin including portions of the Mojave and Colorado Deserts. The southern extension includes some of the hot deserts where creosotebush dominates. Temperature and precipitation data are included. The author believes that shadscale is the American representative of the cold desert. Sagebrush occurs at elevations above 4500 feet in the north and 5500 feet in the south, and occupies an area generally cooler in summer and colder in winter than shadscale.

Biswas, K. and R. S. Rao
1953 Rajputana desert vegetation. National Institute of Sciences of India, Proceedings 19(3):411-421.
On the basis of rainfall the authors divide the desert into three zones: the true desert, the arid zone, and the semiarid zone. Vegetation is listed enumerated under three edaphic types: sand, gravel, and rock communities. BA 29(5)10366.

Black, J. M.
1943- Flora of South Australia. 2nd ed. Government
1957 Printer, Adelaide. 1008 p. in 4 parts.
Part 4 revised by Enid L. Robertson.

Blackall, E.
1954 How to know the western Australian wildflowers. Western Australian Newspapers, Ltd. 321, 90 p.

Blake, S. F. and A. C. Atwood
1942 Geographical guide to floras of the world. I: Africa, Australia, North America, South America, and Islands of the Atlantic, Pacific, and Indian Oceans. U. S. Department of Agriculture, Miscellaneous Publication 401. 336 p.
A list of the floras of the world, including those both general and local in scope. Gives the author, title, place of publication, and a brief resume for each flora. BA 17(1)2509.

Blake, S. T.
1938 The plant communities of western Queensland and their relationships with special reference to the grazing industry. Royal Society of Queensland, Proceedings 49:156-204.

Blake, W. P.
1914 The Cahuilla basin and desert of Colorado in the Salton Sea, a study of the geography, geology, floristics, and the ecology of a desert basin. Carnegie Institution of Washington, Publication 193.
Although concerned primarily with geology, this work provides a very useful description of vegetation as related to geological features.

Blakelock, R. A.
1948- The Rustam Herbarium, Iraq. I: Systematic list.
1949 II: Systematic list (continued). Kew Bulletin 1948(3):375-444; 1949(1):41-65.
Lists of plants collected in Iraq with colloquial names and field notes. The collection includes over 5,000 specimens. BA 23(8)24531.

———

1949 The Rustam Herbarium, Iraq. III: Systematic list (continued). Kew Bulletin 1949(4):517-553.
A continuation of the lists of plants collected in Iraq. BA 24(10)30590.

Blanchard, R.
1929 Asie occidentale. Part I, p. 1-234. A. Colin, Paris. 394 p.
This article covers the area from the Mediterranean to the Indus River. It has information on vegetation, including a colored map showing vegetation types.

Blatter, E.
1919- Flora Arabica. Botanical Survey of India, Records
1936 8:1-519.
Number 6 in a series of publications on the flora of the Indus delta. Describes the more important ecological habitats and gives lists of plants for such different conditions as sand dunes; salty and other kinds of soil; canal, river, and lake banks; ditches and tanks; field and garden crops; ruderals; rocky banks and low hills; and mangrove swamps.

Blatter, E. and J. Fernandez
1933- Flora of Waziristan. Bombay Natural History
1935 Society, Journal 36(3):667-687; 36(4):950-977; 37(1):150-170.

Blatter, E. and F. Halberg
1918a Flora of the Indian desert. Bombay Natural History Society, Journal 26:218-246, 525-551, 811-818, 968-987.

———

1918b On vegetation of Rajputana. Bombay Natural History Society, Journal 26:218-246.

Blatter, E., F. Halberg, and C. McCann
1919- Contributions towards a flora of Baluchistan.
1920 Indian Botanical Society, Madras, Journal 1: 54-59, 84-91, 128-138, 169-181, 226-236, 263-270, 344-352.

Blatter, E., C. McCann, and T. S. Sabnis
1927- The flora of the Indus Delta. Parts I-VII. Indian
1929 Botanical Society, Journal 6:31-47, 57-78, 115-132; 7:22-43, 70-96, 168-175; 8:19-77.

Blatter, R.
1914- Flora of Aden. Botanical Survey of India, Records
1916 7. 418 p.

Blomfield, R. M.
1921 Desert flora of northern Egypt. Horticulture Review (Cairo) 7(49):4-6.
The chief value of this popular discussion of spring flowers in the vicinity of Alexandria is as an aid in identifying plants.

Blumer, J. C.
1909 On the plant geography of the Chiricahua Mountains. Science n. s. 30(777):720-724.
Includes discussion of vegetation of the Lower Sonoran (or Desert) zone, which is considered to include the area below 4500 feet, but may extend up to 6250 feet under certain soil and exposure conditions. Blumer notes that vegetation on transported soils from different sources differs nearly completely, that vegetation on residual soils derived from different materials differs greatly and bears no relation to aspect, and that recent volcanic soils are almost devoid of trees and shrubs.

———

1912 Notes on the phytogeography of the Arizona desert. Plant World 15(8):183-189.
A description of desert vegetation during winter in Arizona.

Bobek, H.
1951 Die natuerlichen waelder und gehoelz-fluren Irans. Bonner Geographische Abhandlungen 8. 62 p.
(The natural forests and bush-steppes of Iran)
This most valuable work deals mainly with the tree and bush vegetation, but contains also much information on the general plant-geographical features of Iran. The attached map shows details with regard to the geographical distribution of many species.

Boelcke, O.
1957 Comunidades herbáceas del norte de Patagonia y sus relaciones con la ganadería. Revista de Investigaciones Agrícolas 11:5-98.
A well illustrated manual on the vegetation of north-

western Patagonia, on the border between the arid steppe and the Cordilleran forests. 112 species are discussed and illustrated, with special reference to their value as forage for sheep and cattle.

Boissier, E. P.
1867- Flora orientalis; sive, Enumeratio plantarum in
1888 oriente a Graecia et Aegypto ad Indiae fines hucusque observatarum. Apud H. Georg, Genevae et Basileae. 5 vols., and Supplement vol. 6.
A basic flora that still serves as a valuable reference for southern Asia.

Bondarenko, O. N. *et al.*
1962 Flora Uzbekistana. Akademii Nauk Uzbekskoi S. S. R., Tashkent. 631 p. Referativnyi Zhurnal, Biologiya, 1964, no. 6V128K.

Bonillas, Y. S. and F. Urbina
1913 Informe acerca de los recursos naturales de la parte norte de la Baja California, especialmente del Delta del Río Colorado. Instituto Geológico de México, Parergones 4(3):162-235.
Gives a comprehensive description of the northern part of Baja California and the delta of the Colorado River. Maps and photos show physiography and vegetation.

Bonner, J.
1950 The role of toxic substances in the interactions of higher plants. Botanical Review 16(1):51-65.
Discusses toxic substances in the interactions of higher plants, including both earlier investigations and recent more convincing investigations. Also reports on the author's studies of guayule and *Encelia,* and discusses the ecological implications. Bibliography includes 41 items. BA 25(1)229.

Borisova, I. V. *et al.*
1961 Spisok osnovnhkh rastenii severnogo Kazakhstana po zhiznennym formam i ekologofitot senoticheskim gruppam. Akademii Nauk S. S. S. R., Botanicheskogo Instituta, Trudy, ser. 3, 13:487-514. Referativnyi Zhurnal, Biologiya, 1962, no. 22V139.
A tabular list of some 400 species of plants of northern Kazakhstan indicating life-forms and ecological types. Vegetation types include desert; desert-steppe; rocky, sandy, and halophyte steppe; and others. BA 44(6)21945.

Botkin, C. W. and L. B. Shires
1944 Tensile strength of yucca fibers. New Mexico Agricultural Experiment Station, Technical Bulletin 316. 30 p.

Botkin, C. W., L. B. Shires, and E. C. Smith
1943 Fiber of native plants in New Mexico. New Mexico Agricultural Experiment Station, Technical Bulletin 300. 37 p.

Boudy, P.
1949 Economie forestière nord-africaine. I: Milieu physique et milieu humain. Larose, Paris. 687 p.
The most recent treatise on forestry in northern Africa and the only one on forest products.

Boulhol, P.
1940 Le pays des gommiers du Sud-Marocain. Société des Sciences Naturelles et Physiques du Maroc, Bulletin 20:60-95.
(The country of the gum-trees of South Morocco.)
A report on the phytogeography and ecology of the gum trees of south Morocco, species of the genus *Acacia.* BA 17(2)4239.

Bouloumoy, R. P.
1930 Flore du Liban et la Syrie. Vigot Frères, Paris. 431 p.

Boyko, E.
1952 The building of a desert garden. Royal Horticultural Society, Journal 76:1-8.
The paper describes the successful development of an experimental garden in Eilat in an absolute desert (rainfall less than one inch). Irrigation water used had a fluctuating total salt content from 2000-600 p.p.m., mainly sulphates. About 200 different species were successfully planted.

Boyko, H.
1931 Ein beitrag zur oekologie von Cynodon dactylon Pers. und Astralagus exscapus L. Akademie der Wissenschaften, Wien, Mathematisch-Naturwissenschaften Klasse, Sitzungsberichte, ser. 1, 140(9/10).
The groundwater relations of many plant species and plant communities of the salt- and sand-steppes east of the Neusiedler Lake are presented by maps and graphs.

1934 Die vegetationsverhaeltnisse in seewinkel. Versuch einer pflanzen-soziologischen monographie des sand- und salzsteppengebietes oestlich vom Neusiedler See, II. Botanisches Zentrallblatt, Beihefte, ser. 2, 51:600-747.
Contains a detailed description of ecological conditions and their relation to the plant communities and their succession for this region.

1946 Plant sociological map of 1:50,000 of the catchment areas between Atlit and Zichron Ja'acov (Central and west Carmel). Ministry of Agriculture, Jerusalem, Department of Ecology.

1946- Checklist of woody plants in Palestine. Imperial
1947 Forestry Bureau, Oxford. 65 p.
A complete compilation of all woody species (described up to 1946) of the region now comprising Israel, Jordan, and the Gaza Strip. It includes also those few non-woody species (such as the annuals *Centaurea hyalolepis* and *Centaurea calcitrapa*) occurring in masses as ruderals and used as fuel by the Arabs and Bedouin, thus diminishing the danger of eradication of the woody plants.

1947*a* On the role of plants as quantitative climate indicators and the geo-ecological law of distribution. Journal of Ecology 35(1-2):138-157.
The decisive influence of the IE-factor (Insolation-Exposure) is discussed on the basis of plantsociological records in the Judean desert and of microclimatic measurements. The results are used as proofs of the "Geo-ecological Law" of plant distribution. This natural law reads in its shortened version: "Micro-distribution of plants is a parallel function of their Macro-distribution, determined by the same ecological amplitudes."

1947*b* Science and erosion problems in the Middle East. Middle East Society, Journal 1(3):82-101.
New ecological methods of studying and measuring erosion in the semi-arid and arid areas of the Middle East as well as of counteractions against its dangers are discussed.

Boyko, H.

1948   Post war situation of plantsociological research in Palestine. Vegetatio 1(1):74-75.
A very brief review of phytosociological research in postwar Palestine, which names the principal researchers and centers of activity including Hebrew University, the Agricultural Research Station of the Jewish Agency in Rehovot, and the government. BA 25(2)3799.

1949a   On the climax-vegetation of the Negev with special reference to arid pasture-problems. Palestine Journal of Botany, Rehovot Series 7(1/2):17-35.
Discusses both semiarid and arid communities. Genuine desert vegetation is characterized by *Haloxylon salicornicum.* Severe overgrazing during many centuries accounts for the current dominance of the most abundant species in southern Israel. Attempts to set up a biological scale of degrees of aridity by plant indicators. Pasture problems are dealt with from various points of view and problems of rehabilitation of half-desert areas are discussed BA 25(9)26398.

1949b   On climatic extremes as decisive factors for plant distribution. Palestine Journal of Botany, Rehovot Series 7:41-52.
Discusses the fluctuations of annual plant populations due to variations of precipitation. The intensity and frequency of extreme climatic factors was found to be important in the interpretation of fluctuations in plant populations. BA 25(9)26399.

1951   On regeneration problems of the vegetation in arid zones. International Union of Biological Sciences, ser. B, Colloquia 9:62-80.
Describes new methods for obtaining plant indicators for determining climatic factors.

1952   Ecological land use map of the central and southern Negev. Ministry of Agriculture, Jerusalem, Department of Ecology.

1953   Ecological solutions of some hydrological and hydroengineering problems. *In* Proceedings of Ankara Symposium on arid zone hydrology. Unesco, Paris. Arid Zone Programme 2:247-254.
Outlines four ingenious methods that may be used to indicate climatic conditions, and discusses indicators of depth of water and of water table lowering. Includes information of value to both ecologists and hydrologists.

1954   A new plant-geographical subdivision of Israel (as an example for Southwest Asia). Vegetatio: Acta Geobotanica 5-6:309-318.
Israel and Southwest Asia are discussed as including parts of 5 principal plant-geographical belts, including the desert belt as one of the 5. The desert belt itself is subdivided into the Central Asiatic or Turanian desert-region, characterized by *Haloxylon persicum* (Saxaul), and the Saharo-Sindic desert-region, characterized by the more thermophilous *Haloxylon salicornicum,* both overlapping in Israel.

1955a   Climatic, ecoclimatic, and hydrological influence on vegetation. *In* Plant ecology, proceedings of the Montpellier symposium. Unesco, Paris. Arid Zone Research 5:41-48.

1955b   Iran, Israel and Turkey. *In* Plant ecology, reviews of research. Unesco, Paris. Arid Zone Research 6:40-76.
A general discussion of the vegetation of Iran, Israel, and Turkey, with an almost complete bibliography for the countries up to 1952. Attached in a folder is also a schematic geo-botanical map showing the pattern of vegetation in Southwest Asia.

1962   Old and new principles of phytobiological climate classification. Biometeorology 1:113-127.
After an historical review on the climatic concept since ancient times, a climatic classification is aimed at by biological yardsticks. Thus in the Negev we can find a region with an *Artemisia herba-alba* climate, another with a *Zygophyllum dumosum* climate, and, in its southernmost part, one with a *Haloxylon salicornicum* climate, all very distinctively different from one another.

Boyko, H. (ed.)

1966a   Salinity and aridity, new approaches to old problems. W. Junk, The Hague. 408 p. (Monographiae Biologicae 16)
Apart from numerous descriptions and ecological discussions of very different arid and/or saline areas the book presents a great number of new principles and methods of how to productivize the sandy and salty deserts of our globe. Boyko's own extensive contributions and those of the other contributors, particularly those of Raheja and Meijering, are also very rich in bibliographical information. Altogether 646 books and papers are referred to and with a few overlappings only, all dealing with deserts or aridity and salinity problems respectively.

Boyko, H.

1966b   Basic ecological principles of plant growing by irrigation with highly saline or sea water. p. 131-200. *In* H. Boyko, ed., Salinity and aridity, new approaches to old problems. W. Junk, The Hague. 408 p. (Monographiae Biologicae 16)
A very thorough review of literature and the experiments of the author on the ecology of plants as related to high salinity in which he discusses the following 15 principles: 1) Quick Percolation, 2) Good Aeration, 3) Easy Solution, 4) Lack of Sodium Adsorption, 5) General Rules, 6) Partial Root Contact, 7) The Viscosity Theory, 8) Subterranean Dew, 9) Biological Desalination, 10) Adaptability to Fluctuating Osmotic Pressure, 11) The Balance of Ionic Environment, 12) Raised Vitality, 13) Microbiological Influences, 14) Global Salt Circulation, 15) The Basic Law of Universal Balance.

Boyko, H. and E. Boyko

1957   A climate map of the Sinai Peninsula as example of ecological climatography. International Journal of Bioclimatology and Biometeorology 1(2)A. 3 p., 6 figs.
This map has been drawn by the new methods of ecological climatography, as an example for other regions. In view of the lack of reliable meteorological data, plant-sociological records and other ecological studies rendered the basic data for it. Graphs explaining the methods are presented in the text accompanying the map.

Boyko, H., E. Boyko, and D. Tsuriel

1957   Ecology of sand dunes. Final Report to the Ford Foundation, Sub-project C-1e:353-399.
A study of dune vegetation and of the ecology of many

single dune species (root systems, evapo-transpiration figures, etc.).

Boyko, H., D. Bugoslav, and N. Tadmor
1957 Pasture research (in the Negev). Final Report to the Ford Foundation, Sub-project C-ld:295-356.
A description of the desert and semi-desert range in the central part of the Negev, with experiments to raise its grazing value.

Boyko, H. and N. Tadmor
1954 An arid ecotype of *Dactylis glomerata* L. (Orchard grass) found in the Negev (Israel). Research Council of Israel, Bulletin 4(3):241-248.
Orchard grass, which normally grows in more humid areas, was found in the central Negev in a region of about 150 mm of rainfall. Additional runoff water was estimated to make the site comparable to one with 250 to 300 mm. of rainfall. Even so, the orchard grass specimens were thought to belong to a very drought-resistant ecotype.

Brand, D. D.
1936 Notes to accompany a vegetation map of north-west Mexico. University of New Mexico Bulletin, Biological Series 4(4). 27 p.
Includes a detailed map of vegetation types and their distribution, an extensive bibliography of articles on the flora of Mexico, and a history of vegetational studies of the region. The region is divided into vegetation areas, which include the Chihuahuan Desert, Sierra Madre Occidental, Sonoran Desert, and the Sinaloa Tropical. The Chihuahuan Desert includes three associations. creosote-mesquite, mesquite grassland, and succulent desert. The Sonoran Desert includes four associations: Colorado River delta, creosote-paloverde-cacti, Sonoran mesquite grassland, and subtropical mimosaceae-cacti.

——— 1937 The natural landscape of northwestern Chihuahua. University of New Mexico Bulletin, Geological Series 5(2). 74 p.

Branscomb, B. L.
1958 Shrub invasion of a southern New Mexico desert grassland range. Journal of Range Management 11(3):129-133.
In a comparison of changes in vegetation between 1915 and 1946 on the Jornada experimental range, it was found that 12 per cent of the total area formerly classed as grassland had been invaded to the point of dominance by undesirable shrubby species. This encroachment was attributed to a favorable climatic pattern, grazing pressure, and possibly the elimination of wildfires which formerly swept the desert grassland.

Braun-Blanquet, J.
1932 Plant sociology, the study of plant communities. Authorized English translation of Pflanzen-soziologie. Translated, reviewed and edited by G. D. Fuller and H. S. Conrad. McGraw-Hill Book Co., Inc., New York and London. 439 p.
The basic work on plant sociology that has become the foundation for phytosociological studies all over the world, especially those of the Montpellier school under the leadership of Emberger.

Braunton, E.
1926 *Clistoyucca arborescens*. Kew Bulletin, Miscellaneous Information 1926(2):49-51.

Bray, W. L.
1901 The ecological relations of the vegetation of western Texas. Botanical Gazette 32(2):99-123, (3):195-217, (4):262-291.
Includes a map of physiographical provinces and another of vegetation provinces of western Texas. Notes mesquite to be an indicator of the lower Sonoran zone and creosotebush present around El Paso and in the trans-Pecos country.

——— 1906 Distribution and adaptation of the vegetation of Texas. University of Texas Bulletin 82, Scientific series 10. 108 p.
Territory between 96th and 98th meridians is the zone of transition between mesophytic and xerophytic vegetation. At Austin, mixture is very evident: Grasslands - (1) semi-humid black-soil prairies 30-35", (2) semi-arid middle plains, (3) arid high plains below 20". High plains west 101st meridian above 2000 feet, rainfall below 20 inches (grass not named). Desert vegetation - the sotol country desert in Texas is due to edaphic rather than climatic conditions. Lower Sonoran zone west of 101st meridian is desert. Sotol country dissected foothills with loose stony debris.

Breitung, A. J.
1959- Cultivated and native agaves in the southwestern
1963 United States. Cactus and Succulent Journal 31 (4):114-117; 32(1):20-23; 34(3):75-77, (4): 112-114, (5):141-144; 35(1):14-18, (2):49-52, (3):74-77, (5):120-122.
A series covering the taxonomy and distribution of agaves in the southwestern United States. The descriptions are complete, well-illustrated, and should be very helpful to anyone desiring to identify North American agaves.

Britton, N. L. and J. N. Rose
1919- The Cactaceae; descriptions and illustrations of
1923 plants of the cactus family. Carnegie Institution of Washington, Publication 248. 4 vols. (Reprinted 1962, in 2 vols., by Dover Publications, New York).
The basic publication on Cactaceae, which, although the authors tended to split genera, is still considered authoritative. Descriptions are excellent and, even in the reproduced edition, the photographs are helpful.

Brooks, C. E. P.
1932 Le climat du Sahara et de l'Arabie. p. 27-105. *In* Le Sahara, publié sous la direction de Masauji Hachisuka. Société d'Editions Géographiques, Maritimes et Coloniales, Paris. 167 p.
(The climate of the Sahara and Arabia.)
Includes tables and maps of various climate elements.

Brosset, D.
1939 Essai sur les ergs du Sahara occidental. Institut Français d'Afrique Noire, Bulletin 1(4):657-690.
(Essay on the ergs of the Western Sahara.)
A discussion of the ergs of the western Sahara and a basic study on the formation of dunes.

Broun, A. F. and R. E. Massey
1929 Flora of the Sudan, with a conspectus of groups of plants and artificial key to families by J. Hutchinson. Controller, Sudan Government Printing Office, London. 502 p.

Brown, S.
1963   World of the desert. Bobbs-Merrill, New York. 224 p.
A very interesting and readable discussion of deserts written by a professional writer: A collection of sketches relating to climate, physiography, vegetation, animal life, and people that may be encountered in desert areas.

Bryan, K.
1928   Change in plant associations by change in ground water level. Ecology 9(4):474-478.
Discusses the change of vegetation along the Santa Cruz and San Pedro Rivers in Arizona from bulrushes to mesquite, as related to a lowering of the water table by a drier climate, arroyo cutting, and overgrazing in the preceding 40 to 50 years. BA 4(1)280.

Bualer, S. B. and C. A. H. Hodge
1964   Observations on vegetation arcs in the Northern region, Somali Republic. Journal of Ecology 52(3):511-544.
Several authors have noted the occurrence of vegetation arcs in northwestern Somalia. This article is a comprehensive study of these arcs, with descriptions based on air photographs and ground observations. Possible reasons are suggested for the formation of these arcs, which are strips of vegetation oriented lengthwise along the contours and separated by bare or less densely covered ground.

Buehrer, T. F. and L. Benson
1945   Rubber content of native plants of the Southwestern desert. Arizona Agricultural Experiment Station, Technical Bulletin 108:3-33.

Buffington, L. C. and C. H. Herbel
1965   Vegetational changes on a semidesert grassland range from 1858 to 1963. Ecological Monographs 35(2):139-164.
A comparison showed that the area occupied by mesquite in 1963 was 10 times as great as in 1858. Creosotebush was dominant on about 600 acres in 1858 and on over 12,000 acres in 1963; it has encroached upon all vegetation types and all soil textures, and was judged to be the best adapted shrub of those studied.

Bullock, A. A.
1952   South African poisonous plants. Kew Bulletin 1952(2):117-129.
An index to poisonous plants recorded in the journals and earlier reports of the Onderstepoort Veterinary Research and Service Organization after 1924. BA 26(9) 25745.

Burbidge, N. T.
1943   Notes on the vegetation of the northeastern goldfields. Royal Society of Western Australia, Journal 27:119-132.

——— 1944a   Ecological succession observed during regeneration of *Triodia pungens* R. Br. after burning. Royal Society of Western Australia, Journal 28:149-156.
A report on a study made in the semidesert savanna of northwestern Australia, south of De Grey River, where *Triodia pungens* is the most important species. Discusses the effects of burning and grazing, and subsequent regeneration. BA 19(8)15465.

——— 1944b   Ecological notes on the vegetation of Eighty Mile Beach. Royal Society of Western Australia, Journal 28:157-164.

Burbidge, N. T.
1945   Ecological notes on the De Grey-Coongan area, with special reference to physiography. Royal Society of Western Australia, Journal 29:151-161.

——— 1953   The genus *Triodia* R. Br. Australian Journal of Botany 1:121-184.
Includes a key to identify 28 species of *Triodia* and maps showing their distribution in Australia. All the species are described and most are illustrated.

——— 1959   Notes on plants and plant habitats observed in the Abydos-Woodstock area, Pilbara district, Western Australia. Commonwealth Scientific and Industrial Research Organization, Division of Plant Industry, Technical Paper 12:3-6.
Discusses the plants and conditions of various habitats, including the spinifex plains, stony rises, granite outcrops, and along the margins of the watercourses. BA 35(3) 6536.

——— 1960a   Further notes on *Triodia* R. Br. (Gramineae) with description of five new species and one variety. Australian Journal of Botany 8:381-398.
A continuation of the 1953 paper on *Triodia;* includes some minor changes due to additional information.

——— 1960b   The phytogeography of the Australian region. Australian Journal of Botany 8(2):75-211.
A discussion, primarily floristic, of phytogeographic relations in Australia and Tasmania. BA 36(1)2450.

Burgess, R. L.
1965   Utilization of desert plants by native peoples; an overview of southwestern North America. *In* J. Linton Gardner, ed., Native plants and animals as resources in arid lands of the southwestern United States. The Committee on Desert and Arid Zone Research, Southwestern and Rocky Mountain Division, American Association for the Advancement of Science, Arizona State College, Contribution 8:6-21.
A summary of the botany of the southwestern United States; discusses plant uses under the headings: food uses, drink plants, building materials, and miscellaneous uses. A very good review of the southwestern desert area. Includes an excellent bibliography.

Burkart, A.
1952   Las leguminosas argentinas silvestres y cultivadas. 2nd ed. Acme Agency, S. R. L. 590 p.
(Legumes of Argentina, wild and cultivated)
An illustrated manual of this large botanical family as represented in Argentina and neighboring countries, many trees and shrubs in arid lands being of this family. Especially interesting is the treatment of important genera of dry regions such as *Prosopis*. Keys for genera and species, and notes on useful properties of plants are included.

Burollet, P.-A.
1925   Considérations dynamogénétiques sur le "salicornietum" de quelques sebkhas tunisiennes. Association Française pour l'Avancement des Sciences, Compte Rendu 49:352-355.
Considers the development of an association of *Salicornia* in Tunisian salt marshes. Depressions in these areas are submerged after rainfall, are exposed in dry periods, and are limited in vegetation to ephemeral halophytes. With

continued absence of submergence an association of *Salicornia fruticosa* develops. The creeping habit of this plant aids in building up the sandy substratum. BA 2 (1-2)291.

———
1927 Le Sahel de Sousse; monographie phytogéographique. Soc. Anon. de l'Impr. Rapide, Tunis. 270 p. Université de Paris, Faculté de Science (Thèse)

Burret, M.
1943 Die palmen arabiens. Botanische Jahrbücher für Systematik 73(2):175-190.
A discussion of Arabian palms useful for identification. BA 19(7)13909.

Burtt-Davy, J.
1938 The classification of tropical w oody vegetation-types. Imperial Forestry Institute, Oxford, Institute Paper 13. 85 p.

Busson, F. *et al.*
1965 Plantes alimentaires de l'Ouest Africain (Etude botanique, biologique et chimique). Impr. M. Leconte, Marseille. 568 p.

Buxton, P. A.
1924 The temperature of the surface of deserts. Journal of Ecology 12(1):127-134.
Surface temperatures obtained by thermocouples and thermometers sprinkled with sand are given. On hard surfaces, paraffin of different melting points was used to determine surface temperatures.

Bykov, B. A.
1959 Geobotanicheskie i floristicheskie issledovaniya v Kazakhstane. p. 7-18. *In* Botanika v Kazakhstane. Akademiia Nauk Kazakhskoi S. S. R., Alma-Ata, Institut Botaniki.
This valuable contribution on the history of flora and geobotanical studies of present-day Kazakhstan has been abstracted in Referativnyi Zhurnal, Biologiya, 1961, No. 1V4. Publications of floras are noted as well as a geobotanical map published in 1933. Bykov notes that at present time much work is being done on large-scale geobotanical mapping and that geobotanical studies are being conducted; he includes a bibliography of 114 references. BA 41(6)24245.

———
1960 K. kharakteristike rastitel' nosti kamenistykh pustyn'. Botanicheskii Zhurnal 45(3):353-368. Referativnyi Zhurnal, Biologiya, 1961, no. 3V260.
Distinguishes several types of stone deserts in the basin of the Ili River and discusses plant associations of these desert types. BA 36(18)58882.

Cabrera, A. L.
1947 Notas sobre la vegetación de la Puna argentina. Academia Nacional de Ciencias Exactas, Físicas y Naturales, Buenos Aires, Anales 12:15-38.
A brief account of the vegetation of the Argentine Puna, with a synopsis of its associations.

———
1955*a* Esquema fitogeográfico de la República Argentina. Museo de La Plata, Revista (n. s., Botánica) 8(33):87-168.
Includes a review of previous phytogeographical studies. The country is divided into 13 phytogeographical provinces and the vegetation and dominants of each are discussed.

———
1955*b* Latin America. In Plant ecology, reviews of research. Unesco, Paris. Arid Zone Research 6:77-113.
The author discusses Patagonia Province which stretches southward from Mendoza Pre-Cordillera, includes western Río Negro and Neuquén, and most of the Chubut and the Santa Cruz. It is bounded on the northwest by the Monte, on the east by the Atlantic Ocean and on the west by the High Andes and sub-antarctic forests. He notes that in the majority of descriptions Ante-Puna Province, Espinal Province, and part of Chaco Province are grouped together and called the "Monte." He outlines the true Monte phytogeographical province as an area in the central part of Argentina running from Catamarca and La Rioja to the extreme north of Chubut territory.

———
1957 La vegetación de la Puna argentina. Revista Investigaciones Agrícolas 11(4):317-412.
Very exhaustive and illustrated study of the Argentine section of the Puna, in the Provinces of Jujuy, Salta and Catamarca, which only in its southwestern half is similar to the Chilean Atacama desert. This region is in the extreme north-west of Argentina, between the high mountains of the Cordillera Real and the peaks of the chain of the Andes. It has a peculiar flora and fauna, adapted to high altitude, cold, and dryness. The types of vegetation found there are listed according to the Raunkiaer method of classification.

———
1958 Fitogeografía. p. 101-207. *In* F. de Aparicio and H. A. Difrieri, La Argentina, suma de geografía, vol. 3. Ediciones Peuser, Buenos Aires.
A well illustrated, more popular account of Argentine plant geography, according to the author's system of 1955.

Cain, S. A.
1950 Life-forms and phytoclimate. Botanical Review 16(1):1-32.
An excellent discussion of life forms in general with some attention to the life forms of arid regions. Reviews various life-form systems, but concentrates on Raunkiaer's life forms. Includes tabular life-form data for Death Valley, California; Salton Sink, California; El Golea, Central Sahara; Ghardaïa, North Africa; Libyan Desert, North Africa; Oudjda Desert, North Africa; Ooldea, Australia; Transcaspian Lowlands; Tucson, Arizona, and other areas.

Cain, S. A. and G. M. de Oliveira Castro
1959 Manual of vegetation analysis. Harper & Brothers, New York. 325 p.
A very thorough and readable 325-page review and discussion of the systems and methods of vegetation analysis. It covers floristics, structure of vegetation, analysis of vegetation, sampling community characteristics, and life forms, and provides extensive information helpful in understanding the methods and terminology used by various authors. Includes an excellent glossary and bibliography of 425 citations.

Calder, R.
1951 Men against the desert. G. Allen and Unwin, London. 186 p.
A popular account of the interactions between men and the desert.

Caldwell, M. E.
1965   Possible medicinal uses of native plants. *In* J. L. Gardner, ed., Native plants and animals as resources in arid lands of the southwestern United States. American Association for the Advancement of Science, Committee on Desert and Arid Zone Research, Contribution 8:22-30.
A discussion of medicinal uses of plants native to the Southwest, including plants found in all plant community types from desert to alpine. Includes a general discussion of the history of plant use and an enumeration of some more important plants of the Southwest.

Campbell, R. S. and J. G. Keller
1932   Growth and reproduction of *Yucca elata.* Ecology 13:364-374.
Notes that *Yucca elata* in the southwest grows an average of one inch per year. The leaves grow rapidly during summer, droop in the second or third year, and die in the fourth; dead leaves persist for many years. The flower stalks are relished by cattle and those in reach of cattle seldom have an opportunity to form seed.

Cannon, W. A.
1911   The root habits of desert plants. Carnegie Institution of Washington, Publication 131. 96 p.
Roots of desert plants differ widely and are of three general types: *(1)* generalized, with both taproot and laterals well-developed (*Franseria deltoidea, Larrea,* and mesquite; and most annuals, whose root systems may be modified extensively by environment); *(2)* taproot type (e.g. *Ephedra,* which obtain water primarily at depth); and *(3)* subsurface-lateral-root type (most cacti, which absorb moisture broadly from even brief rain showers). Perennials with generalized systems are most widely distributed, lateral systems next. Root competition among similar types is severe.

1913   Botanical features of the Algerian Sahara. Carnegie Institution of Washington, Publication 178. 81 p.
Discusses desert characteristics in general, and compares those of southern Algeria and Arizona.

1916   Distribution of the cacti with especial reference to the role played by the root response to soil temperature and soil moisture. American Naturalist 50:435-442.
Notes that cacti usually have very shallow root systems which are subject to the influence of high temperatures but are advantageous in collecting moisture from light rainfall, and that cacti usually occur where rains fall in the warm season.

1921   Plant habits and habitats in the arid portions of South Australia. Carnegie Institution of Washington, Publication 308:1-139.

1924   General and physiological features of the vegetation of the more arid portions of southern Africa, with notes on the climatic environment. Carnegie Institution of Washington, Publication 354. 159 p.
This well-illustrated work discusses climate and general features of the vegetation, and gives detailed information on plant adaptation.

Capot-Rey, R.
1953   L'Afrique blanche française. II: Le Sahara français. Presses Universitaires de France, Paris. 564 p.
The first part of this valuable publication relates directly to flora. Discusses desert environment, limits of the desert, desert landscape, degrees of aridity, general character and changes in climate, and the effects of man in extending desert conditions. Nearly two-thirds of the volume is devoted to the activities of man. Geology and geomorphology are included.

Carles, J.
1948   Le spectre biologique réel. Société Botanique de France, Bulletin 95(7/8):340-343.

Carpenter, J.
1938   An ecological glossary. University of Oklahoma Press, Norman, Oklahoma. 306 p.

1956   An ecological glossary. Hafner Publishing Co., New York. 306 p.
A reprint of the original 1938 edition. Includes nearly 3,000 definitions and references to recent generally available papers in which definitions and concepts are discussed. Appendix includes maps of different systems of life zones, a table of biotic areas, and a table illustrating terms used at present by different schools of plant ecologists.

Carter, D. B.
1954   Climates of Africa and India according to Thornthwaite's 1948 classification. Johns Hopkins University, Laboratory of Climatology, Publications in Climatology 7(4):453-474. Contract Nonr-248(40), Final Report.

Carter, W. T. and V. L. Cory
1932   Soils of trans-Pecos Texas and some of their vegetative relations. Texas Academy of Science, Transactions (including Proceedings) 15:19-32.
A general description of soils and vegetation, including desert types, in western Texas.

Cary, M.
1911   A biological survey of Colorado. North American Fauna 33:1-256.
Includes brief but useful material on the vegetation of the upper Sonoran zone of western Colorado. Sagebrush and shadscale communities are described and discussed.

1917   Life zone investigations in Wyoming. North American Fauna 42:1-95.
Includes a description of the Red Desert of western Wyoming and other information relating to the vegetation of the upper Sonoran zone of western Wyoming.

Castetter, E. F. and W. H. Bell
1942   Pima and Papago Indian agriculture. University of New Mexico Press, Albuquerque. 245 p.
Regardless of the term agriculture in the title, this bulletin given extensive information on native plants of the Sonoran Desert (average rainfall about 10 inches), including extensive information on the uses of native plants.

Chapman, V. J.
1942   The new perspective in the halophytes. Quarterly Review of Biology 17(4):291-311.
A summary of recent contributions relating to plants which attain optimum development in salt concentrations greater than 0.5 per cent. Discusses the effect of the salts on succulence and physiological processes. BA 17 (7)17890.

Chapman, V. J.
1954 The halotype vegetation of the world. Congrès International de Botanique, 8e, Paris, Rapports et Communications, Section 7:24-30.
A brief useful review of the halophyte vegetation of the world. Notes that the zonation of maritime salt marshes is dynamic and of inland halophytic areas is static; but that in both cases, zonation based primarily on salt content can be observed. There is sufficient uniformity around the world to establish seven groups (listed) of inland halophyte areas and tropical salt flats.

1960 Salt marshes and salt deserts of the world. Leonard Hill Books, Ltd., London. Interscience Publishers, Inc., New York. 392 p.
A systematic comprehensive review of salt marshes and salt deserts of the world. Includes a discussion of the salt or alkali deserts, often of vast size, in the arid interiors of continents, and an extensive bibliography. The scope of the work is both physiological and ecological, and is related to agricultural land reclamation. BA 36 (17)54983.

Charley, J.
1959 Soil salinity/vegetation patterns in saltbush (*Atriplex vesicaria*) pastures. Australian Journal of Science 21:301.

Charnot, A.
1945 La toxicologie au Maroc. Société de Scientifiques Naturelles du Maroc, Paris, Mémoires 47:132-602.
A very useful manual which includes brief descriptions of plants (some with line drawings) and information on distribution, medical properties, toxicity, and chemical substances when known.

Chaudhri, I. I.
1961 The vegetation of Karachi. Vegetatio 10(3/4): 229-246.
Discusses the vegetation of this subtropical maritime desert (average monsoonal precipitation of 7.75 inches per year), including vegetation found in creeks and water-logged areas, on coastal dunes, on bare calcareous rock outcrops, and alluvial areas. BA 37(5)16935.

Chevalier, A.
1928 Révision des acacias du nord, de l'ouest, et du centre africain. Revue de Botanique Appliquée et d'Agriculture Coloniale 8:46-52, 123-130, 197-206, 263-270, 357-362, 432-434, 574-579, 643-650, 707-715.
These articles review and revise the taxonomy of the acacias of northwestern and central Africa; include keys, descriptions, synonymy, common names, and distribution of species; and discuss products derived from acacias. The fourth part of this series discusses the wood of the acacias, the ecological characteristics of African acacias, and their geographical distribution. Groups together the acacia species of: the Sahara, the steppes, the thickets of the Sudan, the dense tropical forest, and the dense equatorial forest. BA 3(7-8)15457.

1932 Sur les plants qui croissent à travers le Sahara et le Soudan depuis les déserts et steppes de l'Asie jusqu'au littoral de la Mauritanie et du Sénégal. Association Française pour l'Avancement des Sciences, Bruxelles, Compte Rendu 56:469-474.
This short article on plants that grow throughout the Sahara and the Sudan, from the desert steppes of Asia, to the coast of Mauritania and Senegal, indicates the widespread distribution of plants from Africa to Asia. Notes many indo-pacific plants in the northern Sahara and Sudan, and in contrast, that there are few plants common to the Atlantic and Sudan-Sahara areas.

1933 Le territoire géo-botanique de l'Afrique tropicale nord-occidentale et sus subdivisions. Société Botanique de France, Bulletin 80(1/2):4-26.
This very useful work includes a review of research in various regions of west Africa, and a one-page black-and-white map showing the territory of the Sahara, Sudan, and Equatorial Forest.

1934 Les places dépourvues de végétation dans le Sahara et leur cause sous la rapport d'écologie végétale. Académie des Sciences, Paris, Comptes Rendus 194(5). 480 p.
Chevalier concludes that the decrease of vegetation in the Sahara is due not only to desiccation, but also to the devastating actions of men and domestic animals.

1939 La Somalie française. Sa flore et ses productions végétales. Revue de Botanique Appliquée et d'Agriculture Tropicale 19(217-218):663-687.
A brief discussion of French Somaliland, including the climate, flora, especially trees with nuts or fruit, toxic plants, and forage plants, and notes on plant production.

Chien, S. S., C. Y. Wu, and C. T. Chen
1956 The vegetation types of China. Acta Geographica Sinica, Peking, 22:37-92.

Chikishev, A. G. and S. V. Vikmorov
1963 Indikatsionnaya geobotanika. Priroda 52(12): 45-52.
This paper on geobotanical indicators considers the practical application of plant associations for predicting depth, nature, course, and occurrence of ground waters, especially in arid regions; and also for indicating types of subsoils (including permafrost layers) and the presence of certain minerals. Methods used in mapping are briefly discussed. BA 46(2)5037.

Chiovenda, E.
1929- Flora Somala. Pt. 1, Sindicato Italiano Arti
1936 Grafiche, Rome. 437 p. Pt. 2, Forli, Valbonesi. 482 p. Pt. 3, raccolte Pollacci *et al.* Università di Pavia, Instituto Botanico, Atti ser. 4, 7:117-160.
Considers primarily the plants collected in Somalia, (Italian Somaliland) in 1924. For orientation, presents a sketch of the vegetation of Somalia considered geographically and ecologically, a discussion of the infinity of the Somaliland flora, and a list of wild plants used in Anglo-Italian Somaliland. The main bulk of the work is a detailed enumeration of the plants collected.

1937 La flora. p. 133-184. *In* G. Corni, Somalia italiana, vol. 1. Editoriale Arte e Storia, Milano.

Chiovenda, E. and G. Corni
1929 Le piante alimentari nelle nostre colonie. Società Italiana per il Progresso delle Scienze, Atti, p. 543-558.

Chipp, T. F.
1930a Forests and plants of the Anglo-Egyptian Sudan. Geographical Journal 75(2):123-143.
A narrative description of the chief types of vegetation of Anglo-Egyptian Sudan as encountered on a journey

from north to south. States of the Nubian Desert: "The rainfall of this region is very small and the country is a desert of sand, pebbles, and rocks. There is a general absence of vegetation except the isolated *Acacia* bushes, tufted grasses, and hard desert herbs, which occur along the drainage lines in wadis, or curiously enough on small exposed escarpments. This is the type of country which stretches westward through the Libyan Desert, right across the Sahara, interrupted here and there by areas which are entirely devoid of all plant life." BA 6(11)24418.

1930*b* The vegetation of the Central Sahara. Geographical Journal 76(2):126-137.

A report on an expedition southward from Algiers about 1,500 miles to Tamanrasset. Gives a vivid picture of the scarcity of vegetation, even at elevations up to 5,000 feet in the mountains. Chipp believes that Maire's description of the vegetation of the Hoggar Mountains is the best available. Includes a black-and-white map of North Africa with little detail and another showing routes of travel.

Chippendale, G. M.
1958   Notes on the vegetation of a desert area in Central Australia. Royal Society of South Australia, Transactions 81:31-42.

Describes an area in the vicinity of Alice Springs dominated by *Triodia basedowii* and a smaller area dominated by *Triodia pungens*. Gives a list of plants with frequency, association, and palatability. Provides a good species list for this part of Australia.

1959   Check list of central Australian plants. Royal Society of South Australia, Transactions 82:321-338.

1963   Ecological notes on the "Western Desert" area of the Northern Territory. Linnean Society of New South Wales, Australia, Proceedings 88(1): 54-66.

The western desert area has a precipitation of 9 to 10 inches, and up to 15 to 20 inches at Wave Hill north of Hooker Creek. Plant associations are outlined, principal species are identified and the efforts of grazing and fire are discussed. BA 45(2)4832.

Chippindall, L. K. A.
1947   The common names of grasses in South Africa. South Africa, Department of Agriculture, Bulletin 265. 91 p.

Chouard, P.
1957   Le centre recherches sahariennes de Beni-Abbes et les recherches biologiques et agronomiques au Sahara. Académie d'Agriculture de France, Comptes-Rendus 43(9):477-488.

Describes the Beni-Abbes center of Sahara research, and gives information on the biologic and agronomic research program of this area which is representative of the Sahara.

Christian, C. S. and C. M. Donald
1950   Pasture map of Australia, p. 104-105, *In* The Australian environment. 2nd ed. C. S. I. R. O., Melbourne.

Christian, C. S. and R. A. Perry
1953   The systematic description of plant communities by the use symbols. Journals of Ecology 41: 100-105.

Chu Chen-ta *et al.*
1961   Survey methods of shifting sand topography in desert regions (translated title.) Scientific Press, Peiping. 57 p. (Translation of this Chinese-language article available from JPRS as 16,637, or from OTS as 63-13507, 95 p. English abstract: Technical Translations 9(1):379).

Ciferri, R.
1939*a* Le associazioni del litorale marino della Somalia meridionale. Rivista di Biologia Coloniale 2:5-42.

1939*b* I rapporti floristici tra i distretti della Somalia Italiana. Nuovo Giornale Botanico Italiano 46(2): 344-355.
(Floristics of Italian Somaliland.)

Four phytogeographic districts are recognized in Italian Somaliland, lying from north to south along the coast of the Indian Ocean with their boundaries extending northwest into the interior. As an indication of the heterogeneity of the area, the author notes that only 4 per cent of the species are common to all 4 districts. BA 14(1)1364.

Clements, F. E.
1916   Plant succession—an analysis of the development of vegetation. Carnegie Institution of Washington, Publication 242. 512 p.

A comprehensive discussion of plant succession citing many examples. The principles advanced by Clements have had many followers, but in recent years his concepts have been either modified or replaced by other approaches to the understanding of vegetational dynamics.

1920   Plant indicators: the relation of plant communities to process and practice. Carnegie Institution of Washington, Publication 290:1-388.

A detailed discussion of climax formations of western North America, including extensive descriptions and illustrations of desert vegetation. It is valuable for its description of plant communities; however, many included concepts on successional processes and climax communities have been altered in recent years.

1936   The origin of the desert climax and climate, p. 87-140. *In* T. H. Goodspeed, ed., Essays in geobotany in honour of William Albert Setchell. University of California Press, Berkeley.

States that, in brief, a desert climax is one marked by the absence of forest or grassland, a critical deficit in rainfall, and a high potential evaporation caused by excessive heat and often by high winds also. In general, the 5-inch isohyet marks the disappearances of grasses on the climax level. The desert is characterized by *Larrea franseria* and associates; Death Valley, Mojave, and Colorado regions, and extensions into Mexico are recognized. Clements uses evidence of the past to establish limits of the desert climax. (Some other students of desert vegetation, notably Shreve, do not agree with Clements.)

Clements, F. E. and V. E. Shelford
1939   Bio-ecology. John Wiley and Sons, Inc., New York. 245 p.

A basic text that has been replaced in usefulness by Shelford's 1963 publication, *The Ecology of North America.*

Clokey, I. W.
1951 Flora of the Charleston Mountains, Clark County, Nevada. University of California, Publications in Botany 24:1-274.
Discusses the history of botanical exploration in the area, geology, and plant associations; includes keys to the plants occurring in the area and detailed distribution records. BA 26(4)9508.

Cloudsley-Thompson, J. L., ed.
1954 Biology of deserts; proceedings of a symposium on the biology of hot and cold deserts, organized by the Institute of biology. Stechert-Hafner, Inc., New York. 244 p.
This volume contains the papers presented at the symposium held by the Royal Institute of Biology; the symposium covered many different phases of the biology of deserts, including plant ecology. (Papers relating to vegetation are cited separately under the name of the author.)

Cloudsley-Thompson, J. L. and M. J. Chadwick
1964 Life in deserts. G. T. Foulis and Co., Ltd., London. 218 p.
Discusses plant and animal life in relation to desert environment. Injury, tolerance, and the means of survival of plants is discussed under the headings: drought tolerance, drought avoidance, and drought evasion. A good source of information on desert life.

Clover, E. U.
1938 The Cactaceae of southern Utah. Torrey Botanical Club, Bulletin 65(6):397-412.
Report of a field survey in southern Utah, mostly in the lower Sonoran zone in the vicinity of St. George. Discusses the ranges and distributions of many species. BA 12(7) 12292.

Cochrane, G. R.
1963 A physiognomic vegetation map of Australia. Journal of Ecology 51(3):639-655.
A physiognomic vegetation map based upon structural characteristics rather than upon floristic composition, and intended to aid comparison of vegetation in different areas and to provide a basis for investigating the causes of distributional phenomena. Symbols and formula are used to indicate structural features, and some merits and shortcomings of the map are noted. BA 45(18)76354.

Cockerell, T. D. A.
1900 The lower and middle Sonoran zones in Arizona and New Mexico. American Naturalist 34(400): 285-293.
Discusses the zones, and includes comments on the occurrence of palm trees in the Salt River Valley and interesting historical information on agricultural ventures in the Mesilla and Salt River Valleys.

1945 The Colorado Desert of California; its origin and biota. Kansas Academy of Science, Transactions 48(1):1-39.
A popular article that contains much usable information on vegetation of the region, describes animal life, and includes some remarks on physiography.

Codd, L. E. W.
1951 Trees and shrubs of the Kruger National Park. Union of South Africa, Department of Agriculture, Botanical Survey, Memoir 26. 192 p.

Collenette, C. L.
1931 North-eastern British Somaliland. Kew Bulletin, Miscellaneous Information 1931(8):401-414.
Discusses various types of vegetation encountered in an Anglo-Italian boundary survey. Notes the temperature and rainfall of three zones, and that periodic drought controls vegetation, which is also affected by wild fauna, domestic animals, and fire.

Collier, F. S. and J. Dundas
1937 The arid regions of northern Nigeria and the French Niger colony. Empire Forestry Journal 16(2):184-194.
Concludes that available evidence does not indicate increasing aridity in this region, which is the borderland of an ancient natural desert; however, the extent of this desert fluctuates with oscillations in world climate and was much greater in prehistoric times than now. General character of the region has not altered during the historical period, but human occupation is influencing conditions of runoff and erosion. BA. 12(5)7486.

Collins, M. I.
1923 Studies in the vegetation of arid and semi-arid New South Wales. I: The plant ecology of the Barrier District. Linnean Society of New South Wales, Proceedings 48:229-266.
An excellent description of a desert area with a rainfall of 8 to 10 inches. Includes a detailed discussion of the Barrier Range with a black-and-white geological map; discusses physiography, climate, and the vegetation of several habitats, including rocky hills and slopes, rubble slopes and plains, clay pans, crab holes and flooded flats, creeks, and sandhills. Vegetation is listed by plant families.

1924 Studies in the vegetation of arid and semi-arid New South Wales. II: The botanical features of the Gray Range and its neighborhood. Linnean Society of New South Wales, Proceedings 49:1-18.

Combier, R. P. Ch.
1945 Aperçu sur les climats de Syrie et du Liban, avec carte au 1/1,000,000. Beyrouth.
Includes a summary of the climates of Syria and Libya, with a map scale of 1/1,000,000.

Commission for Technical Cooperation in Africa South of the Sahara
1955 Maps of Africa south of the Sahara. Part 2: Special subjects. Publication 17:71.
Several important vegetation maps have been omitted.

Compton, R. H.
1929a The flora of the Karoo. South African Journal of Science 26:160-165.
Discusses the relationships of the flora of the arid Karroo region of South Africa with both flora types to the north in Central Africa and other antarctic flora types to the south. Notes the chief features exhibited by the Karroo flora as being succulence, geophily (fruiting underground), power of regeneration, unpalatability, spinescence, and resurrectionism.

1929b The vegetation of the Karoo. Botanical Society of South Africa, Journal 15:13-21.
Describes climatic factors and distinguishes six Karroo areas in the western Cape Province. Describes the western Karroo in detail, including streamside and riverbank associations. Discusses the features of succulents,

bulbous and tuberous plants, annuals, and shrubs; protection against grazing by unpalatability and toxicity; powers of regeneration; spinescence; and inconspicuousness.

Contreras Arias, A.
1942   Mapa de las provincias climatológicas de la República Mexicana. Secretaría de Agricultura y Fomenta, Dirección de Geografía, Meteorología, y Hidrología, Instituto Geográfico. Mexico.
This map of the climatological provinces of Mexico includes tables of monthly mean temperature and precipitation. Gives the annual P/E (precipitation, evaporation) index, based on Thornthwaite's 1931 publication, for 377 stations. Includes a climatic map on the scale of 1:5,000,000.

Corti, R.
1942   Flora e vegetazione del Fazzán et della regione di Gat. Tipografia Editrice Mariano Ricci, Firenze. 505 p.
(Flora and vegetation of the Fazzán and the region of Ghât, Italian Sahara)
A valuable contribution to knowledge of the Sahara Desert. Part I provides a catalog of vascular plants found in the area and Part II a statistical analysis of the flora; Part III discusses the general climate and Part IV gives the biological spectrum (after Raunkiaer) and geographic affinities.

Cottle, H. J.
1932   Vegetation of northern and southern slopes in mountains of southwest Texas. Ecology 13(2): 121-134.
This discussion of mountain vegetation in the Big Bend area of Texas was based upon studies near the campus at Alpine, Texas. The density of vegetation varied from 14.5 per cent on northern slopes to 7 per cent on a few bushes; the north slopes had some trees along with grasses.

Coulter, J. M.
1909   New manual of botany of the central Rocky Mountains (vascular plants). Rev. by A. Nelson. American Book Company, New York. 646 p.
Although published a long time ago, this manual of Rocky Mountain flora is still a standard reference for the area. Descriptions are detailed but the text is easy to follow with the aid of the glossary.

Coville, F. V.
1893   Botany of the Death Valley expedition. U. S. National Herbarium, Contributions 4. 363 p.
A basic reference but much of the information contained in this early contribution is more easily available in other sources.

Cowan, J. M.
1930   A botanical expedition to Persia. Kew Bulletin, Miscellaneous Information 1930(2):49-68.
The chief value of this rambling account is that it describes vegetation at known spots. BA 6(5)14164.

Crocker, R. L.
1946a   An introduction to the soils and vegetation of Eyre Peninsula, South Australia. Royal Society of South Australia, Transactions 70:83-107.

———
1946b   The soils and vegetation of the Simpson Desert and its borders. Simpson Desert Expedition, 1939, Scientific Report 8. Royal Society of South Australia, Transactions 70:235-258.

Discusses the general ecology and climate of the Simpson Desert. Soil types include: eolean sands, brown soils (including gibber soils of high salinity), and alluvial soils on flood plains. Describes plant communities of 12 associations. The principal species are *Triodia basedowii* and *Spinifex paradoxus.* Includes a black-and-white map of vegetation.

Crocker, R. L. and H. R. Skewes
1941   The principal soil and vegetation relationships on Yudnapinna Station, north-west South Australia. Royal Society of South Australia, Transactions 65:44-60.
This station, located 50 miles northwest of Port Augusta, in an area with a rainfall of 7.5 inches, was selected as a center for studies of soil erosion, vegetation degeneration, and regeneration by the Waite Agricultural Research Institute. The article discusses soils, vegetation as related to soils, deterioration, and regeneration. Dominant plants were *Atriplex* and *Acacia.*

Crossa-Raynaud, P.
1960   Problèmes d'arboriculture fruitière de Tunisie. Institut National de la Recherche Agronomique de Tunisie, Annales 33:1-263.
An excellent discussion on the cultivation of fruit trees.

Cruse, R. R.
1949   A chemurgic survey of the desert flora in the American southwest. Economic Botany 3(2): 111-131.
A survey of plants that might be used for food, fiber, oils, tanning materials, candy, wine, livestock food, and so forth. Lists products that might be derived from mesquite, cacti, creosotebush, and other desert plants.

Cuénod, A.
1954   Flore analytique et synoptique de la Tunisie. Cryptogames vasculaires. gymnospermes et monocotylédones. In collaboration with G. Pottier-Alapetite and A. Labbe. Office de L'Expérimentation et de la Vulgarisation Agricoles, Tunis. 287 p.
A flora of Tunisia, covering ferns, gymnosperms, and monocotyledons. BA 30(1)2454.

Cufodontis, G.
1953-   Enumeratio plantarum Aethiopiae spermatophyta.
1965   p. 1-1058. In 17 parts, issued as separately paged supplements to Jardin Botanique de l'Etat à Bruxelles, Bulletin 23-35.

Cuny, H.
1961   Les déserts dans le monde. Payot, Paris. 293 p.

Cutler, H. C.
1939   Monograph of the North American species of the genus *Ephedra.* Missouri Botanical Garden, Annals 26(4):373-427.
Various species of *Ephedra* occur in many deserts of the world and their proper identification is important. Thirteen species of the genus are described. BA 14(5) 9131.

Czajka, W. and F. Vervoorst
1956   Die naturräumliche gliederung nordwest-Argentiniens. Petermanns Geographische Mitteilungen 2:89-102; 3:196-208.
Geographical study with 14 vegetation profiles from the Bolivian border, at 22° S to 29° 30′ S.

Dalton, P. D., Jr.
1962 Ecology of the creosotebush *Larrea tridentata* (DC.) Cov. University of Arizona (Ph.D. dissertation). 170 p.
A comprehensive study, which notes the bicentric distribution of the genus in North and South America. Includes a map of the general distribution of *Larrea* in the southern deserts of North America, and another of its distribution in Arizona. Discusses various communities in which it is found, and notes periods of growth, flowering, and seeding. Anatomical studies show ways water loss may be reduced. Notes that extracts from *Larrea* leaves and roots did not inhibit germination and early growth of either *Larrea* or certain grasses, but that mature *Larrea* plants absorb available soil moisture remarkably well; the even spacing of creosotebush appears to result from moisture competition. BA 39(2)4552.

Daubenmire, R. F.
1940 Contributions to the ecology of the Big Bend area of Washington. II: Indicator significance of the natural plant communities in the region of the Grand Coulee irrigation project. Northwest Science 14(1):8-10.
A useful listing of indicators of soil conditions varying from harmful salinity and high water table to deep fertile soil.

————
1947 Plants and environment. John Wiley & Sons, Inc., New York. 424 p.

————
1952 Plant geography of Idaho. p. 1-17. *In* R. J. Davis, Flora of Idaho. W. C. Brown, Dubuque, Iowa.

Davidson, J.
1935- Climate in relation to insect ecology in Australia.
1937   3 parts. Royal Society of South Australia, Transactions 58:197-210; 59:107-124; 60:88-92.
Develops a climatic classification based upon ratio between precipitation and saturation deficit. Includes a bioclimatic map.

————
1937 Bioclimatic zones of Australia. Nature 140:265. Includes a map based upon number of dry months calculated by P/SD ratio (precipitation to saturation deficit).

Davies, J. G.
1955 Australia. *In* Plant ecology, reviews of research. Unesco, Paris. Arid Zone Research 6:114-134.
This comprehensive review of the vegetation of Australia includes maps of Australia showing: vegetation (after Ward and Prescott), pasture, soils (adapted from the map compiled by Prescott), physiography, annual rainfall, variability of rainfall, and departure of mean annual rainfall variability from world mean variability. Discusses physiography, climate, and soils, major plant formations, and pastoral and agricultural use. Desert formations include desert sclerophyll grassland and desert steppe, which occupy areas where the mean annual rainfall is less than 8 inches and monthly evaporation substantially exceeds the monthly rainfall in all months of the year.

Davis, P. H.
1953 The vegetation of the deserts near Cairo. Journal of Ecology 41(1):157-173.
Discusses major plant communities near Cairo. Notes that presence or absence of blown sand was very important in determining the type of community that developed.

Only in sandy areas was vegetation able to develop on slopes below 700 meters, elsewhere it was confined to grooves, valleys, or depressions where soil moisture was sufficient to support vegetation. Notes the Nile Valley as a moderately effective barrier to the east-west dispersal of desert plants; that the Eastern desert has a much richer flora than the Western, due to its greater relief, heavier rainfall, and larger variety of suitable habitats; and that the vegetation of the two deserts is much more similar on sandy areas than other habitats. BA 27(8)21333.

Dawson, E. Y.
1963 How to know the cacti. Pictured keys for determining the native cacti of the United States and many of the introduced species. Wm. C. Brown Company, Dubuque, Iowa. 158 p.
This very useful handbook provides a ready means of identifying the more common wild cacti and most widely cultivated forms. Few little-known or rarer cacti are included. Introductory text discusses characteristic features by which cacti may be recognized, geographic distribution, and morphology. Includes drawings, photographs, and distributional notes. BA 45(15)66044.

Dayton, W. A.
1931 Important western browse plants. U. S. Department of Agriculture, Miscellaneous Publication 101:1-214.
This very valuable treatise describes many shrubs found in desert areas, includes pictures, descriptions of the more common plants, distribution, and notes on their utilization by livestock and native animals. Text can be followed easily by persons with a limited knowledge of botany.

————
1951 Historical sketch of barilla (*Halogeton glomeratus*). Journal of Range Management 4(6):375-381.
Discusses *Halogeton glomeratus*, a very aggressive and dangerous livestock-poisoning plant introduced into the United States, including the botanical characteristics and nomenclature of the plant, and reviews literature covering its toxic properties, habitat, distribution, and life history. Includes a bibliography of 30 titles.

Dayton, W. A. *et al.*
1937 Range plant handbook. U. S. Department of Agriculture, Forest Service. 500 p.
This handbook concentrates on important range plants, but also serves as a means of identifying many common desert plants. Includes many illustrations, which aid identification, and also distribution notes and other information on many plants of the arid and semiarid parts of the western United States.

Delbes, P.
1955 Irak, Jordanie Hachémite, Liban, Arabie Saoudite, Syrie et Yémen. *In* Plant ecology, reviews of research. Unesco, Paris. Arid Zone Research 6:135-150.
This basic discussion of the vegetation of Iraq, Jordan, Lebanon, Saudi-Arabia, Syria and Yemen, includes an English summary. Known climatic conditions for each country are discussed and the major climatic regions are defined. Also discusses ecological characteristics of vegetation of the arid and semiarid zones, and the human and animal environment in some detail. Recommendations are made for improved land use.

Descole, H. R.
1943- Genera et species plantarum argentinarum.
1956 Guillermo Kraft, Buenos Aires. 5 vols. (in 7 pts.)
       to 1966.
A large set of well illustrated floras.

Dewan, M. L. and J. Famouri
1964 The soils of Iran. F. A. O., Rome. 319 p., maps.

Dice, L. P.
1939 The Sonoran biotic province. Ecology 20(2):
      118-129.
Dice recognizes the Sonoran biotic province as an important physiographic province, an important climatic province, and as a vegetation climax. The main emphasis is on fauna, but considerable information on vegetation is given. Includes a map of the Sonoran biotic province. BA 13(4)5367.

1943 The biotic provinces of North America. University
      of Michigan Press, Ann Arbor. 78 p.
A useful publication outlining the biotic provinces of North America. A map is included.

Dickson, V.
1955 The wild flowers of Kuwait and Bahrain. Allen
      and Unwin, London. 144 p.

Diels, L.
1906 Die Pflanzenwelt von West-Australien südlich
      des wendekreises. *In* A. Engler and O. Drude,
      Die Vegetation der Erde, Englemann, Leipzig,
      7:1-413.
A very useful description of the vegetation of west Australia, south of the Tropic of Capricorn.

Diettert, R. A.
1938 The morphology of *Artemisia tridentata* Nutt.
      Lloydia 1:3-74.

Dixon, H.
1935 Ecological studies on the high plateaus of Utah.
      Botanical Gazette 97(2):272-320.
Discusses southern desert plant communities of the lower Sonoran territory, including rock deserts at an elevation of 5,000 feet. BA 10(8)17842.

Dodd, A. P.
1927 The biological control of prickly pear. Australia,
      Council for Scientific and Industrial Research,
      Bulletin 34:5-44.
Notes that prickly pears introduced into Australia do not have natural enemies, have become pests infesting 60,000,000 acres, and (at the time of this publication) were expanding over a million acres each year. Discusses the selection and breeding of insects introduced to combat this range pest. (It is noteworthy that this has become one of the most successful examples of biological control of a plant pest.) BA 5(2)3813.

Domke, W.
1963 Bermerkungen zu der von L. Diels, J. Mildbraed
      und G. K. Schulze-Menz 1939-1942 bearbeiteten
      vegetationskarte von Africa. Botanischer Garten
      und Museum, Berlin-Dahlem, Mitteilungen.
      (Observations of L. Diels, J. Mildbraed and G. K.
      Schultz-Menz 1939-1942. Revised vegetation map
      of Africa.) BA 46(5)18834.

Drake-Brockman, R. E.
1912 British Somaliland. Hurst and Blackett, London.
      344 p.

Drar, M.
1948 A note on the stabilization of the sand dunes of
      Egypt. Ministry of Agriculture, Cairo. 6 p.

1952 A report on *Kochia indica.* Institut Fouad I du
      Désert, Cairo, Bulletin 2(1):54-58.

1955 Egypt, Eritrea, Libya, and the Sudan. *In* Plant
      ecology, reviews of research. Unesco, Paris. Arid
      Zone Research 6:151-194.
A very good review of ecological knowledge of Egypt, Eritrea, Libya and the Sudan, including arid and semiarid conditions, under the main headings: ecological features, taxonomic basis for ecological research, general ecological research, ecological research in relation to physiography, ecology in relation to biotic factors, and others.

Draz. O.
1956 Adaptation of plants and animals. *In* G. F. White,
      ed., The future of arid lands. American Association
      for the Advancement of Science, Washington,
      D. C., Publication 43:331-342.

Dubianskii, V. A.
1928 Peschanaya pustynia yugo-vostochnye Karakumy
      yeyo yestestvennye rayony, vozmozhnosti ikh sel'
      sko-khozyoystvennogo ispolzovaniya i znacheniye
      dlya irrigatsii. Trudy po Prikladnoy Botanike,
      Genetike i Selektsii 19(4):3-285.
Classifies the vegetation of the sand desert in southeastern Kara-Kum and discusses dunes and their control.

Dubuis, A. and L. Faurel
1956 Note sur les *Kochia* observés dans le Nord de
      l'Afrique. Société d'Histoire Naturelle de l'Afrique
      du Nord, Bulletin 47:211-216.

Dubuis, A. and P. Simonneau
1955 Contribution à l'étude de la végétation de la
      région d'Aïn Skrouna (Chott Chergui oriental).
      Direction du Service de la Colonisation et de
      l'Hydraulique de l'Algérie, Service des Etudes
      Scientifiques. Birmandreis. 125 p.

1957 Les unités phytosociologiques des terrains salés de
      l'Ouest Algérien. Section Pédologie et Agrologie
      Minist. Algér, Travaux, Bulletin 3. 23 p.
      (The plant-association units of saline land in west
      Algeria)
Characteristics of the species with regard to soil and salt content are given for two classes (Salicornietea and Phragmitetea) and 10 associations on solonchaks of the sub-littoral plain and in depressions of the Oran Plateau and Chott Chergui region.

1960 Contribution à l'étude de la végétation halophile
      des bassins fermés du plateau d'Oran. Direction
      de l'Hydraulique et de l'Equipement Rural Service.
      Birmandreis. 115 p.

Duisberg, P. C.
1952 Desert plant utilization. Texas Journal of Science
      4(3):269-283.
Discussion of utilization of various desert plants including: mescal, lechuguilla, creosotebush, canaigre, yucca, guayule, jojoba, gourds, devil's claw, mesquite, and cactus.

1963 Industrial utilization of desert plants. p. 139-168.
      In Unesco, Latin American Conference for the
      Study of Arid Regions, 266 p.

A comprehensive discussion of the industrial utilization of desert plants. Although perhaps a bit overoptimistic, this work offers extensive information on possible uses.

Duvigneaud, P.
1946 La variabilité des associations végétales. Société Royal de Botanique de Belgique, Bulletin 78: 107-134.

───── 1953 Les savanes du Bas-Congo, essai de phytosociologie topographique. Lejeunia, Mémoire 10. 192 p. (Université de Bruxelles, Laboratoire de Botanique Systématique et de Phytogéographie, Travaux 7)
An important work on the relation of vegetation to topography and soils.

Dyer, R. A.
1955 Angola, South-West Africa, Bechuanaland and the Union of South Africa. *In* Plant ecology, reviews of research. Unesco, Paris. Arid Zone Research 6:195-218.
Notes that the desert and other arid areas of South Africa have a very distinctive vegetation, in which succulents play a dominant part. Dyer believes the climate has been stabilized for a long time and notes that some of the more primitive plants are well adapted to desert conditions. He notes widespread concern over the effects of man toward deterioration of vegetation, and apparent extension of desert conditions. Discusses the plant geography of the area, and also pasture research and afforestation. Includes black-and-white maps of climate according to Köppen's and Thornthwaite's classifications.

Dyer, R. A., L. E. Codd, and H. B. Rycroft
1963 Flora of southern Africa. Vol. 26. Botanical Research Institute, Pretoria, South Africa. 307 p.

Dyer, R. A., I. C. Verdoorn, and L. E. Codd
1962 Wild flowers of the Transvaal. Illustrated by Cythna Letty. Published by The Trustees, Wild Flowers of the Transvaal Book Fund; distributed by Central News Agency, Johannesburg, South Africa. 362 p.

Earle, W. H.
1963 Cacti of the southwest. Desert Botanical Garden of Arizona, Science Bulletin 4. 112 p.
An excellent publication on the cacti of the southwest, written in easily understood language and well illustrated. Keys are included to aid identification. Cacti of Arizona are emphasized but some representatives of other areas are included.

Edgecombe, W. S.
1964 Weeds of Lebanon. American University of Beirut, Faculty of Agricultural Sciences, Publication 24. 216 p.
A publication useful for the identification of common weeds.

Edwards, D. C.
1940 A vegetation map of Kenya. Journal of Ecology 28(2):377-385.
Map includes desert shrub-grass type under rainfall of 5 to 15 inches where "arid conditions result in preponderance of desert shrubs between which are found widely separated tufts of desert grasses."

───── 1951 The vegetation in relation to soil and water conservation in East Africa. *In* Commonwealth Bureau of Pastures and Field Crops, Management

and conservation of vegetation in Africa, Symposium. Edinburgh. Bulletin 41:28-43.
Describes desert grass-bush vegetation (with a rainfall of 10 to 15 inches) and desert scrub (with 5 to 10 inches). Notes vegetation changes due to misuse. Includes a vegetation map of Kenya showing main communities.

Eig, A.
1926 A contribution to the knowledge of the flora of Palestine. Zionist Organization and Hebrew University, Institute of Agriculture and Natural History, Bulletin 4:1-72.
Lists 50 plants, many not previously reported from Palestine. Discusses changes in the Palestine flora due to increased cultivation, drainage of swamps, etc. Includes a valuable geographical key covering all places mentioned, giving exact locations and distances from well-known points. BA 1(2-3)3556.

───── 1931- Les éléments et les groupes phytogéographiques
1932 auxiliaires dans la flora Palestinienne. Repertorium Specierum Novarum Regni Vegetabilis, Beihefte 63(1):1-200, (2):1-120.
This discussion of phytogeographical groups of Palestinian flora notes that Palestine includes portions of 3 large phytogeographical xerothermic regions: the Irano-Turanian, the Sahara-Sindian, and the Mediterranean, with some Sudano-Deccanian enclaves. Part 2 contains 120 tables presenting the geographical distribution and affinities of all species occurring in the area of the present countries of Israel, Jordan, and the Gaza Strip. BA 9(7) 13143.

───── 1933 Ecological and phytogeographical observations on Palestine plants. Botanisches Centralblatt, Beihefte, Abt. 2, 50(2):470-496.
Discusses the relationship of climatic and edaphic features to phytogeographic regions, notably the rapid decrease of rainfall from north to south and from west to east to the development of 3 phytogeographical regions: *(1)* Mediterranean, characterized by hot and dry summers and generally mild winters; *(2)* Saharo-Sindian, with scanty and irregular rainfall, arid air, and saline soils; and *(3)* Irano-Turanian, with low rainfall and marked temperature fluctuations. BA. 10(1)98.

───── 1938 On the phytogeographical subdivision of Palestine. Palestine Journal of Botany, Jerusalem ser. 1(1): 4-12. Map.
The country is divided into Saharo-Sindian areas (with Sudano-Deccanian enclaves), Irano-Turanian areas, and Mediterranean areas, and the vegetation of each briefly described. The distribution of these phytogeographical units is also noted. BA 20(3)4391.

───── 1939 The vegetation of the light soil belt of the coastal plain of Palestine. Palestine Journal of Botany, Jerusalem ser. 1:255-308.
A very valuable discussion of the vegetation of the lighter soils in the coastal belt of Palestine.

───── 1946 Synopsis of the phytosociological units of Palestine. Palestine Journal of Botany, Jerusalem ser. 3(4): 183-246.
This is a summarization of many previous contributions by Eig on the phytogeography of Palestine. It provides a great deal of valuable information on plant associations, their floristic components, and relationships.

Eig, A.
1955   Systematic studies on Astragali of the Near East (especially Palestine, Syria, Iraq). Israel Scientific Press, Jerusalem; and Interscience Publishers, New York. 187 p.
A comprehensive study of species belonging to the genus *Astragalus*. This very important group includes 164 species in the Near East, and is widely dispersed elsewhere. The study is based upon ecological and geographical conditions, and provides extensive phytosociological information. BA 32(4)13406.

Eig, A., M. Zohary, and N. Feinbrun
1948   Analytical flora of Palestine. 2d ed. 515 p. (in Hebrew).

Ellenberg, H.
1958   Uber den wasserhaushalt tropischer nebeloasen in der küstenwüste Perus. Geobotanisches Forschungsinstitut Rübel, Zürich, Berichte, p. 47-74.
Comprises a bibliography on mist deserts.

Ellison, L.
1960   Influence of grazing on plant succession of rangelands. Botanical Review 26(1)1-78.
A good review of studies of the effects of grazing in various regions, including the northern and southern desert shrub regions.

Elmore, F. H.
1943   Ethnobotany of the Navajo. University of New Mexico Bulletin, Monograph Series 1(7). 136 p.
A very good and comprehensive discussion of the uses of plants by the Navajo Indians. Uses are summarized in tables under the headings: medicinal plants, ceremonial plants, food plants and food accessories, wood plants, dye plants and dye accessories, basketry plants, forage and browse plants, gaming plants, beverage plants, and miscellaneous plant uses.

Emberger, L.
1930-   La végétation de la région Méditerranéenne. Essai
1931   d'une classification des groupements végétaux. Revue Générale de Botanique 42:641-662, 705-721.
A brief discussion of plant classification systems on a bioclimatic basis. Includes maps of the vegetation of Spain, northern Africa, and Morocco.

————
1939   Aperçu général sur la végétation du Maroc. Geobotanisches Forschunginstitut Rübel, Zürich, Veröffentlichungen 14:40-157.
A general outline of the vegetation of Morocco. Types of climate are classified. Emberger believes that typical deserts do not occur in Morocco, because even the desert places receive small amounts of precipitation each year during winter, and even outside the river valleys there is permanent although very scanty vegetation, partly dominated by *Acacia* species on sandy soil, and partly by smaller bushes on rocky soils. True sand dunes do not occur in Morocco. BA. 13(5)7192.

————
1942   Un projet d'une classification des climats, du point de vue phytogéographique. Société d'Histoire Naturelle de Toulouse, Bulletin 77(2): 97-124.
Presents a classification of climates from the point of view of phytogeography (a project on behalf of the International Congress of Botany). Includes a schematic world map of climates on a scale of 1:175,000,000. The first seven pages provide a valuable discussion of desert climates of the world. A one-page black-and-white map shows areas Emberger considers true deserts, and equatorial and tropical dry areas.

Emberger, L.
1950   La phytosociologie et ses applications. Tunisie Agricole 51:65-70.

————
1951   Rapport sur les régions arides et semi-arides de l'Afrique du Nord. International Union of Biological Sciences, Ser. B, 9:50-61.

————
1955   Afrique du Nord-Ouest. *In* Plant ecology, reviews of research. Unesco, Paris. Arid Zone Research 6:219-249.
An excellent discussion of the vegetation and climate of northwest Africa. Includes a detailed discussion of Emberger's aridity quotient and compares it with other methods of expressing degrees of aridity. Gives extensive climatic data for the northwest Sahara Desert. Includes an English summary and a bibliography of 118 items.

————
1957   Les études phytosociologiques entreprises en Afrique du Nord sous le contrôle scientifique et technique du Service de la Carte des Groupments Végétaux de France. Service de la Carte Phytogéographique, Bulletin, sér. B, 2(2): 25-35.

————
1958   Afrique du Nord et Australie méditerranéenne. *In* Climatology and microclimatology, Proceedings of the Canberra Symposium. Unesco, Paris. Arid Zone Research 11:141-147.
(North Africa and "Mediterranean" Australia)

Emberger, L. and G. Lemée
1962   Plant ecology. *In* The problems of the arid zone, Proceedings of the Paris Symposium. Unesco, Paris. Arid Zone Research 18:197-211.
An excellent review of the state of knowledge in the field of plant ecology as of 1960. Discusses the fundamental physical-chemical factors in arid and semiarid zones, biotic relationships of vegetation, and problems to be solved. Concludes with general recommendations concerning the organization of plant ecology research. Includes an excellent bibliography.

Emberger, L. and G. Long
1959   Orientation actuelle au service de la C. G. V. de la cartographie phytosociologique appliquée. Service de la Carte Phytogéographique, Bulletin, ser. B, 4(2):119-146.
A review of the work being done by the Montpellier mapping service group and its associates. Explains the cartographic principles, techniques, and practicalities of the mapping accomplished. Presents details from an agricultural viewpoint on maps of central and south Tunisia, the semiarid region of Doukkala, Morocco, and others.

Emberger, L. and R. Maire
1934   Tableau phytogéographique du Maroc. Société des Sciences Naturelles du Maroc, Mémoires 38. 187 p.

————
1941   Catalogue des plantes du Maroc, p. ix-lxxv, 915-1181. Being vol. 4 of and a supplement to E. Jahandiez and R. Maire, Catalogue des plantes

du Maroc (Spermatophytes et Ptéridophytes). Société Sciences Naturelles du Maroc, Memoires hors série. Imprimerie Minerva, Alger.

Emerson, F. W.
1935　An ecological reconnaissance in the White Sands, New Mexico. Ecology 16(2):226-233.
A general discussion of the gypsum dunes in New Mexico known as the white sands. Notes that seedlings become established only in flats between the moving dunes where the water table is at a depth of 2 to 3 feet and moist sand reaches almost to the surface. The roots absorb water from a saturated solution of calcium sulphate.

Engler, A.
1904　Über die vegetationsverhältnisse des Somalilandes. K. Preussische Akademie der Wissenschaften Berlin, Sitzungsberichte 10: 355-416.
A discussion of vegetation of the Somali area. Political boundaries have changed but the observations on vegetation are still good.

―――――
1910, Die pflanzenwelt Afrikas, insbesondere seiner
1925　tropischen gebiete. Bd. 1, hft. 1-2; Bd. 5, hft. 1. Engelmann, Leipzig. (Die Vegetation der Erde 9)
Presents information on the plant world of Africa, especially of the tropical regions.

Espenshade, E. B., Jr.
1964　Goode's world atlas. 12th ed. Rand McNally. 288 p.

Evans, P. A.
1926　An ecological study in Utah. Botanical Gazette 82(3):253-285.
The region described comprises the greater portion of Salt Lake County, Utah, and includes the narrow strip of the Great Basin from the Great Salt Lake to the western foothills of the Wasatch Range. The soil on the west side of the Jordan River is alkaline and therefore covered by a sparse growth of alkali-tolerant plants; the soil east of the river is higher, well drained, and mostly under cultivation. BA. 2(6-8)9136.

Evenari, M.
1938a　Root conditions of certain plants of the wilderness of Judaea. Linnean Society of London, Journal, Botany 51(340):383-388.

―――――
1938b　The physiological anatomy of the transpiratory organs and the conducting systems of certain plants typical of the wilderness of Judaea. Linnean Society of London, Journal, Botany 51(340):389-407.
The discussion of anatomical structures indicates characteristics of desert plants of the area. The plants vary from herbaceous with xeromophic characteristics, to non-herbaceous xeromorphic plants, and to succulents with xeric characteristics. The life forms of roots of nine perennial and three annual plants were investigated and found to vary from those that penetrated only a few centimeters to those that were deeply rooted. It was noted that the area occupied by the roots of all desert perennials is relatively large. BA. 13(8)12584.

―――――
1962　Plant physiology and arid zone research. In The problems of the arid zone, Proceedings of the Paris Symposium. Unesco, Paris. Arid Zone Research 18:175-195.

In the author's words, "The different branches of botany in conjunction with climatology, meterology, and soil science, are needed to elucidate the ecological relationship between vegetation and environment (synecology) and between the individual plant and environment (autecology) . . . Plant ecology and sociology establish the facts of the ecological relationship between the plant and its arid environment. The role of plant physiology is to find out the physiological mechanism underlying this relationship."

Evenari, M. and R. Richter
1937　Physiological-ecological investigations in the wilderness of Judaea. Linnean Society of London, Journal, Botany 51:333-381.
Includes plant lists, microclimatic data, and extensive material on the physiological relationships of plants.

Everist, S. L.
1949　Mulga (*Acacia aneura* F. Muell.) in Queensland. Queensland Journal of Agricultural Science 6: 87-139.
The area considered lies between the 8-inch and 20-inch isohyets, and is therefore mostly out of the desert area; nevertheless this work provides information useful to the study of deserts. Discusses climate, topography, soils, fodder value, and management. An appendix lists 256 species collected east of Wyandra. The distribution of mulga is shown by a map and associated plants are briefly described.

Exell, A. W. and F. A. Mendonça
1937-　Conspectus florae Angolensis. Vols. 1-3 (in 5
1962　parts). (v. 3, 1962, joint author with Exell: A. Fernandes).

Eymann, J. L.
1953　A study of the sand dunes in the Colorado and Mojave Deserts. University of Southern California (unpublished Master's thesis). 91 p.

Faurel, L., P. Ozenda, and G. Schotter
1953　Les lichens du Sahara algérien. In Desert Research, proceedings of the international symposium held in Jerusalem, May 7-14, 1952, sponsored by the Research Council of Israel and Unesco. Research Council of Israel, Special Publication. 2:310-318.
Lists the lichens of the Algerian Sahara and the principal publications covering the lichen floras. Includes some comments on the lichen flora as related to desert conditions.

Fautin, R. W.
1946　Biotic communities of the northern desert shrub biome in western Utah. Ecological Monographs 16(4):251-310.
Discusses sagebrush and shadscale communities. Notes that sagebrush communities occur along the windward base of mountains or in valleys where the precipitation is greater, or the soil is deep, more permeable, and relatively salt-free; and that shadscale and closely related communities occur in more xeric areas where the soil is often heavily impregnated with mineral salts. Temperature conditions for both communities are similar. The average precipitation is nearly 5 inches for sagebrush, compared to about 8 inches for shadscale areas.

Feinbrun, N. and M. Zohary
1955   A geobotanical survey of Transjordan. Research Council of Israel, Bulletin Section D, Botany 5(1):5-35.
The main physiographic features of the country are described; maps are included showing soil types, rainfall, and vegetation. The country includes three phytogeographical territories: Mediterranean (largely forest associations), Irano-Turanian (steppe associations), and Saharo-Sindian (associations mostly found on stony Hammadas, Nubian sandstone, or granite sand). BA 31 (4)11247.

Fenton, L.
1949   Climate of the Lake Victoria plateau. University of Western Australia, Nedlands, Economics Department, Geographical Laboratory, Research Report 6. 15 p.
Includes maps based upon climate classification by Thornthwaite (1931), Köppen, dry months, and wet months.

Fireman, M. and H. E. Hayward
1952   Indicator significance of some shrubs in the Escalante Desert, Utah. Botanical Gazette 14(2): 143-155.
A report of a study of desert shrubs as possible indicators of agricultural potentialities of new lands. Plants and soils were examined to determine pH of soluble salt content and exchangeable sodium percentage. Soluble salt content was found to be higher under shadscale and greasewood than under sagebrush. The pH value in exchangeable sodium percentage was highest under greasewood. BA 27(7)18882.

1920-   The Flowering Plants of Africa, a magazine containing hand-coloured figures with descriptions of the flowering plants indigenous to South Africa (1920-1944, called Flowering Plants of South Africa). Government Printer, Pretoria. Editors: I. B. Pole Evans (v. 1-19, 1920-1939), E. P. Phillips (v. 20-24, 1940-1944), R. A. Dyer (v. 25, 1945-

Flowers, S.
1934   Vegetation of the Great Salt Lake region. Botanical Gazette 95(3):353-418.
A report of a study of water, swamps, springs, deltas, and salt marshes in the area, and analysis of the vegetation to determine salt content. On the basis of these investigations certain plants can be used as indicators of saline conditions. BA 9(1)159.

1961   Vegetation of the Navajo reservoir basin in Colorado and New Mexico. *In* A. M. Woodbury, *et al.*, Ecological studies of the flora and fauna of Navajo reservoir basin, Colorado and New Mexico. University of Utah, Anthropological Papers 55:15-46.
A good discussion of the flora and fauna of a typical arid area in Colorado and New Mexico.

Flowers, S. and F. R. Evans
1966   The flora and fauna of the Great Salt Lake region, Utah. p. 367-392. *In* H. Boyko, ed., Salinity and aridity, new approaches to old problems. W. Junk, The Hague. 408 p. (Monographiae Biologicae 16)
Discusses adaptation of plants and animals to saline conditions.

Foley, H. and L. Musso
1925   Les plantes du Sahara toxiques pour les animaux. Présence d'un glucoside cyanhydrique dans le *Lotus jolyi* Battandier. Institut Pasteur d'Algérie, Archives 3:394-400.

Follmann, G.
1960   Eine dornbewohnende flechtengesellschaft der zentralchilenischen sukkulentenformationen mit kennzeichnen der *Chrysothrix noli-tangere* Mont. Deutsche Botanische Gesellschaft, Berichte 74 (10):449-462.
A discussion of a lichen association that covers the thorns of succulent plants under conditions of high atmospheric humidity in central Chile.

_____
1961a   Eine dornbewohnende flechtengesellschaft der nordchilenischen sukkulentenformationen mit kennzeichnen der *Anaptychia intricata* (Desf.) Mass. Deutsche Botanische Gesellschaft, Berichte 74(10):495-510.
Presents information on lichens growing on thorns, shrubs, and succulents under conditions of high humidity.

_____
1961b   Acerca de la fitosociología de Chile. Universidad de Chile, Boletín 3(23):31-33.
A review of the most important plant associations of Chile and their economic significance.

Forbes, R. H.
1895   The mesquite tree, its products and uses. Arizona Agricultural Experiment Station, Bulletin 13: 13-26.
Discusses products that may be derived from the mesquite tree, including a handsome durable wood, fuel of high value, excellent charcoal, food and forage, medicinal and industrial gums and resins, and (from the flowers) honey. Although published long ago this is still a valuable reference.

Fosberg, F. R.
1940   The aestival flora of the Mesilla Valley region, New Mexico. American Midland Naturalist 23(3):573-593.
Notes that creosotebush flourishes where drainage is good and develops best on limestone alluvial fans and recent volcanic flows. Along washes it is not abundant but is luxuriant in growth. On porphyritic hills stunted creosotebush is almost the only plant. Grasslands and chaparral are found above the desert area.

Fourneau, F.
1896   Essai de catalogue des noms arabes er berbères de quelques plantes, arbustes et arbres algériens et sahariens ou introduits et cultivés en Algérie. Paris. 48 p.
A catalog of Arabian and Berber names for some plants, shrubs, and trees, native to Algeria and the Sahara, or introduced and cultivated in Algeria.

Fournier, P.
1958   Les "chardons roulants" de divers genres et de divers pays. Société Botanique de France, Bulletin 105(7/8):354-356.
A brief but interesting discussion of the "rolling thistles" of different genera occurring in different parts of the world and often commonly called tumbleweeds. BA 34(3)8384.

Foury, A.
1952 La *Kochia*. Essais de *Kochia scoparia* L. Schrad. var. trichophylla Host. et de *Kochia indica* Wight au Maroc. Terre Marocaine 26(266):1-6.

Fries, R. E.
1905 Zu kenntnis der alpinen flora im nördlichen Argentinien. Nova Acta Regiae Societatis Scientiarum Upsaliensis, ser. 4, 1:1-205.
The first comprehensive exploration of the Argentine portion of the Puna desert; describes its vegetation very carefully, establishes for the first time plant communities and gives the diagnoses of a number of unknown desert plants.

Gabriel, A.
1961 Die wüsten der erde und ihre erforschung. Springer Verlag, Berlin. 167 p.
A general treatise on the deserts of the world giving extensive information on their use and occupancy by man, and many other subjects applicable to deserts. Five small black-and-white maps show the Namib in South Africa, the Atacama in South America, the northern desert belt of the old world, Australia, and North America.

Gahlbach, F. R.
1963 The Guadalupe ecosystem: an approach to basic plant ecological research in the National Park Service. University of Michigan (Ph.D. dissertation).
Includes a discussion of the Chihuahuan Desert and Desert Shrub formations, and their constituent communities. Density, frequency, coverage, height, and distribution data are included.

Galbraith, J.
1959- Australian wattles. Nos. 1-17, 22-34. Victorian
1962 Naturalist 76-78.

García, E., C. Soto, and F. Miranda
1960 *Larrea* y clima. Universidad Nacional de México, Instituto de Biología, Anales 31(1/2): 133-171.
The creosotebush, *Larrea tridentata,* is one of the most characteristic plants of the arid region of northern Mexico. This work discusses its distributional limits in North America and those of the similar *Larrea divaricata* in South America.

Gardner, C. A.
1942 The vegetation of Western Australia. Royal Society of Western Australia, Journal 28:11-77.
An excellent summary of the vegetation of Western Australia, its origins, relationships to other areas, and ecology of various communities. Includes helpful tables and maps relating to plants and physical conditions.

1952a Flora of Western Australia. W. H. Wyatt, Government Printer, Perth. Vol. 1.
Vegetation map of Western Australia. Forests Department, Western Australia, Perth. 1928. 83 x 57 cm. Scale: 1:3,168,000.

1952b The wedge-leaved rattlepod (*Crotalaria retusa* L.), a poison plant of tropical Australia. Journal of Agriculture of Western Australia 1(5):641-647.

1952- Poison plants of Western Australia. Journal of
1958 Agriculture of Western Australia. A series of papers (some with H. W. Bennetts) appearing in various issues beginning with vol. 1 of the 3d ser., and continuing through vol 7.

1952- Trees of Western Australia. Journal of Agriculture
1963 of Western Australia. A series of papers appearing in various issues beginning with 3d ser., vol. 1, and continuing through 4th ser., vol. 4.

1955 New species of toxic plants from Western Australia. Western Australian Naturalist 4(8): 185-187.

1957 The fire factor in relation to the vegetation of Western Australia. Western Australian Naturalist 5(7):166-173.
The author presents evidence to show that fire is a factor affecting plants and has been so in Western Australia for a long time, also that absolute protection from fire in thicket formations has a detrimental effect on the vegetation. BA 32(9)29531.

1959 The vegetation of Western Australia. *In* A. Keast, R. I. Crocker, and C. S. Christian, eds., Biogeography and ecology in Australia. Monographiae Biologicae 8:274-282.
A brief description of the vegetation of Western Australia; various vegetation associations are shown on a black-and-white map. This is largely a floristic discussion and very little text is devoted to the desert.

Gardner, C. A. and H. W. Bennetts
1956 Toxic plants of Western Australia. West Australian Newspapers, Periodical Division, Perth. 253 p.

Gardner, J. L.
1951 Vegetion of the creosotebush area of the Rio Grande valley in New Mexico. Ecological Monographs 21(4):379-403.

Gates, D. H., L. A. Stoddart, and C. W. Cook
1956 Soil as a factor influencing plant distribution on salt-deserts of Utah. Ecological Monographs 26: 155-175.
A report of a study of relatively pure stands of sagebrush, winterfat, shadscale, Nuttal saltbush, and greasewood. Concludes that all were unreliable indicators of specific soil characteristics but in some instances could be used to determine upper limits. Sagebrush and winterfat had lower salt-content tolerance than the other three plants.

Gentilli, J.
1948 Two climatic systems applied to Australia. Australian Journal of Science 11:13-16.
Compares maps based upon Köppen and Thornthwaite (1931) classifications, and discusses their relationships to vegetational regions.

Gentry, H. S.
1942 Río Mayo plants. Carnegie Institution of Washington, Publication 527. 328 p.
A very useful discussion of the flora and vegetation of the southern part of the Sonoran Desert in northwest Mexico, also the vegetation of the higher areas including the Sierra Madre Occidental. Includes good photographs of vegetation and special plants, and an annotated list which gives scientific and local vernacular names for each species, local distribution and habitat, but no plant descriptions. BA. 19(2)3446.

Gerth Van Wijk, H. L.
1909- A dictionary of plant names. A. Asher and
1962 Company, Amsterdam. 2 vols. in 3.

Includes vernacular names of wild and cultivated plants in four languages (English, French, German, and Dutch), also vernacular names for flowers, fruits, and other parts used in medicine and industry. Publication chronology: vol. 1, parts 1-2, originally published 1909-1910, reprinted 1962; v. 2 (index) published 1916.

Giess, W.
1962   Some notes on the vegetation of Namib desert with a list of plants collected in the area visited by the Cape-Transvaal Museum expedition during May, 1959. Cimbebasia 2:1-35. (German summary).
Considers the area as four ecological regions: the red sand dunes, the river beds, the Namib flats, and the mountains. Discusses the vegetation of each region individually, and lists plants collected in the area. Each species is described briefly with respect to habit and habitat. BA 45(5)21283.

Gillett, J. B.
1941   The plant formations of Western British Somaliland and the Harar Province of Abyssinia. Kew Bulletin 1941(2):37-199.

Gilliland, H. B.
1952   The vegetation of eastern British Somaliland. Journal of Ecology 40:91-124.
The precipitation in this area varies from 5 to nearly 20 inches. There is a desert vegetation at the lower elevation and a gypsum-tolerant vegetation. Gilliland believes that desert conditions did not always obtain in their present severity, but that available evidence of past climate indicated greater rainfall than at present. Deterioration of vegetation from grazing of domestic stock is also evident.

Gillman, C.
1949   A vegetation-type map of Tanganyika Territory. Geographical Review 39(1):7-37.
Includes an excellent colored map of Tanganyika Territory (now Tanzania) on a scale of 1:2,000,000, which shows scattered areas of desert in the northeast region of the territory. On areas of desert and semidesert crosshatching indicates areas of vegetation actively induced by natives and actively induced by aliens. Includes very little discussion of desert types.

Githens, T. S.
1949   Drug plants of Africa. University of Pennsylvania Press, Philadephia. 125 p. (African Handbook 8)

Gleason, H. A. and A. Cronquist
1964   The natural geography of plants. Columbia University Press, New York. 420 p.
A well-illustrated and readable discussion of plant geography of value to both layman and scientist. The 233 pages of illustrations depict different plants, plant communities, plant migration, and general plant and area characteristics in North America, and a few examples from other parts of the world.

Glendinning, R. M.
1949   Desert contrasts illustrated by the Coachella. Geographical Review 39:220-228.
Discusses the Coachella Valley portion of the Colorado Desert of California. The valley originally had desert vegetation with some halophytic types near the Salton Sea. Paloverde and smoketree occur on fans and pediments, and some cacti are scattered through the area.

Goldman, E. A.
1916   Plant records of an expedition to Lower California. U. S. National Herbarium, Contributions 16:309-371.
A very well illustrated and useful series of descriptions of some of the more distinctive plants in lower California; includes data on distribution, and notes on habits and habitats.

───────

1951   Biological investigations in Mexico. Smithsonian Miscellaneous Collections 115. 476 p. 71 pl.
A report of a biological exploration by E. W. Nelson and E. A. Goldman in Mexico from 1892 to 1906. A vast store of information is preserved in thousands of pages of manuscript reports. Eight life zones are recognized and 18 biotic provinces. Desert areas, including Baja California, are well represented in their collections, which include more than 10,000 plants.

Goldman, E. A. and R. T. Moore
1946   The biotic provinces of Mexico. Journal of Mammalogy 26:347-360.
Desert provinces include the Sonora, Vizcaíno, and Chihuahua-Zacatecas. Gives brief lists of the common plants of each biotic province.

Golovkova, A. G.
1961   O flore Tsentral'nogo Tyan'-Shanya. *In:* Materialy k X Nauchnoi konferentsii professional'noprepodavatel'skogo sostava. Kirgizskii Universitet Sektsiya biologicheskikh nauk. Frunze. 27-31. Referativnyi Zhurnal, Biologiya, 1963, no. 9V150. (Flora of the Central Tien Shan. *In:* Materials for the 10th scientific conference of the professional teaching staff. Kirgiz University, Biological Sciences Section)
Central Tien Shan has a rich and varied flora because it it located at the junction of various floristic regions. A list is given of the main dominants (74 spp.). The deserts and steppes have a poor floristic composition which includes autochthonic, as well as southeast Asian, Turan, central Asian, arctic-alpine, and Eurasian steppe floral elements. BA 45(6):25797.

Gómez-Pompa, A.
1963   El género *Agave*. Cactáceas y Suculentas Mexicanas 8(1):3-28.
The genus *Agave* has many varied uses and is of great economic importance in Mexico. The genus is exceptionally complex and the taxonomy presents many difficulties, partly because of the extreme variability within species. Species are found from Utah to Maryland, and south to Colombia and the West Indies, especially in dry areas. BA 45(17)74846.

Good, R.
1964   The geography of the flowering plants. 3rd ed. John Wiley, New York. 518 p.
A revised two-part edition with updated information. The first part contains 15 chapters on the floristic regions of the world; the second contains 8 chapters covering factors of distribution and the theory of tolerance. Includes a bibliography of 838 references and an index of plant names. BA 46(2)7961.

Goodspeed, T. H.
1945   Notes on the vegetation and plant resources of Chile. p. 145-149. *In* Plants and plant science in Latin America. Chronica Botanica Co., Waltham, Mass.

A brief account of the principal vegetation types of Chile, with plant geographical notes, followed by a discussion of botanical history, agriculture, and timber resources. BA 20(1)194.

Goodwin, D. L.
1956 Autecological studies of *Artemisia tridentata* nutt. State College of Washington (Ph. D. dissertation). 79 p.
A report of studies of the disseminule, seeding, and mature plant (common name, big sagebrush). Maximum distance of wind dissemination was 33 meters. Temperatures above 25° C. inhibited germination. Field germination began the first week of February and ceased in April. Root systems of seedlings continued to develop even though air temperatures were below freezing. On deep well-aerated soil the root system consisted of a tap root with few lateral roots, but where soil was shallow and contained hardpan, a root system of many widely branching laterals was formed.

Gorschkova, S. G.
1957 Salt cedars (*Tamarix*, Tamaricaceae) of the Soviet Union. Southwestern Naturalist 2(2-3): 48-73.
An English translation of the account of the genus *Tamarix* in *Flora U. R. S. S.*, Vol. 15, 1949. Attempts to identify the American members of this group in relation to the Russian taxonomy. BA 32(5)17231.

Gould, F. W.
1962 Texas plants: A checklist and ecological summary. Texas Agricultural Experiment Station, Miscellaneous Publication 585:3-112.
This publication on vascular plants of Texas summarizes environmental factors and ecological associations in the 10 vegetational areas of the state. Gives scientific and common names, and tells whether the plants are annual or perennial, warm-seasonal or cool-seasonal, and introduced or of native origin. Provides extensive valuable information on the ecological factors of the plants and the associations in which they occur.

Gounot, P.
1958 Contribution à l'étude des groupements végétaux messicoles et rudéraux de la Tunisie. Service Botanique et Agronomique de Tunisie, Annales 31. 283 p.

——— 1961 Les méthodes d'inventaire de la végétation. Service de la Carte Phytogéographique, Bulletin, sér. B, 6(1):7-73.

Graham, E. H.
1937 Botanical studies in the Uinta Basin of Utah and Colorado. Carnegie Museum, Annals 26:1-432.
A useful desert reference as the lower altitude area falls within the scope of desert study. Includes a sketch of physiography, geology, and climate, compares altitudinal vegetation zones of various workers in surrounding regions, and divides the mixed desert shrub into 7 associations, giving a good discussion of plant communities for each.

Granitov, I. I.
1961 Nekotorye bio-ekologicheskie cherty flory Kzyl-Kumov. Tashkentskogo Universiteta (U.S.S.R.), Trudy 187:102-110. Referativnyi Z h u r n a l Biologiya, 1962, no. 16V123.
This work on the bioecological features of the flora of the Kyzyl-Kum desert, gives an analysis of the flora,

noting distribution by habitats, ecological forms, adaptive features, methods of root propagation, times of flowering and fruit bearing, and color of flowers. Gives information on about 900 species. BA 43(2)4360.

Greenway, P. J.
1943 Second draft report on vegetation classification for the approval of the vegetation committee. Pasture Research Conference, Amani, East African Agricultural Research Station. 84 p.

Grenard, F.
1929 Haute Asie. p. 235-394. *In* R. Blanchard, Asie occidentale. A. Colin, Paris.
A regional description including climate and vegetation for central Asia, but unfortunately there is little on vegetation.

Grossweiler, J.
1948- Flora exótica de Angola. Agronomia Angolana 1950 1:121-198; 2:173-255; 3:143-167.
A 3-part treatise on the flora of Angola, a minor part of which is desert. Lists more than 800 species of plants of economic importance, giving notes on origin, geographic distribution, uses, and economic importance. It is believed that many species now in Angola were introduced from India, southern Europe, and northern Africa through the caravan and slave trade before the arrival of the Portuguese. BA 25(1)2652.

Grubov, V. I. and A. A. Unatov
1952 Main characteristics of the flora of the Mongol People's Republic in connection with its districting (translated title). Botanicheskii Zhurnal 37(1): 45-64.
Notes that studies of the Mongolian flora were initiated by Russian scientists in the early eighteenth century. The list of plants prepared by the Botanical Institute totals about 1600. Considers the Mongolian People's Republic to include 16 floral districts, and describes the flora by species. BA 29(7)17054.

Gruenberg-Fertig, I.
1954 On the "Sudano-Deccanic" element in the flora of Palestine. Research Council of Israel, Bulletin 4(3):234-240.
This article has little value except that it advances an idea on distribution relation of species in the area different from that of Eig (1931-1932). Contrary to Eig, the author believes there is little relationship between the flora of Sudan and of the Deccan Peninsula. BA 30(9) 24825.

Guenther, K.
1930 Biologisch-physiognomische landschaftsstudien in Palästina, Syrien, Mesopotamien. Naturforschende Gesellschaft, Freiburg, Bericht 30(1/2):313-334.
A colorful description of the biologic-physiognomic relationship in Palestine, Syria, and Mesopotamia, only a small amount of which pertains to desert. BA 7(9) 20409.

Guest, E. R.
1953 The Rustam Herbarium, Iraq. VI: General and ecological account. Kew Bulletin 1953(3): 383-403.
Presents a general geographical description of the modern state of Iraq, then discusses the physiography of the country, giving descriptions of the main physical regions. Discusses climate, soils, geology, and finally ecology, and

the vegetation of various physical regions of Iraq. Cultivated areas are considered in some detail. BA 28(7) 15377.

Guest, E. R.
1966   Flora of Iraq. Vol. I: Introduction to the flora. An account of the geology, soils, climate and ecology of Iraq with gazetteer, glossary, and bibliography, with assistance from Ali Al-Rawi. Republic of Iraq, Ministry of Agriculture. 213 p., maps.
This is the best concise description of the desert flora of Iraq available. It also includes brief descriptions of Irano-Turanian and Saharo-Sindian regions. The bibliography is comprehensive and the gazetteer and glossary are valuable additions.

Guinea, E.
1945   Aspecto forestal del desierto. La vegetación leñosa y los pastos del Sahara español. Instituto Forestal de Investigaciones y Experiencias, Madrid. 152 p.

1947   Catálogo razonado de las plantas de Sahara español. Jardín Botánico, Madrid, Anales 8: 357-442.
An illustrated detailed catalog of the plants of the Spanish Sahara; brief notes include common names, ecological data, economic usefulness, and general distribution. BA 31(7)22171.

Guinet, P.
1954   Carte de la végétation de l'Algérie. Feuille de Béni-Abbès. Institut Géographique National, Paris.
(Map of the vegetation of Algeria.)

Guinet, P. and C. Sauvage
1954   Botanique. *In* Les hamadas Sud-marocaines. Institut Scientifique Chérifien, Travaux, sér. général, 2:75-167.

Guinochet, M.
1951   Contribution à l'étude phytosociologique du sud tunisien. Société d'Histoire Naturelle de l'Afrique du Nord, Bulletin 42:131-153.
(Contribution to the phytosociologic study of south Tunisia)

Guinochet, M. and P. Quézel
1954   Reconnaissance phytosociologique autour du Grand Erg Occidental. Institut des Recherches Sahariennes, Travaux 12:11-27.

Gupta, R. K.
1966   Bibliography on the ecology (synecology and phytosociology) of the arid and semi-arid regions of India. Excerpta Botanica, B, 7(3): 178-190.

Gvozdeva, L. P.
1960   Rastitel'nost'i kormovye resursy pustyni Sary-Ishik-Otrau. Alma-Ata. 204 p.

Hadac, E.
1966   Bibliographia phytosociologica: Iraq. Excerpta Botanica, B, 7(2):102-104.

Hagerup, O.
1930   Etude des types biologiques de Raunkiaer dans la flore autour de Tombouctou. Kgl. Danske Videnskabernes Selskab, Biologiske Meddelelser 9(4):5-116.
A very good discussion of the desert vegetation near Tombouctou, with a classification by Raunkiaer's life forms. Discusses the life cycle of plants as related to summer rainfall conditions and winter droughts, and relationships with Saharan flora.

Haines, R. W.
1951a   *Haloxylon Schweinfurthii* Asch., Chenopodiaceae, near Cairo. Institut Fouad I du Désert, Cairo, Bulletin 1(1):77-80.
A good description of the plant, its growth, and reproduction. Black-and-white drawings of plants and parts of this important halophyte are included.

1951b   Potential annuals of the Egyptian desert. Institut Fouad I du Désert, Cairo, Bulletin 1(2):103-117.
A discussion of perennial plants that function as annuals in good seasons, including *Diplotaxis acris, D. Narra, Cleome arabica,* and *Gaylusea canescens.* Notes that even *Zilla spinosa* can flower the first season under favorable conditions.

Hall, A. A., R. L. Specht, and C. M. Eardley
1964   Regeneration of the vegetation on Koonamore vegetation reserve 1926-1962. Australian Journal of Botany 12:205-264.

Hall, H. M. and T. H. Goodspeed
1919   A rubber plant survey of western North America. University of California, Publications in Botany 7:159-278.
A report of a survey to discover a source of rubber in native North American shrubs that might be used in time of war. Rabbitbrush (*Chrysothamnus*), a genus widely distributed in western North America, was found to contain a rubber source of high grade. Later investigations, however, disclosed that guayule (*Parthenium argentatum*) showed more promise than *Chrysothamnus.*

Hall, H. M. and J. Grinnell
1919   Life-zone indicators in California. California Academy of Sciences, Proceedings 9(2):37-67.
The authors do not agree entirely with Merriam's temperature factors, but believe that life-zone concepts are useful, and that certain plants and animals could be used as indicators. They noted that in desert regions corresponding zones were lower on large mountains than on isolated peaks, and that rock surfaces were usually warmer than other surfaces. Largely a discussion of floras, including the origins and distributions of floras of 8 separate regions.

Halwagy, R.
1961   The vegetation of the semidesert north east of Khartoum, Sudan. Oikos 12(1):87-110.
Notes that rainfall in this area fluctuates widely from year to year, with a mean of 156 to 166 mm. The vegetation is *Acacia* desert scrub. Sandy substrata favor the growth of grasses and other annuals; clay substrata favor perennials. The hills are nearly devoid of vegetation. BA 38(2)4784.

1963   Studies of the succession of vegetation on some islands and sand banks in the Nile near Khartoum, Sudan. Vegetatio 11(4):217-234.
Includes a notable discussion of the relation of vegetation on islands in the Nile to the accumulation of soil materials. Beginning with newly exposed sandbars, a progressive increase of silt content of the soil and greater soil stabilization is associated with distinct increases in number of species of vegetation, height of tallest species, and amount of plant cover. BA 45(22)94205.

Handel-Mazzetti, H.
1931 Die pflanzengeographische gliederung und stellung Chinas. Botanische Jahrbücher 64(4): 309-323.
Notes that the desert region of the southern Gobi has been extremely dry since the Tertiary period, is contiguous with the western Asiatic and African deserts, and has many species distributed throughout its entire breadth. BA 7(2).

Hanelt, P.
1964 Bibliographia phytosociologicae: China. Excerpta Botanica, B, 6(2):106-134.

Hanson, H. C.
1924 A study of the vegetation of northeastern Arizona. University of Nebraska Studies 24:85-175.
An excellent study of vegetation including the sagebrush zone, which lies below 5200 feet elevation. This area is the southernmost extension of sagebrush (*Artemisia-Atriplex* association). Rainfall is about 7 inches, mostly in summer; April, May, and June are dry.

———
1949 The agroclimatic-analogue (homoclime) technique in plant introduction and distribution of new selections. Agronomy Journal 41(5):186-188.
A very good discussion of the agroclimatic-analogue technique for comparing areas, and as an aid to introduction and distribution of new selections. Describes methods used to identify similar ecological areas in different countries by comparing all available climatological, geographic, and soil data.

Hare, F. K.
1961 The causation of the arid zone. *In* L. D. Stamp, ed., A History of land use in arid regions. Unesco, Paris. Arid Zone Research 17:25-30.
The author believes aridity is dependent upon deep-seated features of the Earth's general atmospheric circulation rather than local or man-made circumstances, that the regime cannot be altered significantly by human intervention, that no past climatic epoch has completely lacked some subtropical aridity, and that the arid zone was probably somewhat constricted at the height of the recent glaciation but not eliminated altogether. BA 38 (6)21347.

Harrington, H. D.
1964 Manual of the plants of Colorado, for the identification of the ferns and flowering plants of the State. 2nd ed. Sage Books, Denver, Colorado. 666 p.
In addition to spp. actually known from Colorado, which are fully described, about 350 spp. from neighboring states, which may be reported in the future are included in the keys. Preceding the keys and systematic descriptions, there is a treatment of "Vegetation zones in Colorado" by David F. Costello. Glossary and index are provided. BA 29(3)6567.

Harris, S. A.
1960 The distribution of certain plant species in similar desert and steppe soils in central and northern Iraq. Journal of Ecology 48(1):96-104.
Compares the distributions of 3 annual and 6 perennial species with soil type and climate. The degree of soil aeration proved to be an important determinant, and also salinity to a lesser extent.

Harrison, M. H. and J. K. Jackson
1955 Map of Sudan. p. 330. *In* Scientific Council for Africa, Report on phytogeography. Yangambi. (unpublished.)
Scale: 1/4,000,000.

Harshberger, J. W.
1911 Phytogeographic survey of North America. G. E. Stechert and Company, New York. 790 p.
A comprehensive report on the vegetation of North America based upon the best knowledge available at the time. Considers the desert area as four regions: (1) Great Basin region, including Oregon, Nevada, and Mojave Desert; (2) Rocky Mountain region, including northeastern New Mexico and west Texas; (3) Chihauhuan Desert region, including parts of west Texas and southern New Mexico, and eastern Arizona; and (4) Western Madre region, in Mexico extending into southern Arizona. Well illustrated with 18 plates, 32 figures, and a vegetation map on a scale of 1:40,000,000. About 4 pages of the extensive bibliography are devoted to desert vegetation.

Harvey, W. H. and O. W. Sonder
1859- Flora capensis. Hodges, Smith and Co., Dublin.
1925 7 vols. in 10.
Continuation, vol. 4-7, by various botanists, edited by Sir William T. Thiselton-Dyer, L. Reeve and Co., Ltd., London.

Hassib, M.
1938 Cucurbitaceae in Egypt. Fouad I University, Cairo, Publication 3. 173 p.

———
1951 Distribution of plant communities in Egypt. Fouad I University, Cairo, Faculty of Science, Bulletin 29:60-261.
The distribution of plant communities in Egypt. A very good discussion of the vegetation of Egypt, largely of the Egyptian-Sinai and the Arabian (Egyptian) deserts. Notes that the major part of this desert area belongs to the Saharo-Sindian province and that a small part, mostly in the mountains of Sinai, belongs to the Irano-Turanian province. Lists 755 species of the Egyptian desert: 46.5 per cent annuals, 7.2 per cent small trees and shrubs, and most of the rest low-growing plants; only 0.1 per cent are succulents.

Hastings, J. R.
1963 Historical changes in the vegetation of a desert region. University of Arizona (Ph. D. dissertation). 499 p.
Concludes that man's influence on the ecology of the area, through introduction of cattle, suppression of natural burning, and control of predators, is not sufficient to account for observed phenomena, but rather that the observed vegetative and hydrologic changes occurred in general response to recent worldwide climatic fluctuations, with trends toward decreased rainfall and increased temperatures, although cultural factors may have reinforced or supplemented the effects of climate. Conclusions are similar to those of Hastings and Turner (1965a), but this work may explain more clearly the various hypotheses relating to the change in vegetation.

Hastings, J. R. and R. M. Turner
1965a The changing mile; an ecological study of vegetation change with time in the lower mile of an arid and semi-arid region. University of Arizona Press, Tucson. 317 p.

Changes brought by a number of factors on the contours and vegetation of the desert region that straddles southern Arizona and northwestern Sonora are recorded in paired photographs and text. Attention is centered pictorially on the last 80 years of change in the three life zones—desert, grassland, and oak woodland—to be found in the Sonoran Desert in one vertical mile above sea level. The 97 picture-pairs were taken from approximately the same vantage point some 80 years apart, and are reproduced on facing pages, with legends that point out and interpret the evidence.

————

1965b Seasonal precipitation regimes in Baja California, Mexico. Geografiska Annaler 47A:204-223.

Hauman, L.
1913 Etude phytogéographique de la région du Río Negro inférieur (République Argentine). Museo Nacional de Historia Natural, Buenos Aires, Anales 24:289-444.
This is a very complete study of the southeastern portion of the Monte vegetation.

————

1926 Etude phytogéographique de la Patagonie. Société Royal de Botanique de Belgique, Bulletin 58: 105-179.
Among other communities discusses the drier portions of Patagonia.

Havard, V.
1896 Drink plants of the North American Indians. Torrey Botanical Club, Bulletin 23(2):22-46.
An interesting and perhaps useful discussion of plants as source of beverages, alcholic and other.

Hayward, H. E.
1956 Plant growth under saline conditions. *In* Utilization of saline water, reviews of research. Rev. ed. Unesco, Paris. Arid Zone Research 4:37-71.
A good review of research relating to the biological problems of plant growth under saline and alkaline conditions. Includes a classification of soils and water quality as related to plant growth. Covers salt tolerance, and notes the occurrence of saline and alkaline soils in Australia, India, and the Western Hemisphere. Includes a bibliography of 256 references.

Hayward, H. E. and C. H. Wadleigh
1949 Plant growth on saline and alkali soils. Advances in Agronomy 1:1-38.

Herbette.
1914 Le problème du dessèchement de l'Asie intérieure. Annales de Géographie, Paris, 23:1-30.

Hernández-Pacheco, E. *et al.*
1949 El Sahara español, estudio geológico, geográfico y botánico. Instituto de Estudios Africanos, Madrid. 808 p.
A comprehensive discussion of the Spanish Sahara, including 89 figures, photographs, maps (some in color), and a bibliography. Part IV, Geobotany, was written by E. Guinea (López). This important 175-page study reviews literature, and discusses deserts, soils of the Sahara, adaptation to small water supply, and plant cover (tapiz). Includes excellent line drawings, showing vegetation profiles for various sites, and lists of important species.

Heumann, M. and H. Winkler
1931 Charakterpflanzen aus Südwestafrika. Vegetationsbilder 21(8):pl. 43-48.
(Character plants from Southwest Africa.)

Illustrations and brief descriptions are given of *Salicornia fruticosa, S. herbacea, Gomphocarpus fruticosus, Euphorbia monteiri, Stapelia* sp., *Harpagophytum procumbens, Drimiopsis* sp., *Tribulus terrestris, T. zeyheri,* and *Buphane disticha.* BA 6(6/7)15333.

Hillel, D. and Tadmor
1962 Water regime and vegetation in the central Negev highlands of Israel. Ecology 43(1):33-41.
An interesting study of vegetation distribution under rainfall of about 100 mm. On rocky slopes with shallow stony and saline soils and a sparse stand dominated by *Zygophyllum dumosum,* it was estimated that 50 mm of water was available for plant use. Loessial plains with deep saline soils dominated by *Haloxylon articulatum* had about 35 mm of water available. Wadi-beds with gravel or loessial soils supporting a Mediterranean-type vegetation had about 400 mm of water available. Sands with deep salt-free soils supporting a stand of assorted shrubs and perennial grasses had about 80 mm of water available. BA 38(2)4787.

Hironaka, M.
1963 Plant-environment relations of major species in sagebrush-grass vegetation of southern Idaho. University of Wisconsin, Madison. (Ph. D. dissertation) 138 p.
Moisture preference of species was determined by frequency of occurrence of individual species in each of the four Great Soil Groups represented in this study. Stands located in the western one-half of the state were treated separately from those in eastern Idaho to determine whether or not distribution of precipitation also has significant effects on sagebrush-grass vegetation. BA 45(2)4840.

Hironaka, M. and E. W. Tisdale
1963 Secondary succession in annual vegetation in southern Idaho. Ecology 44(4):810-812.
An exclosure on abandoned land in south Idaho was first invaded by *Bromus tectorum,* which was replaced by *Sitanion hystrix,* and finally by *Artemisia tridentata.*

Hitchcock, A. S.
1950 Manual of the grasses of the United States. 2nd ed., revised by Agnes Chase. U. S. Department of Agriculture, Miscellaneous Publication 200. 1051 p.
The basic manual of grasses for the United States.

Hoffman, G. O.
1961 Economics of chemical weed control. Southern Weed Conference, 14th, Proceedings: 347-352.
A good discussion with examples of the economic advantages of chemical weed control in range improvement in Texas.

Holland, A. A. and C. W. E. Moore
1962 The vegetation and soils of the Bollon district in south-western Queensland. C. S. I. R. O. Division of Plant Industry, Technical Paper 17:3-13.

Hooker, J. D.
1844- Flora Antarctica. Part 1, 2. Kew Botanic Gardens.
1847 574 p.

————

1875- Flora of British India. L. Reeve and Company,
1897 London. 7 vols.
Includes area now West Pakistan.

Howes, F. N.
1949 Vegetable gums and resins. Chronica Botanica, Waltham, Mass. 188 p.

A good review of the plants containing gums and resins, many of which are found in desert regions.

Hull, A. C., Jr. and W. T. Vaughn
1951 Controlling big sagebrush with 2, 4-D and other chemicals. Journal of Range Management 4(3): 158-164.
A basic study aimed toward developing methods of controlling big sagebrush by chemical means. Various combinations of 2, 4-D and 2, 4, 5-T were used at different times of the year by airplane and ground spraying.

Humbert, H.
1928 Végétation de l'Atlas saharien occidental et additions à l'étude botanique de l'Ari Ayachi. Société d'Histoire Naturelle de l'Afrique du Nord, Bulletin 19(5):204-240.
A study of the vegetation of the western Saharan Atlas area. Lists plants of 9 districts. Describes the general character of vegetation and lists the most interesting species with local vernacular names. Includes some good desert pictures. BA 5(6/7)16505.

Hunziker, J. H.
1952 Las comunidades vegetales de la Cordillera de la Rioja. Revista de Investigaciones Agrícolas 6: 167-196.
Important account of the vegetation of the northwestern Monte and arid Cordillera. It includes a list of 273 plant species of the region, literature, and photographs.

Hurst, E.
1942 The poison plants of New South Wales. Compiled under direction of the Poison Plant Committee of New South Wales. The Snelling Printing Works, Sydney. 498 p.

Hutchinson, J.
1946 A botanist in southern Africa. P. R. Gawthorn, Ltd., London. 686 p.
This 5-part publication, devoted largely to travels in southern Africa, lists plants seen, many illustrated by photographs and drawings. The fifth part reviews South African botanical literature and discusses floral regions of South Africa. BA 25(12)37424.

Hutchinson, J. and J. M. Dalziel
1927- Flora of west tropical Africa. Prepared at the
1936 Herbarium, Royal Botanic Gardens, Kew. Crown Agents for the Colonies, London. 2 vols. in 4.

1895- Index Kewensis, an enumeration of the genera and species of flowering plants from the time of Linnaeus to the year 1885. With supplements nos. 1-13, covering the periods 1866/1895 through 1956/1960, issued from 1901-1906 through 1966, and continuation. Clarendon Press, Oxford.

International Union of Biological Sciences
1951 Les bases écologiques de la régénération de la végétation des zones arides. Symposium, Stockholm, 1950. Secretariat Général, U. I. S. B., Paris. sér. B, Colloque 9. 149 p.

Ionesco, T.
1956a Considérations sur la méthode floristico-écologique appliquée à l'études des milieux dans les Doukkala. Société des Sciences Naturelles et Physiques du Maroc, Bulletin 36(1):1-12.

1956b Sur l'écologie des plantes spontanées dans les Doukkala. Société des Sciences Naturelles et Physiques du Maroc, Bulletin 36(3):243-255.

1958 Essai d'estimation de la valeur indicatrice des espèces psammophiles en pays semi-aride (Doukkala, Maroc). Service de la Carte Phytogéographique, Bulletin, sér. B, 3(1):7-68. (Essay on the estimation of the index value of psammophilic species in a semi-arid country (Doukkala, Morocco).
A very valuable work on indicator value, based upon a study of the general characteristics of the geology, soil, climate, and vegetation of the plain of Doukkala. The relations between plant species and corresponding soil characteristics were studied to determine the index value of these species with regard to depth and percentage of sand in the soil. Includes ecological list indicating soil texture for each species.

1964a La cartographie de la végétation au Maroc. Al Awamia (10):187-221.

1964b Considérations générales concernant les relations entre l'érosion et la végétation du Maroc. Revue de Géographie du Maroc 6:17-28.

Ionesco, T. and C. Sauvage
1962 Les types de végétation du Maroc, essai de nomenclature et de définition. Revue de Géographie du Maroc 1/2:75-86.

Irvine, F. R.
1957 Wild and emergency foods of Australian and Tasmanian aborigines. Oceania 28(2):113-142.
Pertains to north Arnhem Land. The main food of the natives is vegetable. Covers a wide territory and gives some information on desert plants.

Issa, A.
1930 Dictionnaire des noms des plantes en latin, français, anglais et arabe. Cairo. 227 p.
A very useful publication giving plant names in Latin, French, English, and Arabic.

Istituto Agronomico per l'Africa Italiana
1953 Contributo ad una bibliografia italiana su Eritrea e Somalia con particolare riferimento all'agricoltura ed argomenti ani (fino al dicembre 1952). Firenze. 239 p.
A comprehensive bibliography pertaining to Italian studies in Eritrea and Somalia. Useful to ecology and more so to agriculture.

Ivanov, A. F.
1962 Osnovnye peskoukrepitel'nye rasteniya pustyni i polupustyni Vnutrennei Mongolii (Kitaiskaya Narodnaya Respublika). Botanicheskii Zhurnal 47(11):1680-1684.
Gives brief descriptions of major sand-binding plants of Inner Mongolia and northwestern China.

Ives, R. L.
1949 Climate of the Sonoran Desert region. Association of American Geographers, Annals 39:143-187.
Summarizes extensive useful information on the climate of the Sonoran Desert region, based upon field travel by the author and information from various weather agencies. Covers all or part of California, Nevada, Utah, Colorado, Arizona, New Mexico, Texas, Baja California, Sonora,

Chihuahua, Sinaloa, Durango, Nayarit, and Jalisco. Briefly compares climatic systems: concludes that Köppen's original system does not apply as well to the desert as Trewartha's modification. Also discusses factors influencing precipitation and other meteorological phenomena.

Jaeger, E. C.
1941   Desert wild flowers. 2nd ed. Stanford University Press, Stanford, California. 322 p.
Contains descriptions, drawings, and photographs of more than 750 plants of the California deserts, and information on their distribution in other areas. Well illustrated. Gives excellent coverage of desert regions of California and fairly good coverage of Arizona and Nevada. Discusses geographical range, altitude distribution, and landform types upon which the plants occur. BA 16(5)13152A.

1957   The North American deserts. Stanford University Press, Stanford, California. 308 p.

1965   The California deserts, from Death Valley to the Mexican border. 4th ed. Stanford University Press, Stanford, California. 207 p.
History, Indians, animals, birds, plant life.

Jaeger, F. R.
1936   Trockengrenzen in Algerien. Petermanns Mitteilungen, Erganzungsheft 223. 68 p.
This includes description of arid limits in Algeria, a folding map, scale 1:5,000,000, showing the limits of agriculture on the arid margin.

Jafri, S. M. H.
1958   Additions and corrections to the flora of Karachi. (Pakistan) 4(1):10-24.
Lists 158 species of seed plants as additions or corrections to the flora of Karachi, Pakistan. Gives the location and habitat for each species.

Jahandiez, E. and R. Maire
1931- Catalogue des plantes du Maroc. Alger.
1934   3 vols.

Jensen, H. A.
1947   A system for classifying vegetation in California. California Fish and Game 33(4):199-266.
One of the best and most detailed vegetation surveys made in the United States. Describes a system, based on aerial photographs, used for classifying vegetation in California. All vegetation classes described are illustrated by ground photos. Lists approximately 1700 California plants with the symbols used for them in the California Vegetation Type Survey. BA 23(1)204.

Jepson, W. L.
1925   Manual of flowering plants of California. Associated Student Store, University of California. 1238 p.
A standard reference for California plants. Distribution is based upon Merriam's life zones. Includes keys for identifying plants. Each species is described, and its distribution and preferred environment noted.

Jessup, R. W.
1951   The soils, geology and vegetation of north-western South Australia. Royal Society of South Australia, Transactions 74:189-273.
A comprehensive description of an area north of the transcontinental railway, west of Lake Torrens and Eyre, and westward toward the edge of the Nullarbor Plain. Rainfall varies from 4.5 to 7 inches. Soils are developed

from sedimentary rocks. Vegetation consists of chenopodiaceous shrub steppe on heavier soils and acacia woodlands on sandy soils. Gives detailed floristic lists of species for each association and notes their relative palatabilities.

Johnston, I. M.
1929   I: Papers on the flora of northern Chile: 1. The coastal flora of the departments of Chañaral and Taltal; 2. The flora of the nitrate coast; 3. Undescribed species from the Cordilleras of Atacama. II: Some undescribed species from Peru. Harvard University, Gray Herbarium, Contributions 85:1-180.
Includes an excellent description of the coastal flora of northern Chile and a description of species, some not previously described, from the Cordilleras of Atacama and from Peru. The coasts of Chañaral and Taltal, and the nitrate coast to a lesser extent, exhibit features of the Loma zone, well-developed in Peru. Chañaral and Taltal display sharp contrast of mesophytic and xerophytic vegetation; annual rainfall averages only 11 mm, but the ocean fog belt (from 300 to 800 meters elevation on slopes facing the ocean and in valleys extending inland) receives seasonal moisture supporting luxuriant spring vegetation and enabling some xerophytes to persist through the fogless summer. Arid scrub, including hardy deep-rooted xerophytes, extends upward above the belt to 100 meters, above which no plants survive. The nitrate coast is more arid, with an average yearly rainfall of 2 mm and frequent years with no rain. BA 6(1)2106.

1931   The vascular flora of the guano islands of Peru. Harvard University, Gray Herbarium, Contributions 95:26-35.
Higher plants occur on only 4 of the numerous islands: Lobos de Tierra, San Lorenzo, San Gallan, and Viejas. The first apparently owes its small flora to occasional equatorial storms. The other three reach an altitude of 350 to 400 meters, high enough to be bathed by fogs, and so have a flora belonging ecologically and phytogeographically to the Loma formation of the coastal hills of the mainland. Lists 19 species with distribution and descriptive notes. BA 7(4)9310.

1935   The flora of San Félix Island. Arnold Arboretum, Journal 16(4):440-447.
Most of the surface of this island off the northern coast of Chile is devoid of plants. Notes only 7 species of seed plants occurring on the island. BA 11(6)14688.

1943- Plants of Coahuila, eastern Chihuahua, and adjoin-
1944   ing Zacatecas and Durango. 5 parts. Arnold Arboretum, Journal 24:306-339, 375-421; 25: 43-83, 431-453, 133-182.

Johnston, M. C.
1963   The species of *Zizyphus* (Rhamnaceae) indigenous to United States and Mexico. American Journal of Botany 50(10):1020-1027.
Zizyphus is a very important group of desert shrubs and trees. This taxonomic work pertains to the 7 species indigenous to the U. S. A. and Mexico. BA 45(19)83707.

Kachkarov, D. N. and E. P. Korovin(e)
1942   La vie dans les déserts. Edition française par Théodore Monod. Payot, Paris. 360 p.
A valuable compendium of published and original

material on life in the deserts, particularly those of Asia. Includes a map of the principal deserts of Turkestan, a map showing the locations of principal deserts of the world, and a chart showing the relationships between various floristic elements. Chapter four (75 pages) discusses the desert vegetation and gives many descriptions and illustrations of individual plants and plant communities.

Kao Shang-wu

1963 Issledovanie peschanoi pustyni i gobi v Sintszyane. Scientia Silvae 8(1):42-67.

A report of an investigation of the sandy desert and gobi area in Hsing-chiang (in Chinese with a Russian summary). Discusses the sandy and clay deserts of the Dzhungarian and Tarim basins. BA 45(21)89577.

Karamysheva, Z. V. and E. I. Rachkovskaya

1963 Nekotorye zakonomernosti v raspredelenii rastitel'nosti zapadnoi chasti tsentral'-no-Kazakhstanskogo melkosopochnika. Botanicheskii Zhurnal 48(10):1457-1471.
   (Some regular distribution patterns of the vegetation in the western part of the Central Kazakhstan undulating plain.)

Perhaps the most valuable contribution of this article is the precisely drawn boundary between the Eurasiatic steppe region and the Saharo-Gobian desert region. Includes an English summary.

Karschon, R.

1956 Salt conditions in erosion channels in Wadi Araba. Research Council of Israel, Bulletin.

Kassas, M.

1952a On the reproductive capacity and life cycle of *Alhagi maurorum*. Egyptian Academy of Sciences, Proceedings 8:114-122.

This very important and widespread plant is a valuable fodder for camels and other domestic animals, even though it is a wiry, branchy shrub (1 to 3 feet high) armed with pungent spreading spines.

———

1952b On the distribution of *Alhagi maurorum* in Egypt. Egyptian Academy of Sciences, Cairo, Proceedings 8:140-151.

This second paper of a series on this plant notes that it is distributed widely over Egypt and has been recorded in Nubia, Tripoli, Libya, Palestine, Syria, Iraq, Iran, Arabia, Cyprus, and the southern Balkans. The plant depends for moisture upon underground water, is intolerant of high soil salinity, and may be used as an indicator of underground water with relatively low salt content. The plant varies considerably (in spine length, leaf size, growth habit, and succulence) with environmental conditions such as aridity exposure. There are also some physiological variations related to water conditions. BA 29(4)7817.

1952c Habitat and plant communities in the Egyptian desert. I: Introduction. Journal of Ecology 40(2): 342-351.

The first article of a series on various plant communities of the Egyptian desert. Gives a brief description of the rocky plains, wadis, mountains, gravel deserts, and desert plains.

———

1953 Habitat and plant communities in the Egyptian desert. II: The features of a desert community. Journal of Ecology 41(2):248-256.

Notes several factors important to the growth of plants and location of plant communities: (1) topography: the lowest areas receive water (often several times actual rainfall) and soil from extensive higher areas; slopes and higher levels retain the least water and soil; (2) exposure to insulation: the contrast between the north-facing and south-facing sides of a wadi is very obvious; (3) ground surface: compact rock surfaces afford little opportunity for plant growth; hammada deserts and slopes provide other peculiar conditions; rocky surfaces covered with dirt or crust are usually very sterile; soft material will afford favorable seed beds and allow healthy plant growth; (4) geological formation: in arid regions the coincidence of certain plant communities with certain types of rock is often remarkable.

———

1955 Rainfall and vegetation in arid north-east Africa. *In* Plant ecology, proceedings of the Montpellier symposium. Unesco, Paris. Arid Zone Research 5:49-57.

Gives general features of vegetation of Egypt and the northern provinces of Sudan. Discusses climate, water resources, and vegetation. An excellent discussion of vegetation in relation to environmental conditions.

———

1956 Landforms and plant cover in the Omdurman Desert, Sudan. Société de Géographie d'Egypte, Bulletin 29:43-53.

Discusses a desert area near Khartoum, with arid climate, summer rainfall, and high temperatures (Meigs, Ab 34 classification); and which lies within the vegetation belt named "acacia desert scrub" by Andrews. Notes that plant cover changes substantially from season to season and from year to year. Discusses the corresponding vegetational characteristics for each landform, including hills, plains, gravel desert, sand drifts, khors, and qoz.

———

1957 On the ecology of the Red Sea coastal land. Journal of Ecology 45(1):187-203.

Contains a vegetational survey of a coastal belt by the Red Sea in Sudan. The climate is arid with winter rainfall along the shore and summer rainfall inland. BA 31 (10)

———

1959 Habitat and plant communities in the Egyptian desert. IV: The gravel desert. Journal of Ecology 47:289-310.

A very informative report based upon a study of the gravel desert along the Cairo-Suez road, including gravel surfaces and water runnels. Notes that the development of a mature gravel pavement protects underlying deposits against further transportation and allows the development of profile characteristics which can support a reasonably stable vegetation. Four community types are described.

———

1960 Certain aspects of landform effects on plant water resources. Société de Géographie d'Egypt, Bulletin 33:45-51.

Discusses the modification of climate effects by landform. Notes that landform features may modify water revenue or may modify the intensity of water loss by reducing temperature or increasing atmospheric humidity. Examples of landform effects upon plant-water relationships are discussed.

Kassas, M.
1961 Certain aspects of landform effects on plant water resources. *In* Plant-water relationships in arid and semi-arid conditions, a symposium. Unesco, Paris. Arid Zone Research 16:71-78.
Essentially the same as the 1960 paper of the same title. BA 39(2)4562.

———

1966 Plant life in deserts. p. 145-180. *In* E. S. Hills, ed., Arid lands, a geographical appraisal. Methuen and Company, Ltd., London; Unesco, Paris. 461 p.
An excellent discussion of plant life under desert conditions.

Kassas, M. and M. S. El-Abyad
1962- On the phytosociology of the desert vegetation
1963   of Egypt. Annals of Arid Zone (Jodhpur) 1 (1/2):54-83.
Summarizes an ecological survey of the Cairo-Suez desert. Describes floristic composition of 14 community types within the area. Discusses ecological relationships between and within types, and theoretical implications.

Kassas, M. and W. A. Girgis
1964 Habitat and plant communities in the Egyptian desert. V: The limestone plateau. Journal of Ecology 52(1):107-119.
The fifth work of the series. An ecological survey of an area (2000 square km) of the limestone desert east of the Nile Valley. The principal ecogeomorphological systems are: *(1)* the drainage systems (wadis); *(2)* the limestone erosion surfaces; and *(3)* the sand-and-gravel formations (discussed in part IV of this series). The drainage systems are categorized further, by geomorphological units, mostly representing stages in development of drainage runnels. Concludes that the developmental changes of the runnels are accompanied by corresponding changes of vegetation. BA 45(21)89578.

Kassas, M. and M. Imam
1954 Habitat and plant communities in the Egyptian desert. III: The wadi bed ecosystem. Journal of Ecology 42(2):424-441.
Surveys the vegetation of several wadis near Cairo. Several different plant communities are found, according to position in the wadi. On shallow soil, succulent vegetation is most common; deeper soil supports grassland vegetation; woody vegetation is found on wadi terraces. The gradual modification of plant cover proceeds with the gradual accumulation of alluvial sediments. BA 29(6)13048.

———

1957 Climate and microclimate in the Cairo Desert. Société de Géographie d'Egypte, Bulletin 30: 25-52.
The Cairo Desert receives scanty and greatly variable rainfall; except for winter months the year is mostly rainless. Studies of microclimatic features show that adjacent points may differ in temperature and moisture conditions according to topography. South-facing slopes are consistently warmer than north-facing slopes. Lower levels (depressions) receive more water than the higher levels. Microclimatic differences correspond to differences in microhabitat and vegetation.

Kearney, T. H., R. H. Peebles, and collaborators
1960 Arizona flora. 2nd ed., with supplement by J. T. Howell, E. McClintock, and collaborators. University of California Press, Berkeley. 1085 p.
The standard manual for the flora of Arizona. BA 36(10) 32005.

Kearney, T. H. *et al.*
1914 Indicator significance of vegetation in Tooele Valley, Utah. Journal of Agricultural Research 1:365-417.

Keast, A., R. L. Crocker, and C. S. Christian
1959 Biogeography and ecology in Australia. Monographiae Biologicae 8:1-640.
A comprehensive publication on biogeography and ecology written by specialists in various fields. The chapters dealing with flora are cited elsewhere by author.

Keay, R. W. J.
1959 Vegetation map of Africa south of the Tropic of Cancer. Carte de la végétation de l'Afrique au sud du Tropique du Cancer. Oxford University Press, New York. 24 p.
This map was prepared by a committee of the Association for the Taxonomic Study of the Flora of Tropical Africa and published with the aid of Unesco. It is on a scale of 1:10,000,000 and shows major vegetation types as they occur today. The 35 vegetation complexes distinguished are largely physiognomic types. BA 33(10)36456.

Kelsey, H. P. and W. A. Dayton
1942 Standardized plant names. 2nd ed. J. H. McFarland Co., Harrisburg, Pa. 675 p.
The standard authority for plant names in the United States. It includes native flora, introductions, names of certain plant products (e. g. drugs), and some useful specialized lists of plants (e. g. poisonous plants).

Kendeigh, S. C.
1932 A study of Merriam's temperature laws. Wilson Bulletin 44(3):129-143.
Doubts that Merriam's life zones are valid—a viewpoint shared by many botanists and, perhaps less so by zoologists. A substantial critical analysis of Merriam's work.

Khan, M. I.
1954 Water relations of plants in arid regions. Empire Forestry Review 33(2):124-131.
A very good review of the various adaptations plants use to escape or endure droughts.

Killian, C.
1931, Etudes écologiques sur la répartition du chlorure
1935   de sodium dans les psammophytes et halophytes algériens. Annales de Physiologie et de Physicochimie Biologique 7(3):419-468; 11: 70-124.
A report of ecological studies of the distribution of sodium chloride in Algerian psammophytes and halophytes. Notes that salt may be present in these plants in even greater concentrations than in the soil, and that there is no fixed relation between the degree of succulence of a plant and the amount of salt accumulated. BA 7(1)426.

———

1939a Nouvelles contributions à l'étude écologique de quelques plantes rupicoles du Hoggar. Société d'Histoire Naturelle de l'Afrique du Nord, Bulletin 30:413-421.

———

1939b *Anabasis aretioides* Coss. et Moq., endémique du Sud Oranais. Société d'Histoire Naturelle de l'Afrique du Nord, Bulletin 30:422-436.
A monographic treatment of an important plant of the Sahara Desert.

Killian, C.
1941 Sols et plantes indicatrices dans les parties non irriguées des oasis de Figuig et de Beni-Ounif. Société d'Histoire Naturelle de l'Afrique du Nord, Bulletin 32:301-314.
(Soils and plant indicators in the non-irrigated parts of Figuig and Beni-Ounif Oasis.)
A report of a study of soils and plant indicators in non-irrigated oasis areas. *Plantago psyllium* indicated well-drained soils; *Bromus rubens,* sandy soils; *Atriplex halimus,* clay soils and salt; *Peganum,* clay soils with less salt; and *Hordeum murinum,* compact soils with little salt.

1942 *Bromus rubens.* Contribution á l'étude des plantes annuelles xérophytiques du désert. Schweizerische Botanische Gesellschaft, Berichte 52:215-238.
Bromus rubens, an annual grass, was the subject of this contribution to the study of xerophytic annual plants of the desert. The study included morphology, anatomy, edaphology, and ecology. The results throw new light on the whole question of the relation of plants to an arid environment.

1943 Plantes et sols au Sahara et leurs relations mutuelles. Institut de Recherches Sahariennes, Travaux 2:37-54.

1947a Biologie végétale au Fezzân. Pts. 1-3. Mission Scientifique du Fezzân, 1944-1945, Rapport 4. Institut de Recherches Sahariennes, Alger. 107 p.

1947b Le déficit de saturation hydrique chez les plantes sahariennes. Revue Générale de Botanique 54:81-102.
It was found there was no relation between ecological or biological factors and water deficit.

1950 Nouvelles observations sur les conditions édaphiques et les réactions des plantes indicatrices dans les réserves de pâturage de la région alfatière algérienne. Institut Agricole et des Services de Recherches et d'Expérimentation Agricoles de l'Algérie, Annales 5(3). 36 p.
An interesting and useful contribution. Killian developed a polygon by which to plot distribution of species relative to quantity of sand, lime, clay, hygroscopic per cent, moisture equivalent, and amount of nitrogen and carbon (humus), also a polygon for chemical characteristics. Notes a closer relationship of distribution to physical condition and hence a greater indicator between the two.

1951 Observations sur la biologie d'un halophyte saharien, *Frankenia pulverulenta* L. Institut de Recherches Sahariennes, Travaux 7:87-109.
A study of an important Saharan annual halophyte, *Frankenia pulverulenta.*

Killian, C. and G. Lemée
1948- Etude sociologique, morphologique et écologique
1949 de quelques halophytes Sahariens. Revue Générale de Botanique 55:376-402; 56:28-48.
Sociological, morphological, and ecological studies were made of associations of halophytes growing in saline soils near Beni-Ounif in the Sahara desert. Several types of halophytic plants are discussed. BA 25(6)16159.

King, L. J.
1966 Weeds of the world. Interscience Publishers, New York. 526 p.

An excellent discussion of the weeds of the world, beginning with a general outline of the characteristics and life cycle of weeds, and their harmful effects. The second part includes a classification of herbicides, and a discussion of their mode of action, uses of herbicides, and the nonchemical control of weeds. Includes extensive bibliographical listings.

Kinzikaeva, G. K.
1962 Solyanki Tadzhikistana. Akademiia Nauk Tadzhikskoi S.S.R., Botanicheskogo Instituta, Trudy 18:258-285. Referativnyi Zhurnal, Biologiya, 1963, no. 9V166.
A report on a phytogeographical survey of three genera of thistles of Tadzhikistan. Gives keys to the species, and basic data on their ecology and geography.

Kirk, R.
1946 Some vegetable poisons of the Sudan. Sudan Notes and Records (Khartoum) 27:127-152.

Klages, K. H. W.
1942 Ecological crop geography. Macmillan Co., New York. 615 p.

Knuchel, H., Jr.
1947 Über die nebelvegetation an der peruanischen küste. Schweizerische Zeitschrift für das Forstwesen 98(2):81-84.
A study of the Loma vegetation which occurs locally along the Peruvian coastal desert at elevations of 200 to 1000 meters on heights usually covered with clouds from May to November. The flora includes mostly annuals, some bulb and tuberous perennials, and a few shrubs; also, rarely, there may be scattered individuals or groups of *Salix humboldtiana* and *Acacia macracantha.* BA 22(1) 174.

Köppen, W.
1954 Classification of climates and the world patterns. p. 225-226, 381-383. *In* G. T. Trewartha, An introduction to climate. 3rd ed. McGraw-Hill Book Co., Inc., New York.
Trewartha has preserved the essentials of Köppen's classification but added some clarification and minor modifications.

Korovin, E. P.
1927 Zametka o rastitel' nosti central'nykh Kara-Kumov. Sredne-Aziatskogo Gosudarstvennogo Universiteta, Tashkent, Instituta Pochvovydeniya i Geobotaniki, Izvestiya 3:129-150.
Describes fully the vegetation of the Kara-Kum desert region, and gives a list of the plants.

1928 Geobotanicheskii kompleksie jugo-vostochikh Kara-Kumov. Dnevnik Vsesojuznogo Sezda Botanikov, Leningrad, p. 239-240.
(Geobotanical complexes of southeastern Kara-Kum, Turkestan)
The sandy region of Kara-Kum between the Amu-Dar'ya and the Margab Rivers includes the following communities: (1) sandy plains in which *Carex physodes* is characteristic, (2) shores with *Halocnemum strobilaceum* as characteristic, together with *Statice, Seidlitzia, Reaumuria, Haplophyllum, Salsola,* and *Artemisia;* and (3) sandy dunes. Among the dominating plants of the region are *Ammodendron, Aristida, Turnefortia,* and *Heliotropium.* BA 5(6/7):16513.

Korovin, E. P.

1935 Ocherki po istorii razvitiia rastitel'nosti Srednei Azii. I: Pustynia Betpak-dala (tsentral' nyi Kazakstan). Sredneaziatskogo Gosudarstvennogo Universiteta, Biulleten, 20(4): 183-218.

A history of the development of the vegetation of the Bet-Pak-Dala area of central Kazakhstan in Middle Asia (in Russian with a French summary). In this part of Middle Asia, there is a distinction between northern and southern deserts. The article considers primarily the origin and affiliations of present vegetation. BA 12(3) 5446.

1958 Biologicheskie formy i potrebnost' v vode rastitel' nykh vidov aridnoi zony. Sredneaziatskogo Gosudarstvennogo Universiteta, Trudy 136: 79-97. Referativnyi Zhurnal, Biologiya, 1961, no. 1V195.

Concludes that the biological form and water requirements of vegetative species of arid zones, particularly the deserts of central Asia, are jointly determined by: (1) origin and (2) adaptative changes resulting from the arid climate. BA 41(3)8993.

1961a Opyt botaniko-geograficheskogo raionirovaniya Srednei Azii. Tashkentskogo Universiteta, Trudy 186:25-29. Referativnyi Zhurnal, Biologiya, 1963, no. 1V223.

A botanical and geographical division of Central Asia into regions (6 provinces and 31 districts). Vegetation was grouped in 5 categories, the arid category including psammophytes, gypsophytes, halophytes, ephemerals and taiga vegetation. Four other types of vegetation existing under more favorable moisture conditions are also listed. BA 45(5)18443.

1961b Tipy pustyn' Srednei Azii v aspekte ikh sel' skokhozyais-tvennogo osvoeniya. p. 7-10. Pastbishcha Uzbekistana. Akademiia Nauk Uzbek S.S.R., Tashkent. Referativnyi Zhurnal, Biologiya, 1963, no. 4V245.

Includes a brief discussion of vegetation types of Central Asia deserts, their composition, rhythm, and productivity for grazing and various other agricultural purposes. BA 45(2)4848.

1961- Rastitel'nost Srednei Azii. 2nd ed. Akademiia
1962 Nauk Uzbek S.S.R., Tashkent. 2 vols.
(The vegetation of central Asia and southern Kazakhstan)

This monograph, an important contribution to Russian botanical literature, is a revised and greatly enlarged edition of a work published in 1934. An extensive bibliography is appended.

Kramer, P. J.

1944 Soil moisture in relation to plant growth. Botanical Review 10(9):525-559.

This general review of literature on soil moisture covers conditions of desert environment and includes very useful information on the relation of soil moisture to plant growth. Includes a bibliography of 108 titles.

Kreeb, K.

1961 Bibliographia phytosociologica: Iraq. Excerpta Botanica, B, 3(1):78.

Küchler, A. W.

1947a A geographic system of vegetation. Geographical Review 37(2):233-240.

Proposes a system based upon Köppen's classification of climates, using letters for the mapping of vegetation. Küchler revised the system slightly in 1966.

1947b Localizing vegetation terms. Association of American Geographers, Annals 37:197-208.

Discusses the origin of plant names and locally used terms. Provides helpful explanations of terms such as chaparral, garigue, and so forth.

1949a A physiognomic classification of vegetation. Association of American Geographers, Annals 39(3):201-210.

An extension of studies published in 1947.

1949b Natural vegetation. World map in Goode's School Atlas, Chicago, Rand-McNally.

1951 Classification and purpose in vegetation maps. Geographical Review 46(2):155-167. 3 maps.

Küchler compares 3 types of maps: (1) physiognomic system (Küchler), (2) floristic system (K. Hueck), and (3) the physiognomic-floristic system (A. E. Weislander), and concludes each is useful for special purpooses and the first best for use by nonbotanists.

1964 Potential natural vegetation of the conterminous United States. (Manual to accompany the map). American Geographical Society, Special Publication 36. 116 p.

A colored map showing natural vegetation with a description of plant communities.

1966 Analyzing the physiognomy and structure of vegetation. Association of American Geographers, Annals 56(1):112-127.

1967 Vegetation mapping. The Ronald Press Company, New York. 472 p.

Kurochkina, L. Y.

1962a K kharakteristike kustarnikovykh pustyn' Kazakhstana. Akademiia Nauk Kazakhskoi S.S.R., Instituta Botaniki, Trudy 13. Referativnyi Zhurnal, Biologiya, 1964, no. 6V199.

A report of a study of *Calligonum* societies in the Kara Irtis sands between Buran, Karatal, and the Chinese border, which is apparently one of the centers of development of the species. Includes a vegetation map of the area and compares the vegetation with that of other desert regions of Kazakhstan.

1962b K voprosu o slozhenii rastitel'nykh soobshchestv v pustyne. Akademiia Nauk S. S. R., Seriya Botaniki i Pochvovedeniya, Izvestiya 1. 13. 89-95. Referativnyi Zhurnal, Biologiya, 1963, no. 1V226.

This work on the problem of plant community structure in the desert includes a description of the mosaic pattern of plant cover in formations of white *Haloxylon* and *Calligonum* stands in the Kyzyl-Kum desert. The author introduces the "stage mosaic pattern" concept of structure in plant communities where microgroupings are composed of plants with different life forms. BA 45(20)84980.

Langman, I. K.

1964 A selected guide to the literature on the flowering plants of Mexico. University of Pennsylvania Press, Philadelphia. 1015 p.

A comprehensive listing of references relating to the flora of Mexico.

Lavauden, L.
1927 Les forêts du Sahara. Revue des Eaux et Forêts, Juin-Juillet, 1-26.

Lavrenko, E. M. and N. I. Nikol'skaya
1963 Arealy nekotorykh tsentral 'noaziatskikh i severoturanskikh vidov pustynnykh rastenii i vopros o botaniko—geograficheskoi granitse mezhdu srednei i tsentral'noi Aziei. Botanicheskii Zhurnal 48(12):1741-1761. (English summary)
Discusses the ranges of some central Asiatic and northern Turanian species of desert plants on the basis of data from literature and herbarium materials; also discusses the phytogeographical boundary between Central Asia and Middle Asia. BA 45(24)105965.

Le Houérou, H.-N.
1959a Recherches écologiques et floristiques sur la végétation de la Tunisie méridionale. I: Les milieux naturels, la végétation. II: La flore. III: Photos, cartes et tableaux. Institut de Recherches Sahariennes, Alger, Mémoire 6 (i.e.. 8).

_____
1959b Relations sol-végétation en Tunisie méridionale et la mise en évidence des groupements végétaux au moyen de "l'écogramme". Société Botanique de France, Colloque 1:171-174.

Leighly, J.
1952 Dry climates: their nature and distribution. *In* Desert research, proceedings of the international symposium held in Jerusalem, May 7-14, 1952, sponsored by the Research Council of Israel and Unesco. Research Council of Israel, Special Publication 2:3-16.

Lemée, G.
1953 Contribution à la connaissance phytosociologique des confins saharo-marocains. Les associations à thérophytes des dépressions sableuses et limoneuses non salées et des rocailles aux environs de Beni-Ounif. Vegetatio 4:137-154.
A study of associations of annuals on sandy nonsaline depressions and rocky slopes near Beni-Ounif, following an unusually rainy season in this area. Habitats included sandy and loamy depressions without salt, with plant communities determined by soil textures, and rocky slopes with associations closely correlated with climatic and microclimatic conditions. Communities showed a gradation from those with floristic predominance of Saharan species to others containing numerous Mediterranean species. BA 27(12)31441.

Leopold, A. S.
1950 Vegetation zones of Mexico. Ecology 31: 507-518.
This brief article includes a map of vegetation, but the half-page desert discussion is of limited value.

Leredde, C.
1957 Etude écologique et phytogéographique du Tassili n'Ajjer. Institut de Recherches Sahariennes, Alger, Mission Scientifique au Tassili n'Ajjer, Mémoire 2. 456 p.
Describes a relic forest in the center of the Sahara.

Lesueur, H. D.
1945 Ecology of vegetation of Chihuahua, Mexico, north of parallel 28. University of Texas, Austin, Publication 4521. 92 p.

This very thorough discussion of the vegetation north of 28°N latitude includes a vegetation map.

Leyendecker, P. J. and C. A. Kennedy
1956 *Euphorbia antisiphylitica* discovered in southern New Mexico. Madroño 13(5):176.
A distribution note on candelilla, of interest as an important wax producer.

Linchevsky, A. and A. V. Prozorovsky
1949 The basic principles of the distribution of the vegetation of Afghanistan. Kew Bulletin 1949 (2):179-214.
This excellent translation by H. K. A. Shaw of a valuable work provides the best available information on the vegetation of Afghanistan. Covers the desert vegetation very well, gives the distribution of vegetational communities, and includes a bibliography and maps. BA 24(5)13218.

Little, E. C. S. and G. W. Ivens
1965 The control of brush by herbicides in tropical and subtropical grassland. Herbage Abstracts 35(1):1-12.
A very good review of various methods used for control of brush. Although oriented toward tropical and subtropical grassland, the materials and methods discussed are also applicable to desert conditions. Includes a bibliography of 177 references.

Little, E. L.
1950 Southwestern trees, a guide to the native species of New Mexico and Arizona. U. S. Department of Agriculture, Agriculture Handbook 9:1-109.
This handbook includes descriptions and drawings of the principal trees of Arizona and New Mexico. Gives data on distribution and principal vegetation types are tabulated and mapped. An excellent reference for the identification of woody plants. BA 25(10)31771.

Liu, J. C.
1930 Important bibliography on the taxonomy of Chinese plants. Peking Society of Natural History, Bulletin 4(3):17-32.
Cites the principal papers containing descriptions of Chinese plants and, in most cases, gives the approximate number of new Chinese plants described, so that some idea of the value of the work can be obtained. BA 6(1) 2109.

Livingston, B. E.
1913 Climatic areas of the U. S. as related to plant growth. American Philosophical Society, Proceedings 52:257-275.
Includes three black-and-white maps showing the distribution of climatic indices developed by a combination of moisture and temperature elements. The author notes that vegetation types exhibit unequivocal relations to moisture conditions but no relations to conditions of temperature.

Livingston, B. E. and F. Shreve
1921 The distribution of vegetation in the United States as related to climatic conditions. Carnegie Institution of Washington, Publication 284:1-590.
This comprehensive discussion includes many tables and extensive information on the distribution of desert species as related to climatic conditions on the basis of data available at that time.

Logan, R. F.
1960 The central Namib Desert, South West Africa. National Academy of Sciences—National Research Council, Publication 758. 162 p. (Office of Naval Research, Foreign Field Research Program, Report 9.)
An excellent and fairly detailed study of the total geography of the Namib, from Walvis Bay and Swakapmund inland, with considerable attention to the vegetation in the Coastal Namib, the Namib Platform, and the Great Sand Dunes.

Long, G.
1951 Introduction à l'étude de la végétation de la Tunisie centrale. L'intérêt pratique de la connaissance des associations végétales pour la mise en valeur des sols. Cas particulier de la région de Sidi Bou Zid. Service Botanique et Agronomique de Tunisie, Annales 24:101-140.

———— 1954 Contribution à l'étude de la végétation de la Tunisie centrale. Service Botanique et Agronomique de Tunisie, Annales 27(1/2): 1-388.
A fundamental study for central Tunisia. Plant communities are discussed in relation to edaphic conditions and the effects of man.

1963 Glossaire sur les herbages et la production fourragère. Service de Botanique de la Tunisie, Tunis. 122 p.

Lowe, C. H
1964 Arizona landscapes and habitats. p. 1-132, *In* C. H. Lowe, ed., The vertebrates of Arizona. University of Arizona Press, Tucson.
In this publication 110 pages are devoted to Arizona landscape and habitats; in addition, a 32-page bibliography includes many useful references on desert vegetation. The Chihuahuan, Sonoran, Mohave, and Great Basin desert vegetation elements in Arizona are briefly described and illustrated with excellent photographs.

Macbride, J. F.
1936- Flora of Peru. Field Museum of Natural History,
1961 Chicago, Botanical Series 13.

MacDougal, D. T.
1908 Botanical features of North American deserts. Carnegie Institution of Washington, Publication 99:1-111.
This broad review is of some value, but it has been superseded by Shreve (1942*a*).

Macleay, K. N. G.
1951 Ferns and fern allies of the Sudan. Sudan Notes and Records (Khartoum) 34(2).

Madigan, C. T.
1938 The Simpson Desert and its borders. Royal Society of New South Wales, Proceedings 71:503-535.
From the viewpoint of a geographer; includes history, geology, soils, vegetation, and its human inhabitants.. Two black-and-white maps and 14 photographs give a better understanding of conditions.

———— 1946 The sand formations. Simpson Desert Expedition, 1939, Scientific Report 6. Royal Society of South Australia, Transactions 70:45-63.
The chief features of the Simpson Desert are sand and spinifex. Madigan discusses the origin and development of dunes, notes that the barchane formation is absent,

and believes there is no evidence of greater aridity in the past and that because of the spinifex cover no natural expansion of the desert is possible.

Maiden, J. H.
1889 Useful native plants of Australia including Tasmania. Trübner, London; Turner and Henderson, Sydney. 696 p.
Includes an extensive list of Australian plants with notes regarding their uses by aborigines and modern residents.

Maire, R.
1921- Contributions à l'étude de la flora de l'Afrique
1945 du Nord. Fasc. 3, 26, 28, 33, 34. Société d'Histoire Naturelle de l'Afrique du Nord, Bulletin 12:180-187; 29:403-458; 30:327-370; 34:181-193; 36: 85-100.

———— 1926 Carte phytogéographique de l'Algérie et de la Tunisie. 78 p. *In* A. Bernard, Atlas d'Algérie et de Tunisie, fasc. 4. Direction de l'Agriculture, du Commerce et de la Colonization, Algiers, Service Cartographique.
This provisional phytogeographical map represents the natural vegetation, much of which has now been displaced by cultivated crops. Algeria and Tunisia are divided into the Mediterranean and Saharan regions, the Saharan including desert formations. BA 1(6)8693.

———— 1933- Etudes sur la flore et la végétation du Sahara
1940 central. Société d'Histoire Naturelle de l'Afrique du Nord, Mémoires 3:1-433.
These studies of the flora and vegetation of the central Sahara include a report of botanical investigations during a journey of the "Scientific Expedition of the Ahaggar." The first part is a fairly complete catalogue of the flora of the central Sahara, the second gives the native plant names in the Tamacheck dialect, and the third covers the distribution of plants in the area.

———— 1938 La flore et la végétation du Sahara occidental. *In* La vie dans la région désertique nord-tropicale de l'ancien monde. Société de Biogéographie, Paris, Mémoires 6:325-333.

———— 1943 Contribution à l'étude de la flore des montagnes du Sahara méridional. Société de Histoire Naturelle de l'Afrique du Nord, Bulletin 34: 134-141.

———— 1952- Flore de l'Afrique du Nord (Maroc, Algérie, Tunisie, Tripolitaine, Cyrénaïque et Sahara). Paul Lechevalier, Paris. 12 vols. (to 1965). (Encyclopédie Biologique. vols. 33, 45, 48, 53-54, 57-60, 62-63, 67).

Major, J.
1953 A note on *Halogeton*. Journal of Range Management 6(3):186-188.
A translation of material on the description, geographical distribution, and soil preference of three Asian members of the genus *Halogeton*. BA 27(12)32826.

Mallery, T. D.
1936*a* Rainfall records for the Sonoran Desert. Ecology 17(1):110-121.
A report of rainfall at 22 stations southwest and west of Tucson. Much of the information was obtained by a specially constructed rain gauge which prevents evapora-

tion and hence needs to be read only occasionally. Gives data for a 7- to 10-year period.

1936b Rainfall records for the Sonoran Desert. 2: Summary of readings to December 1935. Ecology 17(2):212-215.

A continuation of the earlier article. The accumulated data for several raingauge stations is brought up to date and summarized in a series of graphs and tables. Seasonal rainfall patterns and variability is analyzed for each of 22 long-period raingauge stations in Arizona and Sonora. BA 10(8)17798.

Mann, F. G.
1960 Regiones biogeográficas de Chile. Investigaciones Zoológicas Chilenas 6:15-47. (English summary)
Gives data on climate, vegetation, and animal life in each of 6 biogeographical regions in Chile, one of which includes desert communities. BA 37(2)4911.

Marloth, R.
1913- Flora of South Africa. Darter Brothers and Co.,
1932 Capetown; W. Wesley and Son, London. 4 vols. in 6.

Marsh, C. D., G. C. Roe, and A. B. Clawson
1926 Rayless goldenrod (*Aplopappus heterophyllus*) as a poisonous plant. U. S. Department of Agriculture, Bulletin 1391. 24 p.
A discussion of the poisonous qualities of rayless goldenrod, now more commonly called burroweed.

Marshall, A.
1948 The size of the Australian desert. Australian Geographer 5:168-175.
This paper analyzes the various systems used in the past for delimiting the Australian desert. It includes several maps.

Martínez, M.
1936 Plantas útiles de Mexico. 2. ed. Ediciones Botas, México. 400 p.
This paper replaces an earlier one published in 1928. Lists the most useful plants of Mexico alphabetically by common name, with a bibliography for each. Includes information on where they grow, their cultivation, chemical composition, industrial application, food value, and medicinal value. Includes many drawings and photographs. An excellent reference.

1945 Breve relación de algunas de las principales plantas observadas en el distrito sur de la Baja California. Sociedad Botánica de México, Boletín 2:1-14.
Gives brief descriptions of 45 useful or characteristic plants of southern Baja California, and discusses their uses and value. BA 21(7)17999.

1959 Plantas útiles de la flora mexicana. [3rd ed.?] Ediciones Botas, México, D. F. 621 p.
Descriptions and discussion on useful plants other than those commonly cultivated.

Martonne, E. de
1935 Problèmes des régions arides sud-américaines. Annales de Géographique. 44:1-27.
A description of northwest Argentina and north Chile. Discusses relief, structure, hydrography, climate, and vegetation. Includes an extensive discussion and explanation of aridity. Indexes of aridity are shown on a black-and-white one-page map and discussed in relation to topography. Includes 5 figures (maps of aridity, etc.) and 5 plates showing 2 to 3 good photographs per page.

1942 Nouvelle carte mondiale de l'indice d'aridité. Annales de Géographie 51(288):242-250.
A world map (scale 1:50,000,000) based on de Martonne's index of aridity and an accompanying discussion.

Masson, D. R., ed.
1955 Directory of scientific research organizations in the Union of South Africa. Edited for the South African Council for Scientific and Industrial Research. J. L. Van Schaik, Ltd., Pretoria. 123 p.

Maximov, N. A.
1929 The plant in relation to water. Authorized English translation, edited, with notes by R. H. Yapp. George Allen and Unwin, Ltd., London. 451 p.
One of the earlier comprehensive studies of the physiological basis of drought resistance. It provides a great deal of fundamental informaton on plant-water relations, such as absorption of water by the plant, loss of water by the plant, and water balance and drought resistance of plants, particularly the chapter on xerophytes (p. 249-293).

1931 The physiological significance of the xeromorphic structure of plants. Journal of Ecology 19(2): 273-282.
Notes that there are many very different types of plants with almost no common characteristics included under the name of xerophytes, and that the essential quality of the xerophyte is its ability to resist drought by any means, morphological or physiological. Experimental evidence shows that many xerophytes have very high rates of transpiration, but also have the capacity to restrict water loss to a minimum in time of drought. BA 6(5)12665.

McDonough, W. T.
1964 Reduction in incident solar energy by desert shrub cover. Ohio Journal of Science 64(4):250-251.
This study shows that even defoliated shrubs and plants with very few branches can reduce the solar energy arriving at ground level as measured with a pyrheliograph. For example: creosotebush with leaves reduced it by 57 per cent, blue palo verde by 49, smokebush by 31, creosotebush without leaves by 18, and ocotillo by 10 per cent. BA 46(9)37142.

McDougall, W. B. and O. E. Sperry
1951 Plants of Big Bend National Park. U. S. Department of the Interior, Washington D. C. 209 p.
Includes a key to families, descriptions of seed plants, ferns, and fern allies of the park and 190 photographs of important plants. BA 26(3)6827.

McGinnies, W. G.
1934 The relation between frequency index and abundance as applied to plant populations in a semiarid region. Ecology 15:263-282.

1955 The United States and Canada. *In* Plant ecology, reviews of research. Unesco, Paris. Arid Zone Research 6:250-287.
Includes bibliography of 600 references.

1957 Vegetation. *In* Guide book to research data for arid zone development. Unesco, Paris. Arid Zone Research 9:121-133.

McKay, H. M.
1938 Burchell's index to the aboriginal African and Dutch names of the plants of southern Africa. Journal of South Africa Botany 4(4):129-141.
This index, based on W. J. Burchell's collections in the years 1810 to 1815, includes the present-day names of the districts where the collections were made. BA 13(5) 8443.

McKelvey, S. D.
1938- Yuccas of the southwestern United States. Harvard
1947 University, Arnold Arboretum. 2 vols.
A comprehensive review of the yuccas of the southwestern United States, including California, Arizona, New Mexico, Texas, and Utah. Includes distribution maps for each of the species described.

McTaggart, A.
1936 A survey of the pastures of Australia; embodying ecological information and discussions explanatory of the accompanying pasture map of the Commonwealth. Australia, Council for Scientific and Industrial Research, Bulletin 99:1-71.
Includes a map which outlines and divides the pasture areas of Australia into several zones, such as saltbush type, mulga type, and vast central-interior low-rainfall zones. Discusses soil character and climatic conditions, and mentions floral composition for each area. Includes 18 photographs showing typical types of vegetation. BA 11(4)7937.

McVaugh, R.
1958 Flora of Peru. Field Museum of Natural History, Chicago, Publications, Botany 13(IV-2):569-818.
This part deals with Myrtaceae. Several spp. of *Eucalyptus* have been introduced for shade and for ornament, and at least one has become widespread. BA 33(5).

Meeuse, A. D. J.
1962 The Cucurbitaceae of southern Africa. Bothalia 8(1):1-111.
Reviews of previous taxonomic studies of the Cucurbitaceae (an important group of plants in southern Africa) and discusses their economic importance. Includes a key for identification of species. BA 40(6)24609.

Meigs, P.
1953 World distribution of arid and semi-arid homoclimates. *In* Reviews of research on arid zone hydrology. Unesco, Paris. Arid Zone Programme 1:203-209.
On the basis of Thornthwaite's (1948) classification of climates, Meigs categorized and mapped the arid and semiarid areas of the world by season of rainfall, maximum temperature of the hottest month, and minimum temperature of the coldest month. The original maps which accompanied this paper were dated 1952 and revised in 1960.

1957 Arid and semiarid climatic types of the world. International Geographical Congress, 17th, Washington, D. C., 1952, 8th General Assembly, Proceedings, p. 135-138.

1960 Distribution of arid homoclimates. Map 392: Eastern hemisphere. Map 393: Western hemisphere. Revised. United Nations, New York.
A revision of his original maps published in 1953. Includes some refinements based on additional information not available earlier.

1966 Geography of coastal deserts. Unesco, Paris. Arid Zone Research 28. 140 p. 14 maps.

Meinzer, O. E.
1926 Plants as indicators of ground water. Washington Academy of Sciences, Journal 16(21):553-564.
The term "phreatophyte" is used to designate a plant that habitually obtains its water supply from a zone of saturation. This paper briefly reviews the history of the subject; gives evidence of phreatophytic habitat; discusses relations of these plants to hydrophytes, halophytes, xerophytes, and mesophytes; and discusses their value as indicators of the occurrence, depth, quality, and quantity of ground water. BA 1(6)8697.

1927 Plants as indicators of ground water. U. S. Geological Survey, Water-Supply Paper 577:1-95.
This elaboration of his 1926 paper includes 8 maps of arid regions showing the distribution of certain species in belts with specified depths to the water table.

Merriam, C. H.
1890 Results of biological survey of the San Francisco Mountain region and desert of the Little Colorado in Arizona. North American Fauna 3:5-34.
Merriam's basic study which led to development of the life zone concept.

1893a The geographic distribution of life in North America with special reference to the Mammalia. Smithsonian Institution, Annual Report to July 1891, General Appendix, 365-415.
This paper includes a historical synopsis of faunal and floral divisions proposed for North America. The distribution of plants and animals relative to various climatic conditions is discussed.

1893b Notes on the distribution of trees and shrubs in the deserts and desert ranges of southern California, southern Nevada, northwestern Arizona, and southwestern Utah. North American Fauna 7:285-343.

1893c Notes on the geographic and vertical distribution of cactuses, yuccas, and agave, in the deserts and desert ranges of southern California, southern Nevada, northwestern Arizona, and southwestern Utah. North American Fauna. 7:345-359.
One of the earlier publications on the subject. Notes the characteristics of various plants and gives their distribution, including general range and specific local occurrences.

1898 Life zones and crop zones of the United States. U. S. Department of Agriculture, Division of Biological Survey, Bulletin 10. 79 p.
The author separates the arid zone from the humid along the 100th meridian between 35° and 45° N latitude. He notes that the most conspicuous vegetation of the upper Sonoran area is the true sagebrush (*Artemisia tridentata*) which, however, is equally abundant in the transition zone. Lower Sonoran boundaries are given in detail. The vegetation includes creosotebush, mesquite, acacias, cacti, yuccas, and agaves.

Merrill, E. D. and E. H. Walker
1938 A bibliography of eastern Asiatic botany. Harvard University, Arnold Arboretum, Jamaica Plain, Massachusetts. 719 p.

A valuable reference. *See* Walker (1960) for continuation.

Miller, O. B.
1946 Southern Kalahari. Empire Forestry Review 25 (2):225-229.
A discussion of the vegetation of the Kalahari, noting the tree communities and treeless areas. The author thinks the later condition may be due to recent stabilization of sand, greater aridity, or lower temperatures.

Miranda, F. and E. Hernández
1963 Los tipos de vegetación de México y su clasificación. Sociedad Botánico de México, Boletín 28:29-179.
(Types of vegetation in Mexico and their classification)
Proposes a categorization of 32 different types of vegetation in Mexico, determined mainly upon a physiognomic basis, but also by their relationships to climatic conditions according to Köppen. Includes 107 photographs, which are a valuable contribution to the usefulness of the paper.

Mirov, N. T.
1952 Simmondsia or jojoba, a problem in economic botany. Economic Botany 6(1):41-47.
The jojoba grows in Arizona, adjacent parts of Mexico, and occasionally in southern California. The seeds produce a wax with properties similar to sperm oil; and which has possibilities for use in salad dressing, high-temperature lubricants, and candles. The plants are readily browsed by livestock.

Misra, R.
1955 Progress of plant ecological studies in India. University of Saugar, Botanical Society, Bulletin 7(2):90-101.
The chief value of this paper is its bibliography of 177 entries. BA 30(12)33660.

Momotov, I. F.
1961 Kharakteristika prirodnykh uslovii i rastitel'nosti kyzyklumskoi pustynnoi stantsii. *In:* Akademiia Nauk Uzbekskoi SSR, Tashkent, Pastbishcha Uzbekistana, 88-108. Referativnyi Zhurnal, Biologiya, 1963, No. 4247.
(The characteristic of the natural conditions and vegetation of the Kyzyl Kum desert station. *In:* The pasture grounds of Uzbekistan.)
Describes the natural conditions and vegetation in the area of the Kyzyl-Kum desert station, situated in the southeastern Kyzyl-Kum desert at the foot of the Kul'dzhuktau mountain in the vicinity of the Ayak-Guzhudma springs. The basic vegetative associations consist of xerophytic and halophytic semishrubs. BA 45(6)22925.

Monod, T.
1931 Remarques biologiques sur le Sahara. Revue Générale des Sciences Pures et Appliquées 42 (21):609-616.
Bases the boundaries of the Sahara on flora and fauna, and a precipitation limit of 200 mm. The principal divisions of the desert are related to "vegetation diffus" and vegetation "contracté": "contracté" occurs in areas of very low precipitation, and is constricted to growing only in wadis and other spots of especially favorable conditions; "diffus" is vegetation distributed more generally over terrain in areas of more favorable general moisture conditions.

1932 Mission saharienne Augiéras-Draper, 1927-1928. Museum National d'Histoire Naturelle, Paris, Bulletin sér. 2, 4(6):756-774.
Monod considers the several vegetational divisions of the Sahara and summarizes them in a chart comparing his own classification with those of Engler, Shantz and Marbut, and Chevalier.

1938 Notes botaniques sur le Sahara occidental et ses confins sahéliens. *In:* La vie dans la région désertique nord-tropicale de l'ancien monde. Société de Biogéographie, Paris, Mémoires 6: 351-374.
This very worthwhile discussion starts with a global approach, then proceeds to a local discussion. Discusses Afro-Asian deserts in general and comments upon their relationships to each other. Includes detailed lists of flora.

1953 Exposé liminaire pour la section biologique. *In* Desert research, Proceedings, International symposium held in Jerusalem, May 7-14, 1952, sponsored by the Research Council of Israel and Unesco. Research Council of Israel, Special Publication 2:43-88.
A philosophical discussion of various aspects of the Sahara. The author considers the characteristics of the climate; the bioclimatic limits of the desert, the north and south differences and the relationship of the flora to that of Asia and tropical Africa; various ecological aspects; and a listing of the principal habitats. This discussion, while giving little specific information on the vegetation, is a valuable aid toward an understanding of the ecology of the Sahara and deserts in general.

1954 Mode "contracté" et "diffus" de la végétation saharienne. p. 35-44. *In* J. L. Cloudsley-Thompson, ed., Biology of Deserts; proceedings of a symposium on the biology of hot and cold deserts. Institute of Biology, London. 223 p.
Mainly a discussion of differences of vegetation related to terrain, substratum, and climate. Constricted vegetation found under very low rainfall, is limated to oueds. Diffuse vegetation is found where precipitation is not less than 30 to 50 mm in the north, and not less than 50 to 100 mm in the south.

1955 Sur un cas exceptionnel de sécheresse aréale: les sables de la Mauritanie orientale. Rech. Trav. Lab. Bot. Geol. Zool. Fac. Montpellier, sér. Bot., fasc. 7:63-67.

1957 Les grandes division chorologiques de l'Afrique. Commission for Technical Co-operation in Africa/ Scientific Council for Africa, Publication 24. 147 p.
(The large mapping divisions of Africa.)

1964 A propos de deux publications du Professeur M. Zohary. Institut Français d'Afrique Noire, Bulletin, sér. A. 26(4):1403-1428.

Montasir, A. H.
1951 Studies on the autecology of *Zilla spinosa* (Forsk, Prant). Fouad I University, Cairo, Faculty of Science, Bulletin 29:1-52.
A very useful study.

Montasir, A. H. and A. Abd el Rahman
1951 Root development of *Zygophyllum simplex.* Institut Fouad I du Désert, Cairo, Bulletin 1(1): 21-34.
Comprehensive studies of roots of *Zygophyllum simplex* under dry and wet conditions—roots penetrate 47 cm.

Montasir, A. H. and M. Shafey
1951 Studies on the autecology of *Fagonia arabica.* Institut Fouad I du Désert, Cairo, Bulletin 1(1): 55-76.
Gives geographic distribution, climate and soil habitat, communities, and morphological and physiological features for 10 species of spiny Fagonia. BA 29(1)1629.

Montasir, A. H. and G. H. Sidrak
1952 Etude sur le *Zygophyllum coccineum.* Institut Fouad I du Désert, Cairo, Bulletin 2(1):59-71.
A detailed study on the important desert species, *Zygophyllum coccineum.*

Monteil, V.
1949- Contribution à l'étude de la flora du Sahara
1953   occidental de l'arganier au karité. 2 vols. (Vol. 1, C. Sauvage, joint author). Institut des Hautes Etudes Marocaines, Notes et Documents 5-6.

Monticelli, J. V.
1938 Anotaciones fitogeográficas de la Pampa central. Lilloa 3:251-382.
Contains an enumeration of 302 species found in the political province La Pampa, many of them being from the western part which forms part of the Monte.

Moore, R. M.
1960 The management of native vegetation in arid and semi-arid regions. *In* Plant-water relationships in arid and semi-arid conditions, reviews of research. Unesco, Paris. Arid Zone Research 15:173-190.
An outstanding literature review aimed toward management of native vegetation in arid and semiarid regions. Reviews briefly the vegetation of arid lands. Discusses the effects of grazing and burning, phytosociological relationships in arid-zone communities, and regeneration and management of such communities. Management is subdivided into: control of unpalatable shrubs, artificial reseeding, mechanical methods of range improvement, control of livestock and grazing systems. Includes 297 selected references. BA 38(6)21340.

Moran, R.
1950 Plants of the Todos Santos Island, Baja California. Leaflets of Western Botany 6(2):53-56.

1951 Notes on the flora of Guadalupe Island, Mexico. Madroño 11(4):153-160.

Moran, R. and G. Lindsay
1950 Guadalupe Island. Desert Plant Life 22(1):3-9.
Discusses features of Guadalupe Island, off the coast of Baja California, Mexico. BA 25(4)11642.

1951 San Benito Islands. Desert Plant Life 23(4):78-83.

Morello, J.
1955- Estudios botánicos en las regiones áridas de la
1956   Argentina. Revista Agronómica del Noroeste Argentino 1:301-370, 385-524; 2:79-152.
A study of the anatomy of transpiring organs, habitat, morphology, and variation in transpiring surfaces of 4 resinous species of the Monte, *Larrea cuneifolia, Larrea divaricata, Larrea nitida* and *Zuccagnia punctata.* Includes

habitat pictures, a discussion of xeromorphic characteristics, and a good bibliography. Notes that *L. nitida* was a phreatophyte and that *L. cuneifolia* was found in the driest places (climatic and edaphic). Part 3 deals with the conditions of soil movements (erosion phenomena), erosion and sedimentation in Neuquén, northwestern Patagonia. Many meteorological data are analyzed and then the root-system and rooting habits under the effects of erosion in different shrubs of the desert.

Morello, J.
1958 La provincia fitogeográfica del Monte. Universidad de Tucumán, Instituto Miguel Lillo, Opera Lilloana 2. 155 p.
A very comprehensive publication on the phytogeographical province of the Monte; the best available reference for this area. The paper gives information on the limits, physiography, climatology, floristic composition, ecological types, and types of vegetation of the Monte. The climate of the Monte is discussed in detail in relation to the response of plants to climatological factors. The autecology of the dominant species in each community is discussed in detail. The author states that an effort has been made to gather, in the present paper, the largest possible quantity of exact data on the climate, physiography, ecological types, and types of vegetation of the Monte—this in order to provide other scientists in arid zones such data as will permit them to make comparative studies with similar regions of the world.

Morong, T.
1891 The flora of the desert of Atacama. Torrey Botanical Club, Bulletin 18:39-48.

Mouterde, P.
1966 Nouvelle flore du Liban et de la Syrie. v. 1. Impr. Catholique, Beyrouth. 572 p.

Mueller, F., freiherr von
1858- Fragmenta phytographiae Australiae. Auctoritate
1882   gubern. coloniae Victoriae, ex officina Joannis Ferres, Melbourne. 11 vols., part of a 12th.

Muench, J. R.
1943 Our desert yuccas. Natural History 51(3): 142-145.
This illustrated article discusses four yuccas found in California. Notes that the fruit of *Yucca baccata* is edible, that the fibers of some species are used for cordage, the roots for detergents, and the porous pliable wood for splints. BA 18(1)1496.

Muesebeck, C. F. W. and K. V. Krombein
1952 Life zone map. Systematic Zoology 1(1):24-25.
This map, an adaptation of the U. S. Biological Survey's Fourth Provisional Zone Map of North America, 1910, is designed to assist those who wish to give the range of species by reference to life zones. BA 27(5)12004.

Muir, J.
1929 The vegetation of the Riversdale area, Cape Province. Botanical Survey of South Africa, Memoir 13:1-82.
Includes a discussion of the Klein Karroo which receives 8 to 14 inches of rainfall annually and supports semi-desert vegetation.

Mulay, B. N.
1961 Patterns of plant distribution in Rajasthan. Indian Botanical Society, Memoirs 3:9-12.

The author believes that grazing rather than climatic change may further the encroachment of desert upon other vegetation types.

Muller, C. H.
1937 Plants as indicators of climate in northeast Mexico. American Midland Naturalist 18:986-1000.
Five major climate types are distinguished, including one designated warm and arid occurring on the eastern coastal plain, the broad interior valleys, and the central plateau west of the Sierra Madre Oriental. Describes the vegetation and the method used to interpret it in terms of climate.

1939 Relations of the vegetation and climate types in Nuevo León, Mexico. American Midland Naturalist 21(3):687-729.
Discusses (among other regions) the central plateau desert scrub area with its warm arid climate. Points out that classification of climatic types in Nuevo León is exceedingly inaccurate because of scarcity of observations. Notes that the vegetation types vary from the most scanty scrub to luxuriant forests and lush meadows. Includes landscape photographs illustrating vegetation types, and maps showing relief, vegetation distribution, and climatic types. BA 13(8)12593.

1947 Vegetation and climate of Coahuila, Mexico. Madroño 9(2):33-57.
Vegetation types of Coahuila are described, mapped, and correlated with those of adjacent Nuevo León, and some types of Texas and Chihuahua. One type, Chihuahuan desert shrub, occupies the central plateau region, and is coextensive with the Clima Desértico climatic types of Sánchez. BA 22(2)2864.

1953 The association of desert annuals with shrubs. American Journal of Botany 40(2):53-60.
Reports of a study to determine the relationship between certain shrub plants and annuals. Both *Franseria dumosa* and *Encelia farinosa* have toxic materials in their leaves, but it was concluded that this is not the limiting factor in the growth of annuals—rather that annuals are confined to sites of buried organic debris. Annuals, therefore, occur beneath *Franseria* because of accumulated humus, but are absent beneath *Encelia* because that shrub accumulates insufficient humus. BA 27(6)15301.

Muller, W. H. and C. H. Muller
1956 Association patterns involving desert plants that contain toxic products. American Journal of Botany 43(5):354-361.
It was found that although some shrubs contain water-soluble toxic materials which inhibit growth, this does not seem to determine the survival of shrub-dependent desert annuals; regardless of toxic materials, shrub-dependent herbs grow beneath those desert shrubs that accumulate mounds of wind-blown organic debris.

Munz, P. A. and D. D. Keck
1949 California plant communities. El Aliso 2(1): 87-105.
The authors discuss a tentative classification of California plant communities into 5 provinces, 14 major vegetation types, and 24 communities according to dominant species and climatic conditions. The Nevada division includes a desert scrub, divided further into sagebrush scrub and shadscale scrub. The southern desert includes a desert scrub, divided further into shadscale scrub and creosotebush scrub. In a later publication the authors classed all scrub types under one major scrub type.

Munz, P. A. and D. D. Keck
1950 California plant communities; supplement. El Aliso 2(3):199-202.
The previous classification was revised from 24 to 28 plant communities. The authors consolidated all scrub under one vegetation type, including northern coastal scrub, coastal sage scrub, sagebrush scrub, shadscale scrub, creosotebush scrub, and alkali scrub. The term "scrub" may adequately describe the vegetation found in California, but it is hardly an adequate term to describe the more luxuriant vegetation of the Sonoran and Chihuahuan deserts.

1959 A California flora. Published for the Rancho Santa Ana Botanic Garden by the University of California Press, Berkeley. 1681 p.
A comprehensive manual of the flora of California, covering the thousands of native and naturalized plants that grow in that area. BA 35(1)2249.

Murat, M.
1937 La végétation du Sahara occidental en Mauritanie. Académie des Sciences, Paris, Comptes Rendus 205(5):338-340.

1944 Esquisse phytogéographique du Sahara occidental. Office National Anti Acridien, Alger, Mémoires 1. 31 p.

Murbarger, N.
1950 The great white sands. Natural History 59(5): 228-235.
This 200-square mile area includes dunes composed of 99 per cent pure gypsum crystals completely devoid of nitrogen. The 62 species of plants growing in this area have their roots in the stabilized flats, either beneath or between the dunes. Yucca shows the greatest adaptability. The plants occurring on the flats between the dunes are discussed, and also the animal population of the area. BA 25(2)3761.

Murray, B. J.
1931 A study of the vegetation of the the Lake Torrens plateau, South Australia. Royal Society of South Australia, Transactions and Proceedings 55: 91-112.
The Lake Torrens plateau area has an annual rainfall of about 7 inches. This work discusses briefly climate and soil, then gives details of the vegetation. The rainfall is uncertain: there are no regular wet and dry seasons; sometimes the whole year's rain may fall within a few days, or it may be scattered throughout the year in ineffectual light precipitation. Gives a biological spectrum of the vegetation of the region in relation to habitat.

Muschler, R.
1912 A manual flora of Egypt. R. Friedlaender und Sohn, Berlin. 2 vols. 1311 p.
This early manual is still quite useful.

Nair, N. C. and G. S. Nathawat
1956 Vegetation of Pilani and its neighborhood. Bombay Natural History Society, Journal 54(1): 91-106.
This area is on the boundary line between arid and semi-arid, with a rainfall of less than 15 inches. It is described

as an arid, sun-scorched, sandy area, broken by shifting sand dunes, spotted with trees, and scattered with a meager growth of desert plants. The article is of value here for its list of plants, many of which extend into the desert area. BA 31(9)29185.

Naqvi, S. H. Z.
1961   Some common plants of the arid regions of Nushki and Kharan (Baluchistan). Scientist (Pakistan) 4(1/2):40-43.

Negbi, M. and M. Evenari
1961   The means of survival of some desert summer annuals. *In* Symposium on plant-water relationships in arid and semiarid conditions. Unesco, Paris. Arid Zone Research 16:249-259.
Rapid germination and resistance of seedlings to desiccation are very important in survival under desert conditions. BA 39(2)4568.

Nègre, R.
1959   Recherches phytogéographiques sur l'étage de végétation méditerranéenne aride (sous-étage chaud) au Maroc occidental. Institut Scientifique Chérifien, Travaux, sér. Botanique 13. 385 p.
An ecological and phytosociological monograph covering the arid western portion of Morocco. The major plant communities are discussed in relation to ecological conditions.

———
1961-   Petite flore des régions arides du Maroc Occidental.
1962   Editions du Centre National de la Recherche Scientifique, Paris. 2 vols.
A very valuable flora, compact and well illustrated.

Negri, G.
1940   Per uno schema cartografico della vegetazione dell'Africa Orientale Italiana. Rivista Geografica Italiana 47:2-16.

———
1948   Erbario figuarto; descrizione e proprietà delle piante medicinale e velenose delle flora Italiana, con cenni sulle principali specie dell'Africa settentrionale ed orientale. 4th ed. Hoepli, Milan. 459 p.
A good description of medicinal and poisonous plants of north and east Africa.

Nelson, A.
1898   The Red Desert of Wyoming and its forage resources. U. S. Department of Agriculture, Division of Agrostology, Bulletin 13. 72 p.
This early description of the Red Desert remains a good reference for the area. This area of 85 by 130 miles embraces more than 11,000 square miles. Vegetation is dominanted by sagebrush and saltbushes of several species.

Nelson, E. W.
1921   Lower California and its natural resources. National Academy of Sciences, Memoirs 16:1.194.
This article includes a description, with illustrations, of the vegetation of the area.

Nichol, A. A.
1937   The natural vegetation of Arizona. Arizona Agricultural Experiment Station, Technical Bulletin 68:181-222.
An excellent article on the vegetation of Arizona. It was revised in 1952, but the original publication is still very usable. Discusses the relationships of elevation, temperature, and rainfall to the distribution of vegetation.

Important species of plants are discussed, both separately and in the communities in which they occur. Includes many good photographs.

———
1952   The natural vegetation of Arizona. Arizona Agricultural Experiment Station, Technical Bulletin 127:186-230.
Nichol retained his original text (1937) except for changes in terminology that reflects the work done since 1937. Nomenclature is revised to match the latest edition of Kearney and Peebles. Shows 42 per cent of the state (in the western and southern portions) as desert. The map is the same as in the early edition. Types of vegetation and individual plants are clearly discussed and shown in photographs.

Nichols, G. E.
1923   A working basis for the ecological classification of plant communities. Ecology 4:11-23, 154-179.
A basic work on the classification of plant communities, this largely philosophical publication is valuable to anyone seeking a better understanding of the problems related to the classification of plant communities.

Niering, W. A., R. H. Whittaker, and C. H. Lowe
1963   The saguaro, a population in relation to environment. Science 142(3588):15-23.
An excellent discussion of the saguaro, its relationship to the plant communities in which it occurs, and factors that determine it establishment and survival. The saguaro is a major plant of the Sonoran Desert, occurring in a number of types of desert and extending into the desert grassland. It reaches its maximum population density in the Tucson area at lower elevations on the dry slopes of mountains. It is reproducing well on rocky slopes and in some bajada communities but is failing to reproduce on the finer soils of bajada affected by grazing. The authors believe grazing subjects the population to gradual disaster, with failure to reproduce resulting in slow decline to disappearance. Freezing and disease may cause a temporary setback, or kill older plants. BA 45(11)45128.

Northern Territory Administration, Animal Industry Branch
1956-   Poisonous plants of the Northern Territory.
1959   Extension article 2(1-3).

Novikoff, G.
1958   Relations entre la structure de la végétation et la stratification des milieux halophiles en Tunisie. Service de la Carte Phytogéographique, Bulletin sér. B, 3(1):69-83.
Lists three very different geographical zones where halophilic vegetation occurs in Tunisia. Concludes that coexistence of definite floral and ecological groups at the same location indicates the presence of a complex soil. Pedological studies have confirmed this conclusion. Certain halophilic species can be used as indicators of depth of saline water in the soil. BA 35(5)12409.

———
1964   Contribution à l'étude des relations entre le sol et la végétation halophile de Tunisie. Institut National de la Recherche Agronomique de Tunisie, Annales 34:1-339.
Discusses the relationships between the vegetation of the saline soils that occupy large areas in Tunisia and the principal determining ecological factors. Notes that in the same area there can be two groups of vegetation, reflecting salinity and "hydromorphie." The vegetation corresponds to content of soluble salts and other soil characteristics. Includes a 9-page bibliography.

Nunnayev, A. and S. Veyisov
1965 Natural decline of the black saksaul in the Kara-Kum (translated title). Academiia Nauk Turkmenskoi S. S. R., Izvestiya, Seriya Biologicheskikh Nauk 4:71-75. (English abstract in AD-630 802, 1966, p. 44-45.)

Nuttonson, M. Y.
1946 Agricultural climatology, physical belts and crop ecology of Palestine and Trans-Jordan and their climatic analogues in the United States. U. S. Department of Agriculture, Foreign Agriculture Report 14. 23 p.
A very useful agrometeorological publication, comparing the homoclimatic areas of Palestine and Trans-Jordan with those of California, southwestern Texas, and southern Arizona as a basis for mutual plant introduction. Data are shown in charts and tables that make comparisons easy.

1947 Ecological crop geography of China and its agroclimatic analogues in North America. American Institute of Crop Ecology, Washington, D. C.
This very useful publication includes tables of monthly climatic means for over 200 stations. The comparison between China and North America permits a better understanding of the climate and vegetation of China.

1961 The physical environment and agriculture of Libya and Egypt with special reference to their regions containing areas climatically and latitudinally analogous to Israel. American Institute of Crop Ecology. 452 p.
A very worthwhile publication giving extensive information on comparative conditions. Summarizes information in tables, graphs, and charts, so that analogous conditions are easily seen.

Oberdorfer, E.
1961 Bibliographia phytosociologica: Chile. Excerpta Botanica, B, 3(1):79-80.

Ochoterena, I.
1937 Esquemas biotípicos y sinecias características de las regiones geográfico-botánicas de México. Instituto de Biología, Universidad Nacional de México, Anales 8:463-597.
The desert region is divided into three subregions: the first includes the western part of Mexico; the second includes the Texas-Mexico area; and the third is the sea subregion. Notes that some sun plants grew in shady locations when conditions were severe, and that there was more moisture in the shade than in the bright sunlight. Includes excellent photographs showing types and important species.

1945 Outline of the geographic distribution of plants in Mexico. p. 261-265. *In* Plants and plant science in Latin America. Chronica Botanica Co., Waltham, Mass.
Another of the brief but good descriptions found in this book. The desert regions are discussed with the other major vegetation types in Mexico. BA 20(1)200.

Oppenheimer, H. R.
1940 A contribution to the desert flora south and southwest of the Dead Sea. Palestine Journal of Botany, Rehovot ser. 3(1/2):144-153.
An account of the species and associations observed on a journey from Jebel Usdum to Wadi Fiqra. Almost all the plants found were Sahara-Sindian species.

1951a Light evading plants in the hills and plain of Israel. Palestine Journal of Botany, Rehovot ser 8(1):20-26.

1951b Summer drought and water balance of plants growing in the Near East. Journal of Ecology 39(2):356-362.
A review of 20 years of research on the water ecology of plants, done mainly in Palestine. Distinguishes between the water spendthrifts and water savers, according to average transpiration intensity. Deciduous woody plants are mainly spendthrifts, evergreens mainly savers. Various means of survival under drought conditions are described.

1960 Adaptation to drought: xerophytism. *In* Plant-water relationships in arid and semi-arid conditions, reviews of research. Unesco, Paris. Arid Zone Research 15:105-138.
An outstanding review on adaptation to drought. Considers the ability of plants to survive under aridity arising from various causes, the means and processes by which survival is obtained, and other phases of the subject. Bibliography of 264 selected titles. BA 39(2)4569.

1961 Essai d'une révision des trèfles de la Palestine. Société Botanique de France, Bulletin 108(1/2):47-71.
A general discussion of the clovers of Palestine followed by detailed consideration of each known species from the Republic of Israel and the Kingdom of Jordan. The richness of the region in species of *Trifolium* is indicated by the fact that 38 species are treated. Includes abundant references to literature and bibliography of 53 titles. BA 38(5)19860.

Oppenheimer, H. R. and M. Evenari
1930 Florula Transjordanica. Société Botanique de Genève, Bulletin, Sér. 2, 22. 386 p. (Reliquae Aaronsohnianae 1)
This work and the authors' 1940 paper "Florula Cisjordanica" (*q. v.*) are excellent critical taxonomic studies of the rich herbarium material collected by A. Aaronsohn. Both volumes contain many illustrations and also detailed studies on several Palestinian genera.

1940 Florula Cisjordanica. Société Botanique de Genève, Bulletin, Sér. 2, 31. 432 p. (Reliquae Aaronsohnianae 2)

Orlov, B. P.
1928 K izucheniyu zkologicheskikh usloviy v yugovostochnoy chasti zakaspiyskikh Kara-Kum. Trudy po Prikladnoy, Botanike, Genetike y Selesktsii 19(4):459-401.
Considers ecological conditions in the southeastern part of Transcaspian Kara-Kum, Asiatic Russia. The existence of vegetation in this dune region depends largely on the moisture content of the sand. Below the surface of the sand there are several distinct alternating zones of relatively moist and dry sand down to a depth of about 200 cm, where a uniformity of moisture content is reached. Notes that moisture vapor moves in the soil from layers of high pressure to layers of low pressure caused by differences in temperature. This enables sand to draw moisture from the atmosphere. English summary. BA 4(6)17448.

Orshan, G. and D. Zohary
1955   Vegetation of the littoral salt marshes of Israel. Research Council of Israel, Bulletin 4(4):363-369.
Vegetation of the coastal salt marshes is described, and floristic and ecological relationships discussed. BA 30 (12)33666.

1963   Vegetation of the sand deserts in the western Negev of Israel. Vegetatio 11(3):112-120.
This area, considered an extension of the sandy areas of northern Sinai, has several associations including *Artemisia*. The associated species vary with the characteristics of the sandy material. Characteristic species are Sahara-Sindian with annuals dominant. BA 44(1)458.

Osborn, T. G. B.
1929   On regeneration problems in arid Australia. Pan-Pacific Science Congress, 3rd, Tokyo, 1926, Proceedings 2:1913-1914.
Climatic and edaphic influences are briefly sketched. There are 3 vegetation types: annuals or ephemerals; trees and tall shrubs; and dwarf shrubs, such as *Atriplex* and *Kochia*. Grazing animals, chiefly domestic, have a serious effect, especially on the dwarf shrubs. Various regressive phases are to be noted, culminating in bare soil. BA 6(1)53.

1939   Some comparisons between the vegetation of Morocco and Australia. Geobotanisches Forschunginstituts Rübel, Zürich, Veröffentlichungen 14: 168-191.
The author finds that, in spite of great differences in floristic composition, the general impression of the vegetation is the same in districts of similar climate. Compares climates (graphically), the effects of the activities of man, and soils types. BA 13(5)7209.

Osborn, T. G. B. and J. G. Wood
1923   Some halophytic and non-halophytic plant communities in arid South Australia. Royal Society of South Australia, Transactions 47:388-399.
The area studied has less than 10 inches of rain. *Atriplex* and *Kochia* are more abundant in drier areas and mallee less abundant. The salt content was high in most highly developed communities.

Osborn, T. G. B., J. G. Wood, and T. B. Paltridge
1935   On the climate and vegetation of Koonamore vegetation reserve to 1931. Linnean Society of New South Wales, Proceedings 60:392-427.

Ozenda, P.
1958   Flore du Sahara septentrional et central. Centre National de la Recherche Scientifique, Paris. 486 p.
One of the best descriptions of vegetation and conditions of the Sahara. The first 6 chapters cover: *(1)* desert environment, including world distribution of deserts, characteristics of desert climate, and different types of deserts; *(2)* environmental conditions of the Sahara; *(3)* composition and origins of the Sahara flora; *(4)* biology of desert vegetation; *(5)* vegetative groups of the Sahara; and *(6)* use of plants by man in the Sahara. The second and largest part, an analytical flora, includes general keys to families; brief descriptions of families, genera, and species; and distribution of species. Part III includes definitions of botanical terms used, a bibliography, and an alphabetical index of families, genera, and synonyms. BA 33(8)30868.

Ozenda, P. and P. Quézel
1956   Les Zygophyllacées de l'Afrique du Nord et du Sahara. Institut de Recherches Sahariennes, Travaux 14:23-83.
(The Zygophyllaceas of northern Africa and the Sahara.)

Pabot, H.
1964   Phytogeographical and ecological regions. p 30-40. *In* M. L. Dewan and J. Famouri, The soils of Iran. FAO, Rome.
A brief discussion of the phytogeographical and ecological regions of Iran, useful especially because the discussion is related to soils. The drier portions of Iran are considered under the headings of "subdesert," "steppe," "substeppe," and "xerophilous forest" zones. Saharo-Sindian and Irano-Turanian affinities are discussed.

Palmer, E.
1966   The Plains of Camdeboo. Collins, London. 320 p.
A popular discussion of the Karroo, containing much useful information on the physical and biological characteristics of the vegetation. The graphic descriptions of the individual plant species provide informative and interesting reading. Uses and harmful characteristics of plants are also discussed. An excellent bibliography is included.

Palmer, E. and N. Pitman
1961   Trees of South Africa. Balkema, Amsterdam-Cape Town. 352 p.

Palmer, E. J.
1929   The ligneous flora of the Davis Mountains, Texas. Arnold Arboretum, Journal 10(1):8-45.
The topographical, geological, and climatic features of the Davis Mountains are discussed as a basis for describing the vegetation of various situations and altitudes. The vegetation of the lower and more open portions is described as being more-or-less xerophytic and belonging to the Sonoran province. The second part of the article consists of an annotated systematic enumeration of the the woody plants collected. BA 4(5)16134.

Parker, K. F.
1958   Arizona ranch, farm, and garden weeds. Arizona Agricultural Extension Service, Circular 265. 288 p.
A very readable and useful compendium on the weeds of ranch and farm, and those often found along roadsides. Many illustrations aid in identifying the common weeds. Poisonous and noxious characteristics are described.

Parodi, L. R.
1938   Plantas psamófilas indígenas, que pueden ser cultivadas para consolidar dunas. Jornadas Agronómicas y Veterinarias, Universidad de Buenos Aires. 13 p.
A discussion of native psammophytes, mostly trailing grasses and herbs, which can be used for dune fixation, even in very dry climates.

1945   Las regiones fitogeográficas argentinas y sus relaciones con la industria forestal. p. 127-132. *In* Plants and plant science in Latin America. Chronica Botanica Co., Waltham, Mass.
A description of the phytogeographic regions of Argentina and their relationships with forest industry. Distinguishes major formation, including what the writer calls the "pampas steppe," "Patagonian steppe," and "Andean desert." BA 20(5)7904.

Parodi, L. R.
1950   Las gramineas tóxicas para el ganado en la República Argentina. Revista Argentina de Agronomía 17:163-229.

Passey, H. G. and V. K. Hugie
1962   Sagebrush on relict ranges in the Snake River Plains and northern Great Basin. Journal of Range Management 15(5):273-278.
Compares the kind, amount, and character of sagebrush on various types of soil found in the Snake River Plains and northern Great Basin. Big sagebrush (*Artemisia tridentata*) was the most common and occurred on the greatest number of soils. Includes data useful to any studies in which plant-soil relationships are involved. BA 43(1)406.

Paulsen, O.
1912   Studies on the vegetation of the Transcaspian lowlands. The Second Danish Pamir Expedition. Boghandel-Nordisk Forlag, Copenhagen. 279 p.
A valuable comprehensive report. The area extends from the Caspian Sea to Lake Balkhash, is bounded on the south by the mountains of northern Persia, and excludes the Kirghiz Steppes on the north. Deserts of moving sand cover 88 per cent of the lowland. Precipitation ranges from 91 to 368 mm. Describes in detail each of 5 plant communities: "salt-desert," "clay-desert," "stone-desert," "sand-desert," and "riverside thickets." Includes 77 figures, a map, and bibliography.

Pavlov, N. V.
1961   Osnovny e zakonomernosti vo flore i rastitel' nosti Kazakhstana. Tashkent University, Trudy 187: 28-41. Referativnyi Zhurnal, Biologiya, no. 13V201.
A study of the basic patterns in the flora and vegetation of Kazakhstan. Notes very heterogeneous patterns of flora and vegetation and that the usual statistical patterns, such as latitudinal and vertical zonality, were of secondary importance. The basic factors that formed the flora and vegetation were invasions from adjoining (and sometimes extremely remote) lands, such as Africa and China. BA 42(2)4559.

Paylore, P.
1967   Arid-lands research institutions, a world directory. University of Arizona Press, Tucson. 268 p.

Pechanec, J. F. and G. Stewart
1944   Sagebrush burning—good and bad. U. S. Department of Agriculture, Farmer's Bulletin 1948:1-32.
A good summary of the results of burning in the Great Basin Desert area and adjacent rangeland. Both natural and planned burning are discussed. BA 18(8)15528.

Penman, H. L.
1956   Estimating evaporation. American Geophysical Union, Transactions 37(1):43-46.
An excellent discussion of the physical processes involved in evaporation as they relate to the determination of evapotranspiration.

Pérez-Rosales, S.
1964   Los suelos y la vegetación del campo experimental "La Sauceda" en la zona árida de Coahuila. Instituto Nacional de Investigaciones Forestales, México, Boletín Técnico 16:1-60.
A discussion of the soils and vegetation of the experimental field "La Sauceda" in the arid zone of Coahuila. Vegetation, soils, and topography are discussed for this arid area with summer rainfall.

Perrier de la Bathie, H.
1921   La végétation malgache. Musée Colonial de Marseille, Annales, sér. 3, 9:1-266.

————
1936   Biogéographie des plantes de Madagascar. Société d'Editions Géographiques, Maritimes, et Coloniales, Paris. 156 p.

Perry, R. A.
1960   Pasture lands of the Northern Territory, Australia. C. S. I. R. O. Land Research ser. 5. 55 p.

————
1962   Natural pastures of the Alice Springs area, Northern Territory. C. S. I. R. O. Land Research ser. 6:240-257.

Perry, R. A. and C. S. Christian
1954   Vegetation of the Barkly region. C. S. I. R. O. Land Research ser. 3:78-112.

Perry, R. A. and M. Lazarides
1962   Vegetation of the Alice Springs area. C. S. I. R. O. Land Research ser. 6:208-236.
Concludes that the harsh arid climate is responsible for the area being floristically poor. Important families and representative species are discussed. BA 42(5)16518.

Perry, R. A. *et al.*
1962   Land systems of the Alice Springs area. C.S.I.R.O. Land Research ser. 6:20-108.
Discusses the topography, soils, climate, and vegetation patterns of this area in Northern Territory. The paper is well illustrated and includes maps. BA. 42(5)16519.

————
1964   General report on lands of the Leichhardt-Gilbert area, Queensland. C. S. I. R. O. Land Research ser. 12.

Petrov, M. P.
1933   Kornevye sistemy rastenii peschanoi pustyni Karakumy, ikh raspredelenie i vzaimootnosheniia v sviazi s ekologicheskimi usloviiami. Trudy po Prikladnoi Botanike, Genetike i Selektsii, Seriia 1, 1:113-208.
This article on the root systems of plants in the Kara-Kum sand desert has an English summary. Valuable chiefly for its description of the plants that predominate in each association. Notes that the distribution of moisture in the soil determines the structure of the plants in the associations, and that the roots of trees and shrubs go deeper than those of herbs, which are largely confined to the upper meter of sand. 450 plants are described and illustrated with 5 plates and 45 figures.

————
1935   Problemy rastenievod. Osvoen. Pust. 4:9-66.
(Ecological essay on the vegetation of the Repetek Sand Desert Preserve in southern Karakum.)
The vegetation of the Repetek Preserve is found to be composed of 125 species belonging to 24 families of the higher plants; 19.2% and 12.8% are represented by Chenopodiaceae and Cruciferae respectively. The vegetation is classified according to the Raunkiaer system.

————
1936   On the ecology of saltmarshy and sandy saksauls (translated title). Voprosy Ekologii i Biotsenologii 3:3-46.
A paper on the ecology of salt-marshy and sandy saxauls. Notes that the black or salt-marsh saxaul (*Haloxylon aphyllum*) forms thickets chiefly in the northern provinces of Central Asia and Kazakhstan, and that sandy saxaul

(Haloxylon persicum) grows singly or in association with other psammophytes in the central Kara-Kum and the Kyzyl-Kum. Discusses the physiological and ecological requirements of both.

1939   Ecology of desert plant culture (translated title). Voprosy Ekologii i Biotsenologii 5/6:3-39.
Reviews work at the Repetek Sandy Desert Station in the southeast Kara-Kum Desert since its founding in 1912, and discusses problems of the desert environment and ecological studies describing the desert areas. Includes a bibliography of 65 titles. BA 15(8)16414.

1959   Rastitel'nost' pustyn' Tsentral' noi Azii (Ordos, Alashan,' Beishan') i osobennosti ee raspredeleniya. Botanicheskii Zhurnal 44(10):1387-1408. Referativnyi Zhurnal, Biologiya, 1961, no. 4B262.
This paper (with an English summary) includes a comparison of the characteristics of the vegetation of the Central Asian deserts and review of Russian and foreign literature. Notes that aridity increases from east to west, and also vegetation relationships among the various deserts. BA 36(18)58912.

1960   Geograficheskie isseledovaniya v pustynyakh Tsentral'noi Azii. Leningradskogo Universiteta, Vestnik, seriya Geologii i Geografii 24:118-130. (Issued in translation under the title "Geographic explorations in the deserts of Central Asia," by Joint Publications Research Service, 1961, as JPRS 9221, 31 p.)
A brief but good description of the deserts of Central Asia, with particular reference to sand stabilization.

1962   Types des déserts de l'Asie centrale. Annales de Géographie 71:131-155.
An excellent discussion of the types of deserts of Central Asia, starting from the Ordos in the far east and ending with the Tarim depression and Tsaidam on the west. Most of the rain in this area occurs from June to September. The precipitation is tied to the Pacific ocean and dryness due to the high mountains increases from east to west. Provides a comprehensive discussion of climate, soils, and vegetation of the desert area, and identifies 11 principal types of desert landscapes.

1966-   Pustyni TSentral'noi Asii. Nauka, Leningrad. 2
1967   vols. (Translation of Vol. 1 available from JPRS as 39:145; of Vol. 2 as 42,772.) (The deserts of Central Asia).

Philippi, R. A.
1860   Viage al desierto de Atacama hecho de orden del Gobierno de Chile en el verano 1853-54. Incluso Florula Atacamensis seu Enumeratio Plantarum in Itinere per Desertum Atacamense observatarum, p. 175-236. E. Anton, Halle en Sajonia. 236 p.
Important for the knowledge of the desert flora of Atacama, Chile. Describes many endemic plants. Important also as geographic description. It is a classic used later by Reiche and many other authors.

1891   Catalogus praevius plantarum in itinere ad Tarapacá a Federico Philippi lectarum. Museo Nacional de Chile, Anales, sec. 2 (Botánica), 96 p.

Important for the knowledge of the Tarapacá-Arica desert in northern Chile, many endemic plant species being described. It covers also a part of the western Argentine Puna.

Phillips, J.
1930   Some important vegetation communities in the Central Province of Tanganyika Territory (formerly German East Africa). Journal of Ecology 18 (2):193-234.
A discussion of all the important plant communities. Arid and desert communities are of minor importance.

1956   Aspects of the ecology and productivity of some of the more arid regions of southern and eastern Africa. Vegetatio 7(1):38-68.
Describes the drier regions of southern and eastern Africa, including the Namib, Karroo, and Kalahari. Discusses ecological problems of the area including the need for more information on ecological factors. Includes a bibliography of about 150 references. BA 32(7)22191.

1959   Agriculture and ecology in Africa, a study of actual and potential development south of the Sahara. Faber and Faber, London. 424 p.
A survey of possibilities and problems in agricultural development of Africa as related to soils, climate, vegetation, animal life, and the effects of human population. Includes a map in which the author uses his own set of abbreviations for climaxes, etc. Concentrates on the forest bioclimatic region, but also considers other bioclimatic regions. The subdesert is discussed in 5 pages and the desert in 6 pages.

Pichi-Sermolli, R. E. G.
1955a   Tropical east Africa (Ethiopia, Somaliland, Kenya, Tanganyika). *In* Plant ecology reviews of research. Unesco, Paris. Arid Zone Research 6:302-360.
An excellent and very thorough review of the vegetation of tropical east Africa. Includes the best coverage known of vegetation of the Somali-Chalbi desert area.

1955b   The arid vegetation types of tropical countries and their classification. *In* Plant ecology, proceedings of the Montpellier Symposium. Unesco, Paris. Arid Zone Research 5:29-32.
Proposes a classification, subdividing the vegetation into 7 groups (beginning with the driest): *(1)* absolute desert devoid of vegetation, *(2)* subdesert with shrublets and dwarf trees, *(3)* subdesert grassless scrubs, *(4)* subdesert grass scrub, *(5)* succulent scrub, *(6)* xerophilous open woodland, and *(7)* a group including subdesert shrublets and grass. Each type is described.

1957   Uno schema di classificazione dei principali tipi di vegetazione dell'Africa tropicale. Webbia 12(2).

Pickwell, G.
1939   Deserts. Whittlesey House, London. 174 p.
This popular book is well illustrated with large photographs, some located on the index map of photos. Includes a hachure map of the Mojave, Colorado. and Sonoran deserts and portions of the Colorado Plateau; also a brief bibliography on deserts, and desert plants and animals. The U. S. edition (1939) is published by McGraw-Hill.

Piemeisel, R. L.
1932 Weedy abandoned lands and the weed hosts of the beet leaf hopper. U. S. Department of Agriculture, Circular 229. 23 p.
Describes native vegetation, depletion types, and succession in the Snake River Plains area, Mojave Desert, Escalante Valley, and San Joaquin Valley.

Pilger, R.
1954 Beiträge zur flora von Südwestafrika. I: Gramineae. Willdenowia 1(2):198-274.
(Contributions to the flora of South-West Africa. I: Gramineae.)
A brief characterization and keys are given for subfamilies, tribes, and genera, and for the spp. An index to 64 genera is included. BA 30(10)29444.

Pitard, C. J.
1924 Contribution à l'étude de la végétation du Maroc désertique et du Maroc central. Société des Sciences Naturelles, Mémoire 8:245-278.

Pole Evans, I. B.
1929 The vegetation of South Africa. p. 192-214. *In* South Africa and science, a handbook. Printed for the South African Association for the Advancement of Science, by Hortors, Ltd., Johannesburg.
A good description of the vegetation of South Africa.

———— 1936 A vegetation map of South Africa. Botanical Survey of South Africa, Memoir 15:1-23.
A very good map and accompanying discussion. The desert shrub belt extends from southwest Africa southward to the province of the Cape of Good Hope, where it broadens and extends almost to the coast of Port Elizabeth and Port Alfred; it has a rainfall of 5 to 15 inches, greatest in the southeast. Desert succulent and desert grass occur along the west coast of South Africa, from just beyond the Olifants River in the south to the Union of South Africa boundary in the north. The belt is 10 to 80 miles wide. Average rainfall is 1 to 5 inches. BA 11(7)15575.

———— 1937 The vegetation of South Africa. *In* Official year book of the Union of South Africa 18:58-64.

Polimbetova, F. A.
1965 The problem of experimental investigations in plant physiology (translated title). Akademiia Nauk Kazakhskoy S.S.R., Vestnik 10:13-18. (English abstract in AD-630 802, 1966, p. 49-57.)
Includes an interesting discussion of the phytotron developed in the Soviet Union, described as the largest in the world with the greatest possible diversity of uses. One proposed use is for study of the influence of dry environment.

Pond, A. W.
1962 The desert world. Thomas Nelson & Sons, New York. 342 p.
A popular discussion of the deserts of the world. The coverage is uneven, with more attention given to some deserts than others. The remarks on vegetation are interesting but not sufficiently detailed to be of specific value.

———— 1965 Deserts—silent lands of the world. W. W. Norton Co., New York. 157 p.
Very similar to the author's 1962 publication. Interesting for background material rather than specific value relative to vegetation.

Poore, M. E. D.
1955 The use of phytosociological methods in ecological investigations. I: The Braun-Blanquet system. Journal of Ecology 43(1):226-244.
A very good discussion of the development and aims of the Zurich-Montpellier school of phytosociologists, and of the divergence that has arisen between the phytosociologists of continental Europe and Anglo-American ecologists. Explains techniques for field description of vegetation and for construction of association tables.

Popov, G. and W. Zeller
1963 Ecological survey: report on the 1962 survey in the Arabian peninsula. United Nations Special Fund Desert Locust Project, Progress Report. FAO, Rome. 99 p. (UNSF/DL/ES/6)
Notes that very little is known of the flora of Arabia, which they describe briefly. Includes a black-and-white map of the climatic regions of Arabia, also excellent photographs of specific habitats and their vegetation types. The text includes detailed descriptions of the many habitats pictured, lists important species present in each.

Popov, G. B.
1957 The vegetation of Socotra. Linnean Society of London, Journal, Botany 55(362):706-720.
Gives a brief account of the physical geography, soils, and climate of Socotra. There is no typical desert, subdesert scrub, or xerophilous open woodland. Subdesert shrub and grass covers most of the island. A full list of species is appended. BA 32(9)29540.

Popov, M. G. *et al.*
1929 Wild growing fruit trees and shrubs of Asia Media (translated title; English summary). Trudy po Prikladnoi Botanike, Genetike i Selektsii 22(3):241-484.
Discusses the numerous fruit-bearing trees and shrubs of central Asia. Includes illustrations of more important plants and general views showing types of vegetation. BA 7(7)16924.

Porter, D. M.
1963 The taxonomy and distribution of the Zygophyllaceae of Baja California, Mexico. Harvard University, Gray Herbarium, Contributions 129:99-135.
Gives the geography, climate, and vegetation of Baja California, and discusses 6 genera of this family, with descriptions and keys to species.

Porter, W. L., D. W. Hogue, and W. C. Robison
1955 Analogs of Yuma climate in northwest Africa. U. S. Army, Quartermaster Research and Development Center, Natick, Mass., Environmental Protection Division, Research Study Report RER-3. 26 p., 14 figs.
A valuable comparison of the climates of Yuma and northwest Africa. Identifies the small portions of northwest Africa analogous to Yuma areas in both winter and summer; and larger areas in the Sahara analogous in either winter or summer. Notes that the vast nearly rainless interior of the Sahara except in a few elevated places is drier than Yuma. The seasonality of the rainfall is different than Yuma: the pronounced winter maximum in the north and summer maximum in the south contrasts with the occurrence of both summer and winter maximums at Yuma. The interior Sahara is less humid and more sunny than Yuma, with predominantly lighter

winds than at Yuma, although sand storms are more frequent in the interior Sahara. Of all of the elements studied, mean daily temperature range in the warmest month is the one for which values comparable to Yuma are most widespread in northwest Africa except the immediate coasts.

Portugal. Junta das Missoes Geográficas e de
Investigaçoes Coloniais
1948   Atlas de Portugal ultramarino e das grandes viagens portuguesas de descobrimento e expansão. Lisbon. 110 col. maps.

Post, G. E.
1932-   Flora of Syria, Palestine and Sinai; a handbook
1933   of the flowering plants and ferns, native and naturalized from the Taurus to Ras Muhammad and from the Mediterranean sea to the Syrian desert. 2d ed., extensively revised and enlarged by John Edward Dinsmore. American Press, Beirut. 2 vols. (American University of Beirut, Faculty of Arts and Sciences. Natural Science series no. 1)

An excellent taxonomic work written in English, comprising the flora of Syria, Lebanon, Israel, the Kingdom of Jordan, and the Sinai Peninsula with many illustrations. The taxonomic point of view is that of a wider species concept, but it brings to the subspecies, varieties, etc., the synonyms, thus enabling an easy comparison with other floras of a narrow species concept, where naming of synomyms is in most cases lacking (e. g. the analytical Flora of Palestine by Eig, Zohary and Feinbrun, written in Hebrew).

Prescott, J. A.
1929   The vegetation map of South Australia. Royal Society of South Australia, Transactions and Proceedings 53:7-9.

Consists of two black-and-white maps of South Australia, prepared by the Lands and Survey Department, showing native vegetation prior to settlement for comparison with present vegetation.

Puri, G. S.
1952   The present position of the plant ecology of the desert of Rajasthan and Sanrashtra. National Institute of Sciences of India, Bulletin 1:233-240.

Quézel, P.
1954   Contribution à l'étude de la flore et de la végétation du Hoggar. Institut de Recherches Sahariennes, Monographies Régionales 2. 164p.

————

1954-   Contributions à la flore de l'Afrique du Nord.
1961   Vols. 4, 6. Société d'Histoire Naturelle de l'Afrique du Nord, Bulletin 45:55-67; 47:131-136; 52: 224-232.

————

1957   Peuplement végétal des hautes montagnes de l'Afrique du Nord, essai de synthèse biogéographique et phytosociologique. Lechevalier, Paris. 463 p.

The best work available at the present time on the high mountains of northern Africa.

————

1965   La végétation du Sahara du Tchad à la Mauritanie. Gustav Fisher Verlag, Stuttgart. 33 p., 72 figs., 15 maps.

A comprehensive discussion of the vegetation of the western Sahara including the Hoggar and Tibesti Mountains. Covers climate, distribution of floras, and phytosociology, the latter divided by areas and by edaphic conditions. Much of the material is presented in tables for ready reference and the text is well illustrated. One of the most valuable references for the western Sahara.

Quézel, P. and C. Santa
1962-   Nouvelle flore de l'Algérie et des régions
1963   désertiques méridionales. Centre National de la Recherche Scientifique, Paris. 2 vols.

The most recent manual of the flora of Algeria and the northern part of the Sahara.

Quézel, P. and P. Simonneau
1960   Note sur la végétation halophile au Sahara occidental. Research Council of Israel, Botany Bulletin 8D(3/4):253-262.

Describes the halophyte vegetation in 3 types of situations: valley, steppe, and sebka. Clearly describes the vegetation types in relation to saline conditions. BA 35(23)68039.

————

1963   Les peuplements d'*Acacia* du Sahara nordoccidental. Etude phytosociologique. Institut de Recherches Sahariennes, Travaux 20:80-121.
        (The *Acacia* woodlands of the northwestern Sahara)

Ragonese, A. E.
1951   La vegetación de la República Argentina. II: Estudio fitosociológico de las Salinas Grandes. Revista de Investigaciones Agrícolas 5(1/2): 1-234.
        (The vegetation of the Argentine Republic. II: Phytosociological studies of the great salt basin)

A complete study of the arid land vegetation, including halophytes, which surrounds the "Salinas Grandes," an enormous salt field in northwestern Argentina, on the border between the Monte and western Chaco-vegetations, occupying the corner where the provinces of Córdoba, Santiago del Estero, Catamarca and La Rioja touch.

————

1955   Plantas tóxicas para el ganado en la región central Argentina. Universidad Nacional de La Plata, Facultad de Agronomía, Revista, 3a. ép., 31: 133-336.

Systematic study of poisonous plants, native and introduced, in central Argentina, with details about their toxic properties.

Ragonese, A. E. and R. Martínez Crovetto
1947   Plantas indígenas de la Argentina con frutos o semillas comestibles. Revista de Investigaciones Agrícolas 1:147-216.
        (Indigenous plants of Argentina with edible fruits or seeds)

A systematic account of 233 species of Argentine flowering plants with edible seeds or fruits; a brief description, many illustrations of the edible parts, special references, and bibliography are given; particularly useful for a subsistence manual, includes many species of the arid zones.

Raheja, P. C.
1966   Aridity and salinity, a survey of soils and land use. p. 43-127. *In* H. Boyko, ed., Salinity and aridity, new approaches to old problems. W. Junk, The Hague. 408 p. (Monographiae Biologicae 16)

A worldwide survey of salt-affected soils in arid lands with particularly detailed description of Indian soils, characteristic vegetation, and land use. Contains also an extensive bibliography (261 numbers).

Raizada, M. B. and R. N. Chatterji
1954   A diagnostic key to the various forms of introduced mesquite (*Prosopis juliflora* DC.). Indian Forest Bulletin 14(189):1-6.
A report on two species of mesquite trees introduced into India as species promising to be useful in afforestation of dry and degraded lands. Includes botanical descriptions and notes on their cultivation. BA 32(5) 17208.

Ramaley, F.
1927   Colorado plant life. University of Colorado, Boulder. 299 p.
A semipopular discussion of the vegetation of Colorado. Includes some usable information on the drier portions in the San Luis Valley and on the western slope.

————
1929   Botany of the San Luis Valley in Colorado, I. University of Colorado Studies 17(1):17-44.
This highly arid district of 4000 square miles in southern Colorado has many northern desert characteristics. Native plants are largely grasses and shrubby xerophytes. The valley has been much overirrigated, but remnants of desert remain. Sand dunes in the east of the valley are of great height and extent, and have typical pysammophitic vegetation. BA 4(7-9)20931.

————
1942   Vegetation of the San Luis Valley in Southern Colorado. University of Colorado Studies, Ser. D, Physical and Biological Sciences 1(4):231-279.

————
1952   World deserts, limits and environmental characteristics. U. S. Department of the Army, Office of the Quartermaster General, Research and Development Division, Environmental Protection Branch, Special Report 57. 21 p., 17 maps.

Rattray, J. M.
1960   The grass cover of Africa. Food and Agriculture Organization, Agricultural Studies 49. 168 p.
Principal grass types are listed and their distribution shown. Some genera occur in areas with as little as 2 inches of rainfall. Concentrates on grass types with relatively abundant rainfall but gives some information on desert conditions. A colored map of Africa is printed separately at a scale of 1:10,000,000.

Raunkiaer, C.
1905   Types biologiques pour la géographie botanique. Académie Royale des Sciences et des Lettres de Danemark, Bulletin 5:347-437.
This is Raunkiaer's first comprehensive discussion of life forms.

————
1934   The life forms of plants and statistical plant geography. Clarendon Press, Oxford. 632 p.
This translation contains the papers of Raunkiaer from 1903. Includes life form spectra of some desert regions and perhaps other worthwhile information.

————
1937   Plant life forms. Clarendon Press, Oxford. 104 p.
This small book includes the plant-life-form portion of the earlier publication "The Life Forms of Plants and Statistical Plant Geography," 1934. Especially valuable for individuals desiring to classify plants according to their life forms, or reading publications that list life forms but do not explain the basis of the classification. Describes various classes of life forms and shows the particular characteristics of each by line drawings.

Al-Rawi, A.
1964   Wild plants of Iraq. Ministry of Agriculture, Directorate of Agriculture Research and Projects, Technical Bulletin 14. 232 p.
List of species and their distribution.

Al-Rawi, A. and H. L. Chakravarty
1964   Medicinal plants of Iraq. Ministry of Agriculture, Directorate of Agriculture Research and Projects, Technical Bulletin 13. 109 p.
Distribution, constituents, and uses.

Raychaudhuri, S. P.
1964   Land resources of India, vol. 1. Committee on Natural Resources, Planning Commission, New Delhi.

Razi, B. A.
1957   An annotated list of phanerogamic parasites from India and Pakistan. Lloydia 20(4):238-254.
Discusses the various parastic seed plants of India. BA 33(4)15112.

Rechinger, K. H.
1951   Grundzüge der pflanzenverbreitung im Iran. Zoologisch-Botanische Gesellschaft, Wien, Verhandlungen 92:181-188.
Discusses phytogeographical regions of Iran. Characterizes climate, vegetation, and flora, of all the regions in detail. BA 25(11)32790.

————
1963-   Flora iranica; flora des iranischen hochlandes und umrahmenden gerbirge: Persien, Afghanistan, teile von W. Pakistan, Nord-Iraq, Azerbaidjan, Turkmenistan. Fasc. 1-15 (to 1965). Akademie Druck-u. Verlagsanstalt, Graz.

————
1964   Flora of lowland Iraq. J. Cramer, Weinheim. 746 p.
This very useful manual covering the flora of the drier portions of Iraq has a minimum of technical terms and these are defined in a glossary.

Regel, C.
1954   Phytogéographie de l'Iraq. Congrès International de Botanique, VIIIᵉ, Paris. Rapports et Communications, Section 7:51-52.
This 2-page article summarizes the climate of Iraq. Notes that the north of the country is subdesert and the south is true desert. Gives brief descriptions of types of vegetation found in Iraq. BA 29(10)23149.

————
1956a   Irak und Spanien, ein vergleich. Geobotanisches Institut Rübel, Zürich, Veröffentlichungen 31: 244-349.
Compares common elements of vegetation in Iraq and Spain, and characterizes the ecological associations. BA 31(5)13073.

————
1956b   Zur kenntnis der vegetationsstufen im Mittleren Osten. Geographica Helvetica 11(2):99-103.
Between Amman and Jerusalem, the valley of the Jordan, which is below the level of the Mediterranean Sea, has a peculiar vegetation that does not correspond to the general series of vegetation zones in the Middle East.

The vegetation belts correspond to those in the desert zone to the south. The desert vegetation on the shores of the Jordan and the Red Sea is an isolated occurrence in the Mediterranean region. BA 32(1)483.

Reiche, K.
1907   Grundzüge der pflanzenverbreitung in Chile. Vegetation der Erde 8. 374 p.

Reiche, K. F.
1934-   Geografía botánica de Chile. Imprenta Uni-
1937   versitaria, Santiago. 2 vols.
         (Botanical geography of Chile)

Reichert, J. I.
1937   Steppe and desert in the light of lichen vegetation. Linnean Society, London, 149th Session, Proceedings 1:19-23.
A very interesting discussion of this little known group of plants. Concludes that lichens may define floristic characteristics of steppe and desert and be used to distinguish between the two. Lichens indicate that the deserts of Egypt, Algeria, and Palestine are similar, and that the steppe of southern Russia is different from Palestine and Mesopotamia. For one example, *Diploschistes* species indicate arable steppe soils.

Rempel, P. J.
1936   The crescentic dunes of the Salton Sea and the relation to the vegetation. Ecology 17(3): 347-358.
These unstable crescentic dunes support very sparse vegetation subject to sand blasting and covering by sand. Concludes that stabilization of these dunes by vegetation is impossible.

Renaud, H. P. and G. S. Colin
1934   Tuhfat Al-Ahbab. Glossaire de la matière médicale Marocaine. Institut des Hautes Etudes Marocaines, Rabat, Publications 24. 218 p.

Reynolds, G. W.
1950   The aloes of South Africa. The Trustees, Aloes of South Africa Book Fund, Johannesburg. 520 p.
Gives extensive information on the *Aloe*. Part I relates botanical explorations in South Africa and gives a bibliographic history; part II is a systematic treatment of the genus as it occurs in South Africa. Includes numerous color and black-and-white photographs illustrating various species. BA 25(11)34386.

Reynolds, H. G. and J. W. Bohning
1956   Effects of burning on a desert grass-shrub range in southern Arizona. Ecology 37(4):769-777.
Reports the effects of controlled burn on undesirable species and desirable perennial grasses. Concentrates on semiarid lands, but includes information on the effects of burning plants normally considered desert species. BA 31(8)23427.

Reynolds, H. G. and F. H. Tschirley
1956   Mesquite control on southwestern rangelands. U. S. Department of Agriculture. Leaflet 421. 8 p.
Concentrates on rangelands, but includes information on the susceptibility of mesquite, a common desert plant, to methods of control.

Ricardi, M.
1957   Fitografía de la costa del departmento de Taltal. Sociedad de Biología de Concepción (Chile), Boletín 32:3-9.
A phytogeographical study of the northern region of Chile, including ecology, topography, climate, and relation of the flora to that of other areas. BA 32(8)25903.

Richardson, S. D.
1966   Forestry in communist China. Johns Hopkins Press, Baltimore. 237 p.

Rickard, W. H.
1963   Vegetational analyses in a creosotebush community and their radioecologic implications. p. 30-44. *In* Radioecology, National Symposium on Radioecology, 1st, Ft. Collins, Colorado, 1961, Proceedings. Reinhold Publishing Corporation, New York.
A good example of a research being carried on in radioecology. Detailed vegetational analyses were conducted in a creosotebush community in Jackass Flats, Nye County, Nevada. One result showed that the amount of ground covered by vegetation canopies in the understory is directly related to the vegetation retention of radioactive fallout in desert shrub communities.

Rickard, W. H. and L. M. Shields
1963   An early stage in the plant recolonization of a nuclear target area. Radiation Botany 3(1): 41-44.
Reports on vegetational analyses conducted 3 years after a detonation in a nuclear target area in Yucca Flat, Nevada. Annual plants dominated the early stage recolonization and were quantitatively more abundant in the disturbed areas than in an adjacent undisturbed shrub community. Includes a comparison of recoveries following various degrees of disturbance from nuclear detonation. BA 44(6)21981.

Rikli, M.
1929   Durch die Marmarica zur Oase Siwa. Vegetationsbilder 20(1):1-6.
This very good reference includes a series of pictures, with notes, taken near Siwa, 500 miles southwest of Alexandria, showing vegetation on sand in wadis, and in oasis depressions. BA 4(11)26710.

————
1934   Marokko. Vegetationsbilder 24(4/5):1-11.
Five formation types in Morocco are distinguished, briefly described, and illustrated in the plates. Includes a review of the literature. BA 10(9)20422.

————
1942-   Das pflanzenkleid der Mittelmeerländer. Hans
1948   Huber, Bern. 1418 p. 3 vols.
This important work deals not only with the vegetation of the countries bordering the Mediterranean Sea but also of those into which the Mediterranean flora is penetrating. It is therefore an excellent source of information for many vegetational (particularly plantgeographical) problems, as well as for the desertic regions of Iran, Iraq, Arabia, and the Sahara.

Rikli, M. and E. Rübel
1928   Zur kenntniss von flora und vegetationsverhältnissen der Libyschen wüste. Naturforschende Gesellschaft, Zürich, Vierteljahresschrift 73(15): 190-232.
Includes a brief discussion of climate, a list of important species by areas, and a discussion of plant origins and life forms.

Riley, H. P.
1963   Families of flowering plants of Southern Africa. University of Kentucky Press, Lexington, 269 p.
The families of flowering plants found in Southern Africa are discussed and illustrated. Includes 144 color plates

of individual plants and gives American, European, and Afrikaans plant names.

Rivière, C.
1931 Le sacsaoul du Turkestan, *Haloxylon ammodendron* Bunge. Agriculture Pratique des Pays Chauds, n. s. 7:3-10.
Haloxylon ammodendron, a species of saxaul (French, *sacsaoul*) tree, is a halophyte of the Turkestan Desert useful for wood, food and shade for caravan animals and desert inhabitants, and sand binding.

Robertson, J. H. and H. P. Cords
1957 Survival of rabbitbrush, *Chrysothamnus* species, following chemical, burning, and mechanical treatments. Journal of Range Management 10(2): 83-89.
Gives valuable information on the effectiveness of various methods of control of weedy shrubs of the Great Basin Desert. BA 33(6)20687.

Roberty, G.
1948 Les représentants ouest africains du genre Acacia dans les herbiers genevois. Candollea 11:113-174.

Robison, T. W.
1958 Phreatophytes. U. S. Geological Survey, Water-Supply Paper 1423. 84 p.
A very comprehensive discussion of phreatophytes in the arid and semiarid portions of the United States. Gives the distribution and characteristics of the common phreatophytes: saltcedar, mesquite, baccharis, greasewood, willow, cottonwood, and saltgrass. Includes an extensive tabular summary of phreatophytes in the Western United States, giving common and scientific names, depth to water table, water quality tolerance, and usage of water in acre feet per acre of ground water. Includes a 4-page bibliography. Well illustrated with 32 photographs.

Robison, W. C.
1957 Analogs of Yuma climate in northern Africa. Revised. U. S. Army, Quartermaster Research and Engineering Center, Natick, Mass., Environmental Protection Research Division, Research Study Report RER-2. 20 p., 11 figs.
One of a series of analogs of Yuma climate in various parts of the world. In this case analogous conditions were found in northeast Africa, although there were few places where all climatic elements were found to be closely analogous to those at Yuma.

Robison, W. C. and W. C. Hessen
1954 Environmental handbook for Dugway Proving Ground. U. S. Department of the Army, Head Quartermaster Research and Development Command, Natick, Mass., Environmental Protection Division, Research Report 227.

Rodin, R. J.
1953 Distribution of *Welwitschia mirabilis.* American Journal of Botany 40(4):280-285.
The distribution of *Welwitschia* is analyzed as a guide to climatic and edaphic factors, especially the occurrence of fog and rainfall. BA 27(7)20264.

Rojas-M., P. and M. Rojas-Garcidueñas
1960 Notes on the distribution of the Russian thistle (*Salsola kali* L. var. *tenuifolia*) in Mexico. Weeds 8(3):466-468.
Provides information on the southern distribution of the Russian thistle. Includes a distribution map. BA 36(8)25103.

Rolla, S. R. and K. C. Kenodia
1962- Studies on the vegetation and flora of Jodhpur
1963 Division, Rajasthan State. Annals of Arid Zone 1(1/2):16-46;2(1):25-60.
Includes a list of species by families, with brief annotations on description, habitat, and location.

Rotov, R. A.
1962 Nekotorye osobennosti rastitel' nosti Yugozapadnoi chasti pustyni Muyunkum. Akademiia Nauk Kazakhskoi S.S.R., Seriya Botaniki i Pochvovedeniya, Izvestiya 1(3):77-82. Referativnyi Zhurnal, Biologiya, 1963, no. 1V224.
Discusses the vegetation of the southwestern Muyunkum desert. Includes short descriptions of the basic plant groupings and their floristic compositions. Comparisons are made between Muyunkum and eastern Kara-Kum. Gives a list of species of southwestern Muyunkum by groups of life forms and growth habit. BA 45(5)21289.

Roussine, N. and C. Sauvage
1961 Bibliographia phytosociologica: Afrique du Nord. Excerpta Botanica, B, 3(1):34-51.

Royce, R. D.
1952 The distribution of some of the more important toxic plants of South-Western Australia. Journal of Agriculture of Western Australia 1(6):845-853.
Shows the distribution of 75 poisonous plants on maps. BA 28(1)29422.

Rübel, E.
1930 Pflazengesellschaften der erde. Verlag Hans Huber, Bern-Berlin. 464 p.
This discussion of plant communities of the Earth includes a good standard discussion of the world's deserts, and an excellent colored map showing dry deserts ("siccideserta") and steppes ("steppenwiesen" and "duriherbosa"). Well illustrated. Devotes 28 pages to the world's deserts.

1936 Plant communities of the world. p. 263-290. *In* Essays in geobotany in honor of William Albert Setchell. University of California Press, Berkeley.
Considers an association as a plant phytographical unit indicated by the ending "etum" added to the name of the dominant plant. A federation or alliance has an ending of "ion," and an order or subformation has an ending of "etia."

Ruiz, H. and J. Pavón
1953- Flora peruviana et chilensis. Vol. 4 (in 4 parts),
1959 Vol. 5 (in 2 parts). Instituto Botánico A. J. Cavinilles, Madrid, Anales 12:113-192; 13:5-70; 14:717-784; 15:115-241; 16:353-462; 17:377-495.

Runyon, E. H.
1934 The organization of the creosotebush with respect to drought. Ecology 15(2):128-138.
An excellent monographic treatment of *Larrea tridentata* in North America. Notes that changes in water supply involve striking changes in density and color of foliage and a pecular difference in branching. Naked buds and partially expanded leaves are drought resistant, showing the unique ability to resume growth after prolonged severe drought. BA 10(1)123.

Russell, R. J.
1932   Dry climates of the United States. II: Frequency of dry and desert years, 1901-1920. University of California, Publications in Geography 5(5):245-274.
A very interesting and useful publication showing the frequency of desert years in the United States and the extension of dry conditions eastward.

1945   Climates of Texas. Association of American Geographers, Annals 35(2):37-52.
Discusses climates using both a modification of Köppen's classification and a basis of dry and desert years described in an earlier paper. Considers territory receiving desert years more than 50 per cent of the time to be desert. Notes that desert-year frequency is 100 per cent over parts of California, Arizona, and adjacent areas, and possibly in the Big Bend region of Texas. Includes a map based on Köppen's classification.

Rustamov, I. G.
1961   K kharakteristike rastitel' nosti Zapadnogo Uzboya. Akademiia Nauk Turkmenskoi SSR, Seriya Biologicheskikh Nauk, Izvestiya 4:31-39. Referativnyi Zhurnal, Biologiya, 1962, no. 14V189.
The author believes that the Uzboy Valley with the adjacent sands and plain belongs to the desert zone by virtue of its natural features and vegetative cover. Dominant plants are listed. BA 42(2)4562.

1962   Rastitel' nost' srednei i nizhnei chasti Zapadnogo Uzboya. Turkmensk Universiteta, Uchenye Zapiski 9(4):1-66. Referativnyi Zhurnal, Biologiya, 1964, no. 3V230.
A brief physical and geographical survey of the central lower part of the western Uzboy stream bed. Lists 29 associations with conditions of the habitat, floristic composition, dominant species, abundance, and heights of the belts. Gives a list of the flora of the central lower part of the western Uzboy, and a vegetative map. BA 46(5)18852.

Rutter, A. J. and K. H. Sheikh
1962   A survey of the vegetation of waste lands around Lahore and its relation to soil conditions. Biologia (Pakistan) 8(2):91-121.
A useful discussion of vegetation in relation to physical and chemical conditions of the soil. BA 43(6)21898.

Rzedowski, J.
1957   Vegetación de las partes áridas de los estados de San Luis Potosí y Zacatecas. Sociedad Mexicana de Historia Natural, Revista 18(14):49-101.
A study of the vegetation of arid zones in the states of San Luis Potosí and Zacatecas, Mexico. Describes the plants, their ecology, geographic distribution and relations to climate and soil factors. Gives notes on the most important useful wild plants. BA 41(4)13034.

Sabnis, T. S.
1919   The physiological anatomy of the plants of the Indian desert. Indian Botanical Society, Journal 1:33-43, 65-83, 97-113, 183-205,
The introduction of this article gives the boundaries of the desert area and information on the topography and precipitation, which varies from about 9 to over 13 inches.

1923   The flora of Sind. Indian Botanical Society, Journal 3:151-153, 178-180, 204-206, 227-232, 277-284.

1929   A note on the ecology of the flora of Sind. Indian Botanical Society, Journal 8:263-286.
A very good discussion of the vegetation of Sind, which except for the central alluvial plain, is desert continuous with the great desert of northwest India. Topography and climate are discussed, followed by an analysis of the flora with notes on its relationship with areas to the west and east. Ecological conditions are discussed and lists of characteristic plants are given. BA 6(2)3388.

1940-   A contribution to the flora of the Punjab and
1941   the associated hill regions. Bombay Natural History Society, Journal 42:124-149, 342-379, 533-586.

Safford, W. E.
1921   Peyote, the narcotic mescal button of the Indians. American Medical Association, Journal 77:1278-1279.
A brief description of this narcotic cactus found in the warm arid regions of North America.

Said, M.
1960   Development of range lands in Quetta-Kalat Region, West Pakistan. International Grassland Congress, 8th, Reading, England, Proceedings, p. 220-223.
A good discussion of the Quetta-Kalat region of West Pakistan, a part of which would qualify as desert. The precipitation is given for selected localities.

Sampson, A. W.
1939   Plant indicators: concept and status. Botanical Review 5(3):155-206.
An excellent discussion of plants in relation to climate, soils, grazing use, fire, and other factors. Also an excellent review of literature and an extensive bibliography.

Sánchez-Mejorada, H.
1961   Las cactáceas del estado de Sinaloa. Cactáceas y Suculentas Mexicanas 6(2):27-39.
The state of Sinaloa extends southward from the Sonoran Desert, with rainfall increasing toward the south. Many of the species of cacti here are found also in the Sonoran Desert. A useful publication. BA 41(5)20002.

Sandberg, F. et al.
1957-   Phytochemical studies on the flora of Egypt. 1:
1960   Alkaloids of *Retama raetam* Webb and Berth. 2: The Alkaloids of *Pancratium sickenbergeri* Asch. and Schweinf. ex Boiss, and *P. maritimum* L. 3: The Alkaloids of *Haloxylon salicornicum* (Moq.-Tand.) Boiss. 4: The Saponins of *Anabasis articulata* (Forsk.) Moq.-Tand in DC and *Anabasis setifera* Moq.-Tand. Svensk Farmaceutisk Tidskrift 61:345-352; 63:657-666; 64:541-547, 677-690.

Sanders, E. M.
1921   The natural regions of Mexico. Geographical Review 11:212-226.
Includes a discussion of rainfall, temperature, natural regions, and vegetation, but discussion of vegetation is very limited. There is a 1-page black-and-white map of natural regions.

Sarup, S.
1951   Plant ecology of Jodhpur and its neighbourhood. A contribution to the ecology of northeastern Rajasthan. National Institute of Sciences of India, Bulletin 1:223-32.

Satyanarayan, Y.
1963   Ecology of the central Luni basin, Rajasthan. Annals of Arid Zone (Jodhpur) 2(1):82-97.
A good discussion of the Rajasthan arid area of some 80,000 square miles, west of the Aravalli Range. It is noted that aridity increases from south to northwest, with the greater portion of the area semiarid, becoming arid in the extereme west. Precipitation varies from 500 mm to about 250 mm in the northwest, confined to the summer months June to September. Five plant communities are discussed: (1) mixed xeromorphic thorn forest, (2) mixed xeromorphic woodland or wooded desert, (3) dwarf semishrub desert, (4) psammophytic scrub desert, and (5) succulent halophytic desert. There is a good discussion of structure, physiognomy, and composition of these plant communities.

Saunders, C. F.
1934   Useful wild plants of the United States and Canada. 3rd ed., rev. Robert M. McBride and Co., New York. 275 p.
The author has brought together a great deal of interesting information on wild plants under the heading of: edible tubers, wild seeds of food value, the acorn as human food, wild fruits and berries, wild plants with edible stems and leaves, beverage plants, substitutes for soap, medicinal wildings, and certain poisonous plants. He considers mesquite the most valuable of wild legumes; the sweet pulp of the seed is very nutritious (although the seeds are inedible and indigestible). He discusses many other desert plants including agaves, yuccas, prickly pear, and other fruit-producing cacti.

Sauvage, C. and J. Vindt
1952-   Flore du Maroc. Fasc. 1-2. Institut Scientifique
1954   Chérifien, Travaux 4. Editions Internationales, Tanger. 150, 271 p.

Schimper, A. F. W.
1898   Planzen-geographie auf physiologischer grundlage. Fischer, Jena. 876 p.
This classical work on plant geography on a physiological basis contains a chapter of approximately 50 pages on the Earth's deserts. It was the first systematic classification and map of world vegetation, and is still useful. A detailed regional description of vegetation types is included. Clarendon Press, Oxford, published a 1903 English translation entitled "Plant Geography upon a physiological Basis." (q. v.).

————

1903   Plant-geography upon a physiological basis. Authorized English translation by W. R. Fisher; revised and edited by P. Groom and I. B. Balfour. Clarendon Press, Oxford. 839 p.
This classical work contains a 47-page chapter on the Earth's deserts.

Schimper, A. F. W. and F. C. von Faber
1935   Pflanzengeographie auf physiologischer grundlage. 3. aufl. Fischer, Jena. 2 vols.
This third edition of this publication regarding plant-geography upon a physiological basis has been enlarged and brought up to date. It includes a 165-page chapter on the Earth's deserts.

Schmutz, E. M.
1963   Factors affecting the absorption, translocation, and toxicity of herbicides on creosotebush. University of Arizona (Ph.D. dissertation). 175 p.
This Ph. D. dissertation is the product of a scientist with many years of experience in range research. It is a very comprehensive study aimed toward the determination of the problems involved in the chemical control of creosotebush, *Larrea tridentata,* a major dominant over vast areas of deserts and semidesert rangelands in the southwestern United States and northern Mexico. It was found that susceptibility of creosotebush to 2, 4-D and 2 4, 5-T varied widely from year to year and from season to season, with highest susceptibility generally occurring 12 to 60 days after the first summer rain of at least 0.5 inch and during years of above-average rainfall.

Schulz, E. D.
1930   Texas cacti, a popular and scientific account of the cacti native of Texas. Texas Academy of Science, Transactions 14:1-181.
A popular account of the cacti of Texas including their distribution, ecology, disease and insect enemies, and a description of every species known to be native to Texas. A key to the species of *Opuntia* is included. BA 5(8-9) 21314.

Schwartz, O.
1934   Beiträge zur kenntnis der flora von südwest-Arabien. p 177-211. *In* K. Rathjens und H. v. Wissmannsche, Südarabien-reise, bd. 3. De Gruyter, Hamburg.

Scortecci, G.
1932   Viaggio in Somalia. Natura 23(1):1-30.
A description of Somaliland, its vegetation and animal life, made on the basis of a journey through the country. BA 8(4)7774.

Seifriz, W.
1931-   Sketches of the vegetation of some southern
1932   provinces of Soviet Russia. I: The altitudinal distribution of plants on the Crimean mountains. II: Plant life along the Georgian Military Way, North Caucasus. III: Plant life in the Bakuriani Basin, Minor Caucasus. IV: Autumnal plants at Repetek, Turkmenistan. V: The plant life of the Transilian Mountain range in Semirechje, Eastern Turkestan. Introduction. Journal of Ecology 19 (2):360-382; 20(1):53-88.
Part IV includes a description of the flora of the desert of Kara-Kum and a discussion of the root systems of some of the plants. The desert in the vicinity of Repetek shows great diurnal and annual temperature ranges. Precipitation averages 94 mm, with a minimum of 24 mm and a maximum of 170 mm (no time period given). Rain falls only in winter, a dry period extends from May to September. The maximum period without rain was 250 days; the minimum, 131 days. BA 9(1)186.

Sen, D. N.
1966   Ecology of the Indian Desert. I: On the phytosociology of the vegetation of Jodhpur. Tropical Ecology 7:136-152.
44 plant associations are classified on the basis of Braun-Blanquet, and ecological amplitudes are given for a number of characteristic species.

Shantz, H. L.
1925   Plant communities in Utah and Nevada. U. S. National Herbarium. Contributions 25:15-23.
Shantz prepared the portion on plant communities of this publication on the flora of Utah and Nevada. The desert communities are listed: northern desert shrub, salt desert shrub, and southern desert shrub. These are further subdivided and described.

Shantz, H. L.
1927   Drought resistance and soil moisture. Ecology 8(2):145-157.
A basic discussion of the drought-resistance of plants and the mechanisms by which it is achieved. Includes a classification outline, widely accepted, in which plants are divided into drought-escaping, drought-evading, drought-enduring, and drought-resisting.

———
1938   Plants as soil indicators. p. 835-860. *In* Soils and men. U. S. Department of Agriculture, Yearbook.
A summarization, based on many years of experience, of the use of plants as indicators of temperature conditions, moisture conditions, drought, and soil-moisture conditions. Soil preferences, including soil texture and moisture relationships, are given for many plants and plant communities.

———
1940-   Agricultural regions of Africa. Economic Geog-
1943   raphy. 16:1-47, 122-161, 341-389; 17:217-249, 353-379; 18:329-346, 343-362; 19:77-109, 217-269.
A series of articles on the agricultural regions of Africa in which the vegetation is noted. The articles are not too applicable to the desert, as the main emphasis is on areas of greater agricultural potential.

Shantz, H. L. and C. F. Marbut
1923   The vegetation and soils of Africa. American Geographical Society, Research Series 13:1-142.
An excellent discussion of the vegetation and soils of Africa. The authors note that the desert shrub is what is popularly known as desert, and although the vegetation includes a large number of species and of individuals, the bare ground is always more or less prominent. They also state that extensive areas of absolute desert, from a botanical standpoint, do not exist in Africa, but that portions of the Namib, southwest Africa, and the Sahara approach absolute desert so close that they might well be classified as such.

Shantz, H. L. and R. L. Piemeisel
1924   Indicator significance of the natural vegetation of the Southwestern desert region. Journal of Agricultural Research 28(8):721-801.
This publication, which has been a very valuable asset in the development of irrigation in the Southwest, lists the principal plant indicators of soil conditions. For example, it is stated that a good stand of creosotebush indicates land which has good drainage and is free from alkali. Mesquite and chamise, or chamise alone, indicate a very sandy soil free from alkali. Yucca and cactus lands, and giant cactus and paloverde lands, are too stony or the slope too steep for cultivation. The indicators of saline conditions and poor drainage are also given.

———
1940   Types of vegetation in Escalante Valley, Utah, as indicators of soil conditions. U. S. Department of Agriculture, Technical Bulletin 713. 46 p.
The authors found that the most reliable indicators of soil conditions are the stabilized plant associations in equilibrium with soil and climatic conditions. They noted that little rabbitbush indicates lighter soils, and that progressively heavier soils are indicated by galleta grass, sagebrush, greasewood, shadscale, winterfat, greasewood-shadscale, and saltgrass. Thus it is possible to determine the soil texture, from light sands to heavy clays, by noting the vegetation.

Shantz, H. L. and B. L. Turner
1958   Photographic documentation of vegetational changes in Africa over a third of a century. Arizona Agricultural Experiment Station, Report 169. 158 p.
A series of repeat photographs showing changes in vegetation over a period of more than 30 years. It is of value for the illustrations of types of vegetation as well as for the changes that have taken place.

Shantz, H. L. and R. Zon
1924   Natural vegetation. U. S. Department of Agriculture, Atlas of American Agriculture, Pt. I. Sec. E. 29 p.
An excellent colored map of the natural vegetation of the United States with very good descriptions of plant communities. The authors recognize northern desert shrub with three main associations and a number of minor communities, including sagebrush, shadscale, and saltsage. Their southern desert shrub category includes desert saltbush, creosotebush, yucca, cactus, and California sagebrush mesquite.

Sharma, B. M.
1966   Ecological studies of desert plants: *Prosopis spicigera* Linn. Tropical Ecology 7:54-66.
An interesting ecological study of this arid zone tree growing on coarse, sandy, and alkaline soil. Analyses of soil profiles and foliar analyses from various dune habitats are given.

Shaw, H. K. A.
1947   The vegetation of Angola. Journal of Ecology 35(1):23-48.
An English translation of "Carta Fitogeográfica de Angola," in which vegetation is classified by Rübel's system. Monsoon, woodland, and herbaceous communities occupy 80 per cent of the subject area, and an additional 10 per cent is occupied by desert and heathlike scrub. Each community is described as to composition, distribution, and climatic conditions. BA 22(8)17748 and BA 22(9)19964.

Shelford, V. E.
1932   Basic principles on the classification of communities and habitats and the use of terms. Ecology 13:105-120.

———
1963   The ecology of North America. University of Illinois Press, Urbana, Illinois. 610 p.
The most comprehensive publication on the ecology of North America, which should be standard reference for everyone scientifically interested in the flora and fauna of North America.

Shields, L. M.
1956   Zonation of vegetation within the Tularosa Basin, New Mexico. Southwestern Naturalist 1(2):49-68.
The vegetation on lava and gypsum sand is compared, and the factors influencing the distribution of plants are discussed.

Shields, L. M. and J. Crispin
1956   Vascular vegetation of a recent volcanic area in New Mexico. Ecology 37(2):341-351.
This paper is valuable chiefly for its discussion of the diversity of vegetation found in an area of recent volcanic flow. Detailed information is given for the vegetation of the upper and lower Sonoran zone. It is noted that lava

supports a greater diversity of species than the surrounding plain. BA 31(7)19939.

Shields, L. M. and P. V. Wells
1963 Recovery of vegetation on atomic target areas at the Nevada test site. p. 307-310. *In* Radioecology, National Symposium on Radioecology, 1st, Ft. Collins, Colorado, 1961, Proceedings. Reinhold Publishing Corporation, New York.

A nuclear detonation denuded a zone of desert shrub about 0.5 miles in radius; asymmetrical blast damage to vegetation extended in some cases to beyond a mile, varying with species and stability of the substratum. Gross injury appeared to be largely from blast and thermal effects. The recovery over a 4-year period was studied. BA 45(6) 22933.

Shields, L. M., P. V. Wells, and W. H. Rickard
1963 Vegetational recovery on atomic target area in Nevada. Ecology 44(4):697-705.

A further report of the effects of nuclear detonation at the Nevada test site and subsequent recovery of the vegetation.

Shinn, C. H.
1913 An economic study of acacias. U. S. Department of Agriculture, Bulletin 9. 38 p.

Four hundred fifty species of *Acacia* have been identified, and of these 300 are Australian. Not more than 75 have economic value, and less than 50 are in cultivation. The economic uses include tanbark, forage, timber, medicines, fibers, gums, resins, dyes, perfume, ornamentals, and reclamation of sand dunes.

Shreve, F.
1910 The rate of establishment of the giant cactus. Plant World 13(10):235-240.

It was found that plants less than 1 decimeter high were extremely hard to find and slow growing. It takes 30 years to reach 1 meter in height, 60 years to reach 5 meters.

1911 The influence of low temperatures on the distribution of the giant cactus. Plant World 14(6):136-146.

It was found that a single day without midday thawing and failure of the saguaro to warm up above freezing would result in death. Other species of cacti (*Opuntia versicolor*) can withstand up to 66 hours of freezing. In the Rockies and Canada small succulents have withstood freezing for 13 days or more.

1915 The vegetation of a desert mountain range as conditioned by climatic factors. Carnegie Institution of Washington, Publication 217. 112 p.

This excellent publication is valuable chiefly because of its interpretation of the influence of the interaction of various factors on plant distribution. The author states that the relative richness of the vegetation in this region is due chiefly to the occurrence of 2 yearly seasons of rainfall. He notes that the severe conditions of the desert environment cause the vegetation to exhibit a high degree of sensitiveness to slight topographic and edaphic differences. Heavier stands of vegetation or else particular species of plants can be found wherever the character of the soil or the topographic location is such as to present a degree of soil moisture slightly above that of the general surroundings, or to maintain the moisture for a longer time during periods of extreme aridity, or wherever plants are protected from the most extreme conditions of transpiration.

1917 A map of vegetation of the United States. Geographical Review 3:119-125.

One of the earlier maps of the vegetation of the United States. Various desert types are mapped and discussed, including the California microphyll desert, Great Basin microphyll desert, Texas succulent desert, and Arizona succulent desert.

1922 Conditions indirectly affecting vertical distribution on desert mountains. Ecology 3(4):269-274.

A very good discussion of the factors affecting the vertical distribution of plants, with special emphasis on rocks and their derived soils. The author notes that desert forms obtain a lower maximum elevation on gneiss and granite and that vegetational zones are higher on basalt, rhyolite, and other volcanics.

1925 Ecological aspects of the deserts of California. Ecology 6(2):93-103.

In this publication, Shreve proposed a basic thesis: "In a consideration of the dynamic aspects of the vegetation of a region in which the initial, sequential, and final stages of a succession are characterized by the same species, and often by the same individuals, it is doubtful whether these conceptions, formed in regions with a very dissimilar vegetation, are of much real utility." He notes the extreme climatic conditions where some localities have been subjected to several periods of 12 months or more without precipitation. He also states here that there are very few cacti in the Mojave Desert.

1926 The desert of northern Baja California. Torrey Botanical Club, Bulletin 53(3):129-136.

Includes a description of that region of lower California north of San Felipe Bay and east of the San Pedro Mártir Mountains, one of the most arid in North America. The vegetation consists of a very few species; extensive flats subject to inundation by the Colorado River are devoid of plants. BA 2(6-8)9194.

1934a Rainfall, runoff and soil moisture under desert conditions. Association of American Geographers, Annals 24(3):131-156.

An analysis of a 27-year period showed that drought periods occurred from 2 to 7 times annually, with the longest drought period lasting 149 days. It was noted that in warm months a period of 2 to 3 weeks without rain will kill herbaceous ephemeral plants, but a period of 2 to 3 months without precipitation will be of little consequence to cacti and deep-rooted trees.

1934b Vegetation of the northwestern coast of Mexico. Torrey Botanical Club, Bulletin 61(7):373-380.

An excellent description of the area (which the author characterized as the most arid region in North America), which lies along the lower course of the Colorado River and on both sides of the Gulf of California. In some localities, two species make up 98 per cent of the vegetation, but cover only 4 to 15 per cent of the ground surface. BA 9(6)10918.

1936 The plant life of the Sonoran Desert. Scientific Monthly 42:195-213.

A very readable and useful discussion, briefly covering deserts of the world, effect of deserts on plants, types of desert plants, American deserts in general, and the Sonoron Desert in particular.

Shreve, F.
1938   The sandy areas of the North American desert. Association of Pacific Coast Geographers, Yearbook 4:11-14.
It is pointed out that sandy areas are not common in the North American desert; much less of the area is covered by sand than in the Sahara, and Asiatic deserts. The sandy areas in the southwestern United States and northwestern Mexico are shown on a map, and the types of plants found there are listed.

1939   Observations on the vegetation of Chihuahua. Madroño 5(1):1-13.
One of the best publications on the vegetation of Chihuahua. It includes a map and 4 good photographs. Five physiographic regions are recognized in the state: bajada, enclosed basin, elevated plains, Sierra Madre and barranca. The bajada region is desert, dominated by bushes and small cacti. The enclosed basins are desert, with more or less stabilized sand and open vegetation of low trees, bushes and yuccas, or else are open desert grassland. The flora is listed in detail; relative abundance of species is noted. It is also noted that the types of vegetation resemble those of southeast Arizona and southwest New Mexico, with an infusion of endemic or southern species. BA 13(10)16266.

1940   The edge of the desert. Association of Pacific Coast Geographers, Yearbook 6:6-11.
A good discussion of the basic philosophy on limits of deserts. It includes a complete summary of the distribution of *Larrea* together with some factors related to its distribution.

1942a   The desert vegetation of North America. Botanical Review 8(4):195-246.
A basic study and discussion of the desert vegetation of North America; contains the best overall description, particularly of the warmer desert areas. Desert vegetation, life forms, structure, floristic composition, and geographic areas are discussed for each of the four great desert regions of North America: the Great Basin, the Mojave, Sonoran, and the Chihuahuan.

1942b   Grassland and related vegetation in northern Mexico. Madroño 6(6):190-198.
An excellent discussion of the grasslands of northern Mexico. Although primarily centered on the grasslands, this book is of interest because these grasslands border the desert. As a point of special interest for desert study, the author notes, in the center of the northern plateau, at elevations of 1100-1300 meters the presence of the "*Hilaria* llanos," undrained basins with deep, fine, soil, with a cover of nearly pure *Hilaria*. He believes these should be regarded as a desert association controlled by soil conditions, rather than as a part of the climatic grassland formation. BA 17(6)15363.

1942c   The vegetation of Arizona. *In* Flowering plants and ferns of Arizona. U. S. Department of Agriculture, Miscellaneous Publication 423:10-23.
A very good description. Includes an exceptionally good discussion of desert vegetation, and comparisons with California and Mexican floras. Divides the desert into three types: California microphyll desert, Arizona succulent desert, and Great Basin microphyll desert; describes each briefly and mentions important species.

1944   Rainfall of northern Mexico. Ecology 25:105-111.
A good discussion of amounts and seasonal distribution of rainfall, based upon very limited available records and measurements by Sykes' long-period rain gauges. Includes a half-page black-and-white map of mean annual rainfall.

1951   Vegetation of the Sonoran desert. *In* F. Shreve and I. L. Wiggins, Vegetation and flora of the Sonoran Desert, vol. 1. Carnegie Institution of Washington, Publication 591. 2 vols.
The best available publication on the subject; republished in 1964 as part of a 2-volume publication by Shreve and Wiggins.

Shreve, F. and T. D. Mallery
1933   The relation of caliche to desert plants. Soil Science 35(2):99-113.
An interesting discussion of caliche and its effects upon soil-water and plants, including root penetration. Concludes that the abundance of caliche in the soil of bajadas is important in determining the low and open character of the vegetation, often restricted to *Larrea tridentata*. In pot tests *Larrea* grew best with caliche mixed with the soil.

Shreve, F. and I. L. Wiggins
1964   Vegetation and flora of the Sonoran Desert. Stanford University Press, Stanford, California. 2 vols.
An outstanding 2-volume report. In the first 186 pages Forrest Shreve discusses the vegetation of the area, a critical analysis and description covering physical factors, perennial vegetation, ephemeral herbaceous vegetation, and ecological features of characteristic species. Includes 27 maps: a large map of the Sonoran Desert and its vegetational subdivisions, another showing rainfall distribution by 5-inch intervals, and 24 maps showing the distribution of important species. This vegetation portion is well illustrated, with 37 of the original plates supplemented by additional photographs. The remainder of the 1740 pages is largely a floristic treatment of the vegetation of the area, and includes: keys to families, genera, and species; detailed technical descriptions; local geographic distribution; and critical notes on habitat, time of flowering, and other factors for each species. BA 46(5)21937.

Simonneau, P.
1953a   Note préliminaire sur la végétation des sols salés d'Oranie. Annales Agronomiques 4(3):411-432.
A preliminary description of the vegetation of the saline soils of Oran. Describes plant-soil relationships and includes lists of plants.

1953b   La végétation halophile de la plaine de Perrégaux (Oran). Direction du Service de la Colonisation et de l'Hydraulique, Service des Etudes Scientifiques. Birmandreis. 279 p.

1954a   La végétation des sols salés d'Oranie. Sur quelques modifications de l'association à *Suaeda fruticosa* et *Sphenopus divaricatus* provoquées par la mise en culture dans la plaine du Bas-Chéliff. Annales Agronomiques 5:9-117.
An outline of changes to a *Suaeda fruticosa* and *Sphenopus divaricatus* association in the plain of Bas-Chéliff resulting from cultivation. Includes lists of plants and details of subassociations.

Simonneau, P.
1954*b* La végétation des sols salés d'Oranie. Les groupements à *Atriplex* dans les plains sublittorales. Annales Agronomiques (2):225-257.
Discusses *Atriplex* associations in the sublittoral plains Lists subassociations and notes the effects of cultivation.

Smirnov, L. A.
1935 Kompleksy rastitel'nogo pokrova Zavolzh'ia i puti ikh evoliutsii. Sovetskaia Botanika 5:81-88.
Discusses theoretical postulates and conclusions resulting from a detailed geobotanical investigation of the West Kazakhstan region in 1934, also different types and examples of successions. Gives brief recommendations of agricultural use of the area, and the relationships of concrete and abstract phytocoenological concepts with the concept of the genetic types of complexes.

Smith, A. C. and I. M. Johnston
1945 A phytogeographic sketch of Latin America. p. 11-18. *In* Plants and plant science in Latin America. Chronica Botanica Co., Waltham, Mass.
This brief work is illustrated by a large map and numerous plates. Various zones are distinguished. The terminology and distribution notes on various plant communities do not agree entirely with those of other Latin America writers. BA 19(8)15520.

Smith, J.
1949 Distribution of tree species in the Sudan in relation to rainfall and soil texture. Sudan Ministry of Agriculture, Bulletin 4. 68 p.

Soriano, A.
1949*a* El límite entre las provincias botánicas patagónica y central en el territorio del Chubut. Lilloa 20:193-202.
A report of a careful floristic study of the delimitations and transitions between the Patagonic and central botanical provinces in the territory of Chubut, Argentina. BA 26(10)27085.

———
1949*b* El pastoreo en la parte semidesértica del Chubut. Idia 2(21):8-14.
The title of "Pasturing in the Semidesert Part of Chubut" is somewhat misleading. This is an ecological study of this semidesert region in Patagonia. Soriano notes that the northwest portion of Chubut belongs to the western Monte, has an average annual precipitation of 150 to 200 mm and vegetation is more steppe-like than desertic. Includes brief descriptions of common plants and comments on poisonous plants. BA 28(1)188.

———
1950 La vegetación del Chubut. Revista Argentina de Agronomía 17(1):30-66.
A study of the natural vegetation of the western, central, Golfo de San Jorge, and sub-Andean areas, including a census of plants found.

———
1952 El pastoreo en el territorio del Chubut. Revista Argentina de Agronomía 19:1-20.
The author explored the conditions of sheep grazing in central Patagonia (Chubut, 242.000 sq. km); he gives some censuses of frequency of important species and a systematic list of 63 native plant species which are eaten by stock.

———
1956*a* Los distritos florísticos de la provincia patagónica. Revista de Investigaciones Agrícolas 10(4):323-347.

The floristic districts of the province of Patagonia are described. The area is divided into 5 floristic districts and one of them into 2 subdistricts. For each district the dominant plants are described, and some climatic, edaphic, and physiographic data are also given. Common names for some Patagonian plants are proposed for the first time. BA 31(8)25561.

———
1956*b* Aspectos ecológicos y pastoriles de la vegetación patagónica relacionados con su estado y capacidad de recuperación. Revista de Investigaciones Agrícolas 10(4):349-372.
Describes the ecological characteristics of abundant species; gives data on times of flowering and seed production, amount of seed produced, germination, growth, root systems, and so forth.

Soukup, J.
1959- Los géneros de las monocotiledóneas peruanas.
1961 Biota 2:153-178, 223-237, 234-265, 283-317; 3:14-17, 45-65, 96-122, 172-180, 183-218, 233-239, 332-346.
Discusses the monocotoyledonous plants of Peru, and gives keys, descriptions, and distribution lists for various species.

———
1962- Vocabulario de los nombres vulgares de la flora
1964 peruana. Biota 4(33):205-236; 5(38):45-69.

Spalding, V. M.
1909 Distribution and movements of desert plants. Carnegie Institution of Washington, Publication 113. 144 p.
This study shows that soil water is the most important factor determining local distribution, and that aeration and alkaline conditions are also important. Spalding notes that creosotebush shows a high capacity for adjustment and "perfect indifference" to change of aspect in the vicinity of Tucson, Arizona, that extreme summer heat on south-facing slopes limits the development of some other plants, and that cold temperatures on north-facing slopes limits others, the saguaro for example.

Speck, N. H.
1963 Vegetation of the Wiluna-Meekatharra area. C. S. I. R. O. Land Research ser. 7:143-161.

Speck, N. H., K. Fitzgerald, and R. A. Perry
1963 The pasture lands of the west Kimberley area. C. S. I. R. O. Land Research ser. 8:175-191.

Speck, N. H. and M. Lazarides
1963 Vegetation and pastures of the west Kimberley area. C. S. I. R. O. Land Research ser. 8:140-174.

Spegazzini, C.
1897*a* Plantae patagoniae australis. Universidad Nacional de La Plata, Facultad de Agronomía y Veterinaria, Revista 3:485-589.

———
1897*b* Primitiae florae chubutensis. Universidad Nacional de La Plata, Facultad de Agronomía y Veterinaria, Revista 3:591-633.

———
1898- Nova addenda ad Floram Patagonicam. I: Sociedad
1902 Científica Argentina, Anales 47:161-177, 224-239, 274-290; 48:44- .II: Sociedad Científica Argentina, Anales 53:13-34 et passim. III: Museo Nacional de Buenos Aires, Anales 7:135-308.

Springfield, H. W.
1954　Natural vegetation in Iraq. Ministry of Agriculture, Baghdad, Technical Bulletin.

Standley, P. C.
1920-　Trees and shrubs of Mexico. U. S. National
1926　Herbarium, Contributions 23:1-1721.
The standard manual on the subject. Includes keys, descriptions, and distribution notes. The 5 parts published over a period of years are considered collectively as volume 23 of the Contributions from the U. S. National Herbarium.

Stannard, M. E.
1955　Some fodder trees of western New South Wales. New South Wales Soil Conservation Service, Journal 11:129-136.

Stearn, W. T.
1947　Geographical and other abbreviations in the *Flora U.R.S.S.,* by Komarov and others. New Phytologist 46(1):61-67.
A very useful publication which aids those who do not know Russian to translate the geographic and other abbreviations of the *Flora U.R.S.S.* into English equivalents and thus more easily ascertain the distribution of species described in that work. BA 22(4)9736.

Stephens, E. L.
1953*a* Some South African edible fungi. Longmans, Green and Co., Ltd., Cape Town, South Africa. 35 p.
A guidebook with illustrations and eight color plates.

————
1953*b* Some South African poisonous and inedible fungi. Longmans, Green and Co., Ltd., Cape Town, South Africa. 31 p.
A guide book containing text figures and eight color plates.

Stevens, O. A.
1943　Russian thistle, life history and growth. North Dakota Agricultural Experiment Station, Bulletin 326. 20 p.
A good study of Russian thistle, first observed in the United States in 1873. Gives information on its anatomy, germination, growth periods, flowering, and seeding.

Stevenson, M. C.
1915　Ethnobotany of the Zuñi Indians. U. S. Bureau of American Ethnology, Annual Report 30(1908-1909):35-102.
Discusses the uses of plants by this tribe of Indians living near the desert in the southwestern United States. Includes some information on the characteristics and uses of desert plants.

Stewart, R. R.
1957-　The flora of Rawalpindi District, West Pakistan.
1958　Pakistan Journal of Forestry. 163 p.
A reprint of 2 articles that appeared in the Pakistan Journal of Forestry. Gives the scientific name for each species, also vernacular names, brief descriptions, habitat, and data on time of flowering, uses, associates, and so forth.

Steyn, D. G.
1934　The toxicology of plants in South Africa together with a consideration of poisonous foodstuffs and fungi. Central News Agency, Johannesburg, South Africa. 631 p.

Stocker, O.
1926　Die ägyptisch-arabische wüste. Vegetationsbilder 17(5/6):25-36.
A very good reference on the Egyptian-Arabian desert. Includes pictures of vegetation of the desert, including general views, views of wadis, and closeups of dominant plants, also short discussions including some ecological notes. Briefly describes climatic and edaphic conditions, physiological behavior, and historical factors of the vegetation. BA 3(4-6)4872.

————
1927　Das Wadi Natrun. Vegetationsbilder 18(1). 6 p., 6 pl.
Characterizes the vegetation of the Wadi Natrun, in the desert northwest of Cairo. Gives descriptions and illustrations of swamp, salt marsh, and salt steppe associations. BA 2(9-11)15916.

————
1928　Der wasserhaushalt ägyptischer wüsten-und salzpflanzen vom standpunkte einer experimentellen und vergleichenden pflanzengeographie aus. G. Fischer, Jena. 200 p.
Discusses the water economy of the Egyptian desert and plants of saline areas from the viewpoint of experimental and comparative plant geography.

————
1962　Steppe, wueste, savanne. Geobotanisches Instituts Rübel, Zürich, Veröffentlichungen 37:234-243.
Discusses zonation vegetation (steppe, desert, and savanna) on the north and south sides of the central North African desert, and indicates differences between the two sides. Also makes comparisons with desert and arid lands in North America. BA 45(7)27192.

Svenson, H. K.
1946　Vegetation of the coast of Ecuador and Peru and its relation to the Galápagos Islands. I: Geographical relations of the flora. II: Catalogue of plants. American Journal of Botany 33(5):394-426; (6):427-498.
Discusses temperature and rainfall of this area, influenced by the Humboldt Current. Notes that the Galápagos Islands have climate and vegetation similar to the mainland, and gives (in tabular form) the relationships of the Galápagos vegetation to mainland and West Indian flora. Includes numerous graphs.

Sweeney, G.
1947　Food supplies of a desert tribe. Oceania 17(4):289-299.
Pertains to an area northwest of Alice Springs. Includes a brief account of food plants of the spinifex desert. Gives native and common names, and vegetation types in which the plants are found.

Sykes, G.
1931　Rainfall investigations in Arizona and Sonora by means of long period rain gauges. Geographical Review 21:229-233.
The structure of these rain gauges developed by Sykes permits burial for long periods with little or no loss of moisture by evaporation. Discusses the rainfall of southwestern Arizona, southeastern California, and northwestern Sonora, including both shores of the Gulf of California. Average precipitation was about 10 inches, but varied from 2 inches at sea level to as much as 40 inches on mountain summits (the latter being an exception to the general desert climate).

Sykes, G.
    1937   The Colorado Delta. Carnegie Institution of
            Washington, Publication 460. 193 p., 74 fig., map.
    This irregular T-shaped delta (with the stem upstream)
    includes approximately 3,325 square miles of pre-
    dominantly detrital matter. The soils are alkaline, water-
    segregated with windblown sands, and support a vegeta-
    tion of wild rice, wild flax, mesquite, and salt cedar, with
    tules, cottonwood, and willows growing at the upper-
    ends of fans and along the banks.

Täckholm, V.
    1956   Students' flora of Egypt. Vernacular names by
            M. Drar. Illustrated by A. A. Abdel Fadeel. Anglo-
            Egyptian Bookshop, Cairo. 649 p.
    A very usable and convenient handbook flora of Egypt,
    including many drawings, very good photographs, and
    a map. Includes short simple descriptions, probably less
    complete and detailed than most others.

Täckholm, V. and M. Drar
    1941-   Flora of Egypt. 3 vols. (v. 1 with G. Täckholm).
    1954   Cairo University, Faculty of Science, Bulletins 17,
            28, 30.
    A standard flora of the country, including keys, descrip-
    tions, and distribution notes. By far the most ambitious
    and informative flora of any region between Libya and
    India.

Tadmor, N. H., G. Orshan, and E. Rawitz
    1962   Habitat analysis in the Negev Desert of Israel.
            Research Council of Israel, Bulletin, Sec. D,
            Botany 11(3):148-173.
    Discusses plant-soil moisture and salinity relationships
    for 4 topographically different habitats in a 100 mm
    rainfall area in the southern part of the desert. The
    evapotranspiration was found to be the most important
    factor differentiating between habitats. It ranged from
    as low as 10 mm on hilltops to 600 mm in loessial wadis.
    BA 43(2)4384.

Tadros, T. M.
    1953   A phytosociological study of halophilous Com-
            munities from Mareotis (Egypt). Vegetatio
            4(2):102-124.
    A report of a study of the phytosociology and ecology
    of saline depressions near the Mediterranean coast of
    Egypt west of Alexandria. Two alliances and eight
    associations were recognized, each association having
    its own individuality, occupying habitats at definite
    altitudes, and showing difference in soil texture, salinity,
    water, and organic matter contents. BA 27(12)31445.

Tadros, T. M. and B. A. M. Atta
    1958   Further contribution to the study of the sociology
            and ecology of the halophilous plant communities
            of Mareotis (Egypt). Vegetatio 8(3):137-160.
    Continuing study of the halophytic plant communities in
    the oolitic sand, coastal belt of the western Egyptian
    desert. The zonation of the vegetation is related to the
    accumulation of wind-drifted material over a saline
    substratum, but the vegetation itself helps to accumulate
    surface sands. BA 34(3).

Tanganyika Territory, Survey Division, Department of
Lands and Mines
    1948   Atlas of the Tanganyika Territory. 2nd ed. Dar
            es Salaam.
    Includes maps showing rainfall, areas of interior drainage,
    and vegetation, scale 1:4,000,000.

Tansley, A. G.
    1913   A universal classification of plant-communities.
            Journal of Ecology 1:27-42.
    This philosophical treatment has been important to the
    development of classification concepts.

    _____

    1920   The classification of vegetation and the concepts
            of development. Journal of Ecology 8:118-144.
    A further consideration of the classification of vegetation
    with particular emphasis on development.

Taylor, G.
    1926   Agricultural regions in Australia. Pan-Pacific
            Scientific Congress, 3rd, Tokyo, Proceedings
            2:1657-1662.
    Describes various ecological regions of Australia very
    briefly and includes notes on their agricultural utilization.

    _____

    1937   Comparison of American and Australian deserts.
            Economic Geography 13(3):260-268.
    Compared Australian deserts primarily with the Tucson-
    Phoenix area of Arizona. The comparison would probably
    have been of more value if some other American desert
    areas, more similar to the Australian, had been considered.

Taylor, K. W.
    1951   Guayule, an American source of rubber. Economic
            Botany 5(3):255-273.
    An excellent review of the history of development of
    guayule as a source of rubber, from when it was harvested
    as a native plant in Mexico, through developments by
    the Continental Rubber Company in Arizona and
    California, through the rapid expansion during World
    War II under the direction of the U. S. Forest Service,
    to the decline of interest due to development of synthetic
    sources of rubber. Notes that Russia, Turkey, and Spain
    were probably growing guayule for rubber at the time
    of publication, and that a large area in the United States
    is suitable for guayule production.

Thiébaut, J.
    1936-   Flore libano-syrienne. Imprimerie de l'Institut
    1940   Français d'Archéologie Orientale, Cairo. 2 vols.

Thoday, D.
    1956   *Kochia indica* Wight in Egypt. Kew Bulletin
            1956(1):161-163.
    The identity of the Egyptian plants is confirmed.
    Prostrate habit is generally the result of damage by graz-
    ing or trampling. Diagnostic characters of *K. indica* and
    K. prostrata are given. BA 31(3)8736.

Thomas, H. H.
    1913   The geographical distribution of some plants
            from the Libyan Desert. Cairo Science Journal
            7:205-219.

    _____

    1921   Some observations on plants in the Libyan Desert.
            Journal of Ecology 9(1):75-89.
    Discusses the vegetation of gravelly and sandy desert
    areas 40 km west of Cairo on the edge of the Nile delta.
    It is based upon 1 year's observation and is probably of
    limited value.

Thompson, R.
    1949   A dictionary of Assyrian botany. British Academy,
            London. 405 p.
    A very useful dictionary for persons having occasion
    to identify plants from the names given to them in
    ancient times. Gives plant names in several present and

ancient languages, and also extensive information on ancient uses of the plants. Covers many plants of several types. BA 26(2)4227.

Thornber, J. J.
1906   Alfilaria, *Erodium cicutarium,* as a forage plant in Arizona. Arizona Agricultural Experiment Station, Bulletin 52:27-58.
Discusses the introduction, adaptation, and distribution of alfileria (alfilaria) in Arizona. This native of the Mediterranean region is favored by the mild temperatures, winter precipitation, and soil conditions. The seeds will not germinate in summer in Arizona, except under refrigeration.

———   1911   Native cacti as emergency forage plants. Arizona Agricultural Experiment Station, Bulletin 67:457-508.
A good discussion of the chollas and prickly pears of Arizona, including their possible value as emergency forage plants.

Thornthwaite, C. W.
1931   The climates of North America according to a new classification. Geographical Review 21(4):633-655.
Thornthwaite's basic publication on the climates of North America, later superseded by his publication on an approach toward a rational classification of climate.

———   1948   An approach toward a rational classification of climate. Geographical Review 38(1):55-94.
A key paper in which Thornthwaite advanced the idea of potential evapotranspiration and the methods for computing it. The concept is discussed and illustrated with the use of water balance studies for several stations. Meigs' later classification and distribution of arid homo-climates (Meigs, 1953) uses this concept and the related index derived by Thornthwaite. This article is reviewed in the chapter on weather and climate.

Tidestrom, I.
1925   Flora of Utah and Nevada. U. S. National Herbarium, Contributions 25. 665 p.
The standard flora of these two states. Includes a description of the vegetation by H. L. Shantz.

Tisdale, E. W. and G. Zappettini
1953   *Halogeton* studies on Idaho ranges. Journal of Range Management 6(4):225-236.
Halogeton glomeratus, introduced accidentally into the United States, spread rapidly over the intermountain region during the 15 years preceding this publication and caused serious livestock losses, especially of sheep in winter. This paper discusses the ecology of *Halogeton* and the possibilities of control through management. BA 27(12)31447.

Tits, D.
1926   Le Sahara occidental (contribution phyto-géographique). Société Royal de Botanique de Belgique, Bulletin 58:39-90.
A broad discussion of the steppe and desert districts of the western Sahara lying between the Atlas Mountains and the Atlantic coast. Concentrates on the area south of the Atlas Mountains (which was divided into 4 districts, including the transition to the desert) and on the vegetation of the Hamada du Guir-Saoura and the Grand Erg Occidental. BA 3(9-11)17569.

Torre, A. R.
1962   Leguminosae (Papilionoideae: Genisteae-Galegeae). Instituto Botânico de Coimbra, Lisbon, Conspectus Florae Angolensis 3(1):187.
Keys, references, and distributional data, with some notes on habitat and ecology are given for spp. found in Angola belonging to the tribes Genisteae, Trifolieae, Loteae, and Galegeae. BA 41(4)16070.

Townsend, C. H. T.
1897   On the biogeography of Mexico and the southwestern United States. Texas Academy of Sciences, Transactions 2:33-86.
A very well done early description, still of value. Includes desert areas and others.

Trabut, L.
1935   Flore du nord de l'Afrique. Répertoire des noms indigènes des plantes spontanées, cultivées et utilisées dans le nord de l'Afrique. Alger. 355 p.
A flora of northern Africa. Catalogs native names of spontaneous, cultivated, and useful plants of the area.

Transeau, E. N.
1905   Forest centers of eastern North America. American Naturalist 39:875-889.
Discusses the relationships of temperature and evaporation to the growth of vegetation.

Trelease, S. F. and A. L. Martin
1936   Plants made poisonous by selenium absorbed from the soil. Botanical Review 2(7):373-396.
An excellent review of available information on the relationships between selenium and plants growing in seleniferous areas.

Trelease, W.
1902   The Yucceae. Missouri Botanical Garden, Annual Report 13:27-133.
A classical monograph on the Yucceae. Each species is well illustrated, usually showing the general habit of flowers and fruit. Includes 99 plates, 22 mapping the distribution of various species.

Trewartha, G. T.
1954   An introduction to climate. 3rd ed. McGraw-Hill Book Company, Inc., N. Y. 402 p.
A standard text with a full treatment of Köppen's climatic classification.

Trochain, J.
1940   Contribution à l'étude de la végétation du Sénégal. Institut Français d'Afrique Noire, Mémoires 2. 433 p.
The author categorizes plants, the criterion being whether soil condition or climate is more important to distribution.

Tryon, R.
1964   The ferns of Peru. Polypodiaceae (Dennstaedtieae to Oleandreae). Harvard University, Gray Herbarium, Contributions 194:1-253.
There are 176 native species of ferns in Peru, hence this manual has some reference value, although ferns are not generally abundant in desert areas. BA 46(14)63231.

Tschirley, F. H.
1963   A physio-ecological study of jumping cholla (*Opuntia fulgida* Engelm). University of Arizona (Ph. D. dissertation). 113 p.
A very thorough study of *Opuntia fulgida,* the jumping cholla, by a highly-qualified botanist familiar with conditions in the southwestern United States. Includes information on reproduction, which is largely by vegeta-

tive means (no true seedling has ever been found in the field). Notes that the plant lives about 40 years, has a high invasion potential, is a menace to man and beast, and that the activities of both tend to increase its population. BA 45(7)27196.

Tschirley, F. H. and S. C. Martin
1961 Burroweed on southern Arizona rangelands. Arizona Agricultural Experiment Station, Technical Bulletin 146. 34 p.
A comprehensive review of burroweed in the arid and semiarid Southwestern region.

Turnage, W. V. and T. D. Mallery
1941 An analysis of rainfall in the Sonoran Desert and adjacent territory. Carnegie Institution of Washington, Publication 529. 45 p.
This analysis was based upon a summary of readings from weather stations in the deserts of southern California, Arizona, and Sonora, Mexico. Notes great differences in amounts of winter and summer precipitation at various points in the area, and that within areas rainfall increases with elevation. Differences in total precipitation from south to north and from west to east obscure relationships for the area as a whole. Complete data for the period 1917 through 1937 are tabulated at the end of the article.

Turner, B. L.
1959 The legumes of Texas. University of Texas Press, Austin. 284 p.
A systematic summary of this family which includes many important desert plants of Texas. Includes critical taxonomic notes; observations on growth periods, flowering, fruiting, habitats, and distribution; and a map for each species. Notes present and possible economic significance. BA 35(18)51122.

Unesco
1955a Plant ecology, proceedings of the Montpellier Symposium. Unesco, Paris. Arid Zone Research 5. 124 p.

——— 1955b Plant ecology, reviews of research. Unesco, Paris. Arid Zone Research 6. 377 p.

——— 1958 Climatology and microclimatology, proceedings of the Canberra Symposium. Unesco, Paris. Arid Zone Research 11. 355 p.

——— 1960a Medicinal plants of the arid zones. Unesco, Paris. Arid Zone Research 13. 96 p.

——— 1960b Plant-water relationships in arid and semi-arid conditions, reviews of research. Unesco, Paris. Arid Zone Research 15. 225 p.

——— 1961a Plant-water relationships in arid and semi-arid conditions, proceedings of the Madrid Symposium. Unesco, Paris. Arid Zone Research 16. 352 p.

——— 1961b Salinity problems in the arid zones, proceedings of the Teheran Symposium. Unesco, Paris. Arid Zone Research 14. 395 p.

——— 1962 The problems of the arid zone, proceedings of the Paris Symposium. Unesco, Paris. Arid Zone Research 18. 481 p.

——— 1963 Bioclimatic map of the Mediterranean zone, explanatory notes. Unesco, Paris. Arid Zone Research 21. 60 p.

——— 1965 Methodology of plant eco-physiology, proceedings of the Montpellier Symposium. Unesco, Paris. Arid Zone Research 25. 531 p.

U. S. Army Engineer Waterways Experiment Station
1959 Analogs of Yuma terrain in the Mexican desert. Technical Report 3-630, Report 3. Also cited as AD-478 847.

——— 1960 Analogs of Yuma terrain in the Middle Eastern Desert. Technical Report 3-630, Report 4. Also cited as AD-478 848.

——— 1962a Analogs of Yuma terrain in the northeast African desert. Rev. ed. Technical Report 3-630, Report 1. 2 vols.

——— 1962b Analogs of Yuma terrain in the south central Asian desert. Technical Report 3-630, Report 2. Also cited as AD-478 846.

——— 1963 Analogs of Yuma terrain in the southwest United States desert. Technical Report 3-630, Report 5. 2 vols. Also cited as AD-466 089/450 611.

——— 1965 Analogs of Yuma terrain in the northwest African desert. Technical Report 3-630, Report 6. 2 vols. Also cited as AD-466 206/207.

U. S. Department of Agriculture / Department of the Interior, Range Seeding Equipment Committee
1959 Handbook: Chemical control of range weeds. Rev. Washington, D. C. v. p.
An excellent handbook giving a great deal of information on a large number of plants and their control through chemical means. It was compiled on the basis of information provided by many technicians working in this field.

U. S. Department of the Army, Quartermaster General, Research and Development Division, Environmental Protection Branch
1953 Handbook of Yuma environment. Report 200. 59 p.

University of Southern California
1958 An annotated bibliography for the Mexican desert. Prepared under contract for U. S. Army Engineer Waterways Experiment Station, Vicksburg, Mississippi.

——— 1959 An annotated bibliography for the desert areas of the United States. Prepared under contract for U. S. Army Engineer Waterways Experiment Station, Vicksburg, Mississippi. 387 p.

Uphof, J. C. T.
1959 Dictionary of economic plants. Hafner Publishing Company, New York. 400 p.
A comprehensive listing of economic plants of the world.

Urvoy, Y.
1937 Notes sur la végétation au Sahara-soudanais central. Annales de Géographie 46:270-277.
Describes the distribution of various types of vegetation in the central Sudanese Sahara.

Valentine, K. A. and J. J. Norris
1960   Mesquite control with 2, 4, 5-T by ground spray application. New Mexico Agricultural Experiment Station, Bulletin 451. 24 p.
Discusses equipment and methods.

Vargas C., C.
1940   Formaciones vegetales del departamento de Arequipa, ensayo fitogeográfico. Museo de Historia Natural "Javier Prado," Lima, Boletín 4:338-345.

Velarde Núñez, M. O.
1949   La vegetación y flora de las lomas de la región de Acari. Revista de Ciencias (Lima) 51(467/468):29-38.
Discusses vegetation and flora of the lomas near Arequipa. Lists separately plants which occur above and below 400 meters elevation.

Verdoorn, I. C.
1956   Oleaceae of southern Africa. Bothalia 6(3):549-639.
An important family in arid and semiarid areas. Gives distribution notes, descriptions and keys to the species of 5 genera in the Union of South Africa, Swaziland, Southwest Africa, and Botswana (formerly Bechuanaland), between South West Africa and the Transvaal. BA 30(11)32407.

Vernik, R. S. and I. F. Momotov
1959   Rastitel'nost' del'ty Amu-Dar'i. Materialy po Prozvoditel'nym Silam Uzbekistana (Tashkent) 10:273-294. Referativnyi Zhurnal, Biologiya, 1961, no. 2V279.
The vegetation of contemporary and ancient deltas of the Amu-Dar'ya belongs to 3 types: tugai, halophilic, and psammophilic. The tugai (desert and semidesert river valley) type is most extensive. BA 40(6)21825.

Vesey-Fitzgerald, D. F.
1955   Vegetation of the Red Sea coast south of Jedda, Saudi Arabia. Journal of Ecology 43:477-489.

──────
1957a The vegetation of the Red Sea Coast north of Jedda, Saudi Arabia. Journal of Ecology 45:547-562.

──────
1957b The vegetation of central and eastern Arabia. Journal of Ecology 45:779-798.
One of the few descriptions of the vegetation of the entire Arabian Peninsula. The Red Sea coast has Sudano-Deccanian vegetation (see Vesey-Fitzgerald, 1955, 1957a, for a discussion of coastal areas), and the inland center of the peninsula has largely Saharo-Sindian. The vegetation is largely of mesophytic herbs which grow only after rainfall. Perennials include many halophytes but almost no true succulents. The vegetation is strongly influenced by the character of the geological substratum and the occurrence of wind-piled sand. Rainfall is light, and irregular, averaging less than 5 inches, and occurring during winter. The article includes photographs of important plants and a foldout black-and-white map.

Vest, E. D.
1962   The plant communities and associated fauna of Dugway Valley in western Utah. University of Utah (Ph. D. dissertation). 134 p.
A report of a study of plant distribution in the valley. Describes biotic and edaphic factors affecting the distribution of 8 communities in the various local habitats.

Vinogradov, B. V. and M. P. Petrov
1962   Primenenie aerometodov pri izuchenii rastitel'nosti landshaftov pustynnoi zony. p. 217-231. In Aerometody izucheniya priroduvkh resursov. Geografgiz, Moscow. Referativnyi Zhurnal, Biologiya, 1963, no. 2V190.
Deserts of Central Asia were compared with analogous deserts of the Algerian Sahara on the basis of aerial photographs showing vegetation. Considerable similarity in flora was noted between analogous landscapes of the two areas. BA 45(20)85002.

Volk, O. H.
1954   Klima und pflanzen-verbreitung in Afghanistan. Vegetatio 6:422-433.
A sketch of regionalization according to vegetation, climate, and agronomy (dry farming). Gives the characteristics of the different provinces. All except the extreme east belong to the Irano-Turanian region. (The schlerophyllous wood lands of eastern Afghanistan do not belong to the Mediterranean region; they are different floristically and climatically.) The southern desert is characterized by an *Artemisia herba-alba* plant community.

Vostokova, E. A., A. V. Shavyrina, and S. G. Laricheva
1962   Spravochnik po rasteniyam-indikatoram gruntovykh vod i pochvo-gruntov dlya yuzhnykh pustyn' S. S. S. R. Gosgeoltekhizdat, Moscow. 126 p. Referativnyi Zhurnal, Biologiya, 1963, no. 18V11K.
A handbook of plant-indicators of groundwater and soil types of the southern deserts of the U. S. S. R.

Vostokova, E. A. and D. D. Vyshivkin
1961   Chernosaksaul'niki v peskakh Severnykh Kyzylkumov. Moskovskogo Obshchestva Ispytatelei Prirody otdel Biologicheskii, Byulleten 66(2):98-103. Refertativnyi Zhurnal, Biologiya, 1961, no. 24V207.
Concludes that *Haloxylon aphyllum* can be used in the region as an indicator of the presence of salt-free or brackish water relatively close to the surface (25 to 40 meters). Gives the location of the largest black saxaul thickets. BA 38(5)17370.

Walker, E. H.
1944   The plants of China and their usefulness to man. Smithsonian Institution, Annual Report, 1943: 325-362.
Covers the history of botany in China. Various regions are discussed and information is given concerning the amount, density, and to some extent, the kind of flora. The economic significance of botany is considered. BA 20(2)3539.

──────
1960   Bibliography of eastern Asiatic botany, Supplement I. American Institute of Biological Sciences, Washington, D. C. 552 p.
A fine list of publications. Gives journal titles. Includes a general subject index, geographical index, and a systematic botany index. Does not includes much material relating to deserts. *See also* Merrill and Walker (1938).

Wallmo, O. C.
1955   Vegetation of the Huachuca Mountains, Arizona. American Midland Naturalist 54(2):466-480.
The Huachuca Mountains in southeastern Arizona rise to 9,445 feet from pediments of 5,000 feet. Vegetation types are classified in four zones, more or less conforming with

elevation. The lowest of these is the Desert Scrub and Grassland Zone which is found below 5,000 feet.

Walter, H.

1936a Die ökologischen verhältnisse in der Namib-Nebelwüste (Südwestafrika) unter auswertung der aufzeichnungen des Dr. G. Boss (Swapkomund). Jahrbücher für Wissenschaftliche Botanik 84: 58-222.

———— 1936b Die vegetationsverhältnisse in der Namib-Nebelwüste. Forschungen und Fortschritte 12: 293-294.

Largely a report of the results of the unusually heavy rainfall in the northern part of the Namib, during the summer months of 1933 and 1934. Notes that, except for rocky localities and the erosion gulleys, the Namib is, as a rule, entirely lacking in plant life. The rainfall resulted in a thick covering of grasses, principally *Aristida* species, which had all dried by March 1935.

———— 1962 Die vegetation der erde in ökologischer betrachtung. I: Die tropischen und subtropischen zonen. VEB G. Fischer Verlag, Jena. 538 p.

Important treatise in which the general conditions of desert areas, water-balance, etc., are discussed; the Sonoran, Namib, Chilean-Peruvian coastal, the Karroo, Australian, Sahara and Arabo-Asian deserts are especially studied.

———— 1964 Die vegetation der erde in öko-physiologischer betrachtung. I: Die tropischen und sub-tropischen zonen. 2. aufl. Gustav Fischer Verlag, Stuttgart. 592 p.

This outstanding book contains not only excellent descriptions and comparisons of all vegetation zones but also more than 400 photos and drawings and 114 tables, a great part of them dealing with the deserts and semi-deserts of all continents.

Warming, E.

1909 Oecology of plants, an introduction to the study of plant-communities, assisted by Martin Vahl. Prepared for publication in English by Percy Groom and Isaac B. Balfour. Clarendon Press, Oxford. 422 p.

Waterfall, U. T.

1946 Observations on the desert gypsum flora of southwestern Texas and adjacent New Mexico. American Midland Naturalist 36(2):456-466.

Lists and discusses collections of plants from desert gypsum areas in western Texas and eastern New Mexico. Notes that *Coldenia hispidissima* is characteristic of desert gypsum, and *Larrea divaricata* is characteristic of the adjoining calcareous deserts, also that some plants are obligate gypsophiles and can be used to indicate gypsum.

Watt, J. W. and M. G. Breyer-Brandwijk

1962 The medicinal and poisonous plants of southern and eastern Africa. 2nd ed. E. and S. Livingstone, Edinburgh. 1457 p.

Describes the plants and notes their medicinal and other uses, chemical composition, pharmacological effects, and toxicology in man and animal.

Webber, J. M.

1953 Yuccas of the Southwest. U. S. Department of Agriculture, Agriculture Monograph 17:1-97.

This monograph contains information on yucca ecology, uses, taxonomy, seed and seedlings, root and shoot characteristics, recovery of harvested yuccas, growth rates and age of yuccas, transplantation, and asexual propagation. Includes an index to species and a bibliography. BA 28(7)16775.

Weberbauer, A.

1911 Die pflanzenwelt der peruanischen Anden in ihren grundzügen dargestellt. Vegetation der Erde 12. 355 p.

———— 1912 Pflanzengeographische studien im südlichen Peru. Engler's Botanische Jahrbücher 48: 27-46.

———— 1936 Phytogeography of the Peruvian Andes. *In* J. F. Macbride, Flora of Peru. Field Museum of Natural History, Chicago, Botanical Series 13(1:1):13-81.

———— 1945 El mundo vegetal de los Andes Peruanos. Ministerio de Agricultura, Lima. 776 p.

The second edition of the author's *Die Pflanzenwelt der Peruanischen Anden.* Important reference book on Peruvian plant geography; treats with detail the desert flora of Peru.

Went, F. W. and M. Westergaard

1949 Ecology of desert plants. III: Development of plants in the Death Valley National Monument, California. Ecology 30(1):26-38.

The authors found differences in floristic composition due to salinity, altitude, and other causes. On dry slopes drought-enduring shrubs may be the only flowering plants except at intervals of 5 to 10 years when a moist season brings on a growth of annuals. They found that a rain followed by 30° C. temperature resulted in no germination; by 15 to 16° C., germination in only creosotebush; and by 8 to 10° C., germination of winter annuals but not creosotebush.

Westover, H. L. and C. R. Enlow

1934 Turkistan Turkey Expedition. 3 vols. (unpublished manuscript in U. S. National Archives).

Whaley, W. C.

1948 Rubber, the primary sources for American production. Economic Botany 2(2):198-216.

States that guayule and the so-called Russian dandelion are the only two plants that can be grown in the Americas likely to become important in rubber production. Guayule, *Parthenium argentatum,* is a native of the Chihuahuan Desert.

White, A., R. A. Dyer, and B. L. Sloane

1941 The succulent Euphorbiaseae (Southern Africa). Abbey Garden Press, Pasadena, California. 2 vols.

A study of the South African species of *Euphorbia, Monadenium,* and *Synadenium,* with keys, descriptions, and many photographic illustrations. Includes a glossary, bibliography, and notes on *Euphorbia* culture. BA 19 (5)9136.

Whiting, A. F.

1939 Ethnobotany of the Hopi. Museum of Northern Arizona, Flagstaff, Bulletin 15. 120 p.

One of the better works in this field. Classifies plants by uses and has an annotated list with descriptions of uses. From Indian uses and their beliefs regarding plants may come ideas for uses of plants in other areas.

Whiting, A. G.
1943 A summary of the literature on milkweeds (*Asclepias* species) and their utilization. U. S. Department of Agriculture, Bibliographical Bulletin 2. 41 p.
Notes that those from arid areas have most promise for rubber production, but of low quality, and that milkweeds are valuable also for fibers and oils. Includes an excellent bibliography.

Whyte, R. O.
1950 The phytogeographical zones of Palestine. Geographical Review 40:600-614.
This work follows the classification of Eig. The area was mapped according to Saharo-Sindian, Irano-Turanian, and Mediterranean affinities. Includes a small map showing rainfall and another showing phytogeographical zones, also good photographs of the vegetation.

Wiggins, I. L.
1948 The effects of prolonged drought on the vegetation of southern Baja California. Cactus and Succulent Journal 20(4):49-51.
A report of results of erratic rains in Baja California. Long droughts result in extreme weakening of cacti. When the rains finally return, they invigorate both the cacti and their parasites. The parasites, fungi and bacterial diseases, often develop more rapidly, and may kill the cacti. BA. 23(1)1738.

Wilcox, D. G. and N. H. Speck
1963 Pastures and pasture lands of the Wiluna-Meekatharra area. C. S. I. R. O. Land Research ser. 7:162-177.

Williams, R. J., comp.
1955 Atlas of Australian resources: Vegetation regions. Prepared and published by the Department of National Development, Canberra.
Scale 1:6,000,000. Polyconic projection. 1 sheet.

Williams, L.
1945 The phytogeography of Peru. p. 308-312. *In* Plants and plant science in Latin America. Chronica Botanica Co., Waltham, Mass.
A brief description of the vegetation types of Peru, including the coastal region of deserts and lomas, and the northern coastal region of deserts and semideserts. BA 20(1)218.

Willis, J. C.
1966 A dictionary of the flowering plants and ferns. 7th ed., revised by H. K. A. Shaw. Cambridge University Press, Cambridge. 1214 p.

Wood, J. G.
1929 Floristics and ecology of the mallee. Royal Society of South Australia, Transactions and Proceedings 53:359-378.
"Mallee," a term referring originally to the habit of growth, embraces about 12 species of *Eucalyptus*, is limited in the south by the 20-inch annual isohyet, and in the north by the 8-inch annual isohyet. The supporting soils are all alkaline (pH about 8.0) and contain nodular travertine limestone. Mallee is not usually considered a plant formation of the desert, but of the transition from desert to semiarid. BA 5(4)10467.

———
1936 Regeneration of the vegetation of Koonamore vegetation reserve, 1926-1936. Royal Society of South Australia, Transactions 60:96-111.

———
1937 Vegetation of South Australia. Government Printer, Adelaide. 164 p.
An excellent discussion of the vegetation of South Australia.

———
1950 The vegetation of Australia. p. 77-96. *In* The Australian environment; handbook prepared for the British Commonwealth Specialist Agricultural Conference on Plant and Animal Nutrition in relation to Soil and Climatic Factors held in Australia, August 1949. 2nd ed. C. S. I. R. O., Melbourne. 151 p.

Wooton, E. O.
1895 The Russian thistle. New Mexico Agricultural Experiment Station, Bulletin 16. 20 p.
An early discussion of this unwanted introduction from Asia. This paper, compared with later reports, shows the extensive spread of the plant during the last 70 years.

———
1911 Cacti in New Mexico. New Mexico Agricultural Experiment Station Station, Bulletin 78. 70 p.
Includes keys for identification and information on their value as stock feed. Notes that the tunas or fruits of New Mexican varieties are not as good as Mexican cacti for food.

Wooton, E. O. and P. C. Standley
1915 Flora of New Mexico. U. S. National Herbarium, Contributions 19. 794 p.
The standard flora manual of the state.

Yang, T. W.
1957 Vegetational, edaphic, and faunal correlations on the western slope of the Tucson Mountains and the adjoining Avra Valley. University of Arizona (Ph.D. dissertation). 176 p.
A very careful and comprehensive study in the mountains west of Tucson, Arizona. Found a highly significant correlation between each of the two major vegetation types and specific soil characteristics. The *Larrea* vegetation type is associated with a finer-textured soil, a higher amount of capillary moisture, but a relatively lower portion of that water available for plant use. The *Cercidium* vegetation type is associated with coarser-textured soil, a lower amount of capillary moisture, but a relatively higher portion of that water available for plant use. BA 32(10)32794.

Zapriagaev, F. L.
1938 Dreveshaia i kustarnikovaia rastitel'nost Tadzhikistana. Sovetskaia Botanika 1937(6): 70-95.
(Trees and shrubs of Tadzhikistan)

Zohary, D.
1953 Ecological studies in the vegetation of the Near Eastern deserts. III: Vegetation map of the central and southern Negev. Palestine Journal of Botany, Jerusalem ser. 6:27-36.
This area has extreme desert conditions with precipitation between 25 and 150 mm. The vegetation is mostly Saharo-Sindian, with Irano-Turanian in the uplands. Includes a black-and-white foldout map showing the plant communities.

Zohary, M.
1940*a* Geobotanical analysis of the Syrian desert. Palestine Journal of Botany, Jerusalem ser. 2(1): 46-96.

Describes the geography, geology, soils, and climate. The area includes 3 phytogeographic territories: Saharo-Sindian (the largest), Irano-Turanian, and Mediterranean. Lists the more prominent plant associations found in each territory. Includes illustrations and a map showing the distribution of these phytogeographical territories. BA 19(9)18075.

1940*b* On the ghada-tree of northern Arabia and the Syrian desert. Palestine Journal of Botany, Jerusalem ser. 1(4):413-416.
The author, noting some past confusion of scientific identification of this tree, places it as *Haloxylon persicum*. One of the saxaul trees of Central Asia, it is found in sandy habitats with rainfall less than 100 mm, supplies food for desert livestock, charcoal, and is valuable for sand stabilization.

1942 The vegetational aspect of Palestine soils, a preliminary account of the relations between vegetation and soil in Palestine. Palestine Journal of Botany, Jerusalem ser. 2(4):200-246.
Notes that mature soils are rare, that most are alkaline, and that the nature of the soils is largely determined by the parent rock. The vegetation represents arboreal climax (Mediterranean), steppe (Irano-Turanian), and desert (Saharo-Sindian). Lists the character and distribution of each soil type, and the vegetational associations found on each. Discusses the crop-growing potential of each type in relation to the natural vegetation. BA 18(5) 8005.

1944 Vegetational transects through the desert of Sinai. Palestine Journal of Botany, Jerusalem ser. 3(2): 57-78.
Notes the following 6 types of areas in the Sinai Peninsula: hamada, sand dunes, rocky hills, loess soils, salines, and the central mountain region. Describes the soil types and vegetation of each of the six. BA 22(3)5574.

1945 Outline of the vegetation in Wadi Araba. Journal of Ecology 32(2):204-213.
Wadi Araba, the valley between the Dead Sea and the Red Sea, is remarkable for its abundant vegetation compared to other desert areas of similar climatic type. This paper recognizes 6 soil varieties, each with its characteristic vegetation. Notes large areas of Central Asian saxual forest dominated by *Haloxylon persicum*. BA 20 (1)219.

1946 The flora of Iraq and its phytogeographical subdivision. Directorate General of Agriculture, Baghdad, Bulletin 31. 201 p.
The most comprehensive discussion available on the vegetation of Iraq. Lists species and areas of occurrence, and discusses the vegetation by phytogeographical groups.

1947*a* A geobotanical soil map of western Palestine. Palestine Journal of Botany, Jerusalem ser. 4(1): 24-35.
Essentially a discussion of soils and characteristic vegetation.

1947*b* A vegetation map of western Palestine. Journal of Ecology 34(1):1-19.
The 3 major plant communities include: Mediterranean,

characterized by arboreal climax communities; Irano-Turanian, characterized by steppe; and Saharo-Sindian, the most barren. Describes the vegetation of these, including segetal communities. BA. 21(8)19000.

1950 The segetal plant communities of Palestine. Vegetatio 1949:2(6):387-411.
Analyzes the plant communities of nonirrigated croplands according to Zürich-Montpellier methods. These associations, all on lands under agriculture for centuries, are mapped and described. Also considers their hypothetical original nonanthropic vegetation and return toward that stage upon abandonment. BA 25(9)26426.

1956 The genus *Tamarix* in Israel. Tropical Woods 104:24-60.
Sixteen species are thought to occur in Israel. Line drawings of distinguishing features are given and an artificial key to the species is presented. The distribution of each species or variety is recorded. Includes a discussion of ecological differences and an analysis of present afforestation practices. BA 31(6)18404.

1959 Bibliographia phytosociologica: Palaestina, pt. 1. Excerpta Botanica, B, 1(3):202-212.

1961 Bibliographia phytosociologica: Palaestina, pt. 2. Excerpta Botanica, B, 5(2):157-160.

1962 Plant life of Palestine. The Ronald Press Company, New York. 262 p.
An ecological study of Israel, Jordan, and the Gaza Strip. Discusses climate, topography, and soil conditions. The vegetation is of 3 principal types: Mediterranean tree and shrub; steppe and desert; and coastal sand, swamp, and marsh. Considers man's relationship to the plant communities, and discusses native wild plants used for various purposes. BA 38(5)17376.

1963 On the geobotanical structure of Iran. Research Council of Israel, Bulletin, Sec. D, Botany 11 (suppl.). 113 p.
An excellent phytogeographical discussion of the flora and its affinities. Includes a brief discussion of climate, topography, and soils. A map shows areas of hot desert, empty desert, Irano-Turanian desert, steppe, and includes salt and sandy areas.

Zohary, M. and N. Feinbrun
1951 Outline of vegetation of the northern Negev. Palestine Journal of Botany, Jerusalem ser. 5(2): 96-114.
The northern Negev includes desert and semidesert; rainfall is about 400 mm in the northwest and 100 mm in the southwest. Discusses the vegetation in relation to its phytosociological and ecological relationships. Includes a detailed vegetation and soil map. BA 27(4)8632.

Zohary, M. and G. Orshansky (Orshan)
1949 Structure and ecology of the vegetation in the Dead Sea region of Palestine. Palestine Journal of Botany, Jerusalem ser. 4(4):177-206.
Salt-moisture-air relations of the soil determine distribution of plant communities in this area. The area, one of the largest halophytic centers of the Near East, is characterized by a most intricate vegetational mosaic. Six habitats are recognized. An accompanying map delimits several individual phytosociological units. BA 27(4)8631.

Zohary, M. and G. Orshan

1951　Ecological studies on lithophytes. Palestine Journal of Botany, Jerusalem ser. 5:119-128.

A very interesting article on the ability of some plants to grow on solid rocks. Includes a classification of plants growing on rocks. Some obtain moisture and nutriment from crevices, but true lithophytes have roots that penetrate the rock mass. Rock as a substratum possesses considerable water available and readily-transportable to the plants growing upon it. Notes that moisture conditions may be more favorable than in nonlithophytic habitats. Found lithopytes growing on dolomites, crystalline rock, limestone, and chalk, but most frequently on calcareous crusts. The roots were found penetrating rock with a hardness of 3 to 4 mohs.

1954　Ecological studies in the vegetation of the Near Eastern deserts. V: The *Zygophylletum dumosi* and its hydroecology in the Negev of Israel. Vegetatio 5-6:341-350.

Notes that *Zygophyllum* has great ability to reduce transpiration during dry periods and to produce special roots that penetrate into soil layers not previously exploited for moisture. It is usually found on stony slopes in this area with a rainfall of less than 100 mm. Water relations were also studied. Includes a black-and-white map of vegetation classes.

1956　Ecological studies in the vegetation of the Near East deserts. II: Wadi Araba. Vegetatio 7(1): 15-37.

Climatic data for this area between the Dead Sea and the Gulf of 'Aqaba show an erratic, low (25-50 mm/year), winter precipitation, high temperatures, and low humidity. Five of the vegetation classes in the Saharo-Sindian area of Palestine are described briefly in relation to their edaphic positions, distributions, and component alliances. Ecological data include soil salinity, soil water tension or amount, temperatures, air saturation pressure deficit, and plant transpiration and cell sap osmotic values. BA 32(7)22212.

1959　The maquis of *Ceratonia siliqua* in Israel. Vegetatio 8(5/6):285-297.

The vegetation is discussed as to appearance, composition, and distribution. This whole alliance of the evergreen maquis is thermophilous and is found at the lowest altitudes. All associations are climax communities but at present are relicts and not regenerating.

Zolotarewsky, B. and M. Murat

1938　Divisions naturelles du Sahara et sa limite méridionale. *In* L. Aufrère *et. al.,* La vie dans la région désertique nord-tropicale de l'ancien monde. Societé Biogéographie, Paris, Mémoires 6:335-350.

A comprehensive discussion of natural divisions of the Sahara. The divisions set up by the authors are compared in tabular form with those of Chevalier (1933) and Monod (1932).

FAUNA
OF DESERT ENVIRONMENTS
WITH DESERT DISEASE INFORMATION

CHARLES H. LOWE
Department of Biological Sciences
The University of Arizona

INTRODUCTION

1. Organisms in the Desert

The desert organisms that take the unmodified desert environment head on, in continuous direct exposure for 24 hours a day and 365 days a year, are plants. There are no such animals. By far the single major accomplishment of animals that has permitted them to become true desert species took place long before the evolution of the deserts. This accomplishment is their well-known motility and attendant behavior. They were further preadapted by precise biological clocks that bring them to the surface from their underground and other sheltered retreats at the right time of the day or night during the correct season of the year. By and large, animals, including man, survive within a hot, desiccating desert environment primarily by avoiding it through behavior.

Desert species that are found only in deserts are typically singular in aspects of their physiology, morphology, and behavior that combine as successful, highly adaptive systems not found elsewhere in the living world. In this sense such animals and plants are unique organisms—they have solved a major evolutionary problem in being able to make a successful living entirely within the desert environment.

2. Desert Species and Others

By no means are all the plants and animals that live naturally within deserts in any sense true desert species. Numerous nondesert species occupy partial environments within all arid regions. Such permissive partial environments within the desert are surprisingly many and varied, and the plants and animals that occupy such habitats are commonly those so-called "desert species" that actually have far wider distributions outside of the desert than within it. This fact underlies a major problem in surveying the world literature on "desert fauna," which has more often than not uncritically confused desert and non-desert species.

A proper, however strict, interpretation of the concept "desert species" would greatly restrict the discussion of poisonous animals and pests and would virtually eliminate the topic of desert diseases. Accordingly, it should be understood that here, as in other reviews on deserts, many of the animals discussed are not desert species, but are native species that occur in the desert as well as more widely outside of it in other principal land environments.

True desert species of animals occur in natural desert habitats wholly, or essentially, within the ecological and geographical limits of the desert. As noted, nondesert species of animals occur in deserts in modified environments (smaller or larger micro-environments) such as those occupied by riparian communities, but have wider distributions outside of the desert than within it, extending into the desert from woodland, grassland, savanna, thornscrub, and subtropical deciduous forest. In some local areas within most deserts, therefore, desert species and nondesert species of animals may be found side by side. This situation does not simplify the picture for uncritical observers.

A third distributional pattern involving species in the desert does not fit in a clear-cut way the simple dichotomy of desert species versus nondesert species. The pattern involves animals, relatively few in number, that are at home widely and abundantly throughout one or more deserts and are equally at home in other, semiarid environments. Such species frequently have evolved distinctive races in grasslands, woodlands, *et al.*, as well as in the desertscrub; many of the races are formally described as subspecies. This distributional pattern occurs in both hemispheres, and one of the most remarkable instances is the distribution of the various subspecies of *Varanus griseus,* a varanid lizard ranging across arid and semi-arid lands of North Africa, through the Middle East, and into western India. (see Mertens, 1954). This carnivore is very much at home in the great Saharo-Sindic megadesert with populations in the most severe desert habitats, including the great Eastern Erg and Western Erg of the Sahara and their sand-sea equivalents in the Arabian Desert. Such unusually eurytopic species native to the North American Desert are the teiid whiptail lizard, *Cnemidophorus tigris,* and the iguanid side-blotched lizard, *Uta stansburiana* (See Van Denburgh, 1922; H. M. Smith, 1946; Stebbins, 1954). They are equally at home, widely and abundantly, throughout many of the derived modern communities of the Madro-Tertiary Geoflora, including entire desert subdivisions of the North American Desert (see Shreve, 1942, and Axelrod, 1950, 1958).

Thus, in addition to nondesert animal species and desert-only species, there are in the desert a few exceptional desert-included species. In the present survey I have referred to the latter two groups as *desert species*.

In a sense, the discussion thus far has put the cart before the horse. For, although the concept of "desert" would appear to be of something readily quantified, readily delimited, and readily agreed-upon, such is not the case. Moreover, nondeserts are highly varied Earth phenomena, and include some such as those discussed by Sears (1935), that are frequently referred to as deserts. The animals in such areas ordinarily are not desert species.

3. Where is the Desert

The question: "What is a desert species?" naturally involves the question: "What is a desert?" and "Where is the desert?"* The question of *what* is perhaps the less important at the moment, for it would appear to be the easier to answer. Certainly it has been answered by nearly everyone to his own satisfaction, and with a most remarkable array of "definitions," most of which are useless. *Where* a given desert actually is (extends to), however, in precise and detailed terms of latitude, longitude, and elevation ("altitude"), and how its particular boundaries are to be determined (the boundary criteria for definitions, description, and mapping) are rather important as well as rather knotty questions. One man's answer is not likely to satisfy another.

"Where is the desert?" (usually meaning: "Where is the edge of the desert?") is a perennial desert problem the discussion of which is capable of quickly generating a remarkable metabolic heat production. I have made clear elsewhere (Lowe, 1964) my position that the mappable reality of a particular desert is the mappable reality of the vegetation, and that the edge of the desert is a broad statistical edge that is locatable and mappable on the basis of vegetative statistics. The dream that man-made climate-devices will replace nature-made creosotebushes as total climate-soil integrators must refer to some other planet. It may be a hopeless rejoinder, but far greater efforts should be made to study "climatically" the "creosotebushes" of the world. This is, indeed, a serious proposal, if for no other reason than the fact that the creosotebushes, saltbushes, and their desert

*The question: "Why is the desert?" is discussed elsewhere in this series, principally by Reitan and Green in their chapter on weather and climate.

plant associates on the borders of the deserts are not long for this world.

Animals and plants occur together in desert biotic communities where many animals, as well as the plants, exhibit highly individualistic relationships. But desert animals are markedly less useful than are desert plants for estimating desert parameters. In the desert, the "individualistic" relation of plant to environment is far more striking, and more important, than the "organismic" relation of plant to plant (Shreve, 1915, 1951, and elsewhere). Animal distribution occasionally provides corroborative evidence, and aids interpretation, but as a group of organisms that has evolved high motility and marked avoidance reactions for survival, animals are more secretive and less sensitive climatic integrators and indicators than are the perennial desert plants. In this regard, desert animals do not meet the earlier expectations of bioecologists (see Merriam, 1894, and Shelford, 1945). Certainly for the present, and the foreseeable future at least in the present century, the perennial plants that comprise desertscrub vegetation, rather than animals or climatic indices, offer by far the most fruitful basis for delimiting geographically the deserts of the world.

4. Subjects Discussed and Not Discussed

The present state of knowledge regarding the taxonomy, distribution, and general ecology of native animals (fauna) in the 13 major deserts is estimated and discussed in the present work. Topical discussions center on poisonous animals, food, pests, and disease in the desert. Physiological ecology of native and introduced species in the deserts is an important subject that is not given a topical discussion, although appropriate remarks and conclusions are given. This subject, also referred to in whole or part as environmental physiology, comparative physiology, stress physiology, medical climatology, physiological climatology, bioclimatology, *et al.*, is currently one of the most rapidly growing areas in desert biological investigation. There have been several excellent recent reviews for both animals (vertebrate and invertebrate) and man. Those for animals are : Bodenheimer (1953, 1954, 1957), Cloudsley-Thompson (1954, 1958, 1964), Cloudsley-Thompson and Chadwick (1964), Schmidt-Nielsen (1954; 1959a, b; 1964a, b), Schmidt-Nielsen and Dawson (1964), Schmidt-Nielsen and Newsome (1962), Williams (1954), Wright (1954), Saint-Girons and Saint-Girons (1956), Uvarov (1956, 1962, 1966), Etchecopar and Hüe (1957), Hart (1957), Pradhan (1957), Lee (1958, 1963), Keast, Crocker, and Christian (1959), Edney (1960), Chew (1961), Gates (1962), Kirmiz (1962), Tromp (1963),

Dawson and Schmidt-Nielsen (1964), Hudson and Bartholomew (1964), Macfarlane (1963, 1964), and Folk (1966). Those for man include: Adolph *et al.*, (1947), Newburgh (1949), Selye (1950), Lee (1958, 1962, 1963, 1964), Lee *et al.*, (1951), Ladell (1953, 1957), Kleiber (1961), Gates (1962), Hardy (1963), Tromp (1963), Dill, Adolph, and Wilber (1964), Sulman, Hirschman, and Pfeifer (1964), and Folk (1966); see also reports, publications, and literature cited in Centre d'Etudes et d'Informations des Problémes Humains dans les Zones Arides (PROHUZA) (1960), Unesco (1957, 1958*a* & *b*, 1961, 1962, 1963, 1964), and the several recent symposia in Unesco (1964) and World Health Organization (1958, 1964).

5. Emphases and Limitations

Only one serious information limitation was encountered in the overall attempt (*1*) to sample the faunal work accomplished primarily during the past 100 years, with some emphasis on the present and past two decades, and (*2*) to include all of the 13 major deserts of the world. This single limitation concerns the Takla-Makan desert in the Tarim Basin of northwestern China (Sinkiang Province), roughly midway between the Turkestan Desert and the Gobi proper. The present survey has not examined any important information directly on the Takla-Makan, and, therefore, has not generated an opinion beyond what may be a superficial appearance that something less is known in a scientific way about this particular desert and its fauna. It would be surprising if considerably more is not recorded for the Takla-Makan than what little has been located, in the present instance, most of which is by extension from Russian work in the bordering dry-steppes of the U.S.S.R.

Another limitation has been the inability to identify all of the factors that have contributed to all of the differences in the comparative zoological knowledge of all of the deserts. Major factors identified are discussed under "Conclusions" and "Recommendations."

It would be helpful toward understanding and estimating current levels of comparative knowledge on Earth environments and organisms if values were assigned in an effort to quantify the information for meaningful analysis. This would permit data reductions to some simple and well-understood statistics from which one could then test for sameness or difference (and level of difference), and for trends, in one or both of the relevant dimensions of geography and time. It would also permit calculation of simple coefficients of regression, permitting simple prediction equations for speculation on relevant aspects of the future. The present work has con-

sidered this general problem and includes a beginning toward such quantification.

Literature retrieval is sampling, whether random or not, and whether good or bad. It is felt that the sampling in the present case has been both extensive and intensive enough to justify the conclusions and the recommendations, especially where they appear to have a wide consensus within the living corps of students. The task has not been easy nor is it completed, but some broad generalizations do appear possible regarding where we are, where we have been, and even where we might go in the future.

About the period of World War II, the effort in desert biology experienced a quantum jump. Present interest in the highly ramifying subject of fauna remains strong and appears to be growing stronger each year. This situation is good, for survey indicates that in the deserts we have a long way to go to catch up with knowledge for other major organism-environment systems on the planet Earth.

The animals are the most dependent of all the objects that occur in terrestrial communities. Thus, the subject of a contemporaneous fauna is partly one of weather and climate, of soils and other surface materials, of the flora, and of the vegetation. While desert organisms (plant and animals) are among the most unique of all land organisms, they remain in largest measure the most poorly understood. And we may not have really much longer to enjoy the beauty of work in natural rather than man-made deserts.

6. Acknowledgments

Many individuals, institutions, agencies, and corporations assisted the preparation of this report. Bibliographic assistance was rendered by Mrs. Denise Wolfe (Archives de Institut Pasteur d'Algérie, Algiers), Dr. I. S. Allio (Arabian-American Oil Co., Dhahran), D. S. Anderson, Dr. R. Van Gelder, and Dr. R. G. Zweifel (American Museum of Natural History, New York), Dr. S. A. Minton (Indiana University, Indianapolis), and D. J. C. Bequaert, Mr. R. L. Bezy, Mrs. Kathryn Gloyd, Dr. H. K. Gloyd, Mr. S. R. Goldberg, Dr. W. L. Nutting, Dr. A. R. Mead, Miss Patricia Paylore, and Dr. F. G. Werner (University of Arizona, Tucson). For translations of works in foreign languages I am also indebted to Miss E. A. Halpern (French) and to Mr. O. H. Soule (Russian) of the University of Arizona. The manuscript was typed by Miss S. P. Halpern, Miss K. Wiley, and Mrs. D. Genice Dickerson, to whom I am indebted for careful assistance that greatly aided its preparation.

Both in the United States and in many foreign countries, many persons kindly discussed problems, provided information on current research, and/or arranged for transportation and assistance on field trips. For such assistance I am indebted to the following persons overseas: Dr. Alice Grandison (British Museum, Natural History, London), Dr. J. Guibe (Muséum National d' Histoire Naturelle, Paris), Dr. V. FitzSimons, Transvaal Museum, Pretoria), Dr. C. Koch (Namib Desert Research Station, Gobabeb), Mr. LeRoy Rasmussen (United States Embassy, Algiers), Dr. J. L. Cloudsley-Thompson (University of Khartoum, Khartoum), Mr. Thomas C. Barger (President, Arabian-American Oil Co., Dhahran), Dr. I. Prakash, Dr. G. C. Taneja, Mr. M. Behari, and Mr. R. Singh (Central Arid Zone Research Institute, Jodhpur), Dr. A. R. Main (Western Australian University, Perth), Dr. A. J. Marshall, Dr. T. Ealey, and Dr. A. K. Lee (Monash University, Wellington), Mr. Allan Newsome (C. S. I. R. O., Alice Springs), and Mr. R. Perry (C. S. I. R. O., Canberra). In the United States, the following scientists aided: Dr. W. J. Gertsch, Dr. R. G. Zweifel (American Museum of Natural History, New York), Dr. Kenneth S. Norris (University of California, Los Angeles), Dr. Sherman A. Minton (Indiana University, Indianapolis), Dr. Herndon G. Dowling (New York Zoological Gardens, New York), Dr. Robert C. Stebbins (University of California, Berkeley), Dr. Knut Schmidt-Nielsen (Duke University, Durham), Dr. H. K. Gloyd, Dr. W. L. Nutting, Dr. F. G. Werner, Dr. A. R. Mead, Dr. J. C. Bequaert, Dr. E. H. Spicer, and Dr. L. K. Sowls (University of Arizona, Tucson).

The following individuals read all or a part of the manuscript and many of their suggestions have been incorporated. For this assistance I am indebted to Dr. A. R. Main of Western Australia University, Perth, Dr. J. L. Cloudsley-Thompson of the University of Khartoum, Khartoum, Dr. J. C. Bequaert and Dr. W. L. Nutting of the University of Arizona, Dr. W. J. Gertsch and Dr. R. G. Zweifel of the American Museum of Natural History, New York, and Dr. K. S. Norris and Dr. R. C. Stebbins of the University of California, Berkeley.

DISCUSSION

A. GENERAL

1. Sources of Information

Our knowledge of desert faunas has greatly benefited from the Unesco symposium series on arid research, and all numbers in that series bearing on desert faunas served as important secondary sources during the initial phases of the survey (see Pertinent Publications list at end of chapter, under Unesco). Reports and publications of the World Health Organization (WHO) provided specific, general, and statistical information regarding both desert and nondesert animal species of public health and medical importance in deserts (see Pert. Pubs. list, World Health Organization). Cited references are for reviews, bibliographies and/or original sources that provide a picture either of how little or much is known on a given topic under discussion. The Pertinent Publications list varies widely in sampling representation. As a whole, it cites less than 10 per cent of the subequally pertinent references at hand during the survey, most of which have also been carded and filed. The attempt in discussion and citations has been to be representative and critical rather than encyclopedic.

2. Source Institutions

Several libraries, museums, stations, and other institutions in the United States and overseas served as sources for original documents, specimens examined, and discussions with experts in specific fields. In addition to government agencies, these included the:

American Museum of Natural History, New York City, New York

Arabian-American Oil Company, Dhahran, Saudi Arabia

Central Arid Zone Research Institute, Jodhpur, India

Centre de Recherches Sahariennes, Beni-Abbès, Algeria

Commonwealth Scientific and Industrial Research Organization (C.S.I.R.O.), Division of Wildlife Research, Canberra and Alice Springs, Australia

El Matarîya Research Station, Cairo, Egypt (U.A.R.)

Institut Fondamental d'Afrique Noire (I.F.A.N.), Dakar, Senegal

Institut Pasteur d'Algerie, Algiers, Algeria

Monash University, Wellington, Australia

Namib Desert Research Station, Gobabeb, South West Africa

National Zoological Garden, Riyadh, Saudi Arabia

Scientific Society of South Africa, Windhoek, South West Africa

Transvaal Museum, Pretoria, South Africa

United States National Museum, Washington, D.C.

University of Arizona, Tucson, Arizona

University of Baghdad, Baghdad, Iraq

University of Cairo, Giza, Egypt (U.A.R.)

University of California at Los Angeles, Los Angeles, California

University of Indiana Medical School, Indianapolis, Indiana

University of Western Australia, Perth, Australia

3. Approach

The primary approach to survey involved literature search and review, followed by discussions with area experts, with subsequent literature search, review, and evaluation. The questions on what a desert species is and where the desert edge is arose continually and were sometimes unresolved. The decisions given in table I for state of knowledge, based on this approach to the problem, are the final number weights I have assigned, and provide for ranking. Greater reso-

573

Table I
SUMMARY OF STATE OF KNOWLEDGE OF DESERT FAUNA*

FAUNAL GROUP	DESERT												
	KALAHARI-NAMIB	SAHARA	SOMALI-CHALBI	ARABIAN	IRANIAN	THAR	TURKESTAN	TAKLA-MAKAN	GOBI	AUSTRALIAN	MONTE-PATAGONIAN	ATACAMA-PERUVIAN	NORTH AMERICAN
Arthropods													
Insects													
dangerous	2	3	3	3	2	3	3	2	3	4	3	2	4
harmless	2	2	2	3	1	3	2	0	0	2	1	1	4
Arachnids													
dangerous	3	3	2	3	2	3	2	0	2	4	3	2	4
harmless	2	2	1	2	1	2	2	0	1	2	2	2	4
Crustaceans	0	1	0	2	1	2	2	0	0	2	1	1	3
Molluscs													
Snails	2	2	1	2	2	3	1	?	?	3	1	2	3
Vertebrates													
Amphibians	2	2	1	3	2	3	2	?	?	3	2	3	4
Reptiles													
dangerous	4	3	3	4	3	4	3	2	2	4	3	2	4
harmless	3	2	1	2	1	3	2	1	1	3	2	1	4
Birds	3	4	2	3	2	3	3	1	2	3	2	3	4
Mammals	2	2	2	2	3	3	3	1	3	4	2	3	4
Mean (N=11)	2.3	2.4	1.6	2.6	1.8	2.9	2.3	.64	1.3	3.1	2.1	1.9	3.8
Range	0-4	1-4	0-3	2-4	1-3	2-4	1-3	0-2	0-3	2-4	1-3	1-3	3-4

Legend
 * Apparent state of knowledge: *4* good, *3* subadequate, *2* fair, *1* poor, *0* insignificant
    Question marks indicate information inadequate for estimate.

lution for evaluation is sometimes provided by finer taxonomic categorization, as given in the topic discussions. This improvement is particularly desirable for the invertebrates, which, on the whole, are greatly more varied in both species diversity and life-form diversity than are the vertebrates in the deserts. The literature sources for the estimates of the present state of knowledge are further discussed below.

4. Present State of Knowledge

The survey has enabled some estimates of our present state of knowledge concerning the relatively fewer animal groups, species, and individuals that occur in desert faunas, particularly as regards true desert species. This relative knowledge is summarized in table I, with a scale of *4* to *0*, indicating apparently good (*4*) to apparently insignificant (*0*), with intermediate ranks of subadequate (*3*), fair (*2*), and poor (*1*). The literature sources for the data evaluated for construction of table I vary widely, and obtaining them involved problems that confront literature retrieval in general. In the present case, the extremely wide variation of subject matter encountered has involved matters of currency, size, complexity, and validity of the documents obtained, after running the gamut of problems regarding availability and accessibility, not the least of which have been obscure publishers and places of publication and the usual difficulties with translation and transliteration (more than 15 major languages are involved). The information has proven so highly varied that any discussion of criteria for regarding information as published or not published (*e.g.*, mimeographed *etc.* "proceedings" *etc.* of panels and symposia *etc.*, or of the gamut of reasons and biases involved in what to cite and what not to cite, will not be attempted here other than to say that such decisions were made after due consideration of pertinence, availability, accessibility, usefulness, etc., in relation to other references included in a total of something more than ten times the number cited.

Taxonomic revisions, monographs, checklists, and texts for both the vertebrate and invertebrate animal groups were used, and particularly in this regard the *Zoological Record* was of major assistance in locating many obscurely published and unsuspected papers on the systematics and ecology of desert animals. Extensive "travel surveys," "biologies," and "ecologies" of the faunas *etc.* of deserts, such as those by Tristram (1860), Wallace (1913), Andrews (1932), Kachkarov and Korovin (1942), Scortecci (1940), Capot-Rey (1953), Keast (1961), Vaurie (1964), Minton (1966), and many others provide especially important and often carefully detailed data on animal distribution, relative abundance, population density, and general ecology. Bibliographies, and the bibliographies within bibliographies (such as those of Allouse, 1954, 1956, and that of Field, 1962), have been of much aid to the economy of retrieval. Specialists were especially helpful in the location of key bibliographies on particular animal groups. Maugini (1953), for the Somali-Chalbi Desert, is an example of an extensive, indeed critical, but difficult to obtain bibliography on a relatively little-known desert that required on-the-spot discovery and retrieval in a desert station or in an archive.

Recent reviews, and reviews of reviews, such as those by Cloudsley-Thompson (1954), Bodenheimer (1957), Etchecopar and Hue (1957), Keast, Crocker, and Christian (1959), Khalil (1963), Pradhan (1957), Uvarov (1962) and Schmidt-Nielsen (1964a) give discussions and conclusions (and often recommendations) for faunal groups in arid lands that provide valuable recent overviews. Such contributions have greatly aided the evaluation of both the coverage and the level of the research and knowledge of the fauna in given deserts. One of the strongest boosts to the biological literature on deserts in recent years has come largely through funding by governments interested in pests, disease, and poisonous animal eradication and control. Such subjects are treated in the topical discussions that follow, where a representative part of the literature is also cited.

The many shorter papers on the taxonomy and/or ecology of particular desert animal groups, essential to the estimates of current knowledge given in table I, have been in most but not all cases contributions published during the last hundred years. I refer here to the large number of papers by naturalists of many nationalities. These are usually published in the learned journals, which constitute a major literature source of essentially nonapplied biological research that was investigated both directly and via abstracting media (*Biological Abstracts,* BASIC). The following papers are a small representative sample of the conspicuously wide spectrum of subjects and journals involved, the location and examination of which consumed a large portion of the project time: Andrews (1924), Ahmad (1940),

Akhtar (1958), Allouse (1959), Asplund (1967), Bates (1939), Betham (1904), Biggs (1937), Chapman (1927), Dementev (1962), Di Caporiacco (1939), Dolgushin (1957), Exline (1950), Finlayson *et al.* (1932), Finlayson (1936), Fryer (1955), Heim de Balsac (1925), Janjua and Haque (1955), Kachkarov and Kurbotov (1930), Koch (1961), Krishna, Prakash, and Dave (1956), Kumerloeve (1960), Lane (1962), Lawrence (1959, 1962), Leviton (1959), Lönnberg (1931), Marx (1953), Meinertzhagen (1934), Mertens (1956), Minton (1962), Nambiar (1948), Nutting (1966), Prakash (1963), Read and Jervis (1958), Schmidt and Marx (1956), Steindachner (1903), Taylor and Cavendish (1859), Tregenza (1951), Volsoe (1939), Warburg (1965a, b), Werner, Enns, and Parker (1966), Wiltshire (1940), and Zinovieva (1959). Most such papers are a few pages in length, infrequently over 20. Many such works remain obscurely buried and have yet to appear in reviews or to be incorporated into comprehensive biological syntheses for the deserts. It is not surprising to find, occasionally, that some of the same ground is now being covered by modern workers apparently without knowledge of the earlier work of others.

Birds, mammals, snakes, and butterflies are examples of particular animal groups that have long excited numbers of naturalists. The biological literature reflects greater or lesser interest, by the larger or smaller record, for certain animal groups. This statement is also true of the data for deserts, but the record is relatively thinner for virtually all animal groups in the deserts, and obviously far out of proportion to that apparently deserved by their uniqueness. The animal groups of economic and medical importance, such as locusts, termites, and mosquitoes, have especially large records, although the desert record is skimpier than interest in the groups would lead one to believe. The reason appears to lie in the harshness of the desert environment and the resulting recency of wide penetration within it, with large-scale exploration and development of it by modern man only during the present century.

Two problems immediately arise in evaluating this literature for estimates such as those made in table I. First, it is clearly apparent that for deserts, the literature coverage is more than usually spotty: good in some areas and poor or nonexistent in others in the same desert. The Sahara is a good example. Compared to parts of the Sudan and Egypt (U.A.R.), central Libya has been virtually ignored, a fact that makes Scortecci's (1940) recent *Biologia Sahariana* a spectacularly unusual contribution. Second, the literature coverage for an animal group may be spotty, again particularly accentuated, it seems, for the deserts.

For example, one or two deadly species of spiders in an area may be well known while the vast majority of spider species in the same area remain little known, and some not even worked on in the entire history of arachnology. Such facts make reports such as that by Lawrence (1962) on the spiders of the Namib exciting indeed, as well as extremely valuable. This particular problem, dangerous versus harmless, is simplified in table I by treating the two groups separately.

Reflected in table I is the apparent fact that, except for the insects, knowledge of the invertebrates (represented by three other major animal groups — the arachnids, crustaceans, and snails) in the desert is distinctly less than that for the vertebrates as a group or as separate classes (amphibians, reptiles, birds, mammals). It is not surprising that among the entire fauna, regardless of phylogenetic position, it is the poisonous species that are best known by man throughout the deserts of the world. (An exception is again certain arthropod insects of medical and economic importance.) It should not go unnoticed, however, that even here, there is far more to be learned than is already known. Further comments on data reduction, analysis, and the state of knowledge are given under Conclusions and Recommendations.

B.   POISONOUS (POTENTIALLY LETHAL) ANIMALS

> *Tobacco, coffee, alcohol, hashish,*
> *prussic acid, strychnine, are weak*
> *dilutions: the surest poison is time.*
> —Emerson

There have been several recent reviews, symposia, and bibliographies on venoms and venomous animals that refer or apply in part to desert species and other species which also occur in deserts (Harmon and Pollard, 1948; Sandoz, 1951; Buckley and Porges, 1956; Kaiser and Michl, 1958; Merriam, 1961; Russell, 1962; Beard, 1963; Gennaro, 1963; Keegan and Macfarlane, 1963; Klemmer, 1963; National Academy of Sciences/National Research Council, Committee on Snakebite Therapy, 1963; Keegan *et al.,* 1964; Russell and Scharffenberg, 1964. See also Pawlowsky (1927) and Phisalix (1922). International conferences on animal venoms are scheduled in the near future in Chile and in Israel (S. A. Minton, personal communication).

Only those poisonous species of animals that also are potentially dangerous to man are considered in this section. For man, an important distinction is to be made between the "merely" poisonous animals and the *dangerous* (deadly poisonous, dangerously poisonous, or lethal) animals. The spiders provide a good example: essentially all (99 per cent plus) of the known species of spiders on earth are poisonous, but only a handful of them are deadly to man — the latter are potentially dangerous in addition to being poisonous.

Likewise, not all poisonous snakes are deadly. In addition to the deadly poisonous snakes, of which there may be on the order of 300 out of a total of some 2,500 snake species, there are many kinds that possess venom and inflict bites that are not, for man, dangerous. These are usually relatively small, rear-fanged snakes, some species of which occur in deserts. They are often common snakes with large local populations, as, for example, in the North American Desert (*Hypsiglena torquata, Tantilla planiceps, Trimorphodon lyrophanes*) where — as is commonly the case for rear-fanged snakes — they are not strictly desert species but have wide distributions outside the desert (Smith and Taylor, 1945; Stebbins, 1954; Wright and Wright, 1957). The *large* dangerous rear-fanged species as represented by the common boomslang (*Dispholidus typus*) are confined almost entirely to nondesert Africa; see Pope (1958) for an account of a fatal boomslang bite.

1.   Vertebrates

Amphibians, Birds, and Mammals

There are no poisonous (venomous) birds. The known poisonous mammals are shrews in *Blarina, Neomys,* and *Solenodon* (Pearson, 1942; Rabb, 1959). A poison gland is associated with the movable horny spur on the hind foot of males of the well-known Australian duck-billed platypus (*Ornithorhynchus anatinus*); see Phisalix (1922). The platypus and the known poisonous shrews are not desert species.

The amphibians occurring in deserts are species of frogs and toads, and, occasionally, salamanders. Poison is secreted from poison glands in the skin. For this reason the amphibians are considered to be potentially dangerous and they should be skinned before eating; see section on fauna as human food.

Reptiles

Lizards

There are two species of poisonous lizards that together comprise the family Helodermatidae. These are the Gila monster (*Heloderma suspectum*) and the Mexican beaded lizard (*H. horridum*), both of which occur only in North America (Mexico and U. S.). The Gila monster occurs in the North American

Desert, mainly along the moister eastern edges of the Sonoran Desert and Mojave Desert from southern Sonora northward to the vicinity of St. George, Utah.

A recent monograph by Bogert and del Campo (1956) gives extensive original sources in treating the general biology of the family Helodermatidae, comprised of two species noted above; this work includes information on geographic and ecologic distribution, behavior, the bite, venom, *etc.* See also Tyler (1956), Grant and Henderson (1957), and Lowe and Limbacher (1961).

The "deadliness" of the Gila monster has been greatly exaggerated. It appears that there remains no uncontestable death directly attributable solely to the bite of a Gila monster; nevertheless a Gila monster bite creates a potentially dangerous situation.

Snakes

The following account for the poisonous snakes of the world refers to those that are potentially dangerous to man. They are in four families (Hydrophiidae, Elapidae, Viperidae, Crotalidae) and are commonly referred to as hydrophid snakes (or hydrophids), elapids, viperids, and crotalids. Table II gives the distribution of the major groups of poisonous land snakes (elapids, viperids, and crotalids) in the major deserts of the world. Table III lists numerous works that treat poisonous land snakes dangerous to man that occur in the deserts of the world; the table indicates the deserts to which each work applies. The references in table III are mostly to major works treating mainly identification and distribution (and also relative abundance) of the dangerously poisonous snakes occurring in the deserts.

Hydrophids are the permanently marine sea snakes; they are closely related to elapids. At least one species of sea snake inhabits each stretch of inshore waters of the Pacific and Indian Oceans from southern Japan to southern Africa, and from the Peruvian Gulf on the west coast of South America northward to northwestern Mexico (Smith, 1926; Mertens, 1934; Smith and Taylor, 1945; Volsoe, 1939; Herre, 1942; Cochran, 1943, 1944; Loveridge, 1945; Harmon and Pollard, 1948; Werler and Keegan, 1963; Pope, 1955; Darlington, 1957; Worrell, 1963*b*; Barme, 1963; Klemmer, 1963; Russell and Scharffenberg, 1964, with many original sources; Minton, 1966; and Minton, Dowling, and Russell, 1967). Only one species, *Pelamus platurus,* occurs in the eastern Pacific east of Samoa, reaching Mexico, Central and South America; this single species also extends the distribution of sea snakes to South African shores of the Indian Ocean. One species is landlocked; this is *Hydrophis sempei* in fresh-water Lake Taal, Leyte, Philippine Islands.

Table II

DISTRIBUTION OF THE MAJOR GROUPS OF POISONOUS LAND SNAKES (ELAPIDS, VIPERIDS, AND CROTALIDS) IN THE MAJOR DESERTS OF THE WORLD

Desert	Family		
	Elapidae	Viperidae	Crotalidae
Namib-Kalahari	x	x	—
Sahara	x	x	—
Somali-Chalbi	x	x	—
Arabian	x	x	—
Iranian	x	x	—
Thar	x	x	—
Turkestan	—	x	x
Takla-Makan	—	—	x
Gobi	—	—	x
Australian	x	—	—
Monte-Patagonian	x	—	x
Atacama-Peruvian	x	—	x
North American	x	—	x

Sea snakes are likely to be found along the shore of most of the deserts that have marine shorelines: Sahara, Somali-Chalbi, Arabian, Iranian, Thar, Australian, North American, and Atacama-Peruvian. They do not occur on the coast of the Namib. There is no sea snake found in the Atlantic.

Elapids are the cobras, coral snakes, and their allies. They occur in both the New and Old World (see tables II and III).

In the New World the elapids are largely variations on a single evolutionary theme—the coral snake—and all species but two are treated in the same genus (*Micrurus*), which is primarily tropical and subtropical in distribution. Of the two exceptions, one is a desert species. This is the Sonoran Coral Snake, *Micruroides euryxanthus,* occurring in Arizona and Sonora, in the Sonoran Desert subdivison of the North American Desert and in the adjacent thornscrub at its southern edge in Sonora. Little is known about the venom, or its effects, of this small unobtrusive species that enters the desert (Van Denburgh, 1922; Schmidt and Davis, 1941; Lowe, 1948; Stebbins, 1954, 1966; Wright and Wright, 1957; Russell, 1962; Lowe and Limbacher, 1961).

In the Old World, elapids have radiated widely and are diverse in structure, form, size, color pattern, behavior, venom, *etc.* They are in greatest number in the Australia / New Guinea region; within deserts their greatest diversity is found in the Australian desert areas. Cobras are found in Africa, in southwestern Asia (one species, the Egyptian Cobra also in Africa), and in southeastern Asia. Kraits and Old

Table III

WORKS TREATING POISONOUS LAND SNAKES DANGEROUS TO MAN IN THE DESERTS OF THE WORLD

Work	Desert
Abalos and Pirosky (1963)	Monte-Patagonian
Amaral (1930)	Monte-Patagonian
Anderson (1963)	Iranian
Andrews (1932)	Gobi
Angel (1950)	General*
Barash and Hoofien (1956)	Arabian
Barrett (1950)	Australian
Bogert (1941)	North American
Bogert (1943)	General*
Bogert and Oliver (1945)	North American
Bons and Girot (1962)	Sahara
Boulenger (1896)	General*
Broadley (1959)	Somali-Chalbi
Cansdale (1961)	Sahara
Christensen (1955)	Kalahari-Namib
Cilento (1944)	Australian
Cochran (1943)	Turkestan
Cochran (1944)	General*
Conant (1958)	Takla-Makan
Condamin (1958)	Gobi
Corkill (1932)	Iranian
Corkill (1935)	Sahara
Corkill (1956)	Sahara
Dammann (1961)	North American
de Haas (1950)	General*
Deraniyagala (1960)	General*
Deraniyagala (1961)	General*
Ditmars (1931)	General*
Dodge (1952)	North American
FitzSimons (1921)	Kalahari-Namib
FitzSimons (1962)	Kalahari-Namib
Freiberg (1954)	Monte-Patagonian
Gharpurey (1954)	Thar
Glauert (1957)	Australian
Gloyd (1940)	North American
Hoge (1965)	Monte-Patagonian
	Atacama-Peruvian
Keegan and Macfarlane (1963)	Australian
Kellaway (1932)	Australian
Kellaway and Eades (1929)	Australian
Khalaf (1959)	Iranian
Kinghorn (1956)	Australian
Klauber (1931a)	North American
Klauber (1931b)	North American
Klauber (1936)	North American
Klauber (1956)	North American
Klemmer (1963)	All
Klobustitzky (1960)	General*
Kramer (1961)	General*
	Turkestan
	Takla-Makan
	Gobi
Kramer and Schnurrenberger (1963)	Sahara
Laurent (1950)	Somali-Chalbi
Laurent (1956)	Somali-Chalbi

Work	Desert
Laurent (1964)	Kalahari-Namib
Loveridge (1957)	Somali-Chalbi
Marcenac (1926)	Sahara
Marx (1956)	Sahara
Mendelssohn (1963)	Iranian
Mertens (1952)	Turkestan
Mertens (1955)	Kalahari-Namib
Mertens (1960)	General*
Minton (1962)	Thar
Minton (1966)	Thar
Minton, Dowling, and Russell (1967)	All
Nikolskii (1916)	Turkestan
	Takla-Makan
	Gobi
Oliver (1958)	North American
Owen (1952)	Sahara
Parker (1949)	Somali-Chalbi
Pasteur and Bons (1960)	Sahara
Peters (1959)	General*
Phisalix (1922)	General*
Pitman (1938)	Somali-Chalbi
Pope (1944)	Kalahari-Namib
	Monte-Patagonian
Pope (1955)	Monte-Patagonian
Rooij (1917)	Australian
Saint-Girons (1956)	Sahara
Schmidt (1933)	North American
Schmidt (1953)	North American
Schmidt and Davis (1941)	North American
Schmidt and Inger (1957)	General*
Scortecci (1938)	Sahara
Scortecci (1939)	Sahara
	Somali-Chalbi
Smith (1926)	Kalahari-Namib
Smith (1943)	Thar
Smith and Taylor (1945)	North American
Stanek (1960)	Kalahari-Namib
Stebbins (1954)	North American
Stebbins (1966)	North American
Terentjev and Cernov (1949)	Turkestan
	Takla-Makan
	Gobi
Theodor (1955)	Arabian
Vellard (1944)	Monte-Patagonian
Villiers (1950)	Sahara
Volsøe (1939)	Iranian
Waite (1929)	Australian
Wall (1928)	Thar
Watson (1908)	Australian
Werner (1908)	Sahara
Werner (1922)	General*
Worrell (1963a)	Australian
Worrell (1963b)	Australian
Wright and Wright (1957)	North American

*General: Relevant general information not specifically designated for any desert.

World Coral Snakes are also Asiatic. Elapids extend eastward in diminishing numbers of species, to only one in the Fiji Islands.

Viperids, the "true vipers," are found only in the Old World and are the only poisonous snakes in Europe and immediately adjacent northern Asia. They are widely distributed in Africa and southern Asia. Viperids do not occur in Australia, nor do crotalids (tables II and III). With the elapids, the viperids constitute one of the two major groups of snakes that are dangerous to man in the Old World deserts (table III).

Crotalids, the "pit-vipers," occur in the New World (several genera) and in the Old World (two genera, *Agkistrodon* and *Trimeresurus*). In the New World they occur in North, Central, and South America and are a highly diversified group of snakes. In the Old World they are Asiatic in distribution, reaching from the Japanese islands in the east to the region of the Caspian Sea in the west. The species *Agkistrodon halys* is the only poisonous snake in the Gobi and Takla-Makan Deserts (tables II and III).

No major desert is entirely void of poisonous reptiles. The Takla-Makan and the Atacama-Peruvian are the least known and the North American Desert the best reported with regard to systematic, geographical, and ecological details of the poisonous snakes. Also, the North American is the only desert containing a species of poisonous lizard, the Gila monster.

Surprisingly, and notwithstanding a long written history for the area, the geographic distribution of poisonous snakes in North Africa including the Sahara is not well known. The situation is considerably better for South Africa including the Kalahari-Namib. With a single exception, there are no maps for the distribution of the entire poisonous snake fauna for any of the major world deserts. The exception is the North American Desert, but even in this case not all of the maps cover the entire desert area; see Stebbins (1945, 1966), Wright and Wright (1957), Russell (1962), and Klauber (1936, 1956). Hoge's (1965) recent annotated list of neotropical crotalids also contains maps.

Titles of papers and volumes of varying size and usefulness on one or more poisonous species in one or more of the deserts of the world are given in Russell and Scharffenberg (1964). Klemmer (1963) provides an annotated check list, with major references, for all of the currently recognized species of poisonous snakes in the world. In addition to alphabetical listings under each family, there is a listing of the species found in each of 17 geographical subdivisions of the world. In this excellent work, as in every major work yet published, the basis is geo-

graphical, not ecological; therefore, the deserts are treated, as usual, only by being generally included in the lists for larger geographical areas.

The recent U. S. Navy Manual entitled *Poisonous Snakes of the World* (Minton, Dowling, and Russell, 1967)* treats in varying detail all major groups of poisonous snakes in the world that are potentially dangerous to man and cites major references. Brief species accounts are given for the poisonous species that are responsible for the largest number of bites within the genera, or are believed to be of serious danger to adults. Accordingly, species accounts of many "desert species" are not given. Emphasis is at the generic and family level, and the world is again divided into 10 major geographical regions. Often the distributions of snakes are given in general, sometimes even vague, terms, for it is seldom that exact geographic distributions are known. Klemmer's (1963) nomenclature is followed. This Navy manual is an unusually important work, which, like most others, is necessarily based on the previously existing and incomplete knowledge in the pertinent literature augmented by the knowledge of its authors. Unfortunately, as indicated above, little detailed information has been published on the geographic and ecologic distributions of the poisonous snakes of the world's deserts, particularly for the Old World and South America. A recent exception is Minton's (1966) especially valuable volume on West Pakistan, which treats the Thar Desert.

Species photographs, some in color, are given in Minton, Dowling, and Russell (1967). Klemmer's (1963) work also contains a number of excellent color photographs, including some for little-known dangerous species. Photographs are provided by Pope (1944, 1955) and Ditmars (1931) in popular books on poisonous snakes and other reptiles of the world, and in many of the regional works on snakes, both popular and technical (see Table III).

Poisonous Snakebite and Treatment

Russell and Scharffenberg (1964) give 5,829 titles on snake venoms and poisonous snakes published since the year 100 B. C. and include works on the general biology of venomous snakes, venom apparatus, collection of venomous snakes, prevention of snakebite, yields of venoms, effects of venoms, chemistry and toxicology of venoms, antivenin, snakebite statistics, medical treatment, and other aspects. Harmon and Pollard (1948) give 4,157 titles on animal venoms published since 1863; these include references to poisonous animals in general, including snakes, spiders, and scorpions. Swaroop and Grab

---
* This U. S. Navy volume replaces its predecessor of the same title (Moore, 1963), which was recalled by the Navy.

(1954) give snakebite mortality statistics for the world.

Table IV summarizes information available for treatment of snakebite by species occurring in the various deserts of the world and elsewhere. From Keegan's (1956) table for the world, I have arranged the extractions in table IV by deserts in the usual order followed in the present work. Minton, Dowling, and Russell (1967) is the most recent reference.

The recent important work on poisonous snakes of the world by Minton, Dowling, and Russell (1967) includes what is unquestionably the most up-to-date recommendation for first-aid and medical treatment of snakebite poisoning. These authors have summarized and extended the pertinent data in the earlier references cited by Russell and Scharffenberg (1964), and the works of Keegan and Macfarlane (1963), Reid *et al.* (1963), National Academy of Sciences/National Research Council, Committee on Snakebite Therapy (1963), and Campbell (1964). Information on relative toxicity *etc.* and attendant relative dangerousness is also given, and some desert species are discussed in this regard.

Recently there was much controversy on the potentially dangerous use of cryotherapy (icing or other "refrigeration" of tissue), which was recently revived and recklessly popularized by Stahnke (1953, and elsewhere) in the western United States; accordingly it is especially well-known to residents in the North American Desert and elsewhere in the American Southwest. This is referred to and discussed by Shannon (1956, and elsewhere), Limbacher and Lowe (1959), Emory and Russell (1961), Russell (1962), Lowe and Limbacher (1961), National Academy of Sciences / National Research Council, Committee on Snakebite Therapy (1963), Keegan *et al.* (1964), Minton, Dowling, Russell (1967), and others.

Popularized by Stahnke, mostly in privately published pamphlets, under the name Ligature-Cryotherapy (or L-C) treatment, the peculiar revival of cryotherapy for snakebite followed its rejection and early warnings in American medical journals (Crum, 1906; Allen, 1938, 1949). In short, however, beyond approximately one hour for moderate cooling, tissue "refrigeration" cooling is dangerous and definitely contraindicated as an extensive measure for first-aid or for medical treatment. The following recommendation on the "L-C treatment" (=more than 1 hour) is from the National Academy of Sciences / National Research Council, Committee on Snakebite Therapy (1963): "It is recommended that the ligature-cryotherapy method not be used by military personnel as

a first-aid measure for the treatment of bites of venomous snakes."

2. Invertebrates

Spiders and scorpions are major invertebrate groups that occur in deserts and which include some species lethal to man. Bees, wasps, and ants occur in deserts and are also known to cause human deaths.

The Spider Genus Latrodectus

Listed in table V, Poisonous Desert Spiders, are the ten "species" of "dangerous" or lethally poisonous spiders that account for all or most of the deaths and disabilities resulting from spiderbites in the deserts. Six of the ten are spiders of the genus *Latrodectus* (the black widow and its world relatives). Bogen (1956) estimates that roughly 99 per cent of all serious cases resulting from spiderbite are from bites of *Latrodectus*. The genus was described about two centuries ago (1775), and the lethality of its venom to vertebrates has long been known. Obviously, good as well as extensive data from the genus would be of great interest, and wide taxonomic agreement might be thought to be well established. Unfortunately the facts do not meet all of the expectations.

As this is being written (1966), the taxonomy of the genus *Latrodectus* is in confusion. Keegan's (1955*a*) classification is regarded as incorrect by Levi (1959), whose classification is regarded as incorrect by Gertsch (personal communication); Marikovski's (1956) conclusions are still different, as were those of Chamberlin and Ivie (1935) and earlier workers. Keegan (1955*a*) attempted to apply modern polytypic species concepts but still retained a relatively high number of 11 species in a total of 15 taxa (species and subspecies). Levi's (1959) classification, based on details of internal as well as external morphology, recognizes as subspecies of *Latrodectus mactans* the following taxa that have been treated traditionally as species (see table VI, Classifications for the genus *Latrodectus*):

L. mactans hasselti: India to Australia and New Zealand

L. mactans tredecimguttatus: Europe and the Mediterranean Region

L. mactans cinctus: Southern Africa

L. mactans menavodi: Madagascar and the Seychelles Islands

The nominal subspecies, *L. mactans mactans,* is in North, Central, and South America. This arrangement of five subspecies in part recognizes the desirability of alleviating confusion that would otherwise be created by synonymyzing rather than recognizing the well-known names for the broadly continental

Table IV

ANTIVENIN FOR SNAKEBITE IN THE DESERTS OF THE WORLD

Data in this table is taken primarily from Keegan (1956), who gives additional information on directions for use, units of supply, physical nature, and host animal. The deserts are assigned on the bases of known distributions of the species listed in the column for Venoms Neutralized (data from several authors).

Desert	Venoms Neutralized	Serum	Producer
Kalahari-Namib . . .	All important poisonous snakes of South Africa	Antisnakebite Serum (Polyvalent)	South African Institute for Medical Research, Hospital Street, Johannesburg, South Africa
Kalahari-Namib . . . Sahara . . . . Somali-Chalbi	All African poisonous snakes, including mamba	FitzSimon's Anti-Venomous Serum	FitzSimon's Snake Park Laboratory, Box 1413, Durban, Natal, South Africa
Kalahari-Namib . . . Sahara . . . . Somali-Chalbi	*Naja haje, N. nivea, Sepedon haemachates,* and other African species	Schlangenbiss-Serum Anti-Kobra Serum	Behringwerke, Aktiengesellschaft, Marburg-Lahn, West Germany
Sahara	*Cerastes* and *Naja* species of North Africa	Serum Antivenimeux Antiviperin AN	Institut Pasteur d'Algerie, Algiers, Algeria
Kalahari-Namib . . . Sahara . . . . Somali-Chalbi	*Bitis arietans, B. gabonica,* and *Naja* species	Serum Antivenimeux AO	Institut Pasteur, Paris, France
Sahara . . . . Arabian Desert . . . Iranian Desert . . . . . Thar	*Naja* of Egypt, India, and Indo-China	Serum Antivenimeux C	Institut Pasteur, Paris, France
Sahara . . . . Arabian Desert . . . . Iranian Desert . . . . . Thar	*Echis carinatus*	Schlangenbiss-Serum (*Echis carinatus* anteserum)	Behringwerke, Aktiengesellschaft, Marburg-Lahn, West Germany
Iranian Desert . . . . Thar	*Naja naja, Bungarus coeruleus, Vipera russelli, Echis carinatus*	Polyvalent Anti-Snake	Haffkine Institute, Parel, Bombay, India
Sahara . . . . Arabian Desert . . . . Iranian Desert	*Echis*	Concentrated Anti-Venom	Central Research Institute, Kasauli, India
Turkestan . . . . Takla-Makan . . . . Gobi	*Trimeresurus flavoviridis* and *Agkistrodon halys*	Polyvalent Antivenin Serum	Institute for Infectious Diseases, University of Tokyo, Shiba Shrodane-Daimache, Minato-Ku, Tokyo, Japan
Turkestan . . . . Takla-Makan . . . . Gobi . . . . North American . . . South American . . .	All species of the family Crotalidae (pit vipers), including *Crotalus, Sistrurus, Agkistrodon, Trimeresurus, Bothrops, Lachesis*	Antivenin Crotalidae Polyvalent (This serum replaces the earlier Wyeth product, Antivenin Nearctic Crotalidae)	Wyeth Laboratories, Philadelphia 1, Pennsylvania, U.S.A.
South American . . .	*Crotalus terrificus* (=*C. durissus terrificus*)	*Crotalus terrificus* antivenin	Behringwerke, Aktiengesellschaft, Marburg-Lahn, West Germany
South American . . .	*Bothrops atrox*	*Bothrops atrox* antivenin	Behringwerke, Aktiengesellschaft, Marburg-Lahn, West Germany
South American . . .	*Crotalus terrificus* and *Bothrops atrox* (Recommended when guilty snake is unidentified)	Soro-Anti-Ofidico (Polyvalent)	Instituto Pinheiros, Rua Teodoro Sampaio, São Paulo, Brazil
South American . . .	Species of Bothrops: *atrox, jararacussu, alternata, jararaca, cotiara; Lachesis muta*	Soro-Anti-Botropico	Instituto Pinheiros, Rua Teodoro Sampaio, São Paulo, Brazil

(continues)

Table IV *(Continued)*

ANTIVENIN FOR SNAKEBITE IN THE DESERTS OF THE WORLD

Desert	Venoms Neutralized	Serum	Producer
South American ...	*Crotalus t. terrificus*	Soro-Anti-Crotalico	Instituto Pinheiros, Rua Teodoro Sampaio, São Paulo, Brazil
South American ...	*Crotalus t. terrificus*	Soro-Anti-Crotalico	Instituto Butantan, Caixa Postal 65, São Paulo, Brazil
South American ...	*Bothrops* species	Soro-Anti-Botropico	Instituto Butantan, Caixa Postal 65, São Paulo, Brazil
South American ...	*C. t. terrificus* and *Bothrops* species	Soro-Anti-Ofidico	Instituto Butantan, Caixa Postal 65, São Paulo, Brazil
South American ...	*Lachesis muta*	Soro-Anti-Laquetico	Instituto Butantan, Caixa Postal 65, São Paulo, Brazil
South American ...	*Micrurus* species (coral snakes)	Soro-Anti-Elapidico	Instituto Butantan, Caixa Postal 65, São Paulo, Brazil

allopatric populations (populations that have evolved into reasonably distinct morphological types) that were long thought to be distinct species.

The minor to nonexistent population variations on single continents is questionably assigned subspecific rank in *Latrodectus*. In such an enormously variable animal this might lead to more operational confusion than assistance, as Levi (1959) and his data, and that of others suggests; for example, the subspecies of Chamberlin and Ivie (1935) in the U.S. *(mactans, texanus, hesperus)*.

On the other hand, Levi's (1959) work makes clear his uncertainty in treating the allopatric populations in the Middle East and eastern Sahara that are allied to *L. mactans,* namely *L. pallidus, L. hystrix,* and *L. dahli* (see table VI).

The population (species) diagnoses for these taxa are for slight differences in degree rather than differences in kind. This fact also suggests, along with the rest of the picture, that the whole lot (of few specimens) may represent no more than a set of more or less differentiated allopatric populations of *L. mactans* that are morphotypes, and probably ecotypes to some extent as well. Thus it appears clear, and consistent with regard to Levi's (1959) concern with the polytypic species concept *et al.* (Mayr, 1942, 1963), that in the absence of data on actual or potential gene exchange there are other classifications that remain reasonable for these allopatric taxa (table VI); the name *pallidus* (Cambridge) has priority.

Moreover, the species relationship of *L. mactans* to *L. curacaviensis* in the Americas is not resolved (see also Pirosky and Abalos, 1963). This is another problem in *Latrodectus* that is not aided by the uncertainties concerning chance human distribution of these frequently edificarian* spiders.

Despite a relatively large literature on the cosmopolitan *Latrodectus,* many gaps remain for the deserts, and geographic and ecologic details are particularly insufficient. Levi's (1959) revision gives details and references on distribution (with maps) and on the little information available on ecology. Levi's (1959) map for *Latrodectus* in Australia is representative of our overall poor knowledge of the biota of the Central Australian Desert: apparently there is not a single interior station reported for this genus which is expected to occur there. Recent papers on the red-back spider *(Latrodectus mactans hasselti)* in Australia include those of Keegan (1952, 1955a, 1956, 1963) Keegan *et al.* (1964), Wallace and Sticka (1956), Levi (1959), Southcott (1961), and Wiener (1961a and elsewhere).

Some of the following references for *Latrodectus* and arachnidism (spiderbite poisoning) contain original sources on other species potentially dangerous to man that have appeared since Harmon and Pollard's (1948) bibliography of animal venoms, which contains 4,157 titles of works since 1863. For numerous and/or important original sources see also Bogen (1926, 1956), Savory (1964), Bogen and Loomis (1936), Roewer (1942-1954), Sampayo (1942), Bonnet (1945), Thorp and Woodson (1945), Keegan (1952, 1955a, 1955b, 1956, 1963), Buckley and Porges (1956), Marikovski (1956), Levi (1959), and Keegan *et al.* (1964).

One of the most unusual papers on *Latrodectus* is Cowles' (1937) report that the alligator lizard *(Gerrhonotus)* in California is a successful and natural

---
*Living in association with man-made structures.

Table V

POISONOUS DESERT SPIDERS

Poisonous species of spiders known to be dangerous to man that occur in one or more of the deserts of the world. References are cited in text. A question mark means presence or absence is unknown. Systematics of *Latrodectus* (six "species") in this table follows Levi (1959).

	KALAHARI-NAMIB	SAHARA	SOMALI-CHALBI	ARABIAN	IRANIAN	THAR	TURKESTAN	TAKLA-MAKAN	GOBI	AUSTRALIAN	MONTE-PATAGONIAN	ATACAMA-PERUVIAN	NORTH AMERICAN
Latrodectus geometricus ..	x	x	x	x	—	—	—	—	—	—	—	—	—
Latrodectus mactans	x	x	?	x	—	—	x	—	—	x	x	x	x
Latrodectus pallidus	—	x	—	x	x	—	x	—	—	—	—	—	—
Latrodectus curacaviensis .	—	—	—	—	—	—	—	—	—	—	x	x	x
Latrodectus hystrix	—	—	—	x	—	—	—	—	—	—	—	—	—
Latrodectus dahli	—	—	—	x	x	—	—	—	—	—	—	—	—
Atrax formidabilis	—	—	—	—	—	—	—	—	—	x	—	—	—
Atrax robustus	—	—	—	—	—	—	—	—	—	x	—	—	—
Lycosa erythrogaster ..... (= *L. raptoria*)	—	—	—	—	—	—	—	—	—	—	x	x	—
Phoneutria fera .... (= *Ctenus nigriventer*)	—	—	—	—	—	—	—	—	—	—	?	—	—

predator on the black widow. There is wide agreement on the efficacy of insecticides (e.g., DDT, BHC) against *Latrodectus* (Romaña and Abalos, 1948; Pirosky and Abalos, 1963).

In South America, *Latrodectus* occurs in both the Monte-Patagonian Desert and the Atacama-Peruvian Desert (table V and VI) *Latrodectus* is the only lethal spider in Argentina. The two principal "species" (*L. mactans* and *L. curacaviensis*) are commonly confused (Pirosky and Abalos, 1963). The less dangerous cosmopolitan city-dweller *L. geometricus* is also in Argentina.

Other Spiders

Pirosky and Abalos (1963) state that *Lycosa raptoria* (=*L. erythrogaster*), a dangerous spider in Brazil where a specific antivenin is produced against its venom, is not dangerous in Argentina. Also, *Mastophora gasterocanthoides* and *Loxosceles laeta* are not dangerous in Argentina although they cause serious accidents in Chile, where an antivenin is made for treatment of bites from *Loxosceles* (Macchiavello, 1931; Schenone and Prats, 1961).

Loxosceles is also widespread in the North American Desert (Gertsch, 1958*b*). Micks (1963) recently reported on necrotic arachnidism (brown spiderbite) from the bites of one or more of the four species in Texas. See also the reports on *Loxosceles* by Atkins, Wingo, and Sodeman (1957), Atkins *et al.* (1958), L. F. Schmaus (1929), and J. W. Schmaus (1959).

There are three species of deadly spiders in Australia (table V). The two deadly species of *Atrax* are restricted to Australia. The third lethal species is the world-wide black widow (*Latrodectus mactans*) called red-back spider in Australia (subspecies *Latrodectus mactans hasselti* = species *Latrodectus hasselti*).

Atrax robustus, the funnel-web spider, is apparently more poisonous than *A. formidabilis,* and is also more feared than is *Latrodectus*. Whereas *Latrodectus* occurs widely in arid parts of Australia, *Atrax* apparently does not. The following papers are recent works on *Atrax* or refer to such works: Taylor and Murray (1946), Irwin (1952), Wallace and Sticka (1956),

Table VI

CLASSIFICATIONS FOR THE GENUS *LATRODECTUS*

Keegan (1955a)	Levi (1959)	Other Classifications	
1) *L. geometricus*	1) *L. geometricus*	1) *L. geometricus*	1) *L. geometricus*
2) *L. foliatus*	2) *L. curacaviensis*	2) *L. curacaviensis*	2) *L. curacaviensis*
3) *L. mactans*	3) *L. mactans*	3) *L. mactans*	3) *L. mactans*
L. m. mactans	*L. m. mactans*	*L. m. mactans*	*L. m. mactans*
L. m. texanus	*L. m. tredecimguttatus*	*L. m. tredecimguttatus*	*L. m. tredecimguttatus*
L. m. hesperus	*L. m. cinctus*	*L. m. cinctus*	*L. m. cinctus*
L. m. bishopi	*L. m. menavodi*	*L. m. menavodi*	*L. m. menavodi*
	L. m. hasselti	*L. m. hasselti*	*L. m. hasselti*
4) *L. pallidus*	4) *L. pallidus*	*L. m. pallidus*	*L. m. pallidus*
5) *L. hystrix*	5) *L. hystrix*	*L. m. hystrix*	
6) *L. tredecimguttatus*	6) *L. dahli*	*L. m. dahli*	
7) *L. indistinctus*			
L. i. indistinctus			
L. i. karooensis			
8) *L. menavodi*			
9) *L. hasselti*			
10) *L. katipo*			
11) *L. revivensis*			

Wiener (1957, 1961b, 1961c, 1963), Keegan (1963), and Keegan *et al.* (1964).

Lycosa is a huge cosmopolitan genus that contains many large formidable spiders that are quite toxic and may occasionally cause death. *Lycosa erythrogaster* (table V) is one of these, and an antivenin is prepared for this and allied species in South America (Keegan, 1956; Pirosky and Abalos, 1963). As lycosids are hunting spiders, they frequently come in contact with man. Much of the literature on *Lycosa* refers to "*L. raptoria*" which is a synonym of *L. erythrogaster* (table V). See references for *Latrodectus*, above; see also Bogen (1956), Kaiser (1953, 1956), and Keegan (1956).

South America is especially rich in large spiders that can cause severe and occasionally lethal bites. Singled out in this regard are *Polybetes maculatus, Selenops spixi,* and species of *Mygales* and *Acanthoscurria.* These are not desert species. Similarly, one or more of the hunting spiders in South Africa, in the exclusively South African genus *Harpactirella,* may be potentially dangerous to man (Finlayson, 1956).

Papers on the South American *Phoneutria fera* (= *Ctenus nigriventer*) are cited or are otherwise referred to in Harmon and Pollard (1948), Bogen (1956), Bücherl (1956), Kaiser (1956), and Keegan (1956); see also Steinberg and Ortiz-Luna (1941).

Treatment of Spiderbite

Mortality from black widow (*Latrodectus mac-* *tans*) spiderbite in the U. S. has been estimated at 4 to 5 per cent (Bogen and Loomis, 1936; Thorp and Woodson, 1945). Per cent mortality statistics reflect among other things the sample size and the presence or absence of medical treatment. In a total of 15 cases in Arizona, Noon and Minear (1941) reported 11 per cent mortality (1 in 9) with no treatment, and 0 per cent mortality (0 in 6) with treatment.

Keegan and his co-workers (Keegan *et al.,* 1964) has recently reviewed medical treatment; see also Beard (1963), Horen (1963), and Pirosky and Abalos (1963). Significant seasonal variation in the toxicity of *Latrodectus* venom was reported by Keegan, Whittemore and Hedeen (1960).

Calcium gluconate and species-specific antivenin have proven consistently effective. Russell (1962) recently reported that methocarbomol is even more effective than calcium gluconate for relief of muscle pain and spasms resulting from black widow spiderbite in California.

Producers of antivenins for spiderbite are given by Keegan (1956). Antivenins are prepared for *Latrodectus* poisoning in South America (Pirosky and Abalos, 1963), North America, Europe, and South Africa.

Antivenins for spiderbite are produced in Brazil and in Argentina. Argentina produces an anti-*Latrodectus* serum at the National Institute of Microbiology of Buenos Aires that is concentrated and extremely effective; *L. mactans* is the species used (Pirosky and Abalos, 1963). It is not surprising that antivenin made with *L. mactans* in South America (Buenos Aires) is effective in neutralizing the venom of *L. mactans cinctus* (=*L. indistinctus*) of South Africa, *L. mactans tredecimguttatus* of the Mediterranean, and *L. mactans hasselti* of Indo-Australia (Finlayson and Hollow, 1945; Pirosky and Abalos, 1963).

Scorpions

Scorpions occur on all of the continents and in 11 of the 13 major deserts; scorpions do not occur in the Gobi or Takla-Makan. Structure, classification and distribution are treated by Kraepelin (1899), Lankester (1909), Byalynitskii-Birulya (1917*a,b*), Pocock (1929), Savory (1964), Werner (1934), Berland (1948), Vachon (1952), Cloudsley-Thompson (1958), and others.

All scorpions are venomous, but few are potentially dangerous to man. The notoriously "deadly" species are in five genera that are distributed as follows: *Buthus* and *Parabuthus* in Africa, *Prionurus* in Asia and Africa, *Centruroides* in the United States and Mexico, and *Tilyus* in South America. About a dozen species are involved, and they account for roughly 99 per cent of the serious cases of scorpion envenomation.

The widely scattered literature lacks a modern systematic accounting of all of the dangerous species, much less all of the species in the deserts, and much less all of the species in the world. Since the bibliography of animal venoms by Harmon and Pollard (1948; 4,157 titles) a number of papers have appeared treating aspects of desert genera and species; these include Efrati (1949), Goren (1950), Vachon (1952), Rohayem (1953), Stahnke (1953 and elsewhere), Bücherl (1956), Buckley and Porges (1956), Keegan (1956 and elsewhere), Cloudsley-Thompson (1958), Scott and Pratt (1959), Tulga (1960), Deoras (1961), Whittemore, Keegan, and Borowitz (1961), McGregor and Flanigan (1962), Ridgway, McGregor, and Flanigan (1962), Abalos (1963), Mazzotti and Bravo-Becherelle (1963), Whittemore and Keegan (1963), and Keegan *et al.* (1964). Early important work of Sergent and of Balozet in North Africa is cited by Harmon and Pollard (1948) and reviewed in Balozet (1956).

Treatment of Scorpion Sting

The work on scorpion antivenin and therapy prior to the mid-1940's is cited by Harmon and Pollard (1948). Papers in Buckley and Porges (1956) discuss research completed prior to about 1955. Recent reviews are given by Bücherl (1956), Scott and Pratt (1959), in Keegan and Macfarlane (1963), and by Keegan *et al.* (1964).

Antivenins for treatment of scorpion envenomation are usually very specific in nature, and are produced for local species. Keegan (1956) listed the producers of antivenins for scorpion-sting in North America, South America, the Middle East, North Africa, Egypt, and South Africa. Keegan and his coworkers (Keegan *et al.*, 1964) recently discussed the general problem and reviewed data in pertinent references cited.

Immersion of the stung part (such as a finger or hand) in ice water, or holding ice against it, definitely gives relief from pain and other symptoms caused by some species of "deadly" scorpions, including *Centruroides sculpturatus* of the North American Desert. Freezing of tissue is dangerous, however, and no tissue refrigeration of any kind should be extended for more than a few minutes and certainly not much beyond an hour.

Bees, Wasps, and Ants

Bees, wasps, hornets, and ants are common animals in deserts. Death to humans and other higher animals is usually due to hypersensitivity, and particularly from sensitization from previous stings.

While it is not necessary to warn adults to avoid such insect stings, facts revealed by mortality statistics are often unexpected (see recent reviews by Yaffee, 1959; Beard, 1963; and Keegan *et al.*, 1964). Ant stings have resulted in anaphylactoid shock and death in man (Miller, 1956; Caro, Derbes, and Jung, 1957). The giant bee of India (*Apis dorsata*) has killed humans, elephants (Muttoo, 1956), and water buffalo (Lindauer, 1957). In the report by Parrish (1959) on deaths due to poisonous (venomous) animals in the United States during the years 1950-1954, bees, wasps, and hornets ranked ahead of venomous snakes as causes of human death during that period. Keegan *et al.* (1964) tabulated data from U. S. Army medical records on bites and stings from arthropods and reptiles; they remarked that "snakes have not always been first among venomous animals as causes of admission for treatment."

Keegan *et al.* (1964) reviewed the recent literature bearing on the actual medical problem, which involves *(1)* the emergency treatment for persons showing severe reactions, and *(2)* the prophylactic desensitization of hypersensitive individuals (Mueller, 1959; Mueller and Hill, 1953; Stier and Stier, 1959; Lovelass, 1962; Beard, 1963). Keegan *et al.* (1964) called attention to Archer's (1958) report on the necessity of evacuating infantry cases due to anaphylactoid shock from stings of hornets encountered in the "jungle" in Malaya. Obviously, a major problem for consideration in planning expeditions is whether personnel known to be hypersensitive to insect sting should be allowed to serve in areas where contact with stinging insects could occur. It is not yet known whether this danger is present in all of the deserts.

C. FAUNA AS HUMAN FOOD

There are few living animals that come amiss to the Central Australian aborigines. To mention the names of all that are eaten would be largely to recapitulate the zoology of the district.
— Sterling (1896)

1. Vertebrates

All of the vertebrate animals are commonly known and self-evident as foods of man: fishes, amphibians, reptiles, birds, and mammals. Of these, the fishes and amphibians are in general least available as human food in deserts.

What is true of the very primitive aborigines of the Kalahari-Namib and the Australian Desert as quoted above (Sterling, 1896) is true to equal or subequal degree for early and modern peoples in every desert area in the world, be they Bushmen, Arabs, Mongols, American Indians, or others—the list of desert vertebrate species that serve as human food is essentially or partly the faunal list of the area (see Baegert, 1863; Hartman, 1897; Sterling, 1896; McGee, 1898; Spencer and Gillen, 1899; Fynn, 1907; Hrdlicka, 1908; Carruthers, 1914; Henderson and Harrington, 1914; Miller, 1914; Campbell, 1926; Andrews, 1932; Castetter and Underhill, 1935; Castetter and Oppler, 1936; Hill, 1938; Bailey, 1940; Brygoo, 1946; Scortecci, 1940; Klauber, 1956; Malkin, 1962; Wyman and Bailey, 1964; and Whiting, 1966). For example, in referring to a locality on the edge of the Gobi, Andrews (1932, p. 66) says, "I did not try to do any zoological collecting [in 1922], for my 1919 work had shown that the valley had been virtually denuded of animal life by the Mongols. We did not see even a marmot or a hare, and not a sign of antelope."

Frogs and toads are eaten by aborigines that are primitive food gatherers, and by others, in some parts of most of the deserts of the world. They are skinned to remove the skin poison glands before eating or cooking. They definitely should be eaten when the situation is one of survival, contrary to the U.S. Air Force manual on survival (1962, p. 44) and other works; the advice should be corrected as follows: Eat frogs and toads after completely removing all skin; it contains poison glands.

A recent and more than usually interesting account (with references) of the large and well-known dangerous Colorado River Toad (*Bufo alvarius*) of the Sonoran Desert is given by Wright (1966), who reports that racoons circumvent the skin poison problem by ripping open the abdomen and stripping out the contents of the body cavity.

Marine fisheries (shellfish, fish, sea turtles, marine birds and mammals) border parts of all but three (Turkestan, Takla-Makan, and Gobi) of the 13 major deserts, and the Turkestan Desert borders the Caspian Sea. Limited fresh-water faunas (vertebrate and/or invertebrate) are available periodically, permanently, or both in all of the thirteen major deserts.

Reptiles, birds, and mammals occur throughout the interiors of all of the deserts and constitute the principal vertebrate foods eaten by all aborigines and by others. Poisonous snakes and skunks are not neglected. Rattlesnake flesh as human food is detailed by Klauber (1956), who gives 23 references from 1750 to 1950; rattlesnakes (genus *Crotalus*) are common in the North American Desert, and one species (*Crotalus terrificus*) reaches the northern edge of the Monte-Patagonian Desert in Argentina. Their close relatives, the vipers of the Old World, are common in the African and Middle-East deserts, where they are often equally relished as human food, as are all snakes both poisonous and harmless.

In many of the references cited in this section for the Namib-Kalahari and Australian Deserts, it is stressed that a European would promptly starve to death in these desert areas where the aborigines keep themselves fed and animals appear to be nonexistent. This statement is also (and especially) true for the Sahara, and to some degree for every desert of the world. A nomadic Bedouin and his family who assisted me in the Algerian Sahara a few miles from Beni-Abbès lived at the edge of the Great Western Erg. The Arab family was well supplied daily with fresh meat (mainly reptiles and small mammals) *obtained by hand* from this essentially vegetationless sea of sand. I have had no greater respect for any man, for, in this habitat, this is an impossible feat for a modern American or European, and even when armed with gun and shovel it is essentially impossible.

The situation in which the faunal list is the food list is less true for the insects (species) and other invertebrate animals occurring in deserts (table VII), even though certain insect species are abundantly used as food. The insects and spiders are incredibly diverse (species diversity), the snails less so. There are (specifically for the deserts) fewer actually useful references in the biological literature on vertebrates — which clearly constitute self-evident human food (="animals")—than on insects *et al.* (="vermin") that are used as human food; this situation is probably in part due to the fact that "vermin" are not self-

Table VII
WORKS TREATING INSECTS AS HUMAN FOOD IN THE DESERTS OF THE WORLD

Work	*Desert*	*Work*	*Desert*
Aldrich (1912a)	North American	Calvert (1894)	Australian
Aldrich (1912b)	General*	Campbell (1926)	Australian
Angas (1847)	Australian	Castetter and Underhill (1935)	North American
Anonymous (1935)	North American	Chapin (1924)	Somali-Chalbi
Baegert (1863)	North American	Cobbold (1935)	Somali-Chalbi
Banks (1912)	General*	Cowan (1865)	Sahara
Bargagli (1877)	Turkestan	Cunningham (1827)	Australian
Basedow (1925)	Australian	Cuthbertson (1934)	Somali-Chalbi
Bender (1963)	General*	Daguin (1900)	Atacama-Peruvian
Bennett (1834)	Australian	Das (1945)	Thar
Bequaert (1921)	General*	Dawson (1881)	Australian
	Kalahari-Namib	Dickson (1949)	Arabian
	Sahara	Dornan (1925)	Kalahari-Namib
	Somali-Chalbi	Doughty (1926)	Arabian
	Iranian	Ealand (1915)	General*
	Turkestan	Essig (1934)	North American
	Australian	Eylmann (1908)	Australian
	Monte-Patagonian	Fagan (1918)	General*
	Atacama-Peruvian	Faure (1944)	Kalahari-Namib
	North American	Fladung (1924)	North American
Bequaert (1922)	North American	Frazer (1910)	Australian
Berensberg (1907)	Kalahari-Namib	Frost (1942)	General*
Blunt (1881)	Arabian		Sahara
Bodenheimer (1942)	Turkestan	Fynn (1907)	North American
Bodenheimer (1951b)	General*	Ghesquière (1947)	General*
	Somali-Chalbi	Gourou (1948)	General*
	Arabian	Gray (1930)	Australian
	Iranian	Hanbury (1859)	Iranian
	Thar	Hardwicke (1822)	Iranian
	Turkestan	Harrison (1925)	Arabian
	Takla-Makan	Hartman (1897)	North American
	Australian	Hedin (1918)	Iranian
	Atacama-Peruvian	Hess (1938)	Arabian
	North American	Hoffmann (1947)	General*
Brues (1946)	General*		Takla-Makan
Bryden (1936)	Kalahari-Namib		Gobi
Brygoo (1946)	General*	Hrdlicka (1908)	North American
	Sahara	Hutton (1921a)	Thar
	Atacama-Peruvian	Hutton (1921b)	Thar
	North American	Kolb (1731)	Kalahari-Namib
Burr (1954)	General*	Künckel d'Herculais (1891)	Sahara
	Kalahari-Namib	Leopold (1961)	General*
	Sahara	Lindblom (1920)	Somali-Chalbi
	Arabian	Lumholtz (1890)	Australian
	Iranian	McCook (1882)	North American
	Thar	McKeown (1935)	Australian
	Turkestan	McKeown (1944)	Australian
	Takla-Makan	Morstatt (1921)	Somali-Chalbi
	Gobi	Mountford (1946)	Australian
	Australian	Netolitzky (1920)	Atacama-Peruvian
	North American		

* General: Relevant general information not specifically designated for any desert.

(continues)

Table VII *(Continued)*
WORKS TREATING INSECTS AS HUMAN FOOD IN THE DESERTS OF THE WORLD

Work	Desert	Work	Desert
Nordenskiöld (1929)	Monte-Patagonian Atacama-Peruvian	Skinner (1910)	North American
		Sparrman (1787)	Australian
Palgrave (1865)	Arabian	Spencer (1928)	Australian
Parker (1905)	Australian	Spencer and Gillen (1899)	Australian
Pierce (1915)	General*	Sterling (1896)	Australian
Raswan (1934)	Arabian	Théodoridès (1949)	General*
Rivers (1906)	Thar	Tillyard (1926)	Australian
Robbins (1851)	Sahara	Tindale (1932)	Australian
Salt (1816)	Somali-Chalbi	Uvarov, B. (1948)	General*
Schomburgk (1910)	Kalahari-Namib	Uvarov, B. (1951)	General*
Schwarz (1948)	Monte-Patagonian	Uvarov, E. (1931)	General*
Shaw (1738)	Sahara	Wallace (1952/3)	Atacama-Peruvian
Simmonds (1885)	Atacama-Peruvian North American	Westermarck (1926)	Sahara
		Witherspoon (1889)	North American

*General: Relevant general information not specifically designated for any desert.

evident human foods to most Europeans and Americans, and thus have tended to attract research in part by novelty.

2. Insects and Other Arthropods

In addition to insects in the deserts of the world, spiders, scorpions, centipedes, snails (see below) and numerous kinds of fresh-water and marine invertebrates are eaten. Among the primitive food-gatherers many of these invertebrate animals were, and still are, staples of diet although largely seasonal in availability. They are also widely eaten by natives that have now emerged above simple food-gathering status and are consumed by many civilized peoples in all of the deserts of the world, as well as elsewhere (table VII).

It is an interesting fact that the insects that are eaten in largest quantity, by aborigines and others, such as the locusts and grasshoppers, are rich in animal proteins, animal fats, and calories. The body composition of the Old World desert locust (*Schistocerca gregaria*) is given in table VIII, which is exemplary of more extensive data that are given by E. B. Uvarov (1931), B. P. Uvarov (1948, 1966), and Bodenheimer (1951*b*) for many species from different parts of the world.

The still widely held opinion that entomophagy is primarily induced by famine, and otherwise is simply barbarism, is incorrect. Not only is there an extremely wide and regular use by pantropical peoples of locusts, termites, and honey, but even a real rain forest "honey-civilization" is described by Vellard (1939). In fact, today there is still an almost worldwide incidence of insect consumption by men of all races, and it is now certain that insect food was of very basic importance during the evolution of early man. Of great importance are the insect totems of the primitive tribes in the Australian Desert, for many of the rituals, ceremonies, and traditions of these insect totems have been preserved (Bodenheimer, 1951*b*).

Throughout the deserts of the world, both the sedentary and nomadic peoples include in their diets insects and other invertebrates. It is important to reiterate that insects are important raw or cooked staples, not merely supplementary dietary novelties. For many years Bequaert's (1921) early paper was a major reference on insects and other invertebrates used as human food. The more recent works by B. P. Uvarov (1948) and Bodenheimer (1951*b*) are especially important for the deserts of the Old World. Bodenheimer's (1951*b*) book extends in detail the work of the earlier biologists who expounded the enormous nutritive value of insects (Netolitzky, 1920; Bequaert, 1921; E. B. Uvarov, 1931; B. P. Uvarov, 1948; Hardy and Richet, 1933; Gourou, 1948; and Théodoridès, 1949). Extensive original sources are given in Netolitzky (1920), Théodoridès (1949), and Bodenheimer (1951*b*). In addition to

Table VIII
PER CENT WEIGHT COMPOSITION OF THE
DESERT LOCUST,
*SCHISTOCERCA GREGARIA**

	Sun Dry Weight (Das)	Oven Dry Weight (Guggenheim)
Water	5.0	...
Protein	61.4	75.0
Fat	17.0	3.0
Carbohydrates	...	7.5
Fibre	10.0	...
CaO	0.6	...
P_2O	1.2	...
K_2O	0.8	...

* After Das (1945) and Guggenheim in Bodenheimer (1951*b*)

these and the several works cited above, the following books on insects are among those that have special chapters on insects as human food: Ealand (1915), Frost (1942), Brues (1946), and Burr (1954). It is acknowledged in almost all recent works of depth on insects, both popular (e.g., Lanham, 1964) and technical (e.g., Borror and De Long, 1964), that man is insectivorous as well as carnivorous; however, the subject is little discussed in most of the works even when it is acknowledged.

It should not go unnoticed that in the well-known U. S. Yearbook of Agriculture for 1952, entitled *Insects,* there is a complete lack of reference to this subject (insects as human food) which is of basic importance to mankind at large. This relatively recent U. S. Government publication reflects a provincial attitude toward insects, just as many of the volumes by American authors on conservation and wildlife management of the same recent period also reflect that provincial modern American view, namely, that wildlife as human food was no longer a topic of basic importance because wildlife meat met less than 1 per cent of the meat requirements of the average U. S. citizen.

Survival manuals published by military organizations of the United States and other countries naturally and necessarily take an entirely different and realistic view of the critical value of insects as human food. The following, for example, is from the U. S. Air Force manual on survival (1962, p. 45): "Anything that creeps, crawls, swims, or flies is a possible source of food. People eat grasshoppers, hairless caterpillars, wood-boring beetle larvae and pupae, ant eggs, and termites. Such insects are high in fat. You have probably eaten insects as contaminants in flour, corn meal, rice, beans, fruits, and greens of your daily food, and in stores in general."

Yet, while true enough, this information is merely a recognition of the problem and says nothing about how to solve it — for survival or ordinary diet. Such insect supplies are abundant in the hot deserts, but the real problem lies in knowing where to look for such valuable food and how actually to go about obtaining it; this critical problem is dramatically portrayed in references given in table VII. The essential fact to face is that the natural food animals listed in the survival manuals, as quoted above, are not simply sitting on the desert surface waiting to be plucked. Beyond the aborigines themselves, men who do not publish their results, little is known on this matter for the deserts of the world, and the urgent need for additional large-scale and long-term ecological investigation is clearly indicated. Such important research, leading to knowledge and understanding to enable successful use of animal food resources comparable to the success achieved in primitive food gathering by hand and with wholly improvised primitive tools, should have been long underway.

3. Snails

There is a rich literature on snails as human food. Much of this was recently reviewed by Mead (1961), and essentially all of it refers to nondesert areas. While snails-as-food is largely a nondesert subject, land ("fresh-water") snails do occur in all of the deserts and are eaten by some native peoples, both aboriginal and modern. Snail-eating is apparently a widespread relictual habit among modern Europeans and Orientals, much more prevalent than in the case of the locust, spider, *etc.;* it is by no means restricted to epicureans.

Often snails are in rich supply in deserts, but seldom are they as enormously abundant as in the northern part of the Egyptian Sahara, where aridity is ameliorated by both the Mediterranean, and the Nile, and in northern Libya. A large snail (*Levantina guttata* Olivier) lives in the western Sahara. Algerians, Moroccans, and other North Africans are snail-eaters, but the major species are *Otala lactea* (a Mediterranean nondesert species) and the introduced *Helix pomatia* and *H. aspersa.*

Nowhere in natural desert communities do species of snails reach the size and attendant nutrient value of the large *Achatina* species and their relatives in nearby tropical and subtropical regions; all however, have high nutrient value (Léger, 1925; Moretti, 1934; Mead and Kemmerer, 1953). Extensive original sources on snails as human food are given in Locard (1890), Boisseau and Lanorville (1931), Cadart (1955), Mead (1961), and others; see Mead (1961) for a review.

There is not wide agreement on use of snails as food by desert peoples, and very little is known. Apparently snails are not eaten much if at all by desert Arab tribes of the Saharo-Sindic region. J. C. Bequaert (personal communication) is of the strong opinion that tastes for snails are acquired tastes, not evolved tastes, and, speaking from his own worldwide experience, that desert peoples rarely eat snails. He concedes that the Hottentots and Bushmen of South Africa and the aborigines of Australia probably did so and do so, but also points to the fact that in South Africa all of the nonmarine species of snails are small (Connolly, 1939), and harvesting would be difficult and little rewarding at best in the interior. On the other hand, during certain seasons and during some years, any snail in any amount would be desirable.

Regarding natives of the North American Desert, E. H. Spicer (personal communication) informs me that in the Chihuahuan and Sonoran Deserts (in Chihuahua, New Mexico, Arizona, and Sonora) the Indians apparently did not eat snails, and he suggests that the relative abundance of game in these regions obviously did not necessitate snail-eating. The Papagos did consider as a delicacy one of the caterpillars that was seasonally abundant in the Sonoran Desert (see Castetter and Underhill, 1935).

Bequaert (1950) discusses the snail game laws, season permits, size limits, and antagonism over snail territories in the Gold Coast (Ghana). Mead (1961) also discusses the situation for parts of China, where snails also are eaten, apparently by choice. I know of no extensive study of nonmarine snail-eating by desert peoples anywhere. The literature on ethnobiology has not been thoroughly searched yet in this regard, particularly that of the Old World (works of ethnozoology are much more scarce than works of ethnobotany). More regional reviews of the scope of Whiting's (1966) are greatly needed. Ethnographies subsistence, food customs, *etc.*) are sources that may provide some detailed local information on snail-eating by natives and others in one or more of the major deserts of the world.

D. NATIVE ANIMALS AS "PESTS" IN THE DESERT

What's one man's poison, signior,
is another's meat or drink.
              —Beaumont and Fletcher

1. Poisonous Pests

If it is true that a "weed" is any unwanted plant, be it a tree or otherwise (Parker, 1958), then we may assume that a "pest" is any unwanted animal. From the viewpoint of the species *Homo sapiens,* every other species in the world is a potential "pest," for to qualify, all that it has to do is to be in the way of man at one time or another.

Centipedes, millipedes, urticating caterpillars, vesicating blister beetles, nonlethal spiders, and certain blood-sucking insects are commonly classified as poisonous pests, species of which are occasionally common in deserts. Venom poisoning from these animals appears to be largely if not wholly sublethal. The solpugids, whip-scorpions and false-scorpions are also harmless. In addition to being "pests," all of these organisms are extremely inviting objects for much needed additional scientific investigation in the deserts and elsewhere in the world.

Bees, wasps, and ants are well-known venomous insects, stings from which may be lethal to some persons. These and the spiders and scorpions that are potentially dangerous to man are discussed under B, "Poisonous Animals."

Centipedes

Large carnivorous centipedes of the genus *Scolopendra* occur in Old World tropics and subtropics, and they occur in warm deserts. They are fast-moving nocturnal animals that commonly exceed 6 inches in length. In the deserts they are often household, farm, and ranch pests, although they apparently do not inflict the serious bites for which their still larger tropical relatives (10-12 inches) are known and feared; see, for example, the reports of DeCastro (1921); See also Remington (1950). Lesser species of centipedes are more common throughout the deserts of the world, although few centipedes are as abundant in desert habitats as they are in the bordering thornscrub, savanna, grassland, chaparral, and woodland habitats that are characterized by greater precipitation and lower evaporation.

Centipedes are arthropods in the order Chilopoda. Cloudsley-Thompson (1958) has recently reviewed their general biology. Centipedes live during the day in dark and fairly damp places, and this means underground, or under rocks, foundations, *etc.* in the desert. They forage primarily at night, and while most are carnivorous and mainly insectivorous, some groups occasionally feed on plants and have damaged crops. Some larger *Scolopendra* centipedes can kill small mice and small birds, on which they readily feed. Cloudsley-Thompson (1958) remarks on a large individual of *Scolopendra gigantea* in India that was found devouring the side of a living toad, and another *Scolopendra* that had completely removed about two inches of skin from a small snake writhing in its grasp on the floor of a house in Rangoon.

Recent discussions of centipedes and centipede-bite are given by Cloudsley-Thompson (1958), Keegan (1963), and by Keegan *et al.* (1964), who have reviewed the earlier work by De Castro (1921), Kopstein (1932), Bucherl (1946), Remington, (1950), and Turk (1951). The present concensus reported by these authors is that in spite of the size and aggressiveness of some species, the remarkable quickness with which they are willing to bite, and the intense pain that often follows, the great majority of centipedes are not dangerously poisonous (venomous) for the large vertebrates including man. This conclusion was early recorded by Cornwall (1916) and Baerg (1924). However widespread as pests and feared by people, there appears to be no recorded death due to centipede-bite in a desert region.

Scott and Pratt (1959), Keegan (1963), and Keegan *et al.* (1964) discuss preventive measures for troops in the field and for control around living quarters (chlordane, lindane, malathion). In the North American Desert in Arizona and in Sonora, Mexico, the large native *Scolopendra* (reaching 6 inches) is quickly killed with DDT applied as a direct spray.

Millipedes

In contrast to the flat-bodied carnivorous centipedes, the millipedes are round-bodied vegetarians (order Diplopoda). The diplopods also have been recently reviewed by Cloudsley-Thompson (1958). Keegan and his coworkers (Keegan *et al.*, 1964) comment on a few more recent papers. See also Lawrence (1962) for the Namib and Chamberlain (1920) for Australia.

Millipedes rank as agricultural pests but do not create a serious public health hazard unless handled or eaten. They do not bite. Again in contrast to the quick and continuous movements of centipedes, millipedes ordinarily retire into a tight spiral when they are touched.

Millipedes secrete a fluid that is usually dark-colored, foul-smelling, and caustic. It is emitted defensively from pores on the sides of the body. Some species are able to squirt this fluid a short distance. Halstead and Ryckman (1949) report skin blisters and intense eye pain from contact with millipede secretions. Species of the North American *Chilognatha* are capable of producing irritating effects (Burt, 1947). The secretion of the North American species *Pachydesmus crassicutus* is a defensive fluid mixture of hydrogen cyanide and benzaldehyde (Blum and Woodring, 1962). Scott and Pratt (1959) report good results against house-infesting millipedes by employing the same chemicals used against centipedes (see above: chlordane, lindane, malathion).

Additional comments on millipedes are given by Keegan (1963) and Keegan *et al.* (1964), who suggest quite correctly that troops should be instructed not to touch millipedes. It should be added that simple line drawings or photographs in survival manuals would quickly assist a man attempting to distinguish between the common millipede life-form and the common centipede life-form. Cloudsley-Thompson (1958, p. 53) states that African Arabs devour large centipedes alive when under the influence of religious excitement. For survival eat centipedes after tearing or cutting off the head, but not under any circumstances of survival stress should millipedes be ingested; they should not be touched.

While usually said to be nocturnal, and most millipedes are, some of the largest millipedes are also crepuscular and partly diurnal. The large common millipede (*Chilognatha* sp., Chamberlin and Hoffman, 1958) in the Sonoran Desert subdivison of the North American Desert is frequently called "storm worm." It is periodically active in the early mornings and evenings directly after summer (warm-season) rains, and at such times is frequently seen crossing desert roads and trails during daylight hours in Arizona and Sonora, Mexico. The animal has a distinctive size, life-form, and behavior. A remarkably similar millipede occurs in the Somali desert in east Africa, where it also responds to summer rains in a similar diurnal fashion. In the Somali desert we found that they tended to be even more diurnal than in the North American Desert, and far more so than are other millipedes.

Cloudsley-Thompson (1958) notes that the general response of millipedes to moisture has economic implications, for they are often forced to attack growing crops to maintain water balance during conditions of drought. He concludes that millipede outbreaks tend to be stimulated by a dry spell following a damp period suitable for the reproduction of the species (Cloudsley-Thompson, 1949, 1951, 1958). In a review of the migration of millipedes, he discusses factors that appear to be correlated with reproduction, and provides evidence to support the hypothesis that "mass migration of millipedes is merely an extreme case of the more familiar sudden attacks on crops due to extremely favorable local conditions, followed by drought and possible accompanied by abnormal physiological conditions of reproduction."

Tarantulas

Spiders of any kind are pests to many, perhaps most, people. Entomophobia, a prolonged nervous disorder from fear, anxiety, and worry over insects and other arthropods, is often severe. The large (6 to 7 inches) American spiders called tarantulas are little understood, consequently erroneously feared, and, therefore, they remain little understood; moreover, they are a taxonomically difficult group. They are usually incorrectly considered to be pugnacious and deadly venomous spiders that are prodigious jumpers. One the contrary, the 30-odd species in the United States and almost all species elsewhere in the Americas are quite harmless to man as well as being retiringly shy, and they are by no means powerful jumpers (Baerg, 1929, 1958; Gertsch, 1949).

While several species occur in the American deserts, tarantulas are not a desert group. The majority of the species in the United States occur in the Southwest, i. e., in the natural arid and semiarid region common to the southwestern United States and northwestern Mexico. Here in the American Southwest, in addition to being thought of as pests by some, tarantulas are also occasionally kept as household pets. Certainly it can be agreed that the tarantulas should be, and very likely never will be, regarded as beneficial animals, for it should not go unnoticed that they are efficient insectivores that destroy harmful insects while being themselves harmless to man.

Insect-Produced Poisons

Urticating (Stinging) Moth Hairs and Spines

Stinging hairs and spines of adult moths and their caterpillars and cocoons may cause severe dermatitis, burning pain, swelling, and other symptoms at the site of the skin contact. This is a public problem with outbreaks reported in North America, Europe, Africa, Asia, and Australia.

Weidner (1936) gives a comprehensive bibliography on poisonous insect hairs. Herms and James (1961) list the families, genera, and species of the more important urticating Lepidoptera. Beard (1963) recently reviewed the biological and medical data in a combined total of 23 references dating from 1914 to 1961; see also Matheson (1950), and Kemper (1958). Successful therapy has included 10 per cent calcium gluconate, 1 per cent Dettol, sodium thiosulfate, calamine lotion, ice packs, adrenalin, codeine, morphine sulfate, and meperidine (see especially the references cited in Keegan, 1963). Both temperate and tropical species of moths are involved. Outbreaks have occurred marginal to the North American Desert (New Mexico: Caffrey, 1918; Texas: Micks, 1952, 1960), and the Arabian Desert (Israel: Ziprkowski, Hofshi, and Tahori, 1959).

Vesicant Beetles

Blister beetles in the family Meloidae (order Coleoptera) cause well-known skin blistering on contact with the insect. The blisters, which may be up to several inches long, are caused by cantharidin in the insect's body fluids. The adults are strictly plant-feeders, and have been incriminated in damage to some crops (alfalfa, potatoes, and tomatoes). Some species occur in the deserts of the world, including the North American Desert, and may be sizeable species on the order of an inch long and with conspicuously bright color patterns, such as the desert soldier beetles in the genus *Tegrodera*. Others are inconspicuous and often are concealingly colored. As in the case of other "noxious pests," a local knowledge of the genera and species is desirable. While the family is not easily diagnosed, blister beetles of both the New and Old Worlds are usually easily recognized in the field by their characteristic structure and life-form (Horn, 1885; Champion, 1892; Van Dyke, 1928; Comstock, 1949; Dillon, 1952; Burr, 1954; Imms, 1957; Essig, 1958; Selander, 1958; Giglioli, 1965; and Werner, Enns and Parker, 1966).

2. Nonpoisonous Pests

Biting and Blood-sucking Insects

Aside from being also incriminated as arthropod-transmitters of disease, several flies and bugs are notorious pests. Some of these insects are terrible scourges of man and his domestic animals, although usually in nondesert environments; for example, the fierce blood-sucking blackflies (Simuliidae) that occur in grasslands and savannas that border deserts, as in the southern Sudan and western United States. While few, if any, of these pests can be labeled "desert species," some are prevalent enough in natural desert environments or marginal areas to deserve mention. The problems that they cause are discussed in most volumes on medical entomology.

Assassin Bugs (Reduviidae)

These flying blood-suckers normally live with and feed on native rats (*e. g., Neotoma*), squirrels, and other mammals, and are variously referred to as assassin bugs, conenosed bugs, kissing bugs, Mexican bedbugs, and, in Arizona, Hualpai tigers. They are nocturnal and bite sleeping humans at night. The symptoms appear to be similar on both American continents, where some species are frequent household pests. Our experience with the course of the reaction to the bite of *Triatoma rubida uhleri* in the Sonoran Desert in Arizona indicates that it is similar if not the same as the reaction to the bite of *Triatoma protracta* here in Arizona and in Texas. Both of these species commonly occur together in fresh pack rat middens of *Neotoma albigula* in the Sonoran Desert, where they have different life cycles (P. J. Mehringer, personal communication).

In sensitive individuals severe swelling of body parts follows initial symptoms of burning pain and intense itching. As swelling and pain ensues, reddish blotches and welts spread slowly over the body part. The swelling is often so severe that fingers or toes cannot be bent and arm joints move only with much pain and difficulty. Symptoms may last several days to several weeks, and include excessive irritability and temporary amnesia. Antihistamines are effective in giving relief as is epinephrine in severe cases. Keh (1956) reports that relief from bites of *Rasahus* in California may be obtained by using lotions of menthol, phenol, or camphor.

Sand Flies (Phychodidae)

Phlebotomus flies affect man and other animals in at least two ways, by their bites and as intermediate hosts of parasites. In addition to transmitting disease (see section below, "Leishmaniasis and Phlebotomus Fever") sand flies genus *Phlebotomus* are vicious biters. The bite may be followed by nausea and fever and often results in an inflamed and hardened lesion. Control of sand flies is discussed by Marett (1913), Sabin *et al.* (1944), Hertig (1948), and Hertig and Fairchild (1948).

Mosquitoes

The literature on mosquitoes is extensive. References to the biology of mosquitoes and the mosquito-transmitted diseases of man and other animals, including monographs, reviews, histories, and summaries, are cited extensively in standard works on tropical medicine and medical entomology; see references under section E, "Disease in the Desert," below.

There are tundra mosquitoes, boreal snow mosquitoes, savanna mosquitoes, rain-forest mosquitoes, and others, but the desert has apparently played a lesser role in the evolution of mosquitoes. *Aedes aegypti* Linnaeus ("yellow fever mosquito") is not a "desert species," for although it is widely distributed between roughly 40° N and 40° S latitude it is not a mosquito of hot or cold dry deserts and succumbs to temperatures as high as 37° C and merely as low as 7 to 8° C (Hindle, 1914). True desert species exist, however, including species of *Anopheles,* vectors of malaria (see Hunter, Frye, and Swartzwelder, 1966).

As the distribution of mosquitoes, malaria, and some other mosquito-transmitted diseases is not dependent on heavy rainfall, the potential problem created by irrigation in deserts and by the domiciles of men, as well as by desert streams and by the rivers that course into or through deserts, is self-evident. The mosquito-borne West Nile virus infection in Egypt and the Sudan (Taylor *et al.*, 1956) is a case in point. Mosquitoes occur locally in deserts where adequate water sources are available, and these may be quite minimal and in unexpected natural places. Pradhan (1957) reports that *Anopheles superpictus* (a malaria vector) is a desert species in the eastern Sahara that breeds in streams of running water with gravel beds. We recently discovered a new tree-hole species that was breeding in tree-holes of the saguaro giant cactus (*Cereus giganteus*) in the Sonoran Desert in Arizona, holes that are naturally excavated for nesting by woodpeckers and flickers. During the summer monsoon the giant cactus tree-holes capture and temporarily store rainwater in which the mosquito eggs hatch and the larvae rapidly develop.

Ticks

Ticks are arachnids (Acarina); they are not as well known as the spiders (Araneida). Aside from tick-transmitted diseases and other venom-induced local and systemic disturbances resulting from tick bites, the animals are a nuisance and, indeed, at times may become a blood-sucking scourge, but not in deserts. Ticks lay their eggs on and near the surface of the substratum, and, as the eggs are often relatively exposed to weather elements, most natural desert environments appear to be too harsh for the successful completion of tick life-history.

Solpugids, Whipscorpions, and False Scorpions

These are nocturnal ground-living arachnids that are commonly but erroneously believed to be deadly. Cloudsley-Thompson (1958) has recently discussed this problem and other aspects of their biology in some detail, especially with regard to Old World forms. Especially useful bibliographies include those given in Comstock (1949), Muma (1951), Cloudsley-Thompson (1958), Essig (1958), Lawrence (1962), Keegan *et al.* (1964), and Savory (1964).

Solpugids (Solpugida)

Solpugids are fast-moving insectivores that reach about the size of large scorpions. In the New World the genera and species are concentrated in arid and semiarid lands, and being "lovers of warmth," they are common in deserts. Cloudsley-Thompson (1958) discusses their similar distribution in the Old World and further notes that one species inhabits the 10,000-foot plateau of the Pamir in Central Asia (north of the Hindu Kush mountains). They are treated under pests only because they are much feared.

Solpugids are well-known under different names in different lands. In the Americas they are known as sun spiders, solpugids, genisaros, and others. To Arabs they are wind spiders. They are hunting spiders to the Dutch South Africans, spiders of the sun and kill-deer to the Spanish, and the Russians call them flangas (Essig, 1958).

Whipscorpions (Pedipalpida)

Whipscorpions are ancient animals that are world-wide in distribution; relatively little is known about them. The smaller whipscorpions, with bodies that are little more than a ¼-inch long (6 to 7 mm), are harmless, secretive, and rarely observed inhabitants of deserts and semiarid environments. The larger and better known whipscorpions, usually called vinegarones (also vinegaroons, mule killers, and stinking scorpions) rarely enter the desert proper, but are often abundant in the bordering grasslands beyond the desert edge. The giant whipscorpion of northern Mexico and the southern United States (*Mastigoproctus giganticus*) is a good example; it is distributed across the continent from the Atlantic to the Pacific and is common in the Southwest, but not in the desert proper. It is typical of the group in being a greatly feared species that has long been known to be harmless (Ewing, 1928; see also Cloudsley-Thompson, 1958, and Essig, 1958).

False Scorpions (Pseudoscorpionida)

These are small "tail-less" animals that are even smaller than whipscorpions; some have bodies that are only 1/16-inch long (1 to 2 mm) and seldom are more than 1/3-inch long (8 mm). They lack the conspicuous whip-like or tail-like posterior structure that is so conspicuous on whipscorpions and true scorpions. While none are parasitic, some are myrmecophilous and live in ant nests. Some species are occasionally numerous in nondesert environments, but they tend to be more rarely observed in deserts due to their small size and apparently low population densities in desert habitats.

Woodlice

The woodlice are small, secretive, harmless crustaceans that retreat under rocks, other cover and, in deserts especially, underground. Populations may be exceedingly dense outside of deserts, where diversity is greatest in moist environments. Of the few that occur in deserts, some are "desert species" and their effective microenvironments and nocturnal behavior enable them to avoid desiccation, e. g., species of *Hemilepistus* (Sahara) and *Venezillo* (North American Desert). Nocturnal woodlice may be especially abundant in marine coastal desert sand dunes, in other locally ameliorated environments in the desert and desert-edge, and especially in edificarian habitats. They have vernacular names (e. g., sowbug, pill bug, slater, and cud-worm; see Collinge, 1935, for others). The biology and physiological ecology of woodlice has recently been investigated by Edney (1951, 1954, 1957, 1960), Cloudsley-Thompson (1955, 1958), Den Boer 1961), and Warburg (1964, 1965a,b); see also references in Cloudsley-Thompson (1958) and Edney (1960). Some species are crop pests and all are more or less omnivorous.

Ants and Others

Ants are hymenopterans that are both predaceous and plant-eating. The plant-eating harvester ants, and some other species that are introduced into foreign lands (e. g., the Argentine ant), are occasionally pests in arid lands that have a relatively high annual rainfall; the ground dwelling harvesters are conspicuous in semiarid grasslands, savannas, and woodlands (Wheeler, 1910, 1930; Smith, 1936; Eckert and Mallis, 1937; and Woglum, 1942). Quantitative data are lacking, but the ratio of carnivorous to plant-eating species of ants and other arthropods is apparently higher in desert environments (Wheeler, 1930).

Some species of ants are potentially dangerous to man and his domestic animals, but not usually so in deserts (see section B on poisonous animals). They are also of minor medical interest as mechanical carriers of disease. Workers of fire ants (*Solenopsis*) are reported as carriers of viable dysentery germs on their bodies for at least 24 hours (Smith, 1951) and as mechanical transmitters of smallpox in a hospital in Egypt (Donisthorp, 1945); see also Mickel (1928), Clark (1931), Anonymous (1954), Herms and James (1961), and Jung, Derbes, and Burch (1963), regarding fire ants (*Solenopsis*) and mutillid wasps (Mutillidae).

Ants are undoubtedly the most numerous xerophilous insects in deserts, certainly in numbers of individuals if not in numbers of species. In deserts they are almost invariably underground dwellers, as are other insects, such as tenebrionids, meloids, carabids, scarabids, thysanurans, hymenopterans, and many others, either as larvae, adults, or both (see also Buxton, 1923, 1924; Arnold, 1926; Chapman *et al.*, 1926; Gebien, 1927; Cole, 1933; Uvarov, 1937; Hesse, 1938; Kusnezov, 1952; Bodenheimer, 1957; Pradhan, 1957; Creighton, 1950; Lawrence, 1959; Koch, 1961).

Termites

Termites are secretive, soft-bodied, social insects that comprise the insect order Isoptera. World views are given by Hegh (1922), Grassé (1949), Emerson (1955), Weesner (1965), and Harris (1961); see also Silvestri (1903), Banks and Snyder (1920), Harris (1941, 1957, 1961, 1966), Burtt (1942), Kofoid (1934), Snyder (1948, 1949, 1954, 1961), Cachan (1949), Ahmad (1958), and Sillans (1958).

Cellulose is the basis of termite life and it obviously has played an important role in their evolution. Maximum evolutionary development of the group has been reached in tropical rain forests, where opportunity has been great and termite diversity enormous. Large numbers of taxa also occur in the subtropics between the northern and southern limits of termite distribution, approximated by the mean annual isotherm of 50° F (Kofoid, 1934; Emerson, 1955; and Harris, 1961).

Although termites occur in all of the major deserts of the world except the Takla-Makan and the Gobi, the abundance of termites and termite species decreases sharply from rain forest to desert. Some are true desert species; that is, they occur only within the geographical and ecological limits of the desert. While typically they are either earth-dwelling termites or dry-wood termites, one in the North American Desert is a desert damp-wood termite (Nutting, 1965; see also Light and Weesner, 1948, and Nutting, 1961). The extremes of desert adaptation are reached in the specialized sand-dwelling termites such as *Psammotermes hybostoma* and *Anacanthotermes ochraceus* of the great Saharo-Sindic formation (Scortecci, 1940; Ahmad, 1955; Harris, 1961, 1966; see Synder's 1954 bibliography and 1961 supplement). Weesner's (1965) recent review of the termites of the United States indicates that most of the species occurring in the arid and semiarid Southwest occur partly if not wholly in the North American Desert. Nutting's (1961) recent account of Arizona species indicates that 6 of the 18 total are desert species and that most of the others enter the desert within their wider distributions.

Nutting (1966) recently plotted the field localities of a dry-wood termite (*Pterotermes occidentis*) on Shreve's (1951) map of the Sonoran Desert (in Arizona, Sonora, California, and Baja California) and found the entire distribution of the termite to be contained with the desert. Similar findings may result for the distributions of other species here and, certainly, in other deserts of the world where many true desert species occur, even though it is expected (where not already known) that the ranges of many desert-inhabiting termites more or less spill over the edge of the desert into more ameliorated semiarid environments.

Termites may be found to be an animal group with an unusually high percentage of strictly true desert species among the total species of the group utilizing desert resources. Emerson (1955) recently concluded that temperature and moisture are the major physical limiting factors for the termites of the world, and that these climatic factors exert a major effect on termites indirectly, by determining the vegetation and other aspects of plant communities. Nutting (1966) points out that *Pterotermes* is a monotypic genus that is apparently endemic to the hot-dry Sonoran Desert. He advances the interesting hypothesis "that *Pterotermes* is so restricted [to the desert] not so much by high temperature and low moisture as by the higher rainfall of the surrounding regions." In contrast to the vigorous and healthy *Pterotermes* colonies in extremely desiccated wood of dead desert paloverdes (*Cercidium microphyllum*), a high percentage of individuals apparently succumbed in chambers by drowning or to attack by fungi, bacteria, or both, after unusually heavy winter rains in February. This hypothesis is similar to that recently proposed in relation to the southern (desert edge) distributional limit of another desert plant species inhabited by *Pterotermes*. This is the giant sahuaro cactus (*Cereus giganteus*) that appears to be restricted (in thornscrub) by factors associated with increasing summer rainfall.

Termite "pest control" is reviewed by Kofoid (1934), Chamberlain and Hoskins (1949), Harris (1961), Anonymous (1956), and in government publications (e. g., Anonymous, 1958; and *Insects,* the U. S. Yearbook of Agriculture, 1952). In some deserts, as well as elsewhere, termite control continues to expand into an ever larger field of competitors dedicated, for a fee, to the attempt to remove the termites one may own but may not want. This predator-prey relationship has been growing strong in desert communities during recent years.

Locusts, Grasshoppers, and Other Insects

Pradhan (1957) and Uvarov (1957, 1962) have provided recent important reviews on insect problems of the "arid zone." Some of the literature reviewed by these authors refers to deserts and desert species, but most of it does not. The coverage is greater for the Old World than the New World, and proportionally, more papers are cited for Old World deserts.

A small number of grasshoppers are specialized in having a gregarious habit, with its attendant physiological, morphological, and ecological peculiarities, and while few in number of species they are notorious crop pests. These are the locusts, gregarious grasshoppers that have neither a sharp nor permanent distinction (due to phase polymorphism) from the nongregarious (solitarious) grasshoppers (see Uvarov, 1928, 1966). Uvarov (1957) recently reviewed the locust problems of the Old World, and, more recently, those of both the New and Old World (Uvarov, 1962).

The desert locust *(Schistocerca gregaria)* is a facultative, nomadic species in Africa and western Asia. It has been investigated on a comprehensive international basis, but it has been difficult to control. Such migrant and highly opportunistic species utilize a wide range of plant species, including crops. The successful opportunistic migrations of the desert locust are dependent on weather dynamics. The adults swarm in the direction of the prevailing winds, bringing them to soils and plants concomitantly affected advantageously by summer monsoons and winter-spring rains. Diverse mosaic environments are encountered and different effective microenvironments are necessary for successful completion of life-history events. All of the deserts of the Old World (except the Australian, Gobi, and Takla-Makan) are involved. The invasion area of swarms is the largest known among all locusts, and covers great areas of Africa and western Asia outside of the desert (Brown, 1947; Rainey, 1951*a,b*; Uvarov, 1957; Kraus, 1958; Waloff, 1959; Food and Agriculture Organization, 1959*a, b*; Cloudsley - Thompson, 1962). Aspects of phase polymorphism in locusts in general, including *Schistocerca,* have recently been treated in detail by Uvarov (1966).

On the subtropical edge of the Sahara (Sudan, Senegal, Mauritania), disturbance by cultivation recently has been implicated with swarm-breeding of the desert locust (Popov, 1959, 1960; Popov and Rosetti, 1958). Increases of local water supplies in the desert favor the desert locust, the eggs of which require moist sand soil and the hoppers of which require fresh vegetation for growth as do the adults in order to mature (Uvarov, 1957). Moreover, native grasshoppers and locusts adapted to grasslands are among the insects that quickly become pests of grain crops that become available when farming is initiated, or become pests somewhat later under overgrazing and other land malpractice (Uvarov, 1962; Sudan: Joyce, 1952, Davey, 1959, Popov, 1959; Australia and Soviet Union: Uvarov, 1957; North America: Wakeland and Shull, 1936, Shotwell, 1938, McKinney, 1939, Uvarov, 1947, Anderson and Wright, 1952, Anderson, 1954, Pepper, 1955, Weaver and Albertson, 1956, Smith, 1957, and Cowan, 1958).

In deserts, especially where irrigation is involved, the resulting insect populations may increase suddenly and involve seasonally massive build-ups of both desert and nondesert species. The latter are also aided in crossing deserts by man-made irrigation canals as well as by natural rivers, and by oasis-hopping (Smith, 1957; Uvarov, 1957, 1962, and elsewhere; Pradhan, 1957; see also references below in section E 4 of "Disease in the Desert").

Humid oases concentrate injurious insect species that are both native and introduced (Uvarov, 1943; Bernard, 1954, and Balachowsky, 1954). Moreover, a hazard of oasis cultivation in African and Asian deserts is that of presenting targets for nomadic and migrant insects, such as the desert locust, swarms of which frequently descend upon the oases (Uvarov, 1962).

3.   Introduced Species

Crops of arid lands are not only subject to the onslaught of native insects, but it is well known that they suffer from the large number that have been introduced (Wardle, 1929; Quayle, 1938; Ebeling, 1949; Evans, 1952; Fernald and Shepard, 1955; Metcalf and Flint, 1962; Davatchi, 1955; Rivnay, 1962; Short, 1963; and others). The subject is treated at length in such standard volumes on applied (economic) entomology, primarily in the English language, and in the publications of departments of agriculture, primarily in Britain and the United States where much of the step-by-step development of antipest technology and strategy in arid lands, as well as elsewhere, has been created and recorded.

Australia and California (U. S. A.) were involved in the first successful introduction of a beneficial insect species into another country for the purpose of destroying an insect. This classic example of biological control of one insect by another (entomophagous) insect involved the rapid control in California of the disastrous Australian citrus scale (cottony cushion scale, *Icerya purchasi*) in 1888, by another introduced Australian insect (the lady beetle, *Roadlia {= Vedalia} cardinalis*) that was a natural enemy of *Icerya*. In biological control, management of the ecosystem is attempted through alteration of organism-to-organism relationships, by the encouragement or introduction of predators, competitors, and parasites (Gossard, 1901; Essig, 1931; Sweetman, 1936; Quayle, 1938; Clausen, 1936, 1940; see also: Knowlton and Janes, 1933; Van Volkenberg, 1935; Mead, 1961). The cottony cushion scale was an important stimulus in the United States that led directly or indirectly to the new strategies of biological control, hydrocyanic acid fumigation, oil sprays, and quarantine (Quayle, 1938; Ebeling, 1949).

Control of the date palm scale *(Parlatoria blanchardi)*, introduced into the North American Desert (Arizona and California) from the Sahara (Egypt and Algeria) and successfully controlled by defoliation and torching in a joint U. S. federal and state eradication program, "must be considered as one of the outstanding achievements in applied entomology" (Quayle, 1938; see also: McGregor, 1916; Buxton, 1920; Morrison, 1921; Boyden, 1941; Armitage and Steinweden, 1945; Barnes and Lindgren, 1947; Ebeling, 1949).

The synthetic insecticides constitute one of the most important recent developments (West and Campbell, 1952; Brown, 1951; Shepard, 1951; and Martin, 1959) and possibly one of the most tragic (Egler, 1964; Carson, 1962; and George, 1963). In the United States in 1962 a total of 4.62 per cent of the land was subjected to application of these synthetic contact poisons (DDT, lindane, chlordane, the dinitrophenols, *et al.,*); 3.24 per cent of the total (or 70.1 per cent of the land affected by poison) was in the category "desert, swamp, dunes and wildland" (George, 1963).

Control of introduced injurious pests of fruit crops, field crops, *etc.* has a large literature for temperate and subtropical semiarid environments (general references above), but less so for the deserts (see also: Cockerell, 1899; Quayle, 1929; Clark, 1931; Smith, 1936; Fox, 1938; Bodenheimer, 1940, 1951*a*; Hayward, 1941; Motz, 1942; Wille, 1943; Woglum, 1947; and Platt, 1948). Excellent recent reviews are given by Bodenheimer (1951*a*), Evans (1952), Pradhan (1957), Uvarov (1957, 1962), and Rivnay (1962). All of the deserts of the world are covered by these papers and reviews, except the Takla-Makan for which no specific references are cited; it is assumed, however, that data in papers cited by Pradhan (1957) and by Uvarov (1962) for the Turkestan Desert and the Gobi may have relevance for the Takla-Makan.

In addition to insects, other invertebrates and some vertebrate animals are persistent agricultural and general pests. The recent volume *Cotton Pests of the Sudan* (Ripper and Lloyd, 1965) is a model work in applied zoology in the "arid zone." Vertebrate and invertebrate alien animals and the tragedies created by the "wildlife movers" are reviewed in Laycock's (1966) recent important contribution; see Storer (1931), Anderson (1934), Osborn (1934), Bigalke (1937), Troughton (1938), Day (1948), Duvigneaud (1950), Swanson (1950), Fitch, Goodrum, and Newman (1952), Andrews (1953), Pullar (1953), Allen (1954), Cahalane (1955), Thompson (1955), De Vos, Manville, and Van Gelder

(1956), Hoogstraal *et al.* (1961), Mead (1961), Ratcliffe (1961), Rabbit Control Symposium, 2nd, Sydney, 1960 (1961), and Nosek *et al.* (1962).

The potentially dangerous and often destructive results of the introduction of alien ("exotic") mammal and bird species only rarely affects natural desert communities that are otherwise undisturbed by man. English "sparrows," starlings, house mice, and house rats are essentially followers of men. Unmodified desert land environments are ordinarily too harsh for the successful reproduction and maintenance of populations by aliens, even when transplanted from other deserts to which they are naturally adapted. There have been many predicted failures. For example, the Indian sand grouse from the Thar Desert was released in Nevada in the North American Desert. All of the 1,400 birds released disappeared. Two of them were shot while flying together near Navajoa, Sonora, Mexico, a year and a half after their release. There is no way of knowing how many crossed the international border (Christensen, 1963).

One desert alien, however, remains a well-known and alarming success, unfortunately at the expense of native animals, in the North American Desert. This is the feral burro that has successfully populated some of the most severe habitats in the desert (Anonymous, 1952, 1953, 1961; Davis, 1953; Summer, 1959; Köhler, 1960; and Fulwider, 1965). Even in parts of the Death Valley region in the Mojave Desert in California the burro has successfully reduced or replaced native bighorn sheep. The physiological ecology of the feral burro has not been investigated, nor has that of wild asses, although donkeys as well as camels have recently been studied (see: Adolph and Dill, 1938; Dill, Bock, and Edwards, 1933; K. Schmidt-Nielsen *et al.,* 1957 *a&b*, 1959*a*, 1964*a*; B. Schmidt-Nielsen *et al.,* 1956). The donkey originated in the "dry steppes" and "deserts" of Somaliland, in the Somali-Chalbi desert regions (Bodenheimer, 1957). Andrews (1924, 1932) reported wild asses *(Equus hemionus)* in abundance in parts of the Gobi without water. Camels have been successfully transplanted into many deserts and open semiarid lands where the natives are able camel herders. The very different history of the camel in North America is well told by Laycock (1966). Their general unpopularity with both U. S. Army personnel and civilians, and general failure in the American Southwest during the nineteenth century is well-known. However, the reasons for the final demise of "gone wild" camel herds in the North American Desert toward the end of the century remain unclear.

Recently extinct and vanishing animals are problems in deserts as elsewhere (see Prakash, 1959). The introduced "little Africa along the Rio Grande" in northern Mexico and adjacent Texas (U. S. A.), and the potential for such uncritical intercontinental wildlife moving to expand into plague proportions, is reviewed by Laycock (1966). The well-known introduction of the European rabbit (*Oryctolagus cuniculatus*) and subsequent colossal destruction of many Australian landscapes as well as agricultural enterprises in Australia, New Zealand, and elsewhere is essentially a nondesert problem of semiarid environments. It is worth noting, however, that the resource losses to the Australian public and their continuing financial burden (now over $4,000,000 annually) for control of the rabbits, which are still out of control, has by no means been successfully relieved, either by the hopeful but temporary effects of myxomatosis or by countervailing economic benefits to rabbit trappers and others engaged in a new unexpected fringe-benefit industry founded upon a continuing tragedy.

E.   DISEASE IN THE DESERT

The soul that would rid herself out of all perplexed ways, desireth in her anger even the undoing of this hostile body, only ground of her disease.

—C. Doughty

American coccidioidomycosis is the most serious of three possible candidates for a "desert disease" (desert sore, West Nile infection, and coccidioidomycosis), *i. e.*, in the sense of being endemic to the desert and to some of its bordering and closely related semiarid environments, with a more limited occurrence elsewhere. Coccidioidomycosis (Valley Fever, San Joaquin Valley Fever) is an occasionally fatal fungal disease that occurs primarily in the North American Desert and the Monte-Patagonian Desert of Argentina, and in adjacent subtropical environments. Desert sore is a skin ulceration occurring in Australia, Africa, and the Near East. West Nile infection is a virus disease that occurs in several deserts in the Saharo-Sindic region.

Trachoma is a serious form of conjunctivitis that is especially common in hot dry tropical and subtropical environments. It is a disease that may result in permanent blindness and it is common among native desert peoples, but it has nearly a worldwide distribution.

Tularemia is an occasionally fatal disease in man that involves native rodents, flies, and ticks. It is well-known that it occurs within the North American Desert, but it occurs more widely outside of it, in nondesert environments.

Malaria, schistosomiasis, trypanosomiasis, leishmaniasis, and other human tropical diseases are occasionally found in some parts of some deserts;

however, such diseases of man are typically dependent for their maintenance upon organisms such as snails, flies, and mosquitos that require permanent water or perennially moist microenvironments to serve successfully as vectors and/or intermediate hosts. None is a desert disease. While today such tropical diseases are rarely of wide occurrence in deserts, many most certainly will become so when sea-water is converted on a large scale for irrigating the potentially fertile soils of the subtropical warm deserts that border the oceans and the tropics. What appear to be endemic foci of human disease are widely scattered across the deserts of the world and some certainly date into antiquity. Gelman (1966) has given a recent summary of the world distribution of communicable diseases, based in part on reports and publications of May (1958, 1961), the World Health Organization, Pan American Sanitary Bureau, and the tenth edition of the publication of the American Public Health Association (1965) entitled *The Control of Communicable Diseases in Man*. Standard works on medical entomology, medical mycology, and tropical medicine review in greater or lesser detail the diseases of man that occur, however limited their occurrence, in deserts. Most are amply documented (*e. g.*, Matheson, 1950; Herms and James, 1961; Horsfall, 1962; Emmons, Binford, and Utz, 1963; Steele, 1964; Dubos and Hirsch, 1965; Wilson and Plunkett, 1965; and Hunter, Frye, and Swartzwelder, 1966; see also: Patton and Evans, 1929; Patton, 1931; and Work, 1961). Some otherwise excellent works are not documented (*e.g.*, Adams and Maegraith, 1966).

1.   Coccidioidomycosis (Valley Fever, San Joaquin Valley Fever)

Invasion of the pulmonary system after inhalation of spores of the fungal parasite *Coccidioides immitis* is followed by highly varied syndromes that vary in intensity from asymptomatic to almost explosively fatal. While it is usually a pulmonary disease, an increasing number of primary cutaneous infections have been reported (see Pappagianis, 1967).

In North America, within the United States and northern Mexico, the disease is contained largely, but not wholly, in Merriam's (1894) Lower Sonoran Life Zone (=desert), as recently discussed and partly mapped by Maddy (1957*b*). Roughly 95 per cent of the cases of coccidioidal disease reported in Arizona come from Pima and Maricopa counties, situated in the Sonoran Desert. Only one-third of the Sonoran Desert is in the United States (California, Arizona); two-thirds of it is in the Mexican states of Baja California and Sonora. It is not surprising that it is the state of Sonora that has the highest percentage (67 per cent) of human reactors to coccidioidin that is known in Mexico (Glusker, Fuentes Villalobos, and Gómez del Campo, 1950; Ochoa, in Ajello, 1967).

According to Edwards and Palmer (1957) and Palmer, Edwards, and Allfather (1957) the highest percentages of coccidioidin reactors in a U. S. sample of "48,676 young adults" were located in the Chihuahuan Desert, Sonoran Desert, and Mojave Desert subdivisions of the North American Desert. It is significant that in the great Valley of California (San Joaquin Valley), coccidioidal infection is highest in the southern end, which is a creosotebush desert scrub climax, and that the infection conspicuously diminishes northward into a relatively ameliorated former grassland climax environment.

In South America coccidioidomycosis occurs in the Monte-Patagonian Desert of western Argentina northward into the subtropical semiarid Gran Chaco, which is shared with Paraguay and Bolivia. Local cases are also reported from Colombia, Venezuela, and Central America (references are given in recent reviews by Fiese, 1958; Ajello, 1967; and Pappagianis, 1967). Almost all of the Argentine states with known endemic foci (Catamarca, Córdoba, La Pampa, La Rioja, Mendoza, Río Negro, San Juan, San Luis, and Tucumán) are not in the Gran Chaco, contrary to Albert and Sellers (1963), and Ajello (1967). The significance of this is that all, most, or part, of almost all of the these states lie in the Monte-Patagonian Desert, the South American counterpart of our North American Desert, which is Merriam's Lower Sonoran Life Zone so much referred to by students of coccidioidomycosis since Maddy's (1957b) report and partial zone map. Regarding the wetter and much more mesic Gran Chaco, the one Chaco state in Argentina that is known to be involved (Santiago del Estero) revealed only 19 per cent positive skin-test reactions in a sample of 2,213 children aged 6 to 16 years (Negroni *et al.*, 1952). It is of interest that Gran Chaco environments bordering the Monte-Patagonian Desert in the north are strikingly comparable floristically as well as vegetatively to the thornscrub and short-tree forest environments of our North American Mexican states bordering on the south of the Sonoran and Chihuahuan subdivisions of the North American Desert. Coccidioidal disease also occurs in these North American border areas, particularly west of the Sierra Madre Occidental in Sinaloa, Sonora, and Baja California, but also east of the Sierra Madre Occidental in Durango, Zacatecas, San Luis Potosí, and Nuevo León. Just as the Sonoran Desert (south) and the Great Basin Desert (north) are two of the major subdivisions of the North American desert area, the Argentine Monte (north) and the Patagonian Desert (south) are two major subdivisions of the South American desert area. The geographic term "Monte-Patagonian Desert," within the South American desert area, would be appropriate for what is usually referred to (incorrectly) as the "Patagonian Desert." The Patagonian Desert proper (in Patagonia, as distinct from the Monte) is the South American counterpart of the North American shrub-dominated Great Basin Desert—vegetatively, floristically, and by virtue of the similar higher latitude position (Lowe, 1968, *in press*).

The Phoenix symposia on coccidioidomycosis (1957, 1967) contain numerous papers on clinical, pathological, therapeutic, immunologic veterinary, epidemiologic, ecologic, cultural, and other aspects of investigation of the disease. Fiese's (1958) early comprehensive volume on coccidioidal disease also contains a comprehensive chronological bibliography of 968 papers on coccidioidomycosis from 1892 to 1957. An annual mimeographed bibliography on coccidioidomycosis is published by the Tuberculosis and Health Association of Los Angeles County, Los Angeles, California, and is distributed by the U.S. Veterans Administration/U.S. Air Forec Coccidioidal Study Group.

Primary coccidioidomycosis is essentially an airborne fungal infection; the lesion is a bronchitis, bronchiolitis, or bronchopneumonia in a self-limited disease that is of a few days to several weeks duration. *Secondary* (or *disseminated*) *coccidioidomycosis* is borne by the blood or lymph within the body; the spectrum is wide and the lesion can be any combination of suppuration, necrosis, and granuloma in almost any organ (formerly called *coccidioidal granuloma*). Meningitis is the most significant coccidioidal lesion of the central nervous system, and, among Caucasians, it is the commonest cause of death from coccidioidomycosis. No form of the disease is more invariably fatal (Fiese, 1958; Steele, 1964).

Arthritis, as an allergic response that accompanies primary coccidioidomycosis or as an actual joint invasion by the fungus in disseminated coccidioidomycosis, has given rise to the popular name "desert rheumatism." The almost invariable benignity of the disease should be stressed, rather than the rare hazard of death. Moreover, if the inhabitants of the southwestern United States and western Argentina could be effectively vaccinated against *Coccidioides,* the problem of coccidioidomycosis would be essentially solved (Fiese, 1958).

Autopsy investigations of coccidioidal lesions in native kangaroo rats *(Dipodomys),* pocket mice *(Perognathus),* deer mice *(Peromyscus),* grasshopper mice *(Onychomys)*, and ground squirrels *(Citellus)* provide data that delimit endemic areas (Emmons, 1942, 1943; Emmons and Ashburn, 1942). Infections have been observed also in cats, dogs, coyotes, horses, burros, cattle, pigs, and in captive mice, rats, chinchillas, llamas, monkeys, gorillas, and a tapir. It was earlier thought that animals might be important reservoirs of infection, but it is now evident that wild animals, domestic animals, and man are but accidental hosts (Fiese, 1958; Ajello, 1967). While the mass of evidence appears to favor the conclusion that "all infections are traced to a common source — soil" (Ajello, 1967), see the reports by Wilson, Smith, and Plunkett (1953) and Castleberry, Converse, and Del Favero (1963).

The ecological opportunism involved in the evolution and present geographic concentrations of *Coccidioides immitis* in arid and semiarid areas of North and South America seems fairly clear. A reasonable hypothesis involving the adaptation and life-cycle of this facultative parasite in desert soils, and subsequent infection of vertebrate and invertebrate animals including man, clearly appears in the early work of Smith *et al.* (1946), Egeberg and Ely (1955), Lubarsky and Plunkett (1955), Hugenholtz (1957*b*), and the more recent work of Egeberg, Elconin, and Egeberg (1964), Elconin, Egeberg, and Egeberg (1964), and Maddy (1965).

Smith *et al.* (1946) reported that higher seasonal infection rates occurred during the dry and dusty summer following winter-spring rains in the San Joaquin Valley, California, which is under a winter rainfall regime. In the areas of high endemism in Arizona, New Mexico, and west Texas, a similar seasonal wet-dry regime is present but with the summers wet instead of dry (summer monsoon climate).

Egeberg and Ely (1955) found that a higher percentage of soil samples yielded *C. immitis* at the end of the rainy season than during the dry season. They advanced the hypothesis that scorching heat during a dry season sterilizes the thin layers of topsoil, thereby in some way aiding *C. immitis,* which then flourishes after the onset of rains that provide soil moisture for germination and growth. The hypothesis is supported by the work of Lubarsky and Plunkett (1955), who found that *C. immitis* grows better in sterilized soil than in nonsterilized soil, and by Egeberg, Elconin and Egeberg (1964), who found that 40° C stimulated growth as did high concentrations of soluble salts, one or both of which inhibited competitive soil species of *Bacillus* and *Penicillium*. It is evident that a desert environment offers those climatic and biotic factors that provide the opportunity for a thin surface layer of periodically sterile and relatively alkaline soil, an absent-to-thin vegetative soil

cover, and a seasonally intense isolation at the sandy soil surface producing both high temperature and high evaporation. Similar but less extreme environmental characteristics are shared with the adjacent subtropical scrub communities in which *C. immitis* occurs also and from which the deserts have most recently evolved (Axelrod, 1950, 1958).

Plunkett and Swatek (1957) found viable *C. immitis* at soil depths on the order of 6 to 8 inches during the hot dry summer season in the Mojave Desert in California. They also reported that the natural growth of the fungus occurred only in a certain local soil microenvironment on a transect sampled. Maddy (1965) obtained similar results in the Sonoran Desert in Arizona, and found *C. immitis* in the linings of rodent burrows, a few inches underground, during summer months when the fungus was killed in the soil near the desert surface.

Maddy (1957*b*) early concluded that *C. immitis* grows naturally in soils only in areas exhibiting those climatic characteristics of Merriam's (1894) Lower Sonoran Life Zone (=desert). The endemic areas of coccidioidomycosis do coincide to a convincing degree with the Lower Sonoran Life Zone limits in the southwestern United States and adjacent northern Mexico, but the disease also extends beyond the zone's limits into the adjacent subtropical scrub. Merriam's "Lower Sonoran Life Zone" actually refers to the Chihuahuan Desert, Sonoran Desert, and Mojave Desert subdivisions of the North American Desert (Shreve, 1942), the three "hot desert" subdivisions that widely share creosotebush *(Larrea divaricata)* communities. Rainfall is low (3 to 11 inches annually), seasonal (primarily during winter, summer, or both), and separated by intervening dry and dusty periods with high evaporation. Temperatures are high in the summer, reaching to daily averages on the order of 90° F with extremes in excess of 115° F, and mild in midwinter during which daily minima may fall below the freezing point of water and cold-fronts may bring snow. In California and Nevada the climatic regime is dominated by winter-spring rains followed by a dry summer. In Arizona, New Mexico, west Texas, and adjoining northern Mexico, the climatic regime is dominated by the southwestern summer monsoon (July to October) that is preceeded and followed by foresummer and postsummer droughts.

Hugenholtz (1957*a*) analyzed data for infections of base personnel at Williams Air Force Base in the Sonoran Desert (Lower Sonoran Life Zone) in southern Arizona. He also noted that the records of the Arizona Health Department showed similar temporal peaks. His conclusions for Arizona agree with Smith *et al.* (1946) for California, namely, that relative rates of infection can be predicted on the basis of obvious weather conditions of a preceding season. For example, in southern Arizona, one should expect a relatively low infection rate in an autumn that follows a relatively dry July and August, and a low rate in the spring and summer following a relatively dry winter.

In summary, the most likely hypothetical sequence for growth and infection by *Coccidioides immitis* no longer involves animals. It involves seasonally intense soil surface heating with soil sterilization, followed by seasonal rains producing soil moisture levels permitting rapid germination, growth, and reentry of the fungus into the upper sterile zone of soil. Subsequent dust storms intensify and accelerate distribution of the infectious spores that are inhaled by man and other animals in warm deserts and subtropical semiarid environments.

2. Desert Sore

Desert sore (Veld sore, Barcoo rot) is a skin ulceration, apparently caused by bacteria in connection with skin abrasions, poor hygiene, and perhaps, malnutrition. Its possible relation to the similar tropical ulcer (Naga sore) of the wet tropics is not clarified. Hunter, Frye, and Swartzwelder (1966) summarize the distribution, etiology, pathology, treatment, *etc.* from the data and references in Bettley (1943), Macrae (1944), Henderson (1943), and Anning (1946); see also Adams and Maegraith (1966). The bacteria (staphylococci, streptococci) may be transmitted mechanically by domestic flies and other species under the unsanitary living conditions that prevail in areas where the disease occurs, but otherwise animals are not involved. The problem is one in general medicine and public health, rather than desert biology.

3. West Nile Infection

This is a mosquitoborne arbovirus disease of children in Egypt and Sudan in the Sahara, throughout the Somali-Chalbi, and in ameliorated areas of the Arabian Desert, Iranian Desert, and the Thar. Its candidacy for a truly desert disease is not supported by its wide distribution outside of the desert in Mediterranean North Africa, almost all of East Africa, and central and southern India. The mosquito genus *Culex* is implicated on ecological and epidemiological grounds throughout the distribution of the disease, which is dependent on a cycle in wild birds maintained by transmission through mosquitoes (Taylor *et al.,* 1956). A recent review of relationships with other arbovirus diseases is given by Hunter, Frye, and Swartzwelder (1966). The Russian tickborne arbovirus disease (Omsk hemorrhagic fever)

occurs in the Turkestan Desert, but apparently not in the Gobi or Takla-Makan.

4. Conjunctivitis and Trachoma (Lymphogranuloma Venereum)

There are numerous human eye diseases (ophthalmia) that involve inflamation of the conjunctiva. They are discussed in standard works on tropical disease and medical entomology; see also World Health Organization (1955, 1958, 1962a, 1964) and Auerbach (1955). Conjunctivitis is not a "desert disease," although it is often prevalent in native human populations in both the New and Old World deserts where flies and poor sanitation are a perennial human situation. Conjunctivities, including trachoma, appears most prevalent and is best known in deserts in Africa, the Middle East, and South America, areas in which "dust storms" are also prevalent and may be involved in the etiology. The prevalence is greatest in Egypt and in the Middle East, where over 90 per cent of the population in some villages may be affected. The causative organisms have been usually referred to as viruses; however, they have cell walls and possess both DNA and RNA, and they are more recently referred to as TRIC agents (see Meyer, 1965).

Trachoma is a chronic and contagious conjunctivitis. It is characterized by the presence of inflaming granulations on the conjunctival epithelium that may be eventually replaced by scar tissue, and very early the cornea becomes involved. Partial or complete blindness may result. It was early known that house flies (including *Musca*) and eye gnats *(Hippelates)* were involved as mechanical carriers (Schwartz, 1894, 1895; Howard, 1900). Today it appears generally agreed that the "virus" causing trachoma is transmitted from eye to eye by fingers, fomites, and flies under filthy living conditions (Siniscal, 1955; Lindsay and Scudder, 1956; Adams and Maegraith, 1966; and World Health Organization, 1962a).

The problem with increased native eye gnats *(Hippelates collusor)* and increased catarrhal conjunctivitis in the Coachella Valley of the lower Colorado desert section of the Sonoran Desert in southeastern California (U. S. A.), clearly implicates irrigation in the deserts. In recent decades this was, and is now, a desert area of increasingly intense irrigation-farming on an enormous scale. It has created astoundingly high seasonal populations of eye gnats not previously known (Tinkham, 1952). High populations of this eye pest also occur in other desert areas, farmed and not farmed, in the North American Desert (Mulla, Barnes, and Garber, 1960; Mulla and March, 1959).

Hippelates collusor is the "mal de ojo" of the natives of Baja California (Townsend, 1893). The same or a similar chloropid eye gnat is the "mal de ojo" of Sonora, where this pest increases in abundance as one gradually leaves the Sonoran Desert and almost imperceptibly enters the wetter subtropical thorn-scrub and short-tree forests bordering the desert on the south.

5. Tularemia

Tularemia is a plague-like disease carried from rodent to rodent (squirrels, rabbits, and others), and probably from rodent to man, by the tabanid fly, *Chrysops discalis,* and by ticks (*Dermacentor andersoni* and others). The bacterium *Pasteurella tularensis* is the causative agent. The name comes from Tulare County, California, well outside the desert. The disease occurs widely in the western United States, in Canada, and in many other parts of the world. It occurs in the North American Desert where, as elsewhere, it is usually contracted mechanically by handling rabbits. Lillie and Francis (1936) described the pathology in detail; see also American Public Health Association (1965).

6. Malaria

The definitive hosts and insect vectors of *Plasmodium,* the protozoan parasite that causes malaria in man, are species of the mosquito genus *Anopheles.* Of the more than 200 known species of anopheline mosquitoes, over 60 are incriminated as vectors of malaria. Several of those occur in deserts. The species that occur in the deserts are included in a comprehensive table for the world in Hunter, Frye, and Swartzwelder (1966, table VI. 7, pp. 338-342), which summarizes the geographic distribution, type of breeding place, adult behavior, and efficiency as vector, for the principal anopheline vectors of human malaria. The table is ordered by geographic distribution. It serves well to emphasize the species diversity of the vectors as well as the widespread ocurrence of malaria in desert environments. One or more anopheline species occurs in every major desert of the world. See also Boyd (1949), World Health Organization (1958, 1961, 1964, 1966), May (1958, 1961), Jepson (1963), American Public Health Association (1965), Powell (1966), and discussion of mosquitoes in the section on pests, above.

7. Leishmaniasis and Phlebotomus Fever

Leishmaniasis is a group of infectious diseases most prevalent in tropical environments. Some forms of leishmaniasis occur in subtropical desert-border areas, such as the Gran Chaco in Argentina and the southern edge of the Sahara in Africa, and also well within some of the deserts of the world—the Arabian, Atacama-Peruvian, Sahara, and Thar. With rare exception, it is not a desert disease.

Leishmaniasis, both visceral (kala azar) and dermal, is caused by species of a flagellate protozoan (*Leishmania*). The vectors are species of *Phlebotomus* flies. Dogs are known effective reservoirs, and many mammals are readily infected; these include jerboas, gerbils, rabbits, cats, jackals, and monkeys. There is a high mortality from visceral leishmaniasis, which is characterized by splenic and hepatic enlargements, fever, anemia, and other symptoms.

Dermal and cutaneous leishmaniasis (Aleppo boil, Baghdad boil, Delphi boil, Oriental sore, etc.) may be transmitted by contact with skin ulcers, although the main transmitters appear to be *Phlebotomus* flies (sand flies). One of the most serious forms is the Latin American *espundia* or *uta,* a mucocutaneous form of leishmaniasis that produces an ulcerating infection of the skin that may eventually involve the mucosa of the mouth and margins of the nose. Species of *Phlebotomus* flies are incriminated, and the disease is widespread in southern Mexico and Central and South America (Goldman, 1947).

While arthropod-transmitted diseases such as malaria and leishmaniasis are not expected as endemic desert disease, Dr. R. S. Dorney of the Pan American Union recently informed us that rodent reservoirs and fly vectors of leishmaniasis and malaria have recently been found in the "fog forests" that are interspaced along the Peruvian coast in the Atacama-Peruvian Desert. These natural localized foci within the desert present potential epidemiological problems for serious human disease in the event that conversion of sea-water brings widespread irrigation to this arid Pacific border region.

Other diseases that involve Phlebotomus flies (i. e., other than some form of leishmaniasis), are pappataci fever (or sand-fly fever) and oroya fever (or Carrion's disease). Sand-fly fever, caused by a small filterable virus, is a mild fever ordinarily of three days duration from which mortality is rare. It is endemic in part to the broad Saharo-Sindic desert region. Carrion's disease, caused by a small bacterium-like organisms (*Bartonella bacciliformus*) and characterized by high fever often ending in death, is an important disease in the Peruvian sector of the Atacama-Peruvian Desert above about 2,500 feet.

The taxonomic study of the genus *Phlebotomus* is difficult. References to pertinent works on the taxonomy of these small blood-sucking gnats (Psychodidae, Phlebotinae) are given in Matheson (1950).

8. Trypanosomiasis

African Trypanosomiasis

In Africa, trypanosomiasis is transmitted by the tse-tse fly which is a non-desert-adapted vector and intermediate host, and hence trypanosomiasis does not occur as an endemic disease in the African deserts (Namib-Kalahari, Sahara, Somali). The distribution of the disease, extending to just short of the boundaries of these deserts, is striking; see, for example, the distribution may of African trypanosomiasis in Hunter, Frye, and Swartzwelder (1966); and see World Health Organization (1962b).

Animal Trypanosomiasis (El debab)

El debab is a disease of camels and horses in Algeria, but apparently not widely, at least, in the Sahara proper. The trypanosome is variously referred to as *Trypanosoma evansi, T. berberum,* or *T. sudanese.* The disease is transmitted mechanically on the proboscis of blood-sucking tabanid flies, biting horseflies of the genus *Tabanus* in the family Tabanidae (Matheson, 1950; Herms and James, 1961).

American Trypanosomiasis (Chagas Disease)

Chagas disease is produced by infection through the blood-sucking assassin bugs or conenosed bugs (genus *Triatoma,* and others) in the family Reduviidae (see Usinger, 1944). Although occurring in the American deserts, this is not a "desert disease." Human infections are reported from nearly every country in the western hemisphere (World Health Organization, 1962b).

Trypanosoma cruzi has been isolated from *Triatoma* in California, Arizona, New Mexico, and Texas, and in other U. S. states (F. D. Wood, 1934; S. F. Wood, 1942, 1944 a&b, 1952; Woody and Woody, 1955; Mehringer, Wood, and Anderson, 1961). The degree of infection appears to be considerably greater in South America than in North America. Apparently this is a result of species differences in duration of blood-sucking time and/or other factors associated with time lag between feeding and defecation, and hence in the probability of insect defecation, required for infection, at the site of the bite (Wood, 1951, Tobar, 1952). Woody and Woody (1955) recently reported the only two authenticated indigenous cases of Chagas disease known in the United States, both from Texas. Aside from Chagas disease, the bites of *Triatoma* and some of its reduviid relatives produce serious symptoms in sensitive humans living or visiting in both desert and nondesert environments in the Americas (see the section D, above).

9. Animal Epizootics

Epizootics have not often been studied by ecologists, and when studied have been neglected in the desert. Bodenheimer (1957) recently reviewed the world picture for plague, rinderpest, nagana, and other trypanosome epizootics in the deserts and steppes. There is relatively little information available on the faunas of deserts as reservoirs of infectious diseases and on their ability to sustain epizootics. Almost all the data on arid-zone epizootics comes from semiarid environments (steppe, grassland, and savanna) rather than from deserts.

CONCLUSION

A. DISTRIBUTIONAL PATTERNS OF DESERT FAUNA

Regarding "desert species" in general, there emerges for the desert faunas of the world a picture of three major distributional patterns. There are *(1)* desert-only species, *(2)* desert-included species, and *(3)* nondesert species. The first two groups have wide distribution within desert environments and are regarded as *desert species.* The *nondesert species* have wider distributions outside of deserts than within them. These major distributional patterns are exhibited by both the vertebrates and the invertebrates.

The animal-borne and animal-transmitted diseases in the desert refer preponderantly but not exclusively to nondesert vector species. On the other hand, species that are crop pests and otherwise general pests of man in the desert are frequently native desert species. The same is true for poisonous species dangerous to man. The native fauna as food of indigenous primitive man, and as a survival subject for others, involves either entirely or essentially native desert species.

B. LEVEL OF KNOWLEDGE FOR THE MAJOR DESERTS

Regardless of the numbers and kinds of routes by which the overall knowledge has been obtained, four tiers or levels of comparative knowledge on fauna emerge for the 13 deserts. Estimates of the overall state of this knowledge are summarized in table IX. Sensitivity of the inventory gives accuracy of the estimates of between 1% and 10% of scale (0 to 4), an accuracy of ± 0.04 to ± 0.4. Variation in accuracy is taken into account in outlining the four broad levels of accomplishment.

1. Level I (Best Known)

North American Desert

The North American Desert is alone in the first (best known) level. The knowledge gap between it and the deserts in the second level is on the order of two to several times greater than the gap between any two of the deserts within level II (see table I). The knowledge of the fauna of the North

American Desert, with a mean value of 3.8, is, on the whole, *good,* as further indicated by the high range of 3-4. It should be noted that the designation *excellent* was not used in this system, for nowhere did it appear to apply. Such a category, with a potential value of 5, does not appear in the original table I. Many of the simplest questions regarding fauna, and certainly some of the most important, remain unanswered.

The factor of desert size (geographical extent) is important. It should be appreciated that the area of North American Desert (0.44 million square miles) is small compared to that of many others, and that the entire conterminous United States, an area of nearly 3,000,000 square miles, fits very nicely within the boundaries of the Sahara, which is slightly larger.

Table IX

OVERALL STATE OF KNOWLEDGE OF
DESERT FAUNA RANKED BY DESERT

Desert	Mean*	Range*	Level of Knowledge
North American	3.8	3-4	I
Australian	3.1	2-4	II
Thar	2.9	2-4	
Arabian	2.6	2-4	
Sahara	2.4	1-4	
Turkestan	2.3	1-4	
Kalahari-Namib	2.3	0-4	III
Monte-Patagonian	2.1	1-3	
Atacama-Peruvian	1.9	1-3	
Iranian	1.8	1-3	
Somali-Chalbi	1.6	0-3	
Gobi	1.3	0-3	IV
Takla-Makan	0.6	0-2	

* Mean values and ranges, taken from table I, Summary of State of Knowledge of Desert Fauna, are on a scale of: (4) good, (3) subadequate, (2) fair, (1) poor, and (0) insignificant.

604

One does not have to look far to identify other major factors responsible for the first position of the North American Desert regarding knowledge of the fauna. Although roughly one-half of this desert lies in Mexico (in which country also lie most of the solutions to the evolutionary problems of this fauna) contrary to Bodenheimer (1957), well over 90 per cent of our knowledge of the desert fauna of Mexico comes from the findings of U.S. workers who have spent much time and effort in northern Mexico as well as in the United States.

A larger, dedicated scientific community, greater technological advancement, higher standard of living, and greater educational accomplishment in the United States require no further comment. However, in addition, there is needed a strong interest in natural history among the people, and this has been present in North America. It has led naturally and directly to strong educational institutions with a broad spectrum of opportunities to study natural science and to solve theoretical and evolutionary, as well as natural resource problems. This basic philosophical interest, capitalized upon and further stimulated in feedback fashion by economic and medical problems in general, has played a decisive role historically and appears to be at least maintaining itself if not increasing. The overall picture is well summarized by the observation that while the United States has not been forced to develop extensively its desert lands, the amount of combined work on the taxonomy, genetics, ecology, morphology, and physiology of the desert fauna is greater than that for any other arid region.

2. Level II

The mean level of knowledge for each of the next five deserts in table IX (Australian, Thar, Arabian, Sahara, Turkestan) appears to lie between *subadequate* and *good*. Most of the values are near 3.0 (*good*). The range (1-4), with reference to knowledge of particular faunal groups (table I), is conspicuously wider than for the North American Desert (3-4), and varies from *poor* to *good*.

Australian Desert

The Australian Desert is nearly one-half the size of the conterminous United States and covers much of the continent. In spite of the large desert area involved, second only to that of the Sahara, a good knowledge of the fauna has been obtained and interest in desert problems is accelerating. Causes of this progress in Australia are similar to those for the United States. Moreover, there has been a strong interest in the Australian fauna on the part of foreign investigators. Strong stimulus to investigations of

animal ecology in Australia also recently resulted from the catastrophic devastations by the introduced European rabbit. Through the efforts of C. S. I. R. O. and the strong interests of many universities and scientists, the desert fauna of all but the center of the continent has been investigated. Major blind spots in the biology and geography of the continent are outlined in the excellent contributions of Keast, Crocker, and Christian (1959), *Biogeography and Ecology in Australia.* Many problems remain, not the least of which is a complete inventory of fauna above the level of alpha taxonomy, a fact that could be underscored for virtually every desert in the world.

The Thar

In this, the easternmost sector of the Saharo-Sindic megadesert, the early influence of the British naturalists was important to the development of zoological knowledge of the various Indian desert subdivisions collectively referred to here as the Thar (about 0.23 million square miles). It is natural, therefore, that the British Museum (Natural History), London, is a principal depository for zoological materials. Important materials are also deposited within India, in the zoological laboratories of the Arid Zone Research Association and Zoological Survey of India, Jodhpur, India, and in the collections of the Zoological Survey of Pakistan, Karachi, West Pakistan, from which headquarters faunal surveys and other investigations of the desert fauna are being carried forward in the British tradition. Comprehensive regional monographs with emphasis wholly or primarily on desert species and based on modern systematic concepts (*e. g.,* Minton, 1966) are needed for almost all faunal groups, many of which are now well understood above the level of alpha taxonomy.

Arabian Desert

The area is extensive (0.93 million square miles) in this third largest desert, and the zoological knowledge is spotty both biologically and geographically. The northern countries are, on the whole, better known than interior Saudi Arabia. Faunal bibliographies, checklists, and keys are an important early step in bringing together a faunal inventory of species for a given region. The recent publications by B. E. Allouse for Iraq and neighboring countries are particularly valuable in this regard. The bulk of the contributions for the Arabian Desert, however, are by European authors. The works of the late F. S. Bodenheimer of Israel, including several books and monographs, are not only a major modern contribution to our knowledge of the Arabian Desert but to desert biology everywhere, and a major contribution to the field of general ecology. In Saudi Arabia, the

Arabian-American Oil Company (Aramco) at Dhahran is an incomparable desert research station. In addition to its principal obligations, it is, among numerous other things, an active center of biological and medical research on Arabian problems. Aramco is contributing importantly to our knowledge of the desert fauna including that of the little known Rub' al Khali. The Aramco venture is one of the great sagas of Arabia (see Lebkicher *et al.*, 1960) and it is of major importance to all students of deserts regardless of their field of investigation.

The Sahara

The Sahara alone, with its three million plus square miles, accounts for nearly half of the desert surface of the globe. Thus it is not surprising that we know relatively less about its fauna than that for some other deserts, even though it has been the object of modern zoological expeditions and investigations by many investigators and their parties representing many nations, and contains a relatively large number of cities for a desert, as well as a relatively large number of widely scattered desert research stations (see Paylore, 1967). Information on fauna is actually more spotty, both biologically and geographically, than that for the smaller Arabian Desert. Much of the systematics for the Saharan fauna is at or near the level of alpha taxonomy, and even less is known regarding the general ecology of most species, except in Morocco, Algeria, Egypt, and the Sudan, the countries that appear to be best known zoologically and where the level of knowledge for some faunal groups is good. The nature and probable extent of the Saharan fauna, its uniqueness as well as close relationship to that of the Middle East deserts, and the major evolutionary and biogeographic problems remaining to be clarified have been outlined by several authors during the past 15 years. While it can be said that the major faunal problems are identified for the Sahara, merely to obtain a more or less complete inventory of the animal species at the desired level of taxonomy will require a much more massive cooperative effort than heretofore undertaken for such purposes in any desert.

Turkestan Desert

Important ecological surveys of the Turkestan Desert were initiated by D. N. Kachkarov and his associates during the first half of the century. The work was reported in a series of papers in Russian and in English. The scope and the depth of this early work, and its importance to desert biology then and now, is exhibited in *Life of the Deserts* written in Russian by Kachkarov and Korovin (1942). This is a careful, extensive and well illustrated work of 11 chapters, which covers, in addition to 5 chapters on desert animals, the subjects of desert climate, soils, vegetation, man in the desert, and the principal "forms of desert types" in Central Asia. The intensity and depth of this work in bioecology, as well as its coverage for animal species, can be further appreciated by its inclusion of complex nutritional food-chain analyses of 39 species of animals (including the camel and man) in the "sandy desert of the central Kara-Kum," and data on similar communities studied elsewhere in the desert.

While there have been few efforts comparable to Kachkarov's (above) in this large Asian desert (0.76 million square miles, fourth largest in the world), its fauna has been studied extensively, where not intensively, by many biologists of many nationalities since the turn of the century. The results are published primarily in Russian, French, and English. The origin of the desert fauna by Kuznetosov (1926) is in Russian with a German summary. Of all animal groups, the insects and the birds appear to be the best known, although most groups in the desert appear to have been studied. Many recent papers, especially by Russian authors, written in several languages including English, reveal extensive modern work on desert pests and vectors of disease. There is also an older literature on insects and crop pests to which Plotnikov (1926 and elsewhere) was a major contributor. Some of this work is reviewed in Pradhan (1957) and Uvarov (1957, 1962, 1966).

3. Level III

The next five deserts listed in table IX exhibit somewhat wider variation within the set than for the second level, above. Also, the variation in this set is probably somewhat more extreme than is indicated by the values (table IX) of 1.6 (Somali-Chalbi) 2.3 (Kalahari-Namib). The overall estimate of *fair* is indicated for the entire set. The range (0-4), with reference to knowledge of particular faunal groups (table I and table IX), varies from *insignificant* to *good*. The deserts in this set are uniformly small (0.14 to 0.26 million square miles).

Kalahari-Namib

Before the turn of the half-century, faunal information for the Kalahari-Namib was largely to be found in more general works treating larger areas in southern Africa. Much of the information was for semiarid parts of the Kalahari sector, with less of it for the most arid parts of the Namib. A steadily increasing interest in desert biology in South Africa (Transvaal Museum and Namib Desert Research Association, Pretoria), and in South West Africa (Scientific Society of South West Africa, Windhoek), led to the establishment in 1963 of the Namib Desert Research Station at Gobabeb, South West Africa, under the direction of C. Koch. The station now provides the needed center for research in residence in the central Namib. The fauna is quite unique and is being reported regularly in a series of papers on the general and physiological ecology and systematics of both invertebrate and vertebrate groups. The modest and highly successful research station at Gobabeb should receive strong support for needed growth. Among the faunal-related studies are those involving a string of five weather stations located on a transect from the Atlantic Ocean inland to the station, a distance of approximately 70 miles by road. This is the only weather monitoring activity on the entire Atlantic coast of the Kalahari-Namib desert area.

Monte-Patagonian Desert

The history of the development of knowledge on fauna has been similar in Argentina to that in Chile, Peru, and Ecuador (see Atacama-Peruvian). In addition, during the last 50 years, and particularly during the last 15, there has been a large effort on the part of a small number of scientists to investigate the native desert fauna, entirely apart from applied or economic questions. They have published their results, in part, in Argentina and elsewhere, often in English. Some of this research has centered in Patagonia and some in the Monte, with impressive studies on the desert fauna and flora coming from the Universities of Buenos Aires, Córdoba, and Tucumán. Agricultural problems aside, until recently (circa World War II), Argentina appears not to have enjoyed as high a level of foreign interest in its fauna as has Peru. At the moment, there is high interest in Argentine work among American vertebrate zoologists who are students of desert faunas.

Atacama-Peruvian Desert

The history of the study of the fauna is usual for late-developing countries, in that a major input for zoological knowledge has come via support from government agencies interested in controlling pests and disease, in developing animal husbandry, and in the importance of fish and wildlife to the general economy. The situation regarding entomological investigations is reviewed in Pradhan (1957) and in Uvarov (1962). The vertebrate animals of the desert have received considerable study by North American and European workers, and, more recently, by South Americans; however, the vertebrate animals have not been a subject of review. There are many conspicuous gaps in the knowledge, and these include the important subjects of ecological study of common species and taxonomic study of uncommon groups. While the faunas of Chile and Peru appear to be on the whole fairly well studied, remarkably little zoological work has been carried out within the coastal desert. For two reasons it is important for this situation to be corrected soon. This little known "fog desert" is a unique earth environment, and the distillation of sea water in the near future will certainly destroy it, as civilization "advances" in South America.

Iranian Desert

While knowledge for the Iranian Desert is indicated as fair (table IX), it should be noted that the problem of general field work in many parts of the desert is certainly more aggravated by rugged topography than in other deserts. As a result, large tracts of desert remain either little explored or totally unexplored zoologically. Nevertheless, there is a respectable literature on natural history, particularly on the fauna. Aside from insects of pest or disease significance, this knowledge is primarily the result of work by English, other European, and Indian investigators. Recent papers published on entomology and zoology in the University of Tehran publication series are commonly in Persian with or without summaries in other languages, usually in French when provided. Except for the economic and medically oriented studies on native species, which are substantially studied by Persians and other native peoples in Iran and neighboring countries, the greater bulk of the work on the fauna of the Iranian Desert is that which has been carried forward by European, Indian, American, and other foreign investigators. The insects and the vertebrates are, as usual, the best known faunal groups.

Somali-Chalbi

Serious investigation of the natural history of the desert was apparently initiated as well as advanced by investigators of occupying nations from Europe, particularly the English and the Italians. North Americans have more recently contributed to the work, both as zoologists and as agricultural advisors (U. S. AID = Agency for International Development). A brief review of the Somalian fauna as a whole was given by Scortecci and Tedesco Zammarno (1937). The important bibliography by Maugini (1953) covers the period from the late 1880's to 1951, for Eritrea, Dancalia, and Somalia; all citations are in Italian. From the few papers at hand, the references cited in them, the general difficulty in finding data for the area, and the remaining zoological titles in Maugini (1953), it is clear that, while taxonomy of both the vertebrate and invertebrate faunas of the Somali-Chalbi have been investigated, the amount of work in general has not been exceptional. Ecology has received less emphasis than taxonomy until very recently, and except for "big game" in particular, most animal groups are in need of modern taxonomic revisions. Apparently little if anything of scientific significance has been published on natural history subjects by the Somalis according to U. S. AID personal at Mogadiscio; no papers in the Ethiopian language were examined.

4. Level IV (Least Known)

Gobi and Takla-Makan

Two deserts, the Gobi and Takla-Makan, are included at the least-known level. The knowledge gap between the two, however, appears to be significant in size, with the mean for the Gobi (1.3) roughly twice that for the Takla-Makan (.64). Thus the overall knowledge of fauna appears to be *poor* to *fair* for the Gobi, and *poor* to *insignificant* for the Takla-Makan. Knowledge of particular faunal groups (see table I) appears to vary from *insignificant* to *fair* for the Gobi and *insignificant* to *poor* for the Takla-Makan.

Two points are worth noting in this regard. First, for the Gobi, knowledge of the dry-steppe (semiarid) environments in the Soviet Union was examined but not included in this analysis. If it had been included, and one had, therefore, considered the so-called "arid-zone" rather than the desert proper, the tabular position of the Gobi would lie in the third level (above) rather than in the fourth (bottom) level. Second, the apparent deficiency of knowledge on these two Asian deserts that lie east of the Turkestan Desert may be more illusory than real (see, for example, Wang, 1961). Some literature on the Gobi region is published in non-Russian languages, but, from what could be determined from this material and some references in Russian, apparently there is more extensive and less accessible literature on the Gobi published in Russian than in any other language. Where lies the bulk of the data on the fauna of the Takla-Makan desert per se, if there is such a bulk, remains unknown to the author at this writing. Literature cited in related works, such as that by Wang (1961) on the forests of China, leads one to suspect that there is a respectable scientific literature written in Chinese on the desert fauna of Sinkiang and adjacent Mongolia.

5. Variation Within Levels

Within each set of deserts in the four levels discussed above and shown in table IX, deserts that are listed adjacent to one another in the table may vary slightly or not at all in the mean values determined for them on the scale from 0 to 4. In view of the fact that the accuracy in the system is on the order of $\pm$ 0.04 to $\pm$ 0.4, the orders of the deserts given within each set of deserts in the second and third levels should be regarded as more or less tentative. It is beyond reasonable doubt, however, that major distinctions exist, and that these may be conveniently grouped for further examination into four or more sets.

C. STATE OF KNOWLEDGE BY TOPICS

1. Poisonous Animals

The kinds (families and genera) of venomous snakes that occur in most of the deserts of the world are known in rough outline, although even this most elementary knowledge is far from even, and venomous snakes are nowhere treated as a single unit or problem for the world's deserts. This widely scattered knowledge varies from our area of least knowledge, the Takla-Makan in China, to that of our greatest knowledge, the North American Desert. Next, the knowledge of exact geographic distributions for the species that occur within each of the deserts varies almost without exception from imperfect to nonexistent. Finally, details for the venomous species on their exact habitat (ecological distributions), *habits, behavior,* and *densities* are poorly known to nonexistent for virtually all deserts except, in part, the North American Desert.

The military's twin problems with venomous snakes—troop morale/fear and safety—obtain in deserts as elsewhere, and the same recommendations are appropriate here as elsewhere for (*1*) first-aid instruction and application, and (*2*) medical treatment. However, there remains for both first-aid and successful hospital treatment much more needed research and resulting production of effective polyvalent antivenins that are truly effective over wide geographic areas on all continents.

The literature reveals wide agreement on medical treatment of poisonous spiderbite, particularly for some of the most dangerous species, but equally wide disagreement and confusion on the taxonomy of the responsible spiders, some of which are taxa that occur in deserts. Such a situation provides a measure of false security, for a successful modern medical toxicology requires correct species identification based on satisfactory taxonomy. About 99% of the world's serious cases of arachnidism are caused by members of the cosmopolitan genus *Latrodectus* (the black widow and its relatives), subtropical spiders that are also widely distributed in the warm deserts. However one may criticize Levi's (1959) recent taxonomic result with this group, one cannot criticize his attempt, and his opening paragraph is so exactly to the point that I quote it for those who have an interest in developing greater knowledge of the environmental biology and toxicology of arid regions:

> The poisonous black-widow spiders are notoriously difficult taxonomically and, because arachnologists have been loath to study the group intensively, there is considerable confusion. It is particularly unfortunate in a medically interesting group to find physiological observations based on specimens of uncertain determination (*e. g.,* papers in Buckley and Porges, *Venoms,* 1956). It is hoped that some the facts presented here will stimulate further collecting of *Latrodectus* in those areas from which few specimens are now available, and further study of *Latrodectus* biology directed toward the solution of taxonomic problems.

Dangerous scorpions are a somewhat more diverse group of animals in most of the world's deserts than are the dangerous spiders. Accordingly, the interest in antivenins for treatment of scorpion-sting has been somewhat greater than for spiderbite. Notwithstanding this long interest in the production of scorpion antivenin in Algeria, Egypt, Turkey, South Africa, Mexico, and Brazil, there is relatively little detailed knowledge that is published on the desert ecology of scorpions, and some of the most elementary and important environmental facts for some of the commonest desert species remain totally unknown. In addition, the taxonomy of the lower categories (species and subspecies) and of the genera of scorpions is much in need of major revisions.

Beard's (1963) recent review makes clear enough that much more knowledge is required on (*1*) the biochemistry and physiology of the venom-producing insects ("These questions seem irrelevant to the sensitive victim of a sting, but the answers lie in a knowledge, yet to be acquired, of biosynthesis and metabolism in insect."), (*2*) their taxonomy ("Allergists seem to agree that the yellow jacket is the most potent in sensitizing victims, but perhaps they do not agree as to the wasp species known as the yellow jacket."), and (*3*) their ecology, distribution, and general biology ("Physiological effects in invertebrates other than insects are little known. In vertebrates, human responses are best known simply because of our subjective interest."). In general, there

appears to be less information available for deserts than for any other major land environment.

Regarding the medical aspects of the venomous animals of the deserts, it is clear that the major problems have now been identified and that progress is being made toward their solution on what may be fairly called a worldwide front. That the ranks of this particular scientific medical group are relatively thin at the present time is not surprising. It is a situation that has prevailed throughout the present century and will undoubtedly prevail into the next.

Regarding present knowledge and future work on the distribution and ecology of the venomous animals of the world's deserts, the present outlook and the prognosis are considerably more dismal. The ranks of the workers are especially thin, a small fraction of the number of the still small group of laboratory investigators working on the venom; occasionally the student of venoms is also a serious student of the biology of venomous species, and vice versa. By and large our present sparse modern knowledge has been handed down to us by a few dedicated people who have been and are located at widely scattered places throughout the world. It is both rewarding and frustrating to realize that here also the problems are identified and the *how,* as well as the *what,* is fully understood; all of this only awaits implementation (see the "Recommendations" section). The only remaining question is *when;* for a full understanding of the details of geographic and ecologic distributions and the general biological characteristics of the poisonous animals of the deserts of the world—the surface has been scratched.

Even though this is a public health problem, it has received little help from U. S. Government agencies in the past.

2. Fauna as Human Food

The published data relevant to the use of fauna as food are largely sociological and enormously incomplete, scattered widely and often obscurely through the writings of travelers, ethnographers, ecologists, and others. Thus by their very nature the data are often difficult to analyze, much more so to quantify and evaluate. Nevertheless, there is revealed an inverse relationship between the species diversity of an area and the number of native animals used as food by native peoples of a desert region.

It is clear that the degree to which the food list is the "zoology of the district" depends either directly or indirectly on the relative harshness of the particular desert environment. For the major deserts of the world, the extremes are well represented by (*1*) the central Australian Bindibu who will eat almost any animal species (a very long species food list) and who live yearly under conditions of 0 to 5 inches of rainfall, which produces relatively scanty desert vegetation in biotic communities of relatively low gross primary productivity, and (2) the American Papago who has a highly selective animal species food list (a short list) and lives under 7 to 11 inches of average yearly rainfall, which produces one of the lushest and most diverse desert vegetations on Earth.

Insects are rich in animal proteins, animal fats, and calories. For the deserts, this is a subject on which many have scratched the surface, but very few have worked at depth. Accordingly, beyond such obvious groups as represented by the well-known blister beetles (Meloidae) and conenosed bugs (*Triatoma*), the "civilized" modern knows little concerning poisonous food properties and potential food dangers of the invertebrate faunas of deserts—faunas that have provided, and continue to provide, a very considerable portion of the animal nutrient obtained by primitive man.

Here as elsewhere in our knowledge of desert animals in particular, there are broad gaps in what we know the faunal list must be; I refer to a simple inventory list of animals present. I know of no complete accounting, even a mere listing, of all of the invertebrate animal species — of insects, spiders, scorpions, centipedes, snails, *et al.*—that occur in any desert of the world. It is not likely that such lists for these animals will be easily obtained, and they will not be obtained without conduct of much more needed work on the actual occurrence, taxonomy, and distribution of the invertebrate and vertebrate animals in deserts. Such inventory lists, which do not exist in anywhere near complete form, are the potential food lists for survival in the desert.

A second major fact emerges. It has been remarked by travelers more than a century ago, and it has been verified by modern students, that the Bushmen of Africa, the aborigines of Australia, and the Arabs of the Sahara find daily sustaining animal food sources that the European does not suspect are present, and that he cannot find even when he knows that they exist. For survival in the desert it is more important to know where a natural food source is and how to obtain it than to know almost anything else about it. This is the least known aspect of important desert animal protein food sources. The problem is the serious lack of detailed ecological knowledge for almost all desert environments.

3. Native Animals as Pests in The Desert

In deserts, the wild fauna is an important ultimate source of pests. It is concluded by reviewers of the subject for insects that, prior to widespread agricultural development in deserts, educated estimates (based on predevelopment surveys) of the potential interest of the native animal species in new crop plants can be of critical importance. Disasters can be averted. In deserts, especially where widespread irrigation is involved, the resulting insect populations may increase suddenly and involve seasonally massive buildups of both desert and nondesert species. While this is a problem of the "arid zone," as the term is usually loosely construed, it is no less a problem in deserts than elsewhere. Most of the cases involving actually and potentially injurious crop insects that are cited by Belanovskii (1936), and Jepson (1954), Pradhan (1957), Uvarov (1957, 1962, and elsewhere), and others, are for nondesert species; this fact in no way detracts from their important conclusion that the wild insect fauna of an area sooner or later, and often immediately, produces serious pests for crops in both arid and semiarid lands. While both theory and method are well developed on the scientific side, either apathy, ignorance, or both on the planning side of development in the desert have resulted in rare use of entomological presurvey and prevention, and, therefore, agriculturists and others have been forced to use subsequently the less effective and more expensive kit of controversial entomological cures.

A red flag is up on wildlife-moving into desert environments, even of species native to other deserts. Most animal foreigners cannot successfully establish breeding populations in new desert environments. On the other hand, the few successes have proven dangerous competitors and destroyers of the native fauna in an organism-environment balance system that is more delicate and more easily destroyed than elsewhere. The problem is exceedingly complex and is well known to wildlife management experts in culturally advanced countries practicing conservation and management of native faunas and other natural resources. It is one of the perennial problems requiring education anew for each new generation, members of which think that they found where the last generation failed with wildlife transplantings of exotics (=foreigners). Such public pressure is invariably yielded to in due course by government agencies at both federal and state levels. Major headaches are caused by the unintended disappearances of the introduced foreigners across international boundaries, results not usually widely advertised by the country at fault. The problems are repetitive, the cure well known. The area lies roughly 1 per cent in biology and 99 per cent in politics.

4. Disease in The Desert

Few animals are studied more intensively or extensively than those involved in human disease. The animal vectors of human and animal diseases in deserts, whether such vectors are native species in the desert fauna or not, are under intensive study by medical groups throughout deserts of the world. Rarely, desert species are involved. Native mosquitoes (West Nile disease complex) and ticks (tick-borne Russian complex) are currently implicated in the important and exciting new work with virus diseases in the tropics (see review in Hunter, Frye, and Swartzwelder, 1966). These human diseases may eventually be found to involve desert species as well as other species in the desert faunas of the Saharo-Sindic megadesert and in the Turko-Gobi megadesert of central Asia.

Except in desert areas with high concentrations of humans (causing highly modified nondesert environmental conditions), the major tropical diseases of men and animals that are so prevalent in semiarid environments fall short at the desert edge. The reason for this situation is clear. Each such chain of events has a critical number of links necessary for successful transfer and infection of the obligate arthropod-transmitted and mollusc-borne diseases of man and other animals. Some of the links are particularly vulnerable, and the harshness of a natural desert environment readily breaks such disease chains. The probability of such a chain becoming reestablished in a desert without the advent of man's intervention, is, indeed, extremely low. These disease chains evolved in tropical and subtropical nondesert environments where they remain today. This is apparently the reason that the fungal, wind-transmitted American coccidioidomycosis is the only natural endemic "desert disease" of man. The natural desert environments long ago broke the tropical disease chains involving animals during the evolution of our present deserts out of tropical and subtropical communities with increasing subtropical desiccation late in Earth history.

Aside from animal vectors *etc.* that may or may not make disease in the desert an important problem in medical entomology, the question may be properly raised as to whether disease in the desert is a problem in desert biology rather than in general and veterinary medicine. Certainly most, if not all, human and animal diseases in deserts are extensions of their diseases elsewhere, occasionally magnified by the harshness of desert environments, and occasionally abetted by the meager living conditions of some native desert human populations.

It appears that a fairly strong case can be made for American coccidioidomycosis (valley fever) as primarily a desert disease. In any event, it is concluded that it is beyond reasonable doubt that desert animals (or domestic animals, or others), once thought to be implicated in its etiology, are not involved in this occasionally fatal disease. It is important to understand the comparative ecology of the desert geography that is involved on the two American continents, for it is undoubtedly not coincidence that endemicity of coccidioidomycosis appears to be distributed widely in the Sonoran Desert and its bordering desert areas (Lower Sonoran Life Zone) in North America, and in the Monte of the Monte-Patagonian Desert in South America. The *Monte* in Argentina is the South America counterpart of the *Sonoran Desert* in North America, separated by about 4,000 miles and sharing several of the same plant species (including creosotebush, *Larrea divaricata*), as well as the same life-form dominants. While the floras of these two widely separated areas are very similar, their vertebrate faunas are very distinctive; this fact indicates inability for long-distance dispersal on the part of the animals, before, during, and since the evolution of the deserts.

5. Limitations and Barriers

Regarding inventory or biological research on desert organisms, particularly native desert animals, it is not as important to point to what is known as it is to stress what is not known. There appears to be a unanimous consensus today that the manpower level of investigation in general ecology, behavior, and systematics is grossly inadequate. This is, indeed, a recurring theme in the writing of the current corps of investigators who have taken a world view of our state of knowledge on the increasingly important topic of deserts in general and desert biology in particular.

From the gross inadequacy of the manpower and financing of desert research in general ecology, behavior, and systematics, it is an obvious step to the increasing surge of interest in elucidating the mechanisms of adaptation of desert species in the study of their physiological ecology (environmental physiology, comparative physiology). From there, the next gap, to the technological studies on organisms that are directly in the way of man (involving pests and disease), is an enormously wide chasm, and there is little question that this vast gap between the "pure" and "applied" is ever increasing and will never be closed, whether it should be or not.

The reasons for such a vast and increasing knowledge gap are perfectly clear although infrequently discussed. Regarding the arid lands, the relevant expenditures, worldwide programs, and armies of workers in agriculture alone (that are concerned with species that constitute no more than 1 per cent of the desert fauna) enormously outweigh the skinny ranks of scientists and their puny financial support in their attempt to make fundamental discoveries about the other 99 per cent of the desert fauna. Add to this the human energies and funds poured into medicine and public health, which also aid intensive study of animals and plants of selected species, and the reasons for the pathetic disparity between the small number of animal species in the arid and semiarid environments that are being studied well, and the enormously large number of species that are not being studied at all (the ratio is on the order of several thousands to one) are clearly identified.

The picture can quickly become confused. It was recently stated that arid zone research is perhaps 50 years ahead of its application in the greater portion of the arid and semiarid zones, in the sense that the native desert peoples are, for many reasons, 50 years "behind." Such a completely utilitarian point of view of man's knowledge is, of course, irrelevant to man's search for knowledge in and of his Earth environment and that of other planets. Regarding the urgent need for greater creativity and greater emphasis on nonapplied problems in the study of desert biology, it could be added to the irrelevant argument above that music and art also are considerably more than 50 years ahead of their application in the greater portion of the arid and semiarid zones.

RECOMMENDATIONS

1. General

It should be emphasized that much research is needed on all aspects of the scientific study of desert faunas. In some instances a massive effort will be required to bring the level of knowledge to anywhere near adequate or good. On the basis of the record, which reveals serious inadequacies and gaps, with the general exception of that portion of the North American Desert within the United States, it is recommended that serious efforts be directed toward initiating and extending investigations in all deserts and in all species of environmental biology: taxonomy, morphology, physiology, genetics, ecology, and behavior.

2. Systematics and Ecology

An overall design for synthesis and research should be initiated for the following activities by experts on deserts:

    a) Information retrieval, reduction, and analysis

    b) Synthesis

    c) *Extensive* field survey

    d) Taxonomy

    e) *Intensive* field and laboratory study

    f) Resurvey

This outline for experimental designs to be constructed is recommended for work by one-desert teams, with the effort for all teams coordinated on a realistic time schedule. The concept of a one-desert team might be profitably extended in such cases as the Turko-Gobi megadesert and Saharo-Sindic megadesert to include more than one of the 13 major deserts in a team's work.

3. Poisonous Species

Critical knowledge of the poisonous species themselves commonly lags knowledge of their venoms. Lack of the former compromises the usefulness of the latter. The most important immediate problem is the insufficient knowledge in taxonomy. Awareness of the importance of this has recently penetrated medical ranks. It should be strongly recommended, therefore, that support for obtaining study collections and for their study be provided for the investigation of the distribution, taxonomy, and habits of the major groups of poisonous animals in the deserts. The record shows very clearly, in fact emphasizes in critical fashion, that such activities must be conducted by qualified zoologists and not by ordinary medical personnel. The necessity for this specific recommendation is especially emphasized by some past mistakes made by the United States Armed Forces. This work would be appropriately conducted (and ultimately benefited) as outlined in paragraph 2, Systematics and Ecology, above, allied with intensive programs of specialization.

4. Pests and Disease

Regarding the "transplanting" of foreign introductions (exotics) into natural desert communities, the obviously important recommendation to be made bears on (*1*) the costly process of international wildlife-moving, and (*2*) the unusually large and available record of failure. The government agencies at both the federal and state level, responsible for the sanctions and the funding of such potentially dangerous and worthless schemes, should resist under the shelter of the record and use the funds proposed for such schemes instead to educate the public in a persistent campaign that brings continuously before them the facts of both the dangers and lures of such projects. Insofar as I am aware, there is not a single, inexpensive or otherwise, government pamphlet or other publication directed to the facts in this problem published for public consumption in any country.

Regarding desert animals and desert farming, recommendations in order to anticipate and avert the dangers involved from potential native insect crop pests should follow the two main lines proposed by Uvarov (1962, p. 243):

    1) Before disturbance, the conduct of an intensive survey of the native insect fauna that feeds on wild plants should be undertaken in the region.

    2) A study of the types of land use already practiced in the area, or elsewhere where appropriate, should be conducted to determine the effects of the particular land use on the noxious insect fauna.

With the possible exception of a few especially noxious insects, animals involved in disease in the desert—a subject of general and veterinary medical importance—are undoubtedly the only native animal species in the desert that are receiving sufficient scientific attention.

5. Fauna as Food

Here, as elsewhere for knowledge of desert faunas, it is strongly recommended that long-term research efforts be initiated for needed detailed team-work within the deserts on (1) systematic inventory research, combined with (2) detailed ecological research. Regarding natural food sources in particular, this work is to be aimed at comprehensive knowledge of the occurrence, distribution, cryptic micro-environments, and habits of invertebrate and vertebrate desert animals, and the simplest techniques for obtaining them wholly by hand and with improvised primitive hand tools. Particularly in the Afro-Asian deserts and in Australia, this research should employ the assistance of aboriginal people of the area.

OVERVIEW

During the present century of biological investigation of desert organisms there was a change in emphasis from field work to laboratory work which paralleled that trend elsewhere in biology. More recently, however, and particularly during the present and past decades, there has been fuller recognition of the serious need for greater balance, and whether the questions are primarily genetic, physiologic, ecologic, or systematic in form, the organism-environment system has been given due consideration and examined in greater detail by a sharply increasing number of students of desert problems.

In environmental biology in general, and in the physiological ecology of native desert organisms in particular, it is *genetic adaptation* and *physiologic adjustment* that is being investigated. The functional mechanisms elucidated are those resulting from evolution. These problems are truly desert ones concerning desert species, and the mechanisms are often found to be unique in this unique and most recently evolved of our Earth environments. It is not surprising that information so gained on thermoregulation and water balance of such animals is of obvious importance to animal husbandry and to medical technology in arid lands. Agriculture and medicine benefit, but this is not the immediate objective of such experimental designs that investigate adaptation and evolution of native desert organisms that have already solved the problem of making a successful living in the desert.

The concern of most persons with the subject of poisonous animals, food, pests, and disease in the desert is largely or wholly an important extension of medical and agricultural practice elsewhere, in non-desert environments. In almost all cases, the native animals involved (except in food-gathering by aborigines) present drastically more serious problems in semiarid lands than in deserts. Pests in the desert and diseases in the desert are especially matters of general agriculture and general medicine. Shortcomings are obvious and many, and it can be safely predicted that future headaches and catastrophes during man's future "development" of the deserts will stem largely from his conspicuous lack of basic knowledge of the biology of desert species.

Our present inadequate knowledge of the ecology and systematics of desert animals makes the subject clearly one more for research than review. While there has been a noticeable upswing in physiological, behavioral, and ecological research on deserts, systematics by no means enjoys an equal share of the recent progress in desert biology. It cannot be overemphasized that our systematic knowledge of the faunas of deserts is especially inadequate, and some heroic efforts may now be necessary to correct this deficiency. It is not comforting for a desert biologist to look forward to a comprehensive understanding of desert-adapted organisms in the unique desert environment, and simultaneously recognize that the ranks of the systematists are now so relatively thinned that anything approaching a complete inventory of the great numbers of desert species that actually exist will soon be out of reach unless the situation is corrected. In addition to the land problems, strong emphasis also should be placed on scientific investigations of the desert fresh-water organisms and habitats, some of which have already disappeared from these unique environments in both hemispheres.

What is needed for desert biology is acceleration in both of two major activities in science: synthesis and research. In the biological sciences, synthesis is, on the whole, far more difficult to achieve than analysis. For deserts, the result is obvious—good syntheses for desert biology are rare as well as usually old. Moreover, the uncritical often confuse the mere activity of reviewing with that of synthesizing. The two bear only a temporal relationship in that one follows the other. I know of only one outstanding modern synthesis of data on desert animals. This is Schmidt-Nielsen's (1964a) recent *Desert Animals, Physiological Problems of Heat and Water*. Good modern syntheses, as distinct from reviews, are badly needed for world desert biology in (1) systematics and biogeography, (2) morphology, (3) general ecology, and, in relation to all of these, (4) evolution. One of the great syntheses in desert biology is Axelrod's (1950) discussion on evolution of the desert, based on plant materials.

PERTINENT PUBLICATIONS

This bibliography combines in one alphabetical sequence for simplicity both an annotated bibliography and a more inclusive reference list. Those works which it has been possible to determine are of particular significance or interest to this study within the limitations discussed in the chapter are annotated. Other competent works and best-available works on specific subjects and areas are listed without annotation; lack of annotation should not be construed as *necessarily* indicating a less important publication.

Abalos, J. W.
1963   Scorpions of Argentina. p. 111-117. *In* H. L. Keegan and W. V. Macfarlane, eds., Venomous and poisonous animals and noxious plants of the Pacific Region. Macmillan, New York.

Abalos, J. W. and I. Pirosky
1963   Venomous Argentine serpents: Ophidism and snake antivenim. p. 363-371. *In* H. L. Keegan and W. V. Macfarlane, eds., Venomous and poison animals and noxious plant of the Pacific Region. Macmillan, New York.

Adams, A. R. D. and B. C. Maegraith
1966   Clinical tropical diseases. 4th ed. Blackwell Scientific Publications, Oxford. 582 p.

Adolph, E. F. and D. B. Dill
1938   Observations on water metabolism in the desert. American Journal of Physiology 123:369-378.

Adolph, E. F. *et al.*
1947   Physiology of man in the desert. Interscience, New York. 357p.
Detailed report on a cooperative effort of the Rochester Desert Unit at the time of World War II, stimulated by desert problems in the physiological ecology of foot soldiers. Twenty-one chapters, primarily on water balance and thermoregulation of a large mammal in dry heat.

Ahmad, M.
1955   Termites of West Pakistan. Biologia (Lahore) 1(2):202-264.

————
1958   Key to the Indomalayan termites. Biologia (Lahore) 4:33-198.

Ahmad, T.
1940   A survey of the insect fauna of Afghanistan. I: General features of the country and its fauna. Indian Journal of Entomology (New Delhi) 2(2):159-176.

Ajello, L.
1967   Comparative ecology of respiratory mycotic disease agents. Bacteriological Reviews 31(1):6-24.
See Pappagianis (1967)

Ajello, L., *et al.*
1956   Ecological and epizootiological studies on canine coccidioidomycosis. American Veterinary Medical Association, Journal 129:485-490.

Akhtar, S. A.
1958   The rodents of West Pakistan. Pakistan Journal of Science 10(1):5-18, (2):79-90.

Albert, B. L. and T. F. Sellers, Jr.
1963   Coccidioidomycosis from fomites. Archives of Internal Medicine 112:253-261.

Aldrich, J. M.
1912a Larvae of a Saturniid moth used as food by California Indians. New York Entomological Society, Journal 20:28-31.

————
1912b Flies of the Leptid genus *Atherix* used as food by the California Indians. Entomological News 23:159-163.

Allen, D. L.
1954   Our wildlife legacy. Funk and Wagnalls Company, New York.
This unique volume brings together impressive world data (including much of that which pertains to arid and semiarid lands) bearing on the enormous failure of the international and local wildlife movers, and the threat they represent to stability in the ecosystems with which they tamper.

Allen, F. M.
1938   The tourniquet and local asphyxia. American Journal of Surgery 41:192-200.

————
1949   Venomous bites and stings. American Medical Association, Journal 143:616.

Allouse, B. E.
1954   A bibliography on the vertebrate fauna of Iraq and neighboring countries. I: Mammals. Iraq Natural History Museum, Publication 4.
An example of one of several bibliographies by Allouse on the fauna of the region, providing groundwork for an inventory of the species and a departure point for much-needed greater efforts in research on the biology of the desert species.

————
1956   A bibliography on the invertebrate fauna of Iraq and neighboring countries. V: Mollusca. Iraq Natural History Museum, Publication .8

————
1959   An illustrated key to the non-passerine families of birds in Iraq. Iraq Natural History Museum, Publication 17:1-16.

Amaral, A. do
1930   Lista remissiva dos ophidios da região neotrópica. Instituto Butantan, São Paulo, Memórias 4:129-271.

American Public Health Association
1965 The control of communicable diseases in man. 10th ed., edited by J. E. Gordon. New York. 282 p. This is a reference of major importance on all known communicable diseases in all areas of the world, arranged in four parts: (1) preventive measures, (2) control of patient contacts and the immediate environment, (3) epidemic measures, and (4) international measures. The knowledge for the major deserts is substantial, but very clearly less than subequal.

Anderson, N. L.
1954 Range land grasshoppers. Montana Stockgrower 26:36-37.

Anderson, N. L. and J. C. Wright
1952 Grasshopper investigations on Montana range lands. Montana Agricultural Experiment Station, Technical Bulletin 486. 46 p.

Anderson, R. M.
1934 Effect of the introduction of exotic animal forms. Pacific Science Congress, 5th, Canada, 1933, Proceedings 1:769-778.

Anderson, S. and J. K. Jones, eds.
1967 Recent mammals of the world; a synopsis of families. Ronald Press, New York. 453 p.

Anderson, S. C.
1963 Amphibians and reptiles of Iran. California Academy of Sciences, Proceedings 31:417-498.

Andrews, J. D.
1953 The danger of wildlife introductions. Garden Gossip, March.

Andrews, R. C.
1924 Living animals of the Gobi Desert. American Museum of Natural History, 3rd Central Asiatic Expedition. Natural History 24:150-159.
One of Andrews' several accounts of the Third Asiatic Expedition, on which reptiles, batrachians, fish, and mammals occupied the special attention of the zoologists of the expedition; this report is primarily on large mammals (illustrated).

1932 The new conquest of Central Asia. A narrative of the explorations of the Central Asiatic Expeditions in Mongolia and China, 1921-1930. I: Natural History of Central Asia. The American Museum of Natural History, New York. 678 p.
Provides especially important and carefully detailed data on distribution, relative abundance, population density, and general ecology of the faunas of Central Asia.

Angas, G. F.
1847 Savage life and scenes in Australia and New Zealand. 2d ed. Smith, Edler & Co., London, 2 vols.

Angel, F.
1950 Vie et moeurs des serpents. Payot, Paris. 319 p.

Anning, S. T.
1946 The etiology of desert sore. Royal Society of Tropical Medicine and Hygiene, Transactions 40:313-330.

Anonymous
1935 Locust meal available in Argentina. U.S. Department of Commerce, World Trade Notes on Chemicals and Allied Products 9:42.

Anonymous
1943 Effects of spider bites. Great Britain, War Office, Army Medical Department, Bulletin 27:4.

Anonymous
1952 Wild burros in California. Outdoor California 13(25):4-5.

Anonymous
1953 California's wild burros given legal protection. Outdoor California 14(20):2.

Anonymous
1954 The imported fire ant and how to control it. U.S. Department of Agriculture, Leaflet 350. 8 p.

Anonymous
1956 Protection against decay and termites in residential construction. Building Research Institute, Washington, D.C., Publication 448.

Anonymous
1958 Protection against termites and decay. p. K/11-K/14. *In* Minimum property standards for one and two living units. U.S. Federal Housing Administration, Washington, D.C., Publication 300.

Anonymous
1961 Status of feral burros in California. California Department of Fish and Game.

Archer, T. C. R.
1958 Medical problems of the operational infantry soldier in Malaya. Royal Army Medical Corps, London, Journal 104:1-13.

Armitage, H. M. and J. B. Steinweden
1945 Fumigation of California dates with methyl bromide. California State Department of Agriculture, Bulletin 34:101-107.

Arnold, G.
1926 A monograph of the Formicidae of South Africa. South African Museum, Capetown, Annals 23:191-295.

Asplund, K. K.
1967 Ecology of lizards in the relictual Cape Flora, Baja California. American Midland Naturalist 77:462-475.

Atkins, J. A., C. W. Wingo, and W. A. Sodeman
1957 Probable cause of necrotic spider bite in the Midwest. Science 126:73.

Atkins, J. A. *et al.*
1958 Necrotic arachnidism. American Journal of Tropical Medicine and Hygiene 7:165-184.

Auerbach, H.
1955 Geographic incidence of skin tumors. Argonne National Laboratory, Quarterly Report Biology and Medicine, October, p. 5-7.

Axelrod, D. I.
1950 Studies in late Tertiary paleobotany. VI: Evolution of desert vegetation in western North America. Carnegie Institution of Washington, Publication 590:215-306.
A milestone synthesis in desert biology; data and discussion on evolution of the desert, which is the youngest major Earth environment.

1958 Evolution of the Madro-Tertiary Geoflora. Botanical Review 24:433-509.
This monograph (and Axelrod, 1950) are milestone basic references indispensable to the student of the

systematics and evolution of the faunas and floras of the deserts.

Badcock, H. D.
1932 Arachnida from the Paraguayan Chaco. Linnean Society of London, Journal Zoology 38: 1-48.

Baegert, J.
1863 An account of the aboriginal inhabitants of the California peninsula (translated by C. Rau). Smithsonian Institution, Washington, Annual Report, p. 352-369.

Baerg, W. J.
1924 The effects of the venom of some supposedly poisonous arthropods. Entomological Society of America, Annals 17:343-352.

———
1929 Some poisonous arthropods of North and Central America. International Congress of Entomologists, 4th, Ithaca, Transactions 2:418-438.

———
1958 The tarantula, Lawrence, Kansas. 88p.

Bailey, F. L.
1940 Navajo foods and cooking methods. American Anthropologist 42:270-290.

Balachowsky, A. S.
1954 Sur l'origine et le développement des insectes nuisibles aux plantes cultivées dans les oasis du Sahara français. p. 90-103. In J. L. Cloudsley-Thompson, ed., Biology of deserts. Institute of Biology, London.

Balozet, L.
1956 Scorpion venoms and antiscorpion serum. In E. E. Buckley and N. Porges, eds., Venoms. American Association for the Advancement of Science, Publication 44:141-144.
Reviews early important work of Sergent and of Balozet in North Africa.

Banks, N.
1912 The structure of certain dipterous larvae with particular reference to those in human foods. U. S. Department of Agriculture, Bureau of Entomology, Technical Series 22:1-44.

Banks, N. and T. E. Snyder
1920 A revision of the Nearctic termites, with notes on biology and geographic distribution. U. S. National Museum, Bulletin 108, 228 p.

Barash, A. and J. H. Hoofien
1956 Reptiles of Israel. Hakibutz Hameuchad, Ltd., Jerusalem.

Barden, A. A., Jr.
1941 Distribution of the families of birds. Auk 58: 543-557.

Bargagli, P.
1877 Insetti commestibili. Lettura Nell. Società Entomologica Italiana, Revista Europaea-Riv. Internazionale n. s. 16:1-11.

Barme, M.
1963 Venomous sea snakes of Viet Nam and their venoms. p. 373-378. In H. L. Keegan and W. V. Macfarlane, eds., Venomous and poisonous animals of the Pacific region. Macmillan Company, New York. 456 p.

Barnes, D. F. and D. L. Lindgren
1947 Progress of work on beetle infestation in dates. Date Growers' Institute, Annual Report 24:3-4.

Barrett, C. L.
1950 Reptiles of Australia: crocodiles, snakes and lizards. Cassell, London. 168 p.

Basedow, H.
1925 The Australian aboriginal. F. W. Preece and Sons, Adelaide. 422 p.

Bates, G. L.
1939 Races of *Ammomanes deserti* in Arabia. Ibis, p. 743-746.

Beard, R. L.
1963 Insect toxims and venoms. Annual Review of Entomology 8:1-18.
The chemical and clinical nature of venomous secretions are reviewed and considered together with their physiological effects, primarily on man. The subject of urticating (stinging) hairs and spines is included, as is a section on allergic reactions.

Beck, M. D.
1929 Occurence of *Coccidioides immitis* in lesions of slaughtered animals. Society of Experimental Biology and Medicine, Proceedings 26:534-536.

Belanovskii, I.
1936 Laws of the mass increase of insect pests and meteorological factors (translated title). Zoologischeskii Zhurnal 15:187-216.

Bender, G. L.
1963 Native animals and plants as resources. In C. Hodge and P. C. Duisberg, eds., Aridity and man. American Association for the Advancement of Science, Publication 74:309-337.

Bennett, G.
1834 Wanderings in New South Wales, Batavia, Pedir Coast, Singapore, and China, being a journal of a naturalist. R. Bentley, London. 2 vols.

Bequaert, J. C.
1921 Insects as food. How they have augmented the food supply of mankind in early and recent times. American Museum of Natural History, Natural History 21:191-200.
This early paper was, for many years, a major reference on insects and other invertebrates used as human food.

———
1922 The predaceous enemies of ants. American Museum of Natural History, Bulletin 45:271-331.

———
1950 Studies in the Achatinidae, a group of African land snails. Harvard College, Museum of Comparative Zoology, Bulletin 105:1-216.
Snail game laws, season permits, size limits, and antagonism over snail territories in the Gold Coast (Ghana) are reported in this monograph on giant African snails.

Berensberg, H. P.
1907 The uses of insects as food delicacies, medicines, or in manufactures. Natal Agricultural Journal and Mining Record 10:757-762.

Berland, L.
1948 Les scorpions. Paris. 201 p.
A more than usually useful reference on the general biology, et al., of the scorpions.

Bernard, F.
1954 Rôle des insectes sociaux dans les terrains du Sahara. p. 104-111. In J. L. Cloudsley-Thompson, ed., Biology of deserts; proceedings of a symposium on the biology of hot and cold deserts. Institute of Biology, London. 223 p.

Betham, R. M.
1904 Notes on birds' nesting round Quetta, West Pakistan. Bombay Natural History Society, Journal 16:747-750; 17:828-832.

Bettley, F. R.
1943 Desert sore, a preliminary study. Royal Army Medical Corps, Journal 81:107-112.

Bigalke, R.
1937 The adulteration of the fauna and flora of our national parks. South African Journal of Science 43:221-225.

Biggs, H. E. J.
1937 Mollusca of the Iranian plateu. Journal of Conchology 20(12):342-350.

Blum, M. S. and J. P. Woodring
1962 Secretion of benzaldehyde and hydrogen cyanide by the millipede *Pachydesmus crassicutis* (Wood). Science 138:512.

Blunt, A.
1881 A pilgrimage to Nejd, the cradle of the Arab race. J. Murray, London. 2 vols.

Bodenheimer, F. S.
1940 The ecology of aphids in a sub-tropical climate. Congreso Internacional de Entomología, 6th, Madrid, 1935, 1:49-58.

——— 1942 Studies on the honey-bee and bee-keeping in Turkey. Turkish Ministry of Agriculture, Ankara.

——— 1951*a* Citrus entomology in the Middle East, with special reference to Egypt, Iran, Iraq, Palestine, Syria, Turkey. W. Junk, The Hague. 663 p.
An excellent recent review, and one of the most important on the subject with regard to desert environments.

——— 1951*b* Insects as human food. W. Junk, The Hague. 352 p.
World-wide coverage. An important recent work, especially for the deserts of the Old World. Extends in detail the work of the earlier biologists who expounded the enormous nutritive value of insects. Extensive original sources are given.

——— 1953 Problems of animal ecology and physiology in deserts. *In* Desert research, proceedings International Symposium held in Jerusalem, May 7-14, 1952, sponsored by the National Research Council of Israel and Unesco. Research Council of Israel, Special Publication 2:205-229.

——— 1954 Problems of physiology and ecology of desert animals. p. 162-167. *In* J. L. Cloudsley-Thompson, ed., Biology of deserts; proceedings of a symposium on the biology of hot and cold deserts. Institute of Biology, London. 223 p.

——— 1957 The ecology of mammals in arid zones. *In* Human and animal ecology, reviews of research. Unesco, Paris. Arid Zone Research 8:100-137.
One of the few reviews for a vertebrate class considered across the deserts of the world. Includes discussions and conclusions for faunal groups in arid lands in the broad sense, as well as for deserts in particular. There are 154 references.

Bogen, E.
1926 Arachnidism. Archives of Internal Medicine 38:623.

——— 1956 The treatment of spider bite poisoning. *In* E. E. Buckley and N. Porges, eds., Venoms. American Association for the Advancement of Science, Publication 44:101-105.

Bogen, E. and R. N. Loomis
1936 Poisoning poisonous spiders. California Western Medicine 45:31.

Bogert, C. M.
1941 The Hopi snake dance, American Museum of Natural History, Natural History 47:276-283.

——— 1943 Dentitional phenomena in cobras and other Elapids with notes on adaptive modification of fangs. American Museum of Natural History, Bulletin 81:285-360.

Bogert, C. M. and R. M. del Campo
1956 The Gila monster and its allies. American Museum of Natural History, Bulletin 109:1-238.
A recent monograph giving extensive original sources in treating the general biology of the family Helodermatidae, comprised of *Heloderma suspectum* and *H. horridum;* these are the only 2 poisonous lizards known. Includes information on taxonomy, morphology, geographic and ecologic distribution, natural history, behavior, the bite, venom, etc.

Bogert, C. M. and J. A. Oliver
1945 A preliminary analysis of the herpetofauna of Sonora. American Museum of Natural History, Bulletin 83:297-426.

Boisseau, G. and G. Lanorville
1931 L'escargot; élevage et parcage lucratifs, préparation culinaire et vente. Librairie Hachette et Cie, Paris.
Gives extensive original sources on snails as human food.

Bonnet, P.
1945 Bibliographia Araneorum. Vol. 1. Les Frères Douladoure, Toulouse.
A basic and extremely comprehensive bibliography arranged variously by subject, author and geographical area —for spiders and their allies, and for the major world students (with photographs) of the animal group. Fortunately there are more of these bibliographic monographs for the invertebrates (than the vertebrates) which on the whole have a more diverse if not larger pertinent literature that is more difficut to work.

Bons, J. and B. Girot
1962 Clé illustrée des reptiles du Maroc. Institut Scientifique Chérifien, Travaux, sér. Zoologie 26:1-62

Borror, D. J. and D. M. DeLong
1964 An introduction to the study of insects. Rev. ed. Holt, Rinehart and Winston, New York. 819 p.

Boulenger, G. A.
1896 Catalogue of the snakes in the British Museum (Natural History). III: Colubriadae (Opisthoglyphae and Proteroglyphae), Amblycephalidae, and Viperidae. British Museum (Natural History), London. 727 p.
The three-volume set remains the only work of its kind. It is still one of the most important references from which one is able to construct the outlines of the serpent

faunas of many of the deserts. Such is a repeatedly sad commentary on our state of knowledge for most of the animal groups in most of the deserts of the world. This volume brought to a close a series of works which all zoologists acknowledge today, as they did then, to be of primary importance in the history of systematic science in biology. The series consists of nine volumes: *Catalogue of Batrachia Salientia*, published in 1882; *Catalogue of Batrachia Gradientia*, also in 1882; *Catalogue of Lizards*, vol. i 1885, vol. ii 1885, vol. iii 1887; *Catalogue of Chelonians, Rhynchocephalians, and Crocodiles*, 1889; and *Catalogue of Snakes*, vol. i 1893, vol. ii 1894, and vol. iii 1896.

Bowman, F. T.
1956   Citrus-growing in Australia. Angus and Robertson, Sydney. 311 p.

Boyd, M. F., ed.
1949   Malariology. W. B. Saunders Co., Philadelphia 2 vols.
A comprehensive survey of all aspects of this group of diseases from a global viewpoint, by 65 contributors.

Boyden, B. L.
1941   Eradication of the parlatoria date scale in the United States. U. S. Department of Agriculture, Miscellaneous Publication 433. 62 p.

Broadley, D. G.
1959   The herpetology of Southern Rhodesia. I: Snakes. Harvard University, Museum of Comparative Zoology, Bulletin 120:1-100.
A detailed systematic account, important to the Somali Desert and adjoining regions. It is a good model of the kind of systematic review that is needed for little-known animal groups in little-known geographic areas; maps are provided of recorded localities of the species (in this case only for Rhodesia).

Brown, A. W. A.
1951   Insect control by chemicals. John Wiley and Sons, Inc., New York. 817 p.

Brown, E. S.
1947   The distribution and vegetation of egg-laying sites of the Desert Locust (*Schistocerca gregaria* Forsk.) in Tripolitania in 1946. Société Fouad I d'Entomologie, Bulletin 31:287-306.

Brues. C. T.
1946   Insect dietary. Harvard University Press, Cambridge. 466 p.
Contains a special chapter on insects as human food.

Bryden, H. A.
1936   Wild life in South Africa. G. G. Harrap and Co., Ltd., London. 282 p.

Brygoo, E.
1946   Essai de bromatologie entomologique: Les insects commestibles. Thèse de Doctorat Bergerac, Impr. Trillaud.

Bücherl, W.
1946   Ação do veneno dos escolopendromorfos do Brasil sôbre alguns animais de laboratorio. Instituto Butantan, São Paulo, Memórias 19:181-197.

———
1956   Scorpions and their effects in Brazil. IV: Observations on insecticides lethal to scorpions and other methods of control. Instituto Butantan, Sao Paulo, Memórias 27:107-120.

Buckley, E. E. and N. Porges, eds.
1956   Venoms, papers presented at the first international conference on venoms, December 27-30, 1954, at the annual meeting of the American Association for the Advancement of Science, Berkeley. Publication 44. 466 p.
Papers are highly varied in scope, depth, and usefulness; many contribute summary and/or new information on species that occur in the deserts.

Burr, M.
1954   The insect legion. 2d ed. James Nisbet and Co., Ltd., London. 336 p.
This work contains a special part on insects as human food.

Burt, E.
1947   Exudate from millipedes, with particular reference to its injurious effects. Tropical Disease Bulletin 44:7-12.
Report on species of North American *Chilognatha* capable of producing irritating effects.

Burtt, B. D.
1942   Some East African vegetation communities. Journal of Ecology 30:62-146.

Buxton, P. A.
1920   Insect pests of the date palm in Mesopotamia and elsewhere. Bulletin of Entomological Research 11:287-303.

———
1921   Animal ecology in deserts. Cambridge Philosophical Society, Proceedings 20:388-392.

———
1923   Animal life in deserts, a study of the fauna in relation to environment. Arnold, London, 176 p.
A much referred to, greatly overrated, highly personalized monograph and major reference for a quarter century, which contains much useful and some faulty information.

———
1924   Heat moisture and animal life in deserts. Royal Society of London, Proceedings, Series B, 96:123-131.

Byalynitskii-Birulya, A. A.
1917a   Arthrogastric arachnids of Caucasia. I: Scorpions (translated title). Originally published by Caucasian Museum, Tiflis, as a number of its Annals. Issued 1964 in translation by Israel Program for Scientific Translations, Jerusalem. 178 p.
Treats the scorpion fauna of the Caucasian Region. Contains detailed information on the taxonomy, peculiarities, relationships to related species, and the distribution and mode of life of the scorpions of the region.

———
1917b   Fauna of Russia and adjacent countries. Arachnoidea. I: Scorpions (translated title). Originally published by the Imperial Academy of Sciences, Petrograd, Zoological Museum. Issued 1965 in translation by Israel Program for Scientific Translations, Jerusalem. 176 p.
Summarizes most of available data on the subject from many aspects, and deals in detail with the anatomy, physiology and biology of scorpions as well as taxonomy, ecology and zoogeographical distribution of contemporary and extinct species. Although monographs on the subject have since appeared, mostly on local species, this is the only work of its kind on scorpions. While obviously in need of revision, by the numerous fields encompassed,

the thorough analysis of bibliographical data available at the time, and the critical review on basic principles in taxonomy, this treatise on scorpions remains of considerable importance.

Cachan, P.
1949 Les termites de Madagascar. Institut Scientifique de Madagascar, Mémoires, sér. A (Biologie Animale), 3:177-275.

Cadart, J.
1955 Les escargots (*Helix pomatia* L. et *Helix aspersa* M.); biologie, élevage, parcage, histoire, gastronomie, commerce. P. Lechevalier, Paris. 420 p. (Savoir en Histoire Naturelle, 24)
On the two common European garden snails that are, unfortunately, widely dispersed in the world. Gives extensive original sources on snails as human food.

Caffrey, D. J.
1918 Notes on the poisoning urticating spines of *Hemileuca olivia* larvae. Journal of Economic Entomology 11:363-367.

Cahalane, V. H.
1955 Some effects of exotics on nature. p. 396-405. *In* International Technical Conference on the Protection of Nature, Proceedings. Unesco, Paris.

Calvert, A. F.
1894 The aborigines of Western Australia. Simpkin, Marshall, Hamilton, Kent and Co., Ltd., London. 55p.

Campbell, C. H.
1964 Venomous snake-bite in Papua and its treatment with tracheotomy, artificial respiration and antivenene. Royal Society of Tropical Medicine and Hygiene, Transactions 58:263-273.

Campbell, T. G.
1926 Insect foods of the aborigines. Australian Museum Magazine 2:407-410.

Cansdale, G. S.
1961 West African snakes. Longmans, London. 74 p.

Capot-Rey, R.
1953 L'Afrique blanche française. II: Le Sahara français. Presses Universitaires de France, Paris. 564 p.
Man is the principal animal discussed in this valuable general survey of the Saharan environment, its past and present climate, and the landscapes it controls in conjugation with the desert physiography and soils. This is largely a man-oriented monograph on the Sahara, and Capot-Rey makes a case for man's role in extending the desert.

Caro, M. R., V. J. Derbes, and R. C. Jung
1957 Skin responses to the sting of the imported fire ant (*Solenopsis saevissima*). Archives of Dermatology 75:475-488.

Carruthers, D. (i.e., A.D.M.)
1914 Unknown Mongolia, a record of travel and exploration in northwest Mongolia and Dzungaria. 2nd ed. Hutchinson and Co., London. 659 p. in 2 vols.
Bibliography: p. 635-639.

Carson, R. L.
1962 Silent spring. Houghton Mifflin, Boston. 368 p.
In this indictment of modern man, Rachael Carson summarizes her timely message with a quotation from Albert Schweitzer: "Man has lost the capacity to foresee and to forestall. He will end by destroying the earth." Since the mid-1940's over 200 basic chemicals (synthetic insecticides, herbicides, *etc.*) have been created by man for killing native animals described by him as "pests." The use of these "elixirs of death" in marginally balanced desert ecosystems, as elsewhere, is widespread and enormously destructive. She concludes, "Along with the possibility of the extinction of mankind by nuclear war, the central problem of our age has therefore become the contamination of man's total environment with such substances of incredible potential for harm—substances that accumulate in the tissues of plants and animals and even penetrate the germ cells to shatter or alter the very material of heredity upon which the shape of the future depends." There is little question that *Silent Spring* is one of the most important single studies in ecology and ecosystematics that has been published in the English language.

Castetter, E. F. and M. E. Oppler
1936 Ethnobiological studies in the American Southwest. III: The ethnobiology of the Chiricahua and Mescalero Apache. University of New Mexico Bulletin 297, Biological series 4(5):3-63.

Castetter, E. F. and R. M. Underhill
1935 Ethnobiological studies in the American Southwest. II: The ethnobiology of the Papago Indians. University of New Mexico Bulletin 275, Biological series 4(3):1-84.

Castleberry, M. W., J. L. Converse, and J. E. Del Favero
1963 Coccidioidomycosis transmission to infant monkey from its mother. Archives of Pathology 75:459-461.
If confirmed, this constitutes the first substantial evidence contrary to the established consensus that all infections are traced back to the soil (see Ajello, 1967)—usually the soils of arid and semiarid lands.

Centre d'Etudes et d'Informations des Problèmes Humains dans les Zones Arides (PROHUZA)
1960 Journées d'information médico-sociales Sahariennes. Paris.

Chamberlin, R. V. and R. L. Hoffman
1958 Checklist of the millipeds of North America. U.S. National Museum, Bulletin 212. 236 p.

Chamberlin, R. V.
1920 The myriopoda of the Australian region. Harvard University, Museum of Comparative Zoology, Buletin 64(1).

Chamberlin, R. V. and W. Ivie
1935 The black widow spider and its varieties in the United States. University of Utah, Bulletin, Biological ser. 3:1-29.
An interesting if not entirely successful early attempt to recognize subspecies in the variation of *L. mactans* across the conterminous United States.

Chamberlain, W. F. and W. M. Hoskins
1949 The toxicity and repellence of organic chemicals towards termites, and their use in termite-proofing packages. Hilgardia 19:285-307.

Champion, G. C.
1892 Meloidae. Biologia Centrali-Americana, Insecta, Coleoptera, Heteromera, 4(2):364-450, pl. 17-21.

Chapin, J. P.
1924 Profiteers of the busy bee. Observations on the honey guides of Africa. American Museum of Natural History 24:328-336.

Chapman, F. M.
1927 Descriptions of new birds from northwestern Peru and western Colombia. American Museum Novitates 250:1-7.

Chapman, R. N. *et al.*
1926 Studies in the ecology of sand dune insects. Ecology 7:416-426.

Chew, R. M.
1961 Water metabolism of desert-inhabiting vertebrates. Cambridge Philosophical Society, Biological Reviews 36:1-31.
Amphibians, reptiles, birds, and mammals. Behavioral and physiological adjustments, water balance, thermoregulation, and general ecology. An excellent review.

Christensen, G. C.
1963 Sand grouse released in Nevada found in Mexico. Condor 65(1):67-68.
The Indian sand grouse was imported from the Thar Desert to the North American Desert. All of the 1,400 birds released disappeared. This is a rare report on a common failure—the unintended disappearance of introduced foreign animals across international boundaries, results not usually widely advertised by the country at fault.

Christensen, P. A.
1955 South African snake venoms and antivenoms. South African Institute for Medical Research, Johannesburg. 129 p.
Classification, p. 1.

Cilento, R. W.
1944 Some poisonous plants, sea and land animals of Australia and New Guinea. W. R. Smith and Robertson Pty., Brisbane.

Clark, S. W.
1931 The control of fire ants in the lower Rio Grande Valley. Texas Agricultural Experiment Station, Bulletin 435.

Clausen, C. P.
1936 Insect parasitism and biological control. Entomological Society of America, Annals 29:201-223.

—— 1940 Entomophagous insects. McGraw-Hill, N.Y. 688 p.

Cloudsley-Thompson, J. L.
1949 Notes on Arachnida, 12. Mating habits of *Hasarius adansoni* Sav. Entomologists' Monthly Magazine 85:261-262.

—— 1951 Notes on Arachnida, 16. The behavior of a scorpion. Entomologists' Monthly Magazine 86:105.

—— 1954 Biology of deserts; proceedings of a symposium on the biology of hot and cold deserts. Institute of Biology, London. 223 p.
The volume contains 28 papers, and discussions, presented at a conference, "The Biology and Productivity of Hot and Cold Deserts," London, in a symposium with sessions devoted to climate and physiological environment, plant ecology, entomology and ecology, economic aspects, mammalian physiology and ecology.

—— 1955 The biology of woodlice. Discovery 16:248-251.

—— 1958 Spiders, scorpions, centipedes and mites. Pergamon Press, New York.
This ecology and natural history of woodlice (pillbugs),

centipedes, and arachnids is an excellent work that treats structure, classification, distribution, and physiological and general ecology.

—— 1962 Bioclimatic observations in the Red Sea hills and coastal plain, a major habitat of the desert locust. Royal Entomological Society, Proceedings 37:1-36.

—— 1964 Terrestrial animals in dry heat: Arthropods. *In* D. B. Dill, E. F. Adolph, and C. G. Wilber, eds., Adaptation to the environment. American Physiological Society, Washington, D. C., Handbook of Physiology 4:451-465.
An excellent recent review for invertebrate animals.

Cloudsley-Thompson, J. L. and M. J. Chadwick
1964 Life in deserts. G. T. Foulis and Co., London. 218 p.

Cobbold, E.
1935 Kenya, the land of illusion. J. Murray, London 236 p.

Cochran, D. M.
1943 Poisonous reptiles of the world, a wartime handbook. Smithsonian Institution, Washington. 37 p. (War Background Studies 10)

—— 1944 Dangerous reptiles. Smithsonian Institution, Washington, Annual Report 1943:275-323.
A reprint, with extensive revision and additional plates from Cochran (1943).

Cockerell, T. D. A.
1899 Some insect pests of Salt River Valley and the remedies for them. Arizona Agricultural Experiment Station, Bulletin 32:273-295.

Cole, A. C.
1933 Ant communities of a section of the sagebrush semi-desert in Idaho with special reference to the vegetation (Hymenoptera formicidae). Entomological News 44:16-19.

Collinge, W. E.
1935 Woodlice, their folklore and local names. Northwestern Naturalist 10:19-21.
An account of the numerous confusing vernaculars for these little-known terrestrial arthropods (sowbug, pillbug, slater, cud-worm, *et al,*), which are preadapted and further specialized for successful living in certain desert microenvironments.

Comstock, J. H.
1949 Introduction to entomology. 9th ed., rev. Comstock Publishing Company, Inc., Ithaca, New York. 1064 p.

Conant, R.
1958 A field guide to reptiles and amphibians of the United States and Canada east of the 100th meridian. Houghton Mifflin Co., Boston. 366 p.
This illustrated field guide contains maps and colored illustrations in addition to descriptions, ecological notes, ranges, *etc.,* for species in the eastern U.S. The companion volume for the western U.S. is Stebbins (1966). Overlap in the species treated in the two books is along the 100th meridian (Texas).

Condamin, M.
1958 Snakes collected by the Institut Français d'Afrique Noire in 1956. Institut Français d'Afrique Noire, Bulletin 20A 1:243-262.

Connolly, M.
1939 A monographic survey of South African non-marine Mollusca. South African Museum, Annals 33:1-660.
This is a basic and classical comprehensive monograph on a large terrestrial and fresh water aquatic snail fauna. It is an unusual systematic treatise that illustrates all species yet unfigured, those species previously figured inadequately or in publication of little accessibility, and the especially difficult species where split.

Corkill, N. L.
1932 Snakes and snake bite in Iraq: a handbook for medical officers. Baillière, Tindall and Cox, London, 50 p.

_____ 1935 Notes on Sudan snakes. Sudan Government Museum, Natural History, Khartoum, Publication 3. 40 p.

_____ 1956 Snake poisoning in the Sudan. *In* E. E. Buckley and N. Porges, eds., Venoms. American Association for the Advancement of Science, Publication 44:331-339.

Cornwall, J. W.
1916 Some centipedes and their venom. Indian Journal of Medical Research 3:541-557.

Cowan, F.
1865 Curious facts in the history of insects. J. B. Lippincott and Co., Philadelphia. 396 p.

Cowan, F. T.
1958 Trends in grasshopper research in the United States. International Congress of Entomologists, 10th, Montreal, 1956, Proceedings 3:55-58.

Cowles, R. B.
1937 The San Diegan alligator lizard and the black widow spider. Science 85(2195):99-100.
This unusual early paper on *Latrodectus* reports that the alligator lizard (*Gerrhonotus*) in California is a successful and natural predator on the black widow. Species of *Gerrhonotus* occur in many other western states, although none is a desert species.

Cranbrook, The Earl of
1959 The feeding habits of the water shrew, *Neomys fodiens bicolor* Shaw, in captivity and the effect of its attack upon its prey. Zoological Society of London, Proceedings 133:245-249.

Creighton, W. S.
1950 The ants of North America. Harvard University Museum of Comparative Zoology, Bulletin 104. 585 p.

Croce-Spinelli, M. and G. Lambert
1961 S. O. S. Sahara. Flammarion, Paris. 215 p. (Collection L'Actuel)

Crum, C. W. R.
1906 Treatment of the bites of copperhead snakes. American Medical Association, Journal 46:1433-1444.
Describes the failure and danger of the use of cryotherapy (icing or other "refrigeration" of tissue) for snakebite treatment. This was the first decisive warning published in the *JAMA* itself. This work was known but ignored a half-century later in questionable work by persons outside of the AMA who produced a grave confusion that still persists (*see* Stahnke, 1953).

Cunningham, P. M.
1827 Two years in New South Wales. Henry Colburn, London. 2 vols.

Cuthbertson, A.
1934 Note on the swarming of Pentatomid-bugs. Nada, 38 p. Ann. Native Affairs Department, Southern Rhodesia.

Daguin, E.
1900 Les insectes comestibles dans l'antiquité et de nos jours. Naturaliste: 1-27.

Dammann, A. E.
1961 Some factors affecting the distribution of sympatric species of rattlesnakes (genus *Crotalus*) in Arizona. University of Michigan. 105 p. (Ph. D. dissertation)

Darlington, P. J.
1957 Zoogeography: the geographical distribution of animals. John Wiley and Sons, Inc., New York.

Das, S.
1945 Locusts as food and manure. Indian Farming 6:412.

Davatchi, A.
1955 The obnoxious insects of Persia (translated title). Teheran University, Publication 211. 248 p. In Persian.

Davey, J. T.
1959 Report on a visit to the Blue Nile and Kassala Provinces of the Republic of the Sudan. International Migratory Locust Organization, Paris (unpublished report)

Davis, B. L., R. T. Smith, and C. E. Smith
1942 An epidemic of coccidioidal infection (coccidioidomycosis). American Medical Association. Journal 118:1182-1186.

Davis, C. L., G. W. Stiles, Jr., and A. N. McGregor
1937 Pulmonary coccidioidal granuloma; a new site of infection in cattle. American Veterinary Medical Association, Journal 91:209-215.

Davis, G. S.
1953 Respite for the burro. Nature 46(7):370-374.
This remarkable paper takes an emotional stand in opposition to the recommendations of scientists and wildlife technicians, such as those reported at the Death Valley Desert Bighorn Council (*see* Sumner, 1959). "The wild desert burros are humble but living symbols of the old West and do not deserve the persecution they have been receiving."

Dawson, J.
1881 Australian aborigines, the languages and customs of several tribes of aborigines in the western district of Victoria, Australia. G. Robertson, Melbourne. 111 p.

Dawson, W. R. and K. Schmidt-Nielsen
1964 Terrestrial animals in dry heat: Desert birds. *In* D. B. Dill, E. F. Adolph, and C. G. Wilber, eds., Adaptations to the environment. American Physiological Society, Washington, D. C., Handbook of Physiology 4:481-492.

Day, A. M.
1948 Introduction of exotic species. U. S. Department of the Interior, Fish and Wildlife Service. 13 p.

De Castro, A. B.
1921   The poison of the Scolopendridae, being a special reference to the Andaman species. Indian Medical Gazette 56:207-209.

deHaas, C. P. J.
1950   Checklist of the snakes of the Indo-Australian Archipelago (Reptiles, Ophidia). Treubia 20(3): 311-625.

Dementev, G. P.
1962   Monograph on the ornithology of the Gobi Desert (translated title). Ornithology 4:376-382.
In Russian.

Den Boer, P. J.
1961   The ecological significance of activity pattern in the woodlouse *Parcellio scaber*. Archives Neerlandaises de Zoologie 14:283-409.

Deoras, P. J.
1961   A study of scorpions: their distribution, incidence, and control in Maharashtra. Probe 1:45-54.

Deraniyagala, P. E. P.
1960   The taxonomy of the cobras of South Eastern Asia. Spolia Zeylanica (Colombo) 29:41-63.

———
1961   The taxonomy of the cobras of South Eastern Asia, II. Spolia Zeylanica (Colombo) 29:205-232.

De Vos, A., R. H. Manville, and R. G. Van Gelder
1956   Introduced mammals and their influence on native biota. Zoologica 41(4):163-194.

Di Caporiacco, L.
1939   Scorpioni, pedipalpi, salifughi e chernetidi di Somalia e Dancalia. Museo Civico di Storia Natur di Genova, Annali 59:135.

Dickson, H. R. P.
1949   The Arab of the desert. A glimpse into Badawin life in Kuweit and Saudia Arabia. Allen and Unwin, London. 648 p.

Dill, D. B., E. F. Adolph, and C. G. Wilber, eds.
1964   Handbook of physiology. IV: Adaptation to the environment. American Physiological Society, Washington, D. C. 1056 p.
A critical, comprehensive presentation of physiological knowledge and concepts on genetic adaptation and physiological adjustment (acclimation, *etc.*) in animals and man. Several of the 65 chapters review and interpret reports on desert animals; see especially chapters 29-35 on terrestrial animals in dry heat.

Dill, D. B., A. V. Bock, and H. T. Edwards
1933   Mechanisms for dissipating heat in man and dog. American Journal of Physiology 104:36-43.

Dillon, L. S.
1952   The Meloidae (Coleoptera) of Texas. American Midland Naturalist 48:330-420.

Ditmars, R. L.
1931   Snakes of the world. Macmillan Company, New York. 207 p.
A popular account that was for many years the most available reference (with illustration) on the snakes of the world. It contains information (not with great detail or coverage, however) on species in deserts.

Dodge, N. N.
1952   Poisonous dwellers of the desert. Southwest Monuments Association, Globe, Arizona.

Dolgushin, I. A.
1957   On the history of the avifauna of Kazakhstan translated title). Akademiia Nauk Kazakhskoi SSR, Alma-Ata, Izvestiia, ser. Biologicheskaya 2:3-14.
In Russian.

Donisthrop, H.
1945   Ants as carriers of disease. Entomologists' Monthly Magazine 81:185.

Dornan, S. S.
1925   Pygmies and Bushmen of the Kalahari. Seeley, Service & Co., Ltd., London. 318 p.

Doughty, C. M.
1926   Travels in Arabia Deserta. With an introduction by T. E. Lawrence. Jonathan Cape & The Medici Society, Ltd., London. 623, 690 p. 2 vols. in 1.
Accounts of many animals that are now extinct or nearly so in the Arabian Desert, both invertebrates and vertebrates—cold-blooded and warm-blooded—(*e.g.* ostrich, white oryx, desert stream fishes).
...there is no need at this time of day to commend Doughty to students. They all know of him. It is to the outside public, willing to read a great prose work, the record of the wanderings of an English poet for two years among the Beduins, that this edition must make its appeal, and perhaps with them that the verdict of present-day travellers in Arabia will have weight. I have talked the book over with many travellers, and we are agreed that here you have all the desert, its hills and plains, the lava fields, the villages, the tents, the men and animals. They are told off to the life, with words and phrases fitted to them so perfectly that one cannot dissociate them in memory. It is the true Arabia, the land with its smells and dirt, as well as its nobility and freedom. There is no sentiment, nothing merely pituresque, that most common failing of oriental travel-books. Doughty's completeness is devastating. There is nothing we would take away, little we could add. He took all Arabia for his province, and has left to his successors only the poor part of specialists. We may write books on parts of the desert or some of the history of it; but there can never be another picture of the whole, in our time, because here it is all said, and by a great master . . . .   —T. E. Lawrence

Dubos, R. J. and J. G. Hirsch, eds.
1965   Bacterial and mycotic infections of man. 4th ed. Lippincott, Philadelphia. 1025 p.

Duvigneaud, P.
1950   The introduction of exotic species. *In* International Technical Conference on the Protection of Nature, Lake Success, 1949, Proceedings and Papers. Unesco, Paris.

Ealand, C. A.
1915   Insects and man. Grant Richards, Ltd., London. 344 p.
This book contains a special chapter on insects as human food.

Ebeling, W.
1949   Subtropical entomology. Lithotype Process Company, San Francisco. 747 p.

Eckert, J. K. and A. Mallis
1937   Ants and their control in California. California Agricultural Experiment Station, Circular 342.

Edney, E. B.
1951 The evaporation of water from woodlice and the millipede *Glomeris*. Journal of Experimental Biology 28:91-115.

1954 Woodlice and the land habitat. Biological Reviews 29:185-219.

1957 The water relations of terrestial arthropods. Cambridge, England. 108 p. (Cambridge Monographs in Experimental Biology, 5)
A monograph on the physiological ecology of water-balance and thermoregulation. Physics of evaporation and the saturation deficit, transpiration and cuticle structure, excretion and osmoregulation, water and thermoregulation.

1960 The survival of animals in hot deserts. Smithsonian Institution, Washington, Annual Report 1959: 407-425.

Edwards, P. Q. and C. E. Palmer
1957 Prevalence of sensitivity to coccidioidin with special reference to specific and nonspecific reactions to coccidioidin and to histoplasmin. Diseases of the Chest 31:3-28.

Efrati, P.
1949 Poisoning by scorpion stings in Israel. American Journal of Tropical Medicine 29:249-257.

Egeberg, R. O., A. F. Elconin, and M. C. Egeberg
1964 Effect of salinity and temperature on *Coccidioides immitis* and three antagonistic soil saprophytes. Journal of Bacteriology 88:473-476.

Egeberg, R. O. and A. F. Ely
1955 *Coccidioides immitis* in the soil of the southern San Joaquin Valley. p. 311-315. *In* T. H. Sternberg and V. D. Newcomer, eds., Therapy of fungus diseases. Little, Brown and Company, Boston. 337 p.

Egler, F. E.
1964 Pesticides in our ecosystem. American Scientist 52(1):110-136.
Refers to the faunas and floras of all environments, aquatic and terrestrial, including deserts, An indictment of man who is inexorably destroying the resource base of his life on planet Earth (*see* Carson, 1962).

Elconin, A. F., R. O. Egeberg, and M. C. Egeberg
1964 Significance of soil salinity on ecology of *Coccidioides immitis*. Journal of Bacteriology 87:500-503.

Emerson, A. E.
1955 Geographical origins and dispersions of termite genera. Fieldiana, Zoology, 37:465-521.

Emmons, C. W.
1942 Isolation of *Coccidioides immitis* from soil and rodents. U. S. Public Health Report 57:109-111.

1943 Coccidioidomycosis in wild rodents. A method for determining the extent of endemic areas. U. S. Public Health Report 58:1-5.

Emmons, C. W. and L. L. Ashburn
1942 The isolation of *Haplosporangum parvum* n. sp. and *Coccidioides immitis* from wild rodents, their relationship to coccidioidomycosis. U. S. Public Health Report 57:1715-1727.

Emmons, C. W., C. H. Binford, and J. P. Utz
1963 Medical mycology. Lea Febiger, Philadelphia. 380 p.

Emory, J. A. and F. E. Russell
1961 Studies with cooling measures following injection of *Crotalus venom*. Copeia 3:322-326.

Essig, E. O.
1931 A history of entomology. Macmillan Company, New York.

1934 The value of insects to the California Indians. Scientific Monthly 38:181-186.

1958 Insects and mites of western North America. The Macmillan Co., New York.
This illustrated manual, textbook, and handbook for students, entomologists, agriculturists, foresters, farmers, gardeners, and naturalists contains species accounts of the common arachnids as well as the common insects. This is one of the few general entomologies which give specific information for many species in the North American Desert.

Etchecopar, R. D. and F. Hüe
1957 Données écologiques sur l'avifaune de la zone désertique arabo-saharienne / Ecological data on the avifauna of the Arabo-Saharian desert zone. *In* Human and animal ecology, reviews of research. Unesco, Paris. Arid Zone Research 8:138-163.
An excellent recent review of ecological data on the birds of the Arabo-Saharian desert zone. Includes discussion and some conclusions for faunal groups in arid lands and provides a valuable overview.

Evans, J. W.
1952 The injurious insects of the British Commonwealth. Commonwealth Institute of Entomology, London. 242 p.
The pertinent geographic coverage includes Africa, Asia, Australia, North America, and South America. The following subjects (and others) are treated for each area: insects of medical and veterinary importance, insect and crop associations, insect pests of agriculture and forestry, insect control.

Ewing, H. E.
1928 Observations on the habits and the injury caused by bites and stings of some common North American arthropods. American Journal of Tropical Medicine 8:39-62.

Exline, H.
1950 Spiders of the Rhoicininae (Pisauridae) from western Peru and Ecuador. American Museum Novitates 1470:1-13.

Eylmann, E.
1908 Die eingeborenen der Kolonie Südaustralien. D. Reimer, Berlin. 494 p.

Fagan, M. M.
1918 The uses of insect galls. American Naturalist 52:155-176.

Faure, J. C.
1944 Pentatomid bugs as human food. Entomological Society of Southern Africa, Journal 7:110-112.

Fernald, H. T. and H. H. Shepard
1955 Applied entomology; an introductory textbook of insects in their relations to man. 5th ed. McGraw-Hill, New York. 383 p.

Field, H.
1962 Bibliography on southwestern Asia, VII. University of Miami Press, Coral Gables, Florida. 7,492 titles listed. A particularly useful guide to many works an desert organisms that are published in obscure journals that, unfortunately, are also difficult to obtain even after they are identified.

Fiese, M. J.
1958 Coccidioidomycosis. Charles C. Thomas, Springfield, Illinois. 253 p.
This early comprehensive volume on coccidioidal disease also contains a comprehensive chronological bibliography of 969 papers on coccidioidomycosis from 1892 to 1957.

Finlayson, H. H.
1936 On mammals from the Lake Erie basin. II: The Peramelidae. Royal Society of South Australia, Transactions 59:227-236.

Finlayson, H. H. *et al.*
1932 Heat in the interior of South Australia and in central Australia. Holocaust of bird-life. South Australian Ornithologist 11:158-163.

Finlayson, M. H.
1956 Arachnidism in South Africa. *In* E. E. Buckley and N. Porges, eds., Venoms. American Association for the Advancement of Science, Publication 44:85-87.

Finlayson, M. H. and K. Hollow
1945 Treatment of spider-bite in South Africa by specific antisera. South African Medical Journal 19 (22):431-433.

Fitch, H. S., P. Goodrum, and C. Newman
1952 The armadillo in the southeastern United States. Journal of Mammalogy 33:21-37.

FitzSimons, F. W.
1921 The snakes of South Africa, their venom and the treatment of snake bite. T. M. Miller, Cape Town. 550 p.

FitzSimons, V. F. M.
1962 Snakes of southern Africa. McDonald, London. 423 p.

Fladung, E. B.
1924 Insects as food. Maryland Academy of Science, Bulletin, October:5-8.

Folk, G. E., Jr.
1966 Introduction to environmental physiology. Environmental extremes and mammalian survival. Lea and Febiger, Philadelphia. 308 p.

Food and Agriculture Organization of the United Nations
1959a Report of the FAO Panel of Experts on the Strategy of Desert Locust Plague Control. Rome. 26 p. mimeo.

——— 1959b Report of the FAO Panel of Experts on the Use of Aircraft for Desert Locust Control. Rome. 25 p. mimeo.

——— 1959c Report of the sixth session of the FAO Desert Locust Control Committee. Rome. 32 p. mimeo.

Fox, D. E.
1938 Occurance of the beet leafhopper and associated insects in secondary plant successions in southern Idaho. U. S. Department of Agriculture, Technical Bulletin 607. 43 p.

Frazer, J. G.
1910 Totemism and exogamy. Macmillan & Co., Ltd., London. 4 vols.

Freiberg, M. A.
1954 Vida de batracios y reptiles sudamericanos. Cesarini, Buenos Aires. 192, 44 p.

Frost, S. W.
1942 General entomology. McGraw-Hill Book Co., New York and London. 524 p.
A general work treating, however briefly, insects as food, insects in art and music, and other beneficial aspects of their impact on man.

Fryer, G.
1955 A critical review of the genus Ectocyclops (Crustacea, Copepoda): *E. phaleratus rubescens* from Abyssinia, Egypt, India, Iran. Annals and Magazine of Natural History, ser. 12, 8(96):938-950.

Fulwider, D. S.
1965 Bakersfield's boom in burros. U.S. Bureau of Land Management, Our Public Lands 14(4):14-15.

Fynn, A. J.
1907 The American Indian as a product of environment. Little, Brown & Co., Boston. 275 p.

Gates, D. M.
1962 Energy exchange in the biosphere. Harper and Row, New York. 151 p.

Gebien, H.
1927 Zur erforschung des persischen golfes Tenebrionidae. Supplementa Entomologica 16:121-124.

Gelineo, S.
1964 Organ systems in adaptation: the temperature regulating system. *In* D. B. Dill, E. F. Adolph, and C. G. Wilber, eds., Adaptation to the environment. American Physiological Society, Washington, D. C., Handbook of Physiology 4:259-282.

Gelman, A. C.
1966 Distribution of selected communicable diseases in the tropical and subtropical areas of the world. p. 873-898. *In* G. W. Hunter, III, W. W. Frye, and J. C. Swartzwelder, eds., A manual of tropical medicine. 4th ed. W. B. Saunders Company, Philadelphia.
Recent summary of the pantropical distribution of communicable diseases, based in part on reports and publications of the World Health Organization, Pan American Sanitary Bureau, the tenth edition of the publication of the American Public Health Association (1965), entitled *The Control of Communicable Diseases in Man*, and May (1958, 1961).

Gennaro, J. F., Jr.
1963 Observations on the treatment of snakebite in North America. p. 427-449. *In* H. L. Keegan and W. V. Macfarlane, eds., Venomous and poisonous animals and noxious plants of the Pacific Region. Macmillian Company, New York.

George, J. L., ed.
1963 Pesticide-wildlife studies. A review of Fish and Wildlife investigations during 1961 and 1962. U. S. Department of the Interior, Fish and Wildlife Service, Circulars 67. 109 p.

Gertsch, W. J.
1949 American spiders. Van Nostrand Company, Inc., New York. 285 p., 64 pl.

——— 1958a Results of the Puritan-American Museum Expedition to western Mexico. IV: The scorpions. American Museum Novitates 1903. 20 p.

——— 1958b The spider genus *Loxosceles* in North America, and the West Indies. American Museum Novitates 1907:1-46.

Gharpurey, K. G.
1954 The snakes of India and Pakistan. 4th ed. Popular Book Depot, Bombay, India. 154 p.

Ghesquière, J.
1947 Les insectes palmicoles comestibles. pp. 791-793. *In* P. Lepesme, Les insectes des palmiers. Lechevalier, Paris.

Giglioli, M. E. C.
1965 Some observations on blister beetles, family Meloidae, in Gambia, West Africa. Royal Society of Tropical Medicine and Hygiene, Tranastions 59: 657-663.

Giltner, L. T.
1918 Occurence of coccidioidal granuloma (oidiomycosis) in cattle. Journal of Agricultural Research 14:522-542.

Glauert, L.
1957 Snakes of Western Australia. 2nd ed. Western Australian Naturalists' Club, Perth, W. A. (Handbook 1)

Gloyd, H. K.
1940 The rattlesnakes, genera *Sistrurus* and *Crotalus*. Chicago Academy of Science, Special Publication 4:1-266.

Glusker, D., P. Fuentes Villalobos, and C. Gómez del Campo
1950 Ocurrencia de intradermorreacciones a la coccidioidina, brucelina, histoplasmina, haplosporangia y tuberculina, con relación a los rayos x, en conscriptos del ejército mexicano. Oficina Sanitaria Panamericana, Boletín 29:715-722.
(Occurence of intradermal reaction to coccidioidin, brucellin, histoplasmin, haplosporangin and tuberculin in relation to chest x-rays in Mexican draftees)

Goldman, L.
1947 Types of American cutaneous leishmaniasis; dermatologistical aspects. American Journal of Tropical Medicine 27:561-584.

Goren, S.
1950 Akrepler re Akrep Serumu. Türk Ijiyen ve Tecrübi Biyoloji Dergisi 10:81-93.
(Scorpions in Turkey and antiscorpion serum)

Gossard, H. A.
1901 The cottony cushion scale. Florida Agricultural Experiment Station, Bulletin 56.

Gourou, P.
1948 Les pays tropicaux. Principes d'une géographie humaine et économique. 2e éd. Presses Universitaires de France, Paris. 196 p.
Expounds the nutritive value of insects as human food.

Grant, M. L. and L. J. Henderson
1957 A case of Gila monster poisoning, with a summary of some previous accounts. Iowa Academy of Science, Proceedings 64:686-697.

Grassé, P. P.
1949 Ordre des Isopteres ou termites. *In* P. P. Grassé, ed., Traité de Zoologie 9:408-544.

Gray, J.
1930 Notes on a native tribe formerly resident at Orroroo, S. Australia. South Australian Naturalist 12:4-6.

Guggenheim, J. K.
1951 Body composition of various locusts. p. 32. *In* F. S. Bodenheimer, Insects as human food. W. Junk, The Hague.

Halstead, B. W. and R. E. Ryckman
1949 Injurious effects from contacts with millipedes. Medical Arts and Sciences 3:16-18.
Reports skin blisters and intense eye pain from contact with millipede secretions.

Hanbury, D.
1859 Note on two insects' products from Persia. Linnean Society of London, Proceedings 3:178-183.

Harwicke, T.
1822 Description of a substance called Gez or Manna, and the insect producing it. Asiatic Society of Bengal, Calcutta, Asiatic Researches 14:182-186.

Hardy, G. and C. R. Richet, eds.
1933 L'alimentation indigène dans les colonies françaises, protectorats et territoires sous mandat. Vigot Frères, Paris. 388 p.

Hardy, J. D., ed.
1963 Temperature, its measurement and control in biology and medicine. Vol. 3. Reinhold, New York. 683 p.
A primary reference source on biophysics and the energy exchange involved in animal physiology, physiological ecology, and medicine.

Harmon, R. W. and C. B. Pollard
1948 Bibliography of animal venoms. University of Florida Press, Gainesville. 340 p.
Cites 4,157 titles of animal venoms published since 1863; these include reference to poisonous animals in general, including snakes, spiders, and scorpions.

Harris, W. V.
1941 Termites in East Africa. III: Field key and distribution. East African Agricultural Journal 6:201-205.

——— 1957 Isoptera. British Museum (Natural History) Expedition to southwest Arabia, Report 28:421-433.

——— 1961 Termites, their recognition and control. Longmans, Green and Co., Ltd., London. 187 p.
A modern world view of the termites that is useful in faunistics, being not entirely utilitarian in content.

——— 1966 Risultati delle missioni entomologiche dei Proff. G. Fiori ed E. Mellini nel Nord Africa. XVII: Isoptera from Libya. Università di Sassari, Facoltà di Agraria, Annali 14:1-8.

Harrison, P. W.
1925 The Arab at home. Hutchinson & Co., London. 357 p.

Hart, J. S.
1957 Climatic and temperature induced changes in the energetics of homeotherms. Revue Canadienne de Biologie 16:133-141.
An excellent recent review.

1964 Geography and season: mammals and birds. *In* D. B. Dill, E. F. Adolph, and C. G. Wilber, eds., Adaptation to the environment. American Physiological Society, Washington, D.C., Handbook of Physiology 4:295-321.

Hartman, O.
1897 The Indians of north-western Mexico. Congrès International des Américanistes, 10th, Stockholm, 1894. pp. 115-136.

Hayward, K. J.
1941 Las cochinillas de los cítricos Tucumanos y su control. Estación Experimental Agrícola de Tucumán, Boletín 32. 29 p.

Hedin, S.
1918 Jerusalem. F. A. Brockhaus, Leipzig. 342 p.

Hegh, E.
1922 Les termites, partie générale. Imprimerie Industrielle et Financière, Bruxelles. 756 p.
An early classic giving a world view of the termites.

Heim de Balsac, H.
1925 Mission dans le Sahara central et description d'un oiseau nouveau du genre *Ammomanes* (suivi d'une liste des espèces rapportées pour les collections du Muséum). Muséum National d'Histoire Naturelle, Paris, Bulletin 31:137-144.

Henderson, J. and J. P. Harrington
1914 Ethnozoology of the Tewa Indians. Bureau of American Ethnology, Bulletin 56:1-76.

Henderson, J. M.
1943 The relation of sunlight to desert sores. British Medical Journal 1:657-659.

Herms, W. B. and M. T. James
1961 Medical entomology. 5th ed. Macmillan, New York.
Includes lists of the families, genera, and species of the more important urticating *Lepidoptera*.

Herre, A.
1942 Notes on Phillipine sea snakes. Copeia (1):7-9.

Hertig, M.
1948 Sand flies of the genus *Phlebotomus*; a review of their habits, disease relationships and control. International Congress on Tropical Medicine and Malaria, 4th, Washington, D.C.

Hertig, M. and G. B. Fairchild
1948 The control of *Phlebotomus* in Peru with DDT. American Journal of Tropical Medicine 28:207-230.

Hess, J. J.
1938 Van den Beduinen des inneren Arabiens. Erzählungen, Lieder, Sitten, und Gebräuche, Zürich und Leipzig. 177 p.

Hesse, A. J.
1938 Some adaptive responses of insect life to semi-arid conditions in South Africa. South African Journal of Science 35:69-91.

Hill, W. W.
1938 The agricultural and hunting methods of the Navajo Indians. Yale University, Publications in Anthropology 18:1-194.

Hindle, E.
1914 Flies in relation to disease. Blood-sucking flies. Cambridge University Press, Cambridge, 398 p.

Hoffmann, W. E.
1947 Insects as human food. Entomological Society of Washington, Proceedings 49:233-237.

Hoge, A. R.
1965 Preliminary account on neotropical crotalinae (Serpentes Viperidae). Instituto Butantan, São Paulo, Memórias 32:109-184.
Recent annotated list of the neotropical crotalids. Includes maps.

Hoogstraal, H., *et al.*
1961 Ticks (Ixodoides) on birds migrating from Africa to Europe and Asia. World Health Organization, Bulletin 24:197.

Horen, W. P.
1963 Arachnidism in the United States. American Medical Asociation, Journal 185:839-843.

Horn, G. H.
1885 Studies among the Meloidae. American Entomological Society, Transactions 12:107-116.

Horsfall, W. R.
1962 Medical entomology, arthropods, and human disease. Ronald Press, New York. 467 p.

Howard, L. O.
1900 A contribution to the study of the insect fauna of human excrement. Washington Academy of Sciences, Proceedings 2:541-604.

Hrdlicka, A.
1908 Physiological and medical observations among the Indians of southwestern United States and northern Mexico. Smithsonian Institution, Washington, Bureau of American Ethnology, Bulletin 34. 460 p.

Hudson, J. W. and G. A. Bartholomew
1964 Terrestrial animals in dry heat; Estivators. *In* D. B. Dill, E. F. Adolph, and C. G. Wilber, eds., Adaptation to the environment. American Physiological Society, Washington, D.C., Handbook of Physiology 4:541-550.

Hugenholtz, P. G.
1957a Skin-test survey at Williams Air Force Base, Arizona. *In* Symposium on Coccidioidomycosis, Phoenix, 1957, Proceedings. U.S. Public Health Service, Publication 575:127-131.

1957b Climate and coccidioidomycosis. *In* Symposium on Coccidioidomycosis, Phoenix, 1957, Proceedings. U.S. Public Health Service, Publication 575: 136-143.

Hunter, G. W., III, W. W. Frye, and J. C. Swartzwelder
1966 Manual of tropical medicine. 4th ed. W. B. Saunders, Philadelphia. 931 p.
One of the most recent and excellent manuals and reference texts on the subject. Treated here are all diseases of men and some animals that occur in deserts and are of any significant consequence to mortality or debilitation.

Hutton, J. H.
1921*a* The Sema Nagas. Macmillan & Co., London. 463 p.

———

1921*b* The Angami Nagas. Macmillan & Co., London. 480 p.

Imms, A. D.
1957 A general textbook of entomology. 9th ed., revised by O. W. Richards and R. G. Davies. Methuen and Company, London. 886 p.

Irwin, R. W.
1952 Funnel-web spider bite. Medical Journal of Australia (2):342.

Isakov, Y. A.
1961 Organization and methods of censusing terrestrial vertebrate faunal resources. Moscow Society of Naturalists. Translated, 1963, from the Russian for the National Science Foundation by The Israel Program for Scientific Translations, Jerusalem.
Summaries of 87 reports from a symposium arranged in seven sections: organization of terrestrial vertebrate censuses; principal methods of censusing terrestrial mammals and birds; censusing of ungulates; predatory mammal censuses; censusing rodents and other small mammals; game bird censuses, censusing passerines, raptors and other nongame birds. Methods and data for populations in communities varying from forest to desertscrub, and including some maritime species.

Janjua, N. A. and H. Haque
1955 Butterflies of Karachi, West Pakistan. Agricultural Pakistan 6(3):19-40.

Jasper, D. E.
1953 Coccidioidomycosis in a chinchilla. North American Veterinarian 34:570-571

Jepson, W. F.
1954 A critical review of the world literature on the lepidopterous stalk borers of tropical graminaceous crops. Commonwealth Institute of Entomology, London. 127 p.

———

1963 African fauna: economic aspects of entomology. *In* A review of the natural resources of the African continent. Unesco, Paris. Natural Resources Research 1:317-339.

Joyce, R. J.
1952 The ecology of grasshoppers in East Central Sudan. British Museum (Natural History), Anti-Locust Research Centre, Anti-Locust Bulletin 11:1-97.

Jung, R. C., V. J. Derbes, and A. D. Burch
1963 Skin response to a solenamine, a hemolytic component of fire ant venom. Dermatologica Tropica 2:241-244.

Kachkarov, D. N. and E. P. Korovin
1942 La vie dans les déserts. Edition française par Théodore Monod. Payot, Paris. 360 p.
Provides especially important and carefully detailed data on distribution, relative abundance, population density and general ecology of the faunas.

Kachkarov, D. N. and V. Kurbotov
1930 Preliminary ecological survey of the vertebrates of Central Karakum Desert in western Turkestan. Ecology 11:35-60.

Kaiser, E.
1953 Fermentchemische untersuchungen an spinnengiften. Monatshefte für Chemie 84:482-490.

———

1956 Enzymatic activity of spider venoms. *In* E. E. Buckley and N. Porges, eds., Venoms. American Association for the Advancement of Science, Publication 44:91-97.

Kaiser, E. and H. Michl
1958 Die biochemie der tierischen gifte. Franz Deuticke, Wien. 257 p.

Keast, A.
1959 The reptiles of Australia. *In* A. Keast, R. L. Crocker, and C. S. Christian, eds., Biogeography and ecology in Australia. Monographiae Biologicae 8:115-135.

———

1961 Bird speciation on the Australian continent. Harvard University, Museum of Comparative Zoology, Bulletin 123 (8).
Provides especially important and carefully detailed data on distribution, relative abundance, population density and general ecology of the faunas on the Australian continent.

Keast, A., R. L. Crocker, and C. S. Christian, eds.
1959 Biogeography and ecology in Australia. W. Junk, The Hague. 640 p. (Monographiae Biologicae 8)
Thirty-six chapters follow an introduction by F. S. Bodenheimer on the uniqueness of Australia in biology. Subjects include the environments; primitive man and human ecology; zoogeography and ecology of the marsupial fauna, birds, reptiles, amphibians, freshwater fishes, mollusks, crustaceans, and insects of several orders; vegetation and phytogeography; management, agriculture, and conservation. There are useful maps in several chapters. The central desert is treated in a small part of the overall effort. Fortunately for the desert fauna of Central Australia ("Empty Australia"), there is still less than ⅛ human per square mile.

Keegan, H. L.
1952 Geographic distribution of *Latrodectus hasseltii*. American Journal of Tropical Medicine and Hygiene 1:1043-1046.

———

1955*a* Spiders of the genus *Latrodectus*. American Midland Naturalist 54:142-152.
An attempt to apply modern polytypic species concepts to the enormous worldwide variation in poisonous species —but still retaining the relatively high number of 11 species in a total of 15 taxa (species and subspecies), several of which are desert populations.

———

1955*b* Effectiveness of *Latrodectus tredecimguttatus* antivenin in protecting laboratory mice against injections of *Latrodectus mactans* venom. American Journal of Tropical Medicine and Hygiene 4:762-764.

———

1956 Antivenins available for treatment of envenomation by poisonous snakes, scorpions, and spiders. *In* E. E. Buckley and N. Porges, eds., Venoms. American Association for the Advancement of Science, Publication 44:413-438.
Lists producers of antivenins for spiderbite. Also gives producers of antivenins for scorpion sting in North Amer-

ica, South America, the Middle East, North Africa, Egypt, and South Africa.

————
1963 Venomous spiders of the Pacific Area. p. 133-136. *In* H. L. Keegan and W. V. Macfarlane, eds., Venomous and poisonous animals and noxious plants of the Pacific Region. Macmillan Co., New York.

Keegan, H. L. and W. V. Macfarlane, eds.
1963 Venomous and poisonous animals and noxious plants of the Pacific region; a collection of papers based on a symposium in the Public Health and Medical Science Division, 10th Pacific Science Congress. Macmillan Co., New York. 456 p.

Keegan, H. L., F. W. Whittemore, and R. A. Hedeen
1960 Seasonal variation in venom of black widow spiders. American Journal of Tropical Medicine and Hygiene 10:477-479.

Keegan, H. L. *et al.*
1964 Some venomous and noxious animals of east and southeast Asia. U.S. Army Medical Command Japan, 406th Medical Laboratory, Special Report. 43 p.

Keh, J.
1956 Cone-nosed bugs of California. California Vector Views 3:47-50.
This work reports that relief from bites of *Rasahus* in California may be obtained by using lotions of menthol, phenol, or camphor.

Kellaway, C. H.
1932 Venomous land snakes in Australia. Antivenin Institute of America, Bulletin 5:53-58.

Kellaway, C. H. and T. Eades
1929 Field notes on the common Australian venomous snakes. Medical Journal of Australia 2:249-257.

Kemper, H.
1958 Experimentelle untersuchungen über die wirkung von raupenhaaren auf die menschliche haut. International Congress of Entomology, 10th, Montreal, 1956, Proceedings 3:719-723.

Khalaf, K. T.
1959 Reptiles of Iraq, with some notes on the amphibians. Ar-Rabitta Press, Baghdad. 96 p.

Khalil, F.
1963 African fauna; taxonomy, ecology, and zoogeography. *In* A review of the natural resources of the African continent. Unesco, Paris. Natural Resources Research 1:277-316.
Habitats of the fauna of Africa, the taxonomy and ecology arranged by major phylogenetic groups. African zoogeography of the Ethiopian and Palearctic Zoogeographical Realms. Bibliography: p. 308-316.

Kinghorn, J. R.
1956 The snakes of Australia. 2nd ed. Michigan State University Press, East Lansing. 197 p.

Kirmiz, J. P.
1962 Adaptation to desert environments: a study on the jerboa, rat and man. Butterworths, London. 168 p.
An admirable recent review of vertebrate animal adaptation to desert environments, written by a physiological ecologist who reports on behavorial and physiological adaptations and adjustments as studied primarily in the Egyptian Sahara. Bibliography: p. 149-157.

Klauber, L. M.
1931*a* A statistical survey of the snakes of the southern border of California. Zoological Society of San Diego, Bulletin 8:1-93.

————
1931*b* *Crotalus tigris* and *Crotalus enyo,* two little known rattlesnakes of the Southwest. San Diego Society of Natural History, Transactions 6:353-370.

Klauber, L. M.
1936 Key to the rattlesnakes with summary of characteristics. San Diego Society of Natural History, Transactions 8:185-276.

————
Klauber, L. M.
1956 Rattlesnakes, their habits, life histories, and influence on mankind. Published for the Zoological Society of San Diego by The University of California Press, Berkeley and Los Angeles. 2 vols.
A comprehensive treatise on the rattlesnakes that includes species accounts of all species that occur in the North American Desert, and of *Crotalus durissus terrificus* (the South American rattlesnake) that reaches the northern edge of the South American desert. Includes details on rattlesnake flesh as human food; gives 23 references from 1750 to 1950.

Kleiber, M.
1961 The fire of life, an introduction to animal energetics. John Wiley and Sons, Inc., New York. 454 p.
On biogenetics. A basic reference in the sense of Hardy (1963) and Newburgh (1949) for students of animals in harsh environments.

Klemmer, K.
1963 Liste der rezenten giftschlangen: Elapidae, Hydropheidae, Viperidae und Grotalidae. N. G. Elwert Universitäts-und Verlagsbuchhandlung, Marburg-Lahn. 255-464 p.
This excellent work provides an annotated checklist, with major references, for all the currently recognized species of poisonous snakes in the world. Includes alphabetical listings under each family. Also includes a listing of the species that are found in each of 17 geographical subdivisions of the world. The basis for this work is geographical, not ecological; therefore, the deserts are treated, as usual, only by being generally included in the lists for larger geographical areas. Includes a number of excellent color photographs, including some for little-known dangerous species.

Klobusitzky, D. de
1960 Giftchlangen und schlangengifte. R. Oldenbourg. München. 64 p.

Knowlton, G. F. and M. J. Janes
1933 Lizards as predators of beet leafhoppers. Journal of Economic Entomology 26:1011-1016.

Koch, C.
1961 Some aspects of abundant life in the vegetationless sand of the Namib Desert dunes. Positive psammotropism in Tenebrionid-beetles. Namib Desert Research Station, Scientific Papers 1. 26 p.

Koehler, J. W.
1960 The California undomesticated burro. California Department of Agriculture, Bulletin 49(1).

Kofoid, C. A., ed.
1934 Termites and termite control. 2nd ed. University of California Press, Berkeley. 795 p.

Kolb, P.
1731 The present state of the Cape of Good Hope. Done into English . . . by Mr. Medley. W. Innys, London. 2 vols.

Kong, Y. M. and H. B. Levine
1967 Experimentally induced immunity in the Mycoses. Bacteriological Reviews 31 (1):35-53.

Kopstein, F.
1932 Die gifttiere Java's und ihre bedeutung für den menschen. Dienst de Volksgezondheid in Nederlandsch-Indie, Mededeelingen 22:222-256.

Kraepelin, K.
1899 Scorpiones und Pedipalpi. R. Friedländer u. Sohn, Berlin. 765 p. (Das Tierreich, 8 lfg.)
Treats structure, classification and distribution of scorpions.

Kramer, E.
1961 Variation, sexualdimorphismus, wachstum und taxionomie von *Vipera ursinii* (Bonaparte, 1835) und *Vipera kaznakovi* Nikolskij, 1909. Revue Suisse de Zoologie 68:627-725.

Kramer, E. and H. Schnurrenberger
1963 Systematik, verbreitung und oklologie der Libyschen schlanger. Revue Suisse de Zoologie 70:453-568.

Kraus, E. B.
1958 Meteorological aspects of desert locust control. *In* Climatology and microclimatology, proceedings of the Canberra symposium. Unesco, Paris. Arid Zone Research 11:211-216.

Krishna, D., I. Prakash, and K. C. Dave
1956 On the distribution of reptiles in the desert of Rajasthan. Indian Science Congress, Proceedings 4:34-35.

Kumerloeve, H.
1960 On some birds collected by Mr. Douglas Curruthers in the Syrian Desert. Alauda 28.

Künckel d'Herculais, J.
1891 Les Acridiens (Ecridium peregrinum, *Oliv.*) dans l'extrême Sud Algérien. Les populations acridophages. Académie des Sciences, Paris, Comptes Rendus 112:307-309.

Kusnezov, N.
1952 Algunos datos sobre la dispersión geográfica de hormigas (Hymenoptera, Formicidae) en la República Argentina. Sociedad Científica Argentina, Buenos Aires, Anales 153:230-242.

Kuznetosov, N. N.
1926 Origin of the desert fauna of Turkestan (translated title). Revue Zoologie Russe, Moscow, 6(1):61-82.
In Russian, with German summary.

Ladell, W. S. S.
1953 The physiology of life and work in high ambient temperatures. *In* Desert research, proceedings International Symposium held in Jerusalem, May 7-14, 1952, sponsored by the National Research Council of Israel and Unesco. Research Council of Israel, Special Publication 2:187-204.

1957 The influence of environment in arid regions on the biology of man. *In* Human and animal ecology. Unesco, Paris. Arid Zone Research 8:43-99.

Lambert, G. E.
1964 Modifications des temps de réaction et de l'électroencéphalogramme au cours d'un séjour prolongé en zone aride. *In* Environmental physiology and psychology in arid conditions, proceedings of the Lucknow symposium. Unesco, Paris. Arid Zone Research 24:363-369.

Lane, J.
1962 Insecta patagónica (Diptera: Syrphidae.) Sociedad Entomológica Argentina, Revista 25:17-20.

Lanham, U. N.
1964 The insects. Columbia University Press, New York and London.

Lankester, E. R.
1909 The structure and classification of the Arachnida. Quarterly Journal of Microscopical Science 48:165-269.

Laurent, R. F.
1950 Révision du genre *Atractaspis* A. Smith.. Institut Royal des Sciences Naturelles de Belgique, Bruxelles, Mémoires (2)38:1-49.

1956 Contribution à l'Herpétologie de la région des Grands Lacs de l'Afrique centrale. Généralité Cheloniens, Ophidiens. Musée du Congo Belge, Tervueren, Annales 48:1-390.

1964 Reptiles et amphibiens de l'Angola. Museu do Dundo, Luanda, Publicacoes Culturais da Companhia de Diamantes de Angola 67:1-165.

Lavauden, L.
1926 Les vertébrés du Sahara. Guénard, Tunis.

Lawrence, R. F.
1959 The sand dune fauna of the Namib Desert. South African Journal of Science 55:233-239.

1962 Spiders of the Namib Desert. Namib Desert Research Station, Scientific Papers 9:1-15.

Laycock, G.
1966 The alien animals. Published for the American Museum of Natural History, by the Natural History Press, New York. 240 p.
Bibliography: p. 221-231. This is an important review of man's stupidity in his ageless consideration of himself as capable of improving upon nature by disturbing the natural distribution of organisms. An alarming and forceful message of the havoc that has resulted from the unwanted aliens provided by the wildlife movers, groups of unconscionable men renewed in force with each human generation, who refuse the message which is the massive record of failure and destruction. Deserts are included.

Lebkicher, R., G. Rentz, M. Steineke, with contributions by other Aramco employees
1960 Aramco handbook. Arabian American Oil Company. 343 p.

Lee, D. H. K.
1958 Proprioclimates of man and domestic animals. *In* Climatology, reviews of research. Unesco, Paris. Arid Zone Research 10:102-125.

1962 Applications of human and animal physiology and ecology to the study of arid zone problems. *In* The problems of the arid zone, proceedings of the Paris symposium. Unesco, Paris. Arid Zone Research 18:213-233.

Lee, D. H. K.
1963 Human factors in desert development. *In* C. Hodge and P. C. Duisberg, eds., Aridity and man. American Association for the Advancement of Science, Publication 74:339-367.
One of the better papers (although it contributes nothing new) in a mediocre assemblage (as it pertains to the biological sciences).

———
1964 Terrestrial animals in dry heat: man in the desert. *In* D. B. Dill, E. F. Adolph, and C. G. Wilber, eds., Adaptation to the environment. American Physiological Society, Washington, D.C., Handbook of Physiology 4:551-582.

Lee, D. H. K. *et al.*
1951 Studies on clothing for hot environments, Death Valley, 1950. I: Experiments and results. U.S. Army, Quartermaster Research and Engineering Command, Natick, Massachusetts, Research Report 178. Also cited as PB 163-075. Also abstracted in U.S.G.R.R. 38(3):S-28, 1963.

Léger, L.
1925 La valeur alimentaire et gastronomique de l'escargot de Bourgogne *(Helix pomatia* L). Grenoble, Laboratoire d'Hydrobiologie et de Pisciculture, Travaux 15-16:73-81.

Leopold, A. S. and The Editors of *Life*
1961 The desert. Life Nature Library, Time, Inc., New York.

Levi, H. W.
1959 The spider genus *Latrodectus* (Araneae, Theriidae). American Microscopical Society, Transactions 78:7-43.

Leviton, A. E.
1959 Report on a collection of reptiles from Afghanistan. California Academy of Sciences, Proceedings 29 (12):445-463.

Light, S. F. and F. M. Weesner
1948 Biology of Arizona termites with emphasis on swarming. Pan-Pacific Entomologist 24:54-68.

Lillie, R. D. and E. Francis
1936 The pathology of Tularaemia. U.S. National Institute of Health, Bulletin 167. 217 p.

Limbacher, H. P. and C. H. Lowe
1959 The treatment of poisonous bites and stings. I: Rattlesnake bite. Arizona Medicine 16:490-495.
Includes a discussion on the potentially dangerous use of cryotherapy for snakebite (icing or other "refrigeration" of tissue).

Lindauer, M.
1957 Communication among the honeybees and stingless bees of India. Bee World 38:3-14.

Lindblom, G.
1920 The Akamba in British East Africa. 2nd ed., enl. Archives d'Etudes Orientales. Uppsala, 17. 607 p.

Lindsay, D. R. and H. I. Scudder
1956 Nonbiting flies and disease. Annual Review of Entomology 1:323-346.

Linsley, R. K.
1953 Report on the hydrological problems of the arid and semi-arid areas of the United States and Canada. *In* Reviews of Research on Arid Zone Hydrology. Unesco, Paris. Arid Zone Programme 1:128-152.

Locard, A.
1890 Les huîtres et les mollusques comestibles: moules, praires, clovisses, escargots, etc.; histoire naturelle, culture industrielle, hygiène alimentaire. J. B. Baillière et Fils, Paris. 383 p.
Gives extensive original sources on snails as human food.

Lönnberg, E.
1931 A contribution to the bird fauna of southern Gobi. Arkiv för Zoologi 23A(12):1-18.

Lovelass, M. H.
1962 Immunization in wasp-sting allergy through venom-repositories and periodic insect stings. Journal of Immunology 89:204-215.

Loveridge, A.
1945 Reptiles of the Pacific world. The Macmillan Co., New York. 259 p.

———
1957 Check list of the reptiles and amphibians of East Africa (Uganda; Kenya; Tanganyika; Zanzibar). Harvard University, Museum of Comparative Zoology, Bulletin 110:143-322.

Lowe, C. H.
1948 Effect of venom of *Micruroides* upon *Xantusia vigilis*. Herpetologica 4:136.

———
1964 Arizona landscapes and habitats, p. 3-132. *In* C. H. Lowe, ed., The vertebrates of Arizona. University of Arizona Press, Tucson.

———
1968 Ecologic hierarchy and desertscrub. Arizona Academy of Science, Journal *(in press)*.

Lowe, C. H. and H. P. Limbacher
1961 The treatment of poisonous bites and stings. II: Arizona coral snake and Gila monster bite. Arizona Medicine 18:128-131.

Lubarsky, R. and O. A. Plunkett
1955 Some ecological studies of *Coccidioides immitis* in soil. p. 308-310. *In* T. H. Sternberg and V. D. Newcomer, eds., Therapy of fungus diseases. Little, Brown and Company, Boston.

Lumholtz, C.
1890 Au pays des cannibales, voyage d'exploration chez les indigènes de l'Australia orientale. Hachette, Paris. 499 p.

Macchiavello, A.
1931 La *Loxosceles laeta*, causa del arachnoidismo cutáneo, o mancha gangrenosa, de Chile. Revista Chilena de Historia Natural 41:11.

Macfarlane, W. V.
1963 Endocrine functions in hot environments. *In* Environmental physiology and psychology in arid conditions, reviews of research. Unesco, Paris. Arid Zone Research 22:153-222.

———
1964 Terrestrial animals in dry heat: Ungulates. *In* D. B. Dill, E. F. Adolph, and C. G. Wilber, eds., Adaptation to the environment. American Physiological Society, Washington, D. C., Handbook of Physiology 4:509-539.

Macrae, D.
1944 Desert sore. Royal Army Medical Corps, Journal 83:274-278.

Maddy, K. T.
1957a A study of one hundred cases of disseminated coccidioidomycosis in the dog. *In* Symposium on Coccidioidomycosis, Phoenix, 1957, Proceedings. U.S. Public Health Service, Publication 575:107-118.

1957b Ecological factors possibly relating to the geographic distribution of *Coccidioides immitis. In* Symposium on Coccidioidomycosis, Phoenix, 1957, Proceedings. U.S. Public Health Service, Publication 575:144-157.

1965 Observations on *Coccidioides immitis* found growing naturally in soil. Arizona Medicine 22:281-288.

Malkin, B.
1962 Seri ethnozoology. Idaho State College, Museum, Occasional Papers 7:1-59.

Marcenac, M.
1926 Arachnides, Myriapodes et serpents de la région du Tadla (Maroc). Muséum National d'Histoire Naturelle, Paris, Bulletin 32(5):278-281.

Marett, P. J.
1913 The Phlebotomous flies of the Maltese Islands. Royal Army Medical Corps, Journal 20:162-171. Also: Review of Applied Entomology, B, 1:27-29 (Abstr.)
Includes discussion on the control of sand flies.

Marikovski, P. J.
1956 *Lycosa* and *Latrodectus,* morphology, biology, and toxicity (translated title). Akademiia Nauk Kirgizskoy S.S.R., Frunze, Kirghiz S.S.R.

Martin, H.
1959 The scientific principles of crop protection. Edward Arnold Publishers, London. 359 p.

Marx, H.
1953 The Elaphid genus of snakes Walterinnesia: Egypt to Iran. Chicago Natural History Museum, Fieldiana: Zoology 34(16):189-196.

1956 Keys to the lizards and snakes of Egypt. U.S. Naval Medical Research Unit 3, Cairo, Research Report NM 005 050.39.45. 8 p.

Matheson, R.
1950 Medical entomology. Comstock Publishing Associates. Ithaca, New York.

Maugini, A.
1953 Contributo ad una bibliografia italiana su Eritrea e Somalia, con particolare riferimento all' agricoltura ed argomenti affini. Istituto Agronomico, Firenze. 239 p.
An extensive and difficult to obtain bibliography on a relatively little-known desert, the Somali-Chalbi. Covers the period from the late 1880's to 1951, for Eritrea, Dancalia, and Somalia. All citations are in Italian.

May, J. M.
1958 The ecology of human disease. M. D. Publications, Inc., New York.

1961 Studies in disease ecology. II: Studies in medical geography. Hafner Publishing Company, New York.

Mayr, E.
1942 Systematics and the origin of species. Columbia University Press, New York.

1963 Animal species and evolution. Harvard University Press, Cambridge, Massachusetts.

Mazzotti, L. and M. A. Bravo-Becherelle
1963 Scorpionism in the Mexican Republic. p. 119-131. *In* H. L. Keegan and W. V. Macfarlane, eds., Venomous and poisonous animals and noxious plants of the Pacific Region. Macmillan Co., New York.

McCook, H. C.
1882 The honey ants of the Garden of the Gods and the occident ants of the American plains. J. B. Lippincott & Co., Philadelphia. 188 p.

McGee, W. J.
1898 The Seri Indians. U.S. Bureau of American Ethnology, Annual Report 17(1):1-344.
This remarkable account remains the basic work on the Seri, now numbering fewer than 300 individuals on the Sonoran gulf coast in the vicinity of Isla Tiburon. The flora and fauna are not neglected, nor are food and food-getting, totems, and tools and their uses. The volume is illustrated with 56 plates and 42 additional figures.

McGregor, E. A.
1916 The citrus red mite named and described for the first time. Entomological Society of America, Annals 9:284-288.

1939 The specific identity of the American date mite; description of two new species of *Paratetranychus.* Entomological Society of Washington, Proceedings 41:247-256.

McGregor, T. and J. F. Flanigan
1962 Effects of insecticides on the scorpion *Centruroides vittatus.* Journal of Economic Entomology 55:661-662.

McKeown, K. C.
1935 Insect wonders of Australia. Angus and Robertson, Ltd., Sydney. 252 p.

1944 Australian insects. Sydney.

McKinney, K. B.
1939 Common insects attacking sugar beets and vegetable crops in the Salt River Valley of Arizona. Journal of Economic Entomology 32:808-810.

McMichael, D. F. and D. Iredale
1959 The land and freshwater mollusca of Australia. *In* A. Keast, R. L. Crocker, and C. S. Christian, eds., Biogeography and ecology in Australia. Monographiae Biologicae 8:224-244.

Mead, A. R.
1961 The giant African snail: a problem in economic malacology. University of Chicago Press, Chicago. 257 p.
A review that contains citations of numerous original sources, including those on snails as human food.

Mead, A. R. and A. R. Kemmerer
1953 Amino acid content of dehydrated giant African snails *(Achatina fulica Bowdich).* Science 117:138-139.

Mehringer, P. J., Jr., S. F. Wood, and R. A. Anderson
1961 Conenose bug *(triatoma)* annoyance and *Trypanosoma cruzi* in Griffith Park in 1960. Southern California Academy of Science, Bulletin 60(3): 190-192.

Meinertzhagen, R.
1934 The biogeographical status of the A'haggar Plateau in the central Sahara, with special reference to birds. Ibis, p. 528-571.

Mendelssohn, H.
1963 On the biology of the venomous snakes of Israel. Part I. Israel Journal of Zoology 12 (1/4):143-170.

Merriam, C. H.
1894 Laws of temperature control of the geographic distribution of terrestrial animals and plants. National Geographic Magazine 6:229-238.

Merriam, T. W., Jr.
1961 Current concepts in the management of snakebite. Military Medicine 126:526-531.

Mertens, R.
1934 Über die verbreitung und das verbreitungszentrum der seeschlangens (Hydrophidae). Zoogeographica 2(3):305-319.

1952 Amphibien und reptilien aus der Turkei. Istanbul Üniversitesi Fen Fakültesi Mecmuasi, Revue, ser. B 17 (7):41-75.

1954 Über die rassen des Wüstenwarans *(Varanus griseus)*. Senckenbergiana Biologica 35:353-357.
On the geographic variation of the races (subspecies) of the desert monitor lizard. An example of the many remarkable polytypic species that span the entire Sahara-Sindic megadesert in a series of genetic allopatric ecotypes.

1955 Die amphibien und reptilien Südwestafrikas. Aus den ergebmissen einer in jahre 1952 ausgenfuhrten reise. Senckenbergische Naturforschende Gesellschaft, Abhandlungen 490:1-172.

1956 Amphibien und reptilien aus südost Iran 1954. Vereins für Vaterländische Naturkunde in Württemberg, Stuttgart, Jahresheft 111:90-97.

1960 The world of amphibians and reptiles. G. G. Harrap, London. 207 p.

Metcalf, C. L. and W. P. Flint
1939 Destructive and useful insects, their habits and control. McGraw-Hill Book Co., Inc. 981 p.

1962 Destructive and useful insects. 4th ed. McGraw-Hill, New York. 1087 p.

Meyer. K. D.
1965 Lymphogranuloma venereum agent. p. 1024-1032. *In* F. L. Horsfall, Jr., and I. Tamm, eds., Viral and rickettsial infections of man. 4th ed. J. B. Lippincott Company, Philadelphia. 1282 p.

Mickel. C. E.
1928 Biological and taxonomic investigations on the mutillid wasps. U.S. National Museum, Bulletin 143. 352 p.

Micks. D. W.
1952 Clinical effects of the sting of the "puss caterpillar" (Megalopyge opercularis S. & A.) on man. Texas Reports on Biology and Medicine 10:399-405.

1960 Insects and other arthropods of medical importance in Texas. Texas Reports on Biology and Medicine 18:624.

1963 The current status of necrotic arachnidism in Texas. p. 153-159. *In* H. L. Keegan and W. V. Macfarlane, eds., Venomous and poisonous animals and noxious plants of the Pacific Region. Macmillan Company, New York.

Miller, D. G., Jr.
1956 Massive anaphylaxis from insect stings. *In* E. E. Buckley and N. Porges, eds., Venoms. American Association for the Advancement of Science, Publication 44:117-121.

Miller, J. H.
1914 *In* D. Carruthers, Unknown Mongolia. Hutchinson and Co., London.

Minton, S. A., Jr.
1962 An annotated key to the amphibians and reptiles of Sind and Las Bela, West Pakistan. American Museum Novitates 2081:1-60.

1966 A contribution to the herpetology of West Pakistan. American Museum of Natural History, Bulletin 134:1-184.
Especially valuable volume dealing with the geographic and ecologic distribution of the poisonous snakes of the world's deserts. Treats the Thar Desert.

Minton, S. A., Jr., H. G. Dowling, and F. E. Russell
1967 Poisonous snakes of the world. U.S. Department of the Navy, Bureau of Medicine and Surgery, NAVMED P-5099. *(in press)*
This recent important U.S. Navy volume replaces its 1963 predecessor of the same title by G. M. Moore, which was recalled by the Navy. This work treats in varying detail all major groups of poisonous snakes in the world that are potentially dangerous to man, and cites major references. Most up-to-date recommendation for first-aid and medical treatment of snakebite poisoning is included. Brief species accounts are given for the poisonous species that are responsible for the largest number of bites within the genera, or are believed to be of serious danger to adults. Species accounts of many "desert species" accordingly are not given. Emphasis is at the generic and family level and the world is divided into 10 major geographical regions. Often the distributions of snakes are given in general, sometimes even vague, terms, for it is seldom that exact geographic distributions are known. Includes species photographs, some in color. Gives information on relative toxicity and attendant relative dangerousness is also given. Some desert species are discussed in this regard.

Moreau, R. E.
1966 The bird faunas of Africa and its islands. Academic Press, New York. 424 p.
Bibliography: p. 381-398.

Moretti, G.
1934 Il valore nutrivo degli organi dell' *Helix pomatia* Linn. Bollettino di Zoologia 5:7-15.

Morrison, H.
1921 Red date palm scale. Journal of Agricultural Research 21:669-676.

Morstatt, H. A.
1921 Die stachellosen Bienen (Trigonen) in Ostafrika und das Hummelwachs. Biologische Reichsanstalt für Land-und-Forstwirschaft, Berlin, Arbeiten 10: 283-305.

Motz, F. A.
1942 The fruit industry of Argentina. U.S. Department of Agriculture, Office of Foreign Agricultural Relations, Foreign Agriculture Report I. 102 p.

Mountford, C. P.
1946 Earth's most primitive people, a journey with the aborigines of Central Australia. National Geographic Magazine 89:89-104.
Central Australia; ". . . a tribe of about 300 aborigines who are living probably the most primitive existence on earth today . . . .The menu of my companions was certainly varied; in fact they ate everything that was edible —grubs, lizards, ants, kangaroos, emus, grasses, and seeds of many kinds. I have eaten many of these foods with relish."

Mueller, H. L.
1959 Further experiences with severe allergic reactions to insect stings. New England Journal of Medicine 261:374-377.

Mueller, H. L. and L. W. Hill
1953 Allergic reactions to bee and wasp stings. New England Journal of Medicine 249:726-731.

Mulla, M. S.
1958 Recent developments in the biology and control of *Hippelates* eye gnats. California Mosquito Control Association, Proceedings and Papers 26:78-82.

——— 1959 Some important aspects of *Hippelates* gnats with a brief presentation of current research findings. California Mosquito Control Association, Proceedings and Papers 27:48-52.

Mulla, M. S., M. M. Barnes, and M. J. Garber
1960 Soil treatments with insecticides for control of the eye gnats *Hippelates collusor* and *H. hermsi*. Journal of Economic Entomology 53:362-365.

Mulla, M. S. and R. B. March
1959 Flight range, dispersal patterns and population density of the eye gnat *Hippelates collusor* (Townsend). Entomological Society of America, Annals 52:641-646.

Muma, M. H.
1951 The arachnid order Solpugida in the United States. American Museum of Natural History, Bulletin 97:35-141.
Includes an especially useful bibliography.

Muttoo, R. N.
1956 Facts about bee-keeping in India. Bee World 37:125-133.

Nambiar, T. K.
1948 A brief review of the mosquito fauna of Abadan, Iran. Abadan. 18 p.

National Academy of Sciences/National Research Council. Committee and Snakebite Therapy
1963 Interim statement on snakebite therapy. Toxicon 1:81-87.
Includes discussions on the potentially dangerous use of cryotherapy (icing or other "refrigeration" of tissue). Recommends that the ligature-cryotherapy method not be used by military personnel as a first-aid measure for the treatment of bites of venomous snakes. Pertinent data in this reference has been summarized and extended by Minton, Dowling, and Russell (1967).

Negroni, P. *et al.*
1952 Estudios sobre el *Coccidioides immitis* Rixford et Gilchrist. XII: Cuarta contribución al estudio de la endemia argentina. Revista Argentina de Dermato-Sifilología 36:269-275.

Netolitzky, F.
1920 Kaefer als nahrung und heilmittel. Koloniale Rundschau 8:21-46; 47-60.
This early work expounded the enormous nutritive value of insects. Extensive original sources are given.

Newburgh, L. H.
1949 Physiology of heat regulation and the science of clothing. Saunders, Philadelphia. 457 p.
This product of World War II, prepared at the request of the Division of Medical Sciences of the National Research Council, provides a manual and reference text on heat transfer, thermometry, thermoregulation, physiological adjustments to heat and cold, and regional studies including the desert. This is an important basic reference for students of the physiological ecology of desert, tropical, and tundra animals.

Nikolskii, A. M.
1916 Faune de la Russie et des pays limitrophes. Reptiles, II: Ophidia. Académie Impériale des Sciences St. Petersberg, Musée Zoologique.

Noon, Z. B. and W. L. Minear
1941 Spider-bite. Southwestern Medicine 25:169-175.
Reports, in a total of 15 cases in Arizona, 11% mortality (1 to 9) with no treatment, and 0% mortality (0 in 6) with treatment.

Nordenskiöld, N. E. H.
1929 L'apiculture en Amérique. Anthropologie 39:285-286.

Nosek, J. *et al.*
1962 The role of birds in a natural focus of tick-borne encephalitis. Journal of Hygiene, Epidemiology, Microbiology, and Immunology (Prague) 6:478.

Nutting, W. L.
1961 Termites in Arizona. p. 1-7. *In* University of Arizona Pest Control Conference, 2nd, Tucson, Conference Manual. 104 p.

——— 1965 Observations on the nesting site and biology of the Arizona damp-wood termite *Zootermopsis laticeps* (Banks) (Hodotermitidae). Psyche 72: 113-125.

——— 1966 Distribution and biology of the primitive drywood termite *Pterotermes occidentis* (Walker) (Kalotermitidae). Psyche 73:166-179.
An important paper on one of the few species (perhaps the only species) of termite that occurs wholly in desert habitats within the geographic limits of the North American Desert. Physical and biotic limiting factors are reported and a map of the geographic distribution of this truly desert species is given.

Oliver, J. A.
1958 Snakes in fact and fiction. Macmillan Co., New York.

Ophüls, W. and H. C. Moffitt
1900 A new pathogenic mould (formerly described as a protozoon: *Coccidioides immitis pyogenes):* a preliminary report. Philadelphia Medical Journal 5:1471-1472.

Osborn, T. G. B.
1934 Effect of introduction of exotic plants and animals into Australia. Pacific Science Congress, 5th, Canada, 1933, Proceedings 1:809-810.

Owen, J. S.
1952 Further notes on poisonous snakes. Sudan Notes and Records 33(2):311-314.

Palgrave, W. G.
1865 Narrative of a year's journey through Central and Eastern Arabia (1862-63). 2d ed. Macmillan & Co., London and Cambridge. 2 vols.

Palmer, C. E., P. Q. Edwards, and W. E. Allfather
1957 Characteristics of skin reactions to coccidioidin and histoplasmin, with evidence of an unidentified source of sensitivity in some geographic areas. *In* Symposium on Coccidioidomycosis, Phoenix, 1957, Proceedings. U.S. Public Health Service, Publication 575:171-180.

Pan American Sanitary Bureau
1958 Reported cases of notifiable diseases in the Americas for years 1946 to 1955. *Its* Science Publication 38. *(See also* Science Publications 58, 86, 102, and 114.)

Pappagianis, D.
1967 Epidemiological aspects of respiratory mycotic infections. Bacteriological Reviews 31(1):25-34.
This paper and the one directly preceeding it (Ajello, 1967) are recent reviews on coccidioidomycosis, and provide, together, an excellent summary of the current status of the work and theory on this desert-centered disease.

Parker, H. W.
1949 The snakes of Somaliland and the Sokotra Islands. Rijksmuseum van Natuurlijke Historie, Leiden, Zoologische Verhandelingen 6:1-115.

Parker, K. F.
1958 Arizona ranch, farm, and garden weeds. University of Arizona, Agricultural Extension Service, Circular 265. 288 p.

Parker, K. L.
1905 The Euahleyi tribe, a study of aboriginal life in Australia. A. Constable & Co., Ltd., London. 156 p.

Parrish, H. M.
1959 Deaths from bites and stings of venomous animals and insects in the United States. Archives of Internal Medicine 104:198-207.
Report on deaths due to poisonous (venomous) animals in the United States during the years 1950-1954. States that bees, wasps, and hornets ranked ahead of venomous snakes as causes of human death during that period.

Pasteur, G. and J. Bons
1960 Catalogue des reptiles actuels du Maroc. Institut Scientifique Chérifien, Travaux, sér. Zoologie 21:1-3.

Patton, W. S.
1931 Insects, ticks, mites, and venomous animals of medical and veterinary importance. II: Public health. H. R. Grubb, Ltd., Croydon, England. 740 p.

Patton, W. S. and A. M. Evans
1929 Insects, ticks, mites and venomous animals of medical and veterinary importance. I: Medical. H. R. Grubb, Ltd., Croydon, England. 786 p.

Pawlowsky, E. N.
1927 Die giftiere und ihre giftigkeit. Fischer Verlag, Jena. 516 p.

Paylore, P.
1967 Arid-lands research institutions: a world directory. University of Arizona Press, Tucson. 268 p.

Pearson, O. P.
1942 On the cause and nature of a poisonous action produced by the bite of a shrew *(Blarina brevicauda).* Journal of Mammalogy 23:159-166.

Pepper, J. H.
1955 The ecological approach to management of insect populations. Journal of Economic Entomology 48:453-456.

Peters, J. A.
1959 A bibliography and index of Karl P. Schmidt's papers on coral snakes. Copeia 3:192-196.

Petit, L.
1962 The attitude of the population and the problem of education in the Sahara. *In* The problems of the arid zone, Proceedings of the Paris symposium. Unesco, Paris. Arid Zone Research 18:449-470.

Phisalix, M.
1922 Animaux venimeux et venins: ila fonction venimeuse chez tous les animaux; les appareils venimeux; les venins et leurs propriétés; les fonctions et usages des venins: l'envenimation et son traitement. Masson et Cie, Paris. 2 vols.

Pierce, W. D.
1915 The uses of certain weevils and weevil products in food and medicine. Entomological Society of Washington, Proceedings 17:151-154.

Pirosky, I. and J. W. Abalos
1963 Spiders of the genus *Latrodectus* in Argentina. Latrodectism and *Latrodectus* antivenin. p. 137-140. *In* H. L. Keegan and W. V. Macfarlane, eds., Venomous and poisonous animals and noxious plants of the Pacific Region. Macmillan Co., New York.

Pitman, C. R. S.
1938 A guide to the snakes of Uganda. Uganda Society, Kampala, Publication. 362 p.

Platt, R. F.
1948 Red scale eradication in eastern Riverside County. Exchange Pest Control Circular 159:620-621.

Plotnikov, V.
1926 Insects injurious to agricultural plants in Central Asia (translated title). Tashkent.

Plunkett, O. A.
1955 Ecology and spread of pathogenic fungi. p. 18-24. *In* T. H. Sternberg and V. D. Newcomer, eds., Therapy of fungus diseases. Little, Brown and Company, Boston.

Plunkett, O. A. and F. E. Swatek
1957 Ecological studies of *Coccidioides immitis.* *In* Symposium on Coccidioidomycosis, Phoenix, 1957, Proceedings. U.S. Public Health Service, Publication 575:158-160.

Pocock, R. I.
  1929 Arachnida. *In* Encyclopaedia Britannica, 14th ed., 2:201-208.

Pope, C. H.
  1944 Poisonous snakes of the new world. New York Zoological Society, New York. 47 p.

  ———
  1955 The reptile world, a natural history of the snakes, lizards, turtles, and crocodilians. Knopf, New York. 324 p.
  A recommended popular account on poisonous snakes and other reptiles of the world.

  ———
  1958 Fatal bite of captive African rear-fanged snake *(Dispholidus).* Copeia, p. 280-282.
  An acount of the unanticipated fatal boomslang *(Dispholidus typus)* bite, and death of Karl Schmidt.

Popov, G.
  1959 Some notes on injurious Acrididae in the Sudan-Chad area. Entomologists' Monthly Magazine 95:90-92.

  ———
  1960 Preliminary report on the second survey, Mauritania, Soudan and Senegal. FAO/Unesco Desert Locust Ecological Survey. Mimeographed.

Popov, G. and C. Rossetti
  1958 Preliminary report of the first survey—Chad Territory, Sudan, Ethiopia. FAO/Unesco Desert Locust Ecological Survey. Mimeographed.

Posadas, A.
  1900 Psorospermoise infectante généralisé. Revue de Chirurgie, Paris, 21:277-282.

Powell, R. D.
  1966 The chemotherapy of malaria. Clinical Pharmacology and Therapeutics 7:48-76.

Pradhan, S.
  1957 The ecology of arid zone insects (excluding locusts and grasshoppers). *In* Human and animal ecology, reviews of research. Unesco, Paris. Arid Zone Research 8:199-240.
  A review (649 papers cited) that includes discussions and conclusions for faunal groups in arid and semiarid lands. While the content is largely economic in orientation, it remains one of the major papers that provide estimates of our relative knowledge on the biology of the insects in the world's deserts.

Prakash, I.
  1959 Extinct and vanishing mammals from the desert of Rajasthan and the problem of their preservation. Indian Forester 84:642-645.

  ———
  1963 Zoo-geography and evolution of the mammalian fauna of Rajasthan desert, India. Mammalia 27:342-351.

Pullar, E. M.
  1953 The wild (feral) pigs of Australia, their origin, distribution, and economic importance. National Museum, Melbourne, Memoirs 18:7-23.

Quayle, H. J.
  1929 Citrus fruit insects in Mediterranean countries. U.S. Department of Agriculture, Bulletin 134.

  ———
  1938 Insects of citrus and other fruits. Comstock Publishing Company, New York. 583 p.

Rabb, G. B.
  1959 Toxic salivary glands in the primitive insectivore *Solenodon.* Natural History Miscellanea 170. 30 p.

Rabbit Control Symposium, 2nd, Sydney, 1960
  1961 Conference convened by C.S.I.R.O. and held at Sydney, October 11-12, 1960. C.S.I.R.O., Melbourne. 102 p.
  Thirteen review papers on rabbit control, including an excellent review of the present-day situation by F. N. Ratcliffe (see Ratcliffe, 1961).

Rainey, R. C.
  1951a Flying locusts and convection currents. Anti-Locust Research Centre, London, Bulletin 9:51-70.

  ———
  1951b Weather and the movement on locust swarms. A new hypothesis. Nature 168:1057-1060.
  A discussion of the correlation of the intertropical convergence zone with the distribution of desert locust swarms, and the importance of wind in the dispersal of airborne insects. Convergence also provides the mechanism for the frequently critical simultaneous arrival of rains and locust swarms.

Raswan, C. R.
  1934 Im land der schwarzen zelte. Ullstein, Berlin. 156 p.

Ratcliffe, F. N.
  1961 A review of the 1958 Melbourne Symposium on rabbit control and its relevance to the present-day situation. *In* Rabbit Control Symposium, 2nd, Sydney, 1960. C.S.I.R.O., Melbourne.

Read, S. and H. Jervis
  1958 A provisional check-list of the birds of Iran. Tehran University, Publication 465:1-25.

Reid, H. A. *et al.*
  1963 Clinical effects of bites by Malayan viper *(Ancistrodon rhodostoma).* Lancet 1(7282):617-621.

Remington, C. L.
  1950 The bite and habits of a giant centipede *(Scolopendra subspinipes)* in the Philippine Islands. American Journal of Tropical Medicine 30:453-455.

Ridgway, R. L., T. McGregor, and J. F. Flanigan
  1962 The effect of residual deposits of insecticides on the scorpion *Centruroides vittatus.* Journal of Economic Entomology 55:1012-1013.

Ripper, W. E. and G. Lloyd
  1965 Cotton pests of the Sudan; their habits and control. Blackwell Scientific Publications, Oxford. 345 p.
  This model work in applied zoology in the "arid zone" reports most recent methods for controlling cotton pests and the animals involved in their biological control in the southern Sahara.

Rivers, W. H. R.
  1906 The Todas. Macmallan & Co., Ltd., London. 755 p.

Rivnay, E.
  1962 Field crop pests in the Near East. W. Junk, The Hague. 450 p.

Robbins, A.
  1851 Journal of adventures in Africa in 1815/17. S. Andrus & Son, Hartford. 275 p.

Roewer, C. F.
  1942- Katalog der Araneae von 1758 bis 1940. R. Friedländer und Sohn, Berlin. 2 vols. in 3
  1954

Rohayem, H.
1953   Scorpion toxin and antagonistic drugs. Fouad I University, Cairo. (Thesis, M.D. in Physiology) 56 p.

Romaña, C. and J. W. Abalos
1948   *Latrodectus mactans,* its control. Instituto de Medicina Regional, Tucumán, Anales 2(2):153-161.

Rooij, N. de
1917   The reptiles of the Indo-Australian Archipelago. II: Ophidia. E. J. Brill, Leiden.

Russell, F. E.
1962   Muscle relaxants in black widow spider *(Latrodectus mactans)* poisoning. American Journal of the Medical Sciences 243 (2)1:81-83.
This work includes a discussion on the potentially dangerous use of cryotherapy (icing or other "refrigeration" of tisue). Russell also reports that methocarbomol is even more effective than calcium gluconate for relief of muscle pain and spasms resulting from black widow spiderbite in California.

Russell, F. W. and R. S. Scharffenberg
1964   Bibliography of snake venoms and venomous snakes. Bibliographic Associates, Inc., West Covina, California. 220 p.
This work includes titles of papers and volumes of varying size and usefulness on one or more poisonous species in one or more of the deserts of the world. Gives 5,829 titles on snake venoms and poisonous snakes published since the year 100 B.C., including, works on the general biology of venomous snakes, venom apparatus, collection of venomous snakes, prevention of snakebite, yields of venoms, effects of venoms, chemistry and toxicology of venoms, antivenin, snakebite statistics, medical treatment, and other aspects. Pertinent data in this reference have been summarized and extended by Minton, Dowling, and Russell (1967). Many of the works cited are investigations on desert species.

Sabin, A. B. *et al.*
1944   *Phlebotomus* (pappataci or sandfly) fever; a disease of military importance. Summary of existing knowledge and preliminary report of original investigations. American Medical Association, Journal 125:603-606, 693-699.

Saint-Girons, H.
1956   Les serpents du Maroc. Société des Sciences Naturelles et Physiques du Maroc, Rabat, Variétés Scientifiques 8:1-29.

Saint-Girons, H. and M.-C. Saint-Girons
1956   Cycle d'activité et thermorégulation chez les reptiles (lézards et serpents). Vie et Milieu 7:133-226.

Salt, H.
1816   A voyage to Abyssinia . . . in the years 1809 and 1810. F. C. and J. Rivington, London. 506 p.

Sampayo, R.
1942   *Latrodectus mactans* and Latrodectism. Universidad Nacional de Buenos Aires, Buenos Aires. (Thesis)

Sandoz, A. G.
1951   Bisse und sticke einiger giftiere. Sandoz, Basel.

Savory, T. H.
1964   Arachnida. Academic Press, London and New York. 291 p.
This is an important general reference on the biology of the arachnids (spiders, scorpions, harvesters, ticks, mites, etc.), with particular reference to their classification, structure, and distribution.

Schenone, H. and F. Prats
1961   Arachnidism by *Loxosceles laeta.* Archives of Dermatology 83:139-142.

Schmaus, J. W.
1959   Envenomation in Kansas. Kansas Medical Society. Journal 60:237-248.

Schmaus, L. F.
1929   Case of arachnoidism (spider bite). American Medical Association, Journal 92:1265.

Schmidt, K. P.
1933   Preliminary account of the coral snakes of Central America and Mexico. Field Museum of Natural History, Zoological Series 20:29-40.

——   1953   A check list of North American amphibians and reptiles. 6th ed. American Society of Ichthyologists and Herpetologists, Chicago. 280 p.

Schmidt, K. P. and D. D. Davis
1941   Field book of snakes of the U.S. and Canada. Putnam, New York. 365 p

Schmidt, K. P. and R. F. Inger
1957   Living reptiles of the world. Hanover House, Garden City, New York. 287 p.

Schmidt, K. P. and H. Marx
1956   The herpetology of Sinai. Chicago Museum of Natural History, Fieldiana: Zoology 39 (40): 21-40.

Schmidt-Nielsen, B. *et al.*
1956   Water balance of the camel. American Journal of Physiology 185:185-194.

——   1957   Urea excretion in the camel. American Journal of Physiology 188:477-484.

Schmidt-Nielsen, K.
1954   Water conservation in small desert rodents. p. 173-181. *In* J. L. Cloudsley-Thompson, ed., Biology of deserts. Institute of Biology, London. 224 p.

——   1959a The physiology of the camel. Scientific American 201:140-151.

——   1959b Salt glands. Scientific American 200:140-151.

——   1964a Desert animals. Physiological problems of heat and water. Oxford University Press, London. 277 p.
This is a synthesis of our knowledge on the subject. Following a discussion of man's physiological responses in desert environments, as a basis for comparison with animals, the second chapter treats the most consequential single aspect of an animal's physical characteristics, its body size, a recurrent theme in a fascinating story of genetic adaptation and physiological adjustment of the water balance and temperature regulation of desert animals. Bibliography: p. 253-270.

——   1964b Terrestrial animals in dry heat: Desert rodents. *In* D. B. Dill, E. F. Adolph, and C. G. Wilber, eds. Adaptation to the environment. American Physiological Society, Washington, D.C., Handbook of Physiology 4:493-507.

Schmidt-Nielsen, K. and W. R. Dawson
1964 Terrestrial animals in dry heat: Desert reptiles. *In* D. B. Dill, E. F. Adolph, and C. G. Wilber, eds., Adaptation to the environment. American Physiological Society, Washington, D.C., Handbook of Physiology 4:467-480.

Schmidt-Nielsen, K. and A. E. Newsome
1962 Water balance in the mulgara *(Dasycercus cristicauda),* a carnivorous desert marsupial. Australian Journal of Biological Sciences 15:683-689.

Schmidt-Nielsen, K. and B. Schmidt-Nielsen
1952 Water metabolism in desert mammals. Physiological Reviews 32:135-166.

Schmidt-Nielsen, K. *et al.*
1957*a* The question of water storage in the stomach of camel. Mammalia 20:1-15.

——— 1957*b* Body temperature of the camel and its relation to water economy. American Journal of Physiology 188:103-112.

Schomburgk, H.
1910 Wild und wilde in herzen Afrikas. E. Fleischel, Berlin. 373 p.

Schwartz, E. A.
1894 Notes on *Hippelates pusio* in the southern states. Entomological Society of Washington, Proceedings 3:178-180.

——— 1895 The *Hippelates* plague in Florida. Insect Life 7:374-379.

Schwarz, H. F.
1948 Stingless bees (Meliponidae) of the Western Hemisphere. American Museum of Natural History, Bulletin 90. 546 p.

Scortecci, G.
1938 I "Mamba" dell'Africa orientale italiana. Rivista di Biologia Coloniale 1(2):81-90.

——— 1939 Gli ofidi velenosi dell'Africa italiana. Istituto Sieroterapico Milanese, Milano. 292 p.

——— 1940 Biologia sahariana. Edizioni della Mostra d'Oltremare, Napoli. 205 p.
Provides especially important and carefully detailed data on distribution, relative abundance, population density and general ecology of the animal and plant species, particularly in the little-known remote interior of Libya.

Scortecci, G. and V. Tedesco Zammarno
1937 Somalia: la fauna. *In* G. Corni, La Somalia Italiana, vol. 1.

Scott, H. G. and H. D. Pratt
1959 Scorpions, spiders and other arthropods of minor public health importance and their control. Training Guide, Insect Control Series. U.S. Department of Health, Eucation and Welfare, Public Health Service Communicable Disease Center. Training Branch, Atlanta, Georgia. 27 p.

Sears, P. B.
1935 Deserts on the march. University of Oklahoma Press, Norman.

Selander, R. B.
1958 Melanism in some Meloidae . . . from the Pinacate lava cap in northwestern Sonora, Mexico. Kansas Academy of Science, Transactions 61:77-80.

Selye, H.
1950 The physiology and pathology of exposure to stress, a treatise based on the concepts of the general-adaptation-syndrome and the disease of adaptation. Acta, Inc., Montreal. 822, 203R p.
Bibliography: p. 1R-203R.

Shannon, F. A.
1956 Comments on the treatment of reptile poisoning. *In* E. E. Buckley and N. Porges, eds., Venoms. American Association for the Advancement of Science, Publication 44:405-512.
This is a documented specific warning against the potentially dangerous use of cryotherapy (icing or other local refrigeration of tissue) for treatment of bites and stings of poisonous animals.

Shaw, T.
1738 Travels, or observations relating to several parts of Barbary and the Levant. Printed at the Theatre, Oxford. 442, 60 p.

Shelford, V. E.
1945 The relative merits of the life-zone and biome concepts. Wilson Bulletin 57:248-252.
A biome map for North America, based on Pitelka (1941); includes the Great Basin Desert (shadscale/kangaroo rat biome), and the Mohave, Sonoran, and Chihuahuan Deserts (creosotebush/desert fox biome).

Shepard, H. H.
1951 Insect control by chemicals. McGraw-Hill Company, New York. 504 p.

Sheynermann, A. A.
1941 Clinical aspects and therapy of the bite of "Kara-Kurt" spider. Novyi Khirurgicheskii arkhiv. Tver. Dnepropetrovsk, Ukrainia.

Short, J. R. T.
1963 Introduction to applied entomology. Longmans, London. 235 p.

Shotwell, R. L.
1938 Species and distribution of grasshoppers responsible for recent outbreaks. Journal of Economic Entomology 31:602-610.

Shreve, F.
1915 The vegetation of a desert mountain range as conditioned by climatic factors. Carnegie Institution of Washington, Publication 217. 112 p.
This is an early classic in arid-zone biology that reports on and evaluates the interactions of environment and organisms, and which frankly rejects the organismic theory (of Clements *et al.*) in ecology, in exchange for the very modern concept of an individualistic adaptive response of the geotype to natural selection by the stresses imposed by the environment, in this case primarily arid and semiarid environments. Shreve's concepts and conclusions (1915, 1950, and elsewhere) cannot be improved upon today and form a theoretical framework for explaining the ultimate basis of the existence of the complex biotic (plant-animal) community.

——— 1942 The desert vegetation of North America. Botanical Review 8:195-246.
Map and discussion of the nature and location of the four major subdivisions of the North American Desert: Great Basin, Mohave, Sonoran, and Chihuahuan. This is the modern departure point for the entire subject, both organic and environmental.

Shreve, F.
1951   Vegetation and flora of the Sonoran Desert. I: Vegetation. Carnegie Institution of Washington, Publication 59. 192 p.

This, by far the best available publication on the subject, has been cited by diverse workers (and will continue to be cited) more than any other paper published on the Sonoran Desert at or before the turn of the half-century. It is also used liberally without attribution, as by Jaeger (1957). This work was republished (minus certain photographs) in 1964, to include under the same cover the second part, taxonomy of the flora by I. L. Wiggins.

Sillans, R.
1958   Les savanes de l'Afrique Centrale. P. Lechevalier, Paris. 423 p. (Encyclopedie Biologique, 55).

_____
1959   Les savannes de l'Afrique centrale. Le Chevalier, Paris. 423 p.

Silvestri, F.
1903   Contribuzione alla conoscenza dei termidi e termophili dell'America meridionale. Redia 1:1-234.

Simmonds, P. L.
1885   The animal food resources of different nations, with mention of some of the special dainties of various people derived from the animal kingdom. E. and F. N. Spon, London. 461 p.

Siniscal, A. A.
1955   The trachoma story. U.S. Public Health Report 70:497-507.

Skinner, A.
1910   The use of insects and other invertebrates as food by the North-American Indians. New York Entomological Society, Journal 18:264-267.

Sludskii, A. A. and I. G. Shubin
1961   Aerovisual method of censusing game animals in Kazakhstan deserts. p. 19-21. *In* Organization and methods of censusing terrestrial vertebrate faunal resources. Moscow Society of Naturalists. Translated, 1963, from the Russian for the National Science Foundation by The Israel Program for Scientific Translations, Jerusalem.

Smith, C. E. *et al.*
1946   Effect of season and dust control on coccidioidomycosis. American Medical Association, Journal 132: 833-838.

Smith, H. M.
1946   Handbook of lizards. Comstock Publishing Company, Ithaca, New York.

Smith, H. M. and E. H. Taylor
1945   An annotated checklist and key to the snakes of Mexico. U.S. National Museum, Bulletin 187. 239 p.

Smith, M. A.
1926   Monograph of the sea-snakes (Hydrophidae). British Museum, London. 130 p.

_____
1943   Reptilia and Amphibia. III: Serpentes. Taylor and Francis, London. 583 p. (Fauna of British India)

Smith, M. R.
1936   Distribution of the Argentine ant in the United States and suggestions for its control and eradication. U.S. Department of Agriculture, Circular 387.

_____
1951   Family Formicidae. *In* C. F. W. Muesebeck, K. V. Krombein, and H. K. Townes, Hymenoptera of America north of Mexico, synoptic catalog. U.S. Department of Agriculture, Monograph 2:778-875.

Smith, R. C.
1957   The effects of irrigation on insects and other arthropods. Intersoc. Conf. Irrig. Drainage, San Francisco, Proc. (unpublished typescript).

Snyder, T. E.
1948   Our enemy the termite. Comstock Publishing Company, Ithaca, New York. 257 p.

_____
1949   Catalog of the termites (Isoptera) of the world. Smithsonian Miscellaneous Collections 112:1-490.

_____
1954   Annotated subject-heading bibliography of termites, 1350 B.C. to A.D. 1954. Smithsonian Miscellaneous Collections 130. 305 p.

_____
1961   Supplement to the annotated, subject-heading bibliography of termites, 1955-1960. Smithsonian Miscellaneous Collections 143:1-137.

Southcott, R. V.
1961   Red-back spider bite (*Latrodectism*) with response to antivenin therapy given eight hours after the bite. Medical Journal of Australia 48(1):659-662

Sparrman, A.
1787   Voyage au Cap de Bonne-Espérance. Chez Buisson, Paris. 2 vols.

Spencer, B.
1914   Native tribes of the Northern Territory of Central Australia. Macmillan and Co., Ltd., London. 516 p.

_____
1928   Wanderings in wild Australia. Macmillan and Co., Ltd., London. 2 vols.

Spencer, B. and F. J. Gillen
1899   The native tribes of central Australia. Macmillan and Co., Ltd., London. 671 p.

Stahnke, H. L.
1953   The L-C treatment of venomous bites and stings. Arizona Highways 29(2):35.

One of a number of magazine and newspaper articles, and privately published pamphlets, misguidedly attempting to revive the potentially dangerous use of cryotherapy (icing or other "refrigeration" of tissue) for snake-bite. Warning: do not follow the instructions given for poisonous snakebite; see National Academy of Sciences / National Research Council, Committee on Snakebite Therapy (1963).

Stanek, V. J.
1960   Achtung, giftschlanger (Introducing poisonous snakes, translated by J. Turner). Spring Books, London. 80 p.

Stebbins, R. C.
1954   Amphibians and reptiles of western North America. McGraw-Hill, New York. 528 p.

Covers unusually eurytopic species native to the North American Desert, such as the teiid whiptail lizard, *Snemidophorus tigris,* and the iguanid side-blotched lizard, *Uta stansburiana.*

_____
1966   A field guide to western reptiles and amphibians; field marks of all species in western North America. Houghton, Mifflin Co., Boston. 279 p.

Includes coverage of the "desert species" (both true and

imagined); many of them are highly restricted within the desert, while others are unusually eurytopic species native to the North American Desert and found widely and abundantly throughout most of the modern derivative communities of the Madro-Tertiary Geoflora, including the entire desert subdivisions of the North American Desert.

Steele, J. D,. ed.
1964 The treatment of mycotic and parasitic diseases of the chest. C. C. Thomas, Springfield, Illinois. 259 p.

Steinberg, I. R. and T. A. Ortiz-Luna
1941 Contribution to the study of arachnidism; bite of spider of the genus *Ctenus*. Dia Medico 13: 1062-1064.

Steindachner, F.
1903 Batrachier und reptilien von Südarabien und Sokotra, gesammelt während der südarabischen expedition der Kaiserlichen Akademie der Wissenschaften. K. Akademie der Wissenschaften, Wien, Math.-Naturw. Klasse, Sitzungsberichte 112 (1):7-14.

Sterling, E. C.
1896 Anthropology. *In* B. Spencer, ed., Report on the work of the Horn Scientific Expedition to Central Australia, IV. Dulau and Company, London.

Stier, R. A. and R. F. E. Stier
1959 The results of desensitization in allergy to insect stings. GP 19(3):103-108.

Storer, T. I.
1931 Known and potential results of birds and animal introductions with special reference to California. California Department of Agriculture, Bulletin 20:267-273.

Sulman, F. G., N. Hirschman, and J. Pfeifer
1964 Effect of hot, dry, desert winds (sirocco, sharav, hamsin) on the metabolism of hormones and minerals. *In* Environmental physiology and psychology in arid conditions, Proceedings of the Lucknow Symposium. Unesco, Paris. Arid Zone Research 24:89-95.
An excellent recent review.

Sumner, L.
1959 Effects of wild burros on bighorn in Death Valley. Desert Bighorn Council, Annual Meeting, 3rd, Death Valley, California. U.S. National Park Service, Washington, D.C., Transactions 4.
This is one of three papers on burros in the report of the Death Valley Desert Bighorn Council; the other two are on effects of wild burros on desert water supplies and effects of wild burros on range conditions. These are 3 reports in a total of 18 on problems and present knowledge of the biology and management of the endangered desert bighorn sheep.

Swanson, G. A.
1950 The need for research in the introduction of exotic animals. *In* International Technical Conference on the Protection of Nature, Lake Success, 1949, Proceedings and Papers. Unesco, Paris.

Swaroop, S. and B. Grab
1954 Snakebite mortality in the world. World Health Organization, Bulletin 10(1).

Sweetman, H. L.
1936 The biological control of insects. Comstock Publishing Co., Inc. Ithaca, New York.

Symposium on Coccidioidomycosis, Phoenix, 1957
1957 Proceedings. U.S. Public Health Service, Publication 575. 197 p.

Symposium on Coccidioidomycosis, Phoenix, 1965
1967 Coccidioidomycosis, Papers from the 2nd Symposium on Coccidioidomycosis, Phoenix, Arizona, December 8-10, 1965. Edited by Libero Ajello. University of Arizona Press, Tucson. 434 p.

Taylor, F. H. and R. E. Murray
1946 Spiders, ticks and mites, including the species harmful to man in Australia and New Guinea. Commonwealth of Australia, Department of Health, School of Public Health and Tropical Medicine, Service Publication 6:1-275.

Taylor, J. S. and E. Cavendish
1859 Ornithological reminiscences of Egypt. Ibis, p. 41-55.

Taylor, R. M. *et al.*
1956 A study of the ecology of West Nile virus in Egypt. American Journal of Tropical Medicine and Hygiene 5:579-620.
This study filled the gap between the prevalence of the disease (in Egypt) and the lack of information on the mechanism of its transmission. It details the methods and results for collection and handling of blood specimens, isolation of the virus from the blood of native birds, mammals and men, and the needed attack on sanitation problems in Egypt. It was concluded that the disease is endemic and that the main cycle is through mosquitos *(Culex)* and birds *(Columbia* and *Corvus).*

Terentjev, P. V. and S. A. Cernov
1949 Apredelitej presmykajuschcichsja i semnowodnych. 3rd ed. Moscow. 339 p.
(Distribution of reptiles and amphibians)

Theodor, O.
1955 On poisonous snakes and snake bite in Israel. Jerusalem.

Théodoridès, J.
1949 Les coleopteres comestibles. Naturalistes Belges, Bulletin Mensuel 30:126-137.
A work that expounds the nutritive value of insects, with extensive original sources.

Thompson, H. V.
1955 The wild European rabbit and possible dangers of its introduction into the U.S.A. Journal of Wildlife Management 19:8-13.

Thorp, R. W. and W. D. Woodson
1945 Black widow, America's most poisonous spider. University of North Carolina Press, Chapel Hill. 222 p.
A useful reference on the problem of spiderbite and on the general biology of the black widow spider *(Latrodectus mactans).* A noncomprehensive summary is given of knowledge through the period of World War II. Except for some aspects of treatment and such statistics as those on mortality, it still remains a singular reference in the modern literature on the subject.

Tillyard, R. J.
1926 The insects of Australia and New Zealand. Angus and Robertson, Ltd., Sydney. 560 p.

Tindale, N. B.
1932   Revision of the Australian ghost moths (Hepialidae). I. South Australian Museum, Records 4: 497-536.

——— 1938   Ghost moths of the family Hepialidae. South Australian Naturalist 19:1-6.

Tinkham, E. R.
1952   The eye gnats of the Coachella Valley, with notes on the 1951 larvaciding program. California Mosquito Control Association, Proceedings and Papers 20:83-84.

Tobar, R. G.
1952   Capacidad de ayuno de los triatomideos chilenos. Boletín de Informaciones Parasitarias Chilenas 7(4):56-59.

Townsend, C.H.
1893   On the diptera of Baja California, including some species from adjacent regions. California Academy of Sciences, Proceedings, 2nd ser., 4:593-620.

Travis, B. V. and R. M. Labadan
1967   Arthropods of medical importance in Asia and the European USSR. U.S. Army Natick Laboratories, Technical Report 67-65-ES. 694 p.
Ecological (habitats, activity), distributional, medical, and bibliographical data. Part I includes introductory material and data on mosquitoes. Part II gives data on other arthropods—black flies, sand flies, midges, horse flies, biting and nonbiting flies, fleas, bugs, ticks and mites, verticating and vesicating arthropods. In addition, there is a summary of diseases or disease organisms transmitted by other miscellaneous arthropods.

Tregenza, L. A.
1951   Observations on the birds of the southeastern desert of Egypt. Zoological Society of Egypt, 9:1-18.

Tristram, H. B.
1860   The great Sahara. J. Murray, London. 435 p.

Tromp, S. W.
1963   Medical biometeorology: weather, climate, and the living organism, by S. W. Tromp in cooperation with 26 contributors. Elsevier Publishing Co., Amsterdam, N.Y. 991 p.
A highly readable and detailed recent review covering both animals and men.

——— 1964   Weather, climate, and man. *In* D. B. Dill, E. F. Adolph, and C. G. Wilber, eds., Adaptation to the environment. American Physiological Society, Washington, D.C., Handbook of Physiology 4: 283-293.

Troughton, E. L.
1938   Australian mammals; their past and future. Journal of Mammalogy 19:401-411.

Tulga, T.
1960   Cross-reactions between antiscorpion *(Buthus quinquestriatus)* and antiscorpion *(Prionurus crassicauda),* sera (translated title). Türk. Ijiyen ve Tecrübî Biyoloji Dergisi 20:191-203.
In Turkish, summary.

Turk, F. A.
1951   Myriapodological notes. III: The iatro-zoology, biology, and suplematics of some tropical "myriapods." Annals and Magazine of Natural History, ser. 12, 4:35-48.

Tyler, A.
1956   An auto-antivenin in the Gila monster and its relation to a concept on natural auto-antibodies. *In* E. E. Buckley and N. Porges, eds., Venoms. American Association for the Advancement of Science. Publication 44:65-77.

Unesco
1957   Human and animal ecology, reviews of research. Unesco, Paris. Arid Zone Research 8.

——— 1958a   Climatology, reviews of research. Unesco, Paris. Arid Zone Research 10. 190 p.

——— 1958b   Climatology and microclimatology, proceedings of the Canberra symposium. Unesco, Paris. Arid Zone Research 11. 355 p.

——— 1961   Salinity problems in the arid zones, proceedings of the Teheran symposium, 1958. Unesco, Paris. Arid Zone Research 14. 395 p.

——— 1962   The problems of the arid zone, proceedings of the Paris symposium, 1960. Unesco, Paris. Arid Zone Research 18. 481 p.

——— 1963   Environmental physiology and psychology in arid conditions, reviews of research. Unesco, Paris. Arid Zone Research 22. 345 p.

——— 1964   Environmental physiology and psychology in arid conditions, proceedings of the Lucknow symposium. Unesco, Paris. Arid Zone Research 24.

U.S. Air Force
1962   Emergency rescue, survival. Air Force Manual 64-5. 160 p. U.S. Government Printing Office, Washington, D.C.

U.S. Department of Agriculture
1952   Insects. Yearbook of Agriculture, Washington, D.C. 780 p., 73 pl.

Usinger, R. L.
1944   The triatominae of North and Central America and the West Indies, and their public health significance. U.S. Public Health Bulletin 288:1-83.

Uvarov, B. P.
1928   Locusts and grasshoppers. A handbook for their study and control. Imperial Bureau of Entomology, London. 352 p.

——— 1937   Biological and ecological basis of locust phases and their practical application. International Locust Conference, 4th, Cairo, 1936, Appendix 7:16 p. (361)

——— 1943   Orthoptera of the Siwa Oases. Linnean Society, London, Proceedings 155:8-30.

——— 1947   The grasshopper problem in North America. Nature 160:857-859.

——— 1948   Recent advances in acridology: Anatomy and physiology of Acrididae. Royal Entomological Society, London, Transactions 99:1-75.

——— 1951   Locust research and control 1929-1950. Colonial Research Publication, London, 10:1-67.

Uvarov, B. P.
1956 The locust and grasshopper problem in relation to the development of arid lands. *In* G. White, ed., The future of arid lands. American Association for the Advancement of Science, Publication 43:383-389.

———— 1957 The aridity factor in the ecology of locusts and grasshoppers of the Old World. *In* Human and animal ecology, reviews of research. Unesco, Paris. Arid Zone Research 8:164-198.

———— 1962 Development of arid lands and its ecological effects on their insect fauna. *In* The problems of the arid zone, proceedings of the Paris symposium. Unesco, Paris. Arid Zone Research 18:235-248.
An excellent recent review on problems in the agricultural impact of worldwide arid lands development and the reciprocal interactions with the native insect fauna. Specific recommendations are made for the circumvention of future disasters.

———— 1966 Grasshoppers and locusts, a handbook of general acridology. Vol. 1. Cambridge University Press. 481 p.
Volume one treats the anatomy, physiology, development, phase polymorphism, and introduction to the taxonomy of these important worldwide insects. Volume two is not yet published.

Uvarov, E. B.
1931 The ash content of insects. Bulletin of Entomological Research 22:453-457.

Vachon, M.
1952 Etudes sur les scorpions. Institut Pasteur, Alger. 483 p.

Van Denburgh, J.
1922 The reptiles of western North America. I: Lizards. II: Snakes and turtles. California Academy of Sciences, San Francisco.

Van Dyke, E. C.
1928 A reclassification of the genera of North American Meloidae . . . and a revision of the genera and species formerly placed in the tribe Meloini. University of California Publications in Entomology 4(12):395-474.

Van Volkenberg, H. L.
1935 Biological control of an insect pest by a toad. Science 82:278-279.

Vaurie, C.
1964 A survey of the birds of Mongolia. American Museum of Natural History, Bulletin 127(3):103-143.
Provides especially important and carefully detailed data on distribution, relative abundance, population density and general ecology of the birds of Mongolia.

Vellard, J.
1939 Une civilisation du miel. Les Indians Guayakis du Paraguay. Paris. (Géographie humaine, 13). 188 p.

Vellard, J. A.
1942 Spider bites and anaphylactic accidents. Asociación Médica Argentina, Revista 56:334-335.

———— 1944 Cuatro conferencias sobre animales venenosos, dictadas en 1943 en el Museo Argentino de Ciencias Naturales y en la Facultad de Ciencias Médicas de Buenos Aires. Imprenta J. Belmonte, Buenos Aires. 71 p.

Villiers, A.
1950 Contribution à l'étude du peuplement de la Mauritanie. Ophidiens. Institut Français d' Afrique Noire, Bulletin 12:984-998.

Volsøe, H.
1939 The sea snakes of the Iranian Gulf. p. 9-45. *In* K. Jessen and R. Spärck, eds., Danish scientific investigations in Iran, pt. 1. Copenhagen.

Waite, E. R.
1929 The reptiles and amphibians of South Australia. British Science Guide, Adelaide. (Handbook of the fauna and flora of South Australia). 270 p.

Wakeland, C. and W. E. Shull
1936 The mormon cricket with suggestions for its control. Idaho College of Agriculture, Extension Bulletin 100. 30 p.

Wall, F.
1928 The poisonous terrestrial snakes of our British Indian Dominions (including Ceylon), and how to recognize them. 4th ed. Diocesan Press, Bombay. 167 p.

Wallace, A. L. and R. Sticka
1956 Effect of ACTH on the venoms of *Atrax robustus* and *Latrodectus hasselti*. *In* E. E. Buckley and N. Porges, eds., Venoms. American Association for the Advancement of Science, Publication 44:107-109.

Wallace, A. R.
1852- On the insects used for food by the Indians of the
1853 Amazon. Entomological Society of London, Transactions 2:24-244.

Wallace, H. F.
1913 The big game of central and western China, being an account of a journey from Shanghai to London overland across the Gobi desert. J. Murray, London. 318 p.

Waloff, Z.
1959 Notes on some geographical aspects of the desert locust problem. FAO Panel of Experts on the Strategy of Desert Locust Plague Control, Report, p. 23-26. Mimeographed.

Wang, C.-W.
1961 The forests of China, with a survey of grassland and desert vegetation. Harvard University, Cambridge, Massachusetts, Maria Moors Cabot Foundation, Publication 5. 313 p.

Warburg, M. R.
1964 The response of isopods towards temperature, humidity and light. Animal Behavior 12:175-186.

———— 1965a The microclimate of two isopod species in southern Arizona. American Midland Naturalist 73:363-375.

———— 1965b The water relation and internal body temperature of isopods from mesic and xeric habitats. Physiological Zoology 38:1017-1041.

Wardle, R. A.
1929 The problems of applied entomology. Manchester University Press, Manchester, England. 587 p.

Watson, W. G.
1908 Australian snakes. American Medical Association, Journal 50:293.

Weaver, J. E. and F. W. Albertson
1956 Grasslands of the Great Plains, their nature and use. Johnsen Publishing Company, Lincoln, Nebr. 395 p.

Weesner, F. M.
1965 The termites of the United States. A handbook. National Pest Control Association, Elizabeth, N.J. 70 p.

Weidner, H.
1936 Beiträge zu einer monographie der raupen mit gift-haoren. Zeitschrift für Angewandte Entomologie 23:432-484.
Gives a comprehensive bibliography on poisonous insect hairs.

Werler, J. E. and H. L. Keegan
1963 Venomous snakes of the Pacific area. p. 219-335. *In* H. L. Keegan and W. V. Macfarlane, eds., Venomous and poisonous animals and noxious plants of the Pacific region. Macmillan Company, New York. 456 p.

Werner, F.
1908 The poisonous snakes of the Anglo-Egyptian Sudan. Wellcome Tropical Research Laboratories, Khartoum, Report, 3rd.

———
1922 Synopsis der Schlangenfamilien der Amblycephaliden und Viperiden. Archiv für Naturgeschichte, Berlin, Abt. A. 88(8):185-244.

———
1934 Scorpiones. *In* Bronn's Klassen und Ordnungen des Tierreichs V, 4(8)1-2. 316 p.
Treats structure, classification and distribution of scorpions.

Werner, F. G., W. R. Enns, and F. H. Parker
1966 The Meloidae of Arizona. Arizona Agricultural Experiment Station, Technical Bulletin 175. 96 p.

West, T. F. and G. A. Campbell
1952 DDT and newer persistent insecticides. 1st American ed. Chemical Publishing Company, New York. 632 p.

Westermarck, E. A.
1926 Ritual and belief in Morocco. Macmillan and Co., Ltd., London. 2 vols.

Wetmore, A.
1926 Birds of Argentina, Paraguay, Uruguay, and Chile. U.S. National Museum, Bulletin 133. 272 p.

Wheeler, W. M.
1910 Ants; their structure, development, and behavior. Columbia University Press, New York. 663 p.

———
1930 Demons of the dust. A study in insect behavior. Kegan, Paul, Trench, Trubner and Company, Ltd. London. 396 p.

Whiting, A. F.
1966 The present status of ethnobotany in the Southwest. Economic Botany 20:316-325.
This is a welcome treatment and, indeed, a rare one, that reviews the status of knowledge (123 citations) in an ethnobotanical review of a largely desert and semiarid region, and does not neglect the related ethnozoology of the area. Citations of ten papers are included, on ethnozoology of Indians in the American Southwest (1896 to 1965), that contain much detailed information on the use of native animal species as human food.

Whittemore, F. W. and H. L. Keegan
1963 Medically important scorpions in the Pacific Area. p. 107-110. *In* H. L. Keegan and W. V. Macfarlane, eds., Venomous and poisonous animals and noxious plants of the Pacific Region. Macmillan Company, New York.

Whittemore, F. W., H. L. Keegan, and J. L. Borowitz
1961 Studies of scorpion antivenins. I: Paraspecificity. World Health Organization, Bulletin 25:185-188.

Wiener, S.
1957 The Sydney funnel-web spider (*Atrax robustus*). I: Collection of venom and its toxicity in animals. Medical Journal of Australia 44, II: 377-383.

———
1961a Red-back spider bite in Australia: an analysis of 167 cases. Medical Journal of Australia 2:44-49.

———
1961b The Sydney funnel-web spider (*A. robustus*). III: The neutralization of venom by haemolymph. Medical Journal of Australia 48:449-451.

———
1961c Observations on the venom of the Sydney funnel-web spider (*Atrax robustus*). Medical Journal of Australia 48, II(18):683-699.

———
1963 Antigenic and electrophoretic properties of funnel-web spider (*Atrax robustus*) venom. p. 141-151. *In* H. L. Keegan and W. V. Macfarlane, eds., Venomous and poisonous animals and noxious plants of the Pacific Region. Macmillan Company, New York.

Wille, J. E.
1943 Entomología agrícola del Perú. Estación Experimental Agrícola de La Molina, Lima. 468 p.

Williams, C. B.
1954 Some bioclimatic observations in the Egyptian desert. p. 18-27. *In* J. L. Cloudsley-Thompson, ed., Biology of deserts; proceedings of a symposium on the biology of hot and cold deserts. Institute of Biology, London. 223 p.

Wilson, J. W. and O. A. Plunkett
1965 The fungous diseases of man. University of California Press, Berkeley. 428 p.

Wilson, J. W., C. E. Smith, and O. A. Plunkett
1953 Primary cutaneous coccidioidomycosis. California Medicine 79:233-239.

Wiltshire, E. P.
1940 Insect biotypes in Syria, Iraq and Iran. Entomologists' Record and Journal of Variation, London, 52:43-52.

Witherspoon, W. W.
1889 Collection of honey dew by the Nevada Indians. American Anthropologist 2:380.

Woglum, R. S.
1942 The Argentine ant. California Citrograph 27:155.

———
1947 The citrus black fly campaign in Sonora gets underway. Exchange Pest Control Circular 156: 612-613.

Wood, F. D.
1934 Natural and experimental infection of *Triatoma protracta* (Uhler) and mammals in California with American human trypanosomiasis. American Journal of Tropical Medicine 14:497-517.

Wood, S. F.
1942 Observations on vectors of Chagas' disease in the United States. I: California. California Academy of Science, Bulletin 41(2):61-69.

——— 1944a Notes on the food habits of reptiles with special reference to their possible control of cone-nosed bugs. Southern California Academy of Science, Bulletin 43(2):86-91.

——— 1944b An additional California locality for *Trypanosoma cruzi* Chagas in the western cone-nosed bug, *Triatoma protracta* (Uhler). Journal of Parasitology 30(3):199.

——— 1951 Importance of feeding and defecation times of insect vectors in trasmission of Chagas' disease. Journal of Economic Entomology 44(1):52-54.

——— 1952 *Trypanosoma cruzi* revealed in California mice by xenodiagnosis. Pan-Pacific Entomologist 28 (3):147-153.

Woody, N. C. and H. B. Woody
1955 American trypanosomiasis (Chagas' disease), first indigenous case in the United States. American Medical Association, Journal 159:676-677.

Work, T. H.
1961 The expanding role of arthropod-borne viruses in tropical medicine. Industrial Council for Tropical Health, Conference, 4th, Proceedings, p. 225-248.

World Health Organization
1955 Cases of trachoma reported in various countries since 1945. Epidemiological and Vital Statistics Report 8, 9.

——— 1958 Publications of the World Health Organization, 1947-1957, a bibliography. 128 p.

——— 1961 Chemotherapy of malaria. Report of a technical meeting, Geneva, 1960. Technical Report Series 226. 92 p.

——— 1962a Expert Committee on trachoma, 3rd report. Technical Report Series 234. 48 p.

——— 1962b Trypanosomiasis in Africa and America. Epidemiological and Vital Statistics Report 15(6): 395-423.

——— 1964 Publications of the World Health Organization, 1958-1962, a bibliography. 125 p.

——— 1966 Malaria, 1955-1964. Epidemiological and Vital Statistics Report 19(3):89-99.

Worrell, E.
1963a Dangerous snakes of Australia and New Guinea. 5th ed. Angus and Robertson, Ltd., Sydney.

——— 1963b Reptiles of Australia: crocodiles, turtles, tortoises, lizards, snakes. Angus and Robertson Ltd., Sydney.

Wright, A. H. and A. A. Wright
1957 Handbook of snakes in the U.S. and Canada. Comstock Publishing Co., Ithaca, New York. 2 vols.

Wright, J. W.
1966 Predation on the Colorado River toad, *Bufo alvarius*. Herpetologica 22:127-128.
A recent and more than usually interesting account (with references) of the large and well-known dangerous Colorado River Toad (*Bufo alvarius*) of the Sonoran Desert. Reports that racoons circumvent the skin poison problem by ripping open the abdomen and stripping out the contents of the body cavity.

Wright, N. C.
1954 Domesticated animals inhabiting desert areas. p. 168-172. *In* J. L. Cloudsley-Thompson, ed., Biology of deserts. Institute of Biology, London. 224 p.
An excellent recent review for both vertebrate and invertebrate animals.

Wyman, L. C. and F. L. Bailey
1964 Navajo Indian ethnoenthomology. University of New Mexico, Publications in Anthropology 12: 1-158.

Yaffee, H. S.
1959 Papular urticaria caused by red ants. U.S. Armed Forces Medical Journal 10:26-28.

Zinovieva, I. A.
1959 The biology and ecology of robber flies in the Naryn sands, western Kazakhstan: Diptera, Asilidae (translated title). Entomolgicheskoe Obozrenie 38(3):554-567.

Ziprkowski, L., E. Hofshi, and A. S. Tahori
1959 Caterpillar dermatitis. Israel Medical Journal 18:36.

DESERT COASTAL ZONES

JOSEPH F. SCHREIBER, JR.
Department of Geology
The University of Arizona

INTRODUCTION

A. SUBJECT AND SCOPE

This study of Desert Coastal Zones is an inventory and evaluation of literature and research regarding those areas of the Earth where major deserts meet the sea. Initially the study was limited to coasts with an arid climate (the *BW* type in Köppen's classification as simplified by G. T. Trewartha) but was extended to include semiarid coasts (the *BS* type) where the two climatic types are contiguous along a coast.

The following factors were included for consideration regarding the desert coastal zone in the specifications for "An Inventory of Geographical Research on Desert Environments": nearshore bottom conditions; tides and currents; surf, breakers, and waves; beaches; shore and nearshore erosion and sedimentation; coastal swamps and marshes; and coastal structures and other culture features. The treatment of these factors is not equally extensive because the amount of data available varies widely among the factors. Extent of treatment of individual desert coastal zones varies as well, for the same reason.

The topics of flora, fauna, and weather and climate are covered chiefly by other authors in separate chapters. The few exceptions involve references to coastal vegetation and to climate where climate enters into coastal classification.

B. ACKNOWLEDGMENTS

The author wishes to acknowledge the aid of Dr. Richard J. Russell of the Coastal Studies Institute, Louisiana State University and Dr. Rodman E. Snead of the Graduate School of Geography, Clark University, who reviewed the original manuscript and offered much valuable criticism. Dr. Russell also served as a consultant to the project, and based upon his extensive knowledge of many coastal areas around the world, aided the author greatly in the initial stages of the desert coastal zones study. Dr. Snead, in addition to reviewing the manuscript, supplied valuable information on the West Pakistan coast.

The author also thanks Dr. Donald L. Bryant and Dr. Lawrence K. Lustig, colleagues in the Department of Geology, University of Arizona, for timely discussion of problem areas and the exchange of information. Dr. Laurence M. Gould, also of the Department of Geology, critically reviewed the completed manuscript.

Jan Carol Wilt and Gretchen Luepke, graduate students in the Department of Geology, University of Arizona, and David N. Crowell, a graduate of the College of Liberal Arts, performed most of the bibliographical research in English-, French-, and German-language publications. Their painstaking efforts are greatly appreciated.

During the author's visit to Australia many individuals, and national and state government agencies supplied much information and gave freely of their time. Similar data were supplied by individuals and governmental agencies in South America, Africa, and the Middle East. Within the United States numerous scientists answered the author's many questions regarding past and current research.

C. HISTORICAL DEVELOPMENT

Organized research on coastal zones and desert coastal zones as such does not have a long history. Prior to World War II much of the research was done by a few dedicated individuals with little or no financial backing. The coastal areas covered were primarily the more humid ones, although some desert coastal zones of Africa and Asia were studied by European researchers.

Invasion planning by United States and allied forces during World War II required a knowledge of enemy beaches in a number of climates. Reports were assembled by intelligence teams. The Geographical Handbook Series, Naval Intelligence Division, British Admiralty (described more fully below under "Published Information") is in part an outgrowth of these intelligence requirements.

Research increased in the post-World War II years, but most of the work seems to have been devoted to the more humid coastal areas. The Coastal Studies Institute of the Louisiana State University was founded in the early 1950's and although much of its early research involved Louisiana problems, it later became international in scope, including a few desert coastal areas. Some of its work is cited later.

The Committee on Coastal Sedimentation of the International Geographical Union was established in 1952, but in 1960 the name was changed to Committee on Coastal Geomorphology. The committee has published three bibliographies described more fully below under the subheading "Bibliographies" in "Published Information."

The National Academy of Sciences / National Research Council report of March 1961, entitled *Coastal Geography,* reviewed the entire problem of coastal-zone research.

In October of the same year the First National Coastal and Shallow Water Research Conference was sponsored jointly by the National Science Foundation and the Office of Naval Research. Meetings were held in Baltimore, Maryland; Tallahassee, Florida; and Los Angeles, California. The conference later prepared a directory of marine scientists which was published in 1964.

At the November 1961 meeting of the Geological Society of America in Cincinnati, Ohio, an informal coastal research group was founded. This group endeavors to meet annually.

It should be emphasized again that most of the research covered in these bibliographies or discussed at meetings pertained to the more humid coastal areas.

D. PRESENT INTEREST IN DESERT COASTAL ZONES

The present interest in desert coastal zones is not intense but certainly is greater than it was 25 years ago. The increase of interest stems partly from the rapid advances being made in the desalinization of sea water, because the presence of adequate quantities of fresh water seems to be the key to increased utilization of these lands. As its stands now many of the people living on desert coasts depend upon the sea for a livelihood.

Besides the fish and shellfish catches, seaweeds are harvested and guano is mined. Oil wells have been drilled in the shallow waters of the Persian Gulf. Diamonds are dredged from the nearshore sediments off the southwest coast of Africa. On the northwest coast of Australia existing port facilities are being improved and new ports are being constructed to handle the shipment of iron ore from newly discovered ore bodies located some tens of miles inland. Along many coastal deserts numerous salt pans are in use to evaporate sea water for the valuable salt.

Based upon this study, the persons actually doing research on the desert coastal zone are geographers with a good background in geomorphology, geo-logists, geological oceanographers, marine biologists, meteorologists, engineers, and hydrographers. During World War II the field of military geology came into its own and the U. S. Geological Survey still has a Military Geology branch. The author assumes that at one time or another the military geologist has been confronted with the problems of desert coastal zones.

E. DESERT COASTAL ZONE DEFINED

Two questions must be answered to define the desert coastal zone: what is the extent of the desert zone along a coast, and how wide is the coastal zone? The first question was answered above, i. e., limit the desert coastal zones to the Köppen *BW* type climate and to an extension into the *BS* type climate where the two climatic types are contiguous along a coast.

Determining the width presents many problems because we must deal not only with a strip of land but also a strip of water (in the seaward direction). The zone concerned corresponds to the littoral zone of many marine scientists. The American Geological Institute *Glossary of Geology and Related Sciences* (Howell, 1960) defines littoral zone as follows: "1. Strictly, zone bounded by high and low tide levels. 2. Loosely, zone related to the shore, extending to some arbitrary shallow depth of water." These definitions are probably too restrictive for most geomorphologists and geographers and for many geologists, too.

A panel on coastal geography composed of specialists from the fields of geology, oceanography, biology, engineering, and geography met under the chairmanship of Dr. Richard J. Russell at the Louisiana State University on 20-21 March, 1961. In their report, the coastal zone is described as follows (National Academy of Sciences / National Research Council, 1961, p. 1):

> The coastal zone is not a narrow line between land and sea, but a transition zone of varying width. It may extend far from land, across shallow waters to the limits of major interactions between the land and water interface. This is the domain of green water research, and its problems and challenges are no less complex and significant than those of the deep sea, the realm of blue water. The coastal zone extends inland as far as significant marine influences are active, within reach of coastal fogs, of spray-laden air, and the movement of sea water through tidal channels across the coastal plains. Thus it includes areas of tides, areas of wave action, areas of mixing salt and fresh water, low semiaqueous flats, beaches, and coastal dunes and uplands. Essentially, the coast-

al zone is a region of discontinuities, of sharp breaks or transitional changes in physical, ecological, and cultural patterns and regimes.

Other workers have defined the land to fit their own needs. In the compilation of a coastal landforms map of the world, McGill (1958, p. 402) arbitrarily worked with a coastal strip extending inland five to ten miles. Meigs (1966, p. 13), in his monographic volume entitled *Geography of Coastal Deserts,* poses the question "Just how wide is the 'littoral' or coastal strip?" He footnotes the term "littoral" and writes that " . . . 'littoral' is here used, in accordance with common geographic practice, to denote the strip of land parallel to the coast and with pronounced coastal affinities." Meigs (p. 13) also states:

Some writers have limited it to the narrow strip of coast within reach of salt spray, a few hundred yards wide. Capot-Rey (1953, p. 376) considers the Atlantic Sahara, subject to significantly large amounts of dew and cloud from the sea, to extend inland about 185 miles. Specialized fields of research have come up with their own answers. One physical geographer defined the 'coastal region' as the area between the highest Quaternary marine forms and the outermost Quaternary action of the surf (Valentin, 1952). Such a definition is significant, as the Quaternary plains and terraces are vital sites for development of agriculture, but it makes no allowance for the older geological features that border some coasts, or for the Quaternary plains that extend inland far beyond present-day coastal influences.

From the over-all geographic viewpoint, the criterion for mapping the littoral must include the relationships to present-day coastal influences and some bearing upon actual and potential utilization by man. Sometimes a single factor, such as terrain or climate, can be used to mark off the littoral. Where a narrow lowland along the coast is shut off from the interior by a steep barrier of mountains, as along the Red Sea, the south-western African coast, or the west coast of the Gulf of California, there is no problem. Where a broad plain stretches inland from the coast, there may be no physiographic limit to the littoral, and we must depend upon climate or vegetation for clues. Vegetation mapped on a physiognomic basis, reflecting both climatic and edaphic factors, would provide perhaps the best single basis for delimiting the littorals. The distribution of certain lichens or other plants dependent upon moist air might be as good an indicator as anything. Unfortu-

nately mapping of vegetation has been too incomplete and generalized in most of the coastal deserts to serve the purpose. It is hoped that the publication of Unesco on the plant ecology of the arid zone will partially fill the gap by bringing together the scattered material available. In the meantime, general world maps of vegetation, such as these of Küchler (no date) give some guidance in certain parts of the earth.

Neither McGill nor Meigs deals with or tries to define the seaward limits of the coastal zone, nor can a very specific statement or consensus of opinions be found in the literature as to just how far to extend the coastal zone offshore. In Technical Report Number 4 (U. S. Army Corps of Engineers, Beach Erosion Board, 1961) "coastal area" is defined as the land and sea area bordering the shore line, with the coastal area extending seaward to just beyond the breakers. This suggests a water depth of 5 to 6 fathoms. McCurdy (1947, p. 74), in his instructions to cartographers compiling charts of coastal areas, does cite the need for knowing the location of any dangerous feature inside the six-fathom curve.

For this present study the land strip of the desert coastal zone will be confined to a 5 to 10 mile width, following the procedure of McGill (1958, p. 402) in which he arbitrarily delimited his study of the major coastal landforms to this particular coastal strip width. The width of the seaward strip will be kept flexible to allow for gentle, shelving bottoms on which waves may break far from the actual inshore zone; the presence of coral reefs or other obstructions offshore over which waves may break; and any other unusual feature or structure occurring some distance offshore in a desert coastal zone.

F. LOCATION OF DESERT COASTAL ZONES

Meigs (1966) has described 14 major desert littoral areas. The same general 14 desert coastal zones will be described in this chapter. They are:

1) Northwest Mexico: Baja California and the Sonora-Sinaloa Coasts
2) Peru: The Coast
3) Chile: Northern Desert Coast
4) Argentina: Patagonia Coast
5) Australia: Western Coast
6) Australia: Southern Coast
7) North Arabian Sea: Iran Bordering the Gulf of Oman to the Rann of Kutch/ Kathiawar Peninsula
8) Persian Gulf
9) South Coast of Saudi Arabia: Muscat and Aden Protectorate
10) The Somali Coast

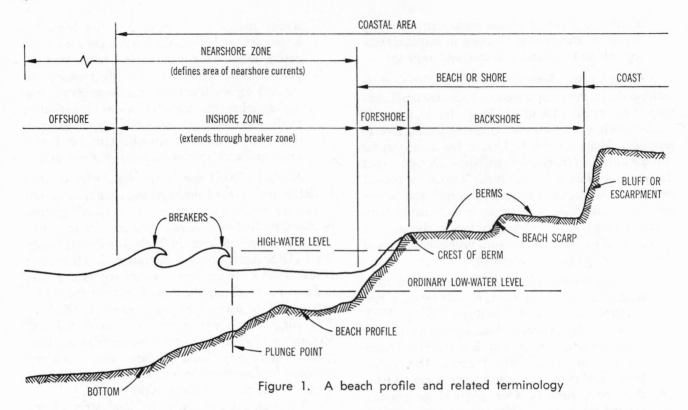

Figure 1.   A beach profile and related terminology

11) Red Sea
12) Mediterranean Coast of Africa
13) Northwest Africa
14) Southwest Africa

G.   TYPICAL FORMS AND TERMINOLOGY

1.   Littoral Zone and Some Related Features

Several definitions and interpretations of the littoral zone have already been given. Figure 1 (taken from U. S. Army, Corps of Engineers, Coastal Engineering Research Center, 1964) illustrates a beach profile which shows the high and low water levels stressed in the geologist's definition. Similar figures may be seen in Shepard (1963, p. 168) and in Putnam *et al.* (1960, p. 6). Some differences in the coastal terminology can also be noted. Putnam *et al.* (1960, p. 6) have commented that:

> Various attempts have been made to set up a rigorous terminology to be applied to shore forms, but unfortunately many of them have resulted only in adding more confusion. This difficulty arises in large part from the fact that almost all the terms applied to coastal regions of the world are taken from the ordinary language and have either a wide variety of meanings or are completely synonymous in people's minds with some other usage of the same word.

The beach is the zone of accumulation of loose sediment which may range in size from sand to boulders. The sediment size in active transit is sand and most studies have been made in the past on sand beaches. Also shown are breaking waves and the berms built by wave action. The U. S. Army, Corps of Engineers, Beach Erosion Board (1961) defines a berm as the " . . . nearly horizontal portion of the beach or backshore formed by the deposit of material by wave action. Some beaches have no berms, others have one or several." The other characteristics shown (inshore zone, foreshore, etc.) are self explanatory. Shepard (1963) contains an excellent chapter on beaches and related shore processes.

Related geomorphic features, not shown in Figure 1 but requiring definition, include the barrier island, longshore bar, and delta. The definitions are taken chiefly from the American Geological Institute *Glossary of Geology and Related Sciences.*

The barrier island is a bank of beach material built up by waves and currents which lies offshore separated from the mainland by a narrow body of water and generally parallel to the coast. The barrier island is similar to the barrier beach but consists of multiple instead of single ridges and may also have dunes and vegetated zones. Barrier islands sometimes help to form a bay or lagoon. In these somewhat protected bodies of water salt marshes may build up as sediment trapping takes place in shore vegetation communities.

A longshore bar is a slightly submerged sand

ridge found offshore paralleling the shoreline and submerged at least by high tides. Many, however, are arranged *en echelon* in a zone paralleling the shore.

Deltas are built by sedimentation at the mouth of rivers where wave and current action are too weak to move the freshly deposited material. Only the larger, more heavily sediment-laden rivers are capable of building deltas on coasts subjected to strong wave action, longshore currents, or tidal scour.

Estuaries, many bays, and some gulfs are indentations extending back from the sea, most commonly along valleys that were cut during lower stands of sea level and flooded as the level rose to its present stand.

2. Waves and Breakers

Waves are important in describing coastal zones because they erode coastal formations, and transport and deposit the shallow-water sediments. Wave generation takes place at sea when wind blows over the water. Although waves may be generated many thousands of miles at sea we are most interested in what happens in shallow water along a coast.

A wave entering shallow water encounters friction with the bottom so that water in the lower part of the waves is slowed down. Water above moves more rapidly toward the shore, piles up, and commonly becomes unstable so that some of it falls forward to become a breaker. The area affected by breaking waves is called the surf zone. It is characterized by a high degree of turbulence and notable entrainment of bottom sediment that increases local turbidity. Entrained sediment is carried forward up the beach by swash (or uprush) and may be deposited there. Water is returned down the beach as backwash.

Closely spaced and steep-fronted waves tend to erode a beach (producing a "winter beach" at any season of the year), whereas widely spaced flat waves transport sediment from the surf zone to restore beach volume and create a steep beach front ("summer beach"). In a minor way each rising tide tends to create a winter beach and each falling tide a summer beach.

Swell resembles waves but is generated during storms up to several thousand miles distant. The wave length of swell is longer and crests arrive more slowly, commonly at intervals of 12 seconds or more, while the period of locally-produced ordinary waves is likely to vary between 6 and 12 seconds. Crests are spaced more closely if the waves have crossed long distances of shallow bottom.

If waves approach a shore at angles of between 90 and 70 degrees, they are reflected out at 90 degrees. At angles of between 70 and 20 degrees, they are reflected at similar angles, as with light reflected from a mirror; in this case longshore currents transport sediment parallel to the shore. At angles of less than 20 degrees, Mach effects arise and a current of tremendous speed is generated along the shore. The current piles up over the more sluggish water ahead, rising several tens of feet in extreme cases. The steep front of a Mach current, called a "king wave" in Australia, commonly rolls large boulders along the bottom; it is characterized by a rumble, increasing in intensity as the front approaches. In spite of this and other warning signs, king waves take a toll of lives in such places as Australia and South Africa, mainly unwary fishermen perched well above the reach of ordinary storm waves. Bascom (1964*a*) has presented a very readable account of the wave battle in the surf zone.

3. Tidal Phenomena

Tides are important in coastal zones because they lower and raise the level at which waves may attack a beach. The amount of erosion and general destruction is intensified when a strong onshore wind accompanies a high tide. Tidal currents flowing into and out of bays and lagoons may also erode as well as deposit sediment.

4. Cold Currents Along Certain Desert Coastal Regions

The numerous maps and charts of the world frequently show warm and cold currents along coasts (see any good atlas or National Geographic Society maps). The true desert and steppe regions include both kinds of currents, but where cold currents flow along desert coasts the climate is changed dramatically from the usual characteristics of high temperatures, low relative humidity, and sparse cloud cover (Trewartha, 1954, p. 276).

The coasts involved, which are chiefly west coasts, and their associated cool currents are the northwest coast of Mexico along which the California Current flows, the Chile-Peru coast and the adjacent Peru Current, the southwest coast of Africa and the Benguela Current, the Canary Current along the northwest coast of Africa, the Falkland Current along the Patagonia coast, and an unnamed, seasonal, cool water upwelling off the east coast of Somalia. Meigs (1966) discusses the cool currents along each of these coastal regions.

The cooler coastal waters are the result of the normal current patterns for their respective latitudes. In addition, it frequently happens that offshore winds displace the surface waters seaward so that even cooler waters from depth may upwell. These cooler waters with their associated richness in planktonic life account for the fishing industries off these coasts. The guano deposits of the Peruvian coastal islands are also indirectly related to the upwelling which supplies food for the very abundant marine bird life.

Trewartha (1954, p. 276) characterizes these regions as having " . . . (*a*) lower - than - average annual temperatures, (*b*) distinctly cooler summers, (*c*) slightly milder winters, and (*d*) smaller annual and diurnal ranges than are normal for most low-latitude dry climates." In addition, and in spite of extremely low rainfall, the coastal regions usually have high relative humidity and abundant fog. The fog results from the cooling of warmer oceanic air by its passing over the cooler coastal waters. The air masses on these coasts remain stable, however, and little rain falls.

H.   THE CLASSIFICATION OF COASTS

1.   General Statement

A number of coastal classifications, including shorelines, are available to the interested investigator today. They are for the most part either genetic classifications or purely descriptive classifications, although several of the classifications have some of the elements of both approaches.

The classification of D. W. Johnson (1919) has been used in many American and foreign textbooks and articles for many years, and is the classification used recently by Strahler (1963). Emmons *et al.* (1960) use Johnson's classification and compare it with those of Shepard (1948) and Guilcher (1958). C. A. M. King (1959), in her *Beaches and Coasts,* describes and criticizes the classifications of Johnson (1919), Shepard (1948), Cotton (1956), and Valentin (1952). Valentin's approach is unique in that he divides coasts into advancing coasts and retreating coasts, which are then subdivided. His classification is partly descriptive and partly genetic.

E. C. F. Bird (1965), in *Coastal Landforms,* describes and comments on the classifications of Johnson (1919), Shepard (1948), Cotton (1956), Valentin (1952), and McGill (1958). Bird's volume and McGill's classification are discussed in more detail herein under the heading "Important Standard Works and Availability."

2.   Some Newer Ideas

C. S. Alexander, a geographer at the University of Illinois, has studied coastal zones in several parts of the world since 1953. Based upon his experience he favors a purely descriptive classification of shorelines (Alexander, 1962). He uses standard terms

and the classification appears to be an easy one to apply to maps.

J. L. Davies (1964) has not presented a new classification but rather focuses attention on the role of wave and tidal activity. Davies describes storm waves, swell, and low energy environments. He states (p. 136-137) that "In the storm wave environment, beaches are dominated by steep, destructive waves which operate with sufficient frequency to control the beach regime." Flat, constructive waves characterize the swell environment " . . . so that beaches tend to show 'summer' or 'fill' profiles, with beach berm platforms much more in evidence." Low energy shores show " . . . a good development of constructional features in sand . . . ," and this suggests to him an ". . . overall dominance of flat waves . . ." He believes that variation in water level is important because ". . . this determines the degree to which wave attack is concentrated on a particular plane and also determines the altitudinal limits within which salt marshes can be built."

3.   Quaternary Eustatic Sea-Level Changes

Sea - level changes during the Quaternary Period were responsible for many geomorphic features along coast lines. Some of these features include terraces, raised beaches, beach ridges, dunes, emerged coral reefs, and buried alluvial deposits. The changes are usually termed "eustatic" because the change is a real worldwide sea-level change. Papers by Fairbridge (1961, 1962), Higgins (1965), and Russell (1964) review the causes and results of these sea-level changes.

For the Quaternary, Fairbridge (1961, p. 173) cites these causes for a eustatic change of sea level:

(*a*) A climatically controlled glacio-eustasy, involving vertical oscillations of a few metres up to 100 or 125 m in periods ranging from 550 years to about 90,000 years.

(*b*) A geodetic change, associated either with the shape of major ocean basins or with the shape of the geoid in respect to the spheroid, perhaps associated with a polar shift . . . .

(*c*) Several minor geophysical effects are to be expected from glacial loading and unbalancing effects on the globe, but their roles have not yet been analysed.

The most striking geomorphic fact pertaining to today's coasts is the effect of the last major rise of sea level by some 450 feet. Estuaries have been pushed up major valleys leading to the ocean, former land areas have been submerged, and former hilltops have become islands. The sea-level rise during the last 8,000 years amounts to approximately 29 feet (Coleman and Smith, 1964). The results of sea-level changes must be recognized and interpreted in studying the coastal zone.

4. Summary

The general problem of classification of coasts has been summarized by McGill (1959, p. 2-3):

Sparsity of information on the coasts of the world is a formidable obstacle to the successful application of any classification, but particularly so for purely genetic schemes. Nearly all coasts are complex in their geomorphic history and thus in the character and associations of their present features. They represent the results of the combined action of many different agents and processes — marine and terrestrial, inorganic and organic—all of which have been highly variable in their efforts in time and space if for no other reason than because of the late Pleistocene instability of sea level. The integrated details of even the recent history of most coasts probably will never be completely known because of this complexity and the fragmentary or inaccessible nature of the record. Generalizations as to origin and development are therefore apt to be extremely misleading and provide an insecure foundation for classification.

DISCUSSION OF STATE OF KNOWLEDGE

A. SOURCES OF INFORMATION

1. Personal Visits

In addition to researching the literature and to corresponding with a number of geographers and geologists in the United States, Africa, Europe, South America, and Australia, the author visited Australia in July of 1965. There he met and conferred with researchers in that country, determined and evaluated sources of data, collected data, and traveled along and observed portions of desert coastal areas.

The writer's visits to Australian universities, state and national agencies, and with many individuals demonstrated the value of personal visits. Many researchers were available for consultation and gave freely of their time and experiences. Such local researchers are often well acquainted with a particular coast and in many cases could be retained to make studies. The libraries visited at five universities in Australia had much better coverage of foreign language journals than many of the American universities of comparable size with which the writer is familiar. These ideal conditions probably do not exist on a worldwide basis, but where deemed feasible, more use should be made of qualified personnel in other countries.

2. Authorities

Those individuals who are regarded, upon the basis of available information, to be primary authorities on desert coastal zones are listed in table I. In part A, individual "desert coastal zones" and "specific locations" within the zones are listed. Opposite each zone and location, primary authorities, where known, are indicated by letter under each of the three headings: "Offshore," "Onshore," and "General." In part B, each authority is listed (by letters corresponding to part A) with the name and address of the institution with which he is affiliated.

3. Libraries

Much material covered in other chapters of this compendium applies as well, in varying degrees, to desert coastal zones and, according to the reader's special interest, he may wish to refer also to the text or depository lists of other chapters of this compendium.

The study of desert coastal zones draws upon several fields, principally geology and geography, and to a lesser extent oceanography and others. Libraries that are regarded upon the basis of available information to be important depositories of literature pertaining to some aspect of the study of desert coastal zones include the following:

Geology and Geography of Coastal Zones:

Coastal Studies Institute
Louisiana State University
Baton Rouge, Louisiana 70803

Geology and Geography:

Columbia University
New York City, New York 10027

Harvard University
Boston, Massachusetts 02138

Johns Hopkins University
Baltimore, Maryland 21218

Library of Congress
Washington, D. C. 20540

Stanford University
Stanford, California 94305

University of Illinois
Urbana, Illinois 61803

University of California at Berkeley
Berkeley, California 94720

University of Michigan
Ann Arbor, Michigan 48104

University of California at
Los Angeles
Los Angeles, California 90024

(Substantial holdings on the deserts of Latin America)

Yale University
New Haven, Connecticut 06520

Geology:

Princeton University
Princeton, New Jersey 08540

U. S. Geological Survey
18th and F Streets, N.W.
Washington, D. C. 20006
(Largest geological library in the
world; card catalog available from

G. K. Hall and Co., Boston,
Massachusetts 02111)

Oceanography:

Scripps Institution of Oceanography
University of California, San Diego
La Jolla, California 92037
(Desert Coastal Zones of
Baja California)

Table I
DESERT COASTAL ZONE AUTHORITIES
Part A

Desert Coastal Zone	Specific Location	General	Onshore	Offshore	Other Comments
Worldwide		y	y	y	General authority on coastal zones
Northwest Mexico	1. Pacific Coast, Baja California	a	a		Lagoonal areas (e) Tidal mud flats of Colorado River delta
	2. Gulf of California	b	d, e, f	b	
	3. Sonora-Sinaloa coast		c	c	(f) Colorado Delta
Peru	1. Entire coast	g	g		
Chile		h	h		
Argentina	1. Patagonia coast	i	i		
Australia	1. Shark Bay, W. A.	j	j	j	(n) General authority on coastal landforms
	2. West coast	k, l	k, l	k, l	
	3. Nullarbor coast	m	m		
	4. See "other comments"				
North Arabian Sea	1. Las Bela coastal plain				
Persian Gulf South Coast of Saudi Arabia		p			
Somali Coast	1. The Horn of Africa	q	q		
Red Sea	1. Egyptian coast	r	r		
	2. Gulf of Aqaba	p		p	
	3. Sudan coast	s, t	s, t		
	4. Ethiopian coast	q	q		
	5. Arabian coast	u	u		
Mediterranean Coast of Africa	1. Egypt	r	r		
Northwest Africa	1. Morocco	v	v		
	2. Senegal coast	w	w		
Southwest Africa	1. Central Namib Desert coast	x	x		

Table I

DESERT COASTAL ZONE AUTHORITIES

Part B

a. Fred B. Phleger
Scripps Institution of Oceanography
University of California, San Diego
La Jolla, California 92037

b. Tjeerd H. van Andel
Scripps Institution of Oceanography
University of California, San Diego
La Jolla, California 92037

c. Joseph R. Curray
Scripps Institution of Oceanography
University of California, San Diego
La Jolla, California 92037

d. Edwin C. Allison
Department of Geology
San Diego State College
San Diego, California 92115

e. Robert W. Thompson
Department of Oceanography
Humboldt State College
Arcata, California 95521

f. Donn S. Gorsline
Department of Geology
University of Southern California
Los Angeles, California 90007

g. J. A. Broggi
Sociedad Geológica del Perú
Apartado 2559
Lima, Peru

h. Juan Bruggen
Instituto Geográfico Militar
Santiago, Chile

i. Horacio A. Difrieri
Sociedad Argentina de
Estudios Geográficos
"Gaea"
Buenos Aires, Argentina

j. Brian W. Logan
Department of Geology
University of Western Australia
Nedlands, Western Australia

k. Rhodes W. Fairbridge
Department of Geology
Columbia University
New York, New York 10027

l. Muarry H. Johnstone
West Australia Petroleum Ltd.
Perth, Western Australia

m. J. N. Jennings
Australian National University
Canberra, A. C. T.

n. Eric C. F. Bird
Australian National University
Canberra, A. C. T.

o. Rodman E. Snead
Department of Geography
Clark University
Worcester, Massachusetts 01610

p. K. O. Emery
Woods Hole Oceanographic
Institution
Woods Hole, Massachusetts 02543

q. P. A. Mohr
Geophysical Observatory
Haile Selassie I University
Addis Ababa, Ethiopia

r. Rushdi Said
Cairo University
Cairo, Egypt (U. A. R.)

s. J. Sestini
Department of Geology
Wayne State University
Detroit, Michigan 48202

t. Leonard Berry
The University College
Dar Es Salaam, Tanzania

u. Desmond Foster Vesey-Fitzgerald
International Red Locust
Control Service
Albercorn, Northern Rhodesia

v. André Guilcher
Institut de Géographie
191, Rue St. Jacques
Paris 5e, France

w. J. Tricart
Institute of Geography
University of Strasbourg
Strasbourg, France

x. Richard F. Logan
Department of Geography
University of California
Los Angeles, California 90024

y. Richard J. Russell
Coastal Studies Institute
Louisiana State University
Baton Rouge, Louisiana 70803

4. Data Centers and Data Processing

Very little has been done toward computer processing of data on coastal zones in general or the narrower category of desert coastal zones, in spite of the recommendations of the panel on coastal geography which convened at the Louisiana State University on 20-21 March, 1961 (National Academy of Sciences / National Research Council, 1961, p. 17). The panel recommended certain facilities for information processing, storage, and dissemination, which included:

a) Clearing house for exchange of data-processing programs and programming advice.

b) Data center, which might be included in the National Oceanographic Data Center.

c) Bibliographic and reference center, with map and photo libraries, and with current information on all investigations in progress in coastal geography.

The National Oceanographic Data Center, located at the Navy Yard Annex in Washington, D. C., seems at present to be devoted chiefly to deepwater oceanographic data. The Science Information Exchange of the Smithsonian Institution supplies summaries of many kinds of research projects. The new Smithsonian Oceanographic Sorting Center, also located at the Navy Yard Annex in Washington, D. C., will supposedly handle samples as well as data. The extent of their present holdings pertaining to the shallow-water coastal zones is not known.

Computer programs are available for sediment

analyses, wave studies, and other kinds of ocean-ographic studies, and are in widespread use by many laboratories.

A data-processing program is needed to handle information on coastal zones, not only on desert coastal zones but on all coastal zones.

5. Published Information

References

Works cited by author and date throughout this chapter are listed in the Pertinent Publications list at the end of the chapter. These listed works were selected from among the more than 3000 initially assembled for this study; most are in English, but works in Spanish, French, and German are also included. Chiefly selected were recent works which either concentrate on coastal zones or provide important information on coastal zones as an included subject. Those works which it has been possible to determine are of particular significance to this study are annotated; many other competent works and best-available works on specific subjects and areas are also listed. Many of the newer works listed include good bibliographies.

Especially important standard works are discussed in some detail below.

Important Standard Works and Availability

The following sections describe specialized sources of information (i. e., maps, charts, tables, and various kinds of publications dealing directly and indirectly with coastal areas) and more general references from the field of geography, geology, and oceanography. All of the material described below was readily available to the author from the following sources: University of Arizona Library; interlibrary loans; reprints from authors; Xerox copies from libraries or individual authors; loans from individual authors; gratis contributions from foreign universities and governmental agencies; direct purchases from universities, U. S. and foreign governmental agencies, and research institutes; and the personal libraries of the author and his colleagues in the Department of Geology, University of Arizona.

U. S. Naval Oceanographic Office: "Sailing Directions"

The U. S. Naval Oceanographic Office is the new name for the former U. S. Navy Hydrographic Office. Although the change became effective on 10 July 1962, the "H. O." abbreviation for Hydrographic Office continues to be used on the newer publications.

The "Sailing Directions" describe coasts, which, for descriptive purposes, are divided into relatively short sections of coast or of bays or gulfs, islands or island groups, or sounds and channels. The divisions are treated in a geographic sequence which is usually illustrated early in the first chapter. Other intro-ductory subject matter usually includes buoyage, pilotage, signals, tides, currents, winds, weather, ice, routes, port regulations, and lifesaving stations. Several of the new editions covering desert coastal areas include a section on oceanography describing tides and tidal currents; sea and swell; and mean sea surface temperatures, salinity, and density. This new oceanography section is accompanied by a section on climatology.

The succeeding chapters cover segments of the coast and their approaches in some detail. Because the underlying theme of "Sailing Directions" is to provide safe passage for any vessel, much of the information presented consists of precautions to be observed. Combined with general information of interest to the mariner, any one description of a coastal segment might include navigational aids and directions; tides, currents, winds, and weather (in-cluding seasonal and local variations); water depths and the distance from shore; landmarks, i. e., cliffs, beaches, a headland; shoals, reefs, and other dangers to navigation; and harbor and safe-anchorage data. A glossary is given in an appendix for the translation of foreign nautical terms. Meteorological data is also appended.

"Sailing Directions" are compiled from a variety of sources. The U. S. Navy makes frequent use of "British Admiralty Pilots," which cover the world, and in appropriate situations also French, Spanish, Portuguese, German, Argentinian, and other pilot information. U. S. Navy vessels, including hydro-graphic survey vessels, obtain data regularly. Other information is assembled from U. S. merchant vessel reports, U. S. consular reports, intelligence studies, port handbooks, maps, charts, tide tables, light lists, and miscellaneous documents. The Coast and Geodetic Survey is responsible for pilot information for the United States and its possessions.

The "Sailing Directions" are perhaps the best general source of information on desert coastal areas in spite of the following shortcomings: They do not contain specific information on the area close in to the beach or on the beach itself when a beach is present. Nearshore bottom conditions may be de-scribed only for safe anchorages. Mention of surf, breakers, or waves is usually confined to the occur-rence of breakers on some offshore feature. Shore and nearshore erosion and sedimentation are not covered.

On the plus side, tidal currents and associated navigational dangers are treated fully. The coastal area behind the beach or shore is also given a very full treatment. This includes the presence of cliffs, hills, rocky points, low flat country, terraces, swamps and tidal channels, beaches, and man-made navigational aids.

The "Sailing Directions" for all desert coastal areas are listed in numerical order, rather than by date, towards the end of the bibliography under U. S. Naval Oceanographic Office: Sailing Directions. In this chapter the "Sailing Directions" are referred to as "Sailing Directions, H. O. Pub. (number)."

U. S. Navy / U. S. Air Force: "Flight Information Publication, Terminal (Seaplane)"

The U. S. Naval Oceanographic Office publishes the *Flight Information Publication, Terminal (Seaplane)* for the U. S. Navy and U. S. Air Force. These loose-leaf volumes contain approach and landing charts and data for seaplanes. In addition to charts, some seaplane landing areas are shown in oblique aerial photographs. The anchorage data includes water depths, tidal range, nature of bottom, beach conditions, currents, sea and swell, and shelter. Unfortunately, due largely to limitations of research and data, known seaplane landing areas on desert coasts are not numerous; however, some data are available for all desert coastal areas except Australia.

U. S. Coast and Geodetic Survey: "Tide Tables, 1965"

The Coast and Geodetic Survey publishes annually, in four volumes, tide tables for the world's coasts. Table I gives high and low water predictions for every day in the year for a number of reference stations. Table 2 gives corrections for obtaining similar predictions for numerous other places along a coast. The world coverage for desert coastal areas is good.

Fourteen countries have provided data for these tables, with Great Britain (British Admiralty) the leader. The British Admiralty publishes similar tide tables for the world. Many other countries that have coastlines and a merchant marine fleet publish tide tables for their areas. In many cases tidal regimes are described as following rules established at some station having many years of record, even though the place may be hundreds or thousands of miles away. For stations without tide gages, actual arrival times of high and low water levels may differ appreciably from estimates.

Bibliographies

The Commission on Coastal Sedimentation of the International Geographical Union was established in 1952. Their first bibliography appeared in 1956, covering 1952 - 1954. The second bibliography, published in 1960, covered 1955-1958 (International Geographical Union, Commission on Coastal Sedimentation, 1960). In 1960 the name of the commission was changed to the Commission on Coastal Geomorphology. This commission issued a third bibliography in 1964 for 1959-1963. These three bibliographies contain very few references to studies of desert coastal areas, but do give the reader an idea of who is engaged in coastal studies and the research organization involved.

John T. McGill compiled the *Selected Bibliography of Coastal Geomorphology of the World*, published in 1960. This bibliography consists principally of references used in the preparation of a map of coastal landforms of the world (McGill, 1958). The references are regional and topical, with many of the regional references covering more than the coastal portion of a given country or region.

The volume entitled *Annotated Bibliography of Quaternary Shorelines* (Richards and Fairbridge, 1965) was prepared for the 1965 congress of the International Association for Quaternary Research (INQUA) held in the United States of America. This bibliography treats the world by countries and includes the desert coastal areas. All abstracts of literature in a foreign language have been translated into English.

The Coastal Studies Institute of the Louisiana State University has published a *Selected Bibliography on Beach Features and Related Nearshore Processes* (Dolan and McCloy, 1964).

"Geographical Handbook Series" of the British Admiralty, Naval Intelligence Division

The Naval Intelligence Division of the British Admiralty first published the "Geographical Handbook Series" during World War I. An entirely new set of books was produced during and after World War II to supply newer information on countries of strategic or political importance. The newer books follow a uniform scheme with but minor modifications. Topics include geology and physical geography, coastal areas data, climate and vegetation, history, administration, ethnology, public health and disease, and resources.

Five volumes cover Iraq and the Persian Gulf, western Arabia and the Red Sea, Tunisia, and the Senegal-Mauritania coasts of former French West Africa. Each contains a chapter on the coastal areas which includes discussions of the geology, general physiography, climate, and ports. Many excellent photographs of coastal areas are included. These volumes are one of the best sources of information for these desert coasts. In the Pertinent Publications list, they appear under Great Britain, Admiralty, Naval Intelligence Division.

Textbooks

A number of textbooks dealing in part or wholly with shoreline features and coastal geomorphology are available in the English language. The oldest, and perhaps one of the better known, is Douglas W. Johnson's *Shore Processes and Shoreline Development* (Johnson, 1919). In this volume Johnson sets forth his genetic classification of shorelines employing the four categories (*1*) shorelines of submergence, (*2*) shorelines of emergence, (*3*) neutral shorelines, and (*4*) compound shorelines. In spite of the difficulties of applying this classification, it is still used in several current geomorphology and geology texts.

Guilcher's *Coastal and Submarine Geomorphology* (1958) was originally written and published in French. Over half of the volume is devoted to coastal geomorphology. Examples are drawn from around the world and include some desert coastal areas. One chapter is on coast classification.

King's *Beaches and Coasts* (1959) is an excellent general treatment of the factors controlling the character of beaches. Other interesting chapters compare the classifications of Johnson (1919), Shepard (1948), Cotton (1956), and Valentin (1952), and present historical data on coastal changes.

Shepard's *Submarine Geology, 2nd edition* (1963) describes well all facets of submarine geology. His classification of shorelines and coasts in chapter VI had its beginning in 1937. Chapter VII, on beaches, is very informative of the newer work being done.

Bird's *Coastal Landforms: An Introduction to Coastal Geomorphology with Australian Examples* (1965) does not cover desert coast areas; however, the general treatment of coastal landform problems, including classification, makes this volume a very useful one.

M. N. Hill is the editor of a 3-volume series entitled *The Sea, Ideas and Observations on Progress in the Study of the Seas* (Hill, 1963). Volume 3 considers *The Earth Beneath the Sea* and contains chapters on beaches and nearshore processes, and on estuaries, deltas, shelf, and slope.

Natural Coastal Environments of the World

Natural Coastal Environments of the World was written by W. C. Putnam, D. I. Axelrod, H. P. Bailey, and J. T. McGill under the overall supervision of Putnam at the University of California, Los Angeles (Putnam *et al.,* 1960). It is best described as a handbook styled for the use of photo-interpreters engaged in terrain studies of coastal areas. Included are chapters on coastal landforms, coastal vegetation, and climates of coastal regions, and three accompanying maps. In the preface (p. v) it states that:

> Putnam . . . wrote the section on coastal landforms of the world; McGill established the classification of coastal landforms; did the necessary bibliographic research and analysis of coastal aerial photography — both military and civilian — and compiled the coastal landform map; Axelrod established the classification of coastal vegetation types, prepared the coastal vegetation map, and assembled the material for the text section on coastal vegetation which was written by Putnam; Bailey designed the climatic classification, coordinated it with the distribution of vegetation types, prepared the coastal climatic map, and wrote the section entitled "Climates of Coastal Regions."

This volume was written with military applications in mind, but would also be useful to non-specialists in the earth sciences. Figures 22, 23, 41, 42, 43, 44, 45, and 46 are excellent photographs of different desert coastal types around the world.

Map of the Coastal Landforms of the World

J. T. McGill published separately the *Map of the Coastal Landforms of the World* (McGill, 1958) which later appeared in *Natural Coastal Environments of the World* (Putnam *et al.,* 1960). This map is on a scale of 1:25,000,000 and shows the major landforms of a 5- to 10-mile wide coastal area. Much additional information pertinent to the analysis of coastal evolution is presented through the use of colored patterns bordered by black print. Generalizations apply to dominant characteristics of coastal segments 25 miles long. After a little study the map is easier to interpret.

McGill (1958, p. 405) states that the map " . . . should prove useful as a guide to the general geomorphologic conditions to be encountered in landward sequence of any given coast from the offshore zone through the coastal strip." A reliability index is not given, but McGill believes the map's reliability to be fair to good.

Photographic Interpretation of Coastal Areas

Aerial photography of coastal areas can provide a variety of information on physical conditions. The numerous amphibious warfare operations of World War II proved the value of preinvasion aerial photography of the beaches and coastal areas to be assaulted. P. G. McCurdy of the U. S. Navy Hydrographic Office prepared the *Manual of Coastal Delineation from Aerial Photographs* (McCurdy, 1947). Shorter papers by Dietz (1947), Coleman (1948), Shepard (1950), and McBeth (1956) deal with various aspects of shore processes, coasts, and beaches.

For the purposes of this chapter, it should not be necessary to discuss the photographic interpretation of coastal areas at length. Probably most coastal areas of the world have been overflown for military or civilian purposes in the past 20 years. Putnam *et al.* (1960, p. *v*) mention the analysis of military and civilian coastal aerial photography, but not the extent of coverage.

U. S. Naval Oceanographic Office: "Nautical Charts"

The U. S. Naval Oceanographic Office issues nautical charts of the entire world. Prior to 10 July 1962 the charts were issued by the U. S. Navy Hydrographic Office. Both names are used in the bibliography, depending upon the issue date of the particular chart. In addition to a name each chart has a number.

Basically the nautical chart shows depth of water (by numerous plotted soundings), the shore line of the adjacent land, topographic features which might serve as landmarks, aids to navigation, and other useful data for the mariner. These basic data make the nautical charts particularly valuable for the investigation of coastal areas. The U. S. Navy compiles the charts from the surveys of other nations and from its own surveys. Some of the pre-World War II charts do not seem to have the onshore detail of the later charts. However, all charts are corrected periodically, so that even charts of areas surveyed prior to 1900 are quite good. Post-World War II surveys are more detailed offshore and inshore. Some areas, like the Persian Gulf, have excellent coverage at several scales.

The nautical charts for all desert coastal areas are listed (in numerical order rather than by date) towards the end of the bibliography under "U. S. Navy Hydrographic Office" or " U. S. Naval Oceanographic Office." In the text the nautical charts are referred to as "U. S. Navy nautical chart H. O. (number)."

Other U. S. Navy Publications

Other publications useful to this study have been issued by the U. S. Naval Oceanographic Office (designated the U. S. Navy Hydrographic Office prior to 10 July 1962) as follows:

1) Chart No. 1. *United States of America*

Nautical Chart Symbols and Abbreviations, 1963. Although more a table than a chart, this publication is essential to the proper interpretation of nautical charts. A number of sections of Chart No. 1 are of particular interest for coastal studies. S e c t i o n A describes the coastline (nature of the coast). Steep coasts with high or low bluffs, flat coasts, cliffy coasts, rocky coasts, sandy shores, nature of the foreshore area, etc., are illustrated. Section B identifies the abbreviations of terms used to describe coastal features. Section C describes the natural features of the land, including topography, vegetation, and water. Section O describes natural dangers (reefs, breakers, tide rips) and man-made dangers (wrecks, submarine piling). Section Q and R cover soundings and depth contours. Section S lists quality-of-the-bottom symbols. (U. S. Naval Oceanographic Office, 1963*a*).

2) Special Publication 56. *The Quality of the Bottom—A Glossary of Terms,* by W. H. Berninghausen (1961). This report defines bottom notations that appear on both U. S. and foreign navigation charts. It also indicates how bottom sediment notations are reconciled to U. S. Hydrographic Office sediment classification.

3) H. O. Pub. No. 150. *World Port Index, 1963.* This publication is extremely useful for quick reference to locations and general descriptions of maritime ports and shipping places, with reference to appropriate "Sailing Directions" charts. (U. S. Naval Oceanographic Office, 1963*b*).

4) H. O. Pub. No. 607. *Instruction Manual for Oceanographic O b s e r v a t i o n s, 2nd edition.* Describes the standard techniques for use aboard U. S. Navy survey vessels and other warships (U. S. Naval Oceanographic Office, 1955). Also see: *Some Techniques in Coastal Oceanography,* by the Council for Scientific and Industrial Research, Union of South Africa, 1964.

5) Technical Report 61. *A Reappraisal of the Tides of the Mediterranean,* by W. E. Maloney and R. E. Burns (1958).

6) Technical Report 55. *Descriptive Oceanography of Kuwait Harbor,* by H. W. Dubach and T. J. Wehe (1959).

7) H. O. Pub. No. 234. *Breakers and Surf, Principles in Forecasting* (U. S. Naval Oceanographic Office, 1944).

8) H. O. Pub. No. 602. *Wind Waves at Sea, Breakers and Surf,* by H. B. Bigelow and W. T. Edmondson (1947).

The *Manual of Amphibious Oceanography* was prepared by the College of Engineering, University of California, Berkeley, under contract to the Office of Naval Research (N7ONR-29535); the editor was Professor R. L. Wiegel. A section on beach characteristics by W. N. Bascom (Bascom, 1951*a*) is extremely useful in that it can provide persons from a variety of scientific disciplines and from the military with a general background on beaches. This section of the manual has been declassified. Wiegel and Bascom and other research team members have pioneered in these kinds of studies following World War II. Bascom (1951*b*) related sand size and beach-face slope in a study of Pacific Coast beaches. Also see Wiegel's glossary of terms for waves, tides, currents, and beaches (Wiegel, 1953) and his comprehensive volume on oceanographic engineering (Wiegel, 1964).

"World Aeronautical Charts" and "Operational Navigation Charts"

The U. S. Coast and Geodetic Survey publishes aeronautical charts of the United States; the U. S. Air Force Aeronautical Chart and Information Center (ACIC) publishes charts of foreign areas. All the charts are distributed by the U. S. Coast and Geodetic Survey. The "World Aeronautical Charts" (WAC) of land areas show cities and towns, principal roads, distinctive landmarks, drainage, and relief. Relief is shown by spot elevations, contours, and gradient tints. Air navigation information includes visual and radio aids, airfields, controlled airspace, restricted areas, obstructions, and other pertinent data. The scale is 1:1,000,000, and the Lambert conformal conic projection is used.

The "Operational Navigation Charts" (ONC) contain about the same information as the WAC series except that relief is shown by shading rather than contours. The ONC series is gradually replacing the WAC series for areas outside the United States.

Both series show the coastal areas well but do not show many offshore features. The ONC charts are larger (42 by 57½ inches compared to the 22 by 29 inch size of the WAC charts) and therefore show more of a coastal area at a glance. The two series definitely complement the nautical charts.

The "World Aeronautical Charts" and "Operational Navigation Charts" covering all the desert coastal areas are listed (in numerical order rather than by date) towards the end of the bibliography under "U. S. Air Force: World Aeronautical Charts (WAC)" and "U. S. Air Force: Operational Navigation Charts (ONC)." In the text they are referred to as "WAC (number)" or "ONC (number)."

U. S. Geological Survey Maps

The U. S. Geological Survey has published geologic, geographic, and topographic maps for Libya, the Arabian Peninsula, and the Kingdom of Saudi Arabia.

The topographic and geologic maps (scale 1:2,000,000) of Libya were prepared by the U. S. Geological Survey (Goudarzi, 1962; Conant and Goudarzi, 1964) under the joint sponsorship of the Kingdom of Libya, the Ministries of National Economy, Petroleum Affairs, and Industry, and the U. S. Department of State. The topographic map shows cultural features, generalized relief, topographic contours in meters, and bathymetric contours in meters; it also includes a short glossary. The coastal areas include numerous sebkhas (*sabkhah*), which are marshy areas and salt flats in undrained depressions. The geologic map describes other formations of the coastal area.

The geographic and geologic maps (scale 1:2,000,000) of the Arabian Peninsula were compiled by the U. S. Geological Survey and the Arabian American Oil Company under the joint sponsorship of the Kingdom of Saudi Arabia, the Ministry of Petroleum and Mineral Resources, and the U. S. Department of State. The geographic map (U. S. Geological Survey, 1963*b*) shows cultural features, generalized relief, spot elevations in meters, coastal cultivated areas, coastal and offshore oil fields, coral reefs, sebkhas, and bathymetric contours in meters; it includes a glossary of Arabic and Persian terms. This map is the base for the geologic map (U. S. Geological Survey, 1963*a*) which shows all formations of the coastal areas. Both maps include the waters of the Red Sea, Gulf of Aqaba, Gulf of Aden, Arabian Sea, Gulf of Oman, and the Persian Gulf.

The U. S. Geological Survey has also prepared a series of quadrangle maps on a scale of 1:500,000. They cover three degrees of longitude by four degrees of latitude, with three exceptions along the Red Sea where about one additional degree of longitude is included. The quadrangle maps are printed in two sheets for each area; sheet A combines geology and geography; sheet B treats geography only. Ten of the maps published to date cover coastal areas and show in greater detail the features depicted in the maps of the Arabian Peninsula mentioned above. Generalized relief is shaded or shown by hachures. Sand is represented by stippling. Four types of sand terrain are distinguished. The maps are of Lambert conformal conic projection and average 104 by 113 centimeters in size.

J. F. Pepper and G. E. Everhart (1963) have compiled a geologic map of the lands bordering the Indian Ocean. This map includes desert coastal areas of Australia, Pakistan, Iran, the Arabian Peninsula, the east coast of Africa, and the west coast of Africa as far north as 28° south latitude. Bathymetric contours show the configuration of the ocean floor. Although the map lacks the detail that might be desirable for some studies, it does present the overall picture. A text of 33 pages accompanies the map and does add a large amount of detail on coastline configuration and nature of the offshore shelf area. Thus the text portion is excellent background reading.

General References

"General references" as used here includes the numerous periodicals and serial publications in geology, geomorphology, geography, oceanography, and related fields; textbooks and reference volumes in the same fields; government publications of more than a dozen nations; specialized bibliographies, including the *Bibliography of Geology Exclusive of North America* published by the Geological Society of America; U. S. Army area handbooks; atlases; and miscellaneous materials.

The *Bibliographie Géographique International* of the Association de Géographes Français, now issued by the Centre National de la Recherche Scientifique, could not be included in this literature search. It has been an outstanding source for 70 years and provides short abstracts of articles appearing in well over 900 periodicals in all countries.

The U. S. Army Map Service in Washington, D. C., prints a number of topographic maps at a scale of 1:253,440 for different parts of the world and is otherwise a general source of maps. These maps are not listed in this survey because the other maps and charts cited cover adequately the desert coastal areas.

B. NORTHWEST MEXICO: BAJA CALIFORNIA AND THE SONORA-SINALOA COAST

1. Introduction

The desert coastal areas of northwest Mexico include the east and west coasts of Baja California and the arid Sonora-Sinaloa coast south to about the latitude of Los Mochis. The total length of this arid coastline is approximately 2700 miles. The name

"Baja California" is used here to include Baja California Norte, which became a state in 1952, and the Territory of Baja California Sur. The geographic-political boundary is in the extreme desert region at 28° north latitude.

Causes of the desert conditions have been discussed previously under "Cold Currents Along Certain Desert Coastal Regions" (IG4). Meigs (1966, p. 102) presents an interesting contrast of the dry climates of the west coast of Baja California and the Sonora-Sinaloa coast to show the influence of the cool coastal current in the Pacific side of Baja California.

Both Baja California and the Sonora-Sinaloa coast are readily reached from California and Arizona cities. Some good and some poor roads either follow the coast or lead to the coast in many places, but not all the coastal areas may be readily reached by land routes; many Baja California shores are more easily reached by ship, small boats, or by amphibious aircraft.

The proximity of Baja California and the Gulf of California to southern California colleges and universities has attracted many investigators from most scientific fields. Prominent among scientific investigations of the area are the expeditions of the Scripps Institution of Oceanography; these have included physical, biological, and chemical oceanographic studies, geophysical work in waters of all depths, submarine geological work in many areas, and numerous sedimentologic studies in shallow to deep waters. The land areas of the coasts have also been studied extensively by other scientists.

The Sonora-Sinaloa coast has been studied least. With isolated mountains and hills reaching the coast at several locations, wide alluvial plains, deltas and associated marshes and flats, and lagoonal areas, studies of this coast could serve as models for similar investigations in other parts of the world. Many areas are now irrigated and produce high quality food and cotton crops. This is also an excellent deep-sea sportfishing region and the coastal resorts are becoming more popular as transportation improves.

The many studies of Baja California Norte and the northern Gulf of California complement similar studies in southern California (U. S.) and Arizona. The coastal area of southern California is well known and therefore is not discussed here. Terry's (1955) bibliography of marine geology and oceanography of the California coast is readily available.

Barrett's (1957) bibliography for Baja California includes the adjacent islands in the Pacific Ocean and the Gulf of California and covers historical, geographical, and scientific literature.

2.   Survey of Information Available: Part I

The U. S. Naval Oceanographic Office "Sailing Directions," H. O. 26, provides good information for the coasts of northwest Mexico, corrected through 3 April 1965. Eight U. S. Navy nautical charts cover the Pacific coast and the Gulf of California waters; they are: H. O. 1149, 1193, 1310, 1493, 1664, 0619, 0620, and 0621. Fifteen larger-scale charts cover the numerous harbors and anchorages; many of these surveys were made prior to 1900. Recent cruises of the Scripps Institution of Oceanography vessels have shown some errors to exist in these charts (Rusnak, Fisher, and Shepard, 1964, p. 60). Landmarks in question should be corrected by triangulation and aerial photography.

Additional sounding lines would be desirable in both the shallow and deep water areas on many of these charts. The American Association of Petroleum Geologists Memoir 3, *Marine Geology of the Gulf of California* (van Andel and Shor, 1964), contains a chart of the submarine topography of the Gulf of California. The shallowest contour drawn is 20 fathoms in the north half and 100 fathoms in the south half. The greatest depth shown in the Gulf of California proper is in excess of 2000 fathoms in Pescadero Basin. The portrayal of landforms is schematic but useful. The onshore topography is better shown by the U. S. Air Force Operational Navigation Charts H-22, H-23, and J-24, and the U. S. Coast and Geodetic Survey World Aeronautical Charts 404 and 405.

Tide tables of the U. S. Coast and Geodetic Survey (1965*a*) provide data for this coastal area. Eight stations are listed for the Gulf of California and 13 for Baja California. Roden (1964, p. 37-43) reports that tidal observations have been recorded from very few locations, but he describes the tides and tidal currents in the Gulf of California and sea-level changes based upon present data. The extreme tidal range near the mouth of the Colorado River seems to be well known to the layman. The *World Port Index, 1963* (U. S. Naval Oceanographic Office, 1963*b*) lists a tide of 23 feet for Punta Peñasco, which is located about 80 miles southeast of the mouth of the Colorado River. Nautical data for 19 ports in the Baja California / Gulf of California area are included in the index.

The U. S. Navy / U. S. Air Force *Flight Information Publication, Terminal (Seaplane)* (1965*a*) gives data for Guaymas and Puerto La Paz.

Meigs (1966) presents an excellent summary of the general geography of northwest Mexico with the most emphasis on Baja California. McGill's (1958) coastal landforms map is excellent for this coastal area. Putnam *et al.* (1960) also describe the

Sonoran type of desert and illustrate the coastal desert with several good photographs. Raisz's (1964) map pictures the landforms of the Sonora-Sinaloa coast.

The second edition of Tamayo's *Geografía General de México* is in four volumes (Tamayo, 1962). Volume 1 contains a chapter on the littoral area and volume 2 contains a chapter on physical oceanography. Both chapters include the Baja California / Gulf of California coastal areas and waters.

Much of the remaining available information comes from geologic studies on land and from oceanographic investigations. Oceanography is an interdisciplinary science, but most of the work described in Part II is chiefly related to the broad realm of marine geology.

3.   Survey of Information Available: Part II
General Geology

A symposium volume entitled *Marine Geology of the Gulf of California* (van Andel and Shor, 1964) presents the results of a massive attack by marine scientists on many problems in the Gulf of California.

Sixteen papers cover general geology, submarine geology, sedimentology, geophysical studies, physical oceanography, and fauna. Six of these papers pertain directly to the shallow water areas and the coast.

Scientists of the Scripps Institution of Oceanography cruised the waters of the Gulf of California in late 1940 to obtain similar types of data; Anderson *et al.* (1950) summarized the results. Many of the problems recognized then were subsequently studied and the results presented in parts of *Marine Geology of the Gulf of California.* Thus the earlier of the two works provides a complementary background to the later.

The best general summary of the geology of the areas that border the Gulf of California is by Allison (1964). Other discussions of general and specific topics are presented by Rusnak and Fisher (1964), Hamilton (1961), Downs and Woodward (1961), Durham and Allison (1960), Mina (1957), Wisser (1954), Anderson *et al.* (1950), Wilson (1949), and Beal (1948).

The geomorphic study of the cape region of Baja California by Hammond (1954) describes the development of coastal features. Two papers by Ives (1951, 1959) describe some of the evidence for sea-level changes along the Sonoran coast.

Studies of offshore islands by Cohen *et al.* (1963), McIntyre and Shelton (1957), Johnson (1953), and Osorio-Tafall (1948) describe coastal features, particularly emerged and s u b m e r g e d terraces.

Many of the above papers contain geologic maps. A conventional geologic map of Mexico has been prepared by the Comité de la Carta Geológica de México (1960). Bathymetry is also shown by contours in meters.

The *Annotated Bibliography of Quaternary Shorelines (1945-1964)* by Richards and Fairbridge (1965) contains rather complete annotations of papers which deal in part with emerged and submerged terraces of northwest Mexico.

Submarine Geology

Many of the submarine geology studies of northwest Mexico concern the deep-water areas. Papers by Curray and Moore (1964*a*) and Moore and Curray (1964) do cover the shallow coastal waters and adjacent land along the Nayarit coast. This is south of the arid coast of Sinaloa by several hundred miles, but important analogies may be drawn. Curray and associates have studied but not published on the arid coast to the north.

Rusnak, Fisher and Shepard (1964) describe the bathymetry and faults of the Gulf of California and Shepard (1964) describes sea-floor valleys.

Sediments

The following cited references, although included under the heading of "Sediments," also contain submarine geology and general oceanographic data. Van Andel's (1964) paper on the "Recent Marine Sediments of the Gulf of California" describes some shallow water coastal areas but is more concerned with the deeper offshore basins. Curray and Moore (1964*b*) describe littoral sands along the Nayarit coast. As mentioned above, analogies may be drawn between this coast and the arid coast of Sinaloa. Curray and associates have studied the subject, but have not published on it.

A number of coastal lagoons and bays on the Pacific Ocean side of Baja California have been studied in the past ten years. Although sediments were emphasized, the studies have yielded a variety of useful oceanographic data. These studies include papers by Emery *et al.* (1957), Stewart (1958), Phleger and Ewing (1962), and Phleger (1965). Nichols (1962) did a similar study for some lagoons along the arid Sonora coast.

Another abstract by Inman, Ewing, and Corliss (1964) describes coastal sand dunes near Guerrero Negro, Baja California. McKee (1939, 1957) has studied sedimentary structures in the sediments of the Colorado River delta and along the northeast Sonora coast. Thompson (1965) studied the tidal mud flats of the Colorado River delta and the coastal plain of the northwestern Gulf of California in conjunction

with the preparation of a doctoral thesis at the Scripps Institution of Oceanography. This study probably will be published as a Special Paper of the Geological Society of America. Gorsline and his students at the University of Southern California are continuing studies in the same general region (Gorsline, 1965).

The sediment studies discussed above are the kind that provide the most useful data for coastal areas because they involve the land near the sea as well as the shallow nearshore waters. The studies are not purely geologic for they include many oceanographic parameters.

Other sediment studies of coastal areas and deeper water areas include those by Grim, Dietz, and Bradley (1949), Emery (1955), Byrne and Emery (1960), Holser (1962), Berner (1964), Calvert (1964), Krause (1964), Taft and Harbaugh (1964), Bouma (1965), and Kirkland, Bradbury, and Dean (1965).

Physical Oceanography

The papers in physical oceanography pertain chiefly to the deeper waters along the Pacific coast of Baja California. These include studies by Dawson (1951), Fleming and Elliott (1956), LaFond (1963), and Reid, Schwartzlose, and Brown (1963). Roden (1964) has summarized oceanographic aspects of the Gulf of California. The observations were made in waters of all depths, but deep or shallow the results apply to the coastal areas. Meteorological aspects, discharge and chemical composition of rivers, tides and sea level, surface currents, and temperature and salinity distribution in surface layers and at depth are also included.

Geophysical Studies

The geophysical studies in the Baja California area chiefly involve the deep-water portion of the Gulf of California. The only study of a coastal area is that of Kovach, Allen, and Press (1962) in the Colorado Delta region. Depths of the Cenozoic section and fault patterns were determined.

Faunal Studies

A number of useful studies of living and fossil faunas of northwest Mexico have been made in recent years. In many instances the studies emphasized general sedimentology and oceanography, but data on living foraminifera also were included because they are very much a part of the environment of deposition (see Phleger and Ewing, 1962; Phleger, 1965). Papers by Walton (1955) and Parker (1964) include faunas of coastal areas and a discussion of the ecological conditions under which they live.

4. Current Research

Current research on the coastal areas of north-west Mexico is largely a continuation of some of the research described earlier. Dr. Joseph R. Curray of the Scripps Institution of Oceanography is completing a project on the Nayarit coast. Dr. Fred B. Phleger is continuing his ecological studies of Baja California lagoons, particularly Laguna Ojo de Liebre (Scammon Lagoon). Dr. Douglas L. Inman is working on coastal dynamics in the northern Gulf of California.

Dr. Donn Gorsline and students at the University of Southern California are continuing their investigation in the northwest Gulf of California area west of the Colorado River delta.

Mr. J. Brian Matthews, formerly of the Institute of Atmospheric Physics, University of Arizona, and now at the University of Alaska, studied the tides at Puerto Peñasco near the head of the Gulf of California. Matthews and Gen. Samuel R. Browning, Project Coordinator of the Numerical Analysis Laboratory of the University of Arizona, programmed the data for computer analysis and produced a 1967 tide calendar for Puerto Peñasco, which is available from the University of Arizona Press.

Biologists of the University of Arizona have been studying the ecology of the northern Gulf of California for several years. More recently they have formed a cooperative marine sciences program with the University of Sonora, resulting in a marine research station at Puerto Peñasco, Sonora. The University of Arizona also has a solar-powered water desalinization plant located here. Future plans call for enlarged facilities and a stepped-up biological studies program plus work in marine geology and physical oceanography.

This attack on the Gulf of California littoral has yielded very useful results and holds great promise for additional useful results in the future if continued and expanded.

5. Suggested Research

In spite of the apparent wealth of information for northwest Mexico, additional data are still needed for the shallow-water areas close to shore, and for the shore and coast areas. This kind of information is particularly lacking for the arid Sonora-Sinaloa coast. The study of a few selected stretches of this coast would provide the models for comparison with analogous coasts.

The U. S. Naval Oceanographic Office nautical charts are not adequate for detailed work. Errors exist in the mapped positions of islands. Many additional sounding lines are needed for deep and shallow waters.

C. PERU: THE COAST

1. Introduction

The entire coast of Peru, about 1,400 miles in length, is a desert coastal area. When the Atacama desert area of the Chile coast to the south is added, the total length is approximately 2,300 miles. Both areas are coastal deserts because the cool offshore Peru (Humboldt) Current combines with south-westerly winds to establish a stable air mass along the coast which produces very little rainfall. Humidity is high and winter fogs (July and August) are frequent. The area's desert climate results from conditions resembling those of the Pacific coast of Baja California (both being related to a cold coastal current) with seasons reversed for the opposite hemispheres.

The Peruvian coastal desert averages about 60 miles in width and is widest at the northwest and southeast ends. Numerous rivers, which head in the mountains to the east and derive their flow from rainfall and melting snow, cross the desert region. Meigs (1966, p. 107) describes the rivers as follows:

> The rivers differ greatly from one another in amount of water, seasonality of flow, fluctuation from year to year, and character of accessible irrigable lands. Maximum flow is during the southern summer (October to April), and many of the streams dry up completely during the winter. The water provided by these rivers, directly or through the intermediary of ground water, supports irrigation agriculture along the valley floors, the deltas by the coast, or the alluvial fans where the streams emerge from the mountains.

Offshore the nutrient-rich cool waters of the Peru Current support a huge fish population. The fish are food for the Peruvians and for large seabird populations. The accumulations of bird guano are mined from the desert islands and more recently from specially prepared nesting areas on the mainland.

Much of the Peru coast is a very low narrow desert plain. The sandy beaches are interrupted by rocky points and cliffs. Sand dunes are common near the coast, but in the northwest extensive areas inland are covered by shifting sands.

2. Survey of Information Available

U. S. Navy and U. S. Air Force publications provide a variety of information on the Peruvian desert coastal area. "Sailing Directions," H. O. 25 covers the entire coast of Peru as well as the coasts of Columbia, Ecuador, and the northern half of Chile. Chapter 1 contains excellent sections on oceanography and climatology. The oceanography section is par--ticularly pertinent for the west coast because of the presence of six major currents. Figures depict the general surface circulation, also cotidal lines, spring tide ranges, and percent frequencies of sea and swell. The latter are shown by rose diagrams for four seasons. Each rose diagram depicts relative frequencies of selected wave-height categories by directions, together with the number of observations making up each rose. The chapter coverage of individual stretches of the coast is good. It is emphasized that the soundings along many parts of the coast are insufficient and that uncharted dangers may exist. Mariners are also warned that errors exist in the actual coastal configuration in many places.

U. S. Navy nautical charts H. O. 1177, 1178, and 1218 cover the coast at a small scale. Soundings close in to the shore are scant and very little is revealed of the onshore topography at this scale. Ten other large-scale charts show ports and anchorages along the coast. Additional hydrographic surveys would be required to depict the nearshore bottom topography acurately. Peruvian government nautical charts were not consulted.

Good coverage of the land portion of the coastal area is provided by the U. S. Air Force Operational Navigation Charts N-25 and P-26, and by World Aeronautical Chart 1101. The "Geologic Map of South America" was compiled by Stose (1950) at a scale of 1:5,000,000. The "Mapa Geológico del Perú" by Bellido B., Narváez, and Simons (1956) is on a scale of 1:2,000,000. Smith's (1957) "Physiographic Diagram of South America" complements the geologic maps. An index to aerial photographic coverage and topographic mapping has been compiled by the Organization of American States (1964a). The coastal area is well covered at one scale or another by aerial photographs and topographic maps.

Tide tables for the west coast of North and South America list 15 stations for Peru (U. S. Coast and Geodetic Survey, 1965a). Marmer (1943) describes the establishment of recording tide gages on the west coast of South America in the early years of World War II.

The Peru (Humboldt) Current is well known from older studies (Sverdrup, 1930; Gunther, 1936). Murphy (1926) and Schott (1951) have described the El Niño current. More recently an undercurrent has been found and studied (Wooster and Gilmartin, 1961). Davies (1964) lists this coast as a "west coast swell environment" where long, low waves dominate the coast. This coastal swell adds to the problem of the lack of good natural harbors along the Peru coast.

The *World Port Index, 1963* (U. S. Naval Oceanographic Office, 1963b) lists 40 ports for this coast. Thirty-eight are classified as very small and even Callao is rated only medium. Many are open roadsteads with fair to poor shelter from the swell mentioned above. Few supplies for ships are available. Tides run from 2 to 5 feet along the coast of Peru. The U. S. Navy / U. S. Air Force *Flight Information Publication, Terminal (Seaplane)* (1965b) gives useful data for Talara, Alferez Huguet (near Ancón), and Callao.

McGill's (1958) coastal landforms map is excellent for this coast. Meigs (1966, p. 107-110) discusses climate and cultural features chiefly, with some emphasis on the northwest Peruvian lowlands. An older but good study by Bowman (1916) describes the coastal desert. The newer study of the arid coast by de Reparaz (1958) discusses the physical and biological geography and has a good bibliography. The *U.S. Army Area Handbook for Peru* (Erickson *et al.*, 1965, p. 48) contains a good 1-page description of the coast. *Peru From the Air* (Johnson, 1930) provides excellent photographic coverage and contains much useful information. Preston E. James also discusses the coast in his book entitled *Latin America* (James, 1959, p. 189-201).

The geology of the coastal area can be obtained from a number of publications. In most instances the coastal area is described as part of a larger mapping problem. The geologic mapping has been aided by the exploitation of oil fields near the coast in northwest Peru and oil company mapping programs in other areas. In spite of the early date of publication, *Geology and Paleontology of North-West Peru* by Bosworth (1922) and "Geology of Northwestern Peru" by Iddings and Olsson (1928) are two of the better references. More recent papers by Broggi (1940), Jenks (1945), and Lemon and Churcher (1961) fill in data for other coastal areas. W. F. Jenks worked in Peru for many years and was the editor for *Handbook of South American Geology* (Jenks, 1956), which discusses the general geology of South America country by country.

J. A. Broggi might be called the "dean" of Peruvian geology because he has written on a variety of problems and areas over a period of many years. Along the coast he has described the terraces (Broggi, 1946a, b), the eolian sands (Broggi, 1952, 1954), and the delta of the Río Tumbes (Broggi, 1946c).

Newell and Wood (1955) have described eolian sandstreams along the coast, and Morris and Dickey (1957) have described the precipitation of gypsum and halite in a restricted marine estuary, the Bocana de Varrila. Dresch (1961) has prepared a paper on his observations of the coastal desert of Peru.

Numerous islands off the coast of Peru are populated by birds, which produce guano deposits. Murphy (1925) has described the Peruvian coast and islands, guano resources, and the influence of the Peru (Humboldt) Current; this work includes many good photographs of the islands with their cliffed shores.

Torrico and Secada (1952) have prepared a number of bathymetric profiles from echo soundings of coastal waters. The soundings usually begin in waters more than 50 feet deep and continue into deeper waters.

Two papers by Schweigger (1943, 1947) on oceanography and the Peruvian littoral were not accessible to the author.

3. Review of Current Research

In the author's study of the Peruvian arid coast it was found that most of the information available pertained to onshore areas. What little offshore data were available centered around the Peru Current. Apparently this interest is to continue because the *Report of the Inter-American Conference on Marine Sciences* (National Academy of Sciences / National Research Council, 1963, p. 15) described a cooperative study of El Niño current with the Peru Marine Resources Research Institute participating. Many kinds of observations would be made on a continuing basis each year. This project would have little to do with the shallow coastal waters, however.

The most useful information of the land areas seems to be a by-product of geological studies. In many situations the geologists were employed by an oil company engaged in exploration in the coastal desert area. Geological research of this kind goes on all the time, but oil companies are usually hesitant about releasing data which might aid a competitor. Doubtless much additional useful information presently in a proprietary status will eventually be made available to the scientific community.

A systematic research on the marine biota of the Peruvian area (along the coast and adjacent sea) was described briefly in *Report of the Inter-American Conference on Marine Sciences* (National Academy of Sciences / National Research Council, 1963, p. 21-22).

4. Suggested Research

Based upon the current study of information available on the desert coastal area of Peru, the area for which we have the least information is the beach and nearshore area. The landward area seems to have been covered adequately by the numerous geologic studies. Detailed studies of beach erosion and growth are needed. Although some tide and wave data of a very general nature are available, detailed observations of wave behavior are needed. Close inshore surveys from small boats and perhaps even from aerial photography might provide some of this information.

D. CHILE: NORTHERN DESERT COAST

1. Introduction

The desert coast of northern Chile merges with the Peruvian coast on the north and extends south to about the latitude of Coquimbo. It includes the coast of the Atacama desert area and an additional coastal strip between about 27° and 30° south latitude. Meigs (1966, p. 111) discusses the reasons for and against extending the desert classification this far south.

The coastal desert is a narrow strip because the Andes are but a few tens of miles inland. Along much of its length the coast is a long line of steep cliffs broken now and then by a river channel. The rivers begin as mountain torrents in the Andes, but many disappear in the desert and never reach the sea. Where possible, the waters are used for irrigation, domestic, and industrial purposes. There are few good natural harbors along the coast. In places, the 100-fathom curve is less than a mile offshore and seldom is more than a few tens of miles offshore. Thus the narrow shelf does not provide good fishing. The ports handle chiefly mineral products from the interior. Bolivia and Argentina, just to the east over the Andes, also use some of the port facilities.

2. Survey of Information Available

The U. S. Naval Oceanographic Office "Sailing Directions," H. O. 25 covers the desert coast of Chile. This volume also covers the Peruvian coast, and the value of the "Sailing Directions" was discussed in the preceding section on Peru.

U. S. Navy nautical charts H. O. 1219 and 1220 cover the desert coast at a small scale. The numerous points and bold headlands, the great depths near shore, and the straightness of the coast are impressive. The entire coast between Arica and Caldera lies between 70° and 71° meridians of longitude. H. O. 2487 shows the Coquimbo-Bahía Tongoy coast at a larger scale. Chilean Navy charts (Chile, Armada de Chile, 1959, 1960, 1965) cover the entire desert coast at a larger scale.

Better coverage of the land portion of the coastal area is found on the U. S. Air Force Operational Navigation Charts P-26 and Q-26. Colors, shading, and contours are effectively employed to show the ruggedness of the coast. Chile has prepared its own geologic map at a scale of 1:1,000,000 (Chile, Instituto de Investigaciones Geológicas, 1960). The "Geologic Map of South America" by Stose (1950) is also available. The entire desert coast is covered by aerial photography; most of the desert coast is covered by topographic maps; and a number of areas along the coast have been mapped geologically at a larger scale (Organization of American States, 1964*b*).

The tide tables for the west coast of North and South America list nine stations on the desert coast of Chile (U. S. Coast and Geodetic Survey, 1965*a*). The comments on tides and swells for the Peruvian coast are also applicable for this coast.

The World Port Index, 1963 (U. S. Naval Oceanographic Office, 1963*b*) lists 22 ports for this desert coast of which 21 ports are small to very small. Antofagasta is listed as medium in size. In general they are better harbors than those of Peru. Tides run from 3 to 4 feet. The U. S. Navy / Air Force *Flight Information Publication, Terminal (Seaplane)* (1965*b*) gives data for Mejillones and Coquimbo. Both anchorages are protected from the southwest swell.

McGill's (1958) coastal landforms map is excellent for this desert coast.

The geological publications pertaining to the desert coastal area of Chile are not numerous, but are sound and to the point. *Fundamentos de la Geología de Chile* (Brüggen, 1950) contains a lengthy section on "Las Formas de la Costa" (p. 171-211); about 24 pages are devoted to the desert coast. The volume also includes a geologic map at a scale of 1:3,100,000. More detailed accounts of local areas displaying the raised terraces that are found along the coast are given by Wurm (1951), Harrington (1961), Segerstrom (1962*a, b;* 1964), and Fuenzalida Villegas *et al.* (1965). Each work emphasizes the fact that many of the terraces have been uplifted very recently.

The *Handbook of South American Geology* (Jenks, 1956) gives broad coverage to Chile. The newer *Geologie von Chile* by W. Zeil (1964) briefly describes the northern desert and coastal area. Muñoz Cristi (1955) has prepared a bibliography of Chilean geology for the years 1927-1953.

3. Review of Current Research

The *Annotated Index of Aerial Photographic Coverage and Mapping of Topography and Natural Resources: Chile* (Organization of American States, 1964*b*) describes several mapping programs that are part of a continuing program. Several desert coastal areas have been mapped and no doubt other areas will be included in the future.

The bibliographies of the International Geographical Union, Commission on Coastal Sedimentation (1960) and the International Geographical Union, Commission on Coastal Geomorphology (1964) did not list any research in progress in any South American countries for the years 1955-1963.

The *Report of the Inter-American Conference on Marine Sciences* (National Academy of Sciences / National Research Council, 1963) mentions two oceanographic projects in Chile, but both involved the coast south of Valparaiso and not the desert coast.

Apparently the deep waters close to shore have not interested the scientist and hydrographer. Studies made are probably geared to economic ventures or have some backing not obvious to the public.

4. Suggested Research

The prevalence of steep cliffs along much of the Chilean desert coast has probably contributed to the apparent lack of detailed studies of the nearshore waters. As in the case of Peru, the landward area has been covered by numerous geologic studies.

The nearshore waters are almost a no-man's-land. Certainly the reader can appreciate the difficulties of working along a cliffed coast with numerous uncharted dangers and a persistent swell moving in from the southwest. To combat these conditions it is suggested that much of the data be obtained by anchoring instrument buoys in the nearshore waters and by installing wave recorders in the cliff face. Periodic observations and photography by trained oceanographers also would be desirable. Aerial photography may reveal bottom conditions in the shallower waters.

E. ARGENTINA: PATAGONIA COAST

1. Introduction

The entire Patagonia coast, extending about 1,000 miles, is a desert. The same conditions prevail inland almost to the foothills of the Andes. In addition the land surface of the territories of Río Negro, Chubut, and Santa Cruz consists of extensive plateaus which slope toward the sea and usually end in cliffs. The only good coastal plain development is found to the north between Bahía Blanca and Golfo San Matías. South of this region the population seems to be concentrated either along the rivers or at one of the coastal ports.

Only a few of the coastal ports could be considered good natural harbors. The tidal range increases southward along the coast and presents problems. The continental shelf is wide (greater than 200 miles) along most of this coast, which is paralleled by the cool Falkland Current.

2. Survey of Information Available

The U. S. Naval Oceanographic Office "Sailing Directions," H. O. 24 covers the south tip of South America, including portions of the coasts of Chile and Argentina. Chapters 2 and 3 describe the Patagonian coast. Meteorological data of interest is found in Appendix II.

The U. S. Navy nautical charts H. O. 5282, 5283, and 5284 provide coverage of the desert coast at a small scale. H. O. 2078, 2104, 3908, 3912, 3913, 5399, and 6540 show portions of the coast and the ports at a larger scale. These larger scale maps also give a better picture of the nature of the cliffed coast. In some instances deeper water occurs just off the cliffed shorelines; in a few areas the cliffs are set back some distance from the water and water depths increase more gradually from narrow beaches seaward.

The U. S. Air Force Operational Navigation Charts R-24 and T-18, and World Aeronautical Charts 1491, 1537, and 1586 cover the land area. Unfortunately, the Argentine coastal area is not contoured like that of Chile. ONC T-18 also includes the Chile coast. The physiographic diagram of South America (Smith, 1957) is useful to compare the coasts of the two countries. Two geologic maps on a scale of 1:5,000,000 are available: Stose (1950) compiled the "Geologic Map of South America"; Argentina, Dirección Nacional de Geología y Minería (1964) published a newer map.

Along the Patagonian coast the tide tables (U. S. Coast and Geodetic Survey, 1965b) list 50 stations between Bahía Blanca and Cabo Virjenes. With the exceptions of Golfo San Matías and Golfo San Jorge, the mean tide level increases southward. This situation creates serious problems for the southerly ports.

The *World Port Index, 1963* (U. S. Naval Oceanographic Office, 1963b) lists 16 ports for this coast; 11 of these are rated very small, and the other 5 small. Maximum tide reported is 26 feet. Seaplane landing areas at Bahía Blanca, Comodoro Rivadavia, Puerto Deseado, San Julián, and Río Gallegos are described in the U. S. Navy / U .S. Air Force *Flight Information Publication, Terminal (Seaplane)* (1965b).

McGill's (1958) coastal landforms map may appear to be distorted for this high latitude, but this appearance is a result of an unfortunate map projection rather than the portrayal of coastal conditions, which is quite excellent.

The best general description of the Patagonian coast is found in the 9-volume series *La Argentina, Suma de Geografía* (Aparicio and Difrieri, 1958). Volume 2 contains a short chapter on the sea and the coast. The marine terraces along the coast have been described by Egidio Feruglio in numerous papers dating back to 1933. The 3-volume series *Descripción Geológica de la Patagonia* (Feruglio, 1949-1950) devotes over one hundred pages in volume three to a description of the terraces. The general geology of Argentina is included in the *Handbook of South American Geology* (Jenks, 1956).

3. Review of Current Research

The current research program seems to be devoted almost entirely to deep - water research (Popovici, 1956; National Academy of Sciences / National Research Council, 1963; Capurro, 1964). The program includes all branches of oceanography and is being conducted in cooperation with United States of America oceanographic research groups.

4. Suggested Research

The bays and port areas along the Patagonian coast are charted on a sufficiently large scale. Periodic resurveys or checks of areas prone to sedimentation or storm damage would be desirable. The other more cliffy stretches of the coast should also be charted on a larger scale. Most of the suggestions for Peru and Chile also apply to this coast.

It would not be necessary to study the entire desert coast in detail. Several typical areas might serve as models from which conditions along the coast could be interpreted.

F. AUSTRALIA: WESTERN COAST

1. Introduction

The desert coastal area of Western Australia extends for a distance of approximately 1100 miles, from just south of Shark Bay on the western coast northward to North West Cape and northeastward to just south of Broome, on the northwest coast. The northwest coast is low and sandy south of Broome to Cape Keraudren and adjoins the Great Sandy Desert. From Cape Keraudren to Exmouth Gulf the coast is more marshy, with many mud flats and tidal creeks. Offshore islands, reefs, and shoals are numerous. This coastal strip is subject to severe tropical storms. Onslow has been severely damaged on many occasions and has the reputation of being hit by every storm. The whole coast is subject to extreme tidal range, at spring tides up to about 40 feet at

Broome, decreasing to about 25 feet at North West Cape. A reported range of up to 40 feet at Port Hedland probably resulted from a combination of spring tides and effects of cyclonic winds.

The coast from North Cape south to Carnarvon is less sandy, more hilly, with cliffs and an offshore reef. Shark Bay has a hilly coast except for the mud flats and mangrove flats south of Carnarvon. The coast from Dirk Hartogs Island south for 230 miles consists of high precipitous cliffs that have not been reliably surveyed. The more hilly and cliffy coasts are part of the Great Plateau of Western Australia (Jutson, 1934).

Denham (Shark Bay), Carnarvon, Onslow, Roebourne, and Port Hedland are the towns or smaller settlements along this stretch of the coast. Their combined population in mid-1965 was less than 5,000 persons. The Carnarvon district is sheep-raising country, but on irrigated land along the Gascoyne River tropical fruits and beans are grown. Carnarvon is also the site of a NASA space-tracking station. North of Carnarvon on North West Cape the U. S. Navy is building a very-low-frequency radio communications station. A permanent town is developing around this project.

Onslow, east of the mouth of the Ashburton River on the Indian Ocean, serves as a shipping center for the adjacent wool-growing area. Hamersley Iron Proprietary, Ltd. is building port handling facilities at King Bay, which is in the Dampier Archipelago west of Nichol Bay. The population can be expected to increase when mining operations expand at Mt. Tom Price, about 190 miles inland. Port Hedland is another shipping port for wool, sheep, and manganese ore. The harbor is being dredged to handle larger ore vessels to carry iron ore from the deposit now being developed 70 miles inland at Mt. Goldsworthy.

A search for oil and gas along this coastal area has been in progress for over 20 years. Although the results have been somewhat disappointing, the recent well completions on Barrow Island, 60 miles off the coast north of Onslow, make the future look better. A number of firms are investigating the possibility of establishing solar salt plants at several locations along the coast between Shark Bay and Broome.

Thus, this western desert coastal area seems to be chiefly an outlet for other activities taking place inland in desert and semidesert regions. Port facilities are being improved at several places and should bring in more permanent residents.

2. Survey of Information Available

The information available on the desert area of the western coast of Australia consists chiefly of very general material. "Sailing Directions," H. O. 74 covers the north and west coasts of Australia from Cape York to Cape Leeuwin. "The Australia Pilot," Vol. V (Great Britain, Admiralty Hydrographic Department, 1959) provides similar information. The following U.S. Navy nautical charts cover the west coast from Cape Leveque in the north, southward, including Shark Bay, to Champion Bay: H. O. 3420, 3421, 3422, and 3436. Nautical chart H. O. 3436 is the only chart of a large scale to show some details of the nearshore bottom conditions, beaches, and coastal marshes and mudflats. The Royal Australian Navy chart of Exmouth Gulf and Monte Bello Islands to Onslow (Australia, Hydrographic Service, Royal Australian Navy, 1955, Aus. 182; and 1956, Aus. 184, respectively) provides some of this kind of detail. Contours are shown at 1, 3, 6, 10, 20, and 100 fathoms. Areas that uncover at low water are designated. Miscellaneous comments on dangers to navigation and shoreline topography are numerous. The coastal area to more than 1 mile inshore is shown in great detail.

The following maps of the Australian Geographical Series (scale of 1:1,000,000) cover the land portion of the coastal area between Broome and just south of Shark Bay: Broome (Australia, 1962), Hamersley Range (Australia, 1959), and Meekatharra (Australia, 1958*a*). The *Tectonic Map of Australia* (Geological Society of Australia, 1960) shows the geology of coastal areas as well as the tectonic features; geological notes (Geological Society of Australia, 1962) explain the tectonic map. Although the *Physiographic Diagram of Australia* (Gentilli and Fairbridge, 1951) is on a small scale, it complements the maps listed above.

Tidal data are provided in the tables for the central and western Pacific Ocean and Indian Ocean (U. S. Coast and Geodetic Survey, 1965*c*). The papers of Curlewis (1915) and Hodgkin and Di-Lollo (1958) make special reference to the tides at Port Hedland. Davies (1960, 1964) discusses the importance of waves on a coast and characterizes the coast from Shark Bay southward as a high energy wave coast. The high cliffs along the coast for some 200 miles south of Shark Bay attest in part to the eroding action of these waves.

The *World Port Index, 1963* (U. S. Naval Oceanographic Office, 1963*b*) gives useful data for the port facilities at Broome, Port Hedland, Balla Balla, Port Walcott, Onslow, Maud Landing, Carnarvon, and Port Gregory. Meigs (1966) discusses briefly the climate and some cultural features of this desert coastal area. McGill's (1958) coastal landforms map is fair for this coast.

Carrigy and Fairbridge (1954) have described the Recent sedimentation, physiography and structure of the continental shelf areas of Western Australia. The sediment types on the bottom have been obtained from notations on British Admiralty charts. The notations are usually too few and too far apart to provide an accurate map, and often the ship gathering the data did not operate very close to the shore. A short section on physical oceanography—tides, winds, and ocean currents—is particularly good.

Another paper by Fairbridge (1955) also considers the continental shelf areas of Western Australia. The treatment is more regional in scope but does provide a good overall picture. Pepper and Everhart (1963) summarize data from many sources to describe the general geology of the west and south coast of Australia. Their map and accompanying text are the best recent summary.

Corals grow on the west coast of Australia. Fairbridge (1950) describes the fringing reefs and corals associated with sandstone reefs that occur along the desert coast.

Konecki, Dickins, and Quinlan (1958) have mapped the geology of the coastal area between the lower Gascoyne River and Murchison River to the south. This account includes many detailed observations on coastal geomorphology and a good bibliography. In Shark Bay, B. W. Logan (1959, 1961) has studied the sedimentary environments of deposition and particularly the occurrence of stromatolites. To the north around Port Hedland, Russell and McIntire (1965) recently completed a study of tidal flats and their sand supply.

3. Review of Current Research

Brian W. Logan, Department of Geology, University of Western Australia, is the principal investigator of a project for the study of carbonate sedimentation in Shark Bay, Western Australia. Dr. Logan's interests in the project stem from his own doctoral research program in Shark Bay during the period 1956-1959 (Logan, 1959, 1961). The current project began January 1, 1964. On July 1, 1964, the American Petroleum Institute funded a portion of the project.

The field investigations in Shark Bay are of the geological oceanography type. An Australian fisheries research vessel was used for the earlier sampling programs. A 23-foot, shallow-draft launch equipped with depth sounder and radar is now in use. Some chemical laboratory analyses are performed at Shark Bay. All other activities are carried out in the laboratories at the University.

Shark Bay is a unique sedimentary environment. The lagoonal waters are mostly shallow but reach depths of up to 60 feet. Runoff into the lagoon is low and evaporation is high, so that there is an increasing salinity gradient from the normal sea water at the north entrance to the hypersaline (6.5%) lagoonal waters in the south. Other biologic factors combine to promote calcium carbonate sedimentation. One objective is to relate many factors controlling the deposition. A second objective is to learn of the nature of the diagenetic alteration that has taken place in some emerged carbonate deposits. A third phase of the project involves the low coastal area between the Gascoyne River and Wooramel River deltas. Mr. Graham R. Davies, a Ph.D. degree candidate at the University of Western Australia, is completing the study.

To date the project has contributed chiefly basic data for a unique carbonate sedimentation environment and holds great promise for additional useful results in the future if continued and expanded. Additional work on faunas particularly is needed. The final ecological synthesis should serve as a useful model, and facilitate the recognition of similar environments in sediments in which oil or gas may have developed.

The project has access to tide gage recordings taken at a point in Denham Sound. They also utilize several portable tide gages. Shallow depth coring is planned for mid-1966. Bottom photography is included in the routine investigations.

Tidal gage, bottom current, and bottom sediment data would be a valuable contribution to our knowledge of desert coastal areas. More studies of the type being conducted by Graham R. Davies are needed as models for desert coastal area analogs.

4. Hydrographic Surveys

The Hydrographic Service, Royal Australian Navy has completed a detailed survey of the King Bay area in the Dampier Archipelago. The chart had not been released as of mid-1965.

5. Suggested Research

The author had the opportunity to view from the air much of the desert coastal area between Shark Bay and Broome in July of 1965. Along the Northwest coast the stranded beach ridges were particularly impressive. The De Grey River appears to have built a large delta into the Indian Ocean; numerous beach ridges are present on the surface of the delta. It is not known why the De Grey River built a delta and the other rivers to the southwest did not. Flow and sediment transport in both cases is seasonal and even during peak seasons is often not intense.

G. AUSTRALIA: SOUTHERN COAST

1. Introduction

The desert coastal area of southern Australia extends approximately from Israelite Bay on the west to Fowlers Bay on the east, a distance of about 600 miles. This semiarid coast is called the Nullarbor Coast after the Nullarbor Plain which extends inland to the north. In discussing some of the geomorphological problems of the Nullarbor Plain, Jennings (1963, p. 44) cites a low annual rainfall of 5 to 12 inches for the area.

Much of the coastline is cliffed, with some cliffs reaching heights of 260 feet. At some places the cliffs are buried by windblown sands (Jennings, 1963, p. 45-46). From the air the cliffs stand out boldly, and where sand is present, the whiteness of the sand contrasts with the blue of the sea and the darker-hued limestones of the cliffs.

The Eucla Basin and Nullarbor Plain coincide approximately (Carrigy and Fairbridge, 1954; Alderman and Parkin, 1958; Pepper and Everhart, 1963); the Tertiary sediments (chiefly limestones) of the basin form the almost flat, featureless surface of the plain.

The Eyre Highway traverses the Nullarbor Plain, beginning in the east at Port Augusta and ending in the west at Norseman. The average distance between the highway and coast is about 20 miles, but the highway reaches the coast at Eucla. Less than 100 miles to the north the Trans-Australian Railway links the state of Western Australia with eastern Australia.

2. Survey of Information Available

The U. S. Naval Oceanographic Office "Sailing Directions," H. O. 77 covers the south coast of Australia. Australian Pilot books are also available. The U. S. Navy nautical charts H. O. 3425 and 3426 cover the coastal and offshore areas at a scale of 1:609,900. The U. S. Air Force charts for the Great Australian Bight, Australia (WAC 1459), and Cape Arid, Western Australia (WAC 1460), provide land coverage. Three maps of the Australian Geographical Series: Esperance (Australia, Division of National Mapping, Department of National Development, 1958b), and Nullarbor Plain and Eyre (Australia, National Mapping Office, Department of the Interior, 1952 and 1953), provide the same coverage on the same scale.

Tidal data are available only for ports on either side of the Nullarbor Coast according to the U. S. Coast and Geodetic Survey (1965c). The *World Port Index, 1963* (U. S. Naval Oceanographic Office, 1963b) does give a figure of 3 feet for the

tide at Eucla. Meigs (1966) has very little to say about the Nullarbor Coast. McGill's (1958) coastal landforms map adequately covers this coast. Davies (1960, 1964) characterized this coast as a high energy wave coast.

Carrigy and Fairbridge (1954, p. 75) describe the Eucla Shelf off the Nullarbor Coast and mention the scarcity of soundings. Pepper and Everhart (1963, p. 27) give a good synthesis of geology onshore and offshore. Alderman and Parkin (1958) outline the geology of South Australia but devote few words to the Eucla Basin.

J. N. Jennings of the Australian National University has best described the Nullarbor Plain and Coast (1963). In an earlier paper Jennings (1961) discusses karst morphology and presents the results of cave mapping of the Nullarbor Plain.

3. Review of Current Research

D. C. Lowry of the Geological Survey of Western Australia is mapping the Tertiary stratigraphy of the western Eucla Basin. A progress report is not available at this time. It is supposed that the coastal areas will be included.

4. Suggested Research

Much basic data is needed for a better knowledge of this coastal area. The starting point might be more detailed hydrographic data from the coastal waters. The other problems lie in the fields of stratigraphy and geomorphology.

H. NORTH ARABIAN SEA: IRAN BORDERING THE GULF OF OMAN TO THE RANN OF KUTCH / KATHIAWAR PENINSULA

1. Introduction

Part of the Iranian coast, all of the West Pakistan coast, and the western part of the Kathiawar Peninsula of India compose the desert coastal area of the North Arabian Sea. This coastal desert is coextensive with the Persian Gulf littoral and at least the Iranian coast faces the Muscat coast of Saudi Arabia. The length of the coast is approximately 1000 miles. Meigs (1966, p. 23-30) has written an excellent summary of this desert coastal area.

Rodman E. Snead of Clark University described this coast as follows (personal communication, 1966):

> This coastal region can be divided into several parts. The Kathiawar Peninsula of India consists of a narrow coastal plain backed by outliers of the Deccan plateau which are capped by sheets of lava. The Indus delta consists of 120 miles of coastline with mud flats, tidal marshes,

and mangroves. Much of this region is an inhospitable wilderness. From Karachi west into Iran the coast consists of uplifted mountains and platforms separated by scalloped bays, wide sandy plains, salt marshes, and lagoons. Six or seven small sheltered fishing ports are found along this very sparsely settled coast of West Pakistan and Iran.

2.   Survey of Information Available

The U. S. Naval Oceanographic Office "Sailing Directions," H. O. 62 describes this coastal area. This volume covers primarily the Persian Gulf but also the Gulf of Oman and eastward. The outstanding features of this publication are, first, its section on oceanography and second, its section on climatology. Appendix 1 contains views of the coast of the North Arabian Sea as well as the Persian Gulf.

U. S. nautical charts H. O. 1588 and 1589 span this coast. Because of their small scale, coastal detail is lacking; however, depth contours are shown on H. O. 1588 starting with the 10-fathom contour. The additional contouring is probably an outgrowth of the extensive hydrographic surveys made in the Persian Gulf in the post-World War II years. H. O. 1589 is based on British surveys made prior to 1900. Newer surveys on this coast are desirable because of the sedimentation that is no doubt occurring near the mouths of the Indus River. H. O. 2844 covers the coast southeast of Karachi for about 180 miles at a scale of 1:300,000. This chart was prepared from Pakistani, Indian, and British surveys made up until 1955. The detail is excellent. H. O. 3658 presents plans for ports and anchorages along the Pakistan-Iran coast. The scales are large (1:25,000 to 1:200,-000), providing a good detailed picture of nearshore bottom and onshore conditions.

The land portion of this coastal area is covered in good detail by U. S. Air Force Operational Navigation Charts numbers H-7, H-8, and J-8. It is suspected that aerial photographic coverage was used to compile these charts.

A geologic map of Pakistan (Abu Bakr and Jackson, 1964) is available on a scale of 1:2,000,-000. The Hunting Survey Corporation, Ltd., of Canada has photographed large areas of Pakistan in the course of preparing reconnaissance geologic maps. Maps on a scale of 1:253,440 are available for the coastal area (Canada, Department of Mines and Technical Surveys, 1958). A geologic map of Iran and the accompanying explanatory notes are available (National Iranian Oil Company, 1959*a* and 1959*b*, respectively).

The tide tables (U. S. Coast and Geodetic Survey, 1965*c*) list 10 stations for the desert coast of India, 5 for West Pakistan, and but one at Jask on the Iranian coast. Mean tide levels do not exceed 6 feet, except for the Gulf of Kutch, where 6 out of 7 stations exceed 11 feet. The *World Port Index, 1963* (U. S. Naval Oceanographic Office, 1963*b*) lists Jask and Chah Bahar on the Iran coast, Karachi on the West Pakistan coast, and 11 small and very small ports on the India coast. The U. S. Navy / U. S. Air Force *Flight Information Publication, Terminal (Seaplane)* (1965*c*) describes the landing facilities at Korangi Creek near Karachi.

McGill's (1958) coastal landforms map accurately portrays this coast.

The regional geography of India and Pakistan is described in a lengthy volume by Spate (1954). Siddiqi (1959) has briefly described the geology and physiography of the Karachi Coast. Snead (1966) has described the physical geography of the Las Bela coastal plain of West Pakistan. This excellent volume covers human settlement on the coastal plain, weather and climate, vegetation and soils, and a geological description of the coastal deposits. No nearshore data are given. The Makran coast to the west has been described by Harrison (1941), Falcon (1947), Ullah (1953), and Field (1959). Wiseman and Sewell (1937) have discussed the character of the coastal regions surrounding the Arabian Sea and their relation to offshore features.

Descriptions of the Iran coast could not be found. Maps for the coast show only one road ending on the coast, at Chah Bahar. Pepper and Everhart (1963) briefly describe this coast.

3.   Current and Suggested Research

The status of current research for this coastal area could not be determined. Qureshi (1957), in a review of oceanography in Pakistan, described the coast and ended by stating that much work is needed in all phases. Certainly much could be learned along the India coast about deltaic sedimentation in an arid climate. Comparisons with the Colorado River of North America would probably prove fruitful. Nearshore studies are notably lacking for this coast.

Snead's study of the Las Bela coastal plain is a good example of what could be done in other areas. He has visited the Makran coast on earlier occasions and is now engaged in further research on this sparsely inhabited and little-known area.

I.   PERSIAN GULF

1.   Introduction

The waters of the Persian Gulf and the adjoining coastal desert area have been studied more intensively in the past 18 years than any other similar area. (The

Baja California and Sonora-Sinaloa coast of Mexico ranks second.) Two factors are responsible for this great wealth of information. The U. S. Navy and other nations have conducted extensive hydrographic surveys and routine oceanographic studies. Secondly, oil exploration has penetrated the offshore waters and thus has required a variety of data on winds, tides, currents, storm activities, and bottom conditions. Many of the papers available on nearshore sediments and coastal geomorphology and sedimentation are a direct product of this oil-company activity.

The Persian Gulf coast is about 2000 miles in length. Along the northeast the Gulf borders Iran; to the northwest at the head of the Gulf are Iran, Iraq, and Kuwait; and to the south the Gulf borders the Kuwait-Saudi Arabia Neutral Zone and Saudi Arabia. Meigs (1966, p. 30-52) has described the entire coastal area in some detail; in fact, this section is perhaps the best of his *Geography of Coastal Deserts*.

Most of the Persian Gulf is shallower than 200 feet. Much of the Iran coast is backed by mountains and has but a few alluvial coastal lowlands. At the northwest and southeast ends of this coast are more extensive alluvial lowlands. The north end of the Gulf also is a low-lying alluvial complex. This is a very productive area agriculturally because of irrigation by waters from streams that receive their waters from the north. The remainder of the coast is rather flat with numerous marshes, mud flats, lagoons, shallow bays, and low rocky shores.

2. Survey of Information Available

The U. S. Naval Oceanographic Office "Sailing Directions," H. O. 62 provides excellent information for the Persian Gulf area. The current volume includes change number three to the fifth (1960) edition and is dated November 14, 1964. A section on oceanography covering currents, tides and tidal currents, sea and swell, and mean sea-surface temperature, salinity, and density is included. (Newer editions of "Sailing Directions" for other parts of the world are adding sections on oceanography; such data were previously lacking or scattered throughout the edition.) The oceanography section is followed by a section on climatology. Appendix 1 of H. O. 62 consists of views of the coast of the Persian Gulf, the adjacent Gulf of Oman, and the northern shore of the Arabian Sea eastward to Ras Muari.

Dubach and Wehe (1959) have summarized a great amount of oceanographic data for Kuwait Harbor, and the U. S. National Oceanographic Data Center has summarized temperature-salinity characteristics of the Persian Gulf (Anonymous, 1964).

The Persian Gulf is well covered by U. S. Navy nautical charts at a small, intermediate, and large scale. H. O. charts 3639, 3641, 3642, 3647, 3648, 3653, 3654, 3660, 3661, 3685, and 6301 provide the main coverage. Twenty-two additional charts cover individual ports and anchorages. The recency of the hydrographic surveys, the use of modern equipment and techniques in the surveys, and the large number of nautical charts made available give the Persian Gulf area the best coverage for any desert coastal area. The detail along the coasts is sufficient to make a variety of geomorphological, engineering geological or marine geological studies.

The land portion of the coastal area is covered by U. S. Air Force Operational Navigation Charts H-6, H-7, and J-7. The usual colors and patterns are employed to bring out topography. Contours are used only in the mountainous areas such as along the Iranian coast. The U. S. Geological Survey has prepared the *Geographic Map of the Arabian Peninsula* (U. S. Geological Survey, 1963*b*), which includes the Persian Gulf. Cultural features, generalized relief, coral reefs, sebkhas, coastal cultivated areas, and coastal and offshore oil fields are shown for the Arabian coast and for Iraq and northern Iran. This map and the accompanying *Geologic Map of the Arabian Peninsula* are on a scale of 1:2,000,000. A geological map of Iran has been prepared by the National Iranian Oil Company (1959*a*); explanatory notes (1959*b*) accompany the map. The map scale is 1:2,500,000.

The U. S. Geological Survey has also prepared a series of geographic and geologic maps of the Arabian Peninsula on a scale 1:500,000. Maps I-203A and B (Bramkamp and Ramirez, 1959*a, b*), I-208A and B (Steineke *et al.*, 1958*a, b*), I-209A and B (Bramkamp and Ramirez, 1961*a*, 1959*c*), and I-214A and B (Bramkamp and Ramirez, 1961*b*, 1959*d*) provides coverage for most of the Arabian Peninsula coast of the Persian Gulf.

The U. S. Geological Survey map coverage is excellent and becomes even more meaningful when combined with the U. S. Navy nautical charts. The physiographic diagram "Landforms of Arabia" (Raisz, 195-), on a scale of about 1:9,000,000, complements these maps and charts.

The A. Sahab Geographical and Drafting Institute (1962) has prepared the "Map of Kuwait and Basrah" which shows mud flats and marshes, stony and sandy areas, sand dunes, ridge cliffs, hills, and depressions.

Tide tables for the Persian Gulf (U.S. Coast and Geodetic Survey, 1965*c*) list 29 stations for the Persian Gulf. Five are on the Iran coast, 2 on the

Iraq coast, and 22 on the Arabian coast. The *World Port Index, 1963* (U.S. Naval Oceanographic Office, 1963*b*) lists 26 ports. Dawhah (Doha) on Qatar, Al Basrah (Basra) on the Iraq coast, and Abadan in Iran are rated as medium in size; the other ports are small or very small. The U. S. Navy / U. S. Air Force *Flight Information Publication, Terminal (Seaplane)* (1965*c*) lists facilities at Abadan on the coast of Iran, and at Bahrain and Kuwait.

McGill's (1958) coastal landforms map is excellent for this coast. One unique feature of the Persian Gulf is the presence of extensive coral reefs and what McGill terms a "narrow-coral plain" along some shores.

A number of papers have been published on the sediments of the Persian Gulf area. These include the deeper water areas and shallow coastal areas. Emery (1956) has described the topography of the coasts, islands, and sea floor, water characteristics (temperature, salinity, sources of salt, currents), and all aspects of the sediments. This paper is the best general summary available for the Persian Gulf; the reference list includes many of the older ones on the geology of the area.

Sugden (1963*a*) discusses some of the aspects of sedimentation in the Gulf, citing the role of eolian sand and dust. In a second paper, Sugden (1963*b*) reviews "The Hydrology of the Persian Gulf and Its Significance in Respect to Evaporite Deposition." Pilkey and Noble (1966) have described the carbonate and clay mineralogy of a number of bottom samples distributed over the Persian Gulf. Groot (1965) describes the appearance of "whitings" in the Persian Gulf, caused by visible precipitation of calcium carbonate.

The Qatar Peninsula area and the Trucial Coast have been described in numerous papers in the past several years. Both are areas of much carbonate deposition. The primary deposition and subsequent changes in mineralogy, along with a description of the coast that includes photographs, are included in the papers by Houbolt (1957), Wells (1962), Illing and Wells (1964), and Illing, Wells, and Taylor (1965)—all about the Qatar area; Evans and Sherman (1964), Evans, Kendall, and Skipwith (1964), Kinsman (1964*a, b*)—all about the Trucial Coast. A portion of the Trucial Coast has been described in a ground-water report by Wiebe (1965).

The British Admiralty, Naval Intelligence Division, has published "Geographic Handbooks" for Iraq and the Persian Gulf (B. R. 524) (Great Britain, Admiralty, Naval Intelligence Division, 1944*b*) and for Persia (B. R. 525).

3. Current and Suggested Research

The author was unable to learn of any research now in progress. It is very probable, however, that much of the same kind of work is going on as described above. Some of the results are a by-product of the studies by American and other oil companies operating in the coastal areas of the Persian Gulf.

The large quantity of data now available needs to be summarized and cataloged so that individual coastal areas can be described in terms of the factors mentioned on the first page of this chapter. Also, the Iranian portion of the Persian Gulf coast requires much additional research on these factors.

J. SOUTH COAST OF SAUDI ARABIA: MUSCAT AND ADEN PROTECTORATE

1. Introduction

The south coast of Saudi Arabia includes (*1*) the Muscat littoral along the Gulf of Oman coast and along the eastern half of the south coast, and (*2*) the western half of the south coast, included in the Aden / South Arabia Protectorate. Total length of these two stretches of coasts is about 1800 miles. Meigs (1966, p. 53-63) has prepared a lengthy description of the two coastal strips. It is noteworthy that he made frequent references to the U. S. Navy's "Sailing Directions" because of the scarcity of information for some portions of this coast.

2. Survey of Information Available

The U. S. Naval Oceanographic Office "Sailing Directions," H. O. 61 contains the most complete description of the coast between Aden and Ra's al Hadd. The description of the Gulf of Oman coast is found in "Sailing Directions," H. O. 62. The western part of the coast is a sandy coastal plain backed by high mountains. Numerous streams drain the mountainous areas along the coast so that the stream alluvium may be cultivated for part of each year. Eastward the mountains become lower hills, lying closer to the coast, and forming bold headlands in many places. The remainder of the coast consists of steep cliffs and sandy lowlands.

U. S. Navy nautical charts H. O. 1586, 1587, 1588, and 2816 cover this coast. Inshore detail is only fair on H. O. 1586 but good on H. O. 1587. Plans of anchorages along the coast are shown in British Admiralty Chart 10, "Anchorages on the Coast of Arabia."

U. S. Air Force Operational Navigation Charts H-7, J-7, and K-6 cover the land portion of this coastal area. The detail for the coastal area is superior to that shown on the nautical charts. Wadis, sandy lowlands, sea cliffs, and rocky areas are indicated in a manner suggesting that the data were derived from aerial photographs. Not all Operational Navigation Charts are this good.

The U. S. Geological Survey has prepared one set of geographic and geologic maps for the Southeastern Rub' al Khali Quadrangle (Maps I-220A and B) (Ramirez, Elberg, and Helley, 1963, 1962), which covers but a small portion of the coast and gives very little geographic information. The *Geographic Map of the Arabian Peninsula* (U. S. Geological Survey, 1963*b*) and the *Geologic Map of the Arabian Peninsula* (U. S. Geological Survey, 1963*a*) also cover this coast. The usefulness of the U. S. Geological Survey maps, the U. S. Navy nautical charts, and the U. S. Air Force Operational Navigation Charts has been emphasized in the previous section on the Persian Gulf.

Tide tables for this coast (U. S. Coast and Geodetic Survey, 1965*c*) list six stations. Masqat (Muscat) is the only station listed for the Gulf of Oman. The *World Port Index, 1963* (U. S. Naval Oceanographic Office, 1963*b*) lists the ports of Aden, Perim Harbour, Mukalla, Masqat, and Al Matrab on this coast. Aden is described as medium in size but is a very important refueling station (coal and oil). The other ports are small or very small. The U. S. Navy / U. S. Air Force *Flight Information Publication, Terminal (Seaplane)* (1965*c*) lists facilities for Aden / Khormaksar.

McGill's (1958) coastal landforms map is excellent for this coast in spite of the fact that the coast is very complex.

The volume entitled *Western Arabia and the Red Sea* in the Geographic Handbook Series of the British Admiralty (Great Britain, Admiralty, Naval Intelligence Division, 1946) contains a short discussion of the Gulf of Aden coasts. Beydoun (1960) has prepared a synopsis of the geology of the East Aden Protectorate. An older and often-quoted paper by Lees (1928) describes the geology of Oman and southeastern Arabia. More recently Morton (1959) described the geology of Oman at the Fifth World Petroleum Congress. Several oil wells have been drilled along this coast in the past and geological investigations certainly were made in association with the drillings, but the whereabouts and contents of the reports of such investigations could not successfully be determined.

During the International Indian Ocean Expedition the British conducted a study of upwelling along the southeast Arabian coast (Royal Society, 1963). Pepper and Everhart (1963) briefly describe the continental shelf off this coast.

The cover photograph (Anonymous, 1965-

1966) of the *Geotimes* magazine for December 1965 / January 1966 (volume 10, number 5) shows the Muscat coast and Oman on the Arabian Peninsula, taken with a hand-held camera from the Gemini 4 spacecraft; altitude was about 120 miles. Many coastal features may be discerned. On page 9 of this issue appears an interpretive map of the entire area. This technique could open up a new means of mapping coastal areas that are otherwise rather inaccessible.

3. Current and Suggested Research

The status of current research for this coast could not be determined. Routine geological mapping is probably going on as before. Specific mention of nearshore oceanographic studies could not be found. Studies of this kind would be desirable for a number of areas. The examination of existing aerial photography would be a good starting point.

K.   THE SOMALI COAST

1.   Introduction

Somalia forms the Horn of Africa and has an east and north coast. Part of the north coast was once British Somaliland. French Somaliland lies to the west, next to Ethiopian Eritrea, and forms part of the south entrance to the Red Sea. French Somaliland is included in this discussion. A brief but excellent discussion of the two coasts is found in Meigs (1966, p. 77-79).

2.   Survey of Information Available

The U. S. Naval Oceanographic Office "Sailing Directions," H. O. 61 describes the north coast, including French Somaliland, and H. O. 60 describes the east coast. U. S. Navy nautical charts H. O. 1586, 1606, 2816, 3881, and 3882 cover both coasts. The charts for the east coast are taken chiefly from Italian surveys of 1938 and 1939. There are no comments printed along the coastal fringe of the chart to indicate the presence of sand dunes, sandy beaches, rocky areas, etc. For this reason H. O. 60 would have to be consulted to determine the nature of the coast. On the other hand, the charts for the north coast have been compiled chiefly from British surveys, and also German, French, and Italian surveys. More onshore coastal details are given, but H. O. 61 would still have to be consulted for an overall picture.

The U. S. Air Force Operational Navigation Chart K-6 and World Aeronautical Charts numbers 687, 688, 808, 911, and 931 cover the land portion of the desert coast of Somalia. Charts 808 and 911 show sandy areas and rocky escarpments for portions of the east coast. A road, little more than a trail in many places, follows the coast for several hundred miles.

Geologic maps are available for the coast of French Somaliland (France, Institut Géographique National, 1947; Besairie, 1946) and for the Horn of Africa (Mohr, 1963*a*). The latter includes the coasts of Eritrea, French Somaliland, the north coast of Somalia, and the east coast of Somalia as far south as about 1° north latitude. McGill's (1958) coastal landforms map accurately portrays this coast.

The Somali coast is about 1800 miles in length. Eleven stations are listed in the tide tables (U. S. Coast and Geodetic Survey, 1965*c*). Mean tide level is slightly over 5 feet on the north coast and less than 5 feet on the east coast. The *World Port Index, 1963* (U. S. Naval Oceanographic Office, 1963*b*) lists the ports of Berbera and Zeila for Somalia, and Djibouti and Obock for French Somaliland; they are rated in the small and very small categories. Djibouti, the largest of the four ports, has limited supplies and repair facilities available.

The U. S. Navy / U. S. Air Force *Flight Information Publication, Terminal (Seaplane)* (1965*c*) lists land facilities at Djibouti in French Somaliland and Hafun South Bay in Somalia.

The geologic data on the Somalia coasts are chiefly derived from papers that deal with more general topics. Blondel (1935) and Dainelli (1943) describe the general geology, mentioning coastal deposits. Hunt's (1942) work on the Zeila Plain, in the former British Somaliland, is a little more specific in its coverage of the coastal area. Pallister (1963) has written a short but excellent discussion of the land strip between Zeila and Bosaso on the Gulf of Aden.

The Somali Current, which flows southward along the east coast was studied as part of the investigations of the International Indian Ocean Expedition (Royal Society, 1965).

3. Current and Suggested Research

The author was unable to learn of any coastal area research in progress. As in the case of other countries in this part of the world, oil and gas exploration programs map a good portion of the country involved and eventually include a coast. A party specifically interested in desert coastal areas would have to "dig out" the desired information. For Somalia there is probably no economic impetus to study the coasts at present.

Geomorphic-geologic study of selected coastal areas would be desirable. The initial phase of such a study could be the examination of aerial photographs to select areas for research, to determine the general characteristics of the coast, and to recognize problems.

L. THE RED SEA

1. Introduction

The Red Sea separates the desert coast of Africa from that of Arabia. The coast around the Red Sea is entirely desert; about 3300 miles long, it constitutes the longest coastal desert in the world.

The waters of the Red Sea have been navigated since the earliest days of exploration and trade in this part of the world. Peoples living near and on the coast today still depend upon the Red Sea for food and as an avenue of transportation. After the completion of the Suez Canal the Red Sea became even more important as an artery for ship traffic between Europe, the United States, and ports on the Indian Ocean and Persian Gulf.

Geologically, the Red Sea is well known as part of the East African Rift System. This system of faults has been described repeatedly in geological literature and many physical geography texts. The best recent discussion of the Red Sea area geologic history is by Swartz and Arden (1960). Meigs (1966, p. 63-76) has summarized many other facets of physical and human geography in this desert coastal area.

2. Survey of Information Available

The U. S. Naval Oceanographic Office "Sailing Directions," H. O. 61 contains the best detailed description of the Red Sea coast. Chapter 1 includes sections on oceanography and climatology.

U. S. Navy nautical charts H. O. 2812, 2813, 2814, 2815, and 2816 cover the Red Sea from northwest to southeast and coast to coast. The scales (1:645,430 to 1:711,850) are such as not to provide detail of the coastal areas. Larger-scale charts for individual ports and for the ends of the Red Sea are available.

The U. S. Air Force Operational Navigation Charts H-5, J-5, J-6, and K-5 and World Aeronautical Charts 687 and 688 cover the land areas adjacent to the Red Sea. Raisz's (1952) "Landform Map of North Africa" accurately portrays the area. For the Arabian Peninsula side of the Red Sea the U. S. Geological Survey has prepared geographic and geologic maps on a scale of 1:500,000. Maps I-200A and B (Bramkamp *et al.*, 1963 and 1962, respectively), I-204A (Brown *et al.*, 1963*a*), I-204B (Brown, Jackson, and Bogue, 1959), I-210A (Brown *et al.*, 1963*b*), I-210B (Brown and Jackson, 1958*a*), I-216A and B (Brown and Jackson, 1958*b, c*) and I-217A and B (Brown and Jackson, 1959, 1958*d*) provide this coverage.

The U. S. Geological Survey has also prepared *Geographic Map of the Arabian Peninsula* and *Geologic Map of the Arabian Peninsula* (U. S. Geological

Survey, 1963*b, a*) on a scale of 1:2,000,000. A variety of cultural features are shown including the coral reefs that lie offshore at varying distances. The geographic map shows the most detail in a coastal belt which averages about 50 miles wide.

Extensive oil exploration, such as has been conducted in Saudi Arabia and on the west side of the Red Sea, commonly involves extensive aerial photography and there is no reason to believe it would not do so in this case; however, the existence and availability of such photographic coverage for this area was not determined.

The tide tables for the Red Sea (U. S. Coast and Geodetic Survey, 1965*c*) list 18 stations. Mean tide levels are under 4 feet. *World Port Index, 1963* (U.S. Naval Oceanographic Office, 1963*b*) lists 29 ports for the Red Sea. Port Sudan and Suez are listed as medium in size; the others are small and very small; however, many of these ports have natural or breakwater-protected coastal harbors. The U. S. Navy / U. S. Air Force *Flight Information Publication, Terminal (Seaplane)* (1965*c*) describes the landing areas at Jedda (Jiddah), Port Sudan, and Kamaran.

The coastal landforms map by McGill (1958) is excellent for this coastal area. The ubiquitous coral reefs stand out along the shores.

The Geographic Handbook Series of the British Admiralty, Naval Intelligence Division, includes a volume entitled *Western Arabia and the Red Sea* (1946). The subject treatment is very much like that in the other volumes of this series, and the reader cannot help being impressed with the thoroughness of the research. This volume includes chapters on geology and physical geography, the coast, and ports. The photographs of coastal areas are excellent.

Another general reference on this area is Furon's (1963) *Geology of Africa*. Pepper and Everhart (1963) include the Red Sea coast south of Port Sudan on their map of the Indian Ocean. Journal-type papers and books best describe the geomorphology and geology of the coastal areas.

Geology of Egypt (Said, 1962) is a modern reference for this coast. The Suez area has been described more recently in *Guidebook to the Geology and Archeology of Egypt* (Reilly, 1964). Ball (1912) has described the geography and geology of the coast farther south. The beach sands of the Gulf of Suez have been characterized by Harris (1959).

Davey's (1948) numerous articles on the southern Sinai Peninsula appeared in *Mining Magazine;* they thoroughly reviewed the geography, geology, and mineral development, including coastal features. The area of coverage naturally laps over into the

Gulf of Suez and the Gulf of Aqaba. Friedman (1964) and Emery (1964) have described the sediments occurring in the Gulf of Aqaba; Emery's paper is the more complete of the two.

The Sudan coast is the subject of a geological study by Sestini (1965) and of a geomorphological study by Berry and Sestini *(in preparation)*. Berry, Whiteman, and Bell (1966) describe the emerged limestone reefs along the Sudan coast. Their introduction reviews other pertinent literature, and they also include a short but helpful bibliography. Earlier, Kassas (1957) described the ecology of a portion of the Sudan coast. His work started in the littoral coral growth and extended inland. The photographs are excellent. Two early papers by Crossland (1907, 1911) also describe the coral reefs of this coast and include sketches, maps, and photographs.

Data on the Eritrea coast (Ethiopia) are not abundant. Porro (1936) has described the Miocene geology north of Massawa (Massaua). Blondel (1935) described the geology and mineral resources of Ethiopa and Somalia. Dainelli's four volumes (1943) give a more detailed picture of the geology of the same areas. Mohr (1963*b*) prepared *The Geology of Ethiopia* as the companion volume to his *Geological Map of Horn of Africa* (Mohr, 1963*a*); the coastal deposits are treated on pages 189-193 (1963*b*).

On the eastern side of the Red Sea the Arabian coast south to Yemen was described by Vesey-Fitzgerald (1955, 1957); the two papers are on vegetation but include good discussions of the beach and foreshore and excellent photographs of coastal scenery.

An older paper by Sujkowski (1932) describes the contribution of the desert clastic sediments to the Red Sea. The deeper water sediments have also been studied by Said (1951) and by many recent oceanographic expeditions. The coral reefs, which occur well offshore in some areas as well as close inshore, have been described recently by Tazieff (1952) and Nesteroff (1955).

3. Review of Current Research

The presence of oil exploration groups in the countries bordering the Red Sea means that much geological data, and some geomorphological and geographical data will be forthcoming. Many of the results already described may be classified as "by-products" of the search for oil and gas.

Professor L. Berry of The University College, Dar es Salaam, Tanzania (personal communications, 1965), stated that the coast of Sudan had been the subject of little study; however, several papers are presently in progress dealing with the geomorphology and hydrology of the coastal zone. When published these papers will provide rather complete coverage for the coast of Sudan.

4. Suggested Research

Extensive data are available on the Red Sea area, scattered throughout the literature. An additional search should be made of Italian geographic and geologic literature, and then all the available data combined into a more usable form. Studies of selected areas could supply missing details of certain parts of the coast and perhaps serve as analog models.

Specific information on waves, breakers, and surf may be available but was not encountered during the research for this desert coastal area.

M. MEDITERRANEAN COAST OF AFRICA

1. Introduction

The Mediterranean coast of Africa constitutes a desert coastal area along much of the east coast of Tunisia and Libya, Egypt, and the Sinai Peninsula. (Inland of the coastal desert is the extremely arid Sahara.) The length of this coast, from south of Tunis to Gaza, is about 1800 miles. Meigs' (1966, p. 79-89) description of the several sections of this coast is recommended. The Nile-Sinai Mediterranean littoral is examined closely. Meigs emphasized the fact that the Libyan littoral ". . . has no extreme desert climate, and only relatively small sections have enough moisture deficiency to be called desert at all." (Meigs, 1966, p. 86).

2. Survey of Information Available

The U. S. Naval Oceanographic Office "Sailing Directions," H. O. 52 covers the Tunisia coast and H. O. 55 covers the remainder of this desert coast. Man has been navigating the waters of the Mediterranean Sea for several thousands of years, and the shores are well known. Chapter 1 in H. O. 52 contains sections on tides, winds and weather, and currents. Chapter 1 in H. O. 55 has separate sections on climatology and oceanography (tides, currents, sea and swell, sea water properties, etc.). As the "Sailing Directions" are revised periodically, it is probable that newer editions will contain similar sections on oceanography. Maloney and Burns (1958) present a study of the tides in the Mediterranean Sea.

U. S. Navy nautical charts H. O. 3974, 3975, 3976, 3977, 3980, 3981, 4290, 4291, 4292, 4293, and 4294 provide good map coverage for this coast. All but the last two of these charts are at a scale of about 1:250,000, which is sufficient to show one or

two contours less than the 10-fathom contour along the coast. H. O. 4293 and 4294 are at an approximate scale of 1:500,000 and include plans of the ports at a larger scale (1:12,750 to 1:51,110). H. O. 3976 and 3975, which show the Nile River delta and the entrance to the Suez Canal, respectively, are particularly good for coastal detail.

U. S. Air Force Operational Navigation Charts G-2, G-3, G-4, H-3, H-4, and H-5 cover the land portion of this coast. The Nile River delta, sanddune areas, salt marshes, and other cultural features are shown, but not all coastal areas are contoured.

The topographic map of Libya (scale 1:2,000,-000) by Goudarzi (1962) is particularly useful because it shows many cultural features, generalized relief, topographic contours in meters, and bathymetric contours in meters, and it includes a short glossary. Geologic maps of Tunisia (Castany, 1951) and Libya (Conant and Goudarzi, 1964) are available. The geologic map of Libya is on the topographic base described above. Lobeck's (1946) *Physiographic Diagram of Africa* gives a general picture of this coast, but in comparison Raisz's (1952) *Landform Map of North Africa* is much superior.

The tide tables for Europe and the west coast of Africa (U.S. Coast and Geodetic Survey, 1965*d*) include the Mediterranean Sea. Ten stations are listed for this desert coast with two each in Egypt and Libya and six in Tunisia. The tides are small in general but may be influenced by wind and atmospheric pressure.

The *World Port Index, 1963* (U. S. Naval Oceanographic Office, 1963*b*) lists 29 ports (Tunis to Daribat El Bahr) for this coast. Port Said and Alexandria are rated large; Benghazi, Tarabulus esh Shan (Tripoli), and Tunis of medium size; and others small to very small. The U. S. Navy / U. S. Air Force *Flight Information Publication, Terminal (Seaplane)* (1965*c*) lists no seaplane landing area for the desert coast but does list one at Fanara, Egypt, a lake on the Suez Canal system some miles south of the coast.

McGill's (1958) coastal landform map depicts this coast accurately in spite of the many geologic-geomorphic complexities. The British Admiralty, Naval Intelligence Division (1945) prepared a well-researched volume on Tunisia as part of its Geographic Handbook Series. Chapters on general geology (relief, drainage, and geology), the coast, ports, and climate make these books extremely valuable.

Furon's (1963) *Geology of Africa* is a general reference for this area. Journal-type papers must be consulted to obtain more detailed information. The desert coast of Tunisia has been treated almost completely; individual works and the areas they treat include: the delta of the Medjerda River (Pimienta, 1954*a*), the Cape Bon peninsula (Allemand-Martin, 1939; Arnould, 1948), the Monastir area (Gobert and Harson, 1956), and the Gulf of Gabès and nearby islands (Allemand-Martin, 1940; Jauzein, 1959).

Recent papers on the Libyan coast show that most of the research effort of late has been concentrated on the Cyrenaica coast in the east (Hey, 1956; Knetsch, 1943). An older paper by Gregory (1911) describes the geology of Cyrenaica, mentioning the coastal areas. Goudarzi's (1959) summary of the geologic history of Libya was not available for evaluation.

The coast of Egypt is well described in a series of papers on ground water in the coastal zone of the Western Desert of Egypt (Paver and Pretorius, 1954), general geology (Shukri, Phillip, and Said, 1956; Shukri and Phillip, 1956; Said, 1958); Pleistocene shore lines of Arabs' Gulf (Butzer, 1960); the Quaternary stratigraphy of the Nile River delta (Pfannenstiel, 1952); and a general review of northern Egyptian coastal stratigraphy (Butzer, 1962). *The Geology of Egypt* by Said (1962) is a monographic compilation based upon Said's extensive field work and a review of the literature.

The coast area of Israel is described in several general papers; some notable examples treat beaches (Emery and Neev, 1960), the coast (Nir, 1959), and the continental shelf (Emery and Bentor, 1960).

Several specific papers on sedimentation along the Tunisia coast include sedimentation in lagoons (Pimienta, 1953, 1954*b*), calcareous sands near Djerba Island (Castany and Lucas, 1955), cyclic fluviatile sedimentation at the mouth of Miliane River (Pimienta, 1956), and dunes bordering playas and and lagoons (Jauzein, 1958). Schwegler (1944) describes loess deposits along the Tunisian and Libyan coasts. Calcareous dunes sands along the Egyptian coast are described by Crommelin and Cailleux (1939) and Schwegler (1948). Hilmy (1951) and Nakhla (1958) discuss beach sand composition for the Egyptian coast. The bottom sediments of Eastern Harbour, Lake Maryut and Nouzha Hydrodrome, all in the neighborhood of Alexandria, Egypt, have been described by El Wakeel (1964).

3. Current and Suggested Research

The author was unable to verify that any coastal desert area research was in progress; however, it is reasonable to assume that research similar to that described above is continuing. Egypt and Israel are the only countries that are likely to become involved in a shallow-water oceanography program. Data of

this kind are needed. Tides do not present a problem, but other information on surf, breakers, waves, currents, and general nearshore bottom conditions is desirable.

It is probable that aerial photographs have been made for much if not all of this coast. The inspection of these would be a good starting point for more detailed studies.

N. NORTHWESTERN AFRICA

1. Introduction

The arid and contiguous semiarid coastal areas of northwest Africa reach from Casablanca about 1,750 miles, roughly southwestward, to Dakar. The semiarid portions lie on the ends of this stretch, in Morocco on the north, and Senegal and southern Mauritania on the south.

The topography inland from the northeastern portion of this coastal stretch differs greatly from the topography inland from the southwestern portion. In the northeast the coast is backed by mountains. These give way to a low plateau in southern Morocco and to low extensive plains along the remainder of the coast. Meigs (1966, p. 91-94) gives an excellent general description of the entire coast.

Proximity to southwestern Europe has resulted in a number of papers on the coastal areas of northwest Africa by geologists and geographers from France, Spain, and Portugal.

2. Survey of Information Available

The U. S. Naval Oceanographic Office "Sailing Directions," H. O. 51 is the best general reference for the northwestern coast of Africa. Chapter 1 contains a brief summary of the physiography of Morocco, Spanish Sahara, Mauritania, and Senegal as well as a discussion of tides, currents, winds, and weather. Chapters 9 and 10 describe in detail this desert coast.

U. S. Navy nautical charts H. O. 1246, 2195, 2196, 2197, 2238, 2239, 3775, and 3776 provide coverage of this coast at both small and large scales. Among the small-scale charts only H. O. 1246 has shaded relief; sandy shores and rocky coasts are indicated, and nearshore 10- and 20-fathom contours are charted. H . O. 3775, of an intermediate scale (1:150,000), also uses shaded relief to advantage and shows good coastal detail. H. O. 2238 and 2239 are at a very large scale with excellent detail in the nearshore waters along the shore.

U. S. Air Force Operational Navigation Charts numbers G-1, H-1, and J-1 cover the land portion of the coast. They lack the contours that many of the charts of this new series carry, but they do show the dune areas, salt lakes and playas, cliffed coasts, the course of dry washes ending at the coast, and the hilly topography away from the coast. Raisz's (1952) *Landform Map of North Africa* gives a good general picture of this coast. Geologic maps are available for the Morocco coast at a scale of 1:500,000 (Morocco, 1946-1955). The numerous papers on the geology of portions of the coast also contain geologic maps; these will be mentioned later.

Tide tables for this coast list 16 stations (Dakar to Casablanca) (U. S. Coast and Geodetic Survey, 1965*d*). The *World Port Index, 1963* (U. S. Naval Oceanographic Office, 1963*b*) lists Casablanca and Dakar as large ports; Safi, Agadir, and St. Louis as small; and Mazagan, Mogador, Villa Cisneros, and Port Etienne as very small ports. Tides of 3 to 8 feet are reported for these ports.

The U. S. Navy / U. S. Air Force *Flight Information Publication, Terminal (Seaplane)* (1965*c*) lists but three terminals: Villa Cisneros, Port Etienne, and St. Louis.

McGill's (1958) coastal landforms map reliably depicts this coast. Guilcher and Joly (1954) have described the Moroccan coast in great detail in their monographic account of the physiographic divisions and principal landforms. Geologic and geomorphic descriptions of other parts of the Morocco coast include those by: Bourcart (1949, 1950, 1952), Casablanca to Mogador; Gigout (1947*a*) on the cliffs between Cape Cantin and Cape Blanc; Gigout (1948) on raised beaches and dunes between Casablanca and Cape Blanc; and Lecointre and Gigout (1948) on the beach and dune deposits south of Cape Cantin. E. Hernández-Pacheco (1950) has described the coastal area farther south in the Spanish enclave of Ifni and F. Hernández-Pacheco (1946) has described the coastal area at Cape Juby (Cabo Yubi).

The Mauritania and Senegal coasts are described in two excellent volumes on the former French West Africa in the British Admiralty Geographic Handbook Series. Volume I (Great Britain, Admiralty, Naval Intelligence Division, 1943) includes a physical description and geology of these coasts as well as a brief discussion of swell and surf. Volume II (1944*a*) gives more details of the coast and climate. The Senegal coast north of Dakar is also well known from the more recent studies of Joire (1947) and Tricart (1955). The *U. S. Army Area Handbook for Senegal* (American University, Foreign Areas Studies Division, 1963) contains an excellent 1-page description of the entire Senegal coast.

Several interesting papers on sand transport in the littoral zone are available. The papers by Lafond (1952) and Gayral and Cauro (1958) concern areas near Tangier and Rabat, respectively, which are along wetter coasts, but the results are certainly applicable to desert coastal areas to the south. Laurent and Rivière (1950) describe sediment transport and dispersion by wave and current action in the Safi area of Morocco. This mission appears to have been a well-organized oceanographic study. The sands of the entire coast of Mauritania were described by Dropsy (1943).

Richards and Fairbridge (1965) in *Annotated Bibliography of Quaternary Shoreline (1945-1964)* list 33 papers pertaining to the desert coastal area of Morocco. Marcel Gigout is the leading contributor.

3. Review of Current Research

The three bibliographies on coastal sedimentation and geomorphology of the International Geographical Union (1956, 1960, 1964) present brief reviews of work in progress for the Morocco coast. French scientists are involved in each study. The 1964 bibliography did not list any projects for the desert coast; however, since this kind of research has gone on in the past, it is very probable that similar work is continuing. The Comité d'Oceanographie et d'Etude des Côtes du Maroc, located in Amirante, Casablanca, Morocco, was cited in the first bibliography of the International Geographical Union, Commission on Coastal Sedimentation (1956), but mention of this committee was not made in subsequent bibliographies.

4. Suggested Research

It appears that the land portion of the desert coastal zone of northwest Africa is well known. Additional research on the nearshore bottom conditions, tides, currents, surf, breakers, and waves would be desirable. Some of these data are already available. First, an attempt should be made to summarize the existing data for the entire desert coast.

O. SOUTHWESTERN AFRICA

1. Introduction

The Namib coastal desert is similar to the Peru-Chile coastal desert in that they are both cool, west-coast deserts. The Benguela Current supplies the cool coastal waters for this strip.

Total length of the Namib coastal desert is about 1,800 miles, extending from just north of Luanda, Angola, southwest to Cape Columbine on the South Africa coast. For much of its length the Namib is less than 100 miles wide. Meigs (1966, p. 94-98) presents an excellent general discussion of the terrain, limits of the desert, fogginess, economic geography, and potentiality.

The most comprehensive study for a portion of this coast and adjacent interior lands is given in *The Central Namib Desert, South West Africa* by Richard F. Logan (1960). This report is certainly one of the best available for a desert coastal area and might serve as a model for other reports.

2. Survey of Information Available

The best account of the coastal configuration is found in the U. S. Naval Oceanographic Office "Sailing Directions," H. O. 50. McGill's (1958) coastal landforms map brings out the many complexities of the long coast. For its entire length the coast is backed by a high plateau, which in places forms cliffs at the shore or forms hills some distance from the shore. Where stream valleys reach the coast, sandy beaches are present. In other locations sand hills and dunes prevail. Good anchorages are rare along the coast because there is little shelter and the water deepens rapidly seaward from the shoreline. The good harbors are related to sand spits formed by sand drifted northward by the Benguela Current.

U. S. Navy nautical charts H. O. 1601, 2203, 2204, 2205, 2206 2267, 6276, 6277, and 6279 cover this coast. The newer editions, H. O. 2203 and 2206, show the land area in shaded relief and the 10-fathom curve; the appropriate symbol for breakers is added. H. O. 6276 shows plans for several ports on the coast of Angola where sand spits are responsible for making good harbors. The large-scale charts are superior for obtaining coastal data.

U. S. Air Force World Aeronautical Charts 1027, 1057, 1150, 1179, 1273, 1302, 1396, and 1422 provide some good coverage for the land portion of the coastal area, although relief data is lacking for parts of the Angola coast. Geologic maps are available for South Africa (South Africa, 1955) and Angola (1951). These maps are on a scale of 1:1,-000,000 and 1:2,000,000, respectively, but geologic maps for portions of the South Africa coast are available on a larger scale. The coastal areas in general seem to consist of bedrock covered with Quaternary sediments. Lobeck's (1946) *Physiographic Diagram of Africa* is presented at a scale too small to provide much detail.

Tide tables for this coast (U. S. Coast and Geodetic Survey, 1965*d*) list 17 stations with a mean tide level of less than 4 feet. The *World Port Index, 1963* (U.S. Naval Oceanographic Office, 1963) describes 12 ports (Luanda to Saint Helena Bay Village), all either small or very small. Walvis Bay has the best facilities in the south and Luanda has the best facilities in the north. Abecasis (1964) has made a study of long-period wave effects on harbor facilities in Luanda Bay. Brongersma-Sanders (1947) and

Clowes (1954) have described both deep and surface currents along the South West Africa coast. Both studies provide good general information.

The U. S. Navy / U. S. Air Force *Flight Information Publication, Terminal (Seaplane)* (1965*c*) gives data only for Walvis Bay and Lüderitz on this desert coast. McGill (1958) has made good use of the literature in compiling the coastal landforms; the coast has many complexities.

Several excellent geographical studies include the desert coastal areas of Angola and southern Africa. Dartevelle (1954) divides the Angola coast into three zones; the two southerly zones include most of the desert coast. Wellington's *Southern Africa: A Geographical Study* (Wellington, 1955) is in two volumes; volume I skillfully combines geographic and geologic facts to depict the coastal areas.

A good general reference on geology is DuToit's (1954) *Geology of South Africa.* This monographic volume includes physical geography, stratigraphy, soils, volcanics, and minerals. The geology of the Angola desert coast is covered in papers by Beetz (1934), Borges (1946), and Soares de Corvalho (1961). The geology of much of the South Africa and South West Africa desert coasts is covered in papers by Haughton (1932) and Gevers (1936). D a v i e s (1959) describes specifically the raised beaches in South West Africa. The numerous dunes are described for the entire west coast of Africa by Jessen (1951).

Diamonds have been mined from coastal deposits along the southwestern Africa coast since 1908. The deposits extend along the coast north and south of Lüderitz, South West Africa, thus engendering the name "Diamond Coast." In the last five years the sediments offshore have been sampled for diamonds. Production is now underway in one subsea area and additional geologic and oceanographic studies are in progress. Bascom (1964*b*) describes some of the activities in a semipopular article. The results of the marine studies are slowly being released to the public. Smith *et al.* (1964) describe the submerged delta and offshore valleys of the Orange River. This area is too far offshore to be considered a part of the coastal zone, but this research gives the reader an idea of what can be done along a coast. Hoyt (1965), who has worked with Smith, describes sediment distribution on the inner continental shelf. More recently Wilson (1965) has described the undersea mining activities. An older paper by Wagner, Merensky, and Haughton (1929) described the coastal diamond deposits between Walvis Bay and the Groen River, including an excellent description of the coast and harbors.

3. Current and Suggested Research

The current research on this coastal area seems to be restricted to the offshore study of sediments that might be diamond-bearing. Whether or not these studies will extend into the more shallow nearshore waters is unknown at this time. The breakers along the sand-dune backed beach are dangerous at all times; under these conditions the study of nearshore bottom conditions might be impossible. Because alluvium containing diamonds extends some distance inland, access to much of the coast of South Africa and of adjacent South Africa is now restricted; it may therefore be difficult to obtain permission to engage in field work.

Tidal studies are probably adequate, but near-shore current studies are needed. The entire coast is one of the most favorable in the world for basic research on waves, breakers, and surf. Many of the good harbors are behind sand spits which are still growing. A study of the factors responsible for this growth would be desirable.

Other basic and applied research in marine geology, coastal engineering, and oceanography has been described by Simpson (1965) and Harris (1966). The projects are located chiefly on the non-desert, populated south coast of South Africa.

EVALUATION

A. GENERAL STATE OF KNOWLEDGE

1. General Comments and Contributions

In section II state-of-knowledge statements have summarized local conditions, and the state of knowledge for various areas is summarized in section IVB; the present section is limited to more general considerations.

Early in this chapter the following factors were specified for consideration in describing the desert coastal zones: nearshore bottom conditions; tides and currents; surf, breakers, and waves; beaches; shore and nearshore erosion and sedimentation; coastal swamps and marshes; and coastal structures and other culture features. Although numerous modern studies of a geographic, geomorphic, geologic, and/or oceanographic nature have been made for coastal areas around the world, the amount of information dealing directly with the "Desert Coastal Zones" was found to be limited. Indeed, data for most of the factors are completely lacking for many of the 14 desert coastal zones studied.

One cause of this paucity of data is the fact that most of the desert coastal zones are considered undesirable places to live and thus lack large population centers and thriving economies. However, towns and smaller settlements are found along or near the coast, because the coastal areas are usually less inhospitable to man than the interior desert. Offshore waters support the existence of some coastal settlements by providing food and serving as avenues of transportation. Other desert coastal zones are quite remote but can be reached by ship unless high cliffs or heavy seas prevent landings. Restrictions on travel in some countries inhibit the study of desert coastal zones.

In contrast, the coastal zones of more humid regions have been studied more intensively because these coastal areas are more favorable for the location of large cities and towns. Agricultural and industrial activities nearby nourish the general economy of the region. A marine research organization or colleges and universities located in these cities and towns often supply the investigators. A good example of this situation exists in South Africa. On-shore investigations and shallow-water offshore investigations have been conducted chiefly on the wetter south coast where the population centers are located. On the arid west coast only in recent years have any studies of this kind been attempted, and then partially because the research was spurred by the possibility of finding diamonds in offshore sediments.

Why have some desert coastal zones been studied more than others? An economic impetus is the reason in many areas. Examples are the occurrence of diamonds in bottom sediments off the southwest coast of Africa, the exploration for oil and gas beneath the waters of the Persian Gulf and the related development of pipeline and other transportation facilities, and the harmful effects of the El Niño current, which kills marine life off the coast of Peru.

Other studies of desert coastal zones belong in the realm of pure academic research. These kinds of studies are numerous and at first glance appear to have no immediate practical value. In many instances a particular desert coast was studied because it had not been investigated before and the coast was accessible. The same reasoning could apply to more humid coasts.

In the United States of America the U. S. Navy has supported much of the coastal-zone research. This includes the continental borders of the United States as well as some foreign shores. Many of these studies appear to have little military significance. During World War II numerous recording tide gages were established on the west coast of South America because of the lack of good data for this coast. This study was of military necessity in order to prepare accurate tide tables for use at that time, but today the tidal data and resulting tables are in use by all nations.

United States of America Contributions

U. S. government publications are an excellent source of much of the available data on desert coastal zones of the world. The most important source is the U. S. Naval Oceanographic Office with its variety of books, manuals, and nautical charts. Other maps, charts, and miscellaneous publications of the U. S. Coast and Geodetic Survey and the U. S. Air Force supplement the U. S. Navy publications. Outstanding among the U.S. Naval Oceanographic Office publications are the "Sailing Directions." The U. S. Navy, through the Office of Naval Research, has sponsored coastal studies in many parts of the world.

All the U. S. Navy publications cited in section II of this chapter were readily accessible to the writer. Correspondence with the U. S. Naval Oceanographic Office in 1965-1966, however, suggested that additional useful information on shallow water coastal areas was held by that office but was not accessible to the general public. No doubt large numbers of aerial photographs of desert coastal areas are also held by other Department of Defense agencies. From time to time collections of photographs are released for instructional and research use.

Contributions from the British Admirality

The British Admiralty publishes pilot books and nautical charts similar to those of the U. S. Navy. In fact, the U. S. Navy obtains data for some of their charts from the British charts. The Naval Intelligence Division of the British Admiralty also has published the Geographic Handbook Series. Existing volumes cover many of the desert coastal areas of the Middle East and the northern half of Africa. The writer found those volumes, in most instances, to be more useful than the U. S. Navy publications.

The Role of "General References"

General references, as used here, includes the numerous periodicals and serial publications in geology, geomorphology, geography, oceanography, and related fields; textbooks and reference volumes in the same fields; government publications of many nations; specialized bibliographies including the *Bibliography of Geology Exclusive of North America* published by the Geological Society of America; U. S. Army area handbooks; atlases; and miscellaneous materials.

The Bibliographie Géographique Internationale is also an excellent guide, covering literature for 40 years before the Geological Society of America bibliography was initiated. Both are currently issued with a time lag of about two years.

Most of the references consulted provide detailed information on a given area. Sometimes they contained only a single or a few details, but in many instances several useful details were obtained to help fill in the picture for a certain coastal desert.

2. Outstanding Individual Contributions

Several outstanding contributions to our knowledge of desert coastal areas are worthy of mention here. W. C. Putnam, D. I. Axelrod, H. P. Bailey, and J. T. McGill, working as a team at the University of California at Los Angeles, prepared a handbook (*Natural Coastal Environments of the World*, Putnam *et al.*, 1960) for the use of photo-interpreters engaged in terrain studies of coastal areas. The handbook includes all coasts, and, although written with military applications in mind, the volume would also be useful to the nonspecialist in the earth sciences. It includes chapters on coastal landforms, coastal vegetation, and climate of coastal regions, plus three accompanying maps. McGill published separately his *Map of Coastal Landforms of the World* (McGill, 1958). One value of this map is that the investigator can obtain a good idea of what a coast is like with but a minimum of study of the explanation. Axelrod compiled the vegetation map and Bailey prepared the climate map.

Meigs' (1966) monographic volume entitled *Geography of Coastal Deserts* is the only one of its kind. He states (p. 9):

> This report does not try to present a complete, detailed picture of all or any coastal deserts. It does present a broad view of world distribution and types of coastal deserts, points out ways in which the potentialities of coastal deserts are being utilized in certain representative localities, calls attention to some of the areas of inadequately used potential, and lists some of the sources of further information. The references make no pretence at completeness. Any one of the thirty-seven coastal deserts is worthy of a large monograph itself.

Additional monographic treatments of the coastal deserts, even by continents, would be useful if based upon adequate field work.

3. Significant Theories and Controversies

Coastal zone research has not produced many theories or controversies. The one subject which does stand out is viewed not so much as a theory now as it is a problem. This problem concerns sea level changes —their causes and recognition—and is described more fully in the introductory section above under the heading IH3, "Quaternary Eustatic Sea-Level Changes." See particularly the papers by Fairbridge (1961, 1962), Russell (1964), and Shepard (1963). These scientists are active in this field of research, and their papers discuss old as well as new concepts. The writer feels that the controversies in this field are those typical of almost any scientific group. Many opinions based upon poor as well as good techniques of observation and sampling still endure, and no doubt this will continue in the future as well.

Classification of coasts also has been a lively subject. Several classifications with slightly different objectives are in popular use now. See the discussion in section IH, "The Classification of Coasts."

4. Nature of the Most Useful Study

Many types of onshore studies can be conducted by one man operating with a low budget. Other types of studies—shallow-depth geophysical work, surveying, or coring for example — require the "team" approach and are proportionately more expensive. Many beach studies, including activities in the surf and breaker zone, would require a research team of only two to five men.

For work in deep waters, whenever a boat or a larger ship is required, the problems increase manyfold and the expense multiplies rapidly. Few individuals in research of this kind have the funds required to conduct such investigations efficiently. Such work is for the larger research organization with a team of specialists.

In section I of this chapter the desert coastal zone was defined to include an offshore and an onshore strip. To be most useful, a study should include both the offshore and onshore strips and should be conducted by a team of specialists.

The best approach to some of the problem areas (see IVC) might be first to send in one or two investigators to perform a reconnaissance study. This study would consist of personal contacts and visits to libraries, research organizations, colleges and universities, and other appropriate agencies, plus field studies onshore and offshore in selected areas. The personal contacts and visits portion of the reconnaissance study should be as exhaustive as time permits.

The field studies should include travel by land where possible. Some desert coasts have roads or trails paralleling the shore; even where such roads are some miles from the water's edge, there are usually side roads and trails leading to beaches, cliffs, or other vantage points on the coast.

Observation from the air is often necessary. In some cases the coasts may be observed from commercial flight routes. In Western Australia the writer obtained excellent cooperation from an airline in order to photograph coastal areas from cruising altitudes of 7,000 to 13,500 feet, and at lower altitudes near the time of taking off and landing. Of course, such flights might have to wait for good weather. In any event inquiries should be made well ahead of time in planning such flights.

Offshore studies present more of a problem. In any study a seaworthy boat or ship will be necessary. For some coasts conditions will be such that a small boat may be used; in other areas a rough sea, breakers, and surf may require a more seaworthy vessel. Some of the desirable observations are best made from the beach or a cliff or hill, but others must be made from a vessel or by wading out from a beach. The investigator cannot operate a boat and make observations at the same time. A reliable boat operator should be engaged and acquainted beforehand with the investigator's purposes. The investigator may have to do his own navigating, which sometimes may have to be somewhat crude; for example, if a depth finder or Fathometer is not available, a lead line will have to be employed.

When a reconnaissance survey has been completed, more detailed studies may be planned according to the findings.

5. Model Studies

Three examples are given of studies that the writer considers to be model studies at different levels of organization. A 100-man operation is not necessarily a hundred times better than a 1-man operation. Objectives are different, and each project must be evaluated by examining all factors involved.

The best example of a large-scale program involving the research-organization / team-of-specialists approach is the Scripps Institution of Oceanography work in the region of Baja California, the Gulf of California, and the Sonora-Sinaloa coast of Mexico. This investigation provided onshore and offshore data that served as the basis for the book *Marine Geology of the Gulf of California* (van Andel and Shor, 1964).

A smaller-scale team approach example is the work of Dr. Brian W. Logan and students in the Shark Bay area of the Western Australia coast. Studies to date have included the shallow bay waters where two men made observations and collected samples while a third team member ran analyses at a shore laboratory. The onshore areas along the east side of the bay have also been studied. Unfortunately the newer data have not been published and are available only as progress reports of limited distribution.

Dr. Richard F. Logan's work on the central Namib Desert of South West Africa was largely a 1-man study (Logan, 1960). Much detailed information was assembled for the offshore and onshore strips as well as the desert farther inland.

B. DEFICIENCIES

1. Current Research

Unfortunately many desert coastal zone studies that begin onshore end abruptly at the shoreline. The move to study the offshore strip is often a big step for a researcher. Offshore, the cost goes up rapidly because of the need for additional equipment and personnel with special training.

Even if the onshore strip study is a geographic-geomorphic - geologic type investigation and the investigator is not necessarily trained in offshore work, some mention can be made and data gathered on tides, currents, surf, breakers, waves, and general beach conditions. Interviews with the local inhabitants familiar with the coastal waters would be beneficial also. After several such interviews the researcher can usually sort out fact from fiction. A landlubber with the curiosity of a scientist can usually pick up the necessary background to make observations in this nearshore area without too much trouble and in a short time.

2.   Deficiencies in the Seven Factors

At the beginning of this chapter and again at the beginning of this evaluation section seven factors were specified for consideration in describing the desert coastal zones. Each factor deserves a comment:

1)   Nearshore bottom conditions: In general the data available are sketchy. Some nautical charts contain many designations; others are rather barren. The need for a more standard system to describe bottom sediments is great. Work in water less than 10 fathoms deep is most desirable.

2)   Tides and currents: The data available are best rated as good. For some coasts tide gages are located too far apart. It should be possible to install recording tide gages on these coasts in order to obtain more complete data. A common datum for comparison of tidal data is also required; the datum now varies from country to country. The nautical charts of Great Britain frequently include tide and tidal current data. This might be a useful addition to the main text pages of the U. S. Naval Oceanographic Office "Sailing Directions."

3)   Surf, breakers, and waves: A number of good general papers on this subject area are available; however, more observations are required for coasts around the world so that analogies may be made. The "Sailing Directions" contain frequent references to breakers, and breakers are shown on certain nautical charts. It is not known by what methods the breakers were observed, whether only with binoculars from a passing ship or by close investigation.

4)   Beaches: Beaches have been well studied in the United States of America and in other countries. With this background much can now be learned from coastal aerial photography. The U. S. Navy probably has a standard operating procedure to evaluate beaches around the world. Detailed studies are always desirable, however.

5)   Shore and nearshore erosion and sedimentation: The status of the knowledge of this subject on a worldwide basis is poor in details. The maps by McGill (1958) and Valentin (1952) are helpful but are presented at too small a scale. Additional studies of new aerial photography plus on-the-spot investigations of selected areas would be the best approach.

6)   Coastal swamps and marshes: These are mostly known but have not been described in any detail on a worldwide basis. Nautical charts present details for a few areas at a good large scale. The examination of coastal aerial photography would help to fill in the information gaps.

7)   Coastal structures and other culture features: This factor covers such features as the presence of piers and breakwaters in a harbor, cities and towns along a coast, railroads, roads, and communications. Much of this information may be obtained from maps, nautical charts, coast pilot books, the U. S. Naval Oceanographic Office "Sailing Directions" or *World Port Index, 1963,* regular geographic atlases, geography texts, gazetteers, and the miscellaneous publications of various government agencies. For example, the writer was able to obtain a variety of data from the state government tourist bureau of Western Australia, a local newspaper office in Perth, and the tourist bureau in the local office of a major oil company. The data covered all facets of industry, agriculture, shipping, and transportation along the west coast of Australia.

Table II.
SUGGESTED RESEARCH FOR DESERT COASTAL ZONES

DESERT COASTAL ZONE	FACTOR 1 NEARSHORE BOTTOM CONDITIONS	2 TIDES AND CURRENTS	3 SURF, BREAKERS, AND WAVES	4 BEACHES	5 SHORE AND NEARSHORE EROSION AND SEDIMENTATION	6 COASTAL SWAMPS AND MARSHES	7 COASTAL STRUCTURES AND OTHER CULTURAL FEATURES	8 REMARKS
Northwest Mexico	C	B	C	C	C	C	B	*Factor 4* particularly Gulf of California
Peru	C	A	C	C	D	C	B	
Chile	D	A	C	C	D			*Factor 6* not very applicable
Argentina	D	A	C	C	C	D	B	
Australia: Western Coast	C	B	C	C	C	C	B	*Factor 1:* A in some areas *Factor 5:* locally better studied
Australia: Southern Coast	D	C	D	D	D		D	*Factor 6:* not applicable *Factor 7:* few people/facilities
North Arabian Sea	D	C	C	D	D	C	C	*Factor 1:* locally B and C *Factor 2:* locally B
Persian Gulf	A	A	A	B	B	B	A	*Factor 1:* some B and C areas *Factor 6:* locally B *Factors 1 & 6:* Iran coast least studied
South Coast of Saudi Arabia	D	C	C	D	D	D	C	
Somali Coast	D	C	C	D	D	D	C	
Red Sea	B	B	B	B	C	C	A	
Mediterranean Coast of Africa	D	B	C	C	B	C	B	
Northwest Africa	D	B	B	C	C	D	B	
Southwest Africa	C	C	C	C	C	D	C	

Legend
A: Well known from studies
B: Studied but requires additional work
C: Studied only slightly, requires much additional work
D: Virtually unstudied

SUGGESTED RESEARCH

A. GENERAL COMMENTS

Promising research has been noted and additional research suggested in the discussion of each of the 14 desert coastal zones. In addition, each of the gaps described under "Deficiencies" above is an area for future research. It cannot be overemphasized that the shallow-water nearshore zone is the one area for which we need the most data. To study this area new techniques are not required. The team-of-specialists approach (probably the best one) has been used before. Care should be taken in selecting a team to gain the optimum amount of information per man; a geological oceanographer seems like a good choice for any team.

Several desert coastal areas have been well studied. Northwest Mexico and the Persian Gulf are probably the two best studied. Coverage is quite good for many shorter sections of other desert coasts. The Shark Bay area of the west coast of Australia, the central Namib of South West Africa, portions of the Red Sea coast, and portions of the northwest Africa and Mediterranean Sea coasts are good examples. Additional research, particularly of the foreign-language literature, will probably turn up new data on many of these coasts.

B. SPECIFIC PROJECT AREAS

Specific project areas may be cited for all 14 desert coastal zones. These projects are indicated in table II, Suggested Research for Desert Coastal Zones, which has been constructed in order to clarify the deficiencies discussed above under "Deficiencies in the Seven Factors." On of four states of knowledge is indicated under each desert coastal zone opposite each of the seven factors, as follows: (A) Well known from studies, (B) Studied but requires additional work, (C) Studied only slightly, requires much additional work, or (D) Virtually unstudied.

For some areas, such as the Persian Gulf, there are fewer suggestions; for other areas, such as the Chilean desert coast, much work is needed.

C. GENERAL COASTAL ZONE RESEARCH

The state of knowledge and research regarding the 14 major desert coastal zones of the Earth are treated in this chapter, and limitations to the seven subject factors for each of the 14 desert coastal zones are summarized in table II, indicating specific project areas needing further research.

However, desert coastal zones, unique in some ways, also have much in common with nondesert coastal zones. Knowledge of wave dynamics, for example, gleaned in research of humid coasts may also apply, in part, to desert coasts, and knowledge of sediment transport obtained in research of a desert coast may apply to humid coasts as well.

To avoid unnecessary duplication, those engaged in study and research of desert coastal zones should take into fullest account the interests, goals, plans, techniques, and knowledge developed by study and research of coastal zones in general, whether arid or humid.

As a most notable example, already cited in the introduction to this chapter, in March 1961 a conference on Coastal Geography, sponsored by the National Academy of Sciences / National Research Council, was held at the Coastal Studies Institute, Louisiana State University, Baton Rouge, Louisiana, under the chairmanship of Dr. Richard J. Russell.

The panel prepared a report of three-fold purpose:

"(a) to identify the coastal zone as an area requiring interdisciplinary research; (b) to focus attention on what now appear to be major problems; and (c) to suggest preliminary steps in the development of an integrated, national research program in Coastal Geography."

The sections of that report headed "Scope and Objectives of Coastal Geography" and "Recommended Research Program" are comprehensive, concise, and eminently pertinent to future research on desert, as well as other, coastal zones, and are therefore quoted below. Future research on desert coastal zones will benefit from full knowledge, communication, and cooperation with related research on coastal zones in general, such as is outlined here.

The following material is quoted from the report of the panel on coastal geography (National Academy of Sciences / National Research Council, 1961).

SCOPE AND OBJECTIVES OF COASTAL GEOGRAPHY

Coastal geography is a distinctive, multi-disciplinary field. It ranges across physical and biological sciences and into social and cultural disciplines, but maintains coherence through the focus on a single, naturally-integrated zone. All the natural and man-made phenomena within the coastal zone, and the ways in which their elements act and react, form the content of coastal geography. Individually, many of these phenomena are objects of study in other highly specialized disciplines, and as such, some have received considerable attention. But scientists concerned with the phenomena of the sea and large lakes, as well as those interested in terrestrial or atmospheric problems, have tended to concentrate their research in areas close to the central cores of their disciplines, rather than attack the complexities of the coastal zone. Coastal geography draws heavily on the traditional disciplines and gains contributions from their specialized research, but the application of the knowledge from these fields to the coastal situation has not reached the point where reliable predictions can be made.

The ultimate goal of research in coastal geography is a basic understanding of the physical, biological, and cultural factors, individually and collectively, that combine to produce the complexes that give the coastal zone its distinctive characteristics and processes. A research program aimed toward this goal has several broad objectives: 1. Characterization of coastal areas and environments, that is, the identification and categorization of those sets of factors that are distinctive and significant in the coastal situation. 2. Understanding of relations and changes across the three major environmental interfaces of water, land, and air. 3. Understanding of the physical, chemical, biological, and cultural processes and interactions within the various coastal zone environments. 4. Appraisal of the coastal zone for its use potential.

RECOMMENDED RESEARCH PROGRAM

An organized, systematic, well-supported research program in coastal geography is essential to achieve these objectives. Such a program calls upon a wide variety of skills not only from geography, but from geology, oceanography, biology, ecology, anthropology, economics, and engineering. In some cases it will be necessary at an early stage to fill existing gaps in the knowledge and research aids in individual disciplines, as by developing taxonomy handbooks of coastal plants and animals, acquiring micro meteorological data on coasts for heat and moisture flux studies, improving chemical and mineralogical information on clays for sedimentation investigations, and

producing better map and photographic coverage. There is a wealth of existing data concerning some coastal phenomena, such as the very long records on tides and on many sites of early civilization and human habitation. These data must be brought together, analyzed, and synthesized to form a coherent body of information available for basic research and other uses.

Advances in interdisciplinary research are urgently needed. Studies which combine and extend the knowledge of separate sciences are essential to the solution of most of the planning and development problems of coastal areas. Many kinds of problems which must be dealt with in the coastal zone call either for individual scientists with competence in more than one discipline or for a cross-disciplinary research group, or both. Problems, such as the prevention or control of pollution of coastal waters, require that the coastal area be analyzed as a complex of interacting physical, biological, and cultural components. A research group with a variety of technical skills could successfully undertake this kind of analysis, assuring that all important aspects of the problem would be considered. Greater accuracy and detail in evaluating and forecasting physiographic changes along coasts are possible when talents of geomorphologists are combined with those of anthropologists, cultural geographers, botanists, and palynologists. These and many other examples that could be cited illustrate that the coastal zone is, in fact, an integrated system of interacting elements. To understand the ways in which the system functions, the changes that take place in the form and matter of the elements within the system, and the various mechanisms that are operative, require analyses involving the concerted efforts of a wide spectrum of scientific specialists.

While interdisciplinary research is at the heart of coastal geography, progress can be accelerated most promptly by basic research in physical coastal geography, ecological coastal geography, and cultural coastal geography. A limited number of competent specialists is available in these areas, and several institutions for some years have concentrated their activities within the coastal zone. From this core could be developed the urgently needed program.

Physical Coastal Geography

Physical coastal geography is basic to all coastal research. It is concerned with the physical framework in which ecological and cultural factors operate, and with the physical processes, in themselves and as they influence and are influenced by the ecological and cultural processes. Progress has been spotty and uneven in understanding the properties and processes within each of the three media that converge at the coast: land, water, and air. For the most part, instruments and rough techniques are available for measuring the significant static properties of the three media, but techniques for obtaining meaningful data on the dynamic properties are still to be developed. This lack seriously handicaps progress toward more precise understanding of processes that interrelate the land, water, and air.

There is also a real need for the development of more adequate sampling systems. In particular, improvement is needed in the methodology and procedures for the design of sampling patterns, and spacing frequency, and location of samples, so that maximum significant information can be obtained with greatest efficiency of operation. Better equipment is needed for the recovery of sediment and water samples, and for rapid and accurate analysis of these samples.

These needs for more incisive techniques and more precise instruments are basic to the solution of a whole array of challenging problems in physical coastal geography. An indication of the scope of these problems is presented here under four headings: geologic framework and upland coast processes; low coast and nearshore processes; beach processes; and meteorological processes and their climatic effects.

1. Geological Framework and Upland Coast Processes

The nature of the regional and local bedrock, its structure and geologic history, have a direct bearing on coastal processes and shore configuration. The characteristics of the sediments reaching the coast depend upon the kinds of rocks in the region and their particular erosional or weathering behavior. The structural attitudes of the coastal rock formations exercise a control over the horizontal plan and vertical profile of a coast. Both the rates and resultant forms of geomorphic processes on upland coasts are closely related to properties of the bedrock, such as erosibility, resistance to shear or vulnerability to landslide, and permeability. Differing erosibility of rocks is reflected in different types of stream patterns, as well as in the resultant shape of the coast, as in the contrasts between long, smooth coasts, and headlands and cliffed coasts.

To extend the general knowledge of the geologic framework, answers to several important questions must be found. For example, why and how are the various rock reduction processes, such as weathering, accelerated in the coastal zone, and what are the process differences under various coastal climates? What are the interrelations of bedrock structures and Recent coastal surfaces, on either side of the strand-line? What are the mechanisms and controlling factors of headland and cliff retreat? How are coastal platforms created? What are the sediment erosion, transportation, and deposition patterns and the water circulation patterns in deep estuaries? What is the chronology and magnitude of Quaternary sea level changes, and how have these altered upland coast processes?

2. Low Coast and Nearshore Processes

Low and deltaic coasts are typically those of expanding land areas; coasts receiving abundant alluvial materials. They are generally of low relief, gradient, and elevation. They are characterized by marshes, swamps, levees and other deltaic landforms, tidal and other flats, interlaced by distributaries, tidal streams, and other waterways, and bordered by shallow estuaries and bays. These are coasts in which the effects of environmental discontinuities have a broad, almost horizontal expression, and boundaries between different sets of conditions are typically wide zones. Balances tend to be delicate, and any change in one element may have widespread effects.

The identification and measurement of the significant elements in the system are basic to understanding processes along low coasts. From the land side there is an input of fresh water and sediments with their particular physical, biological and energy characteristics, and from the ocean side there is an input of salt water with its various properties, including energy of waves, tides and currents, together with transported materials. The internal workings of this system pose many problems; for example, the relation of the salt water-fresh water interface to sedimentation rates and sediment properties; the processes, rates, and results of diffusion and mixing of salt and fresh water; the effect of surface wind and temperature on water characteristics, both at the surface and below; the interrelations of water circulation and sediment patterns and properties; the relations among water properties, biological properties; morphological effects of water exchange; processes of energy dissipation and exchange; the causes and processes of sediment alterations; the effects of tides, storms, earth movements, and works of man on morphology; the characteristics of tidal streams and their morphological effects, processes that create beaches and longshore bars, and the influences of beaches, bars and reefs on coastal processes; the relation between water circulation and sedimentation processes, and bay or other waterbody configuration; and the patterns of diffusion and changes in characteristics of fresh water entering a lake, bay or ocean.

There is also a need to understand the system as a whole, and to determine natural and man-induced local variations, both areal and temporal, and regional variations, possibly as related to different climatic, geologic, and sea-level conditions, past and present.

3. Beach Processes

The beach, the zone of unconsolidated materials subject to wave action, is a resultant of, and an element in, a set of complex interacting variables. These include material shape, size, density, and mineral and chemical composition; nearshore wave height, length, period, velocity, energy, and angle of approach; wind direction, speed, and duration; tide range periodicity and variability; as well as all the dimensional and dynamic components of such factors. The gross ways in which certain composite groups of these elements interact—for example, beach profile and breaker characteristics — have been studied in the field, observed in tanks, and subjected to considerable theorization. But the results of studies even of selected groups of elements are still far short of producing a level of knowledge from which reliable predictions can be made. There is little or no knowledge of the magnitude and patterns of such significant controlling properties as friction, shear, and momentum, and their relation to turbulence. The spatial distribution of the various values or combinations of these properties around the coasts of the world is essentially unknown.

A research program designed to improve the understanding of beach processes should include studies of the following types:

    a. Determination of turbulence patterns of various types of shoaling and breaking wave systems on beaches with different profile, gradient, and material characteristics; interrelationships among turbulence patterns, beach profile, volume of onshore and offshore transport of different sediment types, and wave, tide, and current condition.

    b. Relation of beach profiles to wave types, sediment types, mineral composition of beach materials, tides, and currents; mechanisms and rates of profile change during variations in the characteristics of controlling factors

    c. Transportation mechanisms along shore as related to water properties, currents, wave dimensions, and angle of wave approach; variations in size, location, and depth of sediment transport zone with changes in wave and tidal turbulence; changes in volume of mass transport above and below breakpoint with variations in wave, tide, and sediment conditions

    d. Deposition patterns of transported sediments; processes of origin, growth, perpetuation, and alteration of bars, barrier islands, tombolos,

and other constructional forms; origin of beach cusps; controlling factors and limiting dimensions of nearshore and shore depositional and erosional geomorphic features

    e. Effects of winds, ice, permafrost, plants, and animals on beach processes and morphology; beach sediment lithification

    f. Identification and measurement of properties that indicate trends of beach behavior, both those that reflect cyclic or seasonal changes, and those that integrate cyclic changes over long periods of time; applications of information on current beach forms to an understanding of those produced in earlier geologic periods, and thus to the development of accurate theories of sea level fluctuations

    g. Mechanisms and controls of inlets; behavior of inlets during normal ebb and flow tides, and during special conditions, such as storms, and surges; stability of inlets

    h. Techniques of stabilizing beaches; effects of engineering structures and introduced vegetation

    i. Development of precise techniques for designing and operating physical models of beaches

    j. Development of theoretical models of the action of breaking waves, wave refraction and coastal currents, dune structures and behavior, beach structures, tidal flushing, sediment erosion and transport, and other coastal phenomena

4. Coastal Meteorological Processes and Their Climatic Effects

Coastal regions are characterized by discontinuities which result in distinctive coastal meteorological phenomena. The pertinent discontinuities may be grouped as: (a) those which are a function of the nature of the water and land, such as mobility, transparency, heat capacity, reflectivity, and moisture availability; and (b) those related to surface configuration, such as roughness, mobility of roughness elements, and spatial and temporal variability of roughness. The distinctive process associated with these discontinuities are related primarily to differences of energy and moisture exchange at the air-surface interface. The differences produce moisture and temperature gradients and potential energy distributions which result in distinctive convective and circulative conditions. Differences in surface configuration produce contrasts in aerodynamic drag which in turn affect both locally produced and general circulations. The result is an array of weather phenomena specifically characteristic of coasts, such as fogs, stratus, and the sea breeze.

A program of research on coastal climatology should include studies of the following types:

a. Characteristics of basic variables along coasts, such as turbidity, temperature, waves, radiation, and moisture

b. Distribution and frequency of occurrence of: (1) weather phenomena and conditions which are distinctively different on either side of the strandline, e.g., cloud patterns; and (2) phenomena which are distinctively coastal, such as the sea breeze, coastal convergence, and coastal fogs

c. B a s i c aerodynamics and hydrodynamics; aerodynamic drag over water and typical coastal terrain types; sand-wind dynamics; dynamics of shallow water waves and currents; stratification and convection in water and air

b. Distribution and frequency of occurrence of: of sea and land regimes

e. Development of mathematical models and theory of coastal phenomena, such as the sea breeze, coastal convergence, dune shape and movement, atmospheric structural changes at the coast, and salt spray transfer and fallout

Ecological Coastal Geography

Research on coastal ecology illuminates interrelationships among plants, animals, and coastal environments, and contributes to the understanding of man's place in the physical-biological realm of which he is a part. Knowledge of the coastal ecosystems is necessary for a realistic assessment of the immediate and long-run consequences of man's activities in this zone. For example, such knowledge can aid in the solution of the practical and urgent problems of the detrimental effects of pollutants and radioactive wastes when they are dumped into coastal waters. Among the questions that can be answered through research in coastal ecology are those concerned with man's demand on coastal resources and the extent to which those resources can sustain themselves.

The field of ecology has advanced to the stage of theory-building, backed by *in situ* studies of natural ecosystems, laboratory models of ecosystems, and electronic analogue simulations of geochemical cycles. Much has been learned about biological communities, their structure, functions, and budgets of energy and matter.

These good starts already made in advancing the understanding of both marine and terrestrial ecosystems must be expanded to embrace the coastal systems which straddle the shoreline. This calls for a melding of the knowledge of these two kinds of ecosystems and the techniques by which they are analyzed. Progress toward the understanding of coastal systems is contingent upon a basic descriptive understructure of systematics and ecological surveys, and geological and vegetation mapping. In addition to a broadening of this understructure, there are various fruitful directions of research, such as the following:

1. Effects of organisms on the physical environments, including problems concerning reef building, dune stablization, and the relations between marine angiosperms and sedimentation

2. Biogeography and genetics, such as migrations of warm-water forms, and invasions of harbor parasites; identification, delineation, and changes of biogeographic regions in coastal waters; feasibility of characterizing marine species by racial groupings; comparison of rates of evolution of marine biota and terrestrial organisms; and the implications of such studies for paleoclimatology and reconstruction of past communities

3. Physiological ecology, including tolerances and control of organisms such as borers and undesirable plants; the role of osmo- and thermo-regulatory mechanisms in adaptation; and use of chemical substances to eliminate specific organisms for experimental manipulation of communities

4. Community structure, function, and change in coastal regions; applications of concepts from information theory; and the role of micro-organisms

5. Biological energy budgets; comparisons of energy budgets of various communities; energy budgets of component organisms; and the budget of organic matter accumulation, on a seasonal and regional basis

6. Biogeochemical cycles, including concentrations and transport patterns of trace elements and radioactive waste

7. Ecological boundary phenomena; exchanges of material between sea systems and land systems; and the structure and maintenance of biological boundaries such as occur with reefs or marsh extension and contraction

8. Ecological consequences of various activities of man, such as coastal dredging, upstream regulation of flow, development of aquatic agriculture, and fisheries management practices

Cultural Coastal Geography

In cultural coastal geography the focus is on people — their cultural background and heritage, how and where they live, and how they modify their surroundings, use natural resources, and organize their activities. It is apparent, from the limited research conducted in this field, that human activities and their manifestations and consequences within the coastal zone differ, in varying degrees, from those outside the zone. It is equally clear that man's orientation to the sea, and the extent to which the sea influences the way of life and livelihood of coastal inhabitants varies markedly from place to place along the coast. The contiguity of the strandline adds a variable dimension not found in the wholly land-based studies which typify the field of cultural geography in general. The important advances that have been made in cultural geography in basic methodology and understanding of transportation, land use, manufacturing, trade, population, and urban development, for example, are based primarily on studies of continental places and conditions. Before research in cultural coastal geography can capitalize on these advances, it will be necessary to identify, define, and explain the factors introduced by the proximity of the sea. This is fundamental to the understanding of the human aspects of the zone. It appears in a number of forms in the various approaches to the complex problems of cultural coastal geography suggested here.

1. An "index of marine orientation" should be developed, based on analysis and evaluation of the nature and intensity of land-sea linkages created by human activities. Such an index would make it possible to adapt to coastal problems some of the systems of analysis already developed for other environments. The measure of differentiation caused by land-sea linkage is also likely to provide insights into the physical and ecological process in which human activities play a part.

2. Historical geographic studies should be conducted because they not only identify, trace, and seek to explain changes in man's occupancy of the coastal zone, but also contribute to better understanding of the physical and ecological changes through periods of time too long to permit direct observation. Many lines of approach should be followed in these studies, including the critical examination of hypotheses. One such hypothesis is that the spatial organization of human activities varies with the economic character and development of given societies. From this, the propositions that could be deduced and should be carefully tested in the coastal zone are: (a) The simplest human societies focus on the coastal zone as a source of useful things to be extracted from the environment. (b) At a more advanced level the centers of extraction are likely to be reduced to a few points, such as fishing ports, whereas the shore in general is considered only as a protection against marine invasion of agricultural lands. (c) Finally, in the more highly developed societies, the whole coastal zone again is of interest for its resource values, recreational as well as mineral, nutritional, urban, and industrial.

3. Human ecosystems and their differential impacts on the coastal zone should be examined. The impact might result from deliberate extraction of particular species from the zone or be an accidental product of strictly land-oriented activities. Industrial pollution of coastal waters, heavy deposition effecting shorelines and resulting from accelerated erosion due to some kinds of agricultural practices, and alterations of ecosystems brought about by population pressures are other examples of impacts that require study.

4. Spatial economic interactions across the land-sea boundary, as at ports, should be investigated. Ports are not only places of land-sea transportation linkages; they are also urban-industrial complexes involved in functions and services related to both hinterland and maritime organization. A promising approach to the understanding of ports, therefore, would be the study of mutually related elements, including transportation facilities and patterns, location factors, physical attributes of port city and harbor and other physical, economic, social, political, and technological forces which act together to affect the organization of hinterland, maritime space, and forelands (the land areas, seaward of a port, to which the port is connected by ocean carriers). In these studies various urban space-related theories, such as those concerned with city locations and distribution, urban structure and internal relations, and marketing, would be tested for their validity with regard to ports. Such an approach could also yield needed information on the arrangement and form of specialized functional areas within ports. This would provide a measure of the similarities and differences between ports and other urban complexes. Other needed studies include the development of reliable ways of measuring such aspects as the actual and potential capacity of a port, the degree of a port's efficiency, and the size of a port's hinterlands and forelands.

5. Coasts present research problems in political geography, particularly in the division of coastal waters, both in terms of international boundaries of sovereign waters and of boundaries of local waters. On the international level, the Law of the Sea defines certain bases for delimiting waters that are exclusively

under the jurisdiction of individual nations for various purposes, such as fishing, law enforcement, and defense, but applications of these bases to actual coastlines pose a series of problems that have an impact on the economy, defense, and relations of nations. The magnitude of this impact and the ways in which bases for delineation of sovereign waters change the economic-political structure of nations should be examined. Offshore claims and other water-boundary problems have certain regional aspects related to shore configuration, but these relations and their degree of regionality have not been sufficiently investigated, so there exists no clear-cut sorting or spatial arrangement of demands, interests, and consequences. Studies of the political geography of these aspects might hasten solution of conflicting claims.

6. Another important research area of cultural coastal geography has to do with the use-potentials of coastal areas. Use-potential analyses must be based strongly on an understanding of specific cultural value systems and their dynamic nature. In terms of these value systems a variety of analyses should be made. These would include selection of sites for salt-water conversion plants to meet demands for fresh water supply; exploitative development of marine resources; recreational development of the coastal zone; location of protected natural "laboratories" in all types of coastal areas; and the occupancy and development of coastal zones vulnerable to catastrophes such as tsunamis and hurricanes, to landslides, or to gradual destruction resulting from phenomena such as dune migration or the adding or cutting away of a sand beach. Studies of the vulnerability of coastal areas to catastrophe and the willingness of people to expose themselves and their property to destruction exemplify the interplay of environmental conditions and cultural values.

World-Wide Considerations

To assure that the theories developed under the three preceding headings have a high degree of universality, they should be tested in a variety of representative coastal locations. The extent to which any coastal location can be judged to be representative or typical of a given coastal environment depends upon accumulated, compiled, and organized information regarding the physical, ecological, and cultural characteristics of the coastal zone throughout the world. An immediate requirement is the study and synthesis of available data so that the exact state of knowledge can be ascertained. This should be a starting point for further research. It would also be a guide to the gaps in existing information which need filling. The acquiring, classifying and mapping of

new information is frequently a concomitant of research on processes, but it is also a worthy end in itself. The delimitation and definition of analogous areas and the knowledge of the detailed similarities and differences of coastal areas are fundamental to the improvement of predictions, to the design and pursuit of fruitful lines of applied research, and to the formulation of sound engineering measures for protection and increased utility and value of coasts.

RECOMMENDED FACILITIES

Facilities required for the research program exist to a limited extent in some fifty scattered field stations and in universities. Among these centers, however, there is now a great variety of emphasis and accomplishment. Some are concerned mainly with marine biology, others with coastal engineering. Some are highly localized in programs, aspirations, and experience. Nevertheless these centers are a starting point, and their facilities and staffs should be expanded so that their research programs can contribute importantly to the coastal geography efforts. Equally necessary is the need to increase facilities at universities where capable individuals are present to participate in coastal research.

There is a special need for the establishment of reserved natural areas for laboratory research, with facilities provided for scientists to live and study at the sites. In view of the expanding population and greater exploitation of significant and unique coastal areas for resorts, power plant sites, freeways and other developments, establishment of a national policy for reserving samples of different types of coastal regions for research purposes should be given highest priority. In some instances scientifically valuable areas may be set aside in cooperation with the National Park Service, the Nature Conservancy, and similar organizations.

In addition to the needs for expansion of existing facilities, the development of potential research centers, and reservation of typical natural areas, it is necessary to establish several centralized facilities to provide services that will increase the effectiveness of research. Services that would relieve the expert from undertaking time-consuming, routine, but necessary operations, and that would supply him with the newest equipment and instruments, would ensure greatest efficiency in information recovery. The costs of such services are prohibitive to individual research centers, and it is not economic for the separate centers to attempt to maintain an adequate supply of the newest instruments because the need for any one instrument, or for a boat or plane, is too sporadic to justify its inclusion on a center's inventory. The solution is the establishment and support of service facilities with professional competence that are available to all participants in the coastal geography program. The following service facilities are recommended:

1. For data collecting:
   a. Equipment pools to supply investigators with planes, boats, amphibious vehicles, and measuring instruments. In addition to its own inventory, an index of existing equipment and its location would be maintained so that loans could be arranged and the use of available equipment could be fully coordinated. A very important function of an equipment center would be the designing, building and calibrating of new, specialized equipment, such as sensing devices

   b. Specialized equipment for simulation of complex environmental conditions, such as tanks and physical models

2. For sample analysis:
   a. Sedimentology and chemical laboratories
   b. Biologic identification laboratory, including a library of pollen of plants found in coastal areas
   c. Geochemical dating laboratory

3. For information processing, storage, and dissemination:
   a. Clearing house for exchange of data-processing programs and programming advice
   b. Data center, which might be included in the National Oceanographic Data Center
   c. Bibliographic and reference center, with map and photo libraries, and with current information on all investigations in progress in coastal geography.

The material above was quoted from the report of the panel on coastal geography (National Academy of Sciences / National Research Council, 1961).

PERTINENT PUBLICATIONS

This bibliography combines in one alphabetical sequence for simplicity both an annotated bibliography and a more inclusive reference list. Those works which it has been possible to determine are of particular significance or interest to this study within the limitations discussed in the chapter are annotated. Other competent works and best-available works on specific subjects are listed without annotation; lack of annotation should not be construed as *necessarily* indicating a less important publication.

Abecasis, F. M.
1964 Resonance conditions in No. 1 dock of Luanda Harbour. Conference on Coastal Engineering, 9th, Lisbon, Proceedings, p. 800-831.
Describes a study of long-period wave effects on harbor facilities.

Abu Bakr, M. and R. O. Jackson
1964 Geological map of Pakistan. Prepared as part of the mineral exploration and development programme sponsored by the Government of Pakistan and U. S. AID.
Scale 1:2,000,000.

Alderman, A. R. and L. W. Parkin
1958 Outline of the geology of South Australia. p. 51-59. *In* R. J. Best, ed., Introducing South Australia. Australian and New Zealand Association for the Advancement of Science, Adelaide.

Alexander, C. S.
1962 A descriptive classification of shore lines. California Geographer 3:131-136.

Allemand-Martin, A.
1939 La géologie de la Péninsule du Cap-Bon (Tunisie). Société Linnéenne de Lyon, Bulletin Mensuel 8(5):130-139.

———
1940 Aperçu géographique, géologique et économique sur les côtes orientales Tunisiennes, les îles Kerkenna et la petite Syrte. Société Linnéenne de Lyon, Bulletin Mensuel 9(4):56-63, (7-10):119-125.

Allison, E. C.
1964 Geology of areas bordering Gulf of California. *In* T. H. van Andel and G. G. Shor, Jr., eds., Marine geology of the Gulf of California. American Association of Petroleum Geologists, Memoir 3:3-29.
An excellent discussion of the available information and the problems yet to be solved.

American University, Foreign Areas Studies Division, Special Operations Research Office
1963 U. S. Army area handbook for Senegal. Government Printing Office, Washington, D. C. 489 p.
Good description of Senegal coast north of Dakar on page 34.

Andel, T. H. van
1964 Recent marine sediments of Gulf of California. *In* T. H. van Andel and G. G. Shor, Jr., eds., Marine geology of the Gulf of California. American Association of Petroleum Geologists, Memoir 3:216-310.

Andel, T. H. van and G. G. Shor, Jr., eds.
1964 Marine geology of the Gulf of California, a symposium. American Association of Petroleum Geologists, Tulsa, Oklahoma, Memoir 3. 408 p.

Anderson, C. A. *et al.*
1950 The 1940 E. W. Scripps cruise to the Gulf of California. Geological Society of America, Memoir 43. 362 p.
Presents the results of the first extensive study by Scripps Institution of Oceanography scientists and other specialists. Includes geology of islands and land areas, megascopic paleontology, micropaleontology, marine stratigraphy, submarine topography, bottom sediments, and oceanographic observations.

Angola. Serviços de Geologia e Minas
1951 Carta geologica de Angola. Luanda.
Scale 1:2,000,000

Anonymous
1964 A summary of temperature-salinity characteristics of the Persian Gulf. U. S. National Oceanographic Data Center, Washington, D. C., Publications, General Series G4. 223 p.

Anonymous
1965- (Cover photograph of Oman on the Arabian
1966 Peninsula; explanation, p. 9.) Geotimes 10(5).

Aparicio, F. de and H. A. Difrieri, eds.
1958- La Argentina, suma de geografía. Ediciones Peuser,
1963 Buenos Aires. 9 vols.
A monographic study of the geography of Argentina. Volume 2 contains a short chapter on the sea and the coast.

Argentina. Dirección Nacional de Geología Minería
1964 Mapa geológico de la República Argentina. Buenos Aires.
Escala 1:5,000,000

Arnould, M.
1948 Les formations pliocènes marines de la péninsule du Cap Bon (Tunisie); région d'Oum Douil. Société Géologique de France, Comptes Rendus 11:214-216.

Australia. Division of National Mapping. Department of National Development
1958a Australian geographical series: Meekatharra. 2nd ed. Canberra. SG-50.
Map 50.4 x 84 cm. Scale 1:1,000,000. Lambert conformal conic projection.

——— 1958b Australian geographical series: Esperance, Western Australia. Canberra. SI-51.
Map 50.4 x 65.7 cm. Scale 1:1,000,000. Lambert conformal conic projection. This map is equivalent to World Aeronautical Chart 1460: Cape Arid.

1959 Australian geographical series: Hamersley Range, Western Australia. Canberra. SF-50.
Map 50.7x78.6 cm. Scale 1:1,000,000. Lambert conformal conic projection.

1962 Australian geographical series: Broome. 2nd. ed. Canberra. SE-51.
Map 50.3 x 74.1 cm. Scale 1:1,000,000. Lambert conformal conic projection.

Australia. Hydrographic Service, Royal Australian Navy
1955 Australia. Northwest coast: Exmouth Gulf with approaches. Aus. 182.
Chart 68.7 x 95.5 cm. Scale 1:150,000 (at lat 21°58'S). Mercator projection. Also: Exmouth Gulf / Learmonth anchorage, scale 1:50,000.

1956 Australia. Northwest coast: Monte Bello Islands to Onslow. Aus. 184.
Chart 69.5x110.3 cm. Scale 1:150,000 (mid lat 20°58'S). Mercator projection.

Australia. National Mapping Office. Department of the Interior
1952 Australian geographical series: Nullarbor Plain, Western Australia / South Australia. Canberra. SH-52.
Map 50.5 x 68.8 cm. Scale 1:1,000,000. Lambert conformal conic projection.

1953 Australian geographical series: Eyre, Western Australia / South Australia. Canberra. SI-52.
Map 50.5x65.7 cm. Scale 1:1,000,000. Lambert conformal conic projection.

Ball, J.
1912 The geography and geology of south-eastern Egypt. Government Press, Cairo. 394 p.
A general work that includes coastal data.

Barrett, E. C.
1957 Baja California, 1535-1956; a bibliography of historical, geographical, and scientific literature relating to the peninsula of Baja California and to the adjacent islands in the Gulf of California and the Pacific Ocean. Bennett and Marshall, Los Angeles. 284 p.

Bascom, W. N.
1951a Beach characteristics. 54 p. *In* R. L. Wiegel, ed., Manual of amphibious oceanography. University of California, Berkeley, College of Engineering, for U. S. Office of Naval Research, Washington, D. C. Contract N7ONR-29535.

——— 1951b The relationship between sand size and beach face slope. American Geophysical Union, Transactions 32:866-74.

A series of diagrams is presented, illustrating the variability of sand-size and beach-face slope and the relationship between the two factors as observed on Pacific Coast beaches of the United States. Includes Santa Barbara, Coronado, Oceanside, and Estero Bay.

——— 1964a Waves and beaches, Anchor Books, Doubleday and Company, Garden City, New York. 267 p.
A very readable account of the wave battle in the surf zone.

——— 1964b Exploring the Diamond Coast. Geotimes 9(2):9-12.

Bayard,
1947 Aspects principaux et consistance des dunes (Mauritanie). Institut Français d'Afrique Noire, Bulletin 9(1-4):1-17.
Discusses the principal features of stable and mobile dunes and dune systems of Mauritania.

Beal, C. H.
1948 Reconnaissance of the geology and oil possibilities of Baja California, Mexico. Geological Society of America, Memoir 31. 138 p.
Includes a geologic map and tectonic sketch map. A very intensive treatment of physiography, stratigraphy, structure, and geologic history.

Beetz, P. F. W.
1934 Geology of southwest Angola, between Cunene and Lunda axis. Geological Society of South Africa, Transactions 36:137-176.
Includes geologic map on a scale of 1:1,000,000.

Bellido B., E., S. Narváez L., and F. S. Simons
1956 Mapa geológico del Perú. Sociedad Geológica del Perú. 2 sheets.
Scale 1:2,000,000.

Berner, R. A.
1964 Distribution and diagenesis of sulfur in some sediments from the Gulf of California. Marine Geology 1(2):117-140.
The depth distribution of the following forms of sulfur have been determined from 5 recent sediment cores taken from the central Gulf of California: sulfide, elemental sulfur, sulfate, and pyrite (plus organic sulfur).

Berninghausen, W. H.
1961 The quality of the bottom, a glossary of terms. U. S. Naval Oceanographic Office, Special Publication 56. 11 p.
This report defines bottom sediment notations that appear on both U. S. and foreign navigation charts. It also indicates how bottom sediment notations are reconciled to U. S. Hydrographic Office sediment classification.

Berry, L., A. J. Whiteman, and S. V. Bell
1966 Some radiocarbon dates and their geomorphological significance, emerged reef complex of the Sudan. Zeitschrift für Geomorphologie, n.f., 10(2):119-143.
Describes the emerged reefs of the Sudan Red Sea Coast; general geology is covered in some detail; good discussion of the submarine near-shore topography.

Berry, L. and J. Sestini
The geomorphology of the Red Sea coastal zone of Sudan. Zeitschrift für Geomorphologie (*in preparation*).

Besairie, H.
1946 Carte géologique de la côte Française des Somalis à l'echelle du 1:500,000, Notice explicative. Imprimerie Nationale, Office de la Recherche Scientifique Coloniale, Paris. 15 p.
Explanatory text for coastal map of French Somaliland.

Beydoun, Z. R.
1960 Synopsis of the geology of East Aden Protectorate. International Geological Congress, 21st, Copenhagen, Report 21:131-149.

1966 Geology of the Arabian Peninsula: Eastern Aden protectorate and part of Dhufar. U. S. Geological Survey, Professional Paper 560-H: 1-49.
The area described encompasses the Provinces of Hadramawt and Al Mahrah and part of the Province of Dhufar. Stratigraphy and structure of basement, Jurassic, Cretaceous, and Tertiary rocks are described in relation to the geologic history. The geology is shown on U. S. Geological Survey, Miscellaneous Geologic Investigations, Map I-270 A (1963).

Bigelow, H. B. and W. T. Edmondson
1947 Wind waves at sea, breakers and surf. U. S. Naval Oceanographic Office, H. O. 602. 117 p.

Bird, E. C. F.
1965 Coastal landforms; an introduction to coastal geomorphology with Australian examples. Australian National University, Canberra. 193 p.
This book emphasizes Australian examples, particularly the shore platforms, "surf" beaches, sandy barriers, and estuarine lagoons. No coverage of desert coastal areas is given; however, the general treatment of coastal landform problems including classification makes this volume a very useful one.

Blondel, F.
1935 La géologie et les ressources minérales de l'Ethiopie, de la Somalie et de l'Eritrée. Chronique des Mines Coloniales 4(43):306-317.
Discusses the stratigraphy and mineral resources of Ethiopia, Somaliland, and Eritrea; good bibliography. Includes geologic map on scale 1:10,000.

Bloom, A. L.
1965 The explanatory description of coasts. Zeitschrift für Geomorphologie 9:422-436.
In this explanatory-description scheme the three variables of (1) erosion and deposition, (2) submergence and emergence, and (3) time are represented by three mutually perpendicular axes.

Borges, A.
1946 A costa de Angola da Baía da Lucira à foz do Bentiaba (entre Benguela e Mossâmedes). Sociedade Geológica de Portugal, Lisbon, Boletim 5(3):141-150.

Bosworth, T. O.
1922 Geology and paleontology of north-west Peru. Macmillan and Company, London. 434 p.
An early but very comprehensive treatment of the Tumbes desert. Covers in detail the extensive terraces at four levels, the dry washes and their development, the raised sea cliffs and the episodes of emergence and subsidence, the saline plains and their deposits, coastal mud flats and dunes, and a thorough study of the action of wind, water, and sun in the desert.

Bouma, A. H.
1965 Sedimentary characteristics of samples collected from some submarine canyons. Marine Geology 3(4):291-320.
Describes cores from various submarine canyons off southern California and Baja California, Mexico.

Bourcart, J.
1949 Nouvelles observations sur le Quaternaire du littoral Marocain entre Casablanca et Safi. Société Géologique de France, Bulletin, ser. 5, 19:453.

1950 La théorie de la flexure continentale (with discussion). International Geographical Congress, 16th, Lisbon, Comptes Rendus 2:167-190.
Transgressions and regressions, submarine canyons, sediments of the continental plateaus, and drowned coast lines are explained in the light of the theory of continental flexure. The coast of Morocco is examined in some detail.

1952 Sur le Quaternaire marin de Mazagan à Mogador et sur la non-existence de l'étage "Ouljien." Société Géologique de France, Bulletin, sér. 6, 2(7/9):441-452.
A discussion of the Quaternary marine deposits along the Atlantic coast of Morocco between Mazagan and Mogador.

Bowman, I.
1916 The Andes of southern Peru, geographical reconnaissance along the seventy-third meridian. American Geographical Society, Special Publication 2. 336 p.
Coastal deserts are covered on p. 110-120; coastal terraces are described on p. 225-232.

Bramkamp, R. A. and L. F. Ramirez
1959a Geology of the Wadi Al Batin quadrangle, Kingdom of Saudi Arabia. U. S. Geological Survey, Miscellaneous Geologic Investigations, Map I-203 A.
Latitude 28° to 32°, longitude 45° to 48° E. Scale 1:500,000. Includes the Kuwait and Iraq coast in the northwest Persian Gulf.

1959b Geographic map of Wadi Al Batin quadrangle, Kingdom of Saudi Arabia. U. S. Geological Survey, Miscellaneous Geologic Investigation, Map I-203 B.
Latitude 28° to 32°, longitude 45° to 48° E. Scale 1:500,000. Includes the Kuwait and Iraq coast in the northwest Persian Gulf.

1959c Geographic map of the central Persian Gulf quadrangle, Kingdom of Saudi Arabia. U. S. Geological Survey, Miscellaneous Geologic Investigations, Map I-209 B.
Latitude 24° to 28°, longitude 51° to 54° E. Scale 1:500,000. Includes coast along the central Persian Gulf.

1959d Geographic map of the northeastern Rub' al Khali quadrangle, Kingdom of Saudi Arabia. U. S. Geological Survey, Miscellaneous Geologic Investigations, Map I-214 B.
Latitude 20° to 24°, longitude 51° to 54° E. Scale 1:500,000. Just barely includes the Trucial Coast.

Bramkamp, R. A. and L. F. Ramirez
1961*a* Geology of the central Persian Gulf quadrangle, Kingdom of Saudi Arabia. U. S. Geological Survey, Miscellaneous Geologic Investigations, Map I-209 A.
Latitude 24° to 28°, longitude 51° to 54°. Scale 1:500,-000. Includes the coastal area showing water depths, coral reefs, eolian sand and sebkha (sabkhah) deposits.

——— 1961*b* Geology of northeastern Rub' al Khali quadrangle, Kingdom of Saudi Arabia. U. S. Geological Survey, Miscellaneous Geologic Investigations, Map I-214 A.
Latitude 20° to 24°, longitude 51° to 54°. Scale 1:500,-000. Just barely includes the Trucial Coast.

Bramkamp, R. A. *et al.*
1962   Geographic map of the Wadi As Sirhan quadrangle, Kingdom of Saudi Arabia. U. S. Geological Survey, Miscellaneous Geologic Investigations, Map I-200 B.
Latitude 28° to 32°, longitude 34° 30' to 39° E. Scale 1:500,000. Shows the Gulf of 'Aqaba chiefly.

——— 1963   Geologic map of the Wadi As Sirhan quadrangle, Kingdom of Saudi Arabia. U. S. Geological Survey, Miscellaneous Geologic Investigations, Map I-200 A.
Latitude 28° to 32°, longitude 34° 30' to 39° E. Scale 1:500,000. Shows the Gulf of 'Aqaba chiefly.

Broggi, J. A.
1940   Memoria de la excursión realizada a la zona sur de la costa con los alumnos del 5° año de minas. Boletín de Minas, Industrias y Construcciones, Lima, 3(13):13-24.
Describes geology and mineral deposits south of Lima.

——— 1946*a* Las terrazas, ensayo geomorfológico. Sociedad Geológica del Perú, Boletín 19:5-20.
Discusses coastal terraces along the Peruvian coast.

——— 1946*b* Las terrazas marinas de la Bahía de San Juan en Ica. Sociedad Geológica del Perú, Boletín 19:21-33.

——— 1946*c* Geomorfología del delta Río Tumbes. Sociedad Geográfica de Lima, Boletín 63:3-4.
Describes a desert delta in the extreme northwest of Peru, 3° 30' S., 80° 30' W.

——— 1952   Migración de arenas a la largo de la costa Peruana. Sociedad Geológica del Perú, Boletín 24. 25 p.
Discusses the transport of sand by wind and oceanic currents in the desert coastal zone of Peru.

——— 1954   Pasamayo y la geología. Escuela Nacional Ingenieros, Lima, Boletín 27:28-59.
Discusses the geologic, geomorphic, and other factors that account for the migration of eolian sands along the Roosevelt highway in the Pasamayo coastal region.

Brongersma-Sanders, M.
1947   On the desirability of a research into certain phenomena in the region of upwelling water along the coast of South West Africa. K. Nederlandsche Academie van Wetenschappen, Amsterdam, Proceedings 50(6):659-665.
Discusses the factors that account for the high H_2S and organic content of bottom sediments, phytoplankton production, and periodic mass mortality of fishes in bays along the coast of South West Africa.

Brown, G. F. and R. O. Jackson
1958*a* Geographic map of the southern Hijaz quadrangle, Kingdom of Saudi Arabia. U.S. Geological Survey, Miscellaneous Geologic Investigations, Map I-210 B.
Latitude 20° to 24°, longitude 38° to 42° E. Scale 1:500,-000. Includes the east-central coast of the Red Sea.

——— 1958*b* Geology of the Tihamat Ash Sham quadrangle, Kingdom of Saudi Arabia. U. S. Geological Survey, Miscellaneous Geologic Investigations, Map I-216 A.
Latitude 16° to 20°, longitude 39° to 42° E. Scale 1:500,-000. Includes a portion of the southeast coast of the Red Sea.

——— 1958*c* Geographic map of the Tihamat Ash Sham quadrangle, Kingdom of Saudi Arabia. U. S. Geological Survey, Miscellaneous Geologic Investigations, Map I-216 B.
Latitude 16° to 20°, longitude 39° to 42° E. Scale 1:500,-000. Includes a portion of the southeast coast of the Red Sea.

——— 1958*d* Geographic map of the Asir quadrangle, Kingdom of Saudi Arabia. U. S. Geological Survey, Miscellaneous Geologic Investigations, Map I-217 B.
Latitude 16° to 20°, longitude 42° to 45° E. Scale 1:500,-000. Includes a portion of the southeast coast of the Red Sea.

——— 1959   Geology of the Asir quadrangle, Kingdom of Saudi Arabia. U. S. Geological Survey, Miscellaneous Geologic Investigations, Map I-217 A.
Latitude 16° to 20°, longitude 42° to 45° E. Scale 1:500,000. Includes a portion of the southeast coast of the Red Sea.

Brown, G. F., R. O. Jackson, and R. G. Bogue
1959   Geographic map of the northwestern Hijaz quadrangle, Kingdom of Saudi Arabia. U. S. Geological Survey, Miscellaneous Geologic Investigations, Map I-204 B.
Latitude 20° to 28°, longitude 35° to 39° E. Scale 1:500,-000. Shows a portion of the northeast coast of the Red Sea.

Brown, G. F. *et al.*
1963*a* Geologic map of the northwestern Hijaz quadrangle, Kingdom of Saudi Arabia. U. S. Geological Survey, Miscellaneous Geologic Investigations, Map I-204 A.
Latitude 24° to 28°, longitude 35° to 39° E. Scale 1:500,-000. Shows a portion of the northeast coast of the Red Sea.

——— 1963*b* Geologic map of the Southern Hijaz quadrangle, Kingdom of Saudi Arabia. U. S. Geological Survey, Miscellaneous Geologic Investigations, Map I-210 A.
Latitude 20° to 24° N, longitude 38° to 42° E, Scale 1:500,000. Includes the east-central coast of the Red Sea.

Brüggen, J.
1950 Fundamentos de la geología de Chile. Instituto Geográfico Militar, Santiago, Chile. 374 p.
The coast is discussed on pages 171-211. Includes a geologic map at a scale of 1:3,100,000.

Butzer, K. W.
1960 On the Pleistocene shore lines of Arabs' Gulf, Egypt. Journal of Geology 68(6):626-637.
Discussion of the offshore bar and lagoon topography of the area, and the Pleistocene shorelines southwest of Alexandria.

———
1962 Pleistocene stratigraphy and prehistory in Egypt. Quaternaria 6:451-477.
Describes the coastal stratigraphy on the northern Egyptian coast.

Byrne, J. V. and K. O. Emery
1960 Sediments of the Gulf of California. Geological Society of America, Bulletin 71(7):983-1010.
A study of the sediments of the Gulf of California based on a consideration of structure, climatology, oceanography, organic constituents, and the general areal physiography.

Calvert, S. E.
1964 Factors affecting distribution of laminated diatomaceous sediments in Gulf of California. *In* T. H. van Andel and G. G. Shor, Jr., eds., Marine geology of the Gulf of California. American Association of Petroleum Geologists, Memoir 3:311-330.
Laminated, richly diatomaceous sediments in the central Gulf of California are confined to the slopes of the basins. An investigation has been made of the water, organisms, and sediments in the Guaymas and San Pedro Mártir Basins, which are the sites of most abundant diatom accumulation.

Canada. Department of Mines and Technical Surveys, Surveys and Mapping Branch
1958 Reconnaissance geology of part of West Pakistan. A Colombo Plan Cooperative Project. Surveyed and compiled in 1953-56 by Photographic Survey Corporation, Ltd., Toronto, in cooperation with the Geological Survey of Pakistan. Published for the Government of Pakistan by the Government of Canada, Ottawa. 31 sheets, 29 colored maps.
Maps 46 x 82 cm. Scale 1:253,440 or 4 miles to the inch. Accompanied by text: Hunting Survey Corporation, Ltd. 1960. Reconnaissance geology of part of West Pakistan. Toronto. 550 p.

Capurro, L. R. A.
1964 Geophysical investigations in the western South Atlantic. p. 458-464. In K. Yoshida, ed., Studies on oceanography. University of Washington Press, Seattle.

Carrigy, M. A. and R. W. Fairbridge
1954 Recent sedimentation, physiography and structure of the continental shelves of Western Australia. Royal Society of Western Australia, Journal 38:65-95.

Castany, G.
1951 Carte géologique de la Tunisie. Service des Mines, de l'Industrie et de l'Energie, Tunis.
Scale 1:500,000, 2 sheets.

Castany, G. and G. Lucas
1955 Sur l'existence d'oolithes calcaires actuelles au large de l'île de Djerba (Sud-Tunisien). Société Géologique de France, Comptes Rendus 11-12: 229-232.
The formation of oolitic calcareous sands found off the coast of Djerba Island, Tunisia, is considered due to present-day processes similar to those responsible for formation of oolitic Jurassic deposits. The oolites are composed of aragonite surrounding a nucleus consisting of eolian quartz or detrital limestone grains, foraminifers, or fragments of other organisms, and can definitely be proved not to have been derived by reworking of Quaternary oolitic formations.

Chile. Armada de Chile
1959 Chile. Antofagasta-Caldera. Departmento de Navegación e Hidrografía. Valparaíso.
Map 54 x 96 cm. Escala 1:500,000. Sondas y alturas en metros. Proyección Mercator.

———
1960 Chile. Caldera / Coquimbo. Departmento de Navegación e Hidrografía. Valparaíso.
Map 47 x 86 cm. Escala 1:500,000 en latitud media 28° 35' 00" Proyección Mercator.

———
1965 Chile. Arica/Antofagasta. Instituto Hidrográfico. Valparaíso.
Map 62 x 110 cm. Escala 1:600,000 en latitud media 20° 40' 00" S. Proyección Mercator.

Chile. Instituto de Investigaciones Geológicas
1960 Mapa Geológico de Chile. Santiago.
Map 7 sheets 84 x 77 cm. or smaller. Scale 1:1,000,000. "Proyección policónica modificade de Lallemand."

Clowes, A. J.
1954 Inshore surface currents on the west coast of the Union of South Africa. Nature 173(4412):1003-1004.
Discusses the influence of "inshore setting currents" on the concentration of fishes in the area.

Cohen, L. H. *et al.*
1963 Geology of the San Benito Islands, Baja California, Mexico. Geological Society of America, Bulletin 74:1355-1370.
A study of the petrology, structure, bathymetry, geomorphology, and geologic history of the San Benito Islands.

Coleman, C. G.
1948 Photographic interpretation of coasts and beaches. *In* C. G. Coleman and A. C. Lundahl, eds., Symposium on military photographic interpretation. Photogrammetric Engineering 14:463-472.
Military coast and beach analysis: beach detail, offshore beach approaches, and adjacent terrain.

Coleman, J. M. and W. G. Smith
1964 Late Recent rise of sea level. Geological Society of America, Bulletin 75:833-840.
The eustatic sea-level rise between 7000 and 3650 years B. P. has been approximately 23 feet. Abundant evidence exists for a stillstand in sea level during the past 2,000-5,000 years.

Combier, M.
1935 Carte géologique de Dakar. Comité d'Etudes Historiques et Scientifiques de l'Afrique Occidentale Française, Publication, sér. B, 1, 43 pp.
Detailed study of the geology of Dakar.

Comité de la Carta Geológica de México
1960 Carta geológica de la República Mexicana. Map 120 x 164 cm. Scale 1:2,000,000. A conventional geologic map; bathymetry shown by contours in meters.

Conant, L. C. and G. H. Goudarzi
1964 Geologic map of the Kingdom of Libya. U. S. Geological Survey, Miscellaneous Geologic Investigations, Map I-350 A.
Map 103 x 127 cm. Scale 1:2,000,000. Lambert conformal conic projection. Bathymetric and hypsographic data in meters.

Cotton, C. A.
1956 Criteria for the classification of coasts. International Geographical Congress, 17th, Washington, D. C., 1952, Proceedings, p. 315-319.

Council for Scientific and Industrial Research, Union of South Africa
1964 Some techniques in coastal oceanography, being an outline of methods developed mainly in the course of ocean-outfall studies off the Natal coast. Oceanographic Research Group, Pretoria, Research Report 222. 59 p.
Covers aerial photography, current measurements, use of tracer dyes and phosphorous 32, and mixing in the surf zone.

Crommelin, R. D. and A. Cailleux
1939 Sur les sables calcaires de la côte égyptienne à 50 km à l'ouest d'Alexandrie. Société Géologique de France, Compte Rendu 6:75-76.
Observations and experiments on calcareous sands of the Egyptian coast 50 km west of Alexandria.

Crossland, C. R.
1907 Report on the marine biology of the Sudanese Red Sea. IV: The recent history of the coral reefs of the mid-west shores of the Red Sea. Linnaean Society, London, Journal (Zoology) 31:14-30.
Describes the coast and evidences of elevation, the coral reefs, and the formation of coral-rag. The coastal description is general but useful. Photographs are excellent.

1911 Reports on the marine biology of the Sudanese Red Sea. XVIII: A physical description of Khor Donganab, Red Sea. Linnaean Society, London, Journal (Zoology) 31:265-286.
Includes a detailed account of the Khor Donganab area (marked Donganab Bay on early British Admiralty nautical charts) with sketch maps and photographs of coastal features.

Curlewis, H. B.
1915 The tides, with special references to those of Fremantle and Port Hedland. Royal Society of Western Australia, Journal 1:28-41.

Curray, J. R. and D. G. Moore
1964a Pleistocene deltaic progradation of continental terrace, Costa de Nayarit, Mexico. *In* T. H. van Andel and G. G. Shore, Jr., eds., Marine geology of the Gulf of California. American Association of Petroleum Geologists, Memoir 3:193-215.
Describes the results of a survey by continuous acoustic reflection profiling. Facies interpretations are made from these records and profiles are drawn on the basis of shape, attitude, nature of internal reflecting horizons, and relationships to adjacent facies.

1964b Holocene regressive littoral sand, Costa de Nayarit, Mexico. p. 76-82. *In* L. M. J. U. Straaten, ed., Deltaic and shallow marine deposits. International Sedimentological Congress, 6th, Amsterdam and Antwerp, 1963, Proceedings. Elsevier, Amsterdam.

Dainelli, G.
1943 Geologia dell'Africa orientale. Vol. I: Il progresso delle conoscenze, 464 p.; Vol. II: L'imbasamento cristallino e la serie sedimentaria Mesozoica, 704 p.; Vol. III: La successione Terziaria e i fenomeni del Quaternario, 748 p.; Vol. IV: Tavole, 10 plates and geologic map. Reale Accademia d'Italia, Centro Studi per l'Africa Orientale Italiana, Rome.
Map scale 1:2,000,000. A four volume study of the geology of Ethiopia, Eritrea, and Italian Somaliland.

Dartevelle, E.
1954 Caractères physiques de la région côtiére de l'Angola. Congrès National des Sciences, 3rd, Brussels, 1950, Comptes Rendus 4:148-150.
Three zones are distinguished along the coast of Angola. In the northern part, from the Congo to the Cuanza, the cliffs are formed mainly of Tertiary deposits, with some ancient granite and Upper Cretaceous outcrops; from the Cuanza to the Catumbela (Benguela) the formations are fossiliferous Cretaceous beds capped in places by Miocene deposits; south of the Catumbela the Tertiary reappears, and ancient granite is represented by the Vermelho massif. Noticeable differences in the evolution of the coast between the north and south, particularly the uneven development of the wave-cut platform, are considered a function of the distribution of submarine valleys.

Davey, J. C.
1948 Report on southern Sinai. Mining Magazine 78(1-4):9-20, 76-87, 144-152, 212-214.
A review of the geography, geology and mineral development of the Sinai Peninsula, Egypt. Includes coastal features; much data on Gulf of Suez and Gulf of 'Aqaba.

Davies, J. L.
1960 Beach alignment in Southern Australia. Australian Geographer 8:42-3.

1964 A morphogenic approach to world shorelines. Zeitschrift für Geomorphologie 8:127-142.

Davies, O.
1959 Pleistocene raised beaches in South West Africa. Asociación de Servicios Geológicos Africanos, Actas y Trabajos (International Geological Congress, 20th, Mexico), p. 347-350.

Dawson, E. Y.
1951 A further study of upwelling and associated vegetation along Pacific Baja California, Mexico. Journal of Marine Research 10:39-58.
A temperature survey in the upper 200 feet of the coastal waters from Bahía de Todos Santos to Bahía de la Magdalena has demonstrated the occurrence of upwell along virtually the entire coast. A study of marine vegetation of this coast and the outlying islands has shown a close correlation with the presence or absence of upwelling water.

Dietz, R. S.
1947 Aerial photographs in the geological study of shore features and processes. *In* H. T. U. Smith, ed., Symposium on information relative to uses of aerial photographs by geologists. Photogrammetric Engineering. 13:537-545, 10 figs. (incl. air photos).
Shows photos of various California beaches and discusses use of photography in geological analysis.

Dolan, R. and J. M. McCloy
1964 Selected bibliography on beach features and near-shore processes. Louisiana State University Press, Coastal Studies Series 11. 59 p.

Downs, T. and G. D. Woodward
1961 Middle Pleistocene extension of the Gulf of California into the Imperial Valley. Geological Society of America, Special Paper 68:21 (Abstr.)
Reconstruction of a Pleistocene extension of the Gulf of California based on fossil findings in 215 localities in the Imperial Valley.

Dresch, J.
1961 Observations sur le désert côtier du Pérou. Annales de Géographie 70:179-184.
A short but thorough discussion of the coastal features.

Dropsy, U.
1943 Etude granulométrique sur quelques sables de Mauritanie. Société Française de Minéralogie, Bulletin 66(1-6):251-63.
Granulometric study of sands from Mauritania. Samples taken along the coast between St. Louis and Port-Etienne.

Dubach, H. W. and T. J. Wehe
1959 Descriptive oceanography of Kuwait Harbor. U. S. Navy Hydrographic Office, Technical Report 55. 43 p., 14 figs.
A descriptive analysis of the oceanography of Kuwait Harbor and adjacent waters based up observations taken between November 1948 and May 1949. Temperature, salinity, surface and subsurface currents, waves, and bottom sediment data are included plus other incidental observations and notations of water color, transparency, eddies, etc. Bibliography of 8 references.

Durham, J. W. and E. C. Allison
1960 The geologic history of Baja California and its marine faunas. Systematic Zoology 9:47-91.
A study of the transgressions and regressions of the sea in Baja California with treatment of the faunal provinces, climatology, and general paleogeography.

Du Toit, A. L.
1954 The geology of South Africa. 3rd ed. Oliver and Boyd, Edinburgh-London. 611 p.
Includes a geologic map of southern Africa dated 1950 (scale 1:5,000,000).

Emery, K. O.
1955 Grain size of marine beach gravels. Journal of Geology 63(1):39-49.
Samples were obtained from Pacific coast of southern California and northern Mexico.

1956 Sediments and water of Persian Gulf. American Association of Petroleum Geologists, Bulletin 40(10):2354-2383.
High salinities and seasonally high temperatures of the waters in the Persian Gulf favor deposition of calcium carbonate as shell material and by direct precipitation as oolites, and are considered responsible for the calcareous character of the bottom sediments. The noncalcareous detrital component contributed by streams entering at the head of the gulf and by eolian transport consists mainly of silt and clay; quartz and resistant heavy minerals predominate in the coarser fraction. The modern sediments are similar in many respects to the Mesozoic and Tertiary geosynclinal deposits which extend northwestward from the gulf. A comparative study indicates that "climate is an environmental factor that may rival or exceed in importance the geometry of geosynclines and their environs in controlling the nature of geosynclinal sediments."

Emery, K. O.
1964 Sediments of Gulf of 'Aqaba (Eilat), p. 257-273. *In* R. L. Miller, ed., Papers in marine geology, Shepard commemorative volume. Macmillan, New York.

Emery, K. O. and Y. K. Bentor
1960 The continental shelf of Israel. Ministry of Development, Jerusalem, Geological Survey Bulletin 26:25-40.
"Detailed sounding profiles made across the Mediterranean continental shelf of Israel show the presence of sand, mud, and rock bottom. Some of the rocks are in the form of submerged kurkar ridges which have served as dams to cause the deposition of mud and sand on their shoreward sides. That these sediments have been derived mostly from the Nile River is indicated by a southward shoaling of the flat areas of the shelf. In contrast, the shelf edge, believed to have been eroded across rock bottom, deepens to the south, probably in response to downwarping of the earth's crust under the weight of the Nile delta off Egypt."

Emery, K. O. and D. Neev
1960 Mediterranean beaches of Israel. Ministry of Development, Jerusalem, Geological Survey Bulletin 26:1-24.
"A northward decrease in grain size and a similarity in mineral composition indicate that beach sands of Israel are derived mainly from the Nile River but with some contribution from streams and sea cliffs of Sinai. The sands have been transported from Egypt by a fringe of the general Mediterranean current and by wave-induced currents. Off central northern Israel the Mediterranean current continues its northerly transportation of sand, but curvature of the coast causes the wave-induced current to return some sand to the south-central part of the coast. Particularly in that region some of the beach sand is blown inland to form sand dunes. Similar distribution patterns of sand existed during the Pleistocene epoch, as illustrated by the position and nature of eolianites."

Emery, K. O. *et al.*
1957 Sediments of three bays of Baja California: Sebastian Viscaino, San Cristobal, and Todos Santos. Journal of Sedimentary Petrology 27:95-115.
A study of more than 1350 sediment samples from three bays facing the Pacific Coast of Baja California. Shows that the sediments are closely related to oceanographic conditions.

Emmons, W. H. *et al.*
1960 Geology, principles and processes. 5th ed. McGraw-Hill Book Company, New York. 491 p.

Erickson, E. E. *et al.*
1965 U. S. Army area handbook for Peru. Government Printing Office, Washington, D. C. 707 p.
Good description of the coast on page 48.

Espenshade, E. B., Jr., ed.
1964 Goode's World Atlas, 12th ed. Rand McNally and Company, Chicago. 288 p.
This atlas provides useful maps and other data for all the desert coastal areas of the world. The map of World Climatic Regions shows the "Climates of the Earth" by Glenn T. Trewartha: a scheme of classification modified and simplified from Köppen. This is the classification consulted in defining desert coastal areas as described in this chapter.

Evans, G., C. G. Kendall, and P. Skipwith
1964 Origin of the coastal flats, the sabkha, of the Trucial Coast, Persian Gulf. Nature 202(4934): 759-761.
Describes the coast of the sheikdom of Abu Dhabi, Trucial Coast, including sediments, topography, physiography, and general history.

Evans, G. and D. J. Sherman
1964 Recent celestine from the sediments of the Trucial Coast of the Persian Gulf. Nature 202(4930): 385-386.
Describes celestine occurrences in Recent sediments on the coastal flats of the sheikdom of Abu Dhabi, Trucial Coast.

Fairbridge, R. W.
1950 Recent and Pleistocene coral reefs of Australia. Journal of Geology 58:330-401.

———

1954 Quaternary eustatic data for Western Australia and adjacent states. Pan Indian Ocean Science Congress, Perth, Section F, Proceedings, p. 64-82.

———

1955 Some bathymetric and geotectonic features of the eastern part of the Indian Ocean. Deep-Sea Research 2:161-171.

———

1961 Eustatic changes in sea level. p. 99-185. *In* Physics and chemistry of the Earth, vol. 4. Pergamon Press. 317 p.

———

1962 World sea-level and climatic changes. Quaternaria 6:111-134.

Falcon, N. L.
1947 Raised beaches and terraces of the Iranian Makran Coast. Geography 109:149-151.

Feruglio, E.
1949- Descripción geológica de la Patagonia. Yacimientos
1950 Petrolíferos Fiscales, Buenos Aires. 3 vols.
Marine terraces are described on pages 74-196.

Field, H.
1959 An anthropological reconnaissance in West Pakistan, 1955. Harvard University, Peabody Museum of Archeology and Ethnology, Papers 52. 332 p., figs., maps.
Discusses briefly the Makran and Las Bela coastal areas, citing the desolateness of the region. Also covers the geology, physical geography, and rivers.

Fleming, R. H. and F. E. Elliot
1956 Some physical aspects of the coastal waters of the United States and Mexico. Geographical Journal 122(4):456-465.
Discusses the various geographical and climatological factors that contribute to the marine environment of the nearshore areas of the United States and Mexico.

France. Bureau d'Études Géologiques et Miniéres Coloniales
1939- Carte géologique internationale de l'Afrique.
1952 Paris.
Scale 1:5,000,000 in 9 sheets.

France. Institut Géographique National
1947 Carte de la Côte Française des Somalis. Dessiné et imprimé par le Service Géographique de l'Armée en 1939. Revisé par l'Institut Géographique National en 1947.
Map 108 x 120 cm on 4 sheets 61 x 76 cm or smaller. Scale 1:200,000. "Ellipsoide international. Projection conforme Lambert. Origine L=12°, M=40° Est Paris." Sheets 1, 2, 4 include coastal areas; topography shown by contours, cliffs by hachures, sandy beaches by dot pattern.

Friedman, G. M.
1964 Recent carbonate sediments of the Gulf of 'Aqaba (Gulf of Eilat), Red Sea. Geological Society of America, Special Paper 82:67-68.

Fuenzalida Villegas, H. *et al.*
1965 High stands of Quaternary sea level along the Chilean coast. Geological Society of America, Special Paper 84:473-496.
The Recent low terraces are 8-10 meters above sea level; the highest of Pliocene (?) age are 250-400 meters.

Furon, R.
1963 Geology of Africa. Oliver and Boyd, Edinburgh. 377 p.
A regional geology text.

Gayral, R. and R. Cauro
1958 Observations sur les variations morphologiques et floristiques d'une zone côtière adjacente à l'estuaire du Bou Regreg (rive gauche). Société des Sciences Naturelles et Physiques du Maroc, Bulletin 38(2):59-70.
The periodic removal and redeposition of sand in the littoral zone at the mouth of Bou Regreg (river), near Rabat, Morocco, is controlled by seasonal wind-current relationships and by storms.

Gentilli, J. and R. W. Fairbridge
1951 Physiographic diagram of Australia. Geographical Press, New York. 8 p.
Includes map 43 x 51 cm (drawn by A. K. Lobeck, scale 1:7,500,000).

Geological Society of Australia, Tectonic Map Committee
1960 Tectonic map of Australia. Bureau of Mineral Resources, Geology, and Geophysics, Department of National Development.
Map 165 x 196 cm. Scale 1:2,534,400. Bathymetric contours in feet. This map actually shows geology and tectonics.

———

1962 Geological notes in explanation of the tectonic map of Australia. Bureau of Mineral Resources Geology, and Geophysics, Department of National Development. 72 p.
A handy, concise volume to aid in understanding the map.

Geukens, F.
1966 Geology of the Arabian Peninsula: Yemen. Translated from the French by S. D. Bowers. U. S. Geological Survey, Professional Paper 560-B:1-23.
Describes the geography, geology, and geologic history of Yemen in the eastern Arabian Peninsula. The geology of the area is shown on U. S. Geological Survey, Miscellaneous Geologic Investigations, Map I-270A (1963).

Gevers, T. W.
1936 The morphology of western Damaraland and the adjoining Namib Desert of Southwest Africa. South African Geographical Journal 19:61-79.
A study of the Southwest African coastline for 160 miles from Walvis Bay to the Ugab River in the north and extending some 120 miles into Damaraland. Considers rainfall, drainage, vegetation, causes of aridity, geology, morphology, and the coastal belt in general.

Gigout, M.
1947a Quaternaire du littoral atlantique du Maroc; les falaises mortes entre Cap Cantin et Cap Blanc. Société Géologique de France, Comptes Rendus sér. 5, 17 (3):52-54.

1947b Quaternaire du littoral atlantique du Maroc; les dunes quaternaires du Sahel. Société Géologique de France, Comptes Rendus sér. 5, 17(4):71-73.

1948 Quaternaire du littoral Atlantique du Maroc; traces de la transgression de 5-8 m entre Casablanca at le Cap Blanc. Société Géologique de France, Comptes Rendus sér. 5, 18(2):25-27.
Describes raised beach deposits and dunes (located at levels ranging from 5 to 8 meters along the Moroccan coast between Casablanca and Cape Blanc) attributed to a late Quaternary transgression.

Gobert, E. G. and L. Harson
1956 Les dépôts littoraux de Monastir (Tunisie) et leurs divers facies. International Quaternary Association, 4th Congress, Rome-Pisa, 1953, Actes 1:359-366.

Gorsline, D. S.
1965 Annual summary report of geologic studies of the Colorado delta. Submitted to the Geography Branch, Office of Naval Research in partial fulfillment of the contractual requirements of Contract Nonr 228 (29), NR 388-079, by the Department of Geology, University of Southern California, Los Angeles. 35 p. (Also cited as AD-622 964).

Goudarzi, G. H.
1959 A summary of the geologic history of Libya. U. S. Geological Survey, Open-File Report. 8 p.

1962 Topographic map of the United Kingdom of Libya. U. S. Geological Survey, Miscellaneous Geologic Investigations, Map I-350 B.
Map 106 x 91.4 cm. Scale 1:2,000,000. Lambert conformal conic projection. Bathymetric and hypsographic data in meters.

Great Britain. Admiralty, Hydrographic Department
1959 Australia Pilot. Vol. V: comprising the northern, north-western, and western coasts of Australia from the southern point at the western entrance to Endeavour Strait to Cape Leeuwin. 5th ed. London. 475 p. With Supplement 2, 1964, 40 p.

Great Britain. Admiralty, Naval Intelligence Division
1943 French West Africa. Vol I: The Federation. B. R. 512, Geographical Handbook Series. H. M. Stationery Office, Oxford. 436 p.
Chapter 2 includes a physical description and geology of the coastal area of Mauritania and the Senegal coast north of Dakar. Chapter 3 briefly discusses swell and surf on these coasts. Includes a map of West Africa (1:4,000,000).

1944a French West Africa. Vol. II: The Colonies. B. R. 512 A (Restricted), Geographical Handbook Series. Oxford. 596 p.
Chapter 6 describes Mauritania, including the coast and climate. Chapter 8 describes Senegal coast and climate.

1944b Iraq and the Persian Gulf. B. R. 524 (Restricted), Geographical Handbook Series. Oxford. 682 p.

1945 Tunisia. B. R. 523 (Restricted), Geographical Handbook Series. Prepared by the Oxford Sub-Centre, Oxford. 532 p.
Includes chapters on the coast, climate, general geology and ports.

1946 Western Arabia and the Red Sea. B. R. 527 (Restricted), Geographical Handbook Series. H. M. Stationery Office, Oxford. 659 p.
Chapter 3 deals specifically with coastal areas: geology, general physiography; maps. Chapter 4 mentions coastal climate and vegetation. Chapter 9 discusses ports and towns. Appendix A discusses the occurrence of deep inlets (sherms) in the Red Sea. Many excellent photographs of coastal areas.

Greenwood, J. E. G. W. and D. Bleackley
1967 Geology of the Arabian Peninsula: Aden Protectorate. U. S. Geological Survey, Professional Paper 560-C:1-96.
This report describes pre-Jurassic basement consisting of metamorphic and igneous rocks, and a stratigraphic sequence ranging from Jurassic to Tertiary in age; mineral and water resources are discussed. The geology of the area is shown on U. S. Geological Survey, Miscellaneous Geologic Investigations, Map I-270A (1963).

Gregory, J. W.
1911 The geology of Cyrenaica. Geological Society of London, Quarterly Journal 67:572-615.
A geologic map on a scale of 1:1,267,200.

Grim, R. E., R. S. Dietz, and W. F. Bradley
1949 Clay mineral composition of some sediments from the Pacific Ocean off the California coast and the Gulf of California. Geological Society of America, Bulletin 60:1785-1808.
The results of a study of the clay mineral composition of a series of bottom core samples collected by the Scripps Institution. The minerals were studied by X-ray diffraction, differential thermal, optical, chemical, and electron microscopic methods following particle size fractionation.

Groot, K.
1965 Inorganic precipitation of calcium carbonate from sea-water. (Letter). Nature 207(4995): 404-405.
Discusses so-called "whitings" in the Persian Gulf with examples from Doha Bay (Qatar). Whitings are clouds of calcium carbonate precipitated from sea water that

has become supersaturated with calcium carbonate due to the removal of carbon dioxide by the photosynthetic action of phytoplankton.

Guilcher, A.
1958   Coastal and submarine geomorphology. Translated by B. W. Sparks and R. H. W. Kneese. Methuen and Company, London. 274 p.
Over half of this volume is devoted to coastal geomorphology: forces in action, shoreline movements, coastal features related to sea action, classification of coasts, coastal evolution.

Guilcher, A. and F. Joly
1954   Recherches sur la morphologie de la côte Atlantique du Maroc. Institut Scientifique Chérifien, Travaux, Série Géologique et Géographie Physique 2, 140 p.
A monographic account of the physiographic subdivisions and principal landforms of the Atlantic coastal zone of Morocco. Although many features are considered the product of eustatic changes of level rather than tectonic dislocation, the possibility that faults may have controlled the development of certain landforms is noted. English summary p. 13-19.

Gunther, E. R.
1936   Variations in intensity of the Peru coastal current. Geographical Journal 88:37-61.
Discusses oceanographic investigations in the Peru Current by the Royal Research ship *William Scoresby* in 1931.

Hamilton, W.
1961   Origin of the Gulf of California. Geological Society of America, Bulletin 72:1307-1318.
Discusses the origin of the Gulf of California, probably as a pull-apart feature resulting from a right-lateral strike-slip displacement along the San Andreas fault for 350 miles plus up to 100 miles of cross-strike separation of the continental plate.

Hammond, E. H.
1954   A geomorphic study of the Cape region of Baja California. University of California, Publications in Geography 10(2):45-112.
Includes geology, landform regions and types, development of coastal features.

Harrington, H. J.
1961   Geology of parts of Antofagasta and Atacama provinces, northern Chile. American Association of Petroleum Geologists, Bulletin 45(2):169-197.
Gives a summary account of the geology of parts of the Atacama Desert, between parallels 22° and 26° S. Mentions the steep sea cliffs and that uplift must have been very recent.

Harris, S. A.
1959   The mechanical composition of some intertidal sands. Journal of Sedimentary Petrology 29(3):412-424.
Studies of beach sands in the Suez gulf region show that the effect of wave action consists principally in the removal of the finest grades. The mechanical composition of the parent material rather than the sorting process determines the grading range of the coarser fractions. The data also indicate that it is possible to distinguish between beach and dune sands on the basis of mechanical composition alone.

Harris, T. F. W.
1966   Coastal oceanography and engineering in South Africa. Coastal Research Notes 2(1):12-13.

Harrison, J. V.
1941   Coastal Makran. Geographical Journal 97:1-15.
Discusses an expedition to coastal Makran in 1932-1933, considering climate, geology, and topography.

Haughton, S. H.
1932   The late Tertiary and Recent deposits of the west coast of South Africa. Geological Society of South Africa, Transactions 34:19-53.

Heath, J. A.
1965   Bibliography of reports resulting from U. S. Geological Survey participation in the United States Technical Assistance Program, 1940-65. U. S. Geological Survey, Bulletin 1193. 51 p.
Includes geologic and topographic maps for desert coastal areas of Libya and Saudi Arabia.

Hernández-Pacheco, E.
1950   Morfología y evolución de las zonas litorales de Ifni y del Sahara español. International Geographical Congress, 16th, Lisbon, 1949, Comptes Rendus 2:487-505.

Hernández-Pacheco, F.
1946   Fases de formación de los médanos en las playas de Cabo Juby. Sociedad Española de Historia Natural, Madrid. Boletín 44(3-4):239-242.
Outlines the formation of barchans in the coastal zone of Juby Cape, Spanish Sahara.

Hey, R. W.
1956   The Pleistocene shorelines of Cyrenaica. Quaternaria 3:139-144.
Six shorelines on the north coast of Cyrenaica occur at 6m, 15-25m, 35-40m, 44-55m, 70-90m, and 140-190m without severe warping.

Higgins, C. G.
1965   Causes of relative sea-level changes. American Scientist 53:464-476.

Hill, M. N., ed.
1963   The sea; ideas and observations on progress in the study of the seas. Vol. 3: The earth beneath the sea, history. Interscience Publishers, New York. 963 p.
Chapters related to coastal areas include: 21: Beach and nearshore processes (Bagnold and Inman), 24: Estuaries, deltas, shelf, slope (Guilcher).

Hilmy, M. E.
1951   Beach sands of the Mediterranean coast of Egypt. Journal of Sedimentary Petrology 21(2):109-120.
Data on the mechanical analysis and the mineral content of beach sands from the Egyptian Mediterranean coast. The sands are of two principal types, carbonate and quartz-dominant sands.

Hodgkin, E. P. and V. Di Lollo
1958   The tides of south-western Australia. Royal Society of Western Australia, Journal 41(2):42-54.
Compares tidal observations at Carnarvon with observations at Port Hedland.

Holm, D. A.
1960   Desert geomorphology in the Arabian peninsula. Science 132(3437):1369-1379.
Discusses some factors controlling the emplacement of large sandy deserts such as Rub' al Khali and Great Nafud of Saudi Arabia, the variations in shape and size

of dunes, the origin and distribution of gravel plains, and the formation of sebkhas (sabkhahs), and notes evidence bearing on the age and geomorphic history of the Persian Gulf region.

Holser, W. T.
1962 Diagenetic polyhalite in Recent salt from Baja California. Geological Society of America, Special Paper 73:173-174. (Abstr.)
A study of halite and gypsum now being deposited on extensive tidal flats at Laguna Ojo de Liebre, Baja California.

Houbolt, J. J. H. C.
1957. Surface sediments of the Persian Gulf near the Qatar peninsula. Mouton and Co., The Hague. 113 p.
A detailed petrographic study of the various types of sediment distinguished in the modern deposits of the Persian Gulf, off the coast of the Qatar peninsula (Arabia). For the most part, the sediments are composed of varying amounts of carbonate grains derived from skeletal fragments, mainly molluscan, whose conversion into detritus was caused not only by wave action but by the action of organisms. An increase in the calcilutitic and lutite particles (marl) accompanies a decrease in the calcarenite component. Data on grain-size distribution, the transport and depositional environment of the sediments, and the relief of the bottom (in which four terrace-like levels are distinguished) and a description of *Heterostegina* qatarensis n. sp. (by K. Küpper) are included.

Howell, J. V., ed.
1960 Glossary of geology and related sciences. 2nd ed. American Geological Institute, Washington, D. C. 325 + 72 p.

Hoyt, J. H.
1965 Sediment distribution of the inner continental shelf, west coast of southern Africa. American Association of Petroleum Geologists, Bulletin 49:344-345. (Abstr.)

Hunt, J. A.
1942 Geology of the Zeila plain, British Somaliland. Geological Magazine 79:197-201.
Includes geologic sketch map (scale 1:1,000,000).

Hunting Survey Corporation, Ltd.
1960 Reconnaissance geology of part of West Pakistan. *See* Canada. Department of Mines and Technical Surveys, Surveys and Mapping Branch.

Iddings, A. and A. A. Olsson
1928 Geology of northwestern Peru. American Association of Petroleum Geologists, Bulletin 12(1):1-39.
Discusses the general geology of the oil-producing area of coastal Peru from the Peru-Ecuador border south to about 6° S latitude.

Illing, L. V. and A. J. Wells
1964 Penecontemporary dolomite in the Persian Gulf. American Association of Petroleum Geologists, Bulletin 48:532. (Abstr..)
Describes carbonate sediments that dominate the shallow waters along the arid southwest side of the Persian Gulf. Numerous sebkhas (sabkhahs) are found along the Qatar coast.

Illing, L. V., A. J. Wells, and J. C. M. Taylor
1965 Penecontemporary dolomite in the Persian Gulf. *In* Dolomitization and limestone diagenesis, a

symposium. Society of Economic Paleontologists and Mineralogists, Special Publication 13:89-111.
Describes an area on the west side of Qatar.

Inman, D. L., G. C. Ewing, and J. B. Corliss
1964 Coastal sand dunes of Guerrero Negro, Baja California, Mexico. Geological Society of America, Special Paper 82:99-100. (Abstr.)
A study of the rate of migration and sedimentary structures associated with a field of active coastal barchan sand dunes at Guerrero Negro, Baja California, Mexico.

International Geographical Union, Commission on Coastal Sedimentation
1956 Report of the commission on coastal sedimentation. International Geographical Congress, 18th, Rio de Janeiro, 9th General Assembly. 140 p.
Contains a bibliography for 1952-54, a list of institutions interested in coastal work, and brief reports of work in progress or recently completed on the coasts of each country.

———
1960 Bibliography 1955-58. Louisiana State University, Baton Rouge, Coastal Studies Institute, Contribution 60-2. 148 p.
Second bibliography in the series.

International Geographical Union, Commission on Coastal Geomorphology
1964 Bibliography 1959-1963. Kobenhavns Universitets, Geografiske Institut, Publication 63. 68 p.
Third bibliography in the series.

Ives, R. L.
1951 High sea-levels of the Sonoran shore. American Journal of Science 249:215-23.
Elevated shorelines, tombolo bars, shell banks, and widely distributed marine shells high above present sea level along the Sonoran shore of the Gulf of California indicate former existence of two or more high sea levels.

———
1959 Shell dunes of the Sonoran shore. American Journal of Science 257(6):449-57.
The Great Sand Dunes along the NE shore of the Gulf of California extend from N of Yuma, Arizona to S of Puerto Peñasco, Sonora. W and N of the Pinacate Peaks, the dunes are composed largely of rock fragments and are in part reworked Colorado River sediments; to the S they are composed largely of shell fragments.

James, P. E.
1959 Latin America. p. 189-201. 3rd ed. Odyssey Press, New York. 942 p.

Jauzein, A
1958 Les formes d'accumulation éolienne liées à des zones inondables en Tunisie septentrionale. Académie des Sciences, Paris, Comptes Rendus 247(25):2396-2399.
Observations on loamy dunes bordering playas and lagoons in the coastal zone of northern Tunisia show that their origin is quite varied. Their location in a zone subject to inundation is an important factor.

———
1959 Remarques sur le Quaternaire marin de la côte orientale de la Tunisie. Société Geologique de France, Bulletin sér. 7,1(2):119-122.
In the Gulf of Gabès, Tunisia, only two beaches are visible that postdate the Pliocene transgression, both of which belong to the Tyrrhenian (Pleistocene) cycle.

Jenks, W. F.
1945   La geología de Arequipa sus alredededores. Sociedad de Ingenieros del Perú, Lima, Informaciones y Memorias 46(9):498-509.
Describes the area from the coast inland.

Jenks, W. F., ed.
1956   Handbook of South America geology. Geological Society of America, Memoir 65. 378 p.
Discusses the general geology of South America by country.

Jennings, J. N.
1955   The influences of wave action on coastal outline in plan. Australian Geographer 6(4):36-44.
Discusses the nature and effect of wave action on shore lines, and cites examples from various sections of Australia which support the view that waves are a more important geomorphic agent than currents in the development of constructional features of coasts.

———
1961   A preliminary report on the karst morphology of the Nullarbor Plains. Cave Exploration Group (South Australia), Occasional Papers 2. 45 p.

———
1963   Some geomorphological problems of the Nullarbor Plain. Royal Society of South Australia, Transactions 87:41-62.

Jessen, O.
1951   Dünung in Atlantik und an der westküste Afrikas. Petermanns Geographische Mitteilungen 95:7-16.
Discusses dunes along the west coast of Africa and on islands of the Atlantic Ocean.

Johnson, C. W.
1953   Notes on the geology of Guadalupe Island, Mexico. American Journal of Science. 251(3):231-236.
Indicates that the rock sequence is almost entirely volcanic with an Upper Tertiary or Quaternary marine tuffaceous marl.

Johnson, D. W.
1919   Shore processes and shoreline development. John Wiley and Sons, New York. 584 p.

Johnson, G. R.
1930   Peru from the air, with text and notes by Raye R. Platt. American Geographical Society, Special Publication 12. 159 p.
Provides excellent black and white photographs of coastal valleys and their ports.

Joire, J.
1947   Amas de coquillages du littoral senegalais dans la banlieue de Saint-Louis. Institut Français d'Afrique Noire, Bulletin, Etudes Senegalaises 9(1-4):170-340.
Extensive study of the shell mounds along the coast of Senegal in the vicinity of St. Louis.

Jutson, J. T.
1934   The physiography (geomorphology) of Western Australia, 2nd ed. Geological Survey of Western Australia, Bulletin 95. 366 p.
Coast line and coastal plains, p. 298-295.

Kadib, A.-L.
1964   Calculation procedure for sand transport by wind on natural beaches. U. S. Army, Coastal Engineering Research Center, Washington, D. C., Miscellaneous Paper 2-64. 25 p.
Summarizes available methods for calculating the actual rate of sand transport by wind on beaches.

Kassas, M.
1957   On the ecology of the Red Sea coastal land. Journal of Ecology 45:187-204.
Includes geology and geomorphology of this coastal belt, which includes a littoral coral beach about one mile in width and a maritime plain extending to the foothills of the mountains paralleling the sea. The study area lies between 18° 52' N and 20° 00' N latitude, about 12 x 80 miles, on the Sudan coast. Excellent photographs.

King, C. A. M.
1959   Beaches and coasts. Edward Arnold, Ltd., London. 403 p.
An excellent general treatment of the factors controlling the character of beaches; also has interesting chapters on classification and historical data on coastal change.

Kinsman, D. J. J.
1964a   Dolomitization and evaporite development, including anhydrite, in lagoonal sediments, Persian Gulf. Geological Society of America, Special Paper 82:108-109. (Abstr.)
Describes Recent carbonate sediments on the Trucial Coast.

———
1964b   The Recent carbonate sediments near Halat El Bahrani, Trucial Coast, Persian Gulf, p. 129-135. In L. M. J. U. van Straaten, ed., Deltaic and shallow marine deposits. International Sedimentological Congress, 6th, Amsterdam and Antwerp, 1963, Proceedings. Elsevier, Amsterdam.

Kirkland, D. W., J. P. Bradbury, and W. E. Dean, Jr.
1965   Origin of Carmen Island salt deposit, Baja California, Mexico. Coastal Research Notes 10:9. (Abstr.)
Brief note on the geological history of Carmen Island, which lies 12 miles east off the coastal city of Loreto, Baja California, Mexico, in the Gulf of California. Special attention is given the extensive salt deposits of the island.

Knetsch, G.
1943   Mitteilung über neue beobachtungen zur geologie der Marmarica (Nord-Libyen). Geologische Rundschau 33:409-414.
Describes the coastal area between the Gulf of Bomba and the Gulf of Salûm in western Egypt. Marmarica is in northern Libya.

Konecki, M. C., J. M. Dickins, and T. Quinlan
1958   The geology of the coastal area between lower Gascoyne River and Murchison River, Western Australia. Australia, Bureau of Mineral Resources, Geology, and Geophysics, Report 37. 144 p.

Kovach, R. L., C. R. Allen, and F. Press
1962   Geophysical investigations in the Colorado Delta region. Journal of Geophysical Research 67(7):2845-2871.
Discusses the determination of the depths of the Cenozoic section and fault patterns of the Colorado Delta region by the use of gravity and seismic refraction techniques.

Krause, D. C.
1964 Lithology and sedimentation in the southern continental borderland. p. 274-318. *In* R. L. Miller ed., Papers in marine geology, Shepard Commemorative Volume. Macmillan Company, New York.
Describes the lithology and sediments of the offshore area between Point Conception, California, and Vizcaíno peninsula, Baja California, Mexico. Includes data on bathymetry, terraces, core analysis, and dredging.

La Fond, E. C.
1963 Detailed temperature structure of the sea off Baja California. Limnology and Oceanography 8(4): 417-425.
The detailed temperature structure of the upper 245 meters of the sea provide clues to the dynamic processes occurring in the sea.

Lafond, L. R.
1952 Les phénomènes littoraux dans la zone internationale de Tanger (Maroc). Société Géologique de France, Bulletin, sér. 6, 1(8):657-670.
Analyzes shore processes along the coast in the vicinity of Tangier. Sandy sediment is produced and transported mainly by marine currents and waves, and to some extent by eolian action of the east winds; the fluviatile contribution is negligible. Construction of a break-water has upset the sedimentary equilibrium and cut off the great beach at Tangier from its normal source of supply. As a result, transfer of sand within the bay is limited to the perimeter of the beach; erosion is taking place at the eastern end, sedimentation at the western, and a new beach is being built up east of the jetty. Although some silting of the roadstead has begun, it is predicted that this will diminish and not seriously affect the port.

Laurent, J. and A. Rivière
1950 Resultats scientifiques d'une mission hydro-océanographique à Safi; phenoménes littoraux. Académie des Sciences, Paris, Comptes Rendus 230(23):2037-39.
Discusses transport and dispersion of sediments by wave action and current action, based on observations on the Atlantic Coast of Africa in the Safi area of Morocco.

Lecointre, G. and M. Gigout
1948 Sur le Quaternaire des Djorfs el Ihoudi et er R'eraba (Maroc occidental). Société Géologique de France, Comptes Rendus sér. 5, 18(10):184-186.
Describes Quaternary beach and dune deposits.

Lees, G. M.
1928 The geology and tectonics of Oman and parts of south-eastern Arabia. Geological Society of London, Quarterly Journal 84:585-670.
Includes a geologic map on a scale of approximately 1:3,000,000.

Lemon, R. R. H. and C. S. Churcher
1961 Pleistocene geology and paleontology of the Talara Region, northwest Peru. American Journal of Science 259:410-429.

Lobeck, A. K.
1946. Physiographic diagram of Africa. Geographical Press, Columbia University, New York.
Map 27 x 33.5 cm. Scale 1:30,000,000.

Logan, B. W.
1959 Environments, foraminiferal facies and sediments of Shark Bay, Western Australia. University of Western Australia, Department of Geology (Ph.D. dissertation)

———
1961 Cryptozoon and associate stromatolites from the Recent, Shark Bay, Western Australia Journal of Geology 69:517-533.

Logan, R. F.
1960 The central Namib Desert, South West Africa. National Academy of Sciences / National Research Council, Publication 758. (ONR Foreign Field Research Program, Report 9) 162 p.

Maloney, W. E. and R. E. Burns
1958 A reappraisal of the tides of the Mediterranean. U. S. Navy Hydrographic Office, Technical Report 61. 32 p. 9 figs.
This report proposes that the tides in the Mediterranean Sea are a direct response to the tide-producing forces and not a cooscillation resulting from tidal progression from the Atlantic Ocean. The natural periods of the major subdivisions of the Mediterranean are determined by examining the M_2 and S_2 component tide amplitudes. It is shown that the amplitude ratio H_2/S_2 can be ascribed to the difference between the natural period of the basins and the period of the tide-producing forces. Bibliography of 18 references.

Marmer, H. A.
1943 Tidal investigations on the west coast of South America. Geographical Review 33:299-303.
Discusses briefly a project concerned with establishing tide gauges and suitable datum planes in order to make systematic tidal predictions for this coast. Mentions that there were no regular stations prior to 1937. Three stations each were established on the Peru and Chile coast.

McBeth, F. H.
1956 A method of shoreline delineation. Photogrammetric Engineering 22:400-405.
An empirical method of determining the mean high water line on both beach and rock shorelines.

McCurdy, P. G.
1947 Manual of coastal delineation from aerial photographs. U. S. Navy Hydrographic Office, H. O. 592. 143 p.
Profusely illustrated.

McGill, J. T.
1958 Map of the coastal landforms of the world. Geographical review 48:402-405.
Separate map 80 x 146 cm. Areal Scale 1:25,000,000. Briesemeister equal-area projection.

———
1959 Coastal classification maps: a review. p. 1-21. *In* R. J. Russell, ed., Second Coastal Geography Conference. U. S. Navy, Office of Naval Research, and National Research Council.

———
1960 Selected bibliography of coastal geomorphology of the world. Los Angeles. 50 p.
This bibliography of 933 titles consists principally of references used in the preparation of a recent map of coastal landforms of the world (McGill, 1958); references are regional and topical; many of the regional references cover more than the coastal portion of a given country or region.

McIntyre, D. B. and J. S. Shelton
  1957   Preliminary report on tectonic history of Viscaino Peninsula and San Benito Islands, Baja California, Mexico. American Association of Petroleum Geologists, Bulletin 41(2)352-353. (Abstr.)
Discusses general stratigraphy and structure and the presence of emerged wavecut beaches on the islands.

McKee, E. D.
  1939   Some types of bedding in the Colorado River Delta. Journal of Geology 47:64-81.
Describes the principal types of lamination on the Colorado Delta, and discusses two varieties of pseudo-bedding.

———
  1957   Primary structures in some Recent sediments. American Association of Petroleum Geologists, Bulletin 41(8):1704-1747.
Beach and tidal-flat stratification at Cholla Bay, Sonora, Mexico, are included.

Meigs, P.
  1966   Geography of coastal deserts. Unesco, Paris. Arid Zone Research 28. 140 p., 15 maps.
Identifies the world's coastal deserts in the text and on 15 maps. Discusses in detail climate and terrain. No data for the offshore areas.

Milton, D. I.
  1967   Geology of the Arabian Peninsula: Kuwait. U. S. Geological Survey, Professional Paper 560-F:1-7.
This report describes the surface and subsurface of Kuwait, as shown on U. S. Geological Survey, Miscellaneous Geologic Investigations, Map I-270A (1963).

Mina, U. F.
  1957   Bosquejo geológico del Territorio Sur de la Baja California. Asociación Mexicana de Geólogos Petroleros, Boletín 9(3-4):139-270.
Discusses physiography, petrography, geology structure, and stratigraphy of Baja California Sur on a regional basis.

Mohr, P. A.
  1963a Geological map of Horn of Africa. Philip and Tracey, Ltd., London.
Map 100 x 105 cm. Scale 1:2,000,000.

———
  1963b The geology of Ethiopia. University College of Addis Ababa Press. 268 p.
Describes the coastal deposits on p. 189-193. Excellent bibliography.

Moore, D. G. and J. R. Curray
  1964   Sedimentary framework of the drowned Pleistocene delta of Rio Grande de Santiago, Nayarit, Mexico. p. 275-281. *In* L. M. J. U. van Straaten, ed., Deltaic and shallow marine deposits. International Sedimentological Congress, 6th, Amsterdam and Antwerp, 1963, Proceedings. Elsevier, Amsterdam.

Morocco. Service Géologique, Rabat
  1946- Carte géologique du Maroc.
  1955
Scale 1:500,000. 6 sheets.

Morris, R. C. and P. A. Dickey
  1957   Modern evaporite deposition in Peru. American Association of Petroleum Geologists, Bulletin 41(11):2467-2374.
Gypsum and halite are being precipitated in the saline environment that prevails in the uppermost reaches of a restricted marine estuary, the Bocana de Virrila, in the arid Sechura region on the northwest coast of Peru.

Morton, D. M.
  1959   The geology of Oman. World Petroleum Congress, 5th, New York, Proceedings, Sec. 1:277-294.

Muñoz Cristi, J.
  1955   Bibliografía geológica de Chile (1927-53). Universidad de Chile, Santiago de Chile, Instituto de Geológica, Publicación 5. 121 p.
A classified, partly annotated list of over 600 titles on the geology of Chile.

Murphy, R. C.
  1925   Bird islands of Peru. Putnam's, New York 362 p.
Describes the Peruvian coast, the climate, the islands as guano resources, the Humboldt Current, and marine life. Good photos of the islands showing cliffed shores.

———
  1926   Oceanic phenomena along west coast of South America during 1925. Geographical Review 16:26.
Discusses the causes for a remarkable change in the customary weather of the arid coast.

Nakhla, F. M.
  1958   Mineralogy of the Egyptian black sands and its application. Egyptian Journal of Geology 2(1):1-24.
Major constituents of the black sands on the beaches of the northern parts of the Nile delta are ilmenite, magnetite, augite, zircon, quartz, garnet, monzite, rutile, hornblende, and calcite. The methods and results of fractioning the sand for making quantitative mineralogic determinations are described. The opaque minerals were made into briquettes, polished, and examined in reflected light, and the results tabulated. The sands are thought to be derived from more than one source rock.

Al Naqib, K. M.
  1967   Geology of the Arabian Peninsula: Southwestern Iraq. U. S. Geological Survey, Professional Paper 560-G:1-54.
Cretaceous to Quaternary strata cropping out in southwest Iraq comprise a section about 16,800 feet thick; 27 formations are described in detail. The geology is shown on U. S. Geological Survey, Miscellaneous Geologic Investigations, Map I-270A (1963).

National Academy of Sciences/National Research Council
  1961   Coastal geography, a report of a conference sponsored by the NAS-NRC Committee on Geography, Advisory to the Office of Naval Research, March 20-21. Washington, D. C. 17 p. (Also cited as AD-270 606)

———
  1963   Report of the Inter-American conference on Marine sciences, Key Biscayne, Florida, November 8-10, 1962. Conducted by the Office of the Foreign Secretary and Committee on Oceanography of the National Academy of Sciences. Sponsored by the Office of Naval Research. NAS-NRC, Washington, D. C., Publication 1088. 42 p.

National Iranian Oil Company
  1959a Geological map of Iran. Compiled by the geological staff of the Iran Oil Company.
Map 82 x 83 cm. Scale 1:2,500,000. Polyconic projection.

National Iranian Oil Company

1959*b* Explanatory notes to the geological map of Iran. With stratigraphic tables, index map, and bibliography. Prepared by the geological staff of the Iran Oil Company, 21 pages.

Nesteroff, W. D.

1955 Les recifs coralleins du Banc Farsan Nord (Mer Rouge). Institut Océanographique, Annales n. s. 30:7-55.

A study of coral reefs on the North Farzan Bank based upon the results of the *Calypso* Red Sea expedition, 1951-52. Includes English summary.

Newell, N. D. and D. W. Wood

1955 Extraordinarily coarse eolian sand of the Ica desert, Peru. Journal of Sedimentary Petrology 25(3): 226-228..

Eolian sandstreams along the Peruvian coast locally are composed of well-sorted granules of country rock in which the modal class exceeds 3 mm and the coarsest grains are 617 mm in diameter. Generally this coarse sand is a first generation deposit.

Nichols, M. M.

1962 Hydrography and sedimentology of Sonoran lagoons, Mexico. Geological Society of America, Special Paper 73:210-211. (Abstr.)

Describes the development of lagoons along the arid Sonoran coast, including principal morphologic units, tidal range, sediments, and stratigraphy.

Nir, D.

1959 Etude sur la morphologie littorale d'Israel. Annales de Géographie 68:424-436.

Oren, O. H.

1962 The Israel south Red Sea expedition. Nature 194 (4834):1134-1137.

Notes on the area of Massawa, Eritrea.

Organization of American States

1964*a* Annotated index of aerial photographic coverage and mapping of topography and natural resources: Peru. Pan American Union, Washington. 26 p.

———

1964*b* Annotated index of aerial photographic coverage and mapping of topography and natural resources: Chile. Pan American Union, Washington. 20 p.

Osorio-Tafall, B. F.

1948 La Isla de Cedros, Baja California. Sociedad México Geografía y Estadística, Boletín 66:319-402.

Located off the west coast of Baja California. Includes data on geography, coastal relief, geology, climatology, mineralogy, history, flora, fauna, and inhabitants.

Oxford University Press, Cartographic Department

1957 The Oxford Australian atlas. Oxford University Press, London. 71 p.

The coverage of Australia is quite detailed, and many of the statistical presentations differ from those found in U. S. atlases.

Pallister, J. W.

1963 Notes on the geomorphology of the northern region, Somali Republic. Geographical Journal 129(2):184-187.

A brief but excellent discussion of the land strip between Zaila and Bosaso on the Gulf of Aden.

Parker, R. H.

1964 Zoogeography and ecology of macroinvertebrates, Gulf of California and continental slope of western Mexico. *In* T. H. van Andel and G. G. Shor, Jr., eds., Marine geology of the Gulf of California. American Association of Petroleum Geologists, Memoir 3:331-376.

A reconnaissance study of the zoogeography and ecology of benthic invertebrates has established 11 faunal assemblages which characterize various environments. Comparisons show the similarities in environments throughout the subtropical and tropical regions of the world.

Paver, G. L. and D. A. Pretorius

1954 Report on reconnaissance hydrogeological investigations in the Western Desert coastal zone. Institut du Désert d'Egypte, Heliopolis, Bulletin, Publications 5. 145 p.

Pepper, J. F. and G. E. Everhart

1963 The Indian Ocean, the geology of its bordering lands and the configuration of its floor. U. S. Geological Survey, Miscellaneous Geologic Investigations, Map I-380.

Latitude about 34° N to 54° S, longitude about 15° E to 155° E. Accompanied by a text of 33 pages. Map 94x118 cm. Scale 1:13,650,00 at 15° latitude. Bathymetric contours: 100, 1,000, 2,000, 2,500, and 3,000 fathoms. Mercator projection.

Pfannenstiel, M.

1952 Zur Quartärgeschichte des Nildeltas. Geologische Rundschau 40(1):108-109.

Phleger, F. B.

1965 Sedimentology of Guerrero Negro Lagoon, Baja California, Mexico. p. 205-237. *In* W. F. Whittard and R. Bradshaw, eds., Symposium of the Colston Research Society, 17th, University of Bristol, 1965, Proceedings.

Phleger, F. B. and G. C. Ewing

1962 Sedimentology and oceanography of coastal lagoons in Baja California, Mexico. Geological Society of America, Bulletin 73(2):145-181.

Describes three coastal lagoons of the Ojo de Liebre area, including data on flora and faunal assemblages, currents, sedimentary processes, and general physiographic features.

Pilkey, O. H. and D. Noble

1966 Carbonate and clay mineralogy of the Persian Gulf. Deep Sea Research 13(1):1-16.

Pimienta, J.

1953 La lagune de Tunis considerée comme un milieu de sedimentation à la fois marin et continental. Académie des Sciences, Paris, Comptes Rendus 236(9):946-948.

A study of conditions of deposition in the coastal lagoon region of Tunisia.

———

1954*a* Cycles deltaïques à l'embouchure de la Medjerda. Société Géologique de France, Comptes-Rendus (9-10):204-206.

The present delta of the Medjerda river, Tunisia, was established late in the Quaternary, at the end of the Mousterian. Sedimentation is cyclic, alternately marine and continental, in a steadily subsiding basin, whose rapid rate of subsidence is probably due to the presence at depth of plastic strata similar to the diapiric Keuper (Triassic) beds which occur around the margin of the basin.

Pimienta, J.
1954b Evolution granulométrique exceptionelle de vases littorales en présence de matières organiques. Académie des Sciences, Paris, Comptes Rendus 238(11):1248-1250.
In the lagoon of Tunis organic matter caused a partial deflocculation of alluvial clays, which led to an exceptionally granular condition.

1956 Cycle sédimentaires sur un littoral en déformation tectonique. Académie des Sciences, Paris, Comptes Rendus 243(2):168-170.
Cyclic sedimentation at the mouth of the Miliane river in the coastal zone of Tunisia is due to the interplay of shore processes and present-day deep-seated tectonic activity.

Popovici, Z.
1956 Estudio oceanográfico del Mar Argentino. Revista Geográfica Americana 40(236):63-66.
A preliminary note on investigations of the ocean off Argentina's coast.

Porro, C.
1936 Esplorazione geologica della zone costiera Eritrea a nord di Massaua. R. Accademia di Scienze di Torino, Classe di Scienze, Fisiche, Matematiche i Naturali, Memorie s. 2, 68(1):241-276.
Describes the Miocene geology of the coastal area north of Massaua (Massawa).

Powers. R. W. *et al.*
1966 Geology of the Arabian Peninsula: Sedimentary geology of Saudi Arabia. U. S. Geological Survey, Professional Paper 560-D. 147 p.
An aggregate of approximately 18,000 feet of sedimentary strata ranging in age from presumed Cambrian to Pliocene was deposited on the Arabian shield, a Precambrian metamorphic and igneous complex. Geographic distribution, stratigraphy, geologic history, structure, and economic aspects are discussed. The geology of the area is shown on U. S. Geological Survey, Miscellaneous Geologic Investigations, Map I-270A (1963).

Putnam, W. C. *et al.*
1960 Natural coastal environments, of the world. University of California, Los Angeles, for U. S. Office of Naval Research, Washington, D. C., Contract Nonr-23306. 140 p., maps. (Also cited as AD-236 741)
Written with military applications in mind, the volume serves as a guide to the operational interpretation of coastal landforms. The text and three maps cover the classification of coastal landforms, vegetation, and climate.

Qureshi, M. R.
1957 Oceanography in Pakistan. *In* Unesco Symposium on Physical Oceanography, Tokyo, 1955, Proceedings, p. 207-213.

Raisz, E.
(195-) Landforms of Arabia; prepared for the Environmental Protection Section of the Office of the Quartermaster General. Cambridge, Massachusetts.
Map 50 x 57 cm. Scale ca 1:9,000,000.

1952 Landform map of North Africa. Base map prepared for the Environmental Protection Section of the Office of the Quartermaster General. Cambridge, Massachusetts.

Map 53 x 118 cm. Scale ca 1:5,000,000. Mercator projection.

1964 Landforms of Mexico. 2nd ed., corrected. Prepared for the Geography Branch of the Office of Naval Research. Cambridge, Massachusetts.
Map 69 x 102 cm. Scale 1:3,000,000. The top of the "map" sheet includes a brief but good description of the physiographic provinces; the Sinaloa coast, the coast adjacent to the Sonoran Desert, and the deltas of the Yaqui, Mayo, and Fuerte Rivers are cited.

Ramirez, L. F., E. L. Elberg, and H. H. Helley
1962 Geographic map of the southeastern Rub' al Khali quadrangle, Kingdom of Saudi Arabia. U. S. Geological Survey, Miscellaneous Geologic Investigations, Map I-220 B.
Latitude 16° to 20°, longitude 51° to 54° E. Scale 1:500,000. Includes a portion of the Arabian Sea coast.

1963 Geologic map of the southeastern Rub' al Khali quadrangle, Kingdom of Saudi Arabia. U. S. Geological Survey Miscellaneous Geologic Investigations, Map I-220 A.
Latitude 16° to 20°, longitude 51° to 54° E. Scale 1:600,000. Includes a portion of the Arabian Sea coast.

Reid, J. L., R. A. Schwartzlose, and D. M. Brown
1963 Direct measurements of a small surface eddy off northern Baja California. Journal of Marine Research 21(3):205-218.
Discusses the measurement of the inshore sweep of surface currents off northern Baja California and their significance.

Reilly, F. A., ed.
1964 Guidebook to the geology and archeology of Egypt. Petroleum Exploration Society of Libya, 6th Annual Field Conference. 184 p.
Geology of the Suez area on pages 123-140.

Reparaz, G. de
1958 La zone aride du Perou. Geografiska Annaler 40(1):1-62.
An extensive study of the physical and biological geography of the arid coast, with a good bibliography.

Richards, H. G. and R. W. Fairbridge
1965 Annotated bibliography of Quaternary shorelines (1945-64). Academy of Natural Sciences, Philadelphia, Special Publication 6. 280 p.
This bibliography covers the world by countries and includes the desert areas. Extremely useful for the coverage of foreign literature.

Roden, G. I.
1964 Oceanographic aspects of Gulf of California. *In* T. H. van Andel and G. G. Shor, Jr., eds., Marine geology of the Gulf of California. American Association of Petroleum Geologists, Memoir 3:30-58.

Royal Society, London
1963 International Indian Ocean expedition, R. R. S. *Discovery,* Cruise 1 Report: South east Arabian upwelling region. 36 p.

1965 International Indian Ocean expedition, R. R. S. *Discovery,* Cruise 3 Report: Oceanographic work in the Western Indian Ocean, 15 February to 28 September 1964. 64 p.

Rusnak, G. A. and R. L. Fisher
1964 Structural history and evolution of Gulf of California. *In* T. H. van Andel and G. G. Shor, Jr., eds., Marine geology of the Gulf of California. American Association of Petroleum Geologists, Memoir 3:144-156.

Rusnak, G. A., R. L. Fisher, and F. P. Shepard
1964 Bathymetry and faults of Gulf of California. *In* T. H. van Andel and G. G. Shor, Jr., eds., Marine geology of the Gulf of California. American Association of Petroleum Geologists, Memoir 3:59-75.

Russell, R. J.
1964 Techniques of eustasy studies. Zeitschrift für Geomorphologie 8:25-42.

Russell, R. J. and W. G. McIntire
1965 Australian tidal flats. Louisiana State University, Baton Rouge, Coastal Studies Institute, Contribution 65-6. 48 p.
Includes the results of investigations of tidal flats and their sand supply near Port Hedland, West Australia.

A. Sahab Geographical and Drafting Institute
1962 Map of Kuwait and Basrah. New ed. Tehran, Iran.
Map 54 x 64.8 cm. Scale 1:500,000. Map shows mud flat marshes, stony and sandy areas, sand dunes, ridge cliffs, hills, and depressions.

Said, R.
1951 Organic origin of some calcareous sediments from the Red Sea. Science 113(2940):517-518.
Describes samples taken during the voyage of R. R. S. *Mabaheth* in 1934-35, from the northern Red Sea.

1958 Remarks on the geomorphology of the deltaic coastal plain between Rosetta and Port Said. Société de Géographie d'Egypte, Bulletin 31:115-125.
The shore line of this Egyptian plain is controlled by the balance between Nile sedimentation and marine erosion. The present coast appears to be in retreat. Past coastal advances have been due to the formation of successive offshore bars and infilled lagoons.

1962 The geology of Egypt. Elsevier Publishing Company, Amsterdam. 377 p. maps.
A monographic compilation of data on the geology of Egypt based on extensive field work and a review of the literature. The various parts deal with the general geology and structure of the region, the Arabo-Nubian massif, the stable shelf, the Gulf of Suez taphrogeosyncline, the unstable shelf, and mineral deposits.

Schott, G.
1951 Der Peru-strom. Erdkunde 5(4):316-319.
Discusses the periodic ocean inundations and storms which occur along the Peru coast, with some suggestions as to their cause.

Schwegler, E.
1944 Bemerkungen zum vorkommen von löss im libyschen und tunesischen gebiet. Neues Jahrbuch für Geologie und Paläontologie, Monatshefte 13(1):10-17.
Notes on the occurrence of loess deposits in the coastal zone of Libya and Tunisia.

1948 Vorgänge subärischer diagenese in küstendünensanden des ägyptischen mittelmeergebietes. Neues Jahrbuch für Mineralogie, Geologie und Paläontologie, Monatshefte, Abt. B(1/4):9-16.
Discusses indurated calcareous sands comprising the coastal dunes of Egypt.

Schweigger, E.
1943 Pesquería y oceanografía del Peru. Lima.

1947 El litoral Peruano. Editada por la Compañía Administradora de Guano, Lima.

Segerstrom, K.
1962a High marine terraces in the Coldera region of northern Chile. Geological Society of America, Special Paper 73:237-238. (Abstr.)
Discusses a broad terrace, partly cut in bedrock and partly filled or veneered with clastic deposits, extending along the Pacific coast of Coldera, Chile, for a distance of some 60 km, at varying altitudes up to 235 meters above present sea level.

1962b Deflated marine terrace as a source of dune chains, Atacama Province, Chile. U. S. Geological Survey, Professional Paper 450-C:91-93.
Fine-grained clastic sediments have been eroded from a marine terrace and redeposited in sand streams extending inland through wind gaps. The high terrace has been deflated to expose underlying bedrock, shell beds, and shingle beaches, locally forming undrained basins. The water table is exposed in the deepest depression.

1964 Quaternary geology of Chile: brief outline. Geological Society of America, Bulletin 75(3):157-170.

Sestini, J.
1965 Cenozoic stratigraphy and depositional history, Red Sea Coast, Sudan. American Association of Petroleum Geologists, Bulletin 49:1453-1472.

Shepard, F. P.
1948 Submarine geology. Harper and Brothers, New York. 338 p.

1950 Photography related to investigation of shore processes. *In* Symposium on information relative to uses of aerial photographs by geologists. Photogrammetric Engineering 16:756-769.
Uses of photography in the study of shore processes and tracing the history of shoreline development.

1963 Submarine geology, with chapters by D. L. Inman and E. D. Goldberg, 2nd ed. Harper and Row, New York. 557 p.
Chapter VI, Defining and Classifying Shorelines and Coasts. Chapter VII, Beaches and Related Shore Processes.

1964 Sea-floor valleys of Gulf of California. p. 157-192. *In* T. H. van Andel and G. G. Shor, Jr., eds., Marine geology of the Gulf of California. American Association of Petroleum Geologists, Memoir 3:157-192.
Discusses chiefly the canyons at the south tip of Baja California; also describes numerous canyons in the Gulf of California.

Shukri, N. M. and G. Phillip
1956 The geology of the Mediterranean coast between Rosetta and Bardia. Part III: Pleistocene sediments; mineral analysis. Institut d'Egypte, Bulletin 37(2):445-455.

Shukri, N. M., G. Phillip, and R. Said
1956 The geology of the Mediterranean coast between Rosetta and Bardia. Part II: Pleistocene sediments; geomorphology and microfacies. Institut d'Egypte, Bulletin 37(2):395-427.

Siddiqi, M. I.
1959 The geology and physiography of Karachi Coast. p. 1-6. *In* M. I. Siddiqi, Karachi. University of Karachi, Department of Geography.

Simpson, E. S. W.
1965 South African research in marine geology. South African Journal of Science 61(2):51-54.

Smith, D. D. *et al.*
1964 Submerged delta and off-shore valleys of the Orange River, South and South-West Africa. Geological Society of America, Special Paper 82: 188-189. (Abstr.)

Smith, G.- H.
1957 Physiographic diagram of South America. Geographical Press, Maplewood, New Jersey. 8 p.
Includes map 58 x 41 cm.

Snead, R. E.
1966 Physical geography reconnaissance: Las Bela Coastal Plain, West Pakistan. Louisiana State University Press, Coastal Studies ser. 13. 118 p.
Includes 21 maps and 60 photographs.

Soares de Carvalho, G.
1961 Algunas problemas dos terraços Quaternários do Litoral de Angola. Serviços de Geologia e Minas, Luanda, Boletim 2.

South Africa. Geological Survey
1955 Geological map of the Union of South Africa. Government Printer, Pretoria.
Colored map on 4 sheets 88 x 123 cm. Scale 1:1,000,000.

Spate, O. H. K.
1954 India and Pakistan, regional geography. Methuen and Company, London. 827 p.

Steineke, M. *et al.*
1958a Geology of the western Persian Gulf quadrangle, Kingdom of Saudi Arabia. U. S. Geological Survey, Miscellaneous Geologic Investigations, Map I-208 A.
Includes the coast along the western Persian Gulf north of Qatar. Latitude 24° to 28°, longitude 48° to 51° E. Scale 1:500,000.

1958b Geographic map of the western Persian Gulf quadrangle, Kingdom of Saudi Arabia. U. S. Geological Survey, Miscellaneous Geologic Investigations, Map I-208B.
Includes the coast along the western Persian Gulf north of Qatar. Latitude 24° to 28°, longitude 48° to 51° E. Scale 1:500,000.

Stewart, H. B., Jr.
1958 Sedimentary reflections of depositional environment in San Miguel Lagoon, Baja California, Mexico. American Association of Petroleum Geologists, Bulletin 42(11):2567-2618.
A study of the depositional environment of San Miguel Lagoon, Baja California, Mexico. Includes data on types of sediments, description of areas, lagoon waters, sediment transportation and distribution, foraminifera, calcium carbonate, and general geologic inferences about the nature of coastal lagoon deposits.

Stose, G. W.
1950 Geologic map of South America. Prepared under the direction of a committee of the Geological Society of America, in cooperation with the U. S. Geological Survey from maps contributed by government bureaus of South America countries and other sources. Geological Society of America, New York.
Map 155 x 112 cm on 2 sheets 87 x 120 cm. Approximate scale 1:5,000,000. Bipolar oblique conic conformal projection.

Strahler, A. N.
1963 Physical geography. 2nd ed. John Wiley & Sons, New York. 534 p.

Sugden, W.
1963a Some aspects of sedimentation in the Persian Gulf. Journal of Sedimentary Petrology 33(2):355-364.
Rapid surface water evaporation in the Persian Gulf induces precipitation of calcium carbonate. At the same time eolian sand and dust are deposited in the Gulf and mixed sediments result. In shallow water and on the beaches oolitization and other types of sand modification takes place including the formation of aragnoitic sheet limestones.

1963b The hydrology of the Persian Gulf and its significance in respect to evaporite deposition. American Journal of Science 261(8):741-755.
The hydrological regime of the Gulf is such that the evaporating surface water passes toward the coasts, sinks, and escapes from the Gulf by counterflow at lower levels, the highest salinities, both of surface and bottom water, being in the coastal areas.

Sujkowski, Z.
1932 The influence of desert on the deposits of the Red Sea. Geological Magazine 69:311-314.
A study of bottom sediments which shows the contribution of the desert to the Red Sea. Desertic clay and iron oxide, etc., is mixed with organic material.

Sverdrup, H. V.
1930 Some oceanographic results of the *Carnegie's* work in the Pacific — the Peruvian Current. American Geophysical Union, Transactions 11: 257-264.

Swartz, D. H. and D. D. Arden, Jr.
1960 Geologic history of Red Sea area. American Association of Petroleum Geologists, Bulletin 44(10):1621-1637.

Taft, W. H. and J. W. Harbaugh
1964 Modern carbonate sediments of southern Florida, Bahamas, and Espíritu Santo Island, Baja California; a comparison of their mineralogy and chemistry. Stanford University Publications, Geological Sciences 8(2). 133 p.
A good general discussion of a small area of the Baja California coast (east side).

Tamayo, J. L.
1962 Geografía general de México (Geografía física). 2nd ed. Instituto Mexicano de Investigaciones Económicas, México. 4 volumes.

Tanner, W. F.
1960 Bases for coastal classification. Southeastern Geology 2:13-22.

A preliminary examination of 14 coastal classification schemes leads to a list of 17 types of basic information on which such schemes can be constructed.

Tazieff, H.
1952 Une récente campagne océanographique dans la Mer Rouge. Société Belge de Géologie, Brussels, Bulletin 61(1):84-90.

A short note on the tectonics and coral reefs of the Red Sea.

Terry, R. D.
1955 Bibliography of marine geology and oceanography, California coast. California Division of Mines, Special Report 44. 131 p.

Covers sedimentative, submarine topography, beach erosion and its control, marine engineering problems, coastal sand dunes, marine geophysics, salt-water intrusion, and physical and chemical oceanography.

Thompson, R. W.
1965 Tidal flat sedimentation on the Colorado River Delta, northwestern Gulf of California. University of California, San Diego (unpublished Ph.D. dissertation). 245 p.

Torrico, R. and G. Secada
1942 Notas sobre exploración de la configuración del relieve submarino del litoral peruano en 1939. American Scientific Congress, 8th, Washington, 1940, Proceedings 4:463-465.

Bathymetric profiles start in waters usually over 50 feet and continue into deep waters.

Trewartha, G. T.
1954 An introduction to climate. 3rd ed. McGraw-Hill, New York. 402 p.

——— 1961 The Earth's problem climates. University of Wisconsin Press, Madison. 334 p.

Tricart, J.
1954 Une forme de relief climatique; les sabkhas. Revue de Géomorphologie Dynamique 5(3): 97-191.

Discusses the formation of sebkhas (seasonal saline lakes typical of subarid and semiarid regions) and related geomorphic features.

——— 1955 Aspects sedimentologiques du delta Senegal: Geologische Rundschau, Sonderdruck 43(2): 384-397.

The delta of the Senegal River is typical of large rivers draining a humid region and reaching the sea in an arid region. The development of the delta can be understood only in the light of the Quaternary history of the region, when arid periods (represented by dunes), alternated many times with humid periods (represented by red soils and pebble beds). Eustatic movements also played an important role. Rhythms of sedimentation, both in the geologic past and in the present, have been determined by alternation of rainy and dry seasons. The variations in the fluvial and deltaic, estuarine, and lagoonal sediment are discussed.

Ullah, A.
1953 Physiography and structure of S. W. Makran. Pakistan Geographical Review 9(1).

U. S. Air Force
Operational Navigation Charts (ONC). Aeronautical Chart and Information Center, St. Louis, Missouri:

G-1:
1964 Strait of Gibraltar. 4th ed., rev. 105.1 x 145.4 cm.
G-2:
1965 Strait of Sicily. 5th ed., rev. 105 x 145.5 cm.
G-3:
1964 Aegean Sea. 4th ed., rev. 105.4 x 145.8 cm.
G-4:
1963 Tigris-Euphrates Valley. 4th ed., rev. 105 x 145.1 cm.
H-1:
1965 Algeria, Canary Islands, Ifni, Mauritania, Morocco, Spanish Sahara. 105.3 x 145.5 cm.
H-3:
1967 Grand Erg Oriental. rev. ed. 105.2 x 145.4 cm.
H-4:
1967 Libyan Plateau. rev. ed. 105.2 x 145.4 cm.
H-5:
1960 Sinai Penincula. 2nd ed., rev., 105.2 x 145.4 cm.
H-6:
1959 Persian Gulf. 2nd ed. 105.2 x 145.4 cm.
H-7:
1964 Gulf of Oman. 3rd ed., rev. 105.1 x 145.3 cm.
H-8:
1965 Afghanistan, India, Pakistan. 2nd ed., rev. 105 x 145.2 cm.
H-22:
1965 Gulf of California. 2nd ed., rev. 105.3 x 145.3 cm.
H-23:
1964 Lower Rio Grande. 2nd ed. 104.6 x 145 cm.
J-1:
1964 Levrier Bay. 1st ed. 105 x 145.4 cm.
J-5:
1960 Nubian Desert. 1st ed., rev. 105.1 x 145.3 cm.
J-6:
1963 Red Sea. 2nd ed., rev. 105.3 x 145.5 cm.
J-7:
1960 Great Southern Desert. 1st ed. 105 x 145.3 cm.
J-8:
1965 India—Pakistan. 2nd ed., rev. 105.1 x 145.5 cm.
J-24:
1965 Mexico. 1st ed. 105.4 x 145.6 cm.
K-5:
1967 Ethiopia, French Somaliland, Somalia, Sudan, Yemen. rev. ed. 105.4 x 145.5 cm.
K-6:
1963 Gulf of Aden. 1st ed., rev. 105.5 x 145.5 cm.
N-25:
1964 Bolivia, Brazil, Chile, Ecuador, Peru. 105 x 145.4 cm.
P-26:
1965 Argentina, Bolivia, Chile, Paraguay, Peru. 105.2 x 145.6 cm.
Q-26:
1965 Atacama Desert. 105.3 x 145.4 cm.
R-24:
1965 Argentina, Brazil, Uruguay. 105.1 x 145.3 cm.
T-18:
1965 Argentina, Chile, Falkland Islands. 105.5 x 145.3 cm.

Scale 1:1,000,000. Lambert conformal conic projection.

U. S. Air Force
World Aeronautical Charts (WAC):
No. 404:
1964   Mohave Desert, United States—Mexico. Washington, D. C. 34th ed., rev. 56 x 73 cm.
No. 405:
1965   Gila River, United States—Mexico. Washington, D. C. 34th ed., rev. 56 x 73 cm.
No. 685:
1946   Cape Radressa, Socotra Island, Arabian Sea. Aeronautical Chart and Information Service, Washington, D. C. 55.6 x 73.4 cm.
No. 687:
1962   El Mandeb Strait, Red Sea—Gulf of Aden, 6th ed., rev. Aeronautical Chart and Information Center, St. Louis, Missouri. 55.6 x 73.1 cm.
No. 688:
1957   Mount Po's Dashan, Ethiopia—French Somaliland —Sudan. 4th ed., rev. Aeronautical Chart and Information Service, Washington, D. C. 55.7 x 73.4 cm.
No. 808:
1962   Cape El Cheil, Ethiopia—Somali Republic. 4th ed., rev. Aeronautical Chart and Information Center, St. Louis, Missouri. 55.7 x 73.2 cm.
No. 911:
1961   Giuba River, Ethiopia—Somali Republic. 5th ed., rev. Aeronautical Chart and Information Center, St. Louis, Missouri. 55.5 x 73.1 cm.
No. 931:
1961   Kilimanjaro, Kenya—Somali Republic—Tanganyika. 5th ed., rev. Aeronautical Chart and Information Center, St. Louis, Missouri. 55.6 x 73.3 cm.
No. 1011:
1946   Aguja Point, Ecuador—Peru. 8th ed., rev. Aeronautical Chart and Information Center, St. Louis, Missouri. 55.6 x 73.2 cm.
No. 1027:
1964   Lower Congo, Angola—Congo—Gabon—Republic of the Congo. 7th ed., rev. Aeronautical Chart and Information Center, St. Louis, Missouri. 55.7 x 73.2 cm.
No. 1057:
1964   Cuanza River, Angola—Congo (Leopoldville) 8th ed., rev. Aeronautical Chart and Information Center, St. Louis, Missouri. 55.7 x 73.2 cm.
No. 1150:
1961   Cape Santa Marta, Angola. 6th ed., rev. Aeronautical Chart and Information Center, St. Louis, Missouri. 55.5 x 73.1 cm.
No. 1179:
1951   Tigres Peninsula, Angola—Southwest Africa. 4th ed., rev. Aeronautical Chart and Information Service, Washington, D. C. 55.7 x 73.5 cm.
No. 1273:
1961   Pelican Point, Southwest Africa—Walvis Bay. 3rd ed., rev. Aeronautical Chart and Information Service, Washington, D. C. 55.7 x 73.5 cm.
No. 1302:
1961   Lüderitz Bay, Southwest Africa. 6th ed., rev. Aeronautical Chart and Information Service, Washington, D. C. 55.8 x 73.5 cm.
No. 1396:
1960   Orange River, Southwest Africa—Union of South Africa. 4th ed., rev. Aeronautical Chart and Information Center, St. Louis, Missouri. 55.7 x 73.3 cm.

No. 1422:
1951   Cape of Good Hope, Union of South Africa. 5th ed., rev. Aeronautical Chart and Information Service, Washington, D. C. 55.8 x 73.5 cm.
No. 1459:
1952   Great Australian Bight, Australia, 4th ed., rev. Aeronautical Chart and Information Center, St. Louis, Missouri. 55.6 x 73.4 cm.
No. 1460:
1948   Cape Arid, Western Australia, Australia. 3rd ed., rev. Aeronautical Chart and Information Service, Washington, D. C. 55.5 x 73.3 cm.
No. 1491:
1951   Blanca Bay, Argentina. 9th ed., rev. Aeronautical Chart and Information Service, Washington, D. C. 55.8 x 73.2 cm.
No. 1537:
1952   Valdes Peninsula, Argentina. 6th ed., rev. Aeronautical Chart and Information Service, Washington, D. C. 55.6 x 73.3 cm.
No. 1586:
1949   San Jorge Gulf, Argentina. 7th ed. Aeronautical Chart and Information Service, Washington, D. C. 55.7 x 73.2 cm.
Scale 1:1,000,000. Lambert conformal conic projection.

U. S. Army, Corps of Engineers, Beach Erosion Board
1961   Shore protection, planning and design. Rev. ed. Washington, D. C. Technical Report 392 p.
Later edition is published by U. S. Army Corps of Engineers Coastal Engineering Research Center.

U. S. Army, Corps of Engineers, Coastal Engineering Research Center
1964   Land against the sea. Washington, D. C. Miscellaneous Paper 4-64. 43 p.

U. S. Coast and Geodetic Survey
1965a Tide tables, high and low water predictions, west coast of North and South America including the Hawaiian Islands, 1965. Washington, D. C. 224 p.
Times and heights of high and low waters; data for Chile ports: p. 10-29, 164-166; Peru ports: p. 30-41, 166; west coast of Mexico: p. 66-69, 168.

———
1965b Tide tables; high and low water predictions, east coast of North and South America including Greenland, 1965. Washington, D. C. 289 p.
Times and heights of high and low waters; data for Argentina ports: p. 190-201, 245-247.

———
1965c Tide tables; high and low water predictions, central and western Pacific Ocean and Indian Ocean, 1965. Washington, D. C. 386 p.
Times and heights of high and low waters; data for Australian ports: p. 214-245, 346-347. Pakistan and Arabian Sea: p. 270-273, 348-349. Persian Gulf ports: p. 274-285, 350. Arabian ports: p. 286-289, 350. Suez, Red Sea, Egypt, Ethiopia (Eritrea), and Somalia: p. 290-293, 350-351.

———
1965d Tide tables; high and low water predictions, Europe and west coast of Africa, including the Mediterranean Sea, 1965. Washington, D. C. 210 p.
Times and heights of high and low waters; data for African ports: p. 14-33, 164-168.

U. S. Geological Survey
1963a Geologic map of the Arabian Peninsula. U. S.
Geological Survey, Miscellaneous Geologic Investigations, Map I-279 A.
Latitude about 12° to 32½° N, longitude about 34° to
60° E. Map 127 x 183 cm. Scale 1:2,000,000. Lambert
conformal conic projection. Bathymetric contours and
spot elevations in meters. Also shows coral reefs, coastal
silt deposits, sebkhas (sabkhahs), and coastal sand and
gravel deposits.

1963b Geographic map of the Arabian Peninsula. U. S.
Geological Survey, Miscellaneous Geologic Investigations, Map I-270 B-2.
Latitude about 12° to 32½° N, longitude about 34° to
60° E. Map 122 x 138 cm. Scale 1:2,000,000. Lambert
conformal conic projection. Bathymetric contours and
spot elevations in meters. Shows cultural features and
generalized relief; also coral reefs, sebkhas (sabkhahs),
coastal cultivated areas, coastal and offshore oil fields,
glossary of Arabic and Persian terms.

U. S. Naval Oceanographic Office
1944 Breakers and surf, principles in forecasting. H. O.
234.

1955 Instruction manual for oceanographic observations,
2nd ed. H. O. 607. 210 p.

U. S. Naval Oceanographic Office
Sailing Directions:
H. O. 24:
1965 South America. Vol. II: East and west coasts
between Rio de la Plata and Cabo Tres Montes,
including Falkland, South Georgia, and South
Sandwich. Islands. 5th ed., corrected. 417 p.
(formerly H. O. 173)

H. O. 25:
1964 South America. Vol. III: West coast between Gulf
of Panama and Cabo Tres Montes. 6th ed., corrected. 516 p. (formerly H. O. 174)

H. O. 26:
1965 West coasts of Mexico and Central America; the
U. S. border to Columbian border. 9th ed., corrected. 308 p. (formerly H. O. 84)

H. O. 50:
1964 Southwest coast of Africa; Cape Palmas to Cape
of Good Hope. 4th ed., corrected. 314 p. (formerly
H. O. 105)

H. O. 51:
1965 West coasts of Spain, Portugal, and northwest
Africa and off-lying islands; includes Azores,
Madeira, Canary and Cape Verde Islands, and
Africa southwest to Cape Palmas. 6th ed., cor-
rected. 410 p. (formerly H. O. 134)

H. O. 52:
1964 Mediterranean. Vol. I: Strait of Gibraltar, Spain,
Balearic Islands, and northern Africa to Ras
Agedir. 4th ed., corrected. 346 p. (formerly H. O.
151)

H. O. 55:
1965 Mediterranean. Vol. IV: Libya, Egypt, Israel,
Lebanon, Syria, and southern Turkey, including
islands of Cyprus, Rhodes, Karpathos, and Crete.
3rd ed., corrected. 280 p. (formerly H. O. 154)

H. O. 60:
1965 Southeast coast of Africa; Cape of Good Hope to
Ras Hafun. 4th ed., corrected. 268 p. (formerly
H. O. 156)

H. O. 61:
1965 Red Sea and Gulf of Aden; including Suez Canal,
Gulf of Suez, Africa north of Ras Hafun, Suqutra,
and Arabian coast eastward to Ra's al Hadd, 5th
ed. 375 p. (formerly H. O. 157)

H. O. 62:
1964 Persian Gulf; includes Gulf of Oman and northern
shore of Arabian Sea eastward to Ras Muari. 5th
ed,. corrected. 352 p. (formerly H. O. 158)

H. O. 74:
1964 North and west coasts of Australia; Cape York
to Cape Leeuwin. 3rd., corrected. 372 p. (formerly H. O. 170)

H. O. 77:
1965 South coast of Australia; Cape Leeuwin to Cape
Northumberland. 3rd ed., corrected. 243 p.
(formerly H. O. 167)

U. S. Naval Oceanographic Office
1963a United States of America nautical chart symbols
and abbreviations. Washington, D. C. Chart 1.
25 p.
Standard symbols and abbreviations approved for use on
nautical charts published by the U. S. A.

1963b World port index, 1963; locations and general
descriptions of maritime ports and shipping
places, with references to appropriate Sailing
Directions and charts, 3rd ed. H. O. 150. (formerly
950). 200 p.
Includes data for size and type of harbor; shelter afforded;
entrance restrictions; channel, anchorage, and wharf
depths; tides; pilotage; supplies; repairs; and drydock-
marine railway. Extremely useful for quick reference.

The list of publications that follows includes "Nautical
Charts," issued by the U. S. Navy Hydrographic Office (to
July 1962) and its successor the U. S. Naval Oceanographic
Office. They bear H. O. numbers (from 0619 to 6540),
and are arranged by that number in ascending order.

U. S. Navy Hydrographic Office
1958 Mexico—Golfo de California. Puerto Refugio to
Philips Point. 53rd ed., rev. Washington. H. O.
0619.
Map 63 x74 cm. Scale 1:625,670 at latitude 31° 00' N.
Mercator projection.

1963 Mexico—Golfo de California. Isla Carmen to
Puerto Refugio. 58th ed. Washington. H. O. 0620.
Map 71 x 88.5 cm. Scale 1:644,840. Mercator projection.

U. S. Navy Hydrographic Office
1963   Mexico—West Coast. Golfo de California southern part. 68th ed. Washington. H. O. 0621.
Map 73.5 x 119 cm. Scale 1:667,240. Mercator projection.

U. S. Naval Oceanographic Office
1964   North America. West Coasts of United States and Mexico. San Diego to Bahia San Quintín. 45th ed., rev. Washington. H. O. 1149.
Map 87 x 137 cm. Scale 1:290,000 at latitude 30° 15'. Mercator projection.

1966   South America—Cabo de San Francisco to Paita (Ecuador and Peru). 33rd ed., rev. Washington. H. O. 1177.
Map 72.39 x 94.62 cm. Scale 1:972,600 at latitudes 7° S to 1° 10' N. Mercator projection.

1963   South America. Coast of Peru. Paita to Pisco. 30th ed., rev. Washington. H. O. 1178.
Map 71 x 106.1 cm. Scale 1:962,050 at latitude 9° 00' S. Mercator projection.

1966   Mexico. Baja California. West Coast—Bahia de San Quintín to Isla Cedros. 30th ed., rev. Washington. H. O. 1193.
Map 92 x 120 cm. Scale 1:290,000 at latitude 30° 15'. Mercator projection.

U. S. Navy Hydrographic Office
1964   South America. Coasts of Peru and Chile. Pisco to Arica. 27th ed., rev. Washington. H. O. 1218.
Map 69.3 x 102.2 cm. Scale 1:036,450 at latitude 16°00'S. Mercator projection.

1963   South America. Chile. Arica to Caldera. 29th ed., rev. Washington. H. O. 1219.
Map 68 x 112.7 cm. Scale 1:899,160 at latitude 22° 40' S. Mercator projection.

U. S. Naval Oceanographic Office
1965   South America. Coast of Chile. Caldera to Valparaiso. 26th ed., rev. Washington. H. O. 1220.
Map 70.2 x 93.5 cm. Scale 1:844,150 at latitude 30°00'S. Mercator projection.

1963   Africa—west coast. Cap Cantin to Cabo Juby including the Madeira and Canary Islands. 28th ed., rev. Washington. H. O. 1246.
Map 84.5 x 122.2 cm. Scale 1:844,000 at latitude 30° 00'. Mercator projection.

1966   Mexico—West Coast of Lower California. Cedros (Cerros) Island to Abreojos Point. 27th ed., rev. Washington. H. O. 1310.
Map 84 x120 cm. Scale 1:290,740 at latitude 27° 30'. Mercator projection.

U. S. Navy Hydrographic Office
1945   Mexico—Baja California—West Coast. Punta Abreojos to Cabo San Lázaro. 27th ed., rev. Washington. H. O. 1493.
Map 89 x 117 cm. Scale 1:291,000 at latitude 25° 45'. Mercator projection.

1962   Indian Ocean. Africa—Saudi Arabia. Gulf of Aden and adjacent coasts. 15th ed., rev. Washington. H. O. 1586.
Map 83.8 x 130.8 cm. Scale 1:945,200 at latitutde 14° 0'. Mercator projection.

1962   Indian Ocean. Arabian Sea. Arabian Peninsula—southeast coast. Ra's Al Hadel to Ra's Sajir. 9th ed. Washington. H. O. 1587.
Map 83.5 x 124 cm. Scale 1:921,000 at latitude 19° 00'. Mercator Projection.

U. S. Naval Oceanographic Office
1963   Indian Ocean. Arabian Sea. Gulf of Oman and adjacent coasts from Karachi to Ra's Al Hadd. 9th ed. Washington. H. O. 1588.
Map 73.5 x 127.5 cm. Scale 1:883,200 at latitude 25° 00'. Mercator projection.

1965   Indian Ocean. Arabian Sea. India and Pakistan. Karachi to Bombay including the Gulfs of Kutch and Cambay. 7th ed., rev. Washington. H. O. 1589.
Map 79.8 x 105.4 cm. Scale 1:903,460 at latitude 22° 00'. Mercator projection.

U. S. Navy Hydrographic Office
1964   South coast of Africa. Algoa Bay to Capetown. 1st ed., rev. Washington. H. O. 1601.
Map 80.9x110.6 cm. Scale 1:798, 688 at latitude 35°00'S. Mercator projection.

1963   East coast of Africa. Giuba River to Zanzibar. 5th ed., rev. Washington. H. O. 1606.
Map 65.1 x 84 cm. Scale 1:971,600 at latitude 3° 30' S. Mercator projection.

U. S. Naval Oceanographic Office
1966   Mexico—Baja California Southern Part. Magdalena Bay to La Paz. 24th ed., rev. Washington. H. O. 1664.
Map 96 x132 cm. Scale 1:290,610 at latitude 23° 45'. Mercator projection.

U. S. Navy Hydrographic Office
1932   South America. Argentina. Nuevo Gulf. 2nd ed. Washington. H. O. 2078.
Map 70.9 x 92.1 cm. Scale 1:99,978. Mercator projection.

1960   South America. Argentina, Puerto Santa Cruz. 7th ed., rev. Washington. H. O. 2104.
Map 68.3 x 78.3 cm. Scale 1:50,000. Mercator projection.

1961   Northwest coast of Africa and southern part of Spain and Portugal. 12th ed., rev. Washington. H. O. 2195.
Map 78.6 x 102.6 cm. Scale 1:798,690 at latitude 35° 00'. Mercator projection.

U. S. Naval Oceanographic Office
1964   Africa—west coast. Morocco—Spanish Sahara—Mauritania. Cabo Juby to Baíe de Lévrier, including the Canary Islands. 8th ed., rev. Washington. H. O. 2196.
Map 77 x 109 cm. Scale 1:883,200 at latitude 25° 00'. Mercator projection.

U. S. Navy Hydrographic Office
1965   Africa—west coast. Lévrier Bay to Cape Verde, including Cape Verde Islands. 5th ed., rev. Washington. H. O. 2197.
Map 79.8 x 114 cm. Scale 1:926,562 at latitude 18° 00'. Mercator projection.

U. S. Naval Oceanographic Office
1963   Africa—west coast. Cap Lopez to Luanda. 7th ed. Washington. H. O. 2203.
Map 83.3 x 102.9 cm. Scale 1:970,000 at latitude 5° 00' S. Mercator projection.

U. S. Navy Hydrographic Office
1963 Africa—west coast. Cabo Lombo to Cape Fria, 6th ed., rev. Washington. H. O. 2204.
Map 71 x 116.7 cm. Scale 1:949,134 at latitude 13° 00' S. Mercator projection.

U. S. Naval Oceanographic Office
1964 Africa—west coast. Cape Fria to Lüderitz Bay. 6th ed. Washington. H. O. 2205.
Map 82.1 x 112.9 cm. Scale 1:903,460 at latitude 22°00'S. Mercator projection.

U. S. Navy Hydrographic Office
1964 Africa—west coast. Lüderitz Bay to Cape of Good Hope. 7th ed., rev. Washington. H. O. 2206.
Map 82 x 128.3 cm. Scale 1:835,600 at latitude 31°00'S. Mercator projection.

1959 Africa—west coast. Morocco. 1st ed., rev. Washington. H. O. 2238.
Map 67.6 x 96.8 cm. Scale 1:12,000. Mercator projection. (A) Entrance to Oued Sebou; (B) Oued Sebou [continuation to Kénitra (Port-Lyautey)].

U. S. Naval Oceanographic Office
1965 Africa. Plans on the west coast of Morocco. 8th ed., rev. Washington, H. O. 2239.
Map 66 x 117.5 cm. Scale: Asilah, 1:9990; Baie de Tafelney, 1:24,970; Baie Imsouane, 1:24,990; Larache, 1:9930; Rabat and Salé, 1:9970.

U. S. Navy Hydrographic Office
1962 Africa—southwest coast. Union of South Africa. Walvisbaai. 6th ed., rev. Washington. H. O. 2267.
Map 73.2 x 99.2 cm. Scale 1:25,000. Mercator projection. Local Datum.

1963 Chile. Punta Poroto to Punta Lengua de Vaca. 6th ed., rev. Washington. H. O. 2487.
Map 61.5 x 97 cm. Scale 1:100,000 at latitude 30° 00' S. Mercator projection. (Chart of Bahia Tongoy cancelled.)

U. S. Naval Oceanographic Office
1965 Red Sea. Suez to the Brothers, including Gulf of Aqaba. 4th ed., rev. Washington. H. O. 2812.
Map 76.7 x 94 cm. Scale 1:645,430 at latitude 28° 00'. Mercator projection.

U. S. Navy Hydrographic Office
1962 Red Sea. The Brothers to Jezair Siyal. 5th ed., rev. Washington. H. O. 2813.
Map 14 x 98.8 cm. Scale 1:667,680 at latitude 24° 00'. Mercator projection.

1964 Red Sea. Siyal Islands to Masamirit Islet. 5th ed., rev. Washington. H. O. 2814.
Map 73.3 x 101.5 cm. Scale 1:686,650 at latitude 20° 00'. Mercator projection.

1962 Red Sea. Sheet IV. Masamirit Islet to Zubair Islands. 8th ed., rev. Washington. H. O. 2815.
Map 76 x 95 cm. Scale 1:698,740 at latitude 17° 00'. Mercator projection.

1962 Red Sea and Gulf of Aden. Zubair Islands to Aden. 5th ed., rev. Washington. H. O. 2816.
Map 81.2 x 96.4 cm. Scale 1:711,850 at latitude 13° 00'. Mercator projection.

1964 Pakistan—India. West coast. Ras Muari to Lushington Shoal. 1st ed., rev. Washington. H. O. 2844.
Map 82.8 x 112.9 cm. Scale 1:300,000 at latitude 23° 40'. Mercator projection..

1947 Australia — northwest coast. Bedout Island to Cape Leveque. 2nd ed. Washington. H. O. 3420.
Chart 66.5 x 101.2 cm. Scale 1:687,730 at latitude 18°00'S. Mercator projection. Plans: (A) King's sound — southern portion—scale 1:494,730 at latitude 17° 00' S. (B) Lagrange Bay—scale 1:145,980 at latitude 18° 40' S. (C) Beagle Bay—scale 1:72,290 at latitude 16° 54' S.

1965 Australia—northwest coast. Cape Cuvier to Bedout Island. 2nd ed., rev. Washington. H. O. 3421.
Chart 82.2 x 100 cm. Scale 1:666,860 at latitude 22° 47' S. Mercator projection. Plans: (A) Port Robinson—scale 1:48,490. (B) Port Walcott—scale 1:54,160.

1948 Australia—west coast. Champion Bay to Cape Cuvier, including Shark Bay. 2nd ed. Washington. H. O. 3422.
Chart 66.7 x 100 cm. Scale 1:647,360 at latitude 26°30'S. Plans: Port Gregory—scale 1:20,600.

1948 Australia—south coast. The head of The Great Australian Bight to Doubtful Island Bay. 2nd ed. Washington. H. O. 3425.
Chart 80.8 x 101 cm. Scale 1:609,900 at latitude 30°00'S. Mercator projection.

1965 Australia—south coast. Cape Catastrophe to the head of the Great Australian Bight. 2nd ed., rev. Washington. H. O. 3426.
Chart 85.7 x 103 cm. Scale 1:606,900 at latitude 33°00'S. Mercator projection. Plans: (A) Venus Bay — Scale 1:35,810. (B) Fowler's Bay—Port Eyre—scale 1:146,090 at latitude 32° 15' S. (D) Streaky Bay—scale 1:146,500 at latitude 32° 40' S. (E) Coffin Bay—scale 1:143,370 at latitude 34° 30' S. (F) Waterloo Bay—scale 1:28,630

1947 Australia—west coast. Shark Bay, 2nd ed. Washington. H. O. 3436.
Chart 82.7 x 100 cm. Scale 1:265,700 at latitude 25°30'S. Mercator projection Plans: (A) Gascoyne Road — scale 1:50,180. (B) South Passage—Outer Bar—scale 1:36,490. (C) South Passage—Inner Bar—scale 1:36,490. (D) Naturaliste Channel—Turtle Bay—scale 1:71,980.

1965 Asia. Persian Gulf. Northern part. 2nd ed., rev. Washington. H. O. 3639.
Map 73.1 x 117 cm. Scale 1:350,000 at latitude 26° 00'. Mercator projection. Nahrwan Datum.

1964 Asia. Persian Gulf—Saudi Arabia. Approaches to Ra's Al Tannurah. 4th ed., rev. Washington. H. O. 3641.
Map 68.7 x 100.5 cm. Scale 1:150,000 at latitude 27° 00'. Mercator projection. Nahrwan Datum.

1964 Asia. Persian Gulf. Arabian Peninsula — east coast. Ra's Al Tannurah to Ra's Laffan including Al Bahrayn. 3rd ed., rev. Washington. H. O. 3642.
Map 73.1 x 125.3 cm. Scale 1:150,000 at latitude 26° 15'. Mercator projection. Nahrwan Datum. Also: approaches to Al Khoban—scale 1:50,000.

U. S. Navy Hydrographic Office
1956   Asia. Persian Gulf. 2nd ed., rev. Washington. H. O. 3647.
Map 83 x 110.8 cm. Scale 1:1,00,000 at latitude 27° 00'. Mercator projection. Nahrwan Datum.

U. S. Naval Oceanographic Office
1965   Asia. Persian Gulf. Eastern part. 2nd ed., rev. Washington. H. O. 3648.
Map 73.8 x 130 cm. Scale 1:350,000 at latitude 26° 00'. Mercator projection. Nahrwan Datum.

U. S. Navy Hydrographic Office
1964   Asia. Persian Gulf. North-central part. 1st ed., rev. Washington. H. O. 3653.
Map 80.2 x 130 cm. Scale 1:350,000 at latitude 26° 00'. Mercator projection. Nahrwan Datum.

1963   Asia. Persian Gulf. Ra's Al Buraisha to Al Fuhayhil. 4th ed., rev. Washington. H. O. 3654.
Map 70.8 x 94.5 cm. Scale 1:100,000. Transverse Mercator projection.

1963   Indian Ocean. Arabian Sea—Gulf of Oman. Plans of the coast of Pakistan and Iran. 3rd ed., rev. Washington. H. O. 3658.
Map 71.8 x 91.6 cm. Mercator projection. (A) Iran: Khalij—E—Jack (Jask Bay)—scale 1:50,000. (B) Iran: Khow—E—Rapch—scale 1:25,000. (C) Iran: Khalij—E—Chah—E—Bahar—scale 1:150,000. (D) Pakistan: Gwadar Head—scale 1:150,000. (E) Iran—Pakistan: Govatar Bay—scale 1:150,000. (F) Pakistan: Sonmiani Harbor—scale 1:100,000. (G) Pakistan: Ormara Demi Zarr (East Bay)—scale 1:200,000.

1965   Asia. Persian Gulf. Central part. 2nd ed., rev. Washington. H. O. 3660.
Map 84 x 130.7 cm. Scale 1:350,000 at latitude 26° 00'. Mercator projection. Nahrwan Datum.

U. S. Naval Oceanographic Office
1964   Arabian Peninsula. Persian Gulf. Ra's Al Matbakh to Ash Shariqah. 3nd ed., rev. Washington. H. O. 3661.
Map 67.7 x 123.6 cm. Scale 1:350,000 at latitude 26° 00'. Mercator projection.

U. S. Navy Hydrographic Office
1965   Asia. Persian Gulf. Arabian Peninsula—east coast. Al Fuhayhil to Ra's Bard Halq. 2nd ed., rev. Washington. H. O. 3685.
Map 72.5 x 100 cm. Scale 1:100,000. Transverse Mercator projection.

U. S. Naval Oceanographic Office
1965   Africa. Morocco—west coast. Rade De Safi to Cap Rhir. 6th ed. Washington. H. O. 3775.
Map 83 x 129.3 cm. Scale 1:150,000 at latitude 33° 00'. Mercator projection. European Datum.

1965   Africa. Morocco—northwest coast. Rabat and Salé to Cap Blanc. 4th ed. Washington. H. O. 3776.
Map 84.3 x 129.8 cm. Scale 1:150,000 at latitude 33° 00'. Mercator projection. European Datum. El Jadida — scale 1:20,000.

U. S. Navy Hydrographic Office
1962   Africa—east coast. Somalia. Obbia to Chisimaio. 1st ed., rev. Washington. H. O. 3881.
Map 81.8 x 109 cm. Scale 1:973,000 at latitude 2° 30'. Mercator projection..

1950   Africa—east coast. Italian Somaliland. Ras Hafun to Obbia. Washington. H. O. 3882.
Map 71.2 x 110.7 cm. Scale 1:964,515 at latitude 8° 00. Mercator projection. (A) Anchorage of Eil Marina—scale 1:30,000. (B) Anchorage of Ras Illigh — scale 1:50,000.

1918   South America. Argentina. Cape Tres Puntas to Oso Marino Bay. Washington H. O. 3908.
Map 65 x 89 cm. Scale 1:145,906 at latitude 47° 30' S. Mercator projection. Cape Blanco anchorage — scale 1:7,534.

1938   South America. Argentina. Comodoro Rivadavia to Caleta Cordova. 3rd ed. Washington. H. O. 3912.
Map 69 x 87 cm. Scale 1:25,000. Mercator projection.

U. S. Navy Hydrographic Office
1965   South America. Argentina. Port Gallegos. 3rd ed., rev. Washington. H. O. 3913.
Map 72 x 95.8 cm. Scale 1:41,721. Mercator projection. Port Gallegos anchorage—scale 1:20,861.

1962   Mediterranean Sea. Sur to El 'Arîsh. 5th ed., rev. Washington. H. O. 3974.
Map 69 x 99.3 cm. Scale 1:247,100 at latitude 32° 30'. Mercator projection.

U. S. Naval Oceanographic Office
1964   Mediterranean Sea. Egypt. Damietta to El 'Arîsh. 7th ed., rev. Washington. H. O. 3975.
Map 62.3 x 93.7 cm. Scale 1:249,355. Mercator projection.

U. S. Navy Hydrographic Office
1965   Mediterranean Sea. Egypt. Alexandria (El Iskandariya) to Port Said (Bor Sa'id). 6th ed., rev. Washington. H. O. 3976.
Map 65.8 x 118 cm. Scale 1:235,410. Mercator projection.

1951   Mediterranean Sea. Egypt. Matruh to Alexandria. 8th ed. Washington. H. O. 3977.
Map 69 x 110.5 cm. Scale 1:250,680 at latitude 31° 00'. Mercator projection..

1961   Mediterranean Sea. Tunisia. Mahdia to Ra's El Machbez. 3rd ed., rev. Washington. H. O. 3980.
Map 80 x 121 cm. Scale 1:241,500 at latitude 34° 20'. Mercator projection.

1963   Mediterranean Sea. Tunisia. Ras Engela to Mahdia. 6th ed., rev. Washington. H. O. 3981.
Map 75.5 x 121.5 cm. Scale 1:234,640 at latitude 36° 40'. Mercator projection.

1938   Mediterranean Sea. Libya and Egypt. Ras Azzáz to Marsa Matrûh. Washington. H. O. 4290.
Map 71.6 x 108.7 cm. Scale 1:248,472 at latitude 31° 50'. Mercator projection. (A) Porto Bardia (Marsa Burdi Suleiman)—scale 1:20,000. (B) Bay of Es Sollum — scale 1:35,000.

1965   Mediterranean Sea. Libya. Ra's El Hilal to Ra's Azzáz. 2nd ed., rev. Washington. H. O. 4291.
Map 69.8 x 120 cm. Scale 1:246,450 at latitude 32° 35'. Mercator projection. (A) cancelled; (B) Baia Di Tobruch, scale 1:30,000; (C) cancelled.

U. S. Navy Hydrographic Office
1964 Mediterranean Sea, Libya. Benghazi to Ra's Al Hilal. 1st ed., rev. Washington. H. O. 4292.
Map 72.3 x 110.7 cm. Scale 1:249,300 at latitude 32° 38'. Mercator projection. Port of Benghazi—scale 1:20,00.

U. S. Naval Oceanographic Office
1963 Mediterranean Sea. Libya. Sirte to Tolemaide. 1st ed., rev. Washington. H. O. 4293.
Map 64.6 x 97.2 cm. Scale 1:513,540. Mercator projection. (A) El Aghéila—scale 1:50,860. (B) Ez Zuetina—scale 1:51,110. (C) El Brega—scale 1:50,180.

U. S. Navy Hydrographic Office
1963 Mediterranean Sea. Libya. Ra's Ajdir to Surt. 1st ed., rev. Washington. H. O. 4294.
Map 65.3 x 97 cm. Scale 1:511,650 at latitude 32° 00'. Mercator projection. (A) Zuwarah Anchorage — scale 1:25,470. (B) Marsá Zuwagháh—scale 1:25,320. (C) Al Khums Anchorage—scale 1:12,750. (D) Misratah Anchorage — scale 1:25,500. (E) Al Bu'ayrat — scale 1:50,960. (F) Surt—scale 1:12,780.

———
1963 South America. Argentina. Bahia Blanca to Golfo Nuevo. 1st ed., rev. Washington. H. O. 5282.

———
1960 Argentina—east coast. Golfo Nuevo to Puerto San Julian. 1st ed., rev. Washington. H. O. 5283.
Map 76.7x122 cm. Scale 1:677,740 at latitude 46°00'S. Mercator projection.

———
1964 South America. East coast of Argentina. Puerto San Julian to Magellan Strait with part of Falkland Islands. 1st ed., rev. Washington. H. O. 5284.
Map 82.2x116.8cm. Scale 1:611,970 at latitude 51°00'S. Mercator projection.

———
1926 South America. Argentina. Golfo San Jose. Washington. H. O. 5399.
Map 71.5 x 96.8. Scale 1:80,000. Mercator projection. Plans: Fondeadero Sarmiento — scale 1:40,000; Fondeadero San Roman—scale 1:25,000; Boca del Golfo—scale 1:20,000; Fondeadero Pueyrredon—scale 1:30,000; Fondeadero la Argentina—scale 1:30,000.

———
1961 Africa—west coast. Ports on the coast of Angola. 1st ed., rev. Washington. H. O. 6276.
Map 67 x 69.5 cm. Mercator projection. (A) Pôrto do Lobito—scale 1:20,000. (B) Pôrto Amboím — scale 1:30,000. (C) Pôrto de Luanda—scale 1:30,000. (D) Pôrto de Baia Farta—scale 1:20,000.

———
1947 Africa—west coast. Ports on the coast of Angola. Washington. H. O. 6277.
Map 55.9 x 74.4 cm. Mercator projection. (A) Baía de Benguela—scale 1:30,000. (B) Pôrto do Cuío—scale 1:20,000. (C) Pôrto de Baía Dos Elefantes — scale 1:20,000.

———
1947 Africa—west coast. Ports and bays on the coast of Angola. Washington. H. O. 6279.
Map 65.6 x 80.4 cm. Mercator projection. (A) Pôrto de Mossâmedes—scale 1:30,000. (B) Baía de Santa Maria—scale 1:15,000. (C) Pôrto Alexandre—scale 1:30,000. (D) Baía Das Moscas (Baba)—scale 1:15,000.

———
1962 Asia. Persian Gulf. Saudi Arabia. Bandar Mish'Ab to Jazirat Abu 'Ali. 1st ed., rev. Washington. H. O. 6301.
Map 83.5 x 128.3 cm. Scale 1:125,000 at latitude 27° 45'. Mercator projection. Nahrwan Datum.

———
1965 South America. Argentina. Approaches to Bahia Blanca. 1st ed., rev. Washington. H. O. 6540.
Map 68.7x88.5 cm. Scale 1:100,280 at latitude 39°10'S. Mercator projection.

U. S. Navy / U. S. Air Force
1965a Flight information publication, terminal (seaplane): United States / Caribbean. U. S. Naval Oceanographic Office, Washington, D. C. v.p.
Contains approach and landing charts and text data for seaplanes. Anchorage data include depth, tidal range, nature of bottom, beach, currents, sea and swell, and shelter. Data for Guaymas, Mazatlán, and Puerto La Paz, Mexico, are included.

———
1965b Flight information publication, terminal (seaplane): South America, U. S. Naval Oceanographic Office, Washington, D.C. v.p.
Contains approach and landing charts and text data for seaplanes. Anchorage data include depth, tidal range, nature of bottom, beach, currents, sea and swell, and shelter. Data for Argentina, Chile, and Peru.

———
1965c Flight information publication, terminal (seaplane) Africa—India. U. S. Naval Oceanographic Office, Washington, D. C. v.p.
Contains approach and landing charts and text data for seaplanes. Anchorage data include depth, tidal range, nature of bottom, beach, currents, sea and swell, and shelter. Data for Spanish Sahara, South West Africa, South Africa, Somalia, Sudan, Arabian Peninsula, and West Pakistan.

Valentin, H.
1952 Die küsten der erde; beiträge zur allgemeinen und regionalen küstenmorphlogie. Petermanns Geographische Mitteilungen, Ergänzungsheft 246. 118 p., 9 figs., 2 map pls.
Includes extensive bibliography. Map scale 1:50,000,000; (pl. 1, present coastal configuration of the Earth; pl. 2, present coastal processes of the Earth.)

Vesey-Fitzgerald, D. F.
1955 Vegetation of the Red Sea coast south of Jedda, Saudi Arabia. Journal of Ecology 43:477-489.
Describes the coastal area south of the border of Yemen; excellent photographs.

———
1957 The vegetation of the Red Sea coast north of Jedda, Saudi Arabia. Journal of Ecology 45: 547-562.
Contains a good description of this area, beach and foreshore.

Wagner, P. A., H. Merensky, and S. H. Haughton
1929 Diamond deposits on coast of Little Namaqualand. Geological Society of South Africa, Transactions 31:1-43.

El Wakeel, S. K.
1964   Recent bottom sediments from the neighborhood of Alexandria, Egypt. Marine Geology 2(1/2): 137-46.
Discussion of sediments from 3 basins in the area. Mechanical, mineralogical, and chemical analysis. Areas involved are: Eastern Harbour, Lake Maryut and Nouzha Hydrodrome.

Walton, W. R.
1955   Ecology of living benthonic foraminifera, Todos Santos Bay, Baja California. Journal of Paleontology 29(6):952-1018..
A study of the ecology of Todos Santos Bay, Baja California, Mexico, based on data compiled from samples of sediments, salinity measurements, temperature observations, and faunal assemblages.

Wellington, J. H.
1955   Southern Africa, a geographical study. Vol. I: Physical Geography. University Press, Cambridge. 528 p.

Wells, A. J.
1962   Recent dolomite in the Persian Gulf. Nature 194(4825):274-275.
Carbonate sediments of the intertidal zone in saline lagoons of the Qatar peninsula contain aragonite (up to 95%) in the lower parts of tidal flats and dolomite (generally about 60%) and gypsum on the upper flats. The dolomite and gypsum have apparently been concentrated by evaporation from sea water remaining in the zone between diurnal and spring high tides; the extent to which the dolomite may be of primary origin or a penecontemporaneous replacement of preexisting carbonate has not been established.

Wiebe, K. H.
1965   Ground water in the vicinity of Dubai, Trucial States, Arabian Gulf. Engineering Geology 2(1): 1-6.
The Trucial State of Dubai (or Dubayy) is located on the southeastern coast of the Persian Gulf. The area is characterized by tidal flats and longitudinal sand dunes separated by deflation valleys, and has an average annual rainfall of about 4 inches.

Wiegel, R. L.
1953   Waves, tides, currents, and beaches—glossary of terms and list of standard symbols. Engineering Foundation. Council on Wave Research, Berkeley, California. 113 p.

Wiegel, R. L. ed.
1964   Oceanographical engineering. Prentice Hall, Inc., Englewood Cliffs, New Jersey. 511 p.
Chapter 1: Waves, tides, currents, shores. Chapter 6: Beaches, waves, structures. Chapter 12: Tides, sea-level changes. Chapter 14: Shore and shore processes.

Willis, R. P.
1967   Geology of the Arabian Peninsula: Bahrain. U. S. Geological Survey, Professional Paper 560-E:1-4.
Outlines the geology of the Sheikdom of Bahrain, a group of islands between the Qatar Peninsula and Saudi Arabia. The geology is shown on U. S. Geological Survey, Miscellaneous Geologic Investigations, Map I-270A (1963).

Wilson, I. F.
1949   Buried topography, initial structures, and sedimentation in Santa Rosalia area, Baja California, Mexico. American Association of Petroleum Geologists, Bulletin 32(9):1762-1807.
Discusses the geologic history of the west side of the Gulf of California near Santa Rosalia. Includes structural, stratigraphic and paleographic data.

Wilson, T. A.
1965   Offshore mining paves the way to ocean mineral wealth. Engineering and Mining Journal 166(6): 124-132.

Wiseman, J. D. H. and R. B. S. Sewell
1937   The floor of the Arabian Sea. Geological Magazine 74:219-230.
Discusses the character of the coastal regions surrounding the Arabian Sea and their relation to offshore features.

Wisser, E.
1954   Geology and ore deposits of Baja California, Mexico. Economic Geology 49(1):44-76.
A study of the geography, geomorphology, geologic history, and tectonics of Baja California with particular attention paid to its primary mineral deposits.

Wooster, W. S. and M. Gilmartin
1961   The Peru-Chile undercurrent. Journal of Marine Research 19(3):97-112.
Underlying the Peru Current at depths of several hundred meters is a southward-moving undercurrent. Speed, salinity, temperature, and oxygen content have been measured.

Wurm, A.
1951   Beobachtungen in der wüste nordchiles. Natur und Volk 81(10):239-245.
A brief account of the physiographic and other effects of the extremely arid climate of the Atacama desert, north of Chile, and the occurrence of raised terraces and other evidence of Quaternary crustal movements along the coast.

Zeil, W.
1964   Geologie van Chile. Gebrüder Borntrager, Berlin. 233 p.

A GENERAL SUMMARY OF THE STATE OF RESEARCH ON

GROUND - WATER HYDROLOGY
OF DESERT ENVIRONMENTS

EUGENE S. SIMPSON
Committee on Hydrology
and Water Resources
The University of Arizona

INTRODUCTION

1. History and Evolution of Concepts

The art of well digging is an ancient one, and perhaps just as ancient is speculation concerning the nature and origin of underground water. The ancient Greeks, realizing that springs and wells must somehow be replenished, postulated that sea water entered holes in the sea floor and thence flowed to the land surface via underground caverns or spongelike openings, becoming purified en route. This view was supported by the early Christian theologians. A formulation of the essential idea of the hydrologic cycle is given in Plato's *Critias,* but was thereafter apparently ignored and forgotten (Krynine, 1960). Another Greek theory held that the atmosphere penetrated into underground caverns and was there condensed to water (Meinzer, 1934). The sea-water theory correctly stated that fresh water was derived from the sea, but the mechanisms of purification and transfer were in error. The condensation theory, in one or another modification, persisted into modern times because of a widespread belief that the land surface was too impervious to permit the penetration of rainfall. As recently as 1921 this theory was supported in the technical literature (Ototzky, 1921).

The modern theory of the origin of ground water states that all potable ground water is replenished by rain and melted snow infiltrating into the ground. An early statement of this theory was made by a Roman architect, Marcus Vitruvius, who lived about the time of Christ. After a long hiatus, and apparently independently of Vitruvius, the infiltration theory was restated by Bernard Palissy in 1580 (Palissy, 1957). In the following century Mariotte (1717) demonstrated that rain water infiltrates into the ground and laid the foundation of much modern theory in ground-water hydrology. Since then the evidence in favor of infiltration overcame the combined weight of Greek thought and Christian doctrine, and now it is universally accepted by the scientific community. Hence we may say with confidence that with only insignificant exceptions all potable water in desert aquifers, as well as elsewhere, originally fell as rain or snow sometime in the past. In the case of desert aquifers this past may have been as much as 10,000 or more years ago.

The development of the concept of infiltration illustrates both the mystery that surrounded the study of subsurface waters and the recency of its emergence as a scientific discipline. In the United States the first appropriation by Congress for "the investigation of underground currents and artesian wells" came in 1895 (Follansbee, 1939, p. 93), probably as a result of a drought then prevailing in the western plains. The early investigations were performed almost exclusively by geologists. The first four decades of this century saw the flowering, in both a scientific and an organizational sense, of the study of subsurface waters, largely within the U. S. Geological Survey under the leadership of O. E. Meinzer. During this period the United States led the world in the development of the science. Meinzer is regarded by many as the "father" of modern ground-water hydrology (Hackett, 1964) but he himself gives credit to Mariotte (1620-1684) for being its founder (Meinzer, 1934, p. 12).

In spite of increased understanding, the mystery and importance of subsurface water continues to attract multitudes of nonscientific practitioners in the art of water finding. Dowsers and water-witches could be found in all countries from about the Middle Ages to the present (Vogt and Hyman, 1959; Ellis, 1917, and bibliography therein), and they probably are more active now than ever before. The writer, as a result of his experience in ground-water investigations and of his contacts with dowsers of all kinds, came to the conclusion that neither quality of mind nor of educational background will necessarily prevent a man from becoming a dowser or a believer. He might be anyone from an illiterate farmer to the chief engineer of a municipal water supply. A probable exception is the academically trained specialist in ground-water hydrology; no such person to the writer's knowledge is a believer in dowsing.

2. Scope of the Field

It is useful to discuss the scope (and the various names) of the science of ground-water hydrology. Subsurface water is all-inclusive, referring to all water in whatever state (ice, liquid, vapor) occurring beneath the land surface. Ground water is that portion of subsurface water occurring within a fully saturated confined aquifer or beneath the water table, and the water may be approximately defined as the upper surface of the zone of saturation (see Davis and DeWiest, 1966, p. 41, for a more precise definition). Water yielded to wells or springs comes from ground water, although ground water also exists in formations whose permeability is too low to yield water economically. The science of ground-water hydrology concerns itself with the physical and chemical properties of subsurface water, its laws of motion, the nature of the geological environment through which it moves, and the methods of its recovery and utilization. The main emphasis of the science is on *ground water,* its laws of motion, etc., but to the degree that water in the (agricultural) soil horizon, in the unsaturated zone above the water table, and in surface lakes and streams affects the movement and properties of ground water, these matters also are studied. An alternative definition might be: ground-water hydrology is the science that studies the physical and chemical properties of ground water, its laws of motion, the nature of the geological environment through which it moves, the methods of its recovery and utilization, and the interfaces that form its boundaries.

Various Names

The science encompassed by the above definition also has been variously called hydrology, geohydrology, hydrogeology and ground-water geology (Meinzer, 1942, pp. 3-4; DeWiest, 1965, pp. 1-2; Kazmann, 1965, p. 130; Davis and DeWiest, 1966, p. vii). Davis and DeWiest propose to use the term "geohydrology" when the fluid-flow aspects of ground water are emphasized, and "hydrogeology" when the geologic aspects are emphasized. Kazmann suggests that the term "geohydrology" be applied to the study of ground water within the hydrologic cycle, and "hydrogeology" be restricted to the study of ground waters (mostly brines) that are isolated by geologic processes from the hydrologic cycle. In 1938 the International Association of Scientific Hydrology recognized the term "hydrology" to apply to the study of water that occurs below the land surface (*eaux souterraines*), but Meinzer believed this to be too restrictive a use and proposed instead the term "geohydrology." European usage preference generally is for "hydrogeology." In view of the lack of agreement among workers in the science, the present writer prefers to use Meinzer's older term (Meinzer, 1934) of ground-water hydrology.

Hydrologic Balance

Underlying much of the research in ground-water hydrology is the concept of the hydrologic balance or water budget. In itself this concept is quite simple, being merely a form of the equation of continuity; that is, it is an expression of the law of conservation of matter. Taking an aquifer or an interrelated aquifer system as a frame of reference, the water budget is a statement of the quantity of water entering the aquifer, the quantity leaving the aquifer, and the quantity being added to or removed from storage in the aquifer. In the simplest and most usual approach, the water budget is averaged over a period of years, so that changes in storage may be neglected (excluding man-made withdrawals or additions). The difficulty lies in measuring, directly or indirectly, the quantity of water entering and leaving an aquifer. The problem of aquifer recharge and discharge, which, in spite of some 50 years of research is still in a rudimentary stage of development, will be discussed in more detail below, together with the related problem of the role of the water budget in ground water investigations.

The concept of the water budget has been given greater emphasis in Europe than in the United States. In two recent French texts (Schoeller, 1962, pp. 459-498; Castany, 1963, pp. 91-106) the water budget is treated explicitly and at some length. Out of three recent American texts (Davis and DeWiest, 1966; DeWiest, 1965; Kazmann, 1965) none mentioned the water budget method explicitly. By implication in the treatment of "safe yield," however, this method is utilized by DeWiest (p. 147). DeWiest quotes Todd (Todd, 1959*a*) in giving the following definition: "Safe yield of a ground-water basin is the amount of water which can be withdrawn from it annually without producing any undesired result." The water budget is then calculated in order to help determine safe yield. But the usefulness of the concept of safe yield is also open to question. Kazmann (p. 161) believes that it is a mistaken notion that is unfortunately preserved in the water law of several states, and Thomas (1962, p. 14) declared that it is a "defeasible concept" and would abandon its further use.

Aquifers and Water Storage Beneath Deserts

An aquifer is primarily a subsurface reservoir and only secondarily a conduit through which water is transported. Notable exceptions are those cases where wells are installed near flowing streams or lakes, and where most of the pumped water originated as surface water induced to seep into the aquifer by the lowering of the water table. In such cases the aquifer acts primarily as a conduit. This kind of thing is occasionally of great importance in humid regions, but rarely so in arid regions. It is estimated (Nace, 1960) that ground water above a depth of 2,600 feet represents about one million cubic miles, or over 97 per cent, of all exploitable fresh water in storage on land, not considering glacial ice. If we conservatively estimate that 10 per cent is in storage in arid regions, then there are at least 100,000 cubic miles or 340 billion acre-feet of water in storage beneath Earth's deserts. This is enough water to support the flow of the Nile river for about 1,000 years. Although this estimate is conservative in terms of amount, it probably is not conservative in terms of chemical quality. In many of the deserts much of the ground water is too saline for irrigation or domestic supplies. In some deserts (e. g. Australia) saline water may underlie up to 50 per cent of the total desert area. In most places, not enough data are available to estimate the percentage of saline water.

System Analysis

In any system of ground water exploitation the critical factors to be determined are: (*1*) the geometry of the aquifer, (*2*) the ability of the aquifer to yield water to pumped wells, (*3*) the quality of that water, and (*4*) the interdependence between quality and the manner of exploitation. The magnitude of aquifer replenishment under conditions undisturbed by man is important, but it is not necessarily a limiting factor. The ability of an aquifer to yield water is determined by the transmissivity coefficient, which is a measure of the ease with which water flows through the aquifer, and the storage coefficient, which is a measure of the quantity of water yielded from storage in the aquifer per unit lowering of hydraulic head.

In recent years, largely because of the availability of computers, it has become possible to treat an aquifer as one component in an integrated "systems-analysis" of water supply and water use. Such analyses, in addition to purely hydrologic factors, may consider the economic, legal, sociologic and other variables involved in the optional utilization of aquifers. For the results to be valid, there must be available information on valid functional relationships among the pertinent variables. The functions may be either deterministic or stochastic or a combination of both. In common with the other components of the system, the real aquifer must be simplified and idealized in some kind of mathematical model. It is often found useful to build an electrical model analog of the aquifer, since this provides a convenient method for identifying inconsistencies in hydrologic data and then making whatever modifica-

tions may be indicated. In arid and semiarid regions where aquifers are the principal source of water supply, and where water is the limiting factor in resources development, the construction of model analogs of aquifers and their use in systems analysis is of special importance.

Investigation and research in ground-water hydrology are undertaken primarily by agencies of national governments or their subdivisions, and to a much smaller degree by universities and private groups. Where water is required in large amounts by industry, investigations may be undertaken by personnel of the industry or by their consultants. Also, the petroleum industry gathers information pertinent to ground-water studies as a byproduct of oil exploration; however, water information gained from wells drilled for oil is apt to be sketchy and incomplete because geologic formations above the oil horizons are "mudded-off" in the drilling process and rarely tested for water-bearing properties.

Certain problems related to the data-gathering process are peculiar to ground water. They derive from the fact that most wells that provide the basic data to the hydrologist were originally drilled for someone's water supply and not to provide data. Information may be obtained on the depth of the well and on the nature of the formations penetrated. Ordinarily the depth is accurately known or may subsequently be measured by the hydrologist. The value of the description of formations penetrated, i. e., the log of the well, depends on the skill of the driller and his willingness to impart information. Some drillers regard logs as part of their trade secrets and will impart only the barest minimum of information required by law. Most drillers are reasonably cooperative but vary greatly in their skill and interest in recognizing and describing the characteristics of the formations penetrated. In addition to the depth and log of the well, at the time of drilling a record is also made of the depth to water and yield of the well. The latter figure is often only a rough estimate. Over the years many thousands of these records have accumulated in the files of the various agencies concerned. For the most part, their reliability remains unevaluated.

In addition to the problem of reliability of the data, there is also the problem of access to it. Files are bulky and in many cases poorly organized. Sometimes hours of searching are required merely to find out what data are available for a given area. In order to facilitate data retrieval some agencies are transferring the data to computer cards. In the future we may expect that all major agencies will place these data on computer cards suitable for machine retrieval and printout. This technique solves the retrieval problem, but may worsen the reliability problem. To begin with, the record may reflect the idiosyncrasies of the driller nearly as much as the characteristics of the terrain. The data must be standardized and squeezed into an arbitrary number-system in order to be put on punch cards. A certain amount of judgement is applied in the reduction of each record to the standard form. Many people do this work, and in spite of standard instructions, it cannot be expected that all will make the same judgement in every case. Furthermore, the people that do the reduction are not necessarily or even usually trained in hydrology or geology. Consequently, the unknown uncertainty of the reliability of the original record is increased by an unknown uncertainty arising out of the data-reduction process.

The ground-water hydrologist has sources of data available to him other than those obtained from the drilling and testing of wells. Supplementing his own field observations on geology and soils, the occurrence of springs and seeps, the distribution of vegetation, and perimeter matters, he may consult such sources as aerial photos, and maps of geology and soils which are often available from governmental agencies or scattered through the technical literature. Published and unpublished data on rainfall and air temperature, stream runoff, irrigation practice, and the chemical quality of water also are utilized.

DISCUSSION

A. PERTINENT INFORMATION:
SOURCES, ACCESSIBILITY AND RELIABILITY

In general, collection and dissemination of the various kinds of data pertinent to our subject are the responsibility of different agencies. Usually climatological data are readily available in published form; data on stream runoff usually are published, but often several years after time of acquisition; the publication of chemical data, for which the local public health agency is often the principal respository, is very spotty. Thus, the basic data required by the ground-water hydrologist for resource-appraisal studies, or for research, are scattered among many agencies and often are not available in published form.

A report on ground-water hydrology may or may not be published, depending, in part, on the purpose for which it was written. The U. S. Geological Survey, for example, prepares many "open file" reports in twpewritten or mimeographed form which may be consulted only at Survey offices. In many cases these reports are prepared to satisfy some immediate need, but later may be revised and published. Similar practices exist elsewhere. In some important cases, unpublished reports are not accessible to the public. Arabian-American Oil Company (Aramco), for example, has prepared a number of reports on the ground-water hydrology of areas in Saudi Arabia which are regarded as company-confidential and were nonaccessible to this writer. Engineering and water consultants accumulate in their files information and reports on work done for their clients. Most consultants, with their clients' approval, will make such information available to investigators working for governmental or noncommercial agencies, but no lists of information contained in consultants' files are made public; hence, it is apparent that an important segment of information may be obtained only by personal "digging" by the investigator.

Published reports relating to ground water, while more accessible than unpublished reports, also pose special problems. Because of the large number of agencies responsible for water, both in this country and elsewhere, and the consequent large number of publication sources, very few libraries attempt to maintain complete files of all such publications. Most ground-water reports are in the category of resource-appraisal investigations and are not suitable for publication by technical journals. Nevertheless, many of these reports have aspects pertinent to research. Except for reports appearing in the technical journals, these references are available only in libraries such as the Library of Congress or specialized libraries such as that of the U. S. Geological Survey in Washington, D. C.

Reports of the resource-appraisal type, mentioned above, contain the bulk of available published basic data and are written primarily for use by the nonspecialist and often for the layman. In another category entirely are the research-oriented papers, appearing in a wide range of technical journals, that are written by and for specialists. Reports in the resource-appraisal category are essentially descriptive, emphasizing the location, quantity, and quality of ground water in a specific area, and only incidentally may they contain an examination of hydrologic processes. Papers in the research-oriented category are mainly concerned with processes and methodology, and only incidentally may they contain descriptive information of a given area. The two types of reports are, or should be, mutually interdependent. The state of understanding of hydrological processes should guide data collection programs and, in turn, the degree of availability and reliability of basic data places a constraint on theoretical analysis. For various reasons, interaction between theory and practice is imperfectly realized. An important task facing the ground-water hydrologist is to find ways to increase the efficiency and reliability of data collection.

Ground-water hydrology is also unusual because of the large number of separate disciplines concerned with it in one way or another. Only within the last decade have professional journals appeared that deal exclusively with ground water; however, important papers continue to appear in the journals of the professions of geology, civil engineering, petroleum engineering, public health, chemical engineering, soils science and agriculture, and others. The journals devoted exclusively to ground water probably publish less than half of the total number of important papers in the field. (Trade journals are not considered.) Table I presents a partial listing of professional journals in which research-oriented reports on ground water appear.

It is apparent from the above discussion that even a summary of the availability of basic data, published and unpublished, represents an undertaking of considerable magnitude. Two excellent guides to the availability of data on ground water in the United States are published. One is a report entitled *The Role of Ground Water in the National Water Situation* (McGuinness, 1963), which provides a detailed appraisal of ground water in all of the states on a county-by-county basis. The other is an inventory of federal sources of ground-water data (U. S. Geological Survey, 1966), which provides a state-by-state listing of field offices of all federal agencies having a water responsibility, and the extent and kind of ground-water data available in each, published and unpublished. No other nation has anything approaching this coverage.

For other parts of the world considerable information is available in the library and files of the U. S. Geological Survey in Washington, D. C.; the Foreign Hydrology Branch in particular, through its cooperative program with various countries, has accumulated much information, both published and unpublished (Eakin, 1960; Heath, 1965; U. S. Geological Survey, 1967). Also, the Military Geology Branch of the U. S. Geological Survey makes periodic surveys of water-resource information for most parts of the world.

B. GROUND-WATER RESEARCH

1. Basic Objectives

In appraising research objectives of ground-water hydrology in arid zones, two preliminary statements may be made: (*1*) the research objectives for arid zones are not different in kind from those in more humid regions, but they appear in sharper focus, and (*2*) the objectives of research cannot be separated from the objectives of a water policy. The latter statement is especially true in arid zones where water is the principal limiting factor in the development of agriculture and industry. In the absence of a clear water policy, research will flounder or will be occupied with wasteful and irrelevant matters.

In a general way, the objectives of research fall into two categories: (*1*) how best to describe the aquifer system, its physical properties, and the quality and quantity of its contained water, and (*2*) how best

Table I

PARTIAL LISTING OF PROFESSIONAL JOURNALS

Académie des Sciences Comptes Rendus Hebdomadaires des Séances, Group 2 Gauthier-Villars 55 Quai des Grands-Augustine Paris 6ᵉ	Indus Lahore West Pakistan	Society of Petroleum Engineers, Journal 6300 North Central Expressway Dallas, Texas 75206
	International Association of Scientific Hydrology Jean Jauresbaan 58 Gentbrugge, Belgium	Terres et Eaux Direction de l'Hydraulique et de l'Equipement Rural 117 rue des Poissonniers Paris 18ᵉ
American Society of Civil Engineers, Proceedings 345 E. 47th Street New York, N. Y. 10017		
American Water Works Association Journal 2 Park Avenue New York, N. Y. 10016	La Houille Blanche 20 rue Général Rambaud Box 41 Grenoble, France	
	Journal of Geophysical Research c/o American Geophysical Union 1145-19th St., N. W. Washington, D. C. 20036	Wasserwirtschaft-Wassertechnik VEB Verlag f. Bauwesen Franzosische Str. 13-14 Berlin, W. 8, Germany
British Water Works Association, Journal 341 Park Street London, W. 1	Journal of Hydrology North-Holland Publ. Co. 68-70 Nieuwezijds Voorburgwal Box 103 Amsterdam, Netherlands	Water Moormans Periodieke Pers N. V. Zwarteweg 1 The Hague, Netherlands
Deutsche Gewässerkundliche Mitteilungen Kaiserin-Augusta-Anlagen 15 54 Koblenz, Germany	Journal of Petroleum Technology c/o Society of Petroleum Engineers 6300 North Central Expressway Dallas, Texas 75206	Water Resources Research c/o American Geophysical Union 1145 Nineteenth St., N. W. Washington, D. C. 20036

to manage this resource to satisfy the objectives of water policy. Outside the scope of the present discussion is a third category: (3) how best may a national water policy be developed (usually on the basis of only partial and imperfect resource information). The three research objectives are mutually interdependent.

2. Israel: A Case in Point

Before discussing either of the two research objectives in detail, it will be instructive to refer briefly to the situation in Israel as a case in point. A critical need for water, high technical capability, and a centralized planning authority are essential elements in such a development, all of which are present in Israel, probably to a greater degree than anywhere else. The aquifers in the Negev Desert and along the Mediterranean coast were studied in terms of their roles as: (1) reservoirs for the temporary storage of seasonally surplus water piped in from the Sea of Galilee, (2) sources of "one-time" reserves, which are reserves that may be used up (or mined) pending completion of pipelines, and (3) "live" reserves which are utilized in accord with natural recharge rates. For each role certain processes and properties of the aquifer system had to be investigated, such as mixing and dilution, average flow velocity, chemical exchange, sea-water intrusion, and artificial recharge rates. All of the matters are, and have been, the subjects of research elsewhere. The main difference that distinguishes research conducted in the light of a clear water policy from that conducted in the absence of such a policy is that in the absence of clear policy the work is done on an *ad hoc* basis, often to meet short-term needs, and with little feeling for the amount and kind of data that should be collected to make possible long-term optimum solutions of the water problems in all its ramifications.

Mandel (1967) has provided a discussion of the role of ground water and aquifers in water-resources planning in Israel, in which he states: "Eventually it will be widely realized that scientific management of this vital resource should start systematically from the outset of development and not only by *ad hoc* measures when the situation has almost become desperate. This is essentially a problem of legislation, but that presupposes well-informed legislators and a certain amount of public awareness."

3. Water-Resource Management

Water-resource management is nothing new. What is new is that the pressures of population and industrialization are forcing the management of this resource on a regional and interregional scale. Water pollution, conflicting needs for water, a clumsy, complex, and often obsolete legal code, and a multiplicity of water authorities make the definition of a clear water policy and the optimization process exceedingly difficult.

Beginning about 1960, hydrologists began to adapt the methodology of systems-analysis toward the solution of water management problems. One of the first comprehensive reviews was that of Maass *et al.* (1962), but the discussions in that work emphasized water resource systems in humid areas, and problems peculiar to aquifers received scant attention. Agencies and groups concerned with water in semiarid regions have, however, developed programs where the role of the aquifer is central. The California Department of Water Resources in Los Angeles was responsible for four papers that provide an introduction to the scope and nature of the problem (Fowler, 1964; Tyson and Weber, 1964; Chun, Mitchell, and Mido, 1964; Valantine, 1964). Fowler summarized the basic principles of ground-water basin operation to achieve an optimum management scheme, as follows:

1) The surface and underground storage capacities must be integrated to obtain the most economical utilization of the local storage resources and the optimum amount of water conservation.

2) The surface pipeline system must be integrated with the ground-water basin transmission characteristics to provide the minimum cost distribution system.

3) An operating agency must be available with adequate powers to control or cooperate in the control of the surface water supplies, ground-water recharge sites, surface-water delivery facilities, ground-water extractions. (Fowler, 1964).

Aquifers in Water Management

In the above summary, the aquifer is regarded as a subsurface reservoir with storage and transmission characteristics that must be known and with surface water sources that can recharge the reservoir as required. Chun, Mitchell, and Mido investigated a portion of the coastal plain of Los Angeles County including a ground-water basin (underlying an area of 480 square miles) which is in hydraulic continuity with the Pacific Ocean. Severe overdraft resulted in increased pumping costs and intrusion of sea water into the aquifer. The analysis required extensive use of digital computers, but an electric model analog of the aquifer was first made in order to calibrate the aquifer model fed into the computer and to eliminate, in advance, solutions that either would result in water-logging or undesirable salt-water inflow.

Another group emphasizing the role of aquifers in water management in semiarid regions is at the Israel Institute of Technology in Haifa, under the direction of Jacob Bear. The Institute recently published the first of a series of reports on the optimal utilization of aquifers as elements of water-resource systems (Bear, Levin, and Buras, 1964). The following is quoted from that work, p. 41:

> The main objective of the present research is to analyze design problems and to develop techniques for determining the main components of typical water resource systems in which aquifers play the major role. The aquifer's development and operation are considered from the point of view that the aquifer is an element of the system possessing specified properties and functions, while the system as a whole has a definite objective. Studying the optimal utilization of the aquifer with the above approach requires both a re-evaluation of basic concepts and developing procedures for decision making through analyzing mathematical models which represent the system.

Buras (1964) analyzed a system consisting of Lake Tiberias (Sea of Galilee) and an aquifer in the south of Israel. Water conducted from the lake to the aquifer could be used directly for irrigation or recharged into the aquifer and stored for later use. Buras, however, did not take into account problems arising from the flow of water through the aquifer. Buras (1966) later wrote a theoretical paper on the general subject of programming and optimization procedures. (Other treatments of systems-analysis in hydrology may be found in the following works and the references cited therein: Bower, 1965; Hufschmidt and Fiering, 1966; Technology Planning Center, 1966; Chow, 1964, section 26-II). It is evident that data collection and research in ground-water hydrology, for maximum benefit, should be guided by program goals, and program goals should be tested and made explicit through systems analysis. In this connection it is worth mentioning that according to the director of the recently established Office of Data Coordination, U. S. Department of Interior, a serious and yet unsolved problem facing that agency is to determine which data are meaningful (and by implication which data are not worth collecting) and whether or not there are gaps in the data collection program (O. M. Hackett, personal communication).

Water Budget and Aquifer Recharge

The determination of the natural water budget traditionally has been regarded as the most important factor in planning ground-water policy. In 1964, a meeting of experts convened in Tunis under Unesco auspices (reported in Unesco's *Arid Zone*, No. 25, September, 1964, p. 3) to study the launching of a project for the overall study of the artesian basins in northern Africa. The first of the five subjects recommended for extensive scientific research and applied studies was "(*a*) the problem of the recharge of aquifers in the arid zones, to enable the preparation of policies to govern utilization of water reserves (infiltration, dating, etc.)." Within the context of the report, and also because artificial recharge is usually so labelled, it would seem that natural recharge, i. e., infiltration from precipitation and stream flow, was meant.

The remaining four subjects listed by the committee of experts were the following: "(*b*) the problem of the unification and standardization of methods suitable for the comparison of waters by hydrochemical and isotopic studies; (*c*) studies in applied geomorphology with a view to defining the characteristics of recharge areas or of evaporation from aquifers; (*d*) the problem of the corrosion of casing and silting of screens which leads to the aging of wells and the correlation of this problem with a reduction in supplies; (*e*) problems of fluid mechanics connected with the presence of fine sands in wells and resulting in well plugging." It is seen that item (*c*) is closely connected with item (*a*), and that the remaining items, although important to exploitation, are of a rather narrow technical nature.

The determination of aquifer recharge and the water budget is important to scientific hydrology, but its emphasis, particularly in arid zones, may obscure the study of more important factors in determining water policy. In arid regions virtually all local precipitation, and virtually all streamflow that may come from higher elevations or "humid islands," is returned to the atmosphere by processes of evapotranspiration. In other words, unless engineered structures are built to improve the situation, recharge is a very small fraction of precipitation and is unevenly distributed in time. Also, the procedures for determining natural recharge are quite uncertain, and estimates may be grossly in error. Only by actively exploiting an aquifer may estimates of recharge be evaluated, and by then the water balance is no longer "natural."

Drouhin (1953), in an excellent review of problems of arid-zone research in North Africa, also believed that knowledge of the water balance was a prerequisite to the formulation of water policy, but he was obviously not happy with that constraint. Of the water balance he says: "The production of such a balance sheet is extremely difficult and all that can be hoped for is to arrive at approximate figures with allowance for an ample safety margin." And, again: "It must be admitted that anything of the kind is difficult to secure within a time limit compatible with the needs of practical exploitation and in many cases it is necessary to accept some item or items of the data as provisional only. In such instances extra caution must be displayed."

It is worth repeating Drouhin's general introduction to the problems of arid-zone hydrology, remembering that at the time he wrote, the implications of computer technology were only beginning to be appreciated:

> The relative human significance of water increases in proportion to the aridity of the region concerned. This is an argument in favour of boldness in exploration and exploitation. However, in semi-arid or arid zones boldness must be balanced by caution and good sense for it must never be forgotten that in such regions the need to suspend or restrict ill-judged development and to destroy the life induced to take root, and all for lack of sufficiently thorough preliminary study, is literally catastrophic. The usual outcome is an almost insurmountable psychological—and sometimes political—obstacle to social progress. Properly understood, prudence and boldness, far from being incompatible, go hand in hand.

> In this particular context prudence does not consist in the small-scale investigation of purely local phenomena only assumed to be independent—which they rarely are—for that purpose. Often, indeed, the pressure of immediate needs makes work on a restricted scale for a specific end inescapable. However, an increase of small-scale local developments often results in the growth—usually perceived too late—of utter chaos in irrigation, and in situations well-nigh impossible to unravel. Prudent hydrology consists in setting each point of detail as soon as possible in its true geographical and geological context and then bringing to the study of the system as a whole material and financial resources commensurate with the scope of the overall problems. Experience has shown that this is the way to maximum economy and safety.

What, then, are the principal research problems facing the ground-water hydrologist, and what is the present state of knowledge concerning these problems? Implicit in the foregoing discussion is the belief that these research problems are clustered around a need to refine the aquifer as an element in a total water-resource system. This in turn pre-

supposes the existence of research centers or "hydrologic simulation laboratories" where such systems may be formulated and studied. We are currently witnessing an almost explosive growth of research centers, both governmental and private, oriented toward the study of water problems, employing a systems-analysis approach, and reaching out to handle more and more difficult problems. It is likely that in a few years one of the chief constraints on the solution of water management problems will be a general lack of adequate knowledge of the properties of the individual aquifers and aquifer systems. This statement will be especially true for arid zones where aquifers play a central role in the total system.

Of prime importance is the availability of good hydrogeologic maps, giving the position in space of the aquifer system and of its boundaries and at least a general description of its water-bearing properties. Unfortunately, there seems to be no text specifically devoted to the methods of hydrogeological mapping (at least none has come to the attention of the writer). The standard methods of geological mapping apply, but the special needs of hydrogeology are significant enough to require a special background and outlook beyond that of classical geology. Since the map should give information in three dimensions, thicknesses of formations must be measured or inferred. Other than what may be inferred from surface exposures, this is done by a combination of test drilling and various kinds of geophysical exploration. The petroleum industry has developed such methods to a high degree of efficiency—the extent to which they may be applied to a specific water problem depends on many factors, the most important of which are economic in nature. However, if a model of the aquifer can be formulated at an early stage, it will help to guide exploration so that a maximum of useful information may be obtained from a given expenditure of time and money. In short, the methods of hydrogeological mapping are well established; they are based mainly on classical geology with strong support from experience in petroleum exploration, In any given case, the final product will depend on the skill and experience of the individual hydrogeologist and the organizational support available to him. Still, (whether or not the need may be referred to as a "research gap") there is need for a good text on the subject.

Given a hydrogeological map or, at least, a good geological map, a program may be developed to determine the physical and chemical properties of the aquifer system. The dangers and limitations of relying on data from private wells were outlined in the previous section, but initial estimates often must be based on this type of information.

A basic property of the aquifer is its ability to transmit water, of which the "coefficient of transmissivity" (usually denoted by T) is a measure. Field methods (so-called "pumping" or "aquifer-performance" tests) for determining this coefficient have rapidly developed since C. V. Theis (1935) proposed the nonequilibrium equation which now bears his name. In effect, this equation, and the many elaborations of it developed along the same lines (Hantush, 1964, 1966; Hantush and Thomas, 1966; Ferris *et al.*, 1962; Wenzel, 1942; Bentall, 1963; Muskat, 1937) (see also: Aravin and Numerov, 1953; Polubarinova-Kochina, 1962, for Russian texts on the subject) replaces the real, heterogeneous aquifer having irregular complex boundaries with an imaginary aquifer, having regular boundaries, whose response to pumping reasonably represents that in the real aquifer. The same texts provide a measure of the ability of the aquifer to store water, or the "coefficient of storage" (usually denoted by S). However, the dependence on time of the coefficient of storage is not well understood. These mathematical methods have been elaborated to describe a wide range of possible geological conditions. The accuracy of the results will depend largely on the skill and judgement of the hydrologist in choosing the correct mathematical description to fit his particular case.

By employing all available information on T and S, together with information on the boundaries of the aquifer, an R-C analog may be built whereby electrical resistors and capacitors are made to represent the transmissivity and storage capacity of the aquifer (Brown, 1962; Skibitzke, 1963). It should be noted that for each node point of the analog, a value of T and S must be specified, obtained from field measurement or interpolation. A great deal of averaging is involved. No information on the distribution of hydraulic head or other aspects of the flow regimen are needed in the initial construction of the model. Once the model is built, however, it must be "validated" by imposing on it appropriate hydraulic conditions in terms of electrical voltages, and varying these conditions with time in accord with known events (such as changes in pumping) to discover whether or not the model response imitates the historical response of the real aquifer (for example, the historical record of changes in elevation and shape of the water table). By trial and error, and intuition, the model is modified to minimize discrepancies between model response and the real aquifer. The same information can be programmed for solution by digital computers, or the R-C model may be used in conjunction with digital or other types of computers. The R-C model or its digital counterpart may be used advantageously where water production is of principal concern, and where water quality or the movement and mixing of a contaminant are not important factors.

A recent advance in computer methodology was achieved by workers at the Battelle-Northwest laboratories in Hanford, Washington. It was necessary to determine the movement and dispersion of radioactive contaminants in ground water, and a means had to be found to map the "real" flow lines of the system in detail. This in turn, required the mapping in detail of the distribution of permeability within the aquifer (transmissivity equals average permeability times aquifer thickness). A method was developed whereby the concept of a "permeability integral" made possible the utilization of information on both aquifer properties and hydraulic head distribution to define a computerized model of the aquifer containing the needed permeability distribution (Nelson, 1963, 1966). The important advantage here is that for only a small region does the permeability distribution need to be known. In theory, at least, the distribution of permeability need be known only along a single line crossing the flow lines of the aquifer (in the case of a 2-dimensional model) or along a single surface (in the case of a 3-dimensional model). Suitable fitting functions are obtained for the head distribution measured over the entire aquifer, and the computer, so to speak, does the rest. A model of permeability distribution throughout the entire aquifer is obtained. Thus, the task of modelling the real aquifer is reduced to manageable proportions.

As of this writing, Nelson and his coworkers have applied the method in a 2-dimensional, steady-state study of an aquifer some 400 square miles in area (details as yet unpublished). Its usefulness when applied to the study of the much larger aquifers of arid zones (100,000 square miles and more), in three dimensions and nonsteady state, remains to be evaluated. Small errors in the basic data sometimes lead to physically unrealizable instability in the model solution; hence, it may be necessary to obtain permeability data from more than one line or surface in order to keep errors within prescribed limits. Also, even for the initial study, computers of high capacity were needed; hence, precision in modelling may ultimately be limited by computer capacity.

It does not seem possible to escape the conclusion that the method outlined above, or modifications thereof, eventually will be used to formulate models of aquifers in all parts of the globe. A difficulty arises in the matter of evaluating goodness of fit between model and prototype. The model makes possible the description of mixing and dispersion within the aquifer, but there is at present no technique which makes possible reasonably precise estimates of large-scale mixing based on field measurements. Of course, it is always possible to inject a tracer, but ground-water velocity is slow and years or decades must elapse before motion covers more than a few miles. Besides, the procedures required to intercept a tagged portion of the ground-water body, especially in deep aquifers, are so considerable, that the method of tracer injection is impractical except for special and limited objectives.

Recent work in ground-water chemistry and isotopes in ground water gives promise of a future resolution of this problem. Naturally occurring and bomb-produced radioisotopes, such as tritium and carbon-14, make possible the dating of ground water and certain types of tracing of ground water (see Symposium on the Application of Radioisotopes in Hydrology, Tokyo, 1963, for discussions from various points of view; see also: Begemann and Libby, 1957; Carlston, Thatcher, and Rhodehamel, 1960; Carlston, 1964; Eriksson, 1958, 1963; Feely *et al.*, 1961; Hanshaw, Back, and Rubin, 1965; Libby, 1961; Thatcher, Rubin, and Brown, 1961). Also promising is the utilization of the variation of the relative abundance of certain stable isotopes such as deuterium and oxygen-18 in identifying sources of ground water. This is a very recent development and its possibilities are under investigation by B. R. Payne at the International Atomic Energy Agency in Vienna, Austria, and by A. Nir of the Weizmann Institute of Science, Rehovoth, Israel, among others (Peckham and Payne, 1965; Payne and Dincer, 1965). Another approach has been the study of chemical equilibria relationships between ground water and its solid environment (Back and Hanshaw, 1965) and the study of the distribution of the major chemical elements in ground water by advanced statistical techniques (Smoor, 1967). All of these methods have as a principal objective the identification of source areas of recharge from an examination of the chemistry of the water. The radioisotopes, in addition, offer the possibility of calculating the time interval since recharge occurred. Desert aquifers should be more amenable to this type of study than those in humid regions because recharge to the former usually occurs in relatively well-defined areas that are small compared to the total aquifer area. If a given sample of water may be related to an ultimate source area or areas, it should be possible to employ such data to calculate the mixing properties of the aquifer. This, then, would offer a possibility for validating a computerized model of the aquifer.

Brief reference should be given to work done during the past decade on fluid dispersion through porous media. Dispersion in porous media enters into problems of heat transfer, chemical catalysis, secondary recovery of petroleum, and other areas of engineering, as well as problems in ground-water contamination and artificial recharge. Hence, theoretical treatments and data are found in a wide range of journals. Almost without exception, laboratory experimentation has been limited to homogeneous, isotropic media, and much of the theory contains the assumption of homogeneity. Although a high degree of insight has been achieved (*i. e.,* descriptions of dispersion can be made based on readily measurable fluid and media properties), it is most difficult to apply this theory to a real aquifer which is neither homogeneous nor isotropic. Unlike the property of transmissivity, an averaging procedure gives no useful result. In ground water, dispersion theory has been used mainly in the study of the migration of water of undesirable chemical quality existing naturally within aquifers (brines of all varieties, sea water, high-fluoride water, etc.), or to study the reaction interface between recharge water or contaminated waste water injected into an aquifer and the native ground water of the aquifer. Migration of brines and recharge are of great pertinence in the management of arid-zone aquifers. The computerized aquifer model mentioned above should be a powerful tool in this type of study, but it is by no means certain that the model takes all significant mechanisms of dispersion into account. The model, as presently formulated, assumes that an idealized fluid convection will account for all significant dispersion. Where significant, dispersion caused by physicochemical exchange could also be programmed in, but there may be other mechanisms which should be taken into account. Much basic work remains to be done on fluid dispersion in flow through heterogeneous media. (For accounts of work in homogeneous media see, for example: Bear and Dagan, 1964; Bachmat and Bear, 1964; Bear and Jacobes, 1964; Josselin de Jong, 1958; Ebach and White, 1958; Harleman and Rumer, 1962; Hoopes and Harleman, 1965; Hilby, 1962; Nielsen and Biggar, 1962; Perkins and Johnston, 1963; Saffman, 1960; Scheidegger, 1961; Simpson, 1962).

Turning to the problem of aquifer recharge under natural conditions, which is of prime importance to the determination of water budgets, two preliminary statements may be made: (*1*) The physical processes governing recharge are reasonably well established, at least in qualitative terms (Penman, 1963; Liakopoulos, 1966; Stallman, 1964; Remson and Randolf, 1962; Marshall, 1959; Schoeller, 1962, pp. 395-458), and (*2*) the average annual recharge rate to most arid-zone aquifers is completely unknown. For many such aquifers there is disagreement among hydrologists as to whether or not *any* recharge occurs under present-day climatological conditions. In other words, it is possible that the ground water in these aquifers accumulated during an earlier, and wetter, climatological cycle.

The literature on the subject of measurements of recharge in specific areas is quite scanty and the results achieved are either inconclusive or apply only to a given set of measurements under a given set of climatological and soil conditions. (See, for example: Bergstrom and Aten, 1964; Keppel and Renard, 1962; Linsley, 1953; White, 1963; see also the collection of papers in International Association of Scientific Hydrology, 1961, pp. 535-606.) Nevertheless, some tentative generalizations may be offered: (1) A minimum of between 5 and 10 inches per year of rainfall is required before any recharge occurs, except, perhaps, in fissured rock or in highly permeable sandy or gravelly soil, but even where geology is favorable, recharge is only a small fraction of precipitation. (2) Exceptionally large storms that occur at widely separated intervals of time and space may produce recharge in spite of low average precipitation. (3) The recharge that does occur mostly takes place through channel bottoms of ephemeral streams.

In view of the practical difficulties involved in measuring natural recharge, and of the very few attempts at on-site measurement that have been made, it would seem to be an impossible task to estimate water budgets in this way. It would be far more practical, and in the end more accurate, to determine this unknown from an analysis of a computerized model aquifer. That is, the model would exhibit what the replenishment from recharge would have had to be in order to account for the observed distribution of hydraulic head and other measureable factors. Another advantage to this approach is that the recharge would be averaged out over decades or centuries, since the response of the aquifer to recharge stimuli is sluggish.

Of perhaps greater importance than natural recharge is the possibility of artificial recharge, at least in arid zones. Considerable work along these lines has been done in the United States, in Israel, and in other countries over the past decade. It has been shown that artificial recharge is both technically feasible and economically sound over a wide range of conditions (Todd, 1964). Recharge may be accomplished either by (1) the flooding of pits and basins, with little or no pretreatment of the water except for desilting and chlorination, or (2) injection into "reverse" wells, which generally requires careful quality control of the water. Local conditions will determine which method or combination of methods is best (see, for example: Buchan and Taylor, 1964; Muckel, 1959; Todd, 1959*b*; Schiff, 1963; Schiff and Dyer, 1964; Sniegocki *et al.*, 1965; and Dortmunder Stadtwerke AG, 1966).

Artificial recharge implies the existence of surface flows at or reasonably near the areas of possible recharge. ("Reasonably near" is an economic distance and could be tens or hundreds of miles.) In arid regions surface flows must be temporarily controlled by dams, dikes, pits, or a combination thereof. In order to estimate the quantity of recharge that may be expected and to design the necessary structures, the surface flows must be described. The description is given in probabilistic terms based on the historical record. In arid regions special techniques of analysis must be employed because of the scarcity of the basic record. There is need to design and implement data collection programs compatible with the available analytic techniques (Chow, 1964, section 8) and with the limitations imposed by the low population density and technological backwardness of the peoples in many desert areas.

CONCLUSION

A. THE NEED FOR SYNTHESIS

The general conclusion of this summary of the state of research in ground-water hydrology is that this discipline is on the threshold of an important period of integration. It is a relatively young discipline and has drawn heavily on accomplishments in physics, fluid dynamics, geology, and chemistry, and must continue to do so. Notwithstanding the ever present need for deeper understanding of the functioning of the various parts (McGuinness, 1964), what is now necessary and possible is a synthesis and integration which exhibits the functioning system as a whole. Such a step is possible because the workings of the parts are sufficiently well understood for the purpose and because the technology for synthesis has become available. It is necessary because the ever-mounting pressure for water makes optimum management a matter of life or death for many peoples. The beginnings made during the past decade should now be further implemented and reinforced within the larger framework of all hydrology and with much of life science.

B. RECOMMENDATIONS

The research needs of ground-water hydrology applied to arid zones for which future work is recommended may be summarized as follows:

1) Modern computer technology has placed us past the era of haphazard data collection. There is a need to design and to implement rational data collection programs.

2) The data required for computerized modelling and hydrologic simulation include:

a) The aquifer must be described in space. This is the job of hydrogeologic mapping, and methods for its accomplishment are well developed.

b) The aquifer properties must be described. The methods for determining transmissivity and storage are reasonably well developed, but methods for determining mixing properties are not. The basic relations between water chemistry and aquifer properties are beginning to be explored and should be pursued in all ramifications.

c) The distribution of hydraulic head must be determined both in space and time. The degree to which this is done will depend upon the needs of the individual case and the resources available. It would be useful to develop a recording gage that would operate unattended for a year.

3) Artificial recharge offers a means for salvaging runoff that otherwise would be wasted. Its ultimate potential should be evaluated. This requires a probabilistic description of stream flow for all arid regions.

4) There has been a reluctance to spend the kind of money that is needed to obtain fundamental data. This, more than anything else, is retarding progress in ground-water hydrology. Too much reliance is placed on data from private wells and on surface mapping. Just as oceanography builds research ships and submarines, and meteorology puts satellites into orbit, so must ground-water hydrology drill wells and utilize available technology to collect meaningful data.

PERTINENT PUBLICATIONS

This bibliography combines in one alphabetical sequence for simplicity both an annotated bibliography and a more inclusive reference list. Those works which it has been possible to determine are of particular significance or interest to this study within the limitations discussed in the chapter are annotated. Other competent works and best-available works on specific subjects are listed without annotation; lack of annotation should not be construed as *necessarily* indicating a less important publication.

Aravin, V. I. and S. N. Numerov
1953 The theory of fluid flow in undeformable porous media (translated title). Originally published by State Publishing House for Theoretical and Technical Literature, Moscow. Issued 1965 in translation by Israel Program for Scientific Translations, Jerusalem. 511 p.
An advanced text on ground-water flow from the engineering-mathematical point of view. Based on classical treatises by Muskat and Polubarinova-Kochina. Brings together much useful material in a systematic way.

Bachmat, Y. and J. Bear
1964 The general equations of hydrodynamic dispersion in homogeneous isotropic porous mediums. Journal of Geophysical Research 69(12):2561-2567. *See also* discussions of this paper in Journal of Geophysical Research 69:5432 and 70:2923.

Back, W. and B. B. Hanshaw
1965 Chemical geohydrology. Advances in Hydroscience 2:50-110.
The first general summary of a new approach to the chemistry of ground water, based upon chemical thermodynamics. Very promising.

Bear, J. and G. Dagan
1964 The transition zone between fresh and salt waters in coastal aquifers. Progress Report 3: The unsteady interface below a coastal collector. Technion, Israel Institute of Technology, Hydraulic Laboratory, P.N. 364. 122 p.
Excellent mathematical analysis with possible applications elsewhere along seacoasts.

Bear, J. and M. Jacobes
1964 Underground storage and mixing of water. Progress Report 2: The movement of water bodies injected into confined aquifers. Technion, Israel Institute of Technology, Hydraulic Laboratory, P.N. 264. 43 p.
Valuable contribution to understanding artificial recharge.

Bear, J., O. Levin, and N. Buras
1964 Optimal utilization of aquifers as elements of water-resource systems. Progress Report 1: Basic concepts and program of research. Technion, Israel Institute of Technology, Hydraulic Laboratory, P.N. 4/64. 86 p.
An important contribution to a very rapidly expanding field: optimal management of water resources. Emphasis is on the role of the aquifer.

Begemann, F. and W. F. Libby
1957 Continental water balance, ground water inventory and storage times, surface ocean mixing rates and world-wide circulation patterns from cosmic ray and bomb tritium. Geochimica et Cosmochimica Acta 12:277-196.
A pioneering but controversial paper in its treatment of the continental water balance. Mixing of ground water oversimplified.

Bentall, R., ed.
1963 Shortcuts and special problems in aquifer tests. U. S. Geological Survey, Water-Supply Paper 1545-C. 116 p.
A how-to-do-it manual based on U. S. Geological Survey experience.

Bergstrom, R. E. and R. E. Aten
1964 Natural recharge and localization of fresh groundwater in Kuwait. American Geophysical Union, Transactions 45:52. (Abstr.)

Bower, B. T.
1965 The application of systems analysis in water resources planning. Annual Conference on Water-for-Texas, 10th, Proceedings, p. 36-42. Texas Agricultural and Mechanical College, College Station.
"Overview" of methodology.

Brown, R. H.
1962 Progress in ground-water studies with the electric-analog model. American Water Works Association, Journal 54(8):943-958.
An explanation for the nonspecialist.

Buchan, S. and L. E. Taylor
1964 The problem of ground-water recharge. I: Artificial recharge as a source of water. II: With special reference to the London basin. Institution of Water Engineers, Journal 18(3):239-246.

Buras, N.
1964 Conjunctive operation of a surface reservoir and and a ground water aquifer. International Association of Scientific Hydrology, Publication 63:492-501.
A good practical case history of optimization.

740

Buras, N.
1966 Dynamic programming in water resources development. Advances in Hydroscience 3:367-412.
A contribution to theory in optimization of water resource management.

Carlston, C. W.
1964 Use of tritium in hydrologic research problems and limitations. International Association of Scientific Hydrology, Bulletin 9(3):38-42.
Written from field geologist's point of view.

Carlston, C. W., L. L. Thatcher, and E. C. Rhodehamel
1960 Tritium as a hydrologic tool—the Wharton Tract study. International Association of Scientific Hydrology, Publication 52:503-512.
Indicates some practical possibilities and limitations in use of bomb tritium. In Wharton Tract study most base flow of stream came from upper layers of ground water.

Castany, G.
1963 Traité pratique des eaux souterraines. Dunod, Paris. 657 p.
Based on U. S. practice to a large degree.

Chow, V. T., ed.
1964 Handbook of applied hydrology; a compendium of water resources technology. McGraw-Hill, New York.
A good general reference to bring one up to date on modern techniques in hydrology.

Chun, R. Y. D., L. R. Mitchell, and K. W. Mido
1964 Ground-water management for the nation's future: optimum conjunctive operation of ground-water basins. American Society of Civil Engineers, Hydraulic Division, Journal 90(HY4):79-95.
One of the first applications of optimization techniques to water management in the U. S. Area treated is in southern California.

Davis, S. N. and R. J. M. DeWiest
1966 Hydrogeology. John Wiley and Sons, New York, 463 p.
First American text on the subject in 30 years; written from point of view of a geologist.

DeWiest, R. J. M.
1965 Geohydrology. John Wiley and Sons, New York. 366 p.
Companion volume to Davis and DeWiest, 1966, from point of view of engineer.

Dortmunder Stadtwerke AG
1966 Die künstliche grundwasseranreicherung. Hydr. Forschungsabteilung, Dortmund, Germany, Voröffentlichung 9. 196 p.
A summary of theory and practice of artificial recharge in West Germany from hydraulic, biochemical, and economic points of view. Eleven articles and bibliography.

Drouhin, G.
1953 The problem of water resources in north-west Africa. *In* Reviews of research on arid zone hydrology. Unesco, Paris. Arid Zone Programme 1:9-41.
A sound analysis of problems and prospects. Suggests international cooperation. (The "people-problem" makes one pessimistic.)

Eakin, T. E.
1960 Foreign hydrology program, water resources division. U. S. Geological Survey, Washington, D. C., Administrative Report. 26 p.

Ebach, E. A. and R. R. White
1958 Mixing of fluids flowing through beds of packed solids. American Institute of Chemical Engineers, Journal 4(2):161-169.

Ellis, A. J.
1917 The divining rod, a history of water witching. U. S. Geological Survey, Water-Supply Paper 416. 53 p.
Reprinted 1957; contains extensive bibliography.

Eriksson, E.
1958 The possible use of tritium for estimating ground water storage. Tellus 10:472-478.
A critical examination of use of bomb tritium (tritium discharged into atmosphere as a result of nuclear bomb explosions); probably more accurate in his appraisal than Begemann and Libby (1957).

———— 1963 Atmospheric tritium as a tool for the study of certain hydrologic aspects of river basins. Tellus 15(3):303-308.
A continuation of Eriksson (1958).

Feely, H. W. *et al.*
1961 The potential applications of radioisotope technology to water resource investigations and utilization. Report prepared for Atomic Energy Commission by Isotopes, Inc., Westwood, New Jersey. 2 vols. 340 p.
A comprehensive summary and prognosis. Regarding subsurface water they conclude that "most valuable results may be obtained where duration and range of the experiment are limited."

Ferris, J. G. *et al.*
1962 Theory of aquifer tests. U. S. Geological Survey, Water-Supply Paper 1536-E. 174 p.

Follansbee, R.
1939 A history of the Water Resources Branch of the U. S. Geological Survey to June 30, 1919. U. S. Geological Survey, Washington, D. C. 459 p.

Fowler, L. C.
1964 Ground-water management for the nation's future: Water resources management through ground-water basin operation. American Society of Civil Engineers, Hydraulics Division, Journal 90 (HY4):51-57.

Hackett, O. M.
1964 The father of modern ground-water hydrology. Appreciation of O. E. Meinzer. N.W.W.A., Journal 2:2-5.

Hanshaw, B. B., W. Back, and M. Rubin
1965 Radiocarbon determinations for estimating groundwater flow velocities in central Florida. Science 148:494-495.
A promising beginning. More work will be accomplished with this technique.

Hantush, M. S.
1964 Hydraulics of wells. Advances in Hydroscience 1:282-432.
Best systematic treatment of this subject available.

———— 1966 Wells in homogeneous anisotropic aquifers. Water Resources Research 2(2):273-280.
An extension of Hantush (1964).

Hantush, M. S. and R. G. Thomas
1966 A method for analyzing a drawdown test in anisotropic aquifers. Water Resources Research 2(2):281-286.
A guide to field application of previous theory.

Harleman, D. R. F. and R. R. Rumer
1962 The dynamics of salt-water intrusion in porous media. Massachusetts Institute of Technology, Cambridge, Hydrodynamics Laboratory, Report 55.
A good review of theory plus report of new work.

Harvard Water Resources Group
1963 Operations research in water quality management. Final Report to the Public Health Service, Contract PH86-62-140. Harvard University, Cambridge, Massachusetts.

Heath, J. A.
1965 Bibliography of reports resulting from U. S. Geological Survey participation in the U. S. Technical Assistance Program, 1940-65. U. S. Geological Survey, Bulletin 1193. 51 p.

Hilby, J. W.
1962 Longitudinal and transverse mixing during single-phase flow through granular beds. p. 312-325. *In* Symposium on the interaction between fluids and particles, London, 1962, Proceedings. Institution of Chemical Engineers, London. 351 p.
An excellent summary of experimental work in this field.

Hoopes, J. A. and D. R. F. Harleman
1965 Waste water recharge and dispersion in porous media. Massachusetts Institute of Technology, Cambridge, Hydrodynamics Laboratory, Report 75. 166 p.

Hufschmidt, M. M. and M. B. Fiering
1966 Simulation techniques for design of water-resources systems. Harvard University Press, Cambridge, Massachusetts. 212 p.
An authoritative and pioneering work.

International Association of Scientific Hydrology
1961 Symposium of Athens: groundwater in arid zones. International Union of Geodesy and Geophysics, Publication 56-57. 746 p.

Josselin de Jong, G. de
1958 Longitudinal and transverse diffusion in granular deposits. American Geophysical Union, Transactions 39(1):67-74.

Kazmann, R. G.
1965 Modern hydrology. Harper and Row, New York. 301 p.
A provocative text; analyzes more than a few historical "goofs" in hydrologic engineering.

Keppel, R. V. and K. G. Renard
1962 Transmission losses in ephemeral stream beds. American Society of Civil Engineers, Hydraulics Division, Journal 88(3):59-68.
Area is in southern Arizona.

Krynine, P. D.
1960 On the antiquity of "sedimentation" and hydrology (with some moral conclusions). Geological Society of America, Bulletin 71:1721-1726.

Liakopoulos, A. C.
1966 Theoretical approach to the solution of the infiltration problem. International Association of Scientific Hydrology, Bulletin 11(1):69-110.

Libby, W. F.
1961 Tritium geophysics. Journal of Geophysical Research 66(11):3767-3782.

Linsley, R. K.
1953 Some aspects of precipitation and surface stream flow in ground-water recharge. *In* Proceedings of the Ankara symposium on arid zone hydrology. Unesco, Paris. Arid Zone Programme 2:140-150.

Maass, A. *et al.*
1962 Design of water-resource systems. Harvard University Press, Cambridge, Massachusetts. 620 p.

Mandel, S.
1967 Underground water. International Science and Technology (66):35-41.
A philosophic statement; advocates the "mining" of ground water when part of a systematic plan.

Mariotte, E.
1717 Oeuvres. p. 326-353. P. Vander Aa, ed. Leiden. 2 vols.

Marshall, T. J.
1959 Relations between water and soil. Commonwealth Bureau of Soils, Harpenden, England, Technical Communication 50. 91 p.
An excellent state-of-the-art review.

McGuinness, C. L.
1963 The role of ground water in the national water situation. U. S. Geological Survey, Water-Supply Paper 1800. 1121 p.
More a compendium and summary than analysis; valuable for reference.

────────

1964 Ground-water research of the U. S. Geological Survey. U. S. Geological Survey, Circular 492.

Meinzer, O. E.
1934 The history and development of ground-water hydrology. Washington Academy of Science, Journal 24(1):6-32.

Meinzer, O. E., ed.
1942 Hydrology. McGraw-Hill, New York. 712 p.
Not much on arid zones, but a good general reference. Largely superseded by Chow (1964).

Muckel, D. C.
1959 Replenishment of ground-water supplies by artificial means. U. S. Department of Agriculture, Technical Bulletin 1195. 51 p.
Superseded by later work. (See the works of Schiff and of Todd.)

Muskat, M.
1937 The flow of homogeneous fluids through porous media. McGraw-Hill, New York, 763 p. Reprinted 1946 by J. W. Edwards, Ann Arbor, Michigan.
A classic work in this field and the theoretical foundation for much subsequent work by others.

Nace, R. L.
1960 Water management, agriculture, and ground-water supplies. U. S. Geological Survey, Circular 415.

Nelson, R. W.
1963 Stream functions for three-dimensional flow in heterogeneous porous media. International Association of Scientific Hydrology, Publication 64: 290-301.
This and Nelson (1966) provide part of the theoretical basis for a new advance in making computerized models

of heterogeneous aquifers. Work done at Battelle North-west (Battelle Memorial Institute). This work is significant for problems of subsurface pollution and artificial recharge.

———

1966 Flow in heterogeneous porous mediums. Water Resources Research 2(3):487-496.

See Nelson (1963).

Nielsen, O. R. and J. W. Biggar
1962 Miscible displacement. 3: Theoretical considerations. Soil Science Society of America, Proceedings 26(3): 216-221.

Ototzky, P.
1921 Underground water and meteorological factors. Royal Meteorological Society, Quarterly Journal, p. 47-54.

Palissy, B.
1957 Admirable discourses. Translated by A. LaRocque. University of Illinois Press, Urbana. 264 p.

Payne, B. R. and T. Dincer
1965 Isotope survey of the karst region of southern Turkey. International Conference on Tritium and C-14 Dating, Pullman, Washington.
A promising use of isotopes to locate areas of natural recharge of ground water.

Peckham, A. E. and B. R. Payne
1965 Isotope investigations of the hydrology of Lake Chola and its groundwater system. International Conference on Tritium and C-14 Dating, Pullman, Washington.
A promising use of isotopes to locate areas of natural recharge of ground water.

Penman, H. L.
1963 Vegetation and hydrology. Commonwealth Bureau of Soils, Harpenden, England, Technical Communication 53. 124 p.
An authoritative state-of-the-art review.

Perkins, T. K. and O. C. Johnston
1963 A review of dispersion in porous media. Society of Petroleum Engineers, Journal 3(1):70.

Polubarinova-Kochina, P. Y.
1962 The theory of ground water movement. Translated from the Russian by J. M. R. DeWiest, Princeton University Press. 613 p.
A mathematical treatment of ground water motion. Similar in many respects to Muskat's work.

Remson, I. and J. R. Randolf
1962 Review of some elements of soil-moisture theory. U. S. Geological Survey, Professional Paper 411-D. 38 p.

Saffman, P. G.
1960 Dispersion due to molecular diffusion and macroscopic mixing in flow through a network of capillaries. Journal of Fluid Mechanics 7:194-208.

Scheidegger, A. E.
1961 General theory of dispersion in porous media. Journal of Geophysical Research 66(10):3273-3278.

Schiff, L.
1963 Ground water recharge methods based on site characteristics and on sediment in flood waters. International Commission on Irrigation and Drainage, 5th, Tokyo, R.2: 18.17-18.31.

The third of a series of reports providing the results of much practical field experimentation, mostly in California.

Schiff, L. and K. L. Dyer
1964 Some physical and chemical considerations in artificial ground water recharge. International Association of Scientific Hydrology, Publication 64:347-358.

Schoeller, H.
1959 Arid zone hydrology, recent developments. Unesco, Paris. Arid Zone Research 12. 125 p.

———

1962 Les eaux souterraines. Masson, Paris, 642 p.
A comprehensive text, especially strong in treatment of chemistry of ground water.

Simpson, E. S.
1962 Transverse dispersion in liquid flow through porous media. U. S. Geological Survey, Professional Paper 411-C.

Skibitzke, H. E.
1963 The use of analog computers for studies in ground-water hydrology. Institution of Water Engineers, London, Journal 17.

Smoor, P. B.
1967 Hydrochemical facies study of ground water in the Tucson Basin. University of Arizona, Tucson. 247 p. (Ph. D. dissertation).
A first attempt to apply factor analysis and other advanced statistical techniques to classify and study the chemistry of ground water.

Sniegocki, R. T. et al.
1965 Testing procedures and results of studies of artificial recharge in the Grand Prairie region, Arkansas. U. S. Geological Survey, Water-Supply Paper 1615-G.
Covers practical problems encountered in recharging through injection wells. Generally successful results.

Stallman, R. W.
1964 Multiphase fluids in porous media: a review of theories pertinent to hydrologic studies. U. S. Geological Survey, Professional Paper 411-E. 51 p.
Focuses attention on nonsaturated zone above water table and below soil horizon. Especially important in arid regions where this zone may be several hundred feet thick or more. Excellent treatment.

Symposium on the Application of Radioisotopes in Hydrology, Tokyo, 1963
1963 Radioisotopes in hydrology; proceedings of the Symposium . . . held by the International Atomic Energy Agency, March 5-9, 1963. International Atomic Energy Agency, Vienna. 457 p.

Technology Planning Center
1966 Systems analysis techniques and concepts for water resource planning and management. Technology Planning Center, Inc., Ann Arbor, Michigan, Report C-406.
Provides a good summary of methodology.

Thatcher, L. L., M. Rubin, and C. Brown
1961 Dating desert ground water. Science 134:105.
Water samples from Arabia and North Africa. Carbon-14 method used.

Theis, C. V.
1935 The relation between the lowering of the piezometric surface and the rate and duration of discharge of a well using ground-water storage.

American Geophysical Union, Transactions 16 (2):519-524.

The classic paper that led to modern methods of water-well hydraulics. (See the works of Hantush.)

Thomas, H. E.
1962   Water and the Southwest—what is the future? U. S. Geological Survey, Circular 469. 15 p.

Todd, D. K.
1959a   Ground water hydrology. John Wiley and Sons, New York. 336 p.

———
1959b   Annotated bibliography on artificial recharge of ground water through 1954. U. S. Geological Survey, Water-Supply Paper 1477. 115 p.

———
1964   Economics of ground water recharge. University of California, Lawrence Radiation Laboratory, Report UCRL-7850 Rev. 1. 36 p.

Concludes that artificial recharge is usually economical, assuming a source of recharge water is available.

Tyson, H. N. and E. M. Weber
1964   Ground-water management for the nation's future: computer simulation of ground-water basins. American Society of Civil Engineers, Hydraulics Division, Journal 90(HY4):59-77.

U. S. Geological Survey
1966   Inventory of federal sources of ground-water data. Prepared under auspices of the Subcommittee on Hydrology, Interagency Committee on Water Resources, Bulletin 12. 294 p.

U.S. Geological Survey, Office of International Activities
1967   Interim bibliography of reports related to overseas activities of the Water Resources Division, 1940-67. Open file report. [26 p.]

Contains references to ground-water investigations and appraisals made in most of the major deserts (except Australia) by personnel of the Geological Survey, including references to unpublished, open-file reports. With few exceptions, however, the investigations deal with local or small-scale problems.

Valantine, V. E.
1964   Effecting optimum ground-water basin management. American Society of Civil Engineers, Hydraulics Division, Journal 90(HY4):97-105.

Comments similar to those for Chun, Mitchell, and Mido (1964).

Vogt, E. Z. and R. Hyman
1959   Water witching U. S. A. University of Chicago Press, Chicago, Illinois.

A readable and informative book that examines the psychological and social aspects of the phenomenon. Concludes that water witching does not provide a good means for finding subsurface water.

Wenzel, L. K.
1942   Methods for determining permeability of water-bearing materials. U. S. Geological Survey, Water-Supply Paper 887. 192 p.

Reports on field tests that helped prove the usefulness of the Theis equation (see Theis, 1935).

White, N. D.
1963   Annual report on ground water in Arizona, spring 1962 to spring 1963. Arizona State Land Department, Water Resources Report 15. 136 p.

INDEXES

SUBJECT INDEX

INDEX OF AUTHORS CITED

This index contains names of all primary and secondary personal and corporate authors cited in the chapter texts. Only in those cases where an author's name is included in the pertinent publications list following a chapter but is not referred to in the chapter text is a page reference to the pertinent publications list given in this index. Any name appearing in a pertinent publications list may be found easily, however, if the reader will refer first to the text page indexed here.

Aarons, J., 158
Aaronson, A., 417
Abalos, J. W., 578, 582, 583, 584, 585
Abd-El-Al, I., 139
Abdel-Malek, Y., 319
Abdel-Rahman, A. A., 321, 409
Abdel-Salam, M. A., 295, 333, 334
Abdel-Samie, A. G., 292
Abecasis, F. M., 684
Abel, H., 113
Abell, L. F., 331
Abercromby, R., 257
Abolin, R. I., 426
Abrams, L., 444
Abu Bakr, M., 675
Abul-Haggag, Y., 101
El-Abyad, M. S., 407
Academia Sinica, Peking, 37
——Sand Control Team, 300, 301, 302, 325, 430, 431
Ackermann, W. C., 171
Adams, A. R. D., 601
Adamson, R. S., 394, 400, 436
Addor, E. E., 501
Adejokun, J. A., 35
Adie, R. J., 111
Adkins, W. S., 165, 174
Adle, A. H., 29
Adolph, E. F., 571, 597
Aelion, E., 34
Aellen, P., 501
Afghan Delegation, 143
Afrique Occidentale Française, Service Météorologique, 42
Agafonoff, V., 293
Agassiz, L., 100
Agnew, A. D. Q., 501
Aguilar y Santillán, R., 173
Ahmad, A., 147
Ahmad, K. S., 51, 145, 147
Ahmad, M., 595
Ahmad, M. I., 243
Ahmad, M. S., 51
Ahmad, N., 48, 243, 329
Ahmad, S., 421
Ahmad, T., 575
Ahmed, A., 145
Aitchison, J. E. T., 420, 421

Aizenshtat, B. A., 37
Ajello, L., 599, 600, 616
Akademiia Nauk S.S.S.R., Botanicheskii Institut, 425
Akademiia Nauk S.S.S.R. i Glavnoye Upravleniye Geodezii i Kartografii G.G.K. S.S.S.R., 109, 110, 153
Akademiia Nauk Kazakhskoi, S.S.R., 426
Akester, R., 119
Akhtar, S. A., 577
Akzhigitova, N. I., 329
Alam, S., 145
Al-Ani, H., 319
Albareda, J. M., 339
Albert, B. L., 599
Albertson, F. W., 596
Albertson, M. L., 171, 172
Alderman, A. R., 674
Aldous, A. E., 445
Aldrich, J. M., 587
Alexander, C. S., 654
Alexander, L. T., 334
Algeria. Service de la Carte Géologique de l'Algérie, 127, 213
Alia Medina, M., 124
Alimen, H., 126
Allemand-Martin, A., 682
Allen, C. R., 165, 261, 666
Allen, D. L., 597
Allen, F. M., 580
Allfather, W. E., 599
Allison, E. C., 175, 665
Allison, I. S., 167
Allison, L. E., 333
Allouse, B. E., 575, 605
Almeyda Arroyo, E., 30
Alvarez, J. A., 42
Alvira, T., 339
Amaral, A. do, 578
Ambrose, J. W., 162
Amemiya, M., 331
American Meteorological Society, 56
American Public Health Association, 598, 602
American University, Foreign Areas Studies Division, Special Operations Research Office, 683
Amidon, R. E., 170
Amin, M. S., 118
Amiran, D. H. K., 34, 140
Amstutz, G. C., 156
Ananthakrishnan, R., 36, 43
Andel, T. H. van, 665, 666, 688
Anderson, C. A., 175, 665
Anderson, G. H., 169
Anderson, H. W., 105, 170
Anderson, J. U., 326
Anderson, N. L., 596
Anderson, R. A., 603
Anderson, R. H., 435
Anderson, R. M., 597

Anderson, R. V. V., 126
Anderson, S., 617
Anderson, S. C., 578
Andersson, C. F., 113
Andreanszky, G. v, 502
Andrew, G., 116, 146
Andrews, F. W., 408
Andrews, J., 502
Andrews, J. D., 597
Andrews, R. C., 575, 578, 586, 597
Angas, G. F., 587
Angel, F., 578
Angola. Serviço Meteorológico, 26
——Serviços de Geologia e Minas, 684
Angus, D. E., 45, 54
Aniol, R., 58
Anning, S. T., 601
Anstey, R. L., 145, 151
Antevs, E., 162, 170
Anthony, M. S., 444
Antipov-Karataev, I. N., 329, 331
Anwar, R. M., 292
Aparicio, F. de, 671
Arabian-American Oil Company (Aramco), 731
Aravin, V. I., 736
Archbold, J. W., 35
Archer, T. C. R., 585
Arden, D. D., Jr., 134
Arévalo, P., 124
Argentina. Consejo Federal de Inversiones, 154, 155, 502
——Dirección Nacional de Geología y Minería, 154, 155, 671
Arid Zone Newsletter, 248
Arid Zone Research Institute, Abu-Ghraib, 137, 234
Arifkhanova, M. M., 426
Aristarain, L., 161
Arkell, A. J., 116
Armand, D. L., 430
Armitage, H. M., 597
Arndt, W., 333
Arnold, B., 168, 175
Arnold, D. E., 163
Arnold, G., 594
Arnolds, A., 154
Arnould, M., 682
Arribas, A., 124
Arshad, A., 298
Ascherson, P., 117, 409
Asghar, A. G., 243, 298, 331
Ashbel, D., 415, 418
Ashburn, L. L., 600
Ashby, W. C., 436
Asnani, G. C., 43
Asplund, K. K., 575
Asrarullah, 144
Assad, J. C., 153
Association of African Geological Surveys, 110

INDEX TO SCIENTIFIC NAMES OF PLANTS

Any mention of a plant genus, with or without species, by scientific name in this book is indexed here. Complete scientific names (genus plus species) appearing in the book but not listed in the species summary (pages 473-500) are identified in this index with an asterisk (*).

The index includes page references to some genera without species identification, but when the genus (alone) is mentioned on a page on which the name of a species of that genus also appears, that page number is not given with the genus (alone).

Common names of plants are indexed in the Subject Index, pages 747-760).

* appears only on page given; not listed in Species Summary